THE
LEAGUE

By David Harris

I SHOULDA BEEN HOME YESTERDAY
THE LAST SCAM
DREAMS DIE HARD
THE LEAGUE

THE
LEAGUE
THE RISE AND DECLINE
OF THE
NFL

DAVID HARRIS

BANTAM BOOKS

TORONTO • NEW YORK • LONDON • SYDNEY • AUCKLAND

THE LEAGUE
A Bantam Book / October 1986

*The song "Hoosier Heartland" is by James Irsay, Vice-President and
General Manager of the Indianapolis Colts.*

Library of Congress Cataloging-in-Publication Data

Harris, David, 1946–
   The League : the rise and decline of the NFL.

   Includes index.
   1. National Football League—History.   I. Title.
GV955.5.N35H37 1986   796.332'64'0973   86-47575
ISBN 0-553-05167-9

Published simultaneously in the United States and Canada

PRINTED IN THE UNITED STATES OF AMERICA

FG   0 9 8 7 6 5 4 3 2 1

for Martin Arnold, a friend indeed.

ACKNOWLEDGMENTS

The information I have used to construct this book was obtained along four principal avenues of reporting.

The first was a series of interviews with the principal characters conducted between 1983 and 1986. Most were on an attributable basis. Included among these were Joe Alioto, Jack Kent Cooke, Hugh Culverhouse, Jack Donlan, Keith Fahnhorst, Ed Garvey, Robert Gries, Jr., Lamar Hunt, Jim Kensil, Gene Klein, Don Klosterman, Wellington Mara, Bob Marr, Bill McPhail, Art Modell, Bob Moore, Jay Moyer, Stephen Reinhardt, Joe Robbie, Bill Robertson, Art Rooney, Dan Rooney, Steve Rosenbloom, George Ross, Pete Rozelle, Tex Schramm, Billy Sullivan, Chuck Sullivan, Paul Tagliabue, Leonard Tose, and Wayne Valley. Al Davis refused to respond to two letters and some three dozen phone calls, but his version of events was available in great detail through court records, testimony, and depositions. While Georgia and Dominic Frontiere would not consent to a formal interview, they, too, were available through court records and did allow me some off the record contact that helped me to understand them better. In addition, I conducted some thirty other interviews with individuals who directly observed the principals or the events I have chronicled but were themselves either unimportant or tangential to the story I've told. I thank them all for their cooperation.

The second large body of information was provided by the testimony of a number of the principals under oath both before the United States Congress and in a succession of court cases that have spanned more than a decade. The congressional testimony included *Oversight Hearings on National Football League Labor-Management Dispute, Rights of Professional Athletes, TV Blackout of Sporting Events, Inquiry into Professional Sports, Labor Reform Act of 1977, Sports Anti-Blackout Legislation, Oversight Hearings on Equal Employment Opportunities in the National Football League, Professional Sports Anti-Trust Immunity.* The court testimony was available either from courtroom transcripts, deposition sessions conducted under oath, or affidavits, again submitted under oath. Among the court cases were *LAMCC v. NFL, NASL v. NFL, Mackey v. NFL, Gries Sports Enterprises v. Cleveland Browns, Valley v. Davis, Barrero v. Davis, Coggins v. New England Patriots, Tose v. First Pennsylvania Bank, City of Oakland v. Oakland Raiders,* and *Philadelphia Eagles et al v. Oakland Raiders.* In total, this avenue of research yielded tens of thousands of pages of direct examination on the subjects I have explored. In most cases, the materials were loaned me by various law firms involved and I thank them all very much for their cooperation, but will refrain from naming them lest they be held responsible for what I've written.

The third pillar upon which this book was constructed was an immense store of documentary information made available either through the cooperation of the National Football League, the cooperation of individual owners, or through the evidence process in the above-mentioned legal actions. Again, this avenue yielded thousands of pages of valuable material whose validity was either without question or attested to under oath. Among those materials were the complete National Football League minutes between 1972 and 1984, the SRI Report on Expansion, the letters between Pete Rozelle and Lamar Hunt on the subject of ownership policy, the communications between the commissioner's office and the rest of the League on the same subject, the letters between Pete Rozelle and Al Davis on the subject of Davis's move to Los Angeles, portions of the minutes of the Los Angeles Memorial Coliseum Commission, the internal memos of the banks involved in the restructuring of the New England Patriots, the communications between Carroll Rosenbloom and Cabot, Cabot & Forbes on the subject of Anaheim Stadium Associates and their mutual communications with the city of Anaheim, and the communications between Robert Gries and Art Modell concerning Cleveland Stadium Corp.

The fourth and final informational base was the enormous body of reporting done over the last twenty years by more than 150 newspapers, magazines, and authors. In collecting this reservoir of fact and anecdote, I was aided immeasurably by the cooperation of a number of institutions who opened their facilities or clipping files to my purposes. Among them were the Stanford University libraries, the University of California libraries, the Cleveland Public Library, the Miami Public Library, the Data Center, the National Football League, *The New York Times*, the *Los Angeles Times*, the *San Diego Union* and the *San Diego Tribune*, *The Dallas Morning News*, *The* [Baltimore] *Sun*, *The Boston Globe*, *The* [Philadelphia] *Inquirer*, *The* [Oakland] *Tribune*, the *San Francisco Chronicle*, *The Washington Post*, *The Indianapolis Star* and *The Indianapolis News*, the *Kansas City Times*, *The Phoenix Gazette*, and the *Miami News*. The reportage assembled along this avenue was a critical element in nailing down this story and for that I wish to thank the thousands of reporters who had covered this ground before I reached it. While I didn't necessarily follow their footsteps, knowing where they'd been was of great use.

I also wish to credit the people who assisted me in assembling this body of information. My personal research assistant, Ted Tyson, was invaluable for his insights as well as his research. In addition, a number of other individual researchers aided me in this task: Mary Louise Madigan, Brad Kava, Will Brults, Maria Newman, Chris Wolff, Mel Greenberg, Craig Smith, Virginia Baker, Lucy Anderson-Morshead, Louise Beale, and Liz Davis. My computer services were provided by Peter Golitzen and PKG Systems.

The people who made all this effort worthwhile were my agent, Kathy Robbins, her agency, the Robbins Office, and my publisher, Linda Grey.

Finally, I must thank my wife, Lacey Fosburgh, my son, Gabe, and my daughter, Sophie. This book took me away from our mutual life at critical moments for all of them and they welcomed me back nonetheless. On numerous occasions they were forced to cover my act as a husband and father, so I could pursue this project. In all circumstances, they endured my obsession and comforted me when I needed comfort badly. It all would have been impossible without their support.

—D.H.
April 1986

PART ONE

STATUS QUO ANTE

1

The 1974 annual meeting of the National Football League convened behind closed doors at the Americana Hotel in Bal Harbour, Florida, on February 25 at 10:00 A.M. Scheduled to last a week, this yearly gathering in late winter was traditionally the longest and most significant of the NFL's business year, and the lobby outside was swarming with reporters dispatched from all over America to chronicle the League's private deliberations as best they were able.

By 1974 the long and costly war with the American Football League had been officially over for four years, and the single twenty-six-team professional football monopoly that had emerged from the conflict was already firmly established as the ranking success story of the sports/entertainment industry. Super Bowl VIII, climaxing the NFL's season just a month before, had been the third most watched sporting event in American television history, topped only by the two preceding Super Bowls. Those events' audience included more Americans than had voted in any presidential election in the nation's history. *Christian Century* called it "America's new religion." To most of those who watched, football, as presented to the public by the NFL, was simply "America's game."

Officially, as defined in its constitution and bylaws, the League that assembled in Bal Harbour was an "unincorporated association, not for profit," organized in order "to promote and foster the primary business of League members, each member being an owner of a professional football club located in the United States." Membership was limited to twenty-six franchises, each of whom granted the League "exclusive control of the exhibition of football games in the home territory of each member" in exchange for one vote in the League's innermost councils. All the League's decisions required at least a three quarters majority. To oversee this process, the constitution authorized the League to "select and employ a person of unquestioned integrity to serve as commissioner." The commissioner was in turn granted "full, complete, and final jurisdiction and authority" over "any dispute involving a member or members in the League."

Pete Rozelle had been the commissioner for the last fourteen years and had dominated the football business to an extent unprecedented in more than fifty years of NFL history. His mastery of the commissionership was such that, by the time the League met in Bal Harbour, the position and Rozelle's persona were virtually synonymous. In the chair to call the meeting's opening session to order, Rozelle, forty-seven years old, looked tan and fit. Six feet two inches tall, he managed to seem smaller. His dark hair was receding and long cheeks gave Rozelle's face a hound-dog look that made him seem easygoing and appealing. Pete Rozelle, Clint Murchison, controlling owner of the Dallas Cowboys, noted, was a man with "milk toast all over his high hand" and his years as commissioner had not appreciably altered his style. It was still difficult to find a hard edge anywhere in his demeanor. Rozelle was, everyone agreed, "a nice guy," and his plain vanilla style made him an easy man to underestimate. To do so was, of course, a mistake. Behind that studied inoffensiveness was what one NFL executive called "a consummate public relations man" who was "Madison Avenue slick." The Pete Rozelle who convened the Bal Harbour annual meeting was on top of his world in a way few such public men were. Later, when it all came apart, he would describe 1974 as "the good old days."

At the time, the commissioner seemed without challenge. "In this League," Leonard Tose, majority owner of the Philadelphia Eagles, observed, "Rozelle is the avenue to power. It's more like we work for him than he works for us." Edward Bennett Williams, president of the Washington Redskins, agreed. "Historically," Williams explained, "he has worked his will. There are a number of owners who follow the commissioner and do his bidding, regardless of what their own personal feelings may be. . . . Mr. Rozelle is a very strong commissioner . . . [and] the docility and inertia of many of the members permits him to get policies adopted." Jack Kent Cooke, Williams's partner in the Redskins, painted much the same picture. "Rozelle is as skillful a politician as I have met in my life," he noted. "His capacity to conjure up agreement is sometimes nothing short of miraculous. He's a consummate politician." Al Davis, managing general partner of the Oakland Raiders, summed it up. "Rozelle," he claimed, "is the most powerful man in professional sports." When the League met in Bal Harbour, it seemed Pete Rozelle's dominance would last forever.

It would not.

Over the next decade, he would be denigrated, deplored, challenged, and bested in the most public of ways. The stability he championed would be disrupted by a host of his employers acting both alone and in concert. The unanimity he had enforced behind the League's closed doors would shatter and, in the end, both his vision of the football business and the majesty he claimed for his own office would be torn to shreds.

The end, however, was a long time coming, and 1974 was only its beginning.

That no one in Bal Harbour noticed what was in store for Pete Rozelle and the National Football League was understandable. In those days, it was hard for anyone to look at the League and see much besides unmitigated success, and no single individual was given more credit for that success than Rozelle. Comprised of just twelve teams when he took office in 1960, most of them confined to the northern industrial belt, the League's current twenty-six were spread among each of the nation's major areas, with the sole exception of the Pacific Northwest. The biggest membership jump had come in 1966, when the six-year war with the upstart rival American Football League had been settled by merger into the NFL. Once the merger had been completed and sanctified by the United States Congress, the football business had entered the golden years of what was already being called "the Rozelle era." In the year before Rozelle was hired, the NFL had staged seventy-two games in front of 3,140,000 paid spectators; in 1973 the League presented 182 games cheered from the stands by 10,731,000 fans. The first League-wide television contract negotiated by Pete Rozelle in 1962 had been worth $326,000 a year to each of the franchises. The contract completed with the 1973 season had been worth $1.7 million a year to each of twice as many teams.

As a matter of policy, Pete Rozelle attempted to keep such business matters in the background whenever he could. "The strong public view that professional football is more business than sport," he explained, "can only hurt the game." Instead, Rozelle's League was marketed on another plane altogether. "We sell an experience," he explained. To an audience whose own five-day-a-week struggles were generally confused, mundane, restrained, and without resolution, the weekend battles staged by the League were clear, heroic, uninhibited, decisive, and, at times, even noble. By the time the commissioner and his twenty-six employers gathered in Bal Harbour, consumption of their mutual spectacle was a central requirement for participation in American culture. In 1961, after Pete Rozelle's first year, thirty-four percent of the nation told the Gallup Poll they considered baseball their favorite sport and only twenty-one percent named football. By 1972, thirty-six percent named football and only twenty-one percent baseball. Along the way, Rozelle became the only sports executive ever to be named Sportsman of the Year by *Sports Illustrated,* an honor otherwise reserved for athletes and coaches. Rozelle, the magazine pointed out, was "perfectly cast in the role of a modern executive" and had "decisively and brilliantly guided a great and growing sport." Rozelle's friend Tex Schramm, president of the NFL's Dallas Cowboys franchise and the League's point man in making peace with the AFL, described Rozelle as "a man for the times" and believed the NFL "fortunate to have had him." Lamar Hunt, sole owner of the Kansas City Chiefs, considered Rozelle "the most important person in the history of professional football." Art Rooney, owner of the Pittsburgh Steelers, called Rozelle "a gift from the hand of Providence." By 1974, his skill at handling his employers was legendary. "He lets the owners talk unchecked," one NFL executive noted, "and wear themselves down. Then he goes outside and lobbies and gets things done. By the end of the meeting, he railroads what he wants through when everyone is tired and wants to go home. His patience is infinite and, when the time's right, he's always got all his ducks in a row."

As was his tradition, Rozelle opened the 1974 annual meeting with his "Annual Report and Review," delivered with an earnest touch in typical low-key manner.

A great deal of the commissioner's report this year was devoted to chronicling the League's public relations. Though confident, Pete Rozelle was not sanguine about the future and made a point of repeating what was, by now, a somewhat ritualized warning. At the 1972 annual meeting, he had "again emphasized that self-discipline . . . and strong internal discipline . . . could help avoid problems." In 1973, "the commissioner said that the NFL is looked to by other sports and the media for its harmony and togetherness, but he emphasized that continued cooperation and interchange . . . is more important than ever. . . . He said he felt that internal disputes had increased the past year and urged a major effort be made in the future to eliminate them." Now, at Bal Harbour, he struck the same note again. "The commissioner said 1973 had been a record year for club fines . . . [and] said that, as distasteful as fining and discipline was, members could look for an escalation of disciplinary action should violations continue. . . . Commissioner Rozelle urged that each organization should stress that public statements by anyone associated with the NFL can have serious legal and public relations consequences. Of particular importance, he said, was damage that could be caused by unthinking comments about League matters."

The minutes made no record of how the twenty-six men who employed Rozelle responded to his lecture. By the time he delivered it, a number of them were no doubt distracted. For the League's owners, by far the most interesting part of the commissioner's address had been its first item. "After new club and League personnel were introduced," the minutes observed, "the commissioner reported that agreement had been reached on new four-year television contracts with CBS, NBC, and ABC." It was news the twenty-six had been awaiting eagerly, and Pete Rozelle, as usual, did nothing to disappoint them.

After developing a strategy with Gene Klein and Art Modell, the other two members of the League's television committee, Rozelle had spent the last few months in face-to-face negotiations with the networks as the NFL's sole bargaining agent, empowered to make whatever deal he chose. "As a negotiator," one of the network representatives remembered, "Rozelle was cool as a cucumber and very definitive on the things he wanted. He was as good a TV man as there was. He appreciated what TV could do and had mastered its demographics." Those demographics gave the commissioner enormous leverage over networks in the business of selling advertising time. A 1972 Louis Harris Poll had reported that sixty-five percent of the people making $15,000 a year listed football as their favorite spectator sport. A survey by Simmons Market Research found that among males age eighteen to forty-nine—what *Time* called "the most desirable but hard-to-reach ad target"—six times as many watched the NFL as even the highest-rated television series. As a consequence, Rozelle remembered, "with the networks we were able to stay very close to the numbers we walked in with."

Those numbers were known only to Art Modell and Gene Klein until the commissioner's Bal Harbour speech. Several owners beseeched Modell and Klein to reveal what they knew, but the good news was the commissioner's to break, and once the annual meeting was under way, he was quick to do so.

Over the next four years, Rozelle reported, the three networks would collectively pay the NFL $60 million a year. Split twenty-six ways, that was $2.3 million per franchise per year, an increase of some $600,000 each.

"They were pleasantly surprised," Rozelle remembered. "They always were." At the time, the deal seemed enormous.

Several of those listening to the commissioner's annual report remembered a lot of self-congratulatory chuckles and suckings of breath.

In 1974, it was widely assumed his twenty-six employers were putty in Pete Rozelle's hands.

2

Few had expected such singular achievement from Pete Rozelle when he assumed the commissionership at age thirty-three. He was a man whose pervasive ordinariness masked what would later prove to be extraordinary talents.

Born in South Gate, California, outside Los Angeles, on March 1, 1926, Pete Rozelle's given name was Alvin Ray. Neither of his parents liked the name Alvin, and in the years immediately after his birth, each blamed the other for choosing it. Finally a kindly uncle who worked as a coach at the local junior high school resolved the dilemma by supplying the nickname "Pete" and it stuck. Most of Pete's early life was spent in Lynwood, California, then a separate town of some fifteen thousand southwest of Los Angeles proper. Pete's grandfather had originally moved to the area from Indiana in 1892 to farm one hundred acres along the Los Angeles River. Pete's father, Ray Rozelle, owned a small Lynwood grocery store that went belly-up during the Depression. Ray started over as a shipping clerk at the nearby Alcoa aluminum plant in Compton and eventually rose to purchasing agent.

Pete was the older of Ray's two sons, and his father was the biggest single influence in his life. "He was my role model," Pete remembered. "I think I came out with a lot of my father's attributes. I got my temperament from him. He in particular was a calm person. I got his patience probably. He had a lot of friends and was regarded as a good guy." The most formative single experience Pete Rozelle could remember from his early days in Lynwood happened at a summer day camp in the nearby San Gabriel Mountains. Rozelle was nearly ten at the time and his epiphany came during "a little talk" the counselors delivered to their assembled charges. "I still remember it," Rozelle recounted. " 'Character is what you are and reputation is what people think you are,' they told us. 'But if your reputation is bad, you might as well have bad character.' I've remembered it so much since. Whether it's right or wrong, this is the standard you have when you exist in the limelight. Your reputation is valuable. You might as well have bad character if people think you do." Possessed of an inherited knack for getting along and a precocious concern for the appearances of things, Pete was equipped early for all the public relations to come.

Otherwise, his childhood was fairly standard brand. The family house, built in 1940, had a nice patio in back and a one-car garage. Pete's uncle and cousins lived nearby and much of his growing-up was done in their company. For a good time on weekends, he and his brother and cousins would ride the streetcar into L.A. to catch a movie. Pete remembered himself as "very happy." His favorite excursions were with his father in the Sierra Nevadas, where Ray Rozelle introduced his son to the family camping spot in a place called Long Canyon near the town of Lone Pine.

In Lynwood, much of the Rozelles' time was spent in sports. Pete attended Methodist Sunday school until age twelve, but dropped out to play touch football instead. The world he occupied was "middle class or lower middle class," long on wholesomeness and short on glitter. At nearby Compton High School, Rozelle was a six-foot forward on the varsity basketball team during the early days of World War II and played doubles on the tennis squad with one of his cousins. His first contact with the strata of money and power in which he would eventually find his calling came when the Compton basketball squad was bussed up to Beverly Hills High School for a game. "Beverly Hills High School had an oil well on its grounds," he remembered, "and I'd never seen anything quite so plush before. Their gym had glass backboards and I'd never seen those before. At halftime, when both teams were in the dressing room, the gym floor parted to reveal a swimming pool, and they had an aquatic exhibition instead of song girls. My eyes were like saucers."

Immediately after finishing high school in 1944, Rozelle entered the navy and served as an enlisted man for the duration. In 1946, he mustered out, returned to Lynwood, and enrolled at Compton Junior College. To help pay his way, he worked as the college's athletic news director, and was a stringer covering high school games for the Long Beach and Los Angeles papers. He was paid fifty cents a game to call in details and scores. On Saturdays, he also worked on the sports desk of the *Long Beach Press Telegram*. "I was never a good enough writer to be anything other than a hack," he recalled. "That's what I wanted to do because I was interested in sports and the journalistic side of it."

Pete Rozelle's return from the war also coincided with the arrival of professional football in Los Angeles. That year, the NFL's Cleveland Rams moved west to set up activities in Los Angeles and establish the League's first foothold on the Pacific Coast. It was just one of a number of fortuitous coincidences that marked Rozelle's rise to power. The most fortuitous part was that the Rams chose Compton Junior College to use as a training camp. Compton's young athletic news director quickly made contact and was hired to act as a gofer for Maxwell Stiles, the franchise's public relations director. Rozelle, twenty, was also paid fifty dollars a program to edit the game programs sold at the Rams games in the nearby Los Angeles Memorial Coliseum. In his first encounter with the NFL, he made a good impression, and he continued to work for the Rams until he left town to finish college at the University of San Francisco.

Rozelle's choice of USF had grown out of a chance meeting with Pete Newell, the university's basketball coach, at a Compton basketball tournament. When Rozelle was looking around at colleges, Newell helped him obtain the athletic news director position at USF as a part-time job. Also supported by the G.I. Bill, Rozelle graduated in 1950 and enlarged his news director position to full-time. Again luck was with him. Those were the glory years of USF athletics. The football team was undefeated and nine of its eleven starting players made successful careers in the NFL. The basketball team won the National Invitational Tournament, then the college sport's most prestigious post-season event. "It was a chance to meet a lot of people," Rozelle said.

One of those he met was Tex Schramm, then general manager of Rozelle's hometown Rams. "USF had a very good football team," Schramm remembered, "and I started working with Pete, getting information about their players. He was a very bright young man. I was very impressed with the way he picked things up." In 1952, when the Rams public relations director left to join a short-lived Dallas NFL franchise, Schramm offered Rozelle the job. Rozelle had no qualms about taking it. He had found his niche, and public relations was its name. Rozelle's professional apprenticeship was served with the Rams from 1952 to 1955. Then he went back to San Francisco to join a private PR firm. At the time, Pete Rozelle thought he was saying good-bye to the NFL for good.

The public relations firm he joined was run by Ken Macker, a New York expatriate Rozelle had first met while USF's basketball team was winning the National Invitational Tournament. When Macker moved to the Pacific Coast, the two became fast friends. Macker was Rozelle's best man at his marriage to his first wife, Jane, and godfather to his only child, Anne Marie. "I've never met anybody that has more captivated me," Macker remembered, "then or since. Pete was a bright, interesting young man. I was extraordinarily impressed by him. I needed a strong partner and I talked him into joining." Macker could not have been more pleased with his new partner. "I don't know anybody with an unkind word to say about him," he continued. "He doesn't get blinded or sidetracked. He keeps his thinking process on the road all the time. He was always self-assured, always a man who could make a decision and live with it."

Rozelle's biggest account in his years with Macker belonged to Australia. The country was preparing for the 1956 Olympics at Melbourne and was receiving so much bad press that the International Olympics Committee was threatening to take the games away from them. "Rozelle immediately took the mayor of Melbourne around the country," Macker remembered, "and within two weeks, the feeling was totally reversed." Next, Rozelle took the *Time, Newsweek, Sports Illustrated,* AP, and UPI sports editors to Melbourne for an on-site inspection. Afterward, he was asked to handle the world press for the Melbourne Olympics. The Macker firm was also approached by the Australian government about lifting their image out of the kangaroo-dominated picture currently in vogue. Again, it was Rozelle, the junior partner, who found the solution.

Pete Rozelle's idea was to bring over John Landy, the Australian runner who had been the second man in history to break the four-minute mile, for an American tour. The notion was to make the world think about Australia's athletic accomplishments rather than its marsupials. Landy was the right man for the job. So was Rozelle. The Australians judged the campaign a success— and Rozelle as a certain kind of genius.

In 1957, the National Football League began trying to lure Rozelle back. The League's commissioner, Bert Bell, the former owner of the Philadelphia Eagles who had been hired in 1946, took a personal interest in recruiting Rozelle to rejoin the Rams, largely because the Rams had a problem he thought only Rozelle might be able to solve. In the years since Rozelle had been in San Francisco working for Macker and the Australians, the Los Angeles NFL franchise had been almost paralyzed by inner turmoil. The difficulties grew out of the club's ownership arrangement. Fifty percent of the club was owned by Dan Reeves, and fifty percent by two other partners who could not stand Reeves. The result was total impasse. By 1957, it had reached the point where Tex Schramm, fed up with civil war around him, resigned his general manager's job to join CBS Sports. Bell wanted someone in Schramm's old job who could get along with the two warring factions well enough to get the Rams moving again. Bell was a friend of Macker's and recognized that Pete Rozelle, better at getting along than anybody else Bell could think of, was exactly what Los Angeles needed.

At first, Rozelle wasn't going for the change. "I'm doing what I want to do," he told Bell. Bell, however, did not give up. Among other things, he hired Joe Kuharich, the USF football coach during Rozelle's tenure there, to work full-time convincing Rozelle to move south and take the GM job at the Rams. Eventually, the Macker Company's junior partner was getting four or five calls a week from either Kuharich or Bell. Ken Macker counseled Rozelle, "You won't forgive yourself if you don't at least inquire." Rozelle did, and before 1957 was over had signed a contract as general manager of the Los Angeles Rams.

As Bert Bell had assumed, Rozelle was able to bring relative peace to the franchise, sorting things out with the warring partners enough to make the Rams at least operational. Otherwise, Pete Rozelle was no great shakes as a general manager. As a judge of player personnel, he was too inherently sentimental to excel. His strong suit was marketing. Among other things, he invented the L.A. Rams' sweatshirt, and discounted tickets for children accompanied by an adult in order to help fill the team's mammoth home stadium. Though he now had access to the League's top echelons, he was by no means an NFL power. Dan Reeves represented the Rams at League meetings and, Rozelle admitted, "I didn't know the big boys very well."

That all began to change on October 11, 1959. That Sunday, while attending a Philadelphia Eagles game, Bert Bell dropped dead from a heart attack. The commissioner's job remained vacant for the remainder of the season. "We haven't given any thought to a successor," Carroll Rosenbloom, then owner of the Baltimore Colts, pointed out. "It will take a lot of thinking." In the last half of January, the League's 1960 annual meeting, held at the Kenilworth Hotel in Miami, took up the issue of Bell's successor at the top of its agenda. Rozelle, now thirty-three years old, was in attendance to help out his boss, Dan Reeves. Rozelle was not considered a likely candidate by anyone. In fact, his name did not even come up until the League's owners had been meeting for a week and a dozen other candidates had been considered.

Over ten days at the Kenilworth, the owners had cast twenty-three ballots and gotten nowhere. The leading candidate through most of the balloting was Marshall Leahy, the San Francisco attorney who was the NFL's legal counsel. Leahy, however, had made himself enormously controversial by insisting that, if chosen, he would move League headquarters from Pennsylvania to San Francisco. Leahy needed eight votes to win but could not muster more than seven. The five outstanding votes were split four no, and one abstention from George Halas, patriarch of the Chicago Bears. Halas, head of the expansion committee, hoped to convince the meeting to add two franchises once the commissioner was chosen, and didn't want to antagonize either side. The anti-Leahy faction was led by Art Rooney of the Pittsburgh Steelers and Carroll Rosenbloom of Baltimore's Colts. The leaders of the pro-Leahy group were Paul Brown of the Cleveland Browns, Wellington Mara of the New York Giants, and Rozelle's boss, Dan Reeves.

After ten days of deadlock, however, it was, according to Mara, obvious to the Leahy forces that they couldn't have their man without "seriously dividing the League." On January 26, 1960, Reeves, Mara, and one or two other owners met during a recess and told one another as much. It was at that meeting that Pete Rozelle's name first arose. Reeves suggested his General Manager as a compromise candidate. "Few of us knew Rozelle," Mara remembered, "but Reeves's recommendation was high." Mara was delegated to communicate the name to Art Rooney of the four-vote minority.

"What do you know about him?" Rooney asked.

"Reeves says he's good," Mara answered.

Rooney then reported on what Mara had said to the rest of the minority.

"Rozelle?" Frank McNamee of the Philadelphia Eagles blurted out, "who's he?"

Rozelle learned he was being considered after the January twenty-sixth afternoon session was adjourned. Wellington Mara and Paul Brown approached him, took him aside, and informed him that when the League meeting resumed after dinner, his name would be submitted. "I was quite surprised," Rozelle recalled, "because of my age." He nonetheless knew he had a significant advantage. "I was the only candidate," he pointed out, "who hadn't already alienated most of the people in that meeting." At the evening session, Rozelle was asked to leave the room while he was being considered. He avoided the lobby outside because it was full of reporters and waited, chain-smoking, in the men's room. To camouflage his reasons for being there, Rozelle washed his hands every time one of the waiting reporters came in to use the facilities.

Back in the room where the League was meeting, *Sports Illustrated* reported, the owners were sunk in "stalemate and despair." The tide was turned when Art Rooney declared that if Rozelle was good enough for Mara and Reeves, he was good enough for Rooney. On a motion by Carroll Rosenbloom, seconded by Paul Brown, at 10:35 P.M., the National Football League voted eight for Rozelle, three abstentions, and one for Leahy. As a gesture of unification with the minority group, Carroll Rosenbloom was asked to fetch Rozelle from the bathroom. Rosenbloom found Rozelle at the sink. By then the future commissioner's hands were soggy.

"Well," Pete Rozelle quipped upon rejoining the meeting, "I can honestly say I come to you with clean hands."

When the new commissioner was announced to the press, the gathered sports reporters were even more surprised than the owners had been. Few were impressed. Pencil-necked, skinny, and dog-jowled, Rozelle was also young, relatively inexperienced, and certainly untested. The sports press quickly dubbed him "the boy czar" and, within the hour, bets were being made around the Kenilworth lobby that it would be only a matter of months before Rozelle's notoriously irascible employers had cut their new boy to shreds and proceeded to find more seasoned help.

3

The League Pete Rozelle inherited had been founded in 1920, in a Canton, Ohio, Hupmobile showroom. There, seated amid the fenders and running boards, proprietors of a number of industrial and semi-professional football teams met and formed the American Professional Football Association. Two years later, the name was changed to National Football League. "It was hit or miss," Rozelle explained. "It wasn't very organized. Teams came and they went." Among the original franchises were the Akron Pros, the Canton Bulldogs, the Massillon Tigers, the Hammond Pros, the Muncie Flyers, the Racine Cardinals, the Rock Island Independents, the Decatur Staleys, and the Rochester Jeffersons. By 1926, the League had grown to include twenty-two franchises. By 1931, it was down to ten. Nineteen thirty-six was the first year since the League's founding that did not include a franchise shift of some sort or another. It was also the first year in which all the NFL's teams played the same number of games. Bert Bell became commissioner ten years later, and simple financial survival remained the

League's paramount issue until well into his term. As late as 1952, NFL franchises were still going bankrupt and having to be reorganized. The possibility of actually making considerable sums of money out of their teams became an issue of discussion among owners only shortly before Bell's death. Most still found such an eventuality hard to imagine.

Pete Rozelle's first step was to move the League offices to New York City. During Bert Bell's tenure, the League had been housed in the back room of a suburban bank in Bala Cynwyd, Pennsylvania. Relocating in Manhattan was, his friend Bill McPhail, then President of CBS Sports, noted, "a move into the Madison Avenue mainstream" of American culture, automatically insuring the League's product was at least half again as marketable and newsworthy as it had been a year earlier. In that same spirit, the young Pete Rozelle recognized football's potential future in television and threw himself into the medium. The television policy he inherited was feudal.

"When I came to CBS," McPhail remembered, "college football was the big package. The NFL was just a blue-collar thing, for guys with no college to root for. The first year we decided to go with it, the rights were all scattered around. Chicago had two teams, so it was always blacked out. New York was with the Dumont network. George Preston Marshall of the Washington Redskins broadcast his team on his group of stations throughout the South. Pete changed all that. He and I went around the League together during 1960 and 1961. He became his own TV man so quickly. He understood the industry almost immediately. He would go to affiliate meetings and got to know the big stations. It was hard at first. Local stations made more money then by showing old movies than they did showing professional football games. Pete got friendly with the affiliates and was willing to do things for CBS to help sell them on NFL broadcasts. It was a very smart attitude. At the beginning, people didn't even know about the NFL. Television lifted the League out of the boondocks."

Pete Rozelle knew a good thing when he saw it, and the advent of big-time sports television was the single most fortuitous coincidence of his commissionership. That the NFL might have a genuine national audience had only just been discovered when CBS broadcast the 1958 Baltimore Colts–New York Giants NFL championship game, which went into sudden death overtime and became the talk of the nation for several weeks afterward. At that time, only a little more than half the nation's households owned TV sets and virtually all broadcasts were in black and white. Within two years of leaving the Kenilworth Hotel's men's room, the "boy czar" had used the issue of television to remake the League after his own design. "Pete," Dan Rooney, president of his father's Pittsburgh Steelers, observed, "thought League from his first day on the job."

"League Think" was to soon become the central ideology of the Rozelle era. "One of the key things that a sports league needs," Rozelle would point out over and over in the years to come, "is unity of purpose. It needs harmony. . . . When you have unity and harmony and can move basically as one, you can have a successful sports league." For Rozelle, "the basic objective of the League rules is to reverse the process by which the weak clubs get weaker and the strong clubs get stronger. . . . The entire history of professional football supports the importance of these rules. Leagues do not come and go, and one sport does not gain on another because of the superiority of their stronger teams. Favorable results are a product of the degree to which each league can stabilize itself through its own competitive balance and leaguewide income potential.'' It was a simple premise: "When we stay together on something, we're normally successful and we grow. When we're going to splinter off, we're not as successful." The object of the approach was to transform what had been a feudal organization into a modern corporate combine, "a single entity, like Sears or McDonald's."

League Think was introduced into the NFL cosmos through the television policy Rozelle began to push in late 1960, after less than a year in office. What Rozelle proposed was that the League sell its collective TV rights as a single package, centralize its video marketing, and share its broadcast revenues equally among all franchises. If each franchise were left to shift for its financial and marketing self in the matter of television, he argued, the ensuing division into rich and poor would give a few big market franchises enormous advantages as television grew. This would cause a corresponding imbalance on the field, greatly lessening the marketability of the product created by the League as a whole. That kind of situation would only cost everybody money in the long run. When the League owners finally met in early 1961 and accepted the new commissioner's arguments, *Sports Illustrated* credited Rozelle's "forceful persuasion" and "surefootedness," not to mention patience.

The commissioner's argument was underlined by the policy of the recently organized rival American Football League which, in 1960, incorporated leaguewide pooling of television rights and revenues in its first broadcast contract with ABC. The arrangement was an idea Lamar Hunt, the AFL's founder, had borrowed from Branch Rickey, the legendary baseball entrepreneur. "In 1958," Hunt remembered, "Rickey was working on forming a new baseball league called the Continental League. His motive was to get yet another team in New York City. I attended one of the league's meetings and Rickey mentioned pooled sharing of revenues. It was part of the AFL package from the beginning. After a year, the NFL copied us." In addition to that AFL precedent, CBS was also pressuring the League to adopt Rozelle's proposal. Forced to watch NBC compete with it by paying for only two of the League's teams while it paid for nine and got the same thing, CBS, according to Rozelle, "reached the point where they said, 'We don't want to pay rights to nine teams when we can do what NBC is doing for less.' Some clubs were on the verge of losing all television income. They were about to be dropped."

Pete Rozelle himself credited the League's owners for the innovation. "We were able to do it," he remembered, "because the owners thought League. The Maras in New York, Dan Reeves in L.A., and George Halas in Chicago—the three dominant markets—agreed to share TV equally with the others, which was a major concession. They were wise enough to see the long term and they've been rewarded. All the franchises have seen their money increase from television as a consequence and the League as a whole has remained strong. All of the franchises have remained viable and have the means to compete with the rest of the League. That's what I think sports should be.''

Getting his employers to accept the arrangement was, however, only part of the problem Rozelle faced. Once the owners had agreed to share and share alike, the "boy czar" had to secure a limited antitrust exemption from Congress in order to put the agreement into practice. Apprehensive that such sharing might be considered an illegal monopoly under the Sherman Act, Rozelle had first had the League attorneys pursue a declaratory judgment from the federal courts to the contrary. When the Court ruled against the League, Pete Rozelle spent the summer of 1961 in Washington, D.C., lobbying for legislative help. On September 30, 1961, Congress responded to his pleas by passing a Sports Antitrust Broadcast Act, allowing sports leagues to pool and sell their TV rights. The bright, earnest, vanilla young commissioner had proved one of the better outside operators Capitol Hill had seen in a while.

His work began to pay off immediately. The first Leaguewide television contract Rozelle then negotiated was with CBS Sports for the years 1962 and 1963. Because it already had rights contracts with nine clubs that ran through 1963, CBS was the only network with which the commissioner bargained. It paid the League $4,650,000 a year, some $330,000 per franchise. League Think hit high gear in 1964 when the next contract came up for bids, this time from all three networks. "In a highly publicized bidding contest," Rozelle wrote in *The New York Times,* "sealed envelopes were opened, revealing the amounts offered by these growing and highly competitive electronic leaders. The first envelope opened in front of the network representatives was NBC's. It contained an offer of $10.75 million for each of the 1964 and 1965 seasons. This was followed by the ABC proposal, which was for $13.2 million a year. The final offer read was the winning bid of $14.1 million a year by CBS." Per franchise that was $1 million a year—ten times more than anyone in the League had made from TV under Bert Bell. The sum was considered so astounding that William Paley, CBS's founder and chairman, worried to Bill McPhail that the contract "appears irresponsible to stockholders, worse than Hollywood.''

That contract confirmed Pete Rozelle's claim to power within the League. With this kind of money to share, sharing was easy. In truth, the financial escalation, like League Think, had only just begun.

Ten years later, as the 1974 annual meeting convened in Bal Harbour, Pete Rozelle's League Think was manifest in virtually every economic aspect of the football business. In 1976, testifying before the House Select Subcommittee on Professional Sports, Rozelle would explain just how League Think worked to the profit of all:

The NFL operates with the highest degree of profit-sharing of any professional sport. . . . The NFL, for example, after direct game expenses, splits the gate receipts of each game on a sixty-forty basis—

sixty percent to the home team and forty percent to the visiting team. . . . Every NFL club is thus economically dependent on the successful home business operations of every other NFL club. NFL clubs also pool and divide equally all regular-season and post-season game television receipts. . . . Growth and stability . . . didn't just happen because of the T formation or the speed of wide receivers. It is a product of a carefully studied set of policies designed to give each NFL team the opportunity to compete equally.

Ed Garvey, executive director of the National Football League Players Association, the League's AFL-CIO affiliated player's union, would describe the arrangement as "socialism for management." Rozelle preferred "one for all and all for one." By whatever name, League Think was the lynchpin of the Rozelle era.

If they underestimated his vision, those who doubted the choice of Rozelle as commissioner in 1960 also underestimated the toughness he would employ to implement that vision. Rozelle, one owner later noted, "can be cold as a whore's heart, all the while flashing that PR smile." That, too, he proved early in his career. George Preston Marshall, then owner of the Washington Redskins, and George Halas of the Chicago Bears had, another owner noted, had "run the League" under Bert Bell. Within the first four years of his commissionership, Pete Rozelle butted heads with each of them and forced both into line behind him.

The "boy czar's" conflict with Marshall came during the campaign for a new TV policy. Early on, Rozelle took Bill McPhail along to Washington, D.C., to bring Marshall around. The three men met in Marshall's office. "Marshall was a real character," McPhail remembered. "He had his own individual network around the country and thought of himself as a TV visionary. He was resentful of Rozelle because of that. Pete would ask him a question and Marshall would scream, lecture, and shake his finger. Pete sat there and took it all, and when Marshall finished screaming, took up where he left off. 'Mr. Marshall,' Pete said, 'you still haven't answered my question.' My mind was blown." Rozelle and McPhail left Marshall's office with exactly the agreement Rozelle had set out to get from him.

Halas's turn came in 1964. The Chicago Bears owner was the only surviving League member who had actually been a participant in the 1920 meeting in the Canton Hupmobile dealership. He was not used to being messed with by anyone, especially not a commissioner half his age. During the 1964 season, Halas, still the Bears' head coach as well as owner, made bitter public complaints about the officiating after a game in San Francisco. Such public complaining about the officials was a violation of League rules and Rozelle moved quickly to bring the League's patriarch to heel, ordering the Chicago owner to report to the League's New York office for a disciplinary hearing. Halas responded that if the commissioner wanted to come to Chicago to see him, he would make time on his schedule. Rozelle said come to New York. Halas offered to fly into LaGuardia Airport and meet Rozelle there. The commissioner said come to my office in Manhattan. Halas appeared at Rozelle's office as ordered, was fined, and left with his mouth shut, just as the commissioner had insisted.

Perhaps most important, the new commissioner was proving that when he needed to, Pete Rozelle was very good at getting things done. His antitrust exemption campaign in 1961 had supplied compelling evidence of his strength. Any remaining doubts were quenched in the course of the merger with the AFL in 1966. That merger was the climactic act in forming the League's modern incarnation, and Rozelle's role was central. The merger had come about in response to peace feelers initiated by Rozelle and Tex Schramm. Once agreed to, the merger required Congressional permission. Pete Rozelle delivered it.

Rozelle's two most important 1966 legislative allies were Louisiana's Senator Russell Long and Representative Hale Boggs. Rozelle received their assistance, according to *The New York Times,* after he "dangled an NFL expansion team for New Orleans" in front of them. The specific legislation Rozelle sought was attached as a rider on a Johnson Administration antiinflation bill. An hour before the final House vote on the rider, Rozelle and Hale Boggs met in Washington to touch base a final time.

"Well, Pete," Boggs offered, "it looks great."

"Great, Hale," Rozelle answered, "that's great."

"Just for the record," Boggs continued, "I assume we can say the franchise for New Orleans is firm?"

"Well," Rozelle hedged, "it looks good, of course, Hale, but you know it still has to be approved by the owners. I can't make any promises on my own."

Boggs said nothing for a moment, just staring at Rozelle. "Well, Pete," he finally answered, "why don't you just go back and check with the owners. I'll hold things up here until you get back."

Now it was Rozelle's turn to go silent for a moment. "That's all right, Hale," he finally offered. "You can count on their approval."

Less than an hour later, the NFL had its merger exemption.

Three weeks later, the freshly merged football business added its first expansion franchise, the New Orleans Saints.

Pete Rozelle was not yet forty years old when New Orleans joined the League, but all references to the "boy czar" had ceased for good.

4

Thereafter, Rozelle's luck continued to hold. Among other things, the peace that now descended on the football business transformed the war that had preceded it into an asset. The rival AFL had been with NBC since 1964 and its competition with the NFL had also become a struggle between the nation's two major networks. The merger left the new NFL on both networks and took advantage of the burgeoning interest the twin rivalry had fostered for everyone's product. Now, with the AFL incorporated inside the League as its own conference, and matched against a representative of its old rivals in the Super Bowl, the package with which the NFL would reach its video apex was virtually complete. TV, entering its color era, had uncovered a seemingly unquenchable appetite for what the football business had to offer.

The proof was in the League's invasion of prime time programming in 1970, once the merger's transition period was completed. Rozelle had conceived of the idea in the mid-sixties and, since then, CBS had broadcast on a few Monday nights as an experiment. "The ratings were very good," Rozelle remembered, enough so that the NFL wanted to include weeknight games as part of its regular video package. The idea was offered to CBS first, but CBS declined to make a bid. The commissioner's friend, Bill McPhail, was still president of CBS Sports but McPhail's boss, Frank Stanton, had forbade him to offer for the NFL on Monday nights. At the time, CBS seemed to have Monday night prime time locked up with *I Love Lucy,* and McPhail was told that football would never make it during the week because housewives would not tolerate it. NBC was given the next opportunity, but the network was unwilling to drop *Laugh-In,* its top of the line Monday offering, and take the gamble with a whole new genre of programming.

As it was, Monday Night Football which went to ABC by default, was an integral factor in turning ABC into a true major network, the full equal of CBS and NBC. By the time the League met in Bal Harbour in February 1974, the ABC prime time NFL package dominated its time slot. *I Love Lucy* was long since off the air and *Laugh-In* had disappeared the year before. "What we were after," Rozelle remembered, "was not just the football fans, but the other people." That was, of course, exactly what the League got. The NFL had achieved the status of a national asset. And prophetic Pete Rozelle was the embodiment of the NFL. When the annual meeting convened in 1974, everything had been going his way so long that it seemed impossible that it might ever be otherwise.

"I was lucky," Rozelle said of his success, "and in the beginning, because of my youth, the owners were very kind to me. I replaced Bert Bell,

who had strong powers, only I don't call them powers. I call them responsibilities and obligations because a lot of it is no fun. I've seen it written
occasionally that I'm slick, but I don't think I'm slick. I believe in advance
preparation and knowing what you're going to be dealing with. In everything
I do, I work better by trying to work out of the limelight and behind the
scenes. My public relations background was helpful. All I had to do in the
public relations business was get along with people, which isn't difficult and
is fun. The tough part has been the difficult decisions you have to make. I
found out early on that you're not going to make everybody happy. There
were many times since I became commissioner that as many as ten or twelve
clubs might be upset with me. Fortunately, there's a turnover on it all the
time. You make up with someone and then someone else gets mad at you.
You have to be patient when they're uptight and angry about something.
You've got to stay cool and get as much information on the subject as you can
and try to convince them with logic. . . . It's mainly just patience, calm,
preparation, and, I guess, a degree of political persuasion—the ability to
persuade someone politically."

It was a professional recipe that, by 1974, had taken Pete Rozelle higher
in life than anyone back at Miami's Kenilworth Hotel had ever imagined he
might rise.

Pete Rozelle's personal journey had been a long one as well. His first
marriage had been, according to a Rozelle intimate, an early casualty of his
wife's reported alcoholism and the strains of his commissionership. While his
divorce was being worked out over the course of a long legal separation, he
shared a Manhattan apartment with Bill McPhail. McPhail remembered. With
the exception of his responsibilities to the League, Rozelle was unencumbered
during that period. "Once he and I were having lunch," McPhail recounted,
"and that same day I'd been invited to come down to Houston for some big
VIP event at the new Astrodome that evening. I said to Pete, 'Come along.
We'll leave right after lunch.' He said, 'I can't' and gave for a reason
something that he had to do. 'Come and I'll do it for you,' I said. He said
'O.K.' He went along with me right from lunch, without even so much as a
suitcase."

That footloose quality diminished after Rozelle's divorce came through
and, according to the legal decree, he assumed custody of his daughter, Anne
Marie. He was, all his friends agree, a "conscientious" father. Rozelle set up
a household of his own on exclusive Sutton Place and enrolled his daughter in
school. During football season, he often spent the weekends on the road but
still made a point of taking time to raise his only child. Rozelle was by then a
recognizable face to a lot of people he passed on the street. Though he
accepted it as a "price" of the NFL's success, he found his own celebrity
somewhat confining. A not atypical Rozelle encounter with his own fame
occurred not long after the merger, when he took his daughter to the circus
playing in Madison Square Garden. To escape recognition, the commissioner
wore dark glasses. His disguise lasted about a minute until "some kid"

walked by and said, "Hi, Pete." His daughter laughed. "Daddy," she pointed out, "you just look like Pete Rozelle in sunglasses."

To get away from it all, Rozelle usually left his daughter home and went fishing in the Caribbean. "The ideal location for me," the commissioner reckoned, "is some warm-weather spot where you could both fish and play tennis." Tennis was Rozelle's favorite form of exercise, and he played it whenever he could. "I'm a B minus player at best," he admitted. He sometimes went to the horse races with Bill McPhail but, for years, he refused to place any kind of bet at all. When he finally did, he insisted McPhail go to the window for him. "For Pete," one of his friends noted, "his reputation for honesty was everything; he cherished his credibility." His only vices were his cigarette habit and his predilection for relaxing after work with a couple of Rusty Nails—scotch mixed with Drambuie—on the rocks.

As a personality, Rozelle, a corporate executive friend observed, "was the kind of guy who was acquainted with an enormous number of people, but close to only a few. His friends were an eclectic group, distinguished by their differences. They were all doers. Pete is basically a simple, fine person who will do anything for a friend. . . . He's easy to be with. I can't think of anybody whose word I would bank on more than Pete's. He's a private guy. He doesn't unload his problems on other people. It's rare to see him let off steam, though I have seen him get miffed. . . . In football, he's not a fan's fan, but he understands the business. He's had the remarkable ability to be better known than the owners, but able to be with the owners and let them feel he's working for them."

"Despite his coolness on the outside," another corporate executive friend noted, "he's a lot more sensitive than people realize. He can laugh at himself and has no ego. He doesn't take himself seriously. Pete likes things to be easy. He hates conflict but isn't afraid of it. He sees the humor in a lot of things. He likes the release of humor. If he were in private business and accomplished what he had with the NFL, he'd be worth one hundred million dollars. He's taken that League through its formative years, its adolescence, and now into its maturity. He's made all those shifts of gears and that's unique."

As football's Rozelle era entered its golden years, the only noticeable deficiency in Pete Rozelle's life had been a certain personal loneliness. That vacuum, however, began to be filled at Super Bowl VII, staged in Los Angeles in early 1973. There, at one of the League's many parties leading up to the championship game, he was introduced to one Carrie Cooke, an attractive blond divorcee. Her previous husband had been Ralph Cooke, the son of Jack Kent Cooke, a partner in the Washington Redskins. When the party was over, Rozelle asked one of his friends who she was. He next saw her after the Super Bowl game had been played and he was having a drink with one of his close friends, another corporate executive, in the Polo Lounge of the Beverly Hills Hotel. Carrie Cooke saw him there and came by their table. "Mr. Rozelle," she challenged him, "I'll bet I can beat you at tennis." They were married within the year.

The new Mrs. Rozelle was a Canadian, educated in England, and nicknamed "queen bee" by her intimates. She was outgoing and social and she would soon become a factor in both her husband's life and the life of the League he shepherded. "She has more influence on him than anybody," one of Rozelle's friends explained. "She motivates him to social situations. Their relationship is one of the warmest I've ever observed. They are very close, virtually inseparable." In truth, once married, they would never spend a night apart. "They weren't wedded," another of their friends later observed, "they were welded."

The big change in Rozelle's life did not go unnoticed inside the League. Still a newlywed at Bal Harbour, the commissioner's contract would be altered before the meeting's close so that the League would pay for him to take Carrie along whenever he traveled on NFL business. "Before," one NFL executive observed, "Rozelle was just by himself at League get-togethers. When Carrie entered the picture, she organized a lot of tennis tournament kind of things to entertain the wives at League meetings. She was a little overbearing and more attractive than most NFL wives. She might be a bit of a phony, it's hard to tell." One of the men who would be among Rozelle's stiffest critics when things began coming apart would go further on the subject of the commissioner's marriage. "She comes on so strong that a lot of owners' wives eventually came to dislike her intensely. She's a great charmer and Rozelle was crazy about her. She wanted power through him. There was a distinct personality change when he married Carrie. Before, he was gentle and diplomatic. He was a shy guy and she gave him social confidence. She was a social climber in New York and Rozelle drew his strength from her. She changed him a lot."

Rozelle himself considered Carrie "the best thing that ever happened to me." He would quickly become an active stepfather to her three children by Ralph Cooke and join her on the charity circuit. Once the Bal Harbour meeting was over, they would renovate a five-bedroom home on three acres in Harrison, in Westchester County, New York, and move there with their combined brood. From Harrison, the commissioner would commute to work in a Ford station wagon provided gratis to the League by the Ford Motor Company and driven by a League chauffeur. The Rozelles would do most of their personal entertaining at home on the evenings they weren't in Manhattan for charity events. "The fishbowl is a tough place to live if you have any sensitivity," one of the Rozelles' friends observed. "Carrie's sensational. It's a great marriage."

The wedding took place in December 1973, some two months before the 1974 annual meeting. It was held in the New York apartment of Herb Siegel, chairman of the board and president of Chris-Craft Industries, Inc., the only outside corporation on whose board Rozelle served. It was a private affair to which just twenty couples were invited. The only League members there were Tex Schramm, Art Modell, and Dan Rooney. All were close Rozelle friends.

While still honeymooning, the Rozelles flew to Dallas to watch Schramm's Cowboys battle Max Winter's Minnesota Vikings for one of the two slots in

Super Bowl VIII. The commissioner, Carrie, and Marty Schramm, Tex's wife, sat together in one of the stadium owner's boxes. Tex, as was his habit, watched the game by himself from the press box. Thinking she would be gracious with one of Pete's best friends, Carrie arranged with Marty Schramm for the two couples to have dinner together after the game. When Rozelle was informed, he winced. One of the things she would have to learn as commissioner's wife, he pointed out, was never, under any circumstances, to ask an owner to socialize with them after a game. It was, he noted, "a bad mistake." She saw why when the Rozelles and the Schramms met at Tex's favorite Mexican restaurant after the Cowboys had lost, 27 to 10. Schramm was a figure of somewhat legendary temper, and he was fuming when they all sat down to the guacamole. He thought the officiating had cost the Cowboys the game and his comments were, Rozelle remembered, "dramatic, very emotional, and very personal." Carrie was stunned.

"If he's one of your good friends in the League," she gasped, "what are the rest like?"

5

The twenty-six men with whom Pete Rozelle's future rested were often referred to collectively as the most exclusive club in the United States. Gene Klein, owner of the San Diego Chargers, described them as twenty-six "successful hardworking individualists." Lamar Hunt, owner of the Kansas City Chiefs, called them twenty-six "princes." Leonard Tose, owner of the Philadelphia Eagles, preferred twenty-six "egomaniacs." Art Modell, owner of the Cleveland Browns, chose twenty-six "idiots, myself included." Thanks to Pete Rozelle, television, League Think, and America's Game, each of the twenty-six who gathered in Bal Harbour now owned a barony in modern American life.

Each of the twenty-six had his own way of explaining what brought him to the football business. "It's every sports fan's dream," Art Modell offered, "and I was a fan." Gene Klein pointed out: "It's different from any other business. It's a disease. You've got to be a little crazy to get into it. There's a great deal of ego involved." Leonard Tose agreed: "Every man wants to own a football team. All the people I know want to own one. It's an ego trip and anyone who says it isn't is not telling the truth." Carroll Rosenbloom, by now having switched ownerships from the Baltimore Colts to the Los Angeles Rams, summed it up succinctly: "When I was just rich, nobody knew me," Rosenbloom observed. "Now that I own the Rams, everybody knows me."

Along with their shared status, the twenty-six men convened in the

Americana Hotel in February 1974 shared a psychology. All of them, Gene Klein observed, were "obsessed with the need to win."

"My life and my existence are tied up with the NFL," Tex Schramm admitted. "I get demonstrative." Art Modell was the same. "You should see me when I watch the team play," he confessed, "I call my box the 'padded cell.' " Carroll Rosenbloom ranked near the top on the League's scale of obsessive behavior. One observer noted, "At Rams home games, Rosenbloom doesn't even let the demands of his bladder interrupt his concentration. . . . When nature can no longer be denied, usually toward the end of the first half, Rosenbloom picks up the nearest empty cup in his private box in the L.A. Coliseum and uses it as a urinal."

For their audience's consumption, most of the League's twenty-six characterized their obsession as a public trust. "Nobody really owns an NFL franchise," Gene Klein claimed. "The community owns it—it's a cultural asset of the city." Billy Sullivan, president of the New England Patriots, made the same representation: "Philosophically, I look on sports as a quasi-civic enterprise and with that comes the responsibility to be good public citizens." Art Modell frequently spoke of the franchises' "obligation to put back into the community what they take out." Rarely mentioned by any of them was the business behind it all. While the National Football League, their mutual association, was by charter, not for profit, its individual members were decidedly *for* profit. Despite a vague public image as rich men with time on their hands, for many of the League's more influential members the football business was their principal means of support. Independently wealthy or otherwise, all twenty-six were fond of talking in private about the bottom line.

During the year preceding the Bal Harbour meeting, that bottom line had averaged $6.2 million in gross receipts per franchise—"a gross about the size," one League attorney pointed out, "of a large supermarket." Sixty-one percent of that gross was generated by ticket sales and, under the expiring television contracts, twenty-seven percent from broadcast rights. According to a report by Arthur Andersen & Company, the League's accountants, the average franchise's total operating expenses, including players, front office personnel, travel, and League assessments, totaled $5.3 million. That left more than $900,000 in average operating profit. Collectively, the League's $163 million gross put it $250 million short of ranking in the *Fortune* 500. Any given franchise's tangible assets comprised a very short list, usually including little more than an NFL membership certificate, a lease on a stadium in which to stage games, and contracts with some fifty or so players to perform in the games staged. That relative intangibility had not, however, suppressed those assets' value. A franchise worth $1 million when Pete Rozelle assumed the commissionership was worth in the neighborhood of $15 million when the 1974 annual meeting convened. As a business, Al Davis of the Oakland Raiders observed, any of those franchises was "a very simple operation to run." Edward Bennett Williams of the Washington Redskins said much the same thing. According to him, "any bright, reasonable person could assimilate" everything needed to run such an enterprise "in two days." During the year preceding Bal Harbour, twenty-four League members had made money and two reported losses.

While close to ninety-five percent of the NFL's gross receipts were subject to League Think sharing formulas, profits and losses were not. Each of the League's franchises was a separate legal entity, keeping its own books, and making its own decisions about how its money was spent. The forms of ownership were varied, ranging from sole proprietorships to limited partnerships to private stock syndicates and, in 1974, even included one franchise owned by a community foundation and another whose stock was publicly traded on a regional exchange. Whatever its form, each franchise was required to designate one individual to act on its behalf in the conduct of League business. When those twenty-six "owners" met, as at Bal Harbour, their constitution granted them two modes in which to do so. The first was in general session, when each owner was allowed to be accompanied by two of his front office employees. The second was in executive session, when the owners and the commissioner met alone.

While Rozelle's League Think had centralized much of the NFL's power in the body of the League and, hence, the commissioner's office, there remained large pockets of business activity which were each owner's alone to control. By far the most significant of those in the disintegration to come was each franchise's stadium arrangements. All relations between owners and their landlords was franchise business, in which Rozelle had no voice and the owners had no League obligations other than to file a copy of their lease with the League office. Those leases, unfortunately for Rozelle, remained the nuts and bolts of the football business. Stadiums were still the League's principal financial underpinning. Even with the raises in the new contract, television would account for only some thirty-four percent of the League's gross revenues. "If you can't fill the stadium," Tex Schramm explained, "none of the rest of it works." In the Rozelle era, of course, filling stadiums had already become the NFL's forte. "Of all professional sports," a Brookings Institution study observed, "football is the one with the most obvious excess demand for its product. . . . Since most stadiums, particularly the smaller ones, are sold out, the size of stadium capacity comes very close to predicting the size of attendance."

That land office ticket sale business was split according to League Think's universal sixty-forty ratio, but there were nonetheless some significant variables. One was the lease. According to League rules, the home team was allowed to take a fifteen percent deduction off the top for rent and game expenses. While the rent allowance was uniform and Leaguewide, the leases governing the rents were not. The rents actually paid ran from as low as three percent of the gross to as high as fifteen percent. The difference between actual rent and the League's rent allowance was considered found money, the home team's to keep. Stadium leases were generally longterm but of varying duration, so only a few leases were ever up for negotiation at any given time. Over the next decade, many franchises would be involved in their first lease negotiations since the emergence of the NFL's product as America's Game. When they met in Bal Harbour, the leverage thus afforded each of football's barons over his respective landlord was large and growing steadily.

The most obvious evidence of that leverage in 1974 was an escalating scale of commitments by stadium authorities, usually public entities of one variety or another, to finance and construct new, "modern" stadiums to house what the localities involved still thought of as "our" teams. The momentum of this construction boom was such that the NFL, as part of the AFL merger agreement, had made a home stadium with a minimum seating capacity of fifty-five thousand a condition of membership. By the time the Rozelle era was well on its way to falling apart, twenty-three of the twenty-six franchises who had met in Bal Harbour would be playing in new or remodeled stadiums. *Fortune* called it all "Promoters v. Taxpayers in the superstadium game."

Houston had pioneered the Superstadium Game in 1962 with the construction of the $43 million Astrodome, the nation's first domed stadium and home field to Bud Adams's Houston Oilers. The construction boom took off in the early 1970s. In Michigan, $126 million was committed to build the Silverdome in suburban Pontiac. It would be the home field of William Clay Ford's Detroit Lions. New Jersey had committed $300 million to erect a sports complex on the marshlands across from Manhattan. At its hub was a seventy-five-thousand-seat stadium for Wellington Mara's New York Giants. In Upstate New York, Erie County went the no-frills route and spent $21 million erecting an outdoor stadium for Ralph Wilson's Buffalo Bills. The state of the art superstadium circa 1974 was New Orleans's Superdome, still under construction, but destined to be the home field for John Mecom's New Orleans Saints. The largest fully enclosed stadium in the world, it would be 680 feet in diameter, with a 273-foot-high ceiling and seats for nearly seventy-five thousand football fans. Originally scheduled to cost $35 million, the Superdome would eventually cost almost five times that much. Faced with this monumental overrun, a Louisiana official responded by reassuring the citizenry that "we are not going to let a couple of million dollars stop us."

Still relatively fresh to the big time in 1974, Pete Rozelle's twenty-six employers had yet to take such inflated treatment for granted or realize just how far their leverage might carry them. Most were still just marveling at how the rising tide of superstadia was transforming the watching of the game. What was once played in the mud or trampled sod was now staged on artificial carpets that remained green, clean, and intact whatever season of the year. Where ticket purchasers had once huddled along splintered wood benches, more and more watched from the snug comfort of molded plastic seats as removed from the weather as their own living rooms. The Superdome had even incorporated four giant television screens suspended from its ceiling in order to give the crowd access to the same instant replays, commentary, and advertisements as those watching at home.

With the advent of the superstadium game came the "luxury box." Completely enclosed, these boxes usually held anywhere from eight to twenty people and were generally located along the stadium's best sight lines. The occupants of luxury boxes watched the game below through giant Plexiglas windows, entered their boxes on private elevators, and had their own private bars, kitchenettes, and rest rooms. While only a minority of franchises had such accommodations in 1974, all the League's owners wanted them. Their effect was to add a new, privileged upper echelon to the crowds swarming into the stadiums on Sundays. To join that upper echelon cost not only the price of a ticket to enter the stadium but also a steep fee for proprietorship of the box itself. Each stadium with boxes had its own way of extracting that fee, ranging from longterm leases to outright sales. The fees themselves usually ran from $15,000 to $30,000 per box per year. Each stadium had its own way of handling that income. Some reserved it for themselves, some gave part or all of it to its principal tenant, usually an NFL team. From the standpoint of the football business, the most significant fact about luxury-box income was that it was not covered by any of League Think's sharing formulas. The result was that any owner who could get luxury-box income could keep it all, gaining a financial advantage over his fellows and introducing yet another chink in League Think's armor.

That none of the changes in the football business seemed a significant threat to League Think when the NFL gathered at Bal Harbour was an oversight. In a situation that included the frenzy of the Superstadium Game, a galloping seller's market in football franchises, and twenty-six personalities bound to each other but bent on gaining the individual upper hand, stadiums would easily prove the most volatile element in the League's coming destabilization. Sooner or later, the stadium issue would embroil each of the football barons in a local war in which he was free to call his own shots. The stadium issue would also provide the staging ground for the decisive assault on Pete Rozelle's commissionership when that time finally came.

6

While the stability that reigned in the NFL was identified with Pete Rozelle, it was by no means a single-handed accomplishment. Perhaps the most helpful figure to the commissioner in effecting his agenda was his old friend Tex Schramm, president of the Dallas Cowboys. A number of the twenty-six men gathered in Bal Harbour jokingly referred to Schramm as "Mr. Vice-Commissioner." It was an accurate reflection of Schramm's standing among his peers.

One irony of Schramm's stature was that, technically, he was not an owner at all. Like his friend Pete Rozelle, he was an employee. The Dallas Cowboys were actually owned by a partnership dominated by Clint Murchi-

son Jr., heir to a large piece of the legendary Texas oil fortune amassed by his
father and namesake. In 1982, *Forbes* would estimate the worth of Clint Jr.
and his brother, John, at $260 million. Included in that fortune was ninety
percent of the Cowboys, the remainder being spread between several other
partners. In the Murchison family's internal division of responsibilities, Clint
handled the football and few even knew that John owned an equal share.

Nevertheless, it was Tex Schramm's team. He had run the entire operation since its founding in 1960. His boss, Clint Murchison, was a factor in the
League by reputation only. According to Lamar Hunt, the League's other
legendary Texas oil millionaire, Clint attended only two meetings during his
entire ownership. He was equally distant from the franchise itself and, unlike
most owners, never meddled. "I'd rather let the people who know what they
are doing run things," he observed. "Besides, I'm shy." As Schramm
explained, "The approach he took from the outset was to try to find the
people he felt were the experts in their field and allow them the freedom to
use their expertise and initiative."

It was the kind of relationship Rozelle held up to the public and the rest
of the League as the model NFL ownership. "I suppose ideally you would
have somebody [as an owner]," he said, "who had plenty of money outside
of football and left the running of the team to a competent football man."

Tex Schramm's acknowledged expertise as a "football man" was the
basis of his NFL stature as well as his control of the Cowboys. "I'm very
outspoken, and I have very strong convictions. I have a lot of confidence in
my judgment and make my thoughts known," Schramm declared.

"He's the best," one of the other owners acknowledged. "He's the most
knowledgeable football man in the League. . . . He's a no bullshit kind of
guy."

Another reason for Schramm's influence inside the NFL was, of course,
that he and Pete Rozelle went back a long way.

Texas Schramm Jr. was born in 1920 in Los Angeles. His father, Texas
Sr., had been born and raised in San Antonio, before migrating to southern
California to begin a successful career as a stockbroker. Texas Jr. grew up in
San Gabriel, California, and attended high school in nearby Alhambra, then
enrolled as a journalism student at the University of Texas shortly before the
outbreak of World War II. There he played on the freshman football team and
worked on the student newspaper. After the Japanese attack on Pearl Harbor,
Schramm joined the Army Air Corps and was discharged at war's end with
the rank of captain. Returning to the University of Texas, he finished his
studies and worked as sports editor of the *Austin Statesman* for two years
before abandoning journalism for good. His first job in the football business
developed in 1947 when he learned through his father back in Los Angeles
that the Rams managing owner, Dan Reeves, was looking for a new publicity
director. When he was promoted to general manager in the early 1950s,
Schramm's path crossed Pete Rozelle's for the first time. It would prove a
long association.

Tex Schramm stayed with the Rams for ten years until driven out by the disorder inside the franchise. When the opportunity to go to New York and join CBS Sports arose, he jumped at the chance and was eventually replaced at the Rams by his friend and former employee, Pete Rozelle. At CBS Schramm worked under Bill McPhail as assistant director of sports, obtaining events to televise. Among the contracts he handled were those with the network's assortment of NFL teams.

Tex Schramm's path finally merged with Rozelle's at the 1960 League meeting in Miami at which Rozelle was chosen commissioner. Aside from filling the commissionership, the hottest issue that winter was the prospect of expanding the League by two more franchises, one to be located in Dallas. Schramm had heard about the formation of a Dallas franchise in 1959, and about the same time was recommended to its prospective owner, Clint Murchison, by George Halas.

Murchison hired Schramm to fill the general managership of a franchise that did not yet exist. Schramm notified his employers at CBS and they let him resign contingent upon Murchison actually securing the franchise he sought. Should Murchison fail, Schramm's job at the network would still be waiting for him.

The primary roadblock to NFL expansion into Dallas in 1960 was George Preston Marshall, then owner of the Washington Redskins and one of the most powerful figures in the League. Marshall's television holdings were largely in stations around the South, and he thought of the entire area as Redskins home turf. He had steadfastly opposed any invasion of the region by another purveyor of professional football. In addition, there was no great amount of love lost between Marshall and the rich young Texan, Murchison. During the 1950s, Murchison had sought unsuccessfully to buy Marshall's franchise with the idea of selling it should the NFL expand into his hometown, but the deal fell apart because Marshall insisted on being kept on by the new ownership in a management position and Murchison did not want him. At the meeting in the Kenilworth Hotel, Marshall led the fight to keep the NFL from expanding into Dallas.

Then Murchison played his hole card.

Marshall loved band music at football games and in particular loved his team's fight song, "Hail to the Redskins." He had, however, fired the song's composer from his post as leader of the franchise's in-house band, and in a fit of pique the bandleader had sold the rights to the tune to a Murchison crony. When Murchison threatened to deny the Redskins the use of their theme song, Marshall relented and the Dallas Cowboys were born on January 28, 1960. Not counting the price of the song, the franchise cost Murchison $600,000.

Tex Schramm was immediately announced as the new franchise's general manager, a job he had already held for more than two months. He immediately set about building his reputation as a "football man." Though starting an NFL team from scratch was no small task, the Cowboys would soon be identified by Rozelle as "the most successful modern expansion team in the NFL." At the fore in that rise was Schramm, "one of the game's great innovators."

In 1962, for example, an IBM subsidiary, Services Bureau Corp., approached the fledgling Cowboys franchise seeking to sell it computers to handle its accounting problems. Instead, Schramm challenged them to develop a system to handle the task of choosing which football players to hire. Within a few years, the Cowboys' computerized system was acknowledged as the premier scouting apparatus in the League and the Cowboys were well on their way to being one of the foremost franchises.

In 1964, Murchison expanded Schramm's title to president and gave him the option to buy twenty percent of the team at its 1960 price. In the early 1970s, Schramm exercised that right and then quickly retired his stock for what the *Dallas Morning News* described as "a huge profit."

Though acknowledged as "a driving force" inside the League from the time he entered, Schramm confirmed his central role in the Rozelle era in 1966, when the war with the American Football League had been going on for six long and expensive years. Several different informal contacts between owners of the two leagues had already gone nowhere. The contact that finally led to peace took place between Tex Schramm and Lamar Hunt at Dallas's Love Field airport on April 6, 1966. Hunt was between planes, traveling from Kansas City to Houston. The two men knew each other from the early days in Dallas, when Hunt's AFL franchise was located there and called the Texans. According to the *Kansas City Times,* they had negotiated then about Hunt's eventual move to Kansas City, undertaken after the Cowboys made "financial arrangements" to help pay for the shift.

At the time of their April 6, 1966, meeting, Hunt was headed to the AFL gathering in Houston, where Joe Foss would resign as AFL commissioner and Al Davis would be appointed to fill the post. Hunt and Schramm's first conversation about merger took place inside a parked car in the shadow of the airport's statue of the Texas ranger. "At this point," Schramm remembered, "we did not want to be seen together." Schramm had arranged for the meeting as part of a process he had begun in concert with Rozelle a little more than a month earlier. "Pete and I," he explained, "felt that if the NFL could come up with an acceptable plan that was good for the sport, it could be presented to the American Football League. If they liked it, fine. If not, we could settle down to an all-out war."

In their first brief conversation, Hunt was noncommittal about the plan presented to him, but agreed with Schramm's proposal that the two act as the leagues' intermediaries. A month later, the two met again at Hunt's home near the Cowboys' offices in Dallas, and then again the following week. At that point, Hunt was finally convinced that "any problems could be solved." That conclusion was followed by another month of frantic negotiations between Schramm, Rozelle, and the rest of the NFL owners on the one hand, and Hunt and the rest of the AFL on the other, broken by further meetings between Schramm, Hunt, and Rozelle. All of it was cloaked in secrecy so intense that at one point, Schramm and Rozelle registered under an assumed name in a Washington, D.C., hotel in order to meet with Hunt and then forgot to tell Hunt what name they had registered under. As a consequence, the AFL representative spent two hours in the lobby trying to locate them.

None of it was enough to derail the process. On June 8, 1966, the agreement for merging the two leagues into one was announced to the public. Its three key provisions were the payment of $18 million in indemnities by the AFL, a four-year interim period before commencing business as a single organization, and the retention of Rozelle as the merged NFL's commissioner. In all accounts of the process, Tex Schramm was described as its "architect."

From there, the step to "Mr. Vice-Commissioner" was a short one.

7

At the heart of Tex Schramm's first-among-equals stature inside the League was the success of the franchise he built. The twenty-six franchises gathered at Bal Harbour were collectively America's Game, but among them, Tex Schramm's Cowboys alone were recognized as "America's team"—the most visible and prestigious of the League's franchises. As a history of the franchise noted, "the Cowboys have more avid fans coast to coast than any other athletic team in our history." Among the thousands of T-shirts, mugs, pennants, and ashtrays embossed with team decals licensed by NFL Properties, close to half the annual sales were Dallas Cowboy items. When Schramm arrived at Bal Harbour, their record since merger with the AFL was 83 wins, 27 losses, and 2 ties.

Especially pleasing to Pete Rozelle was the fact the success of his friend Schramm and the Dallas franchise was predicated upon stability. Starting from the ground up in 1960, Schramm had installed a system and stuck with it. The front office he assembled was recognized as "the ablest in the League" and every person in it, from owner to head coach, had remained unchanged throughout the franchise's fourteen-year history.

Schramm's goal at the Cowboys had been to build a model modern football organization and, by all accounts, he had been enormously successful. "It kills him if some other organization does something first," one NFL general manager noted. In addition to pioneering the uses of computers in its talent search, Schramm's Cowboys were also the first to make all its prospective employees take what a later authorized history of the franchise called "a battery of tests measuring intelligence as well as personality and character traits." Schramm was looking for people who, in his words, are "really hurt when they lose or are embarrassed publicly." To find such people, he needed as much information as possible and the Cowboys were the first to put a premium on collecting it. "Nothing escapes us," one Cowboy assistant coach bragged. To handle that information, Schramm's Cowboys kept refining their computers. By 1974, Schramm's approach had made the Dallas franchise into what *Esquire* called "the playing field apotheosis of America's twentieth-century corporate technology."

Not surprisingly for an organization devoted to being on the business's cutting edge, the Cowboys were among the first League members to win big in the superstadium game. Real estate was a subject about which Clint Murchison did not claim ignorance, and securing a new stadium for his team's home games would be his principal personal contribution to the franchise's ongoing operation. He began his quest around the same time Schramm was concentrating on making peace with the AFL. Murchison wanted Dallas to build a downtown sports entertainment complex that would include a stadium and a center for the performing arts. The issue came to a head in spring 1966, when the city government refused the stadium proposal and instead committed themselves to refurbishing the existing Cotton Bowl. Murchison called it throwing good money after bad and decided to pursue his other option.

That other option was land suitable for a stadium site Murchison had already purchased in the suburb of Irving, Texas, immediately west of Dallas's city limits. Murchison was an NFL pioneer in his choice of locations. Though he was the first to discover the leverage afforded by playing the suburbs off against the cities they surrounded, he would by no means be the last. In early 1967, Murchison met with a dozen Irving politicians at a secret gathering in the Dallas Gun Club and got what he wanted. Upon completion, the structure Irving committed itself to build would be christened Texas Stadium. "As I see the situation," Clint later explained, "Irving would like to build the stadium and the city of Dallas wouldn't." Certainly Irving had proved a lot easier to deal with. "Clint Murchison and his high-priced Dallas lawyers are just too much for those country boys," one observer noted. "They get pretty much what they ask for."

The deal Murchison cut in Irving influenced the standards of reward and control in the superstadium game for years to come. Under its terms, Irving financed the $25 million project through the sale of thirty-five-year bonds, but management of the stadium during the life of those bonds was the sole responsibility of Texas Stadium Corporation, a wholly owned subsidiary of the Dallas Cowboys. The contract for constructing the stadium went to J. W. Bateson Co., Inc., owned by the Murchison brothers. The contract to sell concessions at the stadium went to Cebe Corporation, a subsidiary of the Dallas Cowboys. The exclusive right to sell liquor at the stadium went to the Cowboys' Stadium Club. The insurance contract was given to Kenneth Murchison Co., the insurance agency that had belonged to Clint's late uncle and of which Clint owned eight percent. As one critic of the deal put it, "if you mailed a letter to the mayor of Murchison, Texas, it would be delivered to the City Hall in Irving."

Though the rest of the NFL admired Murchison's favorable terms, the most acclaimed aspect of the Cowboys' new stadium was its accoutrements.

While Houston's Astrodome had built the first luxury boxes, it was Texas Stadium that made them all the rage. In total, Murchison built 158, dubbed "the circle suites." The Cowboys advertised their boxes as "your personalized penthouse at Texas Stadium . . . the ultimate in spectator luxury and comfort . . . similar to a second residence, like a lake home, or a ranch." At the time Texas Stadium was being built, Murchison conceived of selling "second residences" to the football upper crust as a way to secure the structure's financing rather than as a generator of longterm income. To acquire a circle suite required the purchase of $50,000 in stadium bonds, the purchase of twelve season tickets at $1300 per ticket per season for thirty-two of the next thirty-five years, and the purchase of twelve memberships in the $300-per-season Stadium Club, where drinks sold for $1.25 apiece. Despite the price tag, the luxury boxes sold like hotcakes, half of them purchased by Dallas-based corporations for expense account entertaining.

In exchange for the minimum expenditure of $663,400 over thirty-two years, the circle suite owner received a sixteen foot by sixteen foot bare concrete shell. Furnishing of the circle suite was at the owner's expense. As the most substantial of the Cowboys legions set about decorating their shells, they also established the public's image of the luxury box for years to come. Decor varied with the individual taste of the owners, but perhaps the top of the line when Texas Stadium opened was a suite described for readers of the *Dallas Morning News,* as featuring "blue velvet Louis XIV couches, gilt armchairs, blue velvet draperies, miniature bar with leather armrests, tufted velvet love seats, crystal chandelier hanging from a vaulted gold ceiling, and hand-painted French panels concealing closed-circuit television sets for instant replays."

Within ten years of Texas Stadium's opening, circle suites without tickets or bonds would be moving on the resale market for as much as $600,000 apiece—$2,343 a square foot.

Murchison applied his financing plan to the rest of the seats in the house as well. Seating between the thirty yard lines required the purchase of one one-thousand-dollar bond per seat and seats outside the thirties and into the end zones went for a $250 bond. The scheme soon led to impassioned newspaper editorials "on behalf of the tens of thousands of fans who dearly loved their Cowboys and now possibly can't afford them." Murchison was unmoved. "What could be fairer than having the stadium financed by the fans who use it?" he asked. The explanation failed to stem the criticism, but Murchison did not have to deal with it. That was Tex Schramm's job and Schramm did it well enough that all the bonds were sold on schedule. Schramm also handled the task of raising the price of season tickets after the bonds had been sold.

Though he did a credible job of insulating Murchison from the heat over Texas Stadium, Tex Schramm was not nearly as emotionally suited to the demands of public relations as his friend Pete Rozelle. "He's so strong," one NFL executive observed, "he makes enemies." Most of those enemies were made by his temper. "Tex burns fast," a friend explained. The description was an understatement to which Schramm added his own: "I love talking and arguing," he admitted, "but I actually don't call what goes on arguments. I call them heated discussions. If a person doesn't feel strongly enough about something to get heated, then it's just really not worth getting into."

Over six feet tall, Schramm had a thick neck, thinning hair, heavy German cheeks, and very cold eyes. He had a tendency to flush when angry. Faced with one of Schramm's bellowing rages, a secretary in the Cowboys offices became so frightened she left work immediately. Schramm was his most notoriously bellicose when dealing with players. In 1970, the year before Texas Stadium opened, he served on the NFL's committee charged with negotiating a new contract with the National Football Players Association. In their most intense phase, the talks lasted through an entire night, hashing over the issue of travel expenses for players who were forced to relocate when traded between teams. At five A.M. one of the player representatives expressed his frustration.

"I don't give a damn about all that crap," the player snapped. "What I want to know plainly is how much money I'll get if I'm traded from say, Green Bay to the Dallas Cowboys."

At this, Schramm exploded out of his seat, almost flying across the table. "That's one goddamn thing you don't have to worry about," the president of the Dallas Cowboys screamed.

Schramm's temper, a friend explained, "derives from him being such a competitor and so stubborn." Not to mention obsessed. In truth, Tex Schramm was a man for whom football was just about everything and who was constantly at the mercy of his obsession.

"I don't think Tex is ever really away from football," Marty, his wife, observed. At the time of Bal Harbour, the Schramms had been married thirty-three years. "I mean it. Last year we went to Acapulco for a week and then came back [to Dallas] to spend more of our vacation. Tex just had to make himself relax, sit around the pool in the sun. But after the fourth day he told me, 'Don't ever let me retire.' The idleness was driving him up a wall."

Schramm's only releases from his obsession were gardening and deep sea fishing. In his neat and orderly vegetable patch in one corner of the yard behind his sprawling brick home off Dallas's Northeast Highway, each row of plants was labeled and obviously well tended. His attachment to working in his garden was, however, strictly therapeutic. "I have to do something when I'm away from football," he explained, "or I'd go crazy."

Tex Schramm's taste for salt water angling was a hobby he shared with Pete Rozelle, though the number of their mutual Caribbean excursions would diminish after Rozelle's marriage to Carrie. Their trips to the islands to relax were a way for Schramm to "get away from football" without ever leaving it. Even on vacation in the tropics Tex Schramm was Tex Schramm. Once, he and one of his fishing parties were walking along the shore in the Bahamas when someone spotted a shark cruising in the shallows nearby. Incensed by its lurking, Schramm immediately grabbed a stick, waded into the water, and beat the maneater over the head.

While Tex Schramm's relentless drive no doubt took its toll on the rest of his life, it made him an effective whip for Rozelle's NFL agenda. Schramm said what he meant, rarely backed off, and the rest of the League listened to Schramm. Where football was concerned, he was thought to be right a lot more often than not, largely because most believed he thought about little else. Rozelle counted on Schramm to use his credibility to further League Think, and Schramm did, even when Rozelle's agenda was in such bad shape that Schramm would make no difference. By then, even the Cowboys' underpinnings would wobble a bit.

8

If an election had been held among the twenty-six men at Bal Harbour for the title of second most powerful man in the NFL, Tex Schramm's only competition would have been Art Modell, majority owner of the Cleveland Browns.

Modell had little of Schramm's stature as a "football man," even though his team was 71-34-3 since the merger. Rather, Modell's influence was a function of style and personality. While Schramm personified a vision of football as an objective discipline which he had mastered, Modell's presence in the League was rooted in his attitude toward the football business as an exclusive club to which he was thrilled to belong. Modell liked being on the inside of things and rubbing shoulders with other insiders. "Art Modell is part of a power clique within the NFL," Al Davis pointed out. "He runs in the pack. He has to because he can't operate if he didn't run in the pack." Belonging was a big thing for Modell, and League Think was simply an extension of what any club ought to be. "He enjoys it," one NFL executive observed, "he enjoys having friends. He doesn't have disputes with other people. He's good at League meetings because he has a great sense of humor. Art goes around, drops one-liners, and they laugh."

For those owners uncomfortable with Rozelle's starched-collar henpecking about the League's image, Art Modell was enough of a "sportsman" in the nineteenth-century barroom sense to put them at ease. Five feet eight inches tall, dark-haired, hawk-nosed, and built like a stump, Modell was, one sportswriter noted, "a hustler kind of guy," easy to have a drink with, jovial, but always playing the angles. At the same time, Modell, in Rozelle's words, "has always been for whatever was in the best interests of the League as a whole." Having friends on both sides of most issues, Modell took the camaraderie approach to League Think. His friendships also let him bridge divisions in a way Schramm's stubborn advocacy and Rozelle's moralizing could not. Like Schramm, Modell was an unflagging booster of Rozelle's commissionership. The two had been close friends ever since Modell bought into the NFL in 1961. During Rozelle's bachelor years, Modell, also then a bachelor, was a regular visitor to New York and the two did what Modell recalled as "a lot of crazy stuff" together.

Ironically, Art Modell was, from the beginning, about as far as he could be from the commissioner's abstract concept of the ideal owner. He had come to the football business with relatively nothing in the bank and, by 1974, football, his principal source of income, had made him rich. Far from retreating offstage like Clint Murchison, Modell assumed the foreground in his franchise whenever possible. He enjoyed the attention and liked what it did for him. Again, it was a question of belonging. Modell was in many ways a classic case study in the kind of civic elevation an NFL ownership could provide. The same age as Rozelle, he had not started life anywhere near the top of the ladder. "I went to the school of hard knocks," Modell said of himself. "I worked my ass off for what I got today. I didn't have anything handed to me."

Indeed, Modell's childhood had been a searing experience, still never far from his thoughts. His father, George, "had a lot of money" when Modell was born, but the wealth all disappeared in the Depression four years later. As a consequence, Modell grew up "poor" in Brooklyn's Borough Park area, while his father "worked his butt off trying to keep the family going." His father was, as Art Modell remembered him, "a great man. He had a great sense of humor. He was handsome, a wonderful, wonderful father. I loved him dearly." Their relationship was terminated abruptly when Art Modell was fourteen years old. By then, George Modell was a traveling wine salesman. While on a trip to Austin, Texas, in the spring of 1939, George Modell was found unconscious and partially clothed in a local hotel and died eight hours later. A woman with whom he had reportedly spent the night had disappeared and could not be found. "It was," as Modell remembered it, "a terrible blow." The circumstances also mingled embarrassment and scandal with grief. To console his mother, Modell promised her then that he would never leave her to marry. In the meantime, George Modell's death left his family "devastated financially."

Art Modell managed to stay in high school until age fifteen and then dropped out to take work as an electrician's helper in Bethlehem Steel's New York shipyards for wages of less than a dollar an hour. He supplemented his income shooting billiards in Pacey's Pool Hall in Brooklyn. During World War II, Modell served in the physical education wing of the Army Air Corps, playing catcher for the Lowry Field baseball team in Denver, Colorado. He was discharged from March Field in Riverside, California, in 1945, an ex-enlisted man with few prospects but enormous dreams. Art Modell's dreams started coming true when he returned to New York and decided to cast his lot with the then newborn television industry. After attending the American Theatre Wing on the G.I. Bill, Modell and another student started a production company. Their first break was a contract with ABC in 1948 that led to *Market Melodies,* New York's first daytime television show. "That started the postwar career of Art Modell," Art Modell later recalled.

In 1948, Modell, twenty-three years old, began "knocking on doors at Grand Union with a novel marketing idea." The idea was to introduce housewives to daytime television by erecting television sets in the supermarkets and broadcasting twelve hours a day of *Market Melodies*. Modell would supply the television sets and the programming, ABC would broadcast, the sales of advertising would generate revenues to pay for it all, and Grand Union would sell more groceries as a result. Grand Union went for it and *Market Melodies* went on the air in 1949. It was, as one reviewer described it, "twelve hours of solid commercial, uninterrupted by entertainment." ABC nonetheless kept it on the air throughout the 1950s.

The only part of Modell's daytime television scheme that didn't pan out was Grand Union's. The delicate televisions of the era lost their tuning whenever a subway train passed the supermarket and had to be constantly readjusted by store personnel. Within four months, Grand Union had removed most of them. The failure did not, however, sour Grand Union on Modell. "He was our account executive for whomever he was with," Grand Union's advertising director remembered. "When he got out of television and into advertising, we stayed with him. Art was a poor boy from Brooklyn and he was going to make it. He was determined to know the right people. This guy was a wonder. He always got along. He always had an angle."

Modell got out of television and into advertising in 1954 and stayed there for seven years. His opportunity to move on to the football business came in September 1960. It was a lucky break and Modell made the most of it.

At the time, the Browns were about to be sold but the deal fell apart three days before the contract of sale was to be signed. Curly Morrison, the former Browns fullback who had been designated by the syndicate which then owned the franchise to find a buyer, called New York theatrical agent Vinnie Andrews looking for someone to pick up the deal where it had fallen. "I know a guy who's a client of mine," Andrews told him, "and a friend. He's a real football nut, Art Modell." Andrews then called Modell and Modell jumped at the opportunity. "I wanted it," he later remembered with great understatement. Within the day, he had committed himself to putting together an offer and immediately began serious negotiations with the sellers. They were asking $4 million for the team, but settled with Modell at $3,925,000, then a record for NFL franchises.

Setting the price was a lot easier than paying it. No bank would loan Modell more than $250,000 on his personal assets and then only because of the intercession of what the *Akron Beacon Journal* described as "the friends Modell had made at Grand Union." That still left him $3,675,000 short. As part of the previous deal, Cleveland's Union Commerce Bank was committed to loaning an additional $2,500,000 against the franchise itself and that loan was still available. Modell's plan for the rest had two stages. The first was to find another major partner to provide the additional $250,000 necessary to make a nonrefundable $500,000 deposit required by early January 1961 in order to seal the deal. The remaining $900,000 Modell figured to raise in a second stage by selling minority partnerships once the first down payment had been made. "I was confident I could sell it to the right people," he later explained.

Modell's original candidate for the other major partner was Vinnie Andrews, the agent who had turned him on to the deal. Andrews agreed and then, the night before a party Modell was throwing to celebrate his ascension to the NFL, backed out. At that point, according to Curly Morrison, "Art turned white." Modell immediately called his attorney, Jack Wells, from a pay phone. Within twenty-four hours, Wells had found brewery heir Donald Schaeffer to take Andrews's place, and Modell was again free to celebrate.

On January 25, 1961, Modell and Schaeffer bought the Cleveland Browns and began issuing stock—twenty-five percent to Modell, twenty-five percent to Schaeffer, with the rest earmarked for future sale. Schaeffer's twenty-five percent was placed in an irrevocable trust voted by Modell, so Modell maintained control. By the time the balance of $900,000 was due, Modell had sold off the remaining fifty percent to eight different minority partners. The most significant of those was the Robert Gries family of Cleveland. Robert Gries Sr. had been a stockholder in the Browns' previous ownership and his participation in the new ownership had been a condition of sale. Gries put up "in excess of $300,000" for twenty-eight percent of the stock.

Eventually the Gries family's involvement would come back to haunt Art Modell. In the beginning, however, "I was a stranger in town and they introduced me to many people and made me very welcome," he remembered. Nevertheless, Modell was "young and didn't know Cleveland" and was suspect in many eyes of being little more than a carpetbagger from New York. It wasn't until 1964, when the Browns won the NFL championship, that he finally turned the corner on his road to civic elevation. "Winning," Modell pointed out, "changes everything."

From then on, Modell's rise in the eyes of Cleveland was steady. Once he established himself as a winner, Modell fit in easily. He was soon a regular in what the *Akron Beacon Journal* described as "a circle of bachelors, businessmen, gamblers, and politicians" who frequented the Theatrical Grill on Vincent Avenue. He was also soon foreman of the Cuyahoga County Grand Jury, a member of the Executive Committee of the Greater Cleveland Growth Association, and recipient of the Cleveland Variety Club's "Super Citizen" award. During the day, Modell could be seen driving his maroon-and-black Cadillac with classical music playing on the stereo at top volume. His home was a five-room twenty-fourth-floor apartment on "swanky" Winton Place with a "spectacular" view of Lake Erie. "Art Modell," *The* [Cleveland] *Plain Dealer* pointed out, "is an intense, successful man who can rarely be found at ease. He is static tension, three packs of half-smoked cigarettes and a peripatetic schedule." Throughout the 1960s, he was also considered Cleveland's most eligible bachelor.

Modell's bachelorhood ended in the summer of 1969, some eighteen months after his mother died. Modell was then forty-four. His bride, Patricia, was an actress in soap operas like *Peyton Place* and *General Hospital*. Their marriage took place in Las Vegas, at the home of "a top official" of Caesars

Palace hotel and casino. Patricia had two sons from a previous marriage whom Modell quickly adopted. The Modells replaced the apartment on Winton Place with a Tudor mansion in the exclusive suburb of Waite Hill.

Waite Hill was a long way from Borough Park and the childhood terror of financial collapse. In his fifth decade of life, Art Modell was finally rich and he owed it all to the National Football League. Despite paying a record price at the time, Modell got into the football business when the getting was good. Once the Rozelle era of television contracts began, the Browns' receipts skyrocketed, as did the value of the franchise. He was now a man who when asked under oath whether he had ever had "a problem raising a million dollars for anything" would answer "no."

Modell used his newfound leverage to consolidate his control over the Cleveland Browns. His first step was to buy Schaeffer out for $1,500,000 in 1965. To raise the capital, Modell wanted the Browns to borrow another $3 million and then pay it out in dividends. His fifty percent share in that dividend would be used to pay off Schaeffer. The only stumbling block to Modell's plan was the Gries family. By now, Robert Gries Sr., who had treated the young Modell "like one of the family," was on his death bed and the rest of the family balked at the arrangement. It was, as one of the Grieses remembered, "the first real hassle" inside the franchise. To convince them, Modell signed an agreement guaranteeing the family two seats on the Browns' seven-man board of directors.

During the late sixties, Modell increased his share of the Browns to "more than seventy percent" and then in 1971 decided to trade in some of that dominance for cash. His plan, as he explained it to the franchise's board of directors, was for Cleveland Browns, Inc., to engage in a "disproportionate redemption" of its own stock. The franchise's bankers were prepared to loan another $7 million. If that money were distributed as a straight dividend to all the shareholders equally, the tax consequences would be much larger than if the redemption was "disproportionate," favoring Modell. As Modell explained it, in order to qualify for special tax treatment, it was necessary for the principal shareholder to reduce his holdings under fifty percent, so he would extract $4 million and reduce his share to forty-eight percent. He also needed the Gries family's agreement to take less. Their holdings were now being overseen by Robert Gries Jr. through an entity called Gries Sports Enterprises. Still on relatively good terms with Modell, Robert Gries Jr. committed Gries Sports Enterprises to forego more than $1 million they might have claimed and settle for a $900,000 redemption and the increase of their share to more than forty-six percent. When a few of the minority partners subsequently sold out, Modell upped his holdings to fifty-three percent, where they stayed throughout the decade and into the next.

One of the odd aspects to these shifts inside the Browns franchise was that throughout it all, few in Cleveland even knew Art Modell had a partner, and even fewer knew his name. One sportswriter who noticed Robert Gries Jr. riding the Browns plane to road games assumed he was "an auto salesman on a promotional junket." No one informed the reporter otherwise and Art

Modell liked it that way. Modell, according to one of his former employees, "wanted to be the Browns and he wanted his name to be associated with the Browns and his name only."

Ignorance about the true state of the Browns' ownership would continue unchecked until League Think started coming apart, relatively late in the decade opened by Bal Harbour. Then the complaints of Modell's partner would finally become a source of public embarrassment that Art Modell, first winner of the Cleveland Sports Media Association's Pride of Cleveland award, could not escape. Until then, however, even most of the men meeting in Bal Harbour assumed their friend Art owned his franchise lock, stock, and barrel. In 1974, Art Modell was still the Browns, the Browns were Cleveland, and Art Modell played the role to the hilt.

9

Art Modell's proficiency at pack-running had made him a principal Rozelle lieutenant, serving as the NFL's president during the merger's transition period. The financial splendors of America's Game had also made the fatherless hustler from Pacey's Pool Hall in Brooklyn into an Ohio dignitary of the first order. Eventually, he would even be mentioned as a possible candidate for governor. In it all, Modell was fond of claiming, his most precious possession was his "good name." For Art Modell, reputation, and the standing which accompanied it, also translated into dollars and cents. As much was apparent in the Superstadium Game Modell played shortly before the 1974 annual meeting convened.

This particular Superstadium engagement was played with a decidedly Cleveland twist. In Dallas, Clint Murchison had pursued his superstadium game in a city on a steady upward spiral of growth and recognition. In Cleveland, a city struggling to keep from sliding into the nation's economic backwater, the issue was how to stop falling apart. Cleveland Municipal Stadium was built downtown on the shores of Lake Erie in 1931, as part of a plan to attract the 1932 Olympic Games to Cleveland, but the games went to Los Angeles's Memorial Coliseum instead. The eighty-thousand-seat stadium sat vacant until the Browns finally occupied it in 1946. The Indians, Cleveland's major league baseball franchise, soon followed suit, but the stadium itself had paid a heavy price for, as Modell put it, being "left dormant down there at the lakefront for a number of years."

Even with tenants, the stadium fared little better. According to Modell, jobs at the stadium were used as "political patronage" and, as a consequence, the facility was "deteriorating at a rapid rate." By 1972, it was a certifiable shambles. "The electrical system," Modell later testified, "was in utter chaos and hadn't been touched in years. Every expansion joint in the stadium was in need of repair . . . chunks of concrete were falling from the ramps to the concourse . . . and the plumbing was in disarray. The main structural beam [primary support of the stadium's entire upper deck] . . . had corroded . . . to a size slightly larger than a pen.''

Modell wanted the structure rehabilitated and demanded as much from his landlord, the city of Cleveland. "Because of the city's lack of funds," according to Modell, "I could not get their attention, let alone get any money for such a rehabilitation program." In 1972, the Browns' lease with Cleveland came up for renewal and Modell's venture into the Superstadium Game began. At first it seemed no more than a run-of-the-mill lease negotiation and in August 1972, *The* [Cleveland] *Plain Dealer* reported "Browns, City Agree." At six percent of gross receipts, less the city's three percent admissions tax, the lease Modell "agreed" to was one of the ten best in the NFL. Modell would operate under the terms of this agreement over the next two years, but would never actually sign a lease.

The most significant signal of Modell's intentions in that unsigned lease was the provision allowing the Browns to "abandon the stadium if the team, a private developer, or the city builds a new stadium." The possibility of such a new stadium was raised frequently during negotiations, usually by Modell. By the time "agreement" had been reached, he had begun taking steps to make his threat clearer. Working through the Bishop Realty Company, Modell bought up some two hundred acres in nine separate parcels in the vicinity of Strongsville, Ohio, near the intersection of Interstate 71 and the Ohio Turnpike, and little more than eighteen miles from Public Square in downtown Cleveland. It had cost Modell about $4,000 an acre, some $800,000 in total.

Eventually, Modell had a "secret" model of a stadium built in Strongsville kept on display in his office at Browns' headquarters.

Robert Gries Jr., Modell's anonymous partner, saw the model there on several occasions. To Gries, Modell implied that his intention was "to shake up the city of Cleveland," not actually to build in the suburbs. Gries asked Modell on several occasions to keep him informed and Modell told him, "I'll let you know when there is anything to report." Though Modell remained uncommunicative at the time, ten years later Gries learned that the studies Modell had commissioned had "found out that the stadium couldn't be done cheaply. It was not feasible. In addition, there was city council opposition in Strongsville. At best, it would have been a battle all the way." None of that was public knowledge at the time.

All the public knew in January 1973 was that the deed to the Strongsville land had just been officially transferred from Bishop Realty Company to Art Modell and, as a consequence, Art Modell appeared to be well on his way toward building a new stadium outside the Cleveland city limits. What happened next, as Robert Gries Jr. saw it, was "Cleveland got panicky." According to Art Modell, "it hit the newspapers like war headlines that the Browns were about to leave downtown Cleveland and it would be a disaster." At this point, Modell was approached by two of the city's most prominent bankers and the head of the Greater Cleveland Growth Association in which Modell was a very visible member and asked to "reconsider" his apparent move. There was, they told him, "a renaissance program going on in Cleveland and the Browns leaving would be a psychological blow."

"I said I would reconsider," Modell later testified, "if I can get the stadium out of City Hall, and the same monies I would put into Strongsville, allow me to put into Cleveland Stadium."

City Hall had already been primed for Modell's request. In November 1972 the Cleveland City Council president had appointed a blue ribbon civic committee to make recommendations about the "immediate and long-range future of the stadium." The committee was headed by George Steinbrenner III, the Cleveland shipbuilding magnate and friend of Modell who would later purchase baseball's New York Yankees franchise. In December, the Steinbrenner committee gave the City Council president its report. The committee's thrust was that Cleveland Stadium had to be improved and that the city of Cleveland ought to get out of the stadium business. Citing Philadelphia, Washington, D.C., Cincinnati, and Kansas City as "cities which have been forced to cut back public programs, especially school sports, to pay for new professional sports facilities," the blue ribbon report urged renovation and "private professional management" as cures to the city's dilemma. "We feel," Steinbrenner's committee advised Cleveland, "that the chances of long-term success would be greatly enhanced if the operation of Cleveland Stadium could be removed from political considerations and placed in the hands of business-oriented management . . . to take over the existing stadium on a long-term lease."

That Art Modell, the stadium's tenant, saw himself as that "business-oriented management" and hence his own landlord, was not immediately obvious. It was not even clear then to the public that he was willing to abandon Strongsville. "What's Modell's Plan?" *The Plain Dealer* asked. Modell's only public hint through the first four months of 1973 was his offer at the end of February to take over Cleveland Stadium's concession contract. In private, however, his plan was much more defined. It was called Cleveland Stadium Corporation, and Modell was about to become involved in what he would later describe as "strenuous" negotiations with the city of Cleveland to bring it about.

Art Modell's original notion for Cleveland Stadium Corp. had been a joint venture with the other major tenant, the Cleveland Indians, creating, in effect, a leaseholders co-op. The original idea went nowhere. Nick Miletti, the Indians' owner, was suspicious, Modell later testified, that Cleveland Stadium Corp. was just a way for the Browns to get a leg up on the Indians and the baseball franchise was in no position to commit itself to any new financial enterprises. As Modell later testified, "the Indians had more financial problems than even the city of Cleveland . . . bank debts up to their eyeballs." His original notion impossible, Modell proceeded to develop Cleveland Stadium Corp. as a corporate entity completely separate from the Browns, which would hold a "net operating type lease" with the city of

Cleveland, allowing it to treat the stadium as its own for the next twenty-five years.

Modell's first partner in this enterprise was Shelly Guren, a Cleveland attorney and head of U.S. Realty Co. As eventually structured, Modell would own "a shade better" than fifty percent of Cleveland Stadium Corp.'s shares and Guren and several partners Guren subsequently recruited would hold the rest. Guren's name first surfaced in Cleveland Stadium developments in March 1973, with no indication at the time that he was Modell's point man. Modell's name joined Guren's in May, and from then on, what would become Cleveland Stadium Corp. was identified as "a group headed by Cleveland Browns owner Art Modell." Modell's proposal was to "invest $10 million in stadium improvements and provide the city with an additional $10 million in revenue" in return for a twenty-five-year lease.

In June, Art Modell and Shelly Guren signed a formal memorandum of understanding creating Cleveland Stadium Corp. In July, Modell and Mayor Ralph Perk reached an "agreement." Typically, that agreement would take another six months of negotiations before being finalized. In the meantime, Shelly Guren filled out his end of the partnership. The most notable among the investors Guren brought in was George Steinbrenner III, the man whose blue ribbon committee report had, as it turned out, started Cleveland Stadium Corp.'s ball rolling.

To finance the corporation's $10 million in stadium improvements, Modell's plan was what Robert Gries Jr. would later describe as a "win/win" deal. After arranging what was planned to be a shortterm bridge loan secured by the partners' personal assets and a new twenty-five-year lease that Cleveland Stadium Corp.'s Modell negotiated with his own Cleveland Browns, Guren would create a real estate investment trust to assume permanent financing. REITs were something of a Guren specialty and once such an instrument assumed responsibility, "Modell and Guren wouldn't be risking a cent."

Though Cleveland Stadium Corp.'s financial underpinning would later be restructured in a major way, Art Modell officially became his own landlord on the evening of October 29, 1973, when the Cleveland City Council passed an ordinance authorizing his takeover of the stadium. The only unpleasant moment in the council's hearing came when one councilman questioned whether Modell in fact had the financial assets to perform as his end of the contract demanded.

Modell bridled at the suggestion that he was less than he represented himself to be and went red in the face. "My signature," Modell informed the city council with an edge on his voice, "is my performance bond."

Art Modell's stature in Cleveland was by then sufficiently elevated that apparently no one wished to insult him by raising the issue again, so the question was dropped. As expected, the lease was approved, and by January 1974 Cleveland Stadium Corp. was in business. Though his fellow NFL owners considered Art Modell a "good businessman" as well as a "good guy," Cleveland Stadium Corp. would become a financial disaster, precipitating the crash of Art Modell's civic reputation and the savaging of his hard-won wealth.

Like the dismemberment of League Think and the problems that would beset his friend, the commissioner, Art Modell's decline seemed unthinkable in February 1974, when he arrived in Bal Harbour to meet with the rest of the League. Things had been getting better for so long, it was hard to imagine they could ever get worse.

10

Carroll Rosenbloom, owner of the Los Angeles Rams, had begun life with all the things to which Art Modell spent most of his life aspiring. The youngest of the eight children of Baltimore work-clothes manufacturer Solomon Rosenbloom, Carroll had been rich since the day he was born in 1907. "I was fortunate in having a father who had worked hard and gave me something to start with," he explained. "And I've had lots of helpful friends. I've just been fortunate—I don't think I ever worked that hard." He may have indeed been lucky and may also have not worked very hard, but Carroll Rosenbloom was nonetheless good enough at what he did to turn the significant inheritance from his father into a positive fortune. After his death, *Forbes* would estimate Rosenbloom's holdings in "land, stock, and oil leases" to be worth "$300 million and up."

Whereas Modell was driven to wealth by the memory of privation, "C.R."—as Rosenbloom was called by those who worked for him—seemed to be driven to even more wealth simply by the competition of it all. His competitiveness was one of the first things people noticed about him. "He liked to win," the Oakland Raiders' Al Davis noted, "and he liked to be number one and he wasn't going to do anything based on just pure emotion or an altruistic experience."

Another of C.R.'s most noticeable traits was his vanity. "Carroll liked to have things his own way," Wellington Mara of the New York Giants remembered. "He wanted to be deferred to and he didn't like to be told he was wrong. He had a very big ego." When the Rams played at home, *Esquire* noted, "their owner enters the L.A. Coliseum like a head of state: fans calling out his name, Coliseum employees rushing up to wish him their best. Once inside, as the crowd starts to swell, Rosenbloom tours the field, chatting with his players. Shouts of 'Carroll' or 'Mr. R' ring out from the stands and friends try to get his attention. The spotlight is on and Carroll Rosenbloom loves it. He is a prince surveying his domain, a star onstage."

A third trait almost everyone noticed in Carroll Rosenbloom was that he could be an unscrupulous son of a bitch if the urge struck him.

According to testimony in a civil suit in the 1950s, he once participated in "bilking a rich businessman, supposedly his friend" by rigging a golf match with two co-conspirators. During the 1960s, four insurance companies sued him for making a false fire insurance claim and his sister sued him for breach of trust in the administration of their father's estate, claiming he "favored his own interests at the expense of the other beneficiaries." When he bought out his last remaining minority partners in the Baltimore Colts, his first franchise, in 1964, C.R. neglected to mention to them that the NFL was about to announce a new television contract that would double the value of their shares. "He took advantage of me," one of those partners remembered. "He gave us a sob story. . . . He pleaded . . . that he wanted the team for his boy [Steve]. The day after we signed the contract, I saw the headlines that the $14 million CBS contract had been announced. We knew nothing. . . . There isn't any question he let us have it with both barrels right between the eyes."

While all these traits were often cloaked by "the horsepower of his unusual charm," Carroll Rosenbloom stepped on people's toes and enjoyed it. "He feuded with everybody," according to Gene Klein. "He was just one of those kind of people." Tex Schramm agreed: "Feuding was part of his style. He was opinionated and strong-willed and he had his disagreements."

"He didn't like things settled," Steve Rosenbloom, his oldest son, explained. "He liked to stir things up." One of the consequences of that predilection was that all Rosenbloom's relationships inside the League were on-again off-again depending on the state of Rosenbloom's itch for combat. Pete Rozelle would later joke about the time when C.R. and several of his fellow owners were talking and one of them asked Rosenbloom if he would get six or seven friends together to vote a certain way. Before Rosenbloom could answer, one of the other owners pointed out to him that he would have trouble finding that many friends.

Rozelle no doubt chuckled nervously when he told the story. Carroll Rosenbloom feuded with everybody, but among those feuds, the one he waged with Pete Rozelle would become his greatest obsession. By 1974, the relationship between the two men had been bad for years. Soon it would get even worse.

The amiability Carroll Rosenbloom had displayed toward the new commissioner when sent to fetch him from the Kenilworth Hotel men's room in January 1960 had lasted roughly three years, to be replaced with a resentment that, though on-again off-again, would never quite recede. The collapse of their relationship came about out of the League crisis in which Rozelle went a long way toward winning his spurs as commissioner.

The crisis began with the new year in 1963 when reports of betting on NFL games by the League's players were confirmed and, as *Sports Illustrated* observed, "rumors of fix and other folly flamed across the land." At issue was the influence of gamblers over NFL games, and, ultimately, the NFL's credibility as a legitimate sporting event. Rozelle's immediate response was to defer action while he investigated. The waiting lasted 102 days, despite a public outcry for speedier action. On the 103rd day, Rozelle convened a press conference at the NFL's offices, then in New York's Rockefeller Center. There was, he announced, "no evidence that any NFL player has given less than his best in playing any game" and "no evidence that any player has ever bet against his own team" or "sold information to gamblers." Rozelle then took steps to make it clear the NFL would henceforth adopt standards worthy of Caesar's wife. He suspended the star halfback of the Green Bay Packers and the star defensive tackle of the Detroit Lions indefinitely for having placed bets on NFL games in which they were not involved. Five players on the Detroit Lions were fined two thousand dollars apiece for having bet on the NFL championship game and the Lions franchise was fined four thousand because its head coach "ignored a police tip that some players had been seen with undesirable characters."

The posture Rozelle assumed, standing slim and solemn before the assembled press, was an overwhelming success. His employers appreciated the performance. "Pete Rozelle's handling of the investigations," Tex Schramm observed, "was the thing that made everybody accept him as commissioner and no longer a boy playing the part. He gained once and for all everybody's complete respect." It had been a masterful display of crisis management requiring "fortitude under extraordinary pressure" and no small amount of finesse.

The aspect of the 1963 gambling crisis that required the most dexterity from the commissioner's office was how to treat his employers under the guidelines he had invoked at his press conference. Few League members resembled Caesar's wife, and no one bore less resemblance than Carroll Rosenbloom. C.R. loved to gamble and most everybody knew it. When American sportsmen gathered in barrooms and told betting stories, one featuring Carroll Rosenbloom was in wide circulation even before Rozelle was selected commissioner. It dated from the December 1958 NFL championship game between Rosenbloom's Baltimore Colts and the New York Giants owned by the Mara family—the exciting sudden-death game that had established NFL football as a television attraction with enormous audience potential.

Rosenbloom attended the game with his "sidekick" Louis Chesler, a Canadian entrepreneur who traveled with the Colts to all their road games. Chesler would eventually be credited by author Robert Pack with "bringing gambling to Freeport in the Bahamas" and by author Bernie Parrish with being "the man who fronted" for Mafia boss Meyer Lansky in that development. Chesler was also described as a "compulsive gambler." As the story went, Rosenbloom and Chesler had together wagered "a bundle" on the Colts. Some tellers of the story placed the figure at $1 million, but no one really knew. Supposedly the bet was the Colts minus three and a half points, meaning Chesler and Rosenbloom won if the Colts' margin of victory was four points or more. The Colts' margin of victory would indeed be one of the game's most memorable aspects. On their way down the field to ultimate victory as day was giving way to night, the Colts surprised everyone by passing up the opportunity to kick an easy field goal and win the game by three points. Instead, they risked everything, scored a touchdown, and won by six. Some tellers of the story insisted the field goal kicker was ready to go in when C.R. himself got on the press box phone to his team's coach and ordered him to go for broke, but there was no evidence of such a phone call on the public record. In any case, the Colts won by six instead of three and Rosenbloom and Chesler were "ecstatic."

In early January 1963, Rozelle had just begun waiting out the gambling crisis' first hundred days. The League was meeting in Miami, the commissioner recalled, when a bellhop entered the meeting room with a stack of envelopes and handed them to an NFL official. Thinking it was something the group had sent out to be copied, the official automatically passed them around the room. The envelopes contained four affidavits from friends and employees of Rosenbloom's, alleging that C.R. not only bet on NFL games but also even bet against his own team, all in complete violation of NFL rules. With them was a cover letter from a Miami private detective stating he had delivered copies of this information to Rozelle's office the previous fall but no action had been taken. The first owner to open his envelope and read the contents suggested they throw it all away.

The affidavits were a heretofore secret outgrowth of a lawsuit against Carroll Rosenbloom filed by one Mike McLaney in 1960 in Federal District Court in Miami. McLaney had been backed by Rosenbloom and Chesler in a Havana casino development before the Castro regime and was suing his backers over another deal for American Totalizator stock in which he claimed to have been denied his rightful finder's fee. The private eye who revealed the affidavits produced in McLaney's suit felt it was his "patriotic duty" to do so despite a judge's order sealing the suit's records. Coming when it did, the new information complicated Rozelle's problems enormously.

McLaney framed the new charges in a deposition: "[Due to] my betting knowledge and background . . . a betting partnership was formed for the purpose of betting large sums of money on football games. It was Mr. Rosenbloom and myself. . . . On some occasions we would not be equal partners because Mr. Rosenbloom had much more money than I had and was able to bet higher. On one occasion, for instance, he bet as high as $55,000 against his own team." Included in the package delivered to the NFL were an additional three affidavits. Robert J. McGarvey, a former Philadelphia policeman who'd worked as Rosenbloom's "friend and personal assistant, performing many confidential and personal services for him" between 1951 and 1954, swore that during that time "Mr. Rosenbloom bet frequently in large amounts on professional football games." Larry E. Murphy, a friend of McGarvey's, swore that Rosenbloom "bet a large amount of money against his own team and, because of the point spread, won the bet." Richard Melvin, a Rosenbloom golfing partner, swore that "during one professional football season, [Rosenbloom] made nine straight winning bets on professional football games."

Rosenbloom denied all the charges, but Rozelle contended he had no choice but to investigate, as he was doing in the other, player-related gambling charges. To do otherwise, Rozelle pointed out to Rosenbloom, would be to admit to a double standard.

Rozelle's investigation lasted until well after his Rockefeller Center press conference, when most of the press were busy praising the commissioner for having saved the NFL's integrity. Rosenbloom, Rozelle remembered, was "upset about the delay and thought he was being left on the hook." The investigation finally reached its conclusion in the summer of 1963, when Mike McLaney called Rozelle and said he wanted to talk. The two men met in a bar across the street from the NFL offices.

McLaney greeted the commissioner by tossing an envelope across the table. "This should help you out," he said with an air of resignation.

Inside the envelope were retractions to the previous charges. Rozelle was surprised and looked at McLaney quizzically. According to Rozelle, McLaney "muttered something about the Irish Mafia being after him." McLaney's comment was obscure but Rozelle knew the "Irish Mafia" was the nickname given the Kennedy political machine then ensconced in the White House and that Carroll Rosenbloom was a good friend of both Joe Kennedy, the clan's patriarch, and Jack Kennedy, the President. "Apparently the IRS was after McLaney," Rozelle concluded.

In any case, the retractions ended Carroll Rosenbloom's role in the 1963 gambling scandals. On July 16, 1963, the commissioner made public his one-page final report on the subject. "No proof whatever has been uncovered," Rozelle reported, "that he [Rosenbloom] ever bet on a National Football League game since becoming an owner. . . . The charges were unfounded."

By then it was far too late for Pete Rozelle to salvage his relationship with Carroll Rosenbloom. After the investigation was over, Rozelle recalled: "Our relationship went into one of its off phases." Steve Rosenbloom explained, "My father had helped Rozelle get his job but Rozelle had considered him guilty until proven innocent." As part of the commissioner's final report, Rosenbloom "freely admitted that he has bet substantial sums on activities other than professional football" but "stated that he has ceased such practices."

It no doubt galled Carroll Rosenbloom to have to make such a claim. He was someone who did not take being jacked around lightly and he had a reputation for holding his grudges a long time. When the NFL met in Bal Harbour in 1974, almost eleven years later, there was no active issue in his feud with Rozelle, and Rosenbloom was content, for the moment, to put a lot of public distance between himself and those League members who were preparing to canonize the man already being called "the best commissioner in the history of professional sports."

"Hell," C.R. was fond of telling people, "with the game we've got, my grandmother could have negotiated those TV contracts."

11

Of the twenty-six men meeting in Bal Harbour in 1974, Carroll Rosenbloom, sixty-seven years old, was one of only four whose membership in the National Football League predated Rozelle's commissionership. In Rosenbloom's iconography, "the commissioner" would always be Bert Bell, someone he considered "a great man." Bell had been Rosenbloom's college football coach in 1927 and, in 1953, was the one who convinced him to join the NFL. While commissioner, Bell was seen over at Rosenbloom's home near Atlantic City "all the time."

Bert Bell brought Rosenbloom into the NFL to solve what had been known as "the Baltimore problem." Professional football first came to Baltimore in 1947 when the soon to be defunct All-America Football Conference established a franchise called the Colts. The Colts and several other All-America Conference survivors joined the NFL in 1950. In 1951, after averaging only sixteen thousand tickets sold per game and losing money hand over fist, the Colts folded. The following year a syndicate started a new NFL team in Dallas, the Texans, but gave the franchise back to the League halfway through the 1952 season, unable to bear ever-mounting financial losses. Bell's solution was to take the Texans franchise, transplant it to Baltimore as the reborn Colts, and this time do it right. The key was to find an owner with plenty of money to lose and enough Baltimore roots to make the franchise a genuine hometown team.

Carroll Rosenbloom had an abundance of both. Born in Baltimore, Rosenbloom grew up on Hollins Street, near the home of journalist H. L. Mencken. "He didn't like kids as a rule," Rosenbloom remembered about Mencken, "but he liked me because I was a mean little so-and-so." Despite his wealth, Rosenbloom attended Baltimore public schools and then Baltimore City College, where he was a football and baseball standout. Rosenbloom finished his education at the University of Pennsylvania, playing halfback for Bert Bell. His collegiate major was psychology. After college, his father asked him to try the family business and Rosenbloom agreed. He spent his first year on the job cleaning lavatories in one of his father's buildings, making $3.50 a week.

The next year, Solomon Rosenbloom's son Carroll began making his own fortune. Dispatched to one of his father's denim mills with orders to close it down, Rosenbloom instead borrowed money from his mother and several banks and purchased the mill himself. A firm of eighty employees and annual revenues of $350,000 when he purchased it, sixteen years later it employed 20,000 and had revenues of $175 million. At age thirty-three,

Rosenbloom was wealthy enough to turn the running of his business over to others and "retire" to a 480-acre farm on Maryland's Eastern Shore. "I never did really care for working," C.R. explained. "I don't know why anyone would work if they didn't have to."

Carroll Rosenbloom's retirement ended when his father died in 1942 and Carroll merged his father's holdings with his own.

During World War II, Rosenbloom served as a consultant to the Philadelphia Quartermaster Depot and the Rosenbloom mills churned out uniforms and parachutes for the war effort. After the war, he merged the family business into the Philadelphia and Reading Corp., one of the nation's first conglomerates, and "walked away with a fortune." By the time Bert Bell approached him with his idea of restarting the Colts, Carroll Rosenbloom was "bored with conventional business" and looking for excitement.

Rosenbloom paid $250,000 for Baltimore's new NFL franchise and upon becoming majority owner, put another $1.5 million in the bank. "That was how much I was willing to lose," he explained. "After that, I'd get out." When C.R. was introduced at a civic dinner honoring his new franchise, the master of ceremonies pointed out it was a good thing Rosenbloom owned a shirt factory because he was about to lose his shirt. In fact, Rosenbloom never had a money-losing season in Baltimore and at the end of the 1950s, his Colts were considered the NFL's premier franchise.

At the same time, Carroll Rosenbloom became a significant power inside the NFL. His closeness with Bell lent him influence in the beginning and his teams' successes enhanced it. Rosenbloom was instrumental in getting the League to accept a players' union. He was also the first to approach the AFL, though unsuccessfully, about a possible merger. While always a man to chart his own course, Rosenbloom wasn't isolated. His relationships with other owners were inevitably there to retrieve when he decided to turn them on rather than off. All of them considered him "cunning" and he, in turn, liked some of them for themselves and some of them for what they could do for Carroll Rosenbloom. By the time of the Bal Harbour annual meeting, Rosenbloom's habit at League conclaves was to have his son Steve sit through the parts he considered "bullshit" and "only come in if it was something of significance."

According to Steve, when Carroll Rosenbloom was considering a move of one sort or another, he kept his own counsel but would "run things by" his owner friends to get "a feel" for the situation without tipping his hand. When he did act, it was usually on his own. He was in many respects a mystery to the rest of the League. "He was an odd person," his friend Art Modell remembered. "His temperament was really even and level. He was very shrewd. I still can't figure him out. He was a team player to a certain point. Al Davis was always the Lone Ranger, but Carroll invoked the League. He gave speech after speech about unity. He looked for an edge but he was fundamentally an NFL man. Except for his vendetta against Rozelle. That was unconscionable."

Despite Modell's left-handed certification of Rosenbloom's standing in

League Think, C.R.'s "vendetta" against the commissioner would start the ball rolling in the NFL's disorder to come. Later, Rosenbloom's final episode in the superstadium game would kick off the scramble for advantage that eventually led to open warfare. Ironically, in 1971, three years before the Bal Harbour annual meeting, it had seemed doubtful that Rosenbloom would play much, if any, of a role at all in the coming NFL decade. Again, he seemed bored with the business he was in. For the last eight years he had been living, for all intents and purposes, in Florida. To keep track of his holdings, he traveled to New York a lot and kept an apartment in the Hotel Navarro. As a rule, he appeared in Baltimore only for home games, arriving on Friday afternoon and staying in the Sheraton-Belvedere's presidential suite. In early 1971, C.R. made his boredom official.

"Steve Rosenbloom Replaces Dad As President of Colts," The [Baltimore] Sun announced in March. Though "retired," Rosenbloom continued as owner and chairman of the Colts' board.

Needless to say, the retirement was an illusion. "I ran all the daily stuff," Steve Rosenbloom remembered, "but Carroll never withdrew. All he needed was a phone and we talked every day." Rosenbloom was indeed bored, but he was, as it turned out, bored with Baltimore, not with football. "Carroll got disgusted," Steve noted. "The press was carrying on every day about 'what's wrong with the Colts.' People began to expect a world championship every year. My father finally said 'Jesus Christ, all we've done is win. What the hell do they want?' "

The first option C.R. explored was moving the Colts to Tampa, Florida. This course led as far as "discussions" with Rozelle and no further.

Then, in July 1972, Carroll Rosenbloom announced a surprise solution to his "Baltimore problem." Instead of moving the Colts, he traded the franchise in toto for the Los Angeles Rams. It was the first and only such franchise trade in NFL history, and with it Carroll Rosenbloom began a second life in the League.

According to Rosenbloom, the idea of taking over the Rams was first suggested to him by Dan Reeves, then the Rams owner, in 1968. Reeves was suffering from terminal cancer. "My number can come up any time now," Reeves told C.R. "I don't think my family will keep the club after I'm gone."

Rosenbloom protested that Reeves would probably last a long time. "Only the good die young," he joked.

Reeves ignored Rosenbloom's attempt to deflect the issue. "I don't think you belong in Baltimore anymore," the Rams owner continued. "If I do go before you do, I hope you'll give serious thought to acquiring this franchise."

Reeves finally died in 1971, the year C.R. "retired," and Rosenbloom spent much of his retirement giving the Rams "serious thought." His initial idea was simply to give the Colts to Steve and buy the Rams himself. Rozelle, however, nixed the possibility. The NFL constitution prohibited any individual from owning more than one franchise, and two members of the same immediate family owning separate franchises was too close for the commissioner's comfort. Realizing that arrangement "wouldn't fly from a League point of view," Rosenbloom again backed off. Rozelle suggested that Rosenbloom instead sell the Colts and buy the Rams.

The principal argument against that option from Rosenbloom's point of view was the tax consequences. A straight cash sale of a property that had increased close to $20 million in value during the term of his ownership would have left C.R. with a $4.4 million tax bill for capital gains. The idea of trading was developed as a way around the tax law. The trade began its tortuous path toward actuality when Joe Robbie, owner of the Miami Dolphins and one of C.R.'s bitterest enemies, fired his director of player personnel, one Joe Thomas. When Rosenbloom learned of the firing, he placed a call to Thomas to offer his condolences and any help Thomas needed. Not long after that Thomas brought C.R. his first candidate for a swap. The candidate was Willard Keland, a former partner in the Miami Dolphins who, according to *Sports Illustrated,* had been squeezed out of the franchise by Robbie. Keland eventually agreed to buy the Rams from Dan Reeves's estate for $19 million and trade the franchise straight across for the Colts.

The deal with Keland began falling apart in its final stages when the former Dolphin partner announced he couldn't raise enough money. By then, time was crucial. A group headed by Florida tax attorney Hugh Culverhouse was preparing its own offer to the Reeves estate. Again, Thomas provided the missing ingredient when he came up with another buyer for the Colts, Chicago heating contractor, Robert J. Irsay. After the swap had been effected, Keland dropped out altogether and Robert Irsay became the one hundred percent owner of the Baltimore Colts. As required by the NFL constitution, the deal received formal approval by League vote and C.R. began looking for a place to live in L.A.

As deals go, Carroll Rosenbloom's swap of the Baltimore Colts for the Los Angeles Rams was a prime candidate for shrewdest in the history of the National Football League. He had paid not a cent in taxes while managing to convert $20 million of accrued franchise value into another franchise, worth potentially a great deal more. In trading franchises, Carroll Rosenbloom had also managed to trade one of the League's lesser media markets for a market second only to New York City in size and visibility. "Owning the Colts is like owning a local brewery, one observer commented. Owning the Rams is like owning Twentieth Century Fox."

Rosenbloom left his old hometown on a final note of on-the-field triumph. In their last season before his "retirement" and subsequent exit, Carroll Rosenbloom's Colts finally triumphed in a Super Bowl, defeating Tex Schramm's Dallas Cowboys 16 to 13 in Miami's Orange Bowl, and soothing one of C.R.'s greatest frustrations. He had been humiliated in the same stadium two years earlier when his Colts were whipped by Sonny Werblin's New York Jets and became the first team in the old NFL to lose a Super Bowl to a former member of the AFL. When that embarrassing situation was finally rectified, it no doubt added to Rosenbloom's sense that it was time to leave Baltimore. The silver trophy emblematic of that last world championship was one of the assets he traded straight across for the Rams. Until early 1973, it was on display in the lobby of the Colts' Maryland training facility.

Exactly who Carroll Rosenbloom thought deserved to have that trophy soon became obvious. The first Super Bowl after his history-making swap was staged in the Los Angeles Memorial Coliseum, Carroll Rosenbloom's new home field. As host owner, Rosenbloom was planning a party at his new Bel-Air home and "borrowed" his Super Bowl trophy from the Colts to use as a centerpiece for the affair. The sterling silver football was hand delivered to Rosenbloom by his nephew, Ed Rosenbloom, who had stayed on in Baltimore as the Colts' business manager. Once it was in C.R.'s hands, he simply kept it.

Rosenbloom kept "his" trophy in his den in Bel-Air. Several years after C.R.'s Super Bowl party, the Colts' assistant general manager saw it there in the course of a visit with Rosenbloom. Not wanting to get mixed up in the controversy, the assistant general manager commented on what a remarkable "replica" it was.

"You're a smart kid," Rosenbloom chuckled.

In 1982, Robert Irsay would finally stop waiting for the trophy to be returned by Carroll Rosenbloom's estate and would purchase an $11,000 copy from Tiffany and Company in New York. The purchase symbolized the attempt Robert Irsay was making to evoke the old Colts glory years before Robert Irsay arrived and solve what was now, thanks to Carroll Rosenbloom and Joe Thomas, *his* "Baltimore problem."

12

C.R. relished the second of his two football lives and loved L.A. "Los Angeles is made to order for Carroll Rosenbloom," an acquaintance observed. The Rams' owner is "an instant celebrity. He's part of the Hollywood–Beverly Hills–Malibu axis. He and his business are the talk of the town."

C.R.'s principal Los Angeles residence was a luxurious estate on five wooded acres in Bel-Air with a swimming pool, tennis courts, and sprawling formal gardens. To keep the Bel-Air house up, he kept a staff of as many as seven or eight. Rosenbloom's "place in the country" was a house at exclusive Trancas Beach, north of Malibu. In both he entertained the likes of Kirk Douglas, Warren Beatty, Jack Lemmon, Walter Matthau, and Dinah Shore. Whenever Ted Kennedy was in Los Angeles, he stayed in Rosenbloom's guest quarters.

In his second hometown with his second NFL franchise, Carroll Rosenbloom was also raising his second family. His marriage to his first wife,

Velma, ended in the mid-sixties after some twenty-five years. They had four children, of whom only Steve was in the football business. In settlement discussions with Velma, Rosenbloom warned her he would not part with any portion of the Colts. "I would never do that," he admonished her. "Especially I'd never give them up to a woman."

C.R. remarried almost immediately. By then his second wife, Georgia, had been his behind-the-scenes companion for a number of years. She was a former lounge singer, musical comedy performer, and TV weather girl. Carroll Rosenbloom was Georgia's sixth husband. Her first marriage, at age fifteen and a half in her native St. Louis, was annulled. Her second husband was killed when hit by a bus in San Francisco. Her third husband, a Fresno, California, resident in the hotel supply business, lost her to the lure of the bright lights of an entertainment career. Her fourth was the stage manager of a traveling music revue she married while working as a chorus girl in Las Vegas. Her fifth was a Miami television personality. It was while she was in Miami working the lounge circuit that Georgia met Carroll in the late 1950s. Her fifth husband claimed to have introduced them.

Georgia contended they were introduced by Joseph Kennedy, patriarch of the Kennedy clan and the only man Rosenbloom's friends ever remembered him addressing as "sir." In any case, the effect was immediate. "She was a dynamite chick," her fifth husband recalled. "She was very much a knockout. Being so attractive, she always had people hitting on her." Carroll Rosenbloom reportedly "hit" on her immediately. "She had the catnip," Georgia's agent remembered. "Men just dribbled over her. [Rosenbloom] was mad about her. He didn't like anything or anyone who took Georgia away from him. He didn't want her out in public with those kind of people looking at her. I got her married. I kept booking her out of the country until Carroll couldn't stand it."

Carroll and Georgia were married on July 1, 1966, less than a month after his divorce from Velma was final. Georgia was then thirty-eight years old, Carroll, fifty-nine. According to later published reports, at the time of Carroll Rosenbloom's second marriage, the younger of the two children he fathered by Georgia was already two years old. The children shared the Bel-Air and Trancas Beach homes with their parents. The Rosenblooms often entertained by erecting a dance floor in the Bel-Air home on which Georgia would entertain their guests with a rendition of songs. "Georgia would get up," a frequent visitor remembered, "and sing to his [Rosenbloom's] eyes. He was like a little boy when she did that. He loved it."

Despite his continuing infatuation with his second wife, Carroll Rosenbloom's Los Angeles obsession was the Rams, and for him football was strictly a male enterprise. Georgia was invited once to the Rams' offices on Pico Boulevard to look around after C.R. had installed his office there and was not invited back. The only other time she showed up at the Pico headquarters was to deliver some papers Carroll had left at home and then he wouldn't let her past the receptionist in the lobby. Steve was sent down to fetch what she'd brought. Women, Rosenbloom lectured his son, should not be meddling in the football business. It was not treatment peculiar to Georgia. C.R. had treated Velma the same way. Wives of the Colts' front office personnel were allowed to sit with the men in C.R.'s owner's box at Memorial Stadium only if the weather was wet or freezing. Otherwise, they sat in a separate section of seats a good distance away.

In Los Angeles, Rosenbloom devoted himself to his football team with renewed energy. Every Thursday during football season he was either flown by helicopter or driven by Mercedes to the Rams' training facility in Long Beach to watch his team's final intense practice and huddle with his coaches. While watching, he sat in a Hollywood director's chair with "C. Rosenbloom" stitched on the back. As he had in Baltimore, C.R. left the daily details of the club to his son Steve, now installed as Rams' executive vice-president. Keeping his family involved in the football business was important to Rosenbloom, and convincing Steve to come west had been one of the most difficult parts of the move. Steve had been, as he put it, "content to stay in Baltimore for the rest of my life." He stayed in Baltimore for a year after his father left, trying to make a go of a dog kennel business, until C.R. finally pressured him into taking the Rams' job.

In Baltimore, C.R. had spent several years haggling with city and state of Maryland authorities over the possibility of constructing a "modern" facility to replace Baltimore's Memorial Stadium. Despite Robert Irsay's later claim that in the course of negotiating the franchise swap Rosenbloom and Maryland's governor had assured him that such a new stadium would be built, none ever was. It was Rosenbloom's frustration with that inaction that led him to consider relocating to Tampa and then reinforced his desire to leave Baltimore any way possible.

In Los Angeles, C.R. inherited a lease that had only two years left to run and a stadium that would later be described as the "Grand Duchess" of American stadiums. Built in 1923 and then remodeled for the 1932 Olympics, the L.A. Coliseum could seat as many as ninety-five thousand and was considered, prior to the rise of superstadia, "one of the great stadiums in the country." By 1974 standards, Lamar Hunt judged it "not a good football stadium" and Pete Rozelle termed it "inadequate." C.R. targeted the "Grand Duchess" for mothballs shortly after arriving in L.A. "If land is made available," he told The [Baltimore] Sun in October 1972, "I will put up a new stadium to replace the Coliseum."

Whatever Rosenbloom's intentions, the L.A. Coliseum would prove to have remarkable staying power. A quasi-independent enterprise, the Coliseum was governed by the Los Angeles Memorial Coliseum Commission, a nine-member board appointed by three different governmental entities. Three of the LAMCC's members were appointed by the Los Angeles County Board of Supervisors, three by the Los Angeles City Council, and three by the state of California's governing board for the Museum of Science and Industry, upon whose land the Coliseum had originally been built. At the time C.R. showed up in Los Angeles, its members were, according to one former member, "usually big political contributors who wanted the glory" of association with the stadium's tenants. Their association with Carroll Rosenbloom, however, would prove considerably less than glorious.

C.R.'s immediate problem was what to do when his current lease ran out after the 1973 season. Early on, Rosenbloom explored the possibilities of playing in Dodger Stadium or at Anaheim's Big A Stadium in neighboring Orange County, but neither was then a suitable option. Building his own stadium was also impossible due to the high price of land and construction. "There was," Rosenbloom noted, "no place else to go." The paucity of options placed him under stringent restrictions in his bargaining, but didn't make him any easier for the LAMCC to deal with. "His sport was hassling with stadiums," his son Steve remembered.

For its part, the LAMCC was under severe financial restrictions as well. They had little money to spend on Carroll Rosenbloom and even less desire to spend it. The LAMCC's difficulties were a function of its disastrous decision in the late 1960s to build the Los Angeles Sports Arena, a companion indoor arena to the Coliseum. In the course of bringing the facility into being, the LAMCC became embroiled in a controversy surrounding the professional hockey and basketball teams it hoped would be the arena's primary tenants. In a struggle between Dan Reeves, late owner of the Rams, and Jack Kent Cooke, later majority owner of the Washington Redskins, over a new Los Angeles hockey franchise, the LAMCC sided with Reeves and Reeves lost. Never one to do business with his enemies, Jack Kent Cooke had proceeded to build his own arena, The Forum, in Inglewood, and to take both his Los Angeles basketball and hockey franchises there. The result was that the Sports Arena was continuously vacant except for an occasional rock concert and had become a white elephant, kept solvent only by the income generated by the "Grand Duchess of Stadiums." There was no money to spare once the Sports Arena's bills were paid.

Rosenbloom opened his negotiations by announcing in August 1973 that he was prepared to "wholly underwrite" a $7 million bond for improvements in the Coliseum. At the top of his suggested improvement list was the construction of luxury boxes and a stadium club for the box holders' entertainment. By November, the LAMCC had rejected C.R.'s offer and accused him of using "pressure tactics." Instead of yielding, the Coliseum Commission was insisting the Rams' rent be raised. "Negotiations" on the issues were at best a distant proposition for C.R. In January 1974, the LAMCC's president complained about his attitude in an open letter released to the press. "For ten months now," the LAMCC pointed out, "we have tried to negotiate a new lease with you, but you have either been too busy . . . or sent someone who could not speak for you. True negotiation requires interested parties."

For his part, C.R. accused the LAMCC of trying to "paint me as the bad boy and I'm not. They have to have more revenue because they have done a bad job of operating the Sports Arena. They chased Jack Kent Cooke out and they've been losing money ever since. I could accept their thinking if they came to me with their cards up. I'd even be willing to assist them out of my charity fund. But they're using a new lease to cover up a losing operation—a mishandled operation.'' A month after his complaint, Rosenbloom gave in and signed a three-year lease with an option to renew. The new deal required him to pay twice his previous rent and to assume the janitorial expenses previously borne by the LAMCC. In Rosenbloom's mind, it was a stopgap solution only.

Already past normal retirement age, Carroll Rosenbloom operated with a constant apprehension that his time might well be running out. ''Some people say I'm too mean to die,'' he told the *Los Angeles Times,* ''but I guess I'll probably die anyway.'' In the meantime, he made a point of not letting his age diminish his vigor. Over six feet tall, fit, square-jawed, and handsome, he wore a custom-made gray-blond toupee, played tennis with ferocity, if not skill, and maintained a hectic daily schedule. Late in life, C.R.'s concern for his football franchise focused on ''continuity.'' ''I don't ever want this football team to leave my family,'' he announced in early 1974.

When Carroll Rosenbloom made such statements about continuity, everyone generally assumed he meant Steve, his heir apparent and proxy at many of the 1974 annual meeting's ''bullshit'' sessions with which C.R. wanted no bother. In conversations with his fellow owners outside the meeting, Rosenbloom ''complained bitterly about how arrogantly the L.A. Coliseum had dealt with him.'' Few were left with any doubts about the smoldering resentment he felt and most assumed it would not be the last they would hear about the LAMCC. No one, however, anticipated that, thanks to Carroll Rosenbloom, the ''Grand Duchess of Stadiums'' would become the decisive battleground in the civil war that would be League Think's undoing.

13

The man who would eventually triumph in that climactic battle, Al Davis, managing general partner of the Oakland Raiders, was one of the few people in the NFL whose relationship with Carroll Rosenbloom was perpetually on rather than on-again off-again. ''I like Al Davis because he is a mean, conniving s.o.b.,'' C.R. explained, ''just like I am.'' Eventually the two men were close enough that they talked ''every day or every other day'' on the telephone. ''I was very fond of Mr. Rosenbloom,'' Davis would later testify.

To much of the rest of the NFL, Al Davis was, as Wellington Mara put it, ''Carroll's boy.'' One of the traits C.R. and Davis shared was their estimate of themselves. Like Carroll Rosenbloom, Al Davis was not the kind to hide his light under a basket.

When the American Football League turned to Davis, then Oakland's coach and general manager, at its meeting in Houston in April 1966 and asked him to be commissioner, he was thirty-seven years old. Unaware that Lamar

Hunt had met with Tex Schramm just the day before at Love Field's Texas Ranger statue and begun to make peace, the choice of Davis by the AFL was a choice to prosecute their war with the NFL to the fullest extent. Later that day, Davis and an AFL publicist prepared the AFL's announcement of Davis's selection. The publicist typed while Al Davis read over his shoulder. When he got to the part describing Davis, the new AFL commissioner leaned forward and penciled the words *dynamic* and *genius* on the top of the page.

"Think you can work these in?" Al asked.

By the time the war was over and Al Davis was back with the Raiders as managing general partner, he was widely identified as "the most hated man in professional football." Typically, the reputation didn't bother Davis a bit. "He's the kind of guy you can't insult," his archenemy, Gene Klein, noted. "You spit in his eye and he says it's raining." While his mentor, Carroll Rosenbloom, often rubbed people both ways, Davis usually settled for the wrong way only. "He has himself paged when he comes into a hotel," one of his fellow owners said derisively, "and he's the kind of man who never passes a mirror without combing his hair. He always was an arrogant son of a bitch and nothing will change until he finally gets his ass whipped."

Whipping Al Davis's ass was, however, a tall order inside the football business. In the years after the 1966 merger, no one's teams would win more games than his. "He is a genius in terms of football," one NFL executive noted. "Very few others understand either the game or the business as well as he does. He's like a hawk who can pick on other birds of prey. Most of the others were just not capable of competing with him."

"He has a remarkable capacity for seeing himself as a victor in confrontations," one of Davis's friends from the early days in Oakland observed. "It pleases him to make sharp trades, he likes to win these little battles. He likes to walk away chuckling and tell his friends, 'I sure jerked the rug out from under that guy but he doesn't even know it yet.' " As another NFL executive complained to *The Saturday Evening Post,* "He'd do anything to win, even if it meant stepping on his mother. He's a ruthless, persistent cuss, full of chicanery. Yet you have to give the devil his due. He's nothing but successful."

In compiling Davis's due, one of the first entries that must be credited to him is the city of Oakland's place on the national map. Few in the National Football League doubted that, without Davis, Oakland's tenuous grasp on big league stature might well have been lost in its infancy.

San Francisco's less glamorous neighbor on the east shore of the bay, Oakland, was not an automatic selection, even to the fledgling American Football League in 1959, and the league's original list of eight franchises did not include it. Until the rise of the Raiders, the city was most famous for Gertrude Stein's description of it as having "no there, there." Oakland's chance finally came at the infant league's first official meeting in Minneapolis in November 1959, when Max Winter's Minnesota franchise withdrew and announced it was expecting to join the NFL. Two months later, Minnesota's NFL membership was confirmed along with Dallas's at the same meeting that chose Pete Rozelle commissioner. It was considered the first skirmish of the AFL war.

Oakland's opportunity came from Lamar Hunt's desperation after Winter's defection. It was Hunt who had put the league together and now he had to fill the hole in its lineup fast. To do so, he floated a rumor that a group in Oakland was interested. An [Oakland] *Tribune* sportswriter, Scotty Stirling, picked the story up and ran it despite being unable to find anyone who was indeed interested. "Hunt was on a fishing expedition," Stirling later remembered. "He wanted to see whether a group would surface. We started running stories and three groups popped up and expressed interest." The group that won the franchise was a limited partnership run by General Partner Wayne Valley, a millionaire California home builder headquartered in San Leandro, Oakland's southern neighbor. Stirling eventually became the club's publicity director.

Wayne Valley got into football because, as one of his friends put it, "Wayne Valley was a football nut." Valley had been an offensive lineman at Oregon State during the Depression, and until he bought into the Oakland franchise, held forty season tickets to the NFL's San Francisco 49er games. He was, as one NFL executive described him, "a tough guy who would come across the table at you." Valley had to be hard-nosed to survive the first years in Oakland.

The initial name chosen for the team was the Senors, but that was soon changed to Raiders. Their first year, they represented Oakland but played their games in San Francisco, lost $500,000, and one of Valley's two other general partners dropped out. After the 1961 season in Oakland's tiny Frank Youell Field, the losses were even bigger and required another reorganization of the Raider franchise by Valley in order to insulate himself from some of the red ink. By the end of 1962, the situation was desperate and there was talk that the Raiders might soon move to Portland, Seattle, or New Orleans. At that point, Wayne Valley found Al Davis and saved Oakland for the big leagues.

At the time, Davis was an assistant coach at the AFL's San Diego Chargers franchise. He would eventually be one of only two men ever to rise out of the coaching ranks to ownership. Asked when in his life he first knew he was going to run a football team for a living, Davis answered, "When I was six."

The son of a successful clothing merchant, Al Davis grew up in Brooklyn. "I really wasn't much of an athlete," he recalled. "I played a little football and baseball, but it would be inaccurate to say I starred or anything like that. I didn't get along with the coaches. You follow me?"

"He wants to be thought of as an athlete," one of Al Davis's former employees told *Sports Illustrated*, "but he isn't even particularly well coordinated. And he may have the skinniest pair of wheels in America, which is why he never takes off his pants where anyone can see. Then there's the Al Davis handshake. It's done with the fingers held apart and rigid so his little hand will seem bigger. He still wears those suits with the big padded shoulders. The players call him 'El Bago.' ''

As much resentment as Al Davis managed to generate, no one in the NFL ever questioned his grasp of the game they all owned. "If I said Al Davis is lovable," Wayne Valley pointed out, "I'd be a liar. But you don't have to love him, just turn him loose." Davis himself told *Sports Illustrated,* "I don't want to give the feeling I'm above and beyond, but I've always had the perception to understand these games. Do you follow me? I was the organizer."

After he'd graduated from Syracuse University with a major in English, Davis's knack took him to Adelphi College as a twenty-one-year-old football coach, but his first significant coaching success came after he entered the army and wangled the job of coaching the Fort Belvoir, Virginia, football team. "He was a private," *Look* magazine observed of Davis's army career, "but he had a car and driver and was the only enlisted man who always wore an officer-type peaked hat." Davis explained, "You know how generals are. They want to win. This general gave me carte blanche. I also had very good contacts in the Pentagon that could move people. You follow me?" According to *Look,* "Davis left Fort Belvoir . . . only a step ahead of a congressional investigation into the coddling of athletes."

After the army, Davis spent a year as a scout for the Baltimore Colts, two years at The Citadel as an assistant coach, three years at the University of Southern California doing the same thing and then landed with the Chargers. He and Valley first made contact in December 1962. By early 1963, Davis, Valley, and the other Raider general partner, Ed McGah, met for a formal job interview in an Oakland hotel room. Davis showed none of the humility or intimidation one might have expected from an assistant coach seeking his first professional head coaching position. Valley invited two Oakland reporters to sit in on the hotel room session. "Al considered owners to be dilettantes," one of the reporters said, "playing with their new toy. The real pros needed to shove them aside, and the sooner they did, the sooner the AFL would be a real league." When Valley and McGah left the room at one point, Davis turned to the press and began making fun of the men who were interviewing him. "They don't even know what questions to ask," he said, smirking.

After turning Valley down twice, Davis accepted the Raider job. "I would have sole and complete control of the operation of the football team," is the way the new head coach and general manager later summarized his contract. On another occasion he explained, "I am not running a school to teach owners football."

One of the noncontractual assurances Davis had insisted upon from Valley was that Oakland would soon provide a better stadium for the Raiders' home field. Valley had been working feverishly for such a stadium since his entry into the football business. The first proposal to build a major league sports facility in Oakland had in fact surfaced in December 1944. A little less than two years later, a proposal to build such a stadium was defeated in a citywide referendum. In 1949, the Oakland Chamber of Commerce backed a new stadium plan but when put to the voters, it, too, lost. In 1956, city officials blamed the departure of Oakland's minor league baseball franchise to Vancouver on the absence of a modern sports facility, and the following year the Oakland City Council appropriated $7500 to study the possibility yet again. "A good stadium would get us back on the map of the sporting world," the vice-mayor contended. Nonetheless, the 1950's stadium agitation died for want of public response.

That agitation resumed in January 1960 with the arrival of the AFL in the East Bay. In March, a bond issue was placed on the coming November ballot for $13.7 million worth of stadium construction. In September, the referendum idea was dropped and, the following month, replaced with a mechanism by which a stadium could be built without risking a public vote—Coliseum, Inc., a private nonprofit corporation which would sell bonds to finance construction of a stadium and then lease the facility back to the city and county for $750,000 apiece per year. The stadium Coliseum, Inc., proposed to build would cost somewhere between $17 and $21 million. County approval finally came in late 1963, during Davis's phenomenally successful first year on the job.

The stadium Coliseum, Inc., would eventually complete was the last to be built before Clint Murchison introduced the superstadium in Irving. One of the sticking points in its development was the question of whether the Raiders would sign a longterm lease. The stadium corporation wanted Wayne Valley to sign up for twenty years. Valley refused. At the time, the AFL was hip-deep in the very expensive war with the NFL, and, as Valley put it, "I was losing my ass. It was not at all clear we were going to succeed." The negotiations over lease terms lasted two years. Coliseum, Inc., finally settled for a five-year lease with five three-year options. They agreed because Valley made what he called "a handshake deal" that he would never leave Oakland as long as the club was successful. At the time the discussions began, such "success" was, of course, highly problematical.

Making success real was Al Davis's job and he did it like a whirlwind. Inheriting a team that had won one game and lost thirteen the year before, Davis immediately bettered the record to ten and four. *Sports Illustrated* described his arrival on the AFL scene: "In flew Al Davis, big-shouldered, with half a scowl . . . eyes that seemed to be reflecting some hidden joke, a kidding voice, a you-and-me-know-about-*them*-don't-let's-kid manner, and with his fingernails mostly bitten off." Before Davis took over, according to one Raider player, "it was terrible. We practiced on lots with rocks and broken glass. There was no organization, no leadership. Then Davis came in and he went out and got it done, all of it, the whole shebang." By 1965, the Raiders were regular contenders for the AFL's Western Division championship and Oakland had begun to fall in love with them.

The rest of the AFL, however, had something of the opposite reaction. "It is not at all certain," *Sports Illustrated* noted, "where Al Davis would finish in a popularity contest among sharks, the mumps, the income tax, and himself." The source of Davis's unpopularity was his reputation for doing whatever it took to win, no holds barred. That reputation would eventually become so entrenched it was central to Al Davis's persona—the stuff of legend itself. As people came to believe Davis capable of anything, they spent a lot of time looking over their shoulders to see what he was up to. That in turn gave an advantage to Davis and further infuriated his opposition. An event typical of this phenomenon took place after Coliseum, Inc.'s stadium had been built and the Raiders were hosting their archrival, the San Diego Chargers. Just before the start of the game, when his team was making its way out into the stadium, the Chargers' coach sat in his team's locker room, alone and apparently deep in thought. When shouts reached him that it was time to take the field, the San Diego coach leaped to his feet and began shouting into the light fixture, convinced there was a listening device hidden in it. "Fuck you, Al Davis! Fuck you! I know you're up there. Fuck you!"

Love him or hate him, almost everyone in the football business agreed that Al Davis would be a considerable asset for any franchise for whom he might work. By 1965, he had turned down several offers to leave Oakland and coach elsewhere in both the AFL and NFL. He approached his task with single-mindedness, and his need to win seemed to provide endless energy. Even after he ascended to the ranks of ownership, he would still spend his evenings during football season studying films of the opposition, looking for cracks in their armor. "Al Davis is a very smart guy who works overtime," Wayne Valley observed. "This is his life, his whole life."

What life Davis actually had outside football was centered on his home in upper-crust Piedmont in the hills overlooking Oakland, where he lived with his wife, Carol, and his son, Mark Clark Davis, named after the World War II general who led the Allied invasion of Italy. Normally penurious, Davis threw a bar mitzvah for Mark Clark that was described as "one of the most lavish in the history of Oakland."

"She worries I don't spend enough time with our son, Mark," Davis said of his wife. "I tell her I didn't spend a lot of time with my daddy, but we were close. I really loved my daddy. It's not how much time you spend, it's what you do with the time you've got." Al Davis's marriage was happy and based on a clear ordering of priorities. "Thank heavens for the movies," Carol once commented. "Otherwise I'd never see Al."

"When we were married," Davis explained, "I said the only thing that would take me away from football was life or death."

Once, after a marathon film study session in the Raiders' offices, Davis returned to Piedmont very late. While Al was undressing, Carol woke up.

"Good God, you're late," she complained groggily.

"You can call me Al," Davis answered.

14

If at the annual meeting in Bal Harbour the other twenty-five members of the National Football League had known they would eventually be in a no-holds-barred battle with Al Davis, no doubt there would have been more than a little consternation. The AFL war was still a fresh memory, and Davis had emerged from it looking like a cross between Robert E. Lee and Genghis Khan.

Al Davis made that reputation during the four months in 1966 he spent as the American Football League's commissioner. His predecessor, Joe Foss, a war hero from South Dakota, was considered by most to be "too nice" for what had to be done. When Valley suggested Davis for the job, "everybody hated his aggressiveness. They said he'd do anything to win. 'That's fine,' I said. 'We need aggressiveness and we sure as hell need a winner.' " Valley's attitude took hold. "Davis would be the perfect choice," another AFL executive agreed. "He'll sit up all night scheming and conniving, trying to find ways to improve our league. He's just the kind of man we need to compete with Pete Rozelle. Pete is smart, ambitious, and dedicated but he doesn't have Al's extreme drive. In fact, nobody else has it either."

Al Davis lived up to all those expectations and more. Entering a conflict that seemed locked in costly stalemate, his response was blitzkrieg, upping the war another quantum level. Davis recognized that in terms of on-field performance, any football franchise's most precious possession was the contract of its starting quarterback. Using a leaguewide war chest, Davis set about raiding the NFL's prize quarterbacks, signing them to record-setting contracts and bonuses to induce them to jump leagues. "He is going to show the NFL that Pete Rozelle doesn't know anything about football," one AFL owner bragged. By June, Davis had seven of the NFL's fourteen best quarterbacks prepared to switch. On June 8, 1966, Pete Rozelle announced the two leagues had agreed to merge. One of the people from whom much of the negotiations leading to that announcement had been kept secret was Davis. "He didn't learn about it until it was announced," Tex Schramm remembered. "Al was displeased, to put it mildly."

The man who broke the news to Davis was Billy Sullivan, president of the New England Patriots. Sullivan had been one of the AFL's secret three-man committee charged with working out terms with another three-man committee from the NFL. Sullivan and Davis met for dinner in New York City. "Mr. Sullivan was kind of emotionally happy we were going ahead with this merger," Davis later testified about their meeting. "[I told him] I thought he had abandoned me and personally had sold me out and that we had the thing won and I thought they gave it away." Later asked on the witness stand if he thought Sullivan had engaged in a "conspiracy" against him, Davis responded, "It is a possibility. I would not deny it."

"I was the general who won the war," Davis later complained, "but the politicians lost the peace." He thought the terms were onerous, particularly the reparations, and bore no resemblance to state of the battle when peace was declared. "We knocked the hell out of the NFL," Davis explained. "We didn't have to give them nothin'." Davis would ever after describe the merger as football's Yalta. Perhaps the bitterest pill for him to swallow was Rozelle's retention as commissioner of the merged league. "Al saw his role as having completely dominated the player war," one of his Oakland friends commented. "He thought he'd showed up Rozelle as an ineffective leader. He expected to be offered the combined commissionership. He didn't recognize then that his methods had offended some of the owners. Even some in his own league were shocked by his piracy. The upshot was that he was so successful, he frightened the owners and ended any possibility of remaining as commissioner. Al had exposed Rozelle as a lesser figure, but it was Al who was left without a ship to steer."

Davis did not stay unemployed for long. In June, in New York at the AFL's offices, he started getting phone calls from Wayne Valley in Oakland. Valley's partners were disturbed he had ever let Davis leave and now wanted him back badly. Davis told Valley he could "relate to" becoming a general partner with "managing control." By July, Valley agreed to such an arrangement. "My philosophy," Valley explained, "is that key men should own a piece of the business." The piece Davis was given was ten percent, second only to Valley's in size. To make acquiring it easy, the book value of the franchise was listed as $185,000 and Davis was sold his share for $18,500. Given that the San Diego Chargers were sold to a group controlled by Gene Klein later that year for close to $10 million, in effect Al Davis bought a million dollars for $18,500.

Davis was also named managing general partner under a ten-year employment contract which specified, according to Davis, that "I would have total and complete operational control. I could do as I see fit. I used Mr. Valley and Mr. McGah [the other general partners] as consultants, a sounding board, but I would use my discretion and do all the things I thought were proper and right." When that contract was signed by all the other Raider partners in August 1966, Al Davis left the ranks of coaching forever. According to Valley, Davis's elevation changed him. "I thought he was aggressive," Valley remembered bitterly, "but if I had thought he was a crook, I would never have brought him back. Within that first year, he was a changed man. He gradually drew away from me, our discussions became limited, and he didn't want to talk about things. Al does things through other people and he built a wall between us."

While walling off Valley, Davis put the finishing touches on the organization he had been building since 1963. Its most notable quality was the degree to which it had been shaped in Al Davis's image. It was he who selected the Raiders' silver and black color scheme and he who provided their motto, "Pride and Poise." To build his team in the days before the merger, Davis had gathered "people who had proven athletic ability but could not be controlled in other cities" and "coaxed first-rate performances out of players who had been given up on." So much did he consider the game in which he employed them to be a "vicious battle" that the Raiders' game day agendas listed starting time as *"We go to war!"* The emblem on the side of Raiders' helmets was a man wearing an eyepatch with a knife clenched in his teeth. The result was an outlaw image that Davis cherished. "I don't want to be the most respected team in the League," he explained. "I want to be the most feared."

However many partners Davis may have had, there was no doubt that the organization behind the team was all his. "In order to run an efficient organization," he argued, "there has to be a dictator. People in an organization have to have the feeling that there's someone there who, if they don't move in the right direction, will chop." Not everyone fit easily into Davis's organizational scheme. He eventually acquired a reputation for going through public relations men at a rapid rate. "I used to go to work every morning with a knot in my stomach," one former employee told *Look*. "I never knew when the next attack was coming." Another former employee explained, "Davis's theory is that people are motivated by fear. He thinks people perform better if they are afraid."

"The goal," Al Davis pointed out, "isn't to be a topflight football team. The goal is to be the number-one football team." Davis's own singleness of purpose was profound. "The real thrill of life comes from setting goals, from meeting challenges, from overcoming adversity. . . . Singleness of purpose, a rational approach to all emotional situations, sound judgment . . . more than make up for huge staffs and computers."

Davis didn't drink or smoke, and lifted weights to keep fit. When offered coffee, he asked for water. He dressed habitually in his team's colors and when he went out to dinner, he inevitably ended up diagramming plays on the tablecloth. "Tell him a joke," one former employee pointed out, "and you'll get a blank look. But if a general manager on another club calls him up and congratulates him on some fast deal he put over, he'll laugh like hell."

Though his style was diametrically different from Tex Schramm's at the Cowboys, the success of Al Davis's system was predicated on information, just like Schramm's. "Davis always acts like he's got some kind of secret information nobody else knows about," one former AFL coach pointed out, "and much of the time it's true."

While the computer was at the heart of Schramm's information-gathering, the telephone was at the heart of Davis's. He once bragged to the editor of *The* [Oakland] *Tribune* that his phone bill was bigger than the entire *Tribune* newsroom's. He told others that he spent no less than five hours a day glued to a receiver. "Al has an amazing information system working for him," a friend commented. "He always knew what was happening. He stayed close to the sportswriter network in the NFL by phone and he had a network of friendly helpers who would go watch teams practice and other things. He called people so often, they expected to hear from him and didn't realize he was getting something out of it. He always laughed at scouting combines. He learned more over the phone.''

"Davis Sees Continued Raider Success" was the headline that announced Al Davis's return to Oakland, and he lived up to it. Within little more than a year, his Raiders were the old AFL's representative in the second Super Bowl, five years after he first came to town to take over the league's doormat team. His Raiders lost to the Green Bay Packers, 33 to 10. At the time, the merger was in its four-year transition stage during which the two old leagues met separately, played separately except for the final game of the year, and continued to negotiate just how the merged schedule slated to begin in 1970 would be organized. Though the merged NFL had no taste for him as a commissioner, Davis was a man of influence among the old AFL faction and played a central role in the drawn-out process of trying to make the peace final.

One of the things Al Davis did in that process was help keep football in Oakland. The advent of competition within their teams' old markets was the hardest pill for the old NFL to swallow. Specifically that meant New York City and the San Francisco Bay Area. On two different occasions during the merger process Davis was approached about moving the Raiders out of California. Both times, he refused. The first time was in response to a proposal by Dan Reeves. According to Davis, Reeves's idea was to have the AFL New York Jets move to L.A., the Rams move to San Diego, the Chargers move to New Orleans, and the Raiders to either Portland or Seattle. Davis's second refusal came in response to a meeting with San Francisco 49er President Lou Spadia during which they discussed the terms and conditions of a possible Raider move to Seattle. Davis went so far as to discuss the idea with Tex Schramm, but his answer was still no.

Davis also helped lead one final successful charge by the old AFL during the final moments of separation. The issue was how to align the new twenty-six-team league. It was agreed that the merged NFL would have two conferences, the National and American, but which teams to put where was a matter of intense disagreement. As *The New York Times* described the situation in early 1969, "Several NFL owners have not yet grasped the point that they must merge. . . . The NFL people drag their feet about integrating the AFL into conferences and divisions, hoping they will not have to give up comfortable rivalries for new arrangements with strangers.'' The NFL wanted, in essence, to continue to play as separate entities with a minimum of games between what were once different leagues.

This diehard position was the conclusion of a joint AFL/NFL Committee report given to the combined owners at a meeting in Palm Springs in March 1969. The loudest opposition to the idea came from Carroll Rosenbloom. He was trying unsuccessfully to move three old NFL teams over to the AFL, his own included. Eventually, after trading what were described as "bitter insults" with Art Modell, C.R.—characterized at the time by *The New York Times* as "considered by some to be the most powerful force in pro football''

—stomped out of the room. The proposal to which he objected needed eight affirmative votes from the old AFL for adoption and was blocked with the assistance of Al Davis, among others.

"Behind the scenes," *The* [Oakland] *Tribune* reported, "Davis was steering strategy. He held the AFL together. . . . Davis played the role of the quiet man for five days but he's lost none of his zeal or skill for infighting and he came away an AFL leader again." A source *The Tribune* would only identify as "one AFL owner" bragged, "The NFL couldn't handle us. We surprised them. They've come to the realization that we have harmony and we're determined to get partial restructure or a new alignment."

The issue of alignment remained unresolved until January 1970, the year the transition period was scheduled to end. Finally Rozelle kept the League convened for a marathon session in New York City, which culminated in a lottery in which three NFL teams were picked to join the old AFL. It was, in essence, Carroll Rosenbloom's original plan and his Colts were also one of the franchises to switch. The others were Art Modell's Cleveland Browns and the Rooney family's Pittsburgh Steelers. Each of the three was compensated with a $3 million payment to ease the transition. With that, the merged NFL became official and the AFL was dead.

By then, however, it was also apparent that the best of its commissioners was not. Al Davis might not be running a league now, but by no means was anyone rid of him. "Davis a Backstage Giant," his hometown paper proclaimed. Regardless of his unpopularity, the headline was accurate.

15

Despite having joined their ranks, Al Davis's opinion of football owners had changed little from the days when Wayne Valley first interviewed him in an Oakland hotel room. "Not all of them are the brightest of human beings," he pointed out.

In League meetings, Davis quickly developed a reputation for obscure statements in pursuit of strategies he rarely chose to reveal. "Mr. Davis is a clever man," Gene Klein complained. "Mr. Davis can talk in half sentences. He can say several things in one sentence. Personally, I think that is by design." Al Davis also had several voices in which he delivered his statements. One sounded as though he hailed from Brooklyn, one sounded as though he were from South Carolina, and another sounded as though he'd moved to California early in life.

Al Davis was not, however, isolated. Later, when questioned under oath, he would identify five of the twenty-six men who met in Bal Harbour as "friends" and claim "cordial" relations with another five. Among his friends was Tex Schramm. The two men worked closely together on the NFL's Competition Committee and Schramm was impressed with Davis's contributions. Davis described his relationship with Art Modell as "circumspect," explaining, "I think he senses that I don't like certain things about him." Al Davis's relationship with Pete Rozelle was even worse. At best, it could be described as uneasy.

Modell would blame Davis's animosity toward Rozelle on Rozelle's selection over Davis as the merged League's commissioner. "That gnawed at him," Modell claimed. "It was a Freudian kind of situation for Davis." Wayne Valley agreed with Modell. "He [Davis] thought he ought to have it [the commissionership]," Valley remembered. "He felt hurt." For his part, Davis denied all such claims. "I didn't want to be commissioner," he told *Look*. "No way. It's a desk job."

Whatever the reason, his lack of deference to Rozelle was a mainstay of League meetings. "Where others tended to tiptoe around Rozelle," one owner remembered, "Davis didn't even try to adopt social graces. When he disagreed, he'd just snap 'that's bullshit' or 'that won't fly.' That there was little respect was obvious." Rozelle remembered, "The antagonism was under the surface, but I knew it was there. I thought Al Davis was a good football man but that was as much as I could say for him."

Davis's public position on Rozelle at the time of the Bal Harbour annual meeting could be described as friendly—within limits. "We've become good friends in recent years," he said of the commissioner. "We have no problems. Of course it takes a long time to heal wounds, but there's no lack of respect, only a lack of camaraderie. Remember, during the war between the leagues, we weren't in the back room. We were in the front lines. It makes a difference."

Another, perhaps even greater difference was the two men's contrary visions of the NFL. To Davis, League Think sounded like " 'my league right or wrong' and I don't believe in that."

Even while Davis was publicly proclaiming his new friendship with Rozelle, the two men were in fact knocking sparks off each other behind the NFL's closed doors. At issue between them was an entity called NFL Properties.

NFL Properties was the League's independent "marketing and promotional company" and as a condition of the merger agreement, all clubs were required to grant it control of NFL copyright privileges. It also printed all the League's game programs and developed "other self-liquidating premium items they would work out with advertisers and sponsors designed to promote the League." NFL Properties generated a relatively small income. NFL Charities had been developed in 1972 to distribute those revenues. "It was," one NFL executive commented, "a good PR gesture."

It was also Pete Rozelle's pet project and during the first two years of NFL Charities' existence, all National Football League teams were members of it.

Then Al Davis withdrew. "I don't like the reason why Charities was formed," Davis pointed out. "If we wanted to give to charity, we would do it on our own as individual partners." From 1974 on, Al Davis demanded separate disbursement of the Raiders' one twenty-sixth share in NFL Properties' revenue and got it. Rozelle was powerless to force Davis but the incident grated on him. Later, when compiling examples of Davis's contempt for the principles of League Think, Davis's response to NFL Charities would be at the top of Rozelle's list.

Others among his fellow owners, when compiling examples of Davis's "ruthlessness," would point to "what he did to poor Wayne Valley."

Al Davis was not the kind of man to share power if he could figure out a way to corner it for himself—and he usually could. With the Raiders, that opportunity arose in 1972, during the seventh year of his ten-year managing general partner agreement. The subject of extending Davis's contract first came up inside the partnership at a 1970 Raiders meeting of all the general and limited partners in an Oakland banquet hall. Valley, Davis, and Ed McGah, the third general partner, sat together at the head of the meeting. At some point, the possibility of extending Davis's agreement arose and discussion moved around the room with each partner saying what he thought of the idea. Everyone was enthusiastic. When it was Valley's turn, he said he'd rather hear what Davis thought first. Davis said he had "no objection" to such an extension for another ten years.

Valley offered no opinion at that 1970 meeting but considered it "too early" to discuss the question. The contract, after all, had five years left to run. That Davis was not content to wait five years to insure his control of the franchise became apparent in 1972.

The organization of the Oakland Raiders Ltd. made his move possible. Under the terms of the franchise's limited partnership, it was necessary only for two of the three general partners to agree in order for the franchise to assume financial obligations such as a contract. As a consequence, Davis didn't in fact need Valley's approval as long as he had McGah's, and Davis had McGah in his pocket. "Al stroked McGah," one of Davis's friends recalled. "He made Ed think he was the best friend Al had. Ed swallowed it." Prior to the contract discussions he had with Davis, McGah "had no interest in the way the club was run. He was almost a silent partner. As long as the team played, he didn't care."

Davis would later claim he informed Valley of his intention to sign a new contract with McGah in the course of a meeting of the general partners on July 6, 1972, convened to discuss possible expansion of the Coliseum, Inc.'s Oakland–Alameda County Coliseum, which had fifty-five thousand seats, and was considered too small for the Raiders' overflow crowds. "I told Mr. Valley," Davis testified, "that I was going to sign the ten-year agreement that Ed was offering. . . . Mr. Valley went on as to how happy he was with the way things were going and wasn't concerned about it [the contract] . . . and just expressed great enthusiasm about the way the Oakland Raiders were going, that he didn't want any operational control, that he had his own business."

Four days later, Al Davis and Ed McGah placed their signatures on a ten-page employment agreement. Davis had to have been pleased with its terms. According to one NFL attorney, "it so broadened Al Davis's control as to not just involve the football operation but also all the business and financial parts of the partnership as well. It virtually relegated Valley and McGah to the status of limited partners." Ed McGah later admitted, first to Valley and then to *The* [Oakland] *Tribune,* that he had never read the document.

For his part, Wayne Valley never saw a copy of the contract until late November 1972. At that point, Valley's auditor was starting the year's audit and Valley got an unexpected phone call from him. The auditor said he had been shown a copy of a new contract for Al Davis by the Raiders' book-keeper. After giving Valley a thumbnail sketch of its terms, he said he'd send over a copy. "You better do something about it," the auditor advised. After reading it, Valley called Rozelle. Since he was already scheduled to be in the Bay Area in a matter of weeks, Rozelle said they could all discuss it then.

Rozelle's meeting with the Raider general partners was delayed several times and finally took place in February 1973. Rozelle was accompanied by Jay Moyer, the League office's in-house legal counsel. In addition to Valley, Davis, and McGah, the Raiders' attorney, Herman Cook, was also in atten-dance. The original purpose of the meeting had been to discuss a suit against the franchise by one of the limited partners. Then "out of left field," Valley announced his grievance. "Very dramatically," Davis later testified, "Valley pulled from a briefcase a newspaper and threw it on the table." The newspaper was the current issue of *Sporting News,* and contained an item about Davis signing a new contract with McGah.

"Is this true?" Valley demanded of Davis.

Caught unprepared, Rozelle and Moyer watched with "our jaws going slack." At the time, they had no idea to what Valley was referring.

When Davis answered that it was true, Valley roared, "How can you do this without me even being aware of it?"

According to Moyer, Davis responded by saying, " 'I can do any damn thing I want,' or words to that effect." According to Davis, "I told him that I had told him about it two different times. . . . McGah reiterated that he had told him about it . . . I said 'You knew about it and I don't know what the hell is bugging you.' "

"I am not going along with this contract," Valley fumed.

"What the hell do you mean, you are not going along with this con-tract?" Davis demanded.

"I'm not going for it," Valley repeated.

At this point, according to Davis, Valley "challenged McGah for taking such a big interest in football all of a sudden." McGah responded by asking Valley "what the hell he was pulling this in front of the commissioner for." Then "there was another little bit of an altercation between Valley and Cook and there was an altercation between Valley and myself."

Finally, Rozelle stopped the meeting and all the parties left the room. Valley cornered McGah outside in the hall.

"Why the hell did you sign it?" Valley demanded. "You never signed a fucking contract in your life."

According to Valley, McGah told him that Davis would have left for another team and he didn't want to lose him.

Valley then asked if McGah had read the damn thing before he signed it and McGah told him no.

Before leaving, Valley informed Rozelle that he didn't desire any intervention by the commissioner's office in the issue. This, he said, "is between me and Davis."

A month after the Oakland Raiders Ltd.'s meeting with the commissioner, the NFL convened its 1973 annual meeting in Scottsdale, Arizona. As usual, both Valley and Davis were in attendance. Both men represented the club during the League's general sessions, and when the League went into executive session in which each franchise was limited to one representative, Davis sat in for the Raiders.

Valley used the forum of that annual meeting to announce that he was suing Davis in California Superior Court. As one NFL attorney described the action, "Valley sought two things. The first was recision or at least amendment of Davis's contract so it at least didn't abrogate the authority of the general partners. Then he went the second mile and said, 'I want Al Davis out of this organization entirely because he's not fit to live with.' "

At the time of the Bal Harbour annual meeting in 1974, the lawsuit was still awaiting a court date. The tension between the two men remained obvious to the other owners. According to one NFL executive, the owners' reactions varied: "It depended on what kind of person you were. If you were a football person, you picked Davis. If you were an owner, you picked Valley."

While the war he was fighting with Wayne Valley added to the edginess the rest of the League felt about Al Davis, there were still no signs of the outright hatred Davis would generate when he later told the League to go to hell and went for Rozelle's throat.

16

When the League began coming apart, Gene Klein, majority owner of the San Diego Chargers, would be the most visible embodiment of implacable antagonism toward Al Davis. Klein's bitterness toward the Raiders' owner would be an NFL truism.

In 1984, Gene Klein would be deposed about Davis as part of a $30 million federal damage suit Klein had filed in San Diego against the man who was by then his archenemy. The attorney for Davis who questioned Klein was as yet relatively unfamiliar with their history and was feeling his way gingerly around the issue. "Isn't it true that you dislike Mr. Davis?" the attorney asked.

"Dislike?" Klein roared, "I hate the son of a bitch!"

At the 1974 annual meeting in Bal Harbour such feelings were not yet apparent to the rest of the NFL. Gene Klein certainly wasn't Al Davis's best friend, nor did he seem his worst enemy. In 1974, despite having been in the League for eight years, Klein himself had yet to really emerge as a figure inside the NFL. He had stature of a general sort through his membership in the exclusive television committee with Rozelle and Modell, but nonetheless lacked a firm place in the League's pecking order. It had been only the previous year that Gene Klein had decided to devote himself exclusively to the business of football, abandoning a meteoric career in the world of big money conglomerates. The career he abandoned had made him one of the richer men in the NFL.

Like Art Modell, Gene Klein had started life in New York City with relatively nothing. "We weren't exactly poor," Klein remembered of his Bronx childhood, "but we were struggling. My father was in the rag business." After graduating from high school, Klein could not afford to go to college full-time so he took work selling encyclopedias door-to-door and studied electrical engineering at NYU night school. Six feet five inches tall when he finally stopped growing, Gene Klein had played in his first sandlot football game at age six and fell in love with it. At NYU, he played end on the school's varsity between his encyclopedia rounds. Klein was in the stands at a New York Giants game on December 7, 1941, when the bombing of Pearl Harbor was announced. The man in the seat next to him asked Klein where Pearl Harbor was and Klein didn't know. The next day, Gene Klein enlisted in the Army Air Corps.

Klein spent the war as a pilot in the Air Transport Command, ferrying bombers to various fronts. At the end of the war, he was stationed in Long Beach, had a wife and baby daughter, and was fascinated with California. He stayed there after his discharge and, using two thousand dollars borrowed from his father, purchased what The [San Diego] Tribune later described as "a seedy little used car lot in the San Fernando Valley." His wife Frances remembered: "I had been so very poor, but I reasoned with Gene that I either would be very poor or very rich."

As it turned out, Frances needn't have worried. Gene Klein had a genuine knack for selling things. Named "Quality Motors," his first used car lot started with four cars, three of which he sold during his first day in business. "I had a buyer for the fourth," Klein recalled, "but I turned him down. I needed something to drive home." It proved to be the opening round in a somewhat legendary rise to the upper echelons of American enterprise. The gimmick that got Gene Klein started in the used car business grew out of Frances's 1946 complaints about the cost of hamburger. Inspired, Klein began weighing his cars and selling them by the pound. "Cheaper Than Hamburger," he advertised. He soon added more lots and then jumped into the new car business when he bought the western states' Volvo distributorship in the early 1950s. The Volvo distributorship made him wealthy. His next step made him rich.

It began on a golf course when a friend of his in the investment business talked him into buying some shares in National Theatres and Television Corp., then just a chain of aging movie houses saddled with a money-losing television production arm. Klein was soon invited onto National Theatres' board and named to a committee to find a new chief executive officer. The committee ended up asking Klein to take the job and he agreed on what he called "a temporary basis." Soon after he became National Theatres' CEO, the corporation was involved in a proxy fight that Klein's side won. "I get my dander up when I'm attacked," Klein explained with great understatement, "and I decided to stay on."

One of Gene Klein's first steps after taking over the reins of National Theatres and Television was to change its name to National General Corporation and write off the television production part of the business. At the time, National General had assets of $40 million, net worth of $8 million, gross sales of $40 million, and net profits of minus $8 million. A dozen years later, National General had $1.1 billion in assets, $270 million net worth, $600 million a year in gross sales, and a net profit of $48 million.

Klein's success had two distinct stages. The first involved making a success out of his firm's movie houses. To do so, he lengthened the intermissions from five to twelve minutes and instructed his employees to put extra salt on the popcorn to sell more drinks as well. By 1968, among National General's assets was what Klein called "the second biggest popcorn producer in the country." He also expanded National General's theater holdings by persuading "shopping centers to build theaters for him with money *they* could borrow on the strength of twenty-year leases with National General." By 1968, National General had 160 more theaters under long-term lease.

With the credit afforded by his movie houses' success, Klein launched his second stage and began making National General Corp. into one of the first of America's conglomerates. This led to what The [San Diego] Tribune called a "wild pyramiding of interests" under National General's roof during the 1960s. By the early seventies, those interests included moviemaking, savings and loans, insurance, book publishing, fruit distribution, and mobile home manufacture.

At the apex of that pyramid was Gene Klein, reviewing as many as five to ten possible acquisitions a day. Later he would regret that he hadn't "spent more time with Fran and the kids when they were growing up. Every day was a highly organized experience. My time was broken down to fifteen-minute segments. There were always thirty or forty calls backed up, always meetings to attend. . . . I was always under pressure to make decisions at what seemed like supersonic speed. . . . There'd be meetings in New York and Boston on Monday, Chicago and St. Louis on Tuesday, Denver and Salt Lake on

Wednesday. . . . Late every afternoon my secretary made up a full agenda of the next day's appointments and I'd take it home and study it at night."

Conglomerates were a controversial development in American business and Gene Klein's conglomerate was among the more controversial. In 1970, one of National General's insurance companies was levied the largest fine ever imposed by the New York State insurance department for alleged instances of self-dealing. *Business Week* noted Wall Street's "distinct coolness towards Klein's succession of complicated deals. The deals smacked more of 'cronyism and self-aggrandizement,' as one broker puts it, than of real interest in the stockholders." Klein defended himself: "I had a lot of support from the stockholders over the years, and I hope they appreciate what I have done to enhance their assets."

One facet of Gene Klein's business career that was not in dispute was the wealth it had brought him. Klein traveled in a chauffeured Rolls-Royce originally built for Queen Elizabeth and a Grumman Gulfstream private jet. His office at National General's Los Angeles headquarters overlooked Beverly Hills, Sunset Strip, and the Hollywood Hills. By the late sixties his two children were grown and Klein's principal residence with his wife, Frances, was a twenty-room house on six and a half acres at 1601 Lexington Road in Beverly Hills, worth some $3.5 million. His house in the country was on Palm Canyon Drive in Palm Springs and cost $500,000. He and Frances belonged to Beverly Hills's exclusive Hillcrest Country Club, where he played tennis with Debbie Reynolds or James Garner and socialized with Bob Hope and George Burns. When National General's stock began to sink somewhat in 1970, Klein convinced Frank Sinatra to buy in and stabilize the price. "The list of his business associates and friends," *Business Week* noted, "reads like a Who's Who of Southern California."

Among all Gene Klein's assets, the San Diego Chargers were closest to his heart. For years he flew his family and friends into town on game days and was, by his own admission, a man obsessed. Given the choice, he once admitted, "I would rather be in the NFL than the [U.S.] Senate." Before finally buying into the AFL Chargers in 1966, he had attempted unsuccessfully to buy into the NFL's Los Angeles Rams and the San Francisco 49ers. His chance at the Chargers arose when Barron Hilton, the Chargers' founder and heir to the Hilton hotel chain, was named president of the Hilton Corp. One of the conditions made by that corporation's board of directors on Hilton's appointment was that Barron give up his controlling interest in the San Diego football club. Klein had known Hilton for years and leaped into the breach with a partnership that bought up much of Hilton's share. The total purchase price of $10 million was, in August 1966, a record for NFL franchises.

A hearty, bluff personality, Klein looked "like a man who trims his hair with a lawnmower." He drew mixed reviews when he arrived on the scene in the League. "When he came in, he didn't understand the business," one owner remembered. "The guys who have the trouble in the NFL," another owner pointed out, "are those who think that because they've made it in the construction business or something, they can make it in pro football. It is not a particularly difficult business, but it's different. I'm not sure that Gene wants to put in the time to learn it." In his early days in the football business, it was not at all clear Klein thought he had anything to learn. "He's an authority on everything," one owner said privately, offering the opinion that "he doesn't know a fucking thing."

Gene Klein demonstrated his capacity to rub people the wrong way at his first meeting with the rest of the AFL in 1966. The decision to merge with the NFL had been made and announced, and now the two leagues were getting down to working out the specifics. It was a tense time. In one discussion about the financial structuring of the agreed-upon reparations, Klein began to lecture one of his fellow owners about limited partnerships. "Look, you son of a bitch," Klein began, "let me tell you about limited partnerships . . ." Klein got no further in his advice because the other owner jumped to his feet and "hit him in the chops."

Prior to his notorious hatred of Al Davis, the most public of Klein's disagreements was with his own partner, one Sam Shulman, and that was just a ripple on the Chargers' corporate surface. Originally Shulman and Klein had each bought 24.5 percent in the franchise, with Klein acting as the club's president and Shulman as chairman of its board. When still on good terms, the two men also bought a share in the Seattle Supersonics professional basketball team, only this time Shulman managed their interests. Shulman was also a member of National General's board. Their falling out came in 1972 when, according to *The* [San Diego] *Tribune,* "Klein's leadership of National General had been challenged by some of the corporation's officers." Shulman was among the dissidents whom Klein then "fired." As part of the breakup of their relationship, Klein bought Shulman's share of the Chargers and Shulman Klein's share in their basketball enterprise. When later asked about his former partner, Shulman said only, "I haven't any comment to make about Gene Klein that I would care to have publicized."

The split with Shulman marked the beginning of the end for Gene Klein at National General. "The heavy pace was getting to me," he later explained, "I grew tired of life at the top." When Frances died unexpectedly in March 1973, Klein decided to get out of the corporate life for good. "It was time to slow down and enjoy what I had," he said.

By fall 1973, Gene Klein had sold all his National General holdings. "I'll never run another business," he told the *Los Angeles Times.* "I've won that game." His only remaining active interest was his NFL franchise and soon he upped his share in it to fifty-six percent. He also added an $850,000 beachfront Spanish villa in La Jolla, just north of San Diego, to his collection of houses, and began living there during football season. Now that he was concentrating on the football business, he had his office in the Chargers' San Diego headquarters done over and the walls papered with what his decorator described as "a fabric with the color and texture of pigskin." He added a four-foot-wide and eight-foot-long burl elm desk and carpet in a geometric design of white and rust. "Mr. Klein is not an informal person," the decorator observed. "He likes quiet elegance. He is very European, very high style." Klein sported a mustache and muttonchops and kept a complete wardrobe at each of his three houses, all of it cut in the fashion then known as "mod."

"Retired" for the first time in his life and without a wife for the first time since World War II, the Gene Klein who attended the Bal Harbour annual meeting was content to drift and enjoy starting over. A little more than a year after Frances's death, he remarried. His birthday present to the second Mrs. Klein was a Mercedes wrapped in a pink bow and his engagement ring a thirteen-karat square cut emerald surrounded by diamonds.

"Now," Klein pointed out, "for the first time in many years, I am getting to know myself. . . . Instead of prowling around relentlessly in the jungle of business . . . I revel in my own discoveries of happiness. . . . The frantic pace is gone. There are no must-do appointments. . . . I just want to be truly free. My obsession is relaxing and avoiding tension."

As a prediction of the actual agenda lurking in Gene Klein's future, "relaxing and avoiding tension" could not have been further from the mark. When later asked to explain the discrepancy, Gene Klein would answer, "Al Davis."

17

In the disorder to come, Gene Klein would be not only Al Davis's worst enemy, he would also be Pete Rozelle's loudest defender, though his alliance with Rozelle was not yet apparent at Bal Harbour. In fact, Gene Klein came to the 1974 annual meeting in the commissioner's doghouse.

The incident that clouded Klein's relationship with Rozelle grew out of Klein's extreme frustration with his team's performance. After winning seasons in his first four years as an owner, the Chargers had nosedived to one of the worst teams in the NFL and Klein was frantic. Since the merger, his franchise had won 49, lost 56, and tied 7. Ordinarily fond of watching the game from down on the sideline of the field, he could no longer do so because he was being booed unmercifully by the San Diego crowds. "What the fuck am I going to do?" Klein roared at one of his employees in the team's locker room after a particularly galling loss. "That was the worst sixty minutes of football that the Chargers have ever played, and I've owned this goddamned organization for . . . years. The fans are rioting out there. I'm not sure it's safe to leave the stadium. We'll be the laughingstock of the League if we aren't already. . . . I've played these games all my life and now I'm stuck with rioting crowds and humiliation. . . . I can't even go into restaurants anymore without getting smiled at. We have to do something."

One of the Chargers' responses to Klein's desperation was to hire Dr. Arnold Mandell, chairman of the psychiatry department at the University of California at San Diego's School of Medicine. The idea was to see if a clinical psychiatrist could discover an edge that might turn losers into winners. Mandell had a particular interest in pharmacological research and it was that interest that ended up getting Gene Klein in trouble with the commissioner's office. What Mandell encountered among Klein's team was a pharmacological nightmare. "A drug agony rages, silently as the plague, through the body of professional football," Mandell later wrote. "It is likely that half the players [in the NFL] are using stimulant drugs to play. . . . Athletes stoked themselves with club-supplied uppers, usually Dexedrine and Benzedrine."

Mandell's discovery was not exactly a secret prior to his arrival at the Chargers for the 1973 season. In the 1960s, the St. Louis Cardinals had been sued by a former player for causing him to take "potent, harmful, illegal, and dangerous drugs . . . so that he would perform more violently." The drugs in question were dextroamphetamine sulfate, chlorpromazine hydrochloride, and sodium pentobarbital. During the 1972 season, one former Oakland Raider player later charged in an Oakland damage suit, the Raiders spent some $6000 on Daprisal and biphetamine that were administered by the club's trainer. By the time Mandell had signed on with the Chargers, the issue had become what Rozelle considered a "problem." That coincidence would eventually lead to the Chargers becoming what Mandell would call "sacrificial lambs."

That the League had a "problem" was made apparent to Pete Rozelle when, in late 1972 and early 1973, "Congress got all excited about it." That excitement took the specific form of a set of hearings about rampant drug use among athletes. At a League executive session in New York City on June 26, 1973, Rozelle took steps to "bring the situation under control," pointing out, "We have to be responsive to what is being learned." During a legal report, an attorney from Covington and Burling, the Washington, D.C., law firm kept under League retainer, "recounted the background of the NFL's concern with drug misuse" and "explained the recent discussions with Congressman Staggers following a study of drug misuse . . . by the Committee on Interstate and Foreign Commerce."

Following that report, according to Rozelle, "I announced to the clubs, this is the way it's going to be." Technically, it was called a "promulgation" and fully within his powers as commissioner. Henceforth, Rozelle declared, all clubs would have to file an inventory of "prescription drugs" with the League office, report "immediately any situation wherein one or more of the team's . . . personnel reportedly are involved in a drug incident," and participate in an expansion of League "educational programs, particularly in the ghetto area, designed to discourage drug use."

"The commissioner," the minutes of the meeting reported, "will take disciplinary action, up to and including suspension from the NFL . . . against team personnel for improper disposition or use of drugs." Rozelle warned, "This is a problem, and we're going to deal with it."

Dr. Arnold Mandell's style of dealing with the same problem insured that the commissioner's new policy would soon have an object lesson. After the fourth game of the 1973 season, the San Diego Chargers' psychiatrist had concluded "there was no way to discuss or manipulate the psychological aspects of pro football without grappling with the pervasive, systematic use of mood-altering drugs." Mandell's approach was to counsel players on the subject and prescribe the drugs people needed "so that they wouldn't go to Tijuana and get the bad stuff."

Rozelle first got hints of what Mandell was doing through the NFL's director of security. This director oversaw investigators under retainer in each of the cities with an NFL team. As the 1973 season progressed, reports began reaching them from Charger players who had been cut or traded since Mandell's arrival. Rozelle instructed Security to investigate further and, according to Mandell, NFL Security soon "had copies of some of my prescriptions, confidential medical records that . . . I had provided to the California State Board of Medical Examiners. . . . When I called the State Board of Medical Examiners [to find out how the NFL had obtained those records], they dismissed it with apologies, talking about 'inevitable cross talk in the intelligence community.' The commissioner was sounding more and more like Big Brother."

At the end of the 1973 season, Klein's team, despite the edge they hoped Mandell would give them, had finished with 2 wins, 11 losses, and 1 tie. For his part, the commissioner was now ready to act. According to Mandell, Rozelle next dispatched a letter to Klein. Mandell, reconstructing the text of the letter in his book, recalls that it said:

> The time has come when we must have a definitive resolution of the drug problems on your team. We have completed our investigations . . . [and] it is clear that you have not acted on warnings that were sent you. . . . You have either disregarded these warnings or have been inept in handling the problems. This situation cannot be allowed to continue. . . . My information indicates that Dr. Arnold Mandell, whom you state you have consulted in these matters, instead of helping may be contributing to the difficulties. . . . It threatens to soil the good name of professional football in this country. Significant punitive measures must be taken. . . .

The letter included an invitation for Klein to bring his attorney and Mandell along to a disciplinary hearing at League headquarters in New York City.

According to Rozelle, Gene Klein arrived at the hearing "upset." The two men then debated in the company of Klein's lawyer for two hours. One of the actions Rozelle proposed taking was banning Klein's general manager, the man responsible for Mandell, from the NFL for life. The proposal made Klein furious. It was reported that he threatened to sell his franchise immediately if Rozelle did it. Had he been willing to even go so far as to fire the general manager, Klein might have escaped a fine, but he wasn't. "I wouldn't make him the scapegoat," Klein explained. According to Rozelle, Klein's worry wasn't about the money a fine would entail "but because of the attitude of the papers in San Diego if I fined him. I told him I had to. We can't have a double standard."

Their meeting was followed by a press release from the League office. "Players and management of the San Diego Chargers were disciplined today for violations of the National Football League drug policies," it announced. "The discipline, imposed by Commissioner Pete Rozelle, consisted of fines totalling $40,000 plus probationary action." Of that $40,000, half the penalties were divided among the general manager and eight players. The other $20,000 was assessed against "the San Diego Charger Football Club" itself, "for supervisory omission by its administrative staff."

"Gene was angry at the time," Rozelle remembered, "but it didn't last too long. Gene did his best to forestall it but once the commissioner had acted, he accepted it and let it drop." The incident did not damage the two men's relationship. In truth, they would just get closer with this behind them. "Rozelle did what he thought he had to do," Klein explained. "We had our differences, but I'll tell you what, I always knew where he stood."

The fines themselves were hailed as precedent-setting, and some even predicted the action would turn the corner on athletic drug abuse once and for all. That, too, was an illusion. In truth, from here on in, wholesomeness was a vanishing NFL resource. While struggling to keep his bosses from savaging League Think, Pete Rozelle would also have to wage a constant campaign of damage control as real life bombarded the image they paid him to protect. By then, of course, Gene Klein was the commissioner's staunchest ally.

18

When war broke out within the National Football League, the front lines would seem to be occupied by legions of attorneys. To casual observers, the lawyers would seem to have suddenly materialized when Al Davis made his break with the League and Pete Rozelle set out to stop him. In truth, lawyers were already regular participants in the NFL's internal life.

Virtually all of the National Football League's serious legal dilemmas had their roots in the Sherman Anti-Trust Act. Passed in 1890, the Sherman Act declared "every contract, combination . . . or conspiracy in restraint of trade or commerce to be illegal." In the hands of the Supreme Court, that stricture was made significantly more vague by the interpretation that all such proscribed combinations and conspiracies had to be "unreasonable." Vague or not, the dilemma such a law posed for the sports business was obvious.

The business's basic form, the league, was on its face exactly such a monopoly to restrain and control the commerce of staging games. The open question of whether or not all its arrangements for doing so were "reasonable" insured a potentially perpetual state of litigation once lawsuits had become a relatively mass American practice.

Professional baseball escaped the dilemma in 1922, while the getting was good. That year, in *Federal Baseball Club of Baltimore v. National League of Professional Baseball Clubs,* the Supreme Court ruled that professional baseball was not interstate commerce and hence was exempt from the Sherman Act. In 1953, the Court sustained that decision in *Toolson v. New York Yankees,* arguing that since Congress had done nothing to change the situation since 1922, it had intended baseball to have an exemption.

Football's first significant encounter with the Sherman Act came in 1957, sixty-seven years after the law was enacted. The case was *William Radovich v. National Football League.* Radovich was a player who had begun his NFL career in 1938 with the Detroit Lions. In 1946, he asked to be traded to Los Angeles to be closer to his dying father and was refused. Radovich then jumped leagues and signed on with the old L.A. Dons of the All-America Conference. When he was offered a job coaching in the NFL after the All-America Conference folded, the League blocked the move. Radovich contended "this blacklisting effectively prevented his employment in organized football and was the result of a conspiracy . . . to monopolize interstate commerce in professional football." When the case reached the Supreme Court, the NFL argued that the Federal Baseball Club exemption ought to cover football as well. The Supreme Court did not agree. It may be inconsistent to include football and not baseball under the Sherman Act, the Court ruled, but it was up to Congress, not the Court, to remedy the situation. Henceforth, the Sherman Act was a fact of life in the football business.

Bert Bell recognized the danger posed by *Radovich v. NFL* and immediately began approaching Congress in search of a blanket exemption from antitrust law. Though he came close in 1959, Bell was unsuccessful. Rozelle took up the cause upon Bell's death. After securing a limited exemption to allow League Think to be applied to television revenues in 1961, Rozelle went back to Congress in 1964 and 1965 in search of something more comprehensive. Like Bell, Rozelle came close, getting bills through different houses in different sessions, but got no closer. Since securing another limited exemption to allow the 1966 merger, Rozelle had not been back to ask for more.

That inaction was a recognition of legislative realities rather than a quiescence on Rozelle's part about the potential dangers posed by the Sherman Act. Given the wrong ruling, he noted, "our whole League and everything it does could be found illegal." At the Bal Harbour annual meeting, he included in the commissioner's opening address his by now familiar admonition that "public statements by anyone associated with the NFL can have serious legal consequences." In 1974 Rozelle was concerned only about the Sherman Act being used against the League by "outsiders." It was still unthinkable then that any member of the League might use the statute against the League itself.

The principal Sherman Act "outsider" Rozelle worried about was the National Football League Players Association. Ironically, the impetus that had led to the League's recognition of a players' union in the first place had come from Bert Bell's attempts to get Congress to declare the NFL exempt. One of the complaints he encountered among politicians was the League's status as a nonunion employer. Bell promised to get the owners to change their stance and convened a meeting to raise the issue to his bosses. The response was less than overwhelming and most were content to let the meeting end without even bringing the union's status to a vote. With adjournment imminent, Art Rooney of the Pittsburgh Steelers took the floor and, according to his son, Dan, "forced the issue to a vote." He was assisted by Carroll Rosenbloom. Pushed to the wall, the League voted ten to two in favor of recognition.

Pete Rozelle's worries about the union on the antitrust front were, by 1974, anything but abstract. Since the filing of *John Mackey, et al. v. National Football League* in 1972, the League and the NFLPA had been at legal war. John Mackey, the principal plaintiff, was a former president of the union and tight end with Carroll Rosenbloom's Baltimore Colts. His suit challenged what the League called "the Rozelle Rule." Under this rule, any franchise whose contract with a player expired had the right to compensation from the player's new employer should that player subsequently work for another franchise. The compensation was to be a player of equal caliber, selected by the commissioner. The effect of the Rozelle Rule was to make competition between franchises for experienced talent virtually nonexistent, thereby suppressing player salaries. Mackey wanted the Court to award free agency, allowing players to sell their services without the penalty of compensation. Anything less, Mackey contended, was a violation of the Sherman Act. *Mackey v. NFL* was still awaiting trial.

John Mackey's name was on the suit but few of the men at Bal Harbour thought he was in fact the man behind it. That man, most agreed, was Ed Garvey, NFLPA executive director. In 1974, Garvey had been with the union for barely three years. Already most of the League considered him anything from an obnoxious nuisance to a dire threat. Even when they could agree on little else, from the time *Mackey v. NFL* was filed, the mention of Ed Garvey's name alone was enough to turn most NFL conversations unanimously ugly.

The owners of football first crossed paths with Garvey at the final stages of negotiations in 1970 for a new four-year union contract. At the time, Ed Garvey was fresh from the University of Wisconsin law school, in his first job with a labor law firm in Minneapolis. John Mackey brought the Minneapolis firm in to help write the actual contract once general agreement on terms had been reached. Garvey was assigned the task. The owners first heard about him from the players. As the actual contract was being written, language was negotiated between the two bargaining committees. One of the conditions of those negotiations was that no attorneys be present, just owners and players. .

Rozelle was present as well, but, according to the NFL constitution, he was "impartial," his role to look out for the interests of football itself rather than for one side or another. When the players wanted to consult their lawyer, they left negotiations and huddled in a room where Garvey was waiting. "You think we're radical," they told the owners back in negotiations, "you should hear what Garvey is saying in the back room."

John Mackey was pleased enough with Garvey's work that he hired him to be the union's new executive director once the contract was signed. His selection was confirmed by vote of the union's executive committee in May 1971. The only owner to congratulate Garvey on his new job was Al Davis. "The whole philosophy changed with Garvey's arrival," Lamar Hunt would later complain. "Now anything management did had to be negative." From Garvey's perspective, the union he inherited was weak and matched against people who "played for keeps." It was that weakness that led him to the Sherman Act. "Without the Mackey case," he later pointed out, "we would have been lost."

While the threat *Mackey v. NFL* posed to the Rozelle era's "all for one, one for all" economics would no doubt have been sufficient to make the owners gathered at Bal Harbour antagonistic to Garvey, the manner in which the case had been filed turned that antagonism vicious. Even Garvey would later call the timing of it all an "unfortunate coincidence."

Immediately before the filing, the League's relations with Garvey had seemed to be on an upswing, largely as a result of the efforts of Carroll Rosenbloom. "Carroll had a lot of confidence in his own ability to work with people," Rozelle remembered. "He talked with Garvey and Garvey agreed to talk to the owners. It was a meeting here in New York at the Waldorf-Astoria that I didn't sit in on. It was supposed to be an olive branch discussion."

"He was a bright young man," Wellington Mara described the Garvey who attended the Waldorf session, "and he was extremely conciliatory." Garvey himself considered the session "fun." He went on, "I enjoyed parrying with Joe Robbie and Billy Sullivan. I talked about the union and how I hoped relations would improve. They hollered about the union's newsletter. I enjoyed it tremendously." There was no mention in any of the Waldorf discussions of the Sherman Act or any possible lawsuit.

The next day, the NFLPA filed *Mackey v. NFL* in Minneapolis Federal District Court. By then Garvey was out of the country on vacation in Ireland and unavailable. "It was," Rozelle noted, "a gesture of absolute disdain. The owners were furious. They all called me about it."

When League Think started coming apart, Ed Garvey would hound the League's flanks, smudging its image, costing it money, and providing the owners with someone besides each other to hate. His decision to pursue *Mackey v. NFL* also presaged the form of the civil war to come. The Sherman Act would be the weapon of choice.

While both sides in football's 1974 legal war waited for a court date, the labor contract upon which Ed Garvey had done his first work for the NFLPA had expired. When the League met in Bal Harbour, *The New York Times* was predicting a strike. Three days earlier, Garvey had called a press conference to condemn the owners' "all-pervasive paternalism."

"Garvey is interested in breaking the NFL," Gene Klein pointed out, "making it impossible for us to exist."

19

When the League discussed its labor relations, it was reconvened as "the Management Council," without Rozelle present. "He is the commissioner of the entire game," Billy Sullivan's son Chuck pointed out, "concerned with the welfare of the owners, the players, and the fans, whereas the Management Council is strictly an owners group." The Management Council in turn hired professional negotiators for the actual negotiation process. Those negotiators were overseen by an elected management council executive committee. In 1974, its chairman was Wellington Mara of the New York Giants.

No single individual in the NFL better fit Ed Garvey's characterization of "all-pervasive paternalism" than Mara. The New York Giants were a family business, and Wellington, like all the Maras before him, treated it that way. "Next to my own family," Wellington, father of ten children, once told a friend, "I care most about the Giant family." Wellington, fifty-eight years old at the time of Bal Harbour, had known little but football for his entire life.

When Wellington was nine years old, his father, Tim, a bookmaker, had bought the Giants for $500. Though he had never seen an NFL game, "his belief," Wellington remembered, "was that an empty store with chairs in it was worth that much." One of Mara's earliest football memories was of standing outside church after a Sunday Mass and hearing his father tell a friend, "Today's the day we see if football can go over in New York." It did, and Wellington Mara had been an officer of the franchise since he was twelve years old. The arrangement came about when his father was putting all his assets in relatives' names in order to escape a court judgment. Wellington's older brother, Jack, was named Giants' president and Wellington secretary. Wellington's favorite team was the 1938 Giants. At the time he had just graduated from Fordham with a degree in philosophy and was resisting his father's demands that he follow his brother, Jack, on to law school. Instead, he asked to take a year and spend it in the football business.

That year turned into a lifetime. During it, Wellington chased balls at practice and roomed with the team's starting halfback. "All the fellows were my age," he remembered. "I was close to them, a part of them. There was an entirely different atmosphere in pro football in those days." In those days, the team all lived together in the Whitehall Hotel on upper Broadway. When they traveled, it was by train with plenty of time for banter and cards and "getting to know a man's character." The average salary on the Giants then was $2500 a season and most of the players had jobs in the construction industry during the off season. Wellington Mara was smitten by it all and, except for three years' duty with the naval reserve during World War II, had been nestled in the Giant family ever since. For most of that time, he had acted as the club's general manager.

His father, Tim, died in 1959, leaving equal shares in the franchise to his two sons, and Wellington's brother, Jack, took over the Giants' reins. "Jack was always the boss," Wellington pointed out. Jack died in 1965, leaving his fifty percent of the Giants to his son Tim. In the family's order of succession, the club was now Wellington's to run. Doing so was the culmination of his life's work, but Wellington's sense of his role and the franchise were still rooted largely in that first season after Fordham that had begun it all. By the time of the Bal Harbour annual meeting, that made him decidedly "old-fashioned" and as such, a poor candidate for dealing with Ed Garvey. The trouble he would have with that role was obvious to his players in 1971.

During that year's football season, Mara became worried that he had gotten out of touch with the team's players and approached the Giants' union representative, a defensive end, with his problem. He wanted the end to survey the team about their opinions of Mara's rapport with them and what they thought of the Giant family. The union rep did as Mara asked and reported back with the survey results one Tuesday at 1:00 P.M. "He asked for an honest report," the end later told *Sports Illustrated,* "and I gave it to him both barrels. I told him, 'You have no rapport with the players and the Giant family image is not there. There is no question about it.' He was crushed when I told him. I wasn't trying to hurt the guy, but to tell him the truth he asked for. He sat back, maybe asked me a couple of questions, and then shook my hand and said, 'At least you gave me an honest answer.' " By 4:30 that same Tuesday, the defensive end who had given Mara the report had been cut from the Giants' roster and was out of the family for good.

Wellington Mara's life-style was also old-fashioned. A self-described "homebody," he lived in Westchester County and commuted to the Giants' Manhattan offices every day after first attending Mass. He had met his wife, Ann, in church, when they both rushed to help an old woman who had fainted. At the time, Ann worked for the Jesuit missions. "It was a sporting courtship," she recalled. "While all my friends were at the Stork Club, I was at the Fordham gym." The Maras had four sons and six daughters. For years they lived in White Plains and most of their friends were Catholic doctors from their old neighborhood. At Wellington's instigation, a priest was appointed the Giants' honorary chaplain. Mara also sent tickets for every game to the rector of St. Ignatius and the faculty at Fordham. One section of seats for Giants games was known as "Jesuit Row."

The tickets Mara distributed were perhaps the most sought after in the business. The Giants had the League's longest waiting list for season tickets and seats at the Giants games were even the subject of hot combat in divorce settlements. Traditionally, the Giants were always a League leader in attendance receipts. That box office success in the League's premier city was the source of most of Wellington Mara's stature inside the NFL. Otherwise, opinions of him among his fellow owners were mixed. "He's from the old school," one noted, "a stubborn Irishman with good instincts." Another said, "He's a staunch League man." Yet another: "He's real gentlemanly." An NFL executive added, "A nice guy," while another said, "He gets on his high horse and preaches sometimes. He's also a little goofy." Another owner offered, "Something of a wimp."

Despite his lack of flash, Wellington Mara was the object of no small amount of envy from his peers at Bal Harbour. He arrived there as perhaps the most successful player ever in the Superstadium Game. Just as Ed Garvey's recent recourse to the Sherman Act presaged the terms of the League's combat to come, Wellington Mara's round in the superstadium game presaged almost exactly the situation in which civil war would erupt.

Mara's opponent was the city of New York, until 1972 his landlord at the city's Yankee Stadium. At the time, John Lindsay was mayor. The wild card in the contest was New Jersey, in the form of Sonny Werblin, head of the New Jersey Sports Authority. Werblin had been the managing owner of the New York Jets until 1969, when his partners Phil Iselin and Leon Hess forced him out. When Sonny Werblin resurfaced in football, he was the guiding light in plans for a new sports complex to be located in the as yet undeveloped marshland just across the Hudson from lower Manhattan. One of the first people Werblin approached was Wellington Mara. Though the two had been bitter crosstown rivals during the AFL war, they were now on good terms. Mara told Werblin that he was "receptive to a possible move."

Mara's receptiveness was a function of his dissatisfaction with both his stadium and his landlord. "Yankee Stadium was built for baseball," he pointed out. Mayor Lindsay recognized as much but insisted that a remodeling job was the answer. Mara disagreed. "It's just a new coat of paint on an old lady," he said of the mayor's plan. While talking with Lindsay, Mara was also talking to Werblin and liked what he heard from New Jersey much better. Werblin's plans called for a seventy-five-thousand-seat outdoor football stadium to be financed by a $300 million state bond issue that would also pay for building a racetrack next door. "Giants Stadium" would also feature theater-style seats, two instant replay scoreboards, a two-story press box, and seventy-two luxury boxes. The luxury boxes would be financed separately by the Giants and would become their private property, initially rented out, mostly to corporations and banks, for $16,000 a year each.

Wellington Mara signed a lease on the as yet unbuilt and unfinanced Giants Stadium in New Jersey's Meadowlands in September 1971. The contract framed what was, by everyone's standards, a "generous" deal. According to *Sports Illustrated,* the Giants "get free office space, free watchmen, free maintenance staff, free cops, free scoreboard crew, free insurance, free water, free heating, free electricity, free sewage and waste disposal, and free transportation for all fans who have to park more than a quarter of a mile away. The Giants pay only for the PA announcer and their phone calls. The

Giants also get twenty-five percent of parking fees, 400 free parking spaces, fifty percent of concessions, all advertising in programs and souvenir books . . . all membership fees in the stadium club, all radio and TV revenue, and up to 2,700 free tickets per game.'' The rent was fifteen percent of gross receipts.

Newsweek renamed Mara's franchise "the Hackensack Giants.'' Mara protested: "New York is not losing a team, but gaining a sports complex.'' The new Giants' home field was just seven miles from midtown Manhattan, he pointed out, only a mile more than Yankee Stadium. The explanation made little headway with the city of New York. The city's first response was to evict the Giants from Yankee Stadium, even though their lease had another three years to run. "If they want to play in a swamp,'' one city politician snorted, "let them play in a swamp right now.'' As a consequence, the Giants spent the three years they had to wait for their new stadium as vagabonds, playing first in Yale Bowl in New Haven and then returning for a short stay at New York's Shea Stadium under Lindsay's successor, Abraham Beame. When Mara first signed his lease with New Jersey, John Lindsay had also threatened to sue over the Giants' continued use of New York in their name, but nothing ever came of it.

The most serious of Lindsay's threats was "to seek another NFL franchise'' to play inside the city limits. For an NFL member to make such a move into an established football market would require, according to the provisions of the NFL constitution's Section 4.3, unanimous approval of all member clubs, giving Mara a veto on any new cross-river competition. Realizing Mara would likely exercise his veto, Lindsay also warned that if the League did block such a move, he would sue under the Sherman Act.

In retrospect, all the rhetoric surrounding the Giants' move to East Rutherford, New Jersey, would sound like premonition. Seven years later the language would all be repeated virtually verbatim in Los Angeles when Carroll Rosenbloom finally decided to give "the Grand Duchess of Stadiums'' what he thought she deserved. The difference between New York in 1971 and Los Angeles in 1978 was that New York did nothing to back up its threat. The Giants kept selling out wherever they played and New York ended up with little more than sour grapes to fall back on.

Most of those sour grapes were hurled in Wellington Mara's direction. Attacking the New Jersey move, a *New York Post* column asked, "What else can you expect . . . from the son of a bookmaker . . . an Irishman named Wellington?''

Mara ignored press comments as a rule, but the *Post*'s derision stung him. Shortly after it was printed, Mara responded angrily at a speech to a Giants' welcome-home luncheon. "I'll tell you exactly what you can expect from an Irishman named Wellington whose father was a bookmaker,'' the Giants' owner lashed out. "You can expect that anything he says or writes may be repeated, aloud, in your own home, in front of your children. You can believe that he was taught to love and respect all mankind—but to fear no man. And you can believe that his two abiding ambitions are that he pass on to his family the true richness of the inheritance he received from his father the bookmaker—the knowledge and love and fear of God—and, second, that the Giants win the Super Bowl.''

Other than vituperation of Mara, New York's only other serious response was to fight a rear guard action, hoping to derail Werblin's nascent plans for New Jersey's swamps and leave Mara nowhere to go. To actually build Giants Stadium, New Jersey had first to sell several hundred million dollars' worth of construction bonds. According to Mara, ''New York bankers were told quietly that if they bought bonds, they would no longer receive any city or state business. Sonny Werblin had to overcome strong opposition. Fortunately, the banks and businesses of New Jersey stepped in.'' It was a close fight and the New Jersey Sports Authority almost didn't make it. At one point, New Jersey's governor even described the plan as ''dead.'' Finally, a month before the Bal Harbour annual meeting convened, the bond issue was completely subscribed and New Jersey's Meadowlands sports complex became a financial reality. ''No public money was spent,'' Mara would later brag, ''and the investment made out like gangbusters.''

On the second day of the 1974 annual meeting, Wellington Mara assumed the chair and, once Rozelle had left the room, convened the Management Council. The NFL's minutes made no note of exactly what the council discussed, but at a press conference later in the week, Rozelle, the ''impartial'' third party, stated that professional football could not function without the Rozelle Rule and that, whether or not there was a strike, the 1974 season would not be canceled.

20

Baltimore was represented at Bal Harbour General Sessions by Robert Irsay, the other half of Carroll Rosenbloom's notorious franchise swap, and Joe Thomas, the man who had found Irsay for Rosenbloom and was now the Colts' general manager. The newest member of the nation's most exclusive club, Irsay was still something of an unknown commodity. Most viewed him as the creature of his general manager, Joe Thomas. Thomas himself shared that view of Robert Irsay and was not reluctant to express his opinion in public. Shortly after becoming general manager for the Colts' new ownership, Thomas hosted a dinner in New York City the night before the Colts were to play the Jets.

''Where's Mr. Irsay tonight?'' a reporter present at the dinner asked. ''If I were he, picking up the tab for this wonderful dinner, I'd want to be here to enjoy it.''

''Forget him,'' Joe Thomas replied. ''You guys are still living in the

Carroll Rosenbloom era, where the owner took you by the hand. The owner counts for nothing. Just don't worry about him.''

"Well, he hired you," the reporter pointed out, "so he counts for something."

"Get this straight," Thomas snarled. "He didn't hire me. I hired him. I could have had six guys for that job and I picked him. He's in the League because I brought him in."

The last statement was accurate. Irsay would likely never have entered the NFL had not Thomas found him for Carroll Rosenbloom at the last minute, when Rosenbloom was desperate to head off a competing bid for the Rams. According to an attorney involved in the transaction, Irsay was called in Chicago and told that if he wanted to own the Baltimore Colts, to "get your ass out here and bring $5 million."

"We have transpired a deal," Robert Irsay proclaimed at the press conference announcing his entrance into the NFL. "Pro football is one of the most exciting things in my life." His only previous contact with the League, he admitted, had been as what was described as "one of those wealthy regulars" at Chicago Bears games. He was a friend of George Halas, their owner, and also knew one of the Bidwill brothers who owned the St. Louis Cardinals. "I think all the owners are great guys," the Chicago air-conditioning millionaire added.

The response of the Baltimore press corps, Carroll Rosenbloom's old bugaboo, was enthusiastic. "New Colt Owner's Approach Refreshing" the News-American headlined. "There was a lot of 'gee whiz' about Irsay yesterday as he stood at the microphones in an upstairs room of the Chesapeake Restaurant. But it was the kind of feeling with which almost anybody in the room could identify. . . . Irsay was pleasingly nervous and wasn't particularly embarrassed by it. . . . He is as naive and enthusiastic about owning a National Football League team as Rosenbloom has become jaded." Robert Irsay was seen, in The Sun's words, as "a sturdily-built, chesty man who nevertheless comes across as less hefty, less imposing than his newspaper photographs. He looks fit for anything, somewhat along the lines of an archetypal military officer. . . . He has a firm handshake and you soon gather, from talking to his friends and associates, that his word is his bond. He's honest they say. For a millionaire, they say, he's a helluva guy."

For Baltimore newspapers, it was a gushy reception. They took Robert Irsay at face value and, indeed, as Irsay described himself, there were a lot of attractive features. "Amazing accomplishments," the Colts' new game programs declared, "are nothing new to Irsay." A self-described "Hungarian tin knocker," Irsay had started life poor in the rough "Bucktown" section of Chicago. Through hard work, the profile Irsay commissioned about himself claimed, he "enrolled in the University of Illinois, where he received a mechanical engineering degree and played 'fourth or fifth or sixth string quarterback.' From 1941 to 1945, he served in the U.S. Marine Corps with the First and Fourth Divisions." Most of Irsay's military career, he claimed, had been spent in combat. "I was wounded once pretty badly in the leg," he told *The Sun,* "in New Guinea, hit by a grenade, but it didn't do any permanent damage."

"Following his discharge as a lieutenant," Robert Irsay spent five years working in his stepfather's "ventilating business." The money Irsay used to buy the Colts came from an air-conditioning firm he had founded with "an initial investment of $800" borrowed from his wife in 1951. "In twenty years, he expanded that investment into one of the world's most famous heating, ventilating, and air-conditioning firms." Irsay was lucky enough to have $5 million cash at his disposal when Joe Thomas found him because he had sold Robert Irsay Company to Zurn Industries for $8.5 million the year before. The rest of the Colts purchase price was borrowed.

Certainly Robert Irsay arrived in Baltimore with all the accoutrements of wealth: an $800,000 home in Winetka, Illinois, a Learjet in which to commute from Illinois for Colts games, a retreat in Florida, and a sixty-five-foot yacht named *The Mighty I.* Eventually he would also buy a condominium in Hunt Valley, Maryland, another house in Dallas, and a fourteen-seat Lockheed Jetstar aircraft to replace the Lear. Normally the wealthy weren't accorded a lot of gratuitous sympathy in Baltimore, but in Irsay's case there was enough visible human pain in his life to make him appear sympathetic.

A devoted family man, Irsay and his wife, Harriet, had three children, Tommy, Jimmy, and Roberta, and by the time Irsay joined the football business, tragedy had overtaken two of them. His oldest son, Tommy, had been born mentally retarded and, at age eight, placed in an institution in Florida. "They bring Tommy home once a year," an Irsay family friend observed, "but it's hard on everyone." In 1971, Irsay's tragedy was compounded when his daughter, Roberta, was killed in an automobile accident on Interstate 294 outside of Chicago. For years afterward, the Irsays would keep Roberta's room intact, "full of pictures of Roberta riding horses" and "rows of ribbons she won." According to his wife, Irsay never got over the loss. "I can't say I have everything I want," the new Colts owner told *The Sun.* "If I could, I would want my daughter back, but that's impossible. They caught the kids who ran her car off the road. They were on drugs when it happened. They got ten to twenty years, but the way things are today they'll probably be out in five. I felt like killing them myself, but that wouldn't help anything."

Such was the tenor of the times when the League met in Bal Harbour that no one had yet bothered to check the facts of Robert Irsay's life as he claimed them to be. It would be another ten years before anyone bothered to do so.

By then, the Baltimore press corps' picture of Robert Irsay had grown decidedly more negative. "The Colts owner is," *The Sun* would write in 1984, "an insecure man who deeply desires to be courted, a man given to royal tantrums when he doesn't get his way, a man prone to titanic swings in behavior. . . . There has been widespread speculation that Mr. Irsay drinks heavily. . . . [He is] a loud, brutish, erratic man who cannot be taken at his word . . . an interfering, miserly, incompetent manager . . . a man who thrives on turmoil no matter the cost." In that mood, *The Sun* finally set out to

find if Robert Irsay really was the man he claimed to be and came up with a
history significantly at odds with the one Irsay had commissioned.

Though Irsay claimed to have graduated from the University of Illinois
with a bachelor of engineering degree, the registrar's office there had records
of him attending only from the fall of 1940 to the summer of 1942 and
leaving without a degree. When asked about Irsay's claims to having been a
combat marine for the duration, a spokesman for the Marine Corps replied
that "records show a man with same name, birth date, and father's first name
enlisted as a staff sergeant in October 1942." That "Robert J. Irsay" had
been demoted for taking a jeep without permission and "getting into a minor
accident." A year after he entered the Corps and without ever having seen
duty overseas, this Irsay was discharged under conditions the Marine Corps
would describe only as "not dishonorable."

The "$800" of his wife's money Robert Irsay claimed he had used to
start his business was not what it seemed either. "It was really a lot more
money than that," Harriet Irsay admitted, and it didn't come from her. "A lot
of older men had faith in him and helped him." Even his story of Roberta's
death turned out to have been significantly embellished. Though Irsay claimed
that "kids on drugs" had forced her car off the road and were apprehended
and sent to prison, "the state police accident report shows no such arrests,
that no other car caused the accident, and that the car in which Roberta was
riding struck a guardrail, rolled down an embankment, and hit another car on
another expressway."

Typically, Robert Irsay would continue to distribute the same biography
even after everyone to whom he gave it knew it was considerably short of
accurate. By then, his reputation inside the NFL would be suffering from the
same problems as the one he had in Baltimore. One fellow owner tried to
defend him. "He makes irresponsible statements and he drinks a lot, but he's
not a bad guy. He's just a little crazy and off the wall sometimes." An NFL
executive offered an even more blunt opinion: "His brain is baked." He
continued, "He's a jerk who says the dumbest goddamn things. You have to
talk to him early in the morning or he's unintelligible."

In 1974, however, Robert Irsay was still largely hidden from view by Joe
Thomas, at least in the League's General Session. In executive session, when
each team was limited to one representative and Joe Thomas was absent, he
revealed more of himself. Still, the Colts "war hero" owner came off as little
more than eccentric to the rest of the owners gathered in Bal Harbour. "No
one paid much attention to him," one owner noted, "but you couldn't shut
him up. It was all heated participation with no substance. You had to suspect
whether he knew his ass from a hole in the ground but, like I said, nobody
paid much attention to him." All anyone in the NFL knew for certain about
Robert Irsay in 1974 was that he had a profound dislike for Carroll Rosenbloom.

In accounting for Irsay's antagonism, some observers claimed Irsay felt
C.R. had misled him about the stadium possibilities in Baltimore and others
pointed out how upset Irsay had been about the details of the player contracts
he inherited from Rosenbloom. The most obvious reason was the swap that

had brought the two men together in the first place. While Rosenbloom was applauded as slick for having pulled it off, Irsay was assigned the role of the sucker who had made it all possible. "He was pissed at my father because the media wrote that Carroll had made a brilliant move," Steve Rosenbloom remembered. "Irsay took heat for that and reacted. He began to resent it after the fact and couldn't see that it was in fact the only way he could ever have got into this closed fraternity." For his part, C.R. considered Irsay "a fool"—"not for the swap," Steve remembered, "but just for the way he was at meetings."

Whenever possible, Carroll Rosenbloom made a point of keeping his distance from the man he'd brought into the NFL. At one of the annual meetings after their swap, however, Irsay cornered Carroll and his son Steve as they waited for the hotel elevator. Irsay reportedly smelled of liquor and that, in itself, turned C.R.'s stomach. "Carroll didn't drink," Steve pointed out. "He had gotten very sick once on prohibition booze and ever since, the smell of a drunk was enough to turn his stomach." While Rosenbloom waited uncomfortably for the elevator, trying not to get queasy, Robert Irsay ranted in his face. "You couldn't even understand what he was talking about," Steve remembered. "He was literally unintelligible." Finally the elevator arrived and Carroll and Steve fled into it, leaving Irsay standing on the threshold, still "ranting."

C.R. shook his head. "Jesus Christ," he muttered to Steve. "Do you believe that guy?"

When the NFL ship later hit rough seas, Robert J. Irsay of the Baltimore Colts would be the loose cannon careening about on its decks.

21

The Executive Sessions in which Irsay was fast making his reputation as an idiot among idiots were reserved for the League's most sensitive discussions. Closeted by themselves with Pete Rozelle in the chair, the owners attended to the business at the heart of their business. Standard items on the executive session agenda were the selection of Super Bowl sites, reports from the League's finance committee, and the most sensitive of the NFL's discussions with its attorneys. The rest of the agenda was devoted for the most part to tinkering with the structure and composition of the League itself. As a consequence, Executive Sessions were also the setting in which, unbeknownst to its audience, all the warfare inside America's Game began.

In the years between the 1966 merger and the 1974 annual meeting, the hottest executive session issue was summarized among members as "owner-ship policy." The designation referred to the League's standards for membership. Prior to 1966, those standards were little more than a loosely enforced, informal, and largely unarticulated understanding rather than a constitutional requirement, enforceable by the commissioner's office. "Just having a policy was enough in those days," Rozelle said of the years before the merger. "On important matters, people just didn't violate them." By the time peace had been reached with the AFL, however, Rozelle had concluded that "it was important that it be specifically reduced to writing." In so doing, the commissioner hoped to formally standardize the character of the League's ownership, much as he had already standardized its marketing and internal economics.

That standardization had been an open Rozelle priority since he and Tex Schramm prepared for Schramm's first peacemaking meeting with the AFL's Lamar Hunt in the spring of 1966. While described by Rozelle as no more than an articulation of what was already a Leaguewide understanding, the attempt to formalize an ownership policy was unprecedented and authorship was for the most part ascribed to Rozelle alone. "It is the commissioner's rule," Edward Bennett Williams observed. "That is why we had it thrust upon us every year."

Rozelle's first such attempt was to have his ownership policy formalized as part of the final NFL/AFL merger agreement. The actual ownership policy the commissioner sought was a further elaboration on the theme of League Think, containing four principal provisions.

The first prohibited "corporate ownership." While entities like Anheuser-Busch, Ralston Purina Corp., and CBS owned franchises in other sports leagues, such were not allowed in the NFL. "A corporation engaged in other business activities owning or controlling one of our football teams would make it impossible for us to control ownership in our League," Rozelle explained.

The second provision of Rozelle's ownership policy prohibited public ownership of NFL franchises, either through purchase by governmental entities or through the issuance of publicly traded stock. Again the issue as Rozelle saw it was control. Public ownership, the commissioner noted, deprived the League of its ability to regulate both who owned a franchise and those owners' other activities. "You would [also] be required to make more disclosures of your business through stockholder reports . . . [and] the stockholders of a public company might well have different views than what might be prudent in operating a football team."

The third provision was called "the fifty-one percent rule," and would require all franchises' ownership to include someone with at least a bare majority, so that franchise control was vested in a single individual. "Virtually in every instance where a team has not had a fifty-one percent rule," Rozelle pointed out, "there has been a problem. . . . There's been disharmony, there have been disputes, and there's been several cases of litigation where clubs did not have one firm, controlling entity. You eliminate internal disharmony within a club if you have one person with that fifty-one percent."

The final provision dealt with "cross-ownership" and was by far the most controversial. At issue was the ownership of other sports businesses by

NFL members. The League's "traditional position" was that "no person having an operating control of a franchise in the National Football League may acquire control of, directly or indirectly, any other team sports enterprise or business." To Rozelle, such prohibitions were appropriate. "I feel," he explained, "that in order to have harmony, unity of purpose and to avoid disruptions which make it more difficult to get things accomplished in a league, you should avoid such cross-ownership conflicts. . . . With the very strong sharing of income . . . you get ill will developing within a league, lack of cohesiveness, when some owners see others they feel are not carrying their proper share in promoting the League."

According to Rozelle, "there were always twenty-one or more clubs in support of the policy" he and Schramm first articulated to Hunt. The only differences, he claimed, were over how exactly to apply it. Nonetheless, those differences were sufficient to doom Rozelle's initial 1966 attempt to reduce ownership policy to constitutional League Think. Instead of a constitutional amendment containing the explicit details of ownership policy, the Supplementary Merger Agreement signed on December 1, 1967, and dated December 1, 1966, bound "all present franchises of the NFL and the AFL" to "present NFL [ownership] policies" but only "with respect to changes of club ownership after February 1, 1967."

Had Rozelle not been willing to settle for the continuance of a vague informality which exempted all violations by those who were members prior to 1967, it is doubtful he would have gotten any written ownership policy at all included in the merger agreement. A number of the new NFL's members were in violation of one or more of Rozelle's ownership standards and in no mood to force the issue:

• Lamar Hunt was an original investor in the Dallas franchise of the North American Soccer League, a founder and fifty percent owner of the WCT professional tennis tour, "indirectly" the sponsor of a professional bowling team, owner of a large piece of a Dallas minor league baseball franchise, and eventually a ten percent partner in the Chicago Bulls professional basketball franchise.

• The Rooney family had "significant" horse racing and racetrack interests and briefly bought into a Pennsylvania soccer franchise.

• Gene Klein shared control of the Seattle basketball franchise with Sam Shulman for several years.

• The New England Patriots NFL franchise of which Billy Sullivan was president had no fifty-one percent owner and had issued publicly traded stock.

• The Green Bay Packers were owned by a quasi-public civic group and had nothing even approaching a fifty-one percent owner.

• Since Wellington Mara had an equal share of the New York Giants with his nephew, the Giants lacked a fifty-one percent owner as well.

• Since half of Clint Murchison's reported ninety percent of the Dallas Cowboys was secretly owned by his brother, the Dallas franchise also failed under the fifty-one percent rule.

• Art Modell briefly dipped below fifty-one percent control of the Cleveland Browns and had also sponsored a golfer and dabbled in horse racing.

• Bud Adams of the Houston Oilers had an interest in a short-lived American Basketball Association franchise.

• Bill Bidwill, the Bidwill brother who would eventually control the St. Louis Cardinals NFL team, also owned a piece of a soccer franchise.

• George Halas, an NFL founder and still owner of the Chicago Bears, had once owned a piece of the Chicago Cubs baseball franchise.

• Jack Kent Cooke, a partner in the Washington Redskins, also owned the professional basketball and hockey franchises in Los Angeles.

While accepting the political impasse created by those realities, Pete Rozelle considered the 1967 solution to the ownership issue to be stopgap at best. He resumed his quest to make ownership policy both formal and comprehensive once the merger's mechanics were at last finalized in January 1970. His opportunity to do so arose at the annual meeting in March of that year, when several owners brought the subject up for discussion. According to Rozelle, the discussion "was prompted by concern about estate sales," which, under the terms of the merger agreement, would be subject to the standards he had developed four years earlier. "Some of the clubs felt that such restrictions as the fifty-one percent requirement and no public stock issuance and no corporate ownership . . . were too restrictive and would hurt the sale of a franchise . . . and families might be forced to divest . . . rather than continue to operate the club. . . . They suggested it be reviewed and I did appoint a committee to make a study of our ownership policies."

Pete Rozelle's power to appoint intraleague committees was a significant one. Its result in this case was an essential reinforcement of his ownership policy agenda. That the commissioner considered the task assigned the three-member "special committee on membership rules and ownership policy" of extraordinary import was apparent in his choice for chairman. The job went to Tex Schramm's boss, Clint Murchison, thus occasioning, when the committee made its report to the membership, one of Clint's rare appearances at a League meeting. The second member of the committee was Gerald Phipps, owner of the Denver Broncos. The third was Edward Bennett Williams, president of the Washington Redskins and the most vocal internal critic of the commissioner's proposed ownership policy. "It was quite clear I was outmanned two to one on the committee at every stage," Williams remembered.

The actual report of the special committee was produced by the League's attorney who, according to Williams, "talked to the members" and then prepared "a report that constituted a consensus of the three." That report was presented to the membership by Clint Murchison at a meeting on May 15, 1970. Its League Think premise was apparent in the first paragraph: "It is the view of the committee that the information [given] most consideration should be the effect the League's rule would have on the League and professional football rather than on the interest of those presently having ownership positions."

The report's principal proposed policy modifications were to the fifty-one percent and cross-ownership provisions. The fifty-one percent rule was loosened to permit "fragmentation" as long as one person still had the right to make a franchise's decisions. The cross-ownership provision, however, emerged in an even more restrictive form. The special committee's proposal would have refused approval of "any future transfers of interests in member clubs" to anyone with "either a majority or minority interest in other professional sports organizations."

The committee's recommendations were tabled pending unspecified further discussions. That a majority supported the general aims of the amended policy, if not yet its particular applications, was a circumstance Edward Bennett Williams ascribed to the fact they were "more susceptible to the domination of the commissioner than others." Whatever the reasons, ownership policy did not stay tabled for long.

In February 1971, Art Modell opened the issue again by circulating his own memo on ownership policy in preparation for the 1971 annual meeting scheduled for March. Modell's "confidential memorandum to members of the National Football League" proposed changes in both the public stock prohibition and the cross-ownership policy. The public stock aspect was motivated by what Modell described as concern "about a liquidity problem" and the additional difficulties the stock provision placed on translating a franchise's accrued value into actual cash. "I was trying to put together an alternate plan," Modell explained, "an idea . . . that might allow us to offer, in limited ways, public stock ownership in a football franchise for the purposes of preserving liquidity." The idea went nowhere when it was discussed by the League in March. "My plan failed for lack of a second," its author remembered. "I had no support in the League."

The same could not be said for his idea on cross-ownership. It amounted to the most serious assault yet, not only on future cross-ownership, but on the heretofore sacrosanct grandfather provisions as well. Those provisions exempted all violations predating the League's formal prohibition. After discussing a "proposed rule that no controlling stockholder, voting trustee, officer, or employee of a member club may own an interest in any other major sports teams or enterprise," Modell proposed that "a period of three years shall be allowed for disposal of present interests inconsistent with this policy." While the Browns owner considered his proposal "generous and fair in giving people a chance to divest," to its more flagrant violators it was remarkable for even raising divestiture at all. "It was quite a departure from the earlier policy," Lamar Hunt remarked.

Art Modell's cross-ownership proposal was not immediately accepted, but it raised the ownership policy stakes geometrically, and in so doing, initiated a new era of internal conflict in the NFL. It also narrowed the issue. Henceforth, discussions of ownership policy would focus virtually exclusively on cross-ownership and so would Rozelle's quest for a constitutional amendment. In the immediate moment, the commissioner succeeded in galvanizing the majority behind his policy and they made their weight felt when the

League met in May 1971, two months after Modell's memo died for want of a second.

The meeting in May was held in the League's New York City offices and ownership policy was a principal part of the agenda. "The commissioner," Joe Robbie of the Miami Dolphins remembered, "reviewed for all the owners . . . the NFL policy with reference to other major team sports and the general nature of the discussion was what the policy should be now." Rozelle himself considered such cross-ownership a "conflict of interest," but as usual said little in the official discussion. The majority who supported his position were not yet prepared to demand as stringent a solution as Modell's, but demanded formal action of some sort soon. At this stage, the discussion "centered on no one acquiring a new interest or increasing a present interest. They," Rozelle noted of the owners, "were satisfied with holding the line while they attempted to work out the other guidelines."

"It was agreed not to take any action now," the minutes of the May 1971 meeting reported, "on the understanding that the present embargo against anyone acquiring a new interest or increasing a present interest in a major league team sport should be continued until the League establishes a policy."

The agreement was, Rozelle pointed out, "another stopgap," and the commissioner's attitude insured that the truce it signaled was only momentary.

22

Pete Rozelle needed three quarters agreement in order to pass a constitutional amendment and in a matter as sensitive as telling his bosses what they could or could not own, marshaling that agreement would prove no small task.

Once the activity generated by Modell's memorandum had spent itself, Pete Rozelle seized the initiative without apparent reservation and included an amendment on ownership policy in the 1972 annual meeting's March agenda. The League's minutes described it as a measure that "would have clarified constitutional language concerning possible conflict of interest resulting from ownership in other team sports." Though a number of other amendments were discussed and acted upon at the annual meeting, the discussion of the amendment number eight on ownership policy was delayed until May, when the League met again in their New York City offices.

The case in favor of prohibition was framed by Rozelle's concern over "conflict of interest." While those arguments were being made, Tex Schramm and Art Modell lined up the commissioner's backing. They were assisted among the old AFL franchises by Billy Sullivan. "A conflict of interest could exist," Schramm maintained. "Even those who were involved in cross-ownerships felt that.'' Among the majority proponents of the commissioner's proposal were the Rooneys, who were now out of soccer and only in horse racing; Gene Klein, who was in the process of divesting himself of his basketball interest; and a good portion of the remaining roster of past, current, or potential violators. While the intensity with which each individual in the majority made his particular argument varied, ''everyone,'' according to Schramm, ''felt a strong necessity to do something about it.''

The premise of the commissioner and his majority was that the football business was in competition with all other sports businesses for a limited pool of ''sports spectator dollars.'' To promote other sports was therefore automatically stripping the NFL of potential revenues. It was, the proponents maintained, a situation that bred conflicts of interest at every turn. What if an NFL owner is involved in another league and the other league takes a position in ''our relations with Congress'' contrary to the NFL's? Precisely that had happened in 1958, Rozelle pointed out, when professional baseball had opposed Bert Bell's initial attempts to get football exempted from the Sherman Act. What if an owner of another sports franchise uses the health and profitability of his NFL holdings to maintain a floundering investment in another league, thereby ruining them both? Again, the commissioner pointed out, exactly that had happened recently when the owner of a prosperous hockey franchise had ruined it by covering the losses of his basketball team. Were that to happen in the NFL, everyone in their common enterprise would suffer. Just as worrisome as the potential dilution of capital was the dilution of operational talent. An owner who had to divide his attention, it was argued, robbed the League of his fullest effort. If that same owner either by accident or design also ''leaked things said at NFL meetings'' to his other sports business, the outcome would be ''a damaging cross-pollination of confidences.''

The proposition's critics included Lamar Hunt and Joe Robbie, but chief among them continued to be Edward Bennett Williams. Already a legendary courtroom attorney, Williams was, as a maker of speeches, easily the most persuasive voice in the NFL. He was also, as one of his fellow owners described him, ''one of the brightest men in the League.''

''I always got along well with Williams,'' Rozelle remembered. ''He was a very authoritative speaker and very helpful at the League meetings. I went to his fortieth birthday party. He's a charming guy. But over this issue we had differences.''

''Differences'' would eventually prove an extensive understatement of the conflict between the two men.

''When this matter was discussed,'' Williams recalled, ''I begged the owners of the National Football League to abandon this thing, this folly, as being prospectively outlandishly costly, and all for nothing. It's just burning the barn down to roast the pig.''

Edward Bennett Williams agreed with none of Rozelle's arguments to the contrary. ''There was no other major sport that could enforce such a proscription,'' he pointed out. ''The same know-how that helps you run one

sports franchise will help you run the other. . . . I don't think there is a
dilution of talent or resources or energies. . . . In 1970, when the mayor asked
me to help him get a baseball team in Washington, I . . . [tried] to importune
a baseball team to move to Washington just as a civic duty. . . . I thought it
was not only good for Washington, it was also good for the Washington
Redskins. . . . It's been proven time and again that it's great for Lord and
Taylor to have a Neiman-Marcus in the same shopping center because they
both benefit. I believe the same thing holds in sports. . . . I thought it was an
imprudent rule [and] that it was not in the interests of the League. . . . To
have such a rule would circumscribe the prospective pool of owners of NFL
franchises . . . and it was in [the League's] economic interest to have the
largest prospective pool of owners that there could be. Furthermore . . . there
were all sorts of people in the National Football League who had other sports
interests, then, now, and at all times.''

Key to Rozelle's strategy was narrowing the number of those interests
covered by the prohibition, thereby minimizing personalized opposition. To
do so, he had confined his proposed amendment to ''major sports.'' Williams
described it as an effort ''to tailor some rule that would sweep in as many
people as possible.'' The language, he pointed out, was ''carefully tailored so
that those people in the League who owned horses or racetracks or dog tracks
or tennis teams or who owned other sports wouldn't be offended by the
proposal and would vote for it. . . . I never understood it. . . . If the rule had
validity, it seemed to me, if there was a sound basis for it, then it would be
equally applicable to all sports, but it was never proposed in that form.''
Though he found any cross-ownership proposal abhorrent, Williams's riposte
in this instance was to unsuccessfully demand the widest and most comprehensive prohibition possible.

Another key to Rozelle's strategy was to gather sufficient momentum to
enter his prohibition in the constitution itself rather than settle for one of the
lesser levels of legality with which his majority might express its approval.
On that front, Williams's counter arguments made headway. Rather than such
a constitutional amendment, Williams endorsed a resolution expressing ''the
will of the majority'' that would ''obtain for the ensuing year.'' The attorney
explained, ''To put such a policy into a constitutional amendment would be
more objectionable to my lights than to have simply a resolution which
required reaffirmation each year. . . . If it had gone into the book as . . . a
bylaw, I would have thought it would take a great deal more in the way of
persuasion to remove it. A bylaw has a certain permanence about it. . . . To
be in breach of a bylaw would carry disciplinary consequences,'' whereas
''breaching a resolution'' was a matter Williams thought considerably more
''amorphous.''

Amorphousness was still attractive among the majority in 1972, and
Rozelle fell short once again. On May 25, according to the NFL minutes,
Rozelle's proposed amendment ''was withdrawn, and in its place, this resolu-
tion was adopted to be effective through the 1973 NFL Spring Meeting:

RESOLVED, that no person owning a majority interest in or direct or indirect operational control of a member club may acquire any interest in another major team sport. Additionally, any person holding such financial interest at the time this Resolution is adopted will in no case increase his percentage of such interest.''

The resolution was moved by Billy Sullivan and seconded by Art Modell. Satisfied its language was vague enough to live with, the pro-cross-ownership minority agreed to make the resolution unanimous.

While a lot less than he ultimately intended to get, the resolution of May 1972 was nonetheless a victory in Rozelle's political ledger. For six years he had sought at least "something in writing" and now he had it. The resolution secured the major team sports limitation essential to maintaining and motivating his majority, and in the course of discussing it, Rozelle had also won a remarkable concession on the issue of divestiture. "All agreed," according to the official record of the discussion, "that there would be a best effort made to dispose of current holdings." While only an informal "agreement" to the vague standard of "best effort," it nonetheless tightened the pressure on the grandfathered interests and insured that divestiture would henceforth be discussed by the majority as a matter of when to do it rather than whether or not it should be done.

When the 1972 resolution came before the League for renewal at their meeting in June 1973, a new element of personal animosity entered the discussion, introduced by Leonard Tose of the Philadelphia Eagles. Tose had said nothing in the preceding seven years of the ownership policy debate, but made up for it in a hurry. He was furious with Lamar Hunt and had been nursing that fury privately for months. Tose's anger had been inspired the preceding January when Hunt journeyed to Philadelphia and held a press conference announcing the formation of a Philadelphia franchise of the North American Soccer League. The end product was a story on the front of *The Philadelphia Inquirer*'s sports page, including a picture of Hunt accepting a check from Philadelphia contractor Tom McCloskey, a friend of Tose's and the new Philadelphia soccer entrepreneur. The gesture infuriated the Eagles owner. "Leonard Tose," Joe Robbie remembered, "was miffed that another owner would come into his city and attend a press conference for another sport."

When Tose expressed his feelings to Hunt, the commissioner and twenty-four other owners were in the room. "I was indignant," Tose admitted. "I confronted [Hunt] personally and tried to stand up close to him so he would get my message. . . . Mr. Hunt is not that big a man alone, but what he has done is taken the prestige of the NFL and turned it into bringing a team into Philadelphia to compete . . . rather than coming into Philadelphia to help me. . . . The mere fact that [Hunt] sits in our meetings and [then reports] whatever we do to the soccer league to me is reprehensible. . . . It turns my stomach. It is against everything I have been taught. It is un-American. . . . I don't have the vocabulary to tell you how disgusting that is to me."

According to Tose's later testimony in court, when he brought up the Philadelphia newspaper story "and confronted Mr. Hunt with it, he denied it, said he had nothing to do with it [so] I sent down to Philadelphia and had copies made from the newspaper. . . . When I passed it around amongst our fellow owners," Tose noted contemptuously, "Mr. Hunt, I think, was still inclined to deny it."

Hunt remained unruffled by the attack. "Lamar is a very laid back seeming guy" an NFL executive noted. "He's hard to get excited." When Tose demanded a report about the state of Hunt's agreed upon "best efforts" to divest himself, Hunt simply offered that he was working on it.

Had they been asked, all of the League's other cross-owners would have answered the same way. No one had sold off anything during the year in which the 1972 resolution and its accompanying agreement had been in place. Instead, the ranks of cross-owners had indirectly grown. The addition was Joe Robbie of the Miami Dolphins and his cross-ownership was indirect because the soccer interest with which he had recently become associated had been purchased by his wife and not himself. Nonetheless, Robbie would personally serve as an ex-officio member on two of the NASL's internal committees. That peculiar twist on cross-ownership "conflict of interest" would eventually cause Robbie to bear the brunt of the commissioner's disapproval, but in 1973 "the Robbie situation" was outside his ownership policy's control. For his part, Joe Robbie had been a vocal opponent of Rozelle's policy even before his wife's purchase.

"This policy through the years has been more honored by ignoring it than enforcing it," Robbie complained. "I haven't gone trumpeting soccer around the country. And when I have been asked questions about soccer, I usually answer the questions I'm asked. . . . I don't consider soccer that highly competitive to professional football." Robbie also scoffed at Rozelle's "selective" notion of conflict of interest. "The first time I ever walked into a North American Soccer League meeting," he pointed out, "the same lawyer who was advising the NFL at that time was on the platform advising the NASL. Covington and Burling . . . were representing both leagues on the same subjects." Robbie, an attorney himself, offered that if the League's lawyers didn't consider the two in conflict, there was hardly much case for the owners treating it any differently.

Despite Joe Robbie's new status, Lamar Hunt's lagging "best efforts," and Leonard Tose's outrage, Rozelle didn't force the issue in June 1973. The expiration of the 1972 resolution itself provoked only a short discussion. "The question simply came up that the one-year resolution was expiring," Joe Robbie remembered, "and it was agreed that the policy be extended for two more years." This time the vote to do so was twenty-one yes, one no, and four abstentions. Edward Bennett Williams cast the one no. Lamar Hunt voted yes, not wishing to "disturb" the rest of the League. Joe Robbie still registered a yes as well, "willing to have the rule continued on a temporary basis." Robbie's sentiment was widely shared, and the NFL executive session minutes for June 26, 1973, recorded the text of a resolution and "agreement" identical to the previous year's, except the expiration date was now 1975. The new two-year term, according to Robbie, "was done to avoid bringing it up the next year."

At that, at least, it was successful. The Bal Harbour annual meeting in 1974 was the first one in five years at which ownership policy was not the subject of belabored discussion. Despite that respite, the crack Rozelle's insistence had already wedged in the League's common front was now a fact of executive session life. Down the line, that same crack would mark the spot where League Think first started coming publicly apart. When it did, Al Davis would have all the precedent he needed.

23

In 1974, Pete Rozelle accepted the "limitations" of the League's continuing resolution and, for the moment, considered ownership policy a dormant issue. The presence of Lamar Hunt in the opposition likely had more to do with the League's "unreadiness" than any other single factor. Forty-two years old at the time of Bal Harbour, Hunt was already enshrined in the Pro Football Hall of Fame and was a legend in the business of staging games for profit. Though not quite the football business power he had been in 1966, he was still a man of significant stature, particularly among former members of the AFL. Most of the owners at the annual meeting referred to him as simply "Lamar."

Despite that familiarity, the first thing anyone ever noticed about Lamar Hunt was his last name.

"Hunt" and "wealth" were already synonymous when Lamar, aged twenty-seven, entered the football business in 1959. *Texas Monthly* described his father, Texas oilman H. L. Hunt, as "the richest man in America," worth "around $2 billion" in 1954, with an "after-tax income of $54 million" a year. Lamar was the sixth and youngest child of H.L. and his wife, Lyda Bunker Hunt. When it was later revealed that H.L. had secretly fathered eight more children by two other women, Lamar and his five siblings were henceforth referred to as Hunt's "first family." They all started wealthy and, for most of their lives, got only more so. Asked on the witness stand to state his occupation, Lamar Hunt, then worth "over $500 million," would find himself momentarily at a loss. "I guess the way you describe it," he finally answered, is "self-employed."

Specifically, the root of Lamar's fortune was the trust established by his father in 1935. Each of H.L.'s first family received a similar arrangement, and between them, the trusts of Lamar and his brothers and sisters controlled Placid Oil Company, "reputedly the world's largest privately held company." In 1978, the worth of Placid's reserves would be estimated at "in excess of $2 billion" with "a gross annual income of $300 million." While each of the first family held a variety of other interests individually, "the most significant thing" about them, according to *Texas Monthly,* "is their cohesiveness." The Hunts did, however, have "their disagreements." As one Hunt friend elaborated, "Family meetings can be a real scene. Bunker says, 'I know how it is, it's like this.' Margaret says, 'No, it's like this.' Herbert says, 'No, it's like Bunker says; I took notes.' Lamar says, 'Why do we always have to go through this?' And Caroline doesn't say anything."

Margaret, the first family's firstborn, was seventeen years older than Lamar and "reigned as queen bee." Haroldson Lafayette Hunt III, the second born, had suffered a nervous breakdown and been institutionalized since Lamar was in junior high school. Caroline, the second sister, "impressed everybody with the gentleness of her disposition." Bunker, born fourth, assumed the mantle of internal first family leadership and became a legendary oilman in his own right. By 1961, at age thirty-five, he was being described as "at least on paper, the world's richest man." Herbert, the next brother, was born three years after Bunker and three years before Lamar. Herbert was considered "the steadying force of the family" and was a partner in a number of Bunker's oil deals. Together with Lamar, Herbert and Bunker also owned Penrod Drilling, one of the world's largest drilling contractors. Both Lamar and Herbert were dedicated joggers. Bunker, on the other hand, was a habitual eater and would eventually balloon to three hundred pounds. Lamar was considered by *Texas Monthly* as "the most preoccupied of the Hunt brothers, the one who is always off in his own world . . . determined to make a name for himself apart from the family."

That he chose the football business to do so no doubt came as little surprise to his brothers. As youngsters, he and Bunker went over the small print at the back of the sports page together, discussing what all the numbers meant. "I read the box scores and the attendance figures," Lamar recalled. "I was always interested in attendance at sporting events." Lamar also "grew up playing football." At Hill School in Pottstown, Pennsylvania, the young Hunt was a halfback and captain of the varsity during his senior year. He returned to Southern Methodist University in Dallas for college. Despite being under six feet, thin, and wearing glasses with thick plastic frames, Hunt played wide receiver for all four of his years at SMU, though never in enough games to earn a letter. A geology major, Lamar started his first sports business while still an undergraduate. It was a batting cage where a swing at ten balls cost a quarter and was very successful, as was the watermelon concession he soon added to it. After that came a miniature golf course, but it failed. "We expanded too fast," Hunt later explained. Two years after bailing out of miniature golf, Lamar decided to get into professional football. "I just felt I had a good understanding of the entertainment world," he explained. "It was a challenge and I think I had some good ideas."

Lamar's quest for a football team was actually set off by a conversation with Bunker in which both brothers agreed that Dallas could support a pro football business despite the failed 1951 franchise which had fled east and become Carroll Rosenbloom's Baltimore Colts. In 1958, Lamar called NFL Commissioner Bert Bell with the idea of expanding into Dallas but Bell said "the League was not interested." In 1959, Hunt resumed his quest by trying to buy an existing NFL franchise with the idea of moving it to Dallas. The franchise was the Cardinals, then in Chicago, and the attempt was unsuccessful. Though the League wanted the Cardinals to leave Chicago, the then owners, the Wolfson family, wanted to stay. Lamar had several meetings with the Wolfsons, but they would not agree to sell more than forty-nine percent and that was of no interest to Hunt. In the course of those negotiations, he learned that three other parties had approached the Wolfsons about their franchise: Bud Adams in Houston, Bob Howsam in Denver, and Max Winter in Minneapolis. All had been run through the same routine as Lamar.

Lamar Hunt's final meeting with the Wolfsons was held in Miami and afterward he caught a commercial flight back to Dallas. On that flight, the American Football League was born. "It was just like one of those cartoons, where the light bulb goes off over the character's head," Hunt remembered. "That is one of the few times in my life that I felt something like that. I just thought, 'Why not start another professional football league?' " Hunt elaborated on the notion: "Why wouldn't a second league work? All the basic information I needed had been supplied by the Wolfsons in the four or five months we had tried to negotiate a sale. They had dropped the names of . . . a bunch of people on the outside wanting in. . . . Why not start a new league? . . . It was all very simple, which is one of the big reasons I think it worked. There were no studies, no marketing reports, because none was needed. Like all successful products, there must be a need, or you must create one. We did not have to create one."

After returning to Dallas, Lamar immediately put in a call to Houston's Bud Adams, a Texas oil scion like himself, and arranged to talk business over dinner. When Hunt got to Houston, Adams was still sore from his treatment at the hands of the Wolfsons and agreed to Hunt's proposal. "From that point on," Hunt remembered, "I was trying to recruit people. I went to Denver and Minneapolis. Nobody turned us down, so now we had four cities. The original thought was to field a six-team league and include New York and Los Angeles. You needed them from an image standpoint. Television wasn't that big a deal then." Realizing the AFL was getting close, Hunt sent an emissary to Bert Bell, "to inform him there was going to be a new league and that we wanted him to be the commissioner of both. I told myself I didn't want to go into this if it meant some kind of battle. Of course," Hunt admitted, "this was one of the more naive thoughts in the history of sports." The emissary returned with Bell's refusal. He thought the new league would fail but wished them luck.

Hunt was still "pondering over what our next step should be" in July 1959, when he received an unexpected phone call from Bell. As part of his continuing effort to secure NFL exemption from the Sherman Act, the commissioner was due to testify in front of Congress at the end of the month. According to Hunt, Bell "wanted permission to mention our league. I'm sure he felt it would be helpful to him if he could. I agreed, but asked that he not mention any names or cities." Hunt then flew to Washington and sat unrecognized in the back of the hearing room when Bell testified. Prior to the NFL commissioner's appearance in front of Congress, the public knew nothing of Hunt's new league. Bell changed all that early in his statement. "I want to tell you about this new league," he volunteered to the congressmen. "I can't tell you any of the details, but there are going to be eight or nine cities." As befitting an entity seeking exemption from antitrust law, Bell promised the NFL would "foster and nourish" its new competition. "The news created an incredible stir," Hunt remembered. "No one had put up a penny and I had no commitments from anybody in New York or Los Angeles, but Bert Bell, the NFL commissioner, had announced it, had said we were in business."

Less than a week later, on Lamar Hunt's twenty-seventh birthday, he and Bud Adams made Bell's announcement official at a press conference in Adams's oil-company office in Houston. Though both men represented the first entry of second-generation Texas oil money into the football business, one looked the role and the other didn't. Adams's office was "the biggest in a business known for offices the size of football fields" and "complete with barbecue pit, lily pond, and a desk as long as a bowling alley." Adams himself was thought "flamboyant" and habitually dressed in white cowboy hats and full-length leather coats. Lamar Hunt could not have seemed more different. Dressed in a business suit and conservative tie, Hunt was "shy, quiet, and frugal, in appearance almost a ringer for Wally Cox," the star of a 1950s television series called *Mr. Peepers*. The two Texans told the thirty reporters in attendance that they were the first of the league's franchise holders and that others would be identified soon.

Over the next few months, Hunt collected and announced six more teams to go along with his Dallas Texans and Adams's Houston Oilers. Bob Howsam took the Denver Broncos and Max Winter the Minnesota Vikings. To fill out the Los Angeles vacancy, Hunt found hotel heir Barron Hilton, a man whose chief previous claim to notoriety was having once had Zsa Zsa Gabor for his stepmother and Elizabeth Taylor as his sister-in-law. Hilton's team was called the Chargers. The hotel heir "really didn't know a lot about football," according to Hunt, "but he enjoyed himself." New York was occupied by the Titans franchise, sold to one Harry Wismer, a former broadcaster. Hunt remembered Wismer as "a lovable rogue who spent everything he had to make his team successful, but he finally ran out of money. He ran his team out of his apartment." Ralph Wilson initially approached Hunt by letter and was hence "the first mail order franchise." A native of Detroit, Wilson had made his money in trucking and wanted a team in Miami, where he kept a winter home. When the city of Miami refused use of its Orange Bowl stadium, Wilson settled for Buffalo and named his team the Bills. The last addition to the original AFL roster, the Boston Patriots, were also its first "phone order." Hunt offered the opportunity to Billy Sullivan during a Sunday long distance call if Sullivan could come up with $25,000 by 4 P.M. the next day. "At that time," Sullivan remembered, "I had eight thousand dollars to my name, not all of it in cash." By Monday, however, he transferred $25,000 to the AFL's account.

The group Lamar Hunt had collected met for the first time as a whole league on November 22, 1959, in Minneapolis. For Sullivan, it was the first time he had actually laid eyes on the league's prodigy founder. "I walked into the meeting," the Patriot president recalled, "and I sat down next to a mild-looking man who turns out to be Lamar Hunt. He was not at all what I pictured. He has one shoe up on the table and there is a hole in the bottom of it. He couldn't help but notice I was staring at it. He raises his other leg and crosses his ankle and this shoe has a hole in it too. He looks at me and says, 'I do twice as well as Adlai.' . . . I wasn't sure how to take it. Stevenson had lost in a landslide."

By then, of course, it was obvious to everyone in the room that they were in for a war. Bert Bell's promise to "foster and nourish" had not lasted a month and, before his unexpected death in October, Pete Rozelle's predecessor had the NFL's first counterstroke under way. Reversing the position he had taken with Hunt the previous year, Bell had announced that the NFL wanted to expand. That "expand" translated as "raiding the AFL" was apparent when Max Winter opened the Minneapolis meeting with the announcement that his Vikings were dropping out and joining the other league. While Winter was still explaining himself, Harry Wismer came running in from the neighborhood newsstand with an armful of local papers announcing the NFL's plans for Minnesota. At that point, Billy Sullivan wondered "if he had spent a lifetime of scrambling and scratching to climb aboard a sinking ship." Hunt, however, didn't panic.

It took Hunt another month and a half to find Oakland's Wayne Valley, fill the hole left by Winter's defection, and bring the infant league's membership back to eight. By then, the NFL had chosen Pete Rozelle as its new commissioner and the AFL had selected Joe Foss, a war hero and politician from South Dakota. The NFL had also announced it was expanding into Dallas to slug it out with Hunt himself. Before doing so, they had offered Lamar the opportunity to defect. Had he, Ralph Wilson noted, the AFL "would have been stillborn." Hunt himself was somewhat angered at the offer. The AFL "was darn important to me," he explained. "I had a lot of money in it. Emotionally, I spent a lot of time, effort, and energy on it. I felt an obligation. A guy like Billy Sullivan had everything he had in it. [Taking the offer of an NFL franchise] wouldn't have been the right thing to do." When Hunt refused, the NFL awarded the Dallas Cowboys to Clint Murchison Jr., and the war was on.

In the six years that war lasted, the NFL and AFL competed head to head in three cities and in all three the AFL came out second best. By 1963, Harry Wismer's New York Titans had been driven bankrupt and had to be restarted as the Jets by Sonny Werblin. Bud Adams visited Wismer as his string was running out. "The heat was turned off," Adams remembered. "It was cold and drafty and the floor was uncarpeted. I stood there in my overcoat and I reached into my pocket and handed Harry ten thousand dollars in cash, ten

thousand-dollar bills. . . . I wanted him to use the money whatever way he
needed. Harry could be very dramatic. He looked at me and said, 'The ship is
sinking.' . . . Then he put his arms around me and started to cry.'' In order to
avoid a similar fate in Los Angeles, Barron Hilton had already moved his
Chargers south to San Diego. The third head-to-head contest was in Dallas,
where the Texans and Cowboys were fighting over a town where one pro
football business had gone belly-up all by itself less than a decade before.
Their struggle had national visibility and was billed as the battle of Texas
millionaires. In his first year in the football business, Clint Murchison lost
$700,000. Lamar Hunt reportedly lost $1,000,000. Lamar's father was informed of his son's football losses by a reporter. Asked for a reaction, H.L.
offered that at this rate, "the boy only has 123 years to go."

    After three of those years, Lamar Hunt had recognized the handwriting
on the wall. He and Bunker had been right that Dallas would support a
football franchise, but the city would not support two. The NFL had hoped
Hunt would resolve the dilemma by agreeing to merge with the Cowboys and
abandon the AFL, but after a series of negotiations with Murchison and Tex
Schramm, Hunt decided to move instead. "We were not helping the League
and we were not helping ourselves," Hunt explained. "I felt that a better
home could be made elsewhere, and really what I wanted to build was a
successful business venture of a football team. I had hoped it would be in
Dallas, but realistically it looked like both teams would go on forever losing a
ton, so we decided to move." Renamed the Chiefs, Hunt's AFL franchise left
Dallas for Kansas City in May 1963. To induce him there, Kansas City had
given the Texas oil millionaire free use of a stadium for two years and a
guaranteed sale of twenty-five thousand season tickets. To make the move
even less painful, Murchison purchased the Texans' old Dallas practice
facility. He and Schramm were "elated" to have Hunt in Missouri rather than
Texas, but the AFL's retreat from Dallas "did not end the problems of
uncontrolled competition." The war would last another three years.

    By the time Tex Schramm and Lamar Hunt began talking peace in spring
1966, the AFL had turned the corner and come of age. "We had the right
product at the right time," Hunt explained. "We helped make pro football a
national game. We opened the gates and the battle caught public imagination." Along the way, the men Lamar had ushered into the football business
formed what NFL Properties' *Pro* magazine called "a bonding, a fellowship,
that may have been unique in professional sports." Lamar Hunt was at the
heart of that bond. "Lamar was always the guy who kept his temper," Bud
Adams pointed out, "who, when things would get out of hand, would bring
everybody back around to making a decision. He was a quiet, quiet force, but
it was his baby, and he cared deeply about it."

    The merger secured Hunt's stature as the nation's premier sports entre-
preneur. "The AFL was an astonishing success," the *Kansas City Times*
pointed out, "becoming the first sports league to reach parity with its more
established rival since baseball's American League started play in 1901." The
success of Hunt's league not only marked a quantum enlargement of the

football business, but was also "the forerunner of an explosion in sports teams, leagues, and interest that gripped this country from the late 1960s to the middle 1970s."

It surprised no one to find the quiet man now known as "the football Hunt" in the forefront of that further explosion. Had he not been, it is doubtful Lamar and the commissioner would ever have crossed swords.

24

Certainly neither Rozelle nor Hunt was the type to pick a fight for its own sake. No one ever described Lamar Hunt's manner as anything but "gentle" and "mild." As one owner put it, "A real sweetheart."

As a rule, Lamar never flaunted his name or his money to the rest of the League. While a number of the men who met in Bal Harbour prided themselves on personal jets and slick wardrobes, Hunt, by far the wealthiest in the room, wore old clothes and flew commercial coach. One of his fellow owners described him as "cheap." Though such habits led to jokes when he was out of earshot, the effect of Hunt's style on the other members of the nation's most exclusive club was by and large positive. "He's almost too good to be true," one owner noted. "He's as regular as an old shoe. He's soft-spoken, sincere. He was looked upon as a leader. Not a forceful, abrasive leader, but leadership by example."

Hunt exercised less of that leadership inside the NFL after the merger, but it was a diminution of his own choosing. Building his league had been all-consuming, but now that it was a success and under Rozelle's stewardship, Lamar was content simply to manage his own franchise and turn the rest of his attention elsewhere.

Among Lamar's preoccupations now that peace had come to football was family business. The late sixties were a trying time for all the Hunts. The family financial picture had doubled in complexity since 1957, when Lamar's widowed father married Ruth Ray, a woman by whom he had already fathered a son and three daughters. Prior to her marriage, Ruth Ray Hunt and her children had lived in a home in Dallas's White Rock Lake area, where the children attended local private schools under the name "Wright." After the wedding, they moved into H.L.'s nearby Mt. Vernon estate and enrolled in new schools under the name "Hunt." The instant establishment of a second official Hunt family complete with offspring ages seven to fourteen apparently "had a powerful effect on the sons and daughters of the first family," *Texas Monthly* reported, "they regarded their half-brothers and half-sisters more like cousins" and, "obviously feeling somewhat displaced from their rightful position . . . the first family apparently saw the second replacing them in the hierarchy of their father's affections.''

In 1968, that "replacement" had become a financial concern as well. H.L. was now "older and dottier" and rumors began to circulate that two of the old man's most trusted Hunt Oil executives "were allied with Ruth in advising H.L. to leave the bulk of his estate to his second family.'' According to *Texas Monthly*, when those rumors were followed in early 1969 by evidence that those same executives had embezzled an estimated $50 million, Lamar's brothers, Bunker and Herbert, decided to act.

The Hunt brothers' first step was to put a listening device on the suspects' phones. When those wiretaps were discovered by the police, Lamar's brothers were eventually indicted for illegal wiretapping. The suspect Hunt Oil executives were indicted for mail fraud and one "acknowledged using his influence on Mr. Hunt to get H.L. to change his will in favor of the second family.'' Whether he had succeeded or not was, at the time of the NFL's Bal Harbour annual meeting, impossible to tell. H.L., now eighty-five, was still living with Ruth at Mt. Vernon, reportedly "fond of munching on nuts spread out on a newspaper and doing 'creeping' exercises on the floor.'' For Lamar, on the edge of events, all of this meant a lot more time in family meetings and phone conferences.

None of those demands, however, was sufficient to have kept Hunt's energies out of the NFL, had that indeed been the place he wanted to put them. In truth, Lamar had been, as he put it, "bitten by the entertainment business bug.'' Once the agreement to merge with the NFL was signed, he immediately began diversifying his heretofore single-minded sports entertainment interests. By 1974, only about twenty percent of Lamar Hunt's working time was spent on football. An equal percentage was now devoted to his other sports businesses. The remaining sixty percent went to the cluster of Hunt businesses in and around Dallas's Placid and Hunt oil companies. While his style made him an easy man to underestimate, as one Hunt friend put it, "Lamar can take care of things.''

In 1966, Lamar had bought an 11.25 percent interest in the Chicago Bulls professional basketball team and founded the Dallas Tornado North American Soccer League franchise. In 1967, he founded the World Championship Tennis tour. Of the three, the tennis tour was the most successful. "The way I got involved,'' Hunt remembered, "is that a man I had known for several years through football, [Dave] Dixon, called me up one day. . . . Dave knew that I was interested in promotion in professional sport and he asked if I would be interested in being an investor.'' At the time, tennis was the monopoly of the International Lawn Tennis Federation and was, in Hunt's words, "closed,'' an "under-the-table type of game.'' Dixon's idea was "to try and sign the players to professional contracts and make them respectable and build a professional tour that was the beginning of what we now know as the pro tennis circuit.''

This tennis venture, flying in the teeth of what had been a monopoly, bore the closest resemblance to the previous AFL assault on the football

market. Both led immediately to promotion wars and in both, Lamar Hunt
eventually won parity. In tennis, it would take ten years. The first step in that
process was taken by Lamar immediately after his conversation with Dave
Dixon, when he called his sister Margaret's husband, Al Hill Sr., and her son
Al Hill Jr.

"I presented Dixon's idea to them," Lamar remembered, "and [said]
that I would be interested in being an investor along with them to the tune of
fifty percent—I would put up twenty-five percent, they would put up twenty-
five percent, Dave Dixon would put up fifty percent." By the time of Bal
Harbour, Lamar's share of WCT was up to ninety-five percent.

The least successful of Lamar's sports diversifications was professional
soccer. "It has been a very broadening experience from the standpoint of
business knowledge," he later said of his North American Soccer League
investment. "In the sense of financial return to date, it has not been a good
financial venture." Like the more successful WCT, professional soccer was
an idea someone else had brought to Hunt. "I was in New York City in a
hotel room at the Waldorf," he recalled, "and I got a call from a man who
was in the lobby. . . . I don't know the man's name [and] I don't really know
his association, but he said he was doing some work on behalf of a group
trying to put together . . . a soccer league and would I be interested in talking
to him? . . . He came up to the room and he had a small brochure, which he
left with me, and [it turned out] I knew the names of several people that were
involved."

It was 1966 and at the moment soccer looked like a growth industry. The
televised final of international soccer's World Cup between England and West
Germany had created a sudden surge of American interest in this "foreign"
game and some thought that the 1966 World Cup would surely prove analogous
to the Giants-Bears 1958 NFL Championship that birthed the televised football juggernaut. Lamar bought in by patching together commitments from
friends and family. During the Dallas Tornado's first year, Lamar himself
owned only 19.6 percent. Three of his children, Lamar Jr., Sharon, and
Clark, owned 9.8 percent each, and his brothers, Bunker and Herbert, were in
for seventeen percent apiece, giving the Hunt family eighty-three percent
control. From that point on, Lamar's share grew—but professional soccer
nosedived. The stampede to get in on the sport's ground floor was so heavy
that the soccer market was glutted from birth. Twenty-two teams in two rival
leagues emerged for the 1967 season; the two leagues merged into the NASL
for the 1968 season. By the time the 1968 season was over, financial losses
had reduced professional soccer to five teams.

It was after that disastrous 1968 soccer season that Lamar Hunt made the
decision that put him on a collision course with Pete Rozelle. "The losses
were considerably higher than some of the partners had expected," Hunt
remembered, and "I was informed . . . that they didn't want to continue. . . .
Rather than let the thing fold, I did take over a larger ownership interest."
That interest increased further in 1970 when one of his brothers abandoned
ship as well. "I felt I had a commitment," Lamar explained, "which I had

made publicly—to attempt to build and help develop a team in Dallas and I didn't feel that two years was a fair trial. I guess I am a little hardheaded from that standpoint and I don't want to be known as a quitter.''

Far from quitting, henceforth, Lamar Hunt devoted a great deal of his sports entertainment time to promoting soccer. He served on the NASL planning committee and, without consulting the National Football League, provided soccer with the names of "people who were interested in . . . an NFL team in their cities." Lamar also became a visible spokesman for soccer as "the sport of the future." Among potential investors in the NASL, Lamar and his wife, Norma, frequently told how even their eight-year-old son was "a total soccer convert." Lamar was fond of repeating the boy's words: "No, Daddy, I am not going to play football. It might ruin me for soccer.''

With Lamar Hunt's shoulder to the wheel, the NASL inched back to six, then eight, then twelve and fourteen teams. Eventually, it would grow as large as twenty-four. Along the way, Hunt located investors in whatever way he could. The Philadelphia NASL franchise which so infuriated Leonard Tose was a case in point. Tom McCloskey, the Philadelphia contractor who bought it from Hunt, had just finished work on a stadium project and, according to *Sports Illustrated*, was "in Los Angeles for the Super Bowl . . . with eight friends and no tickets. He was standing in a hotel lobby when Lamar Hunt . . . learned of his problem. Lamar pulled nine tickets out of his pocket, fanned himself with them and said, 'How would you like to have a soccer franchise in Philadelphia?' ''

Hunt's soccer role was not lost on the rest of the football business. In fact, it had generated irritation even before Leonard Tose blew his top in 1973. Lamar tried to deal with that irritation by participating in the ownership policy debate as little as possible. "Mostly Mr. Hunt was silent when these matters were discussed," Edward Bennett Williams later complained. "When I would make statements against the policy, I would have expected Mr. Hunt to support my statements by saying that he disagreed with the policy. He didn't do that. . . . What he did was pass whenever this subject came up and retained a very, very strong silence on the subject. . . . There may have been occasions when he said that it was very difficult for him to sell but he was not loquacious on this matter. . . . He sort of went along, he didn't say 'I won't.' ''

Despite his silence, Lamar recognized that the anger coming his way over the issue had "damaged my capacity to work inside the League." When later asked why, in 1972, he had agreed to make his "best efforts" to divest all his sports holdings other than football, Hunt claimed the reason was "pressure that was placed on me within the meetings. . . . [I was] in an uncomfortable position which I had no desire to be in. . . . I wouldn't say the pressure was from the League, but pressure from individuals within the League." To the rest of the NFL, however, the "football Hunt" seemed to take that pressure in stride. "Lamar got used to being yelled at," one of the men who was in the room during Tose's 1973 outburst observed. "He didn't really seem to pay much attention to it all."

Hunt was somewhat more attentive in his direct dealings with the commissioner's office and, from 1972 on, Rozelle and Lamar conducted what would become a six-year correspondence on the subject of Lamar's cross-ownerships. For his part, Rozelle was by then annoyed with Hunt's soccer promotion. The 1968 and 1970 increases in his soccer ownership, Rozelle pointed out, were the only violations of the League ownership policy between 1967 and 1972. Once the 1972 ownership policy resolution was in effect, Rozelle began their exchange of letters by inquiring about Hunt's basketball holdings. In a note dated August 11, 1972, addressed "Dear Lamar" and signed "Pete," the commissioner offered that he'd had "inquiries from various clubs" in the wake of the recent sale of the National Basketball Association Chicago Bulls. Rather than taking the opportunity to divest himself of basketball as part of that sale, Hunt had renewed his interest in the new ownership. Rozelle reminded Hunt that "a resolution passed prior to this time had incorporated minority ownership in other teams" in ownership policy prohibitions.

Lamar Hunt had decided to hold on to his basketball interest because he "didn't think that the price was a favorable price." He responded to Rozelle with a letter addressed "Dear Pete" and signed "Lamar." In it, he acknowledged, "I am aware of the best efforts to divest situation. However, I believe the feeling was that no such sale should be [made] under less than desirable circumstances. I hope I am correct in that interpretation."

The correspondence of the two men then ebbed until November 1973, when Hunt resumed it. He was provoked by a phone call he had received from Lou Spadia, president of the NFL San Francisco 49ers. Hunt had recently had a meeting in Spadia's hometown, "with a number of prospective people relative to a soccer franchise in the Bay Area" and Spadia was furious. Hunt listened to Spadia's complaint and then vented his own frustration in a long letter to the commissioner dated November 12, 1973.

"Dear Pete," Lamar began. "A recent call from a professional football club official prompts me to put some thoughts down concerning the question of my investments in other team sports." In defense of himself, Hunt pointed out that he had disposed of his minor league baseball team and had resisted "several offers and even community pressure to invest" in the major league baseball franchise recently arrived in Dallas. "The apparent position of some," he complained, "is that if Hunt has his picture taken with a basketball or if he talks to someone about a promotion of ownership, et cetera, in soccer, he is doing something illegal. . . . Regarding [my sports entertainment] interests and the NFL policy on the subject, I believe many club officials perhaps have an incorrect interpretation. Certainly the position of Len Tose in the League meeting last summer [is] not realistic in view of the circumstances."

"Dear Lamar," Pete answered on November 19. "The points you make are very valid and I do not feel anyone should expect a rapid sale that would involve a sacrifice."

Sensing that Rozelle was backing off a bit, Hunt's next letter was conciliatory and optimistic. The commissioner received it on the eve of the

Bal Harbour annual meeting in February 1974. "Frankly," Lamar admitted, "in retrospect I think I blew it not selling my interest in the [basketball] Bulls a year or so ago. . . . The soccer interest is tougher [to sell] because there really are essentially no buyers for existing teams. . . . I personally, [however], think I see the light at the end of the tunnel and have some ideas that could conceivably accomplish it at the right time."

"That was," Pete Rozelle would point out when reminded of Hunt's letter six years later, "a long tunnel."

25

In the struggle over ownership policy, Leonard Tose's posture as Lamar Hunt's loudest critic was a confrontation of opposites. Tose was everything Hunt was not, and vice versa. Where Hunt was quiet, shy, and unobtrusive, Tose was loud, profane, and pushy. Hunt, astride one of America's greatest fortunes, was frugal. Tose, worth relatively nothing in comparison, was profligate to the extreme. "He thought wealth should always be seen," one of his fellow owners noted about Tose. "He loved the trappings and was extremely arrogant. He tried to be debonair, like an Italian count, but it didn't quite come off. He was still a Philadelphia truck driver's son."

When Leonard Tose was born in 1915, his father, Mike, had recently purchased his first truck. Thousands more would follow. "My father couldn't read or write," Tose remembered. "He came here from Russia and worked as a peddler with a pack on his back. He started a trucking company with a horse and wagon." Before long, Tose Trucking Company was one of the largest common carriers in the midatlantic states, and Mike was wealthy enough to send Leonard, the younger of his two sons, through Notre Dame University during the Depression. After college, Leonard went to work in the family business, first as a truck driver, then as a salesman of trailer rigs. From 1937 on, he was the company's chief labor negotiator.

The Teamsters Union with whom Tose bargained was by no means easy to deal with and some employers could never do so with any success. Leonard Tose, who bragged of his "close relationship" with the Teamsters, had the reputation around Philadelphia as a man who could. Some of his favorite stories were about sitting across the table from Jimmy Hoffa. "At the risk of sounding egotistical," Tose pointed out, "I think I am an expert on labor and labor relations and dealing with union contracts."

Despite his skill as a negotiator, Leonard Tose's principal reputation as he approached the age of forty was as the Tose family's wild hair. After his first marriage failed, according to *Philadelphia* magazine, "to those few Philadelphians with a zest for nightlife, Leonard Tose was one of Philadel-

phia's more playful residents. . . . Handsome, sharply dressed (he favors
continental suits, brightly striped shirts, and shoes with brass buckles) . . . he
escorted beautiful and famous women. . . . Tose was quite a swinger.''
Around the same time, the magazine reported, "there was some difficulty
between Leonard Tose and his father,'' and Leonard left the trucking business
for KS Canning Company, a soft-drink packager. He eventually traded KS to
Walter Kidde & Company, a New Jersey conglomerate, for almost $8 million
in Kidde stock and returned to Tose Trucking when his older brother died in
1963. When his father died two years later, Tose Trucking was Leonard's
alone. Remarried, Tose now "settled down to a life of hard work.''

His career as a Tose Trucking Company chief executive was considerably less than distinguished. One of his first decisions was to commit the
interstate carrier to the Philadelphia package delivery business when United
Parcel Service pulled out of town. While Tose Trucking tripled its gross and
won the ensuing delivery wars when the Teamsters Union fortuitously called a
wildcat strike on his chief competition, the company nonetheless lost money
under his stewardship. He also established a less than favorable reputation
among some of the people with whom he did business. As *Philadelphia*
magazine put it, "he seems to have cultivated more than his share of
ex-friends.'' One of those ex-friends, according to the magazine, which
quoted him, said, "Leonard has an ego problem. If he thought he could get
away with it, he'd have a big picture of himself on every one of his trucks.
You can never convince me that Leonard Tose has partners. He may have
other people's money, but they aren't his partners. That's not Leonard
Tose. . . . He's always telling people that other people love him. He's such
an incredible egomaniac that he expects you to believe everything he says just
because he's such a nice guy.''

One of the arenas in which Leonard Tose's reputation was more elevated
was Philadelphia's sporting circles. There, he "always hobnobbed with the
famous of sport'' and was known as someone "anxious to be associated with
a sports franchise.'' From 1949 to 1963, Tose had owned one percent of the
NFL's Philadelphia Eagles in a partnership known as "the 100 brothers.''
The group of one hundred men with one share apiece was put together by
Philadelphia political boss James P. Clark. When Pete Rozelle assumed the
commissionership in 1960, he considered the Philadelphia ownership situation
a disaster and made changing it a priority. "I guess the original concept was
that [the 100 brothers] would help sell season tickets,'' Rozelle complained.
"But they found that . . . many stockholders merely wanted to get good
tickets for themselves. . . . There was no single person that [sic] could speak
for the club, disputes developed, and also there was no single controlling
person you could look to easily for financial support of the team.'' In 1963,
the 100 brothers were all bought out by Chicago construction phenom Jerry
Wolman. Leonard Tose's $3000 1949 investment was by then worth $60,500.
Tose wanted to buy the club himself but his bid fell far short of Wolman's
and he was instead momentarily out of the football business.

Leonard Tose's chance to get back in again in a big way came when disaster overtook Wolman's construction empire in late 1968 and his holdings ended up in the hands of a federal bankruptcy judge. Rozelle was shocked when he found out. Before approving Wolman's ownership, the commissioner's office had spent "more time and money" checking out Jerry Wolman "than any other prospective owner we've had. We checked lending institutions and contractors. We had a more intensive file on him than any other person," Rozelle told the press. Nevertheless, Wolman's collapse presented Rozelle with a significant dilemma. "We sent our attorneys to see the [bankruptcy] judge," he explained, "because we were afraid that he would auction the club off to the highest bidder." Worried that the high bidder might be a corporation or "an undesirable person that [sic] we wouldn't approve of," the League's attorneys "got the judge to work with us. . . . We retained the right through the judge of approving someone that [sic] would be developed as a potential buyer."

Among those potential buyers were known to be at least four "combines of millionaires." The two most prominent were headed by Leonard Tose and Tom McCloskey, the Philadelphia contractor Lamar Hunt would later induce into the soccer business. Despite his bankruptcy, Wolman remained the wild card in the situation. The judge handling Jerry Wolman's assets was concerned to give the once and former millionaire ample opportunity to reorganize himself, and though his Eagles franchise had to be sold to clear $15 million in outstanding debts, Jerry Wolman still had a lot of say in who would buy it.

Through a mutual friend, Bucks County, Pennsylvania, real estate tycoon Herb Barness, Tose arranged to meet with Wolman at Super Bowl III in Miami's Orange Bowl in January 1969. The two men discussed possible prices and Wolman's plans. Tose's tone was described as that of "a generous businessman coming to the aid of a less fortunate fellow businessman in a time of crisis." Wolman was "heartbroken to sell the club" and "pursuing every conceivable avenue to avoid losing the team." At the moment, Wolman told Tose, he was attempting to float his assets in a new company for which he intended to sell $36 million in public stock. If he was successful in doing so, he wanted the right to buy the Eagles back. Leonard Tose wished Jerry Wolman luck and even offered to purchase the last million of Wolman's new stock offering himself. He also said a ninety-day buy-back agreement was acceptable and could be included in the contract of sale. Because of that Super Bowl agreement between Tose and his Eagles predecessor, the bankruptcy judge eventually gave Leonard Tose the right to top the highest bid. Not surprisingly, his final offer of $16,055,000 was $5000 more than Tom McCloskey's. The price was then an NFL record but Tose was eager to spend the money. "I'm fifty-three," he said. "I don't think there will be another chance in my lifetime. I know I can afford it. What am I supposed to do, wait until I'm eighty?"

Despite Tose's assurances that he could "afford it," most of the $16 million price tag would be paid with other people's money. Eight million came from First Pennsylvania Bank, loaned against the assets of the franchise itself.

Tose's share was $2.9 million, and $2.5 million of that was supplied by First
Pennsylvania as well. It was secured by 90,000 shares of Kidde stock and
Tose's "personal signature." The rest of the funds came from his "combine
of millionaires." Herb Barness, the Bucks County real estate tycoon, came in
for $500,000. Solomon Katz, president of Slick Trailers, took $1 million, and
John Firestone, heir to the rubber fortune, put up $250,000. John Connelly,
chairman of Crown Cork & Seal, put up $1 million, and brought along one of
his executives and his son-in-law for $250,000 apiece. Other, less substantial
partners made up the rest. Such was their eagerness to join Leonard Tose's
football venture, that the men all put up their money without a formal
partnership agreement. The understanding was that Tose "would manage the
day to day operations" and that "the role of the backers, other than Tose,
would temporarily be kept quiet." That silence, Tose assured them, would be
only momentary. "We'll all drive down Broad Street when we win," he
pledged, "we'll all get the calls from the fans when we lose. It's your money
and you'll have as much say as anybody."

For the first six months of 1969, however, Leonard Tose kept a strict
silence about his combine's existence. When he delivered a certified check for
$1.5 million to the bankruptcy court to seal the purchase, he made no mention
that it had been drawn by John Connelly. Instead, he represented it to the
judge as coming from First Pennsylvania Bank.

Tose took a similar approach in March, when he went to New York to be
interviewed by Rozelle, Art Modell, and the NFL attorneys as part of the
League's arrangement with the bankruptcy court. Although the League required all of a franchise's ownership interests, both majority and minority, to
be formally approved by them, the only name Leonard Tose submitted was
his own. Naturally enough, Rozelle and Modell apparently assumed Tose was
buying the Eagles all by himself. As a consequence, the only name presented
to the NFL as a whole for final approval was, once again, Leonard Tose.

The meeting at which Tose was submitted with the commissioner's
endorsement was held in spring 1969 in the League's New York City offices.
Though Tose was granted membership as a matter of course, there were
already some owners who were less than enthusiastic about the development.
After the vote, Vince Lombardi, then president of the Green Bay Packers, and
two other owners were out in the anteroom getting a helping of coffee and
doughnuts. Lombardi was obviously bothered and started to talk.

"I'll tell ya," he offered, "this is the last goddamn Jew I'm going to
vote for. And only because he's replacing another Jew. You get too many of
those sons of bitches and you got a problem."

The other two men, both gentiles, agreed.

Had the rest of the NFL's Jews known that Leonard Tose was the
standard by which they were all being judged, they would have no doubt been
appalled. "He's a weirdo," one of the Jewish owners later observed. "He's
been in money trouble since the day he was born. He's a habitual gambler.
He's got a big mouth and no sense at all. On top of that, you can't take his
word for a damn thing."

That owner's opinion would eventually be shared by virtually everyone who participated in the purchase that brought Leonard Tose into the football business.

The first to be disillusioned was Jerry Wolman. Although his attempt to sell $36 million in stock had come to naught, somewhere Wolman had come up with $16 million and wanted his team back. The deadline on his buy-back agreement was August 1, 1969, and in June, little more than a month after Tose entered the NFL, Wolman notified the new Eagles owner that he intended to buy him out in two months, as per the terms of their agreement. Although already on record saying, "Wolman deserved to keep the team because of the great fight he'd made to remain solvent," Tose now refused to sell. Their buy-out agreement, he pointed out, specified the success of the $36 million stock offering, and when that failed, no other arrangement could be substituted. Wolman appealed to the bankruptcy court, but his appeal was rejected. He then filed two different lawsuits. After losing both of them, Jerry Wolman faded from the sports pages forever.

Wolman's disgust with Tose was next echoed by the faction of Eagles investors led by John Connelly. "Delighted to be partners in an NFL franchise with Leonard Tose," one of them later testified, they had expected "in general terms we would all be partners and we would all share in it. We'd all have fun in it and our friends would have fun in it." At the time they had bought in, Tose had told them their money was "urgently needed if the deal was to go through." A written agreement was to follow, confirming their oral understanding. Instead, "the various agreements given to them by Tose over the next year were greatly at variance with that understanding." All of them proposed an arrangement in which Tose would have "eighty percent of the team and complete authority." During that same year, they claimed, Tose also promised repeatedly to submit their names for approval to the League but never did so. "Tose changed," a source close to Connelly told *Philadelphia* magazine. "When you get to own the Eagles and people recognize you in restaurants, you start getting the feeling people love you and you stop being the considerate person you used to be. Instead of continuing to pander to John Connelly's vanity, he took him for granted. . . . The publicity went to Tose's head."

Disgusted with the treatment they were getting, the Connelly faction eventually appealed to the commissioner's office to force the Eagles "owner" to recognize their full partnership rights. By then, word of the dispute inside the Eagles was already making its way around the NFL and "at least one very prominent football man had raised hell with [the commissioner] for permitting the Philadelphia franchise to get out of joint again." Rozelle applied catch-22 to the situation and ruled the Connelly group was "not considered partners because this only occurs when they are formally submitted to the League for approval."

The Connelly group's next step was a lawsuit in the Philadelphia Court of Common Pleas. There, the plaintiffs, John Connelly, John Luviano, and Buck Riley, charged that Leonard Tose had "refused to honor [their] oral agreement," that he "had represented himself as the sole owner of the Philadelphia Eagles," and had "refused to consult them." Tose defended himself by claiming the $1.5 million supplied by the three men was simply "a friendly loan" and pointing out that the partnership agreement they had refused to sign had been accepted by the rest of the men involved. Their suit was heard in June 1970. On his way into the courtroom, Tose pronounced the threat it posed was "no sweat at all."

Once inside, Leonard Tose was the first witness called by the defense. *Philadelphia* magazine evaluated him as "far and away the worst witness of the case. He came off as either a reckless liar or an incredibly inept business-man. . . . He proclaimed that he, and he alone, ran the Eagles and made the important decisions [then] proceeded to confess ignorance of various basic phases of the Eagles business. . . . He projected arrogance. He attempted sarcasm. Every time [the plaintiffs' attorney] cornered Tose, which he did frequently, Tose either couldn't remember details or claimed the matter had been handled by somebody else. He was, in short, unbelievable."

Despite himself, Tose won the suit. After deliberating for almost two years, the Common Pleas judge ruled that "in order to prove a partnership, plaintiffs had to show more than the fact that they advanced $1.5 million for use in the purchase and operation of the team." Since they failed to do so, Tose did not have to make the men partners. The court did order him, however, to repay their "friendly loan" with interest. Tose was more than happy to do so. On receipt of the court's decision, the Eagles owner launched a round of celebration in Philadelphia's night spots. When those closed, he moved on to South Jersey, where he was seen at 5 A.M., reading the court's decision for the fifth time that evening.

"This gives me complete vindication as far as my intergity," he crowed to *The* [Philadelphia] *Bulletin* the next day. "As far as my reputation is concerned, I've always been a man of my word." Short and dressed to the nines, the silver-haired Tose puffed confidently on a cigarette and couldn't stop smiling. When asked if he was going to have any trouble raising the money to pay the Connelly faction off, Leonard Tose dismissed it as an issue. "The bank," he pointed out, "only says good things about us."

The bank in question was First Pennsylvania and, in truth, it already had its collective doubts about Leonard Tose. Even before the trial with Connelly, the bank had demanded he recollateralize his loan. At the time, Dun & Bradstreet had reported two consecutive losing years for Tose Trucking Company and his Kidde stock had plunged to less than half its former price. To oblige First Pennsylvania, Tose pledged part of the Eagles, a fact the Connelly group claimed he "concealed" from his "partners." The 1970 lawsuit had apparently undermined the bank's confidence in Leonard Tose even further. "We were disturbed by the suit," one of First Pennsylvania's officers later informed Tose's financial adviser, "and the hearings that were going on in court and [that] our name was being mentioned. . . . We thought maybe we'd be better off if we got out of this." First Pennsylvania's shakiness was mitigated by the Eagles' profitability. While everyone waited for the Common Pleas decision, the Eagles' revenues "were pouring in so swiftly" that the original $8 million loan had been paid down to $6.5 million and was ahead of schedule. The other $2.5 million loaned to Tose himself had been entirely paid off from what was described as "other sources." In the end, First Pennsylvania agreed to enlarge the original loan to $9 million, providing Tose with enough to buy out the three Connelly plaintiffs. After a three-year struggle, Tose now owned a clear majority interest in the National Football League franchise he had coveted for most of his adult life. "I've got it," Tose exulted to *The Bulletin*. "I've got it!"

While certainly now the clear owner of record, what Leonard Tose had exactly "got" was extraordinarily compromised by prevailing NFL standards. First Pennsylvania was not about to send its $9 million off to Tose unescorted. The terms of its new loan specified controls on players' salaries, the hiring of coaches, and included a stipulation that Tose could not draw more than $25,000 in salary and $10,000 in expenses. In addition, according to Tose's financial adviser, "the loan is designed so that, for all purposes, the bank gets all the money." In the case of the Eagles, in 1972 that amounted to net profits of more than $1 million a year. As was mandatory League policy in the case of all liens against franchises, an informational copy of Tose's loan was filed with the commissioner's office. When he learned what was in it, Rozelle could not have been pleased. After carefully working the "Philadelphia situation" through the bankruptcy court so that the NFL didn't lose control over its membership process, he was now stuck with an arrangement in which First Pennsylvania Bank, a corporation and nonmember, had "the final word in running the Eagles' business office."

Leonard Tose, on the other hand, at last both "vindicated" and refinanced, couldn't have been more pleased. "Now," he announced, "all my problems are solved."

26

Refinanced or not, Leonard Tose still remained a risky investment by the prevailing standards of Philadelphia banking. The problem, from a banker's point of view, was his life-style. Worse still, as his sixtieth birthday approached, that life-style only seemed to be escalating. "My rule," Tose explained, "is if you can't go first class, stay home." It was the kind of rule that gave bankers nightmares, but even with his lifelong dependency on banks, Tose never considered changing. "The jackals have been at my heels all my life," he shrugged. "They will be until the day I die. They're jealous. Big fucking deal."

Leonard Tose lived to play the role and did so to the hilt. He and his second wife, Andrea, had a mansion in Wayne, Pennsylvania, complete with cook, houseman, and driver for trips into Philadelphia itself. A Cadillac, a Lincoln, and a Mercedes-Benz were parked in the driveway. For air travel, he often chartered planes at $1000 an hour. Tose bought his suits twenty at a time and, insistent that his wife never wear the same dress twice, sent her up to New York on weekly shopping trips. When Tose learned that one of his friends had presented his wife with a huge ring, Leonard took Andrea to the jeweler and said he wanted the biggest diamond ring he could find. The result was a "pear-shaped diamond just under thirty carats" that cost $292,000. On cold days, Andrea wore sable. "My husband always had to have the finest, the biggest, the best, and the most of everything," Andrea Tose noted. "Len's philosophy in life is that nothing is to be banked. Money is to be spent."

In Philadelphia, Tose enjoyed casting himself as a philanthropist as well as sportsman, giving $100,000 to his alma mater, Notre Dame University, $60,000 to his synagogue, $40,000 to a mental health center, and $250,000 to the United Jewish Appeal. On the road, he played traveling potentate. The Toses journeyed to Miami four times a year, to Acapulco regularly, to Europe at least once a year, and to the Caribbean when it struck their fancy. At the airport, they were met by two limousines, one for them and the other for their luggage. At their hotel, the Toses took the penthouse suite. In order to have transportation immediately available, Tose sometimes put the chauffeur in a suite as well. When on the town, he handed one-hundred-dollar bills to bartenders and piano players.

Leonard Tose was a man of numerous indulgences, but perhaps his greatest was gambling. According to Andrea, Leonard spent Monday nights playing poker in an "upstairs room in a downtown restaurant." Thursdays, "he played cards at a country club." It was not uncommon for him to bet $10,000 on a gin game or a round of golf. At the racetrack, the Eagles owner was known to lose money hand over fist. Andrea claimed he had never had a winning day in the nineteen years she accompanied him there, and that he often wagered as much as $5000 on a single race. "He bets five horses at a time," she explained, "[so] even when he wins, he loses. . . . Leonard doesn't know what a two-dollar window is. One time, the man [Tose sent to place his bets] brought back an inch-high stack of daily double tickets. . . . Leonard was an inveterate gambler who never won." He also gave money away to his chauffeur and other members of his entourage so they might bet too, though Tose's time at the track decreased greatly when he took over the Eagles. "He got bored with it," Andrea remembered. He also stopped betting on NFL games, thereby saving himself "between $200,000 and $300,000 a year." The rest of the gambling continued apace.

Normally, none of that information would have come to First Pennsylvania Bank's attention in the course of refinancing a loan, but Tose's life-style stopped being private in spring 1971, when Andrea started proceedings for divorce. She charged her husband with "having committed adultery repeatedly and continuously." For the next eight months, Philadelphia newspapers played up the Tose story with such headlines as, "Nobody Else Picks Up the Tab" and "The Other Woman." Leonard Tose's life-style was writ in bold print.

In this instance, the "other woman" was identified as one Betsy Rubin, a former Miss U.S.A. contestant and wife of Philadelphia "furniture and carpeting tycoon" Mickey Rubin. According to the *Philadelphia Daily News,* "Betsy's big attraction to Len—who is almost thirty years her senior—is the Eagles franchise." One of her friends pointed out, "Betsy likes to sit in the main box. That's the kind of life that impressed her. Football games, yachts, trips to Europe. I think Mickey lost Betsy by spending too much time at the stores." In early 1971, Betsy left her husband, Tose moved out of the mansion in Wayne, and the two became "inseparable." They occasionally ran across Mickey Rubin out on Philadelphia's nightclub circuit and he and Tose ended up in several public shouting matches. Tose eventually sent his driver back to the mansion in Wayne to collect his suits from Andrea; she is reported to have turned them over with a pants leg cut off each one. When the National Football League held its 1971 annual meeting at the Breakers Hotel in Palm Beach, Tose took Betsy along, renting not only a suite at the hotel itself, but also a yacht.

In May 1971, two months after that meeting, it seemed that Leonard Tose had settled his remaining affairs with Andrea amicably. Based on representations by his lawyers that Tose's holdings, including the Eagles, were worth a net of $3.7 million, her lawyers agreed to settle for $1.8 million paid out in annual installments of $100,000. Had Tose then signed the papers her lawyers drew up, it is likely the details of his life-style would have stayed private. Instead, he refused and offered a substitute arrangement for far less money. Andrea struck back quickly.

On June 22, 1971, the still Mrs. Leonard Tose filed a thirteen-page complaint with the Philadelphia Court of Common Pleas, asking the court to take the extraordinary step of declaring her husband "incompetent" to handle his own affairs and appointing a receivership to handle his estate. Andrea claimed any settlement she might eventually receive was in danger of being "dissipated" because "he habitually and compulsively engages in illegal and incompetent gambling, incurring losses of very large sums of money, and makes reckless, ostentatious, and lavish expenditures far beyond his means, without any consideration for the proper payment therefor." In addition to his First Pennsylvania debt, she pointed out, he was also floating $6 million in short term notes, most from friends and payable on demand. He was, she claimed, "liable . . . to become insolvent or bankrupt unless a receiver is appointed." Although the judge dismissed Andrea's action as no more than an "attempt to embarrass" her husband, it set the stage for what was to be a rancorous divorce trial.

That trial commenced in February 1972. For those who were enjoying the scandal, the highlight came when Andrea Tose took the stand dressed in a "heavy gold necklace" and "form-fitting wine-colored wool dress" and cried while telling the story of her $292,000 ring. Leonard, sitting in the front row of seats, laughed out loud. When she got to the part about him blowing $5000 a race at the track, he couldn't contain himself. "Aw, come on now," he shouted. Afterward, he laid his head on the courtroom rail. A week later, the trial was suspended and a settlement announced. "Len Tose Pays Off Wife with 400 G's" the *Philadelphia Daily News* headlined its sports page. Outside the courtroom, the former couple were now all smiles. "See you in Acapulco," Andrea told Leonard as she left. "It's been such an ordeal for the Toses," the *Daily News* explained, "that both are going to Acapulco to rest at separate hotels."

Shortly after Tose returned to the United States, the Connelly suit was finally decided and, despite the aura of public scandal now surrounding the Eagles owner, First Pennsylvania Bank agreed to enlarge his loan under strict conditions. Enforcing those conditions would, however, prove to be no small task. Leonard Tose ran his football team as an adjunct of his now highly public life-style and had little inclination to change, whatever he had promised the bank. To celebrate his new loan, Tose bought a $150,000 helicopter in which to commute to the Eagles' suburban training facility. The aircraft was painted in the Eagles' green and silver colors and had a team emblem painted on the side. The first day he owned it, an Eagles practice session was halted while the boss landed in a rush of wind on the twenty-yard line. When he went to leave after the practice was over, the helicopter developed engine trouble and another had to be dispatched to ferry him home.

By the time the NFL convened for its 1974 annual meeting in Bal Harbour, Tose had established a definite reputation among the League's football playing employees. "I'll never complain again," one New York Giants player told the *Philadelphia Daily News* after a 1972 game in Philadelphia's Veterans Stadium. "Those poor Eagles really know what it's like to work for a slapped ass."

During the first five years of Tose's stewardship, his Eagles won 20 games, lost 45, and tied 5. At one low point, Tose stormed into the team's locker room and berated them personally. "This team has played like it doesn't have any character," he announced. "What good is it if one guy breaks his ass and you've got a bunch of other guys dogging it?" Despite the lavish buffets with free drinks on game days Tose gave them, the Philadelphia press corps tended to locate the Eagles' problems in the franchise's front office. "Is Tose Hurting Eagles?" *The* [Philadelphia] *Bulletin* asked. Yes, the *Daily News* answered. "Leonard Tose bought a sagging franchise to make money out of it to finance his own ego trips. He deserves what he's getting. . . . Pete Rozelle, the merchandiser who runs the NFL . . . must have some kind of secret grudge against Philadelphia. . . . A man like Leonard Tose does not belong in the National Football League."

Belong or not, Leonard Tose was in the NFL and intended to stay there a long time. Until he attacked Lamar Hunt in 1973, Tose was most conspicuous inside the League for his flair for spending money. "He's the kind of guy," one owner noted, "who, if we're having an all-day meeting at the League offices, will hire a limo to take him the four blocks from his hotel. Then, instead of having it come back, he has it wait at the curb all day."

Tose considered the years before 1973 to have been a kind of apprenticeship in League politics. "When you come into this League," Tose pointed out, "you come in as a rookie and you don't say a hell of a lot . . . the first couple years until you get to think you know what you are saying." Once he broke that silence, however, Leonard Tose made a definite impression. "He doesn't pull any punches," one NFL executive noted. "When Leonard came in, there was no longer any reverence. He was very outspoken and would get aggravated. We heard more four-letter words at his first meeting than in the whole previous ten years. I always liked him. He spiced up our meetings." By the time of the Bal Harbour sessions, the Eagles owner had the reputation of someone who had something to say every time the floor was open to comments, whatever the subject.

He remained most voluble, however, on the issue of Lamar Hunt's violations of ownership policy. "Mr. Hunt," Tose raged, "has continually gotten up at our meetings and said, 'I promise you I will divest my interest.' How can I take a man's word for anything when he has totally disregarded his promises in the past? . . . I won't put any more stock in what Lamar Hunt says at our League meetings, based on his performance . . . than I would in the man in the street telling me that was his opinion."

Later, he would say, "Lamar Hunt was a big disappointment. He has no balls."

As usual, Lamar Hunt said little in response.

27

Though Billy Sullivan of the New England Patriots was, in his own way, as significant a violator of Rozelle's ownership policy as Lamar Hunt, nonetheless, Sullivan took little personal abuse for the violations. Leonard Tose, uncompromisingly shrill on the subject, was fond of Billy Sullivan and considered him one of his favorite owners. Tose was by no means alone. With the exception of Al Davis, just about everyone in the NFL liked "Old Billy." Sullivan was the prototype Irish hale-fellow-well-met: short, white-haired, and quick with a funny story or a slap on the back. "He's not smart," one owner noted, "but he is positively the most verbose man you'll ever meet. You ask him for the time and he'll tell you how to make a watch."

Despite that tendency to run at the mouth, Sullivan was a man of no small influence inside the League, a stature first confirmed by his crucial role in the agreement to merge. Sullivan's affability helped make the AFL acceptable to its rivals and put the NFL at ease. Throughout that process, the president of the Patriots had been an outspoken backer of Rozelle's ownership policy, despite the fact that his franchise lacked both a fifty-one percent owner and traded its stock publicly. Sullivan consistently pledged to bring the Patriots franchise in line with policy and asked only that he be given time to do so. One result of Sullivan's plea was the specific grandfathering of the Patriots' violations as part of the final merger agreement exempting the franchise from forced compliance. Another was the development of a close relationship between Billy and Pete Rozelle. "Never was I refused when I went to Pete," Sullivan remembered. "There were times when I felt he couldn't go on with me any longer, but each time he listened, offered any advice he might have, and, in the end, told me to solve my problems, that he'd go along with me as long as possible."

Despite widely divergent styles, Billy Sullivan and Pete Rozelle shared a background that gave them a natural affinity for each other. Like the commissioner, the president of the New England Patriots had made his way up in life through public relations. Born in 1915, one of five children of the city clerk of Lowell, Massachusetts, "Old Billy" grew up in a part of Lowell "where, as the Irish would say, you were rich if you had fruit on the table when nobody was sick." On his eighteenth birthday, Sullivan enrolled in Boston College with the aid of a scholarship and a part-time job, and made a point of praying in the chapel every morning. "Frankly," he later explained, "I wasn't one of the great scholars of history. I figured I needed Divine help." When he graduated, Billy Sullivan was selected to deliver the Class Day address. The speech took him six weeks to write. It was a verse epic that included the names of all 284 graduates, which he memorized and delivered without referring to notes. For the next year, the twenty-two-year-old Sullivan worked nights as a sportswriter with the Lowell paper and days as a salesman at his Uncle Joe's printing business.

Billy Sullivan first entered public relations in 1938, on his twenty-third birthday, when Boston College hired him to be their first public relations director. The job was Billy's idea. Approached with the notion, Father Joseph Maxwell, the dean at B.C., had to be talked into it. "He thought public relations weren't dignified," Sullivan remembered. "He called it a 'burlesque show' until I pointed out that Harvard had a whole department to project the university's image." It was Billy's luck that Frank Leahy, on his way to becoming a legendary football coach and athletic director, arrived at B.C. shortly thereafter. Leahy transformed the school into a collegiate football power, and one of Sullivan's chief responsibilities was flacking that team. Leahy liked Sullivan's work enough that he took him along to Notre Dame as special assistant to the director of athletics in 1940. During World War II, Billy served as public relations officer for the United States Naval Academy at Annapolis.

Billy Sullivan made his move to the world of professional sports in January 1945, when the Boston Braves made him the first full-time publicity director in professional baseball, "effective with his release from the navy." At the Braves, Billy distinguished himself by helping to found Boston's Jimmy Fund charity and producing "Take Me Out to the Wig-Wam," the first promotional film ever made for a baseball team. Sullivan eventually left baseball to join his old mentor, Frank Leahy, in a venture called All-Star Sports, Inc. The company made instructional sports films for television but eventually folded. Billy Sullivan went to work for Boston's Metropolitan Oil Company in 1955, and by 1958 had been named the firm's president.

By then, Billy Sullivan's eyes had already turned to professional football. His first step was to approach the NFL's commissioner, Bert Bell.

"I spoke to Bell about getting a team into Boston," Sullivan recalled, "and he told me to come back when I had a serious plan. So I had an architect draw up plans for a stadium. It was the first stadium with a roof and those executive boxes. . . . We got an option on some land in Norwood adjoining the airport and the [baseball] Red Sox agreed to share the stadium with us. But they said they didn't want any of this to get out until the details were finalized. They didn't want to upset the community. Now a lot of money for this was coming from some beer people in western Massachusetts. One of the fellows was Bissell from Hampton Brewing . . . and he wanted to take the architect's model of the stadium home to show some friends. Well, he paid for it, so we couldn't say no, but we asked him to be very careful about the press and publicity. Then came April 1, 1958. I remember the date because that's the date I became president of Metropolitan. It's also the day I was driving to work and on the radio I heard a report about our stadium and plans. . . . I tried to call [the Red Sox general manager] to tell him we had kept our end of the deal and it wasn't intentional, but I couldn't reach him. . . . Well, the Red Sox were annoyed and walked away from the plan and soon after, Bell died. So I decided to make a try for an AFL team."

On Sunday, November 19, 1959, Billy Sullivan got his first phone call from Lamar Hunt.

A week later, Billy Sullivan was at his first AFL meeting in Minneapolis. "Men like Hunt, son of a millionaire and a millionaire in his own right, and Barron Hilton, whose father started the Hilton hotels," Sullivan marveled. "I wondered what I was doing there."

The Patriots were football's weak financial sister from day one. To help pay for the effort, Sullivan brought in what became a group of nine other investors, most family or friends, each with an equal ten percent of the Patriots' voting stock. Billy would become their president. The franchise started life with no home field in Boston and played its first "home" game at Legion Field in Birmingham, Alabama. It lost money steadily and in 1961, the Patriots issued public nonvoting stock, sold mostly to fans and civic boosters, as a way of raising more capital. Jumping from stadium to stadium around the Boston area without much more than year-to-year leases, the Patriots were rumored to be considering a move on a number of occasions prior to the merger. In fact, during 1964 and 1965, Sullivan twice led unsuccessful drives among the voting shareholders to stem the tide of red ink by selling a majority interest in the club to buyers from California and Rhode

Island. According to one of the partners, Sullivan's interest in selling evaporated when the AFL-NFL merger "made the Patriots financially viable."

It did not, however, insure they would stay in Boston. Despite the
exemption Sullivan had garnered for his team's "ownership situation," he
could not escape the clause in the merger agreement that required all teams in
the merged League to secure a home field with a minimum seating capacity of
fifty-five thousand. The Patriots were, in 1966, no closer to that arrangement
than they had been in 1959, when Sullivan's plans for a top of the line model
in Norwood had collapsed with Bert Bell's death. The Patriots were given
until the end of the merger's four-year transition period to bring themselves
into compliance.

By 1969, Billy had exhausted Boston's supply of ready-made stadiums.
Boston University Field, their first home, dropped them after the franchise
had paid for building a press box and remodeling the locker rooms. Fenway
Park, their next stop, required them to resurface the field and put in a new
scoreboard and then let them go after three years. Sullivan's alma mater, B.C.,
came next, and though the Patriots built a parking lot and put down a playing
field, residents of the area complained about the Sunday traffic and the
Patriots had to move on again. Harvard Stadium, their last stop, required they
put down a new playing surface but would only allow them to use one locker
room. That was given to the visiting team; the Patriots themselves dressed for
games in a nearby Ramada Inn and met under the stands at halftime.

On January 27, 1970, Billy Sullivan announced that his negotiations with
Harvard had fallen through, the city was unwilling to construct a new
stadium, and things looked grim for football in Boston. The NFL annual
meeting was scheduled for Honolulu in the third week of March and, by then,
he pointed out, Boston had to produce or else. There were relocation offers
from Tampa, Memphis, Birmingham, Seattle, Toronto, and Montreal. "We
don't want to leave," Sullivan told *The Boston Globe,* "but we have to come
up with an answer by the time of our next League meeting." Several days
earlier, Sullivan had met with Pete Rozelle in New York. The commissioner
was sympathetic, but he wanted an answer. And Billy had run out of ideas.

Over the next month, a plan to combine the resources of the city and the
state for a new stadium surfaced but, despite being pushed by Massachusetts
Governor Francis Sargent, whose brother owned a large chunk of Patriot
voting stock, the attempt came up empty. On March 4, Billy Sullivan went
back to New York to talk to Rozelle. "I tried to bring him up-to-date on the
situation," Sullivan remembered. "He said he was very pleased by the
governor's response but would be more pleased if the stadium had been voted
into law. I asked the commissioner about the possibility of getting an extension, but I couldn't get an answer one way or another. He just told me that the
owners from the other teams in pro football will have to make that judgment.
If we get to the owners' meeting in Hawaii without an answer, all I can do is
fight for more time. I'll just have to sit down, individually, with every owner
and see if they can give us a break."

When the 1970 annual meeting convened on March 17, no answer had materialized and Sullivan had to spend all his considerable energies fending off "the necessity of a decision on the location of the franchise." He had two things going for him in that attempt. The first was the emergence of yet another stadium possibility in the days just before the meeting convened. The village of Foxboro, about halfway between Boston and Providence, Rhode Island, and the site of Foxboro Raceway, had come up with a proposal. E. M. Loew, owner of the racetrack, was prepared to donate land for a site if someone else came up with the money to build. Just where that money would come from was not at all clear, but it was a possibility and Billy Sullivan made sure everybody in Honolulu knew about it.

Billy Sullivan's second advantage was the continued tolerance of Pete Rozelle. At Billy's request, the commissioner appointed a committee consisting of Lamar Hunt, Art Modell, and Charlie Bidwill—the other Bidwill brother from St. Louis—to study the Patriots' plight. The three men issued their report on the last day of the Honolulu meeting. It recommended that "the Patriots continue to explore every possible method of keeping the franchise in Boston or at least the New England area." While saying a solution must be "prompt," the report set no specific deadline. Billy Sullivan emerged from the NFL's final Honolulu session, the hometown *Globe* noted, "wearing his first smile in days."

While Sullivan was in Hawaii, the Patriots had already begun to explore the possibilities in Foxboro. The pivotal role in that process was played by Dan Marr, one of the two Marr brothers who together owned a chunk of the franchise's voting stock. Since the dilemma was how to pay for what might be built there, the critical question was how cheaply a stadium could be constructed. The Marr family business was erecting structural steel, and Dan had an idea. By sinking two-thirds of the structure in the earth, enormous savings could be reaped. On his own, Marr hired consulting engineers, put together a rough set of specifications, and used his contracting connections to solicit informal bids. The result, he informed Sullivan, was a stadium that could be built for $6 million—relative chickenfeed in the stadium business.

On April 5, 1970, Billy Sullivan called a press conference and announced that the Patriots were moving to Foxboro. Later, they would change their name from "Boston" to "New England." To finance their new home, an independent real estate investment trust (REIT) was being formed for public subscription. The instrument, called Stadium Realty Trust, made use of "Internal Revenue code provisions that allow it to receive income without being taxed, provided that at least ninety percent of all income and return on capital are passed along to shareholders." To qualify, all Stadium Realty's stock had to be subscribed by September 18. To no one's surprise, the stock sale was a cliffhanger. A week before the final deadline, Stadium Realty was still $500,000 short. By then Sullivan had already sold the stadium's name to Schaeffer Brewing Company for $1.5 million. He had also bought a large chunk of stock himself and sold bits and pieces to all his family and friends. On September 18, Sullivan announced the Patriots were "guaranteeing" the unsold stock and the stadium would be built. "The eleven-year struggle of the

Patriots to find a home," *The Boston Globe* noted, had "come to a happy ending."

When "Old Billy" officially announced as much to the next meeting of the NFL, the owners stood and cheered.

The groundbreaking for Schaeffer Stadium was held on September 23, 1970. The Foxboro High School Band played "Let the Sun Shine In" and Governor Sargent called it "one of the most exciting days ever for Massachusetts." Commissioner Pete Rozelle, "tanned and lean and smooth as maple sugar," was visibly relieved. "This stadium," he pointed out, "eliminates a big problem for pro football and adds to its growth. . . . If this stadium didn't come about, the pressure would have been on Billy to move the team next year." The credit, he said, belonged to Billy Sullivan. "Billy isn't a millionaire sportsman like some of our owners," Rozelle elaborated, "but nobody in the NFL has devoted as much time, effort, and money to his ball club as Billy and his family . . . yet he's one of the few people who always thinks of the League first, who pays more than lip service to the good of the game. The New England fans are very, very fortunate to have an owner who cares so much."

As the ceremony marking the realization of the Patriots' dream come true drew to a close, Billy Sullivan, its principal architect, had the last words. "They talked about us going to Tampa, Memphis, Seattle, Toronto, Montreal, Birmingham, and other places," Old Billy crowed. "But there's no place I'd rather be today than in good old Foxboro."

28

Around Boston, Schaeffer Stadium was considered something of a miracle and Billy Sullivan was the miracle maker. That reputation only grew when construction was completed on time and under budget a year after the last Stadium Realty Trust stock was subscribed. Billy Sullivan, now "the man who saved football for New England," cut a considerable civic figure. Still president of Metropolitan as well as president of the Patriots, he and his wife, Mary, had a house in Wellesley and a summer place in Cotuit. They had six children and, by the time Schaeffer Stadium was built, all were close to grown. His son Chuck had served with the army in Vietnam. His daughter Kathleen would eventually be elected to Boston's school board. Billy was also a friend of Congressman Tip O'Neill and a recognizable commodity in the city's Democratic party politics, if for no other reason than he seemed to know everyone in Greater Boston. Sullivan attended Mass every morning and his biggest passion in life was letter-writing. He often wrote more than eighty before leaving for work each day and was renowned for spending more on his personal postage than anyone in Boston except Cardinal Cushing.

In the iconography of the NFL, Billy Sullivan embodied the "rewards of persistence," a notion to which all twenty-six members gave at least lip service. Schaeffer Stadium was, for them, a monument to Old Billy's now legendary doggedness. That persistence was, in turn, one of the primary reasons his fellow owners were prepared to believe him when he promised to comply with ownership policy if given enough time. Having watched Old Billy finally bag a stadium after eleven years, his NFL friends were prepared to believe he was up to keeping any promise he might make. "I've watched this man butting his head against a wall, trying to make things go on a shoestring budget," Lamar Hunt pointed out. "I admire him so much for his stick-to-itiveness and the way he's fought, scrapped, and clawed. . . . Personally I find it very heartwarming to see the success he's having. . . . I think he's done a wonderful job."

Inside the Patriot franchise itself, however, opinions of their President were decidedly more mixed. In the six years between the merger agreement and the passage of the 1972 ownership policy resolution, the team had won only 27 games while losing 54 and tying 3. Billy Sullivan had been the only president in Patriot history, but among Sullivan's partners, there was now a growing feeling that the franchise needed a new approach. They were impatient with his longwindedness and "up to here" with endless speeches about someday making the Super Bowl. Despite his status as a local legend, Sullivan was vulnerable in his own backyard and that vulnerability was a function of precisely the ownership policy violations Billy Sullivan had been promising since 1967 to correct. As the *Boston Herald* put it, the Patriots ownership was "split more ways than a $3 pizza."

Billy Sullivan would later call taking partners into the Patriots "a mistake" and claim that he could have borrowed enough money to make a go of the Patriots single-handedly. Nonetheless, to do so would have meant risking everything he owned and "risk" was probably an understatement. The AFL in 1959 was a shaky investment all over the map, but nowhere more so than Boston. In their first season, the Patriots sold five thousand season tickets, eighteen hundred of them to Billy Sullivan. The franchise lost $1 million during its first four years in business.

In those days, having partners was very useful, though Billy claimed to have approached them all not as investors, but as "friends who had helped me during my life." His original idea was to include four such friends: Paul Sonnabend, son of the president of Hotel Corporation of America; George Sargent, whose brother later became governor; Guido Rugo, a friend from the war who had connected him to the Boston Braves; and his Uncle Joe. Uncle Joe Sullivan was the first of the family to rise to social prominence. His printing business in Lowell was one of the biggest in the area. His two principal clients were the Catholic Church and the racetracks. It was Uncle Joe who convinced Billy to bring in five more partners. Among them were Dom DiMaggio, brother of the baseball legend, and Colonel Dan Marr, whose son Dan later figured out how to build the cheapest stadium in professional football. One hundred thousand voting shares in Patriots, Inc., were issued and, as Billy Sullivan remembered it, he "very foolishly" let all his friends have the same piece of the action as himself. Their ten equal contributions gave the franchise an original capitalization of $250,000.

Sullivan's next group of partners entered the franchise en masse a few months after the first nine, when the franchise sold 120,000 nonvoting shares to their football watching public at five dollars a share. Though these shares did not entitle their owners to any say in the running of Patriots, Inc., they were advertised as "in all other respects . . . equal" to the voting shares purchased by Billy Sullivan and his friends for $2.50 apiece. Over the next decade, 19,000 more five-dollar shares would be issued, raising the total public shares outstanding to 139,000. By the middle 1970s, thirty percent of those shares were turning over each year in local trading at prices between eight and nine dollars.

The turnover in voting shares was nowhere near so rapid and, since all such transactions were private, the prices paid were not revealed. By 1973, however, it was known that the board of directors made up of Patriots, Inc.'s, voting shareholders was an entirely different arrangement from the group of "friends" envisioned by Sullivan in 1960. Billy himself personally owned 23.7 percent and controlled the votes of the additional 12.5 percent owned by Uncle Joe's heir, Mary Sullivan, Billy's cousin. The remainder of the voting stock broke down into three significant blocks. The largest, thirty-four percent, was owned by two New York investors, David McConnell and Robert Wetenhall. Most of McConnell and Wetenhall's daily dealings with the franchise were handled by a Boston attorney, but over the years McConnell gradually took a more direct interest, and by 1973 had become, as one of the shareholders described it, "prominent around the locker room" after Sunday's games. In the last rush to subscribe Stadium Realty Trust, the two New Yorkers had agreed to cover the stadium's $500,000 shortfall in exchange for two more seats on the Patriots' board. Billy would later describe their relationship as "unfriendly, at best."

The second block of voting stock outside Billy Sullivan's control belonged to Bob Marr and Dan Marr Jr., the sons of Colonel Dan Marr Sr. The Marrs had a long history in Boston sports. In 1914, the Marr family firm, then headed by their grandfather, did the steel work for Boston's Braves Field, and when the baseball team didn't have the cash to pay its bills, accepted a piece of the team instead. In his youth, Dan Marr Sr. had played a little professional football and once acted as commissioner of the semi-pro Atlantic Football League. He and Billy had been close and, to Dan Sr., his original Patriots purchase was a "great adventure" that, given Boston's three failed professional football franchises prior to 1960, "looked like a foolish investment." When Dan Sr. died in 1969, he passed on fourteen percent of the franchise to his sons, an inheritance worth in excess of $2 million by 1974. Among the Patriots' second generation of Marrs, Bob, the younger of the two, was the verbal point man. While not particularly close to McConnell and Wetenhall, the Marrs shared the New Yorkers' opposition to Billy. Voting together, the two factions were usually joined by two other minor interests for a total of forty-nine percent. "What you have to remember," Bob Marr pointed out, is that the Patriots franchise, despite being identified in the public mind with Billy alone, "always has been a coalition" and "Billy has never been a unanimous choice for the job."

The swing vote that had kept Sullivan in the Patriots' presidency was a fourteen percent block of Patriots stock owned by the George Sargent Trust. Sargent's widow, Hessie, was the trust's administrator and, like her late husband, an old friend of Billy's and his wife, Mary. While habitually loyal to Billy, she was under increasing pressure to switch sides, primarily from her son, Lee Sargent, football coach and athletic director at Noble and Greenough Academy in Dedham, Massachusetts. In the early days, Lee had been the Patriots' ball boy and by the time Schaeffer Stadium opened, was "more involved" in the Patriots' workings than his mother was. He did not share her attachment to Sullivan's presidency. "Bill had it for a long time," Lee pointed out. "Now maybe it's time for someone else's chance."

By the time the board of directors of Patriots, Inc., met in January 1973, shareholder support for New England's "man who saved football" was, as *The Boston Globe* put it, "shakier than a bathtub of Jell-O." The meeting was held in one of Schaeffer Stadium's utility rooms, a setting that had what the *Globe* called "the waiting room decor of a recently franchised dentist." Once the discussion started, it was apparent that Billy Sullivan's days were numbered.

"The whole franchise was adrift," Bob Marr explained. "The team was not doing well. Boston was down on the team and the sale of season tickets was down. We had to have some changes made." Though Marr's opinion wasn't new, Hessie Sargent was now prepared to go along with it.

Her old friend Billy Sullivan, however, was not about to leave without a fight. When informed he was going to be replaced, Marr remembered, Sullivan "came all apart." If nothing else, Sullivan pleaded to the board, it was a poor way to reward the years of service he had given the franchise. Even if he had to go, this way of doing it was dishonorable. If they would vote him just one more year as Patriots' president, Sullivan promised that he would resign his position when it was done. Billy's emotional plea was aimed at Hessie Sargent in particular and landed on fertile ground. The two had been good friends for too long for her to do less than accede. Faced with Hessie's change of heart, the board made Billy Sullivan's reelection unanimous on the condition he would then resign at the board meeting in January 1974.

The board's decision was "secret" but word of Old Billy's downfall soon reached Greater Boston as a rumor and then as an outright announcement by Sullivan himself. He was indeed resigning next January and had promised as much to the board. "Disenchanted seems like the proper word," he offered in description of his feelings. "I expect to remain with the club in some capacity. I'll just be shedding a lot of responsibilities."

This was not, however, a promise Billy Sullivan meant to keep, and the closer his scheduled resignation got, the more obvious that became. Despite his initial stoicism, Sullivan spent a good part of his last year on the job trying to buy control of the franchise so he wouldn't have to leave. His cousin Mary had agreed to sell her 12.5 percent by March 1973. Then Billy turned to Hessie Sargent again. If she would sell him the Sargent Trust's fourteen percent, he pointed out, his problems would be solved. Hessie said she would talk it over with her son, Lee, and when McConnell and Wetenhall learned of Sullivan's move, they cried foul. The New Yorkers claimed that Old Billy had promised them as part of the deal they cut around Stadium Realty Trust that they would have first refusal anytime the Sullivan family sold any of its interest and also on any further Patriot stock that the Sullivans might buy. Sullivan responded that the first refusal applied only to the sale of his own holdings. At the insistence of Billy's cousin, the issue was referred to Pete Rozelle for resolution.

In the meantime, the Patriot board meeting scheduled for January 1974 was postponed and Billy Sullivan was instead observed at Super Bowl VIII "bubbling over with enthusiasm and confidence . . . not acting like a man about to step down from anything." Shortly thereafter, Rozelle ruled that McConnell and Wetenhall had no right of first refusal but that Sullivan was obliged to offer them the same price he offered Hessie. While considered a Sullivan victory, it was a hollow one. In fact, whatever Rozelle might rule, there was no one besides Billy's cousin who was willing to sell. Lee Sargent was adamantly opposed and his mother agreed with him. "My mother and I have been kind of dependent on each other," Lee explained. "We worked together and we've been quite sure of our position for a year now." The meeting at which that position would be exercised was now scheduled for March 21.

On February 24, Billy Sullivan arrived in Bal Harbour. He represented his by now frantic buy-out strategy to his fellow members as an attempt to bring the Patriots into compliance with the fifty-one percent provision in the commissioner's ownership policy, but admitted he was "backed up against my own goal line." They wished him the best, but most figured this was Old Billy's last appearance in the National Football League.

29

No one in the NFL would miss Billy Sullivan more than Joe Robbie, owner of the Miami Dolphins. Robbie and Sullivan had been close friends since Miami entered the AFL as the last expansion franchise before the merger. At the time, Robbie had replaced Sullivan on the bottom rung of the League's financial ladder. The two were something of an odd couple. The Lebanese Robbie, characterized by *Sports Illustrated* as "tough as a wharf rat and charming as a rent collector," had none of Old Billy's Irish lovableness. Inside the League, he was, with the exception of Sullivan, something of a loner, keeping his business to himself. Nor was he terribly popular. "If someone killed Joe Robbie," one NFL executive observed, "the list of suspects would be the Miami phone book."

One of the few things Billy Sullivan and Joe Robbie had in common was finances. *Sports Illustrated* described Robbie as "the poorest man to obtain a sports franchise in the last twenty years." He was also, by reputation, the cheapest. An attorney with eleven children, he had never made more than $27,000 in a single year before joining the AFL in 1965. "He runs a $2 million business like a fruitstand," one owner observed. His employees described him as someone who counted paper clips and "hardly ever signs checks promptly, if at all." Hook-nosed and squat, with thick-framed glasses, Robbie had none of the glamour usually associated with the NFL, nor any of the flash traditionally associated with Miami. "He looks like a business agent for a labor union," one sportswriter observed, "wears electric-green anklets, and his grip on a cocktail glass is that of a longshoreman holding a schooner of beer." By 1974, Joe Robbie was used to being classed as the least likely member of the nation's most exclusive club. In response, he was quick to point out that he didn't get into the football business to be liked.

"Once," Joe Robbie offered, "people sympathized with the guy who could climb up the ladder, the Horatio Alger thing, you know. But I think in this affluent society, where lots of people have lots of money, they resent a working stiff making it. That kind of thinking exists particularly in the glamorous area of professional sports, which has always been a rich man's plaything in the past. They're big business now and there's going to be more and more of my kind one day. . . . I know how to fight. I come from a town called Hard Times."

More precisely, he came from Sisseton, South Dakota, population 3,218. His father had emigrated there from a village fifty miles outside of Beirut in 1900. His given name was Arabi but the immigration officer wrote it down as "Robbie" and that became the new family name. Robbie's father chose Sisseton because two of his great-uncles had settled there after traveling the United States as itinerant peddlers. Joe was born in 1916. By age fourteen, he was working part-time as the sports editor of the *Sisseton Journal Press*. He then worked his way through Northern State College and the University of South Dakota, finishing with a law degree. While at Northern, he was student body president, and at South Dakota, a debate champion. "I loved to talk," he remembered. "I learned that it could be a weapon too. But it was really enjoyment for me. Debating and the sports pages were my only distractions."

The day after Pearl Harbor, Robbie enlisted in the navy and served in five different invasions in the South Pacific. He was discharged in late 1945 with a bronze star and returned to Mitchell, South Dakota, to practice law. During the next six years, he was elected to the legislature, served as state Democratic party chairman, and ran unsuccessfully for governor. Then, in 1951, he moved to Minneapolis to become regional counsel for the Office of

Price Stabilization. That stint was followed by private practice as a Minneapolis trial lawyer.

Robbie had significant political connections. He was a close friend of Hubert Humphrey from the days when Humphrey's father ran a drugstore in Huron, South Dakota, and he served as campaign manager in the then senator's failed 1960 presidential campaign as well as acting as the then vice-president's personal representative to the 1965 presidential inaugural committee. He kept a photo of himself and John Kennedy on his office wall and never missed a Democratic National Convention. Joe Robbie's political connections had a lot to do with securing his unlikely opportunity to join the NFL. The rest was a matter of being in the right place at the right time.

The particular connection that proved invaluable was his friendship with Joe Foss, still AFL commissioner in 1965. Foss was a much decorated World War II aerial ace who had come home and made a career in South Dakota politics. There he crossed paths with Robbie, another young veteran doing the same thing. In February 1965, lawyer Robbie was hired by a client to approach his friend Commissioner Foss about the possibility of an AFL expansion franchise in Philadelphia. When they talked, Foss informed Robbie that the AFL was indeed going to add a franchise, but that Philadelphia would not be its home. The league wanted no more intra-city combat with the NFL. "If you want a franchise," Foss advised, "make it Miami." Robbie's client wanted nothing to do with Miami, but Robbie, uninhibited by his $27,000-a-year income, decided to pursue the franchise himself.

Despite Foss's advice and backing, Miami was by no means the favorite location for expansion among the members of the American Football League. The south Florida city was a hard town in which to sell a ticket and Robbie, resident of a city two thousand miles away, would have an additional outsider's disadvantage. Lamar Hunt was one of the leading skeptics Robbie tried to convince. Hunt thought that as a resort area, there would be little civic enthusiasm for a football franchise to tap. He also noted that the city of Miami had been less than receptive to previous professional uses of its Orange Bowl Stadium. In response, Robbie pointed out that professional football exhibition games there had drawn well and said that his discussions with the city of Miami indicated their attitude about a professional football franchise had changed. In fact, the deal Robbie eventually cut with Miami would long be considered the best lease in the league.

In 1965, however, Miami was running a poor third in the AFL's expansion discussions. The first choice was Atlanta, but before the AFL could act, the NFL put a franchise there, effectively closing the market. The next choice was New Orleans, but Robbie's luck held. When the AFL 1965 All-Star game was staged there, several black players had been subjected to racial harassment and New Orleans became a potential public relations nightmare no one wanted to risk. At an American Football League meeting in August 1965, Miami was voted in as the upstart league's first and only expansion franchise. On Commissioner Joe Foss's recommendation, the franchise was awarded to Minneapolis attorney Joe Robbie, a total unknown to both Miami and the world of sports. The price tag was $7.5 million, spread out in twenty years of installments.

If convincing the AFL to risk a team in a city heretofore considered a football graveyard was a significant accomplishment for Joe Robbie, his gifts became truly obvious as he went about solving the problem of buying the franchise without any money of his own. The answer was the limited partnership, a form over which Robbie was the football business's acknowledged master.

The limited partnership is, in effect, a two-story legal structure. On the first floor are the general partner or partners, who are personally liable for the partnership's debts and have exclusive decision-making power. The second floor is occupied by the limited partners, who own a piece of the venture but are simply investors with no personal liability. The form was particularly attractive to football owners because of the relatively huge depreciation benefits allowed such enterprises under the Internal Revenue Code. While sheltering significant amounts of income, limited partnership status also insulated the same investor from anything more than paper losses. "I am where I am now," Robbie would later say, "for one reason. That's because nobody wants to put their own money up. They want something for nothing. They don't want to take any risks. That's why I have the club. I took the risk." His twenty-year contract as managing general partner allowed Joe Robbie to run the team as his own. His personal investment was $100,000.

In the first of the three Dolphin partnerships Joe Robbie would form in the course of his first ten years in the football business, he was the only individual general partner. The other general partner was a corporate entity called Danny Thomas Sports, Ltd. Danny Thomas himself was a fellow Lebanese and a very visible and wealthy figure in the television business. His presence would prove instrumental in soothing any worries about Robbie's threadbare finances and, at the same time, in attracting limited partners. During the Dolphins' first year in competition, the space allotted Thomas in the "Meet the Dolphin Owners" section of game programs was the same size as Robbie's and a trifle more prominent. Thomas could also be seen running around on the sidelines with a cigar while Joe Robbie was in the stands hustling prospective limited partners. Although the Miami franchise was "bought" in 1965, it was not until 1967 that its limited partnership was fully subscribed.

In the meantime, the franchise spent as little money as possible and the Robbie reputation for cheapness was made. Despite living in Minneapolis, he signed every check the Miami team wrote. At one point in the team's first season, the franchise's business manager had to come up with the funds for a road trip out of his own pocket. "We never had any money," the business manager remembered. "I couldn't even write a check for a pencil sharpener. Even the paychecks were made out in Minneapolis. I was in charge of business operations but there was no money to run the business." When Joe Foss left the AFL commissionership six months after Robbie joined the league, the new commissioner, Al Davis, confirmed the franchise's shaky finances. "The two general partners were Joe Robbie and Danny Thomas Sports, Ltd.," Davis later testified, "and I remember being greatly concerned about the 'Ltd.' because . . . the general partners are liable for all the expenses of the team and Danny Thomas was supposed to be the money man. . . . We found out [Danny Thomas Sports, Ltd.] was a shell corporation with $25,000 [in the bank]. I was greatly concerned with who was going to end up paying. . . . Danny Thomas, Ltd., couldn't do it or Joe Robbie didn't have the funds to do it. We had a big problem with Miami."

That "problem" eased somewhat when Robbie's limited partnership was finally fully subscribed the following year. At that point, Danny Thomas disappeared from the franchise, bought out by Robbie and Willard Keland, a wealthy Wisconsin developer. The price was not a matter of public record but, judging from Thomas's public response, it was attractive. "Did I lose money?" he chuckled. "You got to be kidding. Did you ever hear of a Lebanese losing money? I don't lose money. I only make money." Though there would be later rumors of a rift between Robbie and the entertainer, Thomas gave no indications of it at the time he withdrew from the Dolphins. "Robbie is a great guy in my book," Thomas told the press, "rough and tough. Joe put the club together. I trust Robbie implicitly."

Joe Robbie's new general partner, Willard Keland, came to a strikingly different conclusion. Their partnership lasted little more than a year. "When we bought out Thomas," Keland claimed, "Joe didn't come up with the money to buy his half, so I figured I was in control. But it didn't work out that way." Keland learned as much in December 1968, when he attempted to fire Robbie. Their dispute soon ended up in Pete Rozelle's lap. When Rozelle upheld Robbie's contract, Keland sold out to a new group of limited partners. "I bear Joe no ill will," Keland said afterward. "He's all right. I learned a lesson from him. If you're going to run with sharp operators, you've got to be smart. He came up with a group from Miami to buy me out, and I guess he's got them doing the same thing for him, supplying the money so he can run the club. When I was there, that club and office were run like a bunch of school kids."

By the time Keland left, Robbie had moved his wife, Elizabeth, and the children who still lived with them to a house in Miami Shores and commuted back to Minnesota when the need arose. South Florida, he pointed out, was now his home. The new partners he brought in also helped him to overcome his outsider image. One was a director of the Hertz Corporation and the Dade County Metro Transit Authority. Another was a director of the Jockey Club and the Ocean Reef resort. The third was a former officer of Pan Am and a director of the First National Bank of Miami. The fourth was a vice-president of the Miami Chamber of Commerce and the fifth was a founder of Burger King. All were Miami residents. "This is what I've wanted for four years," Robbie proclaimed. "This is one of the most vital steps taken to strengthen and develop the Miami franchise." It also marked the point at which Robbie finally gained what *The Miami Herald* called "undisputed operational control of the Dolphins."

Like Leonard Tose, Joe Robbie left a lot of ex-friends in his wake. By 1970, he had already fired four business managers and a number of secretaries. "Nobody thinks much of him," one of his ex-employees told *Sports Illustrated*. "For a big man he's very small." Perhaps the most disgruntled was John O'Neil, the only original limited partner from Miami, in for $500,000 worth of stock. Robbie eventually banned O'Neil from the Dolphins' offices and owners' box for being "subversive to the Dolphin organization." O'Neil in turn sued Robbie for "mismanagement of funds, using club funds for personal use, raising his salary in violation of the partnership agreement, and numerous other practices." The charges were never sustained in court and by the 1974 League meetings in Bal Harbour, Joe Robbie was an established Miami fact. His franchise was profitable and now worth more than twice what it had originally cost. Robbie himself was a recognizable figure along the Orange Bowl sidelines, as *Sports Illustrated* described him, "with his children running behind him, [sprinting] up and down the yard stripes, pounding players on the back, yelling as if he were in the charge at Manassas and banishing people from the area who have suddenly incurred his disfavor." By then he had already served his first term as chairman of Florida's Dade County Democratic party.

He had also won himself something of a reputation inside the NFL. When asked about the move he was then making on Wayne Valley inside the Raider franchise, Al Davis explained that he was taking the "Joe Robbie approach."

At Bal Harbour, Robbie's circumstances stood in stark contrast to those of his friend Billy Sullivan. While old Billy was perceived as a defeated man, Joe Robbie arrived in triumph. Despite all the jokes about his Arab-trader approach, the team he started from scratch and built using willpower in place of cash had just become the first in National Football League history to win two consecutive Super Bowls. It was also the first and only team ever to go the length of a season undefeated.

Yet, among his fellow owners, Joe Robbie's achievement only transformed what had been contempt into a more respectful resentment. "Robbie's a hard guy to like," one of them explained. "You've got to pretend you're talking to someone else."

30

No one in the NFL disliked Joe Robbie more than Carroll Rosenbloom. Their relationship had been perpetually off since 1970, when Robbie had made the uncharacteristic decision to spend some money—at C.R.'s expense.

While Joe Robbie may have been cheap, he was a shrewd businessman and understood that you had to spend money to make it. On game days, Robbie was often seen squiring potential sources of financing around the Orange Bowl, letting them get a feel for his investment at ground level. Robbie was prepared to spend the money he could borrow because the Dolphins had won only three games the previous season, attendance was still spotty, and it was by now obvious that only winning teams would generate the gate he felt he needed.

In the spring of 1970, Joe Robbie made his move. "The Dolphins bought themselves into contention," is the way Al Davis later described it.

What Robbie "bought" was head coach Don Shula.

Shula's name first came up in a conversation between Robbie and Ed Pope, sports editor of *The Miami Herald*, after the disastrous 1969 season had ended. Robbie mentioned he was thinking of changing coaches and Pope recommended Shula. At the time, Shula had three years left on a contract with Carroll Rosenbloom's Baltimore Colts. He had coached the first NFL team to lose a Super Bowl, and when the Colts had followed that with an 8-5-1 season that fell short of making the playoffs, his relationship with Carroll Rosenbloom had soured. By the time Shula's name was mentioned to Robbie, C.R. had already taken steps to reduce the coach's authority inside the Colts and made little secret of the fact he blamed Shula for the franchise's lack of ultimate victory. Even from as far away as Miami, Shula looked ripe for a change of job.

Nonetheless, when Shula received a phone call from a sportswriter friend at *The Miami Herald* the day after Robbie's conversation with Pope, the caller's tone was "very confidential." NFL rules forbade "tampering" with anyone else's coach without first getting his employer's permission, and no one had yet talked to Rosenbloom. The sportswriter wanted to know if Shula would be interested "in coming down to Miami as the head coach and also becoming involved in ownership." Shula said he would call Robbie about it the next day. When he did, his first question was whether Robbie was serious about ownership. Joe Robbie said he was. Shula then said he would inform the Colts.

At the time, Carroll Rosenbloom was vacationing in Bangkok with Georgia and had left his son Steve minding his football business. Steve gave Shula official permission to talk to Robbie and Shula continued to do so. Shula and C.R. finally talked when the Colts owner stopped in Honolulu on his way home. By then Shula had decided Robbie's offer was too good to refuse. "In the beginning," according to Shula, Rosenbloom "was very kind and understanding." Then, "he turned very curt and very businesslike and said he wanted to call the commissioner." Rosenbloom didn't place that call to Rozelle until after Robbie had announced Shula's signing at a ceremony in Miami's exclusive Jockey Club. By then the Baltimore press had jumped all over Carroll for letting Shula get away and he responded by denouncing Robbie to the commissioner and the public at large for "tampering."

While Rozelle found it "hard to believe" that Steve Rosenbloom hadn't secured his father's permission before letting Shula proceed, "the rule said you had to talk to the operating owner," so he awarded the Dolphins' first choice in the next player draft to the Colts. Joe Robbie thought it was too much. Carroll Rosenbloom thought it was too little and made what Rozelle called "a lot of public noise about it." Eventually Rozelle called C.R. and asked him "to bring this to an end." A year or two later, Rosenbloom finally complied.

In the meantime, Joe Robbie attempted to make peace. He placed a phone call to C.R.

"Carroll?" Robbie began, "this is Joe Robbie."

Rosenbloom didn't bother to be polite. "I don't want to talk to you about anything," he snapped. Then he hung up. Later he publicly announced he would never talk to Robbie or Shula again.

In Shula's case that policy eventually changed, but Rosenbloom's distaste for Robbie never lessened. It is doubtful Joe Robbie lost much sleep over C.R.'s attitude, one way or the other. After three years of Shula, the Dolphins were selling out the Orange Bowl and well on their way to making Joe Robbie rich. He was also used to having people mad at him, whatever their reasons. "Joe Robbie is an enigmatic man," *Sports Illustrated* pointed out, "a case study of the type of guy who would pick a fight with Bo Derek on their wedding night." Even Don Shula, the man who put Robbie over the top, was not immune.

At the Dolphins' 1974 team banquet celebrating their second straight Super Bowl, Shula was late and Robbie, who had already been hanging around the head table for a while, found his coach outside the banquet hall, still waiting for his wife. The Dolphins' managing general partner was furious. "It was very evident," Shula told *Sports Illustrated,* "that he had been drinking." Instead of a greeting, the apparently well-lubricated Robbie opened up by yelling at Shula to get the hell into the room. Shula responded in kind. "Yell at me again," he told Robbie, "and I'll knock you on your ass."

Though Shula continued to work for Robbie, it was reported that in private conversations out of Robbie's hearing he referred to his boss as "that asshole." It was a description of Joe Robbie already in wide circulation around the League.

Asshole or not, Joe Robbie was a devoted family man in all his endeavors, including football.

From the beginning, Robbie's Dolphins were a family affair. Robbie invested his wife, Elizabeth's, life savings when he entered the football business and "she participated in virtually every aspect of the Miami Dolphins. . . . My wife and I," he explained, both "have to sign every note that we have ever . . . executed to borrow money. She is in on all the debts of the Miami Dolphins. . . . It's all our family money. It isn't mine and it isn't hers. It's ours."

That "ours" included eleven younger Robbies, most of whom still chased their father down the sidelines on Sundays. The Robbies were by reputation a close family, but not without their tragedies. His daughter

Kathleen, a student at the University of Mexico in Mexico City, drowned in the ocean off Acapulco in 1971. His oldest son, David, a graduate of Notre Dame and the University of California School of Medicine and the only male Robbie not pointed toward the sports business, would jump to his death off the Golden Gate Bridge in 1975. By the early 1970s, his next oldest son, Mike, had graduated from Notre Dame and was working as the Dolphins' director of ticket sales. His other four sons, Robbie was proud to point out, "have the same kind of interest in sports." At the time of the Bal Harbour meeting, they ranged in age from eleven to eighteen.

The Robbie family business's collision course with Pete Rozelle's owner- ship policy was set in 1972, shortly after that policy was first formalized, when Joe and Elizabeth attended a gathering at Miami's Jockey Club, hosted by Harper Sibley, one of Robbie's new limited partners. At the time, Miami had a North American Soccer League franchise called the Gatos and the Gatos' previous ownership had gone bust. Sibley was hosting this party to try to collect a group of twenty or thirty people who might buy in and save soccer for Miami. As Joe remembered it, the Robbies got involved when "Harper Sibley, toward the end of the meeting, pointed to Elizabeth and said, 'We ought to have a woman in this. How about you, Elizabeth?' " Elizabeth said yes and subscribed for a limited partner's "rooting interest." The general partners were Sibley and three other men. Joe Robbie joked he was "happy Elizabeth is in soccer," because now she could "quit running the football team." By the end of the evening, the NASL franchise had been rescued. Renamed the Miami Toros, it would lose some $900,000 over the next three years.

In 1973, Elizabeth dramatically increased her liability for those losses when she agreed with Harper Sibley's request that she step in to replace one of the general partners who was dropping out. When Rozelle learned of Mrs. Robbie's increased NASL role, he would agree that it was at least technically outside the purview of the League's continuing ownership policy resolution. He would also target the arrangement as a potential "conflict of interest" that ought to be formally prohibited whenever the "sense of the meeting" on the subject again heated up. For his part, Robbie found Rozelle's ownership policy arguments specious.

Among other things, attorney Joe Robbie noted, the constitutional amend- ment Pete Rozelle wanted was an open invitation for a lawsuit under the Sherman Act.

31

The only other attorney on the National Football League's membership rolls, Edward Bennett Williams of the Washington Redskins, shared Robbie's assessment. Coming from Williams, however, the opinion carried infinitely more weight.

Edward Bennett Williams was already renowned as the most powerful lawyer in Washington, D.C., perhaps the premier courtroom performer in the nation. Among his more famous and notorious clients were Teamsters President Jimmy Hoffa, Congressman Adam Clayton Powell, *The Washington Post,* the Democratic party, Senator Joseph McCarthy, bookmaker Frank Costello, and CIA Director Richard Helms. By 1974, Williams's personal income from the practice of law was some $1 million a year. A conservative Catholic Democrat, his name was often raised in connection with cabinet level posts but none of the offers was good enough to lure him out of private practice. Even without a post in government, an invitation to Edward Bennett Williams's box at R.F.K. Stadium "was among the most sought after badges of prestige in Washington" and his guests included "a procession of senators, cabinet members, and even a President of the United States."

Williams did little of the day-to-day running of Pro Football, Inc., the incorporated ownership of Washington's NFL franchise. "I delegated that," he explained. "My whole philosophy in running the company was to get the very best people that I could, turn the operation . . . over to them, and do nothing to interfere . . . except to look at the end results and make a judgment at the end of the year. I went to the National Football League meetings when I could and represented the interests of Pro Football, Inc., at those meetings, but I was [also] conducting a full-time law practice." His fellow football owners loved to listen to Williams talk, although, as Lamar Hunt noted, "Mr. Williams has a way of expressing himself where I'm not sure whether you know what you hear after you've heard it."

When in NFL attendance, Edward Bennett Williams was perhaps the only one in the room for whom the power and celebrity of a football owner were actually less than those afforded in the rest of his life. Williams was there at all because he liked to win and made a point of seeking out opportunities to do so. "There are three occupations that involve what I call 'contest living,' " he explained, "sports, courtroom law, and politics." Williams was involved in all three and "in each one you may be absolutely brilliant on a given day, but you still may lose. It's the most agonizing way to live, but it's also the most exhilarating." It was the kind of life Ed Williams had always wanted, and getting what he wanted was a Williams trademark.

Born in 1920 in Hartford, Connecticut, Edward Bennett Williams antici- pated big things for himself from the beginning. His father was a department store buyer and floorwalker who never made much money but was considered a brilliant man. Edward Bennett was the Williamses' only child, for whom his father had high expectations. Williams's sense of his ultimate calling came early in life. As a teenager, he already wanted to be a lawyer and used to mount a chair in the Williams family apartment and imitate Franklin Roose- velt. Williams's high school yearbook described him as "known by everyone, principally for his leadership and scholarship. He always ruled with an iron hand and a dominating will . . . and for this reason accomplished much."

Williams went on from Hartford to a full scholarship at Holy Cross University outside of Boston, and graduated first in his class and summa cum laude. Next came Georgetown Law School in Washington, D.C.

Edward Bennett Williams's stint at Georgetown was quickly interrupted by World War II and an enlistment in the Army Air Corps, lured, he explained, "by being a pilot, getting wings, all that stuff." A year later, the plane he was flying during training in South Carolina crashed and Lieutenant Williams suffered a severe concussion and a back injury that would plague him all his life. Discharged for medical reasons, Williams returned to George- town where one of his professors described him as "the brightest student he had ever encountered."

When Hogan and Hartson, one of Washington's most prestigious law firms, interviewed Williams shortly before his graduation from Georgetown in 1944, they concurred. "I chatted with Ed," the head of the firm's trial department recalled, "and I was so impressed . . . that even though he had a couple of weeks yet left to finish in his school and had not yet taken the bar . . . I made the determination that I wasn't going to let the guy get out of the building except that I had a commitment from him." After two years at Hogan and Hartson, Williams married Dorothy Guider, granddaughter of one of the firm's senior partners. Rather than trade on that connection, Williams left the firm. "When I decided to get married," Williams remembered, "I decided simultaneously to get out of the law firm. . . . I had to leave because I didn't want . . . to have everybody else in the law firm explain whatever success I might have by saying, 'Well, he married the boss's granddaughter.' I didn't need that, I thought, to be successful."

Williams was, of course, accurate. On his own, he had become a visible legal figure by the early 1950s, when he shepherded clients in front of the House UnAmerican Activities Committee. That began three decades of assist- ing a long list of highly visible and generally controversial clients in courts and government hearing rooms. Along the way, Edward Bennett Williams attracted a certain controversy himself. At issue was his willingness to act as anyone's mouthpiece, prepared to say whatever might bolster his client's case. "There was something upsetting about the performance of this lawyer who stands near the top of his profession and commands such respect," a *Chicago Tribune* editorial complained.

However controversial, Edward Bennett Williams's acknowledged legal and oratorical mastery earned him a handsome living. According to Robert Pack's biography, *Edward Bennett Williams for the Defense,* by 1982, the attorney's net worth would be "at least $50 million." Included in that were several office buildings in downtown Washington, a hotel, an estate in Potomac, Maryland, a summer home in Martha's Vineyard, a commanding interest in the law firm of Williams and Connelly, and 14.3 percent of the Washington Redskins' holding company, Pro Football, Inc.

Williams's investment in Pro Football, Inc., had begun in 1962, with the purchase of fifty of the corporation's thousand shares, a five percent interest, for a little more than $75,000. Williams described the purchase as "the most highly speculative investment you could possibly make." At the time, the Redskins' principal shareholder was still George Preston Marshall. Marshall owned 520 shares for fifty-two percent control. Two hundred fifty shares— twenty-five percent—were owned by Canadian millionaire Jack Kent Cooke. The remaining eighteen percent was owned by two Washington attorneys, Leo DeOrsey and Milton King. George Preston Marshall was, as the *Washington Monthly* described him, "an erratic and unpredictable man . . . who had practically disowned his two children when his wife divorced him years before," but he had "a soft spot in his heart for Williams. Williams was like the perfect son to Marshall, the type of son he had always wanted." By December 1963, Marshall was suffering from cerebral arteriosclerosis, emphysema, and heart trouble. "Unable to properly care for his property and interests," Marshall agreed to the appointment of Williams, DeOrsey, and King as conservators of his estate. DeOrsey was made the club's president, the first person other than Marshall ever to hold the position.

When DeOrsey died in 1965, Pro Football, Inc., purchased his 130 shares from his estate for $1.3 million and retired them, leaving only 870 shares outstanding, and Edward Bennett Williams assumed the presidency. That summer, Williams, described by his biographer as a "frustrated jock," showed up at the Redskins' training camp, "wearing shorts, a Redskin T-shirt, and athletic shoes. He proceeded to go through a workout with his players, running laps, doing calisthenics, and impressing squad members by demonstrating that at forty-five he could catch long passes and withstand the rigors of an entire workout." When his team opened the season by losing five straight games, Williams blistered the players with a two-hour speech behind closed locker room doors and they promptly won three in a row.

By then, Edward Bennett Williams's role in the estate of the now incompetent George Marshall had already become the subject of what would be described by *Washington Monthly* as one of Washington's "ugliest" running courtroom battles. The challenge came from Marshall's two children who, under the terms of the will of the senile majority owner of the Redskins, were to be left no more than ten thousand dollars a year apiece. The children charged that Williams and King, the remaining conservators, were "using their dual and conflicting roles" as minority owners charged with looking out for the majority owner's interests "to promote the perpetuation of their personal interests in permanent control" of Pro Football, Inc. They also claimed Williams and King were keeping Marshall "a virtual prisoner" in his home in Georgetown, and doing everything to cut off contact between themselves and their father. Marshall himself was now completely incapacitated, without the ability to speak or even to gesture in a meaningful way.

When Williams had been Redskin president for little more than a year, Marshall's children escalated their objections. They had learned their father's will left the bulk of his estate, including his controlling interest in the Redskins, to a foundation for underprivileged children and, in 1966, set about trying to get him to sign a new will. At one point, Marshall's son went so far as to break into his father's home late at night in order to discuss the subject. According to the younger Marshall, his father was pleased to see him. Edward Bennett Williams, however, was furious and went to court to enjoin the children from "interfering with their father's estate . . . especially . . . from attempting to have him execute legal documents." Ignoring the subsequent court order, the Marshall children and their attorneys showed up at their father's house on July 2, 1966, with a new will for him to sign, that included an express direction that the will be signed by someone else on his behalf. His son and two of the attorneys did so and then left. The new will bequeathed everything to Marshall's children.

Williams responded by demanding the children be cited for contempt of court and ordered to surrender this new document immediately. Marshall's son refused to do so. Williams, he charged, "wants to control the team, as he does now, and wants to maintain control after my father passes on. . . . [He is] stealing a football team for himself." Marshall Jr. was then imprisoned for a total of five weeks until he finally agreed to give up the will.

The terms of George Preston Marshall's two wills became items of active legal dispute in 1969, when the founder of the Redskins died. After further public name-calling, the case was eventually settled in January 1972. Each of Marshall's children was awarded $750,000 plus $10,000 a year and, in return, the 1966 document was declared invalid. Williams and King also resigned their positions as trustees of the estate. To finance the settlement, Marshall's estate sold 260 of its 520 shares in Pro Football, Inc., back to the corporation for $3 million. Pro Football, Inc., then retired the stock, reducing the total number of outstanding shares to 610. To finance the stock reduction, the franchise borrowed close to $3 million from Washington's American Security Bank. By the time of the NFL's 1974 annual meeting at Bal Harbour, Pro Football, Inc., had arranged to borrow another $5.8 million to buy out the Marshall estate's remaining 260 shares. These, too, would be retired, reducing the shares outstanding to 350. Of those, 250 were owned by Jack Kent Cooke, 50 by Milton King, and 50 by Edward Bennett Williams, still Redskins president. Williams had now increased his share to over fourteen percent without spending any of his own money. By conservative estimate, this "highly speculative" 1962 investment of $75,000 was now worth $2.4 million.

When Edward Bennett Williams reported on the status of the Redskin ownership at Bal Harbour, however, that last 260 share buyout had yet to be finalized. Since it would, in effect, create a new majority owner of the franchise, Rozelle had ruled that it required a formal endorsement, even though no new parties were entering the League as a consequence. That endorsement, in turn, was subject to the conditions of the 1972 ownership policy resolution, passed after the first half of Marshall's holdings had been retired.

It was a delicate situation and to resolve it, Edward Bennett Williams's Pro Football, Inc., would eventually become the first and only NFL ownership to comply with the policy of which Williams himself was the most vocal opponent.

32

At issue specifically were the holdings of Jack Kent Cooke, Pro Football, Inc.'s prospective majority owner. Cooke's interests in professional basketball and hockey were clear transgressions of the commissioner's post-1972 cross-ownership prohibition and as far as Rozelle was concerned, to let Cooke move into a controlling ownership position without accounting for that violation was out of the question. Cooke himself had no direct dealings with the League in their deliberations over his elevation and instead left it to his partner, Edward Bennett Williams, to represent his interests.

Williams's first inclination was to dispute the need for a vote at all. "The commissioner took the position that this kind of transfer had to be approved," he remembered. "I disagreed with that. I didn't think it had to be approved because it was an intramural transfer. My understanding of the purpose of transfers of ownership being approved [by the rest of the League] was to keep undesirable persons out of the game. If the transfer contemplated is a transfer of shares to persons already in the game, I didn't think the rule was applicable." Williams went along with its application nonetheless. "We did it," Williams explained, "just so there wouldn't be any dispute. . . . We weren't looking for a quarrel with the commissioner's office." Over a barrel, the nation's foremost trial lawyer recognized the situation would have to finessed.

Apart from his cross-ownership violations, Jack Kent Cooke, then sixty-two, was an ideal candidate for an NFL franchise. Cooke's worth was estimated by *Forbes* as "at least $500 million." Cooke himself admitted only to being "really rich," a stature he defined as having "a lot of liquidity and tremendous credit resources, where you walk into any bank and they say, 'Oh, yes, please let us lend you money.' "

Not surprisingly, Jack Kent Cooke's favorite books featured Horatio Alger. Born in 1912 in Hamilton, Ontario, to which his father had emigrated from Australia, Cooke's family were "awfully well-to-do" throughout his childhood. Young Jack Kent was waited upon by servants and sent to study clarinet at the Toronto Conservatory of Music. In 1929, the Cookes' wealth evaporated in the opening rounds of the Great Depression. Jack Kent immediately dropped out of high school and began earning a living as leader of a band called Oley Cooke and his Orchestra. He also worked as a runner on the Toronto stock exchange and sold encyclopedias door to door. Next he went to work selling soap for Colgate-Palmolive and "sold more soap than anyone in the history of the company."

What Jack Kent Cooke later called "the great break of my life" came when he was hired to manage radio station CJCS in Stratford, Ontario, for $25 a week in 1937. Within two years he had become the partner of the man who had hired him; within four more years he had become a millionaire, with radio stations and magazines providing that wealth. Cooke soon added more companies, including Canada's largest manufacturer of plastics. He purchased his first sports franchise in 1951, taking over Toronto's struggling minor league baseball team. By 1952, he had made it a success and was named Minor League Executive of the Year. Cooke was also a championship yachtsman, a voracious reader, and the composer of more than a hundred copyrighted songs from which he drew royalties.

By 1960, Jack Kent Cooke felt he had exhausted his opportunities in Canada and moved to California, eventually settling in Bel-Air, next to Beverly Hills. His neighbors there included Tony Curtis, Jerry Lewis, and Greer Garson. "A hearty laugh takes the edge off his pomposity," the *San Francisco Chronicle* observed, "and he is frequently interesting if you don't mind all the quotes from Shakespeare and Bismarck. He delights in correcting other people's grammar. . . . His sentences more often than not demand exclamation points." He also soon adopted the Los Angeles habit of peppering his conversations with "dear," "love," and "adorable," used interchangeably as nouns, pronouns, adjectives, or adverbs. Cooke became an American citizen almost immediately upon emigrating by virtue of special legislation that made his residency retroactive to 1950. It was shepherded through Congress by a friendly representative from Pennsylvania who cited Cooke's "fervent pro-Americanism" as reason enough. Cooke's first new enterprises as an American citizen were an investment firm and a cable television company.

In 1961, Jack Kent Cooke bought into the football business. The 250 shares in Pro Football, Inc., that eventually became his had originally been sold by George Preston Marshall to broadcaster Harry Wismer during the 1950s. By the time Cooke purchased them, Wismer had become one of the eight founding owners of the American Football League and needed cash. Wismer was also tired of fighting with Marshall. According to *The Washingtonian* magazine, Wismer's problems with Marshall had begun when he "discovered that instead of paying profits to shareholders, Marshall was spending the team's earnings on himself. Some of the money went to maintain a stable of women in other cities so that when the Redskins played a road game, Marshall could count on finding a friendly face. Marshall also sold his home in Georgetown to the Redskins, but he continued to live in it, paying nominal 'rent,' well below the market rate. . . . He [also] used Redskin employees as his personal servants.'' Wismer sued unsuccessfully for a greater share of the profits and then decided to get out.

Ironically, the first prospective purchaser for Wismer's shares was Edward Bennett Williams. In February 1961, the attorney and Wismer had agreed on a sale price of $250,000. Williams needed Marshall's approval to consummate the purchase, since all partners in Pro Football, Inc., had rights of first refusal on the sale of any stock to outsiders and, though a friend of Marshall's, Williams was still an outsider. In 1961, however, Marshall was still the only owner in football who refused to hire black players, despite the fact that the rest of the League had integrated fifteen years earlier, and Williams had ''strong moral and practical'' objections. ''It was just a terrible and ridiculous position for Marshall to have been in,'' Williams remembered, and Williams told him he would not ''come into the company if he did not break the racial barrier, because I thought it was an absolutely disastrous policy.'' Despite his later fatherlike feelings for Williams, Marshall was furious. ''He not only became angry,'' according to Williams, ''he then told me that under no circumstances would he change and I was not welcome in the ball club.'' A year later, Marshall would hire his first black and sell Williams his initial five percent, but at the time, Williams's deal with Wismer collapsed and Wismer's stock went back on the market.

Jack Kent Cooke learned about its availability by accident, during a trip to New York City, when he shared a cab with a friend who knew of the collapse of Williams's deal. That evening, Cooke and another friend had dinner at Manhattan's ''21'' Club and the friend mentioned he had once worked for Marshall. Before the meal was finished, the friend had called Marshall from their table and secured Marshall's permission for Cooke to buy in. Wismer then agreed to sell for $350,000 and Jack Kent Cooke had his original twenty-five percent. By the time Pro Football, Inc., had arranged the final buyout of the dead Marshall's shares at the franchise's expense, Cooke's investment comprised more than seventy percent of the outstanding stock and was worth at least $12 million.

The basketball and hockey holdings which were the source of the 1974 controversy over Cooke's elevation dated from 1965, four years after his entry into football. The first to have been purchased was the National Basketball Association Los Angeles Lakers. A year later, he'd bought a National Hockey League expansion franchise and named it the Kings. At the time, the only suitable arena in which the teams could play was the Los Angeles Memorial Coliseum Committee's new L.A. Sports Arena, but, as Carroll Rosenbloom would later discover, Cooke found the LAMCC impossible to deal with. Cooke's response was to spend $16 million building his own arena, The Fabulous Forum, in Inglewood. Dismissed as ''Cooke's folly'' when first announced, the Forum would make money from the day it opened and eventually drive the rival Sports Arena to the edge of bankruptcy.

A key influence on the strategy Edward Bennett Williams chose in order to secure NFL approval of the last Marshall buyout was the attitude of Cooke himself, who was battling a string of other difficulties and didn't have the time to bash about with Pete Rozelle. Cooke's run of bad luck had begun the year before, when he suffered a heart attack while having dinner prior to a Laker game at the Forum. To recover, he retired to his ranch in the Sierra Nevada mountains to write songs, only to have that retirement end in September 1973, when his cable television business collapsed.

By then, Cooke's television investments had evolved through merger into a sixteen percent nonmanaging interest in TelePrompTer, Inc., the nation's largest cable television firm. At its high point, TelePrompTer shares sold at forty-four dollars each. Then the summer of 1973 ended with news that the Securities and Exchange Commission had suspended trading in the company's stock. By November 1973, Cooke had moved in to take personal control of the company and try to salvage his investment. At the time, TelePrompTer had fallen as low as two dollars a share. When Pete Rozelle demanded a League vote on the final buyout of Marshall's Redskin shares three months later, Jack Kent Cooke was up to his ears in trimming dead wood out of TelePrompTer Corp., and made it clear to Williams that he had no intention of assuming the prerogatives of a majority owner. His instructions were to settle it all however he could.

The course of action Edward Bennett Williams consequently pursued was strategic retreat. While he agreed with Joe Robbie that the commissioner's ownership policy was an invitation to a lawsuit, Williams did not intend to file it himself. He wanted a compromise and took the best terms he could get. Williams's compromise entailed two concessions, each designed to mollify Rozelle's objections. The first was the establishment by Cooke of a "voting trust" whereby the operational power of his Redskin shares was vested in Williams, his trustee. "It didn't make any difference to Mr. Cooke," Williams explained. "Mr. Cooke lived in California. I lived in Washington. He didn't [like to] fly . . . [and] we didn't want a quarrel with the commissioner's office."

The second concession amounted to the firmest and most definite promise to divest yet offered by any opponent of the commissioner's cross-ownership prohibition. "Mr. Cooke authorized me to say that he would divest his conflicting interests," Williams remembered, "and that he would do it by the time of the next [annual] meeting." According to Rozelle, "on the basis of Mr. Williams's commitment, there was little or no discussion and the member clubs voted approval of this transaction."

Though it amounted to Williams eating a little crow and was accounted a Rozelle victory, the compromise was not necessarily a defeat for Edward Bennett Williams. The last Marshall buyout had been confirmed and his control over the franchise was as secure as it had been when he was trustee of Marshall's stock. Whatever ground he'd given up on the issue of ownership policy would be regained in spades the next time the issue heated up.

33

Though the tensions generated by diverging individual agendas were a familiar factor inside the League, by 1974 the NFL still presented a single face to the world. That face, of course, was Pete Rozelle's. League Think was in its ascendancy and the clamor for the NFL's product gave the exclusive twenty-six-man club which paid Rozelle's salary enormous leverage over how America saw itself. However else a city might try to boost itself, the only sure way to get listed in capital letters on the national map was to have a home team in America's Game. Six years of phenomenal growth had passed since the football business had last added a new location and there was now an impatient assortment of cities outside the League hoping to be let in. All of them insisted they deserved admittance. "Having created an opiate for the people," *Sports Illustrated* noted, the NFL "can no longer deny it to those who can support the habit."

That the membership would be enlarged was by now an accepted NFL fact, but where, who, and under what terms were all still hot issues.

Like ownership policy, expansion had been a League issue since the merger agreement eight years earlier. It was also an issue dominated by Pete Rozelle. To the commissioner, the inclusion of new locations was at the cutting edge of the League's public relations and marketing, both his home turf. It was also the principal currency of the League's political influence, which, under the terms of League Think, was exclusively Rozelle's to spend. The last time he had done so was in the scramble to secure antitrust exemption for the merger with the AFL in 1966. Then, Rozelle had argued to Congress that providing a secure base for the further enlargement of professional football mitigated whatever Sherman Act transgressions might otherwise be involved. The exemption and the cessation of interleague warfare, he assured them, would "guarantee" that football would spread. To prove his point, he promised two new franchises by 1968. The New Orleans Saints and the Cincinnati Bengals were the result. Rozelle had also promised to "study the possibility" of even more expansion after that.

By late 1972, however, no such study had been done. Nor was any then planned. Rozelle wanted "to be sure the League had absorbed the AFL and the two earlier expansion teams" before proceeding any further, and when pressured for a comment on the possibility, said only, "I believe there will be expansion in this decade." The comment did little to assuage the anxiety of the impatient cities, in which Pete Rozelle was fast acquiring a reputation for arrogance.

On September 6, 1972, citizen groups from Memphis, Phoenix, Seattle, and Tampa arrived at the NFL offices to meet with him about redeeming his early congressional promises of future growth. Their appointment had been on Rozelle's schedule for four months and they were all at the commissioner's office at the appointed time. The commissioner, however, was not. Instead of Pete Rozelle, they were greeted by one of his assistants, who informed them, "The commissioner is out of the office today." The assistant listened to the presentations in Rozelle's place. His only response was to admonish the group for having released news of its meeting to the press.

Rather than slackening in response to the commissioner's brushoff, the pressure next became both more official and more effective. As Rozelle remembered it, "Congressmen and senators began hearing from affluent people in their city or state and then the NFL got pressure from politicians for the first time." That pressure included a meeting with Senator Howard Baker of Tennessee at which the commissioner listened to a presentation about the virtues of Memphis as an NFL site. At another meeting, Senator Scoop Jackson of Washington gave the commissioner an earful about Seattle. Both no doubt reminded Pete Rozelle that Congress expected his earlier promises to be kept. Rozelle in turn reminded them it was not his decision, but that of the owners, and added that some of them would be a hard sell. The conversations nonetheless had a visible effect.

When the League met in Scottsdale, Arizona, on April 2, 1973, Rozelle was now convinced that the time had come to expand. It was an issue on which all the initiative was already in his hands. "You ask twelve owners about expansion," Steve Rosenbloom remembered, "and you'd get twelve different answers. They had to be convinced and that was the commissioner's role." According to Leonard Tose, "Rozelle pretty much dictated the policy." In fact, there was never a formal vote to expand or a vote on the number of franchises any expansion ought to include. At Scottsdale, Rozelle simply announced that football could now accommodate two more locations and "it was time to investigate expansion." As the discussion went around the room, there was both "strong, strong interest" and "some resistance."

The resistance centered on the simple economic fact that admitting new members took money out of the current members' pockets. Though any new ownership would have to purchase its franchise from the League, the League would have to split its television revenues more ways. The prospect, according to one League employee, caused several owners to "drag their feet." Rozelle in response "had to sell them on the concept this would benefit the whole League, that we would become stronger as a whole." Congress, he noted, was applying pressure and at the moment were considering some forty-four different pieces of legislation that affected the football business in one way or another. Before executive session adjourned for the day, the minutes noted, the "member clubs" had instructed the commissioner to appoint an expansion committee.

The committee Rozelle appointed included Tex Schramm, Gerald Phipps of the Denver Broncos, Lou Spadia, president of the San Francisco 49ers, and

Dan Rooney, president of the Pittsburgh Steelers. It was not a group likely to throw any surprises the commissioner's way. Dan Rooney was named chairman. "I wanted people on the committee who could make good business judgments," Rozelle explained, "but could also evaluate the various connotations. Dan Rooney was from a football family and had grown up in it." Dan Rooney was also, like Schramm, one of the commissioner's close personal friends. From the day the appointments were made, Rooney functioned as the League's chief representative on the subject of expansion. The procedure worked out by Rozelle and the committee was two-tiered: first, select a city and set a price; then choose specific individuals to whom to sell the new franchises. In all, some twenty-five cities expressed an interest, and Rooney's committee investigated each. By the Bal Harbour meeting, the time had come to narrow the list and start talking about what price was sufficient reward to the NFL for loosening its corner on the market.

Enlarging a monopoly was a process fraught with potential dilemmas and Rooney's assignment was to steer the League's way between them all. While expansion might mean risking overexposure, unsatisfied demand created a vacuum, insuring instability in the market and risking external competition. When Rooney's group started work, the threat of new competition had already added yet another factor to the pressures surrounding the issue and served to push the expansion committee ahead with all due speed. The new factor was named the World Football League, which had officially announced its existence in October 1973. It was the first challenge to the NFL's monopoly since the merger. If the NFL would not heed the public's clamor for franchises, Gary Davidson, the new league's founder, declared, the WFL would. "The NFL has grown arrogant and complacent," he charged. "The doors are open to a rival. The war is on."

Pete Rozelle would later describe the WFL as a minimal factor in the NFL's decision to expand, and expressed great skepticism about the new league's capacity even to wage war, much less win it. Davidson, however, came on strong. "We are far better off than the American Football League was when it was founded," he claimed. The WFL would play its first season in fall 1974 with twelve teams, including Anaheim's Southern California Sun; the Jacksonville, Florida, Sharks; the Portland, Oregon, Storm; the Honolulu, Hawaii, Hawaiians; the Birmingham, Alabama, Americans; the Memphis, Tennessee, Southmen; the Charlotte, North Carolina, Hornets, the Detroit Wheels, and the Philadelphia Bell. According to the WFL master plan, the initial twelve would form the league's American Division. Within five years, a second division would be added in Tokyo, Madrid, London, Munich, Paris, Dusseldorf, Rome, Mexico City, and Stockholm. Initially all games would be scheduled on Wednesdays, ceding the weekend to the NFL, and played using a football with phosphorescent stripes.

Pete Rozelle's skepticism about the World Football League reflected his own sense that while football appeared to be a simple business, it was not nearly as simple as it seemed. It also reflected his sense that Davidson was in it for a quick profit and didn't have the resources to pull it off.

By 1974, Gary Davidson was a familiar face in the sports business. He had already started two new leagues, the American Basketball and World Hockey Associations. In each, he had subscribed all the new franchises, saving one for himself, and established the league with a public relations coup, usually a raid on the existing league for celebrated players. Then Davidson sold his own franchise on the inflated bull market and headed for his next venture. In the case of the World Football League, Davidson peddled his Philadelphia Bell in late 1973, making some $600,000 profit without spending a dime. Then he took a $100,000 a year contract to act as WFL commissioner. He would last barely a year in the job. By the time Davidson bailed out, the WFL's Houston and Washington franchises had fled bill collectors, landing in Orlando, Florida, and Shreveport, Louisiana, and a Birmingham bank was auctioning the foreclosed Americans' game jerseys to trivia collectors. In February 1974, however, Davidson and the WFL had yet to make their initial player raid and still had to be watched.

Of greatest longterm significance to League Think was the signal the mere existence of the WFL, however fleeting, sent in the NFL's direction. Professional football franchises were a commodity for which there was far more demand than supply and the wider the differential became, the more that demand would generate forces at variance with the interests and structure of the National Football League's monopoly. By 1974, more than a few cities were already desperate for a place in America's Game, prepared to do whatever it took to secure a franchise, with or without the League's blessing. Put to the uses of Carroll Rosenbloom, Al Davis, and the players of the Superstadium Game, that runaway seller's market would eventually propel the NFL into what Pete Rozelle called "anarchy" and make his worst nightmares come true.

34

The demographic minefield that would eventually blow the ground out from under League Think had already been uncovered by the 1973 research of the Expansion Committee. The most critical information had been collected by Stanford Research Institute under NFL commission and communicated to Dan Rooney in a December 1973 report, *Socioeconomic Information on Candidate Areas for NFL Franchises*. The document amounted to a detailed map of the football market that remained outside the NFL's 1973 boundaries. In retrospect, it would read like a guidebook to coming battle zones.

At NFL direction, SRI made a preliminary investigation of twenty-four possible locations and then went into fourteen of those in detail. Each was considered as a standard metropolitan statistical area, the geographic urban definition used by the federal government, and evaluated specifically as a potential location in which to stage live football games on the bases of total urbanized population; male population between twenty-five and sixty-five; number of households with relatively high incomes; number of professional and managerial employees; and the number and types of business establishments. Of the cities investigated using those factors, ten seemed promising.

The two weakest candidates for expansion were Honolulu, Hawaii, and Birmingham, Alabama. Honolulu was attractive for its climate but was a long way from the mainland and, though growing fast, somewhat short on population base. While larger than Honolulu, Birmingham was also relatively small and ranked last among the top ten in number of families with an annual income of fifteen thousand or more. Each of the remaining locations had a relatively strong case for membership:

Seattle, Washington, was the capital of the American northwest, one thousand miles from the closest franchise, and encompassed a metropolitan population of almost two million, who already supported professional basketball and hockey franchises. SRI considered it likely a professional baseball club would soon arrive as well. The college football team at the University of Washington regularly drew fifty-five thousand at home games.

Indianapolis, Indiana, encompassed 1.2 million people but another 2.7 million were within a one-hundred-mile drive and more interstate highways converged in Indianapolis than in any other section of the United States. Fully half the American population was within two days' shipping distance. The closest live football was college games in South Bend or Bloomington.

Phoenix, with a population of 1.1 million in 1973, was already the thirty-fourth largest American metropolitan area and growing fast. Phoenix's National Basketball Association franchise ranked fifth in the league's attendance, and the local college football team filled its stadium every Saturday.

Tampa's population was roughly equal to that of Phoenix but the only local supply of football was the University of Tampa's schedule with the likes of Toledo, Florida, A&M, and Southern Illinois. The school averaged only nineteen thousand paid attendance but Tampa had supported "the largest number of [NFL] preseason games played at any neutral site during the last six years." Attendance at those averaged almost forty thousand.

Metropolitan Memphis, Tennessee, the forty-second largest statistical area in the United States, was rated higher than only Birmingham and Honolulu among the final ten. Though promoters of an NFL franchise for Memphis claimed it would draw upon some 191 counties within three hours' drive, enlarging its potential population base to 6.4 million, attendance at NFL preseason games staged there had been "at times disappointing."

The remaining three municipal regions on SRI's top ten were of a somewhat different species than the other seven. While all three represented untapped potential markets, all were within a seventy-five-mile radius of an existing franchise. Yet, their demographics were the most compelling of all:

Nassau and Suffolk Counties on Long Island were already part of a Greater New York market that included more than eleven million residents, currently serviced by the Giants and the Jets. Considered apart from nearby Brooklyn and Queens, Nassau and Suffolk Counties were by themselves the ninth largest metropolitan area in the United States, with a population of 2.5 million. The area ranked first in per capita spendable income and comprised the nation's fourth largest retail market.

Greater Chicago was a metropolitan area of more than seven million, serviced by one franchise, the Bears. While SRI didn't offer a clear geographic boundary as in the case of New York, it noted the untapped potential market there was enormous. The area was the nation's largest producer of capital goods, had an average household income of seventeen thousand dollars, and in the last ten years its "disposable household income after taxes" had increased "more than any other major area of the United States."

The Anaheim metropolitan area in Orange County, twenty-eight miles southeast of Los Angeles, was the eighteenth largest in the country with a population of more than 1.5 million. It was flanked on one side by L.A., the nation's second largest standard metropolitan statistical area, and on another by San Bernadino-Riverside, the twenty-eighth largest. As a county, it ranked seventh in the nation in retail sales and twelfth in the number of households earning twenty-five thousand dollars or more. The only local supply of professional sports was the California Angels professional baseball team based in Anaheim. To consume football, Anaheim had to drive into West L.A. and watch the Rams.

Based on the numbers it had developed, independent of the other "connotations" Rozelle considered so important, Stanford Research Institute's December 1973 conclusions were simple. "According to all the economic and demographic criteria studied," SRI's report observed, "the New York [Nassau and Suffolk], Chicago, and Los Angeles [Anaheim] areas rank substantially above all the candidate areas, even when data are divided by two or three to account for a shared market." Labeled "Client Private," the inch-thick report was circulated inside the NFL by Dan Rooney, usually in the form of excerpts.

The demographics detailed by Stanford Research presented the National Football League's monopoly with two fundamental dilemmas, both of enormous longterm consequence. The first was implicit in the size of the market SRI located. Even after adding two more franchises, some twenty-two percent of the NFL's potentially profitable franchise outlets would remain fallow and the NFL would continue to be significantly smaller than its market. On the plus side, that available reserve of locations created a strong upward pressure on the value of existing franchises and gave NFL members enormous leverage in the Superstadium Game. The negatives were that the pressure that had driven the NFL finally to expand by two in 1974 would remain largely unsatisfied. The potential consequences of that frustrated demand were not, however, a subject on which the expansion committee spent much time. Both Rozelle and Rooney considered expansion a "case by case" situation and made no attempt in 1974 to devise a long-range plan by which the future pressure could be channeled. The principal question as they saw it was to choose from among the current options in a way that "strengthened the League and made it more truly national."

The second of the NFL's dilemmas was crystallized in SRI's somewhat unexpected conclusion that the NFL's best option was to put more franchises into its current three largest markets. Here, the report collided head-on with Rozelle's "connotations." Despite their independent size, Nassau, Greater Chicago, and Anaheim were all still "suburbs" according to the terms of the NFL's monopoly and hence not significant enough for membership. Along this front, the League's structure was at greatest variance with the demographics of its own popularity and though its short-term consequences were minimal, in the long run the stance would insure that the largest untapped markets for live football were not only frustrated at lack of inclusion in the NFL but even further frustrated by the lack of consideration at all. Within four years, that frustration would set off a chain of events that eventually ended with the crushing defeat of League Think at the hands of Al Davis.

There were two reasons for Rozelle's 1974 attitude. The first was television. In the question of "suburbs," the League's broadcast and live gate markets were somewhat at odds. To protect the live gate, the League had always put restrictions on televising games within a seventy-five-mile radius of a franchise's home game. If the home team didn't sell all its live tickets, its game could not be televised, nor could any other games be broadcast into its market. If the home team did sell out, its game could be televised and at least one other as well. Since three games were normally televised into the markets without home teams, simply having a franchise in any market reduced its potential. Having two or more teams in the largest markets of all reduced their TV potential even further. Rozelle considered the television reduction already experienced in New York and San Francisco a "problem" and was not about to add more "problems" to it.

The second reason was built into the NFL constitution and made the possibility of expansion into markets already within a franchise's home turf virtually nil. According to Section 4.3 of the National Football League, the location of a franchise "within the home territory of any other club shall only be effective if approved by unanimous vote." This was the same veto power New York City had encountered in the aftermath of Wellington Mara's move to New Jersey. Eventually Section 4.3 would be the focal point of Al Davis's attack. In 1974, the need to protect each owner's home territory from encroachment was a truism that no one bothered to discuss.

When raised at the expansion committee deliberations leading up to Dan Rooney's report to the Bal Harbour meeting, the possibility of more franchises in the New York, Chicago, and Los Angeles video markets was summarily dismissed. The purpose of expansion was to extend the League's monopoly, not reduce it.

"SRI did a good job," Rooney explained, "but they didn't consider all the factors."

35

Pete Rozelle considered Dan Rooney, president of his father's Pittsburgh Steelers, the "ideal" owner to stage-manage expansion. Young, bright, and articulate, he talked about football ownership as an almost religious obligation. "Our responsibility is the good of the game," Rooney argued. "Owners have to protect the game. That is the owner's function. We are trustees and, unless we're careful, that trusteeship role may get lost in the name of doing business." Trained as an accountant, Rooney was considered by at least one of his owner colleagues the "hardest-working owner in the League" and a devoted backer of League Think. Short and handsome, with dark looks and prematurely graying hair, the younger Rooney was considered level-headed and modest. "In this business," Rozelle noted, "ego can be a narcotic. Dan is a rare exception. You just don't run into very many sports figures who have it under control the way he does."

Rooney was also the leading spokesman for the Old Guard, and the Old Guard was the bedrock upon which League Think and the Rozelle era had been built. The faction's boundaries were somewhat ill-defined but included almost all the ownerships whose presence in the League predated Rozelle, a block of some six votes in 1974. It was a powerful faction not just for its numbers, but also for the influence it accrued as the keeper of the League's tradition. By the time of the Bal Harbour meeting, the NFL had been around for fifty-four years and part and parcel of its marketing under Rozelle had been the mythification of the League's early days. One consequence was that the longer the Old Guard lasted, the more revered it became.

The Old Guard's sacred icon was the Green Bay Packers, the last remaining throwback to the demographics of 1920, when the National Football League had been born. Green Bay, Wisconsin, joined the infant League in 1921 and chose the name Packers after the original owner's Acme Packing Company. When the same League met in Bal Harbour fifty-four years later, Canton, Massilon, Hammond, Muncie, Rochester, Decatur and the rest were long gone, but Green Bay remained. At the time, the city's population was approaching 100,000—off the bottom of the chart as far as standard metropolitan statistical areas went. The town prided itself on being "The Tissue Paper Capital of the World" and included sixty-two churches, fifty-five public schools, forty parks, five golf courses, three television stations, and a branch of the University of Wisconsin. That Green Bay had managed to survive as part of the National Football League was a source of great pride to Pete Rozelle. It was also central to the iconography of League Think. Left to Green Bay's native economic base, Rozelle was quick to point out, the

Packers would have died in the modern age. The town had no media market to speak of, but thanks to the television-sharing policy initiated by the commissioner in 1961, that didn't matter. "Where else could a place like Green Bay play the likes of New York and Los Angeles?" Rozelle asked. "It says a lot for our League that they are still, and will always be part of it." By 1974, Green Bay's franchise was owned by a nonprofit corporation whose stockholders were "barred from receiving dividends and have no stake in the assets that the corporation is accumulating." All of it was grandfathered under the commissioner's ownership policy. At the time of Bal Harbour, the Packers were represented at League meetings by Dominic Olejniczak, considered something of a nonentity whose vote was in Rozelle's pocket.

The Old Guard's two living saints were George Halas of the Chicago Bears and Dan Rooney's father, Art. The reverence now accorded them embodied the League's ritualized yearning for a simpler age. "It doesn't seem too long ago," Art Rooney pointed out, "when we could settle every pro football problem in a quick discussion around a table. The guys who ran the League then were Bert Bell, Tim Mara, George Marshall, George Halas, and myself. We ran it pretty well too. Nowadays, though, the owners don't arrive at a League meeting by themselves as we once did. Each is accompanied by a squad of lawyers, accountants, tax experts, and more advisers than I even can name. When we were struggling to survive, pro football was a fun thing. The bigger we get, the less fun there is in it." Of the Old Guard's living saints, Halas was held in awe, but Rooney, "with his broad Irish face, his frosty white hair, a cigar propped between his lips, and a laugh bubbling up at the least provocation" was, according to Don Kowet's *The Rich Who Own Sports*, "the most beloved figure in all of professional football."

The Rooneys had first come to Pittsburgh from Pennsylvania's rural coal country when Art's father moved there to found Rooney's Saloon, soon the favorite watering hole of the city's Irish sportsmen and politicians. Raised a devout Catholic, young Art was also one of the city's better amateur baseball players and a boxer who reached the quarter finals of the AAU national championships. "I could have gone to the 1920 Olympics," Art remembered, "but I turned pro." After a short professional career, Rooney retired from the ring and went into politics. Throughout the 1920s and 1930s, he was the chief ward heeler for James J. Coyne, Pittsburgh's Republican kingpin. One of his specialties was raising campaign funds by staging semi-pro football games. The games were spirited but informal, with Rooney coaching one or both of the competing teams.

Art Rooney bought into the NFL in 1933. The Pittsburgh franchise cost him $2500, which he'd won handicapping horse races. At first, the team was called the Pirates and its offices were off the lobby of the Fort Pitt Hotel. In those days, one historian of the period noted, "political cronies and gamblers and priests would shuffle in and out, any hour of the day." The Fort Pitt was, by all accounts, a modest beginning. "Once upon a time, I suppose, the Fort Pitt had been a high class hotel," Rooney recounted, "but I can remember guys rushing in, pulling down their flies, and me having to tell them that they had come to the wrong place—the men's room was next door." Art Rooney kept his franchise alive with winnings at the track, the avocation at which he was already a Pittsburgh legend. His most famous exploit was a two-day stretch, one at the Empire City track and another at Saratoga, where he turned two twenty-dollar tickets into an eventual $250,000 payout. Since Pittsburgh's NFL franchise lost money for its first twelve years, Rooney's prowess at the track was essential to its eventual success.

Art Rooney still remembered the NFL's old days well and made no bones that they'd often been a mess. "At one time," he pointed out, "the League had an executive committee of three, rotated among the owners, to screen proposed legislation before each League meeting. One year, Charlie Bidwill [of the then Chicago Cardinals] and George Marshall [of the Redskins] and I were on the committee, and we met in Chicago, just before the League meeting. As usual, Marshall had about a hundred proposals to make to the League. Charlie and I agreed with every one of them and we got finished in less than an hour. Marshall said it was a great thing that the League finally had a progressive executive committee. Charlie and I just wanted to get out to the racetrack. We did, but the next day we met again with Marshall and just as calmly voted against every one of the things he had proposed the day before. And that was the end of that executive committee."

Those memories of Rooney's made him an unalloyed booster of Rozelle. "I didn't know much about him when he was chosen," Rooney remembered, "but Pete Rozelle has had more to do with the growth of this League than anyone else. He was on top of things from the first meeting he ever had. He started well and grew with the job. We were very, very fortunate to have had him. Rozelle made the NFL the strongest of major league sports. He's very honest and very fair. He's been tough when he had to be and compassionate when he had to be. His judgment is just about perfect. I hope Pete stays a long time. It would be very, very difficult to replace him."

The significance of Rooney's endorsement only grew as Art's sainthood burgeoned. By 1974, that status was unquestioned. "He's the finest person I ever met in my life," one owner gushed. At the time, Rooney was seventy-one years old and still lived with his wife, Kathleen, on North Lincoln Avenue across the street from his boyhood home, in the same three-story Victorian he'd lived in when he joined the NFL. Most of the saloons and family homes on the street in those days had long since been replaced with rooming houses and parking lots, but Art, now wealthy, had no desire to move. All of his wealth was mingled with that of his five sons in a company named Ruyanaidh, a Gaelic word pronounced "Rooney." It was the umbrella for some ten different corporations, most of them sporting enterprises. His son Art Jr. was president of the Penn Racing Association. His son Pat was president of Green Mountain Park racetrack in Vermont and helped another son, John, run the Liberty Bell track in Philadelphia. His son Tim ran Yonkers Raceway in New York and was general manager of the Palm Beach, Florida, Kennel Club. Art's oldest son, Dan, was, of course, president of the Pittsburgh Steelers.

Dan had been born the same year as the Steelers and was raised in his father's strict Irish Catholicism. Dan grew up around the Steelers' training camp and was an outstanding athlete himself. As a senior at Pittsburgh's North Catholic High School, he quarterbacked the football team to the city championships. In 1955, after graduating from Duquesne University with a degree in accounting, he went to work in the family football business. His first job was selling ads in the game programs. Over the next ten years, Dan worked in every phase of the Steelers' management. "Dan never thought there was any job too menial," one of his brothers remembered. "Now, with the possible exception of coaching the team, there's not a single facet of this business he doesn't know inside and out." After Dan had been running the team for almost ten years, his father handed over the title of president. "One morning Dad walked into my office," Rooney remembered, "and said, 'As of now you're President,' and that was it."

Dan Rooney's approach to football, like the rest of his life, was notoriously clean-cut and straight arrow. One owner referred to him as "Rozelle's head Boy Scout." He had married his grade school sweetheart and had nine children, ages five to twenty-one, at the time of the Bal Harbour meeting. They lived in a five-bedroom colonial house in Mt. Lebanon, Pennsylvania, "a typical Pittsburgh suburb." His luxuries were skiing in Colorado and a single engine Beechcraft airplane in which he logged one hundred hours a year. His wife Patricia's biggest complaint was that he made himself "so available to the team and the League alike." Physically, Dan Rooney still looked "like a fifties college student" except for the patches of gray growing in at his temples. "This is not a plaything," Rooney said of his franchise. "It demands and deserves everything I can give it. It's my sole livelihood. It may not have been run like a business before my time, but it is now."

While some of the reverence afforded his father overlapped onto Dan, he had also built a significant influence inside the League on his own and brought a great deal of personal credibility to his role as chairman of the Expansion Committee. When asked to name the League's three best "football men," other owners invariably listed Rooney's name with those of Tex Schramm and Al Davis. A second factor in Rooney's influence was his relationship with Rozelle. Close in age, the two men had become good friends when Rozelle was still general manager of the Rams. "I thought highly of him then," Rooney remembered, "but I was surprised when he was selected commissioner. I didn't even consider him a candidate. He was only thirty-three and the League had been talking about guys who were a lot older." Like his father, Dan Rooney was an immediate Rozelle supporter. "Pete's integrity and intelligence carry him," Dan observed. "I've seen him under situations where it's very tough and I've seen him have as much integrity as anyone I've ever met."

Dan Rooney's report to the Bal Harbour meeting on behalf of the Expansion Committee marked the beginning of the formal process of expanding the League. As such, it also marked the end of the period in which expansion was defined by Rozelle's informal sense of what was called for, subject only to the approval of Rooney and three others. Now the League as a whole was involved and, soon, formal votes would be taken. Following the procedure agreed upon by Rozelle and the expansion committee, the questions of location and price would be decided before taking up the issue of actual buyers.

Of the two questions, location proved the least controversial. The Expansion Committee, Rooney announced, had reduced SRI's top ten to five locations for further study: Seattle, Phoenix, Tampa, Memphis, and Honolulu. Honolulu's inclusion was basically a public relations gesture and not a serious possibility, so the list was in fact reduced to four. The hardest part for Dan Rooney had been dropping Indianapolis. "It's the largest city in the country without a football franchise," he observed, "but we had no choice." The committee's hand had been forced by the fact Indianapolis had no suitable stadium. Though boosters of a franchise there had committed the city to building one if NFL membership was approved, the possibility that the city would be unready for games starting in 1976 was not a risk the League could take. Rooney said the committee would be ready to report on the five finalists at a meeting devoted to expansion it recommended the League schedule for April.

The committee's report ran into a lot more rough air on the question of price. Their recommendation was $12 million in a wide spread of payments at interest below prime. Setting the price that low was a particular concern of Rozelle's. The tricky part of expansion, he argued, was making sure the new franchise took. It was counterproductive to weigh it down with too large a debt before it even began operations. The League, he reminded those who might have forgotten, had thrived by nurturing its weakest links. Dan Rooney agreed with the commissioner, as did Tex Schramm, and both argued strenuously for the lower price.

Even so, it was soon apparent the argument wasn't going to wash. "Jesus Christ," Leonard Tose sputtered, "I owe more than that to the bank." Others were clearly uncomfortable with the recommendation as well. Football was a business in which each franchise sale redefined the value of all the rest. In this instance, the committee's recommendation meant that the League itself was officially setting a value of $12 million—$4 million less than Tose had paid for the Eagles and $8 million less than the Rams had been valued at in Carroll Rosenbloom's 1972 swap. A number of men in the room had outstanding loans or tax returns that valued their franchises at prices significantly higher than the one at which the commissioner was prepared to sell. Following Rozelle's lead meant costing themselves money.

No vote on the question of price was taken at Bal Harbour, and after two and a half hours in Executive Session, the committee's recommendations on location were adopted on a motion by Joe Robbie and a second from Edward Bennett Williams. Then, on a motion by Tex Schramm and a second by San Francisco's Lou Spadia, "the membership voted unanimously to meet in the

League office at 10:00 A.M. on Tuesday, April 23 . . . for the sole purpose of discussing the many aspects of expansion.'' Immediately afterward, the Executive Session recessed for the day.

The stage was now completely set for the civil war to come.

36

On the afternoon of February 27, 1974, the National Football League annual meeting gathered in executive session once more before leaving Bal Harbour. The agenda offered no hint of the fate awaiting League Think. If anything, there was only more seeming proof to the contrary. Two such items stood out.

The first was the report of the NFL's finance committee chaired by Denver's Gerald Phipps. The committee, Phipps reported, had finished negotiations on Commissioner Pete Rozelle's employment contract and recommended it be ''amended and extended for ten years from January 1974.'' On a motion by Wellington Mara, the League then unanimously confirmed the committee's recommendation. The extension insured at least another decade in the Rozelle era. The amendments set Rozelle's new salary level at or around $500,000 a year and coupled it to a package of retirement benefits Rozelle described as ''generous.'' Also included was the explicit modification of the commissioner's expense account to cover the travel expenses of the new Mrs. Rozelle. To sweeten the package further, the League agreed to provide a separate $300,000 loan at seven percent interest to help the Rozelles redo their new home in Westchester.

The second apparent proof of Rozelle's firm grasp on the National Football League's reins was a constitutional amendment considered in the last rush of business before adjournment. The amendment added the explicit ''authority to arbitrate'' to the commissioner's existing powers of ''full, complete, and final jurisdiction'' over internal football business disputes. It was passed as proposed. Though the measure was considered a piece of bureaucratic housekeeping that brought forth no discussion, its passage by rote reflected the extent to which Rozelle's dominance was assumed in February 1974. No one seemed to think it could ever be otherwise.

The only hint of the future came up at the commissioner's final press conference on February 28, before he and Carrie made their way back to New York. There, Rozelle had to reassure the press that Robert Irsay's Colts would not leave the city of Baltimore, even though it was now obvious that the new stadium Irsay thought Carroll Rosenbloom had promised was not going to materialize. ''It will be a burden on Mr. Irsay financially,'' Roselle announced to the reporters, ''but the team will stay in Baltimore.''

Aside from that, League Think's horizon seemed remarkably clear. No one recognized any signs that the League everyone called "Rozelle's" would not remain so in perpetuity. The "greatest commissioner in football history" left Bal Harbour tan, in love, and making more money than he had ever made in his life. To all concerned, he seemed destined to sit comfortably in the catbird's seat for years to come.

Things would never look quite that good for Pete Rozelle again.

PART TWO

THE PLOT THICKENS

1

Though internal disorder was the catastrophe lurking in League Think's future, that disorder was still largely concealed from view by the warfare raging outside the NFL's borders. Two such external threats dominated Pete Rozelle's attention when he returned to the League office from Bal Harbour. The more worrisome of them was the National Football League Players Association led by young Ed Garvey. By March 1974, that relationship was enormously bitter on both sides.

As a matter of structure, it was one of the oddest relationships in American labor. Sports unions were the only unions in the United States that did not negotiate their members' salaries. Those were negotiated on an independent contractor basis, club by club, player by player, and by the early 1970s, generally involved an agent to represent the player. The NFLPA restricted its activities largely to retirement benefits and working conditions. Its only role in the League's salary structure was to set minimum levels and establish standardized pay for exhibition games, a minor part of football economics. The union's 1974 grudge dated from the "failed" negotiations on their last contract in 1970. Those had also been the last such contract negotiations in which Pete Rozelle would play a significant part.

Pete Rozelle's posture in 1970 had been to cast himself as the "impartial" representative of the entire game, and therefore in an ideal position to arbitrate. This didn't wash well with the players, who refused to accept his mediation through most of the negotiations. At the time, the union was represented by John Mackey, its president, and Alan Miller, then executive director. Ed Garvey entered the picture when Miller recommended to Mackey that he sign the agreement offered by the owners. Mackey sought out Garvey's Minneapolis law firm for a second opinion, Garvey told him to refuse to sign, and was brought onto the team as a consultant.

The union's attitude was typified by an exchange between Carroll Rosenbloom and Mackey, one of C.R.'s employees. As the possibility of a strike during the 1970 preseason loomed larger on the horizon, Rosenbloom sought to intervene personally. While in Florida, vacationing with Georgia, C.R. called Mackey to point out a strike was hopeless.

"We don't need football," Rosenbloom argued, "but you do."

Mackey responded that the owners needed football in a much worse way than the players did. "If you didn't have tickets to give away," he told his boss, "you wouldn't have any friends."

C.R. hung up.

By August 1970, strike was a reality and players were boycotting preseason training camps. Then Pete Rozelle intervened. The commissioner would later be credited with having locked the two sides in a room together and forced them to find agreement. The room was in the NFL's offices in 410 Park Avenue and the meeting lasted twenty-two straight hours. According to Garvey, "the story of Rozelle's intervention was bullshit. It grew out of his own press release. In order to get the owners to the bargaining table at all, we had to let Rozelle chair the sessions."

The meeting Rozelle scheduled convened at 12:30 P.M. on August 2. The sessions got "grueling" when the building's air-conditioning broke down, but Rozelle kept his coat and tie on throughout. Whenever the sessions split into its respective halves, Rozelle left with the management team. "If you're so goddamn neutral," Mackey groused at him, "why do you always leave with them?" The next time a similar occasion arose, Rozelle stayed in the room with the players until Mackey invited him to get out.

"I thought you said you wanted me to stay," the commissioner explained.

Mackey asked him who he thought he was kidding.

Finally, by 7:00 A.M., an agreement had been reached. "There wasn't any winner," Mackey told reporters waiting outside. Garvey was succinct. "The owners," he remembered, "gave us nothing."

According to one of the NFL's attorneys, "negotiators of the 1970 agreement shook hands, settled their differences, called off the player strike, and left to the lawyers the task of putting their understandings on paper. Mr. Garvey thereafter spent almost a year raising new issues and reopening old ones before the agreement could finally be executed." By then, of course, Ed Garvey, fresh out of the University of Wisconsin, was the National Football League Players Association's new executive director.

His predecessor, Alan Miller, was asked to resign in January 1971 "on the grounds that he didn't seem to have the union's cause sufficiently at heart." Miller's exit, according to *Sports Illustrated*, "may have been brought about by a Mata Hari. During summer 1970 Miller had been introduced to an aspiring young actress by someone close to Cowboy owner Clint Murchison. A romance blossomed. Miller, who was divorced, flipped on the girl to the point where he told friends he was contemplating another marriage. But when the negotiations were finally concluded, the girl was suddenly too busy to see him." The suspicions surrounding Miller and his girlfriend were typical of the attitude the 1970 negotiations had nurtured in the union. "In any negotiation people start getting paranoid and suspicious," Garvey pointed out, "but here an atmosphere of distrust had been created to the point that people began to think that their rooms were being bugged and that they were being spied upon." In elaborating on their fears, union representatives cited the point in the marathon negotiations when Tex Schramm had declared that the owners knew "every detail" of a recent union meeting, "down to who said what."

When news of the union's suspicions became public in 1971, Rozelle was quick to smooth the public waters. "As far as this office is concerned," he announced, "stories that we were spying on the players are totally untrue. Rumors of that sort were just part of the atmosphere. People were getting tense and excited." Privately, Rozelle called John Mackey to complain about the insinuation.

"How could you think we tapped your phones?" the commissioner asked. He also reportedly offered to take a lie detector test.

Mackey told him that was fine and to let the union know when the test was set up.

That was the end of the conversation. According to Garvey, nothing more came of the polygraph offer.

As the NFLPA's new executive director, Ed Garvey was characterized by Pete Rozelle as "a prototypical early sixties radical, a militant ideologue who is unable to see any good, any justice, in any action of management. He is unable to see in any shades of gray, no in betweens. He has no ability to get close to the center of an issue."

Ed Garvey himself could not have cared less what Rozelle thought. From his viewpoint, the situation he faced upon going to work for the NFLPA full-time in 1971 was desperate. He felt the 1970 negotiations had failed for lack of unity and was quite prepared to vilify the owners in order to fill the void. They were, he would later point out, an easy group to make look like bad guys. "The idea of dealing with athletes as equals is obnoxious to them," Garvey pointed out. "These guys are union busters in the classic sense."

Filing *Mackey v. NFL* in 1972 had been the first step in Garvey's strategy and its defiant tone helped turn the situation around. For the rest of the energy he hoped to infuse into the union, he relied on his own not inconsiderable political skills. A Robert Kennedy Democrat, Garvey had considered running for Congress in Wisconsin before accepting the job at the Minneapolis law firm that led him to the NFLPA. The challenge of the task he set for himself was considerable. The union not only negotiated a unique version of labor contract, it was structurally unique as well. The average career of its members was a little over four and a half years, meaning a twenty-three percent annual turnover in the union's composition. Since contracts were negotiated every four years, only some ten percent had a statistical likelihood of having been around during the previous bargaining sessions. "There's no institutional memory," Garvey pointed out. "You have to reorganize the union every year."

While demanding, that particular characteristic of the NFLPA had its advantages. It allowed Garvey himself to provide the continuity and made stamping his identity on the way the union did business a relatively rapid process. His principal vehicle for doing so was the union's system of player representatives, one per team. Those player reps elected a six-man executive committee that handled most of the union's business. "Most reps are just there," one of them observed. "They're not educated enough on the issues, so a lot of decisions were made by Garvey and the executive committee. The executive committee was more or less who Garvey wanted. He liked to have guys who [sic] he could mold. Ed was real skillful at controlling meetings. The more I was around him, the more amazed I was at how good he was at it. He always had his ducks lined up in a row." By 1974, Ed Garvey had made himself the single most critical ingredient in the NFL's labor supply. "Garvey ran the union in every sense," one former union officer noted. "He made all the decisions and then sold them to the membership."

In preparation for 1974 contract negotiations, Garvey took player surveys and made personal visits to each of the teams, trying to whip up enthusiasm. That process culminated in an NFLPA convention in Chicago where the words "strike" and "solidarity" seemed to be on everybody's lips. At the union's final plenary session, new president Bill Curry asked the crowd if they were "willing to stay out until Freedom?" All in favor were to stand. Everyone stood and clapped. "We went into negotiations with a great sense of unity," Garvey remembered. "We were confident we could get what we wanted."

The NFL Management Council with whom he was about to negotiate brought their own grudges to the encounter. The most immediate of those were directed at Garvey himself and dated from the filing of *Mackey v. NFL*. Those had been exacerbated by all the "sniping" at the League he had done since. Rozelle's irritation with Garvey had become such that during attempts to arrange the preliminaries of bargaining that spring, he informed Garvey that Garvey's biggest problem was frustration at not staying on the Wisconsin campus long enough to blow up any buildings.

The second layer of Management Council grudges dated from the 1970 negotiations. One of the concessions granted to the union in that process had been official certification of the NFLPA as the bargaining agent for football. At the time, the NFL had opted to do so by consent rather than force an election that would have postponed bargaining for months. By 1974, there were some in the NFL who wanted to roll that decision back. On the Management Council's executive committee, Joe Robbie was the most vehement proponent of that position. "If a proposed union goes out and gets enough cards signed by employees," Robbie explained, "the employer can accept that card count as a sufficient vote to grant certification to a union and . . . the NFL did this and I thought it was a mistake. . . . I felt at the time that the labor laws were never enacted for the purpose of granting independent contractors, called football players, the right to collective bargaining and no less an authority than [AFL-CIO president] George Meany expressed the same opinion." Ed Garvey considered the Miami owner's labor views "neanderthal."

The two conflicting agendas collided when negotiations began on March 16, 1974. NFLPA President Bill Curry opened the first session with remarks Management Council Executive Committee Chairman Wellington Mara found "encouraging." Then Ed Garvey followed by reading a two-page prepared statement:

> It has been four years since we looked across the bargaining table at one another. We have not forgotten the way you conducted yourself during the 1970 negotiations. . . . Your attitude for the past four years has been to disregard the union, to avoid compromise at any cost . . . and to continue to suppress the rights of individual

players. . . . The players accuse you of taking freedom from the players with no justification. . . . You are guilty of indifference to societal changes which have occurred since the early '60s. You have perpetuated an unjust system of control over athletes headed by those who have demonstrated disdain for the constitutional rights of athletes.

That statement was followed by a list of some fifty-eight demands. Chief among them were "elimination of the Rozelle Rule" and the creation of total "free agency," "a union shop provision for all players from the beginning of their employment," "elimination of the commissioner's authority to discipline players," and a host of "freedom issues." Among the latter were the right of veteran players to veto any trade, the banning of "all psychological and personality testing," and a provision stating that "no player representative or elected officer of the NFLPA shall be cut or traded without his consent."

Wellington Mara was appalled. "Individually and collectively," he responded, "these demands reflect only one thesis—that the experience of generations is worthless, that a structure that has evolved through the years should be torn down and replaced by nothing. You have given us a list for the nongoverning of professional football. They are accompanied by monetary demands which, although still far from complete, we estimate would cost the clubs $100,000,000 more this year. We do not say that our system is the only system. . . . We do not even say that it is necessarily the best system for maintaining the high popularity of professional football. What we do say is that it is a system that has worked. . . . With all the conviction at my command, I urge you to reexamine your values."

On April 4, 1974, the management council executive committee issued a formal answer. The union's proposals were, it argued, "a demolition of the structure which has taken the National Football League more than fifty years to build, with no organization proposed to take its place. That's not freedom; rather, it is freedom-to-do-as-you-please. We are convinced the game cannot be played with no rules at all. . . . We draw the line at a system with no rules, and we cannot be asked to bid against ourselves in altering a structure with which we have no major complaint."

By then it was apparent to everyone in the League that hostilities on the labor front would be longterm at best.

2

The other front monopolizing Pete Rozelle's attention in spring 1974 was the World Football League. Little more than a month after the NFL annual meeting adjourned, Gary Davidson mounted the long-awaited player raid that was his league-building trademark. It came as little surprise that its target was the legendarily cheap Joe Robbie.

The raid had in fact begun in early February when Tom Keating, the agent representing three of Robbie's star employees—Larry Csonka, Jim Kiick, and Paul Warfield—was approached by one of his associates at the International Management Group headquartered in Cleveland. The two men had a drink in the Pat Joyce Tavern and the associate wanted to know how much money it would take for Keating's three clients to sign with the WFL. At the time, the three were considered to be the heart of the Dolphins' success. The agent scratched figures on a cocktail napkin for a while and came up with $2.7 million. "You're kidding," was the associate's response. At the time, Joe Robbie was paying each of the stars between $60,000 and $70,000 a year. By March, the estimate secured by Keating's associate had reached the hands of John Bassett, the principal thoroughbred in the stable of owners Gary Davidson had thus far managed to recruit.

It was already widely acknowledged that the World Football League had no one who brought the financial stature Lamar Hunt had given the infant American Football League, but John Bassett, heir to a fortune based in Toronto, was as close as they got. His father had once been president of hockey's Toronto Maple Leafs, and he was described as "super-rich." Bassett's original intention was to field a team in his hometown, called the Northmen. In the face of the Canadian government's objections to the importation of American football, however, he would quickly move the franchise to Memphis and change the name to the Southmen. Later the name would be changed once again to the Grizzlies, thereby earning Bassett's franchise the trivia distinction of most name changes by a financially solvent member of the WFL. Wherever his team was, Bassett's finances stood out by World Football League standards. Most of the other owners were, in Bassett's words, "a lot of people who wanted to play with other people's money."

The principal financial reason the football business was an attractive investment to men of Bassett's means could be found in the Internal Revenue Service tax codes. "When a team is successful," *Fortune* noted, "its returns are in a class with those found in the sort of real estate deal that generates cash flow, tax benefits, and longterm appreciation . . . a very cost-effective means for enjoying public stature. Professional sports teams qualify for so many tax advantages as to render their . . . 'book' profit or loss figures meaningless.'' For the average NFL team in 1973, those "book" figures had been revenues of $6.2 million and expenses of $5.4 million. After setting aside $400,000 for "taxes that might be owed," the book profit was $400,000. Using the tax codes to maximum advantage, an "average" NFL owner could potentially turn that profit into a $3.6 million tax loss, thereby enabling himself to keep the $400,000 book profit and the $400,000 tax set aside, untaxed. In addition, he could shelter as much as $2.7 million in additional income, saving $1 million or more on his tax return.

There was just one small problem as John Bassett and the rest of the WFL soon found out. The tax magic worked only if the team generated revenues. While an owner was trying to establish a revenue base, the losses were real, not paper. Over the next year, that drain would be in the range of $1 million per club and, given the new league's underfunded character, Bassett pointed out, it would be tough "finding people with enough money to keep things going." Bassett had more to do with setting the scale of those losses than anyone else in the WFL. The escalation was implicit in the raid he undertook for Davidson's league in the spring of 1974.

In late February or early March, John Bassett called Ed Keating. He wanted to talk about Csonka, Kiick, and Warfield. "I've heard about the figure you came up with," the Canadian multimillionaire told the Dolphins' agent. "Are you serious?" Keating said he was and Bassett said he wanted to do business. Formal negotiations were scheduled to begin March 30.

Keating's first step was to check out Bassett's finances. Impressed, he then notified his clients of the approach and arranged for them to come with him to Toronto at the end of the month. Csonka flew there from Los Angeles where he was judging *Playboy*'s Bunny of the Year contest. Negotiation sessions were held in the Prime Minister's Suite in Toronto's Sutton Place Hotel. The night before, Bassett, his general manager, and his attorney went out for drinks and dinner with Keating and his clients. For Keating, it was a critical opportunity to size up his opposite numbers. "Psychology plays a tremendous part in negotiations like this," he later explained. "With some owners you've got to be low key—talk softly, go fishing with them. With others, you might have to pound the table and have a few drinks. The secret is to get the other guy as close to the corner as you can without pushing him against the wall." On the basis of dinner conversation, he decided to use the soft approach on Bassett.

Negotiations commenced the next morning and included Bassett's three-man team and Keating. Keating's clients were there in the beginning but were soon sent down to a clothing store to pick out some custom-made suits courtesy of one of Bassett's minority partners. Keating then presented Bassett with three separate salary demands for each of his clients. The total value as a package was $3.884 million and included a million-dollar signing bonus. Csonka was demanding $1.4 million over three years, Kiick $700,000, and Warfield $900,000. In Csonka's case that was almost eight times what he earned under his current contract with Joe Robbie, not counting a signing bonus.

Keating also presented Bassett with two other documents. The first set out a long list of alterations his clients wanted in the standard NFL player contract. The second was a short memorandum listing a desired set of "extras." Among them were provisions that each of his clients would receive "a fully equipped luxury automobile" every year and a three-bedroom luxury apartment. Keating's palms were sweating when he handed the memos over.

The rest of the morning was spent in seemingly fruitless hashing around of terms. By noon, Keating offered that "it doesn't look like this is going to work out" and stopped the negotiations. At that point, Bassett told him to wait and went into another room to confer with his attorney. Keating had "the sick feeling that it was about to slip away." In the other room, Bassett worried he would lose any chance at the three Dolphins if he quibbled. He also said the signings "would make the club and the league." When he rejoined Keating, Bassett shuffled the papers the agent had given him and then spoke up. "Ed," he said, "you've got a deal." Keating said he'd have to talk it over with his clients.

The next step was to toss the ball into Joe Robbie's court. That evening, Csonka called Don Shula, Robbie's coach and general manager, and told him they might sign unless the Dolphins offered more. Keating was "afraid the Canadians might rescind or lower their offer if we waited too long" and eventually got on the phone with Shula himself. He told Robbie's general manager that time was of the essence and that he had to talk to Robbie himself by the next day. Keating's clients had few illusions that their current boss would match Bassett's offer. "I can't conceive of Joe Robbie giving us a Mustang," Kiick pointed out, "much less a Cadillac."

The next day Robbie and Keating talked on the phone. Robbie refused to negotiate long distance and refused to fly to Toronto to talk. He said he had assumed his players were simply going to Toronto to hear an offer but "I didn't expect them to be spirited off and held for ransom."

Shortly after Joe Robbie hung up, Larry Csonka, Jim Kiick, and Paul Warfield signed with John Bassett's World Football League Northmen/Southmen/Grizzlies. *Time* called it "the deal that astonished sports." Al Davis offered that the new league was taking up where the AFL left off. "The only difference is that they're speeding up the process by six years," the Raiders' managing general partner pointed out. "It took us that long to figure out how the weaker league could bring the stronger league to its knees."

Pete Rozelle, however, remained unimpressed. While admitting the WFL had "raised the price of doing business," there was no evidence the new league could honor the contracts it signed. "In the past," Rozelle pointed out, "Davidson had promised investors either a successful league, a successful merger with the established league, or a successful lawsuit if they failed on the field. I didn't think any of those was a realistic option in our case.''

In the meantime, Joe Robbie had lost the heart of his Super Bowl team and was furious. He considered the whole process ''blackmail'' and complained loudly about having to buy his team all over again.

3

Robbie got a lot of sympathy for his complaint from his friend Billy Sullivan, but, by then, almost all the air was out of Old Billy's NFL balloon. Since the Bal Harbour meeting, Billy had been fighting his last stand. ''Instead of a smooth transition,'' Bob Marr remembered, ''he made it an emotional trauma for everyone. He did everything he could to hang on.''

The object of Sullivan's strategy was still the shares belonging to the George Sargent Trust, which Hessie Sargent controlled. ''Hessie Sargent was one of the most wonderful women I ever met,'' Marr pointed out, ''but she was under terrible pressure by Billy, his wife, Mary, the whole family. Billy was crying on her doorstep every night.'' In depicting the situation, Billy described it as a palace coup ''spearheaded by David McConnell and Robert Wetenhall,'' the Patriots board members to whom he referred derisively as ''the New Yorkers.'' To Billy, they were just interested in money. ''From the first day,'' he pointed out, ''they were trying to buy out other partners and get control. They couldn't get fifty-one percent so they decided to oust me as president.'' There were also hints dropped that the New Yorkers meant to move the franchise once they were in the driver's seat. Bob Marr described the insinuation as ''bullshit.''

In any case, the argument did not make nearly the headway Billy had hoped and with the Patriots' annual board of directors meeting scheduled for March 21, his time was running out. On March 20, he went into Suffolk Superior Court to keep his chances alive. There, Sullivan's personal attorney asked for a temporary restraining order postponing the gathering in order to give him more time to purchase stock. His attorney claimed that the Sargent Trust and Hessie Sargent were prepared to sell to Billy but ''their stock would be voted against him if the meeting were held today.'' The Patriots attorney backed Sullivan's position as well, calling the situation a ''barefaced power struggle'' which was producing ''ping-pong fluctuations'' in the franchise. Billy claimed he would need as much as sixty days but the best he could do was postpone his fate for a little more than two weeks.

Though the Suffolk Superior Court strategy was successful only as a momentary holding action, it marked the advent of another character on the Patriot scene who would prove to be the dominant force in the franchise's future. The new character was Billy's son Chuck. Thirty-one years old in 1974, Chuck was an associate at the Wall Street law firm of Sullivan & Cromwell where, surprisingly enough, the "Sullivan" was no relative. When first contacted by his father about what was going on, Chuck was "surprised" and immediately involved himself in a behind the scenes role in preparing the Suffolk Superior Court request for time. From then on, his involvement became virtually total.

While enormously loyal to his father, Chuck had little of Old Billy's native charm. Moon-faced and balding, his eyes were squinty and his body was short and somewhat pear-shaped. Where Billy was verbose to the extreme, Chuck was circumspect and chose his words carefully. "There wasn't a hint of glitter surrounding him," *Fortune* observed. "His only apparent gleam emanated from his well-polished shoes." As an undergraduate at Boston College, Chuck had promoted campus concerts featuring the Kingston Trio and Duke Ellington. From there he'd gone to Boston College Law School and then to the army after graduation. A captain, Sullivan spent 1968–69 stationed with a logistical group at an air base in Thailand. His job, as he remembered it, was "primarily public relations work." Before rotating home, Chuck served as a project officer and advance man for the Bob Hope Christmas show and President Lyndon Johnson's visit to Saigon. Sullivan & Cromwell was his first job after discharge. There he quickly became adept at the nuances of finance law, an expertise that would prove of no small use to his father.

Chuck Sullivan was an unlikely candidate for the role of football business heavyweight. "He had no idea whether a football was pumped up or stuffed," one acquaintance noted. "He used to go to the Patriots games and sit in the owner's box with his father. When he was there, he was all the time steadily talking about stock deals, legal cases, all that kind of crap, while Billy was trying to watch the game. Finally his father would say, 'Chuck, can't you wait until after the game to talk about this?' Then Chuck would look up like, 'Oh, yah, the football game.' I expected him to ask what all those people were doing down there. He didn't know squat about the game, not at all." That ignorance was inconsequential to the business Chuck Sullivan would eventually do.

In the immediate moment, however, it was too late to do much at all. Try as he might, Billy Sullivan had been unable to bring Hessie Sargent around, and on April 9, 1974, the board of directors meeting he had been fighting to avoid finally took place. The site was again the utility room at Schaeffer Stadium in Foxboro. Billy would later remember that day as one of the low points of his life. As expected, he no longer had the votes to keep the presidency. "He took it very bitterly," Bob Marr recalled. "There were no tantrums or tirades but he expressed bitterness to some of the board who he thought owed him their votes. He attacked some people." It was all to no avail. The new president of the New England Patriots was Bob Marr, the new vice-president, Lee Sargent, Hessie's son. Following the meeting, the new Patriots' management held a press conference.

Marr's goal at the event was to smooth the transition, so he spoke more kindly about his predecessor than he in fact felt, then continued, "Much has been made of the current change in management. We have read a great deal about power struggles and bitter feuds. This is not so."

Lee Sargent also made light of any conflict. "We had disagreements at meetings," the Patriots' new thirty-one-year-old vice-president admitted, "but the disagreements have been nothing like they have been reported in the media. They were greatly exaggerated." Sargent went so far as to claim Old Billy'd had no desire to serve another term.

The fiction was easily penetrated. If that were indeed so, *The Boston Globe* asked, "why wasn't Sullivan at the press conference to wish his successor good luck?"

The reason was that Billy Sullivan had no such generous feelings toward his successors. "I'm not a sorehead," he told the *Boston Herald*, "but I am shocked at the way this was done." In the immediate aftermath, he was most upset by the board's failure to name him to even an honorary post. In the final days before the meeting, Billy's last fallback position had been to ask to be named chairman of the board, where he would have no control of the franchise but would be allowed to represent it at NFL meetings and continue to serve on his NFL committees. "I understood I'd be given the opportunity to serve as chairman," Sullivan went on, "but it was not offered to me at the meeting. I felt I could have done the club a real service by representing it at League meetings. Now that we're doing well, I get thrown out. But I hung in there before and I'll hang in there now. The Patriots have been my real life's work. I had been given every indication I'd be allowed to buy enough stock to own fifty-one percent of the club and had raised the money to do so. Then everything turned around and I was voted out. I don't want to say anything in anger that might hurt the ball club, but my absence from the press conference should speak volumes about how I feel."

While Marr and Sargent were meeting the press, Old Billy was driving home to Wellesley. When he got to his house, his cousin Walter, Uncle Joe's son, was waiting in the driveway.

"What are you doing here?" Billy asked his cousin.

Walter said he was worried about him. "If what happened to you today had happened to me," he explained, "I would have jumped off the nearest bridge."

"You don't know your cousin," Billy Sullivan chuckled grimly. "I guarantee you as sure as I'm standing here today that in another year I'll be back in the driver's seat. Then," Billy promised, "the next Patriots board of directors will have people named Sullivan on it and no one else."

4

When the National Football League convened in its New York City offices on April 23, 1974, for a special executive session on expansion, the first order of business was the introduction of Bob Marr. He was frankly thrilled to be there and was already enjoying being an owner. The feelings of most of the other men in the room, however, were at best mixed. When Marr had been introduced, Ralph Wilson of the Buffalo Bills took the floor and spoke about "the fine record of past service that Bill Sullivan had given." That was followed by a long discussion of the World Football League, during which the NFL's Covington and Burling attorneys answered questions from the floor. Expansion itself did not come up until 3:20 P.M., when the League reconvened after lunch.

The afternoon session was opened by a report from Dan Rooney. His specific charge from the annual meeting had been to further investigate the four serious finalists with an eye to stadium availability. Much of the rest of the day was spent discussing playing fields.

On that subject, Seattle's situation rated at the top of the list. King County, Washington, in which Seattle was located, was already building a new domed facility called the Kingdome, a multipurpose indoor stadium which would seat 64,984 in its football configuration. The facility would be finished by the 1975 football season and, according to the Stanford Research Institute, "officials of King County . . . have indicated that the stadium will be made available to an NFL team franchised in Seattle at reasonable rental rates."

Tampa Stadium was an outdoor, football-only facility with a current capacity of 46,486. Recently the stadium's press facilities had been enlarged and should the NFL commit to locate there, the Sports Authority would implement plans to enlarge the seating to no less than 58,000, perhaps as many as 70,000. They were, SRI noted, "anxious to have an NFL team as a regular tenant." In February 1971 and September 1973, the Tampa Sports Authority had passed and reaffirmed resolutions establishing rental rates of $150,000 a season or ten percent of the gross, whichever was greater, for any Tampa NFL franchise.

Memphis's situation was similar to that in Tampa. Memphis Memorial Stadium had been built in 1965. In March 1973, the Memphis City Council had passed a resolution approving expansion of the stadium from its current capacity of 50,164 to 72,164, contingent on the NFL designating Memphis as an expansion site. "If accomplished," SRI pointed out, the enlargement "would make the Memphis Memorial Stadium one of the largest in the

League." The city of Memphis was also "highly desirous of obtaining a professional team tenant for the stadium. Although a recent feasibility study of stadium expansion indicated that rental rates for a professional team would be on the order of eleven to twelve percent of gross ticket receipts, private conversations have indicated that a somewhat lower rate would be charged an NFL tenant."

Phoenix's stadium availability was the most questionable of the lot. "Phoenix," SRI reported, "has no stadium at present but is in the process of planning the construction of a stadium that would meet NFL requirements." The enabling resolution had been passed by the Phoenix City Council the previous November. Present plans were to create a nonprofit stadium corporation funded by the sale of general obligation bonds and an excise tax on tickets. The stadium itself would seat 55,000. Should the project not be completed in time for the 1976 season, Sun Devil Stadium on the Arizona State University campus was a possible interim site. It seated 50,600 but "has not been available to a professional team in the past." Nonetheless, "opposition from university leaders is not as intense as in the past and state political leaders indicated that the stadium could be made available on an interim basis if required."

Among the four finalists, Seattle was the most obvious choice. Rozelle was its most influential booster and the case he made was strong. "Having grown up on the coast," he remembered, "I respected Seattle as a good sports community. I was high on it as an expansion site, in part because there wasn't a great deal of entertainment competition there." Additionally, Seattle would give the league geographic coverage in the only region of the country with no football franchise at all. That blank spot created what Gene Klein called "a definitive need." However obvious the choice of Seattle might have seemed, it was not an easy one to make in April 1974. The principal hangup was in getting Kingdome officials to translate the "reasonable terms" they had earlier promised into actual "reasonable" numbers. The *Seattle Times* was reporting that King County officials were demanding twenty percent of gross admissions, five percent higher than any other NFL lease. Rozelle himself would only say there were still "stadium problems" there.

The second favorite on most of the NFL's list was Tampa. The League liked Florida, a state where many of them regularly vacationed, and Tampa had a particularly strong backer in Carroll Rosenbloom. C.R. had wanted to move the Colts there when they were still his and considered it a great location. The Tampa Sports Authority had also been on record for three years offering a ten percent lease, which qualified easily as "reasonable," particularly since they would also undertake expansion of the stadium at their own expense. The final factor boosting Tampa was that Joe Robbie, owner of the only current Florida franchise, did not make a fuss about keeping the state for himself. Since ninety-one percent of his tickets were sold to residents of Palm Beach, Broward, and Dade counties immediately around Miami, Tampa represented no lost markets. Joe Robbie would later describe himself as "one of the first to support a new franchise in Tampa." According to Rozelle, "Joe

Robbie had surface misgivings about another Florida franchise but didn't make an issue of it. He probably saw it from the standpoint of a potential intrastate rivalry that would generate a big preseason game every year.'' In any case, Tampa was, if not the place with the most things right about it on April 24, 1974, at least the place with the least things obviously wrong.

Phoenix and Memphis were the clear also-rans, though still attractive. Phoenix's problem was its absence of a reliable stadium. "Otherwise," Tex Schramm noted, "they would have been a strong contender." As it was, there were simply too many ifs involved. Memphis's problem was the World Football League. By then, John Bassett had abandoned the Toronto Northmen for the Memphis Southmen, beating the NFL to Memphis Memorial Stadium. In addition, Pete Rozelle remembered, "the World Football League sent us a wire saying that if we went into any of their cities . . . they would construe it as an attempt to run them out of business and they would sue us." Though Dan Rooney avowed the NFL was "not going in or out of anywhere because of the World Football League," Gary Davidson's threat of a lawsuit in fact ruined what was otherwise a strong Memphis case.

On the issue of location, it didn't take the League long to determine that the only real dilemma left was how best to pressure the Kingdome into getting "reasonable."

The rest of the issues discussed, however, were not nearly so easy to resolve. How, for example, would the expansion franchises be stocked with players? To field a team, the two new entries would have to select from a pool made available by the existing franchises. Just how that ought to be done proved complex and controversial and the subject consumed a major part of the discussion on April 24, produced no resolution, and would have to be postponed to later in the process.

The issue of price, however, could not be postponed. Things got very loud around the NFL offices when it came up. Leonard Tose was demanding $20 million. He was by no means alone. Others jumped the opposite direction and were still sticking obstreperously to Rozelle and Rooney's original recommendation of $12 million. By now, however, Rozelle himself was prepared to accept a $16-million compromise and pushed for it. Young Bob Marr, attending his first NFL executive session, was immediately impressed with the commissioner's technique. "He worked beautifully behind the scenes," Marr marveled. "He had his mouthpieces push his ideas but it was obvious who they were coming from." By 3:45, discussion of the subject was pretty much used up, but rather than try to put something on paper immediately, Rozelle first had Tex Schramm report about some playing rule changes proposed by the competition committee. The effect was to sap the meeting's energy even further. Then, on the verge of adjournment, Rozelle called for a vote.

The resolution on the floor, moved by the New York Jets and seconded by the New Orleans Saints, was,

RESOLVED, that the National Football League grant an expansion franchise to the City of Tampa to begin play in the 1976 season and that the NFL expand by at least one more city before the end of 1974. The price for the franchise is to be sixteen million dollars to be fully paid no later than the spring of 1976. The Expansion Committee is authorized to research potential ownership for the Tampa franchise and to make recommendations to the full membership after discussing the financial terms and method of payment with the parties interested in ownership.

It passed by a 25 to 1 vote, though the minutes of the meeting did not specify who cast the single dissenting vote. Executive session then adjourned at 4:40 P.M.

The news was received with great glee in Tampa.

In Seattle, it provoked impotent rage. "The owners went for the big buck," the *Seattle Post-Intelligencer* complained, and went on to rant about greed and arrogance on the part of the League, as well as to suggest that Seattle take its business to the WFL.

Officially, Seattle remained sanguine and confident. "I would interpret this as meaning," a King County official observed, "that the League wishes to refine the terms on the stadium lease. There is no question that Seattle remains the most attractive possible franchise and . . . barring a totally unreasonable decision, professional football will be here in 1976."

When the NFL's Executive Session reconvened in New York City on June 4, the King County official's prediction finally came true. Again, however, it took all day. The meeting opened at 10:45 A.M. and ran to 5:35 P.M. Shortly before adjournment, a resolution was finally passed:

> RESOLVED, that Seattle be admitted to the National Football League as the 28th franchise under the same terms and conditions under which Tampa was admitted last April and it be reaffirmed that unanimous consent be required of the membership to change the required payment of $16 million no later than the spring of 1976.

The minutes made no record of what new stadium concessions Seattle had offered, but whatever they were, they seemed sufficient. The resolution passed with twenty yes votes, five nos, and one pass.

Commissioner Pete Rozelle announced Seattle's selection. "It's the sixteenth largest market in the country," he pointed out, "and falls into the NFL schedule for the largest cities in the country." Seattle, he said, had been selected over Memphis, Phoenix, and Honolulu. Recognizing the disappointment he knew the also-rans felt, Rozelle went out of his way to indicate that the NFL was not through expanding by any means. "I wouldn't expect another city to be added this week," he continued, "but the expansion committee will explore additional expansion. . . . We are not restricting ourselves from getting into any city, including current NFL cities. There are no limitations on the cities considered. New York, Chicago, and Los Angeles were on our original list as NFL cities to be considered for additional franchises. . . . Any city would be a candidate for future expansion. . . . Future expansion is a totally open deck. Going from twenty-eight to thirty clubs is probably the next logical step.''

While the commissioner's hints about throwing open the NFL doors no doubt gave immediate heart to Memphis, Phoenix, Anaheim, Honolulu, Nassau County, Birmingham, Orlando, and Charlotte, in the long run they would only add to Rozelle's reputation for arrogance. The expansion consecrated on April 24 and June 4, 1974, would be the last in NFL history. The door was now shut for good and, as a consequence, the volatility of the seller's market would increase geometrically over the remainder of the decade.

5

The next step in the expansion process was the actual selection of owners for Tampa and Seattle. Rozelle and Rooney's committee had already begun receiving requests for consideration and would do so throughout the summer.

The commissioner and Dan Rooney had also begun crafting a set of standards for choosing among them. In total, they came up with four key factors. The first was "financial responsibility." Whoever the League's two new members would be, Rozelle wanted assurance they would have the cash to carry most of the franchise by themselves. As a consequence, the first thing Rozelle and the expansion committee did was eliminate "those that indicated that they wanted to put a group together" and were looking to refranchise the franchise once they got it. New NFL members would be required to play with their own money. Hustlers of the Joe Robbie mold need not apply.

The second factor was "where they lived, because," Rozelle explained, "we prefer to have someone living in or in the general geographic area of the franchise itself. . . . We think that home ownership is helpful in the success of the club." The third concern of the expansion committee was to "review the character" of applicants "as best we could ascertain through our investigators." For this task, the NFL security department was dispatched to compile a workup on all serious contenders.

The fourth standard was willingness to adhere to the League's ownership policy. It was no secret to Rozelle that a number of the men interested in NFL ownership might very well already have financial interests in other sports and the commissioner wanted that eventuality accounted for up front. As a consequence, all potential owners engaged in such "conflicts of interest" would be required to promise they would divest their other interests upon entrance.

Although 1974 was shaping up as the worst year for American business in almost two decades and the League's standards additionally circumscribed a great deal of the potential ownership pool, a number of interested parties nonetheless emerged.

Among the list developing for Tampa, the most familiar face was Tom McCloskey, the contractor who had purchased the Philadelphia soccer franchise from Lamar Hunt. McCloskey had also finished second in the bidding in 1969 when Leonard Tose bought the Eagles in Jerry Wolman's bankruptcy proceedings. McCloskey had attended the University of Tampa, still spent a good portion of his year there, and had extensive financial interests in the area. Another familiar face vying for Tampa was Hugh Culverhouse, the Jacksonville, Florida, attorney who had been competing with Carroll Rosenbloom for the Rams in 1972. Though he lived on Florida's northeast coast, Culverhouse was prepared to expand his business into west central Florida and live in Tampa a good portion of the year. Others included Austin Knowlton, a Cincinnati businessman with a minority interest in both the NFL Bengals and baseball's Cincinnati Reds, and Harry Mangurian, a millionaire in partnership with professional golfer Jack Nicklaus, who had made an offer for the Baltimore Colts in 1973 and would briefly own basketball's Boston Celtics. Another was Edward DeBartolo Sr., a Youngstown, Ohio, based shopping center developer with "extensive shopping center interests in Florida."

The list for Seattle, like everything to do with the League's second choice, would develop more slowly and not nearly as smoothly as Rozelle had hoped. The only genuinely homegrown candidate was a partnership built around Seattle's Nordstrom family. Lloyd Nordstrom, board chairman of Nordstrom, Inc., a clothing store chain in the northwest, was the central figure and planned to bring in his brother, three nephews, his daughter, and son-in-law. Other partners in the Nordstrom bid were the chairman of the Alaska Trainship Corporation, the president of a local construction company, and the president of Pay 'n Save Corp. The final member of the group was Herman Sarkowsky, president of Seattle's United Homes Corporation. Sarkowsky had once served as president of professional basketball's Portland Trailblazers, a franchise in which he still maintained an interest, and was scheduled to be the Nordstrom group's chief operating officer. Other candidates were a group headed by Minneapolis millionaire Wayne Field that included former NFL and University of Washington football great Hugh McElhenny and already called itself the "Seattle Kings." Sam Shulman, Gene Klein's old partner in the Seattle Supersonics basketball franchise, was a Los Angeles resident but kept a condo in Seattle and was prepared to give up his basketball interest if the NFL would let him in. Herman Sarkowsky's partner in the Portland Trailblazers, Larry Weinberg, also wanted in badly enough to get out of basketball and according to Rozelle claimed to "have been more or less in the Seattle area for a couple of years." Los Angeles resident Clarence Martin, once a minority owner in the Rams, closed out the list. Martin had grown up in Washington and his father had once been governor of the state.

After sorting these finalists out from the rest, the expansion committee planned to interview each before coming to a final recommendation to take to the membership at large. Those interviews were delayed by the League's continued preoccupation with impasse on the labor front and would not take place until late September.

In June, the only ownership decision immediately confronting Rozelle was Billy Sullivan's final desperate attempt to avoid the inevitable. It was perhaps among the sadder incidents in Pete Rozelle's career to date. Bob Marr would later call it "ludicrous." The thrust of Billy's action was an appeal to the commissioner's office for a ruling on Marr's recent election. Sullivan claimed that the Sargents had violated a previous agreement with him to vote their stock for his candidacy. The agreement, Billy argued, should have precluded them voting for Marr, yet they did. Invoking the full measure of the NFL constitution, Sullivan asked the commissioner to exercise his power to resolve ownership disputes, reverse the decision of the Patriots board of directors, and reinstall him in the presidency. The request led to a hearing in Rozelle's office during June.

Though the Patriots had a corporate counsel who might have accompanied Bob Marr to the meeting in New York City, the man serving in that role was a Sullivan intimate and, with the approval of the Patriots board, Marr hired outside representation from the Boston firm of Hale and Dorr. Billy's case was not a hard one to puncture. According to the Sargents, their agreement applied only to the potential sale of their stock, not to any vote on the board of directors, and their stock was not for sale. In addition, Billy Sullivan's name had never been officially placed in nomination at the April board meeting, therefore any agreement anyone might have had to vote for Sullivan made no difference since doing so was formally impossible. "Sullivan felt he could lobby the owners to put pressure on Rozelle," Marr commented, "but Rozelle played it pretty even. He wasn't obviously partial. He went through it all at Billy's request and was probably embarrassed at being put in that position."

Whatever the reason, Rozelle ruled for Marr and the Patriots board of directors. It was the first and only time the commissioner would ever rule against the Sullivans. Nevertheless, the decision was binding. Billy Sullivan was now officially out of power. Whether that would be a permanent condition, however, remained to be seen.

Billy's son Chuck was already planning his father's comeback. The first key remained Hessie Sargent and the campaign to get her to sell continued unabated. According to Bob Marr, it included calls from Billy's wife worrying that Billy was going to have a heart attack unless all this got "straightened out." His dismissal had been, Billy himself noted, "a terrible, terrible shock." Chuck Sullivan had confidence his father could bring Hessie around, but even then the situation would be far from simple. The further complexities flowed from an interlocking network of buy-out agreements that connected all the Patriots factions. The Sullivans were obliged to offer McConnell and Wetenhall the same price for their stock as they offered Hessie Sargent and, given the bad blood that had arisen between them and Sullivan, "the New Yorkers" would no doubt bail out if it looked as though Billy were returning to power. The New Yorkers also had an arrangement with the Marr brothers whereby they could force the Marrs to sell along with them, should they abandon ship. Once the dominoes started falling, Billy would quite likely have to buy up 63.6 percent of the franchise's voting stock, not counting that owned by his cousin Mary. Since the price would likely be more than $110 a share, Billy's return to power could cost more than $6 million.

Had that power meant outright ownership of the club, Sullivan could have easily collateralized a loan for that sum with the assets of the franchise itself. In the case of the Patriots, that was impossible because of the 139,000 outstanding shares of nonvoting stock, held by some 2,600 different individuals. Their continued presence would mean Billy Sullivan would have to buy his way back to power using his own resources.

As of June 1974, those resources, aside from his $2.7 million in Patriots stock, included $1.2 million worth of liquid assets such as listed stocks, life insurance, and vested pension benefits, and another $600,000 worth of real estate. His net worth was some $4 million. His annual income with which to service any new debt was $96,900.

Chuck Sullivan's dilemma was finding a bank that would loan Billy at least $2 million more than he was worth. First, of course, he would have to convince them that his father could pay it back.

Neither task would prove at all simple.

6

On July 1, labor impasse became open strike and the ensuing fracas at least momentarily obscured the rest of the issues facing the League. While the NFLPA had presented fifty-eight demands in March and added thirty-three more in May, the Rozelle Rule was at the top of both sides' lists. Pete Rozelle and the management council maintained the League could not survive without it and Ed Garvey and the players union were unflinching in their demand it be dropped entirely.

"Players demand freedom," former NFLPA President John Mackey wrote in *The New York Times*. "They demand the rights of citizenship. They demand the Constitutional protections afforded all other citizens of this country. Pete Rozelle will answer that . . . 'the system' would not survive if athletes were free to negotiate with more than one employer. I am appalled that in the United States of America people can still make economic arguments to justify the taking away of a man's freedom. . . . There is no price tag on my freedom. . . . Some say that freedom for athletes will destroy the NFL. I say nonsense. . . . But I also say this: If freedom will destroy the NFL, then the NFL should be destroyed. Then a new and better league run by those who understand free enterprise, based upon freedom of players, would take its place."

"The players association," one of the attorneys negotiating for the NFL answered, "[is] proposing to abolish the entire system governing player transfers and trades that has been built up through fifty years of professional football. . . . The players demand for 'no system' would constitute anarchy." Part of the reason for the League's resentment of the union's attack on the Rozelle Rule was the "unfairness" of Garvey's larger strategy. While on the one hand claiming in *Mackey v. NFL* to need the intercession of the court under the Sherman Act in order to correct a condition the union would be otherwise powerless to change, Garvey was at the same time making the condition an active issue of negotiation backed by a labor boycott. The League didn't feel he should be allowed to do both, but Garvey did both anyway.

The young union leader made no secret of his intention to get the Rozelle Rule however he could. According to Ed Garvey, the rule had existed as a "gentlemen's agreement not to sign free agents" prior to 1963. Then Carroll Rosenbloom violated the agreement in his thirst for championships in Baltimore and signed one R. C. Owens, the NFL's first and only uncompensated free agent. In the aftermath, the League "quietly adopted a new provision, which we now know as the Rozelle Rule, [calling] for compensation for any player who signs with another team." The effect of the arrangement allowed "club owners to control both on-field and off-field conduct of their employees in their industry, to hold wages down. [It also allowed] a team to restrict the right of free expression and deprive the individual of the right to employment of his choice." To Garvey it was a legacy of subjugation with which he intended to break once and for all. "They had stuck it to us in 1966, '68, and '70," Garvey remembered. "This was our turn and our zeal was apparent."

The Management Council noticed Garvey's attitude from the beginning of negotiations. It was his practice to have as many players sitting in on negotiations as possible and, according to one of the League's negotiators, used to play to them as a gallery. Mostly this took the form of tongue lashings across the bargaining table. "The players liked to watch him," the negotiator noted. "They liked to see big management getting jerked around."

Negotiations were broken off on June 26, and on July 1, the union announced that none of the League's veterans would report to training camps scheduled to begin in two days. "I am confident we can hold out until a new collective bargaining agreement is signed," Ed Garvey told *The New York Times*.

The strike's first public skirmish centered around the opening of the San Diego Chargers' training camp on July 3. That day rookies were scheduled to report. Since they had not yet made the team's roster, they were not members of the NFLPA, but the union was nonetheless calling on them to join their boycott. That morning, Ed Garvey led a fifty-man picket line in San Diego to dramatize their request. They were wearing T-shirts emblazoned with a clenched fist and the slogan NO FREEDOM, NO FOOTBALL. Chargers owner Gene

Pete Rozelle (CENTER), commissioner of the
enlarged NFL, Tex Schramm (LEFT),
principal NFL negotiator, and Lamar Hunt
(RIGHT), principal AFL negotiator, after the
announcement of the AFL/NFL merger,
1966. UPI/BETTMANN NEWSPHOTOS

The Boy Czar, 1961. AP/WIDE WORLD PHOTOS

Pete Rozelle testifying before Congress in an attempt to circumvent Al Davis's courtroom assault in Los Angeles, 1985. UPI/BETTMANN NEWSPHOTOS

Rozelle presents the Super Bowl trophy to his longtime friend and ally, Pittsburgh Steelers President Dan Rooney (CENTER) and Steelers Head Coach Chuck Noll (LEFT), 1976. AP/WIDE WORLD PHOTOS

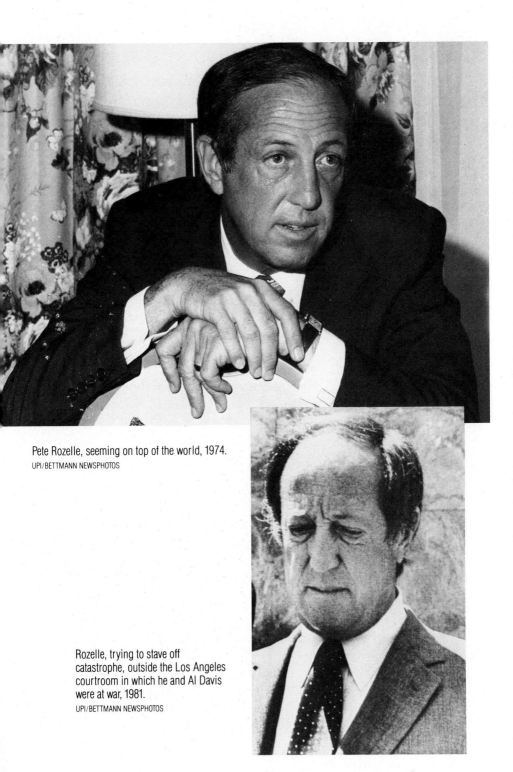

Pete Rozelle, seeming on top of the world, 1974.
UPI/BETTMANN NEWSPHOTOS

Rozelle, trying to stave off
catastrophe, outside the Los Angeles
courtroom in which he and Al Davis
were at war, 1981.
UPI/BETTMANN NEWSPHOTOS

Pete Rozelle and his wife, Carrie, the most important person in his life, outside the San Francisco Federal Building during the early rounds of *LAMCC v. NFL*. UPI/BETTMANN NEWSPHOTOS

Al Davis (SEATED), in 1965, fresh from his brief stint as commissioner of the AFL, signs on as managing general partner of the Oakland Raiders with fellow general partner Wayne Valley (STANDING), later his bitter enemy in the struggle over control of the franchise. UPI/BETTMANN NEWSPHOTOS

Al Davis (RIGHT) "crosses the Rubicon" and signs his Memorandum of Agreement with the LAMCC's Bill Robertson (LEFT), March 1, 1980, initiating six years of open warfare with the commissioner and the League.
UPI/BETTMANN NEWSPHOTOS

Davis and his attorney, Joseph Alioto (RIGHT), outside the Los Angeles court in which they ultimately won a decisive victory, crippling League Think forever, 1982. UPI/BETTMANN NEWSPHOTOS

Davis, complete with Super Bowl ring and other jewelry, 1982. PETER READ MILLER/*SPORTS ILLUSTRATED*

OPPOSITE PAGE: Davis, for whom victory was everything, waits for a Raiders game to commence, 1974. FRED KAPLAN/*SPORTS ILLUSTRATED*

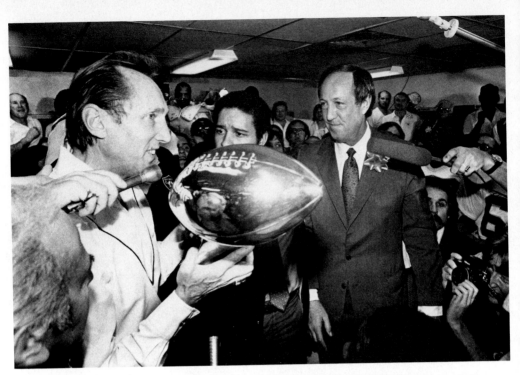

Al Davis receives his second Super Bowl Trophy from Pete Rozelle, New Orleans, 1981. UPI/BETTMANN NEWSPHOTOS

Al Davis receives his third Super Bowl Trophy from Pete Rozelle, Tampa, 1984. AP/WIDE WORLD PHOTOS

Klein was waiting for them at the training camp entrance, dressed in Bermuda shorts and a knit sport shirt replete with Charger emblem on the breast. He considered the display "rather ragamuffin," but cut a street corner deal with Garvey. If the pickets wouldn't enter the training camp grounds or block traffic, the police who had been called would depart. Klein said Garvey agreed but the very next day led pickets into the training camp to talk to the team's rookies. According to Klein, when confronted with his breach of faith, Garvey responded by saying, "This is July Fourth, Freedom Day, and the deal doesn't count." By then, Klein had long since sworn to field a team "if I have to use bartenders."

Wellington Mara had reached the same conclusion in New York. The strike had a deep personal impact on him that was magnified by his role as chairman of the Management Council's Executive Committee. "I never really believed it would happen," he remembered. "The relationship between an owner and a player should be a lot different than the usual employer/employee relationship. Their demands were so outrageous I could only respond with disbelief and indignation. It was a bolt out of the blue to realize players had grievances." On July 11, Mara called all the rookies in the Giants training camp to a meeting and addressed them in somber tones. "I hope we can play this season with veterans and rookies," he announced, "but if we can't, we'll play it with rookies. If you go out, we'll hold a tryout camp and do the best we can. We must operate."

The National Labor Relations Act required granting the NFLPA controlled access to those in training camp, a condition to which both Klein and Mara acceded, but in Mara's case, the patriarch of the Giant family insisted his representatives sit in on the NFLPA's recruiting session. "That's my football team," Mara snapped in explanation. "You wouldn't walk out of your store and leave the cash register untended." *The New York Times* described Mara's stance as "the strongest and most definitive" of any owner in the League.

The most common response by football's owners was to intensify their vilification of Garvey. Though he would later acquire a reputation as a man with his own private channels to the union leader, Carroll Rosenbloom was in the front row of 1974's anti-Garvey chorus. On July 16, he accused Garvey of "using" the players. "This fellow," C.R. claimed, "has told them, 'Look, you should go to a camp where coaches won't be able to say anything but yes, sir, and no, sir. You won't have to practice unless you want to practice. There will be no rules. You can bring your wives or girlfriends to camp.' That's pretty cute. The players themselves will tell you that would destroy the game. It's a strange thing but the players who switched to the new World Football League didn't ask what the freedom issues were there. They just wanted to find out how much money would be paid." The same day Rosenbloom issued his statement, the League office reported seventy-seven union members had thus far crossed the picket lines and gone back to work.

On July 18, the two sides met again briefly in Washington, D.C., rejected each other's demands, and again left the bargaining table. By July

21, the League reported 108 union defections and by July 29, the figure had grown to 248, almost twenty percent of the NFLPA's total membership. Negotiations resumed that same day in the company of a federal mediator, but the mediator almost immediately called for a five-day recess. When the two sides returned to the table, the exhibition schedule had begun, using mostly all rookie teams. The union claimed ticket sales for the first week of exhibitions were down $1.8 million from the year before. On August 5, the NFLPA's board of player representatives met and issued a statement supporting the union's negotiating team. Despite the continued air of public defiance, after thirty-six days on strike, the union's resolve was crumbling and Garvey knew it. The League was applying pressure and finding weak spots all along the solid front Garvey thought he had built. On August 7, the NFL released figures showing 360 union members now in camp.

The heaviest pressure of all was against the twenty-six player representatives upon whom the whole union superstructure rested. Ken Reeves, Atlanta's player rep, was walking a picket line when Falcon owner Rankin Smith drove up in a car with the team's coach and told Reeves to take his picket sign to New Orleans because he'd been traded. The union's president, first vice-president, and second vice-president would either be cut or traded as well. Within a year, a total of twenty union officers and player reps had been cut or traded. Of the seven men on the union's negotiating committee, only two would still have jobs a year after they set up their first picket line. Wellington Mara, Management Council Executive Committee chairman, would set the tone, and by September 15, 1974, "almost every Giant who stayed out during the player strike" would be "gone."

On August 10, after five days back at the bargaining table, the management council sensed the strike's imminent collapse and turned the screws on Garvey by threatening to walk out and not return until the "freedom issues" had been completely dropped. "They smelled blood," Garvey remembered. He responded to management's demand by offering to take the freedom demands off the table and let them wait on the trial in *Mackey v. NFL*. The League said no, it wanted the union to drop *Mackey v. NFL* as well. When Garvey refused, the Management Council walked out of negotiations to let the union appreciate the weakness of its position.

Ed Garvey knew as much already. "The strike collapsed and we lost," he later admitted. "It was time for Plan B."

Ed Garvey's Plan B was to return to work without a contract and "continue the fight in the courts." His player reps were divided on the issue. Some were upset, Garvey explained, "because they knew just by going back in they were going to be cut. The other school of thought was 'live to fight another day.' " At this point in the negotiations, according to Garvey, "the only thing management had agreed to was to no longer force players to shave their mustaches," and then only because several of the players on the negotiating team had hair on their lips. There was, Garvey offered, no option to Plan B except outright surrender. On August 11, Garvey announced Plan B to the public. He caught many observers and the League itself by surprise. At the behest of the federal mediator, he described the return to work as a "fourteen-day cooling-off period," but that fourteen would be followed by fourteen more and evolve into semi-permanent irresolution as both sides geared up to fight *Mackey v. NFL* in Federal Court.

According to Garvey, "management went crazy" at having been denied a definitive victory. "They were vindictive and we had cost them millions of dollars and nothing was settled. They had their camps full of scabs and didn't want to let players back in but they had no choice. They were an inch away from destroying us, then we jumped out of the ring."

At his August 11 press conference, the NFLPA's executive director described "the power of NFL commissioner Pete Rozelle" as "the main issue in dispute." Garvey called the decision to return "tough" but offered that "we have done everything in our power." The decision, he also admitted, had not been unanimous. That point was emphasized when one player stood up and flipped the bird at the assembled press corps before stomping out of the room.

Ed Garvey's first meeting with the union membership after Plan B commenced was in Atlanta, where he addressed the Falcons. He was nervous about it, but one of the Falcons offered him some cogent advice. "Just be honest with them," the player suggested. "Players understand winning and losing, they don't understand ties." Garvey followed the advice. "We didn't stick together," he told the meeting, "so we lost." Now the NFLPA would "raise dues to fight it in court." Garvey considered the approach successful. "Right now it's like we're behind twenty to zero," he offered. "Do we quit or do we still try to win?" While Ed Garvey made it clear he meant to win, he conceded that "it's clear by the attitude here and elsewhere that we will try to avoid another strike." Instead, he would doggedly follow Plan B, hoping the Sherman Act would give him the leverage his union was unable to muster on its own.

While the National Football League and its commissioner, Pete Rozelle, found Plan B enormously frustrating, they had no real choice. All they could do was to hire lawyers—and wait.

7

While the National Football League was still tied up with Ed Garvey, the World Football League had opened for business. To get a jump on the market, the new league started its season in the third week of July and its opening numbers must have sent some tremors through the strikebound NFL. Attendance for that week's WFL schedule was an announced 258,624, an average of better than 43,000 a game. In Birmingham, the game was opened with a prayer to grant the hometown Americans and the visiting Southern California Sun from Anaheim, "the zeal, energy, and ability to make a contest worthy of this football capital." More than 53,000 were in attendance. In Philadelphia, the Bell, thought to be the league's weakest franchise, drew 55,000 to its game with the Portland Storm. The Jacksonville, Florida, Sharks drew 59,112 against the New York Stars. WFL Commissioner Gary Davidson pronounced himself "awestruck" by his league's immediate success.

That patina of vitality lasted for less than a month before collapsing into the infant league's first scandal. At the same time Ed Garvey was launching his Plan B against the NFL, *Sports Illustrated* revealed that of the 120,253 who allegedly attended the WFL Philadelphia Bell's first two games, 100,000 had been admitted free. The inflation of the crowd was the work of the Bell's executive vice-president. "The second game was on TV," he explained. "How would it have looked if no one was there?" To cope with the scandal, Gary Davidson suspended the Bell vice-president for forty-eight hours. By then, the NFL was back to work and the WFL had picked up the nickname "World Freebie League." When the NFL regular season play opened in September, the WFL's credibility was losing altitude each week.

By October, its shaky financial substructure had been exposed. The Detroit Wheels started the month by filing for bankruptcy. During September, the franchise had run out of adhesive tape and couldn't afford to get its uniforms back from the laundry. "They were just thirty-two jerks who thought they'd be millionaires overnight," one Wheel player described the franchise's owners. "They told us only one truthful thing out of fifty thousand lies. That was the fact we were going bankrupt." The owner of the Jacksonville Sharks had been unable to make his payroll for four weeks. At one point, he borrowed $27,000 from his head coach and then fired the coach the next week. The Houston Texans fled Houston for Shreveport, Louisiana, and became the Shreveport Steamer. On their last day in Houston, the team bus driver refused to drive the players to practice unless he was paid his sixty-one-dollar bus rental fee in advance. The New York Stars fled to Charlotte, North Carolina, and the owner of Anaheim's Southern California Sun was indicted on three counts of "making false statements to obtain loans," one of which was for his World Football League franchise. Only Birmingham, averaging a legitimate forty-three thousand a game, and Memphis, fueled by John Bassett's money, were in good shape. "Any new league is going to have problems," Bassett pointed out. "While we have had our problems," Gary Davidson agreed, "we have not ignored them. I feel very positively we have turned the corner."

While the WFL's October pratfall no doubt inspired chuckles and sighs of relief around the National Football League, the NFL was not without its own embarrassments that fall. The year 1974 was, after all, the year Robert Irsay came into his own in Baltimore.

The differences in style between Irsay and his predecessor at the Colts, Carroll Rosenbloom, had been obvious to Baltimore immediately. Tall and stylish, Rosenbloom was a Maryland patrician, accustomed to great wealth, well practiced in a crafty version of noblesse oblige, and capable of generating enormous, if occasionally devious, charm. Squat and bull-necked, Irsay was crude, blunt, and boisterous, raised on the wrong side of Chicago, and incapable of subtlety let alone refinement. "Bob," one of his friends observed, "is a hard, tough, physical man and he likes hard, tough, physical men." Though Irsay had promised to set up a second residence in Baltimore when he took over the Colts in 1972, by 1974 he was still commuting to Colt games from Chicago in one of the three Learjets he now claimed to own. During football season, he was in Baltimore for no more than six days a month but bridled at being described as an absentee owner. "That's more than Carroll had been around," he pointed out.

In 1974, the specter of Carroll Rosenbloom still haunted Robert Irsay in several significant ways, each of which would help turn his feelings toward Rosenbloom even more bitter. First, Irsay was particularly galled to discover in fall 1972 that Rosenbloom had loaned $650,000 of the franchise's money to Colt players so that they could buy businesses for themselves. The practice was C.R. at his most paternal and Irsay disapproved. "I'm no financial consultant, like Carroll Rosenbloom," Irsay told the *Chicago Tribune,* "but I'm a good man. I'm not going to demand payment before the season is over, but I am a little shaky about it. These are some of the highest paid athletes in the country and . . . I'm not in the loan business—I'm in the football business." Despite Rosenbloom's assurances that "we were careful in the giving of our advice and financial aid," Irsay wanted nothing to do with the approach. "We're going back to the good old days," he vowed. "I'll keep the players fired up or I'll fire them, either way."

The second location where Carroll Rosenbloom's shadow continued to fall on Robert Irsay was in Baltimore's Memorial Stadium, the Colts' home field. Essentially a baseball stadium converted to stage football games, it was old, small, rickety, and getting only more so. Since Robert Irsay believed C.R. had promised him that a new stadium was in the works, Irsay would come to view the long string of hassles he would have over his home field as an albatross Rosenbloom had personally hung around his neck. In the fall of 1974, those hassles took the form of a series of unsuccessful negotiations with the city of Baltimore and the state of Maryland over a proposal for a new downtown stadium complex that was still officially dead in the water. "Something ought to be done," the Colts owner complained. "We're really at the tail end as far as new stadiums go. Why, if a town like Buffalo can build a new park, we should hang our head in shame if we can't. If they're not going to put up a new stadium, I would insist they start a complete renovation." He would get neither.

The third arena in which the memory of Carroll Rosenbloom dogged Robert Irsay was in the inevitable comparisons of the franchise's performance on the field. C.R. had left Baltimore with a Super Bowl trophy and, under his ownership, the Colts had acquired the reputation of a League powerhouse. C.R.'s Colts sold out Memorial Stadium every Sunday. Irsay's Colts quickly reversed the trend. Under Irsay, the Colts started badly and were getting worse. During Irsay's first season they won 5 games and lost 9; his second, 4 and 10; his third, 2 and 12. When Rosenbloom pointed out in print that the Colts had been nothing but a disappointment since he'd left for Los Angeles, Robert Irsay's resentment of him turned openly vitriolic and would stay that way long after C.R. himself was dead.

From the beginning, Baltimore's press corps was worried that Irsay, like his predecessor, harbored notions of moving the Colts to another city. "You're gun-shy about moving," Irsay lectured them in 1973. "We have absolutely no idea of moving the franchise. . . . That's not even in our minds. Tell the people to keep the faith, that the Colts will be back as soon as possible." Irsay also prided himself in knowing a thing or two about football. "I was just a little squirt when I was trying to play college football," the Colts owner told *The* [Baltimore] *Sun,* "but that's not the part I'm proudest of. I was also carrying twenty-three semester hours in an engineering course and washing dishes besides. That wasn't easy. . . . We've shown before that we can reach goals. I did it in the Marine Corps and in college and in business and we can do it now."

At the time, Robert Irsay was still claiming to have been a Marine lieutenant who fought at Guadalcanal, Tarawa, and New Britain. He also claimed to have graduated from the University of Illinois with a bachelor's degree in engineering. One of the stories in circulation about Irsay's career in the air-conditioning business recounted the time he walked into a union negotiation conspicuously armed with a .45 caliber pistol. Asked if he would use the weapon, Robert Irsay answered, "Who knows?" The Chicago millionaire took pride in picturing himself as a man who would not back off. "We're here and in this to stay," he pledged. "The Baltimore Colts are going to be winners. The Baltimore Colts are going to the Super Bowl. You have my word of honor."

Baltimore was not yet prepared to question Robert Irsay's word or his honor. In many ways, he was a more natural match for the city than C.R. Baltimore prided itself in being a blue collar town and Rosenbloom was a lot closer to the gold neck chain set. In December 1973, Irsay scored something of a local PR coup when he attended a party of ordinary Colts fans at Gunny's Crab House after a game. According to the organizer of the event, Irsay kept his Learjet waiting at the airport in order to attend and his "humility" had made him the "hit" of the evening. "There were two hundred people here and he talked to all of them." Not knowing anyone's name, Irsay addressed everyone as "Tiger." After a while, the boisterous owner got in a beer-drinking contest with one of his players who was there, and downed three quick bottles. Before leaving for Chicago, Irsay quietly picked up everyone's tab. "He was just like a blue collar worker who made it big," the organizer raved. "He seemed wonderful, strictly a shirt-sleeves kind of guy."

There was, however, a growing body of evidence that under more prolonged exposure, Robert Irsay would seem less wonderful. "He's a liar," Bert Jones, one of his players, complained to *The* [Baltimore] *Sun,* "a cheat, crude, with no manners, and he drinks too much."

Drink was one of the subjects that quickly became a permanent part of Robert Irsay's Baltimore legend, and by 1974, the local press was already speculating that he "appeared intoxicated on Sunday afternoons." One agent who negotiated a player contract with the Colts owner remembered Irsay arriving at negotiations already flushed and then consuming "six or eight vodkas" during the two hours the men talked. "He definitely was not nursing them," the agent observed. "It was boom, boom, boom." Irsay's wife, Harriet, denied drinking played an important part in her husband's personality. "He acts the same if he's had a drink or he hasn't," she explained. "He just hates to lose, and when he does, he gets mad."

Even Robert Irsay's detractors could not deny the intensity he brought to football games. On a typical fall Sunday, he would rise at 7 A.M. in suburban Chicago. Then his Lear would fly him and five or six Chicago friends to Baltimore. He'd usually begin the afternoon in the Memorial Stadium owner's box. "During the game," The Sun observed, "he swears, cheers, criticizes, and exults." By the third quarter, Irsay would make his way through the stands down to the Colts sideline. He was often greeted with catcalls from fans seated along his path. "Stick with us," he'd yell back. "We're trying." To wind down after the game, Robert Irsay would retire to the nearby Hit and Run Club, where he'd have dinner and five or six scotch and sodas before heading back to Illinois.

Like the members of the National Football League, Baltimore had expected Irsay to be little more than the creature of his general manager, Joe Thomas. Irsay himself made a point of reinforcing the assumption. "I've tried to stay out of the limelight," he explained in May 1974. "A lot of owners have tried to run the team by being present all the time. I have chosen to do it through Joe Thomas. I've always felt that if you have two captains making the decisions, you'll have trouble with the crew."

Despite Irsay's representations there was also a growing body of evidence that Thomas was not nearly as in control as he seemed. In 1972, after just four months as an owner, Irsay personally fired the team's head coach. "I've watched this team on the field," the owner pointed out, "and I think a high school team could beat them." In 1973, Irsay stormed into the Colts' locker room after yet another loss and cussed out the team's starting quarterback for a particularly poor performance. "First, everybody thought he was joking," one of the players who observed the scene remembered, "just playing around. We were all laughing, then all of a sudden things got serious. . . . It frightened me. If a guy says those things in front of other people, he might say them in front of your folks." Thomas managed to defuse the situation when he arrived and quickly pulled his boss over to another part of the room. "Anything Irsay said was in jest," the general manager offered in an attempt to smooth things over. "He wasn't in any other kind of mood. If [the quarterback] hadn't been standing there, Bob probably wouldn't have said 'boo.' "

But the incident that finally convinced Baltimore that Robert Irsay was more than Joe Thomas could handle occurred on September 29, 1974, during and after a 30–10 Colt loss to Leonard Tose's Philadelphia Eagles. *The* [Baltimore] *Sun* reported that Irsay was behaving like "a raving, swearing, intoxicated man" at the stadium that day, all of which Irsay later denied. There was, however, no denying he was extremely upset. By the second half, he was down on the sideline, barely able to contain himself. Finally Robert Irsay stormed up to his head coach, interrupted a conversation the coach was having with several players and, with a string of expletives, ordered the man to take the quarterback out of the game. Using his own group of expletives, the coach refused. Irsay stalked away and held his tongue for the rest of the game. Then the Colts owner headed for the locker room in a rage.

Gathering the players around him, he announced that he was firing the head coach. The man was the fourth head coach Irsay had been through in two years, and just ten days before, Joe Thomas had publicly guaranteed the coach's job for at least the rest of the year. Instead, Irsay thrust Thomas into the breach. "Joe Thomas is now the coach," he informed the players. "This fucking ball club will go on that field to win even if I have to play myself." Then Irsay went to the coach's office and informed the man he had lost his job.

The last man to learn of all the changes was Joe Thomas. When he did, he was "visibly shaken and soaked with perspiration." Thomas arrived in the locker room just as Irsay was leaving, "red-faced, with jowls sputtering prophecies, threats, and expletives." The two men passed in the hall.

"You're the coach," Irsay growled at his general manager on the way past, "as of right now."

When Pete Rozelle's office was questioned about Irsay's behavior, it could only point out that the Colts were, after all, Irsay's franchise. "The League is not in a position to decide how an owner operates his team," a spokesman for the commissioner patiently explained.

8

Though neither Pete Rozelle nor Dan Rooney was the kind to say so publicly, both were no doubt looking for people as unlike Robert Irsay as possible when they set out to interview prospective owners for the League's two new franchises. According to the expansion committee's timetable, the League would decide on its two new members at a meeting on October 30 in its New York City offices. Interviews began in September and each city presented an opposite dilemma.

The problem in Seattle was scarcity of the kind of applicants Rozelle had hoped would materialize. That shortage of viable options was exacerbated further when the "Seattle Kings" group headed by Wayne Field dropped out of the running. Of all the applicants, the Kings had been in the hunt longest. The official vehicle for removing themselves was a letter from Field to Rozelle, written with "heavy heart" and relinquishing "all considerations for a franchise for the National Football League in Seattle." The reasons given were financial. "As you know, Pete," Field wrote, "we spent over a quarter of a million dollars in our quest of the franchise, but when the price became sixteen million instead of twelve million, we just could not make the numbers come out right." The particular factors cited for adding to the group's financial worries were the continuing strike by the NFLPA and a recent IRS challenge to the heretofore monumental tax writeoffs granted sports franchises. Though the potential tax law changes were still working their way through the federal court system, the uncertainty of future tax calculations was enough to destroy the group's thin economics. In retiring from the contest, Field recommended the League select Seattle Professional Football, the group clustered around the Nordstrom family and represented by Herman Sarkowsky.

The Sarkowsky group was the only genuinely homegrown Seattle applicant, but nonetheless suffered from what Rozelle considered "significant problems." Most of those were on the ownership policy front. For starters, the group offered no single fifty-one percent owner. The closest thing to such a clear majority were the holdings of the Nordstrom family as a whole, a collection of more than a half-dozen separate individuals. Sarkowsky owned only ten percent but, to help assuage the commissioner's worries, was scheduled to be named the franchise's managing general partner, in much the same manner as Al Davis's arrangement in Oakland and Joe Robbie's in Miami.

But cross-ownership presented an even larger problem. The Sarkowsky group was in fact riddled with such "conflicts of interest." Herman Sarkowsky himself was at the top of the list. At the time of the applicant interviews, Sarkowsky still owned forty percent of the National Basketball Association Portland Trailblazers and was, in Rozelle's words, "active in NBA affairs, serving on some of their committees and attending meetings." In addition, Sarkowsky owned a small piece of the Seattle North American Soccer League club, as did several members of the Nordstrom family. For the purposes of admission in the fall of 1974, Rozelle and Rooney chose to ignore the soccer interests and instead concentrated on Sarkowsky's basketball holdings.

One of the first issues raised in Sarkowsky's late September interview was divestiture. "We said," Rozelle remembered, "that if he were to serve as managing general partner of the Seattle team, even though he didn't have stock control, he would obviously be in a position that came under the heading of an operating head or indirect control of the team." According to Rozelle, Sarkowsky responded that "he would divest himself of the basketball to conform with our policy and said he would . . . sell a rather sizable chunk of [basketball] stock . . . that would place him in a very minority position and then when business or taxwise it made sense for him, he would complete the divesting." The specific promise eventually committed to paper was that "Sarkowsky was to reduce his ownership interest in the Trailblazer basketball team to twenty percent or less by December 31, 1974'' and thereafter "to make every conceivable effort to divest himself of the remaining interest at the earliest possible time." Despite those assurances, the problems attached to the League's Seattle vacancy insured it would sit unfilled much longer than Tampa.

In Tampa, the expansion committee interviewers faced a relative surplus of "viability." Two candidates there ranked almost equally high, though neither was technically "hometown." The first was Tom McCloskey, the Philadelphia contractor and soccer owner. McCloskey had reached the upper echelon of contracting with a series of buildings in Washington, D.C., during the sixties, including the Dirksen Building on Capitol Hill. According to Rozelle, McCloskey "still had the bulk of [his] construction business in the Tampa area" and "was a voting resident of Florida, although he resided in Philadelphia." What made Tom McCloskey particularly attractive to the NFL was his "extended identification with sports." His soccer franchise had won the NASL championship during its first season in existence. Rozelle was familiar with him from the 1969 bidding over the Philadelphia Eagles in Jerry Wolman's bankruptcy case. Prior to finishing second to Leonard Tose, McCloskey had been given a clean bill of health in a League investigation.

This would likely be Tom McCloskey's last shot at a franchise and he was eager to do his best at the expansion committee interviews. He also knew that his soccer team would not be looked on with great favor, champions or not. For advice, he consulted Leonard Tose. Though Tose in particular had been bothered by McCloskey's entry into soccer, his anger over the situation was directed exclusively at Lamar Hunt. "Tom McCloskey and I have been friends for a number of years," Tose recalled. "We were born and raised in Philadelphia. We belonged to some of the same clubs that I was allowed to get into. . . . He came to me at Veterans Stadium, where I have an office . . . for advice about the best way to go about acquiring an expansion franchise. . . . I told him that he should go see the proper people that were on the committee, that I would get him an audience. . . . I said I would advise you to tell him that you were going to divest yourself."

To Tose's great satisfaction, McCloskey followed his advice. Unlike Seattle's Herman Sarkowsky, Tom McCloskey was not about to dicker over the terms of divestiture. Rozelle remembered, "He readily agreed to sell his soccer investments promptly . . . in any manner that the NFL asked him to do." Rozelle himself could not have asked for a more correct response.

McCloskey's principal rival for the Tampa franchise was Hugh Culverhouse, the Florida attorney. At the moment, Culverhouse had offices in both Jacksonville and Miami, though a $1 million estate in Jacksonville was his principal residence. Culverhouse's specialty was tax law, and he was also a director of Barnett Banks of Florida, Inc., the Barnett-Wilson Corp. that operated food services in Tampa International Airport, the George Washington Life Insurance Company, Mode, Inc., condominium developers, the Port Everglades Steel Corp., the Miami International Merchandise Mart, and San Juan, Puerto Rico's, Ivanhoe Insurance agency. In Jacksonville, he cut a considerable civic figure, serving as a trustee of Jacksonville University, a member of the Jacksonville Area Chamber of Commerce, and the Jacksonville Committee of 100. His only previous involvement in sports had been as a collegiate boxer at the University of Alabama, where he fought on the same team as Governor George Wallace.

Hugh Culverhouse was fond of quoting Louis Pasteur to the effect that "chance favors the prepared mind." It was certainly the lesson of Culverhouse's own rise to wealth. Reared in Birmingham, Alabama, during the Depression, Culverhouse, age fifty-five at the time of his Tampa application, had started life in the white collar middle class. In 1947, he graduated from the University of Alabama Law School and went to work as an assistant in the Alabama attorney general's office. In 1949, he joined the Internal Revenue Service and was assigned to Cincinnati, Ohio. His time in the IRS would later be credited with giving him "the tax training that he wanted" and bringing him "in contact with corporate clients on whom he later relied for income and investment advice." Culverhouse's last posting with the IRS was as an assistant regional counsel covering Atlanta and Jacksonville. It was the first time he had lived in Florida and his primary job there was investigating organized crime figures as part of the IRS response to the Kefauver hearings. By 1956 he and his wife, Joy, had become attached enough to Florida that he turned down a transfer to Dallas and went into private practice. At the time he left government service, Hugh Culverhouse was making less than $20,000 a year.

Culverhouse's wealth was a function of "the wise investment of increasingly sizable legal fees" accrued in his private practice. By 1974 he was worth somewhere between $30 and $40 million. Much of that accumulation was in real estate. In 1974, the largest of his land holdings was the 12,500-acre Palmer Ranch in Sarasota County, Florida. He had acquired the entire property for $12.2 million in 1970 and at the time he purchased it already had contracts to sell eight hundred acres of the parcel for $8 million. He kept the remainder and by the mid-1970s, the parcel amounted to seventy percent of the remaining developable land in Sarasota County. Everyone who dealt with Hugh Culverhouse considered him a shrewd businessman with a knack for knowing how to make money. "Hugh takes a piece of everything that crosses his desk," one associate noted, "and more stuff crosses his desk than anyone I ever heard of."

Hugh Culverhouse's application for membership came as anything but a surprise since the Florida lawyer had attempted to buy the Los Angeles Rams two years before. Like Tom McCloskey with the Eagles, he had already come within inches of joining the League. Unlike McCloskey, he had not accepted his shortfall without protest. That history made Culverhouse at least somewhat more controversial than his rival.

Culverhouse had learned of the Los Angeles franchise's availability in late May 1972 from one of his golfing partners while on the course at a Jacksonville country club. His partner knew that the Reeves estate had an offer, but if it fell through, would be looking for new bidders. Over that weekend, Culverhouse and an associate worked up what they thought the numbers of such a business might look like and got excited. He learned the following week that the offer ahead of him in line had fallen through and flew to Los Angeles for discussions with the Rams' general manager, Bill Barnes. After being grilled by Culverhouse for a while, Barnes noted that Culverhouse had done his homework better than anyone who had yet expressed an interest. When Culverhouse then detailed his estimates of what the Rams' balance sheets must look like, Barnes admitted the Floridian was "very close." Culverhouse then reported on the financial worth of himself and the people he planned to bring in with him. Barnes said the asking price was $20 million. Culverhouse said he would be back with an offer, but it wouldn't be for $20 million.

The offer Hugh Culverhouse returned with was for $17 million and, according to him, it was accepted. By June 5, 1972, the understanding had been reduced to writing and on June 6, Culverhouse flew to New York to meet with Barnes and the attorneys for the Reeves estate, sign the sale agreement, and pay the specified $100,000 earnest money to seal the bargain. According to one source close to the deal, while Culverhouse was waiting in the attorneys' outer office, Carroll Rosenbloom was inside finalizing his own last-minute deal for Robert Irsay to buy the Rams for $19 million and trade them to Rosenbloom for the Colts plus $4 million in cash. When the lawyers and Barnes finally met with Culverhouse, they refused to accept his earnest money and said they had decided that the franchise was "best kept within the football family" and were consequently selling the franchise to Rosenbloom.

A month later, Hugh Culverhouse filed suit in the Southern District Court of New York under the Sherman Act, naming Rosenbloom, Barnes, the Los Angeles Rams, the executors of Reeves's estate, Robert Irsay, the Baltimore Colts, the National Football League, and Pete Rozelle as defendants. He claimed Rosenbloom and the others had acted "to further monopolize the monopoly power acquired by them in the business of professional football in the territory of Los Angeles and its environs." Irsay was named as Rosenbloom's "nominee or dummy" in the conspiracy. Rozelle and the League were included because they had approved the deal between Irsay and Rosenbloom. They could do so, Culverhouse claimed, "by reason of monopoly power attained illegally."

Not surprisingly, the suit never reached trial. Hugh Culverhouse was a lawyer who made far more money staying out of court than getting in. In this case, the settlement was initiated when one of C.R.'s friends arranged for Rosenbloom and Culverhouse to meet somewhere in Florida. According to Steve Rosenbloom, the two quickly reached "a meeting of minds." That was in turn formalized at a New York City settlement conference attended by Rozelle. The specific terms under which Culverhouse agreed to drop his suit were not part of the public record. According to Rozelle, "Culverhouse wanted and got assurances that litigation would not be held against him in the future awarding of expansion franchises." According to Steve Rosenbloom, "Carroll had worked out an agreement to help Culverhouse get an opportunity when expansion came along" and when it did, "worked behind the scenes for Culverhouse, talking to people."

Whatever the deal, it did not seem to make much difference when the League met in executive session on October 30, 1974. The meeting was opened by Rozelle with a speech in which he "detailed the various problems confronting the League and pointed out that many of them have been caused internally." It was a familiar speech.

Afterward, Dan Rooney reported for the expansion committee about candidates for ownership. In the case of Seattle, the committee recommended waiting a bit longer until all the options had been further explored and "problems" nailed down. In the case of Tampa, they recommended Tom McCloskey. Rosenbloom, Steve remembered, was "upset" and "a little unnerved" at the announcement. Nonetheless, "without dissent," the League passed the following resolution shortly before adjourning at 5:30 P.M.:

> RESOLVED, that the [Tampa] franchise . . . in the National Football League . . . be granted to Thomas B. McCloskey upon his acceptance in writing of the following terms: McCloskey is to pay Three Million Dollars to the member clubs of the League on December 1, 1974, another Three Million Dollars on December 1, 1975, and an additional Ten Million Dollars in five equal installments of Two Million Dollars plus four percent interest on December 1 of the years 1976, 1977, 1978, 1979, and 1980. McCloskey is to agree to divest himself of his interest in the Philadelphia Atoms of the North American Soccer League. . . . Written acceptance of these terms and conditions is to be accompanied by a minimum One Hundred Thousand Dollars in earnest money.

After the October 30 meeting was over, Rozelle announced McCloskey's selection to the press. Seattle's ownership, the commissioner explained, would be chosen "within a month."

Seattle greeted the League's inaction with a certain nervousness. On October 31, Herman Sarkowsky exchanged several phone calls with the League office. "We were led to believe our decision would come much sooner [than a month]," Sarkowsky griped. "They have come to us with terms but they have not said, if we accept the terms, it's ours. Even the latest conversations have not been that specific." After the phone calls, he described his group's chances as "pretty good."

In fact, the first action the expansion committee took on the matter of Seattle in November was to offer the franchise to Hugh Culverhouse. Fortunately for Sarkowsky's group, Culverhouse declined. "[My wife] Joy and I decided after the Rams experience that we didn't want to move to the West Coast," he explained. "So I told the League, 'No thank you, but I will wait and see where there is future expansion.' "

Culverhouse's wait turned out to be exceedingly short.

Tom McCloskey's tenure was the briefest in NFL history. During his first few weeks in Tampa his performance was unimpressive. "Tom McCloskey seemed an okay guy," the *St. Petersburg Times* observed, "but the Tampa team appeared to be only one of a thousand interests with this construction wheel from Philly. A straight answer wasn't always easy to find. His group was indefinite, slow to organize, and cause for worry." Before Tampa had much chance to be bothered, however, McCloskey suddenly vanished from the scene. At the end of November, he informed the League that he would not be making his required $3 million payment on December 1. Rozelle would later describe the dropout as "a strange thing." Tex Schramm wouldn't "remember the details." Dan Rooney described the reasons as "financial difficulties." One owner explained that McCloskey was in a divorce proceeding, and when his wife learned of the purchase, immediately demanded half the purchase price as her share. "Maybe he was worried about another suit from Culverhouse," another owner speculated. "I assume some pressure was brought to bear, but I don't know what happened behind the scenes." A source close to League business maintained that McCloskey had been a less than serious candidate thrown in place momentarily to conceal the deal Rosenbloom and Rozelle had cut with Culverhouse back in 1972.

The one thing that was certain was that Hugh Culverhouse was now in the NFL to stay. On December 5, Culverhouse's selection to replace McCloskey in Tampa was announced along with the selection of the group represented by Herman Sarkowsky in Seattle.

The Seattle ownership would prove relatively anonymous in the ongoing conduct of League business, but Culverhouse would become increasingly central. Short and obese, with a nose widened by his days as a student boxer, his courtly southern manner and slow drawl concealed what one owner called "a cool slick mind that knows how to operate." The National Football League was now among the business crossing over Hugh Culverhouse's desk and, within a decade, he would amass enough power and influence to rank with the likes of Tex Schramm and Art Modell.

9

By the time Hugh Culverhouse's first check cleared the NFL's bank, Art Modell was finishing up his first year as his own landlord. For tax purposes, his Cleveland Stadium Corp. would report a net 1974 income of $13,789 but its longterm financing was decidedly shakier than it had seemed when first formed.

That shakiness had begun while Modell was in Bal Harbour attending the February 1974 NFL annual meeting. On February 26, Modell's Cleveland office had received a letter formally notifying him that his friend Shelly

Guren's U.S. Realty Company was withdrawing its commitment to form a real estate investment trust to finance Stadium Corp. and was withdrawing from its $8 million commitment to interim financing as well. The reason for U.S. Realty's withdrawal was what Robert Gries Jr. described as its involvement in "a major real estate scandal" called The Hill Deal, the biggest such in Cleveland's history. Lawsuits emanating from it would last another nine years. In the meantime, Guren's partner in U.S. Realty was being driven into bankruptcy by the scandal, and participation in Stadium Corp. was now financially impossible. To cover U.S. Realty's absence, the banks required Modell to assume Stadium Corp.'s financing personally and to do so, Modell pledged all his Browns stock and the land he had bought in Strongsville as collateral. He considered it a temporary arrangement and throughout 1974 was on the lookout for new partners to share his loans.

In early 1975, Art Modell's search focused on Robert Gries Jr., his partner in the Cleveland Browns. Though invisible to the football business's public, Gries had an abiding interest in the Browns and a significant civic standing in Cleveland. Both factors made him seem a natural for Cleveland Stadium Corp. The Gries family had been among the first Jews in Cleveland. His maternal great-grandfather had founded the May Company department store chain and his grandfather was a rabbi at the Cleveland temple from 1882 to 1917. His father had managed the May Company and taken the family into the football business in 1936 when he purchased a piece of the Cleveland Rams. Robert Gries Jr. considered the Grieses the fourth oldest family in the NFL, after the Halases, Rooneys, and Maras. The Rams joined the NFL in 1937 and Robert Gries Sr. remained in their ownership until 1943, when the franchise was purchased by Dan Reeves. In 1946, Reeves moved the Rams to Los Angeles and that same year the Browns were founded in the old All-American Conference. Robert Gries Sr. was among the Browns' original owners and his presence in the new ownership had been a precondition of the sale to Modell in 1963. "To my father," Robert Gries Jr. remembered, "football was a civic kind of enterprise."

Gries Jr. had been educated at an eastern prep school and then graduated from Yale in 1951. Afterward, he returned to Cleveland and worked for the May Company until 1963, when he started Gries Investment Company, his own venture capital business. Despite what he called the business's "very high risk" nature, Gries did well at it and would eventually serve on the National Board of Governors of the Association of Small Business Investment Companies. Thin and handsome, Gries ran marathons for relaxation and served on the boards of fifty civic enterprises from hospitals to universities. He first assumed a seat on the Browns board of directors in 1964. When his father died in 1966, Robert Gries Jr. took the helm of Gries Sports Enterprises, the family's football holding company. Listed as a vice-president in the Browns games program, he had been attending Browns games since age seven and had spent his teenage summers at the team's training camp.

Ironically, it was Gries who initiated contact with Modell over Cleveland Stadium Corp.'s longterm financing. Gries had learned of Guren's withdrawal and thought it presented a potentially lucrative "corporate opportunity" for the Browns, one he considered Modell's fiduciary responsibility as Browns president to pursue. There were, Gries pointed out to Modell, great advantages to the football franchise in controlling its stadium. Since he considered the Browns' twenty-five-year lease "the bulwark of what made this whole Stadium Corp. idea viable," why should the two operations be separate? Why not have the Browns buy in?

Art Modell's response was both negative and, according to Gries, "adamant." The baseball Indians, Stadium Corp.'s other tenant, "would never allow it." Gries claimed he didn't understand. What difference was it to the Indians whether their landlord was Art Modell, president of the Cleveland Browns, or Art Modell, president of Cleveland Stadium Corp.? "The Indians won't allow it," Modell repeated, and on top of that the city "prefers a separate entity" as well. Gries argued that at least the Browns ought to consider it. The Browns, Modell countered, had neither the money nor the credit worthiness for this type of project. They could not afford to get involved in a $10 million obligation. Largely by virtue of the 1971 stock redemption of which Art Modell had been principal beneficiary, the franchise had an outstanding debt of $8 million. He had "worked out an extremely favorable lease for the Browns," Modell pointed out, much better than its previous one with the city of Cleveland, but "under no circumstances" would he consider bringing the Browns into Stadium Corp.

Art Modell's attitude irritated Robert Gries Jr., but over a "period of extensive discussions," Modell continued to hold it. Gries seriously considered taking Modell to court for allegedly violating his obligations to Cleveland Browns, Inc., but eventually decided against it. Instead, he finally suggested that since "between us we own ninety-six percent of the stock" in the Browns, "there are other ways I am sure that we can handle it equitably for, you know, the parties [involved]." Perhaps they should "explore an equitable participation in Cleveland Stadium Corp." Unable to make Modell budge on selling to the Browns, Gries was willing to discuss duplicating the Browns' ownership by having himself and Gries Sports Enterprises buy into Stadium Corp.

That, of course, was what Art Modell had wanted to hear all along. As early as Christmas 1974 he had proposed a seven-point program for involving the Gries family in his stadium venture. Modell wanted Gries to come in for forty-five percent of Stadium Corp. and involve his family in guaranteeing Stadium Corp.'s bank loans. As part of the package, Modell was to be given an "employment agreement providing for reasonable compensation." In addition, Cleveland Stadium Corp. would, at the same time, purchase Modell's 192 acres in Strongsville for $2.1 million, almost three times what Modell had paid for the property three years earlier.

On this last point, Gries took a "vigorous position" and held his ground. He was, he told Modell, interested in Stadium Corp. only as it related to the Browns and did not want to be involved in the land development business in Strongsville. Modell protested that he had bought the land "to protect the

Browns'' and ought to be relieved of that burden. Gries's answer was, ''No way.'' Modell then asked why Gries didn't buy the parcel himself.

''I'm not in the real estate business,'' Gries said, ''and it's not worth two and a half million.''

This time Modell backed off and dropped the Strongsville land from his proposal.

Though it was slow, progress was being made. He and Gries would continue refining the possible terms of Stadium Corp.'s reorganization through much of 1975. The Cleveland patrician and the New York hustler made an oddly matched couple for the very few who knew they were partners, but the way Robert Gries Jr. remembered it, he and Art Modell ''still got along,'' despite the friction of trying to do business.

10

Pete Rozelle led off the 1975 NFL annual meeting with his customary report. ''1974 had included the third largest attendance in League history . . . [and] a Super Bowl game that attracted the largest number of viewing homes for any type of program in the history of television.'' The two principal problem areas identified by the commissioner were the NFLPA and the WFL. To Rozelle, the required response was increased devotion to League Think.

''Although legal, political, labor, and public relations problems ahead were great,'' he continued, ''the answer was an intelligent, well-planned and cool cooperative effort.'' The NFL could continue to be successful, ''if the power, intelligence, and poise the League commands [is] used wisely and without divisive pettiness and purely emotional reactions.''

On the World Football League front, all the news was good. In spring 1975, seventy-five percent of the players from its first year of existence were still owed back salary. Collective losses among the twelve franchises totaled $3.2 million and only five of the original ownerships were still around. *The New York Times Magazine* had dubbed the first World Football League championship game ''Super Flop I.'' It had pitted the Florida Blazers against the Birmingham Americans. The Blazer players had not been paid for ten weeks and their coach personally had to supply toilet paper for the locker room. The Americans, who won the game, had their game jerseys confiscated by creditors while they were celebrating. WFL Commissioner Gary Davidson, who had once claimed ''there is absolutely no way this league can fail,'' was now retired from the football business.

Davidson's replacement was Chris Hemmeter, a thirty-five-year-old Hawaiian who was chairman of the Bank of Honolulu. To salvage the WFL, Hemmeter was pursuing a drastic reorganization. According to his plan, all teams would have to adopt a standard internal economics: 42 percent of gate and television revenues to the salaries of players and coaches, 10 percent to stadium rental, 10.5 percent to league assessments, and 37.5 percent to fixed costs such as offices and travel. During the 1975 off season, each owner was being assessed from $600,000 to $1.2 million to pay league debts, make a down payment on delinquent player salaries, and provide working capital. Seven of the eleven WFL ownership groups now included at least one banker. Hemmeter's style was the opposite of Davidson's and he struggled mightily to rebuild the WFL's credibility, insisting, despite his monumental problems, "This is the league of the future."

The statement was a subject of National Football League laughter. The WFL's revival plan was dependent on the players accepting a percentage of the gross, an unprecedented step, and even if they did accept Hemmeter's forty-two percent figure, the longterm contracts that had been given NFL stars to lure them away were still in force and had to be paid regardless of the WFL's new budget plan. Typically, the contracts of former Joe Robbie employees Csonka, Kiick, and Warfield with Toronto/Memphis Northmen/Southmen/Grizzlies owner John Bassett that had set off the player raids were for "personal services." That meant, one player observed, "even if there's no football team, those guys got to walk around and do whatever the dude say do. But that's cool if they get paid. Especially the way Csonka felt about Miami."

Chuckle as they might, the NFL's own labor relations were almost as problematical.

There had been some hope when the 1974 season first began that NFLPA Director Ed Garvey's Plan B wouldn't be able to sustain itself financially. Without a contract, the union had no automatic dues collection from players' paychecks, which meant Garvey would have to collect his dues himself. That was not always easy and eventually the union would have to offer belt buckles to teams whose dues were paid up. Garvey himself went "in debt up to my keester" and the NFLPA reported $600,000 of losses to the Department of Labor. Nonetheless, Plan B had held into 1975 and deadlock continued to characterize all the negotiations that had followed the return to work. The League insisted that any contract include acceptance of the Rozelle Rule and Garvey held his ground, saying the Rozelle Rule should be left up to courts and *Mackey v. NFL*.

The Mackey case was central to Ed Garvey's strategy. "You had to break the Rozelle Rule to have an effective union," he argued. "If you have absolute control over an athlete, can you expect people subjugated in this way to challenge the situation?" The argument that carried the most weight inside the union was financial. The average National Football League salary had remained at $25,000 a year since 1968. Free agency was the most obvious way to break out. As an attorney, Garvey advised the union that the Sherman Act was their best option. Once they won *Mackey v. NFL*, it would "force them to negotiate with us to get it back instead of us begging for scraps." There was some visible opposition to Garvey's approach inside the union, but it was not yet a significant factor. Much, however, rested on Mackey's Sherman Act suit. "We had to win," Garvey remembered. "If we lost *Mackey,* we were out."

Mackey v. NFL began trial on February 3, 1975, in Minneapolis. Both sides had agreed to have the case decided by a judge rather than by a jury. "We had two attorneys," Garvey recalled, "one of whom was me. The NFL had eight or nine. On the opening day, one of their lawyers said, 'This case is all about young men who've grown rich and famous beyond their dreams who have come to malign the system that made them rich and famous. . . .' The League tried . . . to justify the Rozelle Rule against the rule-of-reason standard. We heard that rich owners would devour the weak by purchasing all the talent, build a superteam, and thus destroy the very entity he seeks to dominate. . . . Rozelle once said Lamar Hunt 'would use the Pro Bowl program like a Sears and Roebuck catalogue.'. . . We heard that elimination of the Rozelle Rule would kill the NFL as we know it today. We heard . . . that poor Green Bay and Minnesota would soon lose their franchises in a free market. In modern times there has never been a free market for professional athletes, so clearly any such speculation is exactly that; nevertheless, it is used to justify all the controls used to deny players their freedom of choice."

All told, *Mackey v. NFL* would consume fifty-five days in court, hearing sixty-three witnesses give more than twelve thousand pages of testimony. On March 17, the 1975 annual meeting was presented with a progress report.

This would be a long process, the attorneys noted. At its current rate, trial would not finish until July and a decision might not be issued until 1976. Any appeals might well consume at least another year after that. In the meantime, the League could only wait.

11

Among the "legal, political, and public relations problems" Pete Rozelle predicted for the National Football League's future in March 1975, no franchise would figure more prominently than the Oakland Raiders, no single person would be more responsible than Al Davis, Oakland's managing general partner. In the months immediately after the 1975 annual meeting, Davis was preoccupied with securing his control over the franchise once and for all. The last stumbling block in that process was Wayne Valley, the man who had hired him in the first place. In May 1975, two years after it was filed, *Valley v. Davis* came to trial in Alameda County, California, Superior Court. It was the second most watched courtroom drama in the NFL that spring.

Valley v. Davis opened with Wayne Valley on the stand. Though he had claimed at the time the suit had been filed that he hadn't learned about Davis's new contract until February 1973, Valley admitted that Davis had made an obscure reference to it some six weeks after Valley's other general partner, Ed McGah, had signed the document sight unseen in June 1972. "In mid-conversation," Valley testified, "Davis stated, 'McGah has given me a ten-year contract.' There was dead air for about thirty seconds. He didn't tell me the terms." Valley claimed he had considered the statement "a trial balloon" with which Davis was attempting to "apply pressure" for a new deal. The next Valley had heard on the subject was in October 1972, when the Raiders were playing the Buffalo Bills and Bills owner Ralph Wilson mentioned to Valley that Davis had claimed McGah had given him a new contract. "I don't believe it," Valley responded. "I would know about it." Valley actually saw the document when his auditor found it among the franchise's business records. When he confronted Davis about it in February 1973, Valley claimed Davis had responded, "Wayne, I could write a twenty-five-year contract myself and you couldn't do anything about it." That Valley considered Davis unscrupulous at best was obvious.

The shadows surrounding the persona of Al Davis darkened dramatically on June 1, after *Valley v. Davis* had been running for less than two weeks and before Davis himself had taken the stand. That morning's [Oakland] *Tribune* featured a front-page copyrighted story about Davis's real estate partnership with one Allen Glick. At the time, Glick, age thirty-three, controlled four Las Vegas casinos and was described by federal investigators as "a straw party controlled by the organized crime syndicate."

The Tribune's story had grown out of the paper's investigation of Glick's organized crime connections. When checking Glick out, *The Tribune*'s reporter had run across the name "Allen R. Davis" as an investor in some of Glick's California real estate holdings. The reporter then took the information to his assistant managing editor, George Ross. Ross had been sports editor during the Raiders' early days and had been a personal friend of both Valley and Davis. Ross had also written the first stories revealing that Ed McGah had never read Davis's new contract. Since those stories, Ross's relationship with Davis had dried up. The reporter asked Ross if the Allen R. Davis at 300 Mountain Avenue in the Oakland suburb of Piedmont was the same Al Davis who ran the football team. Ross said it was. The reporter was puzzled.

"What is he doing in business with Allen Glick?" the reporter asked.

The correct answer, though neither Ross nor the reporter yet knew it, was "making money," something for which Allen Glick seemed to have a knack. Five years earlier, Glick had been an obscure San Diego lawyer and real estate developer. Now, *Business Week* labeled him "a contender to Howard Hughes" for the title "King of the Las Vegas strip." Glick's meteoric rise began with a financial vehicle called Saratoga Development Corp. After serving as assistant to Saratoga's president for two years, Glick claimed to have been "more or less given" a forty-five percent interest in the San Diego based company, though he was less than clear about the circumstances. In 1972, he connected with Al Davis through a San Diego attorney who had once played for the Chargers in the early AFL. At the time, Saratoga

Development Corp. "were very successful developers with a very impressive clientele," the attorney remembered. "They were doing real estate deals with private capital [and] they had a number of professional athletes working for them. . . . I thought Al Davis would be a prospect and so I brought them together."

"I listened to one or two propositions," Davis later recalled. "They involved a minimal amount of investment. Some complexes in La Jolla. I am not sure. I think it was a million or two million dollars. And I liked the deal. . . . I sent an attorney down to see the property, and, et cetera, like that. [Then] I formed a limited partnership with several owners in the National Football League. We invested in the deal." The limited partnership Davis formed to invest in Saratoga Development was Red Dog Investors. Along with Davis, its participants included Carroll Rosenbloom, Buffalo Bills owner Ralph Wilson, and Don Shula, Joe Robbie's coach and minority partner. Davis thought Rosenbloom might also "have gone into business with [Glick] separately." The rewards were apparently high. "That deal became a very profitable situation for us," Davis admitted, "so we formed another partnership. This time, I don't know, we invested somewhere between a million and two million dollars. Again, I brought in several owners and coaches in the National Football League." This second limited partnership was called Blue Chip Investors. Davis also formed his own partnership with Glick, called GWD Associates.

In 1973, Allen Glick began to use the booming Saratoga Development Corp. as a springboard to Las Vegas. His first purchase there was the Hacienda Hotel and Casino. Glick's share of the deal was $2.3 million. Since he was personally worth only $250,000 at the time, the money was loaned to him by Saratoga Development. Shortly thereafter, he also bought the Stardust and Freemont Hotel-Casinos. The financing was supplied to Glick by the Teamsters Union Central States, Southeast and Southwest Areas Pension Fund to the tune of $62,750,000. In one stroke, Glick, age thirty-one, with "exactly four and one half years' experience in the business world," had become the second largest borrower in the history of the Teamsters' pension fund and he was by no means yet done. By 1975, he had also built the Las Vegas Airport Marina Casino, again using Teamster pension fund money. The fund itself already had a reputation for borrowers "who had been jailed by federal authorities for crimes ranging from fraud to kickbacks." When asked by *Business Week* why the fund was so supportive of him in particular, Glick cited his "management ability" and "timing."

By 1974, Allen Glick seemed to stand a significant chance of joining the fund's list of notorious borrowers. He was, *The* [Oakland] *Tribune* revealed a year later, under investigation by the Justice Department's Organized Crime Strike Force, the Nevada Gaming Control Board, the Labor Department, the Securities and Exchange Commission, and the Internal Revenue Service. One consequence of Glick's new notoriety was the withdrawal of all the other football money Al Davis had brought into Saratoga Development through Red Dog and Blue Chip. "I thought it wasn't a good idea for me to be involved in any type of business with Glick,'' one of the departing investors explained. ''Allen became linked with . . . a supposedly federal inquiry into his ties with Central States Fund and the Mafia,'' Al Davis remembered. ''At that time, I . . . got every owner and every coach and everyone out of their investments with all their money back.''

''Everyone,'' of course, but Davis himself. He saw ''nothing wrong'' with Glick's Las Vegas connections. ''Owners in the National Football League own hotels in Las Vegas,'' Davis pointed out, ''and I know that many owners in the National Football League go to Las Vegas or have friends [among] the top hotel owners [there].'' Instead of backing off, Davis loaned Glick's Saratoga Development some $250,000 to help with the liquidation of Red Dog, Blue Chip, and their own GWD.

Al Davis also began a new investment with Allen Glick around the same time called Eastmont Mall Associates, headquartered in Oakland. This Oakland investment was the tip of the iceberg first stumbled over by *The Tribune* in spring 1975. Opened in 1966, Eastmont Mall was a shopping center originally financed with a $25 million loan from the Teamsters' pension fund. Its previous owner had been arrested in a federal gambling raid in 1970 and died in 1973. Glick took over Eastmont in 1974 after agreeing to assume the payments on the pension fund's loan and founded Eastmont Mall Associates, a limited partnership. The deal Glick offered Davis was twenty-five percent of the limited partnership for $5000. ''Allen came to me,'' Davis remembered, ''and told me of a shopping center in the Oakland area that he thought I might like to invest in. When he presented the program to me, I thought it was fantastic. So I went in with him as a limited partner with no management affair in the business. They thought by bringing me in in Oakland, it would somehow or other bring image or stature to the shopping center. . . . It was the most expensive shopping center built in the United States.''

It also generated very profitable tax losses. At one point, the facility's manager would claim Glick and Davis fired him for making the shopping center ''too successful.'' Over the next ten years, though Eastmont made no money itself, Al Davis's $5000 investment would save him an estimated $1 million in taxes. Saratoga Development, his original tie to Glick, filed for bankruptcy in May 1975. One of Glick's original partners in Saratoga would die in prison from a heart attack. Another, who was working as a ''consultant'' to Eastmont Mall at the time *The Tribune* first revealed Davis's ties to Glick, would be found dead in her San Diego living room, shot five times in the head and neck, just six months later.

Neither Davis nor Glick was ''available for comment'' on *The Tribune*'s June 1 story. ''He is extremely reluctant to discuss his business affairs with anyone,'' a ''spokesman for Davis'' explained. In the meantime, the revelations fueled a flurry of headlines along the wire services—''Financier Denies Tie With Crime'' and ''Davis—A Link to the Mob?''

On June 4, Commissioner Pete Rozelle refused any public comment on Davis's connection with Glick. The most *The Tribune* could get was a comment from a "spokesman" for the commissioner that the Davis-Glick partnership "looks like a small investment."

On June 5, Ed Garvey took time out from *Mackey v. NFL* to demand an investigation. "Every time there is the slightest suggestion of a player being involved with 'unsavory characters,' " the union head pointed out, "there's a hue and cry. Typically, the League office focuses only on players." Garvey then went on to focus his attack on Rozelle, telling the New York *Daily News,* "He's always been a puppet of the owners. . . . It's obvious you can't expect anything but a double standard from the commissioner."

While Garvey's acid comments no doubt stung Rozelle, he would maintain his public silence on Red Dog, Blue Chip, Saratoga Development, and Eastmont Associates for another five years. Privately, however, he dispatched "one of the League security guys" to interview Davis shortly after *The Tribune* story came out. The investigator, according to Davis, "found that all it was was a business deal." Later, Davis claimed, he and the investigator would laugh "about the fact that the League . . . was using the Allen Glick association to try and hurt me publicly." In the meantime, Rozelle explained, "the League didn't feel it could do anything. We asked Al to get out but, in effect, he refused. It was never really a League matter."

Al Davis also continued to refuse all public comment. Privately, according to *The Tribune*'s George Ross, "Al let it filter down to me that he would be in touch with my publisher and that I would probably hear from his attorney. I never did. He just passed the word out that I had engineered the whole thing to embarrass him" in the middle of his suit with Wayne Valley.

If that was indeed the intent, it had none of the desired effect. On June 5, Al Davis took the stand in *Valley v. Davis* and showed no signs of intimidation. He had, he maintained, informed Valley in person of his new contract before he and McGah had signed it and over the telephone afterward. There was, he claimed, nothing out of the ordinary about the new powers it granted him and that he had always operated the Raiders with "a free hand." McGah, he pointed out, thought the arrangement was a good deal.

To reinforce that notion, the defense called Leonard Tose of the Philadelphia Eagles to establish Davis's worth. Tose claimed he had tried to hire Davis in 1971 and 1972, immediately before Davis's new Raider contract was signed, and was "so anxious" to do so that he "offered him a piece of the action," ten to fifteen percent of the club. "Al," Tose recalled saying, "you can write your own ticket. I'm in need of a man like you to take over complete charge."

Called back to the stand, Davis admitted he had been "intrigued" by Tose's offer and had also entertained similar proposals from the Houston Oilers and Los Angeles Rams. He also repeated that Valley knew about the new contract ahead of time.

On June 18, the judge heard final arguments and then took the case under advisement. His decision would be delivered two months later. On the face of it, the outcome would appear a tie: the fact that Davis had a new contract was upheld, but the expanded powers it included were thrown out.

"A Solomon-like decision," Wayne Valley offered, "he cut the baby in half." It would not take long, however, for it to become apparent that the real winner was Al Davis. "Al kicked his ass," a Davis associate bragged, "and Valley couldn't take it anymore." Preoccupied with other business and unwilling to stay in the Raiders with a man he no longer trusted, Valley would sell all his holdings in the franchise by January 1976, leaving Al Davis with absolute control. "A lot of people were sorry to see Wayne Valley go," Lamar Hunt remembered.

When Davis arrived at the NFL's next meeting on June 24, 1975, in New York City, he acted as though Valley were already gone. Never short on confidence, he seemed unfazed by having been linked to the mob and called a liar by his partner in open court. If anything, the experience only seemed to have made him bolder. "Al Davis always wanted to be commissioner," Gene Klein pointed out. One of the proofs later offered to support that statement would be Davis's behavior when the NFL discussed the World Football League at that June meeting.

During the preceding spring while the new league was reorganizing, Davis and Carroll Rosenbloom had met with the WFL's John Bassett and, according to Pete Rozelle, "Bassett was hustling the idea of a merger." Neither Davis nor Rosenbloom would ever report to the rest of the League about their discussions, but in June, Davis tried to seize the initiative on the issue. Walking to the blackboard on one wall of the League's meeting room, Al Davis chalked the figure $12 million per franchise and then multiplied it by ten. That, Davis told the group, was how much money they could make by merging themselves with the infant league and putting their war to an end. It was, he claimed, "a great way to make a lot of money."

Gene Klein immediately laughed out loud. Rozelle pointed out that there would be Sherman Act dilemmas, just like the last time. Dan Rooney wasn't sure Davis was serious. Tex Schramm observed that Davis "must have thought he was talking to the World Football League." Leonard Tose thought it was the "dumbest idea Al Davis ever had." Art Modell called it "really Disneyland."

The suggestion went no further. According to one of the NFL attorneys in the room, the predominant response was "snickering."

12

Al Davis made no formal report to the National Football League's June 24 meeting about the status of Oakland's ownership. The only such ownership reports were by Edward Bennett Williams, about the Washington Redskins, and Bob Marr, about the New England Patriots.

Williams's was first and concerned his now one-year-old promise that Jack Kent Cooke would divest his cross-ownership "conflict of interest." Cooke had not, according to Williams, "been able to perform, and the commissioner had been assured that he tried." The problem was not the majority owner's willingness, but the market. No one had yet been found who was prepared to give Cooke what he thought his holdings were worth. In the meantime, Cooke would, of course, continue "to try." The discussion Williams's report set off was, as Lamar Hunt remembered, "related to Mr. Cooke's ownership in other team sports . . . and what he was going to do about it." Williams continued to promise Cooke's "best efforts," but exactly what that meant was "clouded at this point." Though the discussion gave vent to some owners' continued frustration on the issue of compliance with ownership policy, it led to no resolution.

Marr's report followed, and many in the room counted the news as exceedingly welcome. Hessie Sargent had finally given in and Chuck Sullivan's strategy for his father's return had begun to work.

The reason cited by Bob Marr for Hessie's decision to sell the Sargent Trust's Patriot shares to Billy in June 1975 was "loyalty to her departed husband." George Sargent had been the very first outsider involved by Billy in the Patriot ownership, a fact the Sullivans had not let Hessie forget during the fourteen months since she had voted for Billy's removal. With the more than thirteen thousand Sargent shares his, Billy Sullivan would now control a clear majority. The rest of the NFL was first notified officially of the proposed transfer by letter from Pete Rozelle on June 17. In that letter, Rozelle "recommended that the transfer be approved." Rather than wait for the League meetings a week later to pass on the sale, a vote was taken by telex.

Old Billy lobbied hard in advance of the vote. Exile was not a comfortable situation for him. He told anyone interested that he was keeping busy writing a biography of Cardinal Cushing, but it was obvious that football was where he wanted to be. The day votes were wired from around the League, Billy Sullivan took the shuttle to New York. He showed up at the offices of the New York Jets that afternoon at 4:20 and visited his friend Phil Iselin, Jets president. Billy asked Iselin to phone over to Rozelle's office for him and find out the results.

Iselin gladly did so. "I want to be the first to verbally augment my telex vote," the Jets president told the assistant he spoke to.

"You're too late," the assistant responded. "People have been calling all day. Mr. Sullivan has the votes."

Officially the count was twenty-seven yes, one no. The no vote had been Bob Marr's.

By itself, however, the vote was not enough to return Billy Sullivan to the NFL. Two significant roadblocks remained.

The first of those was financial. "The New Yorkers," Billy remembered, "still thought they had me because of the price," since Rozelle had ruled earlier that whoever bought control in the fight between the New Yorkers and the Sullivans would also have to offer to buy out the others. That meant purchasing not only the Sargent interests but those of McConnell and Wetenhall as well. Since McConnell and Wetenhall had an agreement whereby they could force the sale of the Marrs' interest, the Marrs also would have to be paid. The money was thought to be enough in and of itself to stop Billy in his tracks. The New Yorkers had not, however, counted on the presence of Chuck in the Sullivan onslaught. Chuck understood financing from his Wall Street law practice and knew where and how to get it. Buying out the voting shares was only phase one of his strategy.

In order to finance phase one, the Sullivans had to go even further and, in a second phase, buy up all the nonvoting shares, whether their owners wanted to sell or not. In so doing, the franchise itself could be pledged as collateral and the whole package could be financed. The institutions preparing to do so in the summer of 1975 were the LaSalle National Bank of Chicago and the Rhode Island Hospital Trust National Bank. LaSalle was prepared to take the majority of the offering but only under the condition that by October 1, 1976, the Sullivans would offer as additional security the entire assets of the New England Patriots. Those assets were specified as "the franchise granted by the National Football League, all of its contracts with its players and coaches, all proceeds and revenues from television and radio contracts . . . and its rights as lessee to Schaeffer Stadium, Foxboro, Massachusetts, or any other location where it plays its regular season home games." For those assets to be pledged, the franchise had to be Sullivan's personal property. Making it so would amount to phase two, and Chuck Sullivan was confident it could all be pulled off. Once the high ground of voting shares had been taken, there were, he reassured his father, procedures with which to force the nonvoting shareholders to sell. Taking that high ground was phase one and, even with financing in place, it was still, as Bob Marr made clear in his June 25 report to the League, by no means a certainty.

The second remaining roadblock was legal. The Sargent shares were held by the George L. Sargent Trust and their sale would require both the approval of its trustees and the approval of the probate court. The trustees—Hessie Sargent, the New England Merchants Bank, and a Boston probate attorney—

were no problem. The bank had been urging Hessie to sell for years. In its terms, the stock represented a lot of money but generated no dividends. The difficulties were in Suffolk County Probate Court, where McConnell and Wetenhall had decided to make their last stand. "If the court tells the trustees that it would be in the best interest of the Sargent heirs to sell to Sullivan at this time," *The Boston Globe* explained, "then Sullivan would gain enough stock to put him back in command."

For their part, the New Yorkers were asking the court to enjoin such a sale. Though they admitted that the Sargent Trust was bound by a written agreement to sell only to Billy, if the trustees waited until December 1977, when that agreement ran out, McConnell and Wetenhall were prepared to purchase the shares at a much higher price than Sullivan had offered. Ultimately the trust's beneficiaries would be better served, they argued, if the second offer was taken rather than the first. When the argument reached open court, Chuck Sullivan, representing his father, would respond that the New Yorkers' offer was "frivolous." McConnell and Wetenhall's attorney would then produce a certified check for $1,000,000 to offer as a nonrefundable deposit. The stakes were high on all sides. The New Yorkers' case was significantly strengthened when Lee Sargent, Hessie's son and one of the trust's two beneficiaries, joined McConnell and Wetenhall in asking that the earlier sale to Sullivan be blocked. During it all, according to Bob Marr, "politicking was going on all over the place—phone calls, conferences, everybody pressuring or reassuring. I was trying to project stability while all this was boiling, but it was difficult to do."

Marr was nonetheless unwilling to admit defeat on June 25. "This is just another move in a game that has been going on for years," he pointed out for the benefit of those already prepared to celebrate Old Billy's resurrection. "No one, I mean no one, knows how this is all going to turn out. Whatever happens is going to take a long, long time."

13

Whatever happened in New England, the League's dominant concern throughout that summer continued to be *Mackey v. NFL* and defense of the Rozelle Rule from Ed Garvey's Plan B. The courtroom confrontation with the NFLPA continued until July 19. Among the horde of witnesses called to bolster the NFL's position were two former players association presidents, one of its original organizers, and the union's former legal counsel. At the same time, the League managed to maintain its own solid front. Even Carroll Rosenbloom, still the League's most notorious renegade on this issue, fell into line. Rosenbloom testified that the Rozelle Rule was "essential" to maintain football's "competitive balance," echoing the commissioner and the rest of the "member clubs."

Once the judge had taken all the evidence under advisement, however, Rosenbloom went his own way again and, in so doing, set off more than a year of open conflict with Pete Rozelle. When it was all over, the League would remember their series of collisions as a "war."

At the time it began, both men had absorbed the changes that had entered each of their personal lives over the last few years and, at least outside of football, seemed content.

For Rozelle, those changes had revolved around his marriage to Carrie. Gone was the apartment on Sutton Place and the evenings spent catching a movie with Bill McPhail or a few laughs with Art Modell. Gone also were his days as a single parent, trying to stretch himself to provide domesticity while meeting the demands of his job. In their place was the new red brick Tudor house in Westchester and a suddenly bustling family life. In addition to his daughter from his first marriage, Carrie's four children from her marriage with John Cooke, Jack Kent Cooke's son, lived with the Rozelles as well. Her three sons all suffered from learning disabilities and that soon became a focal point in their marriage. Eventually Carrie would use some of her new stature as the commissioner's wife to start the Foundation for Children with Learning Disabilities. "Having to deal with learning disabilities has been an educational experience," Pete pointed out. "It can be very difficult for both the children and their family." By all accounts, the Rozelles dealt with the difficulties well.

The suburban life-style suited Pete Rozelle. There was a swimming pool out the back door and tennis courts on which to battle the bulge at the waist of his once skinny frame. The Westchester red brick Tudor was the first house he had ever owned, and he soon came to prefer quiet evenings there to socializing in the city. As a rule, Pete and Carrie returned to Manhattan after dark only for charity purposes. He described himself as "very comfortable" financially, though he pointed out that "in this type of job—a not for profit corporation—you don't have stock options so you don't have the opportunity for money that say in business you would have."

Asked to describe the most difficult thing he'd done as commissioner, Rozelle answered "the merger with the AFL." Asked to describe his job vis-à-vis the owners, he chose the words "counseling" and "educating." The worst thing about his job was "the loss of privacy." At least for public consumption, he claimed to have adjusted to having to spend an ever-growing portion of his work time in court. "Litigation has become a way of life for me," he explained. "It's an unpleasant way of life, but I'm inured to it now. We get sued all the time. The first time, I was uptight. . . . Now I just ask my attorneys when I have to give my next deposition." There was, however, much worse to come.

For Carroll Rosenbloom, the adjustment to living in southern California had, by all accounts, been easy to make. "He has become," the *Los Angeles Times* pointed out, "a dedicated Californian . . . with a carefully chosen

California life-style." Most of his friends were in the entertainment business and, like Rozelle, C.R. spent a lot of time playing tennis with them. His wife, Georgia, was described as a "dedicated" tennis player herself. They made a point of entertaining a lot, often on the courts. By this point in his life, while not revered like the saints of the Old Guard, Carroll was still considered something of a dean in the football business and he enjoyed the stature.

While in New York for the League's meetings at the end of June, Rosenbloom was the guest of honor at a dinner of the Pro Football Writers Association, where he was awarded the Arthur Daley Memorial Award for long and meritorious service. Previous recipients had been George Halas and Art Rooney. In accepting the award, "Rosenbloom repeated what he has been saying for some time—lashing out at the owners, blaming himself and the others for 'stupidity' in outrageously squandering so much money, and for building up inflated operational budgets." On the labor front, "he urged more cooperation between management and athletes." C.R.'s greatest vituperation was reserved for the litigation process in which the League seemed mired. Unlike Rozelle, he made no noises about having learned to live with it and told the football writers that lawyers were costing each of the NFL's members at least $200,000 a year. "We never get out of court," he complained. "If it isn't with the players association . . . it's hearings in Washington. . . . One day lawyers and accountants may own every franchise in the League."

Back in California, Rosenbloom's life was divided between his estate in Bel-Air and his house at Trancas Beach. Of the two, Trancas was his favorite. He began his days there at 7:00 A.M. with breakfast and business calls to New York. By 8:00, he was on the beach with his dogs, alternately running and walking for two and a half miles. He repeated the routine in the evening and usually managed to get in several sets of tennis in between. It kept him fit and he prided himself in looking much younger than the almost seven decades he had lived. His gray-blond toupee had been custom made in Venezuela and sewn into his scalp in Miami and most everyone who met C.R. considered him handsome. When the Rams were in training camp, he hired a helicopter to ferry him there every morning at 9:00, where he mingled among players and coaches, addressing each by name and having as many as 150 private conversations in a day. During afternoon rush hour, he helicoptered back to Trancas Beach.

One of the great solaces in Carroll Rosenbloom's new southern California life was living next to the Pacific Ocean. The master bedroom at his Trancas house had a thirty-foot ocean view through sliding glass doors that opened onto a porch anchored above the surf. "When night comes," Rosenbloom explained, "I love to go to bed with a good book and listen to the waves." Even when staying in Bel-Air, he went to sleep with the bedroom stereo playing one of "those records that have nothing but the sound of the ocean washing up on the beach." It was, he claimed, perhaps his favorite sound. "I've been a beachcomber all my life. The ocean does for me what the desert does for others. They like the stillness. I never tire of listening to the ocean or looking at it." Four years later, those words would have a haunting quality, but in 1975, they were simply a small item of public interest about one of the most visible figures in Los Angeles.

While Carroll Rosenbloom's relationship with Pete Rozelle had been relatively quiet since C.R. had moved west, the Rams owner's resentment had by no means diminished. He was also considerably vexed about how the League was doing business. "Carroll had a bugaboo about League economics," his son Steve remembered. "There had been assessment after assessment for the League office and all the legal stuff was mounting. The League had hired an in-house attorney and Rozelle had turned him into his personal employee. When Carroll complained, the guy took the position he was the commissioner's attorney, not the owners'. . . . That upset my father. He was also upset that he couldn't get financial information out of the League office. All he could ever get were broad generalities and he wanted to know how the money was being spent. He was a business guy. He didn't go for being brushed off. It got to the point where he was going to have the League audited. Carroll needed a good fight and felt Rozelle and the League office were getting too arrogant. He was one of the few who would stand up to them. Most of the rest of the owners were jellyfish. Carroll had scared the League shitless a number of times." In July 1975, yet another of those times was approaching rapidly.

Carroll Rosenbloom's greatest frustration in life remained his failure to win a Super Bowl with the Rams. The previous season they had fallen one victory short, losing 14–10 to Max Winter's Minnesota Vikings in the final playoff game. Carroll was now convinced he was only one additional player away from the championship and he already knew who the player was. The man's name was Ron Jessie and for the previous six years he had played wide receiver for William Clay Ford's Detroit Lions. Jessie's contract with the Lions had expired with the 1974 season and he was technically a free agent, covered by the sanctions of the Rozelle Rule that C.R. had just finished defending on the witness stand. Despite the united front adopted for *Mackey v. NFL*, Rosenbloom signed Jessie before the trial's closing arguments. Given the circumstances, the commissioner did not want to have to enforce his rule, so at first it was left to C.R. and the Lions to negotiate compensation for Jessie's rights between them. That didn't work, so Rozelle felt he had no choice but to act.

Despite his reputation for smoothing rough edges, Rozelle was not averse to what he called "putting my foot down." Known for not picking fights, he had a surprising record of taking them when offered. In this instance, the penalty he announced was arguably the most severe in the history of the Rozelle Rule. On the four previous occasions Rozelle had invoked his rule since it was formally established in 1963, the compensation awarded had customarily been assessed in future choices at the League's annual draft of collegiate players. Only once, in a 1967 ruling involving the New Orleans Saints and the San Francisco 49ers, had it included a player already in the League and then, the player involved had yet to complete his first year. None of Rozelle's previous compensation awards had involved veteran performers. Looking over his shoulder at the Minneapolis federal court then considering a decision in *Mackey v. NFL,* Rozelle apparently felt the timing of C.R.'s move deserved a precedent-setting penalty. On July 25 the commissioner announced that his award to the Lions was one Cullen Bryant, a promising Ram fullback and two-year veteran. Depending on Bryant's contribution to the Lions during the next season, Rozelle also held out the possibility of giving the Lions some unspecified Ram draft choices as well. "Rozelle Rule Hits Rams," the *Los Angeles Times* headlined.

Carroll Rosenbloom was anything but pleased with the decision. Rosenbloom was convinced Bryant was on the verge of stardom and, as far as he was concerned, the commissioner's ruling left him still one player short in his obsessive quest. When Cullen Bryant filed suit on July 29, attempting to invoke the Sherman Act to void Rozelle's award, it was, as one L.A. sports columnist remembered it, "no secret that Carroll had set up Bryant's fight." Rozelle reached the same conclusion. "Bryant used the same law firm Carroll had used a number of times," the commissioner noted. "The impression was that Carroll was backing the suit." As such, it was received as a stab in the League's collective back. The last thing the NFL needed at this moment was yet another suit over the Rozelle Rule, but thanks to Rosenbloom, that was exactly what it had. Worse still, in its opening round, the suit looked decidedly threatening.

On July 30, at an initial hearing in Los Angeles Federal District Court, the judge delivered what was described as a "stinging rebuke to the National Football League" and temporarily enjoined any enforcement of Rozelle's award. "I think the Rozelle Rule . . . violates Section I of the Sherman Anti-trust Act," the judge declared. "The economic power of the NFL demonstrated by this case truly is awesome. . . . With all power goes correlative responsibility for fair dealing and fair play. . . . The awesome control of the commissioner may be necessary for the effective management of the League. A trial might well show that. But the rule of reason cannot merely be wiped aside by such necessities." Another preliminary hearing was set for August 12.

Pete Rozelle was not about to let *Bryant v. NFL* get that far. He knew he was in a potentially lethal legal crossfire and had no choice but to cut his losses and regroup. On August 2, the League office announced the commissioner was voiding his previous award to the Lions and replacing it with the Rams' first and second round choices in the next player draft. Rozelle himself offered no comment on his change of mind.

The same could not be said of the Lions. Their barrage was opened by the franchise's head coach, Rick Forzano, and aimed straight at Carroll Rosenbloom. Rosenbloom, Forzano told the *Los Angeles Times,* was the "most selfish owner in professional football. Rosenbloom knows the serious nature of the Rozelle Rule in the case with the players association and he could have resolved the situation long before it got this far. . . . I believe Rosenbloom wants to win so badly he would really go as far as this—to cheat another team. He is hurting professional football . . . [and] he could destroy the strong foundation of the game's support."

C.R. gave the criticism short shrift. "If you call 'selfish' attempting to bring the best possible team together for our fans," he replied, "well, yes, I am selfish. The Rams have acted according to the regulations and the spirit of the regulations of the National Football League. All this is a matter of record and nothing further needs to be said."

Ignoring Rosenbloom's admonition, the Lions responded the next day. This time the complaint came from William Clay Ford, their owner, in a letter to C.R. made public the same day Rozelle's turnaround was announced. Ford's presence in the fight was itself extraordinary. Heir to an automobile fortune amassed by his father, William Clay Ford played virtually no active role in NFL affairs and never attended League meetings. His letter on August 2 was one of two cameo appearances he would make there over the coming decade. "It is my opinion," he wrote Rosenbloom, "that you and your organization have done more to harm professional football than anyone in the history of the NFL. Several weeks ago you testified in Minneapolis that the so-called Rozelle Rule was necessary to maintain 'competitive balance' in the League, but this was apparently hypocrisy because the Rams certainly did not live up to the constitution and bylaws of the NFL as called for under the rule. You have made a mockery of the compensation rule. . . . I hope all sports and football in particular have not been too badly damaged."

C.R.'s answer was again short and testy. "The Rams," he announced, "will have no lengthy comment on Ford's letter. The charges therein are ludicrous, irresponsible, and untrue. We will now await word from the commissioner in respect to his judgment concerning Detroit's irresponsible statements."

Rosenbloom was waiting for Rozelle to enforce the section of the NFL constitution that prohibited owners from making public criticism of each other. His wait, however, was fruitless. Rozelle simply let the issue drop.

Carroll Rosenbloom was furious, convinced that if it had been himself in Ford's position, Rozelle would have levied a fine. The incident summoned forth more than a decade's worth of Carroll Rosenbloom's irritation and hostility. Now, not content with having bloodied Rozelle and forced him to back off on the Rozelle Rule, Rosenbloom wanted, as one NFL owner put it, "to get" Pete Rozelle any way he could. To C.R.'s way of thinking, the commissioner had it coming.

Rosenbloom's first step was to hire a private detective to collect whatever dirt on Rozelle he could find before the next meeting of the League, scheduled for the first week of November.

14

When the 1975 season began, the League still awaited a decision in *Mackey v. NFL* and stalemate continued on the labor front. What negotiations there were usually died quickly and always over the same issue. The union continued to demand a contract containing no reference to the Rozelle Rule, and the management council continued to refuse to consider signing anything that didn't have the effect of settling the Mackey case.

In the League's other external war, however, victory was within sight. The reorganized World Football League had begun its second season while Pete Rozelle and Carroll Rosenbloom were going at it over Ron Jessie, Cullen Bryant, and the Rozelle Rule. Reorganized or not, even the WFL's most prestigious owner, Memphis's John Bassett, could offer little optimism about their chances. "It's like a brand new car," he told *Sports Illustrated*. "Once you've wrecked it, no matter how well it's fixed up, it's never the same." By October, impending collapse was apparent everywhere:

First to go was the Chicago Wind, expelled by the league in September for falling beneath the financial floor established by new commissioner, Chris Hemmeter. The precipitating event was the withdrawal of the franchise's two principal investors. Asked to identify those investors, the Wind's vice-president for football operations replied, "George and Rich from California. I don't know their last names, but one's an Arab and the other's a Greek."

When the Southern California Sun played the Philadelphia Bell in Philadelphia's John F. Kennedy Stadium, the scene was stark. "When we came out to warm up," a Sun wide receiver remembered, "I looked around and there wasn't one person in the stands. Not one. I thought, 'My God, aren't we going to have anyone?' I think we ended up with 3,100." The Bell had arrived at the stadium in an old school bus that shook and was losing its back door. At first the stadium guard thought it was a busful of migrant workers and wouldn't let it in. When the bus finally clunked inside, the back door broke open and several players fell out. "To save money," the Bell's quarterback remembered, "we always seemed to arrive at a hotel at one in the morning and then played the game, leaving as soon as we showered. Once we flew commercial to Portland and the flight made eight stops. It was brutal. Then [once] we got on a bus in Philadelphia and it broke down and we had to get out, carry our bags, and hitchhike."

When a storm knocked out power to the Honolulu Hawaiians locker room after a game in Jacksonville, the players assumed it was an economy measure and the coach ordered the team bus to shine its lights through the locker room window. The Charlotte Hornets practice field had no goal posts or yard markers and its locker room had only four showers. Eventually the Hornets were evicted for nonpayment of $1500 back rent. During a game between the Hawaiians and the Sun, a fight broke out on the field and both benches emptied. When the referee threatened to fine anyone who didn't immediately stop fighting, a player yelled, "Fined from what?" and then everyone started laughing so hard the fight died.

By October 16, the death of the WFL was imminent and those who could attempted to jump ship. That day, John Bassett's New York attorneys met with Pete Rozelle and two of his assistants. The attorneys formally notified the NFL that the World Football League was "in danger of financial collapse." At a WFL meeting several days earlier, the attorneys reported, the rest of the league had agreed that Bassett's Memphis franchise and the group running Birmingham would "obtain title to all of the WFL's good players" in the event of the infant league's demise. When the end came, both Bassett and Birmingham intended to apply for membership as "ongoing entities" in the National Football League. Rozelle only noted that anyone who wanted to was free to apply at any time.

On October 22, World Football League Commissioner Chris Hemmeter made the league's end official. After issuing a public statement, Hemmeter dispatched a letter to Pete Rozelle, praising the NFL and sadly admitting there was little possibility a second league could survive. Fittingly, the Hawaiian Hemmeter signed the letter, "Aloha."

The World Football League's capitulation was complete and final. When Hemmeter's announcement was made, the Southern California Sun's phone bank, ringing regularly the moment before, immediately went silent. "We couldn't figure it out," one secretary remembered. "Then someone tried to call out. No dial tone." The San Antonio Wings' public relations man cleaned out his desk immediately after the end was announced and headed for his company car, provided gratis by a local Chevrolet dealer. Before he reached the parking lot, the car had been repossessed.

Though Rozelle said nothing to that effect, it must have been a satisfying moment for him. This was his first victory over a rival league and was at least some counter to Al Davis's sneering claim to have whipped him the last time out. It was also some balm for his recent thumping at the hands of Rosenbloom. Most important, to Rozelle's mind, the National Football League's monopoly over the business of football was once again without exception. On that front at least, his much-cherished "stability" was intact and League Think triumphant.

15

Before the League's November meetings, the commissioner was able to add another entry in his "stability" ledger as well. The subject in this instance was ownership policy. Despite Bob Marr's prediction of endless delays, by the end of October the New England Patriots were about to redeem Billy Sullivan's nine-year-old promise to comply with the fifty-one percent rule.

At the Suffolk County Probate Court hearings, Chuck had reinforced his father's case by invoking the Sullivans' credentials with the NFL. Billy's friend Joe Robbie made a strong witness to that effect. The Miami Dolphins owner argued that it would be a mistake for the Sargent Trust to wait for Billy's buy-out agreement to expire, hoping for a better deal from the New Yorkers. Robbie maintained that the "other NFL owners would never approve McConnell and Wetenhall as majority owners." Billy Sullivan was a "League leader" and his contributions had been a significant factor in the League's growth. McConnell and Wetenhall were an unknown. Given that choice, the National Football League preferred Billy Sullivan "to continue to be the voice of the Patriots." When all the testimony had been heard, the judge took the case under advisement and scheduled another hearing to announce a decision in early October.

Old Billy's breakthrough came before the judge could act. The reason, according to Bob Marr, was that "McConnell and Wetenhall got cold feet" and accepted a last minute offer to sell out. Since they, in turn, had the authority to force the Marrs to sell under their buy-out arrangement, all the club's voting stock would become Billy's and the probate court action would no longer be contested. According to Marr, "McConnell and Wetenhall were afraid that if the court decision went against them, then their stock would lose a lot of value when Billy took control. The way they saw it, they should sell at a handsome profit because otherwise their minority position would be worth less." Marr learned of Sullivan's success on a Sunday when he was in the press box at New York's Shea Stadium before a Patriots game with the Jets. New England's public relations director delivered the news. He had just come from the team's locker room, he told Marr, and Billy Sullivan was down there. Billy was arranging to have his picture taken with the head coach along the sidelines. He was saying, the public relations man continued, that he's back in "control." Bob Marr's tenure in the NFL had lasted for barely a year and a half.

To complete the settlement reached with the New Yorkers, Billy Sullivan borrowed $5.3 million from LaSalle and Rhode Island Hospital Trust national banks. That money would be used to buy the stock of the Sargent Trust, the

Marrs, and McConnell. Wetenhall was paid with a $1.7-million note to be
paid off by 1982. The only other outstanding voting stock was owned by
Billy's cousin Mary, and she assigned its votes to Billy by irrevocable proxy.
She also agreed to eventually sell her shares to Billy, who in turn assigned
that agreement to his son, Chuck. The deal Chuck had cut with LaSalle and
Rhode Island Hospital Trust specified interest at 1.5% above prime and
required the future reorganization of the Patriots to eliminate the nonvoting
stock. Rhode Island Hospital Trust was also to become the franchise's "local
bank" and the Patriots guaranteed to keep fifteen percent of the amount of
Rhode Island's loan on deposit there. Payments on principal and interest to
LaSalle and Rhode Island would run Sullivan roughly $1.4 million a year
until 1981, when they would reduce by half. As of September 1975, $1.4
million was approximately the size of Billy Sullivan's entire collection of
liquid assets.

To secure his new loan, Sullivan pledged 87,320 shares in the New
England Patriots, 7,500 shares of common stock in Pittston Company, a
$500,000 savings investment plan from his job as president of Metropolitan
Oil, and three life insurance policies from Aetna Life Insurance Company. By
October 1, 1976, Sullivan guaranteed to be in a position to pledge all the
assets of the football franchise as well. That, of course, was Chuck's phase
two. In calculating future cash flow, both banks considered it an essential
step. Rhode Island Hospital Trust's credit workup on Billy treated phase two
as an established fact in listing the loan's security. In listing the loan's
"favorable factors," LaSalle noted that though the Patriot franchise was
carried on its own books at a value of $1.5 million, "recent franchise sales
place value nearer to $16 million." It also pointed out that "Sullivan is held
in high regard in the NFL" and that one of the things the loan gave the bank
was a "prospective prestigious relationship with a member team of the
NFL."

As part of the loan's paperwork, NFL Commissioner Pete Rozelle dispatched a letter to LaSalle, establishing the terms under which the bank would
dispose of the franchise should Sullivan default. It was a standard League
procedure whenever NFL holdings were pledged as collateral and in Billy
Sullivan's case it seemed particularly appropriate. The total financial obligation he assumed in the buyout was more than twice what he was worth.
Billy's "financial situation was marginal at the time," Rozelle remembered,
"but this was an individual who had helped found the American Football
League in 1959, and I knew that the member clubs were intending to support
him all the way."

"It's been a long hard struggle," Billy crowed when his victory over the
New Yorkers became public knowledge. "I've put so much into the Patriots
and I just didn't want to give up. This was just a very happy moment for me.
I just had a feeling of tremendous relief that all of this trouble was behind
me." Though the comeback added a whole new chapter to Billy's legend, it
was his son, Chuck, who gained the most stature from the transaction.
"Chuck Sullivan worked out the myriad financial and legal moves for the

family end-around play," *The Boston Globe* pointed out. "He discovered clauses in the agreements to sell stock. He devised ways to apply pressure. He found sources of money. He won." Unlike his father, however, Chuck was well aware the Sullivans' troubles were by no means yet behind them, and quickly turned his attention to phase two. Without it, everything could still fall apart.

In the meantime, Billy's first step was to name a new corporate board of directors. Four of the new board's six members were named Sullivan. Their first act would be to elect Billy president.

For his part, Bob Marr was sad to leave. Though he claimed not to be bitter, he was still convinced that if the New Yorkers had waited for the probate court to decide, everything would have gone the other way. Whatever Marr thought was now, however, of no import. "Billy's back!" the *Globe* exclaimed. "You wonder how Pope Rozelle has run the religion without him. . . . Billy gave us a million laughs, a million tears, a million smiles, a million scowls. Philistine or philanthropist? Messiah or meddler? Who can be sure? . . . Billy's back and we've got him for better or worse. . . . He may be delightful and/or destructive, but he won't be dull."

According to Rozelle, "a lot of people were happy to have Billy back," himself among them.

16

Despite the joy of Old Billy's comeback, the National Football League meetings in November 1975 would not stick in the League's memory as the occasion on which the Sullivans rejoined America's most exclusive club. Rather, the gathering would belong to Carroll Rosenbloom. Still seething, C.R. arrived in New York prepared to go after Rozelle in no uncertain terms.

One of C.R.'s November frustrations was his private eye's lack of success. Pete Rozelle was an exceedingly difficult person upon whom to find dirt. The commissioner didn't run around with women and, though he drank, it was rarely to excess. He had nothing to do with Las Vegas, and his only significant involvement with gambling was navy poker games during World War II. He was scrupulous about his personal behavior and seemed to take to the role of Caesar's wife with an almost religious intensity. With or without a scandal with which to confront Rozelle, however, Carroll Rosenbloom had come to New York to attack.

The November meetings started on the fourth and lasted through four days. Rosenbloom's anger just simmered through two of them. The primary purpose of the gathering was to set up the mechanics of stocking the new franchises in Tampa and Seattle with players. The November 6 executive session convened at 10:00 A.M. and spent the first hour or so considering the technicalities of player contract signings. Then, according to the minutes, "Mr. Carroll Rosenbloom addressed the meeting on many of the complexities and problems facing the club owners and the League."

Carroll Rosenbloom's address lasted for well over an hour. C.R. had been up late the night before working on it and referred to notes he had made on a yellow legal pad. Because all "family" clubs were allowed two representatives in executive session, his son Steve was there with him. "He had stood up several times before and had something to say," Steve remembered. "He got more and more upset that Rozelle's arrogance was not being challenged. Carroll expected business answers to business questions and all he got was the runaround. I knew he was upset. He talked softly and got people's attention. He controlled his anger and said a number of things."

"He gave Rozelle a beating," Leonard Tose remembered. "He was unmerciful. He said Rozelle was a crook, called him everything you could call him. It was so degrading, it was repulsive to me. Everybody was listening to it, though. I don't recall anyone leaving the room."

"Carroll just attacked," Gene Klein agreed. "Then he attacked some more."

According to Wellington Mara, "Rosenbloom denounced Rozelle violently and at great length."

Bob Marr, sitting in on his final executive session prior to the League's formal approval of Sullivan's stock transfer, called C.R.'s diatribe "mostly emotional, not much substance. I got the impression," he noted, "that it had happened before and would happen again."

"Carroll blasted Pete with a slashing attack," Art Modell remembered. "He threatened the League and everybody. I thought it was a totally unjustified attack, but I was impressed with the way Pete handled it, with enormous patience and fortitude."

"I just tried to be cool," Rozelle explained.

Carroll Rosenbloom made no such attempt. His anger seemed to feed on itself as he went along. Toward the end, he made no reference to his legal pad and just rocked back on his heels and railed. A decade and a half of grievances gave him plenty of ammunition. Finally he ended his tirade with a promise: "I will never attend another meeting," he stormed, pointing his finger at the commissioner, "as long as that man is in the chair."

Then C.R. headed for the door. He stopped once along the way for a final threat, addressed straight at Rozelle. "I'll get even," Rosenbloom snarled. "If I can't get you in here, I'll get you out there." His arm waved vaguely in reference to the outside world and then he turned and was gone.

A dead silence followed.

It was Rozelle who finally broke it. "Anyone who would like to talk to me privately about the charges you just heard," the commissioner offered in his calmest voice, "feel free. But for now, let's continue the meeting."

The next item was the formal approval of Sullivan's stock transfer and it was quickly passed by unanimous vote. Then Wellington Mara jumped to his feet and suggested a recess for lunch. C.R.'s outburst had left everyone stunned and Mara "wanted to break the spell."

After lunch, still "looking for something to break the mood," Mara sent over to the Management Council offices for what he hoped was an appropriate cartoon. The drawing was mounted in the office of one of the League's labor lawyers and depicted a cowboy, having been tossed over a cliff by his horse, holding on to a flimsy bush over the lip of the precipice. Above him, another cowboy was assessing the situation. "Hang on, old boy!" he shouted.

When the NFL reconvened, Mara gave the cartoon to George Halas and Halas then took the floor and presented it to Rozelle for having endured the previous item of business. "Everyone laughed," Mara remembered. "It broke the ice."

The laughter was decidedly nervous nonetheless.

17

The "spell" generated by Carroll Rosenbloom's anger was finally broken by what Wellington Mara called "catastrophe" on the League's labor front. The decision on *Mackey v. NFL* came in on December 29 and it could not have been worse.

"The Rozelle Rule constitutes a *per se* violation of the antitrust laws," the federal district court in Minneapolis ruled. It also constituted "a concerted refusal to deal and a group boycott on the part of the defendants. The Rozelle Rule," the court continued, "is so clearly contrary to public policy it is illegal under the Sherman Act. It is also an unreasonable restraint of trade at common law." Even the rule of reason was an inadequate defense. "The Rozelle Rule," according to the Minneapolis court, "is invalid under the Rule of Reason standard. . . . The Rozelle Rule is unreasonably broad in its application . . . [and] is further unreasonable in that there are no procedural safeguards with respect to its employment. There is no hearing or opportunity to be heard. . . . The Rozelle Rule is unreasonable in that it is unlimited in duration. It is a perpetual restriction on a player. . . . He is at no time truly free to negotiate for his services with any club. . . . The Court finds that the existence of the Rozelle Rule and the other restrictive devices on players have not had any material effect on competitive balance in the National Football League. . . . Elimination of the Rozelle Rule would have no significant immediate disruptive effect on professional football. . . . Elimination of the Rozelle Rule will not spell the end of the National Football League or even cause a decrease in the number of franchises in the National Football League."

If that wasn't bad enough, the court went even further and cut off the League's only line of retreat. Even if the NFL were to negotiate an agreement about the Rozelle Rule with Garvey and the NFLPA, it would still be illegal. "There is no labor exemption from the antitrust laws available to the defendants," the decision read.

Ed Garvey learned of the district court's decision from a reporter who called for a reaction.

"Congratulations," the reporter began, "you won the Mackey case."

"Oh my God," Garvey gasped.

The union's response was to throw a big party for the small band of people who "had put it on the line" and made the victory possible. When the union executive committee had voted after "many tough meetings" to file the case, it was assumed by all of them that whoever had his name on the suit would lose his football career. Mackey, then union president, had wanted his name on it nonetheless. An emotional discussion had followed in which, one by one, the others added their names to make it *Mackey et al.* "I have a son," one of them had declared while adding his name, "and I'd like him to play in the NFL as a free man. If this is what it takes, O.K." All the players named when the suit was filed were black except one, but that one left the case when, according to Garvey, "Al Davis got him to drop out." Garvey himself had mortgaged his house to raise money with which to pursue his somewhat desperate Plan B. Now the men who had risked everything seemed to have won everything. Plan B had carried the day.

The National Football League immediately gave notice of its intention to appeal the decision. Then, on January 9, 1976, Pete Rozelle convened the League for two days of special meetings at Park Avenue headquarters to discuss what to do next. The sense of crisis was palpable. Rozelle called it "the most turbulent period since I have been commissioner and very likely in the history of the League. . . . [The Mackey case] attacked the very structure of the game. It attacked the validity of the game."

Rozelle opened the January 9 morning session by outlining the Mackey decision. Then he introduced the League's Covington and Burling attorney to supply further detail. Once the lawyer finished, according to the minutes, "a lengthy discussion followed." Having convened at 9:30, the group didn't break for lunch until 2:15. At that point, "it was agreed that the decision would be appealed to the Eighth Circuit and to the Supreme Court if necessary."

After a brief, forty-five-minute lunch break, the League reconvened. For this session, the subject was the future expansion Rozelle had promised after the selection of Tampa and Seattle had been announced. On the agenda were presentations by the Birmingham and Memphis remnants of the World Football League, officially asking to be let in. The Birmingham franchise, renamed the Vulcans, had sent two representatives. The Memphis Grizzlies had dispatched a six-man delegation led by John Bassett. After another discussion among the members with no decision being made on the application for expansion franchises, at 6:00 P.M., the League broke for the evening.

At 9:15 A.M., January 10, they gathered again. This time, the lengthy discussion concerned "the uncertain future of professional sports in general and professional football in particular, especially in light of the recent Minneapolis court decision.'' New member Hugh Culverhouse, whose Tampa team had been christened the Buccaneers, was insistent on ''the need for an early clarification, in court if necessary,'' of the union's declared position that the League's plans for stocking its two new expansion franchises ''raised antitrust issues.'' There was a lot of talk but the best the twenty-eight franchises could do after more than three hours of discussion was a ''general recognition of a need to study the future direction of professional football.'' Dan Rooney moved that the League found a committee. The motion passed and the National Football League's first ''planning committee'' was born. Rozelle was named chairman. The other members were Tex Schramm, Art Modell, Cincinnati's Paul Brown, Lamar Hunt, and Al Davis. ''The committee was to meet regularly and report back to the membership.'' With that, the League adjourned at 1:00 P.M. and went its separate ways until the 1976 annual meeting, scheduled for San Diego in March.

The 1976 planning committee was, in Rozelle's words, ''very much a spur of the moment thing that grew out of the Mackey decision. There was,'' the commissioner remembered, ''an uncertainty about what we were going to do and the feeling that we ought to talk about this subject somewhere.'' The issue, as he saw it, was ''how certain problems should be resolved and the League get back to a period of stability. It was felt that a think tank team . . . might be able to develop some contingency plans.'' According to Lamar Hunt, one of the members, the 1976 planning committee ''only had one or at the most two meetings [before] the committee more or less just died.''

The man Pete Rozelle would credit with that death was Al Davis. At first, the commissioner thought it might be just the right committee for Davis to serve on. ''Before I put Al on the planning committee,'' Rozelle remembered, ''I suggested he go onto the Management Council. He said no, he worked better solo. I thought he was probably right. Al Davis couldn't fit in a structured thing, thinking just League.'' Rozelle hoped the idea-mongering involved in the planning committee would tap Davis's genius without putting the League in any jeopardy. Davis was already known for his ''original ideas'' about the labor issues that had prodded the committee into existence.

The planning committee's one and only meeting aside from its initial gathering in New York City in January was held in Palm Springs just before the annual meeting convened in San Diego. Al Davis established his presence early. Davis was not one of those owners intimidated by the prospect of free agency. If anything, he expected it would give him an even greater advantage over the rest of the League than he already had. In Palm Springs, he proposed that the League ''just cut everyone, all the players, and make everybody a free agent.'' Davis also had definite feelings about the role of the planning committee itself. It was, he thought, an excellent way to handle the League's business and suggested on several occasions that its future ought to be as an operating executive committee.

Though his peers knew he was power hungry, Al Davis was by no means yet a shunned figure. He and Tex Schramm got along well and that helped ease his dealings with Rozelle. One evening in Palm Springs, after the day's

committee dealings were over, Davis, Schramm, and Rozelle sat out on the
patio watching the sunset. The view of the mountains in the distance, looming
over the desert floor, was inspiring. Davis mentioned that he had always been
fascinated by Mt. Kilimanjaro. He had read a lot of Hemingway, he said, and
the mountain had always intrigued him. When I win the Super Bowl, he told
Schramm and Rozelle, no football for a couple of months and I'm going to
climb Mt. Kilimanjaro.

"Gee, Al," Schramm quipped, "you think it will still be there then?"

Al Davis's greatest frustration was still the absence of a single Super
Bowl victory, but he took the joke at his expense without flinching.

In those days, there was still humor attached to the League's view of Al
Davis. He was still thought of as "a character" who had "his own way of
doing things." There was some lingering resentment of what he'd "done" to
Wayne Valley, but Davis's fellow owners had become accustomed to his
silver and black clothes and his habit of speaking in obscure half-sentences so
the listener could not be sure of his intentions. The rest of the NFL knew Al
Davis always had a hidden agenda, but just what it was still didn't seem to
matter much. Nonetheless, the fear he had inspired ten years earlier when
leading the AFL into battle was still tangible. As much was apparent in the
fate of the planning committee.

The committee's last two hours of existence were in executive session
from 4:10 P.M. to 6:35 P.M. on March 18, the next to the last day of the 1976
annual meeting at San Diego's Hotel del Coronado. "The entire session,"
according to the minutes, "was devoted to the discussion of a possible
planning council." The idea was Davis's and the discussion featured a speech
by Davis himself. On this occasion, the half-sentences were few and the
message clear. Davis's speech, according to one of the men who heard it,
"was about how the planning committee should be made into a full-scale
junta and run the whole League. He clearly saw this as an opportunity for a
power grab. He wasn't just making a proposal. He talked about how the
planning committee was going to run the League. It wasn't the other members
of the committee's interpretation of what the planning committee was supposed to be, but Al had hinted at this kind of role at other meetings. Just
hinting—we ought to do this or we ought to do that—that kind of stuff. When
he stood up at San Diego and spelled out what he thought the powers of the
planning committee ought to be, everybody just looked at him and that was
the end of the planning committee. Everybody said we don't need this
committee anymore and that ended that."

18

"The present overall situation indicates that extreme care should be given to eliminating causes for litigation," the commissioner advised in his opening address to the San Diego meeting. It was a familiar refrain, and the first issue of long-term significance discussed would eventually prove to be just such a "cause for litigation." The issue was ownership policy and, again, it was raised at the commissioner's insistence. It had been three years since the last major discussion on the subject and, in the meantime, the NFL's ongoing ownership policy resolution, prohibiting cross-ownership and pledging League members to their "best efforts" to divest, had been allowed to lapse, much to the commissioner's eventual chagrin. "Our League office fumbled the ball," he explained. Due to an "oversight," the ownership policy resolution had not been reaffirmed upon expiration in 1975. "The acute labor unrest was occupying most people's thinking and . . . that caused us to slip up and not put it on the agenda." The commissioner had not noticed the oversight until the following year. He meant for it to be corrected immediately.

The issue, however, had not become any less touchy in the meantime. The discussion lasted several hours and was loud and occasionally hot. Included was the by now ritualized acrimonious blast at Lamar Hunt from Leonard Tose. "My position has always been the same," Tose pointed out. "Get the hell out [of other sports], you don't belong in it. If you have to take a licking, go ahead and take it. If you don't want to take a licking, let's see what we can do to solve it." As usual, Tose confronted Hunt personally. "I said," Tose remembered, " 'Give us a price for your soccer team,' since he always pleaded poverty and . . . said he didn't want to take a loss. I said, 'Tell us what your price is. Maybe some of us can get together and buy your interest out, or give us a price on your football team, if you want to get rid of that, so that you can make a choice.' His reply was, 'I will think it over,' but, as always . . . there was never ever a corresponding follow-up on it."

"Mr. Tose took exception to [Hunt]," Joe Robbie remembered, "and Lamar Hunt was asked if he still meant to bend his best efforts to sell the soccer franchise and he said that he did still intend to do that. He didn't have a buyer in mind. He was quite clear on that subject. . . . He had invested a lot of money in developing that soccer franchise and wanted to recover it if he were to sell out." As Rozelle remembered it, "many of the owners' tolerance was starting to ebb" and the discussion was "basically directed to Mr. Hunt and the fact that he was promoting a [soccer] league." Those promotional efforts by Hunt still "generated a great deal of ill will and some rather sharp discussion."

For Hunt himself, the March 15 executive session discussion of ownership policy was simply part of the blur the issue had become for him.
"Almost every time the subject came up," Hunt remembered in testimony
later, "there would be a variety of suggestions, some in writing, some verbal,
as to amending it, how it would work, how it could be modified . . . how it
could be handled in the future, whether it should be done away with, whether
it should be continued, but I don't have specific recollection of individual
meetings. . . . It was brought up frequently."

The ownership policy's most implacable critic remained Edward Bennett
Williams, though on March 15 he held his tongue for most of the meeting.
While the discussion raged around him, the nation's foremost trial lawyer
scribbled an occasional note to himself on a pad of paper.

Williams's first note was comical. *"How do you make a small fortune in
sports?"* he questioned. *"Start out with a large fortune,"* he answered.

"That was just a piece of whimsy," Williams later explained, "that I
wrote to myself . . . during the discussion. I didn't intend it as a serious
profound observation . . . just whimsy. I was, I guess, just ruminating while I
was upset during the . . . meeting. I was just writing to myself."

"Sports have a community of interest," Williams next wrote to himself.
"Should have one commissioner's office. Speak with one voice to Congress."

"I don't believe that sports are in competition with each other," the
Redskins president pointed out. "I think [if] there is success in one sport, in
one town, [then there will be] great success in another sport. I believe very
deeply that it is good for a city with a football team to have a baseball team;
good for a city with a baseball team to have a football team. I think it is good
for a city with a hockey team to have a basketball team. I think it is good to
have a soccer team. I think it is good to have people get into the habit of
taking their children and their families to sports events. It is part of the culture
of the city . . . and that they all help each other. . . . I was writing it down
because I was going to say that."

Further into the discussion, Edward Bennett Williams went back to his
notepad and wrote, *"submitted by the commissioner's office"* and then, *"who
is the commissioner's office?"*

"Another bit of whimsy," Williams explained. "If you live in Washington, people always tell you the White House called and I always say, 'Who
in the White House?' and it always ends up being some clerk who called.
When you say the commissioner's office wants this, I say, 'Well, who in the
commissioner's office? Is it the commissioner? Who wants it? Who is proposing it? Why does it say the commissioner's office? Why doesn't it say the
commissioner?' I want to know if it's one of the inside lawyers or who
proposed it. It was my way of saying why doesn't some owner propose this?
Why is it the commissioner who proposes it?"

Williams's next note was two words, *"tennis"* and *"racing."*

"I probably saw people in the room who had tennis interests and racing
interests," he remembered, "and noticed that those [sports] have been carried
out from the proposal, so I wrote that down."

"Don't circumscribe prospective purchasers," he scribbled next. *"Passage deflates value of interest. Distress sale."*

"The people who are interested in sports and who are prospective investors in sports constitute a rather small reservoir of entrepreneurs on the American economic scene," Williams argued. "There is a strong tendency on the part of someone who is an investor in one sport to maybe invest in another sport and . . . if you passed a rule which proscribed this, you would be circumscribing the prospective purchasers. . . . If [a constitutional ownership policy prohibition] were passed and people were required to make a selection as to what they were going to divest, obviously they would be making a coerced or mandated sale and we all know from just the basic rules of economics that a mandated sale produces less in the way of revenue than a voluntary sale."

Williams's last note to himself reaffirmed his complete opposition to all facets of the commissioner's policy: *"Must have corporate ownership, must have multiple ownership. No other sport has such restriction."*

"I have not just been opposed to the ownership policy of the National Football League insofar as it relates to cross-ownership," the attorney reaffirmed, "but also those policies that inhibit a corporation from buying franchises. I've also been opposed to those rules which historically have required a person to own at least fifty-one percent of the franchise. I have been for fragmenting and liberalizing ownership policies. I have said this, but without much response from my colleagues in the League. The ownership policies of the National Football League by my lights are wrong. I believe they are counterproductive to the best interests of the National Football League and to their owners, to players, ultimately to the fans. . . . I think it should be permissible for a hundred people to own a National Football League franchise and each have one percent, or fifteen, and each have seven or eight percent, and I also think you should be able to have ownership in more than one sport. . . . I don't think that there is anything accomplished by keeping people out of investing in the National Football League, making it more difficult to get in."

It was now well past 4:00 P.M. and Williams at last took the floor to level his familiar blast at the policy. His goals were to derail any talk of making this a constitutional amendment and to delay any consideration of the issue as long as possible. His trump card in this instance was his own legal stature. The tactic he adopted was to request a legal opinion. Coming from Williams, the request carried great weight. "I said," Williams remembered, "have we really reflected on the legality of this? Have we really gotten an opinion on it? . . . I just have no expertise in this matter and I think I felt like any layman. I would like to have a view of some reputable counsel with respect to whether there were legal problems in this matter. . . . It was that simple. . . . They agreed to get a legal opinion on it, so I was persuasive, I thought, at the time. At least they would explore whether it was lawful or not."

Edward Bennett Williams had calculated the impact of his request well, and the League couldn't resist the opening it offered. The tactic irritated the commissioner's office. "It was just Ed rattling his chain," Jay Moyer, the League's in-house legal counsel observed. "We sent a legal opinion over to him and never heard another word." Williams claimed never to have seen such an opinion. According to Joe Robbie, "that legal opinion was not forthcoming until after the 1978 [annual] meeting when I asked what had become of the request for a legal opinion."

In any case, the request itself was enough to momentarily derail the ownership policy express until the next League meeting in June. At San Diego, the League did, however, commit itself to "adhere to the terms of the [previous ownership policy] resolution even though it expired in 1975."

When the proposal came off the table in June, it would be stripped of all references to amending the constitution and amount to the same ongoing resolution, first passed in 1973, only this time passed in perpetuity and "subject only to change by 21 votes or amendment by 21 votes." The vote was unanimous and in addition, the minutes noted, "there was general agreement on a moral commitment for strict observance of the spirit of the resolution."

"The resolution ultimately evolved because it was obvious that a constitutional amendment was not going to pass," Joe Robbie pointed out in explanation of the vote's reported unanimity. "We were simply compromising by reducing this to nothing more than a policy. . . . The proposal was to amend the constitution and I didn't want that. I have been practicing law and politics most of my adult life, and I figured that that was the best way to get out of that one at that time. . . . I wanted to get rid of the question."

In 1976, even Pete Rozelle claimed to favor that approach. "At this time," he later testified, "we did have violations of this [policy] and I didn't feel that it made sense to put something in the constitution which was being violated, and it was better to keep it in resolution form until Mr. Hunt, Mr. Robbie, and Mr. Cooke were in compliance."

19

The second issue of longterm consequence raised at the 1976 annual meeting was, once again, expansion. It was a question that simply refused to go away. Encouraged by Rozelle's choice of words during the previous year and the League's irresolution on the issue in New York during January, both Memphis and Birmingham arrived at the Hotel del Coronado in force. Not only did the delegation of potential owners attend, but so did a group of civic boosters and potential fans. The boosters hung around in the Hotel del

Coronado lobby and said good things about their city whenever the opportunity arose.

According to the minutes of the meeting, the discussion was extensive. Worried that it would be years before the League would expand again, both Birmingham and Memphis had, in Tex Schramm's words, "come on strong." Both cities were proud of their relative success in the World Football League and John Bassett of Memphis was aggressively pushing the fact he could deliver a ready-made team. Rozelle, however, was doubtful about growing again so quickly. Tampa and Seattle had yet to be assimilated, and *Mackey v. NFL* was still on appeal. The commissioner's reluctance doomed Memphis and Birmingham to the less than big leagues for the foreseeable future. Before proceeding to other business, the League passed the following resolution on the motion of Tex Schramm:

> RESOLVED, after a thorough review of the major problems presently confronting the NFL, that the member clubs do not believe they can formally commit to specific expansion arrangements at this time. The clubs do, however, reaffirm their desire to bring total League membership to thirty teams as soon as possible after resolution of current problems and assimilation of the new Tampa Bay and Seattle teams. At that time, Memphis and Birmingham, which have most actively sought admission in recent months, will be among the cities receiving strongest consideration for NFL franchises.

The vote was twenty-five to three, with Ralph Wilson, Robert Irsay, and Al Davis voting no.

The door to the NFL had slammed shut once again.

Reactions varied among those remaining on the outside. Perhaps the most bitter was John Bassett, who eventually filed a lawsuit under the Sherman Act, *Mid-South Grizzlies v. NFL*. In it, Bassett and his fellow prospective Memphis owners would accuse the NFL of conspiring to boycott them by refusing Memphis an NFL franchise. The suit would be dismissed in district court and that dismissal would be upheld on appeal. "The exclusion," the appeals court ruled, "was patently procompetitive since it left the Memphis area, with a large stadium and a significant metropolitan area population, available as a site for another league's franchise." *Mid-South Grizzlies v. NFL* would be one of the few Sherman Act suits the League managed to win over the next eight years.

Perhaps the most optimistic response to the NFL's expansion resolution of March 1976 was Indianapolis's. Encouraged by the League's refusal to fill its projected thirty-team membership immediately, NFL boosters in Indiana began a long scramble to be prepared for the unspecified future date when the League would expand again. Indianapolis's 1974 bid had been thwarted by the lack of a big league stadium, and in 1976 a small group of local business leaders began what would become a very long campaign to erect a domed stadium complex in the heart of downtown. Doing so without the assurance of a professional football tenant was a high-risk venture, but within a year after the NFL's 1976 expansion decision, the city of Indianapolis, acting in concert with the Greater Indianapolis Progress Committee, would take an option on a seventeen-acre site between the city's exposition hall and the White River. It was a start.

Phoenix, however, was the first to stake out the strategy of the future. Their logic was simple: The future expansion reaffirmed in the NFL's resolution was indefinite and highly problematical at best. On top of that, since only two more franchises were projected under the promise, competition for the final two spots would be intense and, unlike Birmingham and Memphis, Phoenix had no written promise of serious consideration. The only other option for Arizona was the possibility of an existing franchise abandoning its current hometown and moving there. It was that option Phoenix chose to pursue. In March 1976, a private group of NFL boosters from Phoenix approached Robert Irsay about the possibility of pulling his Colts out of Baltimore. The contact had come about when Irsay was in Phoenix checking out an air-conditioning contract in the construction of the mammoth Paradise Valley shopping center complex. When Irsay was back at his offices in Skokie, Illinois, a group from Phoenix visited him with the move in mind. Irsay subsequently dropped the news to The [Baltimore] Sun in a phone interview. "Phoenix people were in here," the Colts owner announced, "and made an attractive offer."

For Robert Irsay, the approach offered an opportunity to push his effort in the Superstadium Game. His complaints about Baltimore's Memorial Stadium were by now a National Football League truism and he meant to use Phoenix as leverage. At the moment, he told The Sun, he had the Arizona offer on the back burner. "I'm going to be in Baltimore for three months, raising enough hell to get some of the things the stadium needs. I might even go door-to-door explaining our situation. There are things we would like to have done to make the stadium a better place. . . . I will give it ninety days, then I will take another look."

In 1976, few took Irsay's threat to move seriously. "Sources close to the National Football League's New York headquarters" told The Sun that Irsay's chances of doing so were "nil." Under Section 4.3 of the NFL constitution, such a move into new territory would require the approval of three quarters of the membership. "The Pete Rozelle regime prides itself . . . that there has never been a franchise shift during Pete's term as commissioner," one unnamed owner pointed out to The Sun. "Baseball [has] moved franchises all over the place. We don't. Irsay would need the votes of twenty-one owners to get approval to move out of Baltimore. I'd say he has no shot."

The owner's description of the situation was slightly inaccurate. The last shift in location by an NFL franchise, while set in motion by Bert Bell, had in fact been consummated in 1960, during Rozelle's commissionership. The move took the Cardinals out of Chicago and into St. Louis. At the time, it had been considered the solution to a longstanding NFL problem—how to share what was then the nation's second largest market with George Halas's Bears. The two franchises had split the territory since the 1930s under the terms of what was called "the Madison Street agreement." The Bears would play all their games on the north side of Madison, the Cardinals on the south. The problem developed in the late 1950s, when the Cardinals wanted to move north of Madison to play their games in Dyke Stadium. Halas called on Bert Bell to arbitrate and Bell upheld the earlier agreement and prevented the Cardinals from leaving Madison's south side. The ruling heightened the Cardinals' stadium frustrations and, once the Bidwill family assumed controlling ownership, a move was a definite possibility.

The pressure that put the move over the top came from CBS. Chicago was then the League's only shared market and, since TV sets in cities where a home game was taking place were then completely blacked out from football programming, it meant that the nation's number two market was largely inaccessible. Shortly after Pete Rozelle began his commissionership, a deal for moving the Cardinals to St. Louis was finally worked out. According to Rozelle, $500,000 was paid to the Cardinals franchise for "improvements" it had made to Chicago's Soldier Field and then the Cardinals left town for St. Louis. The money came from "several sources." Among them were the rest of the League's owners and CBS.

Since then, however, everyone in the National Football League had stayed put.

In 1976, Robert Irsay professed not to understand why his Colts should not be allowed the privilege of moving. Typically, he raised the issue at the San Diego meeting, but after hours. One evening, long after the day's sessions had adjourned, Pete Rozelle received a phone call in his Hotel del Coronado suite. One of his assistants was calling from the lobby. Robert Irsay, the assistant reported, was at this moment holding forth in the nearby bar. His precise state was undetermined, but he had reached the loud stage. He was talking about "storming the beaches" and "threatening at that moment, even before the bar closed, to transfer the Colts to Phoenix." To hell with the commissioner and Section 4.3 or whatever it was.

"Rozelle," the [Baltimore] *News-American* noted, "prevented any such late night or early morning move" and, for the moment, managed to shut Irsay up.

Like most things about Robert Irsay, however, that silence would prove fleeting.

20

The final issue of great consequence dealt with in San Diego was yet another battle in the war between Carroll Rosenbloom and Pete Rozelle. Despite the boycott of League meetings he had announced the previous November, C.R. came to San Diego and represented the Rams in Executive Session along with his son Steve. Rosenbloom's presence did not, however, represent a change of mind. Carroll had, once again, come to fight.

Nor had his feud with Rozelle cooled in the meantime. Indeed, Rosenbloom's list of grievances had only grown. On Christmas Eve of the previous year, the commissioner made it clear Rosenbloom's threats had not intimidated him when he announced the year's final round of fines. Rosenbloom, Al Davis, and Ralph Wilson were each assessed $5000 for having criticized game officials. Davis made no comment, Wilson made little, but Rosenbloom was icily sarcastic. "Since an agreement exists between the owners and NFL Commissioner Pete Rozelle that fines will not be discussed publicly," C.R. announced, "I am not in a position to elaborate. I helped make the rules and I try to abide by them. In 1971, I was notified by Rozelle on a fine in the Don Shula matter. Abiding by League rules, I refused to discuss the matter publicly. However, Rozelle saw fit to discuss the fine at the next Super Bowl game, when he had a maximum media audience. Therefore, I refer you to Rozelle for any further information. I feel certain if he does not care to elaborate further at this time he will, in all probability, be happy to do so at the upcoming Super Bowl."

That Super Bowl would be yet another for which Carroll Rosenbloom's Rams fell one game short, upping C.R.'s frustration yet another notch. After besting Bill Bidwill's St. Louis Cardinals at the L.A. Coliseum, 35–23, the Rams hosted Tex Schramm's Dallas Cowboys for the right to play in the Super Bowl against Dan Rooney's Pittsburgh Steelers and lost 37–7. It was the game against the Cardinals that put Carroll Rosenbloom on the NFL's San Diego agenda.

The confrontation had begun in the week prior to the game, when the Cardinals had requested use of the Coliseum for a pregame workout. C.R., looking for whatever advantage he could get, said that was impossible due to the terms of the Rams' lease with its landlord, the Los Angeles Memorial Coliseum Commission. The Cardinals complained to the commissioner's office. Since the Rams had filed a copy of their lease with the League, Rozelle instructed the League's treasurer to check it out. In the process of that examination, the treasurer discovered some discrepancies in the way C.R. had handled the question of rent for postseason playoff games. The gate from playoff games, wherever staged, was, once expenses were deducted, forwarded to the League office for equal distribution to all member clubs. Over the previous years, whenever such a game was held at the Los Angeles Coliseum, Rosenbloom had deducted ten percent for rent before sending the receipts along. The treasurer's examination of the Rams' lease revealed that the actual rent C.R. paid was subject to a cap and, once that cap was reached, no further rent was due. Since the Rams had reached their cap before the regular season was over, the franchise had not actually paid anything in rent during the playoffs and Rosenbloom had been billing the League for expenses he never incurred. "He was stealing money from his partners," Gene Klein observed, "pure and simple."

In early 1976, Rozelle confronted C.R. about the discrepancies. "I said it may have been a mistake," Rozelle remembered, "but the fact was you didn't have to pay the Coliseum ten percent rent on this game. If you didn't, then the money should come to the League to be distributed the way the owners decide." Rosenbloom, according to Rozelle, was "very upset."

Trying to avoid any charge of having picked on Rosenbloom because of the incident in November, Rozelle referred the question to the League's finance committee for a report, which was given in Executive Session at San Diego. The finance committee backed up Rozelle and demanded Rosenbloom pay the money back.

Though C.R. engaged in none of the histrionics to which he had resorted in November, according to Rozelle he was "very upset for the next few years." By the time the San Diego meeting was over, Carroll had burned the last of his bridges to Rozelle's camp. Rosenbloom's relationship with Art Modell was already in an "off" stage, and Tex Schramm quickly joined him. According to Steve Rosenbloom, his father's San Diego falling out with Schramm "had to do with a vote at a meeting. He and Schramm had been friends, but he felt that Tex had lied to him. Carroll felt betrayed and when Tex tried to explain his way out of it, it got worse. He didn't talk to Schramm for two years."

After the San Diego annual meeting had adjourned, it was obvious to everyone in the League that the Rosenbloom-Rozelle war was far from over. That spring, according to several NFL sources, Carroll finally redeemed his November promise to "get" Rozelle, "out there" if "in here" wouldn't work.

The incident that gave rise to their suspicion of Rosenbloom was a visit to the National Football League offices on Park Avenue by two investigators from the Internal Revenue Service. They wanted to see Pete Rozelle and the League's treasurer and it was not a casual visit. When the commissioner and his treasurer met with them, the IRS agents read the two men their Miranda rights against self-incrimination and informed them they were under criminal investigation. Though the agents made no mention of what or who had instigated the visit, Art Modell would later note that "it had to have come from within the League ranks."

The object of the IRS's inquiry was the $300,000 loan at seven percent which the League had given Rozelle in 1974 for the purchase of his new place in Westchester. The question in the IRS's mind was whether the "loan" under such favorable terms was simply a way of hiding either a "gift" or "income," upon which Rozelle had failed to pay tax. Certainly the house transaction was one the League had gone to great lengths to hide. Since Rozelle and the finance committee worried that Ed Garvey would make a big deal out of the expenditure in collective bargaining, the title to the Westchester property had been held for the last two years in the name of one of the League's Covington and Burling attorneys. In the course of their investigation, the IRS would subpoena League records and interview all the members of the finance committee. The process took two years before the investigation was dropped without explanation.

Though he would never comment on the incident for the public record, there can be little doubt that Rozelle's own suspicions focused fairly quickly on C.R. It wasn't lost on the commissioner that the man who had brought gambling charges against Rosenbloom in 1963 had subsequently faced a similar IRS investigation. Years later, when Carroll's wife, Georgia, bragged that she had the name of a New York lawyer who could get anybody she wanted investigated by Internal Revenue, Rozelle no doubt had his suspicions even further confirmed.

None of that was, of course, evidence that C.R. had actually instigated the IRS pursuit of the commissioner. Rosenbloom himself had refused to talk when the IRS agents attempted to interview him on the subject. Even so, a number of owners shared Rozelle's suspicions. "Somebody motivated it," Art Modell pointed out, "and it was concurrent with Pete's troubles with Carroll. Someone planted the notion of wrongdoing in the NFL office and it had to have come from inside. I, for one, am sure it started with Rosenbloom. Carroll played for keeps."

On the subject of the rent dispute that touched it all off, Modell, like Gene Klein, considered it a matter of Rosenbloom "stealing from his partners, pure and simple."

21

"Stealing from his partners" was a charge that would eventually be thrown Art Modell's way as well. By spring 1976, the situation from which the charge would emerge was now firmly in place. After more than two years up in the air, Cleveland Stadium Corp.'s longterm financing was at last set and Robert Gries, the young Cleveland patrician, was now, once again, Art Modell's minority partner. Gries's investment did not, however, take quite the form Modell had originally envisioned.

Negotiations between the two men had never ceased being difficult, even when conducted by their lawyers. The final and most telling sticking point was over the issue of how, if Gries were to buy in for a proportion similar to his share in the Browns, the debts of this new incarnation of Stadium Corp. would be secured. Modell's deal with the city of Cleveland required the corporation to spend at least $10 million in improvements over its first ten years as landlord of Cleveland Stadium and that money would, of course, be borrowed. In their discussions through the fall of 1975, Gries, then considering bringing in himself, his family sports corporation, and his brother-in-law, Richard Cole, for a total of forty-six percent, was prepared to guarantee the same percentage of the $10 million borrowing. His idea was that each entity would guarantee its own portion of the debt.

"I don't think the banks will go for it," Modell responded. What he wanted was for the Gries interests to stand as guarantor of the entire amount. The two men discussed a number of "different formulas," but in all of them Modell demanded that Gries guarantee the entire $10 million. Gries kept answering that he didn't see why that had to be. He was prepared to take his share but no more.

The negotiations were still at an impasse in November 1975, when Robert Gries Jr. had to leave Cleveland for a trip to inspect a sugar industry investment in Southeast Asia. Gries had, as he would later testify, "no choice" about leaving, but, in his absence, instructed his attorney and his brother-in-law to "carry on" discussions with Modell and "do the best you can."

On the question of loan guarantees, Richard Cole and the attorneys' best was no better than Gries's and the issue was simply unresolvable. In December, Gries, in Indonesia, received a telegram from his brother-in-law saying they were trying urgently to get in touch with him. Robert Gries then flew to Thailand in hopes of finding a decent phone connection on which to call home. The phone service there was "poor" but he was able to communicate with his negotiators over the heavy static. They reported that negotiations had reached the point where it was proposed that the Gries interests take a simple ten percent of Stadium Corp.'s stock without involving themselves in guaranteeing the bank loans. In addition, Gries, as part of the agreement, would be given "a put"—the right "to get out at a set price" whenever he so chose. Gries's negotiators said it was either take that or proceed with suing Modell for double-dealing and betraying his fiduciary responsibility to the Browns. There were no other options left. Robert Gries, aware he couldn't negotiate from Thailand and couldn't yet return to the United States, simply said "go ahead, wrap it up."

As "wrapped up," ten percent of Cleveland Stadium Corp.'s stock was taken by the combination of Robert Gries Jr., Gries Sports Enterprises, and Richard Cole. Gries later described the interest as a way "to keep a foot in the door and an eye on Modell." Another ten percent went to what Modell described as "employees, lawyers, and others." The remaining eighty percent was Art Modell's. The $10 million would be borrowed at a point over prime, for which Modell pledged "all the leases, assignments on the leases, assignments on all sources of revenue, and my own personal signature and that of my wife" as collateral. "I felt that to preserve my franchise value [in the Browns]," he later explained, "I wanted a contemporary stadium to play in and therefore I had to reach out and gamble my signature, my money, and my life to make it work."

As part of the final agreement, Cleveland Stadium Corp. buttressed Modell's personal finances by purchasing his land out in Strongsville for $4 million, almost five times what he had paid for it three years earlier. Three million dollars of the purchase price was cash, borrowed from Cleveland's Central National Bank. The final $1 million was in the form of a promissory note to Modell to be paid "out of net cash flow of the land [when] developed." Robert Gries still considered the price outrageous and might well have backed out of the deal over it, but at the last moment Modell wrote out a further agreement that the fate of the land in Strongsville would have no effect on "the put price" given the Gries interests. "With that," Gries pointed out, "I really didn't care what he did with the land."

By spring 1976, the word had spread around Cleveland that Art Modell had finished reorganizing Stadium Corp. for the long haul, but just how was an unknown. As with the Browns, only a handful of people even knew Modell had partners. To greater Cleveland, Art Modell was now Cleveland Stadium as well as the Cleveland Browns. Of the two, he claimed to be having the most fun "building something here in the stadium. I'm very proud of what I've done. It's a physical thing I can see and develop. I've had more fun with this thing, despite the gamble, than I've had, perhaps, with my ball club. In retrospect, it's the greatest thing that has happened to me in my professional life, because I do see a renaissance taking place in downtown Cleveland and I'm happy to be a part of it. I'm an activist owner and this is a way I have a slight edge over my competitors."

Stadium expenditures took two forms—structural improvements and what Modell termed "potential income producers." The problem, Stadium Corp.'s chief executive argued, was striking "a balance" between the two. It turned out to be a curious balance. In 1974, sixty-four percent of Modell's $2 million improvement budget was spent on income producers and thirty-six percent on structural work. The following year, eighty percent of $3 million went to income producers and twenty percent to "safety and modernization." Over the next two years, $2 million more would be spent, more than half of it on a scoreboard that would produce as much as $1 million in a year in advertising revenues. It would be the second largest scoreboard in North America, with some twenty-three thousand lamps.

Most of the income producing renovation expenditures went to construct Cleveland Stadium's version of the luxury box, called loges. During Cleveland Stadium Corp.'s first two years of existence, Modell constructed 108, some with eight seats and some with six. They were finally finished at 3 A.M. on the first day of the 1975 baseball season. They were all decorated at the direction of Pat Modell, Art's wife, and she was there herself on the last night, down on her hands and knees putting the final touches on the carpeting. The boxes would generate as much as $2.4 million a year for Stadium Corp.—welcome news, no doubt, to Art Modell's bankers. Perhaps just as important to Modell himself, they also cemented his reputation for having "saved" the stadium and, thereby, helped save Cleveland's downtown. Art Modell loved to hear that kind of talk about himself and took it to heart.

No one in Cleveland talked about Art Modell being an outsider anymore. His knack for running to the head of the pack had, after fifteen years, transformed the former part-time Brooklyn pool shark into a figure high on civic Cleveland's masthead. He was a visible player in the Greater Cleveland Growth Association, "owner" of one of the few Cleveland institutions with the population actually identified, and his short and increasingly chunky figure was immediately recognized when Cleveland's upper echelons gathered to bolster their hometown. Modell's address was as good as could be found in that part of Ohio, and his personal life was inconspicuous and built around his family. His wife, Pat, was by all accounts devoted to him. "I would rather have someone compliment me on my looks than say I'm bright," she explained to The [Cleveland] Plain Dealer, "I think my life is to enhance a man's." To another interviewer, she declared, "I'm there whenever Art needs me. I'm a listening board. He likes me to be with him."

While Art Modell did not have the accumulated generations of philanthropy that stood at the disposal of his silent partner Robert Gries, Art and Pat Modell were a very visible couple in Cleveland's cultural activities. Modell's special passion was the city's symphony. One of his first philanthropic outbursts after his marriage was to stage a fund-raising concert by the symphony in Cleveland Stadium, the week before football season opened. In white tie and tails, the orchestra was to assemble on the fifty-yard line and upwards of forty thousand were expected to attend. The event collapsed when a sixty-mile-an-hour rain squall blew off Lake Erie while the crowd was still filing in. As the audience fled for cover, Modell remained at the railing of the upper deck, out in the weather and refusing to move.

Next to him was his wife, Pat. In one hand she had a walkie-talkie with which to communicate with the concert staff. Her other hand was placed on her husband's arm. "Nice try, darling," she soothed him. "Nice try." Knowing Art was likely to take the failure personally, she kept repeating, "Keep cool, darling, keep cool." His greatest disappointment was that the orchestra had refused to take the field in the face of the storm. Though Modell afterward wondered out loud "whether I'll ever do anything for the orchestra again," his stature as a bulwark of the arts in Cleveland was only enhanced.

In 1976, Art Modell would spearhead yet another civic rescue, enhancing his reputation even further. The precipitating event was the bankruptcy of the Sheraton Cleveland Hotel on Cleveland's central Public Square, an enterprise whose success was considered "essential for the stability of downtown." The bankruptcy judge turned to Modell. The plan Modell developed was to put together eight civic-minded investors to contribute $1 million apiece to establish an equity in the hotel, then borrow an additional $10 million with which to remodel from "all the city's banks." Modell thought that once completed, the old Sheraton Cleveland would be worth some $35 million and, according to Robert Gries, "had hopes of a great profit."

Whatever Modell's motives, even Gries admitted the hotel rescue was "a very fine gesture." Among the Cleveland-based corporations Modell persuaded to pony up $1 million were the Chessie System, Eaton Corp., TRW, Inc., Higbee Company, and Diamond Shamrock. *The Plain Dealer* saw fit to thank Modell in its lead editorial. Such was Modell's visibility that the newspaper found it unnecessary to identify him by anything but his name while extolling his civic virtue. "He used his business expertise and contacts to draft the help of a group of businesses that ensures a new wave of interest by the total community in the future of the once grand Sheraton Cleveland. . . . Modell was the man to do it," *The Plain Dealer* raved.

Among the enterprises anteing up $1 million to save the old Sheraton Cleveland was Cleveland Stadium Corp.—now, much to Robert Gries's discomfort, in the hotel business as well as land development and stadium management.

22

Billy Sullivan was another NFL member about whom "cheating his partners" would be claimed by some of those partners. In the spring of 1976, his son, Chuck, was well into phase two of the family's takeover of the New England Patriots and it would prove exceedingly controversial. The target this time was the 139,000 shares of outstanding nonvoting stock.

On January 16, 1976, Chuck Sullivan met with his father's bankers to discuss how the Sullivans were going to accomplish the complete ownership they had promised by the coming fall. Along with Sullivan, the meeting included representatives of LaSalle National Bank, Rhode Island Hospital Trust National Bank, and their attorney. Sullivan began, a Hospital Trust vice-president later reported in an internal memorandum, by disclosing "that the Patriots' off-field financial success had vastly exceeded their on-field playing record. Whereas they had originally projected $900,000 in pretax earnings for the year ended 12/31/75, the actual looks like $1.1 to $1.2 million. It could be higher by virtue of the Super Bowl game receipts."

The memo went on to note that Chuck spent "some time . . . discussing corporate reorganization of the Patriots." That reorganization would be accomplished by establishing a new Patriots corporation, with which the old Patriots corporation would merge. As a condition of that merger, all holders of old Patriots stock would be forced to sell their interests to the new corporation—owned, of course, exclusively by Sullivans. Chuck anticipated to be done reorganizing by July. In addition, the Hospital Trust vice-president reported, "All assurances were given that everyone's best efforts were being utilized in order to expedite the reorganization which is so key to freeing up cash in order to commence amortization of the bank indebtedness."

Cash was a question about which both LaSalle and Rhode Island Hospital Trust continued to be nervous. Before the meeting adjourned, LaSalle's vice-president "very strongly stated to Chuck Sullivan . . . that the banks expected the first interest payment to be made when due, irrespective to the status of the reorganization, that the interest payment would not be deferred and that LaSalle would not consider capitalizing same. Chuck Sullivan did not seem to be particularly disturbed or surprised, and indicated that although he did not feel that they could borrow money from the Patriots, that other sources of family funds could be tapped to take care of this obligation."

Of the two financial institutions, LaSalle was the less nervous. "As you know," one of its vice-presidents wrote Rhode Island Hospital Trust in February, "LaSalle is the main bank for the Miami Dolphins and the St. Louis Cardinals, as well as the Patriots. Our lending experience in this field dates back to 1968, when we made a loan to Joe Robbie so that he could purchase control of the Dolphins. In 1973, we made a similar loan to Bill Bidwill of the St. Louis Cardinals. . . . When we recently met Pete Rozelle at the Boys' Club Dinner in Chicago honoring George Halas, Mr. Rozelle's first reaction was to thank us for our participation with the teams in the League. . . . We will be traveling to New York sometime in the near future for dinner with Mr. Rozelle to better solidify our position with the League office and get acquainted. . . ."

As well as being quite obviously taken with the idea of becoming the NFL's banker, LaSalle was also quite convinced of the value of the franchise. "I am confident," the LaSalle V.P. continued, "that a minimum price of $12,000,000 to $14,000,000 could easily be obtained [should the Patriots have to be foreclosed and sold]. The recent new franchises given to Seattle and Tampa were at a price of $16,000,000, although for some reason the League broke it down to $12,000,000 principal plus $4,000,000 unstated interest. The Memphis franchise of the WFL and their owner, Bassett, offered the NFL $12,000,000 in cash without any players for a franchise in Memphis. In addition to that, and on a *confidential basis,* the [Chicago] Bears had been offered up to $22,000,000 not too long ago for their franchise. As a note, the First National Bank of Chicago still carries a loan of $17,000,000 to the Baltimore franchise."

Rhode Island Hospital Trust's vice-president was more conscious of the dilemmas posed by their Patriots loan. "One of the continuing risks of this loan," he noted, "is the [possible] cessation of the continued willingness of rich men to pay prices for NFL teams which are in no way justified by the earnings of those teams." Even more disturbing to Hospital Trust was the fact that the merger plan being developed by Chuck Sullivan would, under Massachusetts's existing corporation laws, require the approval of at least two thirds of the affected nonvoting shareholders. The requirement came as news to the

Rhode Island Hospital Trust's vice-president, and on February 12, 1976, he complained that "until today I was under the impression that *no* formal vote of the minority stockholders was required to affect the recapitalization. . . . I clearly remember, in answer to a question at the time of the loan approval, saying it was my understanding that no vote was required."

Chuck Sullivan was also worried about the Massachusetts statute requiring a two thirds vote in order to conduct a forced buyout like the one he was attempting to organize. The Sullivans' strategy in response to that obstacle was to get the law changed. Their first approach for that purpose was to Barney Frank, a liberal Democrat recently elected to the Massachusetts House of Representatives. At the time, Frank was dating Billy's daughter, Kathleen. "We went together for about a year and a half," Frank remembered. "I was at a lot of the family get-togethers. The old man used to like to talk to me about business. He said I was antibusiness."

On Christmas Eve, 1975, however, Billy offered Frank an opportunity to redeem his record. "We were sitting around talking," the representative later claimed, "when Billy came over and said he had a way I could help business in Massachusetts. He told me there was a law on the books that was bad for the businessmen of the state. He said it would really help if someone could change it. This was the law regarding mergers and what kind of vote it took to put through a merger. I really didn't know anything about it. Chuck came over and joined the conversation. He showed me a piece of paper, and out in the margin was a check mark beside the words 'two thirds.' I told them I would look into it."

The papers handed Barney Frank included a proposal for reducing the merger provision to 50.1 percent approval, a bare majority. Frank passed the proposal along to Representative David Schwartz of Haverhill. "I didn't want to file the bill," Frank explained, "because I thought it would be a conflict of interest, going with Kathleen at the same time. Dave knew something about this law and said it wouldn't be bad, that about twenty states had it at fifty percent. . . . [When I learned] what was going on that summer when the bill was about to pass, I felt used."

On June 8, 1976, David Schwartz of Haverhill filed House Bill 5153, an amendment to the state's corporate merger statutes. "I did it for Barney," Schwartz remembered. "Besides, I liked the bill. I thought it would be a good one. It did go through very fast. It's not often you see something go through with unanimous approval of both the House and Senate. . . . I don't even think there was ever a roll call on it." By August, House 5153 would be on Governor Michael Dukakis's desk, awaiting signature.

"I think it very possible that the bill may become effective in time for the Patriots' merger," Rhode Island Hospital Trust's attorney wrote his opposite number at LaSalle. "I have also been told by two or three completely independent sources that this is a bill for the benefit of Billy Sullivan. It seems to be a well-known fact that Chuck Sullivan is leaning heavily. . . . It is now well known that Billy Sullivan is behind all this. One could not hope," the attorney warned, "that this would be excluded as evidence in any lawsuit that might be brought."

When later asked under oath what he had to do with getting House 5153 passed, Billy Sullivan would answer, "Nothing."

23

The National Football League owner with the most pressing partner problems at the time of the 1976 annual meeting in San Diego was Gene Klein, baron of the city's Chargers. By then, Klein was in his third year of just running his football team and trying to "enjoy life."

When in San Diego, Gene Klein stayed in his Spanish-style house overlooking the ocean near La Jolla. Klein kept three Rolls-Royces in the driveway, a sedan, and two $47,000 Corniches. His favorite was the Corniche convertible. For relaxation, he told the *Los Angeles Times,* he liked to "put the top down and take off through the desert or along the ocean." He was known as a big fund-raiser for the Democratic party, but in this year's presidential elections he would serve as California chairman of Democrats for Ford, the incumbent Republican. When Klein first bought his San Diego mansion, he envisioned living there with his second wife, Nancy, whom he had married in 1974, but that relationship soon fizzled and in less than a year he was back on his own.

By the time the NFL arrived in his hometown for the annual meeting, Gene Klein had married his third wife, Joyce, more than twenty years his junior and someone he had known in his days at National General Corp. Subsequently, she had become a stockbroker. Klein had begun dating Joyce in 1975 and, after their marriage, she gave up her job. "There is no way I could work with our life-style," the new Mrs. Klein explained. "It's very unstructured. Gene doesn't make his travel plans in advance, so I have to be flexible. Usually we're together about eighteen hours a day. And that's because we really like each other." Joyce also evinced a great taste for her husband's football franchise. "It's so much fun sitting in our box with our friends and watching the games. I've been going crazy because of all the excitement."

Despite their attachment to the Chargers, the Kleins' principal residence continued to be their mansion in Beverly Hills. There, Gene Klein indulged his passion for collecting modern art, a collection that included Henry Moore, Modigliani, Chagall, Ernst, Picasso, and Degas, among others, in rooms described as "overflowing with paintings and sculpture that read like an exciting modern art lecture."

However many pieces of art he accumulated, Gene Klein's favorite possession remained his football team. It, in turn, continued to perform miserably. In 1974, the Chargers won 5 and lost 9 and in 1975, they fell to 2–12. While still bitter about the drug scandal that had led to Rozelle's 1974 fine, Klein's only continuing grudge from the incident was against Dr. Arnold Mandell. On February 16, 1976, Klein called a press conference at which he charged that two years earlier, Mandell had illegally supplied amphetamines to Charger players and was personally involved in the manufacture of drugs. Eventually, the charges would be the subject of a hearing before a California Board of Medical Quality Assurance. Gene Klein would be the principal witness against Mandell. In response, Mandell's lawyer would threaten to call a witness who would claim that in 1973, Klein had invited the head of NFL Security to his home, got him drunk, and then obtained the League's files about Charger drug use. No such witness would ever be called, but Mandell was "cleared" anyway and returned to anonymity as the co-chairman of the University of California at San Diego's Psychiatry Department.

Gene Klein's partner problems began on February 18, at a meeting of the Chargers' entire ownership group. Klein himself owned only sixty-one percent of the franchise. The rest was in the hands of a group of ten limited partners. The most significant of those was Barron Hilton, the hotel heir and "playboy" who had founded the franchise. When Hilton sold the club's majority to Klein in 1966, he had retained a twenty-percent interest, later enlarged to thirty percent. Among the remainder of the partners, the most visible was John Z. DeLorean, then still the whiz kid of the automotive world. According to Klein, it was DeLorean who engineered the ambush that greeted him on February 18. "It was instigated by DeLorean," he claimed. "DeLorean wanted to sell me his interest and was trying to jack up the price. He didn't like the way the club was going and persuaded the others."

At the time, the most visible figure in the attempted coup was Barron Hilton. According to the hotel heir's attorney, on February 18, "during the course of the meeting, Mr. Hilton brought up the subject of corrective action for the football team's present situation. Mr. Hilton stated that in his opinion, the team while under the direction of Mr. Klein had acquired a bad image in San Diego as well as with the entire League and that a change in management was needed. Mr. Klein responded that he was not going to resign as general partner, that he owned a sixty-one-percent partnership interest, and that he intended to continue to manage the club. When Mr. Hilton suggested that the limited partners had the power to remove Mr. Klein as general partner, Mr. Klein retorted that if so removed, he would appoint a new general partner who would give him a management contract at a big salary to manage the club." The impasse was created by the Chargers' ownership agreement which required two thirds of the limited partners to remove the general partner, but allowed the appointment of a new general partner by a simple majority vote of all the club's stock.

"They were unhappy that we were losing games," Gene Klein remembered, "and thought I should make some changes. I said, 'Fellows, no. As long as I'm running this, we're going to do it that way. In my opinion, we're going to be all right in two or three years. This is a five-year program, and we just have to suffer.' Then they started the lawsuit.''

The lawsuit was filed in San Diego Superior Court on March 12, three days before the NFL's annual meeting convened in the nearby Hotel del Coronado. The plaintiffs were Barron Hilton, John DeLorean, and five others. They sought the removal of Klein as president and CEO of the franchise. "Due to the poor business and management techniques employed by Klein," Hilton told the court, "my partnership has suffered in both financial terms and otherwise. . . . In my opinion, if Mr. Klein is allowed to continue as general partner . . . the ownership interests and the rights of the plaintiffs will be irreparably damaged.''

Gene Klein was furious. "This is obviously a grandstand play before the League meetings," he exploded to the *San Diego Union*. "Those people tried to force me to buy them out and this is an effort to force me to pay the price they want me to pay. I paid Barron Hilton many millions of good American dollars, and now he wants to come back and run the club again. This is quite stunning to me. I think he's taking lessons from Ed Garvey. Most people know Barron doesn't have an overabundance of brains. The smartest thing he ever did was pick his father.''

Among the charges leveled at Klein by his partners was "extravagant" use of the partnership's funds. Cited as examples were the leasing of yet another Rolls-Royce for him to drive, spending more than $1000 on one of his wives' birthday parties, and billing the club for a "twenty-two-day junket to Europe, purportedly to look for a place kicker.'' Both sides charged each other with wanting to move the team out of San Diego.

It was not the first time such a move by Klein had been speculated about. In 1974, rumors had floated around Seattle that he was going to abandon the Chargers and apply for the expansion franchise there. In November 1975, he was approached by Memphis's John Bassett about selling the team to Tennessee. "When the expansion committee seemed negative about our application," Bassett remembered, "I went back to Memphis and said if they don't want to give us an expansion club, let's see if we can buy an established team. Since the Chargers had the worst attendance and the worst record, I had my attorney call Klein. He said the club was not for sale.''

In March 1976, however, Klein claimed the people who wanted to move were his partners. "Some of these people," he told the *San Diego Union*, "and I won't mention names, have urged me to move the club to Phoenix or Memphis. They're not interested in the team or the city, they just want to make money. But I repeat what I have said for nine years. I intend to keep the team in San Diego. I have said unequivocally I will not sell. I've never complained or whimpered about lack of support in San Diego. I know the crowds will come when we give them good entertainment.''

On March 26, a week after the rest of the National Football League left town, the superior court made its first ruling in the suit. The news was headlined "Klein Wins the First Round.'' In that ruling, the judge agreed with Klein's contention that according to the National Football League constitution, Commissioner Pete Rozelle had the authority to resolve the dispute. Gene Klein was jubilant at the decision. "The court has spoken," he crowed, "and I think the court has ruled very well. You've got to have a set of rules in any civilization and I'm a guy who likes to live by the rules. The commissioner has sole power. Whatever he decides will be right. The commissioner knows football. I would say he is an expert."

For more than a year, Rozelle would discuss the problem with Klein and talk to "a couple of the partners" without issuing any ruling. Eventually, according to Rozelle, "they worked it out themselves." On June 30, 1977, sixteen months after Barron Hilton and John DeLorean opened their rebellion, the San Diego NFL franchise would issue a press release stating "there has been an amicable settlement of all differences." The records in the *Hilton v. Klein* lawsuit were immediately sealed.

According to Klein, the settlement had been concluded when "Barron asked for a meeting and, as a gentleman, said he was sorry he started it. He understood what I was doing and [said] let's drop all the animosity. I said, fine. I didn't start it. I was sorry he did, and he was sorry he did. Now we're very good friends."

Hilton concurred. "There is no question in my mind that Gene Klein is the best owner and chief executive officer in the entire National Football League," the hotel heir told *The* [San Diego] *Tribune* after settlement had been reached. "He has done a tremendous job and all of the partners feel indebted to him for his leadership."

24

Despite the abundance of intrafranchise machinations, the League's overwhelming 1976 concern continued to be the war with the players association. On that front, the 1976 annual meeting had yielded the first hopeful signs in almost two years.

The hope surrounded an appearance in San Diego by Dick Anderson, the new NFLPA president. Following an introduction by Wellington Mara, Anderson addressed the League during its Executive Session on the afternoon of March 18. The new union president's attitude was conciliatory. He said the NFLPA could understand the owners' plight and that the two parties had common interests. "We can come up with an agreement," he asserted. Anderson took particular care to take the focus off Ed Garvey, an almost obsessive issue among the owners. "Look," Anderson pointed out, "Garvey is our executive director, he works for us. He is still with us, but our policies are set by the elected officers and a seven-man executive council, all players." The union wanted to discuss issues, not Garvey. "He made the point he was not a puppet of Ed Garvey," Dan Rooney remembered. "At the very least it showed that Anderson was willing to talk and that was progress."

Though it gave no signs to that effect in Anderson's presence, the NFL was also worried that personalities were getting in the way of resolving the situation. "Further complications," *The New York Times* observed, "have stemmed from . . . personality conflicts [by Garvey] with Wellington Mara, chairman of the committee that negotiates for the owners." Mara himself issued a public denial. "Different people with the same positions would reach the same impasse," the Giants owner defended himself. "If I believed that any members of our committee were an obstacle to settling problems, I would do everything I could to get a change." After Anderson's speech had been delivered on March 18, Mara took the floor again, "thanked Mr. Anderson, and stated in behalf of the member clubs that they, too, wished to negotiate in good faith toward an agreement."

Whatever his public position, it was apparent to his fellow owners that Wellington Mara was having trouble handling his role as chairman of the management council's executive committee. "I was close to an emotional breakdown a couple of times," Mara admitted. "It was the first time I had to face this kind of situation. There was enormous frustration. Things just got worse, not better. The things we believed in we were told were wrong. Our good faith was always questioned." Rozelle also recognized that a genuine opportunity was in danger of being lost. The commissioner found Anderson, a Joe Robbie employee, someone "I could talk to. He spoke quite rationally and reasonably and that was a welcome change from the kind of stridency we got daily from Garvey and the people who felt as he did." During the spring, Rozelle had "a number of confidential meetings" with the union president down in Florida. Anderson was, Rozelle noted, "at odds with Garvey on a number of issues." As such, he presented an opening the League could not afford to pass up.

The League's first overt response to Anderson's speech was the appointment of Dan Rooney to take over the management council's negotiations. On May 16, while at his daughter's college graduation, Rooney received a phone call asking him to step in. "They wanted a new face," he explained. "The first thing I did was announce I would meet with the union at any time or place. I had a relationship with Garvey that was O.K. We understood each other. I'm not opposed to unions. Some people in the League called Garvey a Communist, but he was a good person, following what he thinks is the right way to go. He's a unionist, he believes in the union movement, he's sympathetic to the poor. He has two levels of discourse. He'll tell you a lot of things that are just not so, but if he tells me something eye to eye, I believe him. You can't pay attention to the rhetoric."

The person Dan Rooney began dealing with, however, was not Garvey but Anderson. Their conversations began in June 1976, over the phone. "We talked about basic problems," Rooney remembered. "I convinced Anderson that they wouldn't get an agreement if we just continued this way. I said Garvey wants to force total free agency down the League's throat but, given the recent Minneapolis court decision, we didn't need an agreement to get that. Why should we hand out benefits, what do we get out of it? We talked about what the League was willing to do in the way of pension, minimum salaries, and protection for players' rights. In return, the NFL wants preservation of its system of the draft and compensation for free agents. It would be chaos without it." At one point, the two men met face-to-face at Rozelle's house in Westchester. There, according to Rozelle, the discussion focused on the development of a formula for Rozelle Rule compensation that would be acceptable to the union. "It was basically Anderson's idea," the commissioner remembered. "He thought it was a good way of compromising. We massaged it."

While progress remained nonexistent on the public front, privately Anderson and Rooney continued to meet, and by the beginning of August, had reached an agreement. In it, the gains of *Mackey v. NFL* were modified in exchange for a large increase in benefits. If both sides accepted such a modified rule, its illegality would become "unimportant and inapplicable." Neither the NFL nor the NFLPA was bound by the agreement Anderson and Rooney had reached, but both participants signed a letter "admitting our lack of authority but pledging we would both try to sell the arrangement to our two sides." Of the two, Anderson had the toughest selling job by far.

"Anderson stuck his neck out," one NFL executive remembered. "He thought he could get it done, but Garvey didn't like someone coming in the back door and undermining him." Their confrontation came on the last day of August, when Anderson presented the agreement to the union's executive committee meeting in Chicago. By this point, the union's membership had shrunk to sixty percent of its potential because of the lack of an automatic dues checkoff and "the association," according to *The New York Times,* "is torn between anti-Garvey and pro-Garvey forces," with Garvey having "the backing of the more militant of the members." Ever hopeful, the NFL scheduled its own meeting in Chicago for two days later so that the union's acceptance could be ratified.

Ed Garvey, however, would have nothing to do with the deal. Anderson's private initiative amounted to the first serious challenge to Garvey's leadership since the 1974 strike and Garvey moved quickly to dismantle it. "He accused Anderson of making under-the-table agreements," one union officer remembered. "Garvey convinced everyone this was no way to do business. He called them 'secret agreements.' Anderson's proposal was shot down quickly and it would have been voted down no matter what was in it. You can't cut deals without the knowledge of the executive committee. Who knows what is going on? You've got to be aboveboard. There are always people pissed off at every contract and you have to have the perception of fairness, otherwise it won't work. You have to defend a contract for years, and twenty percent always think they got fucked. Garvey was right. It's no way to do business."

Once the union vote was held on August 31, the NFL canceled its Chicago meeting and grudgingly returned to the drawing board.

25

The League's public resentment over the collapse of the Anderson-Rooney agreement naturally enough focused on Ed Garvey. Inside the confines of the NFL's executive sessions, however, Anderson and Rooney's failure also cast an air of suspicion over Al Davis.

Though the planning committee was no longer around to serve as a forum, Davis's ideas about labor were known to be at odds with most of the League's, making him an easy figure to resent. He had also been the only owner to break the NFL's solid front in responding to the *Mackey* decision. "We've got to be intelligent enough to modify, change, and rebuild our rules to deal with what the courts have ruled," he argued. "The judges are placing the rights of individuals above the interests of a group structure like ours so we have to do away with what's illegal."

Suspicion of Davis had been further fueled by the knowledge that Davis had also been working on his own plan to resolve the labor dispute at the same time Rooney and Anderson were working on theirs. To many, it was yet another example of Al Davis "playing commissioner" at no one's request but his own. Davis's idea had been to compensate the signing of free agents with money instead of players and it was thought that he had communicated his plan directly to the union, bypassing the owners' negotiating team. By the summer of 1976, Al Davis was already forecasting "a change in the labor policy in our League" over the coming decade, to grant "much more freedom for the players to move themselves from location to location." While Rozelle was leading the rest of the League in a chorus about how such an eventuality would destroy the football business, Davis simply forecast that the League would be different. Later, Davis would say, "We will find some [owners] who do not have the total wealth of others who still may be able to do a good job, but that will be in the minority. I think that wealth will be the prerequisite for greatness in the eighties."

That attitude made his fellow owners wonder just whose side Davis was on, and with some justification. "Al was a union supporter," one of his employees observed. Then the employee added a qualifier. "That is, of course, as long as he had a guy in the union in a position of power."

That "guy" in this instance was Gene Upshaw, Raiders player representative, member of the NFLPA executive committee, and a rising star in the union's internal politics. Upshaw had played a major role in the devastation of Anderson's proposal at the end of August and his closeness to Davis was no secret. According to Davis, he and Upshaw "discussed the position [Upshaw] would take on every matter I think we have ever had between the players and the owners and the National Football League and et cetera like that.'' In addition, since April 1975, Upshaw had been a "member" of Eastmont Mall Associates, Davis's shopping center partnership with casino king Allen Glick. Upshaw's "owner-management" duties there, according to Eastmont's attorney, were to "work closely with the mall management in developing an extensive community involvement program.'' Davis himself admitted it was "possible" that he had told one member of the now defunct planning committee that "he could get Gene Upshaw to do whatever he wanted.'' Not long after the Raiders' player rep had helped kill Anderson-Rooney, according to Rozelle, "word came through that Al had helped scuttle the deal through Upshaw.''

According to Al Davis, the exact opposite had happened. "The League wanted to push through the Anderson-Rooney agreement,'' Davis remembered, "which was a stacked agreement. I didn't agree with it for a number of reasons, and they wanted me to urge Upshaw to push it through. And I wouldn't do it. . . . I have great influence on Gene. He is a friend of mine and I would never do anything to impugn his integrity, and when I was asked to do that, I wouldn't do it. . . . That is something the commissioner and others asked of me, and I wouldn't do it. . . . Several of the member clubs are still mad at me over it. . . . They wanted to get Ed Garvey out as a power [in the union] and wanted me to use Upshaw to do that. . . . I thought it was wrong, but most important of all, I never thought we would have an agreement without Ed Garvey and several owners, close friends of mine, chastized me on it. . . . We got into violent arguments over it.''

Independent of the maneuvering around Anderson-Rooney, Al Davis remained an easy person for the rest of the National Football League to dislike. "A combination genius and devil,'' his black suit, white shirt, and silver tie gave him a look *Sports Illustrated* dubbed "the appearance of a mobster in an old George Raft movie.'' In that context, *The* [Oakland] *Tribune* noted, "strangers sometimes express surprise when they find he has much charm.''

"I don't know what they expect,'' Davis would observe, "maybe a fat, tough-talking guy with a big cigar in his mouth. I suppose they expect a flashy show-girl type on my arm. I guess it's a shock when they learn I've had the same wife for twenty years.'' Though Al Davis refused to appear on television or radio shows, his image was important to him and he made a habit of stroking the press corps who purveyed it. Every Christmas he distributed binoculars, TVs, stereos, and even cash to the Raiders' regular reporters. Davis called it nothing more than "a little appreciation for the guys who live with us,'' but in at least two instances, reporters were removed from the Davis beat by their editors for having compromised themselves by accepting his appreciation.

Central to the image Al Davis crafted for himself was victory in whatever form it was available. "My kick comes from trying to figure ways for us to win,'' Davis explained, "with the rules that everybody else makes. I'm no rule maker. Football is a game you play to win. Otherwise, like they say, why do we keep score? You play, you win, the money comes; and the recognition, if that's what you want. I didn't make up those rules. That's the way life is.''

While the tension between Al Davis and Pete Rozelle was not yet much of a public issue in 1976, Davis's hostility toward the commissioner was yet another factor that reinforced the "member clubs' " suspicions. "Davis is an implacable enemy of Pete Rozelle," *The Tribune* noted, "though he is more restrained in his criticism of the commissioner than Carroll Rosenbloom, the owner of the Los Angeles Rams. Of the two, Davis represents the more danger to the commissioner. The difference, it is said, is that Rosenbloom wants Rozelle's head; Davis is after his job.''

Before the dust from Anderson-Rooney's rejection had settled, the rest of the League's owners had yet another incident upon which to hang their resentments of Al Davis.

On the opening day of the 1976 season, Al Davis's Raiders were pitted against Dan Rooney's Pittsburgh Steelers on national television. The two teams had a particularly vicious relationship of long standing. The play that set everything off occurred late in the first half. As described by *Sports Illustrated*, "Lynn Swann, the splendid wide receiver of the Steelers, ran a pattern down the right side of the field, then cut to the middle. He was covered by George Atkinson, a tough but hitherto unheralded defensive back for the Raiders. As the play unwound, [Steeler Quarterback] Terry Bradshaw was forced to scramble, eventually firing a pass to [Steeler Running Back] Franco Harris, who thundered downfield. As Harris caught the ball, fifteen yards away Atkinson rushed up behind the unsuspecting Swann and cracked him with a forearm at the base of the helmet. Swann dropped as if he were shot. He suffered a concussion and missed the next two games. No official saw Atkinson's blow, no penalty was levied.''

The game's huge national television audience had witnessed everything, however, and saw it over and over again in slow motion replay as the game progressed. Even the hometown [Oakland] *Tribune* described Atkinson's blow as "dirty football.'' Pittsburgh head coach Chuck Noll was incensed and made it clear after the game that he considered Atkinson's play part of a Raider strategy to maim the Steelers' best players. "You have a criminal element in all aspects of society," Noll charged through clenched teeth. "Apparently we have it in the NFL too. Maybe we have a law-and-order problem.'' Noll also suggested that players like Atkinson should be "kicked out of the League.''

Pete Rozelle had not watched the game but the burgeoning public relations disaster was dumped in his lap by the evening of September 12. One of his assistants had attended, witnessed a confrontation between Noll and several Raider players under the stands after the game, and had a conversation with Dan Rooney about the play that evening. By the following morning, Rozelle's assistant was back at the Park Avenue office to give a report. Rozelle also ordered up film clips of Atkinson's blow to Swann's head. It was a week before he issued any judgment, and in the meantime, the League office was "swamped with calls and letters about Atkinson's hit.'' On

September 20, the commissioner's office announced it was fining Atkinson $1500 for what Rozelle called as "flagrant" a foul as he had seen "in sixteen years in this office." He also fined Noll $1000 for his "criminal element" remarks, under the NFL bylaw that forbade public criticism by a member team of another.

Less than satisfied by the ruling, Dan Rooney fired a private letter back to Rozelle charging "direct premeditated, unemotional efforts by the Oakland Raiders to seriously injure Lynn Swann." These efforts, Rooney charged, involved "the Raiders coach staff" and, by implication, Al Davis.

For his part, Davis's only public stance was to blame the furor on the press. "No one was killed," he snapped when approached by a *Tribune* reporter. "Why get excited? Yet you wrote as though the Pittsburgh game was the My Lai massacre. You guys are the problem. You want us to win. You want us to be tough. But when we're in a vicious game with the Steelers, a team that is notorious for busting up opponents, you seize on an incident involving one of our men and you hammer away. Do you realize what would happen now if we went back to Pittsburgh for one more game?"

Behind the scenes, however, Al Davis had a more aggressive strategy in mind. "Chuck Noll," he pointed out, "had condemned certain individuals playing for the Oakland Raiders and labeled them 'criminals' and I felt it was important that we get rid of that label."

George Atkinson, Davis's employee, did not take kindly to being branded a "criminal" either. For him, the charge had a particular kind of sting. In 1975, Atkinson had been brought to trial in San Francisco on federal charges of embezzlement and larceny for having allegedly convinced two female bank tellers to steal some $3200 from two different Alameda County banks. After one jury deadlocked seven to five for conviction, a second trial in April 1976 had acquitted the football player on all counts. According to one of his Raider teammates, "Al Davis was paying the bills" for Atkinson's defense.

On October 6, Atkinson's attorney announced that the Raider was going to file a $2 million slander suit against Steeler Coach Chuck Noll. "Pro football is on trial here," the attorney argued. "If a jury rules that Atkinson is not slandered by being called part of a 'criminal element' then the term 'criminal' has been judicially certified as a viable, proper, accurate definition of the game. After this, every time a player is injured . . . he could bring a criminal suit for assault. Hell, you could bring a class action suit against showing the 'criminal' violence of football on TV. Pro football could be X rated." The attorney's case would also focus "on the contention that there was a conspiracy on the part of the Rozelle-Rooney establishment to get the outcast upstart Oakland crowd led by Al Davis."

While Atkinson's name was on the suit, Rozelle, for one, was convinced that Al Davis was the one really suing and that the parties really being sued were the Pittsburgh Steelers, Dan Rooney, and the NFL itself. "Al Davis financed and ran the case," Rozelle charged. "Al didn't care how he did it. Hurting the League didn't bother him at all." It was the kind of behavior which Rozelle felt deserved a response, though he took none in the immediate moment of Atkinson's filing. The commissioner's reasoning was simple. "We're a self-governing body," his lieutenant, Art Modell, explained. "We have our way of punishing members. To sue Noll was another attempt to discredit and diminish the office of the commissioner."

Noll's defense would be financed by his employers, the Pittsburgh Steelers. His boss, Dan Rooney, had no illusions about who was suing and considered it an attempt to damage the Steelers on the playing field. "Davis was behind Atkinson," the Steelers' president complained. "In reality, it was Raiders v. Steelers, and that was the way it was fought."

By the time the Atkinson suit came to trial in June 1977, Davis's alleged pivotal role would be the official National Football League position. "Mr. Atkinson was a nominal party in that lawsuit," one of its attorneys would claim. "The Raiders were the real party interest. . . . The action was prosecuted at Mr. Davis's direct direction and . . . a lawyer for the Raiders actually conducted the examination of the principal witnesses . . . and the questions posed by [that lawyer] were the result of notes handed him by Mr. Davis sitting in the courtroom."

Al Davis would claim the opposite was true. "We didn't get into the case," he explained. "We sat there and watched it. . . . Chuck Noll called our players criminals. . . . It was a misrepresentation. It was unfair. . . . I resented it and the commissioner didn't do anything about it. In the confines of the case, we again found out about the close coterie [who ran the League]. . . . Dan Rooney wrote a letter to the commissioner and Rozelle did nothing about it. We had an attorney there to protect our interests."

While *Atkinson v. Noll* was awaiting a place on the federal court trial docket in fall 1976, Dan Rooney began what would be a long string of warnings about the case to the rest of the League. "It was the first suit by one NFL team against another NFL team," he pointed out. "It set a precedent and I pointed this out a number of times at League meetings."

On one of those occasions, a fellow owner responded to Rooney that rather than a precedent, this was really a "unique" case, much more tangled than one team against another.

"No it's not," Rooney snapped. "This is Raiders versus Steelers." Once the precedent of one team taking another to court was set, it would, he claimed, open the doors to potential disintegration of the League.

Three years later, Rooney's prediction would become fact.

26

Nevertheless, in the fall of 1976, the League's trepidations were still focused primarily on Carroll Rosenbloom. The IRS's visit to Rozelle had shocked a number of members and they were well aware that Rosenbloom's anger would not be easily extinguished. Since the San Diego annual meeting, however, C.R. had been relatively quiet.

For most of 1976, Carroll Rosenbloom had his hands full with the second round in his Superstadium Game against the Los Angeles Memorial Coliseum Commission. The three-year lease he had negotiated in 1974 was due to expire at the end of the year. Rosenbloom had long since become totally disenchanted with the Coliseum Commission as a landlord, but still had no other place to go. "They were impossible to deal with," his son Steve remembered. "We wanted something done there, but the LAMCC was the worst kind of political body: it was divided into three parts and the president's position rotated each year. Every year we would tell the new president what we wanted and we'd get lip service but nothing else. Year after year it was the same thing."

In 1976, the president of the LAMCC was one Pete Schabarum, also a Los Angeles County supervisor. He and Rosenbloom had a long series of discussions about the extension of the Rams' lease on the Coliseum. C.R. presented two principal demands, but, according to Schabarum, "was not genuinely interested in a lease extension." The first of Rosenbloom's demands was that the stadium's playing field be lowered, eliminating the running track that currently separated the audience from the game and making room for more seats. This demand made little progress, in part because of the expense and in part because a group in Los Angeles had already begun a drive to bring the 1984 Olympic Games to the Coliseum, for which a running track was an essential. Though the Olympics still seemed an unlikely possibility, the field remained right where it had always been since 1923.

C.R.'s second demand was even closer to his heart. He wanted luxury boxes and, on this issue, negotiations made more headway. The only such convenience currently in the stadium was Rosenbloom's owner's suite. It was two stories high, divided between a suite and a reception area, and sat thirty-six. While any new boxes would not be on such a grand scale, Rosenbloom wanted more than a hundred of them strung along the rim of the Coliseum. Eventually, these suites were portrayed as the kingpin in "securing financing to bring into being [an] overall Coliseum improvement program." As drawn up by architects, that program included lowering the field and squaring the oval shape at one end of the structure as well. Advance sales of the suites, according to Rosenbloom's plan, would underwrite a bond issue for the necessary construction. On a "contingency" basis, the LAMCC agreed to provide design help, a bond counsel, a consultant, and "the initiation of a sales program offering those suites to the public." The contingency, according to Schabarum, was that a 1976 attempt to generate such advance sales would be successful and that Rosenbloom would subsequently sign a longterm lease. Before football season, the Rams and the Coliseum had a joint press conference at which they announced the effort had begun.

"The Los Angeles Memorial Coliseum," the sales brochure raved, "southern California's giant among the world's outstanding sports-viewing complexes, today stands on the threshold of a new era of achievement in stadium design and development. . . . Combining the rich tradition of the Coliseum's fifty-five-year history and a new concept of intimacy and game view improvement, a major renovation program will be completed [by the opening of the 1977 season], enabling the Coliseum to take its place among the nation's finest and most modern. An important feature of the new stadium design is the addition of 138 luxurious, air-conditioned suites which will allow you and your guests to view the game in comfortable, relaxed surroundings. . . . Each suite will have sixteen theater and lounge seats inside the suite for comfortable viewing of the game. Immediately behind the theater-type seats will be the suite area for relaxation and entertaining. . . . Every seat in every suite is a winner! The sight lines between you and the playing field are superb. Every convenience awaits you and your friends, offering the ultimate in spectator luxury. . . . Add to this the advantage of parking spaces close to the Coliseum and private access to your suite!

"Because of the high interest already generated," the brochure claimed, "now is the time to arrange for your Coliseum suite."

In truth, the promotion was an early flop. Only a smattering of commitments were forthcoming, nothing close to the numbers the program needed for success. "L.A. may not have been ready for it," one LAMCC official noted. "Congress was toying with cutting into corporate luxuries and a lot of corporations were reluctant." There was, as Rozelle later described it, "overwhelming disinterest." At that, C.R.'s deal with the LAMCC "unraveled" and he ended up accepting another three-year extension on the lease he already had. The experience helped convince him that the Coliseum would never be the kind of football palace he wanted and thought he deserved.

Not surprisingly, from fall 1976 on, Rosenbloom's concern about stadiums ranged all over the southern California landscape. It was one of the principal subjects discussed in his numerous phone calls with Al Davis up in Oakland. To Davis, he mentioned he had considered Dodger Stadium in Chavez Ravine and the possibility of buying the baseball Dodgers in order to gain access to it. In addition, Rosenbloom had looked into building his own stadium in Inglewood or on a site near Hollywood racetrack, immediately adjacent to Jack Kent Cooke's Forum. On "many occasions," Davis later testified, C.R. also discussed the possibility of moving to Anaheim, the nation's eighteenth largest standard metropolitan statistical area, right next door in Orange County.

While a source of increasing preoccupation for Rosenbloom, the Superstadium Game had not completely diminished his desire to lash out at Rozelle. He loosed his next barrage in the commissioner's direction on the last day of September 1976. It was an elaboration on a theme C.R. had begun working the previous April, when the League's 1976 schedule was announced. At that time, "several people" in the Rams organization called the schedule an "act of retribution." The *Los Angeles Times* reported "a source with Rams connections" as saying, "Everything on the schedule can be explained by NFL policy," and that, "every time the League could have gone one way or another, it went against the Rams." In response, Rozelle "acknowledged [his] problem with Rosenbloom, but denied it had influenced the Rams schedule."

On September 30, Carroll Rosenbloom seized the gauntlet again personally. The commissioner, he charged, had "deliberately" scheduled the Rams to play a 4:00 P.M. game in Miami the following Sunday at the start of Yom Kippur, the Jewish religious holiday. Carroll's wife, Georgia, would later describe the incident as his "Yom Kippur caper." It was one of the few times C.R., a titular Jew, raised the question of religion in his entire public life. Scheduling the game for Miami at that time was, Rosenbloom raged, "insensitive, arrogant, and stupid. But Rozelle has no sensitivity. Yom Kippur is the most important holiday to Jewish people. This is a thing that was done with malice aforethought. They said, 'Let's put the Jew in Miami for Yom Kippur and see how he likes it.' I just know Rozelle and his stooges were giggling about it on the day they released the schedule. It was a stupid thing for the League to do, when it would have been so easy to do it the other way. The game in Miami could have been scheduled at 1 P.M. and a California game could have been scheduled as the second half of the television doubleheader. I make no claim to being a religious man, but I am Jewish and this is an insensitivity that has offended many people.

"The whole schedule of the Rams was based on punishing me," Rosenbloom continued. "It is a punishment and a warning to other teams that if they criticize Pete Rozelle, they will also be punished. Look at our home schedule. Every team that is a contender, we play away from home. Our travel situation is the worst possible. If Rozelle could have arranged to have us play at midnight in Nome, Alaska, he would have done it."

According to the *Los Angeles Times*, "many spectators are expected to leave the [Yom Kippur] game early and several hundred have requested ticket refunds." Rosenbloom, however, "said he would attend."

Rozelle's only response to the attack was a statement issued October 1. "We attempt to avoid scheduling conflicts with all religious holidays," he explained. "Unfortunately, it is not always possible to do so. This League was obligated to provide a national network telecast this Sunday beginning at four o'clock Eastern time. The Rams, by scheduling rotation, play the Dolphins in Miami, and this was the only attractive game available."

Privately, Pete Rozelle managed to chuckle over the attack. "One of the Jewish owners in the League called me," the commissioner noted. "He said, 'I'd hate to have been hanging by my toes since the last time Carroll went to temple.' "

Carroll's son Steve agreed with the gist of the joke. "My father was no more Jewish than you are," he offered to one Protestant reporter. "He really didn't want a late afternoon game and it gave him an excuse to jump on Rozelle."

In the fall of 1976, the commissioner and the League braced itself for the next attack from C.R., but what followed instead was an eerie calm. Once Yom Kippur had been observed, Rosenbloom would put his feud with Rozelle on hold and devote himself to winning his superstadium game once and for all.

27

In 1976, as in 1975, Carroll Rosenbloom's attack on the commissioner was followed by pressing news from the labor front, this time almost immediately. On October 18, 1976, the appeals court sitting in the case of *Mackey v. NFL* announced its ruling. "The National Football League's Rozelle Rule," the appeals court affirmed, "which applies to every League player regardless of his status or ability, which is unlimited in duration, and enforcement of which is unaccompanied by procedural safeguards, as enforced, unreasonably restrains trade in violation of the Sherman Act." The appeals court also tinkered with the district court ruling on the issue of the legal status of the Rozelle Rule if it were a condition specifically accepted in collective bargaining, saying such a labor contract would exempt the arrangement from Sherman Act jurisdiction.

Wellington Mara was in the Management Council's offices in Manhattan, just a short walk from the League's Park Avenue headquarters, when news of the appeals court ruling came in. With him there were Sargent Karch and Ted Kheel, the council's two leading labor attorneys, and several others. At first the response of everyone was depression. "It was another loss," Mara remembered. Only Kheel thought otherwise. "This is not just a victory," he crowed, "but a great victory."

"Everyone laughed at him and called him the captain of the *Titanic*," Mara remembered, "but I soon saw his point. Garvey analyzed the appeals court decision and saw that he should start consolidating his gains."

Kheel's opinion was soon that of the entire League. "The union position," Rozelle explained, "had been that antitrust laws were on one side of the equation, labor law on the other, and that the antitrust law overrode the labor laws. 'Whatever we won in court,' Garvey said, 'we're not going to touch that, can't touch that, even if we wanted to, we can't do it.' The owners felt Garvey always wanted two bites out of the apple—whatever he could get or was entitled to under the labor laws he wanted, then he'd go to court and try and get it under antitrust laws. The *Mackey* appeals court came down saying the issues shouldn't be resolved in court, but instead in collective bargaining. Once the union realized its major legal premise had been pulled out from under it, he decided to bargain.''

Among the other pressures on Ed Garvey at the same time were the effects of more than two years without a payroll checkoff with which to collect NFLPA dues. "Our membership was down to about three hundred," one union source later told *The New York Times*. "You have no idea how close we were to going out of business." According to the NFLPA's Labor Department Annual Report for the period ending November 30, 1976, the union had net assets of minus $233,975, a net loss of almost $1 million since the 1974 strike. While Garvey considered the appeals court decision a "victory," talks with the League resumed before Christmas.

The talks commenced in Washington, D.C., where the union had offices in the Machinists Building. The site was Room 1507 of the Madison Hotel, a suite decorated with red velvet wallpaper. Both sides were well aware of past failures in similar situations. "If you absolutely do not trust them," Garvey explained to *Sports Illustrated,* "and they do not trust you, then you can't get a settlement." The Management Council's chief negotiator, attorney Sargent Karch, arrived with what he hoped would be a new approach. "Settling was just a matter of trust," Karch remembered. "Everybody assumed we could not agree because of Garvey, so I started to think in terms of what was important to Garvey and the union."

The approach began with a somewhat different interpretation of Ed Garvey's position. "We reasoned that the Rozelle Rule . . . was *not* all that important to Garvey," Karch explained. "Getting rid of the Rozelle Rule would help the wealthy players at the expense of the poor ones. The way we began to view it, the Rozelle Rule [was] simply the way Garvey was getting his leverage and he was getting more leverage with every court decision. Then we concluded that three things were important to Garvey: 1) the strength of his union, 2) outside arbitration of player grievances . . . and 3) cash settlements of the lawsuits striking down the Rozelle Rule. . . . I decided to make a last try with Garvey and bring up these three issues. As soon as we started to make sense with Garvey, Garvey started making sense with us."

"For the first time," Garvey agreed, "there was a discussion of things we wanted to talk about instead of just what they wanted to talk about. The whole struggle was to get them to bargain. They'd never bargained before."

The meeting in Room 1507 went well and at its conclusion, Garvey expressed pleasure with their progress. "Sarge," he said to Karch, "I hope you're not kidding me."

"When Ed said that," Karch remembered, "it told me a lot. It was then that I knew a settlement was possible."

More discussions followed in New Orleans in January 1977, and those, too, went swimmingly. Both sides arrived back at Washington's Madison Hotel for a "final" session in February amid predictions that an agreement would be reached by February 15. On February 9, however, everything seemed to come apart. That afternoon, "angered by the owners' sudden refusal to discuss the major issues," Garvey walked out of bargaining sessions and returned to his nearby office. He would later credit Dan Rooney with salvaging the situation. Rooney walked over to NFLPA headquarters shortly after Garvey got there and began talking to him, one-to-one. When dinnertime was reached, the two men adjourned to a nearby steak house and were joined by Karch and two members of the union's negotiating team. "It was the first time we'd ever broken bread together," Garvey remembered. "We managed to talk over a good many things informally and by the time we paid our own checks, we'd gotten back on the track."

Shortly before midnight on February 16, 1977, the two sides agreed on a seventy-six-page contract, ending the longest labor war in football business history.

Perhaps the greatest concession gained by the union was status as what Dan Rooney called "a full-fledged National Labor Relations Board union, an agency shop where you have to pay dues even if you don't join. It was significant to the union," Rooney noted, "and a major issue among the owners. There were some who fought it all the way and there was much argument. I told them, 'We will maintain the system, we will continue to operate. The union will play a bigger role and that is just the way it will be. It's a fact.' "

The union also won concessions on Rozelle's authority over player grievances, a $107-million package of benefits spread over the five-year life of the contract, and a number of the "freedom issues" with which the strike had begun. Henceforth, players would be allowed to have private phones at their own expense when in training camp and the League would have "no arbitrary hair or dress codes." In addition, the NFL would pay $13.65 million over ten years to settle the damages arising from *Mackey v. NFL*. This money would be distributed among some 3,200 active and former players according to a system devised by the union and based on seniority. Payments would range from $147 to $16,500 apiece.

In return, the National Football League Players Association accepted the Rozelle Rule, completely abandoning the free agency it had won little more than a year earlier, and making the NFL's system once again legal. It was the most controversial concession Ed Garvey could have made. One player's agent would later describe the move as "the biggest sellout by a union in sports history." Garvey, however, considered it worth it.

As did Pete Rozelle. Almost three years of continuous external warfare were over and, at last, it seemed as though the forces of "stability" were again on the rise.

28

While both sides were still digesting the appeals court decision in *Mackey v. NFL,* at a New England Patriots stockholders meeting in Schaeffer Stadium on December 8, 1976, the Sullivans eliminated the last publicly traded stock in the National Football League and, under the direction of his son, Chuck, redeemed Billy's ten-year-old ownership policy promises in full. From Rozelle's point of view "stability" in the New England franchise was now "assured."

Chuck Sullivan's phase two had not, however, been easy to pull off. The younger Sullivan would eventually be known throughout the National Football League for his capacity "to get things done," especially where banks were involved, and that reputation was first earned in the last six months of 1976.

The Sullivans' problems began arising when H.B. 5133, reducing the Massachusetts requirements for corporate mergers to 50.1 percent, reached the desk of Governor Michael Dukakis in August. Though they were both on the same political side, the relationship between Dukakis and the Sullivans was uncomfortable. In 1974, when Dukakis was the Democratic party's candidate, Billy had publicly snubbed him at a large party fund-raiser, embarrassing everybody there except perhaps himself. While that didn't by any means ruin the Sullivans' chances for getting Dukakis's signature, there was also increasing opposition to the measure, led by the Boston Bar Association and the Associated Industries of Massachusetts, both of whom had written Dukakis asking him to block H.B. 5133. "House 5133," Associated Industries complained, "would make a major change in the rules of the game which apply to all Massachusetts business corporations for the benefit of perhaps a single party." The Associated Industries of Massachusetts did not need to specify who that "single party" was. "There was tremendous pressure on everyone up there to get this done for Billy Sullivan," one state politician told *The Boston Globe*. "Everyone was in line."

While Chuck Sullivan was confident his family had the juice to secure the governor's signature, timing remained a problem. His father's promissory note to LaSalle National Bank and Rhode Island Hospital Trust had required Billy to pledge the entire Patriots franchise as additional collateral by October 1, 1976. The deadline for accomplishing his "freezeout" was rapidly approaching. Without it, a Rhode Island Hospital Trust vice-president noted, "the loan to Mr. Sullivan cannot be supported." In response to that urgency, the Massachusetts Senate had added a provision to H.B. 5133 making it effective on September 18, 1976. The House, however, struck down that provision, meaning the bill would not become law until ninety days after the governor signed it. Dukakis did so on August 29 but it would not be available for Chuck Sullivan to use until November 26.

As a consequence, the Sullivans were thrown on to the mercy of their banks, a front on which things were not going all that smoothly. Not only did it look as though the Sullivans would miss their deadline, but to finance phase two, LaSalle National Bank and Rhode Island Hospital Trust were to loan Billy another $1.4 million with which to make the bulk of the nonvoting share buyout, and the banks were getting more nervous about their money every week.

Prior to H.B. 5133 becoming law, the banks' principal worry stemmed from Rule 10 (B) (5) of the Federal Securities and Exchange Act. To comply with it, a Rhode Island Hospital Trust senior vice-president noted, "The purchaser must make full and complete disclosure of all facets of the proposed merger," including the corporate purpose for the buyout and the value of the stock if the company were liquidated. The minority stockholders also had the right, even if the deal went through, to sue for the face value of their stock. It was this, Rhode Island Hospital Trust's senior vice-president emphasized, that "causes us the most concern."

On July 30, 1976, that concern was the subject of an internal memo circulated at Rhode Island's highest levels. The memo was developed in response to Chuck Sullivan's initial draft of the prospectus making the required disclosures that would have to accompany all proxy material provided stockholders in the course of the merger. The proposed price was fifteen dollars a share and among the "corporate purposes" allegedly served by eliminating the minority shareholders was compliance with National Football League ownership policy prohibitions of publicly traded stock. "After much careful consideration by counsel for the banks," the memo reported, "it was felt that the business reasons for the merger as set forth in the preliminary copy of the proxy material were misleading as stated because they inferred that the NFL was requiring the Patriots to 'go private.' " In addition, since "the Patriots could reasonably be expected to sell for $12–14,000,000 . . . on a pari passu sharing of the proceeds, the [nonvoting] stock would have a value of fifty to sixty dollars a share. Thus the validity of a fifteen-dollar-per-share offering price is questionable." To Hospital Trust, the shortfall posed an enormous dilemma. "To make the necessary disclosures to the public holders of the [nonvoting] stock pertaining to the value of their stock," the memo gloomily concluded, "would probably kill Sullivan's proposed merger." With it would die the security on Hospital Trust's loan.

Chuck Sullivan was unfazed. "All you have there," he pointed out, "is the opinion of some of the attorneys involved with the banks. We had our own opinions of our own attorneys. We did not try to hide anything. In our opinion, and that of our counsel, everything was put into the proxy statement that should have been there."

On September 8, Sullivan submitted his draft to the SEC. On September 17, they returned to him a six-page list of recommended changes. Again, unfazed, Chuck complied and, though the SEC would eventually investigate the buyout after the fact, nothing it found would be considered actionable.

Reaction among the actual holders of nonvoting shares was decidedly mixed. By November, angry letters had begun arriving at the Patriots' offices in Foxboro. One stockholder, having done an elaborate calculation of the worth of the franchise, concluded that the fifteen-dollar offering price meant the Sullivans were attempting to buy "a $16,000,000 franchise for the total price of $6,743,637." Another angry holder of twenty-five shares declared, "You can tell the Sullivans to go to hell; my stock is not for sale at any price."

By then, the legal worries of LaSalle and Hospital Trust national banks had been enlarged to include the impact of H.B. 5133. The law made it considerably easier for Chuck Sullivan to pull off his phase two, but it also created a dilemma for the banks, which had assumed a vote of sixty-seven percent would be required and "were relying heavily on that protection" in their commitment to loan the Sullivans another $1.4 million. Now, their loan was more legally exposed than ever. The exposure, they worried, would enlarge even further if Billy voted the 11,026 shares of public stock he either owned or controlled. "In the harsh glare of publicity surrounding the recent amendment to the Massachusetts statute," a September memo to Hospital Trust's president advised, "an approval of the merger by a bare majority, particularly if it includes 'insider' votes, gives reason to fear." On September 17, LaSalle National Bank, Sullivan's lead lender, modified its agreement so that it and Hospital Trust would be held free of any possible litigation in the merger. In addition, the banks insisted Sullivan not vote the stock he controlled until after a majority of the publicly traded shares had already been reached.

By October, Billy Sullivan was complaining bitterly. In conversations with LaSalle and Hospital Trust, he claimed the restrictions "would be extremely detrimental to the success of the transaction." On October 8, after a day on the phone with Billy, LaSalle had worked out an agreement "that language would be developed for the proxy that stated that the banks reserved the right to require, but may not actually exercise this right . . . that a majority of outsiders be obtained before the Sullivans vote their nonvoting stock." This compromise lasted less than a month.

On October 28, twenty-eight days after the original deadline had passed, the financing Chuck Sullivan had carefully marshaled for phase two of his father's comeback collapsed. Late that afternoon, LaSalle's executive vice-president called his Hospital Trust counterpart and told him LaSalle "did not wish to continue further in the recapitalization financing." LaSalle's next phone call was to Chuck Sullivan, breaking the bad news. Sullivan, according to a Hospital Trust internal memo, "took the news calmly." He asked if this meant LaSalle was demanding repayment of his father's outstanding loan. The executive vice-president responded that "he hadn't come to that point, but would be studying his bank's position" over the next few days. Chuck's only response was that he would find another bank. At the moment, LaSalle didn't press the issue.

Despite their actions, both LaSalle and Hospital Trust's vice-presidents wanted to give the Sullivans room to save their merger. "LaSalle and we will assess the situation," Hospital Trust's representative noted the following day, "hopefully to the satisfaction of the Sullivans. We both like them very much."

Good will or not, Chuck Sullivan had reached the most perilous position of his entire venture, a moment when the financial structure he had created was quivering. He now not only had to find a new $1.4 million to buy out the nonvoting shares, he also had to find someone to take over the debt left from buying out the voting shares a year earlier. A vote on the Patriots merger was scheduled for December 8, though; if successful, the Sullivans wouldn't actually need the additional $1.4 million until the following spring. In the meantime, he had to keep the existing note from being called.

By November 8, Chuck had convinced LaSalle and Hospital Trust to agree that, while "reserving the right to demand payment on the Note at any time, in order to enable the Patriots to proceed with alternative financing plans, the Banks confirm that they do not have any present intention of demanding payment." In a matter of days, Sullivan was assuring LaSalle and Hospital Trust that First National Bank of Chicago was going to "come in," but the details still had to be worked out. That was welcome news to Hospital Trust. They were worried that a lawsuit might arise as a consequence of the December 8 meeting and wanted to be sure they had a way out. On November 19, the bank's president spoke to Chuck Sullivan on the phone in New York and "indicated that we were rather interested in what kinds of arrangements had been made with the First of Chicago concerning our payout." Sullivan told him that he had "no specific commitment," but that "as soon as the merger is completed [December 8], negotiations in that regard would proceed forthwith. He felt it would be safe to plan a payout by March 31, although he did not feel he could guaranty [sic] it. In his opinion, the possibility of a suit occuring [sic] after the date of the merger, but before the payout, would not mess up the deal."

Chuck Sullivan's placid brushoff did not satisfy the vice-president with whom he had the most dealings. Now there was no talk of "liking the Sullivans very much." Instead, his memo worried about the threat posed by a possible lawsuit and concluded, "As I see it, we stand to lose nothing except the goodwill of the Sullivans . . . if we take a strong stance and clearly get across the message to Chuck that a call of Billy's loan, prior to the merger date, is a realistic possibility unless Chuck can get us a definite written commitment from First of Chicago prior to December 8."

"Realistic possibility" or not, the loan was not called in and on December 8, Chuck Sullivan arrived at the New England Patriots' stockholders meeting in Schaeffer Stadium's largest conference room with his father's financing intact. The meeting was presided over by Billy. Less than one hundred of the twenty-six hundred stockholders attended. A number spoke against the merger, a few spoke in favor. Then the counting of proxies began. Fittingly, it was Chuck Sullivan who announced the results. "The shareholders," he intoned, had "approved a plan of corporate restructuring."

The public credit was all Chuck's. "I don't care for the guy," one of his father's former partners allowed, "but I do admire the way he pulled the whole thing off. This is his deal all the way."

If Chuck himself gave credit, it was in private and likely included a large measure of gratitude to H.B. 5133. The final vote was 84,470 in favor, 34,535 opposed, and 22,795 abstaining. Billy's almost 11,000 shares were voted in the affirmative. With them, the total majority approving the merger was 59 percent. Without them, it was 51.2 percent. Under the Massachusetts corporate statutes that had been in effect until only twelve days earlier, Billy Sullivan's comeback would have collapsed on his son's head, eight percent short of success.

If the Sullivans were grateful to H.B. 5133, their attitude bred no attachment to the statute once it had served its purpose. The Massachusetts merger laws would be changed back to two thirds again in 1981 and the Sullivans would make no protest. At the time, the principal question would be why the reversal had taken so long. "What happened with the bill for the Patriots," one Boston politician explained, "was an embarrassment to a lot of people. Everyone knew what happened and they didn't want to be further embarrassed by changing it back the next year." As it was, the *Boston Herald* described Chuck's 1976 margin of victory a "substantial majority."

The actual payout to effect the merger began before Christmas, using $1.4 million from the First National Bank of Chicago. Within three months, LaSalle, Rhode Island Hospital Trust, and the First of Chicago would all be paid off by a new loan from Industrial National Bank of Rhode Island. The Industrial of Rhode Island loan was at lower interest rates and, according to Chuck, "we ended up with a better situation all around." By then, Chuck Sullivan's burgeoning reputation for finance had made him a rising NFL star in his own right.

Just as LaSalle and Hospital Trust had predicted, several lawsuits would be filed to force the Sullivans to give the stock back, but, just as Chuck had predicted, none of them would prove sufficient to do so. They would, however, take almost another ten years to resolve.

For its part, the National Football League approved the 1976 transaction in short order.

29

If there was any omen of the NFL's future as 1976 turned to 1977, it was the presence of Al Davis and his Raiders in the January 9 Super Bowl XI. The next round of turmoil in the football business would make the previous three years seem tame and Al Davis would be one of those at the heart of the disorder.

For Davis, Super Bowl XI was a personal landmark. His team had played and lost in Super Bowl II and since then, he had not been back, though over that time the Raiders had accumulated the best record in the League. Fittingly, victory came at the end of the first season during which control of the Oakland franchise had been Davis's alone. Wayne Valley was now history, someone Al had beaten and dispensed with. Just as fittingly, the Raiders reached the Super Bowl by thrashing Dan Rooney's Pittsburgh Steelers, his current courtroom adversaries, 24–7 in the conference championship game. The question of why it had taken him so long to reach the Super Bowl was still, however, a sensitive subject. As hoopla for the "Game of Games" mounted, *Newsweek* noted, "Al's boiling mix of ego, tunnel vision, and genius demands that he play down the Super Bowl just a bit."

"Isn't it great to be on top?" someone asked him.

"We've been on top for a long time," Davis snapped.

While his fellow owners might well have disputed the claim, there was no dispute as to what "the top" was. Super Bowl Sunday was the culmination of a four-month period during which an estimated nine billion American manhours had been spent watching the NFL. Super Bowl Sunday was also the biggest single day of the year for bookies and an estimated $260 million would be wagered one way or another. This year's game was being held in Pasadena's Rose Bowl, east of Los Angeles. Over 100,000 people would attend and for the week preceding the game, a ticket to do so was the hottest item in the United States.

Those tickets were also an item of sharp contention inside the League.

The first issue was, of course, their allocation. As of yet, the League had no set formula for distributing tickets to its newly minted classic, so tickets for each Super Bowl were allocated at the preceding year's annual meeting. That allocation had been made on March 16, 1976, in general session in San Diego, and was, in Al Davis's eyes, "unique" and "unheard of." As approved unanimously, each of the twenty-six teams not playing in the game would be given 1,000 tickets apiece, each of the two participating teams would get 15,000, while 10,000 were allocated to the League office, and 8,000 offered for public sale. What Davis found "unique" was that the remaining 30,000 highly prized tickets were all allocated to the host franchise, Carroll Rosenbloom's Los Angeles Rams. Just a day after charging him with "stealing from his partners," the League gave C.R. enough tickets to make it Carroll's Super Bowl, whether his team got there or not.

Al Davis was especially irritated that the League office had "upped their ante for Super Bowl tickets" as well. "The commissioner," Davis later testified, "made a plea that he needed them for Congress. He needed them for people who are sponsors at Super Bowl games, people who are sponsors of our television, and he needed it for League office reasons, for [NFL] Properties, for charities. I began to see that the people who were getting all the Super Bowl tickets were the host city and the commissioner's office, and the two competing teams who might need the most tickets were given an allocation just to satisfy them and keep them in place."

The second issue associated with Super Bowl tickets was their price. Despite being the hottest tickets in the country, their face value was just twenty dollars. As a consequence, scalpers were peddling them for ten and twenty times as much. The bulk of that profiteering was done through travel agencies packaging tours that included a seat for the game. A number of owners wanted to get a piece of that action themselves by upping the ticket's face value, but Pete Rozelle considered it bad public relations and kept the price down. "As far back as 1974," Davis remembered, "different owners in our League have stood up at League meetings and asked why the commissioner has not raised ticket prices for the Super Bowl commensurate with the demand for those Super Bowl tickets. That they were being priced way too low and why was he not raising ticket prices. . . . I remember Lamar Hunt standing up and saying, 'We are selling a twenty-dollar ticket that should be fifty.' And I remember asking one owner in a League meeting, 'Why the hell doesn't he do it?' . . . And the commissioner would always give some far out answer about [how] we don't want to gouge. We don't want to give the country the feeling that we are trying to take advantage of them, and then people would stand up and say yes, but we are not gouging. Everyone else is making a fortune on the sale of Super Bowl tickets from money above the face value. . . . A lot of the tour agencies are making a lot of money on these Super Bowl tickets." At San Diego, the same people had said the same things and the prices remained the same.

In the first week of January 1977, after his Raiders had whipped Rooney's team and were headed for Pasadena, Super Bowl tickets became a source of direct contention between Davis and Rozelle. "At that time," Davis remembered, "I called the commissioner and I said, 'Listen. I have got a tremendous problem here. We have got a minimum amount of tickets. We have a demand that is unbelievable. The fans are in an uproar. I need some more Super Bowl tickets. . . . You have got enough. I don't know why you need as many as you got and certainly the Rams don't need as many as they got, and I would like an allocation of about another three to four thousand Super Bowl tickets.' I told him that if I were playing in Miami, I would understand the amount we were getting. We were playing in Pasadena, which is a short plane trip . . . for our fans, and they wanted tickets. The press was on us tremendously.''

Rozelle, Davis recalled, said ''he would see what he could do about it.''

Two hours later, the commissioner called Davis back and told him he could arrange a ''loan'' of two hundred tickets from Steve Rosenbloom at the Rams.

''What about the League office?'' Davis demanded.

Rozelle said all theirs were gone.

''As commissioner, you do an awful lot of things for 'the good of pro football,' '' the Raiders owner complained. ''You should get us more tickets.''

Rozelle repeated that the Rams would loan him two hundred.

''I was upset,'' Davis remembered, ''[but] I took the two hundred tickets.''

Al Davis would later claim to have been even more upset when he found out just what Carroll Rosenbloom was doing with his ''unheard of'' thirty thousand-seat allotment. It became the subject of a phone conversation between the two men shortly after Oakland's triumph over Pittsburgh. Super Bowl XI had almost been a head-to-head match-up between the two friends, but Rosenbloom's Rams had again fallen short in the conference championship, losing 24–13 to Max Winter's Minnesota Vikings. Had they won, Rosenbloom would have had forty-five thousand seats, almost half the Super Bowl's live gate, at his disposal. As it was, according to Davis, Rosenbloom ''asked me what I was going to do with [the Raiders'] tickets, and I said we are going to give them to our fans, give them to the people we thought were necessary to give them to.''

''What are you going to sell them for?'' C.R. asked.

Davis replied, ''Face value.''

Rosenbloom objected that he was a fool to do so. ''Look,'' the Rams owner offered, ''I have a guy who knows how to handle this. He knows how to market these tickets. We could make a fortune.''

''I said I wouldn't do it, and was committed to go ahead the way we were doing it, and I was quite shocked about it,'' Davis claimed. ''I asked him who the guy was and he said it was a fellow by the name of Harold Guiver. . . . Carroll said Guiver owned a ticket agency.'' Davis also wondered what C.R. planned to do about Rozelle's response. ''You're going to get in a lot of trouble,'' he pointed out.

Rosenbloom, in the derisive tone he used when mentioning the commissioner, asked if Davis was kidding. ''Rozelle is in this up to his neck,'' C.R. claimed. ''He knows what is going on. This is where he makes his big score.''

After the Super Bowl was over, Davis later testified, Rosenbloom would call him again. This time, ''he talked to me about what he had done with the Super Bowl tickets that had been allocated to the host city . . . and told me they made a killing.''

''For Christ's sake, Carroll,'' Davis responded, ''you got a lot of guts.''

''This time again,'' the Oakland owner remembered, Rosenbloom said in roundabout words that Rozelle ''is in this up to his neck. He knows what is going on. What is he going to do about it? He knows about the scalping. He knows about the travel agencies who are making a fortune. . . . He is well aware of it. We talked about it at League meetings. He has never done a thing about it.''

"I was just shocked about it," Davis repeated. "I was then told that other owners are in the travel agency business . . . and that they are using their tickets for their travel agencies. He wanted to know if I would like to start a travel agency. . . . I told him, no, that I didn't want to get involved in it. I didn't want any part of it, and we talked a lot more about the sale of Super Bowl tickets and how much money you could make on it, and I was again led to believe that the commissioner knew about it, was in up to his neck, and was using these tickets not only for his self-gain, but as a way of getting around people throughout the country." Despite his protestations, Davis would fly down to L.A. to discuss the travel agency idea with Carroll face-to-face, but nothing would ever come of it.

It would be almost four years until Al Davis told anyone about C.R.'s 1977 charges against Rozelle. By that time, Carroll Rosenbloom would be dead and the struggle between Al Davis and Pete Rozelle had reached the no-holds-barred stage and gone public. Rozelle would deny every one of the charges and Davis's accompanying insinuations.

At the time of the original conversation, Al Davis said nothing. Indeed, to the public frantically consuming miles of copy and videotape in advance of Super Bowl XI, he was most conspicuous by his invisibility. While Pete Rozelle was throwing a $100,000 party for some two thousand members of the press, Davis was off somewhere in a room that smelled of sweat socks, watching film and diagraming plays. "I have no roundness in my life," he admitted. "I've got to be all football, all sharp edges. If I want something else, I've got to find time at two in the morning."

On the morning of Super Bowl Sunday, he was spotted loitering around the sidelines before anyone but the TV crews had entered the stadium.

"Where have you been?" a reporter asked.

"Aw, you know me," Davis joked. "If I come around, I say something controversial, and the commissioner doesn't get the headlines."

When the game actually began, Al Davis was in his traditional seat in one corner of the press box, jaw clenched, wearing sunglasses with his eyes glued to the field. By halftime, his Raiders led 16–0. With five minutes left to play, the score was 32–7. At that point, *Newsweek* reported, "reporters and well-wishers began to swarm around Davis. They grabbed his hand and slapped his back, probed at him with microphones and even spilled coffee on the ledge in front of him. Aides scurried to clean and shield their dictator's territory. But Davis's gaze never left the field.

"I don't want to lose track of the game," he snapped.

"Hey, Al, congratulations," someone shouted. "Your team's playing great. Really super."

"What bullshit," Davis muttered, eyes still riveted to the game below.

When the final whistle blew with the score 32–14, Al Davis hurried to the Rose Bowl locker room to celebrate with the team and accept the Super Bowl trophy from Pete Rozelle under the TV lights set up there.

Though it never dented his appearance, it must have been a nervous moment for Rozelle. On the other side of the lights, Raiders, covered with turf stains and adhesive tape, were pouring champagne on each other and jumping up and down. Among them, George Atkinson, official plaintiff in *Atkinson v. Noll,* was delivering "a vividly worded diatribe" against the commissioner for everyone to hear. For his part, Davis had the look of a man standing right where he knew he would always be.

"I'm sorry it's not silver and black," the commissioner joked as he handed over the two-foot-tall pedestal topped with a silver football, "but it's close. Al, your victory was one of the most impressive in football history."

Taking the trophy, Davis was exultant. "This is magnificent," he crowed. "I said we'd get it someday and we have." After the obligatory thanking of everyone in the Raider organization, he then addressed the issue of Oakland's fans. "What concerns me," he said, "are the season ticket holders we had to leave home. I'm going to push for more tickets when a Super Bowl team comes from a city near the site. That we upset some of our loyal fans is the only negative part of this whole thing. I hope the fans will forgive us."

It was, of course, a dig at Pete Rozelle, but such was the state of the National Football League's internal politics in January 1977 that only Al Davis, Carroll Rosenbloom, and Pete Rozelle knew it.

Over the next six years, Rozelle would make two more such trophy presentations to Al Davis. With each, the scene would only get more difficult and its portent more dark.

PART THREE
THE
POT
BOILS

1

When the National Football League convened its 1977 annual meeting on March 28 at the Arizona Biltmore in Phoenix, the football business was on the verge of the most damaging sequence of internal struggles in its history, but again, no one seemed to notice. After three years of open warfare with the World Football League, and with Ed Garvey and the players association, the League's own politics seemed little more than random skirmishing of a familiar type. The worries expressed by the commissioner for public consumption still focused largely on the war just gone by. "There have been some negative feelings toward us that began during that turbulent period when new leagues were started," he pointed out to *Sport* magazine. "From that you've had player movement, you've had strikes, you've had a number of things that were turn-offs, but I think we pretty much nipped it in the bud."

In Phoenix, Rozelle's opening "annual report and year's review" was bulging with superlatives. Paid attendance for the previous season had "exceeded eleven million for the first time in history," he noted, "while per game average attendance of 56,582 was the third highest in League history. Overall attendance for regular season, post and preseason was 15,071,846, second only to the record year of 1973." The numbers for television were just as staggering. Among the records produced were "the highest rated Super Bowl game ever," the "highest rated Sunday game ever," the "two highest rated Monday night games ever," and "the highest rated divisional playoff game ever." The Neilsen ratings for Super Bowl XI were 31 million homes, an estimated audience of 81.9 million. Despite all those numbers, the greatest accomplishment of the previous year in Rozelle's eyes was the agreement reached with the NFLPA. "The negotiated agreement," the commissioner reported, "paves the way for intelligent planning and implementation of steps to solidify the franchises and the League."

One of the steps already taken to "solidify" the League was the rewriting of Pete Rozelle's contract as commissioner. The process had begun at a special meeting in the League's Park Avenue office the previous December. There, the owners had created a three-man committee "to negotiate a new long-term contract" with Rozelle. Leonard Tose was named its chairman. The other members were Gene Klein and Herman Sarkowsky, representing Seattle. In the public statement issued at the time, Tose "emphasized that the club owners said their action should be viewed as a strong reaffirmation of the authority of the commissioner in the operation and administration of all phases of the National Football League." The committee's charge was "to meet with the commissioner and work out the specific details." By January

16, they had: a special meeting in Seattle approved a new ten-year contract for Rozelle by a vote of twenty-seven to one. Though the financial terms were not released to the public, it was described by one owner as "another handsome increase." To no one's surprise, the one vote against this "strong reaffirmation" of Rozelle's authority had been cast by Al Davis.

The relationship between Davis and the commissioner was, by now, volatile at best. Rozelle thought Davis needed a comeuppance, and Davis felt much the same way about Rozelle. The antagonism was not lost on the rest of the League, but most still tended to look past Al Davis toward Carroll Rosenbloom when fearing trouble. Al Davis's free-lancing continued to be measured on a scale of personal eccentricity rather than political threat, despite Dan Rooney's repeated warnings to the contrary. Rozelle himself was convinced Davis's transgressions would have to be dealt with by the commissioner and in no uncertain terms. Pete Rozelle had arrived in Phoenix prepared to begin putting the Raiders' managing general partner in his place.

First, Rozelle took steps to cover his own flank. Stung by Davis's Super Bowl barbs about ticket allocation, Rozelle realized that a standardized formula for dividing up Super Bowl tickets would considerably reduce the issue's explosiveness, and on the first day of the 1977 annual meeting, such a proposal was put forward by Herman Sarkowsky and Billy Sullivan. It was among the "steps to solidify the League" the commissioner had heralded in his opening address. Sarkowsky's proposal allocated one percent to each of the League's twenty-six nonparticipants, ten percent to the League office, twenty-four percent to the host city, and twenty percent to each of the participants. The measure passed twenty-one to seven, reaching the required three quarters majority despite the opposition of Davis, Lamar Hunt, Leonard Tose, Gene Klein, Dan Rooney, and Tex Schramm.

Three days later, Rozelle laid the groundwork for his move on Davis, though the step seemed innocuous at the time. On the morning of March 31, according to the minutes, "the member clubs approved by unanimous vote an expression of policy regarding the standing League committees as follows: The commissioner will in consultation with the conference presidents appoint standing committees of the League and would make replacements on an irregular rotation basis." Judging from the reported vote, the import of the expression of policy was lost, even on the wily Davis. It was apparently June before Davis heard Rozelle's footsteps, and then only when Rozelle himself "disclosed that the new owners' committee assignments were being discussed . . . and would be drawn and distributed to member clubs shortly." The March 31 expression of policy formally confirmed the commissioner's power to "irregularly rotate" owners. When it was passed, Rozelle was already preparing to use that power in a dramatic fashion. His target was Al Davis's seat on the powerful Competition Committee.

The Competition Committee, chaired by Tex Schramm, was charged with "recommending all changes in rules in the area of on the field competition." Its purview also included scheduling, roster sizes, and the trading and waiving of players—a majority of the actual mechanics of the football business. One of those most impressed with Davis's contribution there was Schramm, and the two men had formed a close working relationship. "Tex and Al had a good time working on rules together," Rozelle remembered, "but people on a committee should be thinking for the League, what's best for the League. Al had dropped out of NFL Charities, was suing another club using George Atkinson as a straw man, and played a role in the failure of the Anderson-Rooney agreement." In Rozelle's eyes, Davis was using his role on the committee to "give validity to positions contrary to League policy." According to one NFL executive, Rozelle intended to put a stop to it.

Pete Rozelle had made his reputation by getting along, but in spring 1977, he was not looking to smooth things over with Al Davis. The competition committee was the one thing Al Davis wanted that Pete Rozelle could deny him and Rozelle seemed to have no doubts about doing so. If theirs was a fight that Davis made, as Rozelle would later claim, it was also a fight Rozelle chose not to avoid. Such was the intensity of Rozelle's intentions that he did not bother to consult Schramm, "Mr. Vice-Commissioner," about them in advance. In all other instances of the removal of owners from committees, Pete had always talked it over with Tex. This time, Schramm was left in the dark. When the Cowboys president learned of the move, he would publicly describe it as a "disservice" to his committee and to the League. "Tex," Rozelle remembered, "was mad about it." Rozelle had known he would be, but proceeded nonetheless.

At the 1977 annual meeting, Al Davis, like Schramm, was still unaware of what was coming. In principle, however, he no doubt welcomed trading blows with the commissioner. He had bested Rozelle the last time they fought and had great confidence in his ability to do so again. Rozelle's blow would sting when it finally fell, but the impact would only seem to reinforce Davis's contempt and belligerence. "He took me off the Competition Committee," Davis remembered. "Never faced me man to man and told me. Just did it, and then leaked it to the press so that . . . it would be a big story, make him strong."

In March 1977, Al Davis already assumed the commissioner's ill will, but made no moves of his own to reduce it. His first Super Bowl victory had not mellowed him. "You've got to go on," he pointed out. "You keep fighting." He still watched miles of game footage and still saw things his coaches had missed. Even when out to dinner with his wife, Carol, and friends, he often ended up diagraming plays on the tablecloth. Al refused to patronize restaurants in which there was no phone to bring to his table and still spent a huge portion of his day on the line. Davis even bought an interest in a restaurant near the Raiders' practice field to insure he would always have a place nearby where he could both eat and talk on the phone. To relax, he lifted weights, drank ice water, and attended sporting events. "The dictator hasn't lost his drive," The [Oakland] Tribune noted.

Inside the Raider organization, Davis now called all the shots. He still had Ed McGah for a general partner and a dozen or so limited partners as well, but all that meant in practical fact was that he had to pay lip service to an annual meeting. His principal lieutenant was Al LoCasale, a stumpy man who had been with Davis at the San Diego Chargers when Davis was still an assistant coach. "LoCasale was a strong manager," a Davis acquaintance observed. "He took a lot of the day-to-day weight off Al's shoulders without being a threat. LoCasale was a smart man who made himself a very strong colonel to Davis's general. He became Al's voice to the public when Al himself didn't feel like talking. As Al rose in stature, he used LoCasale more and more. LoCasale made himself conversant with Davis's views and made himself a second voice. There was not, however, any doubt about who was in charge."

Davis's organizational model was apparently Germanic. "He was a great admirer of Hitler and the Nazis," Davis's former partner Wayne Valley remembered. "He and I would have these conversations and he'd call them 'a great organization' that 'drove their point home.' "

Given that he was Jewish, Davis's admiration was all the more remarkable. "I didn't hate Hitler," Davis explained. "I was captivated by him. I knew he had to be stopped. He took on the whole world." Al Davis's religion was, like the rest of him, personal and free-lance. "Al was barely conversant in Judaism," one Davis intimate remembered. "It was a personal thing that was largely a reaction to his father's death while he was still in San Diego, before the Raiders. It was somehow a pull on his religious beliefs. He used to say that if he had been there, he could have saved his father. It reaffirmed to Al that if he had been closer to his father, closer to God, he would have known what to do to pull his father through. To my knowledge the only day you can be sure Al will make it to a synagogue is the anniversary of his father's death." Whatever the particulars of Al Davis's theology, it made him neither self-conscious nor timid. "Al was a slick son of a bitch," one of his friends pointed out. "When he wanted to do something, he found a way to do it. I sure wouldn't want to get in a fight with him. He just doesn't back off."

That Al Davis had no intentions of now smoothing Rozelle's feathers was apparent on April 1, when the 1977 annual meeting discussed "the various commitments made to NFL Charities by various clubs." Davis made it clear he intended to continue "requesting receipt of royalties" from NFL Properties "rather than contributing to Charities and would continue in that manner."

When later asked to explain Davis's continued refusal, Rozelle offered, "Because I suggested it."

The rest of the League no doubt agreed with the commissioner's analysis to one degree or another, but on April Fool's Day 1977, few were yet prepared to give Davis's attitude the significance it deserved.

2

The item on the 1977 annual meeting's agenda that drew the most attention was the admission of a new member. The San Francisco 49er franchise was being sold to one Edward DeBartolo Jr., and in Executive Session on the afternoon of March 28, formal League approval was sought to finalize the transaction. The sale had been gestating for more than a year and a half, and a number of familiar characters had been involved in the process.

The first of those was Wayne Valley, Al Davis's ex-partner. Lou Spadia, 49ers president, had notified the commissioner in the summer of 1975 that the Morabito sisters, heirs to the two brothers who had founded the club as part of the All-American Conference in the late 1940s, were looking to sell their ninety percent interest. When Valley decided to sell out his Raiders interest after *Valley v. Davis* had ended in stalemate that August, Rozelle approached Valley and asked if he would be interested in buying the 49ers. Valley's immediate response was "yes." By Christmas, it seemed Valley and Spadia had cut a deal. The price was $11.3 million cash. Valley, however, still had his doubts whether the sale would go through. The Morabitos' minority partner was one Franklin Meuli, owner of the Golden State Warriors professional basketball team, and the terms of Meuli's partnership gave him the right to block any sale by exercising his own rights of first refusal. Meuli, Valley pointed out, was a friend of Al Davis and Davis would not stand by while his ex-partner set up shop right across the bay.

Valley's prediction was on the mark. When word reached Oakland's managing general partner about the sale to Valley, according to *Sports Illustrated*, Davis "convinced" Franklin Meuli "to exercise his first refusal right." The effect of Davis's intervention was to stall the sale for almost a year while Meuli attempted to gather enough partners to make a formal offer. In April 1976, Rozelle tried to get Meuli and Valley together in the hope that the two of them might combine to buy the San Francisco franchise, but the attempt was ill-fated. A meeting was arranged but shortly after it began, according to Valley, Meuli stood up without explanation and left.

The episode was the last in Wayne Valley's football career. Rather than pursue the 49er opportunity, he decided to get out for good. "I talked to my wife about it," he remembered, "and she told me that if I wasn't having fun at it, not to buy. The fun had gone out of it and I didn't buy. The game had changed."

At this point, Al Davis explained, "Valley was knocked out of the purchase" and for the rest of 1976 Franklin Meuli held center stage. Meuli was a former advertising executive with little relative wealth and, though the

Morabito sisters' asking price was more than $4 million less than Leonard
Tose had paid for the Eagles seven years earlier, it was no secret by fall 1976
that Meuli was having difficulties raising capital. As his December 1 deadline
approached, Meuli even made overtures to Valley again, but Valley would
have none of it. Things were not going smoothly between Meuli and the NFL
office either. Rozelle was charged with investigating Meuli's suitability for
membership and Meuli's basketball team was a source of "significant concern."

The commissioner's most formal expression of that "concern" took
place in an October 8 telephone conversation with Meuli. Rozelle pointed out
that the League's continuing ownership policy resolution prohibited cross-
ownership by new members. "I did point out to him the problem presented by
his controlling interest in the basketball team," Rozelle remembered. It was a
critical issue, the commissioner continued, expressing his "ongoing displea-
sure" with "the Cooke situation" because "Mr. Cooke at that point had had
two years to eliminate his conflict and had not done so." Rozelle also
expressed "concern" about Lamar Hunt's continuing relationship to the
North American Soccer League and pointed out that Herman Sarkowsky,
managing partner of the new Seattle franchise, "had had to absent himself
from National Basketball Association meetings" as a condition of entering the
NFL and "immediately sell his equal interest in the basketball Trailblazers."
If Meuli wanted in, the commissioner observed, he would have to get out of
basketball as well.

The effect of Rozelle's conversation on Meuli was unclear, but on
December 1, 1976, Meuli failed to come forward with a solid offer and
disappeared from the picture. While Al Davis was glad Meuli had derailed
Wayne Valley, he was no doubt also pleased at the collapse of Meuli's
position. Davis's continuing problem with the 49er sale was the price. "It
was bigger than a Brinks deal," he pointed out. "The heist was on."

By the end of 1976, the price of football franchises had become an
unsettling issue throughout the NFL and, though most of the League still
preferred Wayne Valley, Davis had done them all a service by blocking the
$11.3 million offer. After close to two decades of continually rising franchise
values, something of a price panic had now set in, instigated by a new tax
law. Under the revised IRS code, only a maximum of fifty percent of any
sports franchise's purchase price could be ascribed to the value of its player
contracts and thus depreciated over a four-year period the tax law's definition
of a player's useful working life. "The new bill will reduce franchise values
substantially," one tax accountant predicted. "There's going to be less
interest in acquiring old franchises and less interest in setting up new ones."
Had the sale of the 49ers to Wayne Valley gone through, that prediction
would have been substantially proven and, on paper, everyone in the League
would have been worth $4 million less. Instead, Davis now moved to
confound the prediction entirely.

Shortly after the Super Bowl in January 1977, the attorney for the
Morabito sisters approached Davis and asked for his assistance in finding a
buyer. Davis proved ideal for the task. "Davis is a man who loves to move

behind the scenes," one Davis associate told the *San Francisco Chronicle*, "set things up, work out details—the more complex the better. This deal was a natural for him." The first buyer Davis produced was, in Davis's words, "not acceptable" and while he was considering other possible buyers, yet another familiar face entered the situation and completed the equation.

The new arrival was Joe Thomas, the man who'd brought Robert Irsay to Baltimore. The 1976 season had been the last one Thomas had worked for the man he'd once claimed to run. On January 20, 1977, two of Irsay's attorneys had walked into Thomas's office and informed him that if he didn't resign, he would be fired. Since Thomas still had a year to go on his contract, he refused and was fired. Back on the streets but undaunted, Thomas set out to find himself another owner. That the 49ers were on the block was by now somewhat common knowledge and in February, Thomas called Edward DeBartolo Sr. and asked if the Ohio construction magnate might be interested in buying the San Francisco NFL franchise. DeBartolo and Thomas had first met ten years earlier in Chicago and had ended up in a friendly three-hour conversation about the football business. DeBartolo had been impressed and the two had kept in touch. That February, DeBartolo told Thomas he would buy the San Francisco franchise only on the condition that Thomas would run it. Thomas was signed to a general manager's contract before negotiations for the purchase of the franchise had even begun. Thomas then approached Al Davis, asking his assistance. At the time, Davis claimed to have been on the verge of approaching DeBartolo himself.

Edward DeBartolo Sr. was already something of a familiar commodity in NFL circles, at least by reputation. He had been considered for Tampa's expansion team and, though he'd lost out to Tom McCloskey and then Hugh Culverhouse, he had impressed the League with his "financial clout." Called "the richest man in Ohio," *Forbes* would later estimate his net worth at "well over $500 million." DeBartolo had made almost all of it himself. Born in 1910 in Youngstown's Italian "hollow," DeBartolo's natural father had died of a heart attack three months before his birth. Taking the name of his stepfather, an immigrant paving contractor who neither read nor wrote, DeBartolo worked his way through Notre Dame and graduated with a degree in engineering. After winning a field commission with the Army Corps of Engineers in the Pacific during World War II, DeBartolo returned to his hometown and founded the Edward DeBartolo Corp., then a fledgling construction company.

By 1977, the DeBartolo Corp. was considered the largest developer in the United States, pioneer of both the shopping center and the enclosed shopping mall. Some seventy different companies in all parts of the country were under its overall umbrella, including thirty-four shopping complexes, a free trade port, four Holiday Inns, hundreds of acres of land, some gas wells, and three Florida banks. Edward DeBartolo ran it all from his Youngstown headquarters, working twelve to fifteen hours a day. His employees called him "The Boss" or "Mr. D." Soft-spoken, short, thin, and well-dressed, Mr. D had never taken a vacation in the history of his corporation. What time off he did take, he spent at home with his family. It was common for him to spend five hundred hours a year flying to his various projects. For short trips, he used a three-passenger Super Helio Courier that took off and landed from the grass field behind DeBartolo Corp.'s two-story brick headquarters. For longer trips, he kept a $1 million Learjet at the Youngstown Airport. He employed three pilots full-time.

DeBartolo's previous participation in sports had been largely through his corporation. DeBartolo Corp. had purchased, renovated, and revived Thistle-down racetrack outside Cleveland, Balmoral racetrack outside of Chicago, and Louisiana Downs near Shreveport, giving it collectively one of the largest betting handles in all of horse racing. It also owned the Pittsburgh Civic Arena. Mr. D's only personal holding was ownership of the Pittsburgh Penguins in the National Hockey League. Now sixty-seven years old, he did not intend to hold the 49ers franchise in his name. It was to be owned by his only son, Edward DeBartolo Jr., known as "Eddie." Thirty years old, Eddie was an officer of the DeBartolo Corp. and, along with his father, mother, and sister, one of the directors of the privately owned corporation. He would become the youngest owner in the NFL.

Like the senior DeBartolo, the junior lived in an enormous house outside Youngstown. Short and chubby, Eddie wore his dark hair thick and over his ears and could be seen driving around Youngstown in a corporation Cadillac. He had married his sweetheart from Youngstown's Cardinal Moo-ney High School in 1970, and his best friend was still a foundry worker with whom he'd hung out since he was a sophomore. Eddie wanted to be an athlete, but at five foot seven and 160 pounds, that was a frustrated yearning. "I didn't treat him like an altar boy," Mr. D pointed out. "He wasn't sheltered. I wanted him to face the world. He's a plain sort of person, like I am." He was also, according to the *San Francisco Examiner,* "a carbon copy of his father in avoiding people on the telephone, forgetting promises, and ducking those whose hopes he has raised through overzealous enthusiasm." Unlike his father, he took an occasional afternoon off for golf, and short vacations in the Caribbean and Las Vegas. The relationship between Eddie and Mr. D was, by all accounts, loving, and Eddie still kissed Mr. D whenever his father returned from one of his innumerable trips.

It was not, however, easy being Mr. D's heir apparent. "People say, 'Well, he got everything from his father,' " Eddie pointed out. "What am I supposed to say? That I wished my father hadn't been successful?" Eddie would later describe the self-imposed pressure of his position as "brutal. It almost broke up my marriage before I realized I can't fill those big shoes. I can't be Edward DeBartolo Sr. and I don't have to be. I have to carry on a tradition, not an identity, and I'll do it in a different way. My father has helped me overcome that pressure by letting me handle things my own way, to be my own man." Part of that process was buying the San Francisco 49ers. In the course of the actual purchase, however, it was Mr. D who carried the ball, so much so that both San Francisco papers would mistakenly identify him as "the new owner" when news of the sale broke. Joe Thomas, as promised, would be the new general manager, though he played almost no role in the actual purchase negotiations and would last little more than two years before being fired.

In this instance, the critical middleman between the DeBartolos and their football franchise was Al Davis. "I kind of brought them all together," Davis later explained, "and kind of advised both of them what I thought was fair." In another instance he would describe his role as "a consultant and conduit between the two parties. Mr. DeBartolo had enough faith in me to ask me to sit down in negotiations and I sat in . . . as we brought the transaction to fruition. . . . I think the transaction took approximately a month and I would say I spent ten to fifteen days on it." To handle the tax planning involved, Mr. D retained Tampa Buccaneer owner Hugh Culverhouse. In the deal's final structuring, the price to the DeBartolos for eighty percent of the franchise was some $18.2 million, placing the total value in the neighborhood of $21 million. For his services, Al Davis was paid a "consultant's fee." For his, Franklin Meuli was offered the option of increasing his minority holdings by as much as five percent. The remainder of the franchise continued to be held by the Morabito sisters.

The last step in the process was securing League approval of Eddie's bid for membership. Pete Rozelle would later claim that NFL Security spent "an extraordinary amount of time" investigating the DeBartolos and "found nothing that would preclude them from ownership in the League."

The "extraordinary" time taken with Eddie's application was likely a reflection of what Mr. D would later call the "innuendo" that already surrounded the DeBartolos. That they were Italians, in the construction industry as a family business, and living in Youngstown, read like the Hollywood recipe for a miniseries about gangsters. Indeed, one of the first questions asked by the *San Francisco Examiner* when Eddie's 49er purchase went public was whether DeBartolo Corp. was connected with the Mafia. Mr. D found the question offensive. "I can't stand people saying we're connected with the mob," DeBartolo Sr. was still complaining years later. "If we were connected with the mob, why would some of the biggest companies in the world—like U.S. Steel and Mellon Bank—be in joint venture with me? I got where I am by working my can off every day of my life. Check our records. We never borrowed a single cent from a Teamsters union or a pension fund. And like everybody else, I had rough times in my career. I could have turned to certain characters in this town. I'm not saying I don't know them. But I solved my own problems."

In 1977, Rozelle's most significant concern about the DeBartolos was with regard to ownership policy. Eddie's NFL franchise and Mr. D's hockey ownership would be a relationship not unlike Joe Robbie's football and Mrs. Joe Robbie's soccer. Though not technically a violation of the current continuing ownership policy resolution, as Meuli's ownership would have been, the DeBartolos' arrangement intimated cross-ownership and potential conflict of interest. In this instance, however, the commissioner's uneasiness was apparently easily satisfied. Rozelle would later testify that he spoke to Eddie only once "briefly" on the subject and Eddie explained that Mr. D had originally become involved in hockey only as a minority partner, but when the other partners withdrew because of the team's losses, DeBartolo Sr. had taken "financial control" and kept the franchise afloat as a "civic duty" to Pittsburgh. Junior added that his father "did want to get out of it when he could reasonably do so."

During the second week of March, Rozelle and the DeBartolos exchanged a series of letters finalizing the commissioner's investigation of Eddie's application. On March 8, the DeBartolos' attorney officially advised the League of the sale's final financial details. Though Eddie was the owner of record and the candidate for admission, the purchase of the 49ers was secured with an "irrevocable letter of credit . . . advanced to Mr. DeBartolo Jr. and the Edward J. DeBartolo Corp., a corporation wholly owned by Mr. Edward J. DeBartolo Sr., the father of the purchaser." On March 11, Rozelle responded by accepting such an arrangement as long as Eddie and Mr. D "each . . . agree, both individually and where appropriate on behalf of the corporation . . . to be bound by the constitution and bylaws, rules and policies of the National Football League."

On the afternoon of March 28, the annual meeting considered Eddie's membership in Executive Session, while Eddie himself waited nearby in the hotel. According to the minutes, Lou Spadia and the 49ers' attorney "presented the request of the 49ers ownership that the transfer of majority interest . . . be approved." According to one of the owners present, "Rozelle pushed it through," though there was little controversy about Eddie himself. "He was a young rich kid," another owner offered, "he seemed basically decent." Discussion lasted awhile before Gene Klein moved the question and Art Modell seconded it. Also among DeBartolo's strongest backers were the Rooneys. Eddie's membership passed by unanimous vote. Shortly thereafter, he entered the room and took Spadia's seat.

The controversy that had prolonged the discussion was about Al Davis's role. Far from thanking Davis for the money his intervention had saved them, a number of League members were "furious" at him for taking a finder's fee as part of the transaction. Art Modell described it as "rather unusual," "appalling," and "outrageous," questioning the "ethics" of the arrangement since the League's constitution forbade any owner to have a financial interest in any franchise other than his own. On that point, Rozelle came to Davis's support. "The financial arrangement with Al Davis was fully explained," he offered. "There's nothing in the constitution against it." Nonetheless, Steve Rosenbloom recalled later, "a lot of owners were upset."

Davis again did nothing to smooth feelings. "Al didn't give a shit what we thought about it," one NFL member observed. "If anything, he figured he was worth a lot more than he'd been paid." In the discussion after Lou Spadia's presentation, Davis told his fellow owners that his fee had been $100,000 and was defiant about having taken it. "I'm no different than Hugh Culverhouse," he argued. "He's a lawyer and he's doing the tax work on this deal. I'm sure he ain't doing it for nothing. . . . I found the DeBartolos. I handled every phase of the sale, including the payoff formula, so I wasn't really a finder as much as I was a consultant." Leonard Tose was Davis's most vocal defender. "It's a little unusual," he admitted to the *Los Angeles Times,* "but Al Davis is an unusual guy. I'm not opposed to the idea. Al obviously rendered a service and was paid for it." Tose's arguments made little headway against the resentment Davis had already provoked.

Al Davis thumbed his nose at the sentiment. The day after the annual meeting adjourned and the League checked out of the Arizona Biltmore, he as much as announced his contempt in the newspapers, though only those who'd sat in on the discussions of Eddie DeBartolo's candidacy could read the comment for what it was.

A reporter asked Davis about the controversy over his "$100,000 finder's fee." The usual finder's fee, the journalist pointed out, was ten percent. In the case of the 49ers, that amounted to something like $1.8 million, not $100,000.

"I didn't receive anything like that," Al chuckled, "but it was," he admitted, "a lot more than $100,000."

That the statement put the lie to what he'd told the Executive Session about his fee four days earlier did not seem to bother Al Davis. Several of his critics would later describe the attitude as "no big surprise."

"That's just like Davis," one of them complained. "After himself, there's not much else Al cares about." The same critic would later say the same thing about Eddie DeBartolo, despite having voted to admit him to the League.

3

Eddie DeBartolo wasn't the only new member admitted to the NFL during the spring 1977 executive session; he was just the only one requiring a vote. The other new member, Leon Hess, required no formal approval under League rules.

Hess had been a partner in the New York Jets since 1964, when he and four other men bought them out of receivership, and his acceptability to the League had been grandfathered as part of the 1966 merger agreement. The franchise was called the Titans then and had been the first casualty of the AFL-NFL war. The purchasing group had been put together by Sonny Werblin and had all been involved in New Jersey's Monmouth Park racetrack together. None of the five held a majority interest, though Werblin and Hess held the most, almost twenty-five percent apiece. Werblin served as Jets president until 1968, when the other partners forced him out of office and bought his share for some nine times what he'd paid four years earlier. The next partner to run the team was Don Lillis, but Lillis died two months after being named president. The next new president was Phil Iselin. Hess, now the largest stockholder, with thirty-three percent, was named vice-president. On December 28, 1976, Iselin dropped dead from heart failure in his Jets office. Hess, shortly to be a fifty percent owner by virtue of buying out Iselin's widow, "reluctantly" accepted the Jets presidency in February 1977.

As with the DeBartolos, there were no doubts Leon Hess could afford a team. *Forbes* placed his "minimum net worth" at $320 million. Like Eddie DeBartolo's father, he'd started with next to nothing.

Mores Hess, Leon Hess's father, had arrived in the United States from Lithuania in 1904. Leon, the youngest of Mores's three sons, was born in 1914. The elder Hess was a meat dealer based in Asbury Park, New Jersey, until 1925, when he bought an old oil wagon and began delivering fuel around New Jersey. By 1933, Mores's fuel company had filed for bankruptcy and been forced to reorganize. The new Hess Oil Company retained Mores as its titular head, but was run by Leon, then eighteen years old and fresh out of Asbury Park High School. Within five years, Leon had made Hess Oil into a major bidder on U.S. government fuel contracts in New Jersey. Leon himself had already acquired a reputation for his toughness and ability to run his family business on a shoestring. While most oil bids were submitted typewritten, Hess still scrawled his with a pen. During World War II, Leon left the company in the hands of his older brother and enlisted in the army. He spent the duration procuring and transporting fuel in Europe to supply George Patton's armored troops and was discharged as a major and awarded a Bronze Star for his efforts. "It taught him about planning," one of his friends said of Leon's military career. "He became very orderly in his way of going about any problem."

Back at Hess Oil, the plan Leon had in mind did not lack ambition. What he wanted to build was a major integrated oil company, just like Standard, Shell, and the rest. To begin, he took Hess Oil into supplying residual fuel for power generation and soon made it the biggest such oil supplier in New Jersey. He also began importing oil, and by 1957 was handling thirty-eight thousand barrels a day. By then, Hess was also into refining, building three refineries in New Jersey, buying one in Texas, and eventually building yet another in the Virgin Islands. In 1960, Hess Oil moved into retail gasoline sales. He started with twenty-eight stations. By 1969, he had more than five hundred, each pumping five times as much as the industry norm. A "fanatic about cleanliness," Hess regularly inspected all the company's facilities and, one of his employees told *Fortune,* "raised hell if everything isn't just right." In 1970, he merged Hess Oil with the Amerada Corp., one of the largest independent producers of crude oil in the world and owner of one billion barrels of reserves in the United States, Canada, and Libya. The new corporation, Amerada Hess, was controlled by Leon, and with its advent, his grand design had been realized.

By then, his business stature was uncontested. "He built a local delivery service into a major integrated oil company," *Fortune* applauded, "in his lifetime, starting with nothing. Hess has been taking more chances than his competitors for the nearly four decades he has been in the oil business and his gambles have paid off with astonishing regularity.'' Though possessed of "supreme self-confidence," Hess, balding and owlish in plastic-rimmed glasses, had surprisingly little ego. Until his father's death in 1965, Leon gave the old man a higher title in the corporation than his own and let him sign all Hess Oil's checks.

Leon also had "an almost pathological aversion to publicity. He is not a recluse on the order of Howard Hughes, but . . . when attending public functions, as he sometimes must, Hess will practically wither at the sight of a camera.''

"Part of his shyness,'' *Fortune* went on to explain, "comes from the fact that he is a strong-minded, volatile man, apt to say things he shouldn't, sometimes in off-color language. Part of it stems from the fact that he is very rich, and has been bothered by cranks and parasites. Hess also explains that his parents, humble Jewish immigrants from Eastern Europe, beseeched him at an early age 'not to toot my own horn' and to 'let my actions speak for me.' ''

Whatever its origins, Hess's passion for invisibility was a trait unusual to the members of the National Football League. The New Jersey oilman had bought into the Jets originally only as a favor to Werblin, a crony of his from their mutual Monmouth Park horse racing investment, Hess's only other sports holding. Over his first seven years as Jets' president, Hess would nonetheless increase his share of the team to one hundred percent—all the while continuing to shun the celebrity trappings that came with owning a piece of America's Game. Once, when spotted by a reporter watching a Jets practice session, he asked that the man not write that the Jets owner had been present. "I'm supposed to be working,'' Hess pointed out. According to the NFL's minutes, it was not until 1982 that Hess personally attended a League meeting as Jets president. When he did, he would quickly acquire a reputation as "one of Rozelle's stalwarts,'' pushing the League's fight with Al Davis because "Rozelle's honor was at stake.''

Despite his initial absence from League gatherings, Leon Hess clearly meant business from the first day he took personal control of the Jets. Running corporate enterprises had few mysteries left for Hess, and after twelve years in this one, he had already formed strong opinions about the Jets' problems. His strongest was about its home field, Shea Stadium, and its lease with the city of New York. A month after Phil Iselin's funeral, the new Jets president set out to better his franchise's position. Though Hess's opening round with New York was inconclusive, it nonetheless foreshadowed the coming escalation of the Superstadium Game into a football business civil war that would leave League Think crippled for life.

Hess's problem in 1977 was not with the physical structure of Shea. Rather, the problem concerned the Jets' lease and Shea's other tenant, the baseball Mets. Completed in 1964, Shea Stadium had been originally built to house a baseball expansion franchise acquired in the civic panic that set in after the Giants and Dodgers left for California in 1958. The deal the city had given that franchise, the Mets, was often described as a "sweetheart" arrangement. Among other things, the lease agreement gave the Mets "the right to restrict the use of the natural grass field from February 20 through the end of baseball season" in October. The Mets, owned at the time by a syndicate whose chairman was New York stockbroker Donald Grant, exercised that right without variance. For the football Jets, that meant having to play all their preseason and their first five regular season games away from home. By the time of their first home game, the turf field at Shea was well on its way to mud and the approach of winter had turned the horseshoe-shaped stadium into a haven for perverse freezing winds.

The 1977 struggle over that arrangement was three-sided, with the city of New York sandwiched between Hess and Grant. Hess's lease then had seven years to run and Grant's had option clauses allowing him to extend its terms well past the year 2000. The Jets had been in discussions with Grant and the city in an attempt to revise the lease terms before Iselin's death, but Hess had inherited a stalemate. Grant's baseball franchise was willing to let the Jets play one preseason and two regular season games while baseball was still on, but, according to *The New York Times,* insisted that those games be postponed if a "baseball game had to be played after a football contest in rainy weather." Such postponement of scheduled games was unacceptable to the Jets and the NFL. To at least mitigate the disadvantages of winter games, the Jets offered an interest-free $4 million loan to the city of New York to install artificial turf, but that was rejected by Grant out of hand.

On February 4, two days after officially becoming Jets president, Hess moved to break the stalemate. That day, officials of the Jets met with New York's Mayor Abraham Beame and Beame, as usual, pointed out that his hands were tied. Whatever changes the football franchise wanted would have to be worked out with the Mets, as required by the baseball team's preferential lease.

Beame's response was unacceptable to Hess, who quickly exercised the leverage provided by the move of Wellington Mara's Giants to New Jersey's Meadowlands several years earlier. Leon Hess was familiar with the advantages of New Jersey and his old crony, Sonny Werblin, was Mara's landlord there. On February 7, Hess wrote Beame a letter. "We do not want to leave New York," the Jets owner maintained, but Grant's offer remained unacceptable. "It is impossible to permit [anyone] other than officials of the National Football League to postpone a game." Without "satisfactory solutions to the problem," the Jets "must explore any and all options, including the use of another stadium. . . . We are New Yorkers and if we are forced to leave New York we voluntarily shall reimburse our city for the net rental income usually realized from our scheduled games in Shea." Love of New York notwithstanding, Hess continued, the Jets had been "forced" into discussions with New Jersey's Meadowlands because the current situation, in effect, compelled them to negotiate with "another tenant" instead of their landlord. By the time

Beame received Hess's letter, those talks with Sonny Werblin in New Jersey had already begun in earnest.

The struggle went public on February 10, when New Jersey Governor Brendan Byrne addressed a Chamber of Commerce luncheon in East Rutherford, site of the new Giants Stadium, and offered that he hoped his state would soon have a second professional football team. The next morning's *New York Times* bannered the story "Football Jets Negotiating Jersey Move" and cited sources close to the Jets as claiming the two parties were "very, very close to a verbal agreement" that would start with the 1977 season. Under the arrangement being discussed, they would alternate home games with the Giants. "We would love to have another professional football team," Sonny Werblin observed. "The Giants are not exclusive. It's up to the Jets. We can certainly accommodate them."

Leon Hess made no comment on the story but Abraham Beame and Donald Grant were not nearly so reserved. "The Jets are absolutely inflexible," Grant complained. "This whole situation is easy to resolve. I have offered Mr. Hess a compromise. I offered to let the Jets play two September games on Saturday nights and one exhibition on a Saturday night. And you know that Leon Hess practically threw his arms around me. He said, 'If you'll do that, then I don't see any reason to go. We'll stay in New York.' I told him there was one thing though: that if it rained heavily enough to damage the field for baseball, the Jets would have to put their game over to the next day. That's all. But he went to Pete Rozelle and Rozelle told him the NFL couldn't do that. I'm very surprised they're talking about going. I think they're trying to put pressure on the city to get us to change our lease."

Grant was, of course, stating the obvious. Hess had tossed a political grenade in Abraham Beame's lap. He knew exactly what he was doing. Recluse or not, Leon Hess was also astute in the mechanics of politics. His father-in-law had been the late David Wilentz, former New Jersey attorney general and a member of the Democratic National Committee, and New Jersey Democrats had been particularly helpful in Congress when Hess secured permission to build his refinery in the Virgin Islands. In election years, Hess spread his money around. In 1968, he donated some $100,000 to Hubert Humphrey's presidential campaign. In 1972, Hess and his corporation donated $250,000 to Richard Nixon. In 1976, Hess voluntarily admitted having paid "substantial" bribes to "a foreign government official." The statement, like all of Hess's, was issued through a corporate spokesman. No such statement was issued in response to Donald Grant's. Instead, Leon Hess waited to see which way the mayor would move. Having already made his way through several decades of the political rough-and-tumble surrounding the oil business, the Jets president had no qualms about playing hardball with Abraham Beame.

Beame knew he was sandwiched. New York City had already lost the football Giants, the North American Soccer League Cosmos, and a good portion of its harness-racing crowds to New Jersey. In addition, the city was convulsed in the worst financial crisis in its history and facing bankruptcy. Losing the Jets would add humiliation to defeat and insolvency. Even if he weren't responsible, Beame knew he would take the blame. His immediate response was noncommittal. "We're extremely concerned," he offered on February 11. "New York shouldn't be without a football team."

By February 14, the mayor had settled on a strategy. "We are determined to use every weapon at our command to insure that the Jets remain in New York and play at Shea Stadium," he announced. Beame had an appointment the following day with Donald Grant and offered that he hoped Grant would prove "reasonable and flexible." Beame did not attack Hess for putting him in that position; he saved his irritation for Sonny Werblin and the New Jersey Sports Authority. "I am particularly incensed at the interference of the New Jersey Sports Authority," the mayor continued. "It is ironic that the same man who signed the original Jets lease is now heading that authority and is trying to induce the Jets to leave the city and the fans who have supported them for years." Beame said the city was exploring the law to see if it had grounds for legal action against New Jersey for "inducing a breach of agreement."

At 3:00 P.M. on February 15, Beame and Grant met. The Mets chairman offered the same arrangement the Jets had already refused, only with the guarantee that any postponement of Jets games would be no more than twenty-four hours. That evening, Grant and Beame were joined at the mayor's Gracie Mansion by Leon Hess. Hess reiterated that the Jets were prepared to offer a flat $2.3 million to buy out their Shea lease. When informed of Grant's latest offer, Hess said he would check with Rozelle about it and get back to the mayor the following day. The meeting lasted an hour and a half and only Grant personally attended the press conference afterward. The mayor sent a spokesman, who announced that "positions remained unchanged." Grant proclaimed that "the Mets' offer is still on the table." Hess said nothing and was nowhere to be seen.

The following day, Leon Hess called Abraham Beame with his response. The NFL would not accept any postponements, he said, and made a counteroffer that was announced to the press immediately thereafter by a Hess spokesman. "The Jets told the mayor that they would be willing to give up the exhibition game in Shea," the spokesman explained. "However, they made it clear that they would not compromise on the two regular season games. The Jets made their offer contingent on the mayor's understanding that it was only the first step—for this year only—in reaching absolute equality with the Mets by 1978 in scheduling games at Shea Stadium." Hess's counteroffer was relayed to Grant by Beame. According to Grant, the mayor was "annoyed" that Hess had made the offer public. Grant himself called it "a backwards step."

Even so, it was one Grant took on February 18, one day later. After a final two-hour evening meeting with the mayor and Hess, the press was summoned to the Blue Room at City Hall and told a deal had been cut. The Mets would accept one exhibition and two regular season games during August and September with no postponement. The artifice crafted to let Grant swallow his hard line was the agreement that the mayor himself would hold the Mets' former postponement rights and the mayor in turn agreed to waive them. "This proposal," Beame pointed out, "was made with the understanding that the Jets would agree to play in Shea Stadium for the duration of their lease and will make no further demands for additional playing dates during the baseball season. I'm very pleased about it. I presume since this is what the Jets and Mr. Hess asked for, they're going to adhere to the conversations we had." The mayor trumpeted the agreement as a victory over the New Jersey Sports Authority. At the press conference, Grant stood behind and to the right of the mayor. The Mets chairman offered that "the mayor made a fair presentation of what the Mets agreed to." Hess had long since left the building and was represented by a spokesman.

Nonetheless, it was the reclusive Hess who got the best press from the affair. "Leon Hess," the *Times* proclaimed, "the New Jets' Muscle." The nation's newspaper of record said, "The oil baron displayed an attribute that had been missing since Sonny Werblin departed—strength." Though the description of Leon Hess may well have been accurate, the assumption that the battle over Shea was over was not.

By the first week of March, Beame's deal had fallen through. Grant initiated the collapse with a five-page letter detailing why the oral agreement could not be accepted. The Mets' major contention was that the mayor could not cede his right to make postponements to save the grass field from damage. Grant's reversal led to a week of frantic negotiations to no avail. Then, on March 16, Leon Hess played his trump card.

At a press conference called by the Jets that morning, a spokesman read a statement from Hess. For the upcoming season, the Jets would play their first two home games at Giants Stadium in the New Jersey Meadowlands and then the rest of their schedule back in Shea after baseball season ended. "We will not completely remove ourselves at this time," Hess's statement read. The Jets would compensate New York with $100,000 for the two missed home dates and should they eventually move altogether, would buy out the remaining years on their lease. "We are choosing not to abandon New York City. That would be an easy course for our minds, but not for our hearts. The ownership of the Jets will not do anything further to further demoralize a city in crisis."

Beame responded by announcing that the city of New York was going to sue the Jets, the Mets, the National Football League, and the New Jersey Sports Authority. The Jets would be forced to play all their home games at Shea, the Mets would be forced to rewrite their sweetheart lease, the National Football League would be enjoined from scheduling Jets games anywhere but Shea, and the New Jersey Sports Authority would be enjoined from inducing the Jets to break their lease. "It's a sad day for major league sports that we must resort to the courts to force parties to fulfill their obligations to the city," Abraham Beame pointed out, "but I am determined to see that those obligations are met."

The City of New York v. New York Jets Football Club Inc., Leon Hess,

Metropolitan Baseball Club Inc., Donald Grant, New Jersey Sports Author-
ity, Sonny Werblin, National Football League, and Pete Rozelle was the first
episode of the Superstadium Game to reach the judicial system. There would
be more, and this first one was by far the shortest.

On May 11, New York State Supreme Court Justice Harold Baer ruled
that the Jets could not play home games anywhere but at Shea Stadium.
"Every business that leaves the city," he ruled, "every major corporate home
office that departs for the suburbs . . . each team that leaves for a larger
stadium is another drop of the city's life's blood." Justice Baer also "strongly
urged" the Mets to accommodate the Jets' September home games. The Jets
immediately appealed.

On May 26, the case was settled out of court. The terms for dropping the
action were hammered out in Baer's Manhattan chambers, all at the Mets'
expense. Baer's plan required Grant to give the Jets two September dates
immediately and, starting the following year, guarantee them two October
dates as well. The Jets would also be allowed to play one game this year in
New Jersey but none for the rest of their lease with Shea. "If you don't agree
to this," the justice lectured Grant's lawyers, "you're going to be sorry."
The justice eventually relayed his threat to Grant directly on the telephone
and, according to one of the attorneys present, "Grant finally caved in."

This time the deal stuck and *City of New York v. New York Jets Football
Club, Inc. et al* was history. Having won what he set out to get, Leon Hess
resigned himself to another seven years at Shea and did his best to resume
being invisible.

4

Others were playing the Superstadium Game in 1977, as well. The seller's
market for football remained volatile even after expansion into Seattle and
Tampa, providing a key strategy for owners who wished to play.

In Miami, Joe Robbie had commenced a fight with the city over the
Orange Bowl that would last another decade before it was resolved. The
stadium, a huge 1930s bowl type inside the city limits, still had wooden
benches for seats and most of its game-day parking area consisted of front
lawns rented in the surrounding neighborhood. As far as Robbie was concerned, all of it cost him money. The seating capacity of nearly eighty thousand
meant Dolphin tickets were easy to get and the stadium's facilities made the
tickets less desirable than they ought to be. The lack of parking lots meant the
Dolphins were one of the few NFL franchises without significant parking

income on game days. When his lease came up for renewal in 1976, Robbie
had demanded that something be done.

Since the Orange Bowl was the only stadium of significant size within four
hundred miles of Miami, Robbie had little leverage. Typically, the Dolphin
owner made the most of what he had. Before his lease negotiations with the
city of Miami began, Joe Robbie announced the Dolphins were retaining a
Minneapolis consulting firm to develop plans for a modern football facility in
Broward County, next door to Dade County and Miami. Robbie claimed such
a facility could be built for $30 million, a figure Miami officials scoffed at. It
was, the *Miami News* offered, "just a dream." The Broward County stadium
idea had gone nowhere by 1977, but by then Joe Robbie had signed a new
ten-year lease which gave him the option to leave for another stadium on three
years notice. Its rental terms were still among the best in the NFL.

The city of Miami also sought to soothe their principal tenant's feelings
about the Orange Bowl by proposing a 1977 bond issue to finance some $15
million in improvements. If the idea was to now make common cause with
Robbie, it was a failed gesture almost as soon as it was made. "I don't think
anyone being nice to Joe Robbie gets anywhere," Miami Mayor Maurice
Ferre observed.

Robbie was quick to oppose the refurbishing measure. By July 1977, the
Dolphins had sold only thirty-six thousand season tickets and their owner was
more adamant than ever about what a white elephant the Orange Bowl was.
He had made it clear that it wasn't fit to hold another Super Bowl in and he
didn't blame Dolphin fans for not wanting to come to it. "I can't go around
telling people this is a great stadium with ample parking," Robbie argued.
"They'd laugh at me. The conditions exist and I am only telling the truth
when I point them out. I can't support this bond issue. I could support it if
there were an alternative proposal to build a new stadium. . . . I definitely
think Broward County will build a stadium and I think Miamians would be
much happier with a superstructure with all the modern conveniences, even if
they have to drive a little farther to get to it. . . . I can't tell the fans that if
they vote for this, I'm staying here. I'd be misleading them."

The lease Joe Robbie had signed was in fact just a truce to buy time
while he waited for his "dream" to ripen.

In Minnesota, the dilemma facing Vikings majority owner Max Winter was
the same, but the setting and circumstances were different. The Vikings' home
field, Memorial Stadium in suburban Bloomington, was the smallest in the NFL,
with only 48,500 seats. As such, it was even less than the League's official
minimum. An open bowl configuration, the field was frozen solid for much of
the last half of the Vikings season and games occasionally featured wind chill
factors of two degrees Fahrenheit. Max Winter had been complaining about the
stadium for more than a decade. His options were either to get a new stadium
built or move to another city, and Max had a lot of roots in Minnesota.

Going on seventy-three years old in 1977, Max Winter had come to Minneapolis at age ten from Mahrishostrau, Austria. His father, Jacob, had owned a meat-packing plant in the old country; in Minneapolis, he dealt distressed merchandise to department stores. Max's earliest memory of America was eating a banana for the first time in his life when the boat docked in New York. Captain of the basketball team at Minneapolis' North High, class of 1922, Max worked nights and weekends as a delivery boy, newshawk, and shipping clerk. He went on to Hamline College but never graduated. Now worth $30 million, "Max," the *Minneapolis Tribune* noted, "has perfected the art of the hustle to a fine degree." His first success was selling women's hair-care products, despite knowing next to nothing about hair care. In the 1930s he made a name for himself promoting local boxing matches. From there, he went into restaurants, real estate, and vending machines. From 1947 to 1957 he was co-owner and general manager of the Minneapolis Lakers professional basketball franchise, Minnesota's first big league team. After Max sold out, the Lakers had left town for L.A. A friend of Art Rooney and George Halas, Winter had first begun approaching the NFL about a Minneapolis football franchise in 1955.

Though Max did not want to leave town, he was more than fed up with the stadium in Bloomington. A new stadium had been an item of loud civic discussion in Minnesota since 1971 but progress had quickly bogged down in the political cross-currents surrounding the issue of where such a publicly funded stadium would be located. Minneapolis wanted it inside the city limits, even though it would cost more that way, while Bloomington and the suburban interests wanted the games to stay in Bloomington. When nothing had happened by 1973, Winter made his first noises about moving the franchise. When the issue finally reached the State Legislature in 1975, the Vikings scheduled an exhibition game in Phoenix, Arizona. In February 1976, a proposal for a $47 million stadium in downtown Minneapolis was formally submitted to the legislature but was almost immediately hamstrung by the pro-Bloomington forces. Shortly thereafter, Winter dispatched the franchise's general manager, Mike Lynn, to New York to discuss the possibility of moving east to play in Yankee Stadium. In March, Lynn paid a visit to Memphis to discuss possibilities there. The Vikings also continued to refuse to sign anything more than a one-year lease on the stadium they had.

In May 1977, the Minnesota House of Representatives voted seventy to sixty-one to start the process again and established the Metropolitan Sports Facilities Commission. The commission was empowered to select a site for a new stadium and then issue bonds for construction. By July, the commission had narrowed the field down to three locations: Minneapolis, Bloomington, and suburban Egan. It would be another year before the field was narrowed to two.

Meanwhile, Max Winter was ready to play his hometown off against whoever was available.

*   *   *

In Baltimore, Robert Irsay was no happier with his stadium than he had ever been. His discussions with the city on the subject had never gone anywhere. Though the lack of a modern football facility was a continued source of frustration to Irsay, he was at the moment basking in the highlight of his career in the NFL. The previous season, his Colts had won eleven and lost three, the best record an Irsay team would ever produce. In spring 1977, Irsay considered himself on the verge of a dynasty that would, he forecast, put the memory of Carroll Rosenbloom's Colts behind him once and for all.

Winning seemed to have softened Baltimore's attitude about Irsay as well. The local papers had little bad to say about Irsay's success and the eleventh annual convention of the Council of Colt Corrals, the Baltimore Colts boosters clubs, even asked Irsay to serve as grand marshal in their Colts parade. The Colts owner flew in from Skokie, Illinois, for the weekend, attending a pep rally and a dance. As part of the festivities, he donated $750 to the Corrals. "I had the time of my life," Irsay observed on his way out of town. "It was just a wonderful bunch of Colts fans. I hope they make me an honorary member of each corral."

Even at his high point, however, Irsay felt no great allegiance to the city of Baltimore. In spring 1977, he made an appointment with Paul Oakes, chairman of the stadium task force of the Greater Indianapolis Progress Committee. At the time, Indianapolis was still trying to figure out what kind of stadium to build, where to build it, and how to pay for it. None of those questions was close to being answered, but Oakes had arranged the meeting anyway. "I had heard he was unhappy with Baltimore," Oakes recounted to *The Indianapolis Star*. "I just took a chance and called Irsay at his office in Skokie. I made an appointment to see him and then I figured out what I was going to say."

Oakes showed up at Irsay's office with a delegation that included Indianapolis's mayor. They told the Colts owner that the city was currently discussing constructing a sixty-thousand-seat stadium downtown.

Irsay's response had little hesitation. "If you break ground," he told the group, "I'll move the Colts there."

Indianapolis's representatives left Skokie ebullient. Another meeting with Irsay was scheduled, but by then the group realized it was way ahead of itself and discussions were dropped at the city's initiative.

Nonetheless, Baltimore's Robert Irsay was obviously ready to listen to all relocation offers and, just as obviously, loved being asked.

In Los Angeles, Carroll Rosenbloom seemed to have ended his Superstadium Game by signing a lease the year before, but that was an illusion. C.R. was determined to find someplace besides the Coliseum to play and would do so shortly.

When Carroll Rosenbloom finally succeeded, all hell would break loose.

5

Though all episodes of the Superstadium Game were accompanied by a litany of alleged financial woes, only one NFL owner, Leonard Tose of the Philadelphia Eagles, was in serious money trouble in spring 1977, and Tose's difficulties were decidedly his own fault. "Tose was just spending money and selling his assets to cover his expenditures," Sidney Forstater, his personal financial adviser, later testified in Philadelphia Federal Court. "For some time, we were able to meet expenditures only by making substantial loans. When the loans became due, it was necessary to sell valuable assets to meet the payments. Mr. Tose said he wasn't going to run out of money. He kept saying he'd be dead before the money ran out."

When making that prediction, Leonard Tose seriously underestimated his own skill at losing money.

Tose's assets, excluding the Eagles, had been worth some $12.5 million in 1969, the year he entered the NFL. By the end of 1976, those same assets were worth $2.5 million and sinking. Tose Trucking, his principal nonfootball worth, had lost $2.5 million since 1973. On paper, Tose's only income during the same period was the combined salaries he drew from his trucking company and football team, some $110,000, about the same amount as the annual costs of his personal helicopter. As a consequence, Tose charged off as much of his life-style as possible to the Eagles franchise, and, despite ranking near the top of the National Football League in attendance, the franchise lost almost $1.3 million in 1976.

Tose's profligacy had also added to the growing list of people who wished they'd never had anything to do with him. By now it included Herb Barness, a man Leonard Tose had once described as his "best friend." Barness owned a twenty-nine percent share of the Eagles and had backed Tose in 1971 when three of the other members of his original group of investors had filed suit. By 1976, he was threatening suit himself and demanding full access to the club's financial records. In September of that year, Barness wrote Tose and accused him of "taking advantage . . . of me and your other partners." By December, he had announced to Tose's lawyers that he was prepared to sell his interest, but in the meantime wanted Sidney Forstater put in financial control of the club. Early in 1977, Barness informed First Pennsylvania Bank, holder of the Eagles' note, that he was considering legal moves to put the football franchise into receivership. By March, Barness and Tose were discussing what Barness's share might cost. Barness was prepared to take $2.5 million. Tose asked if he'd take $2 million cash instead.

"Len," Barness answered, "put it on the table and see what I do." Herb

Barness doubted Leonard Tose could actually lay his hands on that kind of money. In that respect, he was by no means alone.

The most logical place for Tose to find such a sum was First Pennsylvania Bank. Tose had reduced his borrowings there from $10.3 million to $5.3 million and, according to Tose, paid First Penn some $6.2 million in interest over the seven years since the bank had loaned him enough to join the NFL. By 1977, however, First Penn was well on its way to joining the same list as Herb Barness. In December 1976, the Comptroller of Currency had adjudged its loan to Leonard Tose "substandard" and the $5.3 million borrowing with the Philadelphia Eagles as collateral had been assigned to First Penn's problem loan division. First Penn had identified the problem almost two years earlier and forced Tose to sign an amendment to his loan agreement, restricting his salary and expenses, but it had proved a futile gesture. In 1976, Tose exceeded his personal Eagles budget by $200,000 and in the first three months of 1977, he had already drawn and spent more than his entire annual salary. He had also already overspent his annual Eagles expense account by $25,000.

On March 24, 1977, the supervisor of Tose's loan sent a memorandum up First Penn's chain of command recommending that the loan be called. He noted that it was doubtful Tose could get any other bank to refinance him and that calling the loan would then force him to put the team on the market. Herb Barness owned first refusal rights should Tose sell, and the First Penn memo suggested that Pete Rozelle be approached through Barness once Tose's loan had been called. Since Barness was the most likely buyer, the contact might make the foreclosure much shorter lived than the bankruptcy process in which Tose had originally purchased the franchise in 1969. "The rest," the memo noted, "will depend on Rozelle's reaction to the pressure from Barness and the bank."

As a financial institution, however, First Penn was not yet ready to take such a radical step. Though the bank's president, John Bunting, recognized that the Eagles were in "financial chaos," jeopardizing their loan's security and threatening the possibility of repayment, he vetoed the memo's proposed foreclosure because football teams were "not easily resold." He later characterized the March memo he received as "overreacting" on the part of a "saddle sore" vice-president, frustrated with having to deal with Tose. Tose was, First Penn's president noted, "a pretty tough customer."

Instead of calling Leonard Tose's loan, John Bunting summoned him to a meeting at First Pennsylvania Bank headquarters on March 25, shortly before the Eagles owner left for the League's annual meeting in Phoenix. Tose arrived with his attorney. Bunting began by lecturing Tose about the Eagles' financial condition and complaining about Tose's life-style. Tose listened with little interest. "First Pennsylvania wanted us to buy cheaper tape to tape our athletes," he fumed. "They checked lunch boxes. They found there were two pieces of fruit in them and they wanted only one. . . . Bunting said he doesn't like my life-style. He doesn't like my style because he doesn't have any style and I guess if you don't have any style, you don't like anybody's style."

Despite Tose's failings, Bunting continued, First Penn had decided to "try to save the club." Bunting then offered to help Tose buy out Barness once and for all. "We had to get Barness out of there," First Penn's president explained, "because the tension [between Barness and Tose] was creating a cancer," jeopardizing the club, and raising the threat of a protracted public lawsuit. Bunting also meant to use the possibility of buying Barness out as a means to restrict Tose's power to spend the Eagles' money. Any loan to purchase Barness's twenty-nine percent, First Penn's president pointed out, would be conditional upon Tose permitting First Penn to appoint an Eagles financial officer with the power to control expenditures. Tose's attorney would later claim his client was "eager" to accept the proposed exchange of a larger Tose ownership for more First Penn control. Bunting would claim Tose resisted it. In any case, the only concrete result on March 25 was agreement to a succession of meetings with bank officials to discuss ways to remedy the club's financial ills.

The first of those was held in April, after Leonard Tose's return from Phoenix. One of the items discussed was a plan developed by First Penn's problem loan division to cut some of the almost $2 million the Eagles annually spent on administrative expenses. In addition to holding Tose strictly to his agreed upon salary and expenses, it recommended firing or retiring some five front-office employees, including Tose's personal secretary. Tose resisted agreeing to specifics, but promised to adhere to the goals of the plan. Things got testier when Bunting informed Tose and his attorney that the bank had discussed the possibility of buyout with Herb Barness. Tose's attorney responded that he was "shocked" at Bunting's behavior. In March, the attorney had specifically asked Bunting not to inform Barness of the bank's potential willingness to loan Tose more money for fear he would use the knowledge to jack up the price. The attorney later testified in Federal Court that he considered the violation of confidentiality a breach of Bunting's fiduciary responsibility and told him so.

By May, relations between First Pennsylvania Bank and Leonard Tose were even testier. The public accounting firm used to certify the Eagles' internal audit had by then refused to do so, claiming the team had defaulted on the provisions in its loan because Tose had taken more salary than it allowed. At that point, Sidney Forstater had requested those limitations be waived. First Penn had refused, and by May had begun insisting that Forstater be named the club's chief financial officer instead. Replacement was not an option Tose would consider, so everything just sat up in the air. By summer, the Eagles' finances had not improved and the bank made its insistence on financial restraint even louder. First Penn also framed the message in words they were sure Leonard Tose could understand. The man who delivered them was First Penn vice-president John Pemberton. "I've got to treat you like a jackass," Pemberton snarled at Tose. "I've got to mount you and put my spurs in you." Much to the bank's irritation, the effect of Pemberton's rhetoric on Leonard Tose was virtually nil.

First Pennsylvania Bank would have even been more irritated had they known what other financial dealings Tose had been up to that spring. Since First Penn had refused to waive its loan agreement provisions and let the Eagles audit be certified, Tose very quietly looked elsewhere for a loan of $200,000 to repay the Eagles for his 1976 overdrafts. He had a number of short-term personal loans from friends that had to be repaid as well. In the course of his search, Tose was introduced by his lawyer to one Bruce Rappoport, owner of the Swiss-based Grove Corp., a shipping firm. At the time Rappoport was a controversial financial figure, linked to what *The Philadelphia Inquirer* called "allegations that Rappoport had grossly inflated contracts to build oil tankers for Indonesia." That spring, he agreed to loan Tose $1 million. Without informing First Pennsylvania Bank of the transaction, Tose posted his holdings in the Eagles, already completely pledged to First Penn, as Rappoport's collateral. Now, the Eagles were not only in "financial chaos" but, as Tose's attorney later admitted, "doublehocked" as well.

The situation was further complicated in June, when another former football partner of Leonard Tose jumped into the legal ring. The partner, John D. Firestone, had been one of the group of rich "friends" who'd entered football with Leonard Tose and become limited partners several years later. Heir to the Firestone rubber fortune, John had sold his 5.1 percent to Leonard Tose, his former friend, in November 1976. Part of the transaction was a $375,000 promissory note upon which Firestone claimed Tose had defaulted. During the first week of June, Firestone filed suit, charging that during 1976 the Eagles had lost money in large part because of "extravagant and wasteful" spending by Tose on "activities wholly unconnected with and unrelated to the business or interests of the club," all of which was a violation of the limited partnership agreement. Among the "wholly unconnected" activities cited in Firestone's complaint were trips to Acapulco, Beverly Hills, and New Orleans by Tose and a trip to Las Vegas by "a female acquaintance of the defendant and her mother," all billed in whole or in part to the Philadelphia Eagles. The club was also billed for the "female acquaintance's" visits to Bonwit Teller, Henri Bendel, and Giorgio's on Rodeo Drive. To send Leonard Tose to watch the Super Bowl that year had cost the football franchise $10,000, including $3300 in limo rentals, $3000 in hotel bills, and a $2000 tab at one restaurant alone. Tose had also charged the Eagles for $9100 of his helicopter expenses and $2000 so his daughter, Susan, in Miami could buy sixteen season tickets to see the Miami Dolphins. Firestone cited Tose's $200,000 overdraft on his salary as well.

By virtue of *Firestone v. Tose,* First Penn's collateral was now not only "in financial chaos" and "doublehocked." It was, at least momentarily, "legally encumbered." It was not at all what John Bunting had hoped for back in March.

Late on the afternoon of July 28, 1977, First Pennsylvania's president peremptorily summoned Leonard Tose and his attorney to bank headquarters. "I perceived Mr. Bunting sitting behind his desk as being pompous, hostile, and arrogant," Tose remembered, "and I said to myself, 'I wonder what this

meeting is all about?' He told me to sit down like [I was] a schoolboy.''
Tose's attorney described Bunting as "icy calm." The bank president had
decided to get tough and the news he had to deliver was blunt. He had not
called Tose there to hear any more excuses and explanations about the Eagles'
losses, Bunting said. The bank wanted Tose to replace himself as chief
financial officer with Sidney Forstater immediately, and give Forstater full
financial control. If Tose refused, First Penn would call in his loan as of 9:00
A.M. the next morning. The bank would also freeze the $1.25 million cur-
rently in the Eagles' checking account and begin bouncing the franchise's
checks.

Tose asked for two weeks of grace in which to find a new bank, but
Bunting had lost all patience and refused his request. "He said, 'I'm calling
in your loan,' '' Tose later testified, "Five and a half million or something
like that, and I was to have it paid by the next morning. I was sort of
shocked.'' Tose objected that the deadline was illegal but Bunting didn't seem
fazed. "He said [I] might win in court," Tose claimed, "but he said that
before that happens, 'I'll bounce Eagles checks and I'll bury you.' He
threatened me. He said, 'I'll make sure you don't get any financing from any
bank in Philadelphia.' I was stunned and he went on, showing his power, and
said that he would see that I didn't get any financing anywhere in the
country.'' Bunting would later testify only to advising Tose he was "an
undesirable bank client.''

When Tose's arguments failed, his lawyer stepped in. During previous
discussions, he argued, First Penn had promised a ninety-day period in which
Tose could find alternative financing should the bank ever decide to call its
loan. The lawyer demanded the ninety days, telling Bunting that Tose could
find new financing because the franchise was valuable. Just a month earlier,
Tose's attorney pointed out, Herb Barness had offered Tose $21.5 million for
it.

"You should have taken it," Bunting replied.

Leonard Tose and his attorney left shortly thereafter. "Bunting was
adamant," the lawyer explained. "We tried to leave with such dignity as we
could muster." That evening, Tose instructed the attorney to go along with
Bunting. For the moment, he had no choice but to do everything the banker
had ordered.

On July 29, Sidney Forstater became chief financial officer of the
Philadelphia Eagles. It was, The Philadelphia Inquirer noted, "the equivalent
of a second string lineman replacing a charismatic superstar." Though Forstater
had been Tose's financial adviser for a while, he and Tose had been on the
outs for several months. Forstater would later describe Tose's approach to
money as "a philosophy of life that I didn't subscribe to." On August 1, a
delegation from First Pennsylvania arrived at the Eagles' training camp to
inform the coaching staff of the change. Led by John Pemberton, the vice-
president who had once assailed Tose as a "jackass," the bankers read the
coaches a formal letter detailing Forstater's new powers. "Mr. Tose told me
to go along with whatever they have to say," Head Coach Dick Vermeil

remembered, "to make no fuss. But then I asked why financial details of the Eagles operation . . . were leaked to the newspapers. Mr. John Pemberton jumped up and said if we didn't cooperate, he'd 'blow this blankety-blank team out of the water.' " Within hours, Forstater had begun laying off front-office employees and implementing plans to slash expenses to the bone. "They were going to destroy the team," Tose whined.

There was little Tose could do about it in the immediate moment. To recover control, he would have to find new financing and that was proving as difficult as Bunting had predicted. "He tried to borrow from every bank in the city," one Eagles source observed. "And in the state for that matter. Nobody would touch him." Perhaps the closest Leonard Tose came in his first week out of power was with the Belgian bank Brussels-Lambert. Interested in putting together a three-bank consortium to cover Tose's refinancing, the Belgian financial institution queried the London office of Philadelphia National Bank. According to later testimony by a bank official, the Philadelphia bank responded, that Tose was a "dissipated playboy" with a reputation for "squandering and frivolity." The Belgians subsequently dropped out of the picture. The more he was turned down, the more desperate Leonard Tose became. Though he still owned the team, he had been required to pay cash in front for tickets to the Eagles first preseason game. "It was a very difficult period for me," Tose admitted. "I was terribly humiliated and despondent. I couldn't sleep."

It is likely Leonard Tose would have had simply to accept his humiliation if the move by First Penn had not also created severe dilemmas for the National Football League as a whole. For Rozelle in particular it was déjà vu of the worst sort. He had been solving "the Philadelphia problem" since he became commissioner and the Eagles financial collapse in 1977 was a decided embarrassment. Worse, it was also a challenge to ownership policy itself. The Eagles were, in effect, now operated by a corporation, First Pennsylvania Bank, an arrangement Rozelle himself had forecast as the beginning of the end for the NFL. Rozelle was also less than enamored by Sidney Forstater's approach to the football business. One of the commissioner's responsibilities was mediating contract disputes, and within Forstater's first week, Rozelle had intervened in at least one instance and forced Forstater to spend money he didn't want to. Through most of that same week, Forstater was bragging that "Leonard Tose is dead."

Forstater, however, had not calculated on the NFL raising Leonard Tose from the grave. The process began when Tose called Rozelle and, as he explained to The [Philadelphia] Bulletin, said, "Help me." It was, Tose noted, the first time in his memory he had ever used the phrase. The NFL response was immediate. Art Rooney, Bill Bidwill, Wellington Mara, and Art Modell all called the Philadelphia owner to see if they could help find a bank. The most important call came from William Clay Ford, owner of the Detroit Lions. Ford was a director of Manufacturers National Bank in Detroit and suggested Tose try there. To file the necessary paperwork, Tose and his general manager, Jimmy Murray, secretly borrowed the material from the

Eagles' files and conveyed it to Detroit without Forstater's knowledge. "While they were shoveling the dirt on Leonard Tose," Murray noted, "they should have looked in the box. Leonard wasn't there at all. He was alive. Very much alive."

On the afternoon of August 9, Manufacturers National, despite its reputation as a conservative institution, loaned Leonard Tose $5.3 million with which to pay off First Penn. The money was described as a bridge loan, due the following February and designed to buy Tose the time to find longterm financing. Also included in the loan was $1 million to pay off Bruce Rappoport and eliminate the franchise's doublehock. "This arrangement does not mean Leonard Tose is free of debt," John Bunting noted. "He is still very much indebted to someone, although he is free and clear of First Pennsylvania." Asked how he felt when the money actually changed hands, Bunting responded, "As if Santa Claus had just arrived."

In debt or not, Leonard Tose was back in control and relishing the fact. His first step was to fire Sidney Forstater. "Sidney had illusions of grandeur," Tose explained. "I think he was promised big things from First Pennsylvania and probably from Barness. I could [sic] care less now." The next morning, Tose called a press conference and went after John Bunting and First Penn. Bunting was, Tose offered to *The* [Philadelphia] *Bulletin,* "a son of a bitch" and the bank had been part of a "plot from within to get me." The paper described Leonard Tose's return "one of the greatest comebacks in recent Philadelphia sports history" and Tose himself credited "Rozelle and his fellow NFL owners who rallied around him when he was down."

The task of explaining why the National Football League had chosen to do so fell to Art Modell of the Cleveland Indians. "You must understand that there is a great camaraderie among the owners," Modell offered the day Tose's return was announced. "When one of us is in trouble, the others come to his aid. This camaraderie, that's what makes the NFL such a beautiful thing to be part of. While there is no love lost on Sunday [when games are played], it's all for one and one for all the rest of the time. We have strong feelings for Len Tose. We want to see him succeed."

They should have known better. Far from accomplished, the financial rescue of Leonard Tose had in fact only just begun.

6

Only one National Football League owner stood noticeably outside the bound aries of the "one for all, all for one" ethos articulated by Art Modell in the summer of 1977. That one was, of course, Al Davis. By the time the League had rescued Leonard Tose from First Pennsylvania Bank, *Atkinson v. Noll* had been to trial, confirming the Raiders owner in his outcast role. "Al didn't care how he did it," Rozelle claimed. "Hurting the League didn't bother him at all. He just wanted to win that case."

That spring, Davis had dispatched Al LoCasale, his principal assistant, to the League's Park Avenue headquarters to collect evidence for Atkinson's attorneys. The evidence consisted of film clips from the NFL's film subsidiary, all illustrating America's Game at its most violent moments. Their use helped turn the slander suit into what *Sports Illustrated* called "a nasty spitting contest that seemed, at times, to be aimed mainly at proving in court whether the Steelers or the Raiders were the dirtiest team in football." As such, it was a public relations disaster for which the commissioner held Al Davis personally responsible. Davis was not, however, the only owner pushing the confrontation. Dan Rooney, whose Steelers were lined up behind their coach, Chuck Noll, was equally adamant. Rooney's insurance company exerted great pressure on him to settle the suit with a $50,000 payment to Atkinson, but Rooney steadily refused. "We were never interested in making a settlement," Rooney explained. "The wrong people were being sued. If we settled, every player would be suing every time he was criticized. We felt we had to go to court to save the game."

Court opened on July 11 in San Francisco's Federal Building. Noll's attorney argued that Atkinson's hit on Lynn Swann was an "illegal act," violating two clear NFL rules, and provided the context for the Pittsburgh coach's description of Atkinson as among the League's "criminal element." Atkinson's attorney responded that though his client was "no angel and no saint," he was also "not a criminal element." Football was "a game of violent physical contact, rough and tough and injury-producing." Indeed, even the NFL's legal hits were enough to cause permanent physical damage. "It is," Atkinson's attorney pointed out, "legal combat which television shows to sixty to eighty million Americans," every weekend, September to January.

Atkinson's case made excellent use of the footage Al LoCasale had collected from NFL Films. When Chuck Noll was on the stand, he was deluged with video examples of Steelers doing mayhem and ultimately admitted that at least four of his own players belonged on any list of the League's "criminal element."

The commissioner's office was disgusted with the approach and made no bones about it. "The whole thrust of the defense was 'you think this is bad,' " one NFL attorney complained, " 'see how dirty these other bastards play.' That such talk hurt the League is obvious." Rozelle himself was particularly disgusted with Davis. "Al sat near the jury box," Rozelle remembered, "and every time they would show [film clips of] another play, he'd wince and make noises for the jury's benefit."

Atkinson's case also rested heavily on the notion that the League's action against him was the product of what his attorney called "a conspiracy on the part of the Rozelle-Rooney establishment to get the outcast upstart Oakland crowd led by Al Davis." Atkinson's attorney had even written Davis a long warning letter to that effect before the trial began. "Rozelle and Rooney want to dismantle your team," the attorney had observed. "Every official works for Rozelle and every discretionary play from now on could go against you." Though Davis was silent on the subject himself, Rozelle had little doubt he was the argument's architect. "It was," he remembered, "the first example of Al Davis's line."

Al Davis himself took the stand on George Atkinson's behalf on July 17. He was dressed in a white shirt, silver tie, and "dead-black" suit—what Noll's attorney snidely called his "sincere" outfit. Davis now knew that Rozelle was considering his removal from the Competition Committee, but was evidently unfazed. For him, the issue was defending his player and ridding his team of Noll's "label." "Anytime anybody steps on the football playing field," he testified, "there is an element of risk. Every player assumes that. It's part of his contract." George Atkinson's blow to Lynn Swann had been part of that assumed risk and Noll's description of him as "criminal" had diminished his value. "Right now Mr. Atkinson is in limbo," he continued. "Last year I tried to trade him. Right now I'm not because his trade value has lessened. He has an erroneous label that I think has to be reversed." Trying to single Atkinson out was also hypocritical. "In every game that I have ever observed," Davis pointed out, "we have the paradox— the hypocritical thing—that there are some things that are legal that are more violent than things that are illegal. Our problem is to confront this."

Pete Rozelle took the stand on July 18. He had given a lengthy deposition a month earlier and could have substituted it for personal testimony, but nonetheless decided to appear. The reason, according to *Sports Illustrated,* was that "the commissioner had decided that his and the League's reputations were at stake." He looked tan and fit in a business suit and evinced no doubt that his fine of Atkinson had been appropriate. "I am fully convinced that there is no place in professional football for the kind of fouls committed by George Atkinson," Rozelle offered. "Such conduct is clearly outside the rules and calculated either to disable opposing players or to intimidate them into less effective performance." He did not, however, admit to the existence of a "criminal element." He described Atkinson as "an outstanding defensive back" and speculated that Noll's comments might well have enhanced Atkinson's value because they made him more recognizable and hence a candidate for work in commercials. The commissioner's performance would later be described as "unflappable," "strong," and "tranquil," enough so that Atkinson's attorney called him "a professional witness."

Rozelle's cross-examination epitomized the tone of Atkinson's case. Having already described the League's offices as a "castle on Park Avenue," Atkinson's attorney started his questioning by looking over Rozelle's tan and asking if he'd just returned from the Greek isles. The answer was "no." The questioning that followed concentrated on Rozelle's relationship with Dan Rooney and the Steelers. Though admitting that he and Rooney had spoken on the phone some six or eight times since the trial had begun, he denied they were friends and would admit only to being "close acquaintances." Whatever the semantics of their relationship, he denied he had done anything "unusual or unfair" in handling Atkinson's disciplinary action. Pounding on the Rozelle-Rooney axis, Atkinson's lawyer got Rozelle to admit that he had spoken with Rooney perhaps fourteen or eighteen times in the nine months preceding the trial. Rozelle also admitted he hadn't talked with Al Davis once on the phone in the same period. "I have more communication with Pittsburgh than with Oakland," he responded somewhat wryly, "because I get the impression the Oakland organization isn't interested in having much contact with the League office."

Final arguments were delivered on July 22. Noll's attorney went after Atkinson, pointing out that the Raider defensive back had been previously charged with embezzlement, carrying a concealed weapon, and threatening to castrate a man. "Since injury to reputation is the gist of slander," he pointed out, "a bad reputation must be considered." Noll's attorney also sought to lift the onus of violence off the League and onto its audience. He noted that the Oakland crowd had cheered when George Atkinson hit Lynn Swann and called it "a sad commentary on the motives of our generation. It's sadistic," he continued, "this secret love of violence, the spectacle of liking to see others hurt, happiness at pain, enthralled by the love of blood. That's the America of George Atkinson." And, by inference at least, Al Davis.

Atkinson's attorney, whose fees were reportedly being paid by Davis, went after the NFL when his turn came, calling the League "second only to the U.S. government in terms of power, scope, and potential." George Atkinson's mistake had been being "a rag-tag kid brawling with the establishment." He was a "pawn" between Davis and Rozelle, "because he wore a Raider helmet" and "there were differences" between the commissioner and Davis dating back to 1966 and the last rounds of the AFL war. "Glib Rozelle," the attorney warned, "came out here to give aid to his friend, Dan Rooney. He is very smooth and very clever, but he came in and brainwashed the truth."

The jury took the case that afternoon and returned a verdict four hours later: no slander, no malice, no damages for Atkinson. "Raider Star A Loser," The [Oakland] Tribune proclaimed. Al Davis made no comment.

Though hard-won, the victory was also hard for the victors to savor. "This has been the most depressing thing I've ever done," Dan Rooney observed outside the courtroom after the verdict came in. Rozelle, back on Park Avenue, had difficulty celebrating as well. Win or not, he pointed out, "the ugliness of it had stained everything and everyone involved and may well continue to smear the NFL for a long time to come." Damage control was Rozelle's responsibility, and the damage was done. It would not, however, go unpunished. Rozelle would see to that in October, the next time the League met.

In the meantime, Atkinson v. Noll was a victory, hard to savor or not, and it was not without impact inside the NFL. The case set an important emotional precedent, if not a legal one. Davis had been taken on in court at his instigation and Davis had been beaten. Rozelle had been an impressive witness and Davis much less so. Most important, Dan Rooney's decision to "go to court to save the game" had been vindicated. The jury's verdict couldn't help but give Rozelle, Rooney, and the rest of the League confidence in doing the same thing for the same reasons and with the same expectations of success when next faced with a legal challenge from Al Davis.

That confidence would be reinforced by the antagonism toward Davis which *Atkinson v. Noll* escalated to a new level of intensity. Almost everyone in the League enjoyed seeing Davis beaten, whether he had subscribed to all of Dan Rooney's warnings about the case or not. While there was still a wide continuum of feelings toward Davis inside the NFL, from the Atkinson suit on, its principal motion was away from him.

Gene Klein was a case in point. Once indifferent, even friendly to Davis, he was now well on his way to the extreme anti-Davis position he would later hold. His bad feelings had been nurtured by the presence of Klein's Chargers in the Raiders' division and Davis's history of thumping them regularly. Gene Klein was an easy man to offend and to be offended by, and he had done both in his relations with Davis. He knew Davis would go to any lengths to gain an advantage and considered him someone who wanted one rule for himself and another one for everybody else. *Atkinson v. Noll* confirmed Klein's assessment and made him feel his resentment was justified. That resentment was reconfirmed and even further intensified by an incident between the two men during the NFL's slate of preseason games, several weeks after George Atkinson's suit failed.

Klein's team had flown north for an exhibition at the Oakland Coliseum in something of a state of flux. His star quarterback, Dan Fouts, had yet to report and was holding out for a new contract. Because of that star's absence, the Raiders had promoted the game by hyping San Diego's second string quarterback, James Harris, one of the first blacks ever to play that position in the NFL. Given that the city of Oakland was more than half black, it was a natural promotion. Klein's coach, however, pulled the second string quarterback after four plays and used a white third stringer the rest of the game. Davis was furious, feeling Klein had spoiled his promotion and failed to let the Raiders play against top-flight competition, thus diminishing the value of the exhibition. As a consequence, he refused to send Klein his share of the gate receipts, and only did so when Rozelle's office intervened and forced him to.

"He's an asshole," Gene Klein charged, "and he wants to run the whole League. Rozelle had no choice about dealing with him. If you don't put a guy like Davis in his place, pretty soon you got no League left."

7

Pete Rozelle delivered the comeuppance he had been planning for Al Davis on October 13, at a one-day League meeting in the NFL's New York headquarters.

Typically, Rozelle's final assault on Davis's competition committee seat came late in the afternoon, when everyone was tired and sentiments were running very much the commissioner's way. Rozelle delivered his blow without fanfare. It was the next to last item on the agenda and amounted to no more than the distribution of a list of new committee assignments. The list, according to the minutes, included "some changes and additions as called for under the expression of policy adopted unanimously at the annual meeting in Phoenix last March." Some ten League and five Management Council committees with a total of sixty seats were included and Al Davis's name was nowhere to be seen. The minutes noted no discussion of the document, though most members noticed Davis's absence from the new Competition Committee. Al Davis himself was not in attendance on October 13. Apparently anticipating Rozelle's move, he had dispatched his assistant, LoCasale, to New York in his place.

The big winner on the committee list distributed by Rozelle was Hugh Culverhouse, owner of the new Tampa Bay Buccaneers. In the midst of only his second season of fielding a football team, Culverhouse was nonetheless named to both the three-member Congressional Relations Committee and the four-member Finance Committee, two of the more important postings on Rozelle's list. The idea of using the Tampa owner that way had originally come from Carroll Rosenbloom, in his anti-Rozelle tirade two years earlier. "Carroll complained about how people with skills were not being used on committees," Rozelle remembered, "and pointed to Hugh Culverhouse as an example. I thought it was a good idea. Culverhouse is just a real sharp guy who gives of his time." By 1977, several League members had already hired Culverhouse's tax consulting services and, though ambitious, he was a relatively unthreatening presence. "He's the sweetest southern gentleman you could hope to meet," one owner observed, "and in the beginning he played the deferential beginner's role. He was more suited to numbers than speeches, but he was brilliant and he made himself useful."

In the NFL's lexicon, Hugh Culverhouse was a "business guy," not a "football guy." At the time of the October 13 meeting, his Buccaneers had a lifetime record of no wins, twenty-one losses. He also played the role of owner with a decided absence of flash. Already fat when he joined the League, he had added twenty-five pounds since. On game days, he and his wife often wore matching outfits in the Buccaneers' colors and at NFL meetings he was known for wearing gaudy sport coats that clashed with his slacks. He attended all his team's games on the road as well as at home, usually flying on the team's chartered jet and riding one of the team's three buses to the stadium. In Denver the previous year, he had been late getting back to the buses after the game and reached the stadium parking lot just as the last one drove off. Tampa's owner chased after his bus as best he was able, throwing rocks at its back window in an attempt to get it to stop, but it didn't and he was forced to hitch a ride with Denver's team doctor. When Culverhouse arrived at his own team's hotel and caught up with his staff, he delivered what several staffers described as "the worst chewing-out he ever gave us." Henceforth, the last Buccaneer bus was on standing instructions not to leave unless the owner was on it.

Despite the molasses in his public manner, Hugh Culverhouse was not a particularly easy boss to please. He had entered the football business thinking he could rely on "pros to do the job for him" but then, according to his accountant, "found that he and his office had to do more in the daily operations of the team than he had ever suspected." One consequence of that involvement was the departure of the franchise's vice-president of operations, director of administration, director of promotions, business manager, ticket manager, and some six other members of the front office in Culverhouse's first two years in business. During the same period, he acquired a reputation as a "tightwad" among his employees, and was said to complain about items as small as the cost of the paper in the office copying machine. He also "spent many uncounted and painstaking hours doing a personal economic analysis of the future of pro football, taking advantage of financial reports of other teams, interviews with League executives and other owners, and the financial consultation of some of his clients and the many corporations on whose director boards he sits." In the end, rather than rely on "pros," Culverhouse became one himself.

It was precisely that expertise Rozelle sought to tap by putting Culverhouse on the finance committee. Culverhouse in turn made good use of his position. Seven years later, one NFL owner would rate the Tampa owner "right up there power-wise." Another would call him "more the vice-commissioner than Tex Schramm." Culverhouse's rise would coincide with his usefulness. "He did everybody's taxes for them," one NFL observer pointed out, "and he became the commissioner's adviser on finances." He was also the right man with the right expertise at the right time. The cash flow of the football business was about to escalate sharply, making Hugh Culverhouse even more useful than he would have been otherwise.

Pete Rozelle had announced that escalation six hours earlier as the first item on the League's October 13 agenda. Using the superlative TV numbers generated by the 1976 season to great advantage, he had spent the previous six months hammering out a new four-year agreement with the networks. The actual numbers involved had been the owners' favorite subject of speculation since the negotiations began. "The clubs of the League would be calling me as the television negotiations were under way," Rozelle explained, "and they would call Mr. Klein and Mr. Modell [the other TV committee members]. Like a kid at Christmas: 'What do you think it's going to be?' I told everyone . . . we didn't know. You had to deal with three networks. It depends upon the television situation at the time . . . and we just didn't know."

Most of the ensuing speculation assumed the contract would be larger than the $2.2 million a year they were each currently receiving. "I heard three million dollars from a number of sources," Billy Sullivan remembered, "and I think some of the more optimistic predictions were running three and a half. But it was strictly speculation because the commissioner who with his colleagues [on the TV committee], to whom he always gives credit for getting the job done, had, very frankly, at no time indicated what the figures would be, because, frankly, there are critics of the commissioner and some of the people that wanted to hurt him were throwing huge numbers out so if he didn't reach that, they would say he'd done a poor job. . . . One of the owners in the League who was constantly trying to depreciate [sic] the commissioner's position was talking numbers out of sight." Sullivan identified the "out of sight numbers" as "over four million."

Sullivan chose not to identify the "one owner," but Al Davis was the most likely candidate. Davis would later claim to have expected a sharp escalation rather than the incremental growth assumed by the rest of the League. "I took into consideration several factors relative to television," he would explain.

Whether or not Davis had been prescient, he was certainly correct. The new television deals Rozelle announced were worth some $576 million to the League over four years. The new deal would pay each club an average of $5.2 million a year, an increase of 133 percent. In return, the League would go to a sixteen-game schedule, add a "wild card" to the playoff system, and stage at least an additional four prime time games on Tuesday, Thursday, or Saturday nights. The networks, the commissioner noted, had wanted even more games, but he had done "a tightrope act" to avoid "saturation" of the market. *The New York Times* later described the new arrangement as "the biggest deal in television history" and noted that "never before in an industry in which program life is short have such rich long-term commitments been made." It was also a historic moment in the NFL. For the first time ever, the average team's income from the League's shared television revenues would now exceed its income from its own live gate.

Almost everyone who heard Rozelle's announcement on October 13 greeted the numbers with awe. Most were also quick to give Rozelle the credit. The acclaim was predictable and provided Al Davis with another good reason for missing the meeting. He could not have wanted any part of the commissioner's moment of triumph, especially since it coincided with his own comeuppance at Rozelle's hands.

Davis did make his presence felt, however, absent or not, and did so in a manner calculated to piss the commissioner off.

After Rozelle and Art Modell gave more explanation of the agreement and the League's treasurer presented "a summary of the annual club cash flow projections" over the life of the TV contract, the Television Committee presented six proposed amendments to the constitution, designed to simplify the commissioner's job of scheduling games under the new arrangements with the networks. Four of the six were special guarantees given the New York Giants, New York Jets, San Francisco 49ers, and Oakland Raiders at the time of the merger agreement ten years earlier. They required the commissioner to get the permission of those teams in order to schedule their home games any day but Sunday or schedule competing home games on the same day in the same market. The terms had been included in the merger agreement to ease the friction of sharing the same market and had been informally ignored almost since their inception. Their elimination was considered necessary in order to provide Rozelle's office with "more latitude in the development of the playing schedule." It would require a unanimous vote.

The amendments were all moved by Wellington Mara of the Giants and seconded by the general manager representing Leon Hess and the Jets. Eddie DeBartolo, the third of the four affected parties, offered "to waive the provisions at any time to assist in development of the playing schedule." That left the Raiders, represented by Al LoCasale. LoCasale voted no on all four and all four failed by votes of twenty-seven to one.

When asked for an explanation, the minutes reported, "Mr. LoCasale said Oakland was voting no because of insufficient time to examine and study the effect of the proposed amendments." Rozelle no doubt saw the stance as another instance of Raider obstreperousness for obstreperousness's sake, but maintained his veneer of politeness and "asked that he be notified as soon as possible if Oakland were to decide to change its vote."

To no one's great surprise, no such notification was ever forthcoming.

8

While Al Davis no doubt shared some of his darker thoughts about Pete Rozelle with his closest friend in the League, Carroll Rosenbloom, Rosenbloom's own relationship with the commissioner was headed in the opposite direction. C.R., having already raised hell in no uncertain terms, was now content to make peace. The reasons for his turnaround were several.

The first was a certain amount of persuasion applied by other owners. One of those doing the persuading was Hugh Culverhouse. He and C.R. had long since patched up their differences. Culverhouse now helped Rosenbloom with his taxes and had been named by C.R. as one of the executors of his latest will. Culverhouse was also an apostle of getting along with the commissioner. Perhaps the most effective persuasion came from Leon Hess, owner of the Jets. In late 1977, Hess led an NFL peacekeeping mission to Los Angeles that also included Edward Bennett Williams and Chuck Sullivan. The object was to get Carroll to lighten up on Rozelle. "Carroll liked Hess," Steve Rosenbloom remembered. "He and Hess could speak the same language. They were both the same age and both successful businessmen. When Carroll talked to me about the visit, he said Hess hit the right chords. Also I think my father was beginning to get enough satisfaction from the commissioner's office and wasn't nearly so irritated."

A second reason was Carroll's sense of his own mortality and his worry about the legacy he might leave behind.

"I've had a lot of fights with guys in the League," he mentioned to his son Steve after Hess's peacekeeping mission had left town. "I think I should patch things up so you don't have a problem when I'm gone."

"Don't worry about me," Steve responded. "You'll be around for a long time."

Nonetheless, Carroll would remake his relationships with Tex Schramm and Art Modell, as well as the commissioner himself, by early 1978.

The third and perhaps overriding reason for doing so was that Rosenbloom had other fish to fry and it would be a lot easier if Rozelle were on his side rather than against him.

What C.R. wanted more than anything else was out of the L.A. Coliseum. By 1977, he had given up trying to get what he wanted there. "When I came out here in 1972," he pointed out, "I saw that the [baseball] Dodgers had a fine place to play. I saw that the other baseball team [the California Angels] had a fine place to play in Anaheim. And I tried to work with the Coliseum people to get the stadium improved. First, I wanted to spend my own money. I offered to buy the Coliseum. I told them, 'If you can't make these improvements, perhaps you can find a way to sell it to me. Then you'll be free of it.' I didn't know at the time that they couldn't be free of it because they have to support that other thing, the Sports Arena. I've tried every way in the world to get something done . . . and the Coliseum is [still] not that safe and enjoyable."

If anything, C.R.'s description of his home field was charitable. The Los Angeles Times called the L.A. Coliseum "an aging monolithic structure in south-central Los Angeles assaulted on three sides by what socio-economists would call urban blight." Due to several well-publicized muggings in the stadium parking lot, the Rams now employed "a special security force of husky young men in T-shirts and windbreakers" who were "purposefully conspicuous in great numbers" on game days. Even so, the Rams' average attendance had slipped from seventy-six thousand a game in 1974 to fifty-three thousand in 1977, despite fielding teams that consistently won the National Conference's Western Division. When the Rams sent a questionnaire to their ticket holders asking how Rams games could be improved, ninety-nine percent of the respondents complained about the Coliseum. "The parking is bad," Steve Rosenbloom pointed out, "the concessions are inadequate, the sound system is either too loud or you can't hear it, the scoreboard doesn't work half the time, the elevator is out of order too often, and the rest rooms aren't clean enough.''

Rosenbloom still had the dilemma of where to go, and by the time Rozelle announced the League's new television contracts in October 1977, Carroll had decided that the city of Anaheim was his best bet. Twenty-eight miles outside Los Angeles's city limits in neighboring Orange County, it was nonetheless well within the seventy-five-mile radius allotted each NFL franchise for its home turf and, in League eyes, a move to Anaheim would be no different from the Cowboys moving to Irving, the Giants moving to Jersey, or the Patriots moving to Foxboro. Carroll had spotted its possibilities in 1972 when he was still fresh to Los Angeles. He considered its Big A stadium, then housing only a baseball team, to be small at forty-three thousand seats, but "spotlessly clean" and "an enjoyable safe place to go." In 1972, he had even begun preliminary negotiations with the city's stadium manager. "Our proposal to the Rams at that time called for the city to provide the land for Rosenbloom or others to build a stadium he would control," the manager recalled, "a basic football stadium next to the Big A or across the street." Rosenbloom still had hopes for the L.A. Coliseum then, however, and had used Anaheim's offer only to generate leverage on the Los Angeles Memorial Coliseum Commission.

In the fall of 1977, C.R.'s strategy was the reverse. While secretly dispatching an assistant to make contact with Anaheim, he also began discussions with the LAMCC. His lease in Los Angeles ran through 1979, but he wanted to know what the LAMCC was willing to do now to keep him. Before, Al Davis noted, "Carroll got advantages from the Los Angeles Coliseum when he threatened to leave the Coliseum. This time, he used the Coliseum—that he might stay there—as a lever and he got the advantages from Anaheim.''

Anaheim was pleased to be in the bidding. The city had been searching for a football franchise since 1966. That year, Al Davis, then AFL commissioner and in the midst of launching blitzkrieg against the NFL, had selected it for an AFL expansion site in order to wrest control of the country's second largest market from the older league. Before the franchise fee could be delivered, however, merger ended the war and left Anaheim without football. In 1972, Orange County's principal city had tried again with its first offer to Rosenbloom and in 1974, had played host to the short-lived California Sun in the World Football League. The treatment given Anaheim during the NFL's recent expansion had left the city with no hope of obtaining a new NFL franchise, so when Rosenbloom came knocking a second time, Anaheim offered him everything it had that it thought he might want.

Most of what it had was land—ninety-five acres immediately adjacent to Big A, currently used to provide parking for California Angel baseball games. Anaheim had wanted to develop the parcel for a long time and used the inquiry from Rosenbloom to put the idea in motion. What the city suggested was a two-tiered arrangement. Big A Stadium would be expanded to seat seventy to eighty thousand, including luxury boxes, and then leased to the Rams on better terms than Rosenbloom's franchise currently had in Los Angeles. In return, Rosenbloom would also sign a longterm lease with option to buy on the adjoining ninety-five-acre parking lot. There, he would put up a hotel or office complex or whatever development both he and the city could agree on. The way Anaheim had it figured, its rent receipts and the taxes that would be generated by the ninety-five-acre development would cover the costs of redoing Big A and put Anaheim in the big leagues to boot.

Rosenbloom was intrigued by the offer, but by no means sold. "Carroll's concern was to get a new stadium," his son Steve pointed out. "He'd been trying for one for twenty-five years. Anaheim was an attractive possibility. We would have $150,000 more gross a week there. Anaheim also wanted to do something with the parking lot. They'd tried before and failed. They told my father maybe he could get a developer. Anaheim couldn't get a developer themselves. They're Disneyland people. They talked about building a monorail from the stadium to Disneyland and crazy shit like that. Carroll didn't like real estate and was leery of it all. As a businessman, he thought it was a big risk." A developer other than Carroll Rosenbloom would have to be found by the city for the deal to go forward.

Using the possibility of the Rams as fresh bait, Anaheim now went shopping for developers. The most interested party it found was Cabot, Cabot & Forbes, a Boston-based company with projects all over the United States. "It was kind of intriguing to us at that particular point in time," James Kenyon, the senior vice-president then in charge of CC&F's Los Angeles office, explained. "We felt that the property represented pioneering. . . . The economics of the project were really gut-feel. CC&F had some financial difficulty in mid-1976. We had sold a lot of our holdings. We reorganized and we really were looking for a bellwether, high prestige, quality development to do in the western United States. We felt that the draw of the Rams, the modernization of the stadium, the identity, the developer's dream of controlling a large parcel of land so you can properly master-plan it was terrifically egotistically interesting to CC&F."

After inspecting the ninety-five acres, Kenyon had "a get-acquainted meeting" with the city of Anaheim. "The city made it loud and clear that they wanted the property developed," he remembered, "and they wanted a national developer, somebody with some image." For its part, CC&F wanted a joint venture on the project and the partner it wanted was Carroll Rosenbloom. "It was obvious to us," the vice-president explained, "for two reasons: one is that Mr. Rosenbloom was reputed to have a very large net worth, a financially successful guy. Number two, the Rams are the tenant that put the biggest stress on the [proposed] usage. It was logical for us to tie the two of them together." The city showed CC&F its preliminary numbers on the stadium idea, but CC&F made no financial projections itself.

A month after getting acquainted, Cabot, Cabot & Forbes sent Jerry Blakely, its chairman of the board, out to Anaheim to pursue the discussion further. He also helicoptered to Long Beach's Blair Field near the Rams training facility to meet with Carroll Rosenbloom during one of the owner's forays down from Trancas Beach to see his team practice. According to Kenyon, who was present, the CC&F officers "kind of chit-chatted with Mr. Rosenbloom about possibly moving the Rams to Anaheim." C.R. was receptive enough to the possibility that the chairman arranged to meet with him again soon to get more specific.

In the meantime, the developers did more of their homework. CC&F had not been involved in a stadium project since its participation in building the Harvard Bowl in 1907. To update itself, it consulted the architectural firm of Skidmore, Owings and Merrill in Chicago. SOM's design team had done the Oakland Coliseum in the mid-1960s and just completed a stadium analysis for Max Winter in Minneapolis. CC&F's chairman of the board then used the information SOM had provided to make a presentation to Rosenbloom back in Los Angeles. It included "an analysis of the last twenty-seven stadiums built in America, about the parking ratio, the sight lines, all of the various buzz words when it comes to stadiums," and the presentation of pictures and brochures about previous CC&F developments.

The discussion was aided by the rapport between Rosenbloom and Blakely, CC&F's chairman. Their sons had attended the same eastern prep school and they both served on the school's board together. Blakely "told Carroll that we would not move forward with the deal unless he was a partner, for obvious reasons to us. We needed a partner and we felt that the combination of a tenant who potentially is going to average sixty-five thousand people in the stadium was important because you had to work collectively." For his part, C.R. remained enthusiastic but noncommittal. "Carroll was awfully hard to pin down," CC&F's senior vice-president noted, "an excellent businessman."

By the time 1977 had become 1978, however, CC&F felt it had to have some kind of commitment before it could go forward. There were still other developers in the picture who had been approached as Anaheim shopped around, and CC&F wanted some guarantee of exclusivity. "We said," Kenyon remembered, "make a decision about who is going to move forward with development."

Rosenbloom did. On January 20, 1978, C.R. signed a letter of intent with Cabot, Cabot & Forbes. The letter did not bind him to moving to Anaheim, but did bind him to CC&F as his exclusive partner should he move forward "to develop the stadium and develop the peripheral land." The letter specifically stated his intent to form Anaheim Stadium Associates. Fifty percent of Anaheim Associates would be owned by RAMCO, a Rosenbloom holding company, and fifty percent would be owned by CC&F Stadium Properties, a wholly owned subsidiary of CC&F. Together, they would see what kind of terms they could extract from the city of Anaheim.

Now C.R.'s Superstadium Game was in high gear.

News that Rosenbloom was up to something in Anaheim reached the general public in Los Angeles a week later when the *Los Angeles Times* ran a story headlined "Rams Appear Closer to Anaheim Stadium." Though as yet unaware of Anaheim Stadium Associates or the involvement of CC&F, the

Times got the outlines of Anaheim's proposal right and, from the Los Angeles Memorial Coliseum Commission's perspective, the news could not have been worse. The LAMCC had been continuing conversations with the Rams, but was waiting to find out if its bid for the 1984 Olympics would be accepted before committing itself to any improvements. The *Times* story made that strategy dysfunctional. With the Rams publicly identified as "closer to leaving Los Angeles than at any time since they came west in 1946," something would have to be done and done soon. Speaking for the Rams, Steve Rosenbloom pointed out that Los Angeles's options were limited. "If the Coliseum could offer us the same things that Anaheim can offer," Carroll's son promised, "we'd stay at the Coliseum." Otherwise, the Rams were leaving. If they did, the nation's second largest city would be without a football team and the Los Angeles Coliseum and Sports Arena would have to be bailed out of potential bankruptcy. "If we don't get the message this time," the L.A. Coliseum general manager observed to the *Times,* "we're pretty stupid."

While the LAMCC struggled to get a counteroffer together, Anaheim let it know the stakes were high. In early February, a group calling itself "The Committee to Relocate the Rams to Orange County" bought a full page ad in the *Times* for "An Open Letter to the Los Angeles Rams." The committee included representatives of business, industry, and local government, including the mayors of Orange County's twenty-six cities and five of the county supervisors. Their letter described Anaheim as "a modern, attractive place" to watch a game and called on Carroll Rosenbloom to move the franchise there "for the betterment of professional football."

The vice-president of the Los Angeles Memorial Coliseum Commission called the ad "a declaration of war."

At the time, the statement seemed like hyperbole.

Six years later, it would sound like understatement.

9

By the time Anaheim made its declaration of war, Carroll Rosenbloom was back on speaking terms with Pete Rozelle.

The ice had been broken by a series of phone calls in which C.R. reported to the commissioner on developments with the L.A. Coliseum. "He telephoned on several occasions," Rozelle recalled, "and he told me that the Los Angeles Memorial Coliseum Committee would do nothing to improve the stadium. . . . There were a number of things that he wanted to participate [in] with them, he said, in improving the stadium, but they wouldn't do it. His phone conversations with me developed a pattern of growing disenchantment and then he mentioned the possibilities he felt existed at Anaheim to have the stadium . . . refurbished so that it could be a good stadium for football. . . . He told me that he was considering moving there. . . . It was not an extensive discussion. . . . He just said he felt it would be an attractive deal.''

Pete Rozelle would later express feelings of great emotional loyalty to the L.A. Coliseum as "the place where I first watched football games as a kid,'' but in February 1978, he said nothing that might jeopardize his newfound communication with C.R. The commissioner did not treat Rosenbloom's mention of Anaheim as a cloud of war on the League's horizon. Nor did he express concern over just what effects a vacancy in the nation's second city might have on the NFL. Rosenbloom's Superstadium Game was considered his business, not the League's, and simply tracked from a distance by the commissioner's office and Rozelle himself. At the time, it was one of the less pressing developments demanding the commissioner's attention.

Perhaps the most pressing was, once again, the case of Leonard Tose in Philadelphia. The bridge loan supplied by William Clay Ford's Detroit bank in August was coming due on February 9, 1978, and finding a replacement proved no small task. To make sure that it happened, both Tose and Rozelle turned to Chuck Sullivan, Billy Sullivan's oldest son. Chuck's rescue of his father had established his reputation as the best man in the NFL at dealing with banks.

At the moment, Chuck Sullivan was also the League's rising star. Executive vice-president of the New England Patriots, he handled all the franchise's finances. He was also in the process of becoming personal attorney for Carrie Rozelle's family. In June 1977, the rest of the League's owners had voted him chairman of the Management Council, replacing Wellington Mara. The reasons for their choice, according to Rozelle, were "because Chuck stays close, attends meetings regularly, and is based in New York.'' Despite the complete absence of any experience in labor negotiating, Chuck had also been the first person in memory to push himself for the job.

Though he was already reaping the benefits of its success, Chuck Sullivan's brilliant quarterbacking of his father's comeback was not yet complete. Two outstanding items remained unsettled. The first was several suits filed by the nonvoting shareholders who had been forced to sell their interests to Billy, but none of those were yet close to trial in 1978.

The other unsettled item was the Patriots' taxes. Billy's purchase of the Patriots had been calculated under the old tax depreciation laws and the new ones were putting an unanticipated strain on the Sullivans' cash flow. To help ease the strain, Billy hired Edward Bennett Williams's law firm to approach the IRS for an adjustment. Sullivan's argument was that since he had already begun the process of taking over sole ownership in 1975, months before the tax change, he ought to be treated under the old law, even though the takeover had been finally consummated after the new law's deadline. When no adjustment was forthcoming, Billy sought an act of Congress to allow him the benefits of the old depreciation system. The legislation was first introduced by Massachusetts Senator Edward Brooke in 1976 but failed in the House. In

1978, Brooke planned to reintroduce it, this time as a rider on another, unrelated bill. "I'm just asking to be treated like every other sports team," Old Billy explained. "It's a penny-ante thing to Congress, designed to rectify an inequity." Billy's new tax bill was just in the talking stages when Chuck took on the task of finding Leonard Tose a bank loan and, since politics was his father's bailiwick, the effort in Washington required little of Chuck's time.

Chuck Sullivan's involvement with Leonard Tose's finances would later be characterized as an extension of his management council duties, but there was more to it than that. Sullivan was also an attorney who worked for a fee other than the joy of one for all, all for one. "He did it for the money," Tose later explained. Sullivan's fee, calculated in percentage points of the loan, was no doubt considerable, but it was also well-earned. Finding a bank willing to have Leonard Tose for a client was a genuine challenge to Chuck's skills. What Sullivan was looking for was actually two loans. The first, for some $7 million, was to repay Manufacturers Trust in Detroit. The second, for $2.5 million, was to deal with Tose's "personal debts." By January 1978, a dozen New York and Pennsylvania financial institutions had been approached and all of them had turned the loan down. First Provident Bank of Philadelphia was personally requested by both Dan Rooney and the League itself, but still refused to make the loan, citing "bank policy." Even the League's stated willingness to guarantee Tose's borrowings with the Eagles' $5 million a year in television revenues had produced no immediate takers.

There were two significant roadblocks to Leonard Tose's refinancing. The first was his twenty-nine percent partner, Herb Barness. Barness was now in court with Tose over the club finances, charging that his former friend had violated the Eagles' limited partnership agreement. Specifically the charge was "mismanagement of Eagles funds and using them for personal matters." Though no longer "doublehocked," the Eagles were still legally encumbered. "That's why the banks won't lend money to Tose," a "banking source" told the *Philadelphia Daily News*. "They're afraid of the lawsuits Tose may get from his partners. The partners are upset that he's agreeing to too many long-term commitments. He makes agreements with coaches, players, and water boys. There's no question he's up against the wall. Loans are scarce now and he's lost credibility. The League will have to step in for him." Unbeknownst to the *Daily News*'s source, of course, the League already had.

In January 1978, Chuck Sullivan was in Tarpon Springs, Florida, for a special two-day NFL meeting, largely concerned with scheduling and preparations for the upcoming draft of graduating college players, and Herb Barness flew down to talk with him. Art Rooney sat in on their meeting as well. Barness's "main issue," according to Sullivan, was "how much money Leonard can take out as personal salary. He wants Leonard to settle for a $35,000 salary when the other owners take home about $175,000 apiece. We told him we thought his demands were unfair." Despite Sullivan's assessment, on February 2, a Philadelphia Common Pleas Court granted Barness's request for "protective relief" and enjoined Tose from taking more than

$60,000 in annual salary. It also required him to submit an itemized expense account to the court within ten days of the end of each month. The accounting had to be certified by Touche Ross & Co., the Eagles' accountants, and a copy had to be furnished to Herb Barness. Ironically, Tose's reversal in court was at least partially reassuring to those banks still thinking of loaning him money.

Leonard Tose's second major refinancing roadblock was his own reputation as anything but frugal. "The banks aren't worried about the Eagles' ability to pay back money," one Philadelphia banker observed. "They're worried about the personal tab Tose has run up." Tose's previous lenders, First Pennsylvania Bank, did nothing to ease their worries. In December 1977, New York's Citibank had been approached by Chuck Sullivan and began investigating the possibility of a Tose loan. One of its assistant vice-presidents then phoned John Bunting, First Penn's president, asking for his assessment. "He said Tose was 'a big spender,' " the assistant vice-president recalled, "'a 'high liver with debts all over the country and I wouldn't touch him with a 170-foot pole.' "

By the first week of February, with Tose's February 9 deadline rapidly approaching, speculation began to surface around Philadelphia about whether any bank would touch the Eagles owner. It was Chuck Sullivan who surfaced to calm the waters. "Leonard's credit rating with the NFL is Triple A," Chuck contended. "The Eagles are one of the best managed teams in the NFL. Because of the new TV contract, a loan to the Eagles is as strong as a loan to IBM." According to Sullivan, refinancing would not be a problem. "You know," he pointed out, "banks have been making loans to teams since 1922, and no bank has lost as much as a dime on an NFL team. In loans like this, there is a lead bank involved that sells participation to one or more other banks. Several banks have indicated they would be interested as a lead bank and more than that number want to participate."

According to Eagles General Manager Jimmy Murray, Manufacturers National in Detroit was applying no pressure for immediate repayment. "We have an excellent relationship with the Detroit bank," Murray claimed. "I don't know how we'll resolve the issue. Leonard Tose has a lot of options. Maybe he'll just pick up the phone and get an extension. Leonard's the only one who knows what he's going to do, but he's not talking."

In truth, Tose was waiting for Sullivan to do what he was being paid for. Chuck had been negotiating with Manufacturers National since the previous November about possibly rolling the bridge loan over. As their deadline approached, Sullivan flew to Philadelphia for two solid days of meetings with his client. Chuck's immediate goal was simply to buy a little time. After more phone calls with the Detroit bank, he finally succeeded. On February 9, instead of repaying the full $7 million Tose owed in Detroit, a $350,000 interest payment was made. The money, according to the *Philadelphia Daily News,* came from a $1.5 million "personal loan" Tose had secured from an unknown source.

Herb Barness expressed amazement that anyone would make a personal loan to Leonard Tose.

Chuck Sullivan expressed a certain amount of relief. "His personal finances have all been straightened out," Chuck said of Tose. "We paid the interest today and, in view of the fact that several banks have expressed interest in refinancing . . . everything is in great shape." There was still long-term financing to be arranged, but to the press, Chuck was sanguine about that too.

In the meantime, Leonard Tose had the full backing of the National Football League.

The League had bailed him out before, Sullivan pointed out, "and we'll do it again if we have to. We bought Leonard Tose, not anybody else. He's the man the NFL wants to control the Eagles. We will stick by him. Leonard Tose is a very important part of the NFL owners' team. He's chairman of the owners committee on NFL Films, one of the most successful things we have going. He's a vice-chairman in the labor area. Speaking for the rest of the NFL owners, I can say that we will make sure Leonard Tose keeps control of the Eagles until breath leaves his body."

10

Pete Rozelle was also concerned about Joe Robbie in early 1978, but for very different reasons.

The commissioner's worry about Robbie was rooted in the Miami owner's urge to play the rogue elephant on labor issues. That worry intensified when Robbie's labor proclivities combined with his contempt for the commissioner's ownership policy and became, in Rozelle's eyes, yet another potential conflict of interest, threatening the integrity of League Think. At that point, collision between Robbie and the commissioner became inevitable.

Joe Robbie's stirrings on the labor front dated from spring 1977, when the ink on the League's new five-year collective bargaining agreement was hardly dry. The incident that set things off occurred on May 4 in Miami. That evening Miami police arrested two of Joe Robbie's football players, Randy Crowder and Don Reese, in a Ramada Inn near the airport and charged them with attempting to sell a pound of cocaine to an undercover cop. On May 6, Joe Robbie suspended the two from the Dolphins, pending the outcome of their trial, scheduled for the middle of the next football season. After consulting with the National Football League Players Association, Reese and Crowder filed a grievance under the new contract, claiming that Robbie's action amounted to prejudging their case and that all action should await the proof of their guilt or innocence. Under the terms of the League's labor agreement, their grievance was heard by the player-club relations committee, composed of two union representatives, Len Hauss and Gene Upshaw, and two owners, Dan Rooney and Wellington Mara.

The PCRC held its hearing on the grievance on July 28, 1977. Robbie described the procedure as "arbitrarily conducted." The decision the hearing reached displeased him even more than the hearing itself did. On Friday, July 29, the PCRC announced that labor and management had reached a ruling, final and binding to all parties under the terms of the 1977 contract. Robbie's Dolphins, the PCRC ordered, would have until the following Monday at 4 P.M. to either trade, waive, or reinstate the two players. Players association Executive Director Ed Garvey called it "an excellent settlement for all concerned."

Joe Robbie was furious. "It will take virtually a case of mistaken identity before I want Reese and Crowder back on the Miami Dolphins," he stormed. "It's completely unfair to give us a deadline like that. It's obvious nobody's going to trade for them under those circumstances. I am not taking issue with the collective bargaining agreement, but I am taking issue with how the PCRC abused their discretion and authority. . . . The action of the PCRC establishes a dangerous precedent and could rise to haunt the NFL in the future in protecting the integrity of professional football. What will happen if two players are arrested for fixing a football game? Will their owner be prohibited from suspending them until they are tried in court so that they can play while under indictment? What happens in the case of a player who bets against his own team? What happens in a case involving murder or manslaughter? Must the player be paid in jail or out on bail while he awaits trial?"

Robbie immediately took his complaint to Rozelle, calling him three times over the three days between the committee's decision and its deadline. Robbie wanted the commissioner to use his powers to suspend Reese and Crowder for life. "They should never be allowed to play again," he argued. Rozelle, however, had already decided to stay his hand "until the judicial process played itself out" and could offer Robbie no satisfaction. Robbie also called the management council asking for an extension of the deadline and was refused. At 4:00 P.M. on August 1, his Miami franchise grudgingly complied with the PCRC and placed the two players on irrevocable waivers. They were now, Joe Robbie noted, "free agents."

The next day, Joe Robbie announced that he intended to sue the NFL and the NFLPA in an attempt to have the PCRC ruling reversed.

Such a suit was, of course, the last thing the NFL needed. Having struggled for three years to get a contract, it would have been a disaster to now have it sabotaged by one of the League's own members. Fortunately, Robbie's threat of suit became moot when Reese and Crowder pleaded guilty on August 10 and were sentenced to a year in prison. Their suspension for that period was now automatic and Robbie backed off from using the courts to make his point. Nonetheless, Pete Rozelle emerged from the incident with a residual leeriness about the possibility of Robbie rattling Ed Garvey's cage on a free-lance basis. Garvey, the commissioner was quick to point out, was hard enough to deal with as it was.

It had been the commissioner's hope that the new contract, making the

NFLPA more secure and prosperous than it ever had been, would yield labor peace for a while. Certainly the union was no longer struggling for survival. As part of the settlement of *Mackey v. NFL* and *Alexander v. NFL,* a related case, the union had received a $750,000 payment. Coupled with the return of the automatic dues checkoff, the settlement had increased the union's net assets from minus $233,000 to plus $608,000 in one year. Ed Garvey had been paid back the money he had borrowed against his house and his salary had been raised from $56,000 a year in 1976 to $114,000 a year by the end of 1977. Prosperity did not, however, make Ed Garvey easier for the League to get along with. "Garvey took every chance he could to attack, attack, attack," one of Rozelle's assistants complained. "In enforcing the contract, there were a lot of very technical objections. A lot of stuff that was just pure bullshit. We tried to be patient. We listened to him, sifted it out, responded to him, and tried to ignore it all, but it was hard."

By the end of 1977, however, Garvey was not giving the NFL his full attention. Having made football a union shop, he was now looking around for other areas to organize. "Ed envisioned himself being a big man in the AFL-CIO," Bob Moore, one of the NFLPA vice-presidents, remembered. "He thought athletes' notoriety could make them a major force in the labor movement. He envisioned a Federation of Professional Athletes that would include all sports, with Garvey as its head. It would have a big central staff and each sport would have its own skeleton bargaining staff. All contract maintenance, et cetera, would be done out of the central union. The biggest problem it faced was that the union leaders in baseball, basketball, and hockey all hated Garvey, so that part never got off the ground. In the meantime, he went after the unorganized sports." Among the sports Garvey would try to organize into his Federation of Professional Athletes were motorcycle racing, rodeo riding, and soccer. Soccer was the most concerted of those campaigns and was well under way by the beginning of 1978. His target was the North American Soccer League and his new union was named the NASL Players Association. To fund the effort, according to Moore, Garvey's NFLPA loaned his NASLPA some $500,000.

When Ed Garvey took on the North American Soccer League, the would-be sports labor czar soon crossed swords with Joe Robbie again, much to Pete Rozelle's consternation. Robbie was involved in the NASL by virtue of his wife, Elizabeth's, ownership of the league's Ft. Lauderdale Strikers, formerly the Miami Toros. When Mrs. Robbie had taken over the franchise in 1976, she inherited an indebtedness of more than $900,000 and, in so doing, insured a family commitment to making the NASL succeed. "The only way we're ever going to recover the losses that we incurred before Elizabeth became the sole owner," Joe explained, "will be to improve the value of that franchise so that it's recovered in the increased asset value of the franchise."

When questioned by Rozelle or his fellow NFL owners about the soccer franchise, Joe Robbie described it as a separate enterprise, of which Elizabeth was the "sole proprietor." In operation, however, the two franchises blended much more closely together. "My wife and I don't have separate wealth,"

Robbie explained. "As a matter of fact, we don't have joint wealth really. The profits that we make in the Miami Dolphins are available to us for whatever other purposes, including the Strikers. . . . It's all the same jackpot. . . . My wife gets a tickler file, as we call it, of every [letter] that is sent out [by the Dolphins]. I guess I adopted that habit when I was in the federal government as an auditor in the early 1950s. I get a copy of every business letter that is sent from the Ft. Lauderdale Strikers and my wife gets one from the Miami Dolphins and I read that file to keep currently abreast of what's going on." In addition, their thirty-year-old son, Michael, was about to become general manager of the Dolphins, and their twenty-two-year-old-son, Timothy, was assistant general manager of the Strikers.

The aspect of Joe Robbie's soccer involvement that most irritated other NFL owners was not so much the assistance he gave his wife's club as the assistance he afforded to the NASL as a league. In 1976, he had served as an advisory member to the NASL's planning committee and participated in three or four "brainstorming sessions" to discuss "what kind of policy the NASL should adopt with regard to expansion and with regard to information that they might seek and obtain from prospective owners, and about criteria for determining whose applications to become owners should be accepted." He had also furnished the soccer owners with information "concerning the profits per team that an NFL club receives from NFL Properties" and "how much profit each club obtains from NFL Films." All of it was information other NFL owners considered confidential. In addition, Robbie passed on copies of two studies of NFL internal operations by the management firm of Booz, Allen & Hamilton. "We compared notes about how best to operate a professional franchise," the Dolphin owner explained.

Even more irritating in the beginning of 1978 from the NFL's point of view was Robbie's service on the NASL's recently created labor relations committee, again as "advisory member." The committee had been formed, according to Robbie, "for the purpose of dealing with the attempt of Edward Garvey, who represents the NFL players association, to obtain certification of a union to represent the NASL players. I was asked to attend their meetings for the purpose of giving the benefit of my past contact with Mr. Garvey and his union activities." He considered his efforts at those NASL meetings an attempt "to stiffen their backbone and make them stand up and fight Mr. Garvey and the union more so than the NFL did over the years.

"I've told the NASL to avoid our pitfalls," he went on to explain. "In some cases I told them to go see what we did and do it differently. I felt that there was a real need for the NASL to oppose certification based on a card count, to raise issues which hadn't been raised in the past as to what [was] an appropriate unit, for example, to handle the bargaining for the individual clubs. . . . I did not feel that all twenty-four teams in soccer, for example, should have to deal as one with the players union. I felt that the individual club was the appropriate bargaining unit and I wanted that tested, and I felt that was good for every major team sport to have questions raised and resolved. I think had they been raised ten or twelve years ago, before the unions became such an accepted part of the structure of major league sports, that we might have got different answers to those questions. . . . I was intensely interested personally in what was going on between the NASL and Mr. Garvey and his union.''

By the end of 1977, Garvey was already complaining about the outcome of Robbie's NASL involvement. "We now face an interesting recognition question in soccer," the architect of the Federation of Professional Athletes testified to the Senate Subcommittee on Labor. "NASL owners say they believe unionization of the NASL is 'inevitable' and that they don't mind a union in soccer. The problem is that they do not want *this* union in soccer and so we are now before the National Labor Relations Board seeking an election.''

The members of the NFL Players Association were kept up to date about Robbie's "antiunion" soccer activities by pointed coverage in the union's newsletter, *The Audible*. It was actually through the NFLPA that most NFL owners learned what Joe Robbie was up to.

Chuck Sullivan, chairman of the NFL's Management Council, considered the exposure "very adverse," especially since it came during a period when the NFL was trying "to have some semblance of a harmonious relationship with the players union." Leonard Tose, vice-chairman of the Management Council and by far the loudest NFL critic of cross-ownership, was predictably more vociferous about the dangers such behavior posed. "If I was Mr. Garvey," he observed, "and I was negotiating with both the soccer league and the NFL . . . I can realistically conceive that Mr. Garvey or the soccer owners can say, 'We will not pay the players anymore, what we will do is we will give you a piece of the gross.' . . . Garvey would then have, and he has, the gall, to come in and say to the NFL owners, 'Well, the soccer league has given this. . . . You have the same people, why can't you give us the same thing that the soccer league has given us.' '' According to Tose, Robbie was giving Garvey extra leverage, which was, of course, one of the express goals of the NFLPA director's Federation of Professional Athletes scheme.

Across Park Avenue from the Management Council offices, Pete Rozelle was even less sanguine about Robbie's adventurism. "He said . . . in League meetings that his wife had an interest in [the soccer team] and that she was the one involved," the commissioner pointed out, but "from what we've heard of the Robbie situation, it would appear that it is Mr. Robbie who is on the soccer committees, not Mrs. Robbie, and it is Mr. Robbie attending meetings, not Mrs. Robbie. I would say that . . . there is a conflict . . . with the spirit and intent of ownership policy.''

It was not, however, a violation of the letter of the continuing ownership policy resolution then in effect and Rozelle was powerless to do more than observe it. The "Robbie situation" was yet another irritant in the commissioner's open wound over the cross-ownership issue. None of the unspecified promises of divestiture had been lived up to, none of the conflicts of interests eliminated. Rozelle was now sure they wouldn't be until they were meticulously banned and that ban entered in the League's constitution. It had been five years since he had last tried for that solution, but he had not forgotten it.

Joe Robbie provided only the most recent of the reasons Rozelle thought it ought to be done.

On the agenda for the 1978 annual meeting to be held in March in Palm Springs, a "discussion of dual ownership or investment in other major team sports by NFL owners or their immediate families" was scheduled for Executive Session.

From Rozelle's perspective, the time had come to force the issue to its conclusion.

11

The 1978 annual meeting consumed a week of two-a-day sessions at Palm Springs's Canyon Hotel, but most of those in attendance remembered the conclave for the Executive Session discussion of cross-ownership on the morning of March 16. "This is the point where the tolerance had ebbed," Rozelle explained. "It was a very heated discussion about all people getting into conformance with [ownership policy]. There was an escalation of feeling on the part of some members . . . that something should be done about the conflicts [of interest] and the lack of success of those individuals [owning other sports interests] in resolving the conflicts as they had pledged to do."

As had become something of an NFL tradition when this subject was discussed, Leonard Tose opened the issue with a blast at Lamar Hunt. Like the one in 1973, this Tose diatribe was set off by Hunt's ongoing media hype of the NASL. The article that infuriated Leonard Tose this time had appeared in *American Way* magazine, the in-flight publication of American Airlines. Tose carried the magazine in his fist and brandished it like a cudgel when he addressed the rest of the League. "I was flying someplace and I picked up this magazine," Tose recounted, "and I read it and I was glad that my doctor wasn't there to take my blood pressure because I could not believe what I read in this article. What particularly disturbed me . . . was the fact that Mr. Hunt was quoted as saying soccer is going to replace football." Not content with denouncing it, Tose also read the article aloud. Even if Rozelle's ownership policy had no teeth written into it, it should be conformed to. Instead, he railed, waving the *American Way* in the air, "this is the type of thing Lamar is doing."

Hunt was not pleased by Tose's remarks. "There were . . . at least six clubs that had people with ownership interests in other sports," he complained, "and whenever this conversation would come up in the meeting . . . invariably I would be the only one that would be asked to respond. . . . I would look around the room, and [the other cross-ownership violators] wouldn't say a word and wouldn't participate in conversation and yet all of the conversation was pointed at me and asking me questions." Hunt considered Tose's attacks "very disruptive toward the harmony of the League."

Lamar Hunt also thought he'd done nothing wrong. From his point of view, he had made his "best efforts" to divest and had kept the commissioner's office informed of those efforts by letter. The last such letter had been sent a year earlier. He had, he informed Rozelle, made his basketball interest in the Chicago Bulls available, but it was "without real prospective buyers." He had informed the Bulls' attorney, who Hunt considered "able to discreetly find ownership interests," but "had not heard back from him." In the case of his soccer franchise, the Dallas Tornado, Hunt had encountered two interlocking "difficulties." His hope there had been to put together a group of one hundred one-percent owners to replace himself and "assure the stability of the team." Unfortunately, the Tornado was at the moment in a very public dispute with Southern Methodist University over the use of their soccer stadium. "With an ongoing dispute in the newspapers," he explained, he "didn't feel it was practical to even broach the subject" of his one hundred owners plan.

In the meantime, of course, Hunt had continued trying to make the NASL a success. Like Joe Robbie, he served as an ex-officio member of the soccer league's planning committee, and had attended two or three meetings over the previous two years. The goal of the committee was to make a long range plan for NASL success and among the items discussed were soccer's future television policy and how the NASL might "alter the way it marketed its TV rights if and when the NFL shifts to pay TV." In the course of those discussions, Hunt later admitted that he "might possibly" have provided the soccer owners with information about the NFL, but he claimed it was only things that were "essentially public knowledge." He also provided the NASL commissioner with a list of "people who were interested in an NFL team in their cities" but again insisted they had been "people that would not be logical to be considered [by the NFL]." None of it, he insisted, was a conflict of interest.

At the 1978 annual meeting, Lamar responded to Tose by "disallowing" the quotes attributed to him and insisting that he had been making a good faith effort at divestiture. His soccer investment was a "bad" one, he pointed out, and hence quite difficult to unload. Hunt's remarks were brief. "Every year Lamar would just sit and take criticism," Steve Rosenbloom remembered. "Every year he'd say, 'I'm working on it,' and then do nothing."

This year Hunt's response carried less weight than ever and Leonard Tose was by no means the only person prepared to say so. Wellington Mara offered that Lamar should either divest his soccer or divest his football and do it soon. When Max Winter spoke up, he sounded like a Leonard Tose clone. As Winter put it, Tose was "on the same page I was." The two men were "good friends" and talked about soccer regularly. Winter told the other owners that the NASL's Minneapolis franchise, the Minnesota Kicks, "are hurting the Vikings, our sports dollar, and that they are drawing and we are losing ground as far as media exposure and fan participation." Max Winter was also almost as worked up about it as Tose. Winter, Lamar Hunt remembered, "was critical of the fact that the newspaper said I was going to be in Minnesota for some announcement relative to a new group coming into the North American Soccer League. In fact, I wasn't aware of it at all and, in that particular case, had never met the people, did not know who they were." The anti-Hunt onslaught continued nonetheless.

Even the Sullivans, close to both Hunt and Robbie, saw fit to complain about the inequities forced on them by their friends' positions. Since they were considered a "family team," like the Rosenblooms and Rooneys, the Sullivans were allowed two representatives in Executive Session and both Billy and Chuck were there. "We," Chuck explained, "have had the opportunity within the last ten years to purchase the Boston Red Sox [baseball franchise], the Boston Celtics [basketball franchise] were offered to us, the Boston Bruins [hockey franchise] were offered to us, the Boston Tea Men [NASL franchise] were offered to us. In each event we turned these opportunities down because it was our feeling that our family had become identified with the NFL and identification with . . . other enterprises would take away from our primary objective of promoting the NFL. . . . If Lamar Hunt were to devote more time to the promotion of the Kansas City Chiefs and less time to the promotion of other sports interests, I think the NFL would significantly benefit.

"My family made a commitment that we would bring ourselves into compliance with the rules," Chuck continued. "It cost us ten million dollars to do that. We expected Mr. Hunt, who had made the same commitment, would do the same thing and bring himself into compliance." Instead, Chuck went on to note, just as Tose had, that Hunt kept promising to divest but never did so.

Hugh Culverhouse made a similar point to Chuck Sullivan's. He had been offered the opportunity of purchasing a Tampa NASL franchise but had turned it down for very much the same reasons as the Sullivans. Culverhouse was also willing to spread the onus beyond Lamar Hunt. The speculation in the Tampa papers, he pointed out, focused on the possibility that Edward DeBartolo Sr., father of the NFL owner, was a likely buyer of the NASL franchise that Culverhouse had refused. He also noted that the Nordstrom family, central to Seattle's NFL ownership, owned a piece of a soccer team as well. So did Joe Robbie, Culverhouse pointed out.

Joe Robbie was not at the meeting to defend himself. He had left Palm Springs the day before and his seat was silently filled by his coach, general manager, and minority partner, Don Shula. Nonetheless, the "Robbie situation" was, as Rozelle remembered it, "the pivotal family relation issue that was discussed." The majority felt that a situation such as Robbie's ought to be prohibited and that the ownership policy's cross-ownership prohibitions should include "immediate family," an entity the League defined as "husband or wife and sons and daughters of owners."

In the course of that discussion of Robbie, the names of Eddie DeBartolo and his father, Mr. D, came up again. Mr. D already owned a Pittsburgh hockey franchise and the Tampa rumors were not the first time he had been linked to the NASL. In 1977, one of Mr. D's attorneys had approached Art Modell, landlord of Cleveland Stadium, about possibly bringing soccer there. "I thought for a while we had a soccer tenant," Modell remembered, "but that fell through. . . . They didn't come in because they wouldn't pay the minimum rent." Despite that involvement, the DeBartolos came up only as a sidebar on the question of "what ground rules we should have for family conflicts of interest." There was never, according to Rozelle, "a strong case made of it. . . . I think it was raised, but . . . only from the standpoint of whether Eddie DeBartolo Jr. was independently owning and operating the 49ers or whether his father was involved in it." In 1978, the League was apparently satisfied with their separateness. Eddie himself had left the meeting before the discussion of cross-ownership had begun.

The most articulate opponent of Rozelle's ownership policy ideas, Edward Bennett Williams of the Washington Redskins, was absent as well. His place was being filled by Robert Schulman, an attorney with the Williams & Connelly law firm. Schulman pointed out that the Redskins "will conform" to the ownership policy resolution then in effect, but that Jack Kent Cooke, the majority owner, had not yet divested his basketball and hockey interests. The problem, Schulman explained, was, for the moment, out of Cooke's hands. His wife was suing for divorce and until that case was settled, Cooke was under court order not to sell any of his assets.

Of all the excuses for failure to divest, Cooke's was the one with which Rozelle was most sympathetic. Rozelle's wife, Carrie, was Cooke's former daughter-in-law and considered Cooke's wife one of her best friends. It was, Rozelle knew, a sensitive situation. "I didn't want the divorce," Cooke explained. "She did." The dissolution was, the Redskins majority owner admitted, "a very unhappy" turn of events. That evening, when Rozelle happened on Schulman in a Palm Springs restaurant, he communicated his sympathy. "Many of the remarks concerning individuals who had not divested when they had pledged to had become quite heated during the meeting," the commissioner remembered, "and I told Mr. Schulman that I was aware those remarks could not be legitimately directed at the Redskins [because of the court order in Cooke's divorce]. I wanted to convey it to Mr. Williams and Mr. Cooke so that they would not feel that if they got a report of harsh words being said . . . that they were involved."

With Williams and Robbie absent and Hunt maintaining his usual silence on cross-ownership, the most discordant note to Rozelle's ears was sounded by Al Davis.

Davis's complaint was aimed principally at Rozelle's lieutenant, Art Modell. "Al Davis," Modell explained, "who has been an adversary of mine for some time, was jabbing me." At issue was Modell's involvement in cross-ownership conflicts of interest himself. Davis claimed the Cleveland owner was up to his neck in such conflicts and that Rozelle's tolerance of those violations at the same time as he decried others' was a double standard and hypocrisy of the first order.

Certainly Modell's case was an example of the gray areas surrounding the definition of "conflict of interest" for the League.

First, though he was never involved in ownership per se, Modell had, for several years, sought to get an NASL expansion franchise situated in Cleveland. His hope was to find another tenant for his stadium. Modell had tested the Cleveland soccer waters by staging a game in the mid-1970s between the Polish national soccer team and a local Cleveland team called the Cobras. The next year, he followed by scheduling an exhibition between the NASL's New York Cosmos and Lamar Hunt's Dallas Tornado. That exhibition was in turn followed by several meetings between Modell and the NASL's commissioner. They discussed "the needs of the soccer league," according to Modell, and the NASL commissioner "was expressing the hope that I can be of help to him in assembling a group of local investors that would take a soccer franchise in Cleveland and play in the stadium. I made it clear from the beginning [that] the extent of my interest was occupancy for the stadium, but if I can help assemble a group for ownership of a soccer franchise, I will." Nothing ever came of Modell's offer and by 1978, his soccer interest had dissipated.

It was not soccer, however, but baseball that was the principal subject of Davis's objections. Modell was also on the board of directors of the Cleveland Indians baseball franchise, though he had no outright ownership interest. Again, according to Modell, the reason was his stewardship of Cleveland Stadium Corp. By the end of the 1977 baseball season, the Indians, one of Cleveland Stadium's two principal tenants, were "on the verge of bankruptcy" and Modell was admittedly "terrified of losing baseball to New Orleans or some other city and leaving eighty-one playing dates [for Cleveland Stadium] vacant." Were the Indians to leave, Cleveland Stadium Corp. would have been forced "very close" to bankruptcy and that would have meant personal bankruptcy for Modell as well. "It would have been a disaster," he pointed out. Privately, he later admitted, "Had it not been for the NFL's cross-ownership rule, I would have bought the Indians myself."

Instead, he sought to rescue the baseball franchise by finding a new owner who would stay in Cleveland. Modell considered his actions a civic contribution not unlike saving the old hotel on Public Square. The owner he found was F. J. "Steve" O'Neill, described by Modell as "an elderly man who was formerly chairman of the board of Leaseway Transportation." At the time, O'Neill owned a small piece in the New York Yankees baseball partnership headed by Modell's old Cleveland crony George Steinbrenner. "I asked him would he consider taking control of the Indians," Modell remembered, "to save it for Cleveland and, secondly, save it for the stadium." O'Neill agreed and Modell was named to the board of directors in the new baseball ownership. His presence, he claimed, "was designed to ease the transition from one ownership to another. It was designed to give Steve O'Neill some comfort and also to proclaim publicly that this new ownership had my support. It was cosmetic. I did not function on any committees. I did not participate in any player . . . or broadcast negotiations."

Cleveland was appreciative of Art Modell's gesture, if Al Davis was not. Three months before the 1978 annual meeting, *The Cleveland Press* had observed in an editorial that "the most promising sports news these days" was "the reorganization of the Indians by Art Modell, who, despite the burden of problems with the Browns, has factored a new front office structure that promises to make the Indians a respectable organization again."

Al Davis's point was that civic gesture or not, if Lamar Hunt's absentee ten percent ownership of the basketball Chicago Bulls was a conflict of interest, so was Art Modell's presence on the board of the Cleveland Indians, even without an ownership interest.

Pete Rozelle was quick to defend his friend and lieutenant. Davis, the commissioner claimed, "was trying to justify some position he had on some issue. . . . Perhaps that was at the time when Mr. Davis had discussions with people about possibly purchasing an interest . . . in the Oakland baseball team." In any case, "everyone at the time Mr. Modell became a member of the board of directors of the baseball team realized it was part of a business arrangement that Mr. Modell had made with the city of Cleveland to refurbish the stadium." The commissioner went on to say that "it was discussed casually and no one felt it was a serious conflict. . . . I only saw it as a conflict when it gave Mr. Davis an opportunity to bring it up in a meeting. I like to eliminate divisiveness among our people, if possible, and anything that can be used like that and prevent us from going forward with a single voice, I don't think is good."

In the interest of "going forward with a single voice," Art Modell promised the meeting that "rather than get in a problem with Mr. Davis," he would not stand for reelection to the Indians' board when his current term ran out two years hence. It was an act he later described as "my decision to get the hell off." He explained, "It wasn't worth the embarrassment to the League. It wasn't worth the controversy."

Despite Davis's jousting at Modell, when the dust cleared on the March 16 executive session, it was tallied a big victory for Rozelle. The "sense of the meeting" for which he had been waiting five years had arrived. Now, there "was a growing impatience with the inability of several of the clubs to divest their holdings" that was "getting progressively more heated," according to Rozelle. "The consensus was the only way to achieve what had been sought for a number of years was to vote specific sanctions" into the constitution. Ownership policy was at last to be given teeth. "The commissioner," the minutes recorded, "said the League office would develop for the June meeting alternatives to consider regarding penalties for noncompliance with League policy on this subject. In the meantime, he asked for strong best efforts to divest of such holdings before June."

Sensing only long-awaited breakthrough, it apparently didn't occur to Pete Rozelle that he might be opening a Pandora's box in League Think's closet.

12

Carroll Rosenbloom played no significant role in the cross-ownership debate, though his sympathies were apparent in his behavior.

The owner of the Rams had flirted with the notion of owning other sports franchises, but never consummated his interest by making a purchase. The closest he came was to hold substantial stock in Warner Communications, the owner of the NASL's New York Cosmos. In 1976, he and Lamar Hunt had exchanged a series of letters about the possibility of purchasing the NASL's Los Angeles franchise for one of C.R.'s sons. Rosenbloom, Hunt remembered, was "involved in some stadium negotiations and he felt there might be merit in having a combination situation where the Rams . . . and a soccer team . . . would play in the same stadium and might help get some stadium improvements that he was negotiating for." That idea, like the improvements themselves, went nowhere, but in 1977 Carroll had considered another cross-ownership, this time in indoor soccer. The notion was brought to Rosenbloom by two Philadelphia promoters and he tried to draw his friend Al Davis into it. Rosenbloom and Davis met with the promoters on three different occasions, but finally backed away. "I thought the only advantage," Davis explained, "provided we could get it through League channels, would be to use it as a time filler for regular television in the afternoons or the evenings. . . . I thought it had little chance to succeed in that vein to make some money off it and et cetera."

Obviously far less than a fan of the commissioner's ownership policy, Rosenbloom nonetheless kept his peace at the 1978 annual meeting. For him, the Superstadium Game was now everything. Anaheim Stadium Associates had begun hammering out the details of an agreement with the city of Anaheim; Los Angeles and the LAMCC had commenced their last ditch effort to keep his Rams in "the Grand Duchess of Stadiums"; and Carroll had to convert pressure on his second front into leverage on his first. It was a critical stage and he avoided distractions.

In Los Angeles, the LAMCC's drive had begun with reorganization. The critical element in that reorganization was the rotation of Bill Robertson, a fifty-nine-year-old Los Angeles labor leader, into the Coliseum commission's presidency. Over the next six years, Bill Robertson would become arguably the most important external civic figure in the history of the NFL.

Robertson was originally from Minneapolis. After high school, he pitched some Class A professional baseball until what he called his "drinking problem" destroyed his career. That drinking problem would last almost fifteen years. For one four-year stretch, Robertson stayed on the road, living in skid rows and being what he called "a bum." When not on the skids, he worked as an auto worker at the Ford Motor Company's St. Paul plant, as a marine electrician at Bethlehem Steel in San Francisco, and a packinghouse worker for Armour Company back in St. Paul. He'd been a member of the United Auto Workers, the construction trades union, the packinghouse union, and even, for a brief period, the Newspaper Guild. In the mid-1940s he began working as a bartender and manager of bars and restaurants and joined the hotel and restaurant workers union. In 1950, he gave up alcohol altogether and was a "changed man."

Bill Robertson assumed the path that ultimately led him toward a historic intersection with the professional football business in 1953, when he moved to Los Angeles, started tending bar in the San Fernando Valley, and joined Local 694. Four years later, the hotel and restaurant workers international union declared a trusteeship over the local because, according to Robertson, it had "a corrupt administration." Robertson was elected the new president of Local 694 once the international's housekeeping was finished, and served in that post for ten years. In 1967, he joined the staff of the Los Angeles County AFL-CIO Labor Council. One of his first tasks was directing the ten-union strike at the *Los Angeles Herald Examiner*. He was soon the director and chief spokesman for more than six hundred thousand workers in Los Angeles County. Robertson oversaw the union programs for education and safety and the like and helped the four hundred locals who were part of the labor council with their negotiations, but his prime responsibilities were political. As such, he was a key player in California's Democratic party.

Robertson was appointed to the LAMCC in October 1977 by California's governor, Jerry Brown. Originally, Brown had wanted to appoint his labor ally to the board of the state college system, but Robertson, a sports fan, asked for the Coliseum commission instead. The state appointed three of the commissioners at the discretion of the governor, the county of Los Angeles supplied three from the membership of its board of supervisors, and the city of Los Angeles supplied two from its Recreation and Parks Department and one from the membership of its City Council. Two months after Robertson joined the state's contingent, the presidency of the LAMCC made its annual rotation among the three components. It was now the state's turn and Robertson became president.

Bill Robertson and Carroll Rosenbloom first laid eyes on each other in February 1978. The two met in C.R.'s office at Rams headquarters on Pico Boulevard. "I told him how I felt with the change in the composition of the Los Angeles Memorial Coliseum Commission," Robertson would later testify, "that we were determined to do everything possible to make the conditions [to] which he would be receptive to keep him as a tenant." Rosenbloom, he remembered privately, was "decent enough," but "crafty" and tried his best to "stroke" the Coliseum commission president. Robertson had brought a proposal with him that he felt was a "viable vehicle to generate $9 million which would . . . bring the Coliseum . . . up to the standards we thought it should be." Included in the plan was construction of a new double-decked

THE LEAGUE

air-conditioned press box on the north side of the Coliseum, replete with its own kitchen and a new private owner's box. The LAMCC also proposed to build a new "state of the art" scoreboard, larger dressing rooms, larger lavatories, new escalators, and a new "communications center." Rosenbloom told Robertson he "appreciated" the proposal. "He said he would look it over thoroughly and he would be back to us." When Robertson asked about the status of Rosenbloom's dealings with Anaheim, Rosenbloom answered that "he was looking around."

The two men spoke at least twice on the phone during the next month. The proposal Robertson had given C.R. fell short on at least a couple of significant points. Rosenbloom wanted the Coliseum running track eliminated so the playing field could be lowered and the track area filled with seats. That was at the moment impossible for Robertson to promise because L.A. still hoped to host the 1984 Olympics. C.R. also wanted a practice facility closer to his Pico Boulevard headquarters than the current one in Long Beach. Robertson described the practice site as "a reasonable request" that he was powerless to meet. "Because of the political climate in the city," the LAMCC president explained, "it was very difficult to get the things he wanted. It just wouldn't sail politically."

Though expenditures significant enough to satisfy C.R. wouldn't sail, not making them also posed political dangers. The man most threatened by a Rams move was Tom Bradley, Los Angeles's two-term mayor and southern California's foremost Democratic politician. The first black man ever to be elected mayor, Bradley was looking forward to an unprecedented third term and had fought a long battle with the City Council to get the Olympics bid made. Should the city lose that bid and lose the Rams as well, Bradley might face becoming the mayor who lost professional football inside the boundaries of the city and county of Los Angeles.

The mayor and Bill Robertson were close political allies and Robertson did not make light of the difficulties that trying to keep C.R. would pose. His impression from the first meeting was that Rosenbloom already had a deal with Anaheim waiting in the wings. That conclusion seemed reflected in Anaheim as well. "The Anaheim stadium people are bubbling," Jim Hardy, the L.A. Coliseum's general manager, noted. "They think it's a fait accompli." Nonetheless, Robertson continued playing out his end of the negotiations. In March, he arranged a meeting between Rosenbloom, himself, Bradley, Hardy, and City Councilman Gil Lindsay in C.R.'s Pico Boulevard office. Robertson wanted at least to reassure Rosenbloom that Los Angeles wanted him badly.

Part of the obligatory listening on the city's part was a recitation by Rosenbloom of his historical grievances with the LAMCC. He realized Robertson shouldn't be held responsible, but the fact of the matter was that his requests had been legitimate and he was treated cavalierly. In response, according to Robertson, "the mayor and City Councilman Lindsay made a very strong appeal to Carroll Rosenbloom that they as public officials would do all in their power to see that the program that we submitted would come through. . . . Carroll, as [was] his nature, treated us very cordially; but he still said he was looking around, talking. We knew he was talking to Anaheim. . . . So it was clear that there was a real danger of him leaving Los Angeles.''

Not one to shy away from facing up to reality, Robertson directed the conversation to the subject of what would happen should Rosenbloom leave. ''In the event that you decide to go to Anaheim,'' the LAMCC president pointed out, ''we are going to pursue an effort to get an NFL team to replace you. What are your feelings about it? Would you object to it?''

''No,'' C.R. answered, ''I would not.''

That eventuality became an item of public speculation before the end of the month. ''Coliseum Will Try for a New Team If the Rams Leave,'' the *Times* headlined. When Rozelle's office was approached for a comment, one of his assistants pointed out that ''the unanimous consent of League owners would be required to move either an expansion team or existing franchise into Los Angeles.'' The requirement was the same Section 4.3 of the League's constitution that the city of New York had run into when dealing with the Giants, the Jets, and the New Jersey Meadowlands. By virtue of it, Carroll Rosenbloom had veto rights.

Rosenbloom was not answering public questions about the issue of another team in the Coliseum once he left, whatever he had told Robertson. ''If that time ever comes,'' C.R. explained, ''that would be the time to discuss it.''

When Rosenbloom made that remark, he and Cabot, Cabot & Forbes were in the process of drawing up Anaheim Stadium Associates' proposal to the city of Anaheim and Anaheim Stadium, Inc. It was communicated to Anaheim during April. Anaheim Stadium Associates proposed to build an ''approximately twenty-seven-thousand-seat addition'' to Big A Stadium, as well as ''press box, private box, and locker facilities of a character to make the Stadium suitable for use by the Los Angeles Rams.'' Anaheim Stadium, Inc., Big A's official controlling entity, would finance the addition by issuing bonds and lending the money raised to Anaheim Stadium Associates, but Anaheim Stadium Associates would retain title to the improvements and lease them to the city of Anaheim at terms that would cover the interest charges Anaheim Stadium Associates owed Anaheim Stadium, Inc. The city of Anaheim would in turn lease the stadium to the Los Angeles Rams for thirty years under the terms that had been previously discussed. In addition, Anaheim Stadium Associates would lease the city's adjoining ninety-five acres for $4,000 per acre per year with an option to buy the parcel at a price of $40,000 an acre. That property would eventually be developed according to a master plan over which the city would have approval.

With that proposal, serious bargaining with Anaheim began. It was a process Anaheim's city manager described as ''clarifying various points in the proposal and securing modifications where necessary.'' Perhaps the greatest clarifications were required on the lease and option prices on the ninety-five acres. The city of Anaheim thought the acreage had ''a current market value of approximately $170,000 an acre," four times more than Carroll Rosenbloom and his partner, CC&F, had offered. "Adequate compensation," the city manager insisted, "must be obtained once the properties are developed."

For the purposes of making cash flow estimates to Rosenbloom, CC&F assumed Anaheim would settle for $8,000 a year rent and an $80,000-an-acre option price. On the ninety-five acres covered by that arrangement, Anaheim Stadium Associates would, as envisioned in the CC&F master plan, erect 1.5 million square feet of mid-rise office buildings, 350,000 square feet of low-rise office buildings, a hotel complex with five hundred rooms, four theme restaurants, and two "commercial projects" worth some $21 million when completed. They would also erect parking garages to replace completely the twelve thousand parking stalls previously housed on the acreage. If the whole complex was rented and occupied up to certain minimum levels, it would, according to CC&F's estimates, generate a positive cash flow of some $2.5 million a year to Anaheim Stadium Associates.

While those calculations were being developed, Los Angeles was already anticipating the outcome. "Rams to Move to Anaheim Stadium in '80," the *Times* predicted on April 28. According to southern California's principal newspaper, an announcement to that effect would be made "within the month." C.R. would only say that he had made a lease offer to Anaheim but would meet again with the LAMCC before "we arrive at any decision. We owe them that courtesy," he explained. In the meantime, Rosenbloom was said to be looking at homes around Orange County's Newport Beach.

By the first week of June, however, when Carroll and his son Steve left town for two days of League meetings in New York, no such announcement had yet been made.

In the three months since the League had last met, Rosenbloom had phoned Rozelle "a limited number" of times to keep him informed of developments. That information largely involved complaints about the LAMCC's inability to give him what he wanted. There was only passing reference to "some real estate investment." Rozelle's "impression was that it was an office building or hotel or something of that sort." Rosenbloom provided no financial details. "It was not," the commissioner explained, "an extensive discussion."

Rosenbloom was more "extensive" with his friend Al Davis. The two men talked "almost daily" throughout Rosenbloom's negotiations with Anaheim. Among the things they discussed was the possibility that Davis might move his Raiders into the vacant L.A. Coliseum if Carroll should move to Orange County. "I would tell him that my lease [in Oakland] was up shortly," Davis recalled, "and that I might be very interested in the Los Angeles area." Often, Davis's remarks took the form of "teasing that I may come down there with our little 'ol team and we would have a hell of a competitive market and really go at each other and things like that. Sometimes he would think I am serious and sometimes he wouldn't." When C.R. thought Davis was serious, according to Davis, "he would always talk to me about not moving, why I shouldn't move. [C.R. said] that he would help me all he could in the Oakland area to pressure the Oakland people [to improve their stadium]. Certainly he didn't think it was right that I move to Los Angeles and invade his territory." Carroll also mentioned "why he could stop me from moving."

Davis once told Rosenbloom he was "going to come to L.A." during a "social occasion" when C.R.'s wife, Georgia, was present. Later, Georgia asked Carroll about it and he answered that Davis was being "facetious." Georgia disagreed. She thought Al Davis was "serious."

13

To Rozelle's eye in spring 1978, however, the tide still seemed to be running in stability's favor. A seeming sign to that effect was the latest resolution of Leonard Tose's finances. After almost a year of turmoil and uncertainty, Chuck Sullivan had at last found him a longterm loan.

The loan was revealed to the public by Sullivan on April 19. The principal borrowing was for $8 million at an interest rate floating above prime. The main bank was New York's Citibank, the second largest in the world, and the two other participants in its syndicate were Central Penn National of Philadelphia and Midlantic Bank of West Orange, New Jersey. Chuck Sullivan described the loan's structure as a "longterm deal." *The Philadelphia Inquirer* described it as "unique." Divided into two parts, $5 million of the $8 million was to be paid back by Tose and the Eagles within four years. The remaining $3 million was of "indefinite term" and, in effect, perpetual. "The club pays it back," Sullivan explained, but "it can [also] take it back up [to its $3 million ceiling]. It's actually working capital and a credit. It could go on forever and ever." In addition to the $8 million loaned the Eagles, used in large part to pay off the bridge loan from William Clay Ford's Manufacturers National in Detroit, another $2 million was loaned to Tose as a separate personal loan by Citibank and one of the other syndicate members. It was short term and would be paid off in a year, when Tose sold his Tose Trucking Company to Walter Kidde, Inc., a New Jersey conglomerate, for some $4.5 million.

Chuck Sullivan was proud of the deal he had wrought. Leonard Tose, he declared, "is now free and clear. The key is the television revenue. The actual TV money secures the loan, which is the same for eight other NFL clubs."

However, Chuck Sullivan was not yet through. To further stabilize the Eagles and resolve the commissioner's "Philadelphia problem," Sullivan immediately began negotiations to buy out Tose's minority partners and end the threat of legal encumbrance once and for all. The principal immediate target was Herb Barness, owner of twenty-nine percent. Barness had by now settled his own legal action against Tose, but Sullivan was convinced there would be no peace in the franchise until he was gone. Sullivan also began negotiations with Wally Leventhal, the remaining six-percent partner. Both were reported to be in the mood to sell when they learned of Tose's loan. "It wasn't too much news that he could get the Eagles refinanced," Barness pointed out. "The Eagles are worth a lot of money. The thing that surprised me was the $2 million personal loan. Anybody who loans him money personally like that has to surprise you. And that's just to pay off his personal debts." Within two months, Barness would sell his share to Tose for $3 million. Within a year, Leventhal would sell for $1 million and the Eagles would be all Tose's.

The night the Citibank loan was finally secured, Tose took Chuck Sullivan, his general manager, Jimmy Murray, and several Citibank executives to dinner at Brussels, a fashionable New York restaurant. From his point of view, he had a lot to celebrate. Even his enemies admitted Tose had scored a considerable coup just in surviving the previous year. Judging from his public comments, Leonard Tose derived his greatest pleasure from the comeuppance his new financing gave to First Pennsylvania Bank and its chairman, John Bunting. The hatred generated by First Penn's 1977 humiliation was still fresh. "Mr. Bunting said to me, 'I'll make damn sure you won't get any loan from another bank,' " Tose railed, "and he also said, 'I'll bury you.' . . . He did a helluva job. There wasn't a bank in Philadelphia that would even give us an interview or look at our records." The Citibank syndicate, Tose told the *Philadelphia Daily News*, "did a thorough check on me because of the character assassination which was done. They had a thirty-page report." Bunting, Tose maintained to the Associated Press, had been the lynchpin in a "conspiracy" to run him out of football. Other members of the conspiracy besides First Penn and John Bunting were his twenty-nine-percent partner Herb Barness, his former financial adviser Sidney Forstater, his former partner John Firestone, Chase Manhattan Bank of New York, and Provident National, Girard, and Philadelphia National banks of Philadelphia. They meant to deny him credit and make it impossible to keep the Eagles, but, Tose bragged, "that will never happen. I have too many friends in the National Football League and in the banking community."

The most useful of Leonard Tose's NFL friends was, of course, Chuck Sullivan, his hired gun. Even for Sullivan, however, Leonard Tose remained a difficult man to advise, and he proved it with Chuck less than a month after their celebration dinner.

At issue between Tose and Sullivan was the revenge Tose now wanted to seek from First Pennsylvania Bank and John Bunting. Tose believed their "conspiracy" was a violation of the Sherman [Anti-trust] Act and he wanted to sue everybody involved and make them pay him money for what they'd done. Sullivan wanted nothing to do with Tose's strategy and said so. "I think litigation really is self-defeating," he explained. It would most likely make more trouble with the banks than it was worth. For an example he pointed to the fact that being sued, "is one of the things that has galvanized the NFL owners."

Leonard Tose paid no attention and hired a lawyer who agreed with him. The result was *Leonard Tose v. First Pennsylvania Bank et al.,* filed in Federal District Court for Eastern Pennsylvania on May 5, 1978.

Tose's counsel in the suit was Joseph Alioto, former mayor of San Francisco and one of the country's foremost antitrust litigators. Had Pete Rozelle been looking for premonitions of approaching disaster in Philadelphia rather than signs of stability, he might have found one in Tose's choice of Alioto. Though his work for Tose would prove a sideshow, Alioto would soon acquire Al Davis for a client as well and, at Davis's behest, establish himself as a regular feature in League Think's worst nightmares.

In May 1978, the dominant irony of Tose's hiring of Alioto was that while ignoring Chuck Sullivan's advice, the Eagles owner was nonetheless keeping his legal business within the greater Sullivan family. Alioto, one year younger than Chuck's father, Billy, had recently married Chuck's sister Kathleen, age thirty-two. Joe Alioto had divorced his first wife after a failed run at California's governorship in the early 1970s and met Kathleen Sullivan through Democratic party politics. She had a Ph.D. in education from Harvard and had served on Boston's school board.

Leonard Tose had settled on Alioto at the recommendation of several other NFL members. By then, the San Francisco attorney already had a considerable reputation in League legal circles. He was aggressive and relentless and, in previous years, had both cut the League up and defended it to the death.

The cutting up had been in *Radovich v. NFL,* the 1958 suit that had first established the jurisdiction of the Sherman Act over the football business. The suit had germinated from an encounter between Alioto and Radovich when the latter was waiting tables in Los Angeles's Brown Derby restaurant. When he told Alioto his story, the attorney drafted a brief for his case on a napkin. In it, he had attacked the League's "blackballing" of his client as "a conspiracy to monopolize commerce in professional football."

Alioto's defense of the NFL had come in *Kapp v. NFL,* a 1974 suit by one of Billy Sullivan's players claiming the standard NFL player contract was a violation of the Sherman Act and seeking $12 million in damages. On that occasion, San Francisco's former mayor trumpeted on behalf of the NFL's treatment of Kapp, saying "these rules have generated the greatest mass entertainment, not in the history of the United States, but in universal history, in the history of the world. All that can be lost if we let the prima donnas of this game have their way, and if this thing turns out to be a lawyer's paradise instead of a spectator's delight." The jury went with Alioto, awarded no damages, and the NFL was saved from a potential judgment of some $1.4 million per franchise.

In *Tose v. Penn,* Joe Alioto's first duties were to accompany his client at the May press conference announcing the suit. There, Chuck Sullivan's brother-in-law characterized his client as a victim who had been forced to fight back. "There is so much guerilla warfare going on against the Eagles," Alioto explained, "the only way to end it is to bring this kind of suit."

Tose himself cut his usual natty figure at Alioto's side. Still the NFL's best-dressed member, *Philadelphia* magazine described him as favoring "crisply starched French cuffs, fastened by gold Eagles cuff links, well-cut and expensive suits, conservatively striped shirts rakishly set off by white collars and cuffs, and his trademark tie clip placed just a few inches higher than it should be." He lit his cigarettes with a jeweled lighter featuring an Eagle and the number one. After berating John Bunting and First Penn, Leonard Tose characterized his action as a crusade for the average guy. "If this kind of thing can be perpetrated against the Eagles," he pointed out, "God help the poor people. God help my truck drivers. God help everybody." Having already positioned himself, via a press release, as being on the side of the little guy against the big bad banks, Tose went on to say, "Bunting's been to bat and he's struck out and now Leonard Tose is going to bat. I did not seek it, but we'll go all the way." Tose was claiming $12 million in damages and if he won, those damages would be automatically trebled to $36 million.

When Leonard Tose joined the rest of the League at the June meetings in New York, he thanked those who had recommended Alioto. Tose was already calling the attorney "my Italian quarterback" and waxing optimistic about his chances of hitting the jackpot at First Penn's expense. Many of those he talked to were fans of Alioto's and tended to agree with him.

Tose v. First Pennsylvania would not reach trial until spring 1980, however. By then, many of those same men were already wishing they'd never heard Joe Alioto's name.

14

A number of dates would later be offered by National Football League members as they attempted to pinpoint just when League Think actually started coming apart. The earliest of those was the NFL Executive Session in its Park Avenue headquarters on June 7, 1978. At the least, that executive session amounted to the high-water mark of League Think's expansion into the NFL's life. Once the results of June 7 were actually committed to paper, momentum began to shift and Pete Rozelle would go over to the defensive for the duration.

The specific issue for which the June 7 executive session would be remembered was ownership policy. Not on the defensive yet, this time Rozelle raised the issue himself. "Commissioner Rozelle," the minutes noted, "concluded the morning session by reviewing the history of NFL ownership policy in regard to investment in or affiliation with other major professional team sports."

Armed with his "sense of the League" on the subject as reached the previous March in Palm Springs, Rozelle delivered a lengthy presentation, which he closed by again telling the story of Dick Boe, the owner of both the New York Islanders hockey franchise and the New York Nets basketball team who "took money from the successful hockey team to help keep the basketball team afloat and, in so doing, apparently created rather serious problems for both franchises. I pointed out . . . that this could happen in football and that sports are a risky business. . . . They are not like the normal businesses that businessmen would go into in that you are increasing the risk for problems developing if you have one of your people, particularly one who might not be as well-financed as some of the others, involved in a sport other than football."

After a break for lunch, the commissioner announced, "The topic would be discussed fully."

The discussion that raged when the League returned at 2:00 P.M. would be described in the minutes as "lengthy." Rozelle began by opening the floor to what Joe Robbie described as "round-robin discussion" and "called on each club to express itself." Very quickly, "Leonard Tose delivered himself on the subject" again. Tose, Edward Bennett Williams remembered, "spoke with some feeling with respect to the policy and what he said was a commitment on the part of Mr. Hunt to use his best efforts to divest." As usual, Tose maintained Hunt's word was worthless and yelled at him to get out.

Lamar Hunt listened with his usual detached look. "It was basically a criticism," Hunt pointed out, "that these people who were involved in other sports—but basically all the conversations centered around me—that these people, specifically Hunt, should be forced to sell out."

While Robbie and Williams, the two loudest critics of the commissioner's ownership policy, found both Tose and Hunt's behavior predictable, the rest of the discussion was much more unsettling. Most of the men who spoke wanted a deadline for divestiture set and wanted specific penalties for exceeding it as well. The discussion also took up where it had left off in March on the issue of prohibiting cross-ownership by immediate family.

Joe Robbie had missed the March meeting and was outraged by this new aspect. "There had never been mention of familial ownership at any prior meeting," he explained, "and they captured my attention when they went into the matter of extending this policy to families and . . . some of the owners in the room agreed that families should be included. They never got specific as to how far they should go. . . . I got up and took strong exception to the National Football League attempting to tell my family what investments they could make in professional sports. I said that there was no way my five sons could all run the Miami Dolphins. That would be bedlam. I described how [my wife] Elizabeth came into soccer and that she started off with a rooting interest, ultimately to become a general partner . . . and [that] there were several meetings after that at which this policy was extended with no mention of families. . . . I told the NFL that we stood to lose substantial money to sell off the Ft. Lauderdale Strikers as a result of this family policy. . . . I also asked what had become of Mr. Williams's request two years earlier for a legal opinion as to the legality of the rule, even as it related only to owners themselves and not their families. As a result of that I received a letter four or five weeks later enclosing an opinion of Covington and Burling that a policy against dual ownership would be legal.''

Robbie the attorney disagreed with Covington and Burling. ''I think it's illegal,'' he emphasized. ''I think it's contrary to public policy, especially as it relates to family. . . . I don't see any reason why a person can't have an investment in more than one major league team sport.''

Robbie was, however, in a distinct minority. Banning cross-ownership, Tex Schramm remembered, ''was a necessity and to have strength it needed to be in the constitution and it needed teeth.'' It also needed a deadline. Art Modell favored a two-year period in which divestiture should take place, but there were a variety of time frames discussed, from immediate to never. Whatever the total length of time given, Art Modell remembers that Hugh Culverhouse added, ''It should be a January cutoff date to allow a taxable year to commence and give people . . . a chance to attend to their own individual tax problems as they saw fit.'' There were also, Rozelle recalled, ''a number of suggestions made regarding specific sanctions that would be involved after an agreed-upon point in time.''

To Joe Robbie and Edward Bennett Williams, the notion of sanctions was perhaps the most unsettling aspect of all. Robbie noted that ''the discussion got rather heated about the imposition of penalties. There was almost a bidding contest to how much they should be, going from one to another, depending on the depth of his feeling, $50,000 a week or $50,000 a month so long as anybody continued in cross-ownership.''

At this point, Robbie pointed out, ''Edward Bennett Williams also took strong exception. He repeated that he had assured the National Football League on many occasions that Jack Kent Cooke would exert his best efforts to resolve the problem with regard to dual ownership . . . and he said, 'I've made the promise in spite of the fact that I consider your policy to be illegal' and said, 'We are going to keep that promise; as a matter of fact, we hope to resolve it within the next few months, but . . . when you start talking in terms of amending the constitution and bylaws and imposing penalties of the sizes that are being discussed here, then I think you would do better to put down in writing exactly what you have in mind and call a special meeting for that purpose.' '' For Williams, the suggestion served the purpose of at least delaying the procedure. He also wanted to put more pressure on Rozelle's sense of the meeting and suggested a straw vote.

''There were all kinds of divergent views being expressed,'' Williams explained, ''and it was a mélange of confusion and I made the suggestion, why don't we [approach] the subject in stages? Let's ask, number one, how many are in favor of the general policy of cross-ownership, and then, having covered that, let's see how many people want to extend that policy . . . to members of the family, and then later break it down and see what the sanctions should be to enforce it, and finally, how much time should be given to someone who is in violation of the policy . . . to divest himself. . . . They accepted that suggestion and they voted on four different things.''

First there was a brief recess. During it, Rozelle approached Williams to deliver the same message in person as he'd sent through Schulman in March. ''I told him,'' Rozelle remembered, ''that I understand [about Jack Kent Cooke's court order not to sell anything] and would convey to the rest of the members why Mr. Cooke could not comply with the pledge made on his behalf.'' According to Williams, ''Mr. Rozelle told me that the proposed bylaw was not directed against Mr. Cooke or the Redskins; rather, it was directed at Mr. Hunt and his soccer ownership.'' Rozelle's sympathy had no effect on Williams's opposition.

Back in the meeting, the straw vote quickly revealed that Rozelle didn't need Williams's support anyway. The informal poll was organized as a series of four questions, as Williams had suggested.

Edward Bennett Williams approached the vote with the same strategy he'd been keeping to since the issue first arose. ''I voted no on the policy,'' he remembered, ''and then said if you have it . . . it should apply to everyone, because I was anxious to defeat the policy and I thought it would have less chance to pass if it applied to everyone in the family, because that was ludicrous on its face, and then I came out for the minimum sanction and the maximum period to divest.'' On all those issues, he was in an enormous minority.

The question of amending the constitution was the first considered and, in Williams's view, the most critical. The Redskin owner and Joe Robbie cast the only two distinct no votes. Four owners passed, one was absent, and twenty voted yes. Though twenty-one votes would be needed actually to accept an amendment, a quick look at the group who had passed or been absent made it clear the commissioner could easily get the majority he needed. Two of the passes, Lamar Hunt and Al Davis, weren't likely to vote for him, and Seattle, a third pass, might respect its own soccer cross-ownerships enough to deny the additional yes, but the other two were the Sullivans and Max Winter. The Sullivans, Chuck explained, ''had a very close association with both Mr. Hunt and Mr. Robbie. . . . It had been our hope that we could effect a settlement [and] my father and I both felt that we would be in a better position to effect that settlement if we passed.'' Should push come to shove, however, they favored an amendment and would likely give Rozelle the vote he needed. Even if they didn't, Max Winter, who had been out of the room on the phone to Minnesota when the vote was taken, was second only to Leonard Tose in his rabid backing of anything that was against cross-ownership.

The votes on the subsequent three questions were, from Williams's standpoint, just as bad. According to the notes of the discussion kept by one of Rozelle's assistants, the ''consensus'' on them was ''extensive'' coverage of ''family relations,'' sanctions ranging from $10,000 to $50,000 a month, and complete divestiture of all interests in other major league team sports by January 31, 1980. Once they were tallied, the minutes recorded, ''the League office was directed to draft a bylaw proposal reflecting the position expressed by a majority of the member clubs relative to ownership policy.'' Rozelle then informed the meeting that ''the draft would be sent to the member clubs for consideration and comment and as soon as possible thereafter, a special meeting would be convened to act on the bylaw.'' In fact, the lawyers began drafting the amendment the next day.

After eleven years of patient struggle, Pete Rozelle was now on the verge of getting the constitutional amendment he had always wanted.

It was Edward Bennett Williams, however, who would have the final word on June 7. The vote had changed none of his thinking and, in retrospect, a number of NFL members would wish they'd shared that thinking sooner.

''I told them they would have certain litigation if they enacted this,'' Williams remembered, ''I said the League is being led by lemmings into the sea.''

15

There was, of course, another storm brewing on the NFL's horizon that summer besides the one of which Edward Bennett Williams warned. This storm was in Los Angeles and, like the June cross-ownership struggle in New York, its significance went largely unappreciated in the immediate moment. What was going on in L.A. was still, Rozelle noted, ''Carroll's business.''

And C.R. was taking his time in conducting it. By the end of June, the announcement the *Los Angeles Times* had predicted in April still had not been made. The only public stirring on the question of a Rams move that month was a well-publicized June 28 visit by Carroll Rosenbloom to Anaheim's Big A Stadium. It was the third time in his life Rosenbloom had been there and, since he had lawyers handling all the negotiations, the first time he'd met many of the Anaheim city officials. ''I hadn't had the opportunity of meeting anyone,'' C.R. explained, ''and I wanted to see the facility again because we're getting to the point where they need to know and we have to make up our minds, certainly by the end of July.'' Though Carroll was not saying what he planned to do, he did muse on the future of football in both Los Angeles and Orange County. ''There's been a lot of conversation,'' he noted, ''that if the Rams were to leave, the Coliseum would seek another franchise—which I feel they would and should. At the same time, if the people in Anaheim don't get us, they would probably move toward getting themselves a franchise when the NFL expands. . . . No one owner is going to stand up and say, 'Hey, I don't want another team coming in here.' The Anaheim people have been perfect to deal with.''

Rosenbloom's visit to Orange County set the stage for his final face-to-face meeting with Bill Robertson. On July 9, the two men had lunch at Carroll's house in Trancas Beach. Robertson began with a detailed verbal rundown of what the $9 million the LAMCC was committed to raise would buy for the Coliseum. Robertson was also prepared to give his word that the money would indeed be forthcoming.

C.R. didn't doubt Robertson's promise. "I have faith in you," he told the LAMCC president, "and if you had been aboard a year earlier, all of this would not have happened."

"I thanked him for that," Robertson remembered, "but I think he was being very gracious . . . and stroking me a little because . . . I was convinced he already had a deal in his hip pocket for Anaheim."

That, of course, was a subject on which Rosenbloom continued to be noncommittal. According to Robertson, C.R. admitted, "I'm looking at Anaheim. They have made an attractive offer to me, but I'm not ruling out the possibility of remaining in Los Angeles. As I told you before, I haven't decided."

Robertson pushed the issue a little and asked the Rams owner to give some sense of what Los Angeles's chances were.

"Oh," C.R. mused, "I would say it's sixty-five to thirty-five I'm going to make the move to Anaheim." Rosenbloom tried to soften the estimate by again noting that if Robertson "had been here a year or two ago, we would probably be remaining in the Coliseum."

As president of the LAMCC, Robertson pointed out, "my charge is to either retain the Rams or to get another football team. I am going to pursue that with all the vigor at my disposal. Would you oppose such a move?"

"No," C.R. reaffirmed, "I wouldn't."

Robertson left when lunch was over and the remainder of his communications with Rosenbloom were by phone.

The most heartening of those calls came during the week after their lunch when C.R. called the LAMCC president at home. He asked Robertson if he could have the verbal proposals L.A. had made over lunch in writing. Rosenbloom claimed he "wanted a chance to study them." Despite his sense that the die was already cast, Robertson quickly complied.

The letter sent from Bill Robertson to Carroll Rosenbloom on July 17, 1978, included a six-page schedule of where the Coliseum's $9 million would be spent. In the cover letter, Robertson also sweetened Los Angeles's offer. "The Coliseum commission desires to make substantial additional improvements" as well, he pointed out. "These improvements will be funded from a $12,000,000 to $15,000,000 allocation we expect to receive shortly after a contract is executed for the award of the 1984 Olympics to Los Angeles." In closing, Robertson tried to evoke Rosenbloom's loyalty to his adopted home:

> I would like to urge you to give the most serious consideration to the interests of the citizens of Los Angeles. I know that you must be deeply concerned with their welfare, just as I am. As president of the Coliseum commission, I am more than willing to do everything

within my power to make it possible for our football fans to continue to enjoy the finest in professional football. . . . You know, of course, that Mayor Bradley is also fully dedicated to this goal. Under these circumstances, I am confident that, working together, we can overcome whatever difficulties have existed in the past and assure a long and successful future for the Rams in the Coliseum.

Bill Robertson's plea to Carroll Rosenbloom was, in truth, a waste of paper. The day after his Trancas Beach meeting with C.R. and a week before his letter was written, a Cabot, Cabot & Forbes internal memo had noted that an agreement had already been settled upon between Anaheim Stadium Associates and the city of Anaheim. Stadium Associates would build a twenty-seven-thousand-seat addition to Big A "at an estimated cost of $16 million," for which CC&F would act as "construction supervisor" and receive a fee of "six percent, or $1 million, plus fifty percent of cost underruns." The project was to be financed by the sale of $22 million in municipal bonds by Anaheim. The $6 million above the projected cost of the addition would be divided $1 million for "Ram training facilities and offices," $1 million as a "fee" to CC&F, and $4 million for "cost overruns, seed capital for peripheral development, and profit for Rosenbloom, who takes the construction risk." Stadium Associates would hold title to the bulk of the new addition, but Rosenbloom alone would own the stadium's "approximately one hundred" new luxury boxes. The stadium's adjoining ninety-five acre parcel would be rented by Stadium Associates for $8,000 an acre. The option to purchase was set at "$80,000 an acre escalating with cost of living to $100,000 per acre" and was good for fifteen years.

By the time Bill Robertson's letter actually reached Carroll Rosenbloom's Pico Boulevard office, the Rams owner had already notified Commissioner Pete Rozelle of his intentions as well. "He just told me that if he could consummate a deal" with Anaheim, Rozelle remembered, "he wanted to move there and he was going to announce that." Later, Rozelle recalled, "I didn't debate it with him on the telephone. I just listened. I did, however, send him a personal letter on the subject."

That letter, dispatched shortly after Rosenbloom got off the phone, was typed by Rozelle personally and no copy was kept. The typing was all in lower case, a style Rozelle described as "a throwback" to "my PR days." He adopted it because "I wanted Carroll to view it as somewhat of a personal letter and I hoped that he would give it some consideration" as such. Later, Rozelle would explain, "I had some feelings for the L.A. Coliseum. That was the first place I saw football games when I was a youngster. . . . I felt it was more attractive for [Rosenbloom] and his wife to play in the Coliseum. A lot of their friends were in West Los Angeles and I thought they would like the Coliseum better than Anaheim."

There is no evidence that Rosenbloom did—or that he reflected further on the move, as Rozelle had asked him to. On July 21, he had his last phone conversation with Robertson. The Rams owner still maintained that he was only "leaning" toward Anaheim and that the odds of a move were still sixty-five to thirty-five. At that moment, a press conference with Anaheim city officials had been on C.R.'s schedule since at least July 10. On July 21, he promised to call Robertson before announcing any decision one way or another. Bill Robertson never heard from him again.

On July 25, Rosenbloom and Anaheim finally held their press conference at Big A Stadium. C.R. spoke from notes scribbled on stationery from the Disneyland Hotel, where he'd spent the previous evening. "When I came to Anaheim on June 28," Rosenbloom explained, "and met with the men who represent the city, I then began to think of the magnitude and enormity of the decision. Since then, being a poor sleeper at best, I spent most of my nights fast awake. I doubt that anyone can understand what a traumatic experience it has been. It will be with feelings of deep regret that we leave the Coliseum. But we shall look forward to having our playing site, our training facility, our coaches and management together. We believe that this, coupled with a closed, intimate stadium, where fans can be more a part of the game, will help us win." Despite having committed himself to move to the city of Anaheim, county of Orange, Rosenbloom planned to continue calling his team the Los Angeles Rams. "It's our name," he claimed, "and we'll continue to use it."

Rosenbloom also said he would not oppose another NFL team in the soon to be vacant Los Angeles Coliseum. "If my twenty-seven [NFL] partners decide they want to put another team in California, or if they want to put one in Hong Kong," he promised, "I could not vote against it."

Los Angeles bit its public tongue and said nothing. "We made no effort to stop the Rams," Robertson observed. "We didn't try to go to the process of eminent domain. We did not try to generate a ground swell of protest. . . . We believed that Carroll Rosenbloom, like any other businessman in this country under our capitalist, free enterprise system, had a right to move if he so desired."

Of course, that same free enterprise system gave Bill Robertson, the city and county of Los Angeles, and the Los Angeles Memorial Coliseum Commission the right to find another franchise to take the Rams' place, and Robertson immediately set out to do so. The first two steps in his strategy were accomplished within three weeks of Rosenbloom's announcement.

The first step was to nail down Robertson's own negotiating base even further. This he did by tying his search into the stature and office of Tom Bradley, Los Angeles's mayor. The vehicle was the creation of the Mayor's Professional Football Search Committee. Bradley had agreed to it after a lecture from one of his closest advisers. The man had come in to see the mayor to get him to act. The problem, he pointed out, was that the Coliseum had been incompetent over the years. Robertson was the best man for the job, but he'd come on the scene too late to do anything, and his hand had to be strengthened before anything more would get done. Because of its tripartite composition and rotating officials, the LAMCC was dysfunctional.

"Tom," his adviser warned, "if we just let those turkeys handle it, there's going to be no football team and no Coliseum."

The stakes were indeed as high as the mayor's adviser alleged. Unless compensated for during the upcoming final year of the Rams' lease, C.R.'s departure for Anaheim would leave the L.A. Coliseum with a $750,000 annual deficit, the first time in its history it would ever have required public funding. If public money didn't rescue it, "the Grand Duchess of Stadiums" and the LAMCC would be bankrupt. Membership on the Mayor's Search Committee was weighted toward local politicians who would eventually have to foot the bill on a Coliseum bailout, but also included power-broking lawyer Chuck Manatt, thought to be close to a group interested in purchasing an expansion franchise, and entertainment executive Lew Wasserman, a close friend of Pete Rozelle's. The search committee's chairman was Bill Robertson. "The mayor," Bradley's adviser explained, "wanted to give Robertson independent leverage on the LAMCC."

The second step in Bill Robertson's strategy was to find out just where the NFL and Pete Rozelle stood. For this, Los Angeles utilized the services of Kenny Hahn, county supervisor and member of both the LAMCC and the Mayor's Search Committee. Hahn, a longtime L.A. politician, had been an instrumental figure in luring the baseball Dodgers west from Brooklyn twenty years earlier. He also knew Rozelle from the commissioner's old days in L.A., though, Rozelle pointed out, "not well."

Hahn had first made contact with the commissioner's office about the Coliseum's possible vacancy the day before Rosenbloom officially announced his departure, in a telegram requesting the commissioner's help in securing a new team for the Coliseum.

On July 25, immediately after C.R. announced his intentions, Kenny Hahn followed up his wire with a phone call. He was coming to Washington, D.C., on county business, Hahn explained, and wanted to make a side trip to discuss L.A.'s future with the commissioner in person. The issue was a possible expansion franchise. They arranged to meet in early August.

"We had a very cordial discussion," Rozelle remembered. "I told him, 'Kenny, we aren't prepared to expand. I know how the League thinks.' . . . He asked what I thought based upon previous expansion and I said, 'I couldn't pinpoint it, but it would probably be five or six years before Tampa and Seattle were . . . sufficiently established [to warrant further expansion].' So he asked me about L.A. getting a franchise and I said, 'I have always thought highly of L.A. [but] I don't have a vote. I can't say "All right, Kenny, you are going to get a franchise in 1983" because the clubs have to vote. But that I would see that L.A. was given serious consideration.' . . . Mr. Hahn [then] said to me, 'I have some people that I know might be interested in ownership of an expansion franchise.' And I said, 'Fine. I will see that they are given consideration for ownership should we come to Los Angeles.' It was very cordial."

Robertson and Hahn, however, considered Rozelle's response "very negative." The formal letter from the commissioner's office that followed Hahn's conversation was, from their standpoint, even worse. Writing on August 15, Rozelle began by suggesting that "some forthright comment on the Los Angeles situation is called for." He continued:

Decisions as to expansion of the National Football League are made by the member clubs collectively. . . . The National Football League has recently added two new teams. There are already four NFL teams operating within California, more than any other state. . . . Hurried expansion has never served the interests of any sports league. Experience in other professional sports has repeatedly and emphatically demonstrated this. There also exist within the United States other major population centers which do not have a professional football franchise and which have actively sought NFL franchises for many years. Thus, while the League's membership may decide to add additional franchises at some time in the future, and while the Rams themselves have publicly indicated that they will not oppose any form of future expansion which will serve the League's interests, I cannot predict early expansion action by the League. Nor can I provide any assurance as to the direction such expansion will take when and if it is decided upon.

Still further, as NFL commissioner, I cannot in good conscience encourage any existing NFL franchise to leave its present metropolitan market without professional football. While such decisions are not within my control, I take pride in the fact that no NFL club during the League's modern era has taken such an action. Other professional leagues have had a more spotty record in this respect, and have left a residue of ill will in the wake of uprooted franchises.

I fully appreciate the concern which you and the Coliseum authorities have with the prospect that the Coliseum may lose one of its present football tenants. But the Rams' proposed move to Anaheim should not, in my view, be considered a metropolitan area departure. While all stadium shifts within the NFL have differed on their particular facts, the Rams' proposed move is not wholly dissimilar to that of the Patriots' move to Foxboro, Massachusetts, the Cowboys' move to Irving, Texas, the Giants' move [to New Jersey], or the Lions' move to Pontiac, Michigan. . . .

In short, candor compels me to state that I do not believe there is any great prospect that the League will add additional franchises in the near future and I can provide no assurance that Los Angeles will be preferred over other potential franchise sites in any future expansion that may take place. I regret the need for replying to you in this fashion, but I believe it important that we understand each other as clearly as possible.

Sincerely,
Pete Rozelle, Commissioner

The letter infuriated Robertson.

"It was arrogant and an insult," the president of the LAMCC and chairman of the Mayor's Pro Football Search Committee fumed. "He just told Los Angeles to get in line with everybody else."

16

If Pete Rozelle was somewhat deaf to Los Angeles's outrage, it was, at least in part, a function of the uproar his ownership policy initiative had provoked at the same time.

On June 28, while Carroll Rosenbloom was visiting Big A, the commissioner dispatched the draft amendment on ownership policy which his employers had directed him to produce. It was, Rozelle explained, "based upon the informal pool we took [on June 7]." The bylaw proposal was accompanied by a memorandum to the National Football League's membership on the subject of "Ownership in Major Team Sports." While requesting the owners' "thoughts and suggestions on the draft," Rozelle used the bulk of the memo to remake his arguments against cross-ownership. It had been drafted for him by his in-house legal counsel. Prohibition was necessary to avoid the dilution of the resources, energies, and loyalties of NFL owners, he again pointed out. It would prevent "conflicts of interest" and insure "appropriate confidentiality of marketing and other strategies." The commissioner also argued that cross-ownership was "looked at unfavorably by the press" and could very well cost the League money.

"The NFL's success depends on fan interest and loyalty," he emphasized. "The League competes with other major team sports for that interest and loyalty as well as for gate receipts, TV revenues, advertising dollars, and media coverage. Connections with NFL personnel may well enhance these competing team sports, both in fact and in the public's perception, at the expense of the NFL."

The amendment itself would replace Article IX, Section 9.4 of the National Football League constitution. Subsection A of the new 9.4 stated that "No person (1) owning a majority interest in a member club, or (2) directly or indirectly having substantial operational control or substantial influence over the operations of a member club, or (3) serving as an officer or director of a member club, or (4) any spouse or minor child of any such person may directly or indirectly acquire, retain, or possess any interest in another major team sport (including major league baseball, basketball, hockey, and soccer)."

Subsection B expanded A to "also apply to relatives of such persons (including siblings, parents, adult children, adult and minor grandchildren, nephews and nieces, and relatives by marriage) (1) if such person directly or indirectly provided or contributed all or any part of the funds used to purchase or operate the other sports league entity, or (2) if there exists between such person and any such relative a significant community of interest in the successful operation of the other sports league entity." Subsection C gave the commissioner the power to "investigate to the extent he deems necessary or appropriate any reported or apparent violation" and report to the League's executive session as part of the disciplinary process.

Subsection D was the kicker and left little doubt how serious the commissioner was about enforcement. Members had until February 1, 1980, to divest themselves and afterward, any member "found to have violated subsection (A) or (B) above will be subject to fines of up to $25,000 per month for each of the first three months of violations; up to $50,000 per month for each of the next three months; and up to $75,000 per month thereafter." Such extended violations could also be considered sufficient grounds for revocation of the member's franchise. If the fine levied was not paid within twenty days, the League office was empowered to seize the fine as the club's television money passed through its hands.

A special meeting to discuss and vote on the amendment was scheduled for October 4–5 at the Marriott Hotel in Chicago. In the meantime, Rozelle asked his employers to let him know their reactions.

The ensuing uproar came from three parties.

As usual, the most quiet was Lamar Hunt. "The whole tenor of the proposal is considerably different [from previous policy]," Hunt complained. "It asks for the forced divestiture with a time limit that would, to say the least, be punitive. . . . It would make it very, very difficult to sell [my other interests] at a fair price." Hunt considered the policy neither "necessary or reasonable." He did not, however, make his objections to the proposal public. The proposed amendment "probably will be passed," Jack Steadman, the man Hunt employed to run his Kansas City Chiefs, told *The Kansas City Star* in July, and "Lamar would be willing to cooperate. There are a lot of other owners involved in other sports but even they agree it's a good rule. Lamar can see the benefit of concentrating our time on the development of football."

The phrasing of Joe Robbie's objections was much more blunt. "I am flatly, unalterably opposed to it," he responded. Predictably, Robbie's outrage was at the inclusion of relatives in the cross-ownership prohibition. "That wipes my family out in every direction," he said of subsections A and B. It also galvanized his urge to stop the amendment however he could. "I probably would have expressed myself in stronger terms earlier," he explained, if "I'd had before me then [the amendment] subsequently sent me, which would extend this policy not only to my sons and daughters but to my grandchildren and their spouses and with heavy penalties. . . . I suppose if a grandchild of mine at some future time should marry somebody involved in professional sports, that person would have to divest or they would have me paying the penalties because this goes at least into the third generation . . . and involves penalties even if their spouses become investors." Robbie considered Rozelle's draft absurd.

So, too, of course, did Edward Bennett Williams. "The resolution which has been operative through the years covers only those persons who have a majority interest," he pointed out, and "it has no sanctions. The proposal that came forth from the League office . . . [had] very, very heavy sanctions and is very, very broad and sweeping and purports to cover not only majority owners, but members of their families and it causes divestiture of a very sweeping nature by people who are identified with football. . . . It imposes sanctions that go up to $75,000 per month. . . . Seventy-five thousand dollars a month would be a million dollars a year. . . . No company in this League could stand it."

Later in the summer, Rozelle attempted to soothe Williams with a phone call. "The substance of what he said," Williams remembered, "was [that] this proposed bylaw is not directed against Mr. Cooke or the Redskins. . . . It is directed against Hunt [but] he didn't have to tell me that . . . . I heard Tose on the subject and I knew that."

Edward Bennett Williams remained unsoothed and, in July, dispatched a letter to the commissioner repeating his opposition. There was no "conflict of interest," he argued. Nor was there competition for the sports dollar or any damaging lack of "confidentiality of marketing and other strategies." Sports was good business for all sports. Williams also called at least one other owner and repeated his warning of "certain litigation" if the League proceeded any further.

The most likely plaintiff was the North American Soccer League. Indeed, by August 28, the NASL had voted to "retain counsel to seek a preliminary injunction against the NFL." Joe Robbie's wife's Ft. Lauderdale Strikers franchise, represented by his son Mike, voted yes. Lamar Hunt's Dallas Tornado abstained. In September, the NASL's attorneys made contact with Rozelle. "The draft amendment had got into their hands," the commissioner remembered, "and they came marching over here to our [Park Avenue] office. They sat us down for several hours and told us that they were going to sue us unless we voluntarily retracted the amendment. They weren't just going to sue if we passed it; they were going to sue if we put it on the agenda. They, in effect, said if you don't stop it right now, we will sue. We told them we weren't going to stop."

While all that was going on, the League's southern California front was erupting as well. Los Angeles was not going to take no for an answer and was also about to make their intentions a legal issue. This was step three in Bill Robertson's strategy. Rozelle's response to Hahn had made it obvious that the only solution to the LAMCC's dilemma was to convince another NFL owner to do to another stadium what Carroll Rosenbloom had just done to L.A.'s. The chief obstacle in that process was Article IV, Section 4.3 of the NFL constitution. Section 4.3 required that "no member shall have any right to transfer its club or franchise to a different city outside its home territory except with the prior approval of the members of the League." Further, "any transfer of an existing franchise to a location within the home territory of any other club shall be effective only if approved by unanimous vote; any other transfer shall only be effective if approved by the affirmative vote of not less than three fourths."

Bill Robertson knew the veto over the L.A. Coliseum's future given by Section 4.3 to each of the League's twenty-eight members was an impossible obstacle. In September, Los Angeles filed *LAMCC v. NFL,* contending that the section in question was a violation of the Sherman Act. The suit was immediately put on hold by the federal district court because no one had actually yet been prevented from occupying "the Grand Duchess of Stadiums" through the enforcement of Section 4.3, but it served to put Robertson's leverage on the table for all his potential allies to see.

It also served to get the NFL's attention. Shortly after *LAMCC v. NFL* was filed, discussion of the suit was added to the agenda scheduled for the League's special meeting in Chicago on October 4–5.

At the time, the principal subject scheduled for the Chicago meeting was still the commissioner's proposed ownership policy amendment, whatever the NASL's lawyers might threaten. Before the end of September, however, that agenda underwent a drastic alteration. The alteration was provoked by *NASL v. NFL,* a suit charging that the League's proposed ownership policy amendment violated the Sherman Act. Since the NASL was able to quickly win a restraining order preventing the NFL from acting on the proposal, the discussion of it was now confined to discussion of the suit itself. The complaint listed twenty-one of the NASL's twenty-four franchises as plaintiffs and twenty-five of the NFL's twenty-eight as defendants. The unnamed parties were Seattle, where the Nordstroms owned most of football and some of soccer, Miami and Ft. Lauderdale, where Joe Robbie owned football and Elizabeth Robbie owned soccer, and Kansas City and Dallas, where Lamar Hunt owned all of both. All three would be required to foot the legal bills of both sides of the suit. During the NFL's discussions of *NASL v. NFL,* the three would be asked to leave the room so as not to compromise the League's legal strategies.

Edward Bennett Williams didn't need to tell his fellow owners that his prediction had indeed been accurate.

Joe Robbie expressed no regrets. "I am happy enough [the suit] was brought," he observed. "I wasn't consulted but I would have voted for it. . . . It's one way of trying to resolve the issue."

Lamar Hunt said only that *NASL v. NFL* put him in "an awkward position" in which he was "divorced from himself either way." He also pointed to his abstention in the actual NASL vote to sue.

Leonard Tose, the loudest proponent of the contested amendment, was only more adamant about Hunt in response. "Hell," Tose fumed, "I don't know if [Hunt] is a plaintiff on the record, but he is the guy who originated it. He is the perpetrator. Whatever the hell the word is, he is the guy. He started it. . . . I don't think any of this would have happened if Mr. Hunt hadn't started this and I think a lot of things start from where he started this."

For Pete Rozelle, *NASL v. NFL* was a blow to League Think's solar plexus. It was also a dangerous precedent. "I know of no previous instance," the commissioner later testified, "where an NFL owner has been on the minority side of an issue and subsequently played a role in having that decision challenged in court. . . . To [now have to] say [to NFL cross-owners] 'Well, now we are going to excuse you because we have some sensitive subjects to talk about' . . . tears right at the guts, at the foundation, of the harmony and unity that you attempt to build for the success of the League. . . . I can see this leading to anarchy.''

Pete Rozelle was more right than he even knew.

17

The National Football League special meeting that convened in the Chicago Marriott on October 4 would eventually become one of the most minutely examined gatherings in NFL history, but not for the reasons most had anticipated during the previous summer. The NFL was now enjoined by the federal court from voting on Rozelle's constitutional amendment on ownership policy and the discussion of *NASL v. NFL*, the cause of that injunction was inconsequential. Instead, *LAMCC v. NFL* and the "Los Angeles problem" assumed the League's center stage.

Discussion of the issues raised by Los Angeles began at 2:45 in the afternoon of the meeting's first day. By then, Rozelle and the League office had given the suit against Section 4.3 a great deal of their attention. The response they had landed upon was presented to the membership as "bylaw proposal number two," a package of constitutional amendments principally designed to modify Section 4.3 to require only a three-quarter vote for all types of franchise moves. No official advance notice of the proposed constitutional amendments had been given the League members prior to their arrival in Chicago. Since the provision to be replaced required a unanimous vote, a unanimous vote would be required to amend it. To the commissioner, the logic behind such a move was obvious. The LAMCC suit, he remembered, "prompted my thinking about the rule which, of course, I'd say had gone back into probably the founding of the League. . . . I thought it was silly to try to defend in court something that didn't have an important business interest.''

The discussion was opened with a report from Hamilton Carothers, the League's lead attorney from Covington and Burling, whom Rozelle had asked to "describe the factual circumstances'' of the LAMCC suit. The attorney did so and pointed out that the current unanimous provisions of Section 4.3 left the League with "no defense'' should *LAMCC v. NFL* ever be activated.

Rozelle then assumed the floor to bolster the attorney's judgment with his own. He said that he could not guarantee that the LAMCC would drop its suit in light of the proposed changes, nor could he assure them that the changes would necessarily mean victory in court, but he felt "strongly'' that three quarters would be "less offensive than the unanimous vote." In his judgment, the LAMCC wanted "to knock out territorial exclusivity," and the object was to make that principle defensible. The current Section 4.3 was not only indefensible, it was also, the commissioner argued, "no longer necessary." Doubts about its validity could be removed by making it conform to the three-quarters vote used on ninety-six percent of the League's business. "Our teams were strong," Rozelle explained. "We were strong as a League and whatever three quarters felt was good for the League should be satisfactory in today's climate." He then opened the subject up for round-robin discussion.

The commissioner would remember that October 4 discussion as relatively unremarkable. "I don't recall opposition," he later testified. "I recall discussion and a couple of clubs requiring clarification as to what was being done."

Al Davis would remember it very differently. "There were many speeches made on this," the Raiders owner claimed during a pretrial deposition, "many objections, actually violent arguments between owners . . . and this went on for the [whole] first day. . . . To get the [three-quarters vote] rule, the commissioner needed the unanimous consent of all the members of the League. In fact, it was pointed out many times that he couldn't do it without . . . unanimous consent. . . . The commissioner . . . polled the owners approximately five times that day hoping to get the unanimous consent . . . and he couldn't get it."

Leading that opposition was Davis himself. "We had one purpose," he complained, "knock the rule [Section 4.3] down so the L.A. Coliseum would drop the lawsuit." On the subject of the proposed change to a three-quarters vote, he added, "There was no real thought as to whether it was a functional, workable rule relative to someone wanting to move. . . . It was such a dire necessity in their minds to negate that Coliseum lawsuit. They made it sound like it was the most important thing in our lives, and I didn't feel that way."

Instead, Al Davis felt no Section 4.3 whatsoever was a much better option than an amendment. Davis's own attorney had investigated the case and offered Davis the opinion that any required vote about franchise movement would be struck down if taken to court. The Raiders' lease with the Oakland Coliseum would expire at the end of the 1979 season, Davis pointed out, the same time as Carroll Rosenbloom's with the LAMCC. "I told them my lease would be up shortly," Davis remembered. "I told them I may want to move. I told them I don't think I need a vote to move."

Few of the other owners in the meeting evinced much longterm concern with Davis's attitude and figured his stance was another dose of his obstreperousness. "It was just the Al Davis approach," Steve Rosenbloom remembered. Wellington Mara, however, claimed to have seen it coming. "Al," he pointed out, "is a guy capable of bringing the roof down around his own head." While the discussion was raging, he and Carroll Rosenbloom had a short side conversation about what Davis was up to.

"I think what Al is after is the Los Angeles pay TV market," Mara told C.R.

C.R., according to Mara, expressed disbelief. "Al Davis had been his boy," Mara explained. "He said he couldn't believe Davis would do something like move to L.A."

Given that Rosenbloom and Davis had already had a number of conversations about precisely that possibility, C.R.'s response to Mara was less than credible.

For his part, Rozelle claimed he "had no idea the Raiders were thinking of moving to Los Angeles."

Davis was incredulous at Rozelle's claim. "All I was concerned about was Los Angeles," he pointed out. "All the membership talked about for a day and a half was Los Angeles. And I don't think there should have been any question in anyone's mind as to what city I was talking about."

While the meeting was going on, Davis also personally mentioned the possibility of his franchise filling L.A.'s vacancy to Joe Robbie, Tex Schramm, Eddie DeBartolo, Chuck Sullivan, and Leonard Tose.

Certainly Los Angeles was, in one way or another, very much on the minds of the three other owners who joined Davis's opposition in the course of the October 4 discussion.

Joe Robbie thought the proposed amendment would have no effect on Los Angeles at all. When the Rams would move to Anaheim at the end of the next year, he argued, L.A. was not going to allow itself to be left without a franchise, whatever the specific configuration of the League's rule. The situation Carroll Rosenbloom had set off by moving to Anaheim was not like the Giants moving to New Jersey. "There is less difference between New Jersey and Manhattan than between Orange County and L.A.," he warned. "The county of Los Angeles will fight us in the courts, the Congress, and the state legislature." They would keep "the pressure on" until Los Angeles got another franchise, whether or not Section 4.3 was altered as the commissioner wanted. The only solution to the "Los Angeles question," according to Robbie, was "either keep the Rams in L.A. or move another franchise" there. Robbie was the only owner at the NFL's special meeting to suggest keeping Carroll Rosenbloom's Rams where they were.

Buffalo Bills owner Ralph Wilson also considered the Rams move and Rozelle's proposed amendments interrelated questions, and, though he didn't suggest Rosenbloom's Rams be kept where they were, he disapproved of the move. Like most of the owners in the room, Wilson knew nothing of Carroll Rosenbloom's development deal with CC&F and Anaheim, but had picked up on conversations among other owners to the effect the move would "financially benefit" the Rams. In general, Wilson thought no team should move "to get better financial arrangements" unless they were under "dire financial stress," which certainly Carroll Rosenbloom was not. Specifically, Wilson thought the L.A. Coliseum was "a fine stadium," that the Rams had a loyal following there, and that "moving to Anaheim in another county" was not "in the best interests of the League." His feelings that way were strong enough to keep him among the opposition throughout the special meeting's first day.

The opposition's final and loudest voice was Robert Irsay. Seated between Leonard Tose and Wellington Mara, Irsay stood to speak and then launched into a largely incomprehensible address punctuated with pieces of diatribe about Carroll Rosenbloom. "He couldn't make sense," one of the people listening to Irsay remembered. "Everybody looked at each other and thought he was crazy. We just let him rant and rave and tried to pay as little attention to it as possible."

The general drift of Irsay's position was that he "flatly opposed" changing from unanimous vote because he believed that some owners, like Rosenbloom, could get the necessary votes, but others, like Irsay himself, could not. "He did view himself as unpopular," Rozelle later testified. "Mr. Irsay is a high-strung, emotional individual and sometimes it is difficult to understand exactly what he is feeling or saying. . . . He is very florid and vociferous in his speeches. . . . It wasn't clear to me what Mr. Irsay was saying. . . . He was volatile. The impression I got was that he had a dispute with Mr. Rosenbloom and somehow he got this twisted in with the charge it was helping Mr. Rosenbloom. . . . For some reason he felt this might help Mr. Rosenbloom and he was against it for that reason. He seemed to be confused. . . . Some clarification was required for Mr. Irsay to understand that this had no bearing on Mr. Rosenbloom. . . . He was talking without any real . . . consideration of it and he finally ended up and just said, 'I want to talk to my own attorneys.' "

Perhaps the loudest among the twenty-four votes supporting the commissioner's bylaw proposal number two on the special meeting's first day was Gene Klein. Klein addressed his fellow owners on the alteration of Section 4.3 and called it an essential step to put the question of franchise movement "in line with everything else we do." Like Davis, he had raised the question with his own attorneys and they had informed him *LAMCC v. NFL* would be "easy to defend" once Rozelle's amendment had been passed. A longtime resident of Beverly Hills, Klein also knew Bill Robertson of the LAMCC. He had even discussed the Coliseum's vacancy with him recently when the two ran into each other at L.A.'s Friars Club. According to Klein, Robertson had indicated then that the change to three quarters would be sufficient to get the suit dropped.

"Mr. Klein represented to the ownership that he had met with Mr. Robertson," Al Davis later testified, "and that if we changed the vote, [the LAMCC] would drop the lawsuit. That was the theme all day. . . . Gene Klein said it three or four times during the meeting to try and get the ownership to adopt the lowering of the unanimous [vote]. . . . We weren't really amending the rule for the sake of the rule; we were amending the rule . . . because Mr. Klein said the Coliseum people would drop their lawsuit. That was the only reason." Klein himself, under oath, could remember only that he "might have mentioned Robertson" and denied ever having said the LAMCC would drop their suit. In any case, Davis was unmoved by the argument. "Quite frankly," the Raiders owner later admitted under oath, "I had advance information that Mr. Klein would do this."

Throughout October 4, Al Davis continued to hold his ground. "I felt the rule was entirely too restrictive," he pointed out. "I made the statement that we don't need a rule; we need guidelines. . . . I wanted the rule to have outside forces or neutral bodies make that decision as to whether we should move or not. I was not interested in a vote of the members on that particular situation."

Davis's call for guidelines set off the only direct intervention by his friend Carroll Rosenbloom in the discussion of Section 4.3. Rosenbloom was on the other side and supported Rozelle's bylaw proposal number two for reasons of his own. "The change was closing the door after the cows are out," his son Steve explained, "but we didn't want to be accused of blocking any move into the Coliseum after we left." Rosenbloom's intervention was an attempt to find some sort of middle ground that might satisfy Davis. His idea was to craft a definition of home territory that included specifics of "population, geographical area, stadium suitability, economy, travel, demographics, and TV market coverage" rather than just a seventy-five-mile circle. Such an arrangement might very well give Davis the latitude he felt he needed. C.R. advanced his plan in individual discussions around the room.

"These meetings are conducted in a more informal manner than many other meetings," Rozelle noted, "and Carroll particularly had a habit of sitting next to somebody for a little bit, then getting up, sitting next to someone else. At one point . . . he was sitting next to me and he leaned over to me and said, 'Maybe we ought to try to work out a definition of home territory and take into account these [factors].' . . . It was not anything he voiced aloud in the meeting. It was just a sub rosa discussion among us that took maybe fifteen minutes. . . . And then he got up and walked over and sat with somebody else." Rozelle recalled, "If it ever came up, it was rejected immediately because it didn't make sense. We never had a lengthy discussion or any sizable discussion on standards."

Among the other side conversations on May 4 was at least one between Rozelle and Davis. "He and I talked . . . about Los Angeles," Davis remembered. Rozelle said things "like why won't I go along with the vote and what do I think of the franchise and how he himself couldn't believe Carroll would move. . . . He also knew how I felt. . . . He knew my lease was up, that I was in an untenable situation and I wasn't anxious to get this thing into new focus on where no one had before and I expressed this to the membership."

Rozelle remembered that Davis was particularly concerned about a column that had appeared in the *San Francisco Chronicle* sports page the day before, claiming the League was about to change Section 4.3. According to the commissioner, "the thrust of his remarks were that I had leaked to this writer that the League was going to change the vote from unanimous to three quarters." Rozelle denied it and also talked with Davis about more general subjects. "He said some things that made me feel he might change his mind," the commissioner claimed. "He said, 'I don't want to block what

you're doing. I don't want to stop you.' Then he would raise objection.''
Rozelle elaborated, ''It is difficult to know what Al is saying. . . .
I don't know how to describe it. It isn't fair to say he had said one thing at
one time and one thing at another, but he was equivocating. . . . He seemed
to want to stay flexible and to reserve all his options, whatever they might be.''

Rozelle's sense of Davis as obscure about his intentions was corrobo-
rated by Robert Schulman, the Washington attorney sitting in for the absent
Edward Bennett Williams. At one point, Schulman remembered, ''the commissioner asked Al how he was going to vote. He asked, 'Are you going to
vote yes?' and 'Are you going to vote no?' Al waffled . . . did not give him a
definitive answer.''

However obscure Al Davis may have been, Pete Rozelle could read the
handwriting on the wall as the meeting passed 5:00 P.M. and approached
adjournment. Among those he still had listed as holding ''reservations'' were
Al Davis, Joe Robbie, Ralph Wilson, and Robert Irsay. The chances of
getting a unanimous formal vote on October 4 were obviously nil, so, Rozelle
explained, ''I let it go until the next day.''

Discussion of bylaw proposal number two would resume the following
morning, October 5, at 9:45.

18

The October 5 session of the League's special meeting opened with more
uproar. The clamor grew out of a phone call Ralph Wilson had placed to Bill
Robertson in Los Angeles at 2:00 A.M. Wilson wanted to verify Gene Klein's
claims of the previous day.

''Bill,'' Wilson asked, ''did you at any time tell Gene Klein that if the
NFL reduced the requirement [to three quarters] you would back away from
the lawsuit?''

''Absolutely not,'' Robertson answered.

When the League reconvened almost eight hours later, Wilson informed
the other owners of the phone call. According to Al Davis, Wilson also ''told
Mr. Klein that he had misrepresented to the group. Mr. Robertson said they
would never drop the lawsuit.'' At this point, ''Mr. Rozelle and Mr. Carothers
threw their hands in the air with exasperation and everyone yelled at Mr.
Wilson, 'Why did you do that?' ''

Wilson remembered that among the most vocal objectors to his phone
call was Carroll Rosenbloom. C.R., as Rozelle recalled it, pointed out the
League was having a private meeting and Wilson had no business talking to
Bill Robertson about it. Wilson responded that he would talk to anybody he
wanted about anything he felt like.

In the melee that followed, Al Davis pointed out that the principal argument in favor of bylaw proposal number two had just been shown up as an "outright lie" but his point was lost. Most of the ensuing discussion was just more speeches in favor. Al Davis would later characterize their content as " 'this is the most important thing that could happen to this League,' et cetera, and like that."

Whatever Davis thought of the argument, the number of owners now making it had grown since the previous afternoon. The last straw vote on October 4 had been twenty-four in favor and four "reservations." The first poll on October 5 came out twenty-seven yes and one pass. Davis was now alone.

Ralph Wilson had changed his position despite his phone call to Robertson. Wilson later explained that the change had grown out of his concern for "stability" and some "uniformity of rules" within the League. The amendment seemed "in order" because of the widespread use of the three-quarters vote in other League business. Wilson now maintained that going to three quarters on Section 4.3 was "a logical compromise."

Joe Robbie's reservations had apparently been satisfied overnight as well. Robbie himself was now absent and was being represented by his son, Mike. Mike voted yes with no explanation.

Robert Irsay's mind had also been changed. Doing so had been Steve Rosenbloom's assignment, despite Irsay's antipathy for all things Rosenbloom, and Steve called it "tougher than Al Davis." The younger Rosenbloom approached Irsay's general manager after the October 4 session and asked him to talk some sense to his boss. The GM had accompanied his boss to Chicago and was a friend of Steve's. The next day Irsay was absent and his GM had assumed his seat. The general manager voted yes and said he was doing so with the full approval of his boss.

Even alone, however, Al Davis had the upper hand. His refusal to cast the twenty-eighth yes vote still had the commissioner stalemated.

At this point, however, Davis later testified, "someone stood up and made the statement, 'Mr. Davis, this is probably the most important decision we ever had to make. Why can't you give us your vote?' And I told them why. Because I may want to move in the future. I don't think a vote is necessary. . . . I said furthermore the presentation made by Gene Klein the day before, that the Los Angeles Coliseum would drop the lawsuit if we changed the vote . . . we now find is not true. I said, 'So that is another reason.' They will not drop the lawsuit, and I will not give my vote."

Then Davis turned to address Rozelle. "You can't pass this thing," he told the commissioner. "I will not give my vote."

For the remainder of the discussion about amending Section 4.3, the principal topic was whether or not the vote could be considered unanimous without Davis's yes. The question was specifically whether a vote of twenty-seven yeses and one pass constituted universal agreement. Davis was alone in arguing it was not. At close to 11:00 A.M., Rozelle finally called for a formal verbal ballot. "I could see what was coming," Davis later claimed.

To prepare, the Raiders owner turned to Chuck Sullivan of the New England Patriots, who was seated nearby. He asked the lawyer to "give me some language to be sure I made the proper statement." Davis claimed Sullivan wrote it out for him on a piece of paper: *I reserve the right to move my team as I see fit if you are going to declare this unanimous when it isn't.* The piece of paper was later lost and, though he remembered talking with Davis immediately prior to the vote, Chuck Sullivan would later testify to having "no recollection" of ever writing anything.

Davis nonetheless claimed to have used the essence of Sullivan's phrasing when his turn to vote came. First he cast a "pass" and then, he remembered, "I said to the commissioner, 'If you are going to consider that unanimous, and it isn't, then I reserve the right to move the Oakland Raiders as I see fit.' "

Rozelle remembered Davis making his point much more "obliquely." According to the commissioner, Davis said only, "I pass and reserve my rights." Rozelle then asked him what he meant by that and claimed Davis's only response was "half-sentences and mutters" to the effect that he "just passed" and "reserved his rights." When Rozelle asked twice more for clarification, each response by Davis was essentially the same.

The League attorney sitting close to Rozelle remembered listening to Davis and thinking, "I wonder what the hell he means by that?"

Davis himself thought he'd been perfectly clear. "I felt that if they were going to . . . violate my rights, that I would explain to them [that] if they wanted to do it that way, then I would reserve a right . . . to go my own way. And when they didn't respond to it, I felt that they accepted what I said as fact and . . . that they said, in a sense, 'O.K., we will go our way, the twenty-seven of us, and you go your way on this particular issue.' . . . I thought they ratified my right to move."

Pete Rozelle claimed to have interpreted Davis's stance as just the same old Davis approach. "I inferred that Al Davis was doing what he has done on a number of other occasions in League meetings," Rozelle explained. "Rather than voting yes or no on a motion, he will pass and be either oblique or noncommittal as to the reason for his pass. . . . I just concluded that that's the way Al likes to be. He had done it before. The last thing in my mind was that he was saying to the meeting that he was reserving his rights to move to Los Angeles."

Others in the room had their own perspectives:

Leonard Tose agreed with Al Davis. "Al put them on notice," the Philadelphia owner remembered. "He was clear. He was very clear."

Gene Klein agreed with Pete Rozelle. "Al Davis was a great double talker," he observed. "He was a mumbler. He never reserved any right to move."

Jim Kensil, the Jets executive representing Leon Hess, later made a written report to his boss on what transpired. "The proposed reduction passed by a vote of twenty-seven yes and one pass," Kensil reported. "The pass vote was by Oakland [which] claimed it may wish to assert in the future that no votes at all are needed to move a team.''

Robert Schulman, representing Edward Bennett Williams, was taking notes as the meeting progressed. He wrote, *Al Davis on record as not accepting any right to approval of a move. Al Davis reserves rights.* ''When it came to Oakland,'' Schulman remembered, ''Al made clear . . . that he was reserving his rights, whatever they might be, [but] nobody knew what the rights were. We were all vague.''

While it might have been vague, whatever Al Davis was reserving seemed to be a commodity the rest of the League wanted as well.

Gene Klein was the next to vote when Davis was finished. ''I don't think any team in this League should have more rights than any other team,'' Klein offered. ''We'll vote for the amendment, but we want to reserve the same rights, whatever they may be, that Mr. Davis or anyone else has.''

Robert Schulman followed Klein and jumped on the bandwagon. ''Whatever rights San Diego's reserved,'' he said, ''I want to reserve as well.''

At this point, Rozelle intervened. According to the minutes, he ''noted that, upon adoption of the amendment, all NFL clubs would have equal transfer rights regardless of the proposed site of the transfer.'' Afterward, the vote got moving again.

While it proceeded, Schulman jotted down, *Rozelle states flatly everyone has the right to upset new bylaw.*

The final vote was, not unexpectedly, 27–0–1. When it was complete, Rozelle conferred with Hamilton Carothers of Covington and Burling in ''a low voice'' for a moment, and then ruled that twenty-seven yeses and one pass ''constituted a unanimous vote . . . in accord with prior [League] practice.'' Section 4.3 was now officially amended and bylaw proposal number two in the books.

The only remaining item of business on the agenda was officially approving the Rams' move to Anaheim and that took no more than ten minutes. ''We felt there might be some reason in the future that we would want to approve a move from one city to another within a home territory, so Mr. Rosenbloom waited until after that amendment had been made and . . . we called for the first time for a three-quarters vote to move to another city within the same territory,'' Rozelle explained.

The official motion to approve Rosenbloom's move came from Rosenbloom himself. It was seconded by his friend and sometime attorney, Hugh Culverhouse. C.R. gave a brief report on the change but made no mention of the real estate deal involved. ''He only mentioned the gate at Anaheim and what the visiting team could be expected to receive,'' Rozelle remembered. ''He said he anticipated sellout crowds and that the visiting team should get a bigger share.''

During the ensuing vote, Al Davis was sitting next to Ralph Wilson and mumbled to him that he didn't know whether to vote yes or pass. Davis resolved his dilemma by leaving the room. So did Chuck Sullivan.

The final count on the question of whether Carroll Rosenbloom ought to be allowed to leave L.A. was twenty-six yes, zero no, and two absent. It, too, was recorded in the minutes as "unanimous."

At 11:15 A.M. the League adjourned.

The NFL special meeting in the Chicago Marriott on October 4 and 5, 1978, would haunt Pete Rozelle forever after.

"It's a strange thing," the commissioner later mused. "Of all the meetings over which I presided, I will never forget that meeting. We must have been awfully dumb not to realize what Al Davis had in mind."

19

Bill Robertson of the Los Angeles Memorial Coliseum Commission was not surprised by the League's official approval of Rosenbloom's move. Nor was he impressed by their modification of Section 4.3. Robertson never considered dropping the Coliseum's suit in response. "I was committed to this," he remembered. "I knew it was the right thing. The Coliseum had to have an NFL team to stay solvent. I knew the NFL would pull out all the stops to prevent it and I knew it would be extremely tough, but it was the only choice we had." His late summer and early fall had been spent looking for an NFL franchise that might want to move, and the October 4 and 5 NFL meeting in Chicago prompted no interruption.

Robertson's quest had a lot of emotional support around Los Angeles, the most vocal of which was coming from sports columnist Mel Durslag in the *Los Angeles Herald Examiner*. In a series of columns over the summer and fall of 1978, Durslag attacked Rosenbloom for leaving and the NFL for its indifference over L.A.'s coming vacancy. Durslag credited Rosenbloom with "having consummated perhaps the fattest deal in the history of sports" and having "consigned the Los Angeles Rams in 1980 to Wheel-and-Deal, USA, that enterprising niche in Orange County." The other NFL owners, according to Durslag, "are such fat felines today . . . that they can't picture any force big enough to hurt them. You hint that fighting an antitrust case could cost a half-million in legal fees and they shrug it isn't even $20,000 a club. You see the contempt in the League office when it allows the Rams to announce their move to Anaheim before a vote is taken." Durslag also made no secret of his own partisanship. "The territorial battle of southern California is just beginning," he vowed as the 1978 football season opened. "Very lively days are ahead in this little niche of sunshine."

More privately, Mel Durslag also played a key role in the opening rounds of that "territorial battle." He and Bill Robertson had met earlier that year and immediately discovered they shared reactions to what was going on. "Mel believed L.A. was getting screwed," Robertson remembered. "He thought the Anaheim deal was obscene. He became a crusader and was a catalyst.'' Durslag's catalytic influence was a function of what Robertson described as his ''many connections with the NFL owners and such.'' If Robertson was going to find a tenant for the Coliseum, he needed face-to-face access to make his case, something Durslag proved ''invaluable'' in providing.

The closest of Durslag's NFL connections was with Ralph Wilson, owner of the Buffalo Bills. Wilson described Durslag as his ''very, very close friend'' and the two talked to each other at least every week on the phone. Durslag put Robertson in touch with Wilson before the Chicago meeting, and the Buffalo owner and the LAMCC president spoke five or six times during the last six months of 1978. According to Robertson, ''Wilson said that he would love to be playing in Los Angeles . . . because of what he saw as the tremendous potential here because of our population. . . . He was also attracted by the climate.'' Nonetheless, he turned down Robertson's invitation to move.

''Wilson never misled me,'' Robertson remembered. ''He made it very clear that he had a lease in Buffalo and was not looking to break it. He was a decent human being.'' What Wilson provided in his various phone calls with Robertson was advice, none of which offered much hope. ''He said it was clear the commissioner was opposed at that time to a move by any NFL team to Los Angeles,'' Robertson claimed, ''or even an expansion team. . . . He felt that Mr. Rozelle had reasonable control of [the League]. He certainly offered no encouragement.'' While telling Robertson that he would vote yes should L.A. find a possible tenant, ''Wilson also said that he felt it would be impossible for us to get the votes [needed for a franchise to move].''

The next owner with whom Mel Durslag connected Bill Robertson was Gene Klein. Durslag and Robertson attended a 1978 exhibition game at the L.A. Coliseum together and cornered Klein there. Durslag began by ''reintroducing'' the two men. Klein and Robertson had first met some years earlier in a Beverly Hills barbershop. According to Klein, Durslag and Robertson ''tried to convince me to move to L.A. I said 'under no circumstances.' ''

Robertson's version was quite different. ''I asked him how he would feel about coming to Los Angeles,'' the LAMCC president later testified, ''and his response was . . . 'I would be delighted to come to Los Angeles, but I can't. My attorneys have checked my lease [in San Diego]. There is no way to break it.' '' According to Robertson, Gene Klein held out little hope of ''getting any established team or an expansion team into Los Angeles,'' because ''we would be unable in his judgment to get enough votes.'' In addition, Klein admonished Robertson over the Coliseum's lawsuit. ''He didn't think it was wise of us to file an antitrust suit. He thought that would hurt our chances of getting a team [even more].''

Robertson and Klein next saw each other at a banquet at L.A.'s Friars Club. Klein's report of that encounter to the NFL's October 4 discussion would prompt Ralph Wilson's October 5 early morning call to Robertson. While denying he'd said anything to Klein about dropping *LAMCC v. NFL*, Robertson remembered that Klein again gave him ''the distinct impression

Tex Schramm, president of the Dallas Cowboys, the man known as "Mr. Vice Commissioner."
CRAIG MOLENHOUSE/SPORTS ILLUSTRATED

Clint Murchison, controlling owner, Dallas Cowboys, in the days when everyone still thought him one of the richest men in Texas. AP/WIDE WORLD PHOTOS

Hugh Culverhouse (LEFT), owner of the Tampa Bay Buccaneers and the NFL's rising power, in a pregame conversation with Tex Schramm. PHIL HUBER/SPORTS ILLUSTRATED

TOP LEFT: Art Modell, majority owner of the Cleveland Browns, founder of Cleveland Stadium Corp., and one of Rozelle's two principal lieutenants, at the Browns training camp during his bitter court fight with minority partner Robert Gries. UPI/BETTMANN NEWSPHOTOS

TOP RIGHT: Modell leaving a Cleveland area hospital with his wife, Pat, after bypass surgery that saved his life, 1983. AP/WIDE WORLD PHOTOS

RIGHT: Modell, the young Cleveland outsider who had scratched his way up out of the Brooklyn pool halls, shortly after buying the Browns in 1961. AP/WIDE WORLD PHOTOS

Carroll Rosenbloom, Pete Rozelle's longtime antagonist and Al Davis's best NFL friend, shortly after swapping the Baltimore Colts for the Los Angeles Rams in 1972. UPI/BETTMANN NEWSPHOTOS

Rosenbloom, principal partner in Anaheim Stadium Associates, announces his Rams will move from the Los Angeles Coliseum to the city of Anaheim in Orange County, 1978. AP/WIDE WORLD PHOTOS

Carroll and Georgia Rosenbloom, at home in their mansion in Bel-Air, 1977. HARRY BENSON/*SPORTS ILLUSTRATED*

Steve Rosenbloom, Carroll's son and Rams executive vice president, not long after his father's drowning and shortly before his own dismissal by his stepmother and new boss, Georgia.
RICHARD MACHSON/SPORTS ILLUSTRATED

Georgia Rosenbloom Frontiere and seventh husband Dominic Frontiere before Dominic's eventual indictment for IRS violations connected with the scalping of Super Bowl tickets. UPI/BETTMANN NEWSPHOTOS

Gene Klein, owner of the San Diego Chargers and Al Davis's most vehement enemy, 1982.
AP/WIDE WORLD PHOTOS

Wellington Mara, 50 percent owner and reigning patriarch of the New York Giants, 1979.
GEORGE TIEDEMANN/SPORTS ILLUSTRATED

Robert Irsay, owner of the Colts and the loose cannon on the NFL's deck, at the ceremony celebrating the move of his franchise from Baltimore to Indianapolis, 1984.

Leonard Tose, owner of the Philadelphia Eagles and the NFL's most legendary spendthrift, after having successfully staved off foreclosure by First Pennsylvania Bank.

Tose and his daughter, Susan Fletcher, outside a Philadelphia courtroom during the struggle to retract his apparent 1983 sale of the Eagles franchise to a group of his daughter's friends.

that he would love to be in L.A. rather than San Diego." When Robertson asked if he still felt his lease in San Diego was binding, Klein answered, "It is." Klein also "still felt it would be extremely difficult to secure the required votes to get a ball club [for Los Angeles]. It was his feeling that the owners . . . and Pete Rozelle were opposed to it."

Despite the discouragement he and Durslag were getting, Robertson would claim "real sincere interest" from at least two owners by the beginning of 1979.

The first of those was Max Winter of Minnesota. Winter still did not have the domed stadium he wanted and the issue was still hung up in the state legislature. Mel Durslag had known Winter "for years" and called him on the L.A. Coliseum's behalf shortly after Rosenbloom announced his move. Winter told Durslag he was "interested" and Durslag connected him to Robertson. As in the case of Gene Klein, it was a "reintroduction." Robertson and Winter had met in the old days before Robertson left the Twin Cities for L.A. "Max owned saloons and boxers," Robertson remembered. "We met around the local gyms watching fighters." In the summer of 1978, Robertson followed up Durslag's phone call to Winter with one of his own. "I asked him if he was interested in sitting down and exploring the possibility of the Minnesota Vikings coming to Los Angeles," Robertson remembered. "He said he would be receptive to that meeting and we set it up."

The meeting took place in Max's Minneapolis office and lasted about two hours. Robertson began by admitting that he knew Winter would rather stay in Minnesota and that "the only reason to motivate a move would be the fact, if it became a fact, that he couldn't obtain a domed stadium in downtown Minneapolis." Nonetheless, Robertson proceeded to point out the advantages of a move to L.A.—among them "the media value" of the nation's number two TV market, the climate, and the population Winter's franchise would draw upon, some ten million or so.

Winter responded that there was "no question" he would rather stay in Minneapolis, but he "had become very frustrated in his efforts to get cooperation from various politicians" so the stadium he wanted could be built. "He said that he was still pursuing legislation," Robertson remembered, "and he wasn't optimistic on succeeding. He was anxious to see what we could provide. . . . He said he had long recognized Los Angeles as being a good sports city and he constantly said that he would love to remain in Minneapolis. He said he had thought of other possible sites. He mentioned Phoenix, [but] he said to me that if he had to move out of Minneapolis, he felt that Los Angeles would be the place to move if he could get over the obstacle . . . of getting the required votes to permit that move within the NFL." Winter "wasn't in any position to make any type of commitment," but he wanted to "continue discussion" while he waited to see what the state legislature would do.

Bill Robertson and Max Winter next met in the last week of January 1979. This time, the encounter was in Los Angeles. Winter was in town for another NFL special meeting, to be held at the Beverly Hilton on the afternoon of January 28 and morning of January 29, convened in General Session rather than Executive. The agenda was filled with odds and ends. Fittingly, the most time-consuming of those was Max Winter's continuing stadium problems in the Land of Ten Thousand Lakes. The Minnesota legislature's latest stadium financing bill was something with which the entire League had to concern itself. Included in the stadium package as of that January was a provision requiring the NFL to commit itself to "assurances" that a franchise would remain in Minnesota for "as much as thirty years." It also contained a provision "conditioning the new stadium on local telecasting of [Viking] games . . . if ninety percent of the tickets were sold seventy-two hours prior to the game," rather than the NFL's own requirement of one hundred percent.

Robertson and Max Winter had brunch together on the morning of January 28, before the meeting began. The gathering was held at Mel Durslag's house and also included Winter's general manager. Durslag began by saying everything was, of course, "off the record." He was there as a private citizen, not a journalist. Winter, according to Robertson, then "made it clear to us . . . that if he didn't get a domed stadium [in Minneapolis], he was going to look elsewhere. . . . He felt very ominous about securing the necessary votes in that legislature to get the money [necessary to build what he wanted]." Winter was also, Robertson noted, "very cognizant" of Section 4.3 of the NFL constitution.

Should he move the Vikings to L.A., Winter pointed out, "we will have a problem unless I can convince the commissioner and my fellow [NFL] members. However, I think that I'll have a good chance to be able to do that because they recognize my plight."

"He felt that he had the sympathy of the other owners," Robertson remembered, "and for that reason, he could get the votes [to move]. Pete Rozelle had assured him he would do all he could for him if he didn't get that desired domed stadium."

The League formally considered the latest round in Max's Superstadium Game on the morning of January 29. After a lot of legal discussion, the owners authorized Rozelle "to execute a certain form of agreement relating to the continuing of a National Football League franchise in Minnesota." On the question of lifting the local TV blackout, however, the League rejected Minnesota's demand for a ninety percent provision and reinforced its own one hundred percent standards. Afterward, Max Winter, pessimistic about how the Minnesota legislature would respond, "asked that alternative solutions to [his] stadium problems be reviewed in executive session at the [upcoming] annual meeting," scheduled for Honolulu in March.

In the meantime, Bill Robertson had little choice but to watch developments in Minnesota and wait to see which way Max Winter jumped.

Robertson's only other "sincere" prospective tenant in the beginning of 1979 was Al Davis. Robertson had written "at least one letter" and placed "several phone calls" to the Raiders owner, but, prior to the special meeting in Chicago on October 4 and 5, Davis "never responded to any of the letters or any of the phone calls."

During that period, Davis did, however, make contact with Mel Durslag, after the columnist had begun vilifying his friend C.R. in the pages of the *Herald Examiner*. Davis and Durslag had been friends since Davis first moved to California to be an assistant coach at USC in 1957. In making contact, Davis explained, "my first objective was to patch up a tremendous feud that had grown between Carroll Rosenbloom and Mel Durslag. I was fond of both of them. . . . [Durslag] had written a couple articles that were negative and Carroll took exception. . . . I was very friendly with Mr. Durslag and Mr. Rosenbloom and had to walk a tightrope between the two, but I did it." While Davis was unable to patch up things between C.R. and Durslag, Davis and Durslag eventually got around to talking about the coming vacancy in Los Angeles. "We discussed the fact that the Rams had moved," Davis remembered, "and he wanted to know if I would be interested in coming to Los Angeles. I told him no. . . . Mel knew this fellow Bill Robertson and wanted to put me together with Robertson [but] I refused. . . . I didn't want to get involved in that kind of publicity."

After the Chicago meeting, Al Davis made direct contact with Robertson over the phone. Davis began by telling the LAMCC president that he was talking to him now only "because I have been assured by Mel Durslag and others that you are a responsible person and will respect my confidentiality. You must recognize I am in a sensitive position in Oakland."

"He didn't want to do anything to destroy the season ticket sales," Robertson explained, "or create a controversy which would put the ball club in a bad light. I assured him that . . . everything we talked about would be off the record." After that, Robertson "indicated that we were extremely anxious to get a football team here and we would welcome the opportunity to discuss all facets of a possible move."

The two men arranged to meet when Davis came south for the League meeting at the Beverly Hilton on January 28 and 29.

Despite Al Davis's concern for confidentiality, his flirtation with L.A. was a matter of public speculation in Oakland even before he and Robertson ever laid eyes on each other. "The Rams are moving . . . to Anaheim after next [football] season," *The* [Oakland] *Tribune* noted on January 18, and "the Raiders' contract with the Oakland–Alameda County Coliseum runs out at the same time. That might be an unhappy coincidence [for Oakland]. Davis could be using the availability of the larger L.A. Coliseum to negotiate a favorable new lease and stadium expansion with the Oakland Coliseum. Or he really might be hungering for appreciation from the glittering star colony in the southland where he has many friends and where it's said the warmer weather suits him better."

Robertson himself remained puzzled about Davis's intentions after he and Davis met ten days later in Davis's room at the Beverly Hilton. Robertson described the conversation as "informal." For his part, the LAMCC president spoke about L.A.'s "desire to get a football team" and indicated his commission "would do anything reasonable that we could deliver to get Oakland to come here."

Davis responded that "he recognized Los Angeles for a number of reasons as being attractive to him. He likes the area on a personal basis and there was no question in his mind that the area could support his football team. . . . He said that a number of times."

Robertson also stressed that he was not about to try to match Anaheim. "I told Mr. Davis that we were not in a position to give in to any excessive demands by anyone," Robertson remembered. "I don't want to be critical of Anaheim, but . . . if we tried to put together a similar deal in Los Angeles to give to any football team to induce them to come to the Coliseum, we would be run out of town on a rail. . . . I made it clear to him we didn't have a lot of money to deal with. We felt that this area could stand on its own in supporting a football team and that we didn't have to make an attractive economic package for them. He said he understood that, but there were some things he felt he needed."

Among the items Davis needed were luxury boxes, a training site, and "some sort of office comparable to that which he has in Oakland in close proximity to the Coliseum."

Later, Robertson would describe Davis as having both "indicated interest" and acted "not particularly receptive." The only concrete result of the exchange between them, according to Robertson, was that "we did agree to continue talking and we exchanged phone numbers. We both indicated either one would be free to call at any time."

After the meeting was over, Robertson and Durslag discussed just what exactly Davis was up to. The LAMCC president and the *Herald Examiner* columnist had become close friends by now and spoke to each other at least four or five times a week. Robertson readily admitted that he "never had a handle on how serious Al might be." Davis was, he noted, "very cagey" and that January, "I didn't feel a great deal of optimism." Neither did Durslag. Eventually the two friends would bet a coconut cream pie over the question. Robertson wagered Davis was serious and Durslag bet he wasn't.

20

Among the other items covered by the NFL before it left the Beverly Hilton that January was "a brief legal report" about *NASL v. NFL*. All the recent skirmishing over Section 4.3 had somewhat obscured its issues, but the suit was still a topic of great concern. Lamar Hunt and Joe Robbie were excluded for the duration of the legal report, but little of consequence was said. The League's attorneys did not expect to be in court with the NASL for at least another year. After their report, Ralph Wilson raised the subject of cross-ownership for discussion but Rozelle quashed it. Cross-ownership, the commissioner announced, "would be discussed in executive session with legal representation present at the [March] annual meeting."

Perhaps the most noteworthy development on the ownership policy front was Leonard Tose's sudden lethargy on the subject. Though he still fumed in private about Lamar Hunt, he was no longer in the mood to push the question, in part because he was beginning to be disillusioned with the process. "Edward Bennett Williams predicted everything that was going to happen," he later explained. "There was no way to stop cross-ownership. We were kidding ourselves."

No doubt one source of that disillusionment was Leonard Tose's own exhaustion. The fierce financial warfare he'd been engaged in for the last two years had taken its toll in a number of ways. "His feelings of public humiliation linger," *The Philadelphia Inquirer* noted. "He feels removed, distant from city and fans. He realizes that no matter how successful his football team is or how much the image of a winner does for Philadelphia, he probably never will be welcome in the city's loosely knit consortium of power brokers. . . . He remains deeply suspicious, embittered by past events." If Tose had an obsession at this point in his life, it was with *Tose v. 1st Penn,* his revenge against the "conspiracy" that had tried to dethrone him. *Tose v. 1st Penn,* like *NASL v. NFL,* was still more than a year from trial. In the meantime, Tose observed, "the situation hasn't changed a hell of a lot. I probably have one friend."

That one friend was Jimmy Murray, his general manager.

Jimmy, forty-one, was native Philadelphia Irish and a graduate of Villanova University. Overweight and pleasant, he'd worked as a public relations man in minor league baseball for a while and then signed on with the Eagles in that capacity in 1969 for $14,000 a year. In 1974, Tose named him general manager at $25,000 a year. In 1976, as Tose's struggle with First Pennsylvania Bank was picking up steam, Murray's salary was raised to $80,000 a year. He earned it right away. In the battles that July and August, he was Leonard Tose's chief lieutenant. "We were at war," Murray explained. "It was the worst part of my job at the Eagles." It was Murray who created the subterfuges that allowed Tose to sneak off to Detroit with the team's financial records unbeknownst to Sidney Forstater. It was also Murray who championed Tose's cause when Tose retreated into public silence. When Tose finally bought out Herb Barness, the last of the "friends" with whom he had entered football in 1969, he turned around and made Murray a one percent partner. The arrangement gave Tose a more favorable tax status than sole ownership, but it was also an expression of affection.

"He was my best friend," Leonard Tose pointed out. "I used to talk to him three times a day. We were in constant communication. If I can't trust Jimmy Murray, who can I trust?" Tose even went so far as to write an addendum to his will giving the right to operate the Eagles to Murray after his death. "I picked him over my daughter to run the team in my will," Tose continued, "not to own it but to run it. He knew that. He signed it. He was a witness to the will. I treated him like a son. I just turned everything over to him. I trusted him with anything in my life."

No doubt Murray inspired such trust because he understood his boss. "Because people see Len's limousine, his helicopter, his Beverly Hills suit, that's how he's judged," Jimmy explained. "He's a very private person really, and for that reason the public perception of him is superficial. He has a great deal of humility, actually. He's always telling me, 'Don't underestimate me,' and the curious thing is that so many people have underestimated him."

Equally important to their relationship was that Jimmy Murray was by no stretch of the imagination a threat. Leonard Tose's best friend was also his employee and that inequality in status made him the perfect foil to Tose's high-rolling sense of himself.

As one former Eagle employee remembered, "One day the owners were all meeting in New York. Leonard decides to go. It just so happens that Rozelle has a lot of important things to go over. [Rozelle] puts everybody in a lecture room [in the NFL offices]. It looks like a classroom. It has three rows of student desks, the kind with the flip-down arm to take notes. Leonard takes one look at this setup and barks, 'What the fuck.' You know Leonard, he can't go through a sentence without f-sharp. So, he sits down and tries it out. Then he screams again, 'Jimmy, get the fuck over here. What the fuck is this? I can't sit in this. I can't sit here. Are you gonna take care of this? What the fuck? Get me a fuckin' chair.' Now Jimmy's main job is to keep Leonard happy, so Jimmy hustles out and goes looking for a chair on the streets of New York. After lunch, the meeting resumes and in comes Murray, sweating, dragging this huge executive swivel chair with him that he's just gone out and bought. Leonard sits down with a big smile. They clear the desks away and Leonard crosses his legs and leans back. Everybody in the place is roaring by this time. Leonard says, 'That's more the fuck like it.' I think they still have the chair in the NFL offices."

Around the NFL, they still tell that story. But by 1979, the toll Len's troubles had taken on him was already no laughing matter. Football owners were prime heart attack risks, and by the time *NASL v. NFL* was first filed, that risk was dogging Tose's heels. The previous November his personal physician had detected a heart murmur that was increasing in volume. His recommendation was open heart surgery, so Tose and Murray had flown to Houston and checked Tose into Dr. Benton Cooley's Texas Heart Institute. The following morning, Dr. Cooley fitted Tose's heart with a plastic replacement valve. When the Eagles owner came out from under the anesthetic, the first face he saw was Jimmy Murray's. The general manager was kneeling by his boss's bed, praying.

"Leonard has a lot of courage," Murray told the press afterward. Murray also encouraged his boss to sell. As Tose admitted soon after the operation, "Jimmy Murray talked to me many times over the years. He'd tell me, 'For your own sanity and health, why don't you sell?' I knew it was probably the right thing to do. I thought about it many times, but I don't know what I'd do without the Eagles. I have to admit I enjoy owning a football team. I'd be lost without it.''

Leonard Tose's brush with mortality did not significantly affect his life-style. ''It didn't bring me up short,'' Tose noted a few years later, ''I've always believed in living every day like it's your last.'' However, his rehabilitation program was uniquely his own, as his surgeon, Dr. Cooley, learned upon visiting Tose in Philadelphia shortly after the operation. Cooley invited Tose to lunch along with two other Philadelphians upon whom he'd recently performed the same surgery. The subject of how they were taking care of themselves came up early. Cooley's other two patients ordered Perrier and told Cooley they ''run five miles a day, don't smoke, don't drink.''

''What do you do?'' the doctor then asked Leonard Tose.

Tose had ordered a scotch on the rocks. ''I drink ten scotches some nights,'' he answered, ''smoke three packs of cigarettes a day, and go with a lot of young broads.''

Cooley turned to the waiter. ''Give me whatever Mr. Tose is drinking,'' he said.

The special meeting of the NFL at the Beverly Hilton was Tose's first since his surgery, but his passivity there was not wholly attributable to his illness. His recovery had indeed been remarkable. Two months later, when the 1979 NFL annual meeting was held at the Royal Hawaiian Hotel in Honolulu and Tose was even more fully recovered, his attitude was much the same. He and Max Winter had dinner together there one evening, at which Tose railed about how Joe Robbie was still fucking around with Ed Garvey for the NASL, but when the cross-ownership question was brought up as Rozelle had promised, Tose had already flown back to the mainland. ''I heard some nebulous report about it,'' Tose later explained. ''Nothing was done.''

Possibly, Tose's newfound passivity on the subject of ownership policy was emotional, rather than medical. In the football season during which he'd had his heart surgery, his team had found success at last. With it had come a certain mellowness; perhaps he no longer needed to cut up Lamar Hunt to feel good about himself. During 1978, the Eagles won nine and lost seven in the new sixteen-game format, finished second in their division, and were the beneficiary of the new ''wild card'' formula for playoffs. Though they were immediately eliminated fourteen to thirteen by Rankin Smith's Atlanta Falcons, making the playoffs brought Tose the appreciation of Philadelphia and he reveled in it. People who wouldn't talk to him when First Penn was on his back now called for tickets. People who didn't recognize him now did.

Leonard Tose basked in the spotlight. Dressed to the nines, he moved about Philadelphia night life escorting a ''young broad'' and lighting his cigarettes with his diamond-studded lighter. In deference to his doctor, he tried to get to bed by 10 P.M. If he did, he often woke up by 2 A.M. and smoked until he could get to sleep. He averaged about six hours sleep a night. On game days, he woke so nervous he couldn't eat. Suddenly, however, it all seemed worth it.

After one Eagle victory, Tose took his football coach out to dinner at

Philadelphia's exclusive Vesper Club. "We walked in," Tose remembered, "and we got a standing ovation. I never saw anything like that in my life. The Vesper Club is not the kind of club you walk in and get a standing ovation. I was amazed. I was really amazed. That was the first time I got a real feel for what the people think."

At least for the moment, Leonard Tose was having too good a time to pick any fights.

21

The discussion of cross-ownership Leonard Tose chose to skip was held on the morning of March 15, the 1979 annual meeting's fourth day. The session opened at 9:05 A.M. and cross-ownership was the last item discussed before a 1:30 P.M. adjournment. The "discussion" in this case was mostly by Rozelle.

According to the minutes, "the commissioner asked for an expression from the member clubs that the League intends to vigorously continue defense of the antitrust suit brought by the North American Soccer League. He said such an expression would have no bearing on the League's current dual ownership policies and that a vote in favor would not indicate a vote in favor of the proposed bylaw that had been drafted . . . and sent to the clubs for comment in the summer of 1978. The commissioner also said that the League's dual ownership policies continue in effect pending the resolution of the soccer suit for [all] team sports other than soccer, and that violations would be considered conduct detrimental to the League."

The commissioner's reminder that ownership policy remained in effect was aimed principally at the Washington Redskins' Edward Bennett Williams. His franchise's majority owner, Jack Kent Cooke, still owned teams in basketball and hockey. Previously the commissioner had gone out of his way to extend sympathy to Cooke. But as Rozelle and Williams were both well aware, the week before, Cooke and his wife had finally reached agreement on a divorce settlement. Once that settlement was finalized, Cooke would no longer be bound by a court order not to sell his holdings. Earlier in the meeting, Williams had informed Rozelle that Cooke intended to resolve his "conflict of interest" by selling his hockey and basketball interests as soon as he could. If he did, he would be the first owner to do so since the ownership policy resolution had taken effect eight years earlier.

Despite reaffirming Cooke's commitment to obey Rozelle's policy, Williams was long since on record that *NASL v. NFL* was a "bad suit." Once again, Williams's opinion made little difference. On the motion of Hugh Culverhouse, the League passed a formal resolution to "continue to vigorously defend the antitrust lawsuit brought against them by the North American

Soccer League.'' The formal vote was twenty-three yes, two no, three pass. Jimmy Murray voted Leonard Tose's yes for him. Steve Rosenbloom voted his father's and Al Davis voted his own. Edward Bennett Williams and Joe Robbie were the two nos. Lamar Hunt, Herman Sarkowsky, and Eddie DeBartolo were the passes. When the actual vote was taken, DeBartolo voted yes, but then changed it to a pass after the roll call was completed.

Apart from that March 15 resolution, the action at the annual meeting at the Royal Hawaiian was largely dominated by the Superstadium Game. The most publicized episode involved Joe Robbie and the city of Miami. It arose on the morning of March 13 while the League was hearing presentations from various cities and stadiums seeking future Super Bowls. Among those was a delegation from Miami, boosting its Orange Bowl. Having already hosted a record five Super Bowls, Miami was confident of getting at least one of the three years scheduled to be committed in Honolulu. Joe Robbie, however, was not at all pleased with his adopted hometown.

Robbie's antagonism toward his Orange Bowl landlords was a longstanding one, but by March 1979, he was in a particularly irritated state. In January 1978, the city of Miami had repealed a longstanding local prohibition of alcohol sales in the Orange Bowl. The step was one Robbie, the stadium's exclusive concessionaire, had long sought, but it had come with a kicker. In its enabling resolution, the city specifically excluded the change from the purview of its concession lease with Robbie. Rather than automatically award the new arrangement to its exclusive concessionaire, Miami advertised for public bids for the first Orange Bowl beer concession in history. A number of people in the city resented the political roadblocks Robbie kept throwing in the path of the bond issue necessary for any Orange Bowl remodeling and the city's move was guaranteed to piss Robbie off. Robbie immediately filed *Miami Dolphins, Ltd. v. City of Miami,* charging violation of contract. In September 1978, the court ruled in Robbie's favor. Not content to accept that judgment, the city of Miami proceeded to appeal the decision and piss Robbie off even further.

Robbie's irritation had escalated another notch just a week before the 1979 annual meeting when, after a series of ''secret negotiations,'' the city turned down Robbie's offer of a settlement that would have given him both the beer concession and a new scoreboard. The city considered Robbie's offer of thirty-two percent of sales too low. They also wanted to separate the scoreboard from the beer, but still weren't satisfied when Robbie agreed to the separation. When Miami made its Super Bowl presentation, *Miami Dolphins, Ltd. v. City of Miami* was still pending, Robbie still had no beer concession, the Orange Bowl still had a ''bush league scoreboard''—and Joe Robbie meant to make Miami pay through the nose.

After finishing their presentation Miami officials stood there slack-jawed as Robbie interrupted the program to deliver what Miami metropolitan area Mayor Steve Clark described as a ''tirade.'' Robbie claimed he simply recounted the history of his dealings with his landlord and some of the less attractive features of his home field. He considered Clark's account "slanderous." Pete Rozelle described the Honolulu faceoff as "a blowup."

However described, the consequences were clear as soon as the NFL vote on the Super Bowl sites for 1980, 1981, and 1982 were announced. Miami was awarded nothing. The Orange Bowl would never host a Super Bowl again and Joe Robbie made no secret of the fact that he thought it was Miami's own fault. "I've been loyal to the city," he claimed. He explained the boycott as a function of the "damage" the city of Miami had done to "Miami's reputation in the NFL." Robbie also said that if Miami had any sense, it would build a modern stadium suitable for a Super Bowl. In that case, he'd do everything in his power to get the League to select it.

The 1979 meeting also witnessed another presentation from a stadium that would never host a Super Bowl again—the Los Angeles Coliseum. Its delegation was composed of Bill Robertson and Jim Hardy, the stadium's general manager. Even before the L.A. Coliseum's fate was sealed by *LAMCC v. NFL*, the NFL had registered its opinion on L.A.'s "Grand Duchess of Stadiums." The Super Bowl culminating the 1979 season had already been awarded to southern California, but the League had selected the Rose Bowl out in Pasadena rather than the Grand Duchess. To make its point even clearer, on March 13 the League awarded the 1982 Super Bowl to Pasadena as well.

The action came as no surprise to Bill Robertson. His real motive in flying to Hawaii was to look for prospective longterm tenants. Since the first of the year, his list of "sincere" prospects had not grown at all. He had, however, begun a fresh list of prospects who were "less than sincere." Not surprisingly, Baltimore's Robert Irsay was the first one on it.

Irsay had been brought into the L.A. picture by Supervisor Kenny Hahn. It was to be Hahn's last hurrah in his hometown's search for a football team. When the League met at the Beverly Hilton in January, Robertson remembered, "Mr. Hahn set up a small suite with a few hors d'oeuvres to entertain the NFL owners." Robertson came there at 1:30 P.M. on January 27 for a meeting Hahn had scheduled with Robert Irsay. Besides Hahn and Robertson, the meeting also included two representatives of the L.A. City Council.

Robert Irsay had recently reached a verbal agreement with Baltimore to extend his lease through 1981, but Carroll Rosenbloom's departure for Anaheim seemed to have set him off on another direction. Stories were already out that the Colts owner meant to sue C.R. on the grounds that he had made a fabulous deal in Anaheim and therefore owed him more money from their 1972 swap. Irsay denied the stories but allowed that if he had said something about suing Rosenbloom, he was only "kidding." Irsay was also once again fed up with Baltimore. At issue that January were delays on the new Colts training facility in Owings Mills, Maryland, for which Irsay himself was footing the bill. Construction was ready to begin but permits were still snarled in red tape. "Look," Irsay told *The* [Baltimore] *Sun* before the meeting arranged by Hahn, "I like Baltimore. I have said I never plan to leave, but the state and county have run me around the horn on building our training facility. This has been going on for over a year. I have put $300,000 into the plans, that's not counting a couple million for the land. If they don't want me to build my facility, then maybe I should go someplace else.''

At his meeting with Los Angeles, Irsay came on like gangbusters. "I went into that meeting almost a cynic, at least a skeptic of Mr. Irsay," Robertson pointed out. "I must say that he gave an impressive performance."

So much so that Kenny Hahn went overboard making promises. Robertson was L.A.'s official football negotiator and what he had to offer was the $9 million package last developed for Carroll Rosenbloom. "I always believe in trying to be accurate in attempting to preach a case to someone," Robertson explained, "not to go overboard and don't make any promises that you don't have some reasonable assurances you can deliver on." Hahn, however, seemed to subscribe to some other theory. He proceeded to promise Irsay new freeway off ramps, additional parking, and a new training facility to be constructed in what was now a public rose garden—all without assurances Los Angeles would or could pay. Finally, Robertson intervened and shut Hahn up. It was the last L.A. offer made by anyone but Robertson. The incident didn't spoil the meeting, however. Even Robertson felt Irsay was "sincere." The Colts owner seemed to have caught the spirit of Hahn's approach and told the meeting that he was "ninety-five percent sure" he would move to L.A. next season. Hahn and Robertson immediately arranged another meeting for January 29, at which Irsay could make his feelings known to the full LAMCC. Sensing a triumph, Hahn even invited the press.

The politicians and press who assembled in the Coliseum commission's board room to meet Robert Irsay on January 29 waited and waited. Hahn tried to reach the Baltimore owner on the phone, but nothing came of it. Finally, everyone figured he wasn't coming. The LAMCC contingent straggled out with egg on their faces.

For his part, Irsay simply issued a statement before leaving town. "There was no reason to meet again," he said. "We have a commitment to play next season in Baltimore and they still have the Rams playing there in 1979. There will be no further talks until after the season." The day before, he had pointedly drawn "attention to the bureaucratic mess I've run into in Maryland," noting, "We are still going to play in Baltimore as of today, but the state of Maryland and the county have given me no indication that they want the Colts. I think the governor should give me a call."

Though it seemed brief, earlier news reports of Irsay's January flirtation with L.A. had been enough provocation for Rozelle to put himself on record, saying exactly what he felt about L.A.'s chances for any new team. "It's of great concern to me," the commissioner admitted. "Any time a team leaves an area there's a void and we don't like to see it. I don't think any existing team can justify moving into L.A. They are all being adequately supported, they are in the black and have financial stability. There is no reason for them to move. I think one thing that has helped make our League great is the fact that we have had such stability. We haven't had franchises floating around."

In response, Bill Robertson pointed out that the commissioner's statement conveniently avoided the "void" Carroll Rosenbloom had left in the city of Los Angeles when he "floated around" to Orange County.

For his part, Carroll Rosenbloom was still maintaining his public stance that he would refuse to block any move to L.A., but it was by now widely reported that he would expect to receive a generous financial compensation for having to share the nation's second largest market. In this instance, he used Irsay's flirtation as an excuse to pop off at the LAMCC. "I was made all sorts of promises by the Coliseum commission too," he pointed out. "But, like me, Irsay will never get any of them. That group is good at promising things and never doing anything about it."

Irsay responded only to Rozelle. "Nobody can tell me I can't move my own property," he threatened. "A federal judge has said that no one could prevent a man from moving his franchise." The case to which Irsay referred did not exist, but he offered no further clarification.

Bill Robertson did not even bother to approach Irsay when the League met in Honolulu. "After his failure to appear at the Coliseum commission meeting and not receiving any explanation from him," he explained, "I reverted back to my position of being a cynic or a skeptic. I didn't think there was any reason to contact him."

Robertson did, however, breakfast with Max Winter during the 1979 annual meeting. Max's situation was basically unchanged. He was still having problems with the legislature and repeated that if he didn't get his domed stadium, he would move. He was also still optimistic the League would approve that eventuality, telling Robertson that the "League owners and the commissioner were sympathetic to his problems. . . . He got from that assurance that they would help him. In the event he didn't get his domed stadium, they would take a good look at the possibility of him being able to move."

Winter's confidence was reinforced by the executive session on the afternoon of March 13. After approving Leonard Tose's new ninety-nine percent holdings in the Eagles, the League heard a report from the Vikings about the continuing hassles over their proposed stadium. By now the state's stadium commission had chosen Minneapolis for its site and the suburban forces had counterattacked by moving to repeal the two percent liquor tax that would have funded the $55 million venture. In the course of the debate, one Minnesota legislator had flung Rozelle's earlier response to Irsay into the argument, pointing out that Max Winter could not get permission to move and had no leverage. The legislator had wired Winter earlier that day and challenged the Vikings owner to get the League's permission to move.

Winter wanted the League to respond and, according to the minutes, "after discussion, Commissioner Rozelle said he would clarify the situation publicly by stating that while the League was proud of its record of franchise stability, the member clubs would not lock any club into an untenable situation in perpetuity, and that financial condition was only one of the many pertinent considerations in membership evaluation of a proposed transfer. Discussion that followed evidenced agreement with the commissioner's proposed statements and a consensus wholly sympathetic to the Vikings' position." According to Rozelle, "what we wanted to say was that . . . if [a club] had a difficult situation, they could come to the League, and if they had a good enough case, the League could decide whether they were to move or not."

"The League takes pride in the stability of its franchises," the commissioner announced at a press conference following the executive session, "but we don't like our stability being thrown at us. It is untrue that teams never get permission to move. The Vikings are not seeking to move, but the sentiment seems quite strong that the League would not like to be frozen until they lose a million dollars. Metropolitan Stadium [in Bloomington, Minnesota] is below the League guidelines and has been for years. Today, the Vikings are O.K. financially but in sports, changes come dramatically."

After the commissioner's "clarification," Bill Robertson ran into Winter in the Royal Hawaiian and the two chatted, mostly "in general terms about some of the things that we had already discussed." Winter also repeated that the League "already gave a clear indication that they would permit a move." The Minnesota owner was also "confident that they would as a result of a prior conversation with the commissioner."

Robertson still found it difficult to share Winter's confidence. He and Rozelle had their own "very brief" conversation during the Honolulu meeting at a reception thrown for the League by one of the television networks. "I told him that we were certainly disappointed that the Rams made the move to Anaheim," Robertson remembered, but "I couldn't argue with the economics of it because I felt Mr. Rosenbloom made an astute business deal, and that it's his every right to do so and we wished the Rams and the city of Anaheim good luck. We were determined to do all we could to get another football team."

Rozelle responded that he didn't see "any viable likelihood of getting an established team" for Los Angeles. With that, the conversation was over.

Robertson recognized that the commissioner's position might very likely amount to the kiss of death for L.A., whatever clarifications he might issue at this point for Max Winter's sake. Robertson also knew that there was only one owner on record as prepared to buck the League if it came to that. "If I moved my team," Al Davis had told *The* [Baltimore] *Sun* in January, "it would be unilateral. I would not need a vote to make that move."

Davis, however, remained something of a mystery to the chairman of the Mayor's Professional Football Search Committee.

Davis's lease with Oakland would be up at the end of 1979 and he was known to be dragging his feet in his negotiations there. On the other hand, he was still keeping his distance from Los Angeles. Davis and Robertson saw each other in Honolulu, but it was essentially a repeat of their conversation at the Beverly Hilton two months earlier. "Al Davis hadn't changed his posture at all," Robertson remembered. "He didn't indicate anything that would lend us any hope."

22

Had the circumstances remained the same as they were when the 1979 annual meeting adjourned on March 16, Bill Robertson might never have come any closer to finding a tenant than he already was. Rozelle's opposition was enough to make any owner think twice and, if that weren't enough, lurking behind the commissioner was Carroll Rosenbloom—cause for yet another thought or two. Despite C.R.'s public utterances, few in the League felt they knew just what Carroll would do if someone actually tried to move into his territory. Should C.R. disapprove, he would be a formidable foe. Enough, perhaps, to intimidate even Al Davis.

That threat vanished on April 2, 1979, and neither L.A. nor the League would ever be the same again.

C.R. had skipped the Honolulu meeting and sent his son Steve in his place. He had had some oral surgery done, then he and his wife, Georgia, had repaired to a house they kept for winter vacations in Golden Beach, Florida. C.R. mostly played tennis there, ran along the sand, and swam. He tracked his investments on the phone in the morning and went to sleep to the sound of the surf at night. On the morning of April 2, he called Steve in California. They discussed the recent annual meeting. "He sounded relaxed," Steve remembered. "He was enjoying himself." At about 11:00 A.M., Carroll called Rozelle in New York to "chat" about "League business." Rosenbloom noted that the day outside had turned blustery and he'd been driven indoors by it, at least for the moment. "He said he couldn't play any tennis," Rozelle remembered. "It was too windy."

It was not, however, windy enough to keep Rosenbloom out of the water once his round of phone calls was complete. Despite heavy surf, Carroll apparently decided to get his early afternoon exercise in the Atlantic rather than in his own swimming pool. It was a decision that would forever mystify his son Steve. "Carroll was never a good swimmer," Steve explained. "He had a natural fear of the water. He never went in by himself. I used to swim with him. He knew how to react in the water, but he wasn't the kind to just jump in, swim out, and come back. He was just in the water to get wet. To do what he did, he broke the habits of a lifetime. I'm just a son who knew his father, but I'm not satisfied that what happened was ever explained." The water Carroll ventured into was later described by Golden Beach's chief of police as "extremely rough," the undertow as "very, very strong."

The last person to see Carroll Rosenbloom alive was one Raymond Tanguay, a middle-aged French-Canadian tourist. Tanguay was standing on the beach. Rosenbloom was at least 150 yards out to sea, screaming for help.

The Canadian charged into the water and fought his way out to where C.R. was, but his heroism was to no avail. Tanguay later estimated that Rosenbloom had been floating facedown for five minutes before he reached him. "I took out a piece of wood," he remembered. "Three times I put the man on the wood, but every time the big rough wave take the man again into the water. I don't know how far out I was, but the people looked far, far away. I wanted to save him. I did everything I could, but it was not enough. I didn't catch him at a good time. The water was too much rough."

Someone called the Golden Beach police about 2 P.M. and the chief and another officer rushed down to the water. "When we got to the beach," the chief reported, "we saw two men in heavy surf about 150 yards from the beach. One man was trying to support the other. We took off our clothes and went into the water, but by the time we got there, the other man was near exhaustion. There was no apparent sign of life [in Rosenbloom] when we got to him." Before Rosenbloom's body could be brought ashore, the rescuers were dragged almost 150 yards north along the face of the beach by the heavy seas.

Georgia Rosenbloom was notified shortly thereafter. According to one source close to the Rosenblooms, her first phone call was to Hugh Culverhouse, owner of the Tampa franchise and executor of Rosenbloom's estate. Culverhouse soon notified Rozelle. The commissioner, in turn, notified the rest of the League. "Everyone was very shocked that Carroll had died like that," Rozelle remembered. "No one could understand the drowning because Carroll had lived there in Golden Beach off and on for several years. They couldn't understand it." Gene Klein's response was typical. "I was shocked," he admitted. "Carroll wasn't a strong swimmer. It's hard to fathom him going out in the ocean in those circumstances." Still somewhat stunned, Rozelle spoke with the press that afternoon. "Carroll Rosenbloom played a major role in the growth and success of the National Football League," the commissioner observed, "both through the teams he produced and through his active participation in the League's decision-making processes. We had some differences over things in the League that he felt affected his team adversely. I was very pleased that in recent months it was considered past and gone and we had a very close relationship."

Steve Rosenbloom learned of his father's death after returning to the Rams' offices on Pico Boulevard from an errand in the San Fernando Valley. When he walked in, Steve's pregnant wife, Renee, was there crying. Renee had got the news earlier but had been unable to find him. Steve immediately prepared to fly to Florida for a private family funeral in accordance with Jewish ritual. First he met with members of the Rams' coaching and office staff. "There's no danger of any changes," Steve reassured them. "C.R. wanted the team to remain with the Rosenbloom family and he's taken great care to make certain it would."

As Steve flew east, Los Angeles was already eulogizing his fallen father. Even Mel Durslag in the *Herald Examiner* found kind things to say. "The life of Carroll Rosenbloom comprised adventure and character development that would never even be found in the contemporary works of Harold Robbins,'' Durslag wrote. ''A fascinating man, quietly mysterious, he moved in an incredible sphere of excitement, couched in a duality that made him a different individual to different observers. To adversaries, he was ruthless. To those within his social orbit, he was witty and warm. . . . At times, rival owners, incensed by his transgressions, took solemn oaths they never again would speak to Carroll. Some swore revenge whatever the price. But it usually developed they returned to the nest, yielding to the horsepower of his unusual charm. . . . It isn't easy to picture football without Carroll.''

Most assumed the franchise would now pass to Steve.

Like many assumptions about Carroll, it was off the mark. In fact, Rosenbloom left behind no sole heir to his football team. As part of a private inter vivos trust activated before Carroll's death, Steve was charged with ''managerial and operational'' responsibility for the Rams, but actual controlling ownership was left to his widow, Georgia, who inherited seventy percent of the club's stock. The remaining thirty percent was split equally among C.R.'s three children from his first marriage and his two from his second. ''He wanted Georgia to have the income and status,'' Steve explained, ''and he wanted me to run it. Carroll was into continuity. He wanted the Carroll Rosenbloom philosophy to carry on.''

Georgia, however, did not see herself in quite so passive a chief executive role. ''I know what Carroll wanted,'' she pointed out to the *Los Angeles Times* several days after C.R.'s death. ''Carroll knew he'd live through me. He still runs the Rams. I'm just an extension of Carroll Rosenbloom. I don't want to sound kooky, but I feel as close to him as ever. We were never apart, you know. We talked over everything. It was Carroll's wish that the Rams continue as a closely knit family operation and I look forward to working with Steve.''

The two-headed organization Carroll Rosenbloom left behind was on shaky ground from its first day. Steve thought Georgia had been ''good for my father,'' but was not otherwise close to his stepmother. At the family funeral in Florida, he was put off even further. ''She was already into talking about the will,'' he claimed. ''I thought it was in poor taste at best.'' When Steve asked to see his father's body before it was cremated, Georgia objected and Steve viewed it anyway. Steve was even more upset by her behavior at the service itself. To start with, Georgia was more than an hour late and kept everyone else waiting, including Carroll's siblings, all in their seventies or older. Her attitude, according to Steve, was ''less than the grieving widow. She was a grade B actress at best and she couldn't pull it off. She could have pretended to care at least. She didn't even talk to Carroll's brothers.''

If Steve Rosenbloom was upset by what happened in Florida, the memorial ceremony Georgia staged back in L.A. positively turned his stomach. ''C.R. didn't want a service,'' his son complained. ''He told me and Georgia that at the same time. He didn't want a service, period. The thing she had was like a coming-out party. It was the sleaziest thing I've ever been to. There was dancing on the tennis court, for Christ's sake. It was no more like Carroll than the man in the moon. It was pathetic.''

Georgia's memorial service was held on April 11 at Carroll's Bel-Air estate. According to the *Los Angeles Times,* ''the tribute was handled as a celebration of life rather than a mourning over a death. All the music was upbeat and the tone, as set by Mrs. Rosenbloom, was light and loving.'' The eulogies were given beneath a large green and white striped party tent erected on a broad grassy tier behind the house. The NFL was represented by Pete Rozelle, Al Davis, Art Modell, Tex Schramm, Hugh Culverhouse, Gene Klein, Billy Sullivan, Eddie DeBartolo, Leonard Tose, Max Winter, Robert Irsay, Art Rooney, and several others. According to one NFL source, Rozelle had been asked to speak but ''shied away from the circus atmosphere.'' Anaheim, where the Rams were still going, Carroll or not, was represented by Mayor John Seymour. Los Angeles was represented by Mayor Tom Bradley. Hollywood was represented by Warren Beatty, Kirk Douglas, Cary Grant, Jimmy Stewart, Rod Steiger, and Henry Mancini.

All of them waited under the green and white tent almost an hour before Georgia finally made her appearance. She then kicked things off with a welcoming speech. ''Carroll didn't want any tears,'' she said. ''He didn't like sad songs or sad endings.'' Then Georgia turned the program over to the master of ceremonies, comedian Jonathan Winters. ''He was a special man,'' Winters observed of the departed. ''He wanted the Super Bowl more than I did.'' Winters was followed by ten other eulogists, including a rabbi, a priest, three football players, two actors, and two owners of football teams. Carroll was variously described as ''shrewd,'' full of ''excitement, joy, and humor,'' ''a lover of life,'' ''the finest owner in all of sport,'' and ''always on the move to something bigger.'' The rabbi observed that Carroll would have liked this ceremony. The two football owners were Art Modell and Al Davis. Of the two, Davis's remarks were by far the more memorable.

''Among the great people in my world,'' Al Davis observed, ''Carroll Rosenbloom was the giant. It will never be over with me. Come autumn, and the roar of the crowd, I'll always think of him.''

Afterward, the memorial service, according to the *Times,* became ''a buffet party'' on the Rosenbloom tennis court, complete with ''string orchestra,'' ''festive flower-laden tables,'' and ''strolling musicians.'' Georgia Rosenbloom was a charming hostess. Steve Rosenbloom left early.

Whatever Steve thought of his stepmother's ''coming-out party,'' she was now his boss and he set out to make the best of the arrangement. ''We're looking forward to being in this together,'' Steve claimed in May. ''In a sense we are acting as one and I'm sure we'll continue to have a great relationship. My father asked me to take over the operational end, but Georgia owns most of the store and she has a good head for this business. As she's around it more, I'm sure she'll contribute more all the time. Before any step is taken, she and I will have talked it over at length. The thought I'm being guided by is my father's—we have to stick together.''

Georgia evinced the same spirit. ''We're going ahead just as if Carroll were on vacation," she pointed out. "I do have the final say, but the best way to think of this is as a partnership between the children and me. Steve says he enjoys working with me and I like working with him. I am obviously not going to go into the office every day—neither did Carroll—it's also obvious that I'm not now capable of making technical football decisions. But I know what Carroll thought and did for the last twenty years, and why he did it, and I'll learn the technical things. Steve and I are conferring and we'll continue to confer on all the major things."

Behind the scenes, however, Steve found educating his stepmother in the football business an exasperating process. At one point, he went to her because one of their players was about to become a free agent.

"Well," Georgia answered, "if he only has a free agent, why don't we pay to get a professional one for him."

Steve shook his head and found it hard to believe this was happening to him.

Georgia Rosenbloom, president of the Los Angeles Rams, and Steve Rosenbloom, executive vice-president of the Los Angeles Rams, attended their first National Football League meeting together on June 6 in the League's New York headquarters. At that point, Georgia became the first woman in NFL history ever to represent a team in Executive Session. Some found her presence disconcerting. At one point in that day's discussion, Leonard Tose said "fuck" three times in two sentences, and then stopped in midstream, turned to Georgia, and apologized. Georgia laughed and allowed she had already heard some of those words before.

After several other items of business, Georgia Rosenbloom officially introduced herself to the NFL with a speech. Still beautiful and shapely, she spoke in a gentle voice. "It was a general kind of thing," Rozelle remembered. " 'You can count on us to be members of the team,' that kind of thing. 'I will try to operate the way Carroll did. Carroll always supported the League and we will continue. We're only as strong as our weakest link.' " While some of the men in the room were as shocked by Georgia's inheritance as they had been by Carroll's death, she was given a polite and friendly reception.

After Mrs. Rosenbloom had resumed her seat, Hugh Culverhouse suggested that "the owners prepare and present a proclamation to the Rosenbloom family in gratitude to Carroll for his service to the League." The suggestion was adopted unanimously.

> WHEREAS, [the tribute read] the late Carroll D. Rosenbloom established a National Football League franchise in Baltimore in 1953 and, through the application of astute business practices and keen knowledge of football techniques, was the architect of a team which posted the best record in the NFL during the period 1958–71; and . . .
>
> WHEREAS, he became president of the Los Angeles Rams in

1972 and directed that team to six consecutive NFC Western Division titles, and . . .

WHEREAS, he, for twenty-six years, in Baltimore and Los Angeles, played a major role in the growth and the success of the NFL, both through the performance of his teams and through his active participation in the League's decision-making processes; now

THEREFORE, I, Pete Rozelle, Commissioner, on behalf of the other twenty-seven member clubs of the NFL do hereby . . . offer this tribute to the late CARROLL D. ROSENBLOOM, and urge all to honor his memory.

Though the tribute was at best a limp reminder of Carroll Rosenbloom, it didn't much matter. The impact on the League's future of C.R.'s drowning was the same whatever his survivors now chose to inscribe on a plaque. To the vacuum of a vacant Los Angeles Coliseum was now added the further vacuum of Rosenbloom's absence, and there was nothing anyone could do to bring him back.

Nor was there anything Carroll Rosenbloom could now do to keep someone else from filling the spot he'd left open.

23

The most noticeable change Bill Robertson encountered after C.R.'s death was in the posture of Al Davis. The two men made contact again over the phone. Davis was now ready to talk specifics.

Davis and the Oakland Coliseum Commission had been talking intermittently since January, to no avail. The Oakland Coliseum went into the process well aware of what it was in for. Davis was working his way through five three-year options and in previous years when options had come up for renewal, the process had been difficult. "For years," according to one of Davis's former friends, "Al had been engineering a position from which it would look like the Raiders were being abused. He was working on short-term leases and his negotiating always became obstructionist. He would make demands, sit down to talk reluctantly, and then finally sign a new lease after extracting what he wanted."

At the top of Davis's 1979 wish list were luxury boxes. They were a major source of income denied him at the moment and he wasn't at all sure Oakland could even come up with a desirable version of the arrangement. "Unfortunately," Davis noted, "the Oakland Coliseum has a very untenable situation as to building suites because of the structure of the stadium. We couldn't build the suites where I thought it would be intelligent to build them based on the structure. The most we could build . . . was sixty-four suites.'' Davis wanted the Coliseum to loan him the money necessary to build what boxes were possible "so that we could get the depreciation and amortization.'' He also wanted a Raider Hall of Fame located nearby and improvements in the team's practice facility. On top of that, he was irritated at sharing the stadium with the Oakland A's baseball franchise, a situation that meant he could not arrange the Coliseum in its optimum football configuration until well into the football season.

Negotiations were kicked off on January 24 at a meeting of Davis and his lieutenant, LoCasale, with the full Oakland Coliseum Commission, chaired by Robert Nahas. Nahas's idea was to use the baseball team to get what Davis wanted. The A's were threatening to move, but to do so, they would have to buy out their lease. Nahas thought that would bring at least $4.5 million. "Nahas eloquently told me that they would let the baseball team go if I would sign a ten-year lease," Davis later testified. "They would fill in the stadium with approximately ten thousand more seats and do a few other gratuities for me. . . . I told them then that I would like to think about that because I felt I am not in favor of the baseball team moving."

Davis also thought Nahas's buy-out figure was too low. After checking around, he concluded $6 million was a minimum that the Coliseum ought to get. It was his intention to tell Nahas that at their next meeting on February 14, but he never got a chance. "As soon as I came in [sic] the meeting," Davis remembered, "Bob Nahas said, 'The proposal is off from last time. Baseball is staying. We can't move the team.' " The reported reason was the intervention of Oakland Mayor Lionel Wilson. "They told me they couldn't go ahead with it," Davis claimed, because "the mayor put his foot down. He was adamant that it wouldn't happen." The turnaround irritated Davis and he was also irritated that some of the substance of his negotiations were being leaked to The [Oakland] Tribune. At one point he notified the commission that if news of their conversations got into the papers, "that's it"—the negotiations would be over for good.

By February, the Coliseum commission had not yet acquired any cost estimates on the things it thought Davis wanted, but promised to do so quickly. In March, Davis, LoCasale, and John Madden, a former Raider coach turned front office troubleshooter, met with an architect brought in from Kansas City to look the stadium over. The architect told the commission that sixty-four luxury boxes could be added for somewhere between $3.8 and $4 million. Oakland then told Davis it would make the additions he requested, but to do so would require issuing new bonds. New bonds would in turn require a longterm lease. At that point, discussion came to a halt. Al Davis categorically refused to discuss any lease "anywhere" for more than seven years. "From here on," a source close to the Oakland negotiations claimed, "Al started dragging things out, not agreeing to sit down, doing everything through LoCasale rather than personally. He was becoming more and more difficult."

Two weeks after Carroll Rosenbloom drowned, the deadline was reached for Davis to renew under the terms of his previous lease. Davis let the deadline pass without notice. The Oakland Coliseum Commission considered this no more than a standard Davis "negotiating ploy."

Unbeknownst to Oakland, Davis had also begun a parallel set of negotiations with Los Angeles. Both would be protracted. Between C.R.'s death and the June meeting at which Georgia introduced herself to the League, Davis and Robertson had "a number of phone calls" and met face-to-face three times, once at Davis's office in Oakland and twice at the Beverly Wilshire Hotel. In addition, Davis had his first discussion with LoCasale and Madden about maybe moving south and had Madden walk through the Grand Duchess of Stadiums with the LAMCC's architect.

The people in L.A. got a very different impression of Al Davis from the one his current landlords had formed. "He's one of the straightest, clearest people I ever met," one Los Angeles source noted. "His pattern of speech wasn't precise, but he gets the message across. When he was through with a point, you knew where he stood. He was never shy or modest about his demands but he was always guarded. He didn't want to say he was coming until he had a deal. There was no double talk or breach of commitment. If he said it, you could count on it. He was always gentlemanly. He also pushed for the last dime, very tough but completely honest. He always said he wanted to come to L.A., but that he had to deal with Oakland. He told us not to be nervous about it. He said he didn't think Oakland would come up with anything."

The list Al Davis had for Los Angeles once again began with luxury boxes. "There are a lot of people," Davis noted, "who want to be able to go to a game and entertain and have the television and be able to drink and have their own quarters. Seems to be an in thing. Seems to be sweeping the country."

"We had detailed discussions on luxury suites," Robertson remembered. "We came up with different concepts, he came up with different ideas and I came up with other ideas." The version with the most immediate plausibility, according to Davis, "would ring the stadium from goal line to goal line and they would be in the top rows of the stadium's configuration. . . . Once those boxes were sold, we would fill in the end zone by the locker rooms [with more]." That meant some 99 double-deck boxes along the rim and 44 more in the end zone, 143 in total. It was Davis's plan to lease them for $35,000 per box per year for the first four years and then raise the price. He also wanted to lower the field, eliminate the running track, and reduce the total number of seats significantly. "I thought it was more important to fill the stadium and lift the blackout so that we could be exposed to the entire Los Angeles area," he explained, "than it was to sell out the [larger] stadium."

From the beginning, Davis's motives for a move to Los Angeles were entirely financial. The box arrangement he and Robertson discussed would gross $5 million a year when completely rented. The sixty-four less attractive boxes Oakland offered would gross $1.6 million at best. That "substantial added income," Al LoCasale noted, would allow the Raiders to "compete down the road." His boss, Al Davis, liked to think in the long term, and luxury boxes were not the only motivation he found for heading south. "One of the reasons he would like to come here," Robertson explained, was that "he saw significant pay TV somewhere down the line. It is his theory that in four or five years, professional football will be really into pay TV and this being a very large market, this would be an attractive place to be."

Robertson's motives for bargaining were financial as well. With each passing month, the possible insolvency of the LAMCC loomed larger. And by the middle of May, Al Davis was the only "sincere" prospect Bill Robertson had left.

On April 29, the Minnesota state Senate had passed a new financing bill to fund Max Winter's domed stadium in downtown Minneapolis. On May 13, the Minnesota House passed another stadium bill. On May 18, a House-Senate conference committee settled on a common version, but while endorsed by the Senate, it passed the House by only sixty-six to sixty-five, two votes short of the majority required by House rules. The next day, a worried Max Winter called Bill Robertson to update L.A.'s chief negotiator on developments. "They had one day of the session left in which to pick up those two votes," Robertson recounted. "He told me that the governor had taken a list of ten people who had voted in opposition to it and was going to call them. . . . Max said he was skittish about it and very apprehensive. . . . I assured him that he would get the two votes, knowing his political clout with this type of issue."

"Well," Winter continued, "I have another obstacle. I have the City Council."

The city of Minneapolis would indeed have to approve the arrangement formally, but Robertson didn't share Max's worry. "I have known Max for a long time," he chuckled. "I know his political involvement going back many years with the Democratic Farm Labor party and I said, 'Max, you will get the City Council too.' "

As Robertson predicted, the Minnesota House subsequently repassed the stadium bill seventy-four to fifty-nine. The City Council approved it nine to four. Max Winter was now off Robertson's list entirely.

Winter's departure from the scene certainly brought fresh motivation to Bill Robertson in his discussions with Al Davis, but, in truth, Robertson didn't actually have much else to offer Davis. The changes Davis wanted would obviously cost more than the $9 million package originally developed for the late C.R., and even that offer was now shaky. California had passed Proposition 13, an enormous local tax reduction, since C.R.'s offer was first made and Robertson knew full well that the reduction might make it politically impossible to get any money at all from his interlocking network of state, county, and city jurisdictions. At the very least, every dollar would be a struggle. Robertson told Davis as much, but said he wouldn't promise anything that he wouldn't also commit himself to get.

One of the first understandings the two men reached was that "before any final resolution would be made . . . anything we agreed on had to be in writing.'' Robertson additionally pointed out that he couldn't sign anything without the approval of the LAMCC and ''unless I was assured that this area . . . would indeed be available for the entry of an NFL club.'' As a result of that stipulation, the issue of Davis's chances of pulling a move off came up with some regularity.

''I consistently pointed out to him my fear of him being unable to get League approval to move,'' Robertson remembered. ''He responded two different ways at two different times. His first response was that if it came to the mechanics of getting the votes required, he was not at all confident of getting them, but he said, 'Regardless of that, if I want to move, I will just move.' ''

Davis's second response was in answer to a Robertson question.

''You say you will just get up and move,'' Robertson observed, ''but what if the NFL refuses to schedule your games?''

''They can't do that,'' Davis insisted. ''It won't bother me.''

''Later,'' Robertson noted, ''on reflecting on it, that did present a problem in his mind and he said yes, there was a question of getting the twenty-one [votes]. He was apprehensive. . . . He couldn't see fifteen votes out there, if that many. . . . He said there would be some members [who] he felt would not look with favor on his moving. He even at one point said that he knew Pete Rozelle would not favor the move. He said that despite the fact that Gene Klein is eating his heart out that he can't be in Los Angeles, he didn't see Klein voting for him. That's the only name of an owner that I recall him mentioning.'' Though the threat that the League would not approve lurked in the background, it was insufficient to keep Davis and Robertson from trying to work out a deal.

Neither of the two was an easy man to best at negotiating and, as a consequence, their discussions were often a cycle of tests and responses. Typical was the issue of moving costs. ''He expressed a concern,'' Robertson recalled, ''that if he did make the move down here, that he should get some help on moving costs for key personnel. I responded by saying that we would try to work out anything that was reasonable and I didn't know what kind of money he was talking about. . . . He never gave me a specific figure.'' Davis did, however, detail some of the things he expected to be covered under that category. Among them was that ''he would like very much to get a house in the Beverly Hills area or comparable home [to what] he has wherever he lives in Oakland.'' As the list got even longer, Robertson had to interrupt.

L.A.'s negotiator insisted that Davis ''must recognize that some of the things that he was asking for on the moving costs was something that I wasn't going out and beat the bushes . . . trying to get contributions [for]. . . . I wasn't in that line of business. . . . I didn't see how we could do it. And I put it to him almost point-blank, that if he was going to be insistent on this, that we had quite possibly reached an impasse.''

''Well,'' Davis relented, ''I don't want you to feel that way.''

Nonetheless, Robertson remembered, ''he still tried to persuade me to in some manner get some movement going to provide for some moving costs. He said, 'You can do it, you have a lot of ability, you have a lot of friends,' and all that. I told him again, 'Don't depend on it because I am not going to be out there. . . . I am not going to do it.' "

The negotiating process had gotten little further than this kind of jockeying when Al Davis flew to New York for the League meeting at which Georgia Rosenbloom, the new owner of the rights to professional football in greater Los Angeles, was introduced. Al already knew her better than most of the League. Carroll had once told Georgia that if he was dead and she needed help, Davis was the person she should talk to. Georgia Rosenbloom didn't worry Al Davis at all.

24

The Los Angeles Rams were not the only ownership change making news when the NFL met in June. The other big story was the Washington Redskins. On May 29, Jack Kent Cooke, eighty-six percent owner of the franchise, announced that he had reached an agreement to sell his Los Angeles hockey and basketball teams. It was the first and only divestiture in the history of the NFL's formal prohibition of cross-ownership and, as such, the high-water mark of Pete Rozelle's ownership policy.

When the sale agreement was announced, Cooke denied he'd been under any pressure from the League to sell. His motives far transcended divestiture. Cooke meant to get quit of California entirely. The sale included not only the hockey Kings and basketball Lakers, but also his Fabulous Forum entertainment complex and his thirteen-thousand-acre ranch in the Sierra Nevadas. The total price was $67.5 million. The buyer was Jerry Buss, a local real estate magnate. The two men had been talking off and on for several months. Buss, described by the *Los Angeles Times* as a fancier of "fast cars, fast women, and fast scores in business," was asleep when Cooke phoned on the morning of May 29. "I still didn't know whether the deal would go through," Buss claimed. "I expected [Cooke] to call back angry about all the newspaper stories speculating on the sale. I figured, 'Oh-oh, he may call off the whole thing.' Instead, he was extremely congenial. He asked, 'Are you ready?' Even though I felt the deal was imminent, I was in a state of shock. You see, I've been hanging so long. The terms of the deal must have changed something like six times." Both parties announced that it would be "a couple of months" before the sale would be finalized.

In the meantime, Jack Kent Cooke was glad to be leaving the Pacific Coast. His divorce had been a trying and bitter experience about which he did not like to speak. According to one of Cooke's friends, it had split his entire family down the middle. One of his sons, Ralph, allied himself with his mother and stayed in Los Angeles. The other, John, Carrie Rozelle's ex-husband, went with his father. For Jack Kent Cooke, leaving California was a way to cleanse himself of all that. "Jack is a more emotional person than people realize," another Cooke friend explained. "I've gone to restaurants with him, places he'd been to with his wife, and I'd spot a tear in his eye. I think he wants to start fresh in the East. California, to put it simply, reminds him of his wife."

While Cooke's sale was being finalized, Edward Bennett Williams continued as the Redskins' president and chief operating officer. Williams was not particularly pleased that Cooke had kept the promise he'd made five years earlier, but it was kept nonetheless. That submission did not, however, measurably diminish Edward Bennett Williams's sniping at ownership policy.

By the time of the June 1979 League meeting in New York, ownership policy discussions were still largely confined to mounting the defense of *NASL v. NFL,* and Williams ambushed that process during executive session on June 5. His move caught Rozelle unaware. Shortly before the break for lunch, Williams took the floor to give a report about an eight-year-old lawsuit over Washington's RFK Stadium. Then, according to Rozelle, he "attacked the League position on the soccer case. He strongly objected to us defending the case. I was really surprised. It was out of order, out of the blue. He made a very strong advocacy against defending the case." It was a bad suit, Williams warned once again. There would be "big damages" involved and it would end up "screwing the League" and everything the League had going for itself. It was "folly" to persist.

The League minutes summarized the attack as "Mr. Williams . . . asked for discussion of the suit brought against the NFL by the North American Soccer League." Rozelle responded by saying, "such discussion would be part of the Executive Session agenda on [the following] afternoon, when proper legal counsel could be present."

In fact, Rozelle was pissed off and had "harsh words" with Williams during the League's break for lunch.

"Look, Ed," he complained, "when you speak, you speak as an attorney as well as a club member. Now we're going to have to get the Sullivan & Cromwell attorneys over here to explain their views."

Rozelle thought he'd played it fair with Williams and felt he deserved better treatment. From his point of view, the defense of the NASL suit had been discussed and approved in March. This was just useless obstructionism. As promised, the commissioner summoned the Sullivan & Cromwell legal team to the executive session on June 6 and they gave their report shortly after Georgia Rosenbloom's speech. By 4:25 P.M., when the Executive Session adjourned for good, the commissioner had managed to undo some of the damage from Williams's attack, but it took only a little of the edge off Rozelle's irritation.

If the commissioner had any solace, it was, of course, that Edward Bennett Williams's days in the NFL definitely seemed to be numbered. It was commonly assumed that Jack Kent Cooke would now want the Redskins' driver's seat, and the possibility of the two men sharing that seat was commonly dismissed. "Picture the concern when Cooke clashes with Williams," one Cooke friend noted. "People will be evacuated for a hundred miles around. Merely envisioning those two overpowering men residing in the same office is too shuddering to describe." Though Jack Kent Cooke had not clarified his intentions with regard to the Redskins by the middle of June, most signs pointed toward him taking over the actual running of the franchise and leaving Williams a fourteen percent partner along for the ride.

The most obvious sign of impending change inside the Redskins was that Cooke was house-hunting around Washington, D.C. The property he would eventually purchase was Fallingbrook, a fifty-acre estate in the Virginia horse country, thirty miles from the Redskins' headquarters. Cooke would buy the place, originally built in 1750, for $1.3 million and then renovate it according to his own design. When finished, according to *The Washingtonian*, it featured "paintings by the masters and lesser-known moderns; thousands of books, virtually all without dust jackets, which Cooke considers unnecessary; antiques that Cooke has gathered, especially from England; rare rugs; a wine cellar that Cooke is very proud of; a collection of snuff boxes; and sculpture, including a bust of Cooke by his ex-wife." The grounds included, "a large cottage that serves as an office for several accountants, secretaries, and other employees of Jack Kent Cooke, Inc.; a stable that houses five horses; a swimming pool and a small lake stocked with bass; hidden gardens, in one instance linked by a wrought-iron door fashioned by Louis XIV's ironmonger; and topiary gardens filled with shrubs shaped into peacocks, dolphins, and other creatures."

Less obvious, but even more significant as a sign of impending change, was the fact that the five-year voting trust under which Williams had run Cooke's Redskins' interest had been quietly terminated the previous March.

Just what Cooke's advent in Washington would mean for Rozelle and League Think was not clear. While it would certainly get Williams out of the commissioner's hair, Cooke was no less formidable in his own way. Cooke's detractors, according to *Washingtonian* magazine, called him a "pirate" and "highwayman." While possessing great charm, one of his former employees noted that he "constantly plays his employees off against each other" and approached all business with a "tiger's smile." Having already run hockey, basketball, soccer, and minor league baseball franchises, as well as a baseball league, he was not the kind of man who needed to be told how to operate his business. *Sports Illustrated* once dubbed him "the Sol Hurok of sport." Cooke also "loathed" organizations and attending meetings, considering both "a waste of time." Nor was he particularly a fan of Rozelle's. His problems with the commissioner were part of what Art Modell called "family bitterness," directed toward the commissioner's wife, Carrie, his former daughter-in-law. "He hates Carrie," one of Cooke's friends noted. "He can't stand her." Cooke's antagonism toward Rozelle himself was still, however, of the smoldering variety.

Edward Bennett Williams's antagonism was more immediately active. He was indeed destined to leave the inner circles of football shortly, and the way he left pissed off Pete Rozelle even further, effectively ending any remaining personal goodwill between the two men. In essence, Williams used his departure to thumb his nose at the commissioner one last time. The issue, as usual, was ownership policy.

While Jack Kent Cooke was shopping his Los Angeles properties around, Williams had quietly entered the baseball market. His initial foray had been in 1978 when he was hired by former Treasury secretary William Simon to put together a purchase by Simon of the Baltimore Orioles. When that deal fell through, Williams, whose favorite sport had always been baseball, pursued the idea himself. On August 3, 1979, while still the chief operating officer of the Washington Redskins, Williams announced that he had signed an agreement for the purchase of the professional baseball Baltimore Orioles franchise. The deal was to be consummated in November, by which time Williams would have created EBW, Inc., to hold the franchise's stock. Williams would, of course, own one hundred percent of EBW, Inc. The price was $12 million.

When asked by *The Washington Post* if owning a baseball team wasn't in violation of NFL ownership policy, Edward Bennett Williams scoffed. "There is no rule in the NFL on cross-ownership," he pointed out. "There is nothing in the constitution or bylaws on cross-ownership. Therefore, I am not breaching any rules."

Despite that public attitude, Williams privately took steps to make sure he was "meticulously in compliance" with the League's continuing ownership policy resolution. Before November, he and Jack Kent Cooke, the only holders of stock in Pro Football, Inc., the Redskins' holding company, reorganized their corporation. In that reorganization, the functions of the president, Williams, were transferred to the chairman of the board, Cooke. Williams, still president of the Redskins, was nonetheless, as a minority partner, outside the purview of the resolution he had resolutely opposed. He was also, in effect, out of the football business.

None of that lessened Pete Rozelle's anger. In all those speeches Williams had given about saving the League from "folly," the commissioner pointed out, "Ed had spoken with a golden forked tongue." All the while, he had been planning to buy into baseball. "That irritated a lot of club members," Rozelle claimed. "He wasn't speaking for the NFL, he was just speaking for Ed Williams."

After Williams's baseball purchase was finalized, Rozelle would try to do something about it, but the attempt was futile. He would form a committee to investigate "a possible conflict" in Williams's "dual role as a club official" for both the Redskins and baseball's Baltimore Orioles. Gene Klein would be named committee chairman. Their assignment was "to study, make an interpretation, and make a recommendation." In truth, the committee's raison d' être was face-saving.

"I had a meeting with Ed Williams in his office," Klein remembered. "We worked it out amiably." There was no use the NFL kidding itself. There was absolutely nothing they could do about Williams and both Klein and Williams knew it.

25

About the same time Edward Bennett Williams made his leap into baseball, the speculation over which Rosenbloom would actually run the Rams was finally put to rest. C.R.'s two-headed legacy lasted barely four months from the day he was hauled out of the surf. Georgia Rosenbloom and her stepson Steve could not have been less suited for sharing power with each other.

Steve, now thirty-four, was assessed by the *Los Angeles Times* as a "beer-and-pizza guy." His first job with his father's Colts had been picking up dirty towels and socks. While studying toward a degree in business management at Georgetown University, Steve had kept a pig in his dorm room which he took to Georgetown basketball games on a leash. While executive vice-president of the Rams, he was also a long haul trucking buff who subscribed to *Owner-Operator* magazine, had a license to drive eighteen wheelers, and occasionally took the wheel of the team bus. When still in Baltimore, he liked nothing better than to cruise Interstate 695, looking for stranded motorists to assist. "You always see people in trouble," Steve pointed out. "I stop and help them out, maybe change a tire. You meet interesting people that way. They don't know who you are and people in trouble are always friendly. Maybe it's an escape for me."

Steve had originally resisted moving west with his father in 1972. For a year after the Rams-Colts swap, he stayed in Baltimore and ran a dog kennel with his wife, Renee. Carroll had to twist his arm to persuade him to move to Los Angeles and resume the football relationship they'd had in Maryland. Steve and Renee bought a house in Palos Verdes. Four dogs slept on the bedroom floor. Steve started with the Rams as his father's assistant and, according to Rams Vice-President Harold Guiver, "gradually assumed more responsibility and authority until he actually was running the team on a day-to-day basis." Whatever his position, Steve continued personally to select the cold cuts to be eaten on the team plane and made the sandwiches himself. No one ever mistook him for the late C.R. Carroll had dressed impeccably. Steve preferred Levi's jeans and wore his prematurely gray hair tousled in several directions at once. Carroll was infatuated with the glitter of Los Angeles. Steve couldn't have cared less.

"After home games," a man who had worked for both Carroll and Steve observed, "Steve doesn't go to some swank, posh place in Beverly Hills with his Hollywood friends, because he doesn't have any. He goes to Grunyon's, this little bar in Manhattan Beach, where some of his old Baltimore cronies hang out. They shoot the breeze and throw beer on each other if they feel like it. That's Steve. No phony airs. No pretenses. No flaunting his position. Treats everyone the same. Steve Rosenbloom is not a Bel-Air type of guy."

His stepmother, on the other hand, was very much a Bel-Air type of gal.

"During her life with Carroll," one of Georgia's friends noted, "she pretty much had to toe the mark, and it was different. Now she loves the life she's leading. She's free to do what she wants." Georgia Rosenbloom shopped on Rodeo Drive, hired a personal publicist, and kept seven or eight servants at her mansion in Bel-Air. The Super Bowl trophy her late husband had stolen from Robert Irsay remained in the study. Georgia liked to sleep late and stay up a good portion of the night. She conducted much of whatever business she concerned herself with in her bedroom suite, some 2,700 square feet divided into several rooms, one of which was for conferences. A devotee of astrology and numerology, she would claim to "rely" on Carroll for several years after his drowning. "I can't really say I've gotten over his death," she observed. "I don't cry anymore, but I can't sleep more than four hours a night. My brain keeps flashing back to that beach in Florida where he drowned."

To fill the vacuum in her life, Georgia threw dinner parties, always arriving late, even though the events were in her own home. When she made her entrance, according to the *Los Angeles Times*, it was by "sweeping into the room with kisses for all, a carryover from her show business days." She often had crab and lobster flown in from the East Coast for the menu. When all the eating was done, she took the mike and serenaded her guests with a medley of show tunes. It was also "customary for every male present to dance with her on the portable dance floor set up for the occasion."

One of those males invited to dinner with increasing frequency was Dominic Frontiere, the forty-six-year-old Hollywood composer who had written the music for Carroll's memorial service. Among his other credits were the film scores of *Gumball Rally, Pipe Dreams,* and *Freebie and the Bean.* Frontiere had come to L.A. as a teenage musical prodigy from the Italian slums of New Haven, Connecticut, and had spent most of his career creating music for television series. He had first met the Rosenblooms three or four years earlier and become what he discreetly described as "a family friend" shortly after Carroll's drowning. By the time the Rams training camp opened in the middle of July, less than four months after Carroll's death, Dominic Frontiere had moved into the guest house at Georgia's Bel-Air estate. Frontiere would later explain that Georgia "began to receive threats and a great deal of criticism" as the result of owning the Rams and when she became frightened, he agreed to move in "for security purposes." He was described in the *Los Angeles Times* as Mrs. Rosenbloom's "personal lyricist." Steve Rosenbloom described him as "a sleaze bag," and as, simply, "The Frog."

Of course, by the time Dominic Frontiere moved into Bel-Air, the bitterness of his own position had already begun to well up in Steve Rosenbloom. "The way the Rams were set up," he pointed out, "she just had to not touch something that had taken seven years to put together. C.R. had worked for twenty-five years with the same philosophy. My problem was that overnight, one woman turned it all around, took a tradition, and flushed it down the toilet. I saw it coming. She moved faster than I thought she would but it unfolded exactly like I thought. It was apparent from the beginning that she meant to run things. I began to hear things. I knew she didn't want C.R.'s son around. Georgia didn't want any of C.R.'s old people around. She wanted to get her own people in."

Since returning from New York, Steve and Georgia had been knocking sparks with increasing regularity. It often took him three or four days to get hold of her, but she nonetheless insisted on being consulted on everything. Steve soon adopted a policy of acting anyway and that infuriated Georgia. He also took to ignoring some of her requests for information, infuriating her further. On August 6, she attempted to put a stop to Steve's behavior by circulating a memo to the entire Rams staff. It included some twenty-eight items of franchise business that everyone was now instructed to act on only with her full consultation and approval. Among the items on the list were all contracts, anything to do with "budget," "assignment of parking spaces," all hiring or firing, any check "in excess of five thousand dollars," and anything to do with Anaheim.

> I wanted you to know that I am most aware of how difficult the past months have been to you [Georgia wrote to her employees]. The loss of Carroll has been the most traumatic tragedy in my life, but, as you know, he would want us to carry on in the true tradition that he believed in so strongly; and I now share with you all that he has told me countless times in the past years, "If anything should happen to me, I know you will see to it that everyone is looked after; and will see that the Rams are run with protocol, dignity, and good judgment." Since Carroll left me to oversee and be responsible for carrying out his wishes—I have put down the thoughts and desires he shared with me as to how the Rams should be run. . . . We are beginning a new venture together—Carroll wanted us to enjoy the new stadium, practice facilities, offices—and would be proud to see it become a reality. All of these are ahead of anyone in the League in convenience and comfort; and we are starting with a firm foundation so that we can build a cohesive, effective, and most efficient, gratifying organization, where we can all share and be proud of the success that will inevitably follow. . . .
>
> Sincerely,
> Georgia Rosenbloom

It took Steve little more than a week to violate both the letter and spirit of her memorandum, and when he did, she went for his jugular. On August 16, Georgia fired Steve and kicked him out of the organization. "Carroll always told me," she later explained, " 'if the little bastard ever gives you any trouble, get rid of him.' So I did."

The actual firing took place in the Rams' offices. An attorney was with Georgia when Steve walked in. The attorney did the firing and Georgia said nothing. Steve asked to be allowed to go out to the training camp and say good-bye to the players. By the time he got there, Georgia's office had canceled the team meeting Steve had intended to address. Most of the players stuck around anyway. There was talk of a protest strike, but Steve objected to the idea and nothing came of it. "I just wanted to tell them good-bye," Steve Rosenbloom remembered, "wish them good luck, and tell them they had the ability to go to the Super Bowl." Steve himself would eventually be hired to run the New Orleans Saints for a while before being fired again. After that he would flirt with trying to find an expansion franchise. Soon, he would be out of football entirely.

To the press afterward, Georgia described firing Steve as "the hardest thing I've had to do in my life. Right now I'm so exhausted I can hardly think. We love each other, but we can't live together. It's like getting a divorce. If I hated Steve, this would be simpler. I want people to understand the why of this, so they don't think I'm some woman sitting up here with the power to chop someone's head off. I have to think of the business first and I can't be concerned what people think. But I do care. . . . I fear they'll think the worst, that I'm just the ugly stepmother."

Georgia recovered from the experience quickly. With Steve gone, Georgia Rosenbloom didn't have to share the Rams stage with anyone. After a lifetime in show business, it was easily the biggest venue she had ever played. Soon she was dubbed "the Boss Mama of the Rams" by the sporting press. Her style was clearly her own. In her first few months on top, she attended Rams home games but skipped some of those on the road. She visited training camp, but usually for no longer than twenty minutes. Thus far in 1979, the longest time she had spent there was posing for pictures on one end of the practice field while the team was going through its paces at the other end. Her poses involved attempting to kick a football off a kicking tee. To the players, only a bevy of photographers and a shapely blond woman were visible in the distance. "What's going on?" one player was asked by a training camp reporter.

"Some Hollywood broad," he answered, "doing publicity shots."

In fact, Georgia Rosenbloom was, for the moment, the football business's most meteoric figure. In the Rams' 1978 press guide, she had been identified in one sentence of Carroll's biography only as "his beautiful wife." In 1979, her biography ran for 313 words. Written by her personal publicist, it credited the Rams' "Boss Mama" with a six handicap in golf, mastery of skiing and skating, and stardom in light opera and musical comedies. She had, her bio noted, shared with her husband in "the step-by-step building of a championship football team." She was also "a poet of note."

Among Georgia's better poetic efforts was "The Future Is Suddenly Now," a dialogue in doggered among past, present, and future, which concluded,

> Well, I thought & thought and I said at long last
> There's one thing for sure— I can't bring back the Past!
> However, the Future that I dreamed of before
> Is suddenly NOW— and we've settled a score
> So today is all mine— I can clearly see,
> Don't dwell on what's gone
> Or what's yet to be
> Yes, NOW is so perfect
> Except for one goal
> That secret desire to win the SUPER BOWL!!!!!!

Despite her optimism, all was not pleasant for Georgia, alone at the apex of the Rams. As Steve had predicted, she soon began a housecleaning of the franchise's front office in which the entire corps of executives brought to L.A. by Carroll and Steve would eventually be dismissed, one by one. The moves were controversial and she was soon complaining in private about all the bad publicity Steve was giving her. For advice, she talked the situation over with Dominic Frontiere and some of the remaining Rams' executives. She also phoned Pete Rozelle.

According to Georgia's later testimony, she and Rozelle had first met shortly before he became commissioner in 1960. Mrs. Rosenbloom saw the commissioner only on social occasions until she became president of the Rams, but she remembered always trying to convince him she "knew something about football." Since C.R.'s death, she had phoned him several times, but seldom talked just "straight business talk."

"I didn't really advise her," Rozelle remembered. "We discussed things. She would tell me things and we would just talk and I would explain. I had expected that Georgia might want to make some changes. She was going to take a very active role and I knew she would want people working for her with whom she had a close relationship or confidence." In this particular instance, the commissioner claimed to have told both Georgia and Steve to stop any public sniping at the other. "It wasn't helpful," he explained, "to the franchise or the League."

The next problem Georgia Rosenbloom took to the commissioner arose at the Rams opening game of the 1979 season in September. Her franchise's opponent was Al Davis's Oakland Raiders. It was also the kickoff for the Rams' final season in the Grand Duchess of Stadiums. The game was preceded by a memorial eulogy for the late C.R. delivered by Davis. Davis's Raiders then proceeded to win, 24–17. At the time, Georgia was still publicly committed to Carroll's position on anyone moving to fill the coming vacancy in L.A., but her private sentiments were significantly less approving.

That much became clear at the game with the Raiders. For the last month, the Los Angeles papers had been full of speculation that Davis might move his team there the following year and it was now known he was talking with Bill Robertson. Georgia was already having her staff clip any articles that appeared about either the Rams or the Raiders. A host of new clippings was spawned during the course of that opening game when someone hung a banner on the outside of the press box proclaiming WELCOME LOS ANGELES RAIDERS.

Georgia couldn't see the banner from her owner's box, but when reports of it reached her, she was furious and immediately summoned the Coliseum's general manager to demand that it be taken down. She also demanded to know who had put it up there in the first place. It was eventually removed, but not before making the lead photograph in the Monday morning newspapers all over southern California.

Mrs. Rosenbloom called Rozelle shortly thereafter. "She was very upset," he remembered, "it was very embarrassing to her. She felt she was a part of the Los Angeles community. She didn't want to go to Anaheim in the first place. And she was very upset that she was not viewed as the Los Angeles team." She was also worried specifically about the Raiders moving onto her turf and the competition it might bring.

Rozelle tried to calm her down. He told her not to worry.

26

In the fall of 1979, the argument for not worrying about Al Davis still seemed strong and Bill Robertson was the first to admit it. "I'm not confident of getting any team," he pointed out. "Pete Rozelle controls the League and he's adamantly opposed to our getting a team in Los Angeles. Pete's totally cavalier about the big void left in Los Angeles when the Rams move to Anaheim. The NFL is run with a country club attitude. They're not interested in the public, just the almighty buck." As for the intentions of Davis himself, Robertson remained uncertain at best. "I don't know that Al Davis is interested in moving," he admitted. "Al has never said he's coming to L.A. He's exploring his options. We're still a long way from fruition."

In the meantime, the odds against Al Davis ever getting NFL permission to make such a move only increased as more and more owners weighed in with public statements against such an eventuality. "I've never thought the League should be in the business of bartering franchises," Tex Schramm offered. Art Modell agreed. "Our League has built its success on continuity and stability," he pointed out. "If Al Davis came in and said he had a problem, he'd have an attentive audience. That doesn't mean he'll move. I've got problems, too, do I move to Phoenix?'' Herman Sarkowsky of Seattle was even firmer. ''Davis sells out [the Oakland Coliseum], gets tremendous support from the community. Unless there is something I don't know about, I would vote no.'' Gene Klein was firmest of all. A Davis move to L.A. ''wouldn't get my vote,'' he announced, ''and I don't think it will get many of the other owners' votes either. We're not like other sports leagues that are constantly moving. We have stability in our League. The Chargers could move to Los Angeles and we could make more money, but that isn't the object of the exercise.''

In October 1979, only two NFL owners were prepared to commit themselves to public support of a possible Davis move to the L.A. Coliseum. Despite the private panic at the prospect she expressed to Rozelle, one of those was Georgia Rosenbloom. ''I wouldn't oppose it,'' she claimed to *The* [Oakland] *Tribune*. ''We have all the fans we need in Orange County.'' According to Davis, her private conversations with him indicated the same position. ''Georgia told me she would not block a move,'' he claimed. ''In fact, she said she would okay the move.'' Al Davis's other yes vote was Eddie DeBartolo, for whom Davis's departure would mean not having to share the northern California market with anyone. ''I would be for a move,'' he offered. ''I'd be crazy if I wasn't.'' That left Davis nineteen votes short of approval, should he put the issue to a vote.

Al Davis was well aware of the opposition he faced, but it did not drive him back in Oakland's direction. Negotiations on that front were still stalemated. Davis's only public comment about his current arrangements had been made in August after an exhibition game in Oakland. Standing in the Raiders' cramped and shabby locker room, he snapped at a nearby reporter, ''Look at this. This is supposed to be our home stadium. This stadium is so freaking cheap.''

By September, the Oakland Coliseum negotiators were sufficiently frustrated to make a public announcement on the state of the negotiations, a move of which they knew Davis would disapprove. The Coliseum claimed Davis had submitted a list of desired improvements that would cost somewhere between $15 and $20 million and, at the same time, refused to sign any lease for a longer term than three years. ''That's more than it cost to build the stadium in the first place,'' one Oakland official pointed out. It was an impossible figure unless the Raiders made a longterm commitment sufficient to amortize the whole arrangement. Davis's landlord was willing to build the sixty-four luxury boxes he wanted, but, once again, the two sides disagreed on how the financing should work. Davis's proposal called for the Raiders to get all the income rental from them while the Coliseum insisted that income be used to pay off the cost of construction.

In the meantime, Oakland's counteroffer to Davis's demand for a three-year lease was a commitment to spend $1 million over those three years and nothing more. The Coliseum's board was irritated at Davis's tactics and, unlike Bill Robertson in L.A., took heart from their assumption that Davis would never get League approval to leave. They also played down Los

Angeles as a possibility. "We have no evidence to confirm such speculation," the board said in a press release, "nor have the Raiders given the
Coliseum indications that they are considering such a move."

In fact, Al Davis and Bill Robertson had been hard at their negotiations
since June. "Al Davis was edgy," one of the attorneys involved noted. "He
would be risking his entire franchise. On one level, I would have been
surprised if he actually went through with it, but I always thought he wanted
to. As we went on, I got more and more confident that way. The real problem was
that L.A. was in no position to do anything. Bill was really bargaining
without authority. The LAMCC was so badly structured, it was next to
impossible to get anything done. It was not a cohesive group and Robertson
needed their approval. To get money, he had to go to the city, the county, and
the state. The state was a problem because of the North versus South issue.
The city and county were a problem because to get those yo-yos to do
anything is always difficult. There was a real question whether the governmental entities would go through with any deal they made. It would all have to
be done with mirrors and baling wire. The credit goes to Robertson. He did a
fantastic job. He developed a good relationship with Davis and he was
patient. He evaluated Davis properly. He talked to him regularly on the phone
and maintained an even balance throughout. Lots of people would have blown
this deal."

Like Oakland, Bill Robertson figured L.A. would need at least $15
million to land Davis. Davis was also insisting on no lease longer than five
years. Robertson was holding out for at least ten years. "We were a long way
from home," he remembered.

Nonetheless, Robertson began to take steps to try to solidify his financial
position. On September 19, 1979, he wrote a letter to the other members of
the mayor's professional football search committee to alert them to "the
crucial circumstances now complicating the search for a National Football
League franchise to replace the Rams in the coming year." The problem,
Robertson pointed out, was that all the "viable candidates" had "expressed
their unwillingness to relocate in the Los Angeles area while the Coliseum
lacks private boxes and a practice field. . . . If we cannot guarantee the
private boxes will be on line for the 1980 season, the interested NFL
franchises will be forced to exercise other options." As a consequence,
Robertson requested a $15 million loan, "$5 million from each parent authority governing the Coliseum complex" in order that "construction of private
boxes could begin on a timely basis." After noting the Coliseum's possible
bankruptcy if no new tenant were found, Robertson concluded that "we have
reached a point in our negotiations at which aid from the three entities
governing the Coliseum complex is absolutely necessary to the commission of
our task. Without a commitment . . . our work will have been in vain. . . . If
the loan is not forthcoming, the prospects for this area are bleak."

The letter opened discussion of the question but did little more in the
immediate moment. Nonetheless, Robertson and Davis kept talking. From his
side, Davis kept prodding on the financial issues.

"Come on," he was fond of saying, "I have to show my partners something. They keep asking why take the risk." Los Angeles, Al Davis pointed out, had to be willing to risk something too.

The risk he was referring to was, of course, the possible response of the rest of the League. "The real risk," one of the attorneys noted, "was whether Davis would be able to move, not whether he wanted to. The beginnings of all the League opposition was going on."

Pete Rozelle was monitoring the situation from afar. "I know that Al Davis feels unhappy," he admitted that fall, "but I have not explored it with him. I know he feels a number of things could be done to improve the situation [in Oakland]." He and Davis had spoken "briefly and generally maybe on a couple of occasions where," the commissioner remembered, "he may have either told me or inferred [he was interested in L.A.], more than likely inferred because Mr. Davis infers more than he makes declarative sentences."

The commissioner's position had not changed. "Where the team gets support," he declared, "I don't want to see it move unless it's in an untenable situation. I don't like to see movement. We haven't had a franchise change cities since the Cardinals moved from Chicago to St. Louis in 1960. I don't have a vote, but I can recommend." There was, of course, no doubt about what Rozelle's recommendation would be.

Whether or not he would have to exercise that recommendation was, of course, still very much up for grabs. Al Davis was the big question mark, and the risk of moving seemed to be only increasing. "To ever get any kind of deal with L.A. was almost impossible," a source close to the negotiations remembered. "Nobody but Al Davis would have put up with it. The deal was always changing because of the politicians Robertson had to appeal to. He also had no strong allies other than Robertson himself. No owners were on his side and he had no strong city support. L.A. was quivering the whole time. He had to be a little crazy to do it. There had already been times when I thought most normal people would have backed out. But Davis was stubborn and self-confident. He had such a strong ego. He didn't want to let himself be pushed around. He possessed an extraordinary unwillingness to be defeated."

Davis also had motives of his own. "At some point," one of his Oakland friends observed, "Al was impelled to things by the opposition they engendered. He wanted to be the master of his own destiny. But there was also the stature factors. He saw L.A. as one of the two great places in the United States, along with New York. He wanted to be a bigger frog in a bigger pond and there was nothing Oakland could do to satisfy that."

Whatever Davis's internal reasoning, Bill Robertson maintained his faith that Davis was actually serious about coming. Robertson and Mel Durslag discussed the question on a daily basis, but Durslag remained unconvinced. According to Robertson, Durslag "felt that all of the owners in the NFL were out for economic purposes and would take a hard look at any move at all because they were interested in economics. He felt that Davis [currently] selling out [in Oakland] and having some problems . . . in his contracts with the Oakland Coliseum" posed big problems for any League-approved move. Given that opposition, Durslag feared Davis was just using L.A. as "leverage" in his negotiations with Oakland.

Both the Oakland Coliseum and Pete Rozelle tended to agree with Durslag.

Nonetheless, in the middle of October, LAMCC member Kenny Hahn told the assembled L.A. press corps that "the odds are good that the Oakland Raiders will be moving south to Los Angeles next year when the Rams move from the Coliseum to Anaheim." Hahn claimed that "we almost had it wrapped up a week ago, but certain things didn't materialize."

Robertson was quick to contradict Hahn and try, once again, to shut him up. "You can't put a gag on this guy," he noted about his fellow LAMCC member, "but he's never even talked to Al Davis. Al has never said he's coming to L.A."

In truth, even before Hahn shot his mouth off, the process had been put on hold by a near tragedy in Davis's personal life. According to his friends, the incident marked the one and only time Al Davis had even momentarily "abandoned his obsession for football power."

In mid-October, Davis's wife, Carol, suffered a massive heart attack and lapsed into a coma. From then until the end of November, her welfare became his one and only concern. He stopped looking at game films and spent almost all his time in her Oakland hospital room. In the beginning, Carol's prognosis was anything but good. During the initial moments of her attack, she had been technically dead for five minutes, and if she finally managed to survive, her doctors at Oakland's Merritt Hospital worried, it would likely be as a "vegetable" forever after. "When she was lying there in a coma," one of Davis's friends remembered, "and there was nobody who could do anything for her, Al was calling up people, looking for anybody who could help, any doctor with an idea. He went to war."

Al Davis fought death tooth and nail. "We met when I was coaching at Adelphi," he remembered of his struggling wife. "I was a kid. She was a super kid, a man's girl, a little wild. She knew sports, she was smart, well versed in the things that were. She was my kind of woman." Instead of giving her up, Davis moved a cot into a tiny storage room next to Merritt's coronary care unit and spent twenty-four hours a day in the hospital, much of it sitting at Carol's bedside.

"Don't worry," he said to her over and over again. "Everything's going to be fine." She was comatose, but he knew she heard him.

Much of the rest of Davis's time was spent on the phone, consulting doctors around the world. "I'm not gonna let her lie there," he swore to one of his friends. "They tell me they can't do anything for her. I don't believe this. Somebody, somewhere in this world has an idea."

During his vigil, Davis made no contact with either Oakland or Pete Rozelle. He did, however, phone Robertson on several occasions. The first time was on the second day of Carol Davis's coma. Robertson tried to give Davis encouragement and told him about the time Robertson's son had been in an auto accident on the Ventura freeway. The son had been in a coma for thirteen days, but came out of it and was now fine. "Al never gave up hope," Robertson remembered, and that hope eventually panned out. After weeks of coma, Carol Davis regained consciousness and proceeded to make what one surgeon called "one of the most dramatic recoveries I've ever seen."

Once she was out of danger, Al Davis would joke with her about the ordeal. "When we were married, I said the only thing that would take me away from football was life or death," he kidded, "but I didn't think you were going to put me to the test." They celebrated Thanksgiving together in her hospital room.

When Carol Davis finally checked out of the coronary care unit, her husband gave a new color television set to everyone who had helped with her case, doctors, nurses, and bedpan changers alike.

Come December, Al Davis would return to the football business, single-mindedly set on making up for lost time.

27

Even before he withdrew to look after his wife, however, Al Davis had been at least momentarily displaced from center stage in the ongoing drama of franchise moves and the enforcement of Section 4.3. For most of fall 1979, a threat that seemed far more immediate had been posed by Robert Irsay.

Irsay had begun thrusting himself forward on June 11, when he reportedly called the Los Angeles bureau of the Associated Press and announced he would be moving his franchise from Baltimore to southern California as soon as the Coliseum was vacated by the Rams. "Last year was the final year on our contract," he pointed out, "and leases starting now are all on option. In 1980 we will come to Los Angeles. I met with the mayor [Tom Bradley] and the governor [Jerry Brown]. I had a nice conversation with Governor Brown. We will move here next year. We will train here and everything will be here, everything that Los Angeles promised me."

Robert Irsay claimed that his decision had been provoked by the indifference and discourtesy exhibited by Maryland in the person of its governor, Harry Hughes. "The governor doesn't want to talk," Irsay charged, "and [Baltimore Mayor Donald] Schaeffer has promised me a lot of things that nothing ever came of. I canceled my vacation to meet with Governor Hughes on Monday the eighteenth. He called me yesterday and said he was not available until further notice. That's three dates canceled by the governor. I guess Maryland elected God, not a governor. Well, I've had it with Maryland, and the governor can go to hell. My goal is to move to L.A. There will be no more monkeying around."

As usual, Robert Irsay's outburst proved off the wall. While he may have been in Los Angeles, he never met with Tom Bradley or Jerry Brown. Nor had he even so much as notified the LAMCC of his presence. The Coliseum commission had heard nothing from him since he'd stood them up in January. This time, Bill Robertson did not even bother to attempt to find out what Irsay was talking about. Kenny Hahn wondered out loud if "he is using the Coliseum to get a better deal in Baltimore or from the governor of Maryland." For his part, Governor Hughes of Maryland had never had an appointment scheduled with Irsay on the eighteenth and had never called Irsay to cancel it. Nor had he ever canceled any previous meetings with Irsay. Hughes's office had last heard from the Baltimore owner in March, when Irsay promised to call back and make a dinner date with the governor in April.

Irsay's only further clarification concerned his failure to meet with the LAMCC while in southern California. "I haven't talked to anyone from the Coliseum," he admitted, "but it doesn't have to be here. I can go down the road to Phoenix if I have to." Not yet in southern California, he was already threatening to leave there for Arizona.

Predictably, Robert Irsay's outburst in Los Angeles had little impact. "Popgun Effect," The [Baltimore] Sun declared, "New Irsay Blast Fails to Impress Anyone."

It did, however, prompt a series of conversations with Pete Rozelle which lasted, according to Rozelle, "off and on for a period of maybe a month or six weeks." The commissioner's approach was to be patient and try to reason with Irsay. Rozelle pointed out that moving to L.A. would mean that the other members in the NFL's Eastern Division would have to fly all the way across the country to play him. That added travel would more than likely insure that the votes of those franchises would be cast against giving him permission to move. Mostly, Rozelle remembered, the two of them talked "about Los Angeles and his problems in Baltimore. I encouraged him to meet with the Baltimore people—because that city has supported the League for many, many years—and press for improvements."

Irsay listened to the commissioner, but ignored his advice. Instead, he started shopping around for a new home closer than L.A.

The first candidate Robert Irsay came up with was Jacksonville, Florida, former home of the failed World Football League Sharks. In early August, Irsay admitted that he had received an "unsolicited offer" from the Florida city, which was "about the same" as the offer L.A. had allegedly made. "I am very serious," he added. "I'd say it's a good possibility of moving to Jacksonville, based on what I've been told the city can produce. Jacksonville is only one of several cities I'm looking at. I love Florida. In fact, I have a home in Bal Harbour." On August 9, Irsay announced he was flying to Jacksonville the following week for discussions. "I told the mayor [of Jacksonville] that if Jacksonville can match the offers I've received from other cities, then I will be interested in meeting with him. I'm flying there to study the city. In fact, I might stay an additional two or three days." The probability of his remaining in Baltimore past the current football season was, according to Irsay, "one percent. The other ninety-nine percent is divided among Phoenix, Los Angeles, Jacksonville, Memphis, and Indianapolis."

Of the cities Irsay named, Phoenix's offer dated from 1976, Indianapolis's had died in 1977, and Los Angeles no longer took Robert Irsay with any seriousness at all. Aside from Jacksonville, only Memphis actually had an active interest in getting the Colts. Memphis, however, had yet to communicate that interest to Irsay. In August, Jacksonville was first in line and meant to make the most of the opportunity. "I knew Jacksonville would someday be a big time sports town," its mayor, Jake Godbold, gushed to *The* [Baltimore] *Sun,* "but I never thought it was going to happen this fast. I'm prepared to do whatever it takes—as long as it's feasible and reasonable. I think we can meet their requests." To help the city prepare its offer for Irsay, Godbold had secured the services of Hugh Culverhouse, owner of the Tampa Bay Buccaneers and still a Jacksonville resident.

When Irsay actually showed up to look the town over, Jacksonville pulled out all the stops.

At 11:00 A.M. on August 14, Robert Irsay's private jet taxied to a stop at the Jacksonville airport. The city delegation waiting for him at the bottom of the steps included Mayor Godbold, a number of civic dignitaries, and a bevy of curvaceous women wearing T-shirts embossed with I GOT COLT FEVER. Irsay was then ensconced in a silver and black Rolls-Royce and, led by a phalanx of police cars and followed by a fleet of Cadillacs, was driven downtown for a private lunch. The route he took was posted with more than two hundred signs, some of billboard proportions, saying WELCOME BOB.

At the lunch, Irsay made it very clear that he wouldn't come cheap. He wanted Jacksonville to remodel its Gator Bowl stadium completely. He also wanted the city to guarantee the sale of sixty-five thousand season tickets over his first ten years, plus provide a forty-acre parcel for the Colts' training facility, grant him a percentage of parking and concession revenues, and assure him "a profitable radio network." All of this, he pointed out, would have to be forthcoming before the end of October, when the League was scheduled to meet in Dallas. "Although I have not gotten a firm decision from the NFL," he allowed, "I think that Jacksonville would be acceptable to at least twenty-one owners, which is the required number to pass my moving here or someplace else." Afterward, he described Jacksonville's reaction to his proposals as "positive."

Irsay was "positive" as well, especially after Jacksonville's sales pitch reached a crescendo that evening. A public expression of zeal was scheduled for the Gator Bowl and it was unlike anything Robert Irsay had ever seen in Baltimore. Some fifty thousand people were on hand, and another ten thousand were trapped in a traffic jam leading to the stadium. Irsay was landed at midfield in a helicopter. "We want the Colts," the crowd chanted, "we want the Colts." The welcoming ceremony featured sky divers, free food, marching bands, and a galloping horse dubbed the Jacksonville Colt. After watching somewhat dazzled by it all, Irsay took the microphone himself. "Anybody in his right mind has to be very pleased and enthused by the welcome I've had here," he pointed out. "I can't believe all these people came out to see me. This will be a very big part of my decision. Needless to say, it's a little early to say what will or can happen." When his speech was over, the stadium lights were extinguished and each person in the crowd lit a match "to illustrate [sic] a spark to get the Colts to Jacksonville." Then Irsay left for the airport by helicopter.

The next day, Robert Irsay was in New York City and lunched with Pete Rozelle and Chuck Sullivan at "21." "He filled me in on what happened in Jacksonville," Rozelle remembered. "I got the impression, or feeling, that if something were done in Baltimore, he would be happy to stay there. He said he felt frustrated, that he might get trapped in Baltimore. Mr. Irsay didn't mention specifics, but he gave every indication that he had been slighted by the Maryland political leaders and the Baltimore banking community." After their lunch, Rozelle saw fit to take Irsay's side against Maryland—at least partially. "I think they should try harder," the commissioner commented to the press. "I am disappointed that there hasn't been at least more study given [to Irsay's desires]. It has been done elsewhere, sometimes it has been shown to be not feasible and sometimes, like in Minneapolis, they have found a way to do it." In Baltimore, "I have never seen any indication of anything being done on a really serious problem and how it might be resolved."

By then, Baltimore Mayor Donald Schaeffer had already attempted to leap into the breach. He made contact with Irsay on the phone. It was, the [Baltimore] News-American noted, "the first tangible effort by local officials to mend fences with the team owner since he threatened to move the team last spring." Irsay told Schaeffer that "many other cities have made an offer" and that he considered Governor Hughes to be his biggest problem in Baltimore. Schaeffer offered himself as intermediary between Irsay and the governor and also offered to arrange a meeting with Baltimore officials and dignitaries. "It's up to us to show him we want him here," the mayor explained. "I happen to like him. He's a flamboyant individual and he was exuberant over how he was received in Jacksonville. When you have fifty thousand people cheer you, you have to feel good."

The meeting Schaeffer arranged took place on August 29. Robert Irsay flew to Baltimore from Skokie, Illinois, in a rented plane because his own jet was undergoing repairs. Mayor Schaeffer met him at the airport and the two men motored into the city in the mayor's Cadillac limousine. Apparently concerned that the Colts' owner didn't significantly appreciate the way Baltimore had been improving itself, the mayor conducted a tour of the various rehabilitation projects currently under way in the city, including several new expressways and the renewal of the Inner Harbor. Their final destination was the Timonium Fairgrounds. There, Governor Hughes was waiting. The three men had a thirty-minute discussion about improving Memorial Stadium which the governor later described as "very friendly." According to The Sun, "Mr. Irsay was on good behavior. He did not tell the governor where to go, nor did he accuse the Colt fans of nonsupport. He talked rationally and set forth his demands. . . . A tone of cooperation permeated the meeting and all sides agreed to have their intermediaries meet further to work out the details.''

Afterward, Irsay proceeded to the Chesapeake Restaurant for a lunch with city business leaders. He told them that "time is of the essence." The NFL was going to meet again at the end of October, and by then, he had to decide whether or not to ask them to allow him to leave Baltimore.

Maryland's governor and Baltimore's mayor were both at least somewhat sympathetic to Irsay's hurry but, in truth, their hands were tied. The price tag for Robert Irsay's improvements could run as high as $25 million. The state legislature was the only possible source for that kind of cash and the legislature had made it clear that any such appropriation would only be in response to longterm commitments from both the stadium's tenants, Irsay's Colts and the Baltimore Orioles baseball team, recently purchased by Edward Bennett Williams. Williams had been quick to point out that the improvements offered nothing to the Orioles. In his language, they had been "totally excluded" and he was not about to sign any longterm lease on that basis. Until Williams's mind changed, Maryland could only try to mollify Irsay as best they could, while hoping the League held to Rozelle's attitude about "franchise stability."

When, in September, Irsay brought a delegation from Jacksonville up to tour Cleveland Stadium, a facility Irsay had pointed to as his minimum standard, Maryland must have felt cheered. "He's terrible," Art Modell said of the Colts owner. "We owners have a double loyalty, an obligation to protect cities that have been good to the League and the obligation to listen to aggrieved owners. We are not in the business of trafficking in franchises. Irsay came storming in here when the Colts played here and demanded to know how I was going to vote. I asked him, 'Vote on what?' There will be a lot of debate, dialogue, and reflection before there will be a decision on Baltimore."

Irsay's response to the argument was already on the record. "I can go anywhere I want," he pointed out. "It's a free country."

By September 26, Robert Irsay was back in Jacksonville. Again Irsay's jet was met at the airport and he was driven to a private four-hour lunch at Jacksonville's exclusive River Club on the top floor of a downtown insurance headquarters. The occasion was the official presentation of Jacksonville's written offer. The city was willing to guarantee sales of some forty-one thousand season tickets for ten years. It would also spend $14 million to remodel the Gator Bowl. Among the improvements would be 105 luxury boxes, a forty-thousand-square-foot training facility, enlargement to seventy-two thousand permanent seats, brand new press facilities, a ground-level restaurant, and construction of numerous "access roads and pedestrian walkways." Irsay took the offer under advisement. At a press conference afterward, he characterized Jacksonville's presentation as "the first financial offer of any substance" for the purpose of inducing a Colts move, but claimed there were more on the way. Along with Jacksonville, L.A., and Memphis were still in the running. Irsay claimed Los Angeles's offer was due to be mailed the following week and Memphis's would be coming shortly after that. "It is no longer a question of *if* I'm moving," he announced, "but a question of *where*." In case his point had been somehow missed, Irsay repeated the announcement three times before leaving for a post-press conference cocktail party.

As usual, L.A. had no idea it was supposed to be working up an offer to Irsay. Memphis, however, did and was. They were also getting a lesson in the Irsay style of negotiation. In September, he visited the city to meet with civic leaders. "I give you my word we are moving out of Baltimore," he told them. "At this moment, it's either Memphis or Jacksonville." In early October, Irsay and a Memphis delegation met in a Chicago hotel room for the presentation of the city's official offer. "We took a presentation to him," John Malmo, who represented Memphis Mayor Wyeth Chandler, remembered, "and we got a little more than twenty percent through it, at which point certain questions came up. We started discussing the questions and the meeting deteriorated from there." Finally, Irsay halted discussion for a moment, excusing himself to go to the bathroom. The waiting Memphis group heard Irsay close the bathroom door, then heard the toilet flush. Afterward they heard the door to the hotel hallway slam shut. Irsay had walked out and disappeared without so much as a word.

"I thought we were finished," John Malmo explained that October. "Our chances of getting the Colts looked bleak. But having dealt with Mr. Irsay [before], I know that he is a very complex individual, so I decided to call and check with him again. I really felt we were dead, but I have been trying to get a National Football League franchise for our city for the last five years and I wanted to check once more before I wrote off the final chapter in that quest. And I'm glad I did. Irsay said he was still interested in our proposal." The proposal Memphis then proceeded to present would have guaranteed Irsay an annual stadium gross of $7.3 million for nine years, more than $1 million larger than Jacksonville's ten-year offer. It would also build him a training site and increase Memphis's Liberty Bowl stadium from fifty thousand to seventy-four thousand seats. *The* [Baltimore] *Sun* later described it as "the richest commitment ever made by a city to a sports team."

With his offers in hand, it was now Irsay's intention to take them to the NFL's meeting in Dallas at Loew's Anatole Hotel on October 31, and ask for a vote. As that date approached, however, Pete Rozelle began to maneuver the League out of the potential challenge an Irsay request might pose. On October 26, he flew to Baltimore's airport and met there with Mayor Schaeffer and Governor Hughes. Irsay had discussed his Memphis offer with the commissioner and the commissioner now talked to the Maryland officials about what they would have to do to keep him. The package Maryland then came up with called for $22 million in improvements to Memorial Stadium in exchange for a longterm Irsay lease. On October 28, Hughes and Schaeffer discussed the offer with Irsay on a three-cornered conference call. Rozelle noted that he was "very encouraged." Hughes described himself as "satisfied," Schaeffer "did not express any disappointment," but Irsay still planned to ask the League to vote under Section 4.3.

By the time the NFL arrived in Dallas, that request was easily its hottest topic. Robert Irsay was spotted in the Anatole Hotel's lobby and immediately besieged by reporters. Irsay ran up the escalator to the mezzanine in an attempt to escape and tried to hide behind an abutment. When discovered there, he fled into the hotel kitchen, where he was finally cornered in a small utility closet. Irsay then told the reporters to "talk to my wife." His wife, Harriet, in turn told them he had three proposals, from Jacksonville, Memphis, and Baltimore, and that Irsay would "probably ask the other owners to vote on them." She characterized Baltimore's offer as "just talk," since the state legislature would not be meeting until the following January and could then "throw everything out." Memphis's offer was described by Harriet Irsay as "very good."

At this point, Irsay himself intervened. "Harriet has a big mouth," he told the press. "She doesn't know what she's talking about." He and Harriet then disappeared into the elevator en route to their room.

Escaping the press was easier for Irsay than escaping Rozelle. That night, he and the commissioner had an extended meeting at the commissioner's request. Rozelle did not want a vote and made a strong case for the damage such a move would do to the League. Irsay was attracted by Memphis, but Rozelle pointed out that Memphis's Liberty Bowl renovations would not be complete until 1981, so Irsay had nothing to lose by waiting to see what action Maryland was willing to undertake on his behalf. The following morning, Rozelle and Irsay met again before the League convened as a whole. If the commissioner needed any more leverage, he no doubt pointed out that Irsay had no more than six votes supporting him, some fifteen short of what he needed.

Whatever the arguments, the result left the rest of the NFL impressed at the thoroughness with which the commissioner had apparently soothed the League's most savage beast. "Irsay gave a very nice presentation," Gene Klein remembered with a certain astonishment. "He didn't ask for anything and acted totally inside the confines of the League rules." Irsay began his presentation by officially retracting his request for a vote under Section 4.3. Instead, according to Rozelle, "he simply reviewed his discussions with Memphis, Jacksonville, and Baltimore. He said, 'I'm not asking for anything, but I may come back to you again next year or in the future. I'm not talking about moving now, but I might want to come back and ask for permission.' " "He was almost eloquent," another owner gushed. "He made an excellent impression."

Irsay himself explained his turnaround as the best option of the moment. "Even if I had gone through with my proposal to ask the other owners' permission to move the team," he pointed out, "the move probably could not have been made until 1981. As it now stands, I have left the door open to the cities I have talked to in case the [Maryland] legislature turns down the stadium improvements. If the form [the legislature approves] comes up to our expectations and NFL standards, I want to stay in Baltimore. If not, I want to thank Memphis and Jacksonville and the other cities, and I still have them in mind."

The "open door" Irsay left for himself at the October 31 NFL meeting did little to mollify the municipalities with whom he'd been dickering. The "bad news," according to the *Memphis Commercial Appeal,* was that "the Colts are staying in Baltimore." The "good news" was "so is Robert Irsay." "He told us two hundred times he might be coming here," John Malmo complained. "I absolutely don't trust him." Jacksonville now felt much the same way. "He'd cock his head to one side, give us that teddy bear smile, and tell us he was being sincere with us," Jake Godbold remembered. "His name is mud here." Even his "hometown" *News-American* described Irsay's last minute allegiance to Baltimore as no more than a "Sudden Change of Fickle Heart."

In any case, the NFL entered November with Robert Irsay once again safely stashed beneath its decks.

28

With Irsay under control, the focus of Pete Rozelle's uneasiness soon shifted back to Al Davis, who had begun to immerse himself in the football business once again. On November 20, Davis met with Jack Maltester, a member of the Oakland Coliseum's board recently assigned the task of reopening negotiations with the Raiders. The meeting was little more than an illustration of how fervently Al Davis did not want to be nailed down. Davis claimed Maltester elicited a set of complaints from Davis and then afterward sent Davis a letter, listing his various complaints as demands. Davis responded by adamantly refusing to admit to having any list of demands. He also characterized Maltester's letter as "something that shouldn't have been done." Maltester's worst violation was that the letter was "written as a public release," once again violating the secrecy insisted upon by the Raiders' boss.

Maltester had a somewhat different version of events. "I sat down with Al Davis," he remembered, "and I put down notes of what he asked for. He wrote $8.5 million worth of stuff on the blackboard that I hadn't seen before. When I sent him a letter outlining what they were, what I felt we could do, he denied he'd ever proposed them." Maltester subsequently turned the task of negotiating over to a three-man committee, claiming he found further efforts with Davis impossible.

Whichever version of the negotiation was closer to accurate, the most obvious truth about each was the animosity reflected on both sides. "The Raiders owe the people of this area something," Maltester complained to the press. Instead, all Davis did was say, "To hell with the Coliseum and the Coliseum board. They've been sold out for years. Don't they owe anything to these people? They're making money. If they said they were losing money,

I'd be sympathetic. Really, what *do* they want? I know what they want. They want more money and the question is how to get it. They're pulling out all the stops. They're going right down to the wire. They care nothing about the people. It's a greedy organization and I never thought I'd say that. It's a helluva thing for me to say. Most of the limited partners are friends of mine."

Al Davis could not have cared less what Maltester thought. He made no secret of the fact he doubted "the ability and competence" of the people Oakland sent to negotiate. "I don't even know who has the authority," he pointed out, "and I don't think anyone there really wants to deal intelligently." His absence from negotiations while at his wife's bedside also seemed to have provoked some hard thinking on Davis's part about just what it meant to stay in backwater Oakland rather than risking the southern California big time. After Carol was fully recovered, according to one NFL source, he hinted as much in a conversation with one of his owner friends about the possibility of a move. "Would *you* want to bury *your* wife in Oakland?" Davis asked.

Throughout his wife's ordeal, Al Davis had maintained contact with Bill Robertson in Los Angeles. Davis had not maintained any contact at all with Pete Rozelle. At this stage, Rozelle noted, "I still didn't think the move idea was real. I thought it was just a typical case of an owner negotiating with a stadium. I wasn't aware of all the meetings that had been going on. I didn't think Al Davis would attempt to violate the constitution." In the last week of November, Rozelle attempted to make contact with Davis. It had been at least six weeks since the two had last spoken. The commissioner and his wife were flying to Los Angeles and after the weekend there, Rozelle was scheduled to appear at a Press Club luncheon in San Francisco. He had his office contact Al LoCasale at the Raiders and inform him that Mr. and Mrs. Rozelle were going to be in the Bay Area on November 29 and wanted to know if either one or both of them could visit Mrs. Davis in the hospital. The Rozelles would be staying in the Bel-Air Hotel while in L.A.

On the evening of November 28, the phone in their hotel room rang and Carrie Rozelle answered. It was Al LoCasale calling for her husband. LoCasale told the commissioner that "he wasn't certain whether [the Rozelles] would be able to see Mrs. Davis or not the next day." According to Rozelle, LoCasale also "may have said something to me . . . that I would be queried the next day [at the San Francisco Press Club] about [the Raiders] moving and he wanted me to be as soft as I can or, if possible, say yes, the Raiders can move." Specifically, LoCasale wanted what he would later describe as "the Minnesota treatment," in honor of the press conference threat Rozelle had delivered in Hawaii on Max Winter's behalf. The Raiders, LoCasale reminded the commissioner, were in the midst of very sticky negotiations with Oakland.

The next morning, while Rozelle was shaving and Carrie packing for the flight to San Francisco, LoCasale called again. "It was a very short conversation," the commissioner remembered, "because we were going to get a plane. Mr. LoCasale told me that I would be able to get in touch with Mr.

Davis by phone from the Press Club and he would know more about the situation regarding his wife.''

When Pete and Carrie reached the Press Club, LoCasale was already there. Again he requested ''the Minnesota treatment,'' and Rozelle responded he would do his best.

As Davis's assistant had predicted, the possibility of a Raiders move was one of the first items raised during the commissioner's question and answer period. ''I tried to take as soft a line as I could on Davis,'' Rozelle claimed. ''I said that of course the League liked permanency to our franchises, but I hope they can work it out. I was more or less dancing on water there, trying to say I hope they stay here and I hope we can work something out.''

Afterward, the commissioner talked with Davis on one of the Press Club's private phones. It was their first communication since his wife's coma. Most of the talk was, quite naturally, about Mrs. Davis. She had just been moved to another hospital, so a visit was impossible. The heavier issues arose toward the end of their ten-minute talk. According to Rozelle, Davis eventually ''told me he was having great difficulty in negotiating a lease with the Oakland Coliseum.'' He also said, ''I don't think that you helped us out at all at that luncheon meeting.''

''I disagreed with him,'' Rozelle remembered. ''I felt I went as far as I possibly could in trying to help him. I said to Al, 'I helped you as much as I could. I did not have the right to say you could move your franchise. That's up to the member clubs.' I said that Al had not come to me. Al had not asked for a move. That's what I told the press. I said, 'I hope that he can conclude the negotiations with the Oakland Coliseum successfully.' I also said that 'one of our more successful teams is Dallas and I can't say that Dallas is going to be located ten years from now where it is.' So I said all the soft things to the full extent that I could at the time. . . . He wanted me to say more than I did and I told him that I thought that I had gone as far as I could on my own.''

Al Davis was unsatisfied, but, for the moment, dropped the subject. ''I think I might want to sit down with you soon,'' he mentioned in closing, ''and talk.''

''Fine,'' Rozelle answered. ''Just let me know when you are free.''

Though it went unstated, both men now understood that the subject of this conversation would be Los Angeles.

In the meantime, speculation about Davis's dealings with L.A. only escalated. On December 17, the rumor level jumped another notch when the *Los Angeles Times* printed a story claiming that Bill Robertson had at last found a way to wriggle around L.A.'s financial crunch. Ironically, its key element was the 1984 Olympics, the same element that had helped thwart Carroll Rosenbloom three years earlier. Los Angeles had won its Olympics bid and now, according to Olympic Organizing Committee Chairman Peter Ueberroth, was prepared to use its advance revenues to underwrite the $15 million of improvements Davis wanted. ''We have developed, with Bill Robertson,'' Ueberroth explained, ''a plan that we feel would . . . get the facilities needed to attract a team. . . . If a team will come, it assures the viability of financing to make the improvements necessary for them."

The news was received with great uneasiness in Oakland. "There's no way we can get in a bidding match with the Los Angeles Coliseum," Jack Maltester groused. "If they're going to use Olympic money, maybe we'll ask . . . to start a program to send a dollar to the Olympic committee so the Raiders can move to Los Angeles." In its calculations, Oakland was increasingly relying on the assumption that the League wouldn't let Davis move. Otherwise, they had been outmaneuvered. "We don't feel like we're the bad guys," the Oakland Coliseum's general manager observed, "although there has been a strong attempt to make us look that way." Asked how the Coliseum and Davis were getting along, the GM admitted, "It hasn't been very good lately." Asked if the relationship had ever been any good, the GM said, "No comment."

The increased speculation brought some disquiet to Los Angeles as well. Shortly after the *Times* story, Georgia Rosenbloom again called Rozelle. "Have you seen the papers?" she asked. "The Raiders are in the headlines again. They're coming to town." Georgia had not heard from Davis since the first game of the season and was feeling "hurt" that he had not consulted her on his plans.

"Don't worry, Georgia," Rozelle advised. "It won't happen."

"The owners live in a fishbowl," the commissioner later explained. "They are constantly pressed by the media. . . . She was a rookie owner. Her husband had passed away less than a year before and she wanted to know what was going on so that her responses could be accurate from a League standpoint and she wouldn't sound silly. I am sure I used 'Don't worry' because that's the way I get off the phone with owners after lengthy calls. . . . I said, 'Don't worry. Al hasn't come to me. He hasn't said anything about wanting a vote, wanting to move to Los Angeles. . . . I think it's probably at this point just a negotiating ploy.' "

Bill Robertson of the LAMCC had come to the opposite conclusion. In "the latter part of December," Robertson remembered, "my gut feeling was that Al Davis was seriously thinking of coming to Los Angeles." Once, Robertson had considered Davis simply "sincere"; now he upgraded Davis to "a hot prospect." According to Davis, the possibility of Olympic financing had a lot to do with Davis's attitude. "There were certain requirements that we needed to move to Los Angeles financially," he later explained, "and Bill Robertson was trying to put his package together so that the money would be there the day that I agreed to come. . . . In December, we met at the Olympic [Committee] office and every time we would finish the meeting, after we got done discussing details and money, Ueberroth would come up to me and say, 'I want you to know that the minute that you sign, the money will be there. You will have the money.' "

With that assurance, negotiations between Davis and Los Angeles accelerated. On Christmas Eve, Davis, Robertson, and a handful of attorneys and assistants spent the entire day closeted at the Beverly Wilshire, poring over details. According to the L.A. Coliseum's general manager, they discussed "the improvements to be made to the Coliseum and the construction of practice facilities for the Raiders, the cost of these items, and the manner in which these items would be financed." Al Davis was insisting "that he will not move the Raiders to Los Angeles and sign a lease with the Coliseum unless the Coliseum guarantees to make a number of specified improvements." At the time, it was understood that "the Olympic Organizing Committee . . . has agreed that it will advance the Coliseum money owed for the rental of the Coliseum and Sports Arena for the 1984 Olympics to help finance the costs. . . . The remainder of the financing will be through a bank loan [to the LAMCC]."

A week later, on December 30, the two sides met again and got even more specific. "The Raiders and the [L.A.] Coliseum came to an agreement at this meeting," the Los Angeles GM claimed, "regarding VIP executive suites to be built in the Coliseum and other improvements to be made, including the construction of a new press box to replace the present one. An agreement was reached concerning a practice facility for the Raiders, including a clubhouse, training facilities, lockers, weight conditioning rooms, meeting rooms, offices for the Raiders' coaches and executives, two full-sized natural turf practice fields, a seventy-yard Astroturf field, all to be completely fenced in for privacy and security. The parties also agreed on insurance costs, the responsibility for day-of-game expenses, the disposition of income from the VIP executive suites, scheduling dates, and who would pay for moving costs. In addition, the parties reached an understanding without agreeing on specific figures regarding the general amount of rent for the Coliseum, the length of time to be covered by the contract, and the splitting of concession income. The Coliseum expressed its willingness to grant Davis's request for a five-year contract, provided only that the term of the bank financing to pay for the improvements does not exceed five years."

Though the agreement was as yet incomplete and unsigned, Al Davis and Bill Robertson were closer to a deal than they had ever been and Davis more than warranted his new "hot prospect" label. Two "ifs" remained outstanding. The first was if L.A. could really produce the money it was preparing to commit itself to spend. The second was if Davis could really get the League to let him move. Like the agreement itself, those dilemmas were still playing themselves out in private when 1980 began.

Oakland, of course, had no idea Al Davis and Los Angeles had gone as far as they had. By January 3, however, it was apparent something was up. On that day, the suburban *Hayward Daily Review* printed an exclusive interview with the Raiders owner. It marked the first time in the last year that Davis had broken his public silence on the issue of his Oakland lease and the gist of it all was decidedly negative in Oakland's direction. "They have not negotiated with us for ten years," Davis complained. "They still haven't done it. . . . There were a few concessions along the way . . . but when you think of the major stadiums that are being built for $50, $60, and $70 million, the concessions were peanuts. We never got any of the things we deserved. . . . You know who built the Coliseum. They can talk about this guy or that guy, but you know. You know who's had a commitment to excellence. We may not have been as good as we'd like the last two years, but we've done our part. I don't think they've done their part, by any means. That's obvious, otherwise we would have solved the lease. . . . They'd have told us to go stick it except that something came up over the horizon that scared them a little bit." Davis also hinted that Oakland would soon pay for its folly. "I think this thing has gone much further than you assume," he warned somewhat obscurely. "It's like getting ready for a world war and you're still worried about Iran."

Oakland claimed the blast was just more Al Davis. "To me it sounds like just one of their maneuvers," Jack Maltester commented. Oakland and Maltester also took refuge in their faith in the League. "I think the chances are very much in our favor that the League will not let the Raiders move," he argued. "Maybe they can move legally, but it seems to me if Rozelle books the Washington Redskins into Oakland and the Raiders are in Los Angeles, they're going to have a helluva time playing that game."

In the first week of 1980, however, Al Davis was moving on the League front as well.

Over the weekend of January 5, Pete and Carrie Rozelle were in Tampa for the playoff game between the Tampa Bay Buccaneers and the Los Angeles Rams and had dinner in a Tampa restaurant with Georgia Rosenbloom, Dominic Frontiere, Rams General Manager Don Klosterman, and several others on the evening prior to the game. During the course of the meal, Rozelle raised the subject of Davis's designs on Los Angeles. The commissioner now thought Davis was serious about moving there and didn't want Georgia to read about it in the papers. The change in Rozelle's estimate of the situation had grown out of a recent phone call from Davis. The Raiders owner had finally scheduled the meeting he'd mentioned after the Press Club in San Francisco. On Monday, January 7, Davis and Rozelle were to converge in New York at the League's Park Avenue office "to sit down and talk." That the portent of such a talk was ominous went without saying.

29

Al Davis arrived at Pete Rozelle's Manhattan office on January 7, 1980, after taking the red-eye flight from San Francisco the night before. The two men met alone, behind closed doors. "It was not an angry meeting," Rozelle remembered. "It wasn't explosive or vitriolic." Nonetheless, the commissioner would later wish there had been a witness in the room.

According to Rozelle, Davis began by explaining "the difficulties he was having in negotiating what he felt was a satisfactory lease with the Oakland Coliseum people." Davis had brought along a sheaf of correspondence from Oakland to prove his point. "He held the file of papers," Rozelle remembered, "and at one point he wanted to show me [that] there had been a breach of good faith on the part of the Oakland Coliseum negotiators. I believe it involved the length of the lease they were discussing, whether one side or the other had ever offered a three- or a five-year lease, I forget specifically. And he held them up to me and showed me these passages and a couple different letters that he felt were significant. Then he took them back and he said that he felt that they just were not negotiating in good faith and he said, 'I'm strongly thinking of moving to Los Angeles, to the Coliseum.' "

The statement did not surprise Rozelle. "Al," he responded, "if you decide you want to go to Los Angeles, let me know and I'll schedule a League meeting."

"I don't intend to submit this to the League for a vote," Davis announced. His position was the same as in Chicago, more than a year earlier.

"Well, Al," Rozelle shrugged, "it's my job to enforce the constitution, and that's going to present a conflict."

Then, Rozelle remembered, Davis "either said, 'Well, I still don't intend to ask for a vote' or said nothing. I don't recall."

There would later be little dispute over the content of the exchange between the commissioner and the Oakland owner, but much dispute about its tone and the respective postures of the participants. "It was one of the few times Al Davis had ever been humble in his life," one of Davis's Los Angeles associates claimed. "He asked for Rozelle's help. He said he wanted to move to L.A. and needed Rozelle's help. Pete just said, 'You have to put it to a vote.' Al Davis knew who the vote was, he didn't stand a chance." Davis himself claimed that Rozelle "could not give any reason why I shouldn't move and even agreed that L.A. . . . could be the finest franchise in the National Football League."

After their talk was over, Rozelle escorted Davis down one floor to the headquarters of NFL Films, where Davis watched footage for a while and then left. Shortly thereafter, he was on his way back to California.

Once Davis was gone, Pete Rozelle discussed their conversation with his in-house lawyer. That discussion was followed by a phone call to Hamilton Carothers at Covington and Burling in Washington, D.C. "I told Mr. Carothers what Mr. Davis had said to me," Rozelle explained. "That he was strongly leaning toward moving to Los Angeles and did not intend to ask for League approval." Carothers responded that it was "important to go on record promptly, having had that news from Mr. Davis. I think what Mr. Carothers intended to convey . . . to Mr. Davis was that it was a rather serious decision that he was making and that he should be aware of the potential consequences." The result was a letter from Rozelle to Davis, drafted by Carothers and dated January 10, 1980:

Dear Al,

In our conversation last Monday you took the position that no vote by the NFL's member clubs is necessary for you to move the Raiders from Oakland to Los Angeles. Reflection on that conversation suggests that I should make clear what I believe the other clubs' reaction will be if you attempt to take such a step. . . . The requirement of member club approval of a franchise transfer by which the Raiders and every other club in the League are bound, is in the interests of every member of the League [and] I do not know what the membership reaction will be to a proposal by the Oakland club for an immediate transfer of its home operations to Los Angeles. . . . But I think you would be extremely ill-advised to attempt to effect such a transfer without complying with the League's charter and submitting the proposal to the membership for its consideration. . . . When the Raiders entered the NFL, they entered as a franchise conducting their home operations in Oakland. They also agreed to accept the provisions of the NFL constitution and bylaws. The remaining NFL clubs will undoubtedly view the Raiders as contractually committed to remain in Oakland until the charter provisions are followed. . . .

I am, of course, aware of the antitrust litigation pending in Los Angeles [*LAMCC v. NFL*]. But if you are relying on that litigation as a basis for simply ignoring your contractual commitments to the other member clubs of the League, I think you are equally ill-advised. And if your reliance on that litigation is misplaced, which we think it clearly is, the costs, practical problems, and financial penalties inflicted on the Raiders franchise, including possible disciplinary action by the League and the imposition on the Raiders of the costs and expenses incurred by the League, will be quite severe. I therefore strongly urge you to take a responsible approach to the Raiders' interests and the interests of your fellow clubs by submitting your proposal for early consideration by the League's membership.

Sincerely,
Pete

Rozelle sent copies of the letter to all the member clubs and several called him to talk about it. They were, he later claimed, supportive of the stand he had taken.

The letter had no discernible effect on Davis. If anything, he likely found its threats invigorating. Getting hardnosed was something Al Davis enjoyed.

In any case, Davis was obviously making ready to do battle, should it come to that. Before traveling to New York, Davis had retained the services of attorney Joseph Alioto—Billy Sullivan's son-in-law and Leonard Tose's counsel in *Tose v. 1st Pennsylvania Bank*. While not saying whether or not the Raiders were actually moving, Alioto had begun defending their right to do so before Rozelle's letter was even mailed. "We don't think anyone has jurisdiction," Alioto told *The* [Oakland] *Tribune*. "Carroll Rosenbloom moved. He didn't ask anybody. You can't justify that [move] as being in the same area. Moving out to Balloon Land [from Los Angeles] was a major move. That's an entirely different market. If Rosenbloom did it without asking anybody, there's no reason to think Al would have to ask anyone." If the League tried to stop him, Alioto pointed out, it would be a severe violation of the Sherman Act.

Meanwhile, new developments were brewing on both the Los Angeles and Oakland fronts.

In Los Angeles, the focus was on Bill Robertson's continued attempts to nail down financing. What had previously been a $15 million commitment had now grown to $17 million, but, according to Robertson, "by early January, the prospects of the Raiders and the Coliseum committee reaching a mutually agreeable lease looked very probable." As those prospects increased, so did the pressure on Robertson. "Because of the urgency of arriving at an agreement with Al Davis," Robertson remembered, "we had to get some political action which would indicate support of a Raider move" and get it soon. Early in the month, Robertson put Davis together with Mayor Tom Bradley and Bradley made it clear Robertson had his full backing. Robertson also "attended various meetings of the Los Angeles City Council and the Los Angeles County Board of Supervisors which were devoted in part to discussions of the desirability and importance of obtaining the Raiders as the 'home' professional football team for Los Angeles."

According to Robertson's new financial plan, $5 million of the money he needed would be supplied by an advance on rent from the 1984 Olympics; another $5 million would be a loan to the LAMCC by the county of Los Angeles, secured by projected income from advertisement sales on the new scoreboard and the commission's thirty-five percent share of the revenues from Davis's ninety-nine projected luxury boxes; and the final $7 million would be supplied by the city of Los Angeles, which would borrow it from a commercial bank, offering its hotel tax revenues as security. It was an arrangement put together on the run, but it made significant headway. By the time NFL advance men had set up in L.A. in preparation for Super Bowl XIV in Pasadena's Rose Bowl on January 20, Robertson was on something of a political roll. The Los Angeles City Council voted fifteen to zero "in favor of the principle of committing $5.5 million in city hotel tax revenues to underwrite a commercial bank loan to help finance renovations of the Los Angeles Coliseum if a satisfactory arrangement could be arrived at with the Raiders." On January 15, the Los Angeles County Board of Supervisors voted four to one "in principle" to loan $5 million to the LAMCC for remodeling and "to advance the Raiders costs and expenses involved in transferring to Los Angeles," should they decide to move. The *Los Angeles Times* called it "a major step toward bringing the Oakland Raider football team to Los Angeles." L.A. Supervisor Kenny Hahn hinted that Davis might very well announce his move on the Friday before the Super Bowl.

Hahn, however, was off the mark considerably. One significant reason was that, in something of a late civic panic, Oakland had finally responded to L.A.'s challenge. The moving force behind the response was Oakland Mayor Lionel Wilson. Like Tom Bradley in Los Angeles, Wilson was the first black mayor in his city's history and the Raiders now loomed as the most significant challenge of his first term. Though the Oakland Coliseum was an independent entity, its bonds were guaranteed by the city and county and the politician who stood to be blamed if Al Davis actually moved was the mayor. And he would be blamed for much more than just an empty stadium. As *The Tribune* noted, "Snatching the Raiders out of Oakland would rip the heart and guts out of the East Bay. . . . This is an area of volatile social combinations. The Raiders are one subject that keeps the community mind on matters other than unemployment, high taxes, reduced services, and other despairs of present day life. . . . This isn't merely liking a team. It's almost love." The Raiders had put Oakland on the map; Oakland would have to scramble if it meant to stay there.

Wilson began his scramble on January 8 by getting the City Council formally to commission his own intervention in negotiations. He then immediately called for a meeting of all parties, under his auspices, five days hence. Invited were Davis and representatives from the Coliseum, the Oakland City Council, and the Alameda County Board of Supervisors. Davis delivered his RSVP through Al LoCasale. "We're not going to a meeting with twenty-five people on one side and Al Davis on the other," Davis's assistant announced. "We're not interested in a meeting of political people who are ready to run to the nearest microphone the minute it's over. The more people you bring in, the more time you spend discussing past history." Wilson then canceled the larger meeting and arranged to meet with Davis alone on January 14.

On January 13, Davis went public for the second time, but it did little to clarify the situation. The best the Raiders owner had to offer were a few veiled hints. "The environment forces people to act," he philosophized to *The Tribune*. "I always believed I could beat it, I could make the environment work for me. But this time it's forcing me to act in a way I never thought I would. I don't want to blame anyone. I'll survive. No, I'll dominate, not survive." The next day he met with Lionel Wilson for the first time.

Oakland's mayor emerged from that January 14 meeting mouthing optimism. Al Davis, he claimed, "wants to stay here. There was no mention of the terms of the Los Angeles situation. He didn't even mention it. I'm just satisfied that he is trying to find a way to stay here. The meeting was warm, very friendly. I think we've set the stage for further meetings." At the time that meeting ended, however, no such further meetings were scheduled. First Wilson had to put together a new and larger offer to take to Davis. He immediately convened his city/county/Coliseum task force for precisely that purpose. It would take three days.

In the meantime, Al Davis had flown to Los Angeles to join the rest of the League at their Super Bowl festivities. On Thursday evening, January 17, he was at a private party with a number of other owners and Rozelle.

The hottest topic of conversation at that Super Bowl party was a column by Mel Durslag in that day's *Herald Examiner*. It was headlined, "Why the NFL Is out of Line Sermonizing to Al Davis." Starting with the theory that the greatest potential hazard on the NFL horizon was a challenge from Al Davis over the right to move south, Durslag wrote,

> Davis admits readily he could lose the vote in a politically inspired atmosphere in which the commissioner and certain members have begun sermonizing on the evils of deserting fans who have supported a club loyally. . . . In blissful silence, if not with admiration, the commissioner and the owners watched their late brother in Los Angeles use his franchise to make the biggest heist in sports history at Anaheim. . . . Did his colleagues concern themselves with hometown loyalty in Los Angeles, which had supported the Rams since 1946? . . . The owners have gone too far to start sermonizing at this point. Having created the cut-throat environment that they have, they can't sell anyone the notion that their hearts bleed for the suffering fans of Oakland. If they tell the fans of Los Angeles that their football needs are being served in Anaheim, they also can tell the fans of Oakland that their football needs are being served in San Francisco, only a third the distance Los Angeles is from Anaheim.

When Rozelle and Davis spoke briefly at the party, Rozelle brought the column up. "Durslag wrote an article in which he took on the owners . . . for some reason," Davis explained. "I don't remember the article directly [but] Pete espoused to me that a lot of them were upset about it and [said] Georgia was one who was upset about it. . . . She had been taken on quite heavily in the newspapers, and he mentioned that to me [as well]." The two men did not mention Davis's negotiations with either Oakland or Los Angeles.

Back in Oakland earlier on Thursday, Lionel Wilson had been called out of city council meetings on several occasions to speak with Davis on the phone. On Friday, January 18, according to Davis, Alameda County Supervisor George Vukasin called Al LoCasale and arranged for Lionel Wilson and Cornell Maier of Kaiser Industries, Oakland's largest employer, to fly down to L.A. on Saturday "to make certain presentations to me." Wilson had a new proposal to make.

The big news of Friday, however, was on Davis's Los Angeles front. On January 18, the LAMCC dropped a new legal grenade in the League's lap in Los Angeles Federal District Court. Stating that the Oakland Raiders "are on the verge of transferring to Los Angeles" it asked that *LAMCC v. NFL* be immediately revived from legal dormancy. It also asked that the NFL be enjoined from exercising Section 4.3 of its constitution and barred from taking "punitive action against the Raiders." If such relief were not granted, the LAMCC claimed, it would be "prevented from closing a deal" with Davis. The move took the League by surprise but didn't provide any definitive answer to its questions about Davis. Since the Raiders were a defendant in *LAMCC v. NFL*, the NFL's attorneys immediately contacted Davis's attorneys to ask if they should continue to represent him in light of the LAMCC's most recent action. Davis's attorneys, according to Rozelle, "called back and said to continue to represent them until further notice."

Rozelle himself did not learn of the LAMCC's surprise move until late on Friday afternoon. That evening was the commissioner's annual party for the sporting press, a lavish affair for as many as three thousand guests. The new Los Angeles injunction was, according to the commissioner, "a major point of conversation with the owners and others that attended that party." Among the owners Rozelle personally spoke with about it were Art Modell, Herman Sarkowsky, Chuck Sullivan, Wellington Mara, Leonard Tose, Dan Rooney, Gene Klein, Jack Kent Cooke, and Georgia Rosenbloom. "At that time," Rozelle remembered, the most common refrain "was 'What can we do to stop them if they are going to move without approval?' I think there probably were a couple saying, 'What court action can we take to stop them?' I took the position of 'We should give Al an opportunity to come to the League and ask for a vote.' "

Al Davis himself skipped the party. Rozelle did, however, know of his upcoming meeting with the group from Oakland. His source for the information was Lionel Wilson, who had called the commissioner and said the Oakland delegation would also like to talk to him while they were in L.A. Rozelle said he'd be glad to talk with them. "I hadn't heard from Oakland before," he noted. On Saturday, he heard from Oakland again on the phone, but the contact went no further. "They said Davis had gotten wind that they were going to meet with me," Rozelle remembered, "and he had said he would not negotiate with them at all if they met with me." Oakland had "no choice" but to cancel their gathering with the commissioner.

Instead, they met with Al Davis at the Beverly Wilshire. The offer Wilson had brought totaled $8 million, including sixty-four luxury boxes and a $4 million unsecured loan. Two and a half million of the loan was being provided by Kaiser, and the term of the lease was to be five years. While it was not everything Davis wanted, it was a place to start. "They were well on their way to satisfying me," Davis remembered. "They came with a type-written presentation, I don't remember if it was one page or two pages. We took the presentation and we made some notes on the presentation that . . . in essence, said what I was satisfied with or what I thought was do-able. . . . They did too. . . . I was greatly encouraged. It was the first meaningful proposal I had ever had. [Now] I could make an intelligent decision where I couldn't rule them out. Up until the point they came to see me, there was no way. They weren't even close. It was only after my discussions with Cornell Maier and Mayor Wilson that there was a possibility we could make a deal. . . . I gave them . . . the outline of an agreement as I thought it would be, and it was a list of all the things that were necessary for us to evaluate as to whether we stay in Oakland or not. . . . We then both went back to our respective locations."

Davis would later claim the meeting had made a significant impact. "I was pretty solid in the middle of January that I would move," he explained, but then "there was a change in developments that altered my thinking."

Lionel Wilson apparently picked up on the shift in Davis's mindset. Shortly after returning to Oakland, the mayor said the discussion led him "to believe that Davis will remain in Oakland."

Others got the same message from Davis as well. He would tell Tex Schramm that Oakland had made an offer that he might have to take. On Saturday night, not long after Wilson had left, Davis saw Jim Kensil, who ran the Jets for Leon Hess, in the Beverly Wilshire bar. Davis had a glass of ice water and talked. "He led me to believe he was going to cut a deal with Oakland," Kensil remembered.

He did not tell Kensil or anyone else that he had also used his time in L.A. to conduct a more than six-hour meeting with Bill Robertson and the LAMCC's attorney, Steven Reinhardt. To the L.A. contingent he gave the opposite impression. "That day," Robertson remembered, "we knew Al Davis was serious about Los Angeles."

On Sunday morning, Al Davis left L.A. before the Super Bowl game was played. Since his own team wasn't in it, he decided to watch the game on television at home in Oakland with his wife. He gave his game tickets to Robertson. Before leaving town, he also called Rozelle's hotel room. According to Rozelle's later court testimony, Davis told him, " 'A lot of things are being said about the Raiders in the papers and otherwise the last two days that . . . aren't exactly true.' "

Rozelle took the statement as a reinforcement of his own position "that we should give Davis every chance to come to the League for a vote." But, in truth, on Super Bowl Sunday 1980, no one in the League felt he knew just what Al Davis intended to do.

That, of course, was just the way Al Davis wanted it.

30

Perhaps the most anxious of those watching Al Davis at the Super Bowl XIV festivities was Georgia Rosenbloom. The nervousness she'd projected to Rozelle over the phone during December had continued unabated. According to a source close to the Rams owner, some thirty to forty phone calls would be placed between Mrs. Rosenbloom and Rozelle during the first two months of 1980. Some were to Rozelle's office and others to his home in Westchester. Within a day of the commissioner's arrival at the Beverly Hills Hotel for the Super Bowl festivities, Georgia had called him twice. The gist of Georgia's end of the conversation was, according to her secretary's later testimony,

"The Raiders are coming. Why do we have to put up with this? How can it be handled?" Once again, Rozelle told her not to worry, "it would be handled."

There were, however, a lot of other things besides Al Davis on Georgia's mind during Super Bowl week. She and Rozelle also discussed tickets to the game. Georgia had more of them than anybody else in the country—a situation that would have made the late Carroll's mouth water. The Rosenbloom Rams had finally made it to a Super Bowl and as one of the participants, were allotted 22.5 percent of the game's 102,000 seats. Since the game was to be held in Pasadena, the Rams were the official host franchise as well, and as such, allotted another ten percent. That gave Georgia almost thirty-five thousand tickets with a face value of thirty dollars and a resale value of almost four times that much. In addition to being the single largest source of tickets, Georgia was also, according to *Time*, "the star" of the media hype that surrounded this year's NFL championship contest. Georgia nonetheless complained to Rozelle about her press coverage at regular intervals. She considered most things written about her "hatchet jobs."

However unfavorable, none of those stories questioned whether or not she ran the team. As Steve Rosenbloom had predicted, most of the holdovers from her late husband Carroll's organization were either gone or on their way out and Georgia was now charting her own course. One of the people she relied on for advice was her live-in personal lyricist, Dominic Frontiere. Another was Hugh Culverhouse, owner of the Tampa Bay Buccaneers and one of the executors of Carroll Rosenbloom's estate.

For the actual running of the team, Georgia relied on Don Klosterman, the most long-lived remnant of the C.R. days. Klosterman had been hired by Carroll in Baltimore, after Klosterman had worked for the Kansas City Chiefs and the Houston Oilers of the old AFL. Unlike Steve Rosenbloom, Klosterman welcomed the move to L.A. He had grown up in and around Compton and Lynwood with Pete Rozelle, whom he'd known since he was eleven years old. According to Steve, Klosterman was "a survivor. He's like a cat landing on his feet. He doesn't really work, he's just a PR guy who does a lot of name-dropping. He settled into a situation where the others do all the work. He didn't really fit in at either the Colts or the Rams. Eventually we just didn't involve him in things." Steve had wanted to demote or fire Klosterman after C.R.'s death, but his attempt to do so was the final incident before Georgia fired Steve instead. Klosterman was Steve's replacement. There was little doubt he knew upon which side his bread was buttered. "The press has vilified Georgia," he argued. "And what did she do? She made C.R. happy for twenty years."

One of Klosterman's immediate duties after assuming the reins from Steve was liaison with his old friend the commissioner over questions of Davis and an L.A. move. The two had discussed the subject on five or six occasions over the half-year leading to Super Bowl XIV. Klosterman would later claim that he never objected on behalf of the Rams to a Raiders move but did express his feelings that Davis should come to the League for a vote.

At the same time, Klosterman's public position was a little more nebulous. "There's the question of oversaturation of the market," he pointed out in September 1979. "We have four teams in California now. . . . There are other places—Phoenix, Indianapolis, Memphis, Charlotte, and Birmingham— worthy of consideration. Why not spread the wealth around?" Klosterman's private, unofficial position was apparently different as well. Shortly after the Raider banner incident at the L.A. Coliseum, according to one Rams source, Klosterman was fuming. "The fucking Raiders aren't going to make it down here," the Rams GM swore out loud, "no way."

Whatever his true feelings, Don Klosterman was likely of no small assistance to Georgia on the subject. She had only the barest grasp of the issues and strategies involved. Later she would claim she would have supported a Raider move if only Davis had been "nicer to me." When the LAMCC dropped its new legal bombshell on Friday of Super Bowl week, it registered only dimly on Mrs. Rosenbloom. Later, she could only "vaguely remember" the request for a preliminary injunction. She remembered her lawyer calling her with the news that "something" had been filed in conjunction with *LAMCC v. NFL*, but "did not understand what it meant." At the commissioner's party that evening, she claimed to have made no mention of it to Rozelle. Georgia did remember bringing up the subject to Gene Klein of Davis moving south, but Klein "just kind of shook his head and walked away."

Though it was the best role she'd ever played, Georgia was the first to offer that owning the Rams was no piece of cake. "Carroll always wanted the Rams to be fun for me," she claimed, "fun and profitable. That's why he was in it, that's why he gave me the club. I should be having fun. I don't know why I'm not."

One reason might have been the uncomfortable residue of the house-cleaning she'd begun by firing Steve six months earlier. It had generated a ton of bad press and public bitterness and the housecleaning was still continuing at the time of Super Bowl XIV. According to Rozelle, it gave rise to the most "bizarre" incident in the League's entire January sojourn in Los Angeles.

At the center of the incident was one Harold Guiver, C.R.'s "special assistant" and then "vice-president of operations." Guiver had taken a rather circuitous route to membership in the Ram family. From 1953 to 1963, he ran his own southern California real estate investment company and then retired to play on the international tournament bridge circuit. Although Guiver considered himself one of the best bridge players around, he was out of money by 1967 and returned to L.A. to go into partnership with the Lincoln Mortgage and Loan Company. He also became a partner in the Wilton Travel Agency in Long Beach. Harold Guiver and C.R. first got to know each other when Guiver began representing athletes and coaches in 1975. Rosenbloom and Guiver hit it off and, later that year, Rosenbloom helped Guiver finance a shopping center project. In late 1976, Carroll Rosenbloom touted Guiver to Al Davis as the man who could help them make a killing on the resale of Super Bowl tickets. C.R. began trying to recruit Guiver for the Rams around the same time as his discussion with Davis about scalping Super Bowl tickets, and by 1978, had succeeded. Mostly Guiver handled the negotiation of player contracts and similar chores. According to Don Klosterman, when Steve left and Klosterman assumed all the duties of general manager, Guiver was "no longer needed."

Harold Guiver had been a partisan of Steve in the Rams internal power structure and knew his days were numbered. By October 1979, the only question was whether he would resign or be fired. Guiver wanted to be fired, so the Rams would be forced to settle the employment contract C.R. had given him. Georgia wanted him to quit and said she would take care of him as Carroll would have. He ought to trust her, she argued, just like he would have trusted C.R. Guiver didn't, so he and Georgia ended up in negotiations that lasted throughout the fall. C.R.'s previous deal with Guiver contained a number of aspects besides just salary. To lure Guiver to the franchise, Rosenbloom had forgiven a $140,000 note, given him a Mercedes, and promised him a minimum of 1,000 Super Bowl tickets at face value any time the Super Bowl was held in Los Angeles. The biggest fight between Georgia Rosenbloom and Harold Guiver was over those tickets.

On October 24, according to Guiver's later testimony, Guiver met with her in her Bel-Air bedroom suite. At that meeting, according to Georgia, Guiver claimed that Steve Rosenbloom had promised him 3,000 to 4,000 tickets for the upcoming Super Bowl and "to avoid embarrassment" he needed at least 1,000. Mrs. Rosenbloom also claimed that Guiver "kept changing the terms" of the proposed settlement. According to Guiver, Georgia asked him how much Super Bowl tickets were worth. He said it was a matter of "speculation" but guessed $100 apiece, $70 more than their face value. Guiver also claimed that it was Georgia who kept changing the terms under which he would exit. On October 24, by both principals' accounts, a deal was reached. Georgia claims she wanted Guiver to record it verbally on a tape machine but he refused and instead suggested her attorney should draw up the agreement. According to Guiver, he drafted a letter of agreement by longhand that evening and signed it. The note he signed, which later became a trial exhibit, read:

> The Rams will honor the commitment for 1,000 Super Bowl tickets made to me by Carroll Rosenbloom, and after the death of Carroll reaffirmed to me by Steve Rosenbloom. I agree to reimburse the Rams for the cost of the tickets and enclose my check for $30,000 to cover cost of same. These tickets will be used to fulfill the commitment I have made. The tickets will [be delivered] before Dec. 20, 1979.
>
> Harold B. Guiver

Georgia Rosenbloom informed her lawyer of the Guiver conversations and told him that she wanted to get the League's permission to release 1,000 tickets to Guiver. To do so, she phoned Rozelle's office. A copy of Guiver's employment contract was on record there and, after checking with the League's attorneys, Rozelle returned her call. He told her that Carroll's verbal promise of Super Bowl tickets was not in the contract itself but since Steve had confirmed it, he didn't see how she could get out of it. Given that Guiver "would be using them for public relations, clubs, and officials he had promised them to," Rozelle saw "no problem" from the League's standpoint. Subsequent to her conversation with Rozelle, Georgia later acknowledged, Guiver delivered a $30,000 check to her attorney.

By November, according to Guiver, Georgia Rosenbloom had decided to change the terms. He claimed Georgia was now insisting on $100 a ticket instead of face value, an extra $70,000. She wanted Guiver to disguise the payment by agreeing to pay $22,000 for his Mercedes, a "gift" from C.R. the papers for which were still held by the Rams, and $48,000 on his $140,000 note, which he claimed Carroll had already forgiven entirely. Guiver resented the demand, later describing it as an attempt to extort, but agreed to her terms. That agreement was memorialized in a letter from Harold Guiver to Georgia Rosenbloom on November 13, 1979. Guiver agreed to pay the $22,000 car payment and $48,000 loan payment by February 1, 1980, and Georgia acknowledged the receipt of his $30,000 and promised 1,000 Super Bowl tickets would be delivered no later than December 20, 1979. They also acknowledged "there is no ill will between us" and agreed that "each of us will keep this agreement entirely confidential between ourselves." Georgia formally accepted the letter's terms and conditions on November 21. Guiver's advance Super Bowl tickets were delivered shortly thereafter.

By the time Super Bowl XIV moved into L.A., however, Harold Guiver felt Georgia had done less than she had promised and was upset by it. "You have violated the confidentiality clause on probably more occasions than I know," Guiver claimed to Georgia in a January letter later introduced as evidence in court records. "Someone very high in your organization said he knew I received 1,000 Super Bowl tickets in my settlement. A ticket broker told me the same thing and said he could supply locations. I denied any knowledge of this and the person in your organization said he could prove I was lying." Guiver was also offended at how he was being treated by the Rams. He was now, he pointed out, "persona non grata" and thought the treatment unfair. In his letter, Guiver claimed that when he'd called the franchise's office about getting tickets for the big party out in Pasadena celebrating the Rams' trip to the Super Bowl, Klosterman had not only vetoed his request, but did so in language that the secretary who dealt with Guiver was embarrassed to repeat. When Guiver obtained tickets to the Rams party from another source, Georgia was surprised to see him. "What's he doing here?" she asked.

Georgia Rosenbloom had her own worries about Harold Guiver. He was associated with her stepson Steve and the sniping between the Rosenblooms was by no means over. Despite admonitions from Rozelle to cease public comments, Steve was known to have been the source of a lot of information to the press about what had gone on inside the Rams. What to do about Steve had been a subject of discussion among Georgia and her advisers throughout the fall. That January, she may well have been worried that Guiver, too, was funneling derogatory information to the newspapers, though he steadfastly denied it. "I am sure you must know that I have not talked to the press or ever publicly criticized you," Guiver beseeched his former employer in his letter to her. "I have lived up to all the terms of the agreement, and the Rams have not!"

By far the most severe of those Rams violations, according to Guiver, happened on Friday, January 19, the day of the commissioner's giant press bash. It began when someone identifying himself as "Jack Catain" called Guiver at home and said he would like to meet him "on unspecified business matters." A year and a half earlier, Jack M. Catain Jr. had been identified by *The New York Times* as "a key conduit in laundering at least $10 million in organized crime money." The *Times* also claimed "numerous financial and personal links between Mr. Catain and leading organized crime figures or their associates from all over the country. In addition, Mr. Catain has been involved with some of them in such activities as extortion and loan shark-ing." Although Harold Guiver claimed that Jack Catain was a stranger to him, he agreed to meet him later at the Al Brooks Ticket Agency in the Los Angeles Hilton. The owner of the agency was one of Harold Guiver's best friends.

When Guiver arrived for the meeting, Catain had brought along another man whom he identified as "Cohen." Guiver described them both as "swarthy" looking. The three men met in private. According to Guiver, Catain and Cohen told him that someone in the Rams had "set the visit in motion" but that they were not "sent by the Rams." They also told Guiver "he did not want to know who sent them." Their message was simple. Whoever had sent them wanted Guiver to keep "his mouth shut" about the Rams. They also wanted Steve Rosenbloom to shut up as well. Guiver said he could speak only for himself, but that he had not said anything publicly against the Rams and promised he never would. Guiver later described Catain and Cohen in a trial deposition as being "gangsters" from the "Mafia" and claimed they had threatened his life before the meeting broke up.

Guiver made at least two phone calls in response to Catain's visit. The first was to Steve Rosenbloom. Steve said "they should see him if they had any problems." Guiver described Steve as "very upset."

The second phone call was to Pete Rozelle's Los Angeles hotel room on January 22, after Super Bowl XIV was over and Georgia's Rams had lost to the Pittsburgh Steelers, thirty-one to nineteen. Rozelle and his wife were scheduled to leave shortly for Hawaii and the League's final event, a Hono-lulu all-star game. Guiver arranged to meet with the commissioner at the hotel, along with Rozelle's in-house counsel, Jay Moyer. Their conference lasted forty-five minutes. Guiver told Rozelle and Moyer about his visit from Catain and Cohen and now claimed he had "documentation that they were bad people." He wanted Rozelle to talk to everyone and clear it up. Specifically, he wanted the commissioner to arrange for him to meet with Don Klosterman so they could "get things straightened out." According to Guiver, Rozelle was "incredulous," but called Klosterman with Guiver in the room. The commissioner asked Klosterman if he knew Catain and got a negative response. Then Rozelle explained to Klosterman what Guiver had been saying. "I said Guiver was distraught," Rozelle remembered, "he feels threats have been made against him, and he thought that Klosterman had something to do with it. I said I would like Klosterman to meet with him. Klosterman said 'Sure.' Don said he hadn't had anything to do with it. He didn't particularly like Guiver but hadn't encouraged anyone to threaten him."

Not long after leaving the commissioner's hotel room, Guiver met again with Jack Catain, this time at Guiver's instigation. They got together in Monty's Restaurant and Guiver again made it clear he had nothing bad to say about the Rams. Then he told Catain that if it was Klosterman who had sent him originally, he couldn't keep Klosterman from blaming him, but he was doing nothing. "Frightened," Guiver then asked Jack Catain to accompany him to his meeting with Klosterman the next morning "and judge for himself."

For that meeting on January 23, Catain again brought along his friend Cohen. They all arrived at Klosterman's apartment on Oakhurst Drive at 8:00 A.M. According to Guiver, Klosterman expressed surprise at Catain's presence. According to Klosterman, Catain was "uninvited" and Guiver told him he "was concerned people were talking about him in a degrading way." Klosterman claimed he said "let bygones be bygones" and that Catain started to say something but got no further. Klosterman interrupted Catain, said he was an uninvited guest and had nothing to say. Then Klosterman ended the meeting after it had gone on for no more than five minutes. He claimed to have been "very abusive" when speaking to Catain. According to Rozelle, Klosterman also claimed that Catain and Cohen had "threatened him."

In any case, Guiver, Catain, and Cohen left Klosterman's apartment almost immediately and neither Pete Rozelle nor Don Klosterman heard any more from them. Just who had originally dispatched them to shut Guiver up was never clarified. There would later be newspaper reports that Catain had been a guest in Georgia's owner's box, but those were adamantly denied by Dominic Frontiere, now her constant companion. He claimed Georgia did not know Catain at all and that Frontiere himself had heard of Catain only "in connection with his charitable works." Georgia herself had learned of Guiver's charges on January 21 from Rozelle at a birthday party for Don Klosterman in exclusive Jimmy's Restaurant in Beverly Hills. There, she claimed, Rozelle had told her that Guiver was coming to see him the next day and was already maintaining that Klosterman had sent someone from the Rams to "tell Guiver to keep his mouth shut or something would happen to him." Georgia told the commissioner it was a "ridiculous" claim.

Nonetheless, when Harold Guiver was looking for someone to complain to about the affair after it was over, he wrote a letter to Mrs. Georgia Rosenbloom, dated January 28, 1980. "Georgia," Guiver objected, "the person or persons in your organization who instigated this ought to be *very* ashamed of themselves. That is a *dirty, foul* way to act and the tragic part of the whole matter is that the complaints about me are mere figments of someone's imagination. The person who started this is not rational. Since I left, I have refused to talk to . . . anyone about Rams problems. . . . Georgia, I can't be more clear! I have *no* desire to cause trouble to anyone in the Rams organization and I want to be left alone by you, Don, and anyone else to whom I seem to be a problem. . . . I am very hurt by what has happened."

Although Guiver claimed Rozelle had promised to "look into it," he heard no more from the commissioner. Klosterman talked to Rozelle on the phone when the commissioner was in Hawaii and later sent Rozelle a formal memo about the incident, claiming he could not find out who had sent Catain. Klosterman also did an interview with the head of NFL Security. "It was absolutely bizarre," Rozelle remembered, "the entire situation." Nonetheless, the material Security accumulated went no further than a file in the League office.

By the time it had all been gathered, of course, Al Davis's Los Angeles front had broken open once again and Pete Rozelle had a lot more pressing questions to answer than where Jack Catain had come from.

31

While Pete Rozelle was talking with Harold Guiver, Al Davis was back in Oakland negotiating. On January 22, he met with a representative of Mayor Lionel Wilson's task force. The representative was Cornell Maier, head of Kaiser Industries. Maier and Davis had first met down in L.A. at the Super Bowl. After this talk, Davis remembered, "we started to have a meeting of the minds. . . . I was walking around thinking we had a chance to have a deal." That state of mind lasted through January. Davis had his attorneys meet with Kaiser Industries' attorneys to work on language and Davis himself made a tour of the Oakland Coliseum with its luxury box architect. On January 24, Davis announced that negotiations "have gone far enough" and that he now wanted Oakland to produce a formal offer to confirm his dealings with Wilson and Maier. That would have to come from the Oakland Coliseum board. Davis described the initial offer delivered in L.A. as "good" and it had subsequently been improved. "The Los Angeles offer is more substantial," Davis noted, "but what Oakland has going for it is great tradition." Once Oakland's formal offer was in hand, Davis intended to decide where he was going by February 5. "I think it has gone far enough," he offered. "It would be intelligent to get it done by then."

None of these developments was lost on Los Angeles. "This city is about to blow the Raider deal,'' Mel Durslag trumpeted in the *Herald Examiner*. "We've got a chance to get the Raiders. Al Davis is ready to move, believe me. But all he hears is promises, and promises aren't good enough for a smart businessman. Politicians are worried about some cost to the taxpayers but the only cost to the taxpayers here would be if the Raiders do not come to Los Angeles. A little city like Anaheim has the guts to assert itself and get the Rams while Los Angeles is left at the gate while politicians grandstand. Someone has to step forward now, pick up this issue, and run with it, but nobody has shown the guts to take the leadership. This city is losing the Raiders and deservedly so because elected public officials are sitting on their hands.''

The particular object (of Durslag's ire) was the Los Angeles County Board of Supervisors, whose $5 million loan was essential to pull off a Raider move. At their meeting on January 24, a number of supervisors had "complained that they had not been given adequate information about negotiations with the Raiders.'' One even went so far as to call the proposed expenditure on luxury boxes "inappropriate for a publicly owned stadium.'' The strongest opposition argument, however, was simply against going out on a limb. The Coliseum, the *Los Angeles Times* observed, "cannot consummate the deal with the Raiders unless they are certain the Raiders will be allowed to move. Otherwise, they say, they could wind up building the [luxury] boxes and be left without a team to pay for them if the Raiders were denied permission.''

By the first week after Super Bowl XIV, the League's growing anger at Al Davis was a public fact. "I object strenuously to unilateral action,'' Art Modell told the *Times*. "Either we have a structure, a constitution and bylaws, or we don't. Davis has had sellouts for thirteen years [in Oakland]. Maybe there are problems with the Oakland Coliseum Commission. We won't know it until we hear it, but it's wrong to litigate to get a franchise shift.'' Modell was by no means alone. Billy Sullivan took "a dim view'' of L.A.'s "trying to induce'' Davis. Herman Sarkowsky described Davis's approach as "totally wrong'' and claimed "most owners are like I am.'' Even Tex Schramm, who was close to Davis, admitted being "concerned.''

"By early January 1980,'' Davis claimed three months later, "the prospects of the Raiders and the Los Angeles Coliseum Commission reaching a mutually agreeable lease agreement looked very good. From that time, and continuing without interruption through the present, certain members of the NFL and from the commissioner's office, as well as the Oakland [Coliseum] commission, began a concerted campaign to intimidate and prevent the Raiders from transferring to Los Angeles. . . . From that time forward, I received a variety of threats and warnings from NFL Commissioner Pete Rozelle and from certain franchise owners, such as Eugene Klein of the San Diego Chargers and Mr. Sarkowsky of the Seattle Seahawks, that I had better not take any steps to move to Los Angeles without *prior* NFL approval. Mr. Klein, Mr. Sarkowsky, and Mr. Rozelle, among other NFL personnel, stated publicly on a variety of occasions that the Raiders could not obtain NFL approval of their transfer and would have to remain in Oakland.''

While the League's opposition may have still been less than a "concerted campaign" in late January, it was certainly a factor in Los Angeles's thinking. The odds against Davis winning an NFL vote were already considered sufficient to make signing a binding lease before he moved a political impossibility.

The League's known opposition was also a significant factor back in Oakland. There, it helped fuel a fatal counterattack against Wilson and Maier's approach to negotiations. The counterattack was opened by Jack Maltester on January 30. Maltester, president of the Oakland Coliseum board, claimed the mayor and Maier had given Davis a heretofore "secret" deal in which the Coliseum would end up giving so much away that it would have no option but to run in the red. Rumors put the offer in the $8 to $10 million range and Maltester claimed it included a $200,000 a year rent reduction, a flat payment of $1.5 million, and a $5 million loan spread over thirty years at six percent. The loan would be used to construct luxury boxes to which the Raiders would have title, but the loan would be guaranteed for the five years of the lease only, meaning the Raiders could walk away at that point and leave the Coliseum to pay it.

The Raiders responded to Maltester through Al LoCasale. "Jack Maltester has not been a party to negotiations for a number of weeks," LoCasale pointed out. "He is not an involved party in the negotiations and I don't want to give credence to what he says." Maltester's outburst was, however, only the opening round. There was more to come.

On February 1, the Oakland Coliseum board finalized its formal offer to Davis at a five-hour meeting in which Lionel Wilson and Cornell Maier were repudiated as negotiators. The offer was apparently at odds with the one to which Davis and Wilson had already agreed. The most significant change was in the length of the lease from five years to ten. On that same afternoon, Lionel Wilson and Cornell Maier visited Davis at his office near the Coliseum. Wilson and Maier, Davis remembered, "told me they were no longer the negotiating committee, that the offer would have to be withdrawn. They were sorry. They would issue a press release and say they were sorry that they were repudiated."

Sorry or not, Davis's response was immediate and decisive.

"No one in good conscience can question the lousy way we've been treated," Al LoCasale told *The Tribune* on February 2. "We've discovered that the credibility and integrity of the people the Raiders have been dealing with has not changed. It's been this way for twelve years—arrogance, procrastination, deceit, and misrepresentation." A Coliseum official pointed out in response that the Raiders had not even yet seen the Coliseum's offer but that apparently didn't matter. On February 3, the Raiders' PR director announced, "Negotiations are dead. I doubt we would even look at any new offer. Nothing will bring us back to the negotiating table with Oakland."

On February 4, that announcement was confirmed when a young attorney from the Oakland firm of Crosby, Heafy, Roach & May attempted to deliver the Coliseum's formal written offer. The document was some twenty pages long and the attorney took it to the Raiders' offices. Al LoCasale refused to accept the twenty pages and told the attorney to take them away with him. Instead, the attorney left the document on the counter and turned to go. At that point, according to Al Davis, LoCasale grabbed the document and "came over the counter," demanding that the young attorney take it back. When LoCasale chased him into the parking lot and he still wouldn't take it back, Al Davis's principal assistant flung the lease offer on the asphalt and left it there.

Oakland's twenty pages were retrieved from the Raiders' parking lot the following day and read by Davis, but at that point the reading was only a matter of curiosity. His attention was focused on maneuvering with the League.

On February 2, immediately after his visit from Wilson and Maier, Davis had called Rozelle. It was a Saturday and he reached the commissioner at his home in Westchester. Davis informed Rozelle that "Wilson and Maier had come to his office and said the offer they made was no longer available." According to the commissioner, Davis "then asked for a straw vote of the membership to find out where he stood" on the possibility of a Los Angeles move. Davis wanted the polling done over the phone as soon as possible.

Rozelle refused. "I told him that if I were to take a straw vote," Rozelle explained, "there were a number of questions the members would want to know [sic] before they even gave a straw poll opinion and I didn't think I was in a position to answer the questions that they had. I told him I would be happy to schedule League meetings so we could air the entire situation. . . . I urged him to call for a special League meeting. . . . I told him I couldn't call twenty-seven clubs on the telephone and tell them what was being considered . . . when I didn't have all the facts. I felt the best way was for him to ask for a League meeting."

Concerned that any such meeting would end up being used to hold a formal vote which he did not want, Davis requested none. Asked to characterize the way Rozelle treated him at this time, Davis allowed "at times he is pretty good and other times he is just as vindictive as can be." As evidence of this vindictiveness, Davis cited "his public pronouncements, long before I ever considered moving, that I shouldn't move, that I should stay in Oakland; his attitude when I called him on the phone and kept him abreast and [Rozelle's] not telling the other owners as to what I was doing. . . . Instead, [he] polarized them." Bill Robertson in L.A. shared Davis's assessment of the commissioner's attitude. "The League would have let Max Winter move," Robertson claimed. "This was a personality thing, Pete versus Al. Al was not a rubber stamp kinda guy and Rozelle saw him as a threat."

Rozelle steadfastly denied any such motivation. "It's easier for Al to say it's a fight between him and Rozelle than to say it's a fight between him and twenty-seven other owners who disagreed with him," the commissioner explained. "I enjoyed being with Al. The only difference I had with Al was on the League rules. You get a lack of unity, this disintegration, when one person can get away with violating the prime rule of the League. It also sets the stage for others to follow.''

Whichever characterization of Rozelle was accurate, he and Davis settled into an uneasy peace for several weeks after their February 2 phone call. Both were waiting to see how the federal district court would rule on Los Angeles's request for a restraining order on Section 4.3, filed the day of the commissioner's Super Bowl press party. Hearings on the request began on February 4 and lasted until February 21.

In the meantime, Al Davis continued his negotiations with Bill Robertson. Since a firm lease was impossible, the two had decided to draw up a memorandum of agreement that would frame the deal on paper. During Davis's final two-week flirtation with Oakland, the total Los Angeles commitment had grown to $18.5 million: $14.5 million for improvements, including ninety-nine luxury boxes and new locker rooms, press box, and practice facilities; $4 million for the Raiders' relocation expenses. According to the memorandum of agreement, $5 million was to be the county's loan, $5 million from the Olympic committee, and $8.5 million from the city of Los Angeles. The term of the lease called for in the agreement was seven years, with an additional five three-year options to be exercised at the Raiders' discretion. The memorandum also called for the Raiders to be "compensated for the expenses involved" if the League blocked their move. "I knew there was a risk involved to the Coliseum," Robertson acknowledged, but "I felt that this had to be part of the agreement." In truth, the risk to L.A. was slim as things stood.

Legally, the memorandum of agreement was little more than a nonbinding agreement to agree. "The matter was subject to the agreement of the board of supervisors," Davis explained, "which Mr. Robertson assured us was just a formality. [It] was [also] subject to the approval of the Coliseum board, which Mr. Robertson assured us was also just a formality." According to Davis, L.A. Supervisor Kenny Hahn claimed that "he had county approval of the agreement. He named the people, he named the votes." While it was unlikely Al Davis really accepted the notion that any political approval would be a "formality," the situation had intensified enough that he was now willing to accept such assurances. For most of February, the question was not whether Al Davis would sign Los Angeles's memorandum of agreement, but only when.

Pete Rozelle waited for the answer at the League offices in New York, where he continued to monitor the situation, and take phone calls from Georgia Rosenbloom. On some of those calls, Georgia asked her male secretary to listen in silently. Later the secretary would recall the phrases "we have fifteen teams on our side" and "we can depend on San Diego." The conversations in general were about all the votes Al Davis didn't have to support his move. A vote would be held, Rozelle assured Mrs. Rosenbloom, whether Davis requested it or not.

The forces that had been gathered during the first three weeks of February began to unleash themselves on February 21, when Los Angeles Federal

District Court Judge Harry Pregerson granted the LAMCC's injunction against Section 4.3. The League then immediately obtained a stay of Pregerson's order from the federal circuit court. Section 4.3 remained in force.

On February 22, Oakland weighed in with its own action in California Superior Court in Alameda County. Oakland claimed the right to condemn the Oakland Raiders football franchise under the same eminent domain law with which it condemned land for freeways and housing projects. It also sought and got a temporary restraining order preventing the Raiders from moving without a court hearing.

By February 26, Davis remembered, "I was pretty well set [on moving], but I wanted to be sure in my mind that this is the direction I wanted to go one hundred percent." About to risk everything, Al Davis had plenty of reason to pause. Rozelle was already on record threatening the possible loss of his franchise should he fail, and even his support in Los Angeles was already shaky. "No one else would have gone forward at that point," one source close to Davis pointed out, "but Al Davis is built different than the rest of the League. In truth, he didn't have anything he could count on except Bill Robertson." For Davis, that was apparently enough. "I'm going all the way if you are," he told Robertson.

At 1:00 A.M. New York time on Saturday, March 1, 1980, Georgia Rosenbloom called Rozelle's home in Westchester County to discuss the rumors circulating in Los Angeles. At 8:40 A.M. on that same day, Georgia's general manager, Don Klosterman, called Rozelle at home again to tell him the rumors were right. Davis was about to announce his move, Klosterman warned. He was going to sign the memorandum of agreement.

Less than five hours later, Davis did exactly that in the office of Los Angeles Mayor Tom Bradley. The press corps was there to watch the ceremony. Davis told them he had no intention of asking the League for a vote. He planned to move whether the League liked the idea or not.

The most decisive battle in National Football League history was about to commence.

"Al Davis has crossed the Rubicon," Bill Robertson crowed. "Al Davis has made a commitment. He can't go back to Oakland now."

PART FOUR
OPEN WARFARE

1

Pete Rozelle and Al Davis fought their first open skirmish at a special meeting of the NFL's executive session on March 3, 1980, at Dallas's Summit Hotel.

Though the NFL's 1980 annual meeting was scheduled for just a week later in Palm Springs, Rozelle was convinced that this business could not wait. The special meeting had been called by Telex on February 22 in response to the temporary restraining order granted the LAMCC in federal court. Then, on March 1, Al Davis had signed his memorandum of agreement with Los Angeles.

Davis himself had few doubts about what he was in for or how he would handle it. "We know it's going to be tough," he admitted on March 1. "There are going to be a lot of obstacles in the way, but I consider obstacles normal and treat them that way."

Though the coming fight was at its heart legal, Davis left his attorney, Joseph Alioto, behind in San Francisco when he flew to Dallas on March 2. "Al asked me if I would go to the Dallas meeting with him, " Alioto explained, "but I said no because we are not seeking litigation." Nonetheless, Davis was prepared. "Al should just say, 'Gentlemen, I'll take the Rosenbloom deal,' " Alioto noted. "We just want the same approval Rosenbloom got under similar circumstances. Rosenbloom signed his agreement with Anaheim, then had a press conference. Four months later the NFL approved the move. Saturday, Al signed an agreement with Los Angeles and held a press conference. Monday he will seek approval. The NFL is now in the position where if they continue their actions of interfering with that contract, they would be in line for a damage suit by the Los Angeles Coliseum involving millions of dollars. I think the NFL would be well advised to sit down and straighten things out right now because if they take any foolish actions, it could only become worse for them."

Pete Rozelle saw the issues as "apocalypse now." "The greater issue is anarchy," he noted. "The next step a team could take contrary to League rule could be to enter into a pay TV contract . . . or they could sell their team to General Motors or Caesars Palace."

The Dallas special meeting convened at 10:00 A.M. on March 3. The Raiders/Los Angeles "situation" was the primary item on the agenda. The twenty-eight owners had already been given the materials previously distributed at the Raiders' March 1 press conference and Xerox copies of subsequent press accounts of the Davis announcement. Rozelle himself had first seen the actual memorandum of agreement the previous evening after arriving at the Summit Hotel. His first order of business was to procure a further explanation from Davis himself.

Did Mr. Davis wish to make a report?

Mr. Davis was not then prepared to do so, but would consider doing so "after the lunch break."

That being the case, the commissioner noted, the morning would be used "to review the situation . . . so that [the League] could be advised of the legal developments and what options they had."

Quite specifically that meant a report on *LAMCC v. NFL,* a suit to which Rozelle now considered Davis, for all intents and purposes, a party. He was treated as such at Dallas. "Noting that an attorneys' report and discussion was a critical element in the meeting," the minutes reported, "and that in recent weeks the Oakland club had taken a position in the pending Los Angeles Coliseum suit adverse to that of the other clubs, the commissioner suggested, on advice of counsel, that the Oakland representative excuse himself while privileged legal matters were discussed. Mr. Davis then left the meeting."

For the rest of the morning the League and its attorneys discussed their options. At 12:45 P.M., they broke for lunch.

When they reconvened at 2:00 P.M., Al Davis was once again present. He was now, he said, ready to report. The minutes described Davis's speech as "a general recitation of his recollection of the Raiders' negotiating history in Oakland and with the Los Angeles Coliseum Commission, which culminated in the Raiders taking an adversary position in the pending litigation and signing a memorandum of agreement with the Los Angeles Coliseum Commission." According to the *Los Angeles Times,* "Davis talked for about half an hour. He said he told the owners he was 'committed to Los Angeles.' He said he had 'a traumatic feeling about leaving the fans in Oakland' but found himself in an 'untenable position' in negotiations with the Oakland Coliseum. . . . Davis said he thought many owners 'were receptive and wanted to hear me,' but added that it was nothing more than an impression."

Davis's speech was followed immediately with a question and answer period. Predictably, the first inquiries were from Rozelle. "I asked him two questions in front of the membership," Rozelle remembered. "I said, 'Do you intend to move to Los Angeles?' "

"Yes, of course," Davis answered.

Rozelle's second question was, "Do you intend to come to the League for a vote?"

"No," was Davis's second answer.

"I felt that brought it to a head," Rozelle said.

When the other owners' questions for Davis were finished, Rozelle initiated the League's response. Whatever Al Davis's attitude about submitting his move to a vote, "the commissioner commented that under the circumstances more complete information should be made available to the membership regarding all aspects of the proposed transfer, in the event a vote should subsequently be requested by the Raiders *or otherwise.*" To provide the member clubs with this "more complete information," he was appointing a fact-finding committee to investigate the situation and report to the annual meeting one week hence in Palm Springs. Since appointing committees was the commissioner's prerogative, no vote was needed. Rozelle "carried out one of the threats contained in [his] January 10, 1980, letter," Al Davis later attested. The committee he created was unprecedented. Based on my fourteen years' experience in the NFL, and to the best of my knowledge, at no time prior to the transfer by the Raiders did the NFL ever bother to create a fact-finding committee to pass upon the desirability of the transfer of any NFL team. Moreover," he continued, "and over my objections, it stacked that five-man committee with certain persons who were publicly avowed opponents of the Raiders' transfer."

"It was a tough committee to pick," Rozelle admitted. "It was hard to try and find someone with stature, time, and who wasn't already on record as antagonistic to Davis." The criteria the commissioner claimed to have used were whether prospective committee members "had time during the next week," were "knowledgeable in the matters to be investigated," and whether they were the "least objectionable to Al Davis." The group he came up with consisted of Art Modell, Herman Sarkowsky, George Halas, Wellington Mara, and Bill Bidwill. Sarkowsky was named chairman. Of the five-man committee, only Mara and Bidwill were not yet on public record opposing Davis's move.

After their appointment, Rozelle gave his fact finders their assignments. To Art Modell, because of his role on the TV committee, went the task of "ascertain[ing] the views of the three television networks." Because of his presence in New York, Wellington Mara would join him. To Sarkowsky, Halas, and Bidwill went the job of meeting with the L.A. Coliseum representatives to "hear their side of it," with Oakland's representatives to "learn what they were prepared to do," and with the Raiders to "obtain any information the Raiders wished to convey." As the commissioner explained, "I told the committee that it was not to make a recommendation but merely to report on what they had learned."

Al Davis didn't like the committee at all. "I felt it was an unfair committee," he remembered. "I told Rozelle so right there in front of the committee. . . . I said I don't like the composition of the committee. I don't think they are favorable to me. In roundabout terms, I alluded [to the fact that] it was a stacked committee."

Art Modell took umbrage at Davis's inference. "I assume you are referring to me," he interrupted.

Modell's assumption was reasonable. By his own admission, Art Modell had arrived in Dallas with "strong convictions." He already planned to vote against Davis's move, whenever a vote was held, because he felt such "casual moving would hurt the League's image." He also felt Davis was reneging on his contract with the League calling for him to play his games in Oakland and that the League had "a strong moral obligation" to Oakland for its previous support. Most important, Modell noted, he had yet to hear of "a single benefit to the NFL as a whole" from what Davis wanted to do. Modell was convinced any committee of five NFL members would reach the same conclusion.

"If Mr. Davis objects to me," Modell offered, "I will be happy to get off the committee." Perhaps there was someone Davis would rather have.

Al Davis did not fall into the trap. He understood full well that the more he involved himself in the committee's composition, the more credibility he would be giving its conclusions.

According to Rozelle, Davis gave "an unintelligible half-sentence answer" to Modell's offer to resign from the fact-finding committee. "Mr. Davis sometimes speaks in half-sentences," the commissioner explained. "I believe he said something to the effect of, 'Oh, that's all right.' He may have said 'No, that's all right,' or 'It's all bad anyway' or something."

Davis's version was somewhat different. According to him, Rozelle himself was the first to respond to the Cleveland owner's offer.

"No," the commissioner said to Modell, "you stay on."

Then Davis spoke up. "Look," he said to Rozelle, "you picked your committee. You go ahead."

After that, there was nothing left to discuss.

2

That Al Davis's first combat with Rozelle involved Art Modell as well came as no surprise. Davis knew that any attack on the commissioner would be parried by Rozelle's lieutenants, and since Tex Schramm was somewhat neutralized by his relationship with Davis, Modell, who would increasingly become identified as Rozelle's alter ego, bore the brunt. Butting heads with Al Davis was not an altogether unwelcome task for Modell. The Cleveland owner's description of his relationship with Davis as "fair" was an overstatement of major proportions. Al Davis's contempt for Art Modell's pack-running was now obvious and Art Modell's contempt for Al Davis's free-lancing was equally clear. Modell also resented Davis's insistence on going after his friend Rozelle rather than the League as a whole. "Davis tried to make it all a personal issue with Pete," Modell explained, "and Pete's just not that way." Modell was also drawn to the defense of League Think by his own reverence for the League as an exclusive club. "Before Davis," he pointed out, "the constitution was our court and we washed our linen in private."

By the time of the Dallas meeting, Modell had reached the pinnacle of his standing in his adopted home of Cleveland. In 1980, he had already been mentioned as a possible Republican party candidate for lieutenant governor of Ohio and, within a year of his exchange with Davis in Dallas, his name would come up as a possible candidate for governor. To his home in Waite Hill he

had added a vacation house in Palm Beach. As well as owning a majority of
the Browns and eighty percent of Cleveland Stadium Corp., he now had
significant holdings in American Metal Forming Company, the Premier Electric
Company, and the Bede Aviation Corp. He had also founded the Whitney
Land Company to develop some of the acreage in Strongsville he had sold to
Stadium Corp. and had invested heavily in oil and gas leases with Marvin
Davis, a Denver oil millionaire and a close friend. He also owned WJW
Radio with two partners. Whenever Modell's name was linked to political
rumors, his success as a businessman was always cited. In 1978, he had been
appointed vice-chairman of the Greater Cleveland Convention and Visitors
Bureau and in late 1979, after the city went into financial default, he had been
named to the municipal financial supervision board charged with making
Cleveland solvent.

Despite that public acclaim, there was, by 1980, a certain amount of
illusion to Art Modell's apparent financial success, even if Cleveland had yet
to pick up on it. His radio station had lost money for three consecutive years
and the Whitney Land Company had gotten nowhere with its Strongsville
development. American Metal Forming seemed healthy but, in truth, was just
two years away from a collapse that would cost Modell at least $400,000. The
Premier Electric Company had already gone belly-up in 1979, costing Modell
$1 million. The Bede Aviation Corp. had turned a profit, but largely due to a
successful lawsuit against Grumman Corp. By March 1980, Art Modell's net
worth apart from his holdings in the football business had already dropped
substantially and showed little sign of changing course.

Modell's most worrisome investment that spring was Cleveland Stadium
Corp. In 1979, it had reported a $180,000 post-depreciation loss, down from
a $330,000 profit the year before. Two more losing years would follow. "It's
literally a nonprofit organization," Modell claimed in 1980. Later, he would
remember, "I was really becoming concerned about the viability of the
Stadium Corp. project." According to the corporation's treasurer, Stadium
Corp. had been able to make the principal payment on its loan only once in
the previous six years. In the other five, the loan was refinanced and rolled
over. One reason, *The Cleveland Press* noted, was that "the forty-seven-year-
old stadium, built on constantly settling landfill, has required far more
maintenance than originally projected." The previous winter, part of the
stadium's roof had blown off and before that, the pipes froze and burst, the
main concourse sank, and the remodeling work already done had uncovered
even more rusted-out support beams. All of that was costing Modell $200,000
a year more than he'd planned. Another reason for Stadium Corp's financial
shakiness was the failure of the baseball Indians, its second tenant, to draw
more than one million paying customers. Had they drawn two million, the
corporate treasurer claimed, "we'd be out of the woods."

By far the biggest reason for Modell's 1980 worries was interest rates.
He had borrowed significantly to finance the stadium improvements and
Stadium Corp.'s acquisition of his Strongsville land, and that borrowing now
haunted him. "When I entered into my arrangement with the banks," he

noted, "we borrowed at one point over prime. It was fine when it was 6.5 percent prime, but now I'm paying twenty-one percent on $8 million . . . and it's strangling us." Specifically, the interest payments on Stadium Corp.'s rolled-over loans had risen from $400,000 a year to $1.2 million. In addition, Modell was also servicing almost $7 million of personal borrowings from banks and "other lenders." "It just never occurred to me to negotiate for a fixed rate or get a cap placed on the loan," he explained. "Who thought in 1973 that interest rates would be going to twenty percent?"

The value of his controlling share in the NFL Browns insured that Art Modell's assets still significantly outdistanced his liabilities, but he was nonetheless cash poor. To help relieve the pinch, Modell regularly drew interest-free cash advances throughout the year from the Browns, above and beyond his $60,000-a-year salary. At the end of the year, he would deduct the annual bonus voted him by the Browns board from the amount he had advanced himself and "settle accounts." To do so in 1980 had required borrowing $1 million from Cleveland's Union Commerce Bank. By then, Modell was actively considering ways to get out from under the burden of Stadium Corp.'s interest payments. His first attempt was at a breakfast meeting with Cleveland's new mayor, George Voinovich.

"George," Modell offered, "if the city has the wherewithal to reimburse me all my costs, you can have the lease back for $1 and I'll stay here with the Browns."

Voinovich declined.

By the time the League met in Dallas, Modell was considering the possibility of selling Stadium Corp. "I wasn't feeling too good," he claimed, "and I was concerned about my estate." His first thought was to have the Browns purchase Stadium Corp. from him, but, in 1980, he took no steps to pursue that possibility.

Despite his financial pressures and concerns for his health, Art Modell handled his fact-finding committee duties with dispatch during the week before the annual meeting in Palm Springs. He and Wellington Mara met first with ABC, the League's Monday night prime time broadcaster. The ABC representatives, according to Modell, "were reluctant to become involved in the NFL's problem" but did allow that they would "not be happy" if Monday night football ended up blacked out in Los Angeles as a consequence of Davis's move. CBS met with Modell and Mara the same day. Their attitude was much the same as ABC's only they were "even more reluctant to engage in any dialogue" over Al Davis's plans for Los Angeles. NBC offered that "it would be a plus to have another representative team in the L.A. market," but made "no recommendation" one way or the other.

At the same time Modell and Mara were convening with the networks in New York, the other three members of the fact-finding committee were carrying out their chores on the West Coast. Herman Sarkowsky handled the logistics for that part of the operation. For health reasons, George Halas sent his general manager, Jim Finks, to represent him. Bill Bidwill represented himself. Davis sent his lieutenant, Al LoCasale, to talk to them and then the committee met with Oakland and Los Angeles. The L.A. meeting took place over lunch. "We went through a charade," Los Angeles's attorney remembered. "The lunch was a joke. There was no warmth but no unpleasantness either. Everyone was being polite, going through the motions. It was absurd, an obvious farce. It was just done so they could make a report and say Davis shouldn't move." Bill Robertson felt the same way. "It was a *Playhouse 90* that Pete put together," the LAMCC negotiator claimed. "It was like dealing with someone who has all the cards and their marching orders. We wasted a couple of hours and were stupid enough to pick up the check."

By the time Los Angeles and the fact-finding committee broke bread together, it was obvious to all concerned that the League had no intention of waiting for the committee's report. Neither, of course, did Al Davis. Instead, Rozelle had launched a new attack as soon as the Dallas meeting was over and Davis had responded in kind.

The attack was *Philadelphia Eagles et al v. Oakland Raiders Ltd.*, a suit filed on March 4 by NFL attorneys in Oakland's superior court, charging Davis with breach of contract and asking that he be restrained from moving his franchise. Eventually, it would also ask that Davis's franchise be removed from his control and placed in receivership. "We wanted to stop their action," Rozelle explained, "and we took every step we could think of to achieve that." All twenty-seven franchises were party to the action though just why Leonard Tose's was picked to lead the list was never fully explained. A likely explanation was that Tose, like Davis, was represented by Joseph Alioto and the overlap might well force Alioto to rule himself out over a conflict of interest. "We were all kind of surprised it was the Philadelphia Eagles who instituted the lawsuit," Davis remembered, "because the Philadelphia Eagles have always espoused that I should have the right to move. . . . I was told it was instituted to see if they could put pressure on my attorney. . . . The Eagles themselves didn't know that their name was put on the top of it." According to Davis, the step had been taken by Chuck Sullivan and one of the League's Covington and Burling attorneys.

According to Pete Rozelle, *Philadelphia Eagles v. Oakland Raiders Ltd.* was a step a number of League members had been pushing since before Dallas. "Many owners were urging such action right up to the time of the [special] meeting," he claimed, but "I said . . . I think it's important to give Al Davis every opportunity to ask for a vote." Even so, Rozelle had prepared for other contingencies. He had already retained an attorney in Oakland on behalf of the League and warned him "that we might wish to file a suit if Mr. Davis does not come to the League for a vote." During the privileged legal discussion in Dallas, Rozelle did not mention that specific suit, but asked for and was given "clear authorization to do whatever I see fit to stop the Raiders from doing this and violating the constitution." When Davis refused to request a vote, Rozelle consulted with the League's attorneys immediately after the meeting and decided to file a state court action on breach of contract the next day. The papers for doing so had already been drawn up. The rest of the League was notified by Telex after the suit had been filed.

"It was a directly related attempt to move the lawsuit out of the theater it belonged in," Al Davis objected. "It was just another attempt to bring more attorneys into the case to put pressure on me financially. . . . There was no breach of contract. . . . There was no reason for the receivership."

On March 6, while receivership motions were still being prepared, the judge in *Philadelphia Eagles v. Oakland Raiders Ltd.* granted a temporary restraining order barring the Raiders from actually setting up shop in Los Angeles. At that point, according to Davis, two private detectives on retainer to the NFL had been staking out Raider headquarters, watching "every move that the organization made," for several days.

But Al Davis was still one step ahead.

Before the temporary restraining order in the *Eagles* suit was issued, Davis dispatched a March 6 telegram to Pete Rozelle saying he had already moved.

> This communication is to notify you respectfully that the Raiders have legally and formally moved to Los Angeles. Our contract with the Los Angeles Coliseum is in precisely the same posture as the Rams at the time they held their widely covered press conference in July 1978, announcing their move to Anaheim. Moreover, the statements at our press conference were in substance similar to theirs. In fact, our move is in the same posture as all other recent moves. The Rams and the others were not charged with fomenting anarchy . . . nor should we be so charged in following their example. Our love and dedication to professional football . . . will continue to endure. The facts are that the Oakland politicians have effectively closed out negotiations by repudiating their own negotiators and their commitments as well as resorting to tactics favoring sham litigation. But in any event, it is imprudent in the highest degree in all of these circumstances to deny the historic Los Angeles Coliseum a right to life after the League itself ratified the Rams' move from Los Angeles County to the different world of Orange County.
>
> I trust that you will view our actions in the same spirit that you viewed the others.
>
> Sincerely,
> Al Davis

When Alameda County sheriff's deputies arrived at the Raiders' Oakland offices on March 6 to enforce the restraining order, the only items left to impound were the telephones. All the rest of the Raiders' business was loaded in vans that had long since left for the University Hilton in Los Angeles, where Davis had rented a temporary headquarters.

A [Oakland] *Tribune* reporter found Davis in the lobby of the dark and abandoned building that evening, looking "bleary-eyed, his tousled hair flopped over his forehead, and he sported several days' growth of beard on his chin."

"I feel a lot of nostalgia about it," Davis offered in a soft voice. "I've lived here for eighteen years. I love Oakland and the fans, I really do. I feel passive about it. I just think that you take a certain direction in life and you make things happen and you hope it all works out for the best. You anticipate the roadblocks and see various ways around them and you make it happen."

3

The 1980 annual meeting was held at Marriott's Rancho Las Palmas resort outside Palm Springs. Pete Rozelle arrived there with Carrie late on the afternoon of Saturday, March 8. Their bungalow was very close to that given Al Davis. On Sunday, Davis was sitting out on his veranda, near the weight lifting equipment he'd brought along for exercise, and saw Art Modell go into Rozelle's quarters. Davis continued to occupy his vantage point and would later claim that Gene Klein, Don Klosterman, Wellington Mara, Bill Bidwill, and Chuck Sullivan consulted with the commissioner as well. Most of those meetings, according to Rozelle, were brief.

The longest was with Herman Sarkowsky, chairman of the fact-finding committee, who, Rozelle remembered, "told me that based upon . . . what they had been told and what they had seen in the way of papers, he felt there probably was some fault on both sides [of the Oakland-Davis negotiations]." Sarkowsky also reported that the television networks "did not want to get very involved."

Perhaps the most telling of the commissioner's Sunday consultations, at least in terms of Rozelle's strategic intentions, was his talk with Chuck Sullivan. Rozelle told Billy's son that he was through waiting for Davis to ask for a vote. There was, he explained, "no language in the constitution that states how and by whom a motion for the transfer of a franchise may be made." Whether Davis wanted it or not, Rozelle "intended to see that a vote was taken." According to the commissioner, Chuck Sullivan was in accord with his intention, and offered to make the motion whenever Rozelle wanted the vote.

Pete Rozelle opened the annual meeting in general session at 10:00 A.M. the following morning. The first item of business was the commissioner's annual report and, as usual, it was full of superlatives. Regular season live gate had passed thirteen million for the first time in history, an average of 58,848 a game. Super Bowl XIV in Los Angeles had drawn an audience of more than one hundred million, making it the most-watched sporting event in the history of television. His report was followed by a long report from Tex Schramm and the Competition Committee. During much of the morning session, small groups of owners caucused on the side in preparation for the afternoon's executive session at which Al Davis was to be discussed.

Davis himself spent a good portion of the morning on his veranda, holding court with selected reporters. He claimed his team had sold more than thirty thousand season tickets during its first five days of business in Los Angeles and rented seventy of its projected ninety-nine luxury boxes. "I'm not for anarchy," Davis offered in his own defense. "I love the NFL. But I'll be damned if I'm going to let those Oakland people hold me hostage."

Back at the general session, according to *Sports Illustrated,* the commissioner "already looks tired and it's only Monday." Eventually, Rozelle left the meeting room for a cigarette, was cornered by reporters, and used the opportunity to fire his opening salvo. "Al says he's not for anarchy and I'm sure he wants a stable League," the commissioner pointed out. "He just wants anarchy for himself. I don't know why he didn't seek League support when he was having trouble over his lease with the politicians in Oakland, and I know his trouble was very legitimate then. I don't know why he didn't let the other owners know what was happening. When Bob Irsay had a problem in Baltimore, I had a meeting with the governor and the mayor. They said they'd move on it. Same thing in Minnesota last year. The Vikings are going to play in a new domed stadium in 1982. There are ways of working these things out and if you can't, then you go to the other owners. They know what stadium problems are like. But Al chose to do things his own way. I guess the carrot was just too big down there in L.A."

The League's executive session finally convened at 1:45 P.M. The first item of business was a legal report on the Davis move. Since its content was "privileged," Davis was immediately asked to leave until the League's lawyers were finished. At 3:50 P.M., Davis was readmitted to the meeting. Next on the agenda was the report by Herman Sarkowsky's fact-finding committee.

Art Modell and Wellington Mara led off with a description of the television end of the committee's investigation. According to Rozelle, "the television report was inconclusive because the networks said . . . we don't want to tell you how to run your business. In effect they said, 'You take your chances.' " Davis interpreted Modell's report as "they didn't want to get into it. . . . The only thing some of them were concerned about [was] whether we could sell out in Los Angeles."

At that point, he raised his hand and interrupted. "I assured him," Davis remembered. "The applications [for tickets in L.A.] were so great that they would be sold out."

Mara went slightly further than Modell. He, Rozelle remembered, "said that one or more of the networks . . . expressed concern about this entire situation if the League was not going to have control over where its franchises were located. They expressed concern for the future." As Al Davis remembered it, Mara held up a copy of the NFL's constitution, and said the networks' concern was for the future of "this little book, this constitution and bylaws."

"I was shocked," Davis claimed. "[What Mara] came back with was that the networks were interested in preserving our constitution, that little book. That is what they were interested in. And that they were concerned that someone might be violating the constitution and bylaws."

Next, Herman Sarkowsky "reviewed meetings and conversations with interested people in Oakland and Los Angeles." To accompany his presentation, he had large display graphs of Oakland's offer but none of Los Angeles's. "Sarkowsky had a note pad," Davis remembered, "and he read off about his meeting with the Los Angeles people and he discussed the character of Robertson and Reinhardt [L.A.'s attorney]. . . . He told what they were going to offer and it was a very fine deal and it was a very lucrative deal, and he brought in the fact that they kind of threatened [that] if [the League] didn't go along, [the League] would be sued. Then [Sarkowsky] went into the meeting with the Oakland people. And it was very subjective. It was not all the facts that were given to them."

"Does Oakland wish to be heard on this?" the commissioner asked Davis when Sarkowsky was finished.

The answer, of course, was yes. Al Davis stood and cut loose. His remarks were addressed to the fact-finding committee who had collected this report. "I told them that the thing was totally subjective," Davis claimed, "that I didn't like it and it wasn't fair. . . . I told them . . . in no uncertain terms, that they are not men. . . . I told Modell that I didn't appreciate what he had done. . . . I didn't think he acted with any courage or truth. Sarkowsky, I told to his face I didn't appreciate what he did because I didn't think he did an honest job. Mara, I never said a word [to] about it. I understand Wellington. . . . Bidwill at least had the courage to tell someone that he hated to do it but he did it."

Davis went on to the subject of the deals available to him. "I thought it was an unfair report," he continued, so "I explained to them about my negotiations with . . . Cornell Maier and Mayor Wilson and how they were repudiated and . . . went into the reason why I thought I ought to be allowed to move to Los Angeles." At this point, "some gentleman from Buffalo, an attorney, Halpern, stood up and said, 'Mr. Davis, are you going to abide by this constitution and bylaws? Are you going to ask for a vote?' And I said I didn't think a vote was necessary. He [again] said, 'Are you going to ask for a vote?' I said, 'I tell you what I will do, as we so often do in this membership. Commissioner Rozelle, you poll the members. A straw vote. And see what the vote will be. . . .' I said I am not going to ask for a vote if I can't get a polled vote."

Rozelle turned quickly to his legal counsel seated nearby. The lawyer recommended against any straw vote. It was a conclusion Rozelle himself had already reached. "The Rubicon had been crossed," he explained. Davis "had already sent me a message on March 6 saying that the Raiders were now the

Los Angeles Raiders . . . and he said he . . . would not submit to the League." As Rozelle saw it, Davis was asking for a privilege he had already forfeited. Rozelle also claimed that he made no recommendation on the move himself, but "just chaired the meeting and acknowledged people that [sic] wanted to speak, attempting to move the meeting along."

According to Rozelle, virtually everyone who spoke offered arguments against Davis's move. "There were a variety of reasons expressed," the commissioner remembered. "One was the theory of self-governance. They felt that having a team move without a vote . . . was a very unhealthy precedent for the League. . . . Two, the business uncertainties, because the matter had not been carefully explored. . . . The other uncertainty was [that] Oakland had been selling out in Oakland and Los Angeles, when the Rams played in the Los Angeles Coliseum, has not been selling out. . . . Also . . . the League had the right to derive the benefits of an expansion franchise . . . in Los Angeles. I think an expansion franchise in Los Angeles would be worth more than the other cities in the League. . . . That money should be shared by the twenty-eight partners and they felt that they would be precluded if Oakland took it." On top of that, "a number of them were concerned about what they felt was the erosion of goodwill for the League to have a team that had sellouts at the gate . . . leave it because it could do better elsewhere."

Perhaps the most emotional of the speeches was delivered by George Halas, dean of the Old Guard. Halas, now eighty-five, leaned heavily on the nurse who was constantly at his side. "He brought up stories from the 1920s and 1930s," Rozelle recalled, "to illustrate some early problems the League had on violations and how they were handled. . . . He was very concerned about the preservation of the solidarity of the League as represented by, in his mind, observance of the constitution. He was very upset that a team would attempt to move from its location without asking for a vote and then just saying, as the Raiders did on March 6, that they had already moved. And he said that he could foresee deep problems for the League in the future if that sort of conduct were to be condoned."

When Halas was done, Chuck Sullivan took the floor and called for a vote. The resolution he offered was "whether the transfer of the Oakland franchise from Oakland to Los Angeles should be approved pursuant to Article 4.3 of the constitution and bylaws." Rozelle would later admit that he knew Sullivan was going to make such a motion but denied having personally asked him to do so. That chore had been handled by one of the League's attorneys.

Though he knew Rozelle and Sullivan had met on Sunday before the annual meeting convened, Al Davis claimed the move took him by surprise. "Is this a legal motion?" he asked. "I never heard of someone else being able to ask for a vote," Davis explained. "The commissioner led me to believe that no one could ask for a vote without asking me. Chuck did it and someone else seconded it." For his part, Rozelle confirmed its legality.

Before any votes could be cast, however, Leonard Tose attempted to intervene. He said he had an idea he wanted to discuss, but that would require a "privileged conversation." At that point, Davis remembered, Rozelle "asked me to leave, and he said, 'Will you come back when I am done?' and I said, 'I will think about it.'. . . . I said, 'Look, I will leave the room if you people want me to leave,' and . . . I left the room. . . . I thought the whole meeting was orchestrated. . . . I was called after I left and told I could come back and I said, 'No, I don't want to come back.' "

With Al Davis out of the room, Leonard Tose spoke to the membership about the need to explore compromise and find a peaceful settlement. His proposal was that Davis be allowed to move but fined $1 million for doing so. After brief consideration, Rozelle remembered, "the consensus was that they did not feel that would be a satisfactory solution." Some even doubted Tose's motives. "At the time," Gene Klein remembered, "Davis was close to Tose. Tose was just being his stooge."

Whatever his motives, the vote was only briefly delayed. Davis was notified of what was about to happen, but stayed on his veranda. He considered the outcome a foregone conclusion and claimed the owners "were inflamed by someone before the vote."

The actual polling took forty-five minutes and included a number of explanatory speeches.

Art Modell voted "no" for reasons everyone was by now familiar with.

Tex Schramm also voted "no," but was ambivalent. He told Rozelle that "he would have voted for it if the Raiders had properly submitted it to the League," but as it was, "he felt that an opposition vote would support the constitution, which he felt strongly about."

Gene Klein's negative vote was delivered in no uncertain terms.

Billy Sullivan voted the Patriots' "no" after delivering an address describing how the first game in Oakland had been played at a high school and how "the franchise had been developed and supported there. . . . He did not feel it was proper to pull the franchise."

Don Klosterman, representing Georgia Rosenbloom, abstained "upon advice of counsel."

Eddie DeBartolo abstained for similar reasons.

Leonard Tose abstained because he still thought his plan was the best.

Paul Brown of the Cincinnati Bengals also abstained without explanation.

The only "yes" vote was cast by the Miami Dolphins, represented by Joe Robbie's son Mike. After the vote was tallied, however, Mike changed his family's vote and abstained. "I voted yes on the question of whether he should be allowed to move," the younger Robbie explained. "I thought he should, but within the constitution. I changed my vote because if that's what the League wanted, I might as well go along."

The vote as recorded was 0 yes, 22 no, 5 abstenations, and one absent, and the March 10 executive session adjourned at 6:20 P.M. It was apparent to all concerned that the National Football League had now crossed a Rubicon of its own.

Afterward, Al Davis doubted the League's capacity to make the fight to which they'd committed themselves. "We'll see what happens when this thing gets down to punitive damages," Davis sneered. "You'll see how many guys will back down rather than fight."

Dan Rooney gave the League's answer. "I think he'll find that we're committed to go all the way on this thing," the Pittsburgh owner predicted. "Our constitution, our whole League, is at stake."

The coming conflict was now impossible to avoid. "It's a case of NFL capitalism vs. NFL cannibalism," one franchise executive observed. "The League will remain firm and not back down. Davis will remain firm and not back down."

"What does this mean?" the executive was asked.

"Hardball," he answered, "all the way."

4

The National Football League had a lot of throw weight at its disposal in this "hardball" game. Al Davis felt the impact on his Los Angeles front as soon as the March 10 vote had been reported in the papers. There, the League's official disapproval collapsed the fragile coalition on the board of supervisors that Bill Robertson had spent months building.

Even before that vote, however, the Los Angeles County Board of Supervisors had become something of a political quagmire for Al Davis and his memorandum of agreement. For that agreement's terms to have substance, the board had formally to approve a $5 million loan to the LAMCC *in fact,* rather than *in principle* as it had in January. Securing that approval proved an embittering experience for a number of those involved. "Everybody gave their assurances to Davis," one Los Angeles participant noted, "but nothing happened with any of them. Once we started dealing with the supervisors, we found we couldn't count on them. Hahn had promised to deliver, and in the end we couldn't even count on Hahn. Everybody was taking a new position each day and the board ended up being used as a forum from which to launch attacks on Davis."

The first of those "attacks" had been launched even before Davis signed his memorandum of agreement. Its author was Supervisor Baxter Ward. On January 14, Ward had been the lone dissenting vote against approving the loan in principle, arguing at the time that it wasn't a proper use of public funds. "In mid-January," he informed the board in a motion filed later that month, "I became aware of rumors circulating that there was at least one business relationship between Al Davis, principal owner of the Oakland Raiders, and Alan [sic] Glick, who is said to be the subject of various federal investigations." Ward then suggested that the LAMCC "should ask Mr. Davis for a forthright statement regarding the allegations."

On February 26, Davis was invited to a meeting of the board of supervisors to discuss Glick and other subjects, but Al LoCasale declined over the phone, citing the limitations placed on the Raiders by the restraining order then in effect from the city of Oakland's recently filed eminent domain suit. According to a memorandum on the conversation filed by Los Angeles County's chief administrative officer, "Mr. LoCasale also indicated that Mr. Davis wants to inform the board of his business relationship with Mr. Al Glick, namely: that Mr. Davis is a limited partner and investor in an Oakland shopping center, of which Mr. Glick is the general partner. Mr. LoCasale indicates that that is the extent of their association and that the association is winding down. Mr. LoCasale stated that any implications of wrongdoing would be totally irresponsible."

Baxter Ward found the explanation insufficient and at the meeting Davis declined to attend, Ward offered a resolution. "Clearly," his motion read, "it should be within keeping with public policy to inquire into the relationship between a key figure in the current Coliseum transaction and a person who is reputed to be 'the Chicago mob's main front man in Nevada and California.' . . . THEREFORE, as a matter of civic responsibility, I MOVE that the board of supervisors request the district attorney to inquire into the allegations and prepare a public report as to their truth or falsity." The motion to inquire was passed.

Al Davis considered Ward's attack to be a form of character assassination. "It's the same old stuff," he later commented. "A long description of Allen's notoriety and no real link between us. I'm a limited partner at twenty-five percent. The thing isn't worth much. It's losing money. It's a hell of a tax shelter. As soon as the tax ramifications are worked out, I'll divest. Look, it's a well-to-do shopping center in a black neighborhood near the [Oakland] Coliseum. It was built by the Teamsters. Allen got a good deal on it—that was before the notoriety. Some of our former players work there and help run it." Davis also refused to cooperate with Ward's investigation. On March 3, the Los Angeles County counsel wrote him at the Oakland headquarters he was preparing to abandon and asked the Raiders' owner to release information from his tax returns to L.A.'s district attorney. The letter was not answered.

Despite his persistence, Ward was a fringe player on the board and would likely have remained isolated if the only issue were whether or not the L.A. Coliseum's new tenant had a relationship with a Las Vegas gangster. The board did nothing when Davis refused to cooperate with the district attorney, in effect letting the investigation die.

Of much greater concern to the other four supervisors was the League's vote on March 10 and Rozelle's subsequent announcement that the NFL would refuse to schedule any Raiders games in Los Angeles. Bill Robertson noticed the effect on March 11. "I talked to some politicians," he remembered, "and they were extremely skittish as a result of that." And their skittishness could not have come at a worse time. That same day, the supervisors were scheduled to have a second and final reading of the proposal to loan $5 million to the Coliseum. On March 12, the first payment of moving expenses to Al Davis under the terms of the memorandum of agreement was due and if it was to be made, board approval on March 11 was essential. When the meeting convened, however, it was obvious to Robertson that his base had eroded significantly. Robertson and Coliseum Attorney Stephen Reinhardt did their best to reverse the slippage but had little success.

The two votes they were losing belonged to Supervisors Yvonne Braithwaite Burke and Ed Edelman. "Despite my strong belief that Los Angeles County would benefit by the proposed arrangement," Burke explained, "I have had to seriously reassess my position in light of recent actions taken by the NFL. I have learned through public media coverage and otherwise that the NFL recently voted twenty-two to nothing against approving the transfer of the Raiders to Los Angeles and that in connection with that vote the NFL has taken the position that it will refuse to schedule or play any games against the Raiders in Los Angeles. Obviously, if the Raiders are not able to play their home games in Los Angeles, many of the benefits which I believe justify the county's commitment of $5 million would not materialize. Because of the NFL's threatened boycott, and the concerns which that engendered, I acted with Supervisors Ward and Edelman to oppose the immediate commitment of certain county funds called for by the memorandum of agreement."

Edelman's objections were similar. "Suppose the Raiders don't get here?" he asked Robertson and Reinhardt. "What happens to that $5 million?" Edelman didn't go for Robertson's answer that Los Angeles had to take some risks too. Instead, he introduced a resolution "forbidding any advance of county money until the Los Angeles Olympic Organizing Committee first puts up the $5 million it pledged as part of the package to lure the Raiders to Los Angeles."

Stephen Reinhardt argued strenuously against Edelman. "I can tell you the effect of your refusing to act today," the attorney warned. "It is not an understatement that we are in a war of nerves with robber barons who are sitting there trying (to see if, that by) flexing their muscle, they can show strength and that we won't." The League had "thrown down the gauntlet" and was trying "to intimidate the county."

"Nobody is going to intimidate the county," Edelman shouted. "I'm for the loan. I'm for bringing the Raiders here, but I don't want to sit here two years from now and feel that we've paid $5 million and we have no Raiders, no football team, and we can't get the money back."

"We're really getting out there on a limb," Burke agreed.

The best Reinhardt and Robertson were able to do was to reduce Edelman's motion to a decision to postpone the vote for a week. Despite all the promises made to him, Al Davis's money would not be delivered on schedule. "We're disappointed with the delay," Bill Robertson admitted, "but we've had many delays."

Once again, Robertson was whistling in the dark. Before the week's delay was up, the League had hit Davis with another salvo.

This time the blow was struck on the Oakland front in *Philadelphia*

Eagles v. Oakland Raiders Ltd. It was a graphic illustration for all concerned that the NFL and Pete Rozelle were playing for keeps. On March 17, they formally filed their request that Davis be removed from control of his football franchise and replaced by a receiver of the NFL's choice. It was an act unprecedented in NFL history. The reason for it, according to Rozelle, "was that no action was being taken to sell tickets in Oakland" for the upcoming season, despite the fact the League was already scheduling games there.

One of those games was a preseason affair with Billy Sullivan's Patriots. The receivership motion was provoked by Sullivan, Rozelle remembered. "Mr. Sullivan suggested, because he felt he would suffer in the check he would receive when he went into Oakland for this game, that if the League wasn't going to do it, he would. . . . We either at that point had to try to get a receiver or file a motion saying that Al Davis should go to jail, which we did not want to do." While it made no immediate response to the receivership request, the court did continue the temporary restraining order Davis had escaped from on March 6.

The same day receivership papers were filed, Rozelle also authorized Jay Moyer, the League's in-house attorney, to write a letter to the LAMCC, the mayor, and the board of supervisors "telling them of the Oakland restraining order in the hope they would bring things to a grinding halt." The commissioner also had the League's lead litigator for *LAMCC v. NFL* send a letter to fourteen major banks. A copy of the Oakland order was enclosed. "We didn't want anyone to lend money to anyone and have the League be the fall guys," Rozelle explained. "We wanted them to be on notice what our position was." The ultimate purpose was "to stop any loans [to finance the Raider move] that might be in process or at least give those banks serious cause to think about it."

On March 18, the Los Angeles supervisors postponed their loan vote once again. "There are still a lot of loose ends in this thing," Ed Edelman explained.

Those loose ends would remain untied for a long time. Soon after this second postponement, Robertson and Reinhardt went back to the drawing board in their search for financing. "We gave up on the board of supervisors," Reinhardt remembered. "We just dropped the original deal. As soon as the Raiders got here, they started raising questions. It was supposed to have been approved quickly. We finally withdrew the proposal after about three weeks of trying. Nothing the county had promised was ever delivered on."

On March 25, the Oakland court hearing *Philadelphia Eagles v. Oakland Raiders Ltd.* enjoined the Raiders from soliciting "ticket sales for games anywhere other than Oakland" or taking "any final action to move the franchise." As a legal maneuver this was the Eagles suit's high-water mark: Davis's Raiders would have no choice but to play their home games in Oakland. Their offices and training facilities, however, remained in L.A. and the team would commute four hundred miles north on game days. Pinned down, Al Davis would not abandon ground he had already seized.

Davis also fired back. On March 25, he, too, went into court, filing a

$160 million damage suit under the Sherman Act and joining that suit to *LAMCC v. NFL*. To escape the potential conflict-of-interest trap set by the League for his attorney Joseph Alioto, the Raiders' action left only one franchise unnamed—the Philadelphia Eagles, Alioto's other NFL client. Davis's suit also raised the stakes. Not content just to challenge the League as an anonymous entity, he also named specific individuals as having conspired to violate his economic rights, forcing them to defend themselves as well. The three he named were Pete Rozelle, Gene Klein, and Georgia Rosenbloom. Now the case could be personal. Its new official title was *LAMCC and Oakland Raiders Ltd. v. National Football League, Alvin Pete Rozelle, Eugene V. Klein, and Georgia Rosenbloom.*

"It became a personal issue," Tex Schramm remembered, "because Al Davis made it a personal issue. He framed it that way. . . . It didn't surprise me that Al did it like that. It was obviously a tool he felt he could use to distract attention and it was Al's nature to fight by whatever means are available."

5

In the public furor surrounding the face-off between Al Davis and the rest of the League, Davis was often mistakenly credited with being the first owner ever to sue his fellows. That description ignored the precedent already set by Lamar Hunt and Joe Robbie in *NASL v. NFL*, but such ignorance was by then common. Virtually from the beginning, the suit over ownership policy, once the most pressing issue on the NFL agenda, had been overshadowed by Davis and Los Angeles. In April 1980, *NASL v. NFL* came to trial in Federal District Court in New York City and almost no one outside the League noticed. Even for the NFL, it was considered something of a dry run for the battle to come.

The North American Soccer League case had two significant thrusts. The first was that the NFL's proposed ban on cross-ownership was starkly anticompetitive in intent. As proof, the soccer league offered what it termed the "smoking pistol"—a statement made by Pete Rozelle to the owners in his June 28, 1978, ownership policy memo. "The NFL's success depends on fan interest and loyalty," the commissioner had argued. "The League competes with other major team sports for that interest and loyalty, as well as for gate receipts, television revenues, advertising dollars, and media coverage. Connections with NFL personnel may well enhance those competing team sports, both in fact and in the public's perception, at the expense of the NFL." On its face, the NASL argued, the NFL's proposed ownership policy amendment was an "unreasonable" attempt by a combination of owners to reduce competi-

tion among major sports leagues and hence a violation of the Sherman
Act.

The NASL's second argument was that it and the NFL also competed in
a "limited submarket" for "sports ownership capital and skill." There were,
according to soccer's logic, only so many people either capable of or interested in owning sports franchises of any sort and the NFL's current membership comprised a "significant part" of that potential pool. For the League to
deny the NASL access to that group was another contravention of the Sherman Act.

The NFL's attorneys responded to those arguments with two thrusts of
their own. The lesser of them was to maintain that there was no identifiable
submarket in sports ownership capital. In effect, they argued that a member of
the National Football League was no more capable of purchasing and running
a soccer franchise than any other person with comparable wealth or resources.

Far more important to the NFL's case and Rozelle's sense of the football
business's unique identity was what would later be described as "the single
entity defense." The Sherman Act specifically exempts the internal operations
of "single economic entities" from all its provisions. The National Football
League claimed to be such an entity. Its proof was League Think itself. The
League's economic organization was constructed around sharing income and
maximizing the economic viability of the members' mutual enterprise. As
such, its desire to prohibit the membership from buying into other sports
leagues was legally no different from Sears requiring standard servicing
warranties from all its stores or McDonald's requiring all its franchisers to
serve Big Macs on sesame seed buns. What the NASL was seeking protection
from was simply a more efficient, better organized, and stronger competitor,
not an unfair combination. To find otherwise, the League argued, would
restrict competition rather than enhance it.

When those arguments were tried in April 1980, the rifts running along
the NFL's inner surfaces officially entered the public domain, noticed or not.

The first National Football League owner called by the NASL plaintiffs
was Lamar Hunt. By then, of course, Lamar had already acquired a certain
personal familiarity with the courtroom process. He had spent a good portion
of 1977 and 1978 litigating with other Hunts. The case had grown out of the
death of Lamar's father, H.L., in November 1974. The old man had spent his
last days, according to *Texas Monthly,* "crazed by old age and troubled by
what he could see of the turmoil within his empire." As Lamar and the rest of
H.L.'s first family had feared, the bulk of H.L.'s bequest had gone to his
second family, by his second wife, Ruth. Though it was significantly less
than the bequest already left the first family through his earlier trusts, the first
family was "still suspicious that someone other than their father had helped
write the will" and "seriously considered a challenge, despite [an] automatic
disinheritance clause [should they do so]. Then tempers cooled, and the
family decided to avoid a public feud."

Instead, a "third family" entered the fray in the person of Frania Tye,
the woman H.L. had kept, and her four children whom H.L. had sired before

taking up with Ruth. Their union had never been blessed by a recorded marriage, though Frania claimed such a ceremony had actually taken place. In November 1975, she and her children filed suit in Shreveport, Louisiana, Federal Court, asking for an equitable share of the moneys left the second family after H.L.'s death as well as the moneys provided the first family in their earlier trusts. To fight the charges, the first and second families made an uneasy alliance, though at the trial in Shreveport in January 1978, the two groups of Hunts watched from different sections of seats. Lamar, of course, sat with his wife and his siblings. Lamar did not testify, nor did any of the rest of the first family. While a lot of other testimony was heard before any decision could be reached, the two sides agreed to settle by awarding Frania Tye and her children $7.5 million.

Back in court two years later, this time on the stand as part of the North American Soccer League's case, Lamar would testify during most of April 2 and 3, 1980. He was defensive about being labeled an opponent of the NFL for doing so, claiming, "I am not testifying *for* or *against*. The things I'm saying are factual, I hope. [At least] I think they are." Among the "facts" Hunt helped establish on the stand was the importance of ownership for the success of a sports league. "Probably the most important reason" for the old AFL's success at starting from scratch, Hunt stated, "was in having a solid ownership group. . . . Not all were of the same resource capability, but they were pretty well all of the same dedication toward getting the job done. . . . Sound ownership is very important to a sports team operation and I believe success in one [sport] leads to success in another."

Lamar defended his own previous votes in favor of ownership policy resolutions as a simple unwillingness "to be disruptive to the general tenor of the League." He also defended having furnished the names of potential owners accumulated by the NFL to the NASL. "I may have mentioned some name here or there," he testified, "but it was public knowledge in many cases. . . . They were people that . . . would come and attend cocktail parties at League meetings and bring eight or ten people from their city and have a private drawing room. They might have a setup showing the stadium plans in their city. . . . It was in many cases a . . . Chamber of Commerce type operation."

For Hunt himself, perhaps the most embarrassing part of his testimony came when he was cross-examined about the "best efforts to divest" he had promised the League over and over again. At the same time that he was making those promises in 1978, he had also received three separate leaguewide communications from the NASL commissioner asking to be notified if anyone in the soccer league wanted to dispose of his franchise. In none of the cases had Hunt responded. Hunt denied that failure to respond meant he was lying to his NFL colleagues; it was just good business. "I don't believe that that is the way to sell the team," Lamar offered before leaving the stand.

On April 7, the NASL called Edward Bennett Williams. Williams, chief executive officer of the Washington Redskins when the events in question had occurred, now identified himself as the owner of the Baltimore Orioles baseball franchise as well as still an owner of approximately fifteen percent of the football team. The Redskins were a named defendant and Williams was served a subpoena to testify, but was adamant that such steps were unnecessary. "If I have information that is useful to the adjudication of any issue in any court," he pointed out, "as an officer of the court, I will come to the court and give it. I don't need a subpoena."

To no one's surprise, the nation's foremost trial counsel proved a superb witness.

"I think that an investment in professional sports is such a highly speculative investment that there are very few people who are willing to take the gamble that it entails," he testified. "When you invest your money in real estate or in stocks and bonds of a solid company, there is a certain solidity. I had it very much impressed on me one time [when] the Redskins went to Cleveland one Sunday to play football and a disgruntled ex-player had brought a suit . . . on a workman's compensation claim and there was [an] attachment before judgment . . . and the sheriff came out and attached our equipment and there it sat in the middle of the room. There were shoulder pads and jerseys and towels and balls and helmets and it was a graphic demonstration to me. Those were all the assets we really owned in the world, tangible in nature. . . . All of the rest of the things we have are contractual in nature: leases, player contracts. And that, that kind of thing . . . drives away all but a very few prospective investors."

Williams was quick to disassociate himself from the policy the League was attempting to defend. "It's the commissioner's rule," he bristled. "It's the real Rozelle Rule. That is why we had it thrust upon us every year. . . . I had deep concerns when I saw [the constitutional amendment] that was circulated [in June 1978] and I spoke out very strongly. . . . I told them they would have certain litigation if they enacted this." Williams defended the Redskins' eventual compliance with the policy as simply a necessary step to keep the peace, but never an endorsement. When confronted with a copy of the League minutes from May 1972 that recorded a unanimous twenty-six-member vote for ownership policy, Williams dismissed the document's accuracy. "When it says the vote was twenty-six to nothing and it records that I was present, then I say it was in error. Somebody missed it. There was maybe a chorus of yeses but I always said no." When confronted with the minutes of June 1976, claiming the League had reached "general agreement on a moral commitment for strict observance" of the ownership policy resolution, Williams dismissed that as well. "I don't recall any such discussion ever taking place," he claimed. "There was never a spirit of moral commitment. There was a resolution. It got passed, so we abided by it."

Edward Bennett Williams's most obvious contempt was reserved for the commissioner's argument that his ownership policy was essential to maintain the secrecy of the League's internal business. "My experience in twenty years at these [NFL] meetings is that there were no secrets," he maintained. "There were two or three hour head starts, but no secrets. . . . Within three or four hours, whatever took place at a meeting would be in the public domain. . . . We are not operating a covert, clandestine intelligence apparatus for the nation. We are not the CIA.''

When the NASL eventually rested its case, Williams's Redskins would be dismissed by the soccer league as a defendant in recognition of his longstanding opposition to the policy they were suing to block. As Rozelle remembered it, ''the Redskins went solo.''

The last National Football League owner called by the NASL was Joe Robbie. He took the stand on April 9. Robbie, also an attorney, was familiar with courtrooms and admitted that he had welcomed the soccer league's suit as a way to clear this question up, once and for all. He also evinced sympathy for those football owners who resented the NASL's competition. ''I can understand their feeling about the competition with soccer in their communities,'' Robbie noted, ''and if I felt strongly about that, I guess I would certainly want my family to be in soccer in Miami so somebody wouldn't be competing against us.'' Nonetheless, he argued, ''you hurt yourself more than competition hurts you if you let your product fall apart. The best way to sell tickets is to win.''

Joe Robbie characterized his own relationship to the soccer business as a natural outgrowth of his family approach. ''My wife is also interested in sports,'' he claimed, ''and was extremely helpful to me in the early years of the Miami Dolphins, when we had a number of difficulties in establishing the professional sport for the first time in Miami. We had five sons and four daughters who are all interested in sports. . . . I told [the NFL] that Elizabeth had the choice of folding a franchise in front of all the fans of the Miami Dolphins . . . or of continuing it. . . . I told them that we stood to lose substantial money to sell off the [NASL] Ft. Lauderdale Strikers as a result of the [NFL's] family policy.''

''Have you ever told Commissioner Rozelle or anyone else that you intended to ask your wife to sell her [soccer] interest?'' Robbie was asked.

''No,'' Robbie grinned, ''I am waiting for her to come home and tell me I have to sell the football team because she is in soccer.'' The NFL's policy had, he noted, ''been more honored by ignoring it than enforcing it. . . . I never saw any 'best efforts' to dispose of anything until Jack Kent Cooke sold his entire empire in Los Angeles.''

Before leaving the stand, the Dolphins' owner also buttressed the NASL's contention that there were, in truth, a lot fewer potential sports owners than it often seemed. ''I may have more experience than almost anybody in professional sports about people coming around wanting to buy a pro franchise,'' he claimed, ''because there were twenty or thirty of them in the early years of the Dolphins and I generally found that if the conversation got serious, then the prospective purchaser wanted to go out and syndicate the interest that he was going to acquire so he could come in free. I don't put a lot of stock in lawyers calling saying they have clients who are interested in buying a pro franchise.''

In its defense, the National Football League called Bill Bidwill, Leonard Tose, Charles Sullivan, Art Modell, and, of course, Commissioner Pete

Rozelle. Rozelle was the League's most substantial witness and stayed on the stand for the better part of four days, from April 16 through April 22.

The ownership policy in question, he testified, was an expression of "the philosophy that the League has had that certainly predated my taking my present position over twenty years ago, and it was based upon the fact that you are only as strong as your weakest link. . . . One of the key things that a sports league needs is unity of purpose. It needs harmony. Because they have to . . . hash out sometimes very serious matters on which there is a division of opinion but a decision must be made. When you have unity and harmony and can move basically as one, you can have a successful sports league. But when you have to eliminate some of your colleagues in a meeting in order to have private discussions . . . it's a very unpleasant, unsettling situation." Whatever Edward Bennett Williams might say, the commissioner emphasized, ownership policy was not his. "If this were just my policy," he complained, "I see no way this suit would have come about. . . . The decision to defend this policy . . . could not have been made by myself unilaterally.

"Unlike some other team sports," Rozelle continued, "we have been fortunate in that the National Football League has basically moved as one. They have had a unity of purpose [and] that spirit . . . has pervaded the NFL and been helpful, very helpful in us moving ahead. . . . It is seldom that we have twenty-eight people agreeing, all voting yes on something, even on adjournment, but up until now, they have accepted the voting procedure and abided by it and moved ahead as one."

Al Davis, currently the most glaring example of the League's lack of oneness, was not at issue in this trial, but his name came up anyway.

The first time was in Rozelle's cross-examination. The reference flowed from a discussion of Herman Sarkowsky's cross-ownership situation.

"Is the reason you have not enforced the ban against Mr. Sarkowsky," Rozelle was asked, "because Mr. Sarkowsky is part of a 'small coterie of close associates' whom you favor, as alleged in the complaint in the Oakland Raiders case by Mr. Davis?"

"No," Rozelle answered.

Later, Rozelle made reference to Davis himself while bemoaning the dangerous precedent *NASL v. NFL* had set for the League's internal workings. "I know of no [previous] instance where an NFL owner has been on the minority side of an issue and subsequently played a role in having that decision challenged in court," Rozelle claimed. "The problem in California stems to some extent from what happened in this litigation. . . . The California litigation was triggered by someone saying, 'Well, if others are going to be selective in their observance of matters put to a vote by the NFL, then I am going to be selective.' . . . I can see this leading to anarchy."

The commissioner was followed on April 22 by Bill Bidwill, who provided little of import, one way or the other. Later the same day, Leonard Tose gave a similar performance. Mostly Tose just confirmed his own quite vocal role in ownership policy's history. "There has never been a meeting where this subject was discussed," he bragged, "that I didn't express my views in terms that I would not offend His Honor with. . . . I was very definitive in my suggestions about what should be done about it and to those people."

On April 23, Chuck Sullivan was called to the stand. His principal contribution was to paint the Patriots as a franchise that had gone out of its way to obey ownership policy, starting with its stadium problems in the early 1970s—"We built our own stadium in Foxboro. . . . It was built for a cost of $7 million and $1 million of that money was provided by my family." Progressing to the battle to reinstate Old Billy, Chuck testified, "My family made a commitment that we would bring ourselves into compliance with the rules. It cost us $10 million to do that."

The last NFL owner to take the stand, also on April 23, was Art Modell. He claimed Edward Bennett Williams was all wrong about the competition between sports leagues. "We have argued that point many times," Modell testified, "and I think he's wrong. He is a personal friend of mine, he served as my attorney from time to time, but I think he's wrong about sports feeding on each other's success. It doesn't happen that way. . . . We compete for the consumer dollars, we compete for space in the newspapers, we compete for the first item on the news show . . . and perhaps most importantly . . . we compete for the emotions of the people. I consider professional sports to be a continuing love affair with the public at large and the one that grabs the heart the earliest and holds on to it will maintain that hold for some time."

Modell also pointed out that, as of the previous March, he had ceased serving on the board of the baseball Indians. "I decided when the problem was raised by Al Davis at a League meeting," Modell explained, "that this may indeed be a violation of our cross-ownership rule. I said, why beg the problem? I will not stand for reelection and I did not."

Like Rozelle, Art Modell ended his testimony with a warning about the precedent this case had already set. "The very fact that we are in this courtroom right now is a cause of concern to me," he argued. "I believe that there is a pattern taking place in the National Football League which I find most disturbing of all. We have operated in the League on a three-quarters-vote principle for as long as I have been in football and many years before that and we have a self-governing system, and we have abided by it. I think it's a scary prospect to have an owner who may not get his vote, get his way, and looks to twenty-two teams, with others abstaining, takes them to court and tries to upset the voting of the League. It's happening in California right now . . . in the case of Al Davis."

When all the testimony had been heard, the judge took the case under advisement. It would be November before his decision was announced, but to the NFL, at least, it would be worth the wait. The federal district court sustained the single entity defense and agreed with the NFL that there was no significant submarket in football owners. The League's elation would last until January 1982, when a federal appeals court reversed the lower level, found for the NASL, and banned any ownership policy amendments forever.

In 1980, however, *NASL v. NFL* was a significant confidence-builder for the League's legal strategists. Their single-entity arguments seemed to have worked. They would see no reason not to use them again when it came time to go to the mat with Davis.

6

In June 1980, there was another legal warmup of sorts in Philadelphia when *Tose v. First Pennsylvania Bank* was finally heard in federal court. Because Leonard Tose's case was being handled by Joseph Alioto, it was something of a trial run for Davis's side of the aisle. Rozelle and the other defendants in *LAMCC v. NFL* had already knocked a few sparks with Alioto as the long pretrial process of affidavits and depositions ground forward. Now, the legal gunslingers had the chance to size up the quickness of Alioto's draw. Since he'd first entered the NFL's legal life in the 1950s, the League had yet to see Joe Alioto lose. That was, of course, the reason Leonard Tose had hired him in the first place.

Tose entered the courtroom that June in the best shape of his football life. The interest rates on his Citibank loan had risen beyond twenty percent, like Art Modell's with the banks in Cleveland, but he was current on his payments and his financing was stable. Even more important, at least from Tose's point of view, his team continued to win football games. In 1979, the Eagles had won eleven, lost five, and advanced to the second round of the playoffs before losing to Hugh Culverhouse's Tampa Bay franchise. One result was an $800,000 profit for the Eagles, but Leonard Tose maintained to the public that he was unconcerned about making money. "I don't dwell on figures," he pointed out. "It's not my goal to be the richest guy in the cemetery. I still believe you go first class or you stay at home. What the hell. I really believe that. And I don't stay at home."

His steady companion continued to be Caroline Callum, a former stewardess half his age. As he explained their courtship to *The Philadelphia Bulletin*, Tose had met her four years before, on a flight when she was working the first class compartment. "You've got a beautiful ass," he offered. They had been together ever since. "I don't like her," Tose maintained, "I love her. I'm not happy being alone. I'm not for going out with one hundred different girls. I'm still old-fashioned." Tose also claimed to be taking care of himself better than ever. "I get finished work at 6, 6:30. I pick Caroline up. We have one or two scotches. She makes dinner. That's our nightlife that everyone is so excited about. We eat at home five nights a week. I don't socialize. . . . I try to get six hours sleep a night. I try to get away, relax.''

Leonard Tose also claimed to have significantly reduced his gambling. "I haven't played gin rummy for big money for years," he explained, "not since that thing with Andrea.* I used to play for big stakes, more than a buck a point. But no more. Same way with golf. I'd play $1000 nassau, but in recent years I'd play $10 nassau or a buck a hole. And the last two years, I've hardly played at all.''

Tose had not, however, lost his taste for luxury. He was still in the habit of giving $100 bottles of champagne to people he saw in restaurants celebrating birthdays or other occasions. The catered meals he provided the press corps on game days were described by The [Philadelphia] Bulletin as "lavish.'' He continued to commute to practices in his helicopter. "My life-style is that I go first class all the time,'' Tose explained. "I go to an away game, I have a limo meet me at the airport. I do everything for my comfort. I have lunch for my friends at the home games. King's caterers does a first class job. We feed the press. So what's wrong with that? I don't think we're extravagant. Being first class means doing the right thing. We're not pissing away money.''

Among the benefits winning football games had brought to Leonard Tose was an escalation of his standing in the League's inner circles. "When I first came into the League,'' he claimed, "I couldn't even talk at the meetings. I now think I've gone from one of the least respected guys in the League to one of the leading guys getting respect.'' Along the way, Leonard Tose claimed to have become "very close'' with Hugh Culverhouse and William Clay Ford, owner of the Detroit Lions. "Ford is the one guy who saved my butt,'' Tose admitted. "He did it nicely, where I didn't know who was involved. He said, 'I'll have this guy call you.' Later, I found out that the Ford family owned the bank.'' It was a favor Tose returned when the League decided to give the Super Bowl culminating the 1981 season to Detroit. "I paid Bill Ford back,'' Tose noted. "How much chance do you think Detroit had of getting the Super Bowl? Pete Rozelle was against it. But for Bill Ford, I busted my butt. Got him eight votes. Bill Ford thanked me. Five years ago, I'd have only gotten my own vote.''

One of the League roles in which Tose asserted himself was the Management Council executive committee, on which he was serving as Chuck Sullivan's vice-chairman. "I speak out now,'' Tose noted. "I think we must maintain the prerogatives of management. We can't surrender them to the union. I've had more experience with unions than anybody else. We face no problems until the end of this contract, two years from now. Then, I anticipate problems that the owners must face up to. They can't sit back. They have to attack.''

Leonard Tose's confidence in his League clout had been apparent on the stand in NASL v. NFL. There, he'd asserted his independence from Rozelle as

---

*Tose's earlier divorce trial, when his former wife testified as to his gambling habits.

well. "Mr. Rozelle is a good commissioner," he'd testified, "but Mr. Rozelle works for Leonard Tose and twenty-seven other members. I do not work for Mr. Rozelle. When he's right and makes a suggestion, I consider it. If I don't like it, he above all people knows exactly where I stand and I guarantee you that most of the time we disagree."

That testimony was a dry run for Leonard Tose. He would be the plaintiff's central witness in *Tose v. First Penn,* starting in June.

The case Joe Alioto made in Tose's name leaned heavily on Sections 1 and 2 of the Sherman Act. The defendants were First Pennsylvania Bank, John Bunting—now its former chairman, John Pemberton—still its vice-chairman, Provident National Bank, Girard Bank, Chase Manhattan Bank, Philadelphia National Bank, and Sidney Forstater—Tose's former financial adviser. Together, Alioto argued, they had "entered into conspiracies to unreasonably restrain trade." Their alleged purposes "were: 1) to form a 'banking boycott' which would deny plaintiffs access to the credit market in the Philadelphia area, and 2) to fix the prime interest rate so that all defendant banks would charge 'a uniform noncompetitive prime rate.' " In addition, "the plaintiffs allege that the defendants' activities constitute malicious interference and conspiracy to interfere with advantageous contractual relations and business prospects under Pennsylvania law." The ultimate object of all this had been, of course, to drive Leonard Tose out of the football business once and for all.

On June 24, 25, and 26, Leonard Tose, sartorially splendid in a custom-made gray western suit, took the stand on his own behalf and began by describing how he had worked sixteen-hour days in the 1960s "to transform his father's debt-ridden trucking company into a million-dollar operation." Then, his voice quavering with emotion, he told how John Bunting had called in his loan. "I was stunned," Tose testified. "I guess he felt his power growing because he said, 'I'll even do better than that. I'll make sure you don't get financing at any bank in the country.' " Tose recalled how John Pemberton had insulted him. "He told me, 'I've got to treat you like a jackass. I've got to mount you and put my spurs in you' . . . but the good Lord gave me the strength not to respond to that." He had managed to save his life in football, Tose claimed, only with a "desperate" last minute "bid for help" to William Clay Ford in Detroit. "I was totally humiliated," Tose shuddered. "I was despondent. I was a physical wreck. I couldn't sleep. I felt inside me that I should sell the team and not embarrass the players."

To no one's surprise, cross-examination bore in on Leonard Tose's life-style. At one point, First Pennsylvania Bank's attorney interrogated the Eagles owner about a series of American Express charges billed to the Eagles by Caroline Callum. One was for $1238 at Giorgio's on Rodeo Drive in Beverly Hills.

"I think it's a shop," Tose explained.

Then the defendants' attorney wanted to know about $189 billed in St. Tropez, France. Tose said he couldn't remember it.

"Maybe she was there and you didn't know about it," the attorney suggested.

"You don't mean that," Tose snarled.

"Sure I mean that."

The judge interrupted. "Stick with the law case," he admonished.

"Wasn't one of the things Mr. Pemberton wanted you to do was lift Caroline's credit card?" the attorney continued.

"We did," Tose answered.

Then the defense questioned a $9100 bill in helicopter expenses.

"That's the only bill [for helicopter expenses] that was ever rendered to the Eagles," Tose explained, "and if the true figures were ever billed to the Eagles, it would be much more."

During his final day on the stand, Leonard Tose was questioned about his borrowing habits. The defense counsel, *The Philadelphia Inquirer* noted, "attempted to depict Leonard Tose as a man who went deeply in debt to support a flamboyant life-style that included a chauffeured Rolls-Royce and a private helicopter." First Penn's attorney also pointed out that he had once, in his desperate search for money, doublehocked the franchise.

"It was like a second mortgage," Tose maintained.

"Did you tell the bank [about it]?"

"No," Tose answered, "I did not."

Leonard Tose's 1976 tax return indicated that he had paid some $42,000 in interest on his personal loans, the defense attorney noted. "Do you remember what was causing you to borrow all those monies?"

"To live in the style that I am accustomed to."

"And what is that style?"

"Graciously," Tose answered.

First Penn's attorney wanted to know what that meant.

"That includes me being comfortable, sir."

"And is that still true?"

"Still true," Leonard Tose answered with a certain visible pride.

On re-direct examination, Joseph Alioto tried to undo some of the damage done by the defense. "Has any bank ever suffered the loss of a dime in dealing with you?" he asked.

"No, sir," Tose replied.

"And how many stockholders of First Pennsylvania Bank have suffered the loss of money because of Mr. Bunting?"

"All of them," Leonard Tose answered.

That Joe Alioto's effort was insufficient became apparent on June 30. By then, the plaintiff's case had been heard and the judge ruled there was insufficient evidence to send the issue to a jury. After spending some $500,000 on making his case, the best Leonard Tose got was a legal bellyflop.

From the League's viewpoint, the only significant contribution of *Tose v. First Penn* was the comfort of knowing that Joe Alioto was by no means unbeatable.

7

When Leonard Tose finished his day in court, *LAMCC v. NFL* was still almost a year from going to trial. The League's focus in the meantime was on the struggle over public reputation that pitted Al Davis against Pete Rozelle, Gene Klein, and Georgia Rosenbloom, the three individuals Davis had charged with conspiracy. Each side's object was to paint the other in as black and sinister a visage as possible, hoping to make the other backpedal and spend its energies defending its good name rather than its legal flanks.

In Gene Klein's case, the process had begun even before Davis's memorandum of agreement. In October 1979, Klein was already identified by *The [Oakland] Tribune* as someone "who becomes irritated even at the suggestion of the Oakland Raiders moving to Los Angeles."

"It wouldn't get my vote," Klein had pointed out while Davis's wife was in the hospital, "and I don't think it would get many of the other owners' votes either." In February 1980, Klein went after the LAMCC in an interview with the *Los Angeles Herald Examiner* and predicted that he "wouldn't be surprised if taxpayers suits arise if the Oakland Raiders are permitted to move to Los Angeles." Bill Robertson responded immediately on a radio talk show in L.A. Klein, Robertson pointed out, had "personally told me during 1978 he would love to move the Chargers to Los Angeles" but "there was no way to break the San Diego lease." Robertson also charged that in the early 1970s, Klein had seriously investigated moving his franchise to Seattle. Klein's public contention that the L.A. Coliseum could have kept the Rams if they had only agreed to Carroll Rosenbloom's original demands was a statement that made Robertson "want to vomit." Klein was "a hatchet man for Pete Rozelle and the National Football League." Ever since "he was involved in the San Diego drug scandal and got off easy with that $20,000 fine," Robertson argued, Gene Klein had been nothing but "a puppy dog for the League office."

Rozelle stuck up for Klein the next day. "That's funny," the commissioner pointed out from his Westchester home, "Robertson's getting emotional, isn't he? To say Klein is anybody's lackey is ludicrous. Gene is and always has been his own man." Gene Klein also stuck up for himself. "It's pretty obvious that the Ayatollah Robertson is trying to divert attention from the ridiculous actions of the Coliseum commission," he maintained. "All this yelling and hollering is an attempt to cover the commission's tracks. It's ridiculous. They've lost one hundred percent of their tenants. They're really inept. If they were a private enterprise, I'm sure the shareholders would demand an explanation. Robertson is Al Davis's lackey and he obviously is saying the things Davis wants him to say.''

According to Bill Robertson, the proof of his contentions about Gene Klein came on March 3. While the League was meeting in Dallas, a young attorney from the Los Angeles firm of Wyman, Bautzer, Rothman & Silbert filed a taxpayer suit asking that the LAMCC, L.A. County Board of Supervisors, and city of Los Angeles be prohibited from signing any loan agreements for the purpose of fulfilling their deal with Al Davis. The suit arose, Al Davis pointed out, just as Gene Klein had said it would less than a month earlier. ''You just don't have your average citizen walking into Wyman, Bautzer and saying, 'I want you to sue the Coliseum commission for me,' '' LAMCC attorney Stephen Reinhardt observed. Eugene Wyman, Wyman, Bautzer's late founder, had been a Democratic National Committeeman and a close friend of Gene Klein's. Wyman, Bautzer also continued to list Klein among its clients. Reinhardt thought it was easy to see his hand in this behind the scenes.

Klein himself steadfastly denied any involvement. Predictably, Al Davis found the denial less than credible. He assumed Klein's enmity and considered it one of the more obvious facts of the case. As much was apparent when the first of Davis's depositions was taken on March 14, the last day of the 1980 annual meeting at Palm Springs. Accompanied by Joe Alioto, Davis met with League attorneys at a hotel called The Spa to be questioned under oath.

''Do you believe that the management of the San Diego Chargers has a personal animosity toward you?'' an NFL attorney asked.

Alioto immediately interrupted. ''You have got to be kidding,'' he laughed. ''Even you can testify to that one.''

Much of the public mudslinging that characterized developments in *LAMCC v. NFL* during 1980 was rooted in the deposition process. Under oath, but out of the presence of a judge, the questions could be wide-ranging and provocative. The most embarrassing information offered or solicited in that process also had a way of leaking to the press afterward.

In the course of Al Davis's three deposition sessions, the League's principal interest was the exploration of Davis's relationship with the ''Mafia front man'' Allen Glick. When their business dealings had first surfaced four years earlier, the relationship had been handled in a relatively perfunctory fashion by Rozelle's office, but now the League wanted a lot more details from Davis under oath. Joe Alioto called for a break when the subject was first raised, and huddled with the NFL's attorneys. He warned them not to continue. If they did, he pointed out, two could play the same game. The NFL attorneys ignored his warning.

''Many of the people in the National Football League . . . were associated with Mr. Glick at one time,'' Davis explained. ''The commissioner, Rozelle, had run an investigation of this association and found it to be business dealing. Any representation that there was something other than just a simple business deal was purely irresponsible and misrepresented. . . . In early 1971, one of the players who played for the San Diego Chargers and

one of the players who played for the Los Angeles Rams, namely Lance
Alworth and John Hadl, came to me and told me they were working for a
gentleman by the name of Dennis Wittman and a gentleman by the name of
Allen Glick. They were in the real estate business and they had some very
good real estate properties that I might be interested in, and they wanted to
know if I would come down and meet with these people."

Was Wittman, Georgia Rosenbloom's lawyer asked, "the chap that died
playing basketball in jail?"

"Yes."

Alioto interrupted at this point. "Anybody playing basketball at fifty
years old deserves to die," he snapped.

"Ask Mrs. Rosenbloom about Dennis Wittman," Davis added. "He did
a lot of work for Carroll."

In any case, most of Davis's contact had been with Glick himself and
even that was minimal. "Allen was an attorney," Davis continued in his
usual rambling fashion. "He was a war hero, decorated with honor. And he
was a very bright land developer and tax attorney. Now, whether he was or
not, I don't know, but this is what the young people who came to me who I
had coached, recruited, learned to live with, love, and assured me that these
people were outstanding young people in the business world. This was not the
first time I had been with young people who were developers in the business
world and that was my observation of Allen. . . . I don't know Mr. Glick
very well. . . . I think I have seen Mr. Glick two or three times in the last
four years. I have had very little dealing with him and, based on my
experience in life and the fact that I was taking down our investments, et
cetera, like that, I thought nothing of it. . . ."

"Did you become aware that in addition to the fact that Mr. Glick owned
casinos in Las Vegas in which gambling activities existed," Georgia's attorney asked, "that it was publicly reported that he had associations with
organized crime?"

"Yes."

"When did you become aware of that?"

"Oh," Davis answered, "I would say somewhere around 1977, '78. . . .
I even welcomed the commissioner's investigation of my business dealings
with Mr. Glick, and if you are trying—maybe I can rest your mind—if you are
trying to find out was I concerned about it, I was concerned to the point that I
was doing everything I thought was right to eventually disassociate myself
with [sic] Mr. Glick in a proper business manner, see to it that all our clients
and constituents who were in the thing were dealt with fairly, and certainly
uphold everything that we believe in in the National Football League."

After several hours on this subject, the League knew little more than
what it had previously read in the papers. Allen Glick was deposed as well,
but spent most of the time taking the Fifth Amendment and provided no fresh
weapons to use against Davis.

Davis himself was quick to strike back, as Alioto had promised. The
subject he chose was ticket scalping. That an owner would claim anyone in

the League was involved in it was an embarrassment in and of itself, but Davis went even further and claimed it was also done with Rozelle's knowledge and tacit consent. First he told about C.R.'s approach in 1976, looking for tickets to scalp, and repeated what he swore were Rosenbloom's conclusions about Rozelle's relationship to such behavior. Then he made it clear that the approach had not been a one-time-only endeavor. In December 1977, Davis swore, Rosenbloom had approached him again.

"I was again asked if I got into the Super Bowl would I like to use my tickets in a different manner than I had in the past and be thinking of charging above face value for the tickets and making a killing," Davis explained. "I again said no, I wouldn't do it, but how the hell are you going to do it this year if you are not in the Super Bowl because we are only allocated as teams who are not in the Super Bowl—a thousand tickets? He [C.R.] told me that he had talked to the New Orleans owner and the New Orleans owner had gone along with the plan to use their host city tickets in a way of selling them above face value and using travel agencies, et cetera. . . . In February or March of 1978, there was a public announcement that John Mecom [owner of the New Orleans Saints] had arrived in Los Angeles to discuss a potential coach with Carroll Rosenbloom. . . . I learned at the time he was there not only to discuss a potential coach but how to handle the Super Bowl tickets because those two teams were going to be the host city teams for a number of years to come. . . . I was shocked. I was told that everyone in the League is doing it and everyone is doing it. I said doesn't he [Rozelle] know about it? I was totally shocked. Again, I am told he [Rozelle] is aware of it."

Above and beyond that awareness, Davis continued, Rozelle was also enmeshed in the world of travel agencies and Super Bowl tickets himself. In 1979, Davis claimed under oath, "a fellow by the name of Ross from an Ask Mr. Foster travel agency which I later found out was owned by [Los Angeles Olympics Organizing Committee President] Peter Ueberroth [and which] the commissioner has been pushing for years . . . contacted me and said that they had the full approval of the commissioner of the National Football League, that he had investigated their tour package, thought it would be advisable that the League use this tour agency as their official agency and they wanted to meet with me in Hawaii [at the 1979 annual meeting]. I would not meet with the individual in Hawaii. I know that several clubs did. . . . Ross from Ask Mr. Foster [also] has told people in Los Angeles that he gets his Super Bowl tickets from Pete Rozelle.

"When you look at the history of . . . the Super Bowl scandal which we are all well aware of," Davis concluded, "and the statements made to me by different people in the League relative to the commissioner's actions with Super Bowl tickets and his tremendous interest in the Super Bowl, [this examination] leads me to believe that he certainly didn't want me in Los Angeles as the host team in a city that seems destined to have the Super Bowl in Pasadena at least five of the next ten years." Davis also intimated that another reason Rozelle did not want him in L.A. was that he was reserving that franchise for himself whenever he retired from the commissionership.

The NFL bristled at Davis's claims. "You knew how dirty this was all going to be when they started all this bullshit about the Super Bowl tickets," an NFL attorney remembered. It was dirty enough, Gene Klein claimed, "that it even surprised me. I never thought Davis would stoop that low. On a scale of one to ten, he has a character of zero."

Even so, Pete Rozelle felt he had no choice but to respond when Davis's insinuations seeped into the press. Rozelle considered his reputation to be his principal asset and could not sit still while it was sullied. "I can't understand all the statements Davis makes over and over," he was still complaining several years later, "but there's no proof. I'm not interested in an L.A. franchise. Among other things, that would be the quickest way for me to get divorced. My wife doesn't want to live in Los Angeles. That's the last thing I want to do."

Rozelle considered the ticket scalping insinuations preposterous. "I was absolutely unaware [of] what Carroll was doing," he claimed. "Davis offered no shred of evidence to the contrary. No word of it ever reached my office. I never heard of the arrangement between Mecom and Rosenbloom. As for the Ueberroth story, Davis heard it from Durslag, and Durslag heard it at a cocktail party. Ueberroth said he gets his tickets from Rozelle. Ueberroth had a travel agency and Don Ross worked for him. I've known Ross for thirty years. Ross has helped me a lot over the years with various tasks like collecting television information, so I would sell Ross between six to ten tickets. Most of those went to Ueberroth. What Ueberroth was saying was that he got his *personal* tickets from me. Ross explained that to me for Ueberroth. There was no substance whatsoever to what Davis was saying."

Nonetheless, Davis's charges had accomplished his initial objective. Rozelle was now pinned down, defending his reputation. Furthermore, Al Davis had found a critical chink in the commissioner's armor. Innocent or not, the commissioner's sense of himself made him vulnerable simply to the fact of an attack. "It was the first time Pete's personal integrity had ever been challenged," one of his old friends observed. "Having his integrity attacked really hurt Pete in a personal way and, as a consequence, I guess he sort of lost his cool over the Davis thing. It took a big toll on him."

Rozelle began the fight at a disadvantage. It would only get worse. Sensing the commissioner's soft spot, Davis applied pressure to it relentlessly.

8

Georgia Rosenbloom, the third of Davis's alleged conspirators, was by no means exempt from the public relations assault either.

Georgia, of course, had public relations problems to begin with. Her ire at the Los Angeles press corps remained intense. She felt victimized by her coverage and once the Pasadena Super Bowl was over, refused to speak to reporters for the next eighteen months. She touched on her attitude in a poem called "Cynics and Critics":

A cynic is a critic that has lost his optimism.
His brain is filled with knives and barbs and petty pessimisms.
The muck and the mire that he sees as his news can hurt or destroy, divide and confuse.
While hiding behind the freedom of the press, he gloats with great glee at someone's distress.
We must try to reunite and resist the temptation, to build and enhance this fool's reputation.

Georgia Rosenbloom later enlarged upon that theme in a speech in Los Angeles, telling the story of a recurring dream she'd had. In it, she meets with her staff and they convince her to have lunch with the press, so Georgia has them all over to her house in Bel-Air for a meal by the swimming pool. During the gathering, Georgia decides to put on her swimming suit and then steps out of the cabana and into the pool. The water is solid and she walks on it. "I walk across," Georgia recounted, "and nobody says anything. Then I walk back and nobody says anything. Everyone leaves. Then the next morning's headlines are 'Georgia Can't Swim.'"

For Georgia, the public catfight she was about to enter with Al Davis was, first and foremost, the end of a relationship. When Carroll had still been alive, she and Davis had been friends. He had been a guest at their home and they had known each other since 1961. It was a "social" relationship, Davis remembered, but "she used to, once in a while, sing something [to me] over the telephone or something like that."

Now, of course, Carroll was dead and nowhere was that more obvious than inside the front office of the Rams. Georgia's housecleaning was close to complete. Virtually the last vestige of Rosenbloom in L.A. was Georgia's name and in July 1980, that changed as well. On July 21, Georgia Rosenbloom

took Dominic Frontiere for her seventh husband. Henceforth she was Georgia
Frontiere. The ceremony was held in Jacksonville, Florida, and Hugh
Culverhouse, in his role as a notary public, presided. Pete Rozelle was one of
the few guests invited. The newlyweds had traveled to Florida from New
York and, afterward, honeymooned in Europe.

Upon their return in August, the Frontieres oversaw the grand opening of
the Rams' new Anaheim home field. Though the Anaheim city attorney had
overruled making Carroll or his heirs contractor, forcing a modification of the
original deal cut with Anaheim Stadium Associates, the construction had been
completed in time for the 1980 season, as promised. None of the real estate
options for the adjoining ninety-five-acre parking lot had yet been exercised,
but the Rams had new offices, new practice facilities, and, of course, new
luxury boxes. Georgia's suite left few doubts who the owner was. The
size of three normal luxury boxes, it was a split level with a private entrance,
a forty-five-foot viewing window, and seats for fifty. The two levels were
connected by a spiral staircase. Upstairs there was a Jacuzzi, downstairs, a
bar and buffet in knotty pine. The entire suite was decorated in shades of
lime, mint, and jade, Georgia's favorite colors.

In September, the newlyweds also entered the entertainment production
business together, forming Empress Productions with a reported capitalization
of $250 million. Dominic Frontiere was named the CEO and executive in
charge of production. Their first property would be the staging of *Partridge in
a Pear Tree,* a play by Leslie Stevens about the trial of a scullery maid
in London. Currently in production, they announced, was a musical about
the life of baseball legend Babe Ruth scored by Dominic Frontiere. The
Babe Ruth production was "intended as the first of a sports musical
trilogy," the *Los Angeles Times* reported. Dominic was also reported to
be one of the more important advisers Georgia huddled with in trying to
run the Rams. "He attends meetings and he offers advice," the Rams
new club attorney, Terry Christensen, an old friend of Dominic's, observed.
"And the first and last thing he says to me is, 'What am I doing in those
meetings? What do I know about football?' The thing to remember is that
Georgia is still learning the ropes and she finds it helpful having him
participate. However, I don't see him making any decisions in Georgia's
domain and I don't see her backing away from those responsibilities. She's
head of the organization and runs the team. Any press speculation to the
contrary is simply wrong."

One source of such speculation about Georgia's leadership ability was
her stepson Steve Rosenbloom. In August, he had been invited to the opening
of the almost new Anaheim Stadium, but the invitation had been revoked by
the city of Anaheim after Georgia insisted that if Steve was there, she would
not be. "What has happened to that organization is a shame," Steve later told
the *Los Angeles Times.* "It makes me sad. And the problem isn't only that
she can't make a decision, it's that she has everyone else scared of making
one too. There's a hundred people at her ear, but she doesn't listen to anyone,

even those people that know what they're talking about. I'm also hearing more and more that she can't make a decision without Dominic helping her. I mean what's he know? He's an accordionist.''

Perhaps even more important than Dominic among Georgia's inner circle was Hugh Culverhouse, the man who had married them. He flew out from Florida for some of the meetings Georgia called at the time of Davis's move. At the same time, he was also assisting her to dissolve the trust in which the Rams had been left to C.R.'s children as well as to Georgia, so that Georgia could buy the children out and become sole owner. Within a year, the *Los Angeles Herald Examiner* would note that "it's now quite apparent that Hugh Culverhouse is playing a prominent role with the Rams [and] that Georgia Frontiere doesn't dare make a major move without consulting him." Steve Rosenbloom would call Culverhouse's role "a curious conflict of interest. Owners always talk among themselves," Steve explained, "but Georgia was getting more than the usual advice. The other owners were a little uncomfortable about it. Here a guy, in effect, has two teams all of a sudden."

The commissioner, however, expressed no reservations about the arrangement. "Hugh Culverhouse has a close relationship with Georgia," Rozelle noted. "He was executor of Carroll's estate and that went on for several years. He and Georgia exchanged financial information about club operations. He was just more conversant than she was with the specifics of running a club. There was no conflict of interest as far as I was concerned. Culverhouse was very sensitive to such a conflict. He wanted to settle the estate and get out of that role as soon as possible." Culverhouse himself explained that "once the [Rams] stock was liquidated I never had any authority."

Authority or not, Hugh Culverhouse did have considerable influence. In October 1980, a source identified as "one high-ranking Rams official" told the *Times* that "Georgia thinks Hugh Culverhouse is the smartest man on the face of the earth. Maybe so, but he's also very cheap. This may be the direction we're heading in. One of Culverhouse's people came out here to set up the business end of the Rams organization." Whether or not it reflected Culverhouse's approach to the football business, on a road trip to St. Louis that month, the Rams were housed in "a rundown old hotel whose best days were in the 1940s and '50s" that was twenty dollars a head cheaper than the other options. "Next week we'll probably stay at the Y," one player observed.

The franchise itself, however, was still run with a style noticeably Georgia's. "Mrs. Frontiere has had limited contact with the players," the *Los Angeles Times* noted, "and refused to meet with those with contract problems. She did tell one player she wanted to provide free singing and dancing lessons for those interested in show business careers after football." The approach was highlighted by a somewhat unique executive technique. "Reporting to Bel-Air," one Rams employee explained, "you are ushered into the study, where you usually are kept waiting one to two hours. One time, I was seated in the study waiting when she telephoned me from her room. Our whole meeting was conducted on the phone. Why, I asked myself, did I have to drive all the way from Anaheim for this?''

At best, Georgia's football efforts produced a mild levity among her NFL peers. Once, when she made her first personal venture into the player market, acquiring a quarterback from Baltimore, the deal was widely trumpeted as having been personally arranged between Georgia and Robert Irsay. That in turn became a joke in wide League circulation. "The announcement was impossible," the joke went. "Georgia doesn't get out of bed before noon and by then, Irsay is too drunk to talk."

A more common reaction to Mrs. Frontiere's football prowess was offered by another owner. "She's a crazy cunt," he fumed. "Her head rattles when she shakes it yes or no."

Whatever Georgia Frontiere's peers might have thought, she was one of the four most visible figures in the NFL fight over the L.A. Coliseum and would end up heavily splattered in the deposition slinging set off by *LAMCC v. NFL*. The worst of it began in August 1980, when one Mel Irwin approached L.A. County Supervisor Kenny Hahn. Irwin and his wife, Dottie, had been employed by Georgia and the Rams between June 1979 and July 1980, when they were let go as part of a cost-cutting effort. Hahn and Mel Irwin had been high school classmates. Irwin told the supervisor that "the newspapers did not have the full story," that he thought Los Angeles should have a team, and he thought he could help. Hahn called Bill Robertson and Robertson and Irwin had lunch at L.A.'s Papachoux Restaurant several days later.

"Mr. Irwin," Robertson remembered, "told me that his wife had been employed, as well as himself, by the Rosenblooms, and that after Carroll's death, she had been assured by Georgia . . . that her employment would be permanent and shortly after that . . . she was abruptly terminated. . . . He said that he owed no allegiance to Georgia and had some information that might be beneficial to us. He said that the [Frontiere] residence was taped and all phone conversations in the place were bugged. . . . He implied all conversations [there] were taped." Irwin also mentioned that Georgia had assigned him to listen in on "very confidential conversations" between herself and Rozelle. Robertson immediately asked what the content of those conversations was, but "he wouldn't reveal them to me. He wanted to pursue it with responsible people. . . . I asked him if he would talk to attorneys and he said yes, so that's where I left it. . . . Either that evening or the next day I had occasion to be talking to Al Davis and I suggested to Al that maybe his lawyers might want to talk to him."

Robertson discussed the development with Mel Durslag and after Robertson informed Davis, Davis talked with Durslag about Irwin as well. Durslag, Davis remembered, said that "he had heard that Mel Irwin wanted to talk to me. . . . Someone else had called me about would I be willing to talk to Mel Irwin and I asked Durslag if he knew Mel Irwin. . . . I was squeamish about talking to Mel Irwin. Quite frankly, I thought he was a plant. . . . [Durslag] felt [Irwin] was an O.K. guy, what he knew of him."

Shortly thereafter, Irwin flew to Oakland for a private meeting with the Raiders owner. Davis asked him about the conversations between Georgia Frontiere and Pete Rozelle that he'd mentioned to Robertson. Irwin recounted Georgia's panic at the possibility of a Raiders move to L.A. and how Georgia'd had him listen in. He had listened to some six to ten such calls over the previous year. Before Davis's move, Rozelle had always reassured her that Davis could not muster the votes to do it and that she shouldn't worry.

This first meeting with Davis, according to Irwin, was "not very long." Two weeks later, Irwin flew back to Oakland for a second meeting of similar duration. This time, Joe Alioto was also there. After listening to Irwin repeat what he'd earlier told Davis, Alioto agreed that the information would be of some value and asked if Irwin would consent to a deposition.

On October 8, 1980, Mel Irwin was deposed in Los Angeles. The resulting document was a somewhat startling window into Mrs. Frontiere's otherwise private operations. Irwin had begun his employment as director of community relations for the Rams, writing press releases with Georgia's publicity director and working mostly out of the house in Bel-Air. His wife, Dottie, was Georgia's personal secretary. After Dottie suffered a heart attack, Mel took over her duties. According to Mel Irwin, Georgia Frontiere had something of an obsession with getting everything on tape. Irwin drove her from Bel-Air to Orange County whenever she needed to be at the Rams offices or training camp, and on the way, she listened to tapes of phone and other private conversations often recorded, he related, without the knowledge of other participants. The house in Bel-Air included equipment to record both phone calls and gatherings in her meeting room secretly, and there was even a member of the staff designated to keep the equipment functioning properly.

"How come you are taping those phone calls?" Irwin once asked the resident soundman.

According to Irwin, the soundman replied he had orders from "the boss." Georgia was also referred to as "Mrs." Irwin claimed that "Mrs." had confirmed the soundman's assignment to him personally and instructed Irwin not to "butt in." When she wanted to record conversations outside her house, Mrs. Frontiere carried a transmitter in her purse that broadcast to a tape recorder in the trunk of her car. Irwin swore under oath that she had taped Steve Rosenbloom on several occasions before Rosenbloom was fired. He also said that while cleaning up her bedroom once he found two or three cassettes which Georgia had labeled "Rozelle." Once when Georgia was meeting with Harold Guiver during their dispute over Super Bowl tickets, the taping system broke down, and his boss asked Irwin to take Guiver out to see the tennis courts while the machine was surreptitiously repaired. When Irwin had maneuvered Guiver out to see the courts, Guiver pointed out that he had seen them a number of times already, having played tennis there when Carroll was still alive. Obviously, he noted, someone wanted him out of the house for a while.

"What's the matter?" Guiver asked. "Tape machine busted?"

"Yes," Irwin admitted, it was.

While Mel Irwin's claims were titillating, it was Harold Guiver himself who provided the most scandalous contribution to the battle of depositions. Guiver, who had been officially terminated at the Rams earlier in the year, called Mel Durslag. "He told Durslag he wanted to go public about many of the things of the Rams," Al Davis testified. Among those things were Georgia's "ticket scalping," his visit from Jack Catain, and threats that had been made against him at the direction of some unknown benefactor of the Rams. Durslag told Davis about the conversation and that he had advised Guiver not to do it. Durslag proceeded to fill Al Davis in on Guiver's background and what Harold had to say. As Davis recalled, "I think it was [Durslag] who told me that the intrigue of this thing is so great and the whole thing is so big [it] rivals those two fellows Woodward and Bernstein [who exposed the Watergate scandal]."

Harold Guiver and Al Davis talked "about three times" on the phone before Guiver was deposed on October 14. "He wanted to know more about what we were going to discuss," Davis said. "I told him we were going to discuss generally his relations with the Rams and I did tell him . . . that we were going to discuss the Super Bowl tickets." Joe Alioto also promised that "out of respect to Carroll," they would not ask him questions about Super Bowls prior to the 1980 one for which Georgia had allegedly charged him one hundred dollars a ticket.

Davis and Guiver met face-to-face on the day of Guiver's deposition for about forty-five minutes in L.A.'s Bonaventure Hotel. By that time, Guiver had already met with the League's lawyers. "What I told him," Davis testified, "was that I know Pete [Rozelle] is involved in this, and I know you are going to have to try and protect him. He told me that [the NFL attorney] had come to see him and what [Guiver] was interested in was getting at Georgia, nothing else. And I said to him . . . I am interested to find out if Rozelle is involved in the ticket scandal. I know he is, you know he is, and the question is, can he be implicated. [Guiver] said he couldn't do it. . . . He said that [the NFL attorney] was interested in protecting the commissioner and the League [and] didn't care much about anything else." Guiver then entered the deposition hearing and told the story of Georgia and his one thousand tickets to Super Bowl XIV.

When Al Davis was next deposed on November 25, 1980, he pointed to Guiver's testimony as proof that Georgia was marking up tickets for resale and offered it as a motive for her involvement in the conspiracy to prevent a Raiders move. The commissioner, Davis reiterated, "is locked in on this . . . and I think the Harold Guiver situation certainly shows that he has been well aware of it."

The news of Georgia Frontiere's Super Bowl ticket machinations was broken to the public on December 10 by Mel Durslag's paper, the *Los Angeles Herald Examiner*. Her attorneys immediately announced that they would seek to exclude the allegations from the upcoming trial of *LAMCC v. NFL* because they were "sensational, inflammatory, and fundamentally irrelevant.'' Mrs. Frontiere's lawyers would eventually be sustained, but in the meantime, Rozelle again felt he had no choice but to respond. ''Rozelle: Scalping Allegation Is a Hatchet Job,'' the *Los Angeles Times* headlined on December 11. ''It is apparent the *Herald* has access to information from a party to the litigation,'' Rozelle noted, ''which chose to use the *Herald* to misrepresent the litigation in the L.A. area.''

Pete Rozelle was convinced ''the party'' was Al Davis and dismissed the move as a tactical ploy. ''Davis knows that the League as a whole does not like distasteful publicity,'' he told the wire services on the day after Christmas. ''It's a form of intimidation. He figures that the League will get so tired they'll say, 'Al, you go to Los Angeles without a court case.' ''

That, Rozelle pointed out, was not about to happen.

9

By the beginning of 1981, *LAMCC v. NFL* was as much blood feud as lawsuit. Each party saw it as an ultimate test of just what the League was, each claimed the other was bullying him, and both sides vowed to never allow themselves to be pushed around.

That mindset was apparent during the January playoffs leading up to the NFL's American Conference championship. At stake was a spot in Super Bowl XV to be staged in New Orleans at the end of January. The three principal contenders were Art Modell's Cleveland Browns, Gene Klein's San Diego Chargers, and Al Davis's Raiders. Of the three, Davis's team was the decided underdog. The Raiders had only barely qualified for the last playoff wild-card spot but, according to *Sports Illustrated*, ''were a typical Oakland playoff team—mean and ugly and hungry.''

The first face-off was Raiders v. Browns in Art Modell's Cleveland Stadium on January 4. The game was played on an icy field and into the teeth of a freezing wind off Lake Erie. With fifteen seconds left, the Raiders were leading fourteen to twelve, but the Browns were on the Raiders' thirteen-yard line, within range of a three-point field goal. Instead of immediately electing to try for the three points, the Browns made an attempt at a seven-point touchdown, throwing a wobbly pass toward the corner of the end zone. The pass was intercepted by a Raiders defensive safety and the game was over.

The Raiders' victory was the subject of Mel Durslag's column in the *Herald Examiner* the following day. ''Considering what happened to them in Cleveland,'' Durslag wrote, ''the Raiders should begin the championship round by asking for a change of venue, arguing that they can't get acceptable officiating within the confines of the fifty states.'' He went on to make a case against the way the officials had called the game, saying, ''This was a day on which a team suing the League for $160 million and rocking the boat with charges of ticket scalping wasn't going to get the better of anything,'' and concluding, ''Certainly no proof exists the officials were groping for a way to beat the Raiders, but to be on the safe side, Oakland should ask for a change of venue [for the game in San Diego with Klein's Chargers], and, failing, should request an officiating crew from Canada.''

Among that column's readers was Gene Klein. Klein's response was immediate and unmitigated fury. On January 8, he convened a press conference in San Diego and let fly in Davis and Durslag's direction. ''The afternoon newspaper in Los Angeles is an Oakland Raider mouthpiece,'' Klein fumed. ''One of its columnists writes huge lies and makes incredible accusations. This is a devious plot to undermine the officials and intimidate the officials. That's exactly what it is.'' Klein then picked up a copy of Durslag's column and gave a melodramatic reading of it, interspersed with his own sarcastic comments. ''It wouldn't have been a call from somebody in Oakland who asked him to write this—that couldn't happen, could it?'' Klein observed. ''I ask you, gentlemen of the press, if that's fair, equitable, honest reporting or is the writer in somebody's pocket? And for what reason? It casts aspersions on the integrity of the National Football League from top to bottom.''

Klein refused to mention Al Davis by name, but went after him anyway. ''You know where it came from,'' he told the press. All of this was a ''ridiculous smokescreen,'' fueled by ''a group of people who are practicing the big lie, the same thing that Hitler's people practiced, and Mr. Goebbels. You keep telling the big lie over and over again and pretty soon, people start to believe it. Throw enough of it at a wall and hope some of it sticks. That's nonsense. . . . Nobody can play God. No owner has the right to say, 'I like rule one, two, three, four, five, but I don't like rule six, so I won't obey it. I'll do what I want.' . . . All of this intrigue, all of this extraneous matter . . . When I was in business, we had a saying, 'Losers litigate.' All this smokescreen, all this nonsense about scalping Super Bowl tickets has nothing to do with the merits of the case. . . . One man made an accusation which was denied by the people he accused. But he's the only one who *admitted* he scalped Super Bowl tickets. He has admitted in his deposition that he sold Super Bowl tickets to Las Vegas hotels—he says for face value—but he also says he and his employees get in return free rooms, free meals, all kinds of comps. All sorts of questions arise. Was income tax paid on the free rooms? Who knows? I certainly don't. . . . I live by the rules and that's the way most of the owners think it should be. . . . As Commissioner Rozelle told me several years ago, the only thing we have to fear is ourselves.''

Al Davis made no response, though he had in fact confirmed Klein's Las Vegas charges in his November 25 deposition. The arrangement dated from 1977 and the casinos involved were the Riviera, Caesars Palace, the Las Vegas Hilton, the Aladdin, and the Sands. Each year, they split seventy-five to one hundred tickets acquired from the Raiders. At the time the arrangement was first made, Davis testified, he called both C.R. and Max Winter ''and asked them what they thought about it and they told me they were all doing it.''

Mel Durslag issued a public response to Klein as soon as word of the press conference reached him. "Mr. Klein," Durslag observed, "is a deliciously scurrilous individual who takes the position that if you are not on his side, you must be crooked. There is no reason for any logical person in Los Angeles to be on the side of the National Football League in the current argument. The National Football League is not above reproach, nor is Mr. Klein. All are fully capable, if not inclined, to punch to the pelvic region, describing people as being in the enemy's pocket, merely because they reject the political conspiracy that is keeping football out of Los Angeles. Klein voted for the Ram move to Anaheim, openly embarrassed by the land heist involved in the deal. He told me personally it was embarrassing. He would tolerate such a caper and then turn around and call me a Coliseum and Raider house man for trying to encourage a replacement for that team. Klein should be ashamed of himself.''

On January 11, a warm day in San Diego, Davis's Raiders handled Klein's Chargers thirty-four to twenty-seven. Afterward, the Raider players awarded the game ball to their owner. The man doing the presenting was Gene Upshaw, Raider captain and union rep. "This game ball goes to the one man in the organization who has taken more from the fans, the media, and the League than anyone in sports," Upshaw announced. "If anyone deserves a game ball, Al Davis does." Upshaw also made it clear that the team endorsed the larger struggle in which its owner was involved. "One thing that gave me great pleasure was coming down here and sticking it to Gene Klein," he told the press. "The only thing that's left is to win the Super Bowl, to stick it to our commissioner. I'm waiting for him to come into our locker room and present the trophy to us and find out what it's like to be booed.''

That Super Bowl was scheduled for January 25 in the Louisiana Superdome. This time, the Raiders' opponents were Leonard Tose's Eagles and the matchup, Eagles v. Raiders, read the same as the Oakland court case in which the League had unsuccessfully sought to have the Raiders placed in receivership.

For Tose, of course, being in the Super Bowl was the culmination of what once had seemed an impossible dream. "There was a time," he pointed out before the game, "when I said if we ever made the Super Bowl, I'd probably get out. We haven't been there yet, but we're close enough that if you do it once, I can see where you might want to do it two or three times. I don't say that ten years down the road I won't think differently. I'll be sixty-six in March. I feel terrific now, but who knows how a guy is gonna feel at ninety. I do know one thing, I sure as hell have no intention of leaving right now. I certainly don't consider myself the perfect owner. If I get passing grades, I'll be satisfied. You can't expect any better when you've been at it for eleven years without delivering. I feel a responsibility to Philadelphia. I always have. Hey, these fans supported me when we were winning two games a year and if you don't have feelings for people like that, what kind of man would you be?''

Philadelphia would, of course, find out the answer to the question, but that would take a while yet. In the meantime, much of what this Super Bowl meant to Tose himself was buried in the avalanche of pregame hype anticipating the possibility that Pete Rozelle might be forced to award the NFL's greatest prize to his archenemy and legal foe, Al Davis. Rozelle prepared for his Super Bowl week press conference by meeting for an hour and a half with the League's attorneys. In response to a question about whether he'd rather give the trophy to Leonard Tose, the commissioner said, "It makes no difference to me. I totally divorce from my mind problems I and the other twenty-seven owners have with the Raiders when the game begins."

Those problems, however, were the major subject of Super Bowl discussion. If the League lost *LAMCC v. NFL,* he told the reporters, it would have "a very damaging effect" on his power as commissioner, but he would decide then whether or not to resign as a consequence. The commissioner claimed he felt defamed by the ticket scalping accusations. "It hurts me because I care about my integrity," he explained. "I have never scalped a ticket and I don't believe there's any evidence that I ever did." According to Rozelle, it was all part and parcel of Davis's strategy. "Al's attorney, Joseph Alioto, likes to find a villain in the case," the commissioner offered, "and I—as the authoritarian commissioner—was an easy figure. My differences with Al resulted from business matters. It's nothing personal." Those differences had, however, changed his opinion of Davis. "I've always considered Al like a charming rogue," Rozelle admitted, "but in my business judgment, he's gone to outlaw."

Once again, Al Davis said nothing and, once again, Gene Upshaw, leader of the Raiders players, spoke freely. "I may not give Rozelle a chance to present the trophy," Upshaw said. "I may snatch it away from him. Rozelle sees me as the right arm of Al Davis and, if he can slap that arm, he will. I want to see him, standing in that locker room. He'll probably wonder why I'm still in the League. Maybe I'm blowing this out of proportion. Maybe he doesn't care. Maybe he's at a tennis club or on his yacht. Maybe he's worried who's going to get his Super Bowl party tickets, the ones for the party he has with his three thousand closest friends and none of the players. . . . I know the players will say, 'Oh, wow, that's Pete Rozelle, the commissioner.' But if they knew him the way I do, they wouldn't be as impressed. He is a PR guy cloned as a commissioner. With that in mind, he doesn't want to do anything to disrupt anything. In the Atkinson thing,* the players were guilty until they proved themselves innocent. Now, I know Rozelle can play hardball, but I can play hardball too. . . . I know he's in a bitter fight with Al, but I know the ballpark I'm playing in."

The Super Bowl game itself was a thumping from beginning to end. "We're not a bunch of choirboys and Boy Scouts," Upshaw observed of his Raider mates. "They say we're the halfway house of the NFL. Well, we live

---

* The commissioner's 1976 firing of Raider George Atkinson for excessively violent play in a game with the Pittsburgh Steelers.

up to the image." While more than 100 million Americans watched, Davis's Raiders were, he later pointed out, "relentless." At halftime in the Eagles locker room, their coach observed, "There was just an eerie feeling, an eerie quiet feeling. There was a faraway look in a lot of people's eyes. All of a sudden, there was a feeling of shock, a feeling that we had lost it." The final score was twenty-seven to ten. Among the very last people to leave the victors' locker room afterward were Gene Upshaw and his boss, Al Davis.

An hour earlier, the moment they'd both been waiting for had come. With 100 million Americans watching, Commissioner Pete Rozelle put on his best smile and gave Al Davis his second Super Bowl trophy. Davis took it. "Thanks very much," he mumbled. "Thanks very much, Commissioner."

Despite Upshaw's prediction, there was no booing from the Raiders players. Instead, most of them raised the cameras they'd brought just for this occasion and snapped away, recording forever the day they stuck it to the commissioner.

There was, of course, still a great deal more sticking to be done.

If Pete Rozelle wasn't worried, he should have been.

10

Art Modell, like much of the League, worried that the public skirmishing that pitted his friend Pete Rozelle against Al Davis was an uneven match, weighted to Davis and hence unfair. While Rozelle had access to vast resources that Davis did not, on a personal basis, the sentiment was somewhat accurate. Davis was free to do what he wished, whatever anyone else thought. Rozelle, still married to Caesar's wife, had to keep his demeanor dignified throughout. Davis could be inaccessible, Rozelle could not. Davis had only to look out for Al Davis. Rozelle had to look out for League Think as well. Davis could snipe and bludgeon as the occasion arose. Rozelle was bound by both his personality and job description to downplay and soothe. Davis had only to fight. Rozelle also had to clean up the battlefield during intermissions.

In the first few months of 1981 there was little that Modell could do to help out. Everything now hinged on the trial of *LAMCC v. NFL*, scheduled for May. Art Modell continued to defend the commissioner at every public opportunity, but he also had significant problems of his own to look after that spring. The problems were financial and they were mounting. By January 1981, Modell had outstanding personal bank loans of $7.5 million, above and beyond the moneys owed by the Browns and Cleveland Stadium Corp. To service the interest on that personal borrowing would require $2.2 million over the next fifteen months, and Modell was cash poor. Concerned, as he phrased it, to "put my estate . . . in proper shape," Modell described himself as "anxious to consolidate the assets and reduce debt where possible."

Among the assets Modell wished to consolidate, Cleveland Stadium Corp. was his most significant financial albatross. It was carrying some $6.1 million in bank debt, not counting the $1.5 million in improvements it was still obliged to make in Cleveland Stadium and another $1 million it owed Diamond Shamrock Corp. The Diamond Shamrock debt was a result of Modell's agreement to buy out that corporation's share in the hotel on Public Square, a civic gesture that was a less than stellar investment. Cleveland Stadium Corp. reported a $232,000 profit for 1980 tax purposes but would have to pay more than $1 million in interest charges before the year was over. Modell was already worried that it would not be able to pay its debts before the stadium lease with Cleveland ran out in the 1990s.

Part of the reason was the continuing deterioration of the physical condition of the stadium. Despite Stadium Corp.'s expenditure of some $8.5 million to fix it, a new generation of problems seemed to be growing out of the fix itself. Typical was the playing field. The stadium Modell took over in 1974 had been previously improved with new baseball dugouts and immediately adjacent box seats in 1967, but both had been built too low. Players in the dugout could see only the heads of those on the field and fans in the field boxes could barely see over the people in front of them. To remedy that problem, Cleveland Stadium Corp. lowered the field—and opened a Pandora's box.

Cleveland Stadium was built on a landfill substructure and when Stadium Corp. scraped off nine inches of topsoil and another three inches of underlying cinders, the field began gobbling money that Stadium Corp. didn't have. The remodeling had left as little as two inches of silty sand separating the surface and the landfill in some spots. The new field had drainage problems so a drainage system Modell had not calculated on had to be installed. Even that didn't alter the field's spongy character. After particularly heavy rains it was treacherously unstable and prone to collapse in sink holes. In 1981, Modell was still trying to cope with it with no success. Later that year, after a torrential downpour on the eve of a Browns preseason game, the stadium's groundskeeper was inspecting the sideline area when the dirt beneath him gave way and he fell six feet into the landfill. "I would not do it again if I was asked to," Modell commented with a certain disgust about his stadium. "I wouldn't touch it with a ten-foot pole. I would be happy to get out as landlord."

Worse, Cleveland Stadium Corp. was also carrying the burden of its nonstadium investments, particularly the land in Strongsville it had bought from Modell himself six years earlier. Stadium Corp.'s outstanding debt of $2.6 million dated from that purchase. "When he sold that parcel to Stadium Corp.," Modell's minority partner Robert Gries remembered, "Modell had studies done, including the possibilities of shopping centers, industrial parks, and hotel chains. He was going to have an exit off the freeway made. But nothing happened. There was a housing boom in Strongsville between 1977 and 1979, so he went into residential housing instead. He developed about a quarter of the property out there, putting in roads and sewers, and sold it off to two developers. Modell was very bullish about developing the whole thing. He said Stadium Corp. could make $6 million. The boom in Strongsville ended in the middle of 1979 with the rise in interest rates, however, and never revived. The builders Modell had sold the developed piece to went broke, and half the houses they built didn't sell. It was a complete disaster.''

Although Robert Gries owned slightly less than half of the Browns and ten percent of Stadium Corp., he was unaware of Modell's financial pinch. "I knew nothing about Modell's finances," Gries explained. "I knew Premier Electric had gone bad through the talk in the venture capital industry. I knew he also owned a radio station and was in oil with Marvin Davis. He had taken $7 million out of the Browns besides his normal salary and bonuses. My assumption was having $7 million over ten years would be a huge amount of money. I had no idea he was in financial trouble."

That "trouble" was the subject of a series of communications between Art Modell and Central National Bank of Cleveland during March. Modell had borrowed $1.7 million from Central National in order to go into the oil business with Marvin Davis. His interest payment on that loan was due that month and Modell's principal financial adviser, James Bailey, made contact with Cleveland National Vice-President William Huffman, seeking a ninety-day extension on what Modell owed. Bailey advised Huffman that Modell was going to sell off his oil and gas interests because of the rise in interest rates and didn't want to make a "forced liquidation" of the properties.

The extension was granted, and on March 27, Bailey and Huffman met face-to-face to discuss Modell's finances. After the topic of the sale of his oil and gas interests was covered, the conversation proceeded to the subject of the larger financial picture. Modell had the beginnings at least of a plan for financial consolidation. His idea was to merge Cleveland Stadium Corp., of which he currently owned eighty percent, with the Browns, of which he owned fifty-three percent. There were two ways to accomplish that. The current Browns ownership could purchase Stadium Corp. outright, or Modell could buy out all his minority partners so he owned one hundred percent of both enterprises. That would allow him to use the one to pay for the other and consolidate both with the rest of his personal assets. The disadvantage to the latter plan, Modell admitted, was that "I would have needed additional borrowing." The disadvantage to the former, Bailey told Huffman, was that he didn't think the minority partners would approve it.

On April 7, Modell, Bailey, Huffman, and Bill Simon, manager of Central National's Cleveland division, met to continue the discussion. According to Huffman, one of the principal topics was "restructuring the Browns debt and making available new funds" to the tune of $7.5 million. The money would be used to buy out the Gries family and the other Browns partners. Modell and Bailey were hoping for a "sub prime loan" and argued that owning one hundred percent of the Browns would give Modell "more flexibility." It also might result in a Browns merger with Stadium Corp. at "a later date." Art Modell described the proposal as "part of the consolidation of my assets and estate planning."

On April 14, Bailey and Huffman met again, this time with Browns Treasurer Gordon Helms. The discussion centered on the proposed $7.5 million loan. Bailey told Huffman he was to meet with Goldman Sachs in New York within a week, to get the financial house to appraise the value of the outstanding Browns stock. Helms wasn't "overly optimistic" of the minority shareholders "receptiveness," whatever numbers Goldman Sachs came up with. Robert Gries had refused to sell on previous occasions, and there was nothing to indicate he felt any differently now. If that was the case, Bailey pointed out, the alternative was for the Browns to buy Stadium Corp. He told Huffman that would probably cost them $5 to $6 million. Since Modell owned eighty percent of Stadium Corp. and only fifty-three percent of the Browns, the transaction would reduce his net obligations for Stadium Corp. and also gain him a significant influx of cash.

Not long after the meeting, Goldman Sachs estimated that the one hundred percent option would cost at least $9.5 million—$2 million more than originally thought—and Modell dropped the idea for good. On April 24, Bailey informed Huffman that the dominant possibility now was that the Browns would buy Stadium Corp. He would be meeting soon with Cleveland's McDonald & Company for an appraisal. He anticipated a price somewhere between $5.5 and $7 million.

The man whose share of Stadium Corp. would, in effect, increase more than fourfold in such a transaction, the patrician investor Robert Gries, had as yet no idea such a purchase was even being contemplated. It would be months more before he learned about it.

While Modell explored those possibilities behind the scenes, he continued to use his public status as an elder statesman in the NFL to defend Rozelle and League Think. "Right now, it is a complex legal issue," Modell explained in phrases worthy of the commissioner himself. "I consider myself a National Football League man. I believe in the constitution and bylaws. You can't be selective in the rules you want to obey. . . . Oakland has been a great franchise and has sold out its games for thirteen years. Los Angeles is a large enough market to be considered in the future for an expansion team, along with Phoenix, Memphis, Portland, possibly Birmingham, and possibly even Jacksonville. If it's made to sound as if I have a vendetta against Al Davis, I can only reply that such talk is fallacious. . . . Our biggest problems are internal. Sometimes we have nothing to fear but ourselves. I think we are going through a turbulent period. We ourselves, meaning ownership, need to keep the sport healthy. I hope we achieve a measure of stability."

11

Ironically enough, the only signs of rising stability in the NFL in spring 1981 came from Baltimore. Like all situations involving Robert Irsay, however, it had been reached only after a long succession of twists.

By now, Irsay's penchant for bizarre behavior was the stuff of NFL legend. According to accounts in the press, immediately after one Colts loss in which the team's kicker had missed four field goal tries, Irsay announced he was giving the man a ten-thousand-dollar raise "for trying." Shortly thereafter, the kicker was fired. After another Colt loss in Seattle, Irsay attacked the game's officiating, claimed the Seattle ownership had locked him into a luxury box during the game and would not let him leave, and threatened to sue the NFL for $5 million. "To hell with Rozelle," Irsay fumed, "let's see what a federal court has to say." No such suit was ever filed. During yet another Colt losing streak, Irsay began calling the team's plays from the press box, with no success whatsoever. When criticized for doing so, he pointed out that Al Davis did the same thing. "Irsay has never contributed anything to the League since he's been in it," one owner told *Playboy* magazine. "We would be better off without him." After the quote was printed, Irsay announced he was suing the magazine for $10 million. Again, no such suit was ever filed.

Unstable as he was, at least Robert Irsay was now confining his activities to Baltimore rather than shopping for a new home for the Colts.

The talks between Robert Irsay, the city of Baltimore, and the state of Maryland initiated in the mad rush to head off Irsay before the October 31, 1979, NFL meeting had been continuing on a sporadic basis ever since. At the end of February 1980, Baltimore Mayor Schaeffer, Maryland Governor Hughes, and Irsay met in a hotel room at the Baltimore/Washington International Airport. True to their promise, the two politicians had been pushing a $23 million stadium renovation bond issue in the state legislature. To assure its passage, they told Irsay, they needed his agreement to sign a fifteen-year lease. Noting that the same demand was not being made of Edward Bennett Williams, owner of the stadium's other tenant—baseball's Baltimore Orioles—Irsay refused and demanded parity with Williams. Irsay also told *The* [Baltimore] *Sun* he made a counteroffer. If the bond issue was raised to $35 million, Irsay offered, "give me the whole $35 million bond issue and I would buy the stadium."

Later that same day, Irsay told *The Sun* he had never said anything about buying the stadium. "I don't want to buy the stadium," he claimed. "They asked for my personal guarantee on the [$23 million bond package]. Evidently they feel the stadium bill is in trouble. I told them I couldn't guarantee that kind of money. I won't do it and my banks won't let me do it." What Irsay had said was that if the bond issue were raised to $35 million, "I'd guarantee the difference between the $23 million and the $35 million and the state would loan the money to me at low interest, about 6.5 percent." A spokesman for Governor Hughes described the meeting as "tentative" and the situation as "tenuous."

Irsay's refusal to sign a longterm lease without a matching commitment from Edward Bennett Williams had thrown Hughes and Schaeffer back into a dilemma. Williams would have nothing to do with such a longterm lease. He had made that clear at a meeting in the governor's mansion several days before the hotel room rendezvous with Irsay. Far from committed to Baltimore, Williams was known to be privately considering building a new baseball park next to Interstate 95, halfway between Washington and Baltimore. He was also discussing the possibility of managing such a stadium with Art Modell. Publicly, Williams maintained that he would keep the Orioles in Baltimore as long as the town "supports" the team, but refused to define what he meant by the term. According to *The Washington Post*, "because of the conflicting nature of Irsay's and Williams's demands and also because of their apparent dislike of one another, Baltimore city officials have grown pessimistic about their ability to keep both teams."

On April 4, 1980, the state legislature ignored the dilemma and passed a $23 million bond issue to build luxury boxes, new locker rooms, and thirteen thousand new seats in Memorial Stadium. In order for the bonds to be issued, the legislation required Irsay's Colts to sign a fifteen-year lease.

On April 9, Irsay told *The Sun* both that he was personally responsible for the bill's passage and that he would refuse to sign the lease it demanded. "The only way we got it was because I fought for it," he pointed out, "but I'm not going to sign anything he [Williams] doesn't sign." Williams only evinced disgust. "I am in Baltimore," he repeated. "I want to stay in Baltimore. I didn't ask anything from the state or city. I didn't want anything. I supported them in their efforts to please Mr. Irsay. But I find his reaction to what the state and city have tried to do for him so outrageous that I can't comment."

On April 10, Robert Irsay reversed course again, claiming that reports that he was demanding anything from Williams were inaccurate. "I think the reporter was twisting words," he told *The Sun*. "I never said the Orioles had to sign a lease as a condition of my signing a lease. The only thing I said is that I wanted parity with the Orioles. It's not fair for me to be required to sign a longterm lease if the Orioles do not have a similar arrangement, but it is not a condition. I never said I would sign a fifteen-year lease, but the fact remains that this will wash itself out. We haven't talked any further on the lease, but I see no problems."

The "further" talk would consume the rest of 1980 without going anywhere.

In the meantime, Robert Irsay continued to run his team as he saw fit and make sporadic visits to his "hometown" of Baltimore. On May 23, he attended the city's annual Saints and Sinners Roast to benefit the police Boys Club. The subject of the roast was Irsay himself. One of Irsay's players regaled the crowd with the story of how his boss had come to the locker room looking to congratulate his star black running back and congratulated a white second stringer by mistake. The mayor of Memphis described his city as "the cotton capital of the world and Robert Irsay's memorial sewage treatment plant." The toastmaster noted that he would "hate to see Baltimore without a baseball franchise because it would mean we would be without a major league team." Another of Irsay's players joked about how his boss "goes out early for a liquid lunch." Even Irsay's wife, Harriet, got into the act. "He can't afford to divorce me," she noted. "He's not a cheap guy. Players get paid so much we just don't have any more money." Irsay took the jokes in good spirit and donated $1000 to the pot before flying back to his home in Skokie, Illinois.

Despite Irsay's intermittent acts of public goodwill, the popularity of his franchise continued to plummet as the 1980 football season progressed. The Colts won seven and lost nine, better than their five to eleven record of the year before, but the people of Baltimore avoided Memorial Stadium as though the Colts had the plague. In a stadium seating 60,000, Irsay's attendance averaged barely 41,000. On the final day of the season, they drew 16,941, the smallest crowd in the twenty-eight-year history of the franchise. On January 3, 1981, Irsay's general manager announced the franchise was losing money but would not say how much. Even Rozelle now had to admit that Irsay "would have a stronger case for moving than he would have had in the past."

Instead of threatening again to move, however, Robert Irsay headed off on a new tack. On January 16, he mailed a personal appeal to Colts season ticket holders. "There have been matters attributed to me," Irsay wrote, "I know, that have upset many of the fans in the area. For this reason, I have refrained from public comment for most of this past year. Unfortunately, many have interpreted this silence incorrectly. We are the Baltimore Colts. We want to play here, and we want to give you the kind of team you can be proud of again. This is our commitment. I'm a competitive person. I want to win. I've said some things maybe I shouldn't have. If I have offended the fans here, I apologize."

At his Super Bowl XV press conference on January 23, Pete Rozelle went out of his way to praise this fresh approach. "I'm very pleased with his letter to the fans," the commissioner pointed out. "I think it was a good thing and strongly indicates Mr. Irsay's position in regard to Baltimore."

To further indicate his seriousness about staying put, Robert Irsay purchased a condominium near the Colts' new training facility for a home away from home. During most of the football season, it would be occupied by his son Jimmy, recently graduated from Southern Methodist University, where he'd aspired unsuccessfully to play linebacker, and now an aide to the Colts' college scouting department and the team's photographic assistant.

On February 10, Irsay met with Mayor Schaeffer again. The mayor's press aide called it "a very good meeting." Irsay himself made no comment on the meeting but told a reporter from *The Sun*, "Keep on your toes, there are going to be big things happening in a couple of weeks." At the time, there were rumors Irsay might be about to sell his franchise, but he scotched those emphatically. "The Colts aren't for sale," he explained. "About twenty people want to buy the franchise. I got a call from Steve Rosenbloom about selling the club and I told him, 'You would be the last person I would sell the team to.' "

In fact, the "big news" Irsay predicted took almost four months to materialize and wasn't all that big. On June 9, 1981, Irsay signed a two-year lease that would keep him in Memorial Stadium through 1983. The terms— one percent rent on the first $1 million, two percent on the second $1 million, three percent of the third million, and ten percent of anything above $3.5 million—were the best in the NFL. Though the lease was short term, Irsay characterized it as the first step to a longterm lease that would be signed sometime in the coming year. In his ebullience of the moment, he even called Memorial Stadium "one of the best built stadiums in the country."

"The Colts are here to stay," Robert Irsay announced.

By the time of the announcement, of course, the trial of *LAMCC v. NFL* was under way, and few in the League were paying much attention to anything else.

12

Perhaps the most critical pretrial legal skirmish in *LAMCC v. NFL* was the fight over where the trial ought to be held. The League was seeking a change of venue out of Los Angeles. Davis and the L.A. Coliseum were opposed. On March 17, 1981, Davis and the Coliseum won. Judge Harry Pregerson ruled that court would convene in the Los Angeles Federal Courthouse as soon as possible. The NFL appealed his ruling but succeeded only at delaying trial for another two months. According to Joe Robbie, the loss of the venue motion was a critical turning point. "Once we lost the change of venue," he later commented, "we should have settled the case. Your options narrow as courts hand down decisions. We should learn from our experience in the courts and tread carefully and not confront. The obvious resolution is a franchise for both Oakland and Los Angeles. It could have been settled but both sides bowed their necks."

Inside the NFL in spring 1981, Robbie's opinion was a distinct minority. There was more sentiment among the League for expelling Davis than for finding a way to cut a deal. Settlement possibilities were discussed at the League's annual meeting on the island of Maui in March, but, according to

one NFL source, "nothing proposed ever had any real prospect of flying."
Other NFL members were willing to give Los Angeles an expansion franchise
in 1984, but knew that Davis and the Coliseum had "a blood pact" to stick
together and refuse such a blandishment.

"The League had no option," Tex Schramm observed. "There was no
alternative in the League's mind to fighting Davis. It couldn't be kept out of
court." Jay Moyer, Rozelle's in-house lawyer, agreed. "Settlement," he
noted, "was never a realistic possibility at any time I can recall."

Nonetheless, there were several attempts. The man pushing for them was
Harry Pregerson, the trial judge. On January 13, he summoned both sides to
San Francisco for a settlement conference in the chambers of the federal court
of appeals. Aside from attorneys, the NFL was represented by Pete Rozelle,
Wellington Mara, and Billy Sullivan. Sullivan and Mara were included,
Rozelle noted, "because I wanted Pregerson to understand that it wasn't just
Rozelle versus Davis." On the other side were Al Davis, Bill Robertson, and
their attorneys. The meeting lasted for five and a half hours and, Rozelle
remembered, "was organized like shuttle diplomacy. We might all be together with Pregerson sometimes, then just me, then just Al, then the other
two owners." Pregerson was pushing the idea of keeping the Raiders in
Oakland but creating an expansion franchise in Los Angeles that would be
awarded to Davis.

"Why are we talking about giving Davis an expansion team in Los
Angeles?" Joseph Cotchett, Georgia Frontiere's attorney, asked. "He won't
come down here on those terms."

"Why do you say that?" Pregerson asked.

"Judge," Cotchett answered, "I'll prove it to you." He turned to Joe
Alioto, Davis's lawyer. "Joe, I'll sell you the Rams right now. Would Davis
like to buy the Rams?"

"No," Alioto responded, "you're right. Al wouldn't do it. He'll only
come down here with the Raiders."

Nonetheless, Pregerson insisted the discussion of possible compromises
continue. His idea had evolved into splitting the Raiders in half, with one
piece going to L.A. and the other staying in Oakland under new ownership.
Though both sides promised to continue to think it over, Pregerson's efforts
went nowhere on January 13. "I thought the meeting today was not particularly productive," Bill Robertson commented afterward to the *Los Angeles
Times*. "I'm not too optimistic, but we all agreed we'd try to come up with
creative ideas and get back to the judge."

Robertson and Rozelle next saw each other at Super Bowl XV in New
Orleans, a week and a half later. In their brief conversation, according to
Robertson, the commissioner offered L.A. an expansion franchise if they
would drop the suit.

"It's too late," Robertson answered.

It may well have been, but Pregerson continued to push his formula for
compromise throughout the spring. The closest it came to success was in a
series of private meetings that began when Bill Robertson attended a political

fund-raiser in Los Angeles and was seated next to Lew Wasserman, head of Universal Studios and an old friend of Rozelle's. Robertson and Wasserman had been on friendly terms since Robertson's union organized the workers who sold snacks to the tourists on Universal's guided tours. Wasserman had also been a charter member of the mayor's pro football search committee. "We started talking about the situation," Robertson remembered, "and someone suggested Wasserman talk to Rozelle. Later I met with Wasserman and I told him up front that I thought something might be done. The best thing was for he and I [sic] to meet with Al Davis."

Wasserman gave one of the people involved in the negotiations the "impression he was there with the knowledge and consent of Rozelle," but Robertson remembered him as "clear that he was an ambassador without portfolio." He was, however, game to try. "Wasserman was torn by his friendship with Rozelle," Robertson remembered. "He wanted the Coliseum to have a football team and tried to function as a mediator. He was sincere in his efforts."

Sometime in late March, Wasserman and Robertson met with Davis at the Beverly Wilshire Hotel. "We were trying to work out some formula for splitting the Raiders," Robertson claimed. "Al was courteous without indicating he was receptive." According to Mel Durslag, "Wasserman [was] attempting to bring peace with a plan that would call for Al Davis to sell his interest in the Oakland Raiders and take a similar position with an expansion team in Los Angeles. . . . But the conditions under which Davis even would consider the idea [were] clearly specified. First, he would have to be guaranteed half . . . of the current Oakland roster. Second, he would have to be granted the same control of the L.A. operation that he has in Oakland. . . . And the third provision would be that the Los Angeles Coliseum would follow through with the . . . promises it made to Davis when Al previously attempted to shift the Raiders to this city." Robertson also maintained that Davis had to be part of any future L.A. ownership. "If it weren't for Al," Robertson pointed out, "Los Angeles would have no case at all. Davis became our sole hope, and ethics demand that we stick with him to the finish."

Wasserman's effort died not long after Durslag wrote in his column that "prospects for a settlement of the most volatile legal case ever to visit sports are beginning to brighten."

"Wasserman got mad because Davis didn't call him back after their meeting," one source claimed. "Davis didn't really trust Wasserman and they both had huge egos." According to Robertson, "word came that Rozelle was not receptive and nothing ever came of it."

Either way, by May 1, the possibility of the case being settled was dead. On May 13, jury selection commenced. League Think's decisive battle was under way. The trial was expected to last four months, feature more than one hundred witnesses, and cost at least $5 million in attorneys' fees before any possible appeals would be completed.

Privately, attorneys from both sides described the outcome as "up for grabs."

13

Though the case was composed of complex series of interlocking pieces, the issue that divided the two sides who faced each other in Los Angeles Federal Court was simple at its core. The LAMCC contended that the NFL's Section 4.3 concerning franchise movement was "illegal in that it restricted the individual teams from moving and . . . anticompetitive in that it did not allow stadiums to compete for NFL teams." Davis's Raiders joined in that contention and also claimed that Davis "was not bound by the rule since he had an oral contract that he could move without a vote," given to him at the League meeting in Chicago on October 4 and 5, 1978. In addition to NFL's having acted in "bad faith" as a whole, Davis contended, Georgia Frontiere, Gene Klein, and Pete Rozelle "conspired individually to keep the Raiders out of Los Angeles."

In response, the League argued that there had been no conspiracy on the part of the individual defendants and that Section 4.3 was "valid, not anticompetitive, and a reasonable rule for leagues to have for the betterment of fan loyalty and stability." Most important of all, the League maintained, the NFL was "a single economic entity with a unitary product and [therefore] could not conspire together to commit an antitrust violation."

Pete Rozelle would be one of the most important witnesses in the trial. He and Carrie moved to a hotel in Beverly Hills for the duration. Most days they sat together in the first row of the courtroom on the right hand side. When Carrie wasn't there, she was taking tennis lessons back at the hotel. On the very few occasions when Pete wasn't there, he was over at the Los Angeles office of NFL Properties, trying to conduct the ongoing business of the League. Every evening after court adjourned, he would return to the hotel with the League's attorneys, order dinner from room service, and review the legal material for the following day. He also talked on the phone with the League office and various owners who called, wanting to know what was going on. He looked tanned and composed in the courtroom, but the experience was enormously wearing. Usually a sound sleeper, he now woke often in the middle of the night and paced back and forth, thinking.

Rozelle was the first of the NFL's inner circle to be called to testify. He had been preparing for the performance for weeks and his attorneys acknowledged his would be the most difficult task of the entire trial. "He had a burden that I'm not aware of any other witness in any other trial having to carry," a League lawyer observed. "Pete had to answer hostile questions about literally anything and everything that had happened in this League for the previous twenty years." He would be on the stand for more than a week, with a weekend off and a half a day's break in the middle. In sum, the *Los Angeles Times* noted, "Rozelle's polished performance . . . was about what had been expected. His reputation as an exceptional witness had preceded him. While he lived up to it, he did not surpass it. . . . Rozelle, sometimes known affectionately and otherwise as 'Pope Peter,' was an urbane, cautious, well-spoken, persuasive advocate of the League position."

Rozelle's advocacy began with a two-hour stint on Thursday, May 21. He evidenced irritation only at the very end of the day, when Joe Alioto was questioning him about his telephone conversations with Mrs. Georgia Frontiere in the fall of 1979. Using material gleaned from Mel Irwin's deposition, Alioto wanted to know if Georgia hadn't said she wanted the Raiders stopped because she couldn't stand "the competition." His voice rising, Rozelle said he didn't think he'd ever heard Mrs. Frontiere use the word "competition."

"That's a buzzword used for the purposes of this case," the commissioner snapped. "I don't think that word is in her vocabulary."

Alioto then hammered at Georgia's reactions to the "Welcome L.A. Raiders" banner hung in the Coliseum that September.

"She didn't know what it all meant," Rozelle answered. "I just knew she was under pressure, thrust into the limelight for the first time in her life." She was "angry and upset," but calls from owners in that state were part of his routine as commissioner. "One of my roles is to play psychiatrist," he explained.

"In your role as psychiatrist," Alioto wanted to know, did Rozelle realize her real problem was "she had a vehement objection to the notion of the Raiders moving?"

Rozelle answered that he avoided diagnoses of that depth, "perhaps because I'm not a schooled psychiatrist, just a lay psychiatrist."

"Did you say, 'Don't worry'?"

Rozelle said that phrase was a routine part of dealing with owners. "It's my fastest way of getting off the phone at night," he explained.

On Friday, May 22, Rozelle and Alioto butted heads over Davis's alleged oral contract made at the League meeting in Chicago in October 1978. According to Rozelle, Davis had "absolutely not" been given assurances he could move during the vote on Section 4.3. He had merely said, "I reserve my rights." Just what those rights were, the commissioner testified, "was never clarified for me."

When court resumed on Tuesday, May 26, Alioto badgered Rozelle about the League's motives for halting Davis and got Rozelle to admit that there were other violations of the constitution besides Davis's and some of them had gone unpunished. On May 27, Alioto turned the witness over to Maxwell Blecher, the LAMCC's counsel, and Blecher slashed away at the notion of the NFL as a single entity. While Rozelle pointed to the NFL's internal sharing as proof, Blecher kept hammering at the fact that there were significant differences in income between the member clubs, making some more competitive than others. When court was over for the day, Al Davis took up the same theme with reporters on the steps outside. He claimed that the Rams had $2 million more annual ticket income than the Raiders and, counting their luxury box rentals, had made somewhere between $3.5 and $7 million more than he had the previous year.

Pete Rozelle got a break for most of Thursday, May 28, when Gene Klein was called to the stand. Klein's appearance was taken out of order to accommodate his schedule and it lasted almost four hours. "Testimony Proves Klein Is Class Act," his hometown *San Diego Union* headlined, and went on to praise his performance for its self-possession, wit, and eloquence.

Klein's lengthy testimony was broken by several recesses, during which he mingled with reporters in the hall outside. Complimented on the job he was doing, Klein chuckled, "Boy, these lawyers can kill you." The remark would soon qualify as the most ironic of the entire trial.

Certainly Gene Klein seemed at the very least drained during his final fifteen minutes on the stand. He began sweating profusely and answering hesitantly. "I was going to tell the judge I wasn't feeling well," he remembered, "and then the questions were over." When dismissed, Klein rose and walked straight out of the courtroom. "He didn't stop or say anything," Rozelle recalled. "I remember thinking it was strange, he can't have anything that important to do. I thought he would stay for at least the rest of the session and my testimony."

"I barely made it across the courtroom," Gene Klein explained.

Once outside the courtroom doors, Klein told one of the reporters who had followed him, "I'm not feeling well. I really feel awful." He had pains in his left arm and shoulder and violent feelings of nausea. "I don't think I can make it," he said at one point. A security guard called the paramedics and Klein waited for them in a witness room, his head slumped on his hands, his shirt drenched with sweat. Ten minutes later Gene Klein was wheeled out to an ambulance, strapped to a gurney and an oxygen mask, and rushed to Queen of Angels Hospital. He had suffered a massive heart attack. By evening he was listed in "satisfactory condition" in intensive care, but over the next week, his condition was made "almost desperate" by a mysterious infection. Klein would run a 105 degree temperature and lose all lucidity. When the infection was finally in hand, he would be transferred to Cedars of Lebanon Hospital, where his recuperation lasted another four months. "It was as tough a period as I ever had," he remembered. "I had trouble even walking across a room."

Pete Rozelle learned of what had happened from Judge Harry Pregerson. The commissioner had resumed the stand but not yet begun to testify. Pregerson caught Rozelle's eye and Rozelle leaned toward him to hear better. "Mr. Klein has had a heart attack," the judge whispered. After trial was done for the day, Rozelle went out to Klein's hospital but no one was allowed to visit with him. "I'm shocked," Rozelle told reporters. "It's hard to believe. He was so vibrant on the witness stand." Henceforth, however, Gene Klein would be no factor whatsoever in *LAMCC v. NFL*.

On Friday, May 29, as Klein lapsed into feverish incomprehension, Pete Rozelle spent his last day on the stand. It was arguably his worst. He looked tired and, at times, uncomfortable. Perhaps the most uncomfortable moments surrounded the letter he had written Al Davis in January 1980, warning him of the potential consequences should he move without League permission. The first line of the letter included the statement "you took the position that no vote by the NFL member clubs is necessary." The word "necessary" was what Joe Alioto was interested in. Heretofore, Rozelle had maintained that he knew nothing of Davis's belief that he had been given an oral contract allowing him to move on his own until after Davis had filed suit. "Necessary," however, implied that Davis had explained why he wasn't going to ask for a vote. "What he told me," the commissioner insisted, "was, 'If I decide to go, I do not intend to go to the League for a vote.' " There was no discussion at all about what was "necessary" and its use in the letter was a "false" account of what had transpired. The letter had been drafted "quickly" by the League's attorney, Rozelle explained, and he had signed it "because I wanted to get it out to him."

Al Davis, the "him" in question, watched Rozelle squirm from the middle of the courtroom's first row. Like Rozelle, he had moved into a local hotel for the duration and spent his evenings talking legal strategy with lawyers. He would also be in court, watching, every day the trial was in session. While most observers gave the commissioner's testimony relatively high marks, Davis was contemptuous. "He's good at a press conference when he's got control of the situation," Davis noted, "but when he was on the witness stand, I wasn't impressed with the way he handled himself under pressure. . . . He was caught being incorrect on several cross checks or said on numerous occasions that he didn't remember."

Al Davis's turn would come soon. During the recesses out in the hallway, Davis told several reporters he was "nervous" about testifying. Most of them found that hard to believe.

14

Al Davis was preceded on the stand by Georgia Frontiere. Though not as regular in her attendance as either Rozelle or Davis, she and her husband, Dominic, were often seen in the back row on the same side as the commissioner. She later reflected on her experience there in a poem, "Courting a Sport":

> I think we are missing one thing in this case
> The rules have been made so we won't lose our place. . . .
> The truth is a weapon that each side can use
> But the fact still remains a half truth will confuse

And so while the pages are transcribed each day
There is no way of knowing just who's gone astray
For, blending the truth with unbelievable lies a bitter result
will most surely arise. . . .

Georgia took the stand on June 8 and finished her testimony on the morning of June 9. She was wearing a periwinkle blue suit and her blond hair fell onto her back. On her way to the witness chair she gave Al Davis a long "how-dare-you" stare. There had been a lot of wondering just how Georgia would do, matched against Joe Alioto, but she acquitted herself well. "Her background as an entertainer showed," the *Los Angeles Times* observed. "She was a poised witness. She didn't devastate anybody, but she didn't walk into any manholes either."

When Alioto intimated she had been a show girl, Georgia took it in stride. "I was an aspiring opera singer," she answered in a frosty voice, "but I learned I couldn't make a living singing opera, so I went to singing more popular songs."

When Alioto noted that she had fired some twenty-seven Ram employees since taking over the L.A. franchise, she looked convincingly sad. "I don't keep count," she noted. "I never liked firing anyone."

Georgia admitted that she had not been well prepared for some of the business and legal aspects of running a football team. "I couldn't get in my head what 'pecuniary' and 'fiduciary' meant," she remembered. "I'd go to the dictionary afterward and look up the word."

Al Davis and her late husband, Carroll Rosenbloom, had been close. "He loved him," she said of Carroll's feelings for Davis, "as much as one man can love another man." Prodded by Alioto, she also testified that Carroll had told her that after his death, "if you ever need any help and someone you can really trust, it will be Al." She had not consulted Davis because "I felt he was rejecting me. Maybe he couldn't see a woman as being equal, as an owner of a football team." On the day of the banner incident in 1979, Davis had been "withdrawn, cool, not the usual exuberant, affectionate Al." As a consequence, she had called Rozelle afterward. She had indeed been upset. "I didn't think that was a nice thing to do for Carroll's memory," Georgia testified about the banner and her subsequent call to the commissioner. "I hated to bother him, but I felt that I needed moral support . . . that perhaps I wasn't being accepted. He reassured me everything was fine . . . and said to keep your chin up and I wondered how that would help me. I was hurt and angry that someone wanted to hurt me. . . . They were calling us a lame duck team and I didn't even know what that meant." She had not told Rozelle that she couldn't stand the "competition."

Asked if the commissioner's surmise that the word "competition" was not in her vocabulary was true, Georgia hedged somewhat. "Well," she answered, "up until recently, I thought the only competition would be if a girl came along and tried to take my husband."

Since Judge Pregerson had ruled all the material provided by Harold

Guiver was inadmissible as evidence, Georgia had to answer no questions about it, but she did have to respond to the deposition of Mel Irwin. "I have [recording] equipment," she admitted, "not to record telephone conversations, but to get information off the telephone."

"You've lost me," Alioto pointed out.

"I didn't tape phone conversations unless it was something I had to remember," Georgia explained.

And what about the two tapes marked "Rozelle" that Irwin had seen?

Georgia thought one of them might have been from one of his press conferences and the other was "one with his favorite songs on it."

During much of her testimony, Georgia stared straight at Al Davis in the front row. After it was over, she was relieved. "It's a bit like an operation," Mrs. Frontiere told a reporter out in the hall. "You don't know what they're going to remove."

The most controversial aspect to Georgia Frontiere's testimony emerged after she had left the stand. On June 10, Judge Harry Pregerson received word from his clerk that two of the jurors thought something untoward might have been going on when Georgia was testifying on June 9. Pregerson immediately called a halt and spent two hours interviewing the two jurors and then Dominic Frontiere in his chambers. According to the *Times* account, "a woman juror noticed on Tuesday [June 9] that Mrs. Frontiere was pausing and looking into the spectator section before answering questions. The juror followed Mrs. Frontiere's line of sight . . . and saw Frontiere moving his head, sometimes up and down and sometimes sideways. . . . The woman juror was reported to have nudged a male juror and called his attention to Dominic Frontiere's head movements. One of the jurors later told the court clerk that the movements might have been signals."

Dominic Frontiere denied the allegations. He said he had noticed that his wife "was not completing all her sentences in her last hour on the stand Monday. He said he'd told her about it that evening and noticed improvement when she resumed her testimony Tuesday morning. Inadvertently, he said, he may have nodded approvingly.

Waiting in the hallway while this was going on in the judge's chambers, Georgia was outraged. "It's utterly ridiculous," she insisted. "It's preposterous. No one has to tell me what to say."

Pregerson apparently agreed with her. "There was some concern about conduct that occurred in the spectator section of the courtroom during proceedings held on Tuesday," he finally reported. "The court has talked to the parties involved and . . . concluded that nothing improper took place. . . . So as far as the court is concerned, the matter is closed and we'll move on as we have before."

It was now Al Davis's turn on the stand and he'd been there since Georgia finished on June 9. His testimony would last through June 18 and his short appearance on his first day was considered "preliminary." He confirmed what Georgia had said about his relationship with her late husband, Carroll Rosenbloom. "I was very fond of him," Davis offered. "He was a close personal friend of mine.'' As he testified about Carroll, Georgia Frontiere rose from her seat in the spectator section and left the courtroom ''distraught.'' Her attorney later informed reporters that ''she was in tears and spent thirty minutes in a witness room outside the courtroom regaining her composure.''

The Al Davis visible to the jury in *LAMCC v. NFL* was, at least on the surface, a different man from the one the rest of the League was familiar with. Gone was the black suit, white shirt, and silver tie; gone was the amulet from oddsmaker Jimmy the Greek. At one of his depositions, Al Davis had arrived dressed in a black and silver workout suit emblazoned with Raiders symbols, but that, too, was nowhere in evidence. In their place were tasteful suits of blue and gray, sometimes with modest pinstripes, light blue shirts, and quiet blue ties. His only jewelry was a single Super Bowl ring. His voice dropped often into southern tones as he testified and he always addressed Joe Alioto as ''sir'' and ''Mr. Alioto.''

The approach, according to the hometown *Times,* worked every bit as well as Rozelle's had. ''Davis,'' the paper reported, ''sometimes known affectionately and otherwise as 'the Genius,' was more blunt and less grammatical, but just as sharp and forceful. Rozelle was thought by some to have been too evasive too often. Davis, on the other hand, was said by NFL loyalists to have such sweeping recall that he could remember things that hadn't even happened. Rozelle, a seasoned witness, looked more at ease on the stand than Davis. But Davis did not look nervous, just intense. He was never close to cracking up.'' The NFL's attorneys agreed with much of the assessment and one called Davis the ''most ringwise'' witness he had ever encountered. Writing for the area Davis was seeking to leave, the *San Francisco Chronicle* offered a theory for his success. ''Davis could be a convincing witness,'' it commented, ''because . . . he believes what he's saying. This is classic behavior: Al Davis against the world. Much of his behavior over the years has been predicated on his belief that everyone else is out to get him. He has always believed others capable of the kind of action he would take. . . . Based on that kind of reasoning, it is only a short jump to the conviction that his fellow owners are united against him.''

On June 10, after the interruption to assess whether or not Dominic had been giving signals to Georgia, Davis testified about the oral contract he had received from the League in October 1978. Of the Chicago meeting's final day, after the other owners had attacked him for holding out, he testified, ''I said, 'If you fellows want to do what you want to do . . . I'll change my vote to abstain for the right to move without approval.' '' At that point, he continued, ''someone from the other side of the room shouted, 'That's it! ' '' Before the actual vote had been taken, he had a ''private meeting'' with Rozelle in which ''I told him I might want to move down the road and I mentioned Los Angeles.''

On June 11, Davis claimed that the Rams, by virtue of their new stadium acquired at lucrative rates, had made at least $4 million more than the Raiders in 1980. ''I just want parity, or close to parity, with top teams,'' he claimed.

By way of an example, Davis offered international politics. "If Russia has so many nuclear weapons, I want America to have at least a near equal number." On Friday, June 12, Davis testified that San Francisco 49ers owner Eddie DeBartolo had told him in early 1980 that "he'd give us the buses to move, that it would mean five to ten thousand more season tickets for him immediately."

With about an hour of court time left before the weekend, Joe Alioto handed his star witness over to the NFL for cross-examination. The first attorney to go after him was Patrick Lynch from the Los Angeles firm of O'Melveny and Myers, hired to lead the League's case. Earlier in the trial, Lynch had referred to Davis's oral contract claim as "trumped up," and Davis had responded that Lynch's statement was a "falsehood."

"I apologize for saying you trumped it up," Lynch offered in a quiet voice. The attorney paused a beat before continuing. When he did, his jaw was set and his voice raised to a shout. "When did you trump it up?" Lynch demanded.

Joe Alioto was on his feet in a flash, bellowing that Lynch ought to be cited for misconduct. Then, according to one courtroom observer, Alioto "snarled some contemptuous words at Lynch out of the side of his mouth."

Before trial broke for the weekend, the tone for Al Davis's next week had been set.

From June 14 to June 18, the NFL's lawyers went at Davis in shifts.

"Didn't it strike you as puzzling," Lynch asked, that the commissioner's letter on January 10, 1980, made no reference to any oral contract?

Davis answered that the only thing that "struck" him was "that the letter was written by a lawyer, and it was written to protect Pete."

When the defense attorneys hammered on the other testimony that contradicted Davis's version of the October 1978 meeting, Davis stood his ground. "I've found a lot of people here under oath made statements related to that October meeting," he pointed out, "and I dispute their integrity." The truth of the matter was, Davis insisted, that the NFL's own attorneys had called Section 4.3 illegal.

"I don't know that, sir," Lynch snapped.

"Oh, you don't," Davis snapped back. "Well, I'll tell you then."

By all accounts, Davis's toughest day on the stand was Wednesday, June 17, and his most effective tormentor was Joseph Cotchett, Georgia Frontiere's attorney. Cotchett noted that Davis had testified that the future possibility of pay TV had played no role in his decision to move but that his testimony was contradicted by Bill Robertson's, who claimed Davis had mentioned it among his reasons for wanting to come south. "Who is telling the truth?" Cotchett thundered. "Is it Mr. Robertson under oath, or is it you under oath?"

Joe Alioto was on his feet immediately and forced Cotchett to withdraw the question and ask instead if Robertson was "mistaken."

"It is conceivable in the discussion the words 'pay TV' could have come up," Davis admitted, "but it was never discussed." Robertson's testimony expressed only "his feeling. It wasn't my state of mind."

Noting Davis said, like a southerner, "ah" instead of "I," Cotchett asked, "Is that accent an affectation of yours?"

Davis said it dated from the 1950s, when he was a coach in South Carolina.

"You have told people you can charm anyone," Cotchett continued, "haven't you?"

"I have told people I can charm people if I have to, yes," Davis admitted. "I can charm if I have to . . . but I'll follow through with anything I say I'll do."

Cotchett also wanted to know what was "the primary thing" in Davis's life.

"To win," he answered without hesitation, "outside of life, health, and death—to win."

As Wednesday was waning, Cotchett scrambled to score his last points of the day. He began quizzing Davis about an interview he had given *Inside Sports* magazine. In it, Davis was quoted as saying, "I didn't hate Hitler. He captivated me. I knew he had to be stopped. He tried to take on the whole world." Cotchett introduced the quote via overhead projector, so it was blown up on a giant screen.

After court was out for the day, Joe Alioto called the move "a cheap shot" and "a stab in the back." On June 19, Judge Pregerson agreed with him and ordered the jury to ignore all references to that quote about Hitler. Later that Thursday, Davis finished testifying and left the stand.

It had been an impressive performance. "I thought he would be a good witness," one observer remarked to the *Los Angeles Times,* "but he's even better than I expected." Judge Harry Pregerson was reportedly among those most impressed. According to a federal court source, he later described Davis in private as the best witness he had ever seen.

"I sort of hate to see you leave," Pregerson noted as Davis stepped down.

"I'll see you around," Davis answered.

The courtroom audience laughed, but for many, it was more nervous gesture than spontaneous mirth.

15

Though Al Davis, Pete Rozelle, Georgia Frontiere, and Gene Klein were the focus of the trial, a number of other NFL members participated in one way or another. Some came to testify and others just visited for a while, sitting in the courtroom, and left. Leonard Tose was one of the latter. He arrived with a well-developed cynicism about the legal process. "Lawyers are all full of shit," he observed. "The only thing they agree on is how much to charge."

Nothing Tose saw in Judge Harry Pregerson's court changed his attitude. The experience also further soured him on Pete Rozelle. "It didn't take me long to decide we couldn't win," Tose remembered, "so I met with Al Davis. Davis was reluctant to come, but I got him to agree to meet with Rozelle. Then I called Rozelle and suggested he meet with Davis and me. Davis would have settled, he was willing to go back to Oakland. He would have settled for money and stadium improvements there. He was reasonable and prepared to cut a deal. Rozelle called me back the next morning. He said he wasn't interested. Our problem was that nobody had balls enough to take Rozelle on. He made the decision to pursue the lawsuit. Davis would cut a deal, but Rozelle wouldn't even consider it."

Unlike Tose, the other League members who came to the trial did so to offer Rozelle moral support in his vigil there. Some testified as well, but their contributions were at best a mixed blessing. "There is a perception," the *Los Angeles Times* noted, "that the testimony of NFL witnesses has, at times, been more helpful to the other side than to their own."

Tex Schramm's was a good example. Though the NFL's case was to portray Davis as someone who had dealt in bad faith with Oakland negotiators from beginning to end, Schramm supported Davis's version. When the offer from Lionel Wilson and Cornell Maier had been made, Schramm testified, Davis had told him "he felt it was something he was going to have to accept."

Herman Sarkowsky's testimony had worked to a similar effect. The chairman of the NFL's fact-finding committee on Davis's proposed move admitted that his impression was that Davis had bargained hard with Oakland, but not dishonestly.

"You don't accuse him of bad faith in negotiating a hard bargain?" the LAMCC's Maxwell Blecher prodded.

"No," Sarkowsky answered, "I just consider him a hard bargainer."

Chuck Sullivan's testimony was abortive as well. He claimed that at the March 3, 1980, League meeting in Dallas, Davis had approached him and stated that both Davis and Sullivan's brother-in-law Joe Alioto were "concerned" at Sullivan's opposition to Davis's move. Then Davis had threatened him. "If you don't lay back," Chuck Sullivan claimed Davis said, "we're going to have to go after you."

Al Davis laughed that one off in the hallway outside. "I've never thought of Mr. Sullivan as someone I'd go after," he noted. "I don't give him that much credibility. Mr. Sullivan is very young, he's immature."

Perhaps the most conspicuous blunder on the stand was made by Rozelle's friend, Art Modell. Modell had been the most present of all the nondefendants and spent at least two months in Los Angeles, often sitting next to the commissioner in the front row. "It's an important case to the future of football," he explained. "Either we have a set of rules or we don't. If the jury says these rules are illegal, then we have to start all over."

Modell's testimony lasted two days, most of it spent fending off the assaults of Joe Alioto. "He's a very bombastic person," Modell remembered, "and he and I went at it pretty good. Neutral observers say I won, but I don't know." Modell's slip-up came under the pressure of Alioto's badgering during his second day on the stand. Throughout his appearance, the Cleveland owner had been adamant in refuting Davis's claim to an oral contract and Alioto swarmed all over his version of the events in the Chicago League meeting in October 1978.

During the roll call vote in Chicago, hadn't Davis said, "I reserve my rights to move"?

No, Modell insisted, he had said only, "I reserve my rights."

Alioto asked the same question over again and got the same answer. Undeterred, Alioto asked yet again and at last struck paydirt.

"Mr. Alioto," Modell answered, "you can keep me here all summer long. I am not going to change my testimony. All he said was, 'I reserve my rights to move.' "

As soon as the last two words were out of Modell's mouth, a stir moved through the courtroom. Sensing the stir, Alioto asked for the court reporter to read back the transcript. Modell had indeed said, "I reserve my rights *to move.*"

The audience laughed.

"I misspoke myself," Modell explained in chagrin. "All he said was 'I reserve my rights.' "

Despite occasional appearances by other football moguls, the six weeks that followed Al Davis's departure from the stand were torpid. "NFL vs. Raiders," the *Times* bemoaned, "Will It Ever End?" Most of the testimony concerned the precise shape of the football business, with one side claiming a single entity and the others attacking that notion.

Once during that period, unbeknownst to the bored onlookers, the whole affair came within inches of being declared a mistrial. The incident commenced when the NFL team began having questions about one particular juror. The judge had ordered, as part of jury selection, that the jury would be made up of a certain proportion from L.A. County. The juror in question had a residence in Los Angeles but reportedly spent most of his time at his girlfriend's house outside county limits. Looking for possible mistrial grounds, an NFL functionary had, according to a source close to the case, approached a part-time security guard the League had hired on a temporary basis and asked the guard to call the juror at his girlfriend's. The idea was to acquire proof he was not, in fact, a true resident of Los Angeles County. Instead of making the phone call, however, the security guard informed the Raiders and the whole mess ended up in being hashed out with Pregerson in judge's chambers. The discovery gave Joe Alioto the opportunity to move for a mistrial then and there, but he declined to push it. Convinced he was winning his case, Alioto did not want to stop and start over. His refusal ended the incident, the parties returned to the courtroom to slog onward, and the public remained oblivious to the allegation of jury tampering.

The trial's final six weeks were exceedingly dry except for two legal rulings handed down by Pregerson. Both were critical in shaping the final outcome.

The first came on June 26, after the plaintiffs, Davis and the LAMCC, had rested their case and the NFL had responded with a motion to drop all charges. After a submission of briefs on the question, followed by two hours of oral arguments, the judge ruled that the trial of the NFL would continue. The trial of the individual defendants, however, would not. Charges against Pete Rozelle, Gene Klein, and Georgia Frontiere were dropped for lack of evidence and would not be submitted to a jury. "Reasonable jurors would not find that the three named individuals conspired," Pregerson ruled. When the ruling was finished, the *San Francisco Chronicle* noted, "Al Davis stalked out of the courthouse and declined to comment to reporters."

Pete Rozelle, on the other hand, was jubilant. "I feel like $160 million," he gushed. "Now Carrie can have another baby." Regaining his composure somewhat, he gave a more sober assessment. "The case has been cluttered with personal issues," Rozelle explained, "but the judge has done a fine job of carving them out." Pregerson had removed "the scurrilous material that they've tried to personalize this with. . . . Maybe the main thing is that now they can't use all this junk stuff in cross-examination and closing arguments, and we can get down to the actual case."

Georgia Frontiere broke into tears when the ruling was made. "I'm most happy for Pete Rozelle and Gene Klein," she told reporters out in the hall. "They did not deserve to be here and neither did I. I learned a lot about the justice system. There's justice after all. I believe in justice and I'm thankful I live in America."

Even increasingly feisty Gene Klein made a statement over the phone. "Al Davis is a master of throwing crap against the wall and seeing what sticks," the recuperating Klein told the *San Diego Union*. "There was not a shred of evidence against myself, Pete Rozelle, or Georgia Frontiere. It was all part of the game Davis plays of putting extraneous things in orbit so he can take the focus away from the real issue. . . . Al Davis is really a bully . . . but he wasn't dealing with the new kid on the block."

After that flurry of activity at the end of June, the trial resumed its humdrum pace, unbroken even by legal rulings. Though it often seemed to be going nowhere, there was a drift to the trial's progress, and by July 20, the *Los Angeles Times* was reporting "a growing impression among observers at the National Football League antitrust trial that the wind has shifted and that the NFL is now sailing more or less into the teeth of it."

That conjecture was confirmed on July 24, when Judge Pregerson made his second major ruling. In it, the *Times* noted, Pregerson "demolished the League's first line of defense."

"The undisputed facts preclude treating the NFL as a single entity for the purposes of this lawsuit," the judge ruled. "On its face, the NFL certainly appears to be an association of separate business entities rather than one single enterprise. The twenty-eight member clubs are all separate entities—some corporations, some partnerships, and some sole proprietorships. No two clubs have a common owner. The clubs share a large part . . . of their revenues [but] do not share profits or losses. They are managed independently. . . . They do not exchange or share their accounting books or records.'' The effect of the ruling was to bar the jury from considering the single entity question, but the jury still had to decide whether the NFL response to Davis was a restraint of trade and unreasonable. Nonetheless, the League case had been severely injured.

''The single entity defense was the primary defense argument,'' one of the League's lawyers complained. ''We had pitched our case narrowly on that basis. Through the whole term of the litigation, Pregerson had refused to rule on that point, saying it was a jury question. Then, days before the end of the trial, he says he'd been thinking about it and decided it wasn't a jury question and ruled against us. It was very damaging to the NFL case. After the trial, the foreperson on the jury said, 'That was a pretty good defense and if the judge hadn't taken it away from us, we might well have found you were a single entity.' ''

The League used its summation to regroup as best it could, and on July 29, *LAMCC v. NFL* was finally given to the jury to decide. The wait on their deliberation lasted almost two weeks. Then on August 11, the impasse was broken and the trial, now eighty-four days old, began a rapid collapse.

The catalyst was juror Thomas Gelker, a sixty-six-year-old retired plastics manufacturer from Anaheim. On August 11, a reporter informed Judge Pregerson that he had learned that Gelker's cousin had once owned a team in the defunct World Football League. Since, as the *San Francisco Chronicle* pointed out, ''all ten jurors were selected on a primary criterion of having virtually no knowledge or interest in professional football and no relations or friends involved in the NFL,'' the revelation raised a legal storm. When informed about Gelker by Pregerson, Joe Alioto and Max Blecher argued that the information had been concealed by Gelker himself and that he should be dismissed from the jury. Pregerson took their motion under advisement and then interviewed each of the jurors individually.

Thomas Gelker claimed he was not at all close with his cousin and hadn't seen him in ten years, since before the cousin ever got into football. According to ''a source'' of the *Los Angeles Times,* ''three jurors told the judge that Gelker displayed extensive knowledge of football though he had represented himself during jury selection as uninformed about the sport. . . . Gelker identified NFL Commissioner Pete Rozelle in a pretrial questionnaire as a 'baseball official' but later gave his fellow owners a 'lecture' on how Rozelle's office distributes Super Bowl tickets.'' The jury foreperson, Carole Slaten of Big Bear, said Gelker had ''made a statement on the first day that indicated to me personally that it wouldn't matter what we said, or what evidence was taken out of the files, that that's it.'' She also later claimed that ''Tom Gelker was biased against Al Davis.'' In the poll Pregerson took as he interviewed jurors, the split was eight for the plaintiffs, two for the defense, and Gelker was one of the two holdouts. Few jurors had any optimism at all that a unanimous verdict was possible.

Late in the evening of August 13, Judge Pregerson announced that the "likelihood of the jury arriving at a unanimous verdict is nonexistent" and declared a mistrial. The most decisive battle in the history of the NFL had ended in no decision and would have to be replayed.

At his press conference the following day, Al Davis charged that juror Thomas Gelker had been "planted" by the NFL. "I anticipated this type of thing," he noted, "that the NFL would do everything it could to win. It's the law of the jungle." Davis was gratified that his "credibility" had been sustained by the vote of eight to two. He also intended to continue the case. Asked if that wouldn't hurt the League, Davis was defiant. "I am the NFL," he boasted. "I am the establishment. I believe in it. I'm not trying to make anyone squirm—but if I did, I think it would have been fun. I'm sure there is some animosity among the other owners, but I really don't think there's that much. There's a couple of owners who try to act tough, but I don't think they're tough."

It was likely that one of those owners to whom Davis referred was Art Modell. Modell, back in Cleveland when the verdict came in, was more ebullient about it. "Naturally," he pointed out, "I would have preferred a clear-cut victory, but the jury could not reach a decision so, so be it. . . . I consider it to be total vindication of Pete Rozelle. . . . It represents a victory in that it vindicates Pete's credibility, integrity, and honor, as well as the credibility, integrity, and honor of the other twenty-seven owners in the League. . . . Now we'll take our chances in a retrial."

But Pete Rozelle did not act vindicated. "I'm disappointed we didn't win it," he commented. "That's what we came here for. But considering it's a local issue and it was tried here in Los Angeles, it would be like Ronald Reagan breaking even with Jimmy Carter in Plains, Georgia."

When he met with the press after Davis's press conference, the commissioner was, in fact, as agitated as any of the reporters covering the trial had ever seen him, so much so that he attacked the press themselves, violating a cardinal rule of public relations. The articles that had run about Thomas Gelker set him off. "The message is," Rozelle complained, "if you're on a jury involving the city of Los Angeles and the Los Angeles Coliseum, you better be supportive . . . or you're just going to be castigated by the media." Rozelle went on to note that the "tone" with which the reporters had approached Davis at his press conference was "friendly and supportive," while Rozelle himself had been fielding questions that were markedly unfriendly. "I've had friends in the media I've known for thirty-five or forty years who are cutting the hell out of me," the commissioner complained. "It's like Alioto cross-examining me." Such treatment was an example of why the retrial should be held "any place" but L.A. Support for Davis "permeates the entire area" and a fair trial was impossible. "You people want a football team here," Rozelle whined.

Shortly thereafter, Pete Rozelle and his wife headed back to Westchester and the New York office. Al Davis flew to Green Bay, Wisconsin, where his team was about to play an exhibition game.

Of the two, Rozelle looked decidedly the worse for wear.

16

Bedraggled or not, there was no respite for Pete Rozelle. *LAMCC v. NFL* would not convene again until April 1982, and, in the meantime, though the Davis case was still the greatest of the commissioner's nightmares, there were other threats on the League's horizon that also demanded his attention that fall. Fittingly, the most significant of those, like the problem of Al Davis, was yet another subject about which he could do little but worry. Once again, the National Football League Players Association was stirring, and doing so in ways that made everyone in the League uncomfortable.

The 1981 football season that commenced shortly after the Los Angeles mistrial would be the last one conducted under the 1977 contract that had finally settled the Mackey case and brought labor peace. The union had been making noises about the coming expiration of the contract since 1979, and by now, Ed Garvey was giving it his full attention. Garvey's notion of a federation of professional athletes had long since collapsed in red ink and he had retrenched, retreating back to his established turf of football. The losses the NFLPA had incurred from Garvey's adventure nonetheless played a significant role in the 1981 situation. When the union accepted an agreement in 1977, the idea had been to use a portion of the damage settlement of *Mackey v. NFL* and *Alexander v. NFL* to accumulate a strike fund for the day when the contract was over. Next time, Garvey had pledged, they would go into their battle against management well armed. Unfortunately, the cash didn't accumulate the way they had imagined. Quite the contrary.

The union executive committee had first been informed of the dilemma at a meeting in Miami during Super Bowl Week in January 1979. One of those present was Bob Moore, a former Oakland Raider and Tampa Bay Buccaneer tight end who had played college ball for Stanford. Moore, recently retired as a player, was one of the union's vice-presidents and its assistant director. He was also one of Garvey's closest personal friends. Their families socialized together and Moore was one of the NFLPA's key organizers. In Miami, Moore remembered, "Garvey came in looking white. 'What's wrong,' I asked. He then tells the executive committee that we're $1 million in the hole. 'What are you talking about?' everyone asked. Garvey had spent everything, including the $750,000 [from the Mackey settlement]. We asked Garvey, 'Where'd it go?' Garvey didn't know where it went."

Upon receipt of the news, Bob Moore and Len Hauss, union president, flew to Washington, D.C., and rushed to union headquarters to look at the books. "Some of it was explained," Moore remembered, "but I can't explain where the $750,000 went to this day. There were no major expenditures listed to explain it. I kept after the bookkeeper, but I never got a full explanation."

Keith Fahnhorst, player rep of the 49ers, confirmed Moore's version. "There was supposed to be a $1 million strike fund," he explained, "but it wasn't there. The money from the settlement had been poorly invested and a lot of debt was hidden in the books." Certainly no such $1 million loss showed up in the union's 1979 financial report to the Labor Department. That form indicated the NFLPA's total assets had risen from $950,000 to $1.1 million and its net assets fallen from $313,000 to $297,000. In 1978, net assets had fallen to $313,000 from $607,000. During the three reporting periods since the strike had been settled, net expenditures on union employees had risen from $306,000 to $751,000.

Whatever the reasons, as the union prepared for new contract talks in 1982, they knew they would have no strike fund to see them through. One immediate effect was to add to the pressure on Ed Garvey when the union began designing its approach to negotiations during 1979 and 1980. He was already under pressure for having traded away all the rights to free agency won by the Mackey case and his critics claimed the players had nothing to show for it. Their average pay was still the lowest of the nation's three leading professional sports, largely because football was still the only one without any form of free agency to bid prices up. There had been assorted attempts to vote Garvey out of his executive director job since 1977, but all of them had been relatively easily handled. By 1980, however, it was widely believed that would not continue to be the case if Garvey did not deliver in 1982.

Ed Garvey's response to that dilemma was a bold one. Rather than turn back in the direction of free agency, he pushed for taking the issue to its logical conclusion by seizing a piece of the business itself. The mechanism for doing so was called percentage of the gross. Instead of demanding free agency, the union would demand that fifty-five percent of all NFL clubs' gross income be allocated to player salaries. Those salaries would be distributed by the union according to a formula taking into account position and seniority. According to the union's figures, players' salaries currently amounted to only thirty percent of the gross. Operating expenses accounted for thirty-four percent and owners' profits, thirty-six percent. In effect, Ed Garvey was suggesting that the union abandon its traditional position of negotiating only minimum levels and benefits and demand the right to negotiate salaries for all its members. Coupled with a percentage of the gross, Garvey argued, such an arrangement would be worth much more than free agency ever was.

The history of the NFLPA's adoption of percentage of the gross as a primary demand was also the history of the disintegration of Ed Garvey's friendship with Bob Moore, the NFLPA's assistant director. "At one point I thought he was my closest friend in the world," Moore later remembered with some bitterness. "Now, I can't stand him. He was in it for the visibility and ego. He would never answer his phone calls personally unless it affected his personal standing. He'd never talk to the average guy. He was a great speaker with a great sense of humor, but he was trying to be a senator."

Their falling out was not over the idea of demanding a piece of the action. Moore considered the idea a good one but it had become apparent to him that "the players didn't like it. Every guy believes he's the next superstar," Moore explained. "By the end of 1980, I became aware that percentage of the gross was a losing cause. I told Garvey, 'We don't know where we stand and we're going to have to go to war on this with the owners.' Garvey said no, the idea had vast support." On the eve of a series of early 1981 membership meetings to refine the union's strategies, Moore and Garvey also disagreed on what should be the union leadership's approach. Moore proposed to Garvey that they present a series of options but, he remembered, "Ed didn't like doing it that way. His approach was that percentage of the gross was the best and we had to sell it to the players."

That selling was the last straw for Bob Moore. "He was like a fucking used car salesman," Moore complained. "The way Garvey sold percentage of the gross to teams was he would go to the chalkboard and do 'the numbers.' He would estimate teams' costs and figure percentages. Then he'd say, 'Here's what percentage of the gross means.' The way he figured it everybody would make three times as much as they were making then. After that, Garvey would ask the players, 'What do you think?' Everyone agreed with him. He was amassing an overwhelming majority."

Bob Moore made a last ditch effort to derail the Garvey express at a meeting of player reps held in Chicago about the same time Al Davis was testifying in L.A. "Things had come to a head," Moore explained. "There were four or five guys on the executive committee who wanted Garvey's ass, who felt we couldn't go on strike with him, and I called them. I told them this was our last chance to dump Garvey before it was too late." The four men Moore called were Gary Fencik of Chicago, Dewey Selman of Tampa Bay, Keith Fahnhorst of San Francisco, and Len Hauss, the union's outgoing president.

"Bobby Moore called me," Fahnhorst remembered, "he said, 'Things are going on that you need to know about.' "

"Do we need to fire Garvey?" Fahnhorst asked.

"Yes," Moore answered.

The dissidents met in Fencik's Chicago apartment the night before the player reps' meeting and discussed who else might be on their side. Later that evening, according to Moore, "Garvey got word of what we were up to. We made some serious mistakes. We thought we'd just go in with our core group and fight it out, but he pretty much cut us off at the pass." Fahnhorst agreed. "Garvey blew us out of the water," he remembered. "We didn't seriously understand how powerful Garvey was."

The next morning, before the meeting began, Ed Garvey approached Bob Moore.

"They're after us," Garvey warned his friend.

"I'm one of them," his friend answered.

According to Moore, Garvey offered to resign but then refused to do so when the meeting began. "The fight was on," Moore remembered. Moore started it by resigning his post as assistant director, arguing that he couldn't keep the post and try to oust the director. Then he launched his argument for dumping Garvey, emphasizing what he called the poor management of the union, Garvey's lack of respect in the eyes of players, and that the union could not get a good contract with him at the helm. The opposition to Moore was led by Gene Upshaw, employee of Al Davis and the Eastmont Mall and incoming union president. According to Moore, there were three principal arguments for keeping Garvey but "no one said Garvey was the right man for the job." The first argument was that Garvey had announced the whole staff of some forty employees would resign if he were ousted. "That scared the shit out of a lot of players," Moore remembered. The second argument was that it was "too late" to fire Garvey. Negotiations would soon begin and there was no time to regroup. The third argument was that the attack on Garvey was "racially motivated," based on resentment of Garvey's multi-racial policies. "Garvey presented it as a black/white thing," Moore claimed, "and Upshaw got the blacks together behind it."

The result was a walk-over. "What we wanted wasn't even voted on," Fahnhorst remembered. "We ended up with a vote on whether or not to extend Garvey's contract, not terminate it." The vote to extend passed eighteen to seven, an overwhelming Garvey triumph.

Afterward, Ed Garvey and Bob Moore met outside the meeting.

Garvey was very friendly and told Moore he wasn't going to accept his resignation as assistant director.

Moore told his former friend that he was resigning anyway.

By the end of June, Bob Moore had severed his ties to the NFLPA and returned to California to finish law school.

Traveling in the opposite direction, Pete Rozelle got back to New York a month and a half later to find percentage of the gross was entrenched as the union's position. By then, of course, management's position was fairly well set as well. The work of putting the position together had been done by the management council's new director, Jack Donlan. Formerly a vice-president in charge of labor relations at National Airlines, Donlan had been hired after an interview with Chuck Sullivan, the management council chairman, in July 1980. Donlan arrived with a reputation as a "union buster," although he denied the description. While at National, he had helped steer the airline through a bitter fourteen-month strike with the Machinists Union, one of the NFLPA's closest labor allies. "Donlan was a hit man," Ed Garvey later complained, "not a negotiator. He was brought in to bust the union."

According to Garvey, the first time he and Jack Donlan met was in the summer of 1980, not long after Donlan was hired. To get acquainted, he visited Garvey in the Washington, D.C., offices the NFLPA rented from the Machinists. "The first words out of his mouth," Garvey remembered, "were that they were canceling a joint labor/management career counseling program because they didn't think it made sense. I said, 'Fine, get the hell out of here. You're just here for show anyway.' It's Rozelle, Schramm, and Modell who decide everything. I was so ticked off.''

Donlan has a different version of the encounter. ''I hadn't heard of Garvey before I looked at the management council job,'' Donlan remembered, ''and during the month before I went on payroll, I collected information. I was struck that Garvey was already talking about a 1982 strike in August 1978. I thought that was strange. Unions use a strike threat to get something, usually at the last stage. They don't talk about it early. After three weeks on the job, I called Garvey and went to D.C. to meet him. He says to me that the biggest problem we have is we're supposed to have two arbitrators for injury grievances and we only have one because labor and management couldn't agree on a second. So when I got back to New York, I looked at the union's list of acceptable arbitrators and picked one. Then I called Garvey with his name. Garvey went off the wall. He says, 'Where do you get off choosing a neutral?' ''

During the first eight months of 1981, Donlan and the management council executive committee made the rounds of a series of ''mini-meetings with groups of owners. We picked their brains for the best ideas,'' Donlan explained. ''Then we put all those ideas together and presented them to the executive committee. They adopted the outlines of a negotiating position. We talked among ourselves about opening negotiations early, during the 1981 season, but Garvey's attitude vetoed that. Garvey was bound to put the worst face on everything we did, so we didn't want to negotiate during the season. It would just detract. By then, the owners were convinced Garvey wanted a strike.''

Perhaps the most notable exception to that generalized sentiment was Al Davis. ''I don't think there will be a breakdown in labor negotiations if we handle it intelligently,'' Davis observed. ''Sometimes we have in the past. Sometimes we haven't.''

Pete Rozelle said nothing about the gathering impasse, preserving his self-proclaimed ''neutrality,'' but worried nonetheless. After all the disastrous publicity being generated by *LAMCC v. NFL,* the last thing the League needed was a labor war.

His friend and lieutenant, Art Modell, was more vocal. ''There's always a possibility of a strike next fall,'' he told reporters before a September 1981 speech at the City Club Forum in Cleveland. Modell hoped there wouldn't be, but percentage of the gross was an ''unworkable'' proposition.

In private, Donlan passed the same message to Garvey. ''Look, Ed,'' he said, ''the owners are not going to let you in their knickers. There's no way. It's just not going to happen.''

Ed Garvey ignored his advice completely.

17

Of all the NFL owners, Art Modell had the most immediate and personal reasons for fearing a labor war. Professional baseball had gone through a player strike in the summer of 1981 and, as the landlord of a baseball team whose rental was collected as a percentage of gate receipts, he had experienced the grim reality of a financial dislocation that was, for the rest of the League, only abstract. Cleveland Stadium Corp.'s revenues had dipped significantly as a consequence of the baseball strike, and, at the same time, the interest rates Art Modell's stadium company was paying rose from seventeen percent to more than twenty-one percent. Though "I was totally preoccupied with the Oakland Raiders case in Los Angeles" while this was going on, Modell admitted, the situation "shook me." As he put it, "the whole ballgame changed" that summer and, back in Cleveland, Modell began scrambling to prop up Stadium Corp. and find someone to sell it to.

The most obvious candidate for a buyer continued to be Modell's football franchise, the Cleveland Browns. On June 3, while Modell was at the commissioner's side in L.A., James Bailey, Modell's financial adviser, had met with an officer of Cleveland's Union Commerce Bank to discuss Modell's finances again. Union Commerce held a good portion of Modell's debt, mostly in one-year notes secured by Browns stock. These notes were customarily rolled over when their due dates came. The bank considered Modell a "longtime customer" who had "never missed any interest payment on any loan" and the bank "wanted Modell's business." Bailey reported that Modell was in the process of selling his oil and gas holdings. He had also commissioned McDonald and Company, a prestigious local financial house, to ascertain Stadium Corp.'s value in preparation for sale. "One of many plans considered at that time" was for the Browns to then buy it, generating immediate cash with which Modell could pay off his personal debts. Modell himself would later testify he didn't "seriously consider" that option until the late summer or early fall.

Preparations for some sort of sale, however, had begun the previous spring, when Modell set things in motion by calling Joseph Thomas, the managing partner at McDonald and Company. Thomas and four other partners in the firm also owned small bits of Browns stock. Then he conducted Thomas and another partner on a tour of the stadium itself. In preparing their report, McDonald and Company had basically three assets to evaluate. The first and principal asset was Stadium Corp.'s lease with the city of Cleveland allowing it to treat the stadium as its own until 1998. The second was the parcel of vacant undeveloped land in Strongsville. The third was Stadium Corp.'s two-ninths interest in the hotel on Public Square. By July, that hotel had been sold to a limited partnership based in Milwaukee in exchange for a note payable in full after twenty-three years. At that point more than two decades down the line, Stadium Corp.'s two ninths would be worth $4 million.

On August 12, 1981, while *LAMCC v. NFL* was teetering on the doorstep of mistrial, McDonald and Company dispatched its initial report, addressed to Art Modell, president of Cleveland Stadium Corporation. It valued Stadium Corp. at between $5.2 and $5.9 million after deducting its outstanding debts. Modell responded by asking for an "updating" on Stadium Corp.'s value if sold to the Browns rather than any other buyer. He also called Joseph Thomas. "I do not accept your values," Modell told him. "I think they are inadequate, but I asked you for the record and I will live by your recommendation." Nonetheless, McDonald and Company was soon working on a revision of its Stadium Corp. report.

In the meantime, Modell took two significant steps to pave the way for a sale. The first was to meet with his minority partner Robert Gries in September. The subject of their discussion was the Browns, of which Gries controlled some forty-three percent. Modell mentioned that there was an "interest by an outside party" in Gries's football holdings. Though Modell did not identify him, the "outside party" was his oilman friend, Marvin Davis. In any case, Gries once again responded that he had no intention of selling. Most of their time was spent discussing the diversification of Cleveland Browns Football Company, Inc. Modell wanted to start a newspaper, the *Browns News Illustrated,* and had plans to put the Browns in the travel agency business, "to service our fans that go on road trips." In that context, he also mentioned the possibility of the Browns purchasing Stadium Corp. The mention itself, Modell explained, was "just conceptually . . . as part of an overall discussion concerning diversification." In any case, the mention was made and Gries apparently made little in the way of response.

Art Modell's second step that September was to pursue stabilizing Stadium Corp.'s finances. On September 1, a memo on that subject from one of his employees reached Modell. It specifically recommended that an independent concessionaire be approached about buying or leasing those rights from Stadium Corp. Modell gave the go-ahead shortly thereafter, "to see what avenues would be afforded to us." By October 9, discussions were under way with three different possible concessionaires, and final bids were expected to be forthcoming shortly.

By October 9, McDonald and Company had checked back in again with better news. In answer to Modell's original question, a McDonald partner indicated that Stadium Corp. would be worth $1 million more to the Browns than any other buyer because of the peculiar advantages that arrangement would afford. In addition, McDonald had redone its figures and boosted Stadium Corp.'s worth by yet another $1 million for all buyers. The new figures had been reached by assuming the stadium lease with Cleveland would be renewed on the same terms until the year 2018, then assuming that the cash flow they had projected for the lease's original term would continue as a constant for an additional twenty years, and finally discounting the calculation by twelve percent. Robert Gries, a venture capitalist himself, would later describe the process as "one of the strangest ways of trying to justify a million dollars I have ever seen in my life." As of yet, however, Robert Gries knew nothing of what Modell was planning.

Art Modell was more forthcoming with Union Commerce Bank. On October 13, he and Bailey met with the head of the commercial loans division. The good news, Modell announced, was that his oil and gas interests were being bought by his friend Marvin Davis for some $4.9 million. That sale would close in February 1982. Modell was also enthusiastic about progress on the concession front at Stadium Corp. When the concession sale was made, he would have enough to pay at least a good portion of the corporation's $6 million debt, with $1.5 million left over to pay for the repairs still due to be made under the terms of his Cleveland lease. Next the discussion moved to the sale of Stadium Corp. to the Browns. Modell contemplated realizing such a sale by March 1982 and indicated that he expected to net approximately $5 million from it, enough to "extinguish" his debts at Union Commerce and, combined with the sale of his oil holdings, extinguish his borrowings at Central National and National City as well. He and Union Commerce discussed the financial package that would be necessary for the Browns to make the purchase. Finally they discussed the fact that Modell had interest to pay in the meantime to cover his personal obligation and might need a temporary loan in the immediate future.

On October 22, Modell had the Browns' treasurer work up a schedule to see how the terms of a possible concession sale might fit into the larger financial game plan that was emerging. According to that schedule, the Browns' debt then stood at roughly $2 million, Stadium Corp. owed $6 million to banks plus an outstanding $1 million note owed Modell from the earlier purchase in Strongsville, and Modell himself owed $8 million. Two possible concessionaire scenarios were mentioned. The first was an outright grant of $3 million. That money would reduce Stadium Corp.'s debt to around $4 million, a remaining obligation that could "ultimately" be repaid from the sale of the lots in Strongsville. The second scenario called for the concessionaire to loan $7.5 million at favorable rates. Six million of that would pay off the banks and the other $1.5 million would meet the corporation's obligations to Cleveland. Stadium Corp. would be left with a more manageable $8.5 million debt. If the Browns then bought Stadium Corp. at a price that realized the expected $5 million net for Modell, the Browns majority owner would be left owing less money than he would get from the oil sale and by March 1982 would be out of debt altogether. In the process, the Browns would have increased their indebtedness eightfold.

On November 11, Cleveland Stadium Corp. announced that a tentative agreement had been reached with Servomation, Inc., a national concessionaire. Under the terms of the agreement, Servomation would lend Stadium Corp. $6 million at nine percent over eight years on a schedule of accelerating payments. In addition, Servomation would put $1.5 million into capital improvements to satisfy Cleveland, all of them to the stadium's concession facilities. According to Modell, it wasn't until Servomation had entered the picture that he had become convinced that Stadium Corp. was the right purchase for the Browns.

Art Modell informed Robert Gries of that conclusion on November 24, two days before Thanksgiving. Modell telephoned Gries and asked him to come down to the Browns office and bring his brother-in-law, Robert Cole. Cole was in the process of being divorced by Gries's sister, but the relationship was "still very amicable" and, for the moment, Cole was still a director of Gries Sports Enterprises and still filled one of the Gries seats on the board of the Browns. Two months earlier, Gries had loaned Cole $250,000 to see him through "a very severe financial difficulty" and "still considered him at that time as part of the family."

Down at the Browns office, Modell informed Gries and Cole that he wanted the Browns to purchase Cleveland Stadium Corp. and expected to present such a proposal to the board by early 1982. He gave Gries the two evaluations by McDonald and Company and indicated that yet a third evaluation was on the way, designed to reflect the addition of the Servomation refinancing. Verbally, Modell pointed out, McDonald and Company had indicated that the increase to the original report would now be $1.5 million. The Browns, the Browns president contended, were the "logical" buyer. As president of Stadium Corp., he was prepared to make the corporation "available" for $6 million. That offer was followed by what Robert Gries remembered as "a big build-up as to why he thought this should be done."

Gries took the McDonald and Company reports and said he would like time to look them over. "I couldn't comment much," he remembered. "This was the first I'd learned that reports had even been made." Noticing the August date on the initial McDonald and Company document, Gries asked why he hadn't been shown the report before, since he was a stockholder in both the Browns and Stadium Corp. Modell answered that he hadn't decided on the move until now. The addition of Servomation had finally made it the right course for the Browns to take.

When the meeting ended, Gries said he would look the reports over and get back in touch. Modell said he would keep Gries posted.

It had apparently been a good meeting from Modell's perspective. On December 1, his financial adviser, James Bailey, met with a vice-president at Central National Bank about Modell's finances and stated that he "felt confident the merger [of the Browns and Stadium Corp.] would succeed."

By then, Robert Gries had read the McDonald and Company reports. He shared none of Bailey's confidence. "When I first read the October report," Gries remembered, "I laughed out loud. It seemed obviously just a way to get the value up to $6 million. Its reasoning was a little atrocious. When I looked at the report, I saw the land in Strongsville valued at $3.8 million. So I called a developer I knew and had a meeting. He knew the land in question. I said, 'What's it worth?' He said, 'Take a half a million dollars if anyone offers.' I also had an appraisal done of the hotel notes. They were overvalued by more than half a million. At that point, I knew I had problems." By Gries's own estimate, the whole operation was worth no more than $2 million net. Over December, he expressed his objections to James Bailey.

Gries's objections seemed to have little impact on Art Modell's plans. On December 23, he and Bailey met again with Union Commerce Bank, where the Browns owner had a note coming due in eight days. The principal subject of the discussion was the possible consolidation of Modell's personal debts, including not only those with Union Commerce but also his notes at Central National and National City. While bringing all those together at Union Commerce, Art Modell also needed a new loan of $1.5 million "to cover year-end funding of miscellaneous investments, internal advances, interest, and other requirements." The "internal advances" referred to the money he had been fronting himself from the Browns and paying back at the end of the year, a practice about which Robert Gries as yet knew nothing. The total "consolidation" Modell asked for was $10 million. The term would be less than a year.

Asked how he intended to pay $10 million so quickly, Modell answered that part of the money would come from the sale of his oil and gas interests for $4.9 million in March 1982. The rest he intended to generate from the sale of Cleveland Stadium Corp. around the same time.

18

Despite his preoccupation with meeting his Cleveland debts, Art Modell also managed to participate in the major drama surrounding *LAMCC v. NFL* as it waited to be retried. The dilemma facing the League was how to break out of its current legal encirclement. There was still another trial to go through, but it would be held in L.A. and the last jury there had voted eight to two for Davis. The next trial would also be subject to the legal rulings made by Pregerson, making "single entity," the NFL's defense of choice, inadmissible from the beginning. One way out of the trap was to split Los Angeles away from Al Davis before the next trial started. Art Modell, commuting between Cleveland and L.A., was a central player in the League's exploration of that option.

Modell's efforts began in response to an opening provided by Los Angeles Mayor Tom Bradley in the last week of September 1981. By then, Bradley was in the first stages of his campaign to become the state's first black governor, trying to answer the question of whether he could rally support outside the Los Angeles basin. On Friday evening, September 25, his campaign took him to San Leandro, next door to Oakland, to address a banquet of the Alameda County Building Trades Council. It was suspected he might encounter significant resentment from the crowd because of his city's enticement of the Raiders, and Bradley came prepared to mollify. "I'm not here to pirate away a team from any city," he told the labor leaders. Bradley claimed he did not want to see a second trial of *LAMCC v. NFL* and that he intended to approach Pete Rozelle to see "if there isn't some way to reach a settlement of the lawsuit." For his kicker, Bradley announced that he planned to ask Rozelle to "get an expansion team down in Los Angeles and leave your Raiders alone." The crowd cheered. Los Angeles reporters ran for the telephones.

The *Times* trumpeted Bradley's dramatic reversal of stance: "Won't Try to Get Raiders, Bradley Says." Oakland's Lionel Wilson had nothing but praise for the announcement. "Now that Tom's got the message and he really understands that the Raiders have got to stay here," Wilson applauded, "I'm going to give him all I have in terms of making him the next governor of California." The LAMCC's current president, Mike Frankovich, confirmed that Bradley had already discussed the plan with him. "Until Rozelle makes the move," he cautioned, "there is nothing we can say. Until the NFL makes an approach to us, there is nothing we can say. I don't try to approach Rozelle. It would be weakness on my part." Immediately after Bradley's speech, Bradley and Wilson announced they would be making a conference call after the weekend to the commissioner to ask him to "get going on negotiations."

Tom Bradley's move caught the Raiders' other Los Angeles allies totally by surprise. "The speech was a mistake," one source close to Bradley explained. "He got carried away. It wasn't a prepared remark and the people traveling with Bradley were shocked." When the story of what Bradley had said ran in the Sunday morning *Times,* Bill Robertson was on a vacation in the Far East and attorney Stephen Reinhardt was holding down the fort. He immediately called Bradley at home and asked him if that was what he'd really said. The mayor admitted it was, but it wasn't what he'd really meant. He'd meant that Oakland deserved a team, but not the Raiders. Reinhardt said he had to straighten the confusion out the next day or risk the Raiders' move falling apart.

Next Reinhardt tracked down Robertson in Hong Kong and woke him up with a phone call at 4:00 A.M. local time. "Bill," he said, "you've got to get back here." After getting a transpacific account of what Bradley had set off, Robertson placed some calls to Los Angeles and then caught the first plane back, determined "to try to square things up."

That Reinhardt had successfully plugged the gap in the meantime was apparent during the heralded conference call linking Bradley, Wilson, and Rozelle on Monday morning. The discussion lasted ten minutes. Afterward, Bradley announced that he and Rozelle had agreed on "the possibility of beginning negotiations that will settle this issue." Bradley had imposed only two conditions. The first was that Al Davis had to be part of the ownership of any expansion team in Los Angeles. The second was that the team be stocked by the League with players who would make the team immediately "competi-

tive with any team in the League." According to Lionel Wilson, the conditions amounted to yet another reversal of position. "I did not know he was
going to attach the conditions that he did," Wilson explained. "I was frankly
taken by surprise." The conditions "tended to belie any reasonable chance of
settlement," largely, the Oakland mayor noted, because of the insistence
upon the inclusion of Davis. The NFL had already made it clear that Davis
controlling any franchise in L.A. was "unacceptable."

Nonetheless, the negotiations Bradley had promised were actually begun.
Each side sent representatives. L.A.'s were Robertson, Mike Frankovich, and
Stan Sanders, another LAMCC member. The NFL's were Art Modell and
Tex Schramm. "It was all to be very quiet," one source close to the
negotiations pointed out. "No one was supposed to know. I was surprised
Rozelle had appointed Schramm and Modell. I didn't expect someone with
authority." The process culminated at a meeting in the Ramada Inn on Pico
Boulevard that lasted three or four hours. In essence, the discussion went
nowhere. "Their demands were excessive," Art Modell explained. "They
wanted a cash settlement and an expansion team." According to Robertson,
the League's problem was Al Davis. "Rozelle was going down the line on
this thing," he claimed. "He wouldn't let Al Davis in Los Angeles under any
circumstances."

The failure of those first abortive efforts induced by Tom Bradley's slip
of the tongue did not put the issue to rest. It was now obvious to all concerned
that Davis's control of his Los Angeles front was deteriorating rapidly. "A lot
of L.A. support was ready to sell Al Davis out," Robertson remembered.
Robertson's friend and confidant, Mel Durslag, went further. "Rozelle was
working very coolly," Durslag noted, "and had split the Coliseum commission. He had one faction convinced to drop Davis for an L.A. expansion
franchise. Robertson was frantic. He'd lost a lot of votes on the commission.
For a while Robertson had only three or four votes out of nine." According to
Robertson, that erosion came because "the Coliseum commission was uptight
about the financial situation involved in continuing the trial. Their attitude
was: if a deal was possible, let's do it. I thought it wasn't possible."

Whatever Bill Robertson thought, he was clearly no longer in control of
things. "At one time," Robertson remembered, "I was the Coliseum's sole
negotiator. I got a lot of heat. I also got a load of publicity and others wanted
in on it. My opposition on the commission insisted we needed broader
representation, so I added Stan Sanders and Mike Frankovich and made a
negotiating committee." Robertson would later describe his creation as "a
Frankenstein." To the NFL it seemed like a possible opportunity and they
concentrated their efforts on Frankovich, working through Art Modell.
Frankovich, a movie producer, and Modell, who had joined the board of
directors of Twentieth Century Fox after Marvin Davis bought the studio, had
known each other for a long time.

Not long after the Bradley talks dissolved, Frankovich called Robertson.
Frankovich claimed to have obtained "new information from the NFL" that
made him think a deal could be worked out. Would Robertson be willing to

meet with Rozelle? Robertson told Frankovich he would, on the condition that they meet in Los Angeles.

The next Robertson heard of the proposal was several days later when he was in Oakland for a meeting of the State Federation of Labor's executive board. After the board meeting, he was scheduled to have dinner with Al Davis. Between the two appointments, Robertson called his L.A. office and learned that Frankovich and Sanders had agreed to meet with Rozelle the next day, but, ignoring his instructions, had scheduled the meeting for Dallas. The location was a compromise because Rozelle was insisting they come to New York. "I was furious," Robertson remembered. At dinner, he told Al Davis what Frankovich had done.

"The sons of bitches set up a meeting with Rozelle in Dallas," Robertson explained. "I'm not going."

Davis's reaction was instantaneous. "You gotta go," he exclaimed. Davis was worried the two others would cut a deal if left to their own devices. Davis used the restaurant phone to arrange for a car to take Robertson to San Francisco International in time for a plane to L.A. that allowed him to fly to Dallas with his fellow negotiators.

"We have to have an understanding among ourselves," Robertson told them on the plane. The understanding he proposed was that "we all have to agree to any proposal made and that there would be no deal unless it satisfies Al Davis." According to Robertson, both Frankovich and Sanders agreed with him. One of them said that the deal they should ask for would be an expansion franchise for Davis in L.A. and $8 million. "Don't put it on the table," Robertson admonished. "Let's see what they put on the table first. Don't say anything about it." Again, Robertson claimed, the other negotiators agreed.

The actual meeting was held in a hotel room near the Dallas airport. Robertson opened for L.A. "We need an understanding on one point right away," he announced. "Otherwise there's no point in talking. Whatever we're able to work out here has to be acceptable to Al Davis."

According to Robertson, Rozelle immediately "balked" and shortly thereafter, Robertson was undercut by his fellow Los Angeles negotiators. They suggested putting Robertson's demand aside for the moment and working on other things. They could come back to the issue of Davis. While Robertson looked on with irritation, one of the other L.A. negotiators then said they wanted a deal for an expansion franchise and $6 million. "He'd even reduced the figure he'd agreed not to talk about," Robertson noted with irritation. "I stopped things and called a caucus. 'What nonsense is this?' I asked." Robertson described the rest of the session as "a dog and pony show" that even "Rozelle knew was a nothing thing. It was just a bullshit session. Because of the conversations between Frankovich and Modell, Rozelle thought that the Coliseum was weakening and caving in." Robertson also claimed that he was able to convince Frankovich and Sanders to that effect and that they reported to the LAMCC afterward that there was no chance of a settlement. "Al Davis was the stumbling block," he explained.

According to other sources close to the negotiations, however, the talk in Dallas went further than Robertson thought. One source claimed Frankovich and Sanders "came back prepared to take an expansion franchise for L.A. It fell apart because Rozelle changed his mind about offering one. He didn't want to reward the Coliseum. He thought he could keep getting a hung jury and Davis just wouldn't be able to continue. A deal had been tentatively set up. There had been no promises yet by anybody, but Rozelle knew they were ripe and backed off."

Another person close to the negotiations claims that, in fact, Robertson had "lost control. Frankovich and Sanders would have done anything," he explained. "They were like puppies with Rozelle. A deal had been discussed that they expected to be made. It wasn't acceptable to Davis but everyone thought it was going to be made anyway. It gave the League most everything it had wanted. L.A. would have gotten an expansion franchise and it wouldn't include Davis. The L.A. Coliseum would get $2 to $3 million and an expansion franchise within two years." The source claims the deal was actually "voted down unanimously" during confidential discussions of *LAMCC v. NFL* at the League's 1982 annual meeting. "The League was ready to accept it," he says, "but then they decided they had to fight. Someone scotched the deal."

Joe Alioto, Davis's attorney, endorsed this version. "The plan was to give the L.A. Coliseum an expansion franchise," he explained, "and have the Coliseum settle the case out of court. It would leave the Raiders out to spit in the wind. There are a lot of angles to this thing. You have to recognize that Georgia Frontiere is represented by the law firm of Hugh Culverhouse and . . . Culverhouse took an active role in killing this thing because Georgia doesn't want another team out there. That's obvious to everybody. It's what the fight was about to begin with." According to statements made by Alioto to *The* [Cleveland] *Plain Dealer*, the new expansion franchise would have been awarded to Art Modell, who would have then sold the Browns and moved west. Modell denied any such intentions.

Whichever version was the more accurate, the conclusion was the same. No settlement was reached.

"By this time," one participant explained, "things had gotten too personal for that."

19

The pattern of animosity generated by *LAMCC v. NFL* had long since become wide, deep, and readily apparent throughout the League. In the case of the Sullivans in Boston, it had even driven a wedge within the family. The schism centered on Billy Sullivan's son-in-law, Joe Alioto. As Al Davis's hired gun, Alioto was a particularly resented figure among the circle to which Billy was allied. Alioto admitted that he and Billy never talked about the case and that it was never brought up at family gatherings. "We're on opposite sides, no doubt about it," Alioto joked. "I tell people it's the generation gap—Billy's a year older than I am."

For his part, Billy Sullivan was open about the case's family impact, though he found it hard to laugh. "When Kathleen and Joe and I sit down," he explained, "we never discuss it. We couldn't possibly discuss it. Joe and I are too far apart on the issue. He's a wonderful man, but he's on the other side. We can't talk. The three of us and Joe's son, Joe Jr., had lunch [once] and Joe Jr. started talking to his father about the case. I told Kathleen, 'I think I should leave.' I couldn't sit there with them talking about the case like that. So I went and sat in a corner by myself. Kathleen came over with tears in her eyes. She said, 'Can't we even sit together?' And I had to tell her no, we couldn't. It just wasn't right for me to sit there while they were talking about the case."

Despite what Kathleen Sullivan Alioto described as the "very private, deep, and very emotional feelings" the rift inspired within her family, not to mention the disruption it brought to the League in general, the Sullivan empire nonetheless expanded while *LAMCC v. NFL* was going on. Again, the growth was due principally to the energies of Kathleen's brother, Chuck. This time his target was Schaeffer Stadium in Foxboro, where his father's franchise played its games.

Originally considered a miracle that Old Billy had somehow managed to produce at the last minute out of thin air, Schaeffer Stadium was controlled by Stadium Realty Trust, the REIT Billy had constructed in 1971 to procure the necessary financing to build in Foxboro. To float the trust, Billy had bought more of its stock than any other individual and the Patriots more than any other organization. By 1981, however, the limitations of the arrangement they'd created were considered a "problem" by both Billy and Chuck. "I had been instrumental in raising a lot of money for the stadium," Billy remembered, "but in the beginning I had decided against having a Patriots member on the board, so of the original five on the board, none had ties to our franchise. After several years it became apparent that Stadium Realty Trust wasn't getting other events at the stadium to help the income of the stockholders. Also, the income from the Patriots alone was insufficient for sound maintenance, so the Patriots had to subsidize the stadium to try to keep it from falling apart. Because it wasn't a public facility, we had the second highest rent in the League. We subsidized the railroad to bring people out but because of traffic jams, we had the largest police payroll in the League, which the Patriots had to pay. When we still saw no efforts by Stadium Realty Trust to get other events to defray some of those costs, we decided to try to buy it."

Once again, Billy pointed out, the takeover was "a family affair" following a strategy designed and quarterbacked by Chuck. The plan was revealed to the public on April Fool's Day, 1981. "The problem," Chuck explained to the *Boston Herald*, "is that we've had an erosion of our season ticket holders from fifty-five thousand to forty thousand. So we surveyed our fans and the general reaction was that they are high on the team and the game, but not on the facilities. This is no knock against the Stadium Realty Trust, which has done a fantastic job, but the stadium is ten years old and needs a major overhaul and a real estate investment trust is not a desirable financing vehicle.'' In part, Chuck was speaking generously of the trust at this point because he had just made them an offer. Chuck's proposal to the trust's board was $12 a share for stock then selling at $7. The stock would be purchased by Stadium Management Corp., a vehicle wholly owned by Sullivans. To finance the transaction, Stadium Management Corp. intended to borrow $7 million dollars, of which $4.9 million would be used to buy the outstanding Stadium Realty stock, $1.5 million to take over the trust's outstanding debt, and another $600,000 to make immediate improvements. Down the line, it was the Sullivans' intention to refinance and, in Billy's words, ''make it one of the best facilities in the NFL.''

The board did not exactly jump at Chuck's offer. Even Bob Marr, no friend of the Sullivans, considered the board ''not an easy group to deal with.'' For the Sullivans, relations with them were further complicated by the fact that Billy himself had originally asked some of them to serve. By June, the board had rejected Chuck's offer as ''inadequate.''

The setback barely caused a pause in the Sullivan strategy. By July, a dissident slate of trustees had been nominated to replace the current board and a proxy fight had begun. The Sullivans' proxy statement informed shareholders that the current board had to be replaced ''to provide a more hospitable home for the Patriots at Schaeffer Stadium and to eliminate the increasing distrust and disputes which have in recent years plagued the relationship between the Patriots and the management of the trust.'' The current trustees responded that the Sullivan offer which the dissident slate intended to recommend to the shareholders ''was not fair, adequate, or reasonable.'' *The Boston Globe* described the fight between the two positions as ''nasty, even vengeful.'' By the middle of July, Billy had made some 173 phone calls rounding up votes and Chuck thought he had more than enough to get the two thirds necessary. Balloting was scheduled for July 28.

Before the vote could be held, however, a new bidder jumped in. The bidder was Nelson Skalbania, who owned some $50 million worth of sports teams around Canada. His offer for Stadium Realty Trust was $16 a share and seemed to appear out of nowhere. As of the time it was made, the Canadian had never even seen Schaeffer Stadium. Nonetheless, the sitting trustees postponed the scheduled vote to ''give the trust an opportunity to continue discussions with N. M. Skalbania Ltd., which has offered to purchase the trust's assets.'' Chuck Sullivan reacted angrily to the move. ''Calling it an offer,'' he fumed, ''is a misnomer. It is more an expression of interest.''

Whatever it was, Chuck acted quickly to remove it. Within four days Skalbania had received a phone call from Chuck and a letter from Billy. Though the contents of those communications were not revealed, on August 4, the Canadian ''reluctantly'' withdrew his offer for Stadium Realty because of "business aspects" and some "nonbusiness problems." The men the Sullivans were seeking to depose thought they knew where those problems had come from. "The trustees," their spokesman announced, "believe opposition by the Sullivans played an important role in Skalbania's decision." Even so, the trustees' days were now numbered. The day Skalbania withdrew, Chuck Sullivan already claimed to have proxies in hand for more than 203,000 of the trust's 382,000 outstanding shares.

On August 13, a formal shareholders meeting was convened in Boston for final summations by each of the two sides. On August 14, the proxy count would be announced. Billy Sullivan spoke for the dissident slate. "I appear here today not as a father of two girls that served on the [Boston] school committee," he began, "but as a substantial stockholder in the Stadium and as owner of the prime and, I think, only tenant in the facility. . . . This is not the ordinary garden variety form of stockholder proxy fight . . . our guys versus their guys. [The current trustees] are friends of mine since well before the stadium was built. Indeed, in some cases, answered my invitation to serve as trustees. This is not the Sullivan family versus the trustees." Confident of victory, Billy thanked his opponents for their "dedicated services." He also thanked the lawyers engaged by both sides and the shareholders in general. However they voted, Old Billy noted with a twinkle, "they participated in a very great part of democratic society, the proxy fight."

The next day, the Sullivans' slate won. Now there was only one remaining hurdle to Chuck's takeover. That was a formal vote by the same shareholders to approve the trust's liquidation and sale to Chuck Sullivan's holding company. The vote was held on November 6 and once again Billy called all the major shareholders personally. Chuck needed 255,000 shares to gain approval and got 263,000. "I'm just delighted with the vote," he beamed afterward. He also credited his father with being "very significant in the success we were able to achieve." Football and Sullivan were now synonymous throughout New England. Once the owners of less than forty percent of a football franchise with no stadium, they now owned the football team completely. The team had a stadium, and the Sullivans owned all of the stadium as well.

While enlarging the family empire, Chuck Sullivan also continued to play a major role in League affairs. Between the trials of *LAMCC v. NFL*, most of Chuck's NFL energies went into his job as chairman of the management council executive committee. The management council was attempting to ready the League for potential labor war and its chairman's contribution behind the scenes was critical. While the union was headed for the confrontation with no strike fund to speak of, Chuck was busy arranging a $150 million unsecured line of credit from a syndicate headed by Crocker Bank. This owners' strike fund would be in place not long after negotiations began. As a matter of policy, those face-to-face negotiations were left in the hands of Jack Donlan, the management council's hired help.

The management council's opening session with the NFLPA was held in Miami's Diplomat Hotel on February 16, 1982. The council was represented by Donlan and four other negotiators, none of them owners. The union was represented by Garvey and some thirty others, most of them players. The negotiations took place around a square table and the union took up three of the four sides. Gene Upshaw, now NFLPA president, noted the absence of owners and described the management group as "virtually a subcommittee." Ed Garvey was "disappointed." Nonetheless, they proceeded to present their demands. "They had a twelve-page document," Jack Donlan remembered, "and they all took turns reading it aloud. It was like a high school pageant." According to one source in the room, the most embarrassing moments came when two of the players couldn't pronounce the words Garvey had written for them.

The part the management council had been waiting to hear, dealing with percentage of the gross, came last. It was a disappointment and a frustration. After a long explanation of why the concept was essential to the well-being of players and justified by the shape of the League itself, Garvey's document stopped short of actually saying what percentage the union wanted. Instead, it demanded to see the owners' books so it could determine for itself what percentage it intended to ask for.

The recitation was followed by a counterproposal from the management council side that Gene Upshaw described as "an insult to our members." It refused access to management's books, demanded new player dress codes, and refused to improve the pension plan. By the end of the opening session, people were shouting at each other.

On February 18, the two sides met again for ten hours, once again ended up shouting, and suspended negotiations.

Before leaving Miami, Ed Garvey described the February 18 meeting as "the worst experience I've been through in my twelve years of dealing with the NFL."

Chuck Sullivan, chairman of the management council executive committee, made no comment.

20

Pete Rozelle, of course, took no direct role on the League's labor front, explaining that he was "the commissioner of all of football," not the representative of one interest over another. At the time, he also had his hands full with other League business.

There were two items that preoccupied Rozelle between trials. One was the negotiation of a new television agreement with the networks, a contract he intended to announce at the 1982 annual meeting in March. The other preoccupation was breaking out of his *LAMCC v. NFL* encirclement. Once Rozelle had developed a strategy on that front, he pursued it single-mindedly.

The commissioner's plan to break out was remarkably daring for a man with Rozelle's cautious reputation. Rather than seek a piecemeal victory, he went for the whole ball of wax—eliminating the League's Sherman Act vulnerability once and for all. To do that, he shuttled back and forth between New York and Washington, D.C., campaigning for a "sports bill" that would exempt the NFL from many of its current antitrust dilemmas. It had been more than a decade since he had last petitioned Congress for a limited exemption and almost two decades since he had sought anything as broad as what he now had in mind, but it was a natural strategy from the commissioner's standpoint. He had confidence in his ability to convince politicians and it was in front of Congress that he had previously made his reputation as a witness. If not exactly home turf, Capitol Hill at least afforded more possibilities than were available in front of a judge in L.A. The congressional strategy had great allure: If he was successful, he would have beaten Davis and saved League Think once and for all.

The commissioner's campaign was scheduled to kick off with congressional hearings in October 1981, but those were postponed until December. In the meantime, he worked privately, meeting with congressmen and senators to discuss the issues, dancing the political dance that made Washington work. At that level of politics, the operative principle is quid pro quo and the League made its case accordingly. What it had to offer was expansion, and Rozelle was not averse to pointing that out in private or in public. "A lot of cities have talked to us about expansion," the commissioner explained, "and we're ready to expand. But the situation is this. We can't expand without fear of litigation. We've said that as soon as the sports bill has passed, which gives us the same rights as multidivisional corporations, we'll expand. We've told people that if you pass this sports bill, we're ready to expand. You can call it dangling if you wish, but all we're saying is that as soon as the sports bill is passed, we'll appoint an expansion committee to give us two more teams for a total of thirty."

With the concept of expansion in his back pocket, Rozelle met in November with Senate Republican Leader Howard Baker of Tennessee. Baker, according to the *Memphis Commercial Appeal,* had "been spearheading Memphis's attempts to get into the exclusive NFL club for a couple of years." He was, needless to say, more than happy to discuss expansion with the commissioner. Baker also invited Tennessee's governor, Lamar Alexander, and two wealthy residents of Memphis who were interested in buying any hometown franchise that might develop. Though their meeting of minds was not complete, Baker and the commissioner made some headway. According to one of the people present, the meeting ended "in a posture of Rozelle saying there'll be expansion when they get their antitrust exemption and Baker saying there'll be antitrust exemption when Memphis gets a team." Nonetheless, Senator Baker emerged optimistic enough to tell his constituents that Memphis "has the best chance of any city in the country" to be included in NFL expansion. "Rozelle didn't promise anything," he pointed out, "but he just left me with a good, strong, positive feeling."

On December 10, Pete Rozelle formally launched his campaign with a tour de force in front of the House Judiciary Committee's subcommittee on monopolies and commercial law. The subject was "the effects of antitrust laws and policy on professional sports leagues," a field, the commissioner pointed out, "that remains utterly confused and unsettled after three decades of constant litigation." There was, however, a solution. "In my view," the commissioner read from his prepared text, "the time has come for Congress to directly address this subject with legislation.

"I will attempt to summarize why this is so," Rozelle continued. "If some of my statements today are strong, it is because the case for legislative clarification is overwhelming. Put simply, professional sports leagues are at a point where—because of the novel business form of sports leagues—every league action, every league business judgment, and every league decision can be characterized as an 'antitrust' issue, so that every league activity can be second-guessed in antitrust, often on conflicting grounds, by outside parties, league members themselves, and courts. . . . I am not a lawyer, but I have probably spent more time in litigation matters than many members of the bar. I have thus acquired more than a passing knowledge of the present subject. In my judgment, it is clear that the antitrust laws, as now applied to sports leagues, do more to frustrate the very consumer and public interests that they were designed to promote than to serve them."

The commissioner's case for different treatment was, in essence, the same single entity defense that had been disallowed in the last L.A. matchup with Al Davis. "The relationship among the clubs within the League is unique," he emphasized. "It is found nowhere else on the American business scene. On the playing field, the teams are clearly competitors. But in producing and marketing the NFL product, the clubs are co-producers and co-sellers, not competitors. They are partners acting together in a common enterprise. . . . The problem arises from the absolute novelty of the League business relationship and the complete lack of antitrust guidance for identifying what leagues can and cannot do. . . . The antitrust straw is thus about to break the camel's back unless antitrust doctrine comes to recognize the true novelty of the sports league economic relationship. . . . If sports leagues cannot act as unified business operations, if they cannot establish and apply equal operating principles to all of their members, and if they cannot make and keep their promises to communities, stadiums, Congress, and the public, then responsible league sports can be added to the endangered species list."

The reason, Rozelle noted, was that "the antitrust courts are in the process of rendering leagues powerless to act. They are putting leagues in a catch-22 situation—where the individual clubs are regarded as separate, independent entrepreneurs, outside the plane of League decision making, while all of the rest of the League's members remain obligated to conduct all of their operations on whatever conditions are established by the individual club or sought by some outside party. The inability of the League to make and enforce operating principles equally binding on all members threatens many serious consequences for professional football and the public.''

Rozelle suggested several such consequences. "For one thing," he continued, "it risks foreclosing future expansion of the NFL. . . . If we find ourselves with antitrust ground rules where the League's choice of location and decision to create a new partner can be challenged as a 'conspiracy' with antitrust consequences, then there is simply no practical way to continue to enlarge the League. Nor can we assure that other NFL operating principles will survive current antitrust thinking. The NFL has always operated with a policy of franchise stability. . . . But it is unlikely that the NFL's pattern of stable team-community relationships will continue if antitrust concepts are used to make leagues powerless to influence or control team location decisions. . . . There is not even the assurance that the NFL's established patterns of revenue sharing will survive.''

Perhaps the most irritating aspect to the current antitrust dilemma, Rozelle testified, was that "leagues are regularly damned in antitrust if they do, and damned in antitrust if they don't.'' He offered four examples. The first was a succession of suits over television in 1960, when the NFL was first sued for placing its broadcasts on more than one network and then, when it moved to unify on just one network, sued for failing to place their programming with more than one. The second example dated from the World Football League when the WFL had threatened suit if the NFL expanded into Memphis and the NFL "carefully avoided" that eventuality. Then, the following year, the League had been sued for declining to expand there. The third example was *LAMCC v. NFL,* where the League had been sued for failing to permit a transfer. If they had permitted it, Oakland was preparing a suit against doing so. The fourth example was *NASL v. NFL,* which Rozelle claimed was in compliance with antitrust law "prohibiting interlocking directorships" but nonetheless subject to litigation for precisely that prohibition.

Rozelle also offered further illustrations of the confusion inherent in legal thinking on this subject. The federal court in Philadelphia, he pointed out, had ruled that the NFL is "a unique type of business" and its clubs "must not compete too well with each other in a business way.'' The federal court in Minneapolis, on the other hand, ruled the NFL is "like any other business" and "open unfettered competition must take place among its clubs.'' In St. Louis, judges called the NFL "unique" and "novel," yet in Washington they called it "no different" from a trade association. The federal court in New York deemed the NFL a single economic entity and the District of Columbia court of appeals ruled that NFL teams "are not competitors in any economic sense" and "operate basically as a joint venture,'' but the federal court in Los Angeles had most recently declared them "business competitors" and not a single economic entity.

That court in Los Angeles was, of course, the subject of some of Rozelle's most intense attention. "Now," the commissioner lamented, "the NFL is involved in exhausting litigation over whether the League's executive committee could evaluate the Oakland Raiders' proposed move to Los Angeles—

and, ultimately, prevent an NFL club from abandoning its home territory when the League's membership believed the club had no sufficient reason for walking out. The recurring antitrust confusions and contradictions are illustrated in this litigation. Before the Raiders tried to abandon Oakland, antitrust law as to League decisions regarding location of franchises seemed clear. The National Hockey League and National Basketball Association had each been confirmed in their antitrust right to decide where their teams would be located and who would own them. In 1976, the Department of Justice told the House Select Committee on Sports, chaired by Representative Sisk, that team transfer issues probably did not even present an antitrust issue.

"Yet," Rozelle went on, "when the Los Angeles Coliseum challenged the NFL's decision not to endorse the Raiders' effort to abandon Oakland, prior antitrust learning went out the window: the local Los Angeles area federal court found not only an antitrust issue but an antitrust violation. It did so on preliminary injunction; and it did so without a trial on finding that 'irreparable injury' to the Los Angeles area in not immediately having the Oakland Raiders transfer to Los Angeles would outweigh any injury to Oakland in losing its Raiders after many years of consistent, enthusiastic support. Fortunately, the court of appeals reversed the preliminary injunction and set the case for a full trial. But we had to try the case in Los Angeles, because the judge there refused to transfer the case to a neutral city. After three months of trial, the jury could not reach a verdict, and unless the courts sharply change their view, we must try the case again in Los Angeles. . . . Under ever-changing antitrust concepts, the League is now tied down like Gulliver in its efforts to keep the Raiders in the Oakland community."

As he wound up his testimony, the commissioner's plea for help was adamant. "Let me be unequivocal," he asked of the congressmen. "I do not regard all sports league antitrust issues as requiring a legislative solution. . . . The greatest danger lies in the use of the antitrust laws to attack the internal structure of a sports league and to permit even league members to second-guess every league operating principle. In managing League affairs and in producing and marketing their league entertainment, sports leagues simply need to be recognized as the common economic enterprise that they are. This would accord the leagues antitrust treatment equivalent to that already received by other single enterprises. . . . Today the only way a sports league could avoid antitrust involvement and treble damage exposure is to cease operations altogether and simply turn the whole thing loose. . . . I can guarantee the committee that if that occurs, the results will not serve NFL fans, League cities, the players, the participating clubs, the League's expansion potential, or the public interest generally. But we have already arrived at the stage where wrongly transplanted antitrust concepts are going to make the leagues powerless to prevent such results."

Having identified the problem, the League's next step was to start shaping the solution and, in the first few months of 1982, Covington and Burling began drafting possible legislation. "We approached it from the angle of what it would take to clear things up," the League's attorney explained, "more than what would pass. First we came up with a concept."

According to the lobbyist for the NFLPA, the first draft the League came up with was "an extraordinarily broad exemption" that covered almost every situation anyone could think of. That draft went through a number of alterations. Meanwhile, Rozelle was assembling a team to push the legislation that would eventually include nine different Washington PR and legal firms, all working the Hill every day. Included among them were former senator Marlowe Cook, former chairman of the Democratic party Robert Strauss, and former Carter administration insider Anne Wexler.

As impressive as the League's show of force would be, opposition quickly developed around two aspects of their proposed sports bill.

The first was from the union. Rozelle had tried to anticipate this response in his remarks to the House subcommittee. Pointing out that antitrust issues between sports management and labor were "controlled by collective bargaining agreements" and "labor laws," Rozelle called on the congressmen to turn their "focus" to antitrust law "outside of the labor-management area." That disclaimer was certainly not enough to satisfy Ed Garvey, and by the end of January, the NFLPA had begun a steadily rising drumbeat of negativity about the proposal. "If this law had been passed in 1970," its newsletter pointed out, "the NFLPA would have lost the Mackey case . . . and no one could have challenged the draft. The NFL could then concentrate on breaking the NFLPA and all players' rights would be gone." Garvey's attitude eventually meant that the AFL-CIO would lobby against the measure as well.

The second focus of opposition was to a particular provision that the League insisted on including in all versions of its sports bill. That provision made its exemption retroactive to include court cases then under litigation. According to Paul Tagliabue, the League's new Covington and Burling chief counsel, such retroactivity was guaranteed to be controversial. "If we got it," he admitted, "we'd probably face lawsuits over it. There are precedents both ways: cases saying it's fine, cases saying it's a problem. Several years ago, a bill was passed specifically to overturn a series of court cases the FTC had won against the bottling industry, so it's been done even though a lot of people say it's not been done. The Civil Rights Act was retroactive. Remedial legislation of that type is usually retroactive to pending cases, even when on appeal. When it's still in the courts and not yet final, Congress can do what it wants. Once it's final, it can't do a thing about it."

The issue created two types of problems for the League. The first was one of timing. During the same session that the League's sports bill began testing congressional waters there was also, Tagliabue remembered, "a big debate going on about applying antitrust legislation retroactivity to exonerate a bunch of companies in the paper industry who had been convicted of price fixing. They had a big bill up there and there was a lot of opposition to that. It had a major impact. People who would privately say we support you would also say, but I can't do it openly because I'm opposing the paper industry bill and I'll be contradicting myself if I oppose them on retroactivity and support you on retroactivity."

The second problem with the League's position was that it increased both the number and intensity of the opposition. Retroactivity was the League's new last line of defense in *LAMCC v. NFL* and immediately recognizable as such. It gave Los Angeles and Al Davis no choice but to add their not inconsiderable weight to Garvey's. With this provision, Joe Alioto thundered, the NFL was "giving even arrogance a bad name." It was "the worst kind of special interest legislation" that the League hoped "to sneak through" and overturn "well-reasoned court decisions." The political deals involved would amount to "a sale of votes for football franchises. Don't ever underestimate the power of the NFL," he warned, "particularly when they're out there dangling franchises that are worth $250 million."

Pete Rozelle's in-house counsel, Jay Moyer, issued the League's response. "Alioto's allegations," he noted, "as usual, are pretty strong stuff, but are completely unsupported by the facts. . . . There is not, and has never been, any atttempt to sneak through legislation. . . . The legislation we seek would not be special interest legislation. It would be public interest legislation. . . . I would view Alioto's comments as another in a long series of efforts to poison the well against the National Football League."

Nonetheless, the problems retroactivity posed for Rozelle's breakout strategy would only escalate. That the notion would still never be jettisoned was a testimony to how obsessive the League's civil war had become. "Rozelle insisted on retroactivity," Steve Rosenbloom remembered. "The exemption would have had a chance without retroactivity. The only real reason for it was that he and Al Davis hate each other so much. If Rozelle had let retroactivity go, he would have closed the door. Instead, he got caught up in the battle with Davis. It was an arrogant approach and Rozelle demonstrated an inability to cut his losses. His attitude was 'pro football is second to God, maybe first.' It didn't work."

That judgment was, of course, in retrospect. By the time of the 1982 annual meeting in late March, momentum was still growing behind the commissioner's exemption—just not at quite the pace for which he had hoped.

21

While his friend Pete Rozelle spent most of January 1982 on Capitol Hill, Art Modell was in Cleveland trying to put his financial game plan over the top.

Just how pressing Modell's debt had become was highlighted in a letter he dispatched to Union Commerce Bank on January 6. Enclosed was a statement of his net worth. If none of his assets was sold by April 1, his personal debt would have risen to $11.5 million. At the same time, he had less than $1 million in assets he could convert readily into cash. This nadir had been reached, his minority partner Robert Gries pointed out, despite drawing "a quarter million dollars a year average in salary and bonuses from the Browns over the last four to five years. He'd lost and spent millions. Interest was the big factor. It was costing him $1.5 million a year and he was just rolling it over into his debt. It was a $13 million swing in thirteen years."

In his letter to Union Commerce Bank, Modell included an explanation of how he hoped to escape from that vicious cycle. The first element was the sale of his gas and oil holdings for $4.9 million. Modell noted that the sale price was "substantially less" than the value of those holdings as originally listed on his financial statements, but observed that "the discount was necessary to eliminate the high cost of indebtedness." As projected through March, the oil and gas transaction would reduce Modell's debt to $6.6 million, $4.8 million of which he already owed and $1.8 million he would need to borrow to survive the next three months. Even reduced by that much, his interest burden would still be in excess of $1 million a year. Aside from more borrowing to cover himself, Modell's only other option was the sale of Cleveland Stadium Corp., the second element of the plan he presented to Union Commerce. The Browns, Modell told his banker, would acquire Stadium Corp. for $6 million. Of that price, $4.8 million would go straight to Modell, reducing his debt to a manageable $1.8 million. Modell's letter projected that transaction would close by February 1.

That date proved overly optimistic, but it reflected Art Modell's confidence that he could handle what was still a relatively dicey situation. He expected opposition from Robert Gries and unless handled carefully, Gries could still torpedo the deal. Modell had begun to anticipate those difficulties even before his communication with Union Commerce. His first step was to isolate Gries from the rest of the Browns' board, who would have to approve the purchase.

The board was composed of seven members, two of whom, under the terms of a previous agreement between Modell and Gries, were appointed by Gries. Gries's other appointee besides himself was his brother-in-law Richard Cole. Cole held a small piece of Browns stock personally and a small piece of Stadium Corp. as well, but the financial difficulties Robert Gries had helped him cope with the previous fall had continued to plague him and were exacerbated by his impending divorce from Gries's sister. In late December 1981, unbeknownst to Gries, Cole visited Modell in his office at Cleveland Stadium. Cole told Modell that he wanted to sell his interest in the Browns and noted that the franchise itself had right of first refusal. Modell responded that he would arrive at a value for Cole's interest and he would recommend the repurchase to the Browns board. If the board didn't want to buy the shares, Modell guaranteed he would purchase them himself. Relieved to have found a buyer and apparently intent on ingratiating himself with his new benefactor, Cole also provided Modell with information about Gries's intentions. His brother-in-law was opposed to the Stadium Corp. purchase, Cole explained, and he intended to sue Modell and the Browns if they proceeded with it.

By January 13, 1982, Art Modell and Richard Cole had arrived at a formal understanding and signed a letter of intent. The deal it framed was conspicuous for its generosity toward Cole. In return for his 4.3 percent of the club's stock, the Browns would pay Cole $661,000. Cole would remain a director of the Browns for the next five years, despite owning no stock. He would also continue to receive the salary and Blue Cross coverage of a Browns vice-president until August 1987. On top of all that, the Browns would also purchase Cole's Stadium Corp. holdings for $192,000 and if they had failed to do so by March 1, Modell would purchase the Stadium Corp. interest himself.

That same day, Art Modell received yet another report from McDonald and Company, reflecting the value the new Servomation loan had added to Stadium Corp., and forwarded it to Robert Gries. Modell also retained the law firm of Jones, Day, Reavis & Pogue. He had, Modell remembered, a "strong feeling" there might be litigation. The new McDonald and Company report reached Gries on January 15. Shortly thereafter, he called Modell and said he was ready to meet. A discussion was scheduled for January 19. It was in that discussion, Gries remembered, that "it all hit the fan."

"This was wrong from beginning to end," Robert Gries claimed, "and I told him that." Gries was "very, very upset because no one represented the Browns in this transaction. Who was fighting to get the best possible price on behalf of the Browns?" His answer was no one. "If we are going to spend $6 million," he told Modell, "I guarantee you we won't be simply having one report and saying O.K."

Art Modell responded that McDonald and Company was a good firm and their report was a good report.

McDonald and Company was a "good firm," Gries agreed, but "this report is not a credible report." He then launched into an attack on the particulars of McDonald's evaluation. Its estimate on the worth of the Strongsville parcel was "outlandish." When he had first read the report, Gries remembered, that valuation had "jumped out" and left him "incredulous." McDonald and Company had first admitted their "lack of expertise in land valuation" but, instead of hiring an outside expert, nonetheless insisted on coming up with a valuation themselves. They used two methods. The first one Robert Gries "couldn't believe." Starting with a 1975 appraisal, they added an inflation factor for the years since, then discounted it, with no investigation of what had happened to the Strongsville market in the meantime. The second method started with the projected revenues from Strongsville based on a lot price supplied by Modell, calculated the costs involved in generating that revenue plus the financial carrying charges, subtracted that total all from the projected revenue, and produced a value. Both methods yielded a figure of $3.8 million.

Robert Gries had procured his own evaluation of Strongsville since he and Modell had met the previous Thanksgiving. He began reading it aloud.

"I don't want to hear all this," Modell interrupted. "Give me the bottom line."

Gries continued reading anyway. His evaluator had used two different methods to assess Strongsville's worth. One came up with $400,000, the other with $700,000. That part of Stadium Corp., in Gries's estimate, was overpriced by at least $3.1 million.

Cleveland Stadium Corp.'s other nonlease asset, its notes from the sale of the hotel on Public Square, was, according to Gries, overpriced as well. Later, he would testify extensively in Cleveland's Court of Common Pleas about their disagreement.

"Unless the Browns have surplus money," Gries argued, "they should not be getting into things that have nothing to do with football. I can't, in my wildest imagination, conceive of why the Cleveland Browns . . . would invest millions of dollars in something that is nothing but a twenty-three-year note payout." McDonald and Company had said the hotel note was worth $2.1 million; Gries's consultant said the value was no more than $1.3 million. "We can solve this disagreement right away," Gries challenged Modell. "We don't have to argue about its value. Ask McDonald and Company to go out and sell it right now."

"This is worth more with the land and notes as part of the whole package," Modell objected.

"I can't agree," Gries emphasized. "I don't understand what relationship these have."

"Well," Modell said with some irritation, "they are part of the deal and it's going to be sold as one deal."

"There's no rationale for it."

"Well, that is the way it's going to be."

Robert Gries also raised objections to McDonald and Company's conclusion that Stadium Corp. was worth $1 million more to the Browns than anyone else. "This makes no sense," Gries badgered, gesturing at the letter in which McDonald and Company had set forth the notion. "You don't pay for things based on that."

"Control of the stadium by the Browns is really the important thing," Modell argued. He then launched into what Robert Gries described as a "very strong and impassioned, emotional speech about why the Browns must control their own destiny." The real issue, according to Modell, was to avoid the problems that had plagued other franchises who did not control their stadiums. The Rooney family's Pittsburgh Steelers were in that position and, according to Modell, "couldn't even raise ticket prices because the city wouldn't let them."

"What has that got to do with here?" Gries interrupted.

"Suppose someone else owned the stadium?" Modell asked back.

Gries pointed out that in any case they were not going to control Browns ticket prices. "Even if you could sell that right to somebody, you won't," he noted.

"Suppose I sell the stadium to somebody and they let the thing fall apart?" Modell pressed. "Then what will the Browns do?"

The Browns had a valid lease, Gries replied. "You told me it was a very favorable lease. I am sure it provides protection against a landlord if they let things run down. I am not convinced we have to buy protection because there is nothing appearing that we have to protect against."

Quite the contrary, Gries argued, from the standpoint of protecting the Browns, the purchase itself posed the most immediate danger. "I strongly objected to increasing the Browns' debt," Gries explained. The franchise had paid down the $7 million it had borrowed to make a payout in 1971 to just $2 million of basic bank debt. If the Browns bought Stadium Corp., they would add "another $15.5 million of potential debt." The transaction "made no sense whatsoever for the Browns at this point in time." Labor negotiations were about to begin, Gries pointed out, and the NFLPA was already talking strike. In the face of that, "you just don't go out and take the Browns and load them up with this huge amount of debt."

Modell responded that "maybe everything will get settled."

Gries scoffed. "No corporation," he pointed out, "would rush into doing something like that in the face of that kind of instability in their operation."

After listening to all Gries's objections, Art Modell remained unmoved. He was going to present the transaction to the Browns board, he informed his minority partner, and he hoped Gries would reconsider his opposition.

Later asked on the witness stand how the January 19 meeting ended, Robert Gries answered, "Acrimoniously."

While Gries was still considering his options during the following week, Art Modell phoned him and asked if he could come down to the stadium for another meeting. That meeting took place on January 26. "I was anxious to avoid litigation at all costs," Modell remembered. He began by telling Gries that his complaints were "all wrong" and that he did not agree. "The McDonald and Company report is a good report," Modell affirmed, "and I will stand on it. We are going ahead. But, to give you comfort, I am going to give you a guarantee that the Gries family isn't going to come out any worse with this deal than if we didn't make the deal."

Gries called it an "interesting concept" and asked how it would work.

"I haven't worked out the details," Modell admitted. He thought Gries would be able to "figure something out" in consultation with Modell's financial advisers.

"I'll give it a shot," Gries promised.

Modell thought Gries had been pleased with the guarantee offer and described him as "cordial" when the meeting ended. Shortly thereafter, Modell flew to Detroit for the Super Bowl and then on to L.A., where he stayed for the next six weeks while his assistants dealt with Gries.

While in southern California, Modell vacationed, met with the rest of the League's television committee about the network negotiations, and participated in some of the League's settlement flirtation with the LAMCC. It was

during this stay that Joe Alioto became convinced Modell meant to move to
L.A. permanently. "Beverly Hills is a glamorous place," Davis's lawyer
pointed out. "Art likes to be around glamorous people and his wife, Pat, is a
former actress and is thinking about going into some film production. Art is
on the board of directors of Twentieth Century Fox. Life out here with all the
glamorous people is heady stuff, real heady stuff. And when you finish
making all the money you want and have everything else, you start looking
for something else."

"All I will tell you about Joe Alioto," Modell responded, "is that he
never lets facts interfere with a good story."

Alioto, of course, had no idea just how far Art Modell really was from
having made "all the money you want." Debt was still socked in around him
on all sides and, in Cleveland, his negotiators were making little headway
with Robert Gries.

The negotiations had begun immediately after Modell left the January 26
meeting and continued with some intensity over the next two weeks. Gries's
proposal was to drop the Strongsville land from the transaction altogether and
if the hotel was to be included, do so under provisions for selling it off in "a
reasonable time." In that framework, the two sides could then "find a price
we both can agree is justified." If Modell's more optimistic projections
actually happened, then there would be provisions for getting him more
money. Those ideas were rejected by Modell's men, who instead concentrated
on finding terms for Modell's proposed guarantee. Their idea was, according
to Gries, the "most unfair guarantee I've ever seen, ever." The formula
Modell's representatives advanced was "as long as the Browns get $6 million
over the term of the lease, you're guaranteed. Even if I got my money back,"
Gries pointed out, "it amounts to an interest free loan of seventeen years.

"That is not a guarantee for us," Gries exploded. "That's a guarantee
for Modell."

By the end of the first week in February, Modell's negotiators had called
him in L.A. and told him Gries found none of their guarantees acceptable.
"What [Gries] wanted was guaranteed profit return," Modell explained,
"contrasted with my offer of a guarantee against losses and if profits were to
develop, so much the better."

Art Modell and Robert Gries didn't square off again face-to-face until the
third week of March, shortly after Modell returned from California intent on
finishing off the Stadium Corp. transaction once and for all, whatever Gries
thought. That finishing off occurred at a meeting of the board of directors of
the Cleveland Browns Football Company, Inc., on March 16. When Gries
arrived in the company of his attorney, the six other directors were already
there, having met privately ahead of time. Among the six were Modell, his
wife, Richard Cole, and James Bailey. All of them had received a long letter
from Gries several days earlier, stating his continuing objections to buying
Stadium Corp. The first point Gries raised at the meeting was his right to have
legal counsel present. Modell considered the request "unusual" and left the
room for a phone consultation with his own attorney.

"O.K.," Modell told Gries's lawyer when he returned, "you can stay, but don't talk."

The Browns president and majority owner then opened the issue of purchasing Stadium Corp. with a reference to Gries's letter and turned the floor over to its author. Gries, according to Modell, "expounded at length as to his views." The presentation lasted an hour and a half.

Much of it was the same thing he had already told Modell in January. "This transaction was absolutely wrong," Gries remembered, "the whole procedure was wrong. . . . You can't arrive at a fair price without anybody representing the Browns. . . . To assume all this debt at that time was absolutely outlandish." Gries also presented the reports he had received contradicting the one drawn up by McDonald and Company, citing some fifteen experts he had consulted. As usual, his greatest complaint was about including Strongsville in the purchase. He had looked into land out there, he pleaded. There were still fifteen hundred developed lots that had been unsold for a long time. There were also "some repossessions or the builders had not completed their projects and some of them were in trouble." Gries had commissioned yet another appraisal of the property and this one said it was worth $335,000—$3.5 million less than the Browns were about to pay.

At the mention of Gries's new report, Modell and his financial adviser, James Bailey, looked at each other and chuckled. Modell then proceeded to give his only ground of the whole encounter. There was "a problem" with the McDonald and Company evaluation of the Strongsville parcel, he admitted. James Bailey had procured another real estate appraisal that lowered the value to $2.5 million. To make up for that potential shortfall and give more "comfort" to Gries, Modell announced that he was going to forgive the $1 million note he still held from Stadium Corp. That note had been part of the original purchase of the Strongsville parcel and Modell's offer did not impress Gries in the least. "The note was only payable off the profits of the land," he pointed out, "which hadn't been realized to date, might never be realized, and if realized, it would be long in the future and hence, of far less value than $1 million."

Modell also presented a twenty-page document spelling out the guarantee he was willing to furnish his minority partners. Gries's attorney then asked if the meeting could recess long enough to let him study the document. Modell refused. "It's absolutely unnecessary," he told the attorney. "There's no reason for it. We're going on with the meeting." Later, Modell was more forthcoming about his motivation. "I honestly thought he was going to file suit the moment he got out of that room," he explained.

Much of the remainder of the meeting was spent questioning Gries. The exchanges became particularly sharp between Gries and Modell's wife, Pat.

At one point, she demanded that Gries tell the rest of them the names of all these experts he had consulted. "Why don't you identify the names of your evaluators and appraisers?" she asked.

Gries refused "to give a laundry list of every person I had talked to."

That wasn't good enough for Pat Modell. "Well, we did," she complained. "We gave you ours. Why don't you make them available?"

"I'll make them available in court," Gries snapped.

Robert Gries was convinced that Stadium Corp. was worth no more than $2 million, a third of its price tag, "even if you accept management's figures, which is a big if." By now, however, it was more than apparent that the rest of the board wasn't much interested in what he thought. Before an actual vote was held, he requested a short recess so he could consult his attorney.

When the board meeting reconvened, Modell remembered, Gries "made a statement that all his remarks were extemporaneous and he reserves his rights." Next came the vote. To maintain appearances, both Modell and his wife abstained. The tally was nonetheless four votes in favor of the purchase and only Robert Gries against.

It was now late in the afternoon, but the actual documentation for the transaction had been finalized that morning. Once the board had given its approval, Central National Bank, carrying seventy-five percent of the loan with which the Browns would pay Stadium Corp., would transfer $4.8 million to Art Modell's personal account. Modell would then transfer $4 million of that to Union Commerce Bank, settling his debts there. At Union Commerce, a vice-president cleared his schedule for the day to be available should assistance be required. At 5:00 P.M., not long after the board meeting, Union Commerce's legal department informed the vice-president that there "might be an attempt to file a temporary restraining order to block the transaction on the following morning." Shortly thereafter, the vice-president spoke on the phone with Modell and his money man, James Bailey. Both apparently urged speed in completing the exchange.

At 7:45 A.M. the following day, Central National Bank dispensed its funds to Modell. Robert Gries filed suit shortly after the courts opened at 10:00 but was too late to block a dime.

His business done, Art Modell left Cleveland again, this time for Phoenix, where the 1982 annual meeting was scheduled to convene at the Arizona Biltmore on March 21.

22

The 1982 National Football League annual meeting was full of both good news and bad news. The good news was delivered in executive session on the morning of March 22 when the League's television committee reported on the outcome of its negotiations with the networks.

Tactically, this television pact was of prime importance to Pete Rozelle, more so perhaps than any he had ever negotiated. The commissioner had been entrapped in trench warfare since shortly after the last TV agreement was announced in 1978 and, as yet, had few, if any, victories to show for an enormous expenditure of effort on several fronts. Rozelle did not have to be told that if that pattern continued, his position would eventually be ravaged by attrition. A big win now would bolster his backers and provide fresh financial incentive to keep the League's solid front intact. It was also Rozelle's first opportunity in a long time to break away from legal quibbling and, after two years of public battering at the hands of Al Davis, once again demonstrate just how valuable he and League Think actually were.

As usual, he had entered the negotiations well armed. The 1981 season had been the NFL's best year ever for combined television ratings. Both ABC and CBS had logged all-time highs during the regular season, ABC up four percent from its previous record and CBS up fourteen percent. The National Conference Championship Game pitting Eddie DeBartolo's 49ers against Tex Schramm's Cowboys in January had been the eighth most watched sporting event of all time. Super Bowl XVI, two weeks later, had been the third most watched program of any type in television history and the most watched live production ever. More than 110,000,000 Americans saw Eddie DeBartolo's franchise win its first Super Bowl over Paul Brown's Cincinnati Bengals and 14,000,000 more listened on the radio. The NFL's average live gate for the season topped 60,000 for the first time in history as well.

Normally, final statistics for the last year of a television contract had little effect on negotiations because negotiations were usually finished by the time such numbers were available. However, 1981 had been a very different kind of year. *LAMCC v. NFL* had set the timing of everything back and, as a consequence, Rozelle and the rest of the TV committee did not begin their final preparations for bargaining until after Super Bowl XVI was over. Then Rozelle, Art Modell, and Gene Klein huddled for a week at Klein's house in Beverly Hills. Klein was now fully recovered from his heart attack and, according to Rozelle, showed no lasting effects from his brush with death. At the end of that week, the trio had come up with the figures they wanted and sent Rozelle back to New York to tell the networks. Their demands were rumored to be "enormous" by all previous standards.

Another difference between the 1982 negotiations and those of earlier years was the role of the TV committee. Until now, Modell and Klein had been an offstage presence when the deal was being cut, but this year, Rozelle remembered, "they had more involvement than ever before." At one point, Modell and Klein flew to New York and joined Rozelle in some network meetings. At another, a CBS executive flew to L.A. and negotiated with Klein alone, the first time since 1960 that any network representative had ever negotiated football programming outside of Rozelle's presence.

Klein's unprecedented involvement was one of several attempts to break the most significant logjam of the process. All the networks were stunned when told what the League wanted. "We had been expecting a one hundred percent increase," one television executive explained, "but he hit us with 150 percent from the start and that was a surprise." Nonetheless, Rozelle at first found the going relatively easy. Taking the networks one at a time, he started with ABC and relatively quickly got them to agree to pay $680 million over five years. Next came NBC, who demanded a share of ABC's prime time slot but soon "knuckled under" and agreed to $640 million. CBS was the first of the three to put its foot down. Rozelle wanted $770 million from them and they categorically refused. The CBS executive flew out to see Klein in the middle of the dispute. "CBS didn't want to pay," Klein remembered, "so we went at it head to head. I had to convince him that those were the numbers we really wanted." The CBS executive left L.A. still unconvinced and, back in New York, told Rozelle that CBS would drop the NFL entirely if their price didn't come down. "They stood eyeball to eyeball for a while," a source close to the negotiations remembered. "Then Pete blinked." The League dropped $50 million from its asking price and CBS signed for $720 million on March 20, little more than a day before the annual meeting convened.

The package Rozelle had to present on March 22 was still beyond almost everyone's fondest imaginings. Before laying out the contract's specifics, he first singled out Art Modell and Gene Klein with praise for their efforts. Then came the numbers. The three networks had agreed to pay the League a total of $2 billion over five years. Split the usual twenty-eight ways, that was $14 million per club per season, almost three times their current $5.2 million. "There were lots of smiles," the commissioner remembered. "They were very happy." For good reason. At the time, the average total annual expenses of an NFL club was in the neighborhood of $11 million. The new television contract thus meant the average club was guaranteed a profit before it even began counting the live gate. "Once again," *Sports Illustrated* declared, "the wiliest sports commissioner of them all had gone to the network treasuries and come back loaded with untold riches." When it came time to vote on the package, Rozelle remembered, "it was the quickest yes vote we've gotten from the Raiders in a long time."

Just how happy the owners were with Rozelle became apparent immediately after the TV committee's report was finished. "At noon," according to the minutes, "the commissioner and League office employees were asked to leave the room." Gene Klein then took the floor to make a motion. During the negotiations, Rozelle had remarked that "this is the last time I'll be doing this," a reference to the fact that his own contract would expire a year before the networks'. Klein wanted to eliminate that possibility immediately and submitted the following motion:

> RESOLVED, that a committee of owners be chosen and authorized to negotiate and execute a contract for the further employment of Pete Rozelle as NFL commissioner.

The motion was seconded by Billy Sullivan and passed by a vote of twenty-seven to one, with, once again, only Al Davis dissenting. Following the passage of the resolution, "the membership then nominated and approved

a three-member committee.'' The members were Hugh Culverhouse, nominated by Dan Rooney; Gene Klein, nominated by Robert Irsay; and Leon
Hess, nominated by Billy Sullivan. This executive session was the first Hess
had attended since assuming one hundred percent ownership of the Jets and he
spoke for the committee. The three said they would accept the assignment on
''the proviso we can finalize the deal without coming to the membership for a
vote.'' Such authority was given, twenty-seven to one. In essence, the
committee was now free to give Rozelle whatever it felt was appropriate. The
''secrecy'' surrounding their subsequent negotiations with Rozelle was such
that it would be two years before most of the owners even learned what was
in the contract.

"We corrected some terrible financial injustices to Pete,'' Gene Klein
remembered. ''If he was a standard CEO, he would have had stock options
so that the success of the enterprise would have made him a lot of money.
Pete can't do that, so we tried to make up for it. Only Al Davis objected.''

While Pete Rozelle no doubt felt a certain vindication in the glory
surrounding the new television deal and his employers were certifiably richer
than ever, none of that changed the fact that the rest of the news facing the
1982 annual meeting was bad. Three issues in particular dominated the
League's worries.

The first was, of course, *LAMCC v. NFL*. Privileged legal conferences
were held on three different days in Phoenix. To the great frustration of the
NFL's attorneys, none of the new change of venue motions they'd made had
proved successful and less than a week after the meeting adjourned, trial
would resume in Los Angeles. The prospect was ominous and already there
was talk about winning this one on appeal. Bolstered by the prospects of a
television bonanza, however, the League was in a fighting mood, and on the
morning of March 23, the executive session minus Al Davis voted unanimously ''to give no further consideration to settlement.''

The second concern was Ed Garvey and the NFLPA. At that point, labor
negotiations were looking like a replay of 1977, only worse. Even the
League's optimists were counting on Garvey's position collapsing rather than
modifying. ''I was convinced,'' Art Modell remembered, ''that Ed Garvey
. . . had no consensus whatsoever within his own ranks as to what approach
to take about a work stoppage.'' Modell thought that the worst that could
happen was ''a show of unity'' by the union during next season's training
camps. A number of other owners, however, were already convinced there
would be a full-fledged strike because that's what Garvey wanted.

The third item of foreboding that March was also the newest. For the
first time since 1975, the League was about to face the prospect of external
competition. Within two months, a new football business calling itself the
United States Football League would announce its existence. That such an
announcement would be made was common knowledge at the Phoenix meetings. Both rumors and accurate information about the USFL had been in
circulation for the last year. Perhaps the first NFL owner to learn about the
plans for a new league was Al Davis. Davis had been approached by one of

the league's initial organizers shortly after the 1980 annual meeting in Palm Springs. The approach was in response to a statement Davis had made to the press shortly after walking out of executive session while the rest of the League voted on his move to L.A.

"I've just been thinking about . . . starting a new football League," Al Davis told a reporter while lounging by the pool. The idea would be to field eight teams to stage eight games a month. The broadcast rights would be sold to cable and pay television outlets. "There are 17 million cable TV sets in the U.S. and 7 million cable pay televisions. By 1981, they project 30 million cable and 12 million pay cable. If, in 1981, we play eight football games a month, we could charge $10 apiece to show those games on each cable TV. If the stations kept $5 and we kept $5, we would get $20 per set, per season." If twenty percent of those sets tuned in, the league would net $48 million, $6 million per team. "I'm not planning this or anything," Davis had pointed out. "I'm just thinking about it. You know, just talking . . ."

Shortly thereafter, Al Davis received a phone call from one George Allen, former coach and general manager of the Washington Redskins under Edward Bennett Williams. Now out of the NFL, Allen was enthusiastic about Davis's comments. "George called me," Davis remembered, "and said, 'Why don't we do it?' And I would talk to him about it and then he was very interested in it and, from time to time [after that], he would ask me questions about budgets and things like that, which I would help him [with] and even went with him a couple of times to listen to what people had to say about it and [I] advised him what I thought he would have to do to make a new league work. . . . I told him how much money he would have to get from the networks per team to succeed." When his fellow NFL members eventually learned of Davis's cooperation, it would become yet another reason to resent him.

In March 1982, however, it was not yet clear just how much of a challenge the USFL was going to pose. Rather than go head to head, the new league's intention was to play a schedule of games in the spring and summer. It would not compete directly for audience, which was good news, but they might well compete for players, which decidedly was not. That March, it was the USFL's organizers' stated position not to try to buy away NFL talent but to build a league on the leftovers, almost like an NFL farm team. The League's optimists saw their competitors' plans as reason to expect a bidding war could be avoided. "As far as competing for players," Art Modell noted, "they have limited payroll budgets, according to their [plans], so that should not be a problem." Modell thought there was a future for the new league as a "feeder" organization for the NFL big time. The pessimists noted that there had never been two football leagues without a bidding war between them and that the USFL was recruiting owners with money to spend. The pessimists were right. Just as the NFL seemed to have found the goose that laid the golden egg, the cost of doing business was about to go through the roof.

Euphoria from their television contract apparently blinded a number of the participants at the Phoenix meeting to the actual direness of their situation, but, on paper, it looked like Pete Rozelle's worst nightmare. For the next year, the League would have to fight a trade war, a labor war, and a civil war all at the same time. Rich or not, League Think was in deep trouble.

23

The most immediately pressing of those potential disasters was *LAMCC v. NFL*.

Certainly, there was no one most of the League wanted to whip more in March 1982 than Al Davis. The extent that sentiment had reached was apparent at the Phoenix meetings, where one owner had a parrot trained to squawk "Fuck you, Al Davis" stationed near the check-in counter when Davis arrived.

Despite such behavior, Al Davis's detractors claimed the issue was much larger than Davis himself. "You can't have a rule and then abide with it when you agree and say the hell with it when you don't," Art Modell argued. "I feel as deeply about this as Pete Rozelle does. We fought it tooth and nail. This is a far more important thing than merely if the Oakland Raiders move or not."

Davis himself remained largely silent between trials, but there was little doubt he found the rest of the League's arguments specious. "It's stupid," he told *Sport* magazine. "It's ridiculous. It's the same lament and cry from Rozelle and the other owners in the NFL for the last ten or fifteen years. When Congress lifted the TV blackout, Rozelle told Congress it would destroy the home gate. On the contrary, it's grown. Every time one of our illegal rules is struck from our constitution, it's meant 'doom' for the League. But in reality, it's always been a new beginning and the NFL has become a better League. . . . It's the old fear package, something that's typical of Rozelle."

According to Davis, Rozelle was the reason for it all. "He had a nickname for a while, Sneaky Pete," Davis told *Sport*. "He was called that in the League and he knows that. And that's the way he operates. . . . Rozelle is the most powerful man in professional sports and he does not want to give up his power base. This [trial] is a challenge to it. He tried to destroy my negotiations in Oakland. He's sent me letters threatening disciplinary action that would, in essence, take my team away from me. He's sent letters to banks in Los Angeles, telling them not to loan me any money. All of those things are personal, there's no question about it. . . . The League has what we call its police force. It's a thing that started out as a security force to protect the League from gambling influences and things like that. Instead, it has become a personal gestapo for the commissioner that he uses unfairly on owners and players. . . . He has used it to threaten owners. And he has used it to look into people and harass them. God, the investigations that we've gone through. I know one owner in particular, I don't want to mention his name, who was called in within the past two years and told to get in line or else. And he has gotten in line. . . . My life has been gone over with a fine-tooth comb.''

Al Davis still claimed that Rozelle's motive was in part a lust for Los Angeles for himself. ''He said in court that he wanted it for the owners, but a lot of them say that they never even discussed it. They asked Tex Schramm on the stand. He never heard of it. They asked Billy Sullivan and he never heard of it either. I really don't think that I would have had any problems if I wanted to move my team to Phoenix. I strongly believe that he wanted the territory for himself. I have my perceptions and I know Pete. Pete lived there, his family lived there. He wants equity. He doesn't want to be an employee, to have his salary docked. He's gotten older and he's reached a stage where he wants to play tennis, be a big socialite.'' According to Davis, Rozelle's own needs had even affected the new TV contract. ''I think we might have made a mistake in signing a five-year contract, I really do. It was my opinion that we should have signed a shorter contract. But it was a victory at the time and he watches his life very carefully on victories. He wanted that $2 billion figure. It gives him a chance to look for a new contract for himself. It also gives him a power base with the networks that he wants very badly when he has to influence Congress or the country on certain issues. The League probably has the most massive media control of any entity in America other than the President.''

Pete Rozelle, of course, continued to maintain his decorum and ignore Davis's sniping. ''As commissioner of the National Football League,'' *The New York Times* would note, ''Rozelle has been its most visible and peripatetic spokesman . . . the League's symbol of integrity and honesty and prosperity, some said its conscience, and, above all, the embodiment of its carefully constructed and neatly maintained image. . . . Rozelle is supposed to look good, never ruffle, be a staunch adversary, keep his nose shiny, and, crucially, see to it that the League's financial figures perform a pleasing dance on the bottom line.''

By March 30, the day the *LAMCC v. NFL* retrial's opening arguments began in Judge Harry Pregerson's Los Angeles Federal District Court, the difficulty of the commissioner's role was also becoming apparent. The battle was now etched under Rozelle's eyes in shadows and puffy ridges. There was more sag to his cheeks and there was already a sense of something battered about him. The year 1982 would be his third straight one without a vacation, and there was yet another to go after that. ''Of course it has taken its physical and mental toll on him,'' his friend Art Modell explained. ''How could it not? Just read any fifty of Mel Durslag's columns and you can see what's been heaped on Pete.''

Though the retrial process would not be as physically grueling as what had happened the previous year, it would prove just as wearing or even more so. The new trial was essentially a severely foreshortened version of the first. Since personal charges against Rozelle, Klein, and Frontiere had been previously dismissed, there was no need on their parts to either prove or disprove a personal conspiracy. The same, of course, was true for the NFL's single entity defense. Even the jury was smaller, having been reduced by mutual agreement from ten to six members, all of them women with no discernible knowledge of football. The one constant from the first trial was that Al Davis and Pete Rozelle remained the star attractions.

The issue both would be measured by was framed by the LAMCC's Maxwell Blecher in his opening statement. "The real subject matter is monopoly and monopoly power," the attorney argued. "All the Oakland Raiders and the Coliseum commission have done is to request an equal opportunity to compete on the merits in the marketplace. . . . We say the NFL does not own Los Angeles. They cannot make the decision who will play in our ballpark. . . . The NFL is fighting about money and property rights. We're here fighting about freedom."

Rozelle's testimony lasted four days, starting April 1, and had few variances with what he'd sworn to in 1981. Those few discrepancies, however, were picked at mercilessly by Alioto and Blecher.

During the commissioner's first day on the stand, he sought to modify his earlier testimony that the Los Angeles Rams had benefited more than any other party from the League's refusal to allow Davis to move south. Upon reflection, he pointed out, he had noted that the Rams games in Anaheim had been sold out and the absence of any other unsold home team tickets in the L.A. media market meant the Rams home games could be televised. "The biggest winners," he now observed, "were the followers of professional football in southern California."

Naturally enough, Blecher wanted to know why the commissioner had omitted such calculations the previous year.

Rozelle's reply was sheepish. "I guess I have a lot to think about," he explained.

The change that did the most damage to the NFL's own case emerged on Rozelle's last day on the stand. Heretofore, he had resolutely refused to admit that the League had any pecuniary motive of its own for refusing Davis. Before going on the stand that morning, however, the League's attorneys instructed him to add one. Their reasoning was that the admission would somehow be useful in the appeal process once the trial was over. Whatever the motive, Rozelle's new testimony was like a crowbar in Joe Alioto's hands.

"The League has a right to derive benefits of an expansion franchise in Los Angeles," the commissioner pointed out. He also noted that such a franchise would be worth "considerably more" than one in Oakland or any number of other cities. "It's a corporate right of all twenty-eight clubs if all have contributed to the growth of the NFL. They're entitled to share the benefits." That right, Rozelle admitted, allowed the rest of the League to say that Davis "must stay where a franchise is worth less money."

Did this NFL rule, Alioto probed, mean that eight owners could say "we want a franchise for ourselves and we'll divvy up the money" and then "vote their pocketbook against Mr. Davis?"

"Yes," Rozelle admitted, "but Mr. Davis would share equally."

So if Section 4.3 of the NFL constitution, granting them that right, were invalidated, Alioto continued, "it would be competitive to your right to put a franchise in and divvy up the money?"

If Section 4.3 were invalidated, Rozelle retorted, "we couldn't put a franchise anywhere."

"What stops you from putting a franchise in Oakland?"

"We might be sued by Chicago," the commissioner claimed, "for not putting it there."

Try as Rozelle might to put his statement in context, the next morning's headlines were ominous for the League. "Testimony by Rozelle May Hurt NFL," the *Los Angeles Times* noted. "He Tells of League's Financial Motive in Blocking Raider Move."

Al Davis himself took the stand some two weeks later. The closest the defense came to catching him in a contradiction came on April 21. At issue was Davis's testimony that the Los Angeles Coliseum, Grand Duchess of Stadiums, was "superior" to Oakland's newer stadium for the staging of football games. Once he was on record to that effect, the defense sprang its ambush.

So you have never been critical of the L.A. Coliseum as a place to watch football? one of the NFL attorneys asked.

"Never," Davis answered.

The attorney then produced the clipping of an interview Davis had given to the *Los Angeles Times* in 1973. In that interview, Davis was quoted as saying the exact opposite. "The [L.A.] Coliseum is tough on football games," he had told the *Times*. "You don't really see the game in the Coliseum, because the seats are too far from the playing field. Los Angeles fans sit so far away they don't feel involved. It's like looking at a parade from a helicopter. Most of what you see is a blur. . . . Football as a spectator sport was meant to be played in an intimate, closed-up stadium. When the spectators are on top of the players, the game is never dull. Every play is exciting when you're in the thick of the action, when you feel involved. . . . At the [L.A.] Coliseum, everybody has to look across that running track and even the best seats are remote. So the fans don't really see and hear the violent and artistic things that make football what it is. . . . If a Rams fan could attend a game sometime in Oakland, he'd understand what I mean."

Davis's immediate response was to deny the quote entirely. "I would never say that," he claimed. "That's not me. That's not my language. I didn't say it." Under pressure he admitted he had probably talked to the reporter, but continued to deny the quote itself. Though described as "stunned" by the clipping when the attorney produced it, Davis could not be shaken any further and that was as close as the NFL came to breaking him the second time around.

On May 7, the case went to the jury and both sides began their familiar ritual of anticipation. Rozelle retired to the Los Angeles Biltmore, where the League had set up temporary offices. His wait was short. The jury in the first trial had hung after more than twelve days in deliberation. This new jury took just six hours. It had two counts to decide. The first was whether Section 4.3 violated the Sherman Act. The second was whether the League had also breached its contractual duty of good faith and fair dealing with Davis. The jury found for Davis and the LAMCC on both counts.

The news reached Rozelle when the League's PR man called from the courthouse. Jay Moyer, the commissioner's in-house counsel, took the call.

"What happened?" he asked.

"It's not good."

"Both counts?"

"Yah."

Moyer turned to Rozelle, shook his head from side to side, and made a downward motion with his thumb.

When the court clerk read the verdicts aloud, the *Times* reported, "Al Davis was sitting in his usual front row seat and beamed."

Pete Rozelle immediately issued a press release saying the League intended to appeal the verdict and fight all the way to the Supreme Court. "If the jury's verdict and related rulings of the court are sustained," he explained, "sports leagues will have been told that league objectives and community commitments are of no legal consequence in antitrust cases. The long range effects could include a serious erosion in the competitive balance that makes sports entertaining. The final result could be a loss of both fan support and public goodwill."

Joe Alioto called the verdict "a smashing victory over a very worthy and very resourceful opponent," but his boss, Al Davis, objected to the use of "victory."

"It's just an injustice that has been rectified," Davis claimed. "I'm not emotionally elated. I wish I could say it's a victory, but I can't look at it that way. . . . I thought we were going to win all along." Warming to the subject, Davis did note who the loser was. "I think we showed Mr. Rozelle that he can't treat people like that," he added. "He can't push people around like that."

The League's optimists thought the verdict would not affect its immediate behavior, and Art Modell, who flew from Cleveland to L.A. the day after the verdict came in, went so far as to predict there was "no chance" the Raiders would play in L.A. for the upcoming 1982 season. "The game isn't over," he pointed out.

In response, Joe Alioto explained the risk the NFL would be taking if it didn't allow Davis to move while the appeal was being made. *LAMCC v. NFL* would be reconvening in the not too distant future to hear testimony on what damages should be awarded the plaintiffs as a consequence of the verdict. "It's going to compound damages," Alioto observed, "which are running about $8 million a year." Since antitrust damages were, as a matter of federal law, automatically trebled, the actual price would be $24 million a year. Given those numbers, the lawyer added, "You can understand why a lot of those people are getting nervous."

Despite Modell's prediction, the League dissolved its own temporary restraining order barring such a move and, within a month of the verdict, included the new Los Angeles Raiders in its 1982 schedule.

A little more than two years after he set out to make the move, Al Davis was at last free to do so. For the moment, at least, Los Angeles was his.

24

Returning quickly to New York once the jury had dispensed its bad news, Pete Rozelle fell back on his breakout strategy in an attempt to make good his now considerable losses. On May 21, Congressmen Fortney Stark and Don Edwards of California and Henry Hyde of Illinois introduced the Major League Sports Community Protection Act of 1982. The legislation would prohibit "a franchise from using antitrust laws to attack a sports league" and required "teams to receive league approval before moving to another city." On July 12, S. 2784, a similar version of the Major League Sports Community Protection Act of 1982, was introduced in the Senate.

The Senate bill was the focus of the most legislative attention. It was submitted by Senators Dennis DeConcini of Arizona, Howell Heflin of Alabama, Alan Simpson of Wyoming, and Lloyd Bentsen of Texas with the stated purpose of allowing Congress "to clarify the application of antitrust laws to professional team sports leagues [and] to protect the public interest in maintaining the stability of professional team sports." It specifically exempted votes on franchise relocation and "rules for the division of League or member club revenues" from the Sherman Act. It applied "to all actions commenced under the antitrust laws of the United States prior to the date of enactment" unless "the judgment in an action is final and unappealable on or before the date of enactment." If Rozelle could convince Congress to pass S. 2784 before the *LAMCC v. NFL* appeals ran out, the day would be saved.

To effect that rescue, Rozelle called out the League's lobbying blitz. In addition to the nine firms it retained for that purpose, a number of the League's owners participated directly as well, visiting senators and making political contributions. By August, Senate Democratic party leader Robert Byrd of West Virginia had received the maximum legal campaign contribution of $1000 from Georgia Frontiere, Hugh Culverhouse, Joe Robbie, Gene Klein, Bud Adams, Rankin Smith, and Leonard Tose. "Now the League is stepping up the fight in the only other arena left to them," Joe Alioto complained. "Rozelle and his people are trying to make an end run around the courts. They're trying to buy an antitrust exemption that would nullify the courts' carefully written regulations. They're dangling franchises in front of states with influential congressmen, they're making campaign contributions to powerful U.S. senators, and they're hiring some of the most expensive lobbyists in Washington."

Alioto's client, Al Davis, was more succinct. "The NFL is trying to bribe its way through Congress," he said.

One of those "bribers," Leonard Tose, would later claim that Davis needn't have been so worried. Despite the League's enormous mobilization, Tose remembered, "there was no organization. It was amateur night. I went down and saw a couple senators and, frankly, they had more important things to do than help the NFL. I talked to one senator I know well and he told me, 'You guys are just playing with yourselves. You're not going to get anything.' "

If Tose communicated that information to Rozelle, it did not dent the commissioner's effort. When the Senate Judiciary Committee held hearings on S. 2784 in August and September, Rozelle was again the League's lead witness. The substance of his argument was much the same as he had offered to the House the previous December, only now *LAMCC v. NFL* was at the top of his list of complaints. If that decision were allowed to stand, he pointed out, "it would be anarchy. It would be a terrible situation. We sit down at a League meeting, and under the decision in Los Angeles, that can be called a conspiracy. We have some of our owners that do not even want to come to League meetings. They will send an attorney or they will send someone else on their staff, because if we are not a single entity or a joint venture, everything we do—I include picking where we are going to have a League meeting—could be a conspiracy. That is the chief problem that we are confronted with in a situation like this. Everything you do can be a conspiracy."

Rozelle's principal opponents at those hearings were Ed Garvey of the NFLPA, Bill Robertson of the Los Angeles Coliseum, and Al Davis of the Los Angeles Raiders.

Ed Garvey testified immediately after Pete Rozelle on August 16. Six days earlier, the union's membership had voted strike authorization, although no date for the strike had been set. "I guess it is fair to say," Garvey told the senators, "that we would not envy a senator from the states that are considering expansion, or at least hoping to have an expansion NFL team in their particular states. There is enormous pressure on them to try to accommodate the NFL so that the NFL will indeed expand. But in a real sense, I think what the NFL is saying to the Congress is what each team says to its city: 'Unless you do certain things, we will move or we will do something else.' . . . To just trust the monopoly I think is folly." Even League Think's revenue sharing was not out of bounds for Garvey. "We suggested to the House Committee on the Judiciary," Garvey continued, "that it was time to take a long hard look at revenue sharing because it has hurt the player market pool and we do not see that it has helped competition. More importantly, it has given the NFL enormous power to make sure that other leagues could not form, and it allows them to decide when and where to expand.''

Ed Garvey also made it clear that he did not buy the League's claims that S. 2784 would not affect its labor/management relations. "We also hear," Garvey continued, "that somehow or other the commissioner . . . is now a labor expert and that they are very concerned to make sure that this bill does not in any way impact adversely on the players. Anyone who looks at the antitrust laws and the history of sports litigation could not reach that conclusion, and they know that that is not the conclusion they want to reach. If the Congress declares [the NFL] to be a joint venture, then by . . . force of law, they will be able to successfully argue their way out of Section 1 of the Sherman Act. They tried it in the Mackey case . . . they tried it in the Los Angeles Coliseum case. They have tried it every time they have had a case come before the court. . . . The courts have said, 'Follow the rule of reason: come up with something less restrictive: negotiate with the union, and you have no problems.' And, indeed, that is what happened. Yet, if this bill passes, they know perfectly well then they have an incentive not to reach agreement with the union, but to continue what they have been trying to do for years, and that is not to have a union at all.''

Bill Robertson testified shortly after Garvey.

"NFL Commissioner Rozelle has maintained that the NFL is the proper determinant of what constitutes public interest as it applies to professional football," Robertson complained. "The Los Angeles Coliseum Commission finds such an assertion incredible. . . . The NFL owners could easily manage their affairs so as to avoid running afoul of the antitrust laws. If they are chronic violators—and indeed I submit they are—it is only because of their arrogant and willful insistence that they should be above the law. . . . Given a choice between letting the free market decide versus twenty-eight NFL aristocrats, we believe the public interest is best served by a free market economy and the laws of the United States which protect the free enterprise system.''

Al Davis testified on September 20 and then only because "forced" to do so by Joe Alioto. "This is my first experience before a Senate committee," he began nervously, "and I accept the opportunity to be here and I appreciate it very much to talk about my opposition to [S.2784] presented by Senator DeConcini. I am very much opposed to it. . . . I have spent seven months in the courtroom out in Los Angeles and had a trial by jury, two different trials, the first was a hung jury in which the case of the Raiders was won by eight to two and the second trial was in Los Angeles and we won unanimously six to nothing. . . . We won in every court decision, so far, between the National Football League and the Raiders. . . . The DeConcini bill is a bill that has no objective standards or guidelines that I think are necessary for any bill to make it fair and it should not be based on whim or caprice of individual owners. . . . When the Los Angeles Coliseum [first] sued the League . . . I was the one who said we ought to have objective standards and guidelines so that individual owners cannot vote based on money, friendship, loyalty.

"For example," Davis continued, "this bill would now give the National Football League, the owners, the opportunity to go back to unanimity, unanimous vote before somebody could move or eight people could decide they didn't want somebody, based on any reason whatsoever. Pete Rozelle admitted, under oath, that the reason they did not want me to move to Los Angeles was that the Los Angeles franchise was worth a lot more money than the Oakland franchise and that by my moving to Los Angeles, I would get a valuable piece of property that other owners thought they should have and they should divvy up amongst themselves. . . . I do not think it is fair. I do not think it is necessary. I think that the National Football League is twenty-eight individual owners who are individual competitors and I would go a little further and say vicious competitors. . . . We do have common rules. We have common scheduling, but we do not share profits and losses. We do not share them at all. And to make us a single entity is totally unfair because that is what we are not."

Under questioning by the senators, Davis contested the idea that he was trying to live outside the rules. "I do abide by the rules," he insisted, "especially if they are legal rules, but if you remember this, when we won the trial in Los Angeles, the Raiders, at the beginning, did not contest Section 4.3. What I contested was that even if the rule was legal, they acted in bad faith and unfair dealings, and we won that unanimously, that they did not give me proper consideration, that they did act in bad faith and unfair dealing. . . . They put every type of harassment in front of me, and I have abided by the rules all the way and I think the court bears that out. . . . I really do not think these sports bills are necessary for the good of the National Football League and the good of the American public. I think that these sports bills take away the right of cities to protect themselves. They give us a hammer and a wedge to do whatever we want."

"Are you telling this committee," one senator persisted, "that if these pieces of legislation were amended to include standards and guidelines that that would be acceptable to Al Davis . . . ?"

". . . I have won in court," Davis responded. "I won on the good faith and fair dealing and I won on the rule being illegal . . . but I am willing to do anything that is reasonable. . . . I do not want a continuing confrontation with the commissioner. In fact, I am willing to let him win in some way, if that is what he needs, a victory. I am willing to let him win."

Pete Rozelle, quite predictably, found Davis's claims to "reasonableness" laughable.

Even Rozelle, however, had to admit that by the time Davis testified, the League's bill was facing significant problems. Most of those flowed out of deterioration on the League's labor front. On September 20, the morning Davis testified, Ed Garvey had announced the NFLPA was on strike and the three-week-old football season came to a grinding halt. "As soon as the strike was first announced," Rozelle remembered, "some people who had been supportive of the legislation said to hell with it.'' No one on Capitol Hill wanted to intervene in a labor dispute.

The news could not have been worse. While Pete Rozelle had been intent on breaking out of Davis's encirclement, League Think had been taken from the flank by the NFLPA. The League had no choice but to drop its business in Congress and square off with Ed Garvey for the fight of its life.

25

The 1982 strike marked the first time in history that an NFL regular season game had ever been canceled by a labor dispute. Though the League's relations with the union had always been conflict-ridden, the events of 1982 were a quantum leap beyond simple animosity and irritation. This time, the fight cost the League large amounts of money, threatened the marketability of its product, and even its status as America's Game. Coming as it did, when League Think was reeling from civil war and the League had been exhibiting its dirty laundry in federal court for two years, the strike culminated in a public relations disaster of enormous proportions. It was also the climactic episode of the National Football League's decade-long relationship with the NFLPA's Ed Garvey.

From the owners' viewpoint, it was Garvey's strike and, as such, only confirmed what they had always felt about him. "Garvey is a horse's ass," Leonard Tose railed. "He promised the young people in the union the moon and they thought he could deliver. He never gave them the true story." Gene Klein complained to the *San Diego Union*, "This is Ed Garvey's strike. Simply, he has overpromised so much, he can't deliver." Hugh Culverhouse blamed Garvey "unequivocably." "I think when Mr. Ed Garvey wants a settlement," he fumed, "you'll have settlement. It's that plain."

From Ed Garvey's viewpoint, there was little surprise at being vilified. He had taken this approach into account when developing his own tactics. Recognizing, as *Time* put it, that "his is a face that does not exactly warm the cockles of football fans' hearts," Garvey stayed in the background and let union President Gene Upshaw issue most of the statements that had to be made. "It's a tragic situation to be dealing with these people," Upshaw said of the management council. "They don't care about you. We're replaceable parts." Garvey himself pointed out how much better prepared the union was now than it had been in 1974. "Our communications are far superior than they were then," he explained. "The input from players is better than before, our staff is large and experienced enough to handle essential contacts in a union so spread out, and we've worked carefully . . . to communicate our need for assistance to the entire labor community. And the key point is, we have the right issue. All the players can see how much is involved. . . . They can see a percentage of the gross will help virtually every player. If it means strike, it means strike. We're not going to get it unless the owners believe the players will strike. No one gives up money or power for the fun of it.''

As of September 20, of course, there was no longer any doubt about whether the NFLPA would walk out. Nor was there any doubt that Garvey began that strike with the backing of his union. The shutdown was complete and would remain that way for fifty-seven days. "It was the first time the players recognized the union as a viable force," one of its former officers claimed, "an organization you could take seriously. It was the first time the union went after wages. The attitude was if you're serious, you go after the whole deal and now was the time to do it.''

The strength of the union's solid front grew out of two parallel and mutually reinforcing attitudes on the part of its membership. The first, and most important, was a righteous sense of being underpaid. "While there is only a twenty percent difference in the average revenue generated by each NFL player and players in baseball and [basketball]," a union flyer pointed out, "there is more than a 150 percent difference in average salary levels." Baseball and basketball generated some $610,000 per player per year and the NFL generated $476,000. Baseball had an average salary of $240,000, basketball, $215,000, and football, $95,000. The union claimed that the owners made an average gross profit of $5 million, more than their average total expenditure on player salaries, making the owner more valuable than all his players put together. Ed Garvey had no problem generating agreement among the players that the disproportion was intolerable.

He had also been eminently successful at selling his notion of percentage of the gross. Such a mechanism would, the union claimed, make the owners spend twice as much on salaries, raising the average to $200,000. Those calculations were based on fifty-five percent for the players, the level Garvey was currently demanding as an absolute minimum—fifty-five percent because, according to the union's figures, that was the level player cost had risen to at the high point of the old NFL/AFL war. The arrangement was justified, Garvey explained, "because of the economic structure of the National Football League. The NFL owners decided many years ago that they would share all revenues with one another equally. That has brought economic stability, but it eliminates any economic reward for winning or signing star players. A team that never has a winning season makes as much money from the playoffs as teams that are in the playoffs every year. The system is pure socialism. We want fifty-five percent of all revenues put into a fund from which all players would be paid. Of that fund, seventy percent would go to base wages. You'd start with about a $90,000 base for rookies and work on up, on a basis of seniority, to about $450,000 base pay for a player with, say, fourteen years of experience." Garvey's proposal also included a complex system of incentives for individual and team performance. "We are fighting socialism with socialism," he pointed out. "What else can we do?''

The League's response to Garvey's demand for a piece of the action remained the same in September as it had been in February. "The percentage of the gross concept is alien to American business," management council negotiator Jack Donlan argued. "It would turn over control of the business to the players. The owners believe pro football is the most successful of all sports entertainment businesses because of the business decisions made by the owners over the years, and the owners don't want to give up the right to make those decisions." Management was prepared to negotiate over money but not over power. According to Donlan, in 1981, some forty-eight percent of football's gross had been allocated to "player costs, which includes salaries and other benefits," but Garvey's fifty-five percent demand was for salaries alone, independent of "pensions, insurance, deferred compensation, signing bonuses, and so forth." Donlan's strategy was to turn the negotiations away from structure and toward money. Management's final offer before the strike began was a package of immediate payments and salary level pledges it valued at $1.6 billion over its five-year term.

Ed Garvey and the union negotiators rejected the offer the same day it was made. "I am convinced they're offering $1.6 billion," Garvey explained, "about as much as I'm convinced there is a tooth fairy." Garvey's counteroffer was to drop fifty-five percent of the gross in exchange for a $1.6 billion payment over four years into a player's compensation fund administered by the union. The management council rejected the offer and talks broke off on September 17. Garvey wanted to restructure the football business and that was the last thing the League intended to allow.

The strike began after the League's third regular season game. The starting date allowed the players to draw three paychecks and the union hoped the partial pay would compensate for the lack of any significant strike fund. Negotiations resumed on September 26, the first Sunday without a game. What followed was a long series of starts and stops without much discernible progress at all. There was no shortage of animosity in the process.

The union bargaining team was always no less than six: Garvey, Upshaw, three other players, and another attorney. When negotiations began, the other attorney refused to shake hands with Donlan and the management team. Garvey, Donlan remembered, "was the same as in 1974. He was always putting a show on for the players, always trying to put the owners on the defensive." At one point, the two sides sat across the table from each other in absolute silence for more than an hour. At another, Garvey and management council aide Vince Lombardi Jr. ended up almost jaw-to-jaw yelling at each other. The yelling quickly turned to threats of physical violence. Then Gene Upshaw, six foot five and 265 pounds, intervened. "Hey, Vince," he thundered in Lombardi's direction, "if you're looking for some action, here it is." At that point, threats of bodily harm ceased. "If Lombardi ever hit Upshaw," Garvey joked, "and Upshaw found out about it, Vince would be in trouble."

Donlan found negotiating with Garvey as frustrating a venture as he had ever been in. Usually, Donlan pointed out, labor negotiators keep their real position to the last. "Garvey didn't try to pull the wool over our eyes,"

Donlan explained. "He was very predictable. The things he said were the things he kept saying. We kept waiting for his real position and it turned out to be the first one. He talked a lot about his membership, but he decides what the union wants and then sells it to them. I said to him over and over, 'Ed, we can't afford your promises.' "

Garvey was frustrated as well, particularly at the continued absence of any owners at all from the bargaining table. Finally, in response to Garvey's complaints, Donlan arranged a secret meeting of Garvey and the management council executive committee on October 9, in North Andover, Massachusetts, but Garvey didn't show up. He claimed he had never been informed of the time. The meeting was eventually held as a one shot affair at which the management council executive committee told Garvey that Donlan spoke for them and to negotiate with him. In the meantime, the owners also kept the pressure on. "I would say that if the union persists in its demands for a wage scale," management council Chairman Chuck Sullivan told *The New York Times*, "it will leave us no option but to seriously consider shutting down" for the entirety of the 1982 season. Sullivan also noted that there was "a lot of enthusiasm" on the part of "many" owners to open up training camp and put together new teams out of scabs and NFLPA defectors. "No matter what time we schedule a meeting," management council Vice-Chairman Leonard Tose complained to the Associated Press, "they're at least an hour late. . . . Many times they have rejected our proposal without reading it. These meetings have lasted as short as three minutes. . . . I can say without fear of contradiction that the players have been misled, lied to, subjected to distorted information continuously by their own union leadership."

The League's solid public front toward Garvey had only one serious defector. That, of course, was Al Davis. He thought the management approach all wrong and, by the time the strike was two weeks old, had begun saying so. "The idea should not be to defeat the players," he complained. "I see one owner [Gene Klein] saying the season is over and others talking about getting new players to play under the banner of the NFL. To my way of thinking, that's not the way to approach the problem. The players are the game. We own it, but they play it." Davis also called on Pete Rozelle to intervene in the discussion.

Rozelle, of course, was powerless to do so. Because of his position as "the commissioner of all of football," Rozelle had no function in the management council and could only join negotiations as an impartial intermediary, a role, as Davis no doubt knew, the union would never permit him. Rozelle tried nonetheless, approaching Ed Garvey and Gene Upshaw privately during October. The trio met in a Washington, D.C., hotel room.

"From all I can gather," Rozelle told the two union men, "the owners are never going to accept percentage of the gross. I just want to tell you that. The strike has started and I know these guys and in my opinion, they feel they can't live with it and say why should we make an agreement we can't live with? Right or wrong, I'm telling you, I don't think they'll ever accept it."

Rozelle also told them, "I hope to be an escape valve and anytime I can help, please use me."

According to Rozelle, Garvey responded, "The only way we see your involvement is in negotiating on behalf of the owners."

"They have Jack Donlan for that," Rozelle pointed out.

Garvey just shrugged, and for all intents and purposes, the commissioner's intervention was a dead issue. Though, according to Hugh Culverhouse, "Rozelle stayed in daily contact with the owners" and, according to Leonard Tose, "attended meetings of the management council and there were occasions when he helped modify a position," Rozelle could do nothing on a commissioner's traditional scale. That powerlessness was yet another diminishment at a time when he needed a victory fairly badly. "I couldn't do much during the strike," Rozelle admitted. "I was just frustrated along with everyone else."

Ed Garvey's most significant problem as the strike wore on was keeping his membership together behind percentage of the gross and a union wage scale. "It is our legal right to bargain over wages," he insisted. "With all the money they're getting from the networks, we are standing firm in our bargaining position." Behind the scenes, however, Garvey's support was diminishing as the absence of a strike fund began to be felt by the membership. Their malaise was accentuated by the very public collapse of one of Garvey's schemes to supplement the strikers' finances by staging their own football games. The union had gone to federal court for an injunction allowing them to stage a succession of strikers' All Star Games which would both raise money to keep the strike going and demonstrate that the players were indeed the game. Their first effort was held in Washington's R.F.K Stadium on October 17. While the NFLPA claimed to have sold more than 8,700 tickets, the Associated Press estimated the crowd at 2,500. Though the October 17 match had been projected as the first in a nineteen-game series, the rest of the games were soon dropped as pointless.

The League was, of course, well aware of the pressures on Garvey. "Garvey had told the players the owners would fold after two games," Jack Donlan claimed. "After that, his position had to weaken." On October 31, the sixth straight Sunday the NFL had failed to stage games, the NFLPA summoned all its player reps to the Summit Hotel in New York City for what would prove to be the final extended round of bargaining. That same day, the NFL made what it described as a "$1.28 billion," four-year offer. The offer was rejected by the union, but described as a "possible basis for future discussions." By November 4, the League had made its "best offer"—$1.313 billion over four years plus $60 million in "money now" bonuses that would pay every veteran $60,000 as soon as an agreement was settled upon. At that point, according to Dan Rooney, "everyone thought the strike would end. Everyone was ready to make a deal, but the NFL made a mistake." The mistake was the League's attitude toward the union's desire for a formal gesture that established their right to negotiate wages. Garvey had now abandoned fifty-five percent of the gross, but the NFL refused to allow him some face-saving. On November 5, negotiations collapsed and management walked out.

"We began to realize that Garvey didn't know how to solve the situation he'd gotten himself into," Donlan explained. "He wanted to meet to be able to hold off the players. Our strategy was to have no meetings. When he couldn't get meetings, Garvey called Rozelle and was shut off. He also called individual owners and was shut off there. We put Garvey under pressure and he couldn't hold off the players anymore." The League's final freeze out of Garvey lasted more than a week. During that same time, the League mailed copies of its final offer to all the players for their "informal discussion." Four days later, players on the New Orleans Saints, Cincinnati Bengals, Los Angeles Rams, and Houston Oilers all voted to accept the League's offer by overwhelming margins. "The rank and file," Dan Rooney noted, "was ready to cave in."

By the weekend of November 12, Ed Garvey was in somewhat desperate straits as well. He called his one "friend" among the owners, Dan Rooney, to commiserate. "Ed was down," Rooney remembered, "real down and upset. He kept saying the thing was blown. Both of us were talking that the season was over and we both kept asking 'What can we do?' Wasn't there someone we could get to mediate?" The name both Rooney and Garvey came up with was Paul Martha, a former player who now worked in the front office of Eddie DeBartolo's 49ers. The next morning, Rooney and Garvey talked with Martha on a conference call. That night, they talked with the rest of the management council executive committee on a similar phone hook-up and on November 14, Martha and Rooney flew to New York, where negotiations were reopened in the St. Regis Hotel. Even Garvey soon admitted "progress is being made." Additional impetus had been added to the process by the failure of Garvey's last gambit, a request to the National Labor Relations Board to intervene and force management to negotiate on his wage scale plan. The NLRB announced its refusal to intervene the same day negotiations resumed.

That first day's negotiations were nonetheless rocky. "The NFL people talked to Garvey and his people all day," Dan Rooney remembered, "and it wasn't working. The union people even said on TV that Martha didn't know what he was doing. Martha called me that evening and said, 'We have to get together with Garvey.' "

"Haven't you seen what they've been saying about you on TV?" Rooney asked.

"Don't pay any attention to that," Martha responded.

The next morning, Garvey, Upshaw, Donlan, Rooney, and Martha all met and after hours of negotiations with Martha as mediator reached a tentative agreement. That evening, the owners met to ratify it. Both Dan Rooney and Chuck Sullivan played key roles in persuading them to do so. "Nobody did any handsprings," Art Modell noted of the owners' vote, "and there was no elation. But nobody voted against it either."

On November 17, *The New York Times* ran "Strike Is Ended in Pro

Football; Games Sunday'' on its front page. "The contract,'' the "impartial''
Pete Rozelle explained, "contains no major changes from our last offer.''

    Certainly the outcome was nothing for Ed Garvey to brag about. "It was
bizarre there at the end,'' one of the assembled player reps remembered.
"Garvey had a terrible cold and it was obvious he'd just had it. The strike
collapsed from the top down.'' The contract Garvey initialed ran some sixty-
eight pages, not counting appendixes. Having set out to get fifty-five percent
of the gross and the right to act as the sole bargaining agent for players,
paying salaries out of a collective fund according to a seniority scale, Garvey
had settled for an owners' guarantee to spend $1.6 billion over four years on
players' salaries, including $60 million in "money now'' bonuses for ending
the strike. There would be no collective fund, but there would be minimum
salary levels that went up with seniority and the union had won the right to
approve the agents who negotiated players' individual contracts. The $1.6
billion was indeed, as Rozelle had pointed out, the same the owners had
offered before the strike began.

    "The strike was a complete failure,'' one player rep noted. "If we'd
kept the old agreement, we would have been better off.''

26

Though the League "won,'' there was little for Pete Rozelle to celebrate
when the strike finally ended. He tried to contain the damage, patching
together a foreshortened schedule for the remaining six weeks of football
season, but as the League limped into 1983, it was obvious that its accumulated damage was on a scale far beyond anyone's immediate control. The
losses could be calculated any number of ways, and all of them bid ill for Pete
Rozelle.

    In dollars and cents, all sectors of the football business of which he was
commissioner showed heavy debits. The fifteen hundred players lost $72
million in wages. Employees at football stadia lost $4.5 million and conces-
sionaires lost $17 million. Overall business in NFL cities was down by $110
million and surrounding municipalities lost some $11 million in taxes and
rent. The twenty-eight owners lost a total of $240 million in television and
gate revenues. While the owners' losses may have been a worthwhile investment that, according to *Sports Illustrated*, "preserved their way of life for
half a decade,'' their losses nonetheless had to be covered with borrowed
money that would have to be repaid with interest. Though football players
would continue to draw the lowest average salaries in professional sports
under their new contract, salaries would go up and take the price of doing
business with them.

The League was also faced with a legacy of labor ill will that would be slow to disappear. A significant faction of the NFLPA had a great deal of trouble digesting the crow they'd been forced to eat. Faced with the final deal cut in the St. Regis, the union's player reps had voted nineteen to six to put the deal to a membership vote and go back to work, but only three of them recommended acceptance. The Detroit Lions' players boycotted their first day of practice and Ed Garvey had to fly up to Massachusetts to dissuade the New England Patriots from calling their own wildcat strike. The membership as a whole ratified the pact by a margin of three to one, but few had good feelings about it. "I noted how the players kept their distance from me when I went out to practice," Art Modell observed of his team's second day back on the job. "None of them even acknowledged I was there. I guess many of them are angry and bitter."

An even worse legacy, from Rozelle's perspective, was the residual ill will among the League's audience—an attitude he described as "fie on both your houses," that showed up in reduced attendance for the patched together second half of the season and reduced television ratings as well. The strike had in fact culminated in a development Rozelle had been warning the League about since 1977. After half a decade of lawsuits and the worst labor war in its history, there was now little doubt that the National Football League was first and foremost a business. With that conclusion, much of the mystique Pete Rozelle had spent two decades building crumbled in a heap at his feet.

Though he was a prisoner of events, the commissioner's image sustained significant damage as well. "Rozelle was a loser in this strike," *Sports Illustrated* observed. "The world had come to look on him as some kind of savior. He wasn't."

On top of that, Rozelle's embarrassing powerlessness was only deepened by the strike's impact. Rozelle learned as much when he got back to Washington in late November 1982. He was there to revive the League's efforts to escape their hamstringing at the hands of Al Davis. He got a chilly reception. There were no antitrust exemptions available. The failure of his breakout strategy, Rozelle remembered, "started becoming clear when the strike lasted into November. Some people in Washington were saying if you can get the strike resolved by November 1, there would be a positive reaction and it might well be possible to do something. There was a lot of support for it. If the strike had been forty days instead of fifty-seven days, there might still have been time to do something in 1982. There was a lot of support, but as it was, even when the strike was over, the response was not euphoria. By then everyone had been beaten to death with it. Instead of a positive reaction, the attitude was, 'It's finally over, so to hell with them for a while.' " By early 1983, the League was laying off lobbyists and abandoning its quest for a sports bill. "We will make additional efforts at the right time," Rozelle explained, "it just doesn't seem worthwhile doing now."

With his breakout strategy dead in the water, Pete Rozelle's last hope of dislodging Al Davis and saving League Think rested with the appeals court, for whom he could only wait and wait. In the meantime, *LAMCC v. NFL* was the law and Rozelle, by his own description, was surrounded on all sides by legal minefields and unable to act. In his terminology, "anarchy" now had the firm upper hand and, for the first time in more than two decades, there was nothing the commissioner could do about it.

If there was any consolation for Rozelle and the League in the dismal situation they faced in 1983, it was that Ed Garvey was a casualty of the 1982 strike as well. "The cocky majordomo," *Sports Illustrated* noted, "became the beleaguered commander of a little garrison at New York's Summit Hotel, desperately trying to hold out as his treasury dwindled and his strength eroded." By January 1983, several clubs' players had voted to oust Garvey. Most also asked for an outside audit of the union's books. According to Garvey's most recent financial report to the Labor Department, the NFLPA finished 1982 with assets of minus $962,000. Some of the dissidents placed the union's debts at closer to $2 million. For public consumption, Garvey denied the union was in financial trouble. "Running a union is not like running a business," he explained. "You build up to negotiations and spend what you have to [in order to] carry on negotiations effectively. . . . There's no danger of going into bankruptcy. Unions don't do that." Garvey also downplayed the dissent. "When you go through a negotiation," he pointed out, "some people are disappointed and you settle the problem internally. I think that's healthy. This sounds like a big problem, but it isn't."

The showdown came in February, when the union's player reps met in Florida. The leader of Garvey's opposition there was Keith Fahnhorst, representing the San Francisco 49ers. Fahnhorst was a veteran of the abortive 1981 rising against Garvey and claimed his forces were better organized than before. They were not, however, successful in bringing Garvey down immediately. "I called the other reps," Fahnhorst remembered, "and as we got close to the meeting, I saw we didn't have the votes. Then, when I walked into the meeting, I saw Garvey's wife was there and I knew Garvey's people were pulling out all the stops. A number of people had been approached and told that Garvey had decided he wasn't going to stay on, but he didn't want to be fired. The argument was that he was going to resign, so don't force him out. Some of his opponents voted for him because of that." The official vote split two to one in Garvey's favor but afterward, according to Fahnhorst, "Garvey was real subdued and quiet. He realized he was finished. He couldn't hide things anymore."

In June, Ed Garvey made his resignation official and left Washington to take an assistant attorney general's job with the state of Wisconsin. "He feels he has pretty much exhausted his potential in his job," one of Garvey's friends explained to *The New York Times*, "and his family has gone through enough vilification. He wants to embark on his career. He feels that he has finished his business with the players association, and his mind is made up. Ed hopes to move through the mainstream of Democratic politics in Wisconsin and wants to be a congressman. He must move before he is too old. His present job is a one-way street."

The NFLPA's new executive director was former Oakland/Los Angeles

Lamar Hunt, owner of the Kansas City Chiefs, whose entrepreneurship in a variety of other sports eventually led to a bitter ownership policy fight with the commissioner which culminated in *NASL v. NFL*. UPI/BETTMANN NEWSPHOTOS

Billy Sullivan (RIGHT) and son, Chuck (LEFT), celebrate the family's recapture of the New England Patriots after a protracted stockholders fight and search for bank financing, 1975.
UPI/BETTMANN NEWSPHOTOS

Billy and Chuck after Chuck's takeover of Sullivan Stadium and before his disastrous venture into rock'n'roll production, 1985.
CARL IWASKI/SPORTS ILLUSTRATED

Joe Robbie, the owner of the Miami Dolphins, "poorest owner in the NFL," and a principal foe of Rozelle on the issue of cross ownership, announcing plans for his own stadium outside of Miami, 1985.
AP/WIDE WORLD PHOTOS

Edward Bennett Williams, president of the Washington Redskins and the commissioner's most articulate opponent in the fight over ownership policy, before abandoning the NFL's inner circle with a final thumb of the nose in the commissioner's direction.
AP/WIDE WORLD PHOTOS

Art Rooney, owner of the Pittsburgh Steelers and the living saint of the NFL's Old Guard.

Jack Kent Cooke, majority owner of the Washington Redskins, Carrie Rozelle's former father-in-law, and an outspoken critic of the commissioner once Al Davis's victory was virtually complete.

Ed Garvey, executive director of the NFL Players Association, whose irritating style made him a widely disliked figure among the NFL's inner ownership circle. UPI/BETTMANN NEWSPHOTOS

Mr. D.—Edward DeBartolo Sr.,
whose 1983 investment in the rival
USFL brought the DeBartolo family
to the center of the League's
ongoing ownership policy dispute.
AP/WIDE WORLD PHOTOS

Eddie—Edward DeBartolo Jr.,
who purchased the San Francisco
49ers in 1977 with the assistance
of Al Davis and the backing of his
father's corporate finances.
UPI/BETTMANN NEWSPHOTOS

Leon Hess, owner of the New York
Jets, "the NFL's Howard Hughes," and
architect of the move that left the city
of New York without a football tenant
for any of its stadiums.
NEW YORK *DAILY NEWS* PHOTO

George Halas, the founder of the
Chicago Bears and the last
surviving veteran of the 1920
meeting in a Canton, Ohio,
automobile showroom at which the
National Football League was born.
AP/WIDE WORLD PHOTOS

Pete Rozelle, battered by a decade of internal warfare, is inducted into the Pro Football Hall of Fame, 1985.

Raider Gene Upshaw. Once Garvey's staunchest ally, Upshaw nonetheless took steps to distance himself from the previous regime. "It's reconstruction, sort of like after the Civil War," he explained. "I think we need a change in philosophy in our approach. When people think of the National Football League Players Association, it doesn't rank up there with some of the most credible organizations in the country. I want our image changed." Once Garvey was gone, according to Keith Fahnhorst, it became popular to refer to him around NFLPA circles as "that bastard."

While he must have been gratified to have Ed Garvey off his back at last, Garvey's departure would be the only piece of good news Pete Rozelle would have to report in 1983. As the year began, the commissioner already sensed that the careful structure he had crafted was collapsing around his commissionership. "What's happening," Ed Garvey observed from his Wisconsin retirement, "is that it is all coming home to roost. Rozelle, Tex Schramm, and Art Modell have run the League and the League has to pay the price of their rigidity. The Davis case cost at least $9 million in legal fees and they may have to pay $50 million in damages and all Rozelle has succeeded in doing is making Al Davis the most powerful man in sports. As one owner told me during the strike, 'Pete is losing his fastball.' He's lost his grip on the situation. I suspect his days are numbered. He's just taken one body blow after another."

Ed Garvey underestimated Rozelle's staying power but was correct in identifying *LAMCC v. NFL* as the heaviest of the body blows the commissioner continued to absorb. While the 1982 strike was a landmark of financial devastation, the defeat in Los Angeles changed the very rules on which the business was built. By the time the NFL 1983 annual meeting convened at the Rancho Las Palmas Resort in Palm Springs on March 20, the full impact of what Al Davis had wrought was beginning to sink in.

"Davis's litigation has caused a substantial problem," Gene Klein observed. "Tremendous damage has been done and won't be undone." Chuck Sullivan offered that the suit posed "a big problem" that could create "a difficult situation." Lamar Hunt called it "a negative" that "I can't quantify yet." Hugh Culverhouse worried that "the Davis suit strikes at the crux of the League's ability to govern itself." Tex Schramm called it "a destabilization that creates the possibility that the clubs are not obligated to live by the rules and regulations which were responsible for the growth of the League. If anybody can do what they feel they must, then there's no League." Art Modell called "the Davis litigation" a "debilitating process, particularly for Pete." If sustained on appeal, it would surely lead to "a form of anarchy." All admitted that it left Rozelle's commissionership in severe flux. "The trend is discomforting," Modell noted. "There has been a significant erosion of authority. The important thing for Pete now is to bring the rank and file of ownership back into line so they act as a single unit. His powers will disappear without that."

By March 1983, the challenge Art Modell posed was no mean trick. The commissioner's powers to enforce agreement were at a low ebb. The eight years leading up to the current disorder had indelibly altered the character of the League he would have to persuade once again to agree. "In the old days," Steve Rosenbloom remembered, "during the fifties, ownership wasn't so ego-oriented. They were mostly football guys who weren't all that impressed with themselves. They didn't get involved in it for the money and they'd had the experience of trying to keep the League from going under. I went to League meetings as a kid. There were just twelve owners. Football was what they enjoyed doing and they saw themselves as providing a team for their city. These days, everything is different. The sports page has little sports on it anymore. The business of football has changed dramatically. It has unraveled to the point that the owner is egotistical and self-centered and thinks only of money. The people making the decisions now are all lawyers, business people, and accountants."

Rosenbloom was at the 1983 meeting and the transformation made a deep impression on him. Now out of the NFL, he had come as part of a delegation from Indianapolis seeking ownership of an expansion franchise. "I was outside the meeting room," he remembered, "and the doors opened and the first fifteen guys to come out I had never seen before. They were all lawyers and accountants. At first, I thought I had the wrong room."

The final handicap under which Pete Rozelle labored at the 1983 annual meeting was himself. The last three years had been one long, caustic fight in which he lost and lost and then lost again. "He looked terrible," one friend said of him at the time. "He was nervous. The whole thing with Davis had gotten to him in a very personal way. He was letting his mishaps dominate his life. That stage passed, but it took a while and was hard for Pete."

In the meantime, Rozelle had little choice but to hang on while bad went to worse.

27

Pete Rozelle tried to dress up the annual report he delivered at Palm Springs as best he was able, but the material he had to work with was slim by his usual standards. The previous season's opening week of games had set a League record and, even with the strike's bad aftertaste, average per game attendance had been the fifth highest in NFL history. Television ratings were down "marginally" from the record year of 1981, ABC by five percent, CBS by six percent. Super Bowl XVII, pitting Joe Robbie's Dolphins against Jack Kent Cooke's Redskins, had nonetheless been "the second highest rated live TV program of all time." As a consequence, now all of the top ten highest rated live programs in history were NFL broadcasts.

The commissioner's recitation did little to lift the League's grim mood. It hardly seemed possible that only the year before the same group had thought themselves the owners of a goose that laid golden eggs. Some of the bad news overshadowed by the television contract at the 1982 annual meeting now had a price tag attached to it and everyone was worried about money. Everyone also knew that the bills from that bad news had only just begun to come in. Of particular concern that March was the United States Football League, the NFL's freshly minted competitor. No one at Rancho Las Palmas still harbored doubts as to whether or not this would be a war too.

A week earlier, the USFL had kicked off its premier season with franchises in Los Angeles, Oakland, Tampa, Denver, Detroit, Philadelphia, Boston, Birmingham, Phoenix, Memphis, Chicago, and New Jersey. By then, it was obvious that the original notion of leaving the "big time" to the NFL and operating as a frugal spring feeder league had been abandoned. "What you have to understand about our league," General Manager Bruce Allen of the new Chicago Blitz warned, "is that we're a whole league of Al Davises. Most of our guys had been promised NFL expansion franchises but had never received them. Most of our people are just as rich as the NFL owners, if not richer, but our guys are hungry. Hungry and imaginative."

While the USFL would not compete directly with the NFL for audience, or for television ratings, it would compete for players. The bidding war began over the most glamorous of incoming college players and would soon widen as the USFL waged raids on the NFL's established talent. The effect was to do for the players everything the NFLPA had failed to and then some. Over the next year, several NFL teams would more than double their expenditures on players' salaries and Rozelle would claim all but a few franchises had been driven into the red by the escalation.

"The USFL," Art Modell warned on March 20, "because of what it has done and is doing, has added a dimension to our meetings. There's no doubt about it. They have attacked our system and we've got to defend ourselves. We must review our options. We must protect ourselves and maintain our competitive stance."

Just how to do so, of course, was another problem altogether. For the League actually to consult about how best to cope with its competition might well be in violation of the Sherman Act, and the League's minutes at Rancho Las Palmas made no mention of any response to Modell's call for a joint review of "our options." Instead, the USFL war would be fought owner by owner, as each saw fit. As such, the USFL challenge was yet another of the forces sucking power away from Rozelle's commissionership. It also provided the commissioner with yet another of his worst dreams come true. This time the perpetrator was Eddie DeBartolo, the League's youngest member.

Now starting his sixth year in the League, the thirty-eight-year-old DeBartolo was less than a regular at NFL meetings, though he did come to Palm Springs that year. It was his more regular practice to send someone else to represent him. On March 22, however, Eddie himself was an item on the executive session agenda. The bone the League had to pick with him was over newspaper reports that his father, Mr. D, was about to purchase the Pittsburgh expansion franchise in the USFL. "It's a smash at the guts of the League," a source in the NFL offices argued. "It would violate a sensible conflict of interest agreement. Even worse than the Al Davis case, this invasion of a long-established territory could, down the road, cause a franchise war." Had the federal courts allowed the League to enter the commissioner's ownership policy contested by *NASL v. NFL* into its constitution, Rozelle would have had an automatic mechanism with which to respond. As it was, the League had to tread on thin legal ice. "As of yet it's not a problem," NFL counsel Jay Moyer pointed out, "but we are aware [it] could be. There is nothing now in our bylaws that legislates against owning another football team, but we feel that the League is covered by our rule that states we do not want our owners to be majority owners in another sports team." That "rule" was a continuing resolution and whether or not the League could enforce it, given the additional precedent of *LAMCC v. NFL*, was very much up in the air.

For the DeBartolos, buying into the USFL in Mr. D's name was a logical step. "We're going to continue to concentrate on sports," DeBartolo Sr. had pointed out, "and make it a major division of our company. Sports in this country will get greater and greater." Pittsburgh was also the focus of much of that DeBartolo Corp. development. In addition to the hockey franchise they had owned there before Eddie got into football, they also owned the indoor soccer franchise, the Civic Arena, and cable TV for much of the Pittsburgh metropolitan area. That family expansionism can hardly have come as a surprise to the NFL in 1983. In 1980, Mr. D had purchased the Chicago White Sox professional baseball franchise in the name of his daughter, Marie Denise DeBartolo York, only to have the takeover blocked, much to Pete Rozelle's relief, by baseball Commissioner Bowie Kuhn. Kuhn's official reason for doing so was DeBartolo's interests in horseracing tracks. Unofficially, the *San Francisco Examiner* noted, Kuhn's "real reason" was "the suspicion of a Mafia connection." Eddie considered the allegation nonsense. "I suppose it's a stereotype that Italians who are successful just can't overcome," he complained. "You hear it all the time about any guy whose last name ends in *i* or *o*."

Pete Rozelle had heard rumors of the family's new spring football interest several months before the 1983 annual meeting. "Eddie Jr. made a couple of appointments to come to New York to talk about it," Rozelle remembered, "and subsequently canceled both. I first learned about it in the newspaper." The rest of the League's owners learned what the DeBartolos were up to the same way and, according to Rozelle, "expressed considerable concern."

In executive session on March 22, the League demanded an explanation. There, the minutes noted, Eddie, and Paul Martha, the DeBartolo executive who had mediated the end of the 1982 strike, "were introduced and a discussion followed pertaining to reports that the DeBartolo family was planning to invest in and/or operate a USFL franchise in Pittsburgh." At this point, Mr. D had already signed a USFL letter of intent. Martha explained that entry into the USFL was "a business decision." The DeBartolos wanted the spring team so a "sports package" including its hockey, soccer, and USFL football holdings could be sold on its cable television network in greater Pittsburgh. Among its options, Martha pointed out, the family would consider "either buying into the USFL and risking whatever recourse the NFL might have or divesting itself of its interest in the 49ers." One owner remembered that Eddie himself said he was going to talk to his father about it, but couldn't control what his father did. "Eddie did assure us that he wants to resolve this," Rozelle commented to *The New York Times*, "that he would like to see the conflict resolved and eliminated. I wouldn't want to discuss our options until I hear back from Eddie, but, in effect, he will probably tell his father that the conflict puts him in an embarrassing conflict arrangement, at least in the opinion of the other teams in the NFL."

The League had already assumed a solid front on the matter, as an owner explained: "The feeling was virtually unanimous. No one wants clubs involved in the same family in the NFL and the USFL. Their objections are even stronger with a city that has an NFL franchise." On March 22, however, all they could do was wait and see what Eddie's father said.

"Wait and see" was the watchword of the 1983 annual meeting. Immediately after the DeBartolo discussion ended, the League went into "privileged" executive session to hear a report on *LAMCC v. NFL,* where the attorneys' advice was in essence the same. A number of the country's finest lawyers had participated in putting together the League's appeal brief and had produced a document in which they had great confidence. A decision could be expected sometime toward the end of the year. In the meantime, however, the League might very well be receiving more bad news. While the NFL was in session in Palm Springs, court was in session in Los Angeles and the jury was hearing evidence on the damage portion of their verdict. The only NFL member who had skipped the annual meeting to be there was Al Davis, represented in Palm Springs by Al LoCasale. LoCasale was, of course, asked to leave the room when the legal discussion began.

The bad news the attorneys warned about was finally delivered twenty-one days after the annual meeting adjourned.

On April 13, the jury of six women found that the NFL had damaged Al Davis by some $11.5 million and the LAMCC by some $4.9 million by delaying Davis's move south for two years. Because of the antitrust violation, those damages would be automatically tripled. The total bill was almost $50 million in damages. On top of that, the League would also have to pay another $10 million in the plaintiffs' accumulated legal fees. It was, one NFL source noted, the first time Pete Rozelle had ever cost the League money.

The League immediately appealed the damages and began work on yet another brief. In April, it was just one more hope to wait for—and Pete Rozelle continued to wait harder than anyone else.

28

Life in the NFL continued while Rozelle waited. In Philadelphia, that life still centered on Leonard Tose. By spring 1983, Tose was once again in deep financial trouble and everybody in Philadelphia knew it.

The financing Chuck Sullivan had found for Tose in 1978 had apparently stabilized his finances for little more than two years. By July 1980, Tose was looking for more personal borrowing and arranged a $400,000 loan from Tampa owner Hugh Culverhouse. That money had been repaid in April 1981, when Tose sold some 34,000 shares in the American Bank and Trust Co. of Pennsylvania and wired the proceeds to Culverhouse's bank in Jacksonville. By October 1982, however, Tose had to go back to the well again. This time, Culverhouse guaranteed a $3 million personal loan for Tose from Merrill Lynch Private Capital, Inc. Between March 1982 and April 1983, the Eagles also borrowed $7 million from Crocker Bank in two separate transactions and another $4 million from the management council's strike fund. Although both Culverhouse loans were in apparent violation of the NFL's constitutional provision banning any loans by one member to another, the League took no action. "If it is a violation," Jay Moyer pointed out, "and the words [of the constitution] seem to say that, it would amount to a technical violation that didn't cause any harm to anyone." Both transactions were consummated with the full knowledge of the commissioner and the League's finance committee. Rozelle himself claimed to have "ignored" the apparent conflict "because of Tose's promise to refinance in a short period." Tose noted that Culverhouse had taken a fee for his assistance.

There were, as usual, a myriad of indulgences responsible for Leonard Tose's financial shortfall, but one stood out. Casino gambling was now legal in nearby Atlantic City, New Jersey, and, despite his 1980 claims to have all but given up such activity, the temptation proved too much. The year 1982 had been particularly hard for Leonard Tose, and during it, his wagering flared to an all-time high. When in Atlantic City that year, according to *The Philadelphia Inquirer,* "it was not unusual for Tose to win or lose $500,000 in one night." His favorite game was blackjack, at which he was known to wager as much as $70,000 on a single hand. That preference insured he lost far more than he won. "He's probably one of the worst blackjack players I've ever seen," a casino source confided. Nonetheless, Tose acquired a reputation for paying his gambling debts quickly and remaining "unflappable," even when he lost. "He was a sweetheart to deal with," another casino source pointed out. "He paid us like he was a man with no worries."

An evening in April 1982, not long after Tose learned of the League's upcoming television bonanza, was typical of his nocturnal odyssey at the tables. According to the records of one Atlantic City casino cited by *The Philadelphia Inquirer*, at 12:45 A.M. Tose signed a marker and borrowed $25,000. At 12:53, he signed for another $25,000. At 1:00 A.M., he borrowed $50,000 more, then borrowed yet another $50,000 just three minutes later. At 1:30, he added $15,000; at 1:31, $35,000; at 1:35, another $50,000. By 3:07 A.M., Tose had switched tables and borrowed another $50,000. By 3:30, he had borrowed yet $100,000 more. Before he finally left as the sun was coming up, Leonard Tose had lost some $400,000, not counting whatever money he'd brought along to start with. In November, according to reports by a Philadelphia radio station, not long after the settlement of the strike, Tose had hopped over to Atlantic City for a night and lost more than $1 million at an assortment of casinos.

None of this was a very hidden diversion. When Tose was in one of his betting frenzies, people would come from all over the casino to watch. "The guy sat there in front of 150 people," a source told the *Inquirer*. "The whole world saw him. He used to walk out of the pit and say, 'Do you think anyone saw me?' You could tell he loved the attention, the allure. Anyone could have seen that kind of gambling display and it was awesome." One casino eventually began to discourage Tose from gambling there because it was afraid it would be accused of taking advantage of him. "He became a kind of loaded cigar and we just didn't need that," a casino official explained. "He had constant losses." By January 1983, rumors around the National Football League depicted Tose as having at least $2 million in outstanding casino markers to pay back.

By the end of January, the public reports circulating about Tose's gambling had become loud enough that Pete Rozelle felt obliged to comment. On January 28, Rozelle announced that he planned to talk with Tose. "I don't know what I'll say to him," he explained. "Legalized gambling is a sort of hard thing to get in perspective, except when people talk about it and tie it into the instances we've had this year. But it's not good for the League or for Leonard. . . . I would be a hell of a lot more concerned if I knew that [a player] had bet at the casinos. . . . An owner doesn't control the outcome of a game. So when you talk about the credibility of the game, anyone close to football knows that an owner does not interfere with the coaches and players. He's not going to send in plays, except in infrequent situations, but he's not going to have a big effect." Rozelle did not plan to tell Tose to stop gambling, rather just to ask, "Why cause trouble for yourself, the Eagles, and the League?" The low priority Rozelle placed on the discussion was apparent in the fact that the meeting with Tose did not take place until April.

In the meantime, Leonard Tose publicly denied his financial difficulties.

"Is the team for sale?" a Philadelphia reporter asked him in January.

"No, the team's not for sale," Tose answered.

"Are you in financial trouble?"

"No," Tose exclaimed. "I don't have any financial trouble. Not from gambling. Not from the strike. Honest to God."

Despite his denials, that January Tose took dramatic steps to reorganize his principal asset, the Philadelphia Eagles. He also began a quiet, behind-the-scenes search for a buyer to bail him out. Both moves were spearheaded by Tose's daughter from his first marriage, Susan Fletcher. After a career as a child equestrian, two failed marriages, and a failed fashion design business, Fletcher had enrolled in Villanova University Law School and earned a reputation as a brilliant student. As an attorney, she was considered a tough litigator. Forty-two years old in 1983, she was described by *Philadelphia Magazine* as "attractive," "small," and "fiery." On January 12, the Eagles announced that Fletcher was being brought on as a vice-president and house counsel. By then, Tose's private financial crunch was such that he was trying to sell part of his personal luxury box in Veterans Stadium to several casino operators in order to raise some quick cash.

"What he intends to do," Susan Fletcher said of her father's appointment of her, "is sometime down the road eventually take some time off and give me more responsibility in the day-to-day operation." Fletcher pointed out that she had been involved in Eagles' legal affairs for several years already, "including League matters," and added, "I think that I have all the skills that are necessary and the energy and enthusiasm. I have a business background. . . . I have a familiarity with football, since I've been involved since I was a young child." Tose personally confirmed that he intended to leave her the team in his will. "Of course I want to leave it to her," he explained. "What does every Jewish father want?" Fletcher's immediate responsibilities were extensive. "What I do here," she later explained, "is handle the business end with a lot of help and advice from my father. I don't intend to have anything to do with football decisions. . . . I am here to make this team as fiscally sound as possible. That's why I do what I do."

The advent of Susan Fletcher caused some confusion in Philadelphia, and most of it centered around the question of Jimmy Murray. Murray, whom Tose had often referred to as "my adopted son," had previously been designated to control the franchise after Tose's death. Many of Murray's responsibilities also seemed to overlap with those just given Fletcher. There was public concern about Murray's fate because, as general manager for more than a decade, he had become a popular local figure. "Jim Murray was the link between the Eagles and the neighborhoods," the *Philadelphia Daily News* pointed out. "He knew Philly; he felt its pulse. As GM, he set the tone for the classiest, most civic-minded front office in this or any other city. Leonard Tose got most of the applause for that but Jim Murray was the man who did the legwork. Murray gave heart to a tin woodsman of a franchise." In January, Tose tried to reassure Philadelphia about Murray's fate. "Jimmy will always be a big part of the team," he explained.

In the meantime, Susan Fletcher had taken over the Eagles' front office. "What you had here when I took over," she explained, "was an old organization where everybody was somebody's best friend. There had been very little movement for years, and I think any organization needs new blood." Fletcher instituted a time clock, tightened expense accounts, and had all the club's executives write job descriptions. Using those, she began to fire people. One of the things she discovered in the process was that many were covered by ten-year contracts given out by Murray two years earlier. "No NFL employees outside of coaches have contracts like that," one Eagles source pointed out. "Susan got upset at the idea of so many people in the organization locked into multiyear deals. Leonard accepted it, but she doesn't like cronyism." By the middle of March, rumors of the housecleaning had reached the public and again, questions were raised about Murray's status. This time, Susan Fletcher did the reassuring. "I think he will be back as general manager," Fletcher told a local television station on March 14. "I think Jimmy Murray is very happy with the situation here. I think it's been a very tough couple of years for Jimmy. We told him to take some well-deserved time off and relax and get himself physically in much better shape, because he's had a very trying year."

In fact, Fletcher had already fired Murray thirteen days earlier. "It was like a punch in the heart to me," Tose said of firing his best friend. "I couldn't believe it. I'll tell you this, honestly and truthfully—if it weren't for Susan, I would have sold at that point. I would have sold for anything, it wouldn't have mattered. I was so disillusioned and heartsick that I didn't want to come back to my office again. That's not being dramatic. That's being truthful." Philadelphia at large wouldn't learn about Murray's firing for another two months. When the word got out, Tose said he had been "disappointed" by the Eagles' financial excesses under Murray and the fact that "he wasn't able to graciously accept Susan." By the time Murray's fate became news, he had taken his contract to Rozelle for arbitration. Rozelle upheld the document and ordered the Eagles to pay it off in full.

On March 19, while Philadelphia was still assuming Murray had just taken "some well-deserved time off," Leonard Tose and his daughter flew to Palm Springs for the 1983 annual meeting. On March 22, when the League went into executive session, the Eagles claimed the right to two representatives as a "family club" and Susan Fletcher became the second woman to sit in the League's innermost council. Georgia Rosenbloom Frontiere, of course, had been the first. "It's a rough road for a woman in sports," Tose observed of the League's reaction. "Women have it tough in any business—it's a chauvinistic world—and that prevails especially in this one. The membership as a whole was nice to Susan. Some can't change, but fuck them."

In early April, Leonard Tose flew up to New York by himself for the meeting with the commissioner about gambling that Rozelle had promised in January. "There's nothing against it," the commissioner pointed out. "It's legal. Players can do it, owners can do it, but I talked to Leonard about how when it reaches the point where this publicity could be embarrassing to you or the club, then it becomes a different problem. Leonard immediately volunteered, 'I'm not going to bet in a casino again. I may go there for a show, but I'll never bet.' He tended to agree with me and said, 'I'm just not going to do it anymore.' " With that, the subject was dropped altogether.

Not long after his meeting with Rozelle, Tose also succeeded in stabilizing his personal finances for at least the immediate moment. The technique he used was, once again, refinancing. In April, he borrowed another $5 million from Kidde Company, the conglomerate that had bought his trucking firm and to which he already owed $1.8 million. Some of Tose's new loan was used to finish paying off the $3 million from Merrill Lynch that Hugh Culverhouse had guaranteed. Under the terms of the Kidde loan, the entire sum owed them by Tose had to be paid in full by January 1984. Should the sum not be forthcoming, Kidde had the right to force the team's sale. In that liquidation, Crocker Bank, to whom the Eagles owed $19 million, would be first in line. Kidde would be next in line for its $6.8 million plus one percent of the franchise's sale price. Another one percent of that sale would go to Chuck Sullivan, who had negotiated the original Kidde loan. Interest on the Kidde refinancing was set at 4.5 points above prime.

One of the reasons such a deadline was acceptable to Tose in April 1983 was that under his current game plan, he would have sold the franchise long before the Kidde loan came due. It was an option, of course, that Tose had long rejected. "After all the fucking problems I went through to get this team," he once pointed out, "after all the fucking charges, all the fucking plots, all the problems with the fucking banks, my fucking broads, my fucking ex-wife, my kids. . . . Now I am finally in a position where I can relax and I'm going to sell the team? No fucking way." Nonetheless, Susan Fletcher had been working that option out since she'd come on the job. By May, she had made significant progress.

The first concrete offer Fletcher turned up was from Ed Snider, owner of the Philadelphia Flyers hockey franchise. In addition to assuming some $33 million in Eagles' bank debt and longterm contractual obligations, Snider offered to guarantee Tose an $8 million income over eight years and $650,000 a year for the rest of his life after that. Snider would also loan Tose $8 million immediately and another $2 million over the next four years. In total, the offer was valued at $52 million. It also contained a provision allowing Fletcher to buy twenty percent of the franchise and giving her a ten-year contract to manage the Eagles' business affairs. On June 6, the details of the pact had been hammered out at the offices of Snider's tax attorney with Susan Fletcher and two other Tose lawyers. Afterward, Snider left thinking he'd made a "handshake deal" to join the NFL. A final meeting was scheduled for June 17.

Unbeknownst to Ed Snider, however, there was another potential buyer maneuvering in the wings. This buyer was a five-person syndicate. The five included Louis Guida, a Merrill Lynch executive and racehorse owner who had once arranged the sale of Caesars Palace in Las Vegas; Ira Lampert, another racehorse owner and a senior partner in a Great Neck, New York, accounting firm; and Dr. Julius Newman and his wife, Sandra. Dr. Newman was the plastic surgeon who had redone Susan Fletcher's nose and Sandra Newman was an attorney and Susan Fletcher's "best friend." The fifth member of the syndicate was Fletcher herself. In the offer they finally structured, Fletcher would be loaned money by the other members of the syndicate with which to buy twenty percent of the franchise. In addition, she would be hired as the team's general manager at no less than $125,000 a year and was guaranteed ten percent of the team's net profits.

Susan Fletcher began negotiations on her father's behalf on June 13, four days before her scheduled meeting with Snider. She and some of the other syndicate members met in a Philadelphia restaurant for lunch. At one point, according to *The Philadelphia Inquirer,* "Tose stopped by the table, shook hands and exchanged greetings, but did not stay." That evening, the group met again at the Newmans' home. "I'd like to sell the Eagles to you," Fletcher told them. Then she described the offer Snider had made in some detail and discussed how to structure an alternative bid. "She laid the whole deal out," Louis Guida remembered. The offer, as finalized, would include taking on $33 million in team debts and lending Tose $9.1 million to settle his personal debts. The money would have to be repaid by his estate after his death. Tose would continue to hold a title with the franchise and represent it at NFL gatherings until his death as well. In addition, he would be paid $1 million in consulting fees during the first year after the sale, $600,000 a year for the next three, $400,000 of which would be immediately advanced to Tose as a down payment, and $400,000 for year five and every year thereafter until his death. The offer's total value to Tose was placed at $42.1 million.

On June 17, the day she had originally been scheduled to meet with Snider in pursuit of his $52 million offer, Susan Fletcher instead joined the rest of her syndicate in Sandra Newman's limousine and drove out to Longport, New Jersey, where Tose was renting a summer home. They carried with them a draft document described as a "memorandum of understanding." Not an actual sale agreement, it was an agreement to negotiate a sale agreement based on the terms it included. As the day was later reconstructed by *The Philadelphia Inquirer,* Tose greeted the group and immediately suggested opening some Dom Pérignon champagne he had in the icebox. Tose, Louis Guida later testified, just wanted to sign the papers and "get on with the celebration." Fletcher, however, insisted that her father read the papers before signing them.

Donning his glasses, Tose went through the memorandum, asking questions and suggesting alterations. At the section specifying payment of $100,000 cash immediately and $200,000 by July 1, Tose told Guida that he had a $296,000 interest payment due the same day and asked that the second payment be raised to $300,000. Guida agreed. The draft document also called for Tose to be paid $250,000 a year from year five onward. "I can't live on that," Tose pointed out. He wanted $400,000 and again, Guida, on behalf of the syndicate, agreed. The draft's original "no binding effect" paragraph, giving Tose a way out if he changed his mind, had been scratched out. Tose initialed the deletion and told Guida he could understand why it had been made. According to Guida, Tose told him, "If I was in your shoes, I'd want it the same way. Frankly, I've been trying to sell this team for six months . . . and I want it binding as much as you do." When he was finished reading, Leonard Tose signed the last page of the memorandum, then opened the champagne, and the group celebrated. Before the syndicate left, Tose distributed Philadelphia Eagle cuff links and necklaces among them. "The minute I met you," he told Guida in parting, "I knew we had a deal. You're my kind of guy."

Negotiations toward a final sale document continued until June 28 and then suddenly fell apart. On that day, Sandra Newman arrived at Eagles' headquarters to meet with Susan Fletcher. While Newman waited outside, Fletcher went into her father's office for a few moments and then returned. Her father wasn't going to go through with the deal, Fletcher said. "He has a better offer from Ed Snider." The Snider offer, of course, had already been rejected by Fletcher herself some two weeks earlier.

On July 1, all the syndicate's members except Susan Fletcher filed suit against Leonard Tose, contending their memorandum of understanding was binding and had been violated.

Leonard Tose's attorney responded that his client thought he was only taking the team off the market while he and the syndicate negotiated. The $400,000 down payment was his to do with as he pleased until September 15, at which time he was obligated either to sign a sale agreement or return the money.

Tose himself claimed that parts of the memorandum he signed had been illegible and that he had never considered it binding. He called the memorandum only a "first step" in the negotiating process. "I never envisioned giving up control," he claimed. "They shoved it under my face and said, 'Sign it, sign it.' It was like a kangaroo court. Everyone was surrounding me saying it's not binding, it's not this, it's not that. I told them I couldn't read the damn thing. It wasn't legible. I read parts of it and there were some changes I made after I signed it. It was certainly a vigilante group."

A source in the National Football League office told the *Inquirer* shortly after the "vigilante group" filed suit that even if the syndicate won, they were in violation of the League's fifty-one percent ownership requirement and hence, stood only a "one thousand to one" chance of being approved.

Later in July, Tose was found in contempt of court for having used his disputed Eagles stock as collateral for a $400,000 personal loan obtained the previous month from Fidelity National Bank of New Jersey.

On September 20, the parties agreed to settle their differences. Under the terms of the settlement, Leonard Tose would retain uncontested ownership of the Eagles in exchange for an immediate cash payment to Guida, Lambert, and the Newmans, of $1.75 million. Tose admitted that he borrowed the money, but would not say from where. "I didn't have it in my cellar," he pointed out.

Back in the saddle, Leonard Tose would also find a loan to pay off Kidde and even further secure his hold on NFL membership. Susan Fletcher, having been given a proper Tose introduction to the business of football, returned to her job at the Eagles somewhat chastized and would continue to run the franchise's daily financial operations for the duration of her father's tenure.

"At this point," Pete Rozelle observed once Tose's obligations to Kidde had been met, "I am satisfied Leonard has stabilized his finances."

29

Art Modell, the owner who in 1977 declared the NFL had "strong feelings" for Leonard Tose and wanted to see him "succeed," said little about the Philadelphian's difficulties in 1982 and 1983. Modell now had his own very pressing concerns with which to occupy himself in Cleveland. It had been a bad year for Art Modell as well. The purchase of Cleveland Stadium Corp. was now out of the back room and onto the front page and Modell's reputation suffered severely in the process. "Modell Enters Fight for Integrity," *The* [Cleveland] *Plain Dealer* declared. With his own civic good name suddenly up for grabs and the League under constant attack as well, Art Modell got no respite and the unrelenting pressure eventually took a severe toll.

Modell's "fight for integrity" had begun on March 17, 1982, the day after the Cleveland Browns purchased Cleveland Stadium Corp. and got Modell out of debt. That day Cleveland, heretofore operating under the assumption Art Modell owned the Cleveland Browns all by himself, suddenly learned that he had a partner of considerable proportions, that the partner was Robert Gries, scion of one of the city's oldest, most respected, and well-heeled families, and, even worse, that Gries claimed in no uncertain terms that Modell had been cheating him. The accusations came in *Gries Sports Enterprises v. Cleveland Browns,* filed that morning in Cleveland Common Pleas Court. In order to make a personal $4.8 million killing, Gries charged, Modell had led the Browns to pay $6 million for an enterprise with a book value of no more than $385,000. "We're aiming to protect the financial viability of the Cleveland Browns," Robert Gries announced, "and we're aiming to protect our interests as forty-three percent owner of the Browns. This is not a frivolous suit . . . and we mean to pursue it to a fair and equitable conclusion."

Art Modell issued a response before flying off to the 1982 annual meeting. The suit, he told *The Plain Dealer,* was "totally frivolous, unwarranted, and without foundation." The purchase of Cleveland Stadium Corp. had been legitimate Browns business, he claimed, and "the terms of this transaction have been determined by independent appraisers to be more than fair and reasonable." The charges infuriated Modell but, in truth, the shit had only just begun to hit the fan.

Robert Gries was serious and dogged about his pursuit of the Gries family's ownership rights and seemed to hound Modell's reputation everywhere he turned. By May, Modell had learned Gries was making plans to attend the next NFL meeting in June and when Gries showed up uninvited at the Browns' press preview of their (annual highlights film) on May 5, Modell's anger and irritation escalated another notch.

Dear Bob, [Art Modell wrote Gries the following day in a letter that later showed up in court]

I consider your uninvited attendance at our highlight film press preview last night to be the most impudent of your actions to date. Functions such as that are sponsored to enhance the Browns' public relations and to foster camaraderie and staff morale. Your name was very intentionally excluded from the invitation list precisely because of the chilling and negative impact that your presence had. You have chosen to create an adversary relationship and to publicize it to the hilt. Surely you cannot be so insensitive to human relations not to have known full well the impact of your actions. I have no idea what your motivations are and, frankly, don't care. You have laid down the gauntlet in court and we are fully prepared to meet and prevail in that challenge. In fact, I welcome the opportunity.

However, I will not allow the diversion of your legal actions to detract from the successful operation of this football team. Staff and media functions are just that, and are by invitation only. They are not stockholders' or directors' meetings. Whatever your rights in those capacities, they do not include the right to be where you are not invited. I would be derelict in the exercise of my authority as president and chief executive officer of this organization if I did not do everything in my power to protect it from such encroachments. I tolerated your attendance last night because I did not want to tarnish the image of the Cleveland Browns at what was supposed to have been an upbeat function by causing a scene. From this point forward, I will insist that you do not attend any staff, media, or team activities unless invited, and will enforce my authority to do so if it becomes necessary.

In addition, I have learned through counsel that you plan to attend the NFL meeting in June. As a shareholder and director, you have no legal right to do so, and you have no function to perform on behalf of the Browns at such meetings. As I have for the past twenty-one years, I fully intend to enforce my exclusive contractual right to conduct and manage all relations with the NFL on behalf of the Browns. You therefore are not to attend this or any other NFL meeting.

Very truly yours,
Art

Robert Gries responded to Modell's letter as soon as it was received on May 7.

Dear Art,

Despite my firsthand experience with your quick temper and your insistence on always being in total command, it was more in sadness than in anger that I read your letter of May 6. Surely you are not suggesting that I, as an officer, director, and a forty-three percent owner of the Browns, had no right to attend the media party of May 5, a party which I have attended often in the past and which, incidentally, was attended this year by many nonmedia types, including my teenage nephew.

I totally reject your suggestion that my presence had a "chilling and negative impact" on those present. Perhaps I had that effect on you, and on some of those who are dominated by you, but it had no such effect on others, especially the media. My discussions with staff and media that evening were most cordial and in no way touched upon any difficulties between us. Or are you perhaps suggesting that my very presence serves as a reminder of the fact that you are not the sole owner of the Browns, that as majority shareholder you owe me a duty of fairness and that you have made it necessary for me to enforce that duty in court. Nor is there justification in suggesting that it was I who "threw down the gauntlet" or that it was I who created the adversary relationship which you presume to exist. To the contrary, we both know that I tried for four months to avoid the step which you forced upon me. I offered one compromise after another in an attempt to equitably resolve the Cleveland Stadium Corp. matter and I let you know, right up to the day of the directors' meeting, that I was willing to listen to any reasonable proposal of yours. It was you who slammed the door, not me.

I can understand your personal discomfort over press reports of the litigation. But you are not the Cleveland Browns, a team the Gries family helped to found, and which we nurtured and supported over thirty-seven years. Your embarrassment over the suit should not be confused with the image of the team which I have not tarnished one iota. And my motives are precisely what they appear to be, a pursuit of equity, fairness, and decent treatment. Faced with your actions, I intend to protect my interests and those of my family and those of the Browns. I intend to fulfill my responsibility as a director and as an owner. I expect to be present at such team functions as I deem appropriate in the fulfillment of those duties. Any unwarranted attempt on your part to block me will be added to the growing list of actionable conduct by you, and will be met with such necessary, proper, and lawful measures as are called for under the circumstances. If there is any disruption, any "scene," it will be your doing not mine.

I do, indeed, plan to attend the NFL meetings in June and thereafter, just as other owners and part-owners are entitled to do. I have no intention of encroaching on your right to speak for and act on behalf of the Browns. But I also have a right to be there. . . .

> Very truly yours,
> Bob

Each man sent a copy of his letter to Pete Rozelle and sought a ruling on the dispute. Rozelle allowed Gries to attend the social functions at all NFL gatherings, but none of the business sessions. Gries's first such attendance was on June 2 and 3, 1982, when the League met at New York's Grand Hyatt Hotel. Robert Gries would continue to attend all those that followed, shadowing Modell on what had heretofore been Modell's exclusive turf.

On June 11, in Cleveland, Gries filed *Robert D. Gries and Gries Sports Enterprises v. Arthur B. Modell,* subsequently labeled "Gries II." This suit charged that Modell had violated a 1965 agreement with Gries to hold regular meetings of the Browns board of directors. Modell responded that the 1965 agreement was "unenforceable" because the Browns were registered as a corporation in Delaware and, under Delaware law, shareholder agreements could not last longer than ten years. "The record will show that my personal and professional conduct during twenty-one years of Browns' ownership has been beyond reproach," Modell bridled. "I do not understand what the man is talking about, nor, more importantly, do I understand his motives." From that point on, Robert Gries says, he was specifically excluded from all activities of the Cleveland Browns.

Unintimidated, Gries filed what would be "Gries III" on October 29, 1982, the thirty-ninth day of the NFL's strike. *Robert D. Gries and Gries Sports Enterprises v. Arthur B. Modell and Cleveland Browns Football Company, Inc.,* challenged Modell's conduct as president of the Browns in four new ways. The first was Gries's charge that Modell had let the option on his previous contract as Browns president lapse, then negotiated a new arrangement with himself for more than triple the pay and an increased bonus. The raise was from $60,000 a year to close to $200,000 and Gries alleged that he would now receive "as much money as the heads of businesses one hundred times larger" than the Browns. Gries also complained about Modell's "lack of accountability for expenses paid by the Browns," his "autocratic one-man control of the Browns, disregarding corporate procedures," and his "abuse of power in attempting to bar our family . . . from virtually all contact with the Browns organization."

"If Modell seemed upset at Gries I," *The Plain Dealer* noted, "and exasperated at Gries II, he was downright furious this time." Modell immediately called a press conference in his attorney's office and appeared noticeably "red-faced and angry." He described Gries's new charges as "outrageous" and "irresponsible and scandalous . . . especially during what is probably the NFL's darkest hour. . . . I have received the same $60,000 base salary for twenty-one years, since purchasing the team in 1961—which, by the way, places me at the bottom thirty percent of all NFL players. I have no apology that the board of directors saw fit to give me my first raise in twenty-one years. I do not need Gries to approve my business expenses. Arthur Anderson & Company [accountants] has verified our books each year without so much as a question as to my business conduct. The record is clear. My personal and professional conduct during twenty-one years of Browns' ownership has been unblemished. Gries has no moral or legal right to question that record. I do not understand Gries's motivations, but I can tell you, he will be held responsible for damaging the Browns organization and the Modell name. I have instructed our attorneys to hold him accountable.''

These latest charges came at an embarrassing moment for Art Modell. The "NFL's darkest hour" to which he referred had hurt the Browns as much or more than any franchise in the League. Just as Gries had warned, the Stadium Corp. purchase was a millstone around its neck in the face of labor war. Now with more debt to service than ever in their history, the Browns also had a piece not only of the League's strike losses, but those of the concessionaires and stadium authorities as well. On November 11, while the League was still freezing out Ed Garvey in the Summit Hotel, Modell announced that all seventy front-office employees of the Browns and Stadium Corp. would henceforth work half the hours at half the pay, a reduction that would ''continue indefinitely until our future can be more clearly defined.''

Even with the strike over, the pressure continued on Art Modell and by early January 1983, the pace was telling on him. The Browns were in the playoffs and he flew on the team plane to Los Angeles for a game in the Coliseum with Al Davis's Raiders. When the flight arrived in southern California, Modell collapsed and was taken to an Ontario, California, hospital, where he remained three days for tests. The doctors concluded his collapse had been due to ''fatigue, lack of oxygen on the plane, and a reaction to high blood pressure medication.'' While Modell was in the hospital, the Browns lost to the Raiders, twenty-seven to ten.

Out of the playoffs and back in Cleveland, Modell immediately donned his hat as Stadium Corp. president and reentered a long-standing and acrimonious set of negotiations with the Cleveland Indians baseball franchise, his other principal tenant. By this time, there was little love lost between the baseball club's general manager, Gabe Paul, and Modell. Paul had been demanding a significantly better deal for several years and Modell had been pleading poverty. The combination had already produced considerable friction, as evidenced by their correspondence later introduced in the Court of Common Pleas.

Dear Gabe [Modell had written Paul in January 1982],

I am writing this letter out of sorrow and resignation. You have created an adversary relationship between our two organizations to such an extent that mutual trust and understanding is nonexistent. . . . You and I have absolutely no meeting of the minds as to what we should be trying to accomplish here. I can no longer be bound by spirit and concepts in responding to your continual demands because there is no reciprocation from you. I know you don't

care or give a damn about the Stadium Corp.'s problems, but for the
record . . . whether you choose to believe it or not, our economic
arrangement with the Indians provides us with the bare minimum
required to meet our commitments. . . . Having taken all the risk of
the stadium venture and made it work, I very much resent being put
in a position of continually defending the lease and my motives,
especially to a prime beneficiary of the effort. From this point
forward, we will view our stadium lease arrangements purely as a
business proposition. . . .

> Very truly yours,
> Cleveland Stadium Corp.
> Arthur B. Modell
> President

By April 1983, when the Indians' lease was just eight months from
expiration, the talks were locked in stalemate. On the 21st, Modell met with
Cleveland's mayor to present a dramatic offer to the city that he hoped would
break the logjam. To satisfy the Indians' constant harping at him, he was
prepared to withdraw Stadium Corp. from the lease picture altogether, turn
the stadium back over to Cleveland, and let the Indians and the city find some
agreement. In exchange, Modell wanted $10.1 million for the improvements
Stadium Corp. had installed, plus the right to lease back the stadium's luxury
boxes, the principal such improvement, from the city for $1.25 million a
year. As president of the Browns, he would also commit the football franchise
to extend its current lease to match any agreement Cleveland and the Indians
could work out. One of the proposition's major advantages to Modell was that
it would likely thwart Gries I, then making its way slowly toward a 1984 trial.
The mayor turned Modell's offer down, saying the city had better uses for its
$10 million.

On April 26, the Indians made their own move to break the stalemate
and filed *Cleveland Indians Company v. Cleveland Stadium Corp. and
Servomation Corp.* in Cleveland Common Pleas Court. The suit alleged that
Stadium Corp. had cheated the Indians on concession revenues during the ten
years of its current lease and set the figure they'd been shorted at $1.25
million. They also demanded that Stadium Corp. and Servomation, the concessionaire that took over in late 1981, open their books to an outside audit.
"This is not casting aspersions," Indians GM Gabe Paul claimed. "We are
entitled to an audit and we want an audit. It says so, big as life, in the
[current] lease. Who's afraid of an audit?"

The lease did indeed require Stadium Corp. to open its books, but
Modell balked at allowing Servomation's books to be examined as well. "It is
a sham and a disgrace," he thundered, "that the Indians, with only months
remaining on a ten-year lease, should file this frivolous lawsuit . . . purely and
simply as a negotiating ploy." Cleveland Stadium Corp. immediately informed the Indians that no more negotiations would take place until the suit
had been dropped and the Indians issued a public apology. In a later deposi-

tion, Gabe Paul conceded that privately he referred to Modell as a "crook" and Modell called him a "no good, lousy son of a bitch."

Art Modell stood his ground but, by the beginning of June, was straining to do so. It had been a long stretch of uninterrupted combat of one sort or another for Modell and he often looked flushed and less than well. He was still a civic heavyweight in Cleveland, whatever Robert Gries and Gabe Paul might say, and he still moved easily in the city's upper circles and met his political and social obligations faithfully, however exhausted he might be. On June 6, former Secretary of State Henry Kissinger stopped in Cleveland for a speech and Modell took him to the airport. Afterward, Modell felt a tightness in his chest, but it went away shortly.

Then on June 10, the Indians filed a second suit, *Cleveland Indians Company v. Cleveland Stadium Corp. and Cleveland Browns, Inc.,* in federal district court. The Indians claimed that their landlord's refusal to negotiate violated the Sherman Act and asked that he be forced to do so. "A disgraceful performance," Modell fumed, "bush league." It was the fifth lawsuit against the owner of the Cleveland Browns in the last fifteen months.

That evening, Art Modell and his wife, Pat, attended a black tie event in the city and then returned to their suburban Waite Hill mansion. Modell complained of indigestion and was unable to sleep. By the time the sun was coming up, his indigestion had turned into a "viselike pressure" in his chest. Finally, his wife rushed him to the Cleveland Clinic Hospital. An EKG determined that he was in the midst of a massive heart attack and he was put into intensive care. On June 17, surgeons performed a quadrupal bypass operation on his heart. Two days later, he suffered a pulmonary failure and was rushed back to surgery to correct several complications. Art Modell survived the second operation and spent the rest of the summer regaining his strength.

In the meantime, the battle over his good name was put on hold.

30

The last meeting of the National Football League Art Modell attended before his heart attack was held at the Saddlebrook Resort outside of Tampa on May 25 and 26. Again, the topic of greatest interest was Eddie DeBartolo and his father. The controversy now surrounding them was on the agenda for executive session on the afternoon of the 25th. Mr. D's ownership of the new USFL Pittsburgh Maulers was now an established fact and Modell was one of those most put out by the arrangement. "It's a disgrace," he fumed, "and that's the general sentiment of the entire League. But what can we do about it? Everyone is gunshy of litigation now and it's not clear we have any legal powers to force either DeBartolo to divest. It's a perfect example of what has happened to us. It flies in the face of the unanimous sentiment of the League. This never would have happened years ago and we have Al Davis to thank that it's happening now."

Whoever was responsible for its dilemma that May, the League's response was to continue to act as though it did have powers with which to handle Eddie and Mr. D, though everyone was at best unsure just what they might be. "I'm concerned," Pete Rozelle admitted. "The clubs feel that there is a clear-cut conflict of interests. I can't say what the clubs might do. The range of possibilities, from a purely academic standpoint, is to disqualify him from votes by asking him to leave the room, all the way up to attempting to throw him out of the League. I'm not saying that's feasible, but that's the range of possibilities, I guess."

The option presented to the commissioner and the League by Paul Martha, Eddie's employee, was that the NFL and USFL jointly agree to rules that would prohibit Eddie's franchise and Mr. D's franchise from owning the negotiating rights to the same players. "I think the two commissioners are going to have to talk about this," he explained, and "the executive committees of the two leagues are going to have to get together and try to reach some sort of accommodation." That option was, of course, anathema to the NFL. "We have no intention of sitting down with the USFL," Rozelle declared. "We'll make our own rules."

In the discussion on May 25, sentiment ran high against Eddie DeBartolo. "He's a spoiled rich kid," one owner groused. "He doesn't know his ass from second base."

That sentiment, of course, did not affect the question of what they could or could not do. Eddie himself was adamant and unworried. "The USFL team in Pittsburgh is the responsibility of Edward DeBartolo Sr.," he pointed out to the *San Francisco Examiner*, "I have nothing to do with it. I'm Eddie Jr. I own the 49ers. That's the only team I care about. . . . I don't care what Pete Rozelle thinks. He's a terrific guy and he's been great for the NFL as commissioner, but that's not the issue. If they couldn't do anything to Al Davis, then they aren't going to do anything to me."

On May 25, Pete Rozelle resolved the issue by appointing a three-man committee, headed by Judge Robert Parrins, representing the community-owned Green Bay Packers. The other two members were Wellington Mara of the New York Giants and Eddie leBaron, the general manager of Rankin Smith's Atlanta Falcons. Their task, as defined by the minutes, was "to study conflicts that might result from members of the same family owning controlling interests in competing professional football leagues." As Rozelle remembered it, the group was to "evaluate options." Alike in form and purpose to the fact-finding committee he had sent after Al Davis in 1980, this committee was given more time in which to do their work. After naming its members, the commissioner told his employers that "the committee would be asked to submit a report within sixty days." In fact, it would be October before any report was available, and Rozelle left Saddlebrook with little to show but one more thing for which he had to wait.

If the commissioner was looking for omens on the value of perseverance that summer, he could have found one in Foxboro, Massachusetts, on June 29, when the crowning touch was put on Old Billy Sullivan's dogged rise to football power in New England. The occasion was a celebration of the remodeling Chuck Sullivan had promised for Schaeffer Stadium. It had cost some $18 million altogether and was, Billy remembered, "a family affair." Chuck, of course, had raised the money and Billy Jr. had handled the liaison with the contractor. Billy's daughter Nancy had decorated the new luxury boxes, which Billy called "the best in the League." The Patriots' board of directors also helped. That group included Miss Mary H. Sullivan, Mrs. Mary T. Sullivan, Jean Sullivan McKeigue, and Walter Sullivan. Perhaps the most noticeable alteration in Schaeffer Stadium was its name. The Schaeffer Brewing Company, which owned advertising rights in the structure, had sold its rights back to the Sullivans. They, in turn, had resold them to Budweiser beer and Budweiser wanted a change. The brewer's suggestion, according to Billy, was "William Sullivan Stadium." Billy would have nothing to do with it, insisting a simple "Sullivan Stadium" was enough. On June 29, "Sullivan Stadium" was unveiled in fifteen-foot-tall letters over the stadium entry.

The ceremony was a luncheon for several thousand at the new Sullivan monument's brand new Stadium Club restaurant. A brass plaque featuring a bust of Old Billy had been attached to the structure and, in the distance, a brand new enormous DiamondVision scoreboard flashed a highlight film of the family's franchise in action. "The inmates at Walpole [State Prison] were evidently the only people not included on Billy Sullivan's guest list," the *Boston Herald* noted. "Tuxedoed waiters shuffled through the milling crowd bearing trays laden with crab claws, shrimp, lamb chops, and bloody Marys, which they tried not to spill into the sea of white suits. It looked like a sort of cross between a Roman orgy and one of those mass ceremonies the Moonies periodically hold in Yankee Stadium."

The program featured a few speeches and sportscaster Howard Cosell as master of ceremonies. Cosell lauded "the contributions made to the progress of our society" made by his "old friend" Billy and introduced the dignitaries seated up by the dais. Max Winter of the Minnesota Vikings made a few short but boring remarks. "I wish I could say that you're a hard act to follow, Max," Cosell quipped when he came back to the mike. Then came Old Billy. Billy's remarks were, in the *Herald*'s estimation, "miraculously brief, consuming a record eleven minutes and one second." To thank his son Chuck, Billy quoted the Bible, to the effect, "this is my beloved son in whom I am well pleased." He also thanked Budweiser. "We're delighted with this arrangement," Billy observed. "My grandmother, God rest her soul, once said, 'Tell me the company you keep and I'll tell you what you are.' The King of Beers is awfully good company to keep." Billy called the stadium and its new name, "an impossible dream type of thing. Some people hang around pool rooms and some people hang around churches and some hang around taverns, but I've always kind of hung around stadiums." Afterward, the crowd mingled to the serenading of the Boston Pops orchestra. Billy circulated, pumping hands, slapping backs, and beaming.

Perhaps the most remembered incident from Sullivan's stadium bash was Howard Cosell's introduction of Georgia Frontiere among the dignitaries. Georgia, the master of ceremonies confessed, was someone for whom he had long had a "naked lust." He then called the owner of the Los Angeles Rams to the mike and gave her a wet and long-winded kiss on the lips. When Cosell turned to the audience, looking, according to the *Herald,* as though he "thought he was the first man ever to do it to the woman," the crowd laughed.

Georgia took it all in good fun. Sullivan's celebration was her kind of NFL event. She had long since tired of the League's seemingly endless meetings and usually sent a hired hand to take her place. It was no doubt a welcome relief for her to have something to celebrate. That it came somewhere other than Los Angeles was, from her point of view, predictable. The "negativity" of her home turf was still a sore point with Georgia. On the field, her Rams had slipped badly from the standards set in C.R.'s day and Georgia took the blame. "Current Management Has Presided Over a Major Collapse," the *Los Angeles Times* pointed out. "It went from first class to just garbage," an NFL executive agreed, "I don't know why anyone would want to be part of that organization." One obvious explanation for the collapse was Georgia's continued insistence on acting as her own general manager. "She actually believes she can go one-on-one with people like Al Davis and Tex Schramm," a source close to the Rams told the *Times,* "and hold her own. . . . You're dealing with someone whose perception is not reality."

By February 1983, the criticism had driven Mrs. Frontiere to name a new head coach to whom she planned to turn over all football responsibilities. It was a "new" Georgia at the press conference announcing the change. First, she was on time, and second, she took the blame herself. Asked if all the negative publicity was bothering her, Georgia answered, "Not really. I can't say it didn't enter my mind. I'd have to be stupid to say that. Whenever there's negative publicity, there's a reason for it. Whoever is to blame, me or the gremlins out there, perhaps we deserved some of the negative publicity. Perhaps I tried to do too much myself." With that, Georgia withdrew into the background to wait for her team to come back.

Georgia Frontiere also waited on *LAMCC v. NFL.* Though she seemed to have a dim understanding at best of the mechanics of legal appeals, it was a way to get back at Al Davis and that was an opportunity she no doubt wanted more than ever. Her life was still shadowed by the case and, for her in particular, the reverberations of the deposition fights of 1980 were still a quite active practical fact. Though the ticket scalping allegations made by Al Davis and Harold Guiver that year had played no subsequent role in the trial and had set off no League action, they had not been lost on the Internal Revenue Service. An IRS investigation into Georgia and her husband Dominic's involvement had been smoldering since December 1980. At that time, the IRS investigation centered on "circumstances involving the sale of 1980 Super Bowl tickets" and evidenced an apparent curiosity about Jack Catain, the man who had put the arm on Harold Guiver on behalf of an unknown third party. According to police intelligence, Catain had bragged that he was Dominic's friend on at least one occasion. Through their attorney, both Georgia and Dominic denied any such acquaintance.

In spring 1983, that investigation gained new life when the IRS and the Los Angeles federal attorney turned over two new witnesses. Both men were associates of Catain's and both claimed to have taken large blocks of Rams Super Bowl tickets to several southern California ticket agencies and resold them for as much as six times their face value. While Georgia was in Massachusetts, IRS accountants were conducting an audit of the Rams' books, looking to confirm or deny "allegations that there may have been hundreds of thousands of dollars in unreported income from the illegal sale of tickets." Georgia's attorney denied any significance to the audit. "The IRS looks at the Rams all the time," he contended.

But the IRS was looking at more than just the Rams' books. One of the people they interviewed during the summer of 1983 was Steve Rosenbloom. "They were concerned about Georgia and Dominic," Steve recalled. "Since I was gone during all that, there wasn't much I could tell them. I wasn't surprised they were asking, though. I was hearing about it out on the street. It was handled real sloppily. They might as well have taken an ad in the paper." The IRS also called on Rozelle and a number of other owners. "They came to us and a lot of clubs for records," Rozelle remembered. "They mainly wanted to know how many tickets each club got." Much of the information was passed on to a federal grand jury that had been convened in L.A. and, in conjunction with that, Leonard Tose noted, "the FBI interviewed everybody." According to one NFL source, several owners and franchise employees were also subpoenaed to give secret testimony. Yet another probe at the same time was being conducted by the Justice Department's organized crime strike force, "focusing on the role organized crime figures may have played in the alleged ticket scalping scheme."

Whether or not all those federal agents would turn up anything of significance was, like much of the NFL's life in the summer of 1983, just another case of wait and see.

31

Georgia Frontiere's co-defendant in the original *LAMCC v. NFL* case, Gene Klein, still carried considerable baggage from the proceedings as well, though in a wholly different way. For him, it remained more a personal obsession than a legal threat.

Al Davis was by no means popular anywhere inside the League, but many had by now adopted a grudging but passive acceptance of his presence among them, at least until they learned what the appeals court had to say. Gene Klein, however, still wanted Davis's scalp in the worst way, whatever the courts said, and it ate at him. "He's an egomaniac," Klein raged about his nemesis. "He loves to bitch and complain and throw smokescreens. He loves to hear himself talk and tries to get the spotlight at our meetings. He loves to expound about anything. The son of a bitch has been trying to take power ever since I've been in the League."

By 1983, Gene Klein had sold his mansion in Los Angeles, now Al Davis's hometown, and moved full-time to San Diego County. His home there was up on the desert mesa northeast of San Diego proper, in the exclusive suburb of Rancho Santa Fe. Klein's estate, El Rancho del Rayo, was a four-hundred-acre horse farm overlooking the wide, sandy, and largely dry bed of the San Dieguito River. The front yard of his adobe mansion was decorated with sculptures by Miro, Moore, Rickey, and Hepworth, and 350 acres of the ranch was reserved for Klein's growing passion: the buying, breeding, and racing of Thoroughbreds. His wife, Joyce, had begun the endeavor with three mares that January, and shortly thereafter, Klein himself rushed into the venture whole hog, hiring Wayne Lukas, one of America's best-known trainers. "There are pressures in everything," Klein told the *San Diego Union* about his own life, "running a football team, having a racing stable, but I think the pressures I've surrounded myself with now are good pressures. There's excitement, but it's good excitement. I don't have to worry about 8,000 employees, 40,000 stockholders, and here I am living out in the country, breathing the fresh air, able to pick up and go to Palm Springs for a few days anytime I want to."

"Good pressure" or not, Gene Klein was much more vulnerable to it than he had been as a conglomerate executive turning salty popcorn into a financial empire. His heart was still fragile from his 1981 attack and, in late spring 1983, Klein was reminded of that medical fact while out for his daily walk along the nearby county road, dressed in a Charger blue jogging suit and shoes. Often Klein would see no one in the entire course of his walk. Had that been true on the walk in question, it might have been Gene Klein's last.

Topping a rise, Klein remembered, "I suddenly felt severe chest pains." Klein recognized the sensation and immediately sat on a rock by the road, hoping the pain would go away. At that moment, a Mercedes came along the road and stopped. Klein opened the passenger door. The driver had a stethoscope around his neck.

"Are you a doctor?" Klein asked. "I'm in trouble."

"Yes, Mr. Klein," his neighbor the physician answered. Klein got in and the doctor drove him to the hospital. The heart attack was contained and he was released after observation. No surgery was required.

Few in either the general public or the League knew of Gene Klein's second heart attack. There were certainly no signs of either convalescence or retirement on Klein's part during that time. During the summer of 1983, he paid $2.2 million for a new horse and $1 million for breeding rights to another. He also fought the summer's major battle with the USFL.

Klein had been one of the first League members to confront the USFL's potential challenge in no uncertain terms. Threatening to move his franchise to Tulsa, Oklahoma, should the USFL come to town, Klein had helped persuade the San Diego City Council to vote five to three on January 15 to bar any USFL franchise from use of the city's Jack Murphy Stadium, the Chargers' home field. His summer fight had actually commenced on April 26, when the Chargers used their first pick in the NFL draft to choose a running back from the University of Arkansas, Gary Anderson. Anderson was represented by Houston agent Jerry Argovitz, and until the Chargers' move, had drawn only lukewarm attentions from the new league. On May 3, Argovitz told his client that the Chargers had offered a three-year contract worth $830,000. He also said someone from the USFL would be in Houston the next day to make another offer. Argovitz did not tell Anderson that Argovitz himself had been awarded the Houston USFL franchise more than a month earlier.

The USFL representative who talked to Anderson on May 4 was John Bassett, the Toronto millionaire who was the only World Football League veteran who had come back for another try with the USFL. Bassett owned the Tampa franchise called the Bandits. He offered the young running back $1.375 million over four years. While Bassett waited, Argovitz then called the Chargers' general manager, John Sanders. Anderson's agent said he was calling with a "final" proposal, $975,000 over three years. Sanders, ignorant that Bassett had even made contact, refused Argovitz. When the phone call was over, Gary Anderson made a handshake deal to be in Tampa on May 9 to sign a contract. In the meantime, Argovitz sent Anderson to his mother's house in Columbia, Missouri, and told him not to answer the phone. When Charger officials were subsequently unable to reach their first-round pick, they called Argovitz and the agent said he had no idea where Anderson was. Gene Klein then ordered Sanders to "send out a dragnet," spending some $30,000 on unsuccessful attempts to locate their future star. When Anderson surfaced in Tampa on the scheduled date and signed a USFL contract with Bassett, Klein was furious. "It's not over yet," Klein vowed. "There was no good-faith bargaining whatsoever between us and Anderson. . . . One day Gary Anderson is going to wake up and realize what Mr. Argovitz did to him and Mr. Argovitz is going to be in for one sizable lawsuit.''

Round two of Gene Klein's summer fight featured exactly the lawsuit Klein had predicted. The road to the courtroom began when Anderson was befriended shortly after his USFL signing by one Lloyd Wells, a former scout for the Kansas City Chiefs. In mid-July, Anderson signed a contract naming Wells as his new agent, despite the fact that Wells had negotiated only one contract in his life. Wells immediately contacted the Chargers and Gene Klein loaned the agent $5000 with which to fly his client to southern California. Klein subsequently loaned Wells $25,000 more. All the loans were unsecured, without interest, and of no specified duration. After southern California, Wells and Anderson flew to Houston where, on August 3, Anderson's attorney filed suit against Argovitz, Bassett, and the Tampa Bay Bandits and asked for a temporary restraining order to prevent the USFL from interfering with Anderson's dealings with the Chargers. That evening, Anderson and Wells were back in San Diego, where the running back signed a series of four one-year contracts worth $1.5 million, $800,000 of which would be deferred until after 1986. On August 12, a Houston judge lectured the Chargers for having "financed" Anderson's "cause" and found no evidence that "Argovitz or anyone else entered into a conspiracy against Gary Anderson." The highlight of the court hearing had come when Anderson's attorney revealed that his client, having earned 82 units toward the 142 required for a college degree, nonetheless "cannot read" and had no ability to understand any of the documents he had signed. Once the judge ruled, Anderson returned to Tampa and the USFL, ending Gene Klein's summer battle.

The defeat did little to diminish Klein's pugnaciousness. By October, he was in another skirmish, this time with Al Davis, his target of choice.

Al Davis had been active himself. While the commissioner and the League had the luxury of waiting for the appeals court for salvation, he had been back in court again, "fighting to save my team." The case was *City of Oakland v. Oakland Raiders,* Oakland's attempt to seize Davis's franchise under the California eminent domain statutes. It had finally come to trial in May 1983, in the "neutral" court of Salinas, California. Oakland was trying a unique legal argument. Under California law, intangible property could be condemned in the same manner as more tangible items like real estate, if the city could demonstrate a bona fide "public use." The public use in Oakland's argument was, in essence, the identity of the city itself. "I know of nothing else in the city that is more important to Oakland than the Oakland Raiders," Mayor Lionel Wilson testified. "I have never seen such a phenomenon in my lifetime. Everywhere I went, regardless of what was the subject of my appearance, all I could get out of people was 'Are we going to be able to keep our Raiders?' . . . It covered every segment of the community. It covered all ages. It covered all racial lines. It covered all economic lines, the lame, the sick, the disabled.''

The Raiders' counterargument had four principal facets. The first was that Oakland's attempt was an abuse of any real notion of public use. "This is how the Nazis collected art treasures," Mel Durslag noted. The second was that any such public ownership was an overt violation of the National Football League constitution. The third was that Davis's team was in fact part of a single national network, not a part of Oakland, and as such, out of the city's jurisdiction.

League attorneys observing the case were infuriated by the first three arguments. "The Raiders have been taking different positions in different courts," one of them complained. "In Oakland, they're claiming there's no public purpose, no public use in taking a sports team. In L.A., they had to justify a $21 million expenditure by the Coliseum which happens to be a public authority and the California constitution says that no public authority can spend money except for a public purpose. The L.A. Coliseum argued that this is an exquisite public use and they won that before Pregerson. They then go up to northern California and say there's no public purpose. In L.A., we said we were a partnership or an interlocking web of joint ventures or a single entity or whatever you want to call it. They said, 'We're just the Raiders and we're competitors of these people. It's Al Davis's team and he can move it just like the gas station.' Then they went up to Salinas a few months later and said, 'Take the Raiders? How can the city of Oakland take the Raiders? We're not even in Oakland. We're part of an interlocking web which is nationwide, the National Football League. The Raiders are inseparable from the rest of the League. We're so inseparable from the rest of them, we're not even in Oakland for jurisdictional purposes.' "

To no one's surprise, Davis's fourth argument was that the attempt to condemn his property was a conspiracy between Oakland and Rozelle's NFL. "The National Football League and the city of Oakland were in bed together," one of Davis's attorneys argued. Davis considered the proof to his point was found in how the League had dealt with the issue of its constitution in this particular case. Despite the constitution's clear prohibition of any ownership by not-for-profit entities and Rozelle's absolute opposition to such minimal forms of public ownership as the issuance of traded stock, the commissioner had submitted an affidavit saying that as long as Oakland then resold the franchise quickly to another private owner, condemnation would be acceptable to the NFL. In Salinas, Jay Moyer, Rozelle's in-house counsel, testified to that effect as well. "In a perfect world," the attorney admitted, "eminent domain is not something the League would look at with kindness. However, we do not live in a perfect world."

"The Raiders really drew us into that testimony by going to court," Moyer later explained, "and throwing the League's constitution up as a defense. We found it the supreme irony, that the Raiders of all people would hide behind the League, but they did so. They said, 'Look here, the League's constitution says a city can't own a team and that's the end of it because if the League says a city can't own a team, then a city can't own a team.' Part of our problem was the recognition that the power of eminent domain in any jurisdiction is a pretty damn fundamental sovereign power and we thought it was dangerous at best for any element of the NFL to go to court taking that kind of position. We thought that it was certainly possible that as a result of that a court could say, 'To hell with your private associations and your constitution. Your constitution can't override the law of the land.' I tried to make the point that while we're not that excited about the law of eminent domain being applied to a sports league, we weren't arrogant enough to say to the court, 'Just because we say that you can't exercise a power, therefore you can't exercise it.' We were there to do what we had to do or what the court said we had to do to salvage whatever parts of our constitution that we could.''

To solidify their conspiracy argument, the Raiders called a surprise witness to end their case. The witness was Joseph Alioto, Al Davis's attorney. Alioto testified that despite the League's claim to having had no knowledge whatsoever of Oakland's intentions to file this suit, his brother-in-law, Chuck Sullivan, had warned him of what Oakland was going to do before the suit was even drawn up. "Eminent domain is an awesome power," Alioto told the press, "and it was sprung on us very quickly. It is obvious Pete Rozelle is still working with Oakland officials. It's a strange brand of socialism.''

On July 22, the judge, whom both sides had agreed could hear the case without a jury, ruled in favor of the Raiders. Oakland appealed, but it was yet another Davis victory in the meantime. Joseph Alioto did Davis's talking for him afterward. "To be corny," the attorney observed, "I think the American flag flies proudly over Salinas today. It's a great day, not only for the Raiders, but for the American dream and free enterprise.''

By then, the Los Angeles Raiders preseason training camp had opened in Santa Rosa, California, and Davis was up there, watching films, observing practices, and working the phone in search of the one or two players he thought he needed to go back to the Super Bowl. Outside of court now, he was inaccessible except by invitation and screened his press contacts carefully. On July 26, C.W. Nevius from the *San Francisco Chronicle* managed to arrange an interview. Davis picked the reporter up that evening at his Santa Rosa hotel and drove him to a local restaurant in a long black Cadillac, complete with telephone. "The owner [of the restaurant]," the reporter remembered, "leaped to his feet to shake hands and the waitress giggled nervously. Davis's table was ready. It is next to the door, so he can watch everyone come and go. On the table were a pitcher of water and a black telephone." Davis looked "tired" and mentioned that his doctors had told him to take a couple of weeks off to get away from it all, but he doubted whether that would be possible. Since Davis's "dislike of tape recorders is legendary," the reporter took notes by hand.

Was Davis worried about the USFL? "It's like putting in ten McDonalds," he pointed out. "It's easy to do when the time is right. The question is whether they will survive or prosper. I wish them luck. At least it will get our commissioner off the social circuit." Had his attitude toward Rozelle changed at all? "I never have respected him," Davis pointed out. "I've seen him flirt with the truth too often. But that's not important. I beat him. . . . Obviously they felt they could win in the courts. The commissioner thought settlement would be a defeat. I have often said if there was some way he could win and we could settle, we'd do it. I don't begrudge them doing what they wanted to do—Argentina took the Falklands because they thought they could hold them—but I think they should have negotiated instead of litigated."

While the two were talking, the *Chronicle* reporter noted, "more than once Davis called attention to the reaction of other diners. He is a distinctive figure, dressed in white pants and black and white pullover with a Raider badge on the chest. No one asked for an autograph, but several people stared and did double takes. It pleased him no end."

"See," Davis chided, "and you say people hate me so much."

Did he have any apologies to make to Oakland?

"What do I have to apologize for?" Davis asked. "My conscience is totally clear."

As Al Davis and the reporter were leaving the restaurant, Davis had a question of his own. "Do people ever ask you what I'm like?" he inquired.

"All the time," the reporter answered. "All the time."

By then, of course, Davis was perhaps the most recognizable owner in the National Football League. Both his persona and that of his team had become synonymous with a very particular approach. "Attack, fear, pressure," Davis summarized the Raider ethic. "Don't take what they give you. They're not going to stop you by design or location. They have to do it on the field. Screw it. You say you can stop us. Prove it."

The strategy was illustrated once again in October, when Davis locked horns with Klein and the commissioner. The incident grew out of Davis's unceasing search for talent to add to his team, even though the season was already well under way. Davis thought he needed a new defensive cornerback to be truly championship caliber. The man he had his eye on was one Mike Haynes, an all-pro who had sat out the season thus far because of a salary dispute with his employer, Billy Sullivan's Patriots. Haynes wanted $1.5 million over three years and the Patriots were looking for a trade. Patrick Sullivan, the Patriots GM, wanted a first- and third-round pick in the next collegiate draft in exchange for negotiating rights to Haynes and would not come off his price, as hard as Davis tried to budge him. The two were still dickering at 4:00 P.M. Eastern Standard Time on October 11, the League's deadline after which no trades could be made. Several minutes after 4:30 P.M., they settled. Davis would get Haynes and the Patriots would get the first and third picks they wanted.

In the meantime, Gene Klein had called Patrick Sullivan at 4:30 P.M. to see if the deal had been consummated and Sullivan told him it hadn't been. When Klein then learned that the trade had been made, he immediately protested to Rozelle and asked him to void the deal because it had been made after the trading deadline had passed. "I assume we are all playing by the same rules," Klein explained. "Even though that little fellow up there doesn't like to play by the rules, he's going to have to learn that he must." In a matter of hours, Rozelle had agreed with Klein and voided the trade. Patrick Sullivan protested the decision, but then changed his mind the following day. "After sleeping on it," Billy's son noted, "I realize it wouldn't be fair. You set up rules in order for things to be done in certain ways. I was mad at them last night, but they certainly have made the right decision in this case." Al Davis, however, did not back off at all. "The trade should still be allowed," he insisted. "We asked for an extension." Davis also pointed out that Haynes's agent was now about to meet with the USFL. "It would be insane not to allow this trade," he argued, "and let Haynes go to the other league."

In less than two weeks, Mike Haynes filed suit under the Sherman Act in Los Angeles, claiming Pete Rozelle had blocked the deal with an "arbitrary and capricious" trading deadline. In addition to seeking an injunction to let the trade proceed, the suit asked $5 million in damages and charged that Rozelle had used the trading deadline as part of a vendetta against Davis for his "past dealings with the NFL." In addition to the League, Pete Rozelle and Gene Klein were named as individual defendants.

Within another two weeks, the League had given in and settled the case exactly as Davis and Haynes wanted it. The deal would be allowed to go through and Haynes would drop his lawsuit. Gene Klein was now zero to two for the year and Al Davis's winning streak continued.

The settlement became final when Haynes's agent and several NFL attorneys met in the courthouse lobby and signed the papers. The agent was startled by the paranoia the League's men had about Al Davis that fall. "One of the League lawyers said, 'What if Al refuses to give New England his first-round pick?' " the agent remembered. "But that wasn't the height of the paranoia. That came when my fifteen-year-old son went downstairs to Xerox the contract. Two NFL guys went with him. They didn't want to let it out of their sight."

32

The Superstadium Game that had thrust Al Davis into the foreground of the football business had abated during the trial portion of *LAMCC v. NFL*, but by the fall of 1983 was once again flourishing throughout the League.

In Miami, Joe Robbie had finished off 1982 by helping defeat another city of Miami–sponsored referendum for refurbishing the Orange Bowl. In the course of it, Robbie accused Miami Mayor Maurice Ferre of having "misrepresented the facts to the public" and of "hurting, rather than helping, the chance of keeping professional football in Miami." Robbie wanted a new stadium and was by no means subtle in his hints that he might leave Miami altogether to get it. "Mr. Robbie is bluffing," Ferre insisted. "He will not

leave a major franchise [location]. I will do all I can to get him to stay.''
Undeterred by the renovation measure's 1982 defeat, by the fall of 1983 the
city of Miami was preparing yet another such ballot proposal, again to Joe
Robbie's intense objections. On September 1, 1983, Robbie announced that
the Dolphins would leave the Orange Bowl when their lease expired in 1986,
whatever the city did to the structure. If a new stadium wasn't built in the
meantime, he would leave for another city. "Who says you can't fight city
hall?" Robbie exclaimed. "They haven't done a pleasant thing for us since
the Dolphins came to town. They have not just been ungrateful, they have
been hostile and antagonistic.''

In Baltimore, Robert Irsay had spent 1982 in on-again, off-again negotiations aimed toward a longterm lease that would activate the state legislature's
$22 million renovation financing for Memorial Stadium. Though Irsay contin-
ued to refuse to sign any kind of longterm agreement, he also steadfastly
maintained he had no desire to move elsewhere. Few believed him. "He hates
the city, he hates the state, and he hates the governor,'' one source close to
Irsay explained before the League's defeat in *LAMCC v. NFL*. "You know
why he didn't sign that lease? Because he's waiting to see the outcome of the
Davis case. If the courts let Davis move, then Irsay won't be far behind,'' the
source said, and predicted, "He'll take the Colts to Phoenix within two
years.''

Phoenix was the first on the list of Irsay's possibilities for 1982 and
1983, followed closely by Indianapolis. In Arizona, one Phoenix source
pointed out, "The governor wants a team here, the business community wants
a team here, and the public has demonstrated that it wants one here over-
whelmingly. This is a conservative community, though, and while we'd love
to have an established team here, we wouldn't try to lure them, because that
looks like piracy to many people. But we intend to get some NFL team here
before too long.'' In Indianapolis, also on Irsay's list, 1982 had been opened
with groundbreaking on a sixty-three-thousand-seat enclosed stadium called
the Hoosier Dome. Scheduled for completion in 1984, it would cost some $65
million to build, complete with luxury boxes. As yet, the Hoosier Dome had
no football tenant.

Robert Irsay continued to insist that he was staying put throughout 1983,
the last year of his short-term agreement with Baltimore. "The Colts could
move tomorrow," Irsay pointed out on June 3, "if they wanted to. They
could have moved six months ago, a year ago. When Al Davis moved, we
could have moved. We are not moving. We didn't move. We're not moving. . . . I could stand on my head, but I don't think that's going to help. The
proof is that I haven't moved. I'm here, aren't I? I wouldn't be here if I was
going to move, would I? I'll tell you what I could do—and don't think it
hasn't crossed my mind—but I'm not going to do it. I could pull up thirty
vans and be out of here Sunday and you'd never know who was here, but I
haven't done it. The other thing is, the Colts and the people here will never
get in a situation such as the gentleman [Al Davis], I won't mention names,
who picked up his candy store. That is not the way my family and I've been

living all my life. As I told you before, we're here to stay unless you throw us out.''

On September 1, Irsay met again with Baltimore's mayor—another ''good meeting,'' according to the mayor, that reached ''no conclusions.'' Said Mayor Schaeffer, ''We were just staying in touch.''

The most visible of 1983's superstadium games was played in New York City by Leon Hess of the Jets. Since beginning to attend NFL meetings the year before, Hess had made both friends and enemies among his fellow owners. ''He's very competent,'' one of Hess's admirers noted, ''a very shrewd businessman. He's piss poor with his team, but I like and respect him.'' The feeling was not universal among NFL owners. ''He's an arrogant son of a bitch,'' one of his detractors observed. ''He's only come to about three meetings and he doesn't know what he's talking about. He's become one of Rozelle's staunchest backers. He said we should fight this Al Davis thing to the end because Rozelle's honor was at stake.'' His detractors suggested that Hess's ''sucking up to the commissioner'' was motivated by his plans for New York, though it is not at all clear he needed the commissioner's help to pull off what he had in mind.

Hess's latest round with New York City had entered the preliminary stage in 1980. The mayor he now had to deal with was Ed Koch. While the Jets' lease at the city-owned Shea Stadium did not expire until the end of 1983, the city was already eager for negotiations to begin. ''Three years is not that long away when you're talking about negotiating complicated leases,'' one New York source noted. ''It usually takes a year to negotiate a sports lease. Then you want to have that lease a year before you're ready to move or to stay put. So we're not talking about three years from now. They're going to start talking about the lease in the next twelve months.'' Hess, with his ''obsession for neatness,'' was known to be troubled by the difficulties involved in keeping Shea looking ''attractive'' and to have already had some discussions with the New Jersey Sports Authority about moving to Giants Stadium in the Meadowlands. Hess himself had little to say. ''I haven't made up my mind what we'll do,'' he told *The New York Times*. ''I've made no commitment either way. But the more the mayor and the governor go public with this, the more I'm going to dig in.''

By February 1983, little progress had been made. On February 25, Mayor Koch received a letter from Hess, addressed ''Dear Ed.'' He gave the city until March 15 to submit a proposal to him for remodeling Shea. By that same date, Hess informed the mayor, New Jersey would have submitted its lease proposal to him as well. ''I . . . find it incomprehensible that the city at this late date should need additional time to submit a proposal,'' Hess wrote. Hess also rejected Koch's suggestion that the city's corporation counsel, F.A.O. Schwarz Jr., should personally tour Shea with Hess to get a sense of what the Jets owner wanted. ''I appreciate and consider it regrettable,'' Hess continued, "that you are not personally familiar with the physical and operational problems at Shea during games so that you could familiarize Mr. Schwarz with the subject, since during your five years in office you attended only one Jets game, in the company of Governor [Hugh] Carey, and then only stayed for a brief period."

On March 14, Koch responded and mailed Hess an outline of what the city was prepared to do. The proposal, worth an estimated $43 million, called for the addition of ten thousand new seats, plus luxury boxes. "A first class stadium used by first class teams is good for this city," Koch wrote. "We look forward to working with you for many years."

Leon Hess waited until April to answer. This letter began, "Dear Mr. Mayor." In it, Hess complained that the city's proposal lacked "specific information" about when the improvements would be made and demanded more "specific assurances" that the city actually had the money to make it happen. Hess had by now compared the city's offer with New Jersey's. Even with New York's improvements, New Jersey's offer yielded the Jets about $2 million more gross a year, not counting parking and concessions. If that weren't enough, Hess was also attracted to New Jersey by the fact that New York's lease still left the Jets a secondary tenant to the baseball Mets. The Mets were no longer run by Donald Grant and were now much "friendlier" and sympathetic toward the Jets, but that made little difference in the football club's bottom line. The Mets, as number one tenant, still received all concession and parking income from Shea year-round, including proceeds from the sale of Jets' programs.

By July, the city and Leon Hess had yet to meet for face-to-face negotiations, and Koch, worried, wrote Hess on the 12th. "It is important," he pleaded, "that you or your designee start work with us on implementation." Koch noted that Hess had promised him a copy of the New Jersey proposal and complained "that has not happened." Koch assumed that was the case because Hess found New York's offer "first rate."

"Let me say again," the mayor continued, "that New Yorkers in general—and I in particular—very much want you to stay. . . . On the verge of another real shot at the Super Bowl, we are particularly anxious to continue together with the Jets. New York City will not ever be without an NFL team and the Jets are our favorites." Koch closed the letter with a handwritten "Hope to see you soon."

He didn't. Instead, Hess waited sixteen days and then answered with a short and official letter. "We do not encourage the city nor the New Jersey Sports Authority," Hess noted, "to assume that a successful bid has been tendered by either party."

The two men continued to exchange letters through August and into September, but made no discernible progress. Koch was beginning to panic. "It's vital that we sit down," he wrote on September 9, "and attempt to deal with your concerns. . . . The key is that we meet and meet soon." Koch added another handwritten postscript under his signature. "Honest, Leon," the mayor wrote, "I'm beginning to love football—and the Jets are number 1."

On September 12, Leon Hess and Ed Koch finally talked briefly on the phone. According to sources in the mayor's office, Hess was angry over the condition of Shea and made his anger felt. He told Koch he would announce his decision about where to play after the Shea lease would expire next January. "The mayor was rebuffed," one of his aides noted.

The following day, Koch wrote another letter. "I was very disappointed in our telephone conversation yesterday," the mayor began. He went on to note that he still had not received a copy of New Jersey's offer and he still had not met face-to-face with Hess himself. "Are you willing to meet," Koch demanded, "or must we begin to explore other options toward our aim of having first class facilities for all major league sports in the city?"

On September 15, Hess answered. The city had not received New Jersey's offer, he explained, because the city was supposed to have a representative in Hess's office on March 15 when its proposal was submitted and "neither you nor any representative attended at my office." As for meeting face-to-face, Hess claimed he had decided against it because the mayor had released to the public information about the Shea lease. That, Hess noted, "prompted my refusal to meet with you thereafter."

Koch's return letter of September 19 made little attempt to hide New York City's irritation. "I cannot simply wait around for you to announce your decision at the end of January, as you suggested in our telephone conversation last week," Koch wrote. "The issue of where a sports team plays is a matter of concern to the public. Cities should not be abandoned for suburbia. Given the profits that you made in the city and the even greater profits you can make in the future, I do not believe that you should analyze the issue with a green eyeshade. I cannot believe that is how you want to behave. . . . Please give me a call. As you know, many of my calls have gone unanswered."

On September 26, Leon Hess and Ed Koch met face-to-face for the first and last time. The encounter lasted seventy-five minutes. Hess, Koch remembered, "talked about Donald Grant a lot and also about dirty bathrooms." According to Koch, Hess also said, "No matter what you do, we will not stay in Shea." On September 28, Koch called a press conference and announced that negotiations had broken down and that the Jets would be playing in New Jersey once this football season was over. Hess said nothing and could not be reached for comment.

On October 5, the National Football League met in executive session at New York's Grand Hyatt Hotel. That afternoon, the minutes stated, "Mr. Hess reported to the membership on his negotiations with New York City about the team's lease at Shea Stadium . . . and his discussions with the New Jersey Sports Authority about the possibility of the Jets playing games beginning in 1984 and beyond at Giants Stadium in East Rutherford, New Jersey." No permission to relocate was asked and no votes demanded.

On the following day, Leon Hess dispatched his last letter to Koch. The mayor's announcement had "forced the issue," he explained, and since Shea was "unsuitable," he was moving to New Jersey.

New York City immediately appealed to Pete Rozelle for help and got none. "I would prefer to have a team in New York," the commissioner admitted, "so we don't have all the flak." Nonetheless, he was powerless, given *LAMCC v. NFL*. "We went to bat for Oakland," Rozelle complained, "and it could cost the League $50 million. It's probably moot whether we have any opinion at all about a club moving."

That being the case, the Big Apple quickly announced plans to lure another NFL team inside the New York city limits. The two most obvious candidates were Joe Robbie and Robert Irsay. When approached for a comment, Robbie's office released a short statement. "Mr. Robbie is en route to Vancouver, British Columbia, to attend the North American Soccer League meetings in advance of the Soccer Bowl," it read. "He has heard today's announcement that the New York Jets will move to the Meadowlands next year. He has not yet read the reaction of Mayor Koch or any other New York officials. He has no comment at this time."

Robert Irsay had two different responses. "I don't rule out any move," he told the *New York Post*. "At the same time, I don't rule any move in." He was more blunt with *The* [Baltimore] *Sun*. "I have no interest in moving," he claimed, "and especially in moving to New York. I hate New York and you can quote me on that."

The closest thing to a positive response New York received was from Joseph Alioto, Al Davis's attorney. Alioto informed an aide to Governor Hugh Carey that in the "unlikely" circumstance that the courts should bar the Raiders from L.A., his boss would be willing to consider Shea as a possibility.

By November, New York officials were admitting they did not "expect" any football team to move into Shea in the "forseeable future." The *Times* lamented, "City Unable to Find New Football Team."

The refrain was by now a familiar one.

33

The October 5 League meeting in New York City at which Leon Hess made his report about New Jersey had been understandably preoccupied with other issues. First and foremost among them was the DeBartolo situation, the most serious challenge to the will of the commissioner and the League since the *LAMCC v. NFL* decision.

Pete Rozelle convened the meeting in much better personal shape than he'd been in six months earlier. His depression had apparently run its course. The process culminated in early September with the death of his father, Ray Rozelle, in a Rancho Granada, California, nursing home. During the second LAMCC trial in 1982, Pete had brought his father in to watch one of the sessions but it was, Pete remembered, "difficult for him to understand."

Rozelle had last seen his father alive during the summer of 1983, when he and Carrie visited Ray at the nursing home and took him into the mountains behind San Diego for a drive. "We took him up on Poway Ridge," Rozelle remembered, "and sat on the grass and talked. I don't know how much my father comprehended, but I talked." Ray Rozelle's death seemed to focus Pete's disappointment in a very specific grief and the effect was cathartic. "He's happier and healthier now," one of the commissioner's friends noted. "He doesn't let things get so personal anymore. We talked about it and I think he has it all in perspective. He's come to terms with what's happened. He understands you can't let mishaps dominate your life. Pete's cheery and confident again."

The light that had appeared at the end of the commissioner's personal tunnel was not, however, yet reflected in his professional life. *LAMCC v. NFL* was still being deliberated upon by a three-judge panel from the Ninth Circuit Court of Appeals and, in the meantime, continued to cast a long shadow over League Think. He could still hope, nonetheless, and did so with regularity. Rozelle wanted very badly to have confidence in the appeals process, and the longer it lasted, the more his confidence seemed to grow. He considered the League's arguments sound and now that the personal sting had gone out of his Los Angeles defeat, it was easier to believe those arguments would hold sway, free of the district court's local encumbrances. While Rozelle would make no predictions of the outcome that fall, he thought the League's chances on appeal were "good."

In October, however, that was still just wishful speculation. Reality beckoned in the form of the DeBartolos, with whom Pete Rozelle had to deal right away. The Parins Committee's report was ready and, on the afternoon of October 5, was presented to the entire League. To no one's surprise, it concluded that the concern over "conflicts of interest that might result from Edward DeBartolo Jr. and Edward DeBartolo Sr. owning teams in competing football leagues" was justified. There was, the committee noted, "sufficient cause" to make that assumption because of "the existence of two competing football leagues" in which each DeBartolo held a franchise and "the existence of respect and trust" between father and son. That was almost enough to guarantee that the sanctity of the NFL's inner councils might be violated. It was, after all, Mr. D who had originally guaranteed Eddie's purchase of the 49ers in 1977. How could the two of them not look out for each other in a business they were now both in?

Rozelle himself did not speak on the question at the October 5 meeting, but his feelings were no secret. By now, the vocabulary had become familiar. "Anarchy could develop," he had warned, "and one indication of it that we've never had before is the DeBartolo situation. For example, you always have litigation between competing leagues. We've had it already between San Diego and Tampa over Gary Anderson. In the history of two-league competition in professional football, going all the way back to the All-America Conference, then the AFL, then the World Football League, it always develops litigation. You always have it. It's just automatic. That places a terrible burden on Eddie to act against his father." At the same time, Rozelle did his best to cast his opposition in a sympathetic tone. "It's a tough situation for Eddie," the commissioner pointed out to the San Francisco press. "He's put in a very embarrassing position, a very difficult position. The situation that he's involved in is not necessarily of his doing, but it exists. He said it was uncomfortable for him. He said it to the full membership. It's not a thrill for him to go through this, obviously."

The DeBartolo position was presented on October 5 by Eddie and the family's Youngstown attorney, Carmine Policy. Eddie made no secret of his frustration. "I think the owners are trying to make a decision based on fiction," he complained. "The facts are that I own my team and my father owns his team and never the twain shall meet. Hell, I don't even care if the Pittsburgh Maulers win a game this year. Look, I'm competitive in business and in football. And that means I intend to be competitive against any other football team, including the Pittsburgh Maulers. Why should I compromise the excellence of my team for any other team? I can't even comprehend what they mean by conflict of interest. I haven't even discussed the legal positions or ramifications. I just think it's all very absurd and I know I'm within my rights." Carmine Policy framed the dispute as an unfortunate misunderstanding. "We anticipated more understanding and sympathy for the situation," Policy explained. "Eddie likes the NFL. He is not a rebel. He enjoys being part of the fraternity. He does not want to be part of, or in any way interact with, the USFL, but he loves his father. I think what he'll try to do, if it does not conflict with his father's deep-seated interest or substantial, long-range plans, is to try to get his father to disengage himself from the USFL."

However they were presented on October 5, the DeBartolo arguments made little headway with the rest of the League. The discussion that followed DeBartolo and Policy's explanations was "emotional" and "blunt" and no one took Eddie's side. Among the most vehement opponents of the DeBartolos' situation was Al Davis. "We've got these rules," he argued, "and we have to live up to them." At that, Gene Klein "laid into him" for being a fine one to talk. If it weren't for Davis, the League wouldn't be in this fix. Despite that sniping on the side, all the League besides Eddie DeBartolo felt the same way. The fact that his father's USFL franchise was located in Pittsburgh, home of the NFL's beloved Art Rooney, only added to many owners' feelings. "I think a lot of people are going to be thinking of the Rooney family," Billy Sullivan noted, and it was no secret Art Rooney was very displeased. "Mr. Rooney can't believe that DeBartolo would come in his own backyard with a team from the league we're at war with," a source close to the Rooneys explained, "especially after Mr. Rooney endorsed the DeBartolos when they wanted to buy the 49ers. Anyone with a brain in his head can see the conflict. Who are they kidding?"

"I don't want to make this thing a bloody mess," Eddie pleaded. "I just want to run the 49ers. I want to operate this franchise independent of my family's business, of our corporation, of the USFL team, and if everybody leaves me alone, everything will be fine. . . . I just don't feel as though I'm doing anything wrong.'' Eddie's plea fell on apparently deaf ears. After the League's discussion had lasted two hours, Eddie walked out of the meeting room, huddled briefly with Carmine Policy in the men's room, and then left to catch his company jet back to Youngstown, refusing all comment to the reporters gathered in the hotel's lobby.

After DeBartolo walked out, the rest of the League took steps to deal with their latest hot potato. The possible penalties, Rozelle pointed out again, ranged from nothing to forcing Eddie to divest his team and leave the NFL altogether. By twenty-seven to zero vote, the League then passed a resolution.

> RESOLVED, that if the commissioner finds that the ownership of the 49ers has either violated the constitution and bylaws or is engaged in conduct detrimental to the welfare of the League, the commissioner is authorized to develop and implement appropriate remedial actions or discipline within the League itself . . . to eliminate the prospect of continuing damage to League interests.

In effect, the owners tossed the dilemma into Rozelle's lap.

Rozelle did his best to toss at least part of it back. ''There's always the fear of legal action,'' he pointed out, ''and that will be an evaluation that I will take into account, against what we feel might be the consequences of doing nothing. . . . The owners will have to decide for themselves whether this is an important enough issue to take a stand on.''

After the October 5 meeting had adjourned, Eddie DeBartolo quite angrily put his finger on what had everyone else in the League worried. ''The League can't hurt me,'' Eddie blustered. ''It's not big enough. They don't like it? That's the way it is. Nobody's going to take this team away from me, including the League. Because, I tell you, the League can't afford the lawsuit. I can. Enough of this bullshit about conflict of interest. That's ridiculous. They can't afford a lawsuit because I'll bury them.''

That warning wasn't lost on Pete Rozelle. Though he had promised that DeBartolo would be summoned to his office for a hearing within thirty days, no such hearing was ever held. Instead, the commissioner decided to back off and continue waiting for the appeals court to effect his rescue.

34

While the Sherman Act continued to enforce a vacuum at the core of the National Football League, the football business itself had turned an invisible corner and become something markedly different from the institution Pete Rozelle had made his name dominating. Rozelle's job was secure, but the era he had personified was on its last legs, even while he waited. Super Bowl

XVIII, the finale to the 1983 season held during January 1984, in Tampa, Florida, was, in several ways, emblematic of the transformation that had overtaken League Think.

First, Tampa was by far the smallest city and smallest stadium ever to host a Super Bowl. That it did was a tribute to the ascension of Hugh Culverhouse inside the NFL. "It was a plum for Culverhouse," one owner said of the site, "pure and simple. He'd earned it." Most of the League now ranked the Tampa owner as the equal in influence to Tex Schramm and Art Modell, hitherto Rozelle's chief lieutenants. In the spring of 1983, Culverhouse was named the new chairman of the management council executive committee, replacing Chuck Sullivan. He was already finance committee chairman and from that position had begun a significant restructuring of the League's internal fiscal practices. He had created a standardized mechanism for handling deferred contract payments which required the clubs to deposit a set percentage of their longterm obligation in a League fund, and, by 1984, was setting out to devise a formula for sharing revenues from luxury boxes. Culverhouse, the management council's Jack Donlan noted, was a man who "marshals all his arguments based on logic because he knows early on where he wants to go. He has the ability to identify the problem early, analyze it, and try to see about getting a solution." Donlan also observed that Culverhouse was "very effective at getting his way."

Indeed, Hugh Culverhouse seemed to pop up behind the scenes just about everywhere. He had commissioned the computer software a number of the clubs used to manage their money and consulted with a number more about tax matters. In the nine years since he had entered the NFL, he had also participated in the sale of the 49ers and the Denver Broncos, acted as executor of Carroll Rosenbloom's estate, helped Georgia Frontiere reorganize the Rams, and bailed Leonard Tose out by guaranteeing one of his loans. Though he was a staunch Rozelle partisan, Culverhouse's rise was also an indication of how much the foundation of the football business had shifted. "Sure it's changed," Tex Schramm admitted. "The people who've been in a long time say it's not as much fun. The reason is the distractions. It's become so big and complex and lawyers, accountants, and courts are so much a part of it now. Before, we always had the ability to close together when faced with problems, but now our problems are more created from within than without." Hugh Culverhouse, the epitome of the inside operator, half attorney and half accountant, was the mechanic of football's new age. Where Schramm had risen by understanding the game and preaching professionalism, and Art Modell had risen by appreciating the League's fraternity and preaching all for one, one for all, Culverhouse rose by understanding litigation and preaching liquidity. Though the commissioner made a strong alliance with it, this new technocracy made football a very different business from the one Rozelle was used to.

The second way the Super Bowl staged in Hugh Culverhouse's hometown reflected the League's shifting larger picture was in the participant representing the National Conference. By virtue of a twenty-four to twenty-one victory over Eddie DeBartolo's 49ers in the conference title game, Jack Kent Cooke's Washington Redskins, the defending NFL champions, were the first half of the Super Bowl billing. Cooke himself was emblematic of the new opposition to Rozelle that had grown up over the last year. Rozelle had always faced opposition here and there over a specific issue, but never had it been so generalized or so attached to his leadership per se. "There were doubts about Rozelle among owners now," one NFL insider observed privately. "He'd committed them to a long costly fight and now they had treble damages hanging over their heads." Art Modell described the disaffected as "a group who don't think favorably of the League office," rather than an actual "opposition." Whatever their description, by the end of 1983, their number was fast reaching eight—the critical mass that would allow them veto power under the NFL's three-quarter vote rules.

Jack Kent Cooke was often listed at the head of this group. He was not an NFL insider, rarely attending meetings personally, but he was rich and successful—and still pissed off at Rozelle. His "family bitterness" toward the commissioner's wife was an ongoing resentment. In addition, Cooke still smarted from his forced divestiture under the commissioner's ownership policy and made no secret of the fact that he was in the market for a baseball team to buy and bring to Washington, D.C. He also objected, like Carroll Rosenbloom before him, to the way Rozelle spent the League's money.

Joining Cooke in that attitude were Al Davis, of course; Joe Robbie, who still smarted from the events leading up to *NASL v. NFL* and thought the League had overreached itself in *LAMCC v. NFL;* Eddie DeBartolo, who spoke nicely about Rozelle in public but was obviously quite prepared to go his own way and particularly disliked the commissioner's policy on corporate ownership; and Leonard Tose, who was upset at the money Rozelle had cost them, tired of being lectured to, and eager to get on Al Davis's good side while the getting was good. In addition to that block of five votes, there was a group of at least four "floaters" who, in Art Modell's words, "were not in opposition to the commissioner, but not in support either." Those included Lamar Hunt, who, one of his fellow owners noted, "was conservative and penurious and found the legal expenses Rozelle had run up appalling"; Ed McCaskey, who had inherited the Chicago Bears from his late father-in-law, George Halas, and was reportedly obsessed with the bottom financial line; Paul Brown of the Cincinnati Bengals, who had long hated Art Modell and was glad to go against him when he could; and Ralph Wilson, who was a friend of both Pete Rozelle and Mel Durslag and consequently, according to one NFL observer, "played it both ways."

The minority had two principal bones of contention with Rozelle in December 1983 and January 1984. Both were financial. The first of those was the League office's lack of fiscal accountability and the size of its budget. The League office was overseen by Culverhouse's finance committee, and the only information the rest of the League received about its operations was a rough financial breakdown that included no details about the actual cash flow. The report for the year ending in March 1983 included items like "legal" for

$5,862,000, "commissioner's office" for $3,204,000, "general office" for $2,467,000, and "public relations" for $740,000. In all, Rozelle's jurisdiction accounted for "total cash disbursements" of $17,942,000. A number considered the expenses bloated and one accounted himself "amazed" that more details had not been furnished. Another criticized Culverhouse for his "secrecy" and included the commissioner in the criticism. "If any owner wants to see the books," Culverhouse answered, "they can come up and see them. They're no big secrets. We have nothing to hide. I don't know any business that publishes line-by-line items."

The minority's other bone to pick was about Rozelle's contract, drawn up in 1982 by Culverhouse, Gene Klein, and Leon Hess. Most owners had still never seen a copy of it and had little idea what it provided. "The owners aren't allowed to look at it," Leonard Tose complained. "I've never seen a copy. Letting that get by is just stupidity on the part of the owners." By January 1984, Jack Kent Cooke was quite privately leading a chorus of demands that the contract be made available for their inspection.

Publicly, Cooke was content to keep his mouth shut about Rozelle and play the role of visiting mogul appropriate to a Super Bowl owner. Now worth a fortune estimated by *Forbes* at $600 million, Cooke could easily afford to do so. For the Tampa Super Bowl, he chartered a Boeing 747 airliner and footed the transportation and hotel bills of more than one hundred personal guests. Among them were former CIA Director Richard Helms, columnist Carl Rowan, Senator Paul Laxalt, former Democratic party chairman Robert Strauss, and former presidential candidate Edmund Muskie. Cooke was enjoying himself immensely. "I'd say the satisfaction I have had from the Redskins transcends by far the satisfaction I've had in total from all the other teams I've owned," he gushed to *The Washington Post*. "It's fantastic." Going into Super Bowl XVIII, his Redskins were favored to win, but no one expected it to be easy.

Cooke's opponent from the American Conference was the third and by far most visible reflection of the League's larger change in Tampa that January. With the NFL at yet another critical juncture, Al Davis and his Raiders were back in the Super Bowl once again. The difference was that now they were representing Los Angeles for the first time, having soundly thrashed League Think in the process.

If League Think's partisans could take any solace from Davis being in Los Angeles, it was that his relationship with the Coliseum there was still informal and tenuous and that the local following for his team was still problematic. On the Coliseum front, nothing had in fact changed since March 1, 1980, when he and Bill Robertson initialed their memorandum of agreement. By January 1984, he and the LAMCC had still signed no binding lease despite having been landlord and tenant for almost two years. They had originally been prevented from doing so by the Coliseum's fears about their court case, but after the verdict in May 1982, they had still made little progress. By then, Bill Robertson had left the Coliseum commission and Al Davis was content to pay rent under the terms of the memorandum and in no hurry to reach a longterm understanding with Robertson's replacements. "There is no pressure on Davis," the *San Francisco Chronicle* observed. "If he doesn't sign, what are they going to do in Los Angeles—kick him out? They need Davis more than he needs them."

The terms Davis had to live with in the meantime were not, of course, hurting him. During the strike-shortened 1982 season, his first in town, his franchise yielded the Coliseum a net return of only $93,000 due to an annual rent credit of some $675,000 that ran until 1986. One consequence of that credit was a 1982 Coliseum deficit of some $84,000. By 1983, some Los Angeles County politicians were complaining about the rates Davis paid, as well as his delays in signing a longterm lease. Bill Robertson defended Davis. "No final agreement has been executed yet," Robertson pointed out, "because we still owe Al Davis $4 million under the terms of the last agreement. He put out a hell of a lot of money moving, establishing offices, putting together a practice field and a local staff, and fighting this litigation. Until he gets the money coming to him, he's not going to finalize a deal." A source close to Mayor Tom Bradley agreed with Robertson. "Los Angeles has no complaints," the source explained. "If anyone does, it's Al Davis. L.A. never kept its agreement. Kenny Hahn told Al Davis the day before the Raiders moved, 'If you come down here, I'll fly to [the League meeting in] Palm Springs and deliver a $2 million check.' Al Davis still hasn't got the money. What happened is we got a guy down here and then broke all our promises. L.A. never made a deal earlier in the game when it could have and they haven't delivered. Al Davis doesn't owe anybody here anything."

Of much more concern than the LAMCC to Davis himself was his team's attendance in their new home. During the strike year, the Raiders established an eight to one record as compared to Georgia Frontiere's two to seven Rams, sold some forty-nine thousand season tickets and drew an average game day attendance of fifty-three thousand, about half the Coliseum's capacity. In their final unsuccessful playoff game against Leon Hess's Jets that year, the Raiders drew ninety thousand and seemed to have turned the corner going into 1983. Instead, they only slipped backward. For the 1983 season, only forty thousand season tickets were sold. The cancellations, the *Los Angeles Times* noted, were largely because the Raiders "distributed them poorly and bungled seat assignments so badly that they infuriated thousands of their customers. Promised good seats, those customers instead got end-zone seats—and rude talk and the runaround from the Raiders. Coliseum officials said there was one stretch when they were getting as many as five hundred complaints daily. The Raiders blamed the mess on a computer foul-up. . . . Executive assistant Al LoCasale, accustomed to wearing many hats in the Raiders' bare-bones front office setup, had to be hospitalized with exhaustion in the midst of the ticket rush, and Davis was so upset by the ticket snafu that LoCasale was almost fired." After the first four of their eight 1983 home games, the Los Angeles Raiders were in first place in their division at six to three, but were averaging only forty-six thousand tickets sold.

In response, Davis threw himself into marketing. The biggest innovation made on that front during 1983 was the adoption of a new Raider motto. While "Pride and Poise" continued to be a team dictum, the new Raider bottom line, Davis announced, was "Commitment to Excellence." The slogan, accompanied by a Raider logo, was displayed in silver and black on billboards and the sides of buses all over Greater Los Angeles. When he reached the Super Bowl, Davis also bought up billboard space all around Tampa and did the same thing.

While the billboards were a new touch, Al Davis still placed his ultimate marketing faith in the team itself. Winning football teams would draw crowds, sooner or later, and it was as simple as that. Despite his attendance trouble, Davis didn't bother to hire a franchise public relations man. "People say the [Los Angeles] Dodgers [baseball team] do well here because they promote their product," one Raider insider noted, "and Al got tired of hearing that. He finally said, 'I don't care about the Dodgers. I just want to win.' " Under the banner of "Commitment to Excellence," the Raiders did just that, going twelve to four and crushing their two playoff opponents. They did so with the usual Raider attitude. "In 1983," Al LoCasale observed to *Sports Illustrated,* "our team battled not only opponents on the field, but a powerful combination of the NFL's propaganda machine, the federal courts, the state courts, the halls of Congress. I can assure you their campaign to prevent the Los Angeles Raiders from being the world champion Los Angeles Raiders will not go unchallenged. Our goal is the same in the courts or on the field." Being underdogs in Super Bowl XVIII suited the Raider personality to a T.

Al Davis, the architect of that personality, played the mogul role in Tampa on a scale that matched Jack Kent Cooke. He, too, chartered an airliner for his guests, who included actor James Garner, singer Frank Sinatra, and actress Jane Fonda. While Cooke spent the week in Tampa partying, however, Davis worked, going over films, lifting weights, and secluding himself from the press. His confidence was apparent to everyone he had contact with. Uncharacteristically, he predicted to his friends that the Raiders would win and win big.

The biggest media event of that week leading up to the championship game was, as usual, the commissioner's press conference on January 20. There, in front of at least three hundred reporters, he answered questions about the state of the League. It did not take long for *LAMCC v. NFL* to be raised. "While the case on the Coast is on appeal," the commissioner noted, "free agency has been created in football franchises. The League is not in a position to take cognizance of the public trust, and pending the Los Angeles appeal, we have nothing to say about franchise shifts."

Asked about a report that Robert Irsay was at that moment in Phoenix, perhaps negotiating such a move for his Colts, Rozelle answered that he had talked to Irsay the previous Monday and "he didn't mention it. But, as I said earlier, while the Los Angeles case is still out, there's franchise free agency."

Asked about the DeBartolo situation, Rozelle claimed "DeBartolo's attorneys are submitting briefs." He would "analyze" them, he said and "schedule a hearing" before the League's 1984 annual meeting in Hawaii that March.

The most asked question, Rozelle pointed out, "is how I'll feel about possibly giving the trophy to Al." It was, of course, a question he was now quite used to. "As far as Al is concerned, I have great admiration for his work developing a fine football team. I can set aside the fact Al is responsible for five pieces of litigation against the League. I have no problem presenting the trophy to Al."

On January 22, Super Bowl Sunday, Davis could be seen during the last half hour before kickoff down on the stadium floor dressed in a long black leather jacket and dark glasses, shaking hands with each of his players. Then he made his way by elevator to the press box to watch the contest by himself. At halftime, his team led twenty-one to three. With 8:51 left to play in the final quarter, the lead was thirty-eight to nine. Davis shook both fists in the air. "That's it," he exulted.

In the locker room, he and Rozelle faced the television lights together. "Davis," Rozelle remembered, "was hyper. He was more caught up in the emotion of it all than I'd ever seen him." Nervously, the Raiders owner kept popping his jaw, as though trying to unplug his ears.

"Congratulations, Al," Rozelle said as he handed over the championship trophy. He also praised Davis for "putting this cast together." Then, as he'd promised the press earlier in the week, Rozelle shook his nemesis's hand.

"Thank you, Mr. Commissioner," Davis offered. Then he began a disjointed but intense monologue, at one point noting, "This is a great credit to an organization after all the outrageous things the League has done to it."

Off camera, the Raiders' players cheered.

Davis responded immediately. Looking past the TV lights toward the sound, the managing general partner of the Los Angeles Raiders raised a fist in the air and sounded the call to arms of football's new age.

"Just win, baby," Davis shouted. "Just win."

Thirty-five days later, the Ninth Circuit Court of Appeals upheld the verdict in *LAMCC v. NFL* by a vote of two to one. The League appealed to the Supreme Court but the Supreme Court refused to hear the case.

Pete Rozelle's wait was over.

Al Davis had won it all.

PART FIVE
EX POST FACTO

1

The advent of football's new age cut across the League's members in different ways.

Texas Schramm managed to land on his feet, though as a League man, Tex considered the new state of affairs an abomination. "If anybody can do what he feels he must," Schramm reiterated, "there's no structure at all. Sports leagues must be able to make rules and structures to live by. You take that away and there's no league. Competition within a league must be contrived, not natural. To compete on an equal basis you need to make that contrivance possible." Despite his friendship with Al Davis, Schramm had fought on the League side throughout the three-year battle just completed. Of the second trial of *LAMCC v. NFL*, Joe Alioto noted, "Schramm even ran the NFL show. Rozelle hadn't gone over so he moved toward the background and Tex sat in the front row." In the end, it only meant Schramm shared in the diminishment of his friend the commissioner. The two were still good friends, although not, Rozelle admitted, in as close touch as they'd once been. Tex was still a powerful figure, now virtually synonymous with the competition committee, but few rated him the second most powerful in the League anymore. As one of the owners privately noted, "Mr. Vice-Commissioner" had been dropped from his informal titles. A "football man" par excellence, his skills were no longer so central to the business. "Anarchy" had moved the action elsewhere.

As 1983 became 1984, the "instability" about which Pete Rozelle had warned over and over again seemed to be symbolized even within the Dallas franchise that the commissioner had long held up as a model of ideal League Think ownership. The way Clint Murchison had sat back and let Tex Schramm run things was a central piece of the commissioner's carefully crafted iconography, as was the fact that there had been no changes in the organizational end of the Cowboys since they'd come into the League at the same meeting at which Pete Rozelle had begun his commissionership. Stability, as everyone now knew, had a shelf life and, in Dallas, time had caught up with Clint Murchison. "America's team" was for sale.

The precipitating event that eventually put the Cowboys on the block was the death of Clint Murchison's brother John from an asthma attack in 1979. John and Clint had managed their inheritance jointly through a partnership called Murchison Brothers. Their partnership agreement required the surviving brother to liquidate the company. Liquidation posed severe difficulties for Clint. Like their father before them, the brothers had made [heavy use] of borrowed money and their own reputation for wealth. "For years," *Newsweek* noted, "a Murchison signature was considered as bankable as a proven oilfield." Their heavily leveraged investment portfolio included oil, gas, railroads, high technology, newspapers, and lots of speculative, big ticket real estate developments. Extended as the brothers were, liquidation might very well bring the whole structure down before its estimated total value of some $260 million could be extracted. That vulnerability was enhanced when rising interest rates began to put a number of the real estate ventures in trouble.

Clint attempted to hold off executing the partnership agreement as long as he could but, in 1981, his nephew, John Murchison Jr., filed suit contesting the way Clint was managing the family assets. Among other things, Clint and John Sr. had apparently pledged the assets of trusts set up by their father for his grandchildren as collateral on some of their loans. That suit was settled out of court in April 1983 with a payment to John Jr. of some $20 to 30 million. At the time, Clint's affairs were reported by Newsweek to be so "tangled" that he'd had trouble raising the cash. Later, aides to John Jr. would brag they'd forced Clint to sell the Cowboys.

That was not, of course, the official reason given for the Cowboys sale when the possibility was first admitted by Tex Schramm in November 1983. Few people in Dallas or anywhere else at that point could imagine that Murchison could possibly be prey to financial problems. "It's just unbelievable all the things Clint owns," Schramm had once pointed out. "You just couldn't put a number on it." Once Schramm and his boss had been riding in an elevator, the Cowboys president remembered, and it broke down. "Clint looked over at me and said, 'Somebody ought to get the people who own it to fix it.' And somebody in the elevator said, 'Wait a minute, Clint, you own the elevator company.' "

The stated reason for selling the Cowboys was Clint Murchison's health. In 1982, Murchison had begun losing his sense of balance, forcing him to use a cane and then confining him to a wheelchair. The cause was a degenerative brain disease that also attacked his powers of speech. While it did not affect his ability to think, by November 1983 he was unable to stand or speak in anything more than a laborious effort to make a few words come out.

On November 14, Tex Schramm confirmed that the franchise might be sold. "It's a consideration because of Clint's illness," Schramm explained. "Selling the team is one of the things being considered. It's just in the initial discussion stage," he said, adding, the next day, "There are some people who have shown varying degrees of interest. But we do not have time constraints and we don't want to rush into anything. On the other hand, if exactly the right people come by, there will be no reason for us to delay the proceedings."

The announcement was the biggest news in Dallas. Nowhere was an NFL franchise more central to a city's sense of itself. Hosting "America's team" was perhaps the city's most cherished claim to fame. Those who dared oppose the Cowboys' wholesome image, W. A. Criswell, pastor of the local First Baptist Church, declared, were "the same bunch" who support "socialists, liberals, communists, pinkos, Ted Kennedy, Washington, and Moscow." Anyone who worried that the Cowboys might deteriorate, however, was no doubt comforted to learn that the sale itself would be managed by Tex Schramm, the same man who'd built the club from day one. "I'm going to try and find people that fit the parameters Clint is looking for," Schramm explained. "Obviously the final decision will be the Murchisons'. The Murchison family wants the present organization to continue without disruption. There are two things I want to be very specific about, number one is I am not part of any group, and number two is I am not seeking to form any group. If the new ownership felt it would be beneficial to include me, I'm prepared to do anything to keep the organization functioning as it is. I fully hope to remain with the team."

Tex Schramm, of course, had good reason to "fully hope." In fact, continuation of Schramm's contract in which he was granted exclusive control of all football operations was a condition of any potential sale. By December 14, he had opened the franchise's books to "five or six" groups of potential investors. He had screened those groups carefully. "There were a lot of non-serious applicants," Schramm remembered. "They didn't understand. They weren't trying to do anything to mislead, they were just misinformed as to the financial requirements." Asked by *The Dallas Morning News* how long this would take, "Schramm said the NFL stipulation that one person, not a corporation, have a controlling fifty-one percent interest, could be slowing the process." Nonetheless, by January 8, 1984, the Cowboys president reported, "We have been making some headway. You could definitely say that. But I don't think the sale is imminent at this time. We have some people who are interested and we're interested in some people."

Said to be at the top of that list were a combine headed by Dallas businessmen Vance Miller and W. O. Bankston. Bankston was a friend of Schramm's and would make no comment on the possibility. He did say, however, that should he and Miller purchase the club, "Tex knows that we'd stay out of the way and let him run it." Tex himself was sidelined from the process during the second week of January, when he was hospitalized briefly for a stomach ailment. By January 18, Schramm was back in the saddle and submitted Miller and Bankston's names to Rozelle's office for investigation. "Pete will check it out," Tex explained. "They are the only names at the present time to be submitted, but they are not the only ones that will be." Despite that disclaimer, speculation that Miller and Bankston were first in line was additionally fueled when the two men flew to Tampa to watch Super Bowl XVIII from Tex Schramm's box. Miller especially seemed convinced. "As far as the price goes," he told the *Dallas Times Herald,* "we've reached an agreement. Right now I'd say I'm feeling pretty positive about the deal. We need to get the lawyers from both sides together, and we need to get the approval of the NFL owners. We have some technical things to work out. But I feel we have the blessings of the Cowboys." Tex Schramm, embodiment of the Cowboys, refused all comment.

Within a week, Miller's confidence seemed something of an overstatement. Instead of an announcement that Miller and Bankston had been accepted, there was talk about a new name that had popped up. The name was

H. R. "Bum" Bright, oilman and chairman of the Texas A&M University board of regents. Though he was well known in Texas money circles, Bright's only brush with national notoriety had been as a signatory of the inflammatory "Welcome Mr. Kennedy" ad in the Dallas papers on the morning President John F. Kennedy was assassinated. "I contribute to conservatives and right-wing causes," Bright explained, "always have and still do." Tex Schramm would say only that Bright was "one of the people I've talked to. I'm not saying anything more beyond that point." During February, Bright's name was also submitted to the League for checking, along with at least one other. That other may have been Boca Raton, Florida, land developer George Barber, with whom Schramm also admitted negotiations were under way. While this bidding war went on behind the scenes, Clint Murchison was, as usual, invisible.

At the end of January, he appeared in public as Cowboys owner for the last time. The occasion was a dinner in his honor. While Clint sat listening in his wheelchair, unable to say anything himself, Tex Schramm gave him much of the credit for the Cowboys' success. "Clint gave us much more than the freedom to operate efficiently," Schramm said. "He also gave us the support and the counsel and the understanding that makes a great organization. A lot of people have said that Clint's greatest contribution was staying out of the way. Well, that isn't true. His contribution was his support and counsel." At the time, it was thought Schramm would finalize a sale within a month and was on record as saying whatever transaction was made would be presented to the NFL's annual meeting for approval during the week of March 19 in Honolulu.

Sale negotiations in fact continued until the last minutes before Schramm's deadline. On March 10, Miller and Bankston were frantically restructuring their offer to match Bright's. On March 16, Schramm denied that any sale to Bright had been made. "There has been no resolution today on who will be the next owner," he pointed out. "Bum Bright is one of the many people we've talked to about buying the team, but he is just one of the people." On March 18, Schramm again refused to confirm that a deal with Bright had been made. "It's going to happen pretty fast now," was all the Cowboys' president would say.

On March 19, Schramm submitted Bright's name to the League's executive session. The part of his report that drew the most attention was the price tag. Bright's consortium would pay $80 million to Murchison—$60 million for the franchise, and $20 million for its operating lease on Texas Stadium and associated real estate. The sum was almost twice what had been paid for any franchise in NFL history. While there was no doubt an immediate urge among the members to confirm that their franchises were indeed worth that much, to do so would require violating their own rules. Schramm had surmounted the problems posed by the fifty-one percent provision of the commissioner's ownership policy by, in essence, ignoring it. Bright would own only seventeen percent. Two other partners would own fifteen percent apiece, another ten percent, another five percent, and the rest split between a half-dozen or so others. To compensate for having no majority owner, the group had designated a managing partner, much as the Los Angeles Raiders partnership worked. The managing partner with absolute control of the franchise's League operations was Texas Schramm, in for three percent.

In the course of trying to make the sale, Rozelle remembered, "Tex found that people of means didn't want to have control over the franchise. They didn't want their peers either to think that they were bad businessmen, paying that much money for a football team, or didn't want their peers to think they'd done it for the self-aggrandizement. It was the first time we'd experienced that. All of the potential purchasers had wanted Tex to run it." Both Pete Rozelle and Hugh Culverhouse recommended acceptance. "It was a change from existing League policy," Schramm admitted, "but the quality and substance of the individuals concerned was very attractive and made it acceptable to the commissioner and other members of the League."

"Aren't we eroding the constitution?" Leonard Tose complained.

"Yes we are," Leon Hess agreed.

Nonetheless, the vote was taken quickly and the Cowboys sale was passed twenty-four to zero. No one wanted to turn down either $60 million or Tex Schramm, and in NFL Year One After Davis, all things were indeed now possible.

Most of the money Clint Murchison received from the sale was taken almost immediately by creditors. After that, Clint's fortunes continued to plummet. "It's as if someone found out the emperor had no clothes," one of his friends lamented. That discovery prompted a run on Clint's assets that resembled a stampede. By the end of 1984, banks and financial houses were lined up in court seeking foreclosure on what they said Murchison owed them. Among the group were Continental Bank and Trust for $75 million; Citicorp Real Estate for $10 million; First Federal Savings of Arkansas, $15 million; Merrill Lynch Private Capital, $13.5 million; the Marriott Corporation, $6 million; California First Bank, $14 million; Wells Fargo National Bank, $11 million; Midwest Federal Savings and Loan of Minneapolis, $20 million; the Arab Banking Corp., $18 million; and the European American Bank, $18 million. "Clint's problems to a great extent are like that of any bank in the U.S.," one of his partners pointed out to *The Wall Street Journal*. "If everybody wants their [sic] money today, they can't do it." Despite Clint's extreme difficulties with speech, one of Murchison's friends noted in early 1985, "he is on the phone around the clock and he is very determined that everybody get paid."

The Dallas Cowboys, first of Murchison's assets to be jettisoned, were unaffected by the crash. Nothing but the name at the top had changed and even that was still misleading. It was now Tex Schramm's franchise more than ever. "If you think Clint Murchison was an invisible owner," Bum Bright explained, "my group and I are going to be even more invisible." The announcement surprised no one, but Texas Schramm least of all.

2

To the surprise of almost no one, Robert Irsay was the first member of the League to take full advantage of the victory Al Davis had won. He did so with typical Irsay flair.

The question asked about Robert Irsay at the commissioner's Tampa Super Bowl press conference was substantively correct. Robert Irsay had in fact been conducting secret negotiations with various individuals in the city of Phoenix since January 4. The Arizona principals were Anthony Nicoli, a wealthy Phoenix businessman, and Arizona Governor Bruce Babbitt. Irsay flew to Phoenix to meet with them. Most of his time was spent with Nicoli. "We spent the day with one another," the Phoenix businessman remembered. "All we did was go to my home and visit for two hours. We ate lunch and visited for another four hours. Then we went to dinner with his wife and from there they flew on to Chicago." In the course of their "visit," Nicoli told Irsay he wanted to buy the Colts and move them to Phoenix. Irsay's first response was to say the franchise would cost $50 million.

On January 11, Nicoli and his accountant flew to Chicago to meet with Irsay and his attorney. The four of them met all day January 12, going over the Colts' books. On January 13, the discussions continued when Irsay flew everyone to Philadelphia and then to Baltimore in his Jet Star. In the Colts' hometown, Nicoli and Irsay toured the team's training facility, ate at a restaurant, and then flew back to Chicago. There, on January 14, they started to talk price again. "At that point," Nicoli remembered, "he wasn't prepared to release one hundred percent of the club. He would entertain very seriously to sell me forty-nine percent, and as a matter of fact, on a very tempting reasonable basis. The problem was, I wasn't interested in forty-nine percent. So I said, 'Let me stop negotiating for myself and put on a hat as a citizen for the people of the Valley of the Sun. Let's bring the team to Phoenix in 1984.' "

Nicoli left Chicago with a list of instructions from Irsay. He was to find temporary office space for the Colts, a suitable practice field, arrange a meeting with Arizona State University officials to discuss using their stadium until a new one could be built, and arrange a meeting with Governor Babbitt, legislative leaders, university officials, and local business leaders. Irsay also had told Nicoli to reserve five giant Mayflower Moving and Storage vans for use in his eventual move. Irsay wanted vans from outside of Maryland and said his plan was to leave Baltimore in the middle of the night and announce it after the fact. It was arranged that Irsay would fly to the meetings Nicoli had set up on the Tuesday after the Super Bowl. It was originally thought it would take that long to carry out Irsay's instructions but Nicoli was faster than that. Irsay then told his Phoenix contact, "Let's do it during the week of the Super Bowl. So much attention is on that that people won't know what we're doing."

The meetings were moved up to Thursday of Super Bowl week. Then, on that Thursday morning, Irsay called from Las Vegas. He'd flown there from San Francisco. He wanted to cancel the meetings and reschedule them for Friday afternoon and Nicoli agreed. At 5:00 A.M. Friday morning, Robert Irsay was awake in his Las Vegas hotel room, watching television, and saw a news report that he was scheduled to be in Phoenix to meet with the governor later that afternoon. At 5:30 A.M., Irsay's attorney called Nicoli and told him there was a "security leak" and the deal was on hold. Nicoli asked him to think it over and call him back. He and the attorney talked three more times on the phone that morning. "The last time he called, he said, 'We'll get back to you,' " Nicoli pointed out the next day. "I haven't heard from him since."

By then, Irsay's Jet Star was warming up at the Las Vegas airport, taking on enough fuel to get him to Baltimore. The late edition of *The* [Baltimore] *Sun* announced the Colts owner was on his way to town to hold a press conference and meeting with Mayor Donald Schaeffer. At 7:30 P.M., Irsay's plane taxied to a stop and he bounded into the terminal to be greeted by Schaeffer and a swarm of reporters. "My name's Irsay," he said to the mayor. "How do you do?" Robert Irsay and Donald Schaeffer then stepped over to a bank of microphones and met the press.

The first question was from an AP reporter, but Irsay didn't like the man and refused to answer. "Let the mayor have a chance, will ya?" Irsay snapped.

"There was a story," Schaeffer opened, "that said Robert Irsay is in Arizona. . . . I've told everyone that you told me if you were going to move the team, you'd tell me personally."

"Let me," Irsay broke in. He was at his most belligerent and waved his hands angrily. "We'll get this over real fast. I haven't been in Arizona. I haven't been in zero. I've been in three, four places where I got plenty machines, my own companies. I haven't been in Phoenix. I give you my word of honor. I'm a good Catholic. I haven't been in Arizona. Where the hell did this all come from? Who started this? . . . I didn't have any meetings planned. I don't know where this comes from. Don Schaeffer is my friend."

"You say the Arizona governor's a liar?" the AP reporter asked.

"I don't want to talk to you," Irsay snapped.

"Is there any thought about moving the Baltimore Colts to Arizona?" another reporter asked.

"I don't know where all this comes from," Irsay complained again. "Now, somebody started this. I don't know who did it. We are negotiating [with Baltimore]. . . . Now, why would I want to go to Arizona? . . . I have not any intention to move the goddamn team. If I did, I would tell you about it. . . . I flew a lot of miles today. That's my plane out there. And that bird

burns a lot of fuel. I come over to tell you I don't know what the hell this is
about. . . . If you love the Colts, why don't you treat me right? . . . You want
me here, why do you hang me? Why do you hang me for? . . . I flew over
here just to answer you guys. I don't know what the hell you're doing
here. . . ."

"Why did you come to Baltimore tonight?" a reporter asked again.

"Because jerks like you, jerks like you put things in the paper that I'm
moving to Phoenix."

When the press conference was over and he and Schaeffer had met
privately, Irsay flew off for parts unknown, probably Chicago, where he
lived. "He's one of the most interesting men I've ever met," Mayor Schaeffer
noted. "I am encouraged. I really am. I don't think he's made a deal
[elsewhere] . . . I think he would have told us."

Within a month, Robert Irsay was back in serious negotiations, this time
with Indianapolis. On February 27, *The Indianapolis Star* announced, "Deal
to Move Colts Here at 'Decision Stage.' " Indianapolis, negotiating through
Mayor William Hudnut, had already offered Irsay a package that included
free rent in the brand new Hoosier Dome, the building of an accompanying
practice facility, and a large loan to Irsay at an annual interest rate of eight percent. By March 2, negotiations were reported to have reached the point where
Irsay's attorney was flying into Chicago with final documents to move the
franchise. Only Irsay's signature was needed.

That same day, the National Football League convened a special meeting
at the Chicago O'Hare Airport Hyatt Regency Hotel. When Irsay showed up
there, he was mobbed by the press. Pushing his way through the crowd, Irsay
grunted "No information," and then disappeared behind closed doors. Inside,
"Mr. Irsay addressed the membership," Pete Rozelle told the press afterward, "and said he has not made up his mind what he wants to do. He
acknowledged the discussions that he's had with other cities and that there is a
possibility he would move, but he stressed he had no firm commitment from
anybody." The rest of the League membership, Rozelle later explained, "all
felt Irsay would have to make his own best decision. We had to leave it in his
hands because of the judgment in L.A." All the League could ask of Irsay
was that he make his decision by April 1, one of the owners confirmed, so
that the League's 1984 schedule could be drawn up.

Robert Irsay would meet the League's deadline, but March was a busy
month for him. On March 3, the [Baltimore] *News-American* revealed that
Irsay was again talking with Phoenix. "It's hard to figure out," Indianapolis's
Mayor Hudnut admitted. "I don't know what's going on. It may work out, it
may not work out." Irsay's communications with Phoenix were scheduled to
culminate in a meeting at Caesars Palace in Las Vegas on March 14 at which
a new offer would be made. When word of the meeting leaked out, however,
the meeting was canceled. Instead, Phoenix officials were told that meeting in
Vegas was now impossible and that Irsay was flying elsewhere. When he got
there, he would call them and they would fly to meet him there. The place
Irsay flew to was nearby Bakersfield, California, and on March 15, a five-

man Phoenix delegation headed by Governor Babbitt flew up by private plane and met him there. Afterward, Babbitt admitted that the meeting had taken place, but refused all other comment.

Indianapolis was still mystified. The final papers they'd drawn up in a great rush for March 2 remained unsigned on Robert Irsay's desk. "Nobody here had heard anything," a source there explained. "Irsay's lawyer lived with these guys for two weeks and now it's like it all didn't happen."

Baltimore, more accustomed to Irsay, continued to plug along while all this was going on. Robert Irsay and Donald Schaeffer continued to exchange phone calls and on March 12, Schaeffer and Governor Hughes had led a delegation to Chicago and made a revised offer to match those of Phoenix and Indianapolis.

When the NFL met again for its annual meeting in Hawaii on March 19, Robert Irsay stayed away and sent his twenty-five-year-old son, Jimmy, to represent him. Jimmy had recently been named the franchise's general manager and was, at this point, perhaps Robert Irsay's only public defender. "I see him as a sensitive person," Jimmy said. "He comes from a tough background—the Bucktown section of Chicago and the Marines—and I think that has shaped his personality. He's had to fight for everything he's got. He's a simple man in that he appreciates the little things and family pleasures. He's a very simple man. . . . He's sixty-two now. He's had some hardships and he's paid his dues. When people really get to know him, I think they'll find he's a sensitive, generous person." For example, Jimmy was fond of pointing to an incident that happened after a Colt victory in 1979, when Jimmy, home from college, was eating dinner with his folks. "All of a sudden," Jimmy remembered, "Dad got up from the table and left. He went across the street to an ice cream store, made a deal with the manager, and put on the guy's hat and took the ice cream scoop and invited every kid to come in off the street and have free ice cream. It must have cost him four hundred dollars. That's a side of him others don't see."

At the Honolulu meeting, all Pete Rozelle could do was to remind Jimmy that the League had to know where his father's franchise was going to play next season by April 1. "All his options are open," Jimmy answered. "He'd like to take his time because it's such a big decision."

By then, Robert Irsay had three offers to choose from. If Irsay would agree to sign just a six-year lease, Baltimore was prepared to spend $7.5 million on stadium improvements, and give Irsay a ten-year loan for $15 million, subsidize his payments on that loan to the tune of $500,000 a year, grant him $4.4 million in cash and $2.2 million in industrial revenue bonds, and guarantee the sale of at least forty-three thousand tickets per game for the duration of the lease. Phoenix offered a $15 million loan at eight percent with no payment on the principal for ten years, free stadium rent for up to twenty years, and an agreement to underwrite the Colts in any instance their annual gate revenues should dip below $7 million. Indianapolis, the only one of the three with a brand new luxury-box-equipped stadium, offered a ten-year, $12.5 million loan at eight percent, a $2.5 million line of credit, a brand new

$4 million training facility, the first $500,000 of luxury box income for the first twelve years, fifty percent of the suite income thereafter, exclusive right to sell programs and novelties, and a guarantee of $7 million in ticket income for the first twelve years.

Then, on March 28, Phoenix withdrew its offer, saying it could no longer wait for Irsay to make up his mind. By that time the Maryland legislature was hurriedly working on a law that would permit the Colts to be seized under eminent domain. Later that evening, Robert Irsay chose Indianapolis.

In the darkness of the early morning hours of March 29, moving vans were loaded with all the Colts' records and equipment and sent west. When they were long gone across the Maryland state line, Indianapolis Mayor William Hudnut announced the Colts were coming to town. "We are going to welcome them with open arms," he beamed. Hudnut's Baltimore counterpart, Donald Schaeffer, voiced only disgust. "That's the final humiliation," he noted.

Colts General Manager Jimmy Irsay composed a song to celebrate the occasion, which he later helped record in a rendition he described as "very Bruce Springsteen-like." It was called "Hoosier Heartland":

Daddy called me up on the telephone.
"Son, is there anybody listening? Are you alone?
It's goin' down tonight around 9 P.M.
The trucks are on their way as soon as I say when."

Well, the trucks pulled up to Baltimore.
The people 'round there didn't want us no more.
So we packed up our bags and drove out of town.
And 12 hours later we were Indy bound.

Well, the Colts we had it tough a couple of years,
Just a lot of empty seats.
Lord, there was no one to cheer.
But we heard about a place that had a big white dome.
And it didn't take long for us to find a new home.

Hoosier Heartland, that's where we do roam.
Hoosier Heartland, gettin' down in the Hoosier Dome.
Hoosier Heartland, and the Indy Colts have found their home.

While the Colts' move provoked a storm of criticism throughout the country, Al Davis, the man who had opened the door Irsay walked through, claimed it didn't bother him. "I have no misgivings," he explained. "This is America and industries can move. But the difference is that Baltimore made an honest effort to keep the Colts. I gave Oakland the best operation in football—and it wouldn't even give me $11 million in stadium improvements. The League will use this to say, 'We told you so,' but they could have stopped it if they wanted to.''

Pete Rozelle, of course, claimed exactly the opposite. "I talked to Irsay," the commissioner explained. "I can't say I put heavy pressure on him because of what our attorneys said. He knew that our rules on franchise moves have been suspended because of the Oakland situation. We just weren't in a position to stop him." While Rozelle did place the blame with *LAMCC v. NFL,* as Davis predicted, he was careful to distinguish Irsay from his predecessor. "As far as the League is concerned," Rozelle pointed out, "Bob hasn't caused trouble. At meetings, he goes along with the majority on things. He's very supportive of staying together and operating as a League. He was really self-conscious about going to Indianapolis. He didn't want to move like Al Davis. He wanted to have a vote. He told me he didn't want to be viewed as an Al Davis."

On April 2, 1984, some seventeen thousand local residents showed up at the Hoosier Dome to welcome Robert Irsay officially to town. At the accompanying press conference, Irsay was blunt. "It's not your ball team," he warned Indianapolis. "It's mine and my family's ball team and I paid for it and I earned it." The line drew applause from Indianapolis's reporters.

On January 4, 1985, shortly after the close of his first season in Indianapolis, Robert Irsay was driving his car through the north side of Chicago when unknown assailants fired two gunshots through his window. Irsay was unhurt. Reporters seeking more information about the shooting located Robert Irsay's eighty-two-year-old mother. She knew nothing about it and claimed she had not seen her son in thirty-five years. "I got a big heartache," Mrs. Irsay told United Press. "After I put him through school, he goes and marries that Polish girl, I forget her name already. I pay five thousand dollars for the wedding. He's the devil on earth." By June 1985, "that Polish girl," Mrs. Harriet Irsay, had come around to her mother-in-law's point of view and filed for divorce. The precipitating event came when Mrs. Irsay, vacationing alone at the couple's home in Bal Harbour, Florida, called back to their home in Illinois and spoke with her maid. Mrs. Irsay then learned that her husband had, without announcement, taken up with a widow twenty years younger than herself. "All his clothes were gone," Harriet told *People.* "He [even] took the fifty-five-gallon fish tank we kept behind the bar. Did he think I was going to take it out on the fish?''

Instead, Harriet Irsay sued for divorce, demanding, among other assets, the Indianapolis Colts. Her husband, she alleged, was, in *People*'s words, "a drunkard and a compulsive gambler." Harriet Irsay also claimed he had used Colts funds to buy himself a $1 million home in Indiana and had done "a lousy job" of running the football franchise. "All the time Bob was scheming to move the Colts," she complained, "he was also scheming to get rid of me.''

3

The second most visible superstadium game in the opening months of the League's Year One A.D. was played by Joe Robbie in Miami. Rather than utilize the Davis precedent, however, Robbie took his own singular approach.

By the time of the League's March 2 special meeting in Chicago to review Irsay's situation, Joe Robbie was hip-deep in yet another bond issue fight with the city of Miami. On January 27, the Miami City Commission had put a $55 million bond to redo the Orange Bowl on the city's March 13 municipal ballot. But Joe Robbie wanted nothing more to do with a refurbished Orange Bowl now than he had before and while the League met in Chicago, Robbie stayed home and launched a daring counterstrategy. He was, he announced on March 2, going to build his own $90 million, seventy-two-thousand-seat football stadium, in which the Dolphins would play. Even if the city got its $55 million for the Orange Bowl, his franchise would not be a tenant once its lease ran out after the 1986 season. The city of Miami described the announcement as nothing more than a pre-election ploy. "He's made promises and promises," Mayor Maurice Ferre observed, "but not delivered. If he can do it, he should get a prize as sugar daddy of the year."

Four days later, Robbie announced he had arranged for a site on which to build his stadium. The location was on the edge of Dade County, a mile from the Broward County line, in a sandy, barren track east of 27th Avenue and south of the Snake Creek Canal. It was currently owned by one Emil Morton. According to the plan worked out between Morton and Robbie, as reported by the *Miami Herald,* Morton would donate 160 acres to Dade County, which would in turn lease the land back to Robbie for a "nominal fee" on the condition he build a stadium on it. In addition, Morton would sell Robbie and "partners to be named later" 142 adjacent acres for "an undisclosed sum." There Robbie intended to develop "a hotel, shopping, and entertainment complex." Another 130 acres along 27th Avenue would be sold by Morton to "an unnamed New England group of investors" where an "amphitheater and restaurant complex" would be constructed.

Robbie also claimed to have found a way to pay for it all. "We have disclosed our financial projects to at least seven investment bankers," he explained, "three commercial bankers, two major insurance companies, and other prospective lenders. We have received written financial proposals. We are confident that we will obtain financial commitments within weeks, hopefully days, to provide construction money and permanent financing based upon our target goals in marketing luxury suites and preferred seats in loge areas." Joe Robbie's plan was to lease luxury boxes and the stadium's best seats in advance of construction. "Based upon our financial projections," he noted, "we will soon launch a campaign to market sufficient luxury suites at annual prices ranging from $25,000 to $65,000 and market sufficient luxury loge seats at annual prices ranging from $600 to $1400 which, combined with revenues from stadium operations, will retire a longterm mortgage or bond issue for the stadium."

If those announcements were not sufficient to kill the city of Miami's bond issue, Robbie moved to put the finishing touches on his obstructionism with a last minute pre-election letter to Miami's forty-two thousand season ticket holders. In it, Joe Robbie urged "all season ticket holders, all fans, and all supporters of the Miami Dolphins to join with all other oppressed taxpayers to vote no on the bond issue. City Hall intends to rule or ruin the Miami Dolphins. They threaten to damage or destroy our financial base in this community unless we consent to be held prisoners in the Orange Bowl. We will not be intimidated. We will not be shoved around. We will continue to campaign for a modern, new stadium for our fans rather than have $55 million of taxpayers' dollars poured down a gopher hole to repair a half-century-old, archaic football museum."

"He's doing what I call the 'Robbie rhumba,' " Mayor Ferre taunted in response. "You move to the left, you move to the right, you go in a circle and stay in the same place. I am more convinced than ever that Joe Robbie basically doesn't want anything to happen."

Nonetheless, the "Robbie rhumba" worked. On March 13, Miami voters rejected the Orange Bowl bonds by a two to one margin. Robbie described the vote as a "resounding defeat" for City Hall and told the *Miami Herald* he was "gratified." The renovation, he noted, had been a plan to "torpedo" his new Dolphin Stadium. Now that it was defeated, he could get about the business of making his dream a reality.

Joe Robbie took charge of marketing that dream himself. "In effect," one of his advertisements for the project noted, "the Dolphin Stadium effort is a high stakes game of planning, finance, and construction played out with a game plan that calls for the Dolphins coaches and players to watch from the sideline while the Dolphins fans and supporters perform alongside the Dolphins management." What Robbie had to sell in specific was a seventy-three-thousand-seat stadium with sixteen thousand parking spaces, a tier of "luxury club seats," and 234 "executive suites" in ten-, twelve-, or sixteen-seat configurations. These luxury boxes were all to be "air-conditioned and fully furnished with a choice of three decorator designs . . . [featuring] plush carpeting, lounge furniture, refrigerator and icemaker, lockable liquor cabinet, closed circuit television, and optional telephone connections. Food and beverages will be catered to the suites upon request." Robbie planned to contract Billy Sullivan's daughter Nancy to do the actual decoration. First, of course, the boxes had to be sold.

Joe Robbie could think of no better way to kick off his sales campaign than to announce that his stadium's inaugural season would be culminated with hosting the January 1988 Super Bowl. He took his case to the rest of the

League at a two-day meeting convened in Washington, D.C., on May 25, 1984. One of the items on the agenda was the selection of Super Bowl sites for 1987 and 1988. Both years proved to be tough battles. The two contestants for 1987 were the Rose Bowl in Pasadena, the home turf of Georgia Frontiere and Al Davis, and Veterans Stadium in Philadelphia, Leonard Tose's hometown. For 1988, contenders were Jack Murphy Stadium in San Diego, Gene Klein's home field, and Robbie's projected Dolphins Stadium. In both cases, the owners were unable to reach a three-quarters majority as their constitution required and had to suspend the three-quarters rule in order to decide. The vote on the 1987 site took thirteen ballots before Pasadena beat out Philadelphia, sixteen to twelve. The site for 1988 required eight ballots, most of which were split fourteen to fourteen. Finally Robbie lost a vote and San Diego was selected. Although he had argued strenuously that the Super Bowl would be of great assistance to his stadium project, he denied it was a setback when he lost. "The Super Bowl would have been a splendid event to have in the stadium's first year," he noted, "but since it didn't occur, I'm going home to sell boxes and build the stadium. It doesn't alter or interrupt our plans."

For the rest of 1984, Joe Robbie was first and foremost a salesman and kept busy at it. "I feel like I'm sailing into space at the rate I'm going," he noted in June. "I'm really on a treadmill. I know we have a long trail to travel to meet our marketing goals, but we are plugging along at the speed it requires." He also claimed to be doing a land office business. He had already sold twenty-nine of his luxury boxes and had commitments for twice that many. Among the purchasers was Hugh Culverhouse, who kept an apartment and law office in Miami as well as in Tampa. Robbie also evinced high hopes for future sales. "The unusual thing," he explained, "is we haven't started getting orders yet from the law firms, the accounting firms, the major corporations and civic groups that we figure will form the nucleus of our sales. Our sales have come from many people we don't even know. A conservative estimate is that we'll double our figures within the next two weeks."

Joe Robbie's goal was lease sale deposits of $9 million, the accumulation of capital required to trigger his construction financing. At the "Meet the Dolphins" breakfast in Ft. Lauderdale's Marriott Hotel on July 6 Robbie gave a typical performance. There, the *Herald* reported, "the estimated 725 aqua-and-orange-dressed fans heard encouraging words about the new season from Coach Don Shula. . . . Autographs were available from the relatively few players on hand. . . . But the morning belonged to Robbie, the owner, who came armed with a six-minute film about the stadium he wants to build near Calder Race Course in North Dade. No matter that fans' boisterous cheering at the appearance of game highlights at times obliterated the voiceover. With the backdrop of a large banner that read 'Dolphin Stadium—First & Goal 87,' Robbie made his points. Stadium pamphlets were placed on every table. Stacks of twenty-three-page contracts were out in the lobby. Robbie was in high gear. . . . By the time he yielded the microphone some twenty minutes later, he was talking to a receptive crowd about building 'the finest stadium in America.' ''

In Ft. Lauderdale, Robbie claimed to be twenty-five percent of the way to his goal. "By New Year's Day," he told the breakfast, "I want to announce that we'll break ground by next May or June and start actual construction."

On July 29, Robbie announced he had reached thirty-three percent. "We're so close to something so important," he claimed, "I would never let up for a moment for fear it might slip away."

On October 8, he told the *Herald* he was "within a hair of the halfway mark," and noted, "The money . . . is coming in at a steady, if not over-whelming pace. I told Jack Kent Cooke about this and he said, 'You mean to tell me you're charging sixty-five thousand dollars a year? Who the hell would ever pay that?' Well, I'm here to tell you those sell first. The top-priced boxes and loge seats are nearly gone."

On November 15, the Dade County Industrial Development Authority guaranteed the stadium's longterm financing by approving an $85 million issue of tax exempt industrial development bonds. They would be paid off solely with stadium revenues and would be activated once Robbie produced a letter of credit certifying he could pay them off should the stadium fall short. On November 28, Robbie claimed to be at sixty-four percent and rising.

On January 9, 1985, Joe Robbie's subscriptions were at seventy-two percent and still rising. It was close enough to his goal to convince what was described as a ["consortium of bankers"] to back the stadium's construction financing. Joe Robbie called a press conference at Dolphin headquarters on Biscayne Boulevard. "This is a signal day in the history of the Miami Dolphins," he trumpeted. "We can now announce the stadium will be built. . . . The dream is coming into the field of reality."

On March 17, at the 1985 annual meeting in Phoenix, the League awarded the as yet unconstructed Dolphins Stadium the January 1989 Super Bowl.

Thanks to Joe Robbie, Joe Robbie's dream had come true.

4

If anyone in the League doubted that NFL business was running by new rules in Year One, they had only to look to the [resolution] of the "DeBartolo situation" announced by the commissioner at the 1984 annual meeting in Honolulu. "I had a number of discussions with Eddie DeBartolo Jr. and his attorneys," Pete Rozelle explained at his press conference on March 19, "and they felt that rather than have a formal hearing, they would prefer to recognize that . . . the conflict of interest was created. And for that reason, they would like to volunteer steps that they should take to lessen the conflict that exists between Eddie's owning the 49ers and his father the Pittsburgh Maulers.''

The concrete form that alleged admission and voluntary submission took was a three-page letter from Eddie to the commissioner. It was significantly less than the commissioner claimed for it. "In truth," the *San Francisco Examiner* observed, "DeBartolo Jr.'s letter does little more than mildly address points of concern brought up by the League's conflict of interest committee chaired by Judge Parins. It is three pages of elusiveness. . . . Rozelle accepted it for the League—without even calling for a vote of the other owners—because it was the NFL, not the 49ers, who needed to surrender.''

What Eddie specifically agreed to do was withdraw the 49ers from the scouting combine they shared with several other teams—a step they were already planning anyway, not sign any Pittsburgh Mauler players, not attend NFL discussions of the USFL, and not participate on any NFL committees. As far as admissions of any conflict went, DeBartolo wrote something less than that. He agreed that his franchise would "maintain individuality . . . from entities associated with the USFL," but put the rest off to peacemaking. "No matter how often I may profess my total removal from the Pittsburgh Maulers," Eddie wrote, "the situation is very evident that I am deeply involved with my father in certain other business interests as well as in our close family relationship. If I were in the position of my fellow owners, I would be hard pressed to accept the feasibility of total detachment and noninvolvement. . . . I recognize that this is not a final solution . . . but it will at least create a higher degree of comfort and respect for all concerned as we try to work together as partners." In effect, Eddie DeBartolo agreed to say that the commissioner had won and the commissioner agreed to drop the issue for good.

With that, the League could stop, at least for the moment, fighting among themselves and get on to fighting the USFL, what it really had in mind that March. By then, the NFL had lost some forty-eight of its own players and seventeen highly sought college players to its challenger. "The situation was reminiscent of the first year of the late, unlamented World Football League," the *San Francisco Chronicle* noted, but "that has all changed. Now the situation is reminiscent of the last couple years of the AFL-NFL war. The USFL is going after established NFL players, especially quarterbacks, and it is all-out war." A good portion of the League was eager to commit itself to that war. "We have a lot of guys who have the means to fight back," Leonard Tose pointed out. "You certainly have Leon Hess, who according to *Fortune* magazine is worth $500 million. You have Bill Ford, who owns most of the stock in Ford Motor. You certainly have Lamar Hunt, who's got a billion dollars. I believe the Maras are ready to fight. I believe there are maybe twelve to fifteen owners who are not only willing to fight, but have the means to fight.''

As a League, however, they still had to tread lightly around the Sherman Act, and the only step they took that March was tangential. On March 22, the commissioner announced he was appointing a six-man "planning committee" along the same lines as he had attempted in 1976 until it had been undermined by the other members' suspicions of Al Davis. Ironically, it was a move Davis had been advocating. He called it a "watchdog" committee. Among its assignments was to study "how League finances could be affected by the USFL."

"It's not a go-to-war committee," Rozelle cautioned. "We just want to take an overall look at our future." In fact, the committee was quite the opposite. The goal was to make sure owners didn't throw the League's salary structure totally out of whack in their impatience to crush the USFL. Its membership included three general managers and three owners—Lamar Hunt, Ed McCaskey, and Wellington Mara. All three were known to feel that the best way to deal with the USFL was to let it spend itself to death.

If restraint was in fact their mission, the committee's job was by no means easy. The bidding war had long since begun and eventually reached a point beyond anything ever experienced in the history of the football business. At the end of it, NFLPA would claim that their share of the NFL's gross had risen well past the fifty-five percent Ed Garvey had been unable to win. Joe Robbie gave his starting nose tackle $515,000 a year to stay. Hugh Culverhouse's starting quarterback, making $180,000 a year in Tampa, jumped to the other league for $400,000. The USFL offered William Clay Ford's best running back $3.5 million over four years and the Lions matched it with $4.5 million over five years. Edward DeBartolo Sr. paid $3.3 million over three years to a running back fresh out of the University of Nebraska. The apex of the process was reached when the USFL's L.A. franchise paid a college senior a $2.5 million bonus to sign a contract that would pay him $1 million for the four seasons it lasted and then pay him a total of $30 million in deferred payments between the years 1990 and 2027.

Ironically, the leader of the NFL's every-man-for-himself signing blitz against the USFL was Eddie DeBartolo. By the end of 1984, he had given his quarterback a raise to $1.1 million a year, his best wide receiver $550,000 a year, and his best defensive lineman $500,000. His best defensive back was given a new $2.3 million four-year contract and his first choice in the 1984 draft signed for $2 million over four years. Eddie was also one of the first to use his own inside information and announce that the NFL was winning the war. "There are [USFL] teams losing $12 million and $8 million," he claimed in July 1984. "Throw my father into this. That team's losing a lot of money. Those men aren't successful in business because they like to lose money. I don't think the USFL can make it. I really, personally, truthfully don't. I don't think they can buck us even if they play in the fall. I'll give them two years."

DeBartolo's enthusiasm for the fight won him no fans on the commissioner's planning committee. "San Francisco is doing more harm than the USFL in escalating salaries," one of its members complained. "The philosophy of a lot of clubs is win at any cost, and clubs that have that philosophy escalate salaries and bring other clubs to their level. So everybody gets in the

red quicker than if everybody would just run things in a prudent manner."
During the early fall, the planning committee convened a series of regional
owners' meetings, the purpose of which was, according to Pete Rozelle, "to
point out that if this escalation continues, you are going into the red." At the
League meetings in New Orleans in the last week of October, the planning
commission reported that at current rates, the League would lose $90 million
collectively by 1986. Since they concerned the USFL, Eddie DeBartolo was
not allowed to attend any of the conclaves. "DeBartolo himself lost $10
million," Gene Klein complained. "It was madness. We were losing money
for no reason. We didn't have to match the USFL. There was a great deal of
bitterness over what some of our owners have done."

Regardless of Klein's change of heart about the need to bid with the
USFL, the competition was certainly having its desired effect on the other
league. After the completion of its second spring-summer season, the USFL
Boston franchise had moved to New Orleans and then on to Portland. Its
Washington franchise went to Orlando, and Philadelphia to Baltimore. The
Oklahoma franchise merged with the Arizona one and Detroit did the same
thing with Oakland. "NFL teams may switch towns to make more money,"
Sports Illustrated noted, "but in the USFL you switch towns to keep breathing." One of the casualties was Edward DeBartolo Sr.'s Pittsburgh Maulers,
who dissolved before the USFL's third season. Much to the NFL's relief, Mr.
D was out of the football business and henceforth, Eddie DeBartolo went his
way and the USFL its—just as Eddie claimed he had wanted it in the first
place.

For the USFL, the downward spiral only continued. In October, the new
league announced that after its 1985 season, it would no longer stage its
games in the spring and summer, but starting in 1986 would play in the fall,
head to head with the League. During the switch, the USFL would go
dormant everywhere except the courtroom. Invoking the Sherman Act had
been the second decision made by the USFL in October 1984. Filed in federal
district court in Manhattan, *USFL v. NFL* charged the League with "monopolizing and conspiring to control the business of major league professional
football." The three television networks were listed as "involuntary co-
conspirators." It would come to trial in May 1986.

Though he had been freed of the USFL albatross after a year and a half
of skirmishing with the commissioner, Eddie DeBartolo had acquired a taste
for the maverick's role. His pet peeve soon became the commissioner's
ownership policy, which he wanted altered to permit him to vest ownership of
the 49ers in DeBartolo Corp. Doing so would allow him to write any of the
franchise's losses off against his father's corporate tax bill. He had begun that
campaign before his father's divestiture but became even more forceful about
it after that. Eddie raised the issue at the League's 1985 annual meeting in
Phoenix, but it went nowhere.

In the meantime, Eddie also played a quick round of the superstadium
game with the city of San Francisco. Eddie wanted $30 million worth of
improvements in the city's Candlestick Park and it was basically no contest.

The only time he ran into political difficulties over the issue, Eddie knew just what precedent to invoke.

"Maybe we'll have to get somebody else to negotiate for us," he offered, "like Al Davis."

DeBartolo got his $30 million in improvements shortly thereafter.

As hard as it was for some of the League to accept, for Eddie, playing the game by its new rules came easily.

5

To no one's surprise, the owner who had the greatest difficulty accepting the new order of things was Gene Klein. Unwilling to live with the League's defeat as the last word, Klein opened Year One by filing his own lawsuit against Al Davis, hoping to find at least personal revenge.

Filed on January 30, 1984, in State Superior Court for San Diego County, *Gene Klein v. Oakland Raiders Ltd., Allen Davis, and John Does I through XX, inclusive* charged Davis with "malicious prosecution" for having named Klein an individual defendant in *LAMCC v. NFL*. Klein asked $3 million in actual damages and $30 million in punitive damages. Davis, Klein alleged, had made the charges "without probable cause" and in a "wilfull, wanton, malicious, vexatious, and oppressive" manner. As a result, Klein had "suffered loss of goodwill, loss of reputation, humiliation, injury to his health, strength, and activity," and had been caused "great mental, physical, and nervous pain and suffering," including, "but not limited to, plaintiff suffering a heart attack when testifying in the underlying action to defend himself from said malicious charges."

Al Davis called the action "frivolous and a sham" and filed a countersuit in March, *Los Angeles Raiders Ltd. v. Eugene Klein*, charging "malicious abuse of the court process." Davis and his franchise alleged that "if Klein's claimed loss of health and business opportunities and feigned emotional distress can ridiculously be attributed to an event, there are numerous events, rather than the Los Angeles Raiders trial" which caused Klein's distress. Davis offered a list of six possibilities: "1. a large fine levied [in 1974] against Klein by Commissioner Rozelle for drug-related activities; 2. a [1983] national television program which gave details of Klein's association with notorious underworld figures; 3. a well-known [1962] California civil case which found Klein guilty of malicious prosecution and assessed actual and punitive damages against him of more than $800,000; 4. a [1976] lawsuit by Barron Hilton and other minority partners against Klein for mismanagement. . . ; 5. the [1983] $60 million damages award against the Chargers and other NFL teams for antitrust violation . . .; 6. the numerous altercations that Klein has had with the city of San Diego, former Chargers coaches, players, administrators, and owners while Klein served as the Chargers' executive head.''

Davis's countersuit was eventually dismissed and Klein's original action was scheduled for trial in September 1986.

By then, Gene Klein was long since out of the football business. He first told Pete Rozelle of his intentions privately while in Honolulu for the 1984 annual meeting. ''He said if someone made a good offer,'' Rozelle remembered, ''he would sell. It was because of the stress. He was really torn but he said he could buy a box in the stadium and watch as a fan and make his horses his avocation.'' Klein himself doubted ''I would ever have gotten out of football if it hadn't been for that second heart attack.'' As it was, the bother had gotten too much for him. After informing the commissioner, Klein called a press conference on March 23 in San Diego. There, he explained that he would [entertain bids] for his controlling interest in the franchise. ''There is no purchase to which I have agreed,'' he told the press, ''but if someone wants to be in the NFL and wants to acquire the San Diego franchise, I would, for very personal reasons, have to give it consideration. That is not to say that I would sell it. But for the first time, that is not to say that I wouldn't.''

Gene Klein's ambiguity was fairly quickly resolved. On July 5, 1984, Dallas developer Carl Summers Jr. offered him a reported $40 million for his fifty-six percent interest, setting a value on the whole franchise of some $72 million—$10 million more than America's team had sold for some four months earlier. Klein accepted immediately and, as required under the Chargers partnership agreement, notified his minority partners. Under that agreement, the partners had a month to exercise their right of first refusal and match any offer for Klein's share. Among those partners in the summer of 1984 was one Alex Spanos, who was of Greek ancestry and a wealthy developer from Stockton, California. Reportedly worth some $175 million, Spanos had considered buying the 49ers before Eddie DeBartolo bought them in 1977 and had entered the Chargers partnership in 1983 when he bought ten percent from Barron Hilton. Spanos had known Al Davis for ''ten, maybe twelve years'' and considered him ''a great football man.'' At 11:00 A.M. on the last day of July, Spanos notified Klein that he was exercising his right.

Notifying the commissioner that Alex Spanos was the new Chargers owner was particularly easy. Rozelle was visiting at Klein's Rancho Santa Fe home on the day Spanos called. Rozelle was quick to praise the departing Klein. ''He was always thinking League,'' Rozelle told the *San Diego Union*. ''I think he was a major influence on the National Football League, always very constructive.'' Art Modell also chimed in from Cleveland. Praising Klein's contribution on the television committee, Modell claimed ''he also offered a moderating influence in our League meetings when they got heated and spirited, owner-to-owner or owner-to-Rozelle. Gene always had the ability to calm the disputants and bring about a peaceful resolution to whatever problem we were facing. He was always an NFL man, and I can't say that about all the owners in the League.''

The only public objections to Klein's leaving were raised, ironically enough, by Al Davis. He objected that there were ''legal impediments'' to the sale ''at this time.'' ''No bond has been posted in the federal case [*LAMCC v. NFL*],'' Davis pointed out. ''Klein as an owner is vulnerable for the damages. We want to be sure that the franchise is not in hock.'' Davis hinted he might file suit to stop the transaction, but nothing came of either his objections or the hint.

On August 3, Gene Klein introduced Alex Spanos to the San Diego press as the new owner of the Chargers and said his own very quick good-byes. ''The man had his points,'' the *Union* observed afterward, ''some good, some bad, all interesting. It will not be the same without him.''

For Gene Klein, Year One was time to get out while the getting was still good.

6

The Old Guard entered football's new age considerably diminished in both number and influence. Of the owners who predated Pete Rozelle, Halas was dead, as was Carroll Rosenbloom. Billy Bidwill soon adopted the new ways and the Green Bay Packers were largely irrelevant. That left only the Maras and Rooneys to uphold the old traditions. Both had supported Rozelle throughout the Davis fight and continued to do so. In Year One, both were quite openly worried about what was going on.

''The situation now is getting harder and harder on the Old Guard,'' Wellington Mara observed sadly. ''We're people who use football for our primary income and we're getting crowded like the corner grocery faced with a supermarket across the street. Greater capitalization is required. I don't know how to cope with the rise in salaries, the rise in operating expenses. The new owners now are people who've been successful in other areas. They don't depend on football for money. Many of the great fortunes have now come to the game. They're better at business than the founding fathers, but when someone isn't concerned with the bottom line at the end of the year, it sets the salary standards for all the others.'' For Wellington Mara, Year One was a whole different planet from that first year he took off from school and joined the Giant family living together in a downtown hotel.

Art Rooney felt much the same way. ''The NFL had a constitution that started with the start of the League,'' the League's last living saint pointed out. ''When the NFL lived by the constitution, it prospered. We never sued each other. But that's the whole world now. What Davis did won't make it easier and this could just be the start of things. A lot of the new people haven't lived with the constitution. It's a wholly different game. It's the way of life nowadays. I hope Commissioner Rozelle stays a long time. Pete used excellent judgment. His judgment has been just about perfect. It's a lot tougher to handle twenty-eight guys than eleven. Pete is very honest and calls them as they should be called. He's very fair. Through Rozelle, we made the NFL the strongest of major league sports. It would be very difficult to replace him."

Art's son Dan was equally adamant in continuing to back the commissioner. "Rozelle approached the Davis problem with the idea it was a problem against the League," Dan Rooney explained. "He went into it that way. After all the court cases, where Davis put out his story and Pete being called names and things like that, he had to feel those things. He still tried to treat Davis fairly. If it were me, I'd be tougher on Davis. The commissioner's job is Pete's as long as he wants it. Pete has never said he wants to do anything else, but the problem is, how long does he want it? If he can't operate, why put up with it? All these outside forces affecting the game are difficult to fathom. The biggest thing we have to do now is protect our game. Decisions have to be made with that in mind."

For Dan Rooney, Year One was as good a time as any to start all over again. "I think ownership in this League itself might be the most important particular that should be handled. The influence of owners is crucial. For the good of the game, the owners have to protect the game. That is the owner's function. Judgments have to be made about what's best for the game. That might mean decreasing TV, that might mean paying less because it's not good for the game to lose money. We're entering the most critical point in our history. TV's not going to bail us out. We've reached the limit other than inflation. We have to be more businesslike. Ownership is so important and so is how people get voted in. We have to have the courage to say no to new owners. Just because someone wants to sell, we just say O.K. We've never turned anyone down. I haven't voted for everybody, myself. I think there is a potential of the trusteeship role being lost. The game is at a crossroads. In the current situation, the economics are skewed, people are near the choking point. We need to find a new structure of ownership intelligently. An antitrust exemption would help, but we don't have to have it. A lot of our antitrust problems are internal. Owners isolate themselves now. It's better to have it out face-to-face. Then at least you're involved. As it is, people don't even come to the meetings anymore. We have to continue to encourage them to come. Our problem is all twenty-eight of us never sit down together. We have to have goodwill, understanding, and courage by owners to make the decisions that have to be made."

In Year One, however, it was not at all clear how many others were still listening to Dan Rooney.

7

Lamar Hunt was another figure whom the previous decade had significantly diminished. Once the boy wonder of the football business, Hunt now carried little weight at all inside the League. He was still "personally close to the owners from the old AFL days," especially Billy Sullivan, and had hewed to the League court position against Davis faithfully, even retaining additional League legal counsel for the second trial to represent the American Conference, of which he was titular president. Nonetheless, *NASL v. NFL* and the ownership policy fight leading up to it had left him outside the lines of heavy influence. He still retained his holdings in the North American Soccer League, the Chicago Bulls, and the WCT tennis tour, as well as his NFL Kansas City Chiefs, but his personal involvement in the sports business had been reduced significantly. "I made the mistake of getting involved in too many things," Lamar admitted. Still a regular at NFL meetings, he was nonetheless spending the majority of his sports energy as of Year One on the WCT.

Lamar Hunt was also suffering from a less severe but nonetheless formidable bout with the same financial disease that had afflicted Clint Murchison's Texas-based empire. The affliction had been acquired through his brothers Herbert and Bunker. During the early 1970s, his two older brothers had begun buying up large amounts of silver bullion and silver futures contracts and by 1975 were flying immense amounts of it to a stockpile in Europe. The shipments were escorted by ranch hands from the brothers' Circle K Ranch. Herbert and Bunker reportedly convinced Lamar, not yet financially involved himself, to ride shotgun on several of the shipments. From 1976 to 1979, Bunker and Herbert reduced their buying and concentrated on finding a partner with sufficient capital to make a corner on the world silver market possible. On July 1, 1979, Lamar's older brothers formed a partnership in Bermuda with two Saudi sheikhs called International Metal Investments. When the Hunts made their run for a corner, International Metal Investments would purchase some $900 million worth of silver to match the $450 million Bunker and Herbert had already collected.

By fall 1979, all that buying had the desired effect and began to drive the price of silver up, from $8 an ounce to $17.88 by October 1. After that, the price began to spiral even further upward. By December 31, it reached $34.45 and Bunker, Herbert, and the Saudis controlled 220 million ounces now worth $7.57 billion. In part, the Hunts had continued to enlarge their stake between October and December by involving their younger brother, Lamar. Eventually Lamar pledged himself for some $300 million worth of the brothers' escalating obligations. Since most of Lamar's silver was bought on margin and the price was rising, he had been able to secure that holding with only an immediate $15 million investment. Several sources later claimed Lamar did so because he was tired of being ragged by his brothers for missing out on the big silver killing.

By January 17, 1980, the high water mark of $50 an ounce was reached. Since 90 million ounces of the Hunts' bubble were future contracts deliverable in March 1980, all of those who had opposed the Hunt move and bought short faced possible bankruptcy. Among those in that position were a number of members of the New York COMEX exchange, on which much of the brothers' silver trading was done. According to a report by the Federal Commodities Futures Trading Commission, COMEX's directors collectively had $1.88 billion gambled on going short. On January 21, COMEX ordered that all trading in silver be halted. On January 22, silver had fallen to $34. On March 14, it was down to $21, reducing the value of the Hunt and Saudi investment by more than $2 billion in the space of a month. During that same month, Lamar had to borrow $50 million to cover his own now burgeoning margin calls. The Hunts had used a dozen brokers to make their run and in March, the margin calls from just one of them were running about $10 million a day.

On March 25, 1980, Bunker wired a three-word message to Lamar. It read, "Shut it down." When the Hunts' largest broker reported a margin call of some $135 million, the Hunts informed him they did not have the cash to cover it. At March rates, the three brothers were losing $4,687.50 per second. On March 27, the price collapsed to $10.80, leaving the Hunts with combined debts to brokers and banks of some $1.75 billion. "Word that the Hunts were strapped," *Fortune* reported, "sparked fears of Wall Street bankruptcies and talks of national financial calamity." To allay those fears, the Hunts paid off their most significant creditor, to whom they owed $665 million, with 8.5 million ounces of silver and a twenty percent interest in a Canadian oil property worth about $700 million, and the Federal Reserve Board put together a consortium of banks to make the Hunts a ten-year, $1.1 billion loan.

Since then, the brothers had spent much of their financial energy trying to reduce that debt. The interest alone ran at $220 million a year. To secure that bailout, the three brothers had been forced to post even their personal property as collateral. For Lamar, that included his Rolex watch and his National Football League franchise. Bunker, once thought to be worth perhaps $10 billion, was now described by *Forbes* as "worth probably still about $1 billion." Lamar, described as having "about $1 billion" in 1982, was pegged in 1984 at "more than $500 million." By 1985, the brothers still had 59 million ounces of silver stashed in a Delaware bank, now worth $5.80 an ounce—and Lamar's football franchise was still in hock.

Though hardly broke, Lamar emerged from the experience seared and it showed in the narrowness of the posture he brought to the NFL's Year One. "The League has to take steps so that the business will remain financially successful," he warned. "We cannot let costs get out of hand. Professional football will not continue to grow. Most stadiums are already full. TV ratings only have so far they can grow. We just can't continue our previous growth and there's not a lot of room left for expansion. We're at a saturation point from the standpoint of logical growth. The battle now will be to keep the relative position the NFL has. The single most important thing we have to deal with is to take the steps necessary to keep this business on a sound business basis."

For Lamar Hunt, the bottom line was the bottom line—especially now.

8

New age or not, the football business still had a Philadelphia problem and that problem was still personified by Leonard Tose. The year 1984 had begun on an upbeat note for the Eagles owner. On January 30, he announced that he had met the deadline on his Kidde Corp. loan and paid back the entire $6.8 million. The new money had come in the form of yet another loan, this time from a bank whose name Tose refused to disclose. "Everything has been worked out," he explained, without having to sell his franchise. "I still own ninety-nine percent of the Eagles and I intend to own the club as long as I live."

But as Year One began, even Leonard Tose evinced worry about whether too many feathers were falling out of the goose that laid golden eggs. During the 1983 season, Leaguewide paid attendance had not regained the pre-strike record levels of 1980 and 1981. In Philadelphia, long an attendance leader and considered an automatic sellout, the dip in season ticket renewals during the first months of 1984 was glaring. Tose's answer to the dilemma was what he called "promotion." It was a solution he recommended to the whole League. "If they'll get off their ass at 410 Park Avenue," he complained, "this deterioration will stop. It's no longer automatic to fill the stadium and the biggest thing in our business is to fill the stadiums. We've worked at promoting but Rozelle doesn't believe in promoting. We're not allowed giveaway days or anything like that. We can't give away anything."

In late March, Tose even participated in the Eagles' promotion, appearing personally to help plug flagging season ticket sales at one of the working class hangouts that were the backbone of the franchise's Sunday afternoon crowds. The promotion was staged at the Red Lantern Bar in Folcroft. "The ambiance of the place did not seem to fit Leonard Tose," the *Inquirer* noted, "but the Eagles owner was nothing if not comfortable." Tose, his recently acquired fourth wife, Julia, and some of his accompanying staff distributed team pictures, media guides, and Eagles stickers. Tose also bought a round of drinks for all seventy people in the bar. "When I was active in the trucking business," he noted, "I used to do this kind of thing almost every day at one of the terminals. I don't know why I didn't think it'd work in football." Tose was apparently a big hit. "I think Leonard Tose is a gentleman," one patron observed. "He bought everybody in the place a drink." Before Tose left, the crowd performed a spontaneous Eagles cheer. "I'll drink to that," the ebullient Leonard Tose responded. "I'll drink to anything."

Tose's crack at Rozelle's office about promotion was not an exception. One obvious difference Year One meant for Leonard Tose was a change in his expressed attitude toward the commissioner. "People don't understand Pete Rozelle's great ability to have patience," Tose had said of the commissioner in 1983. "He performs the miracle of making our League cohesive." In 1984, Tose's line was altogether different. "Rozelle's a compromiser," Tose bitched. "I don't think much of him and I don't care who knows it." Tose's disillusionment with Rozelle had been growing for a while and a number of reasons could be advanced for his change of stripe. The most pecuniary of those was that his Eagles had been the one NFL franchise not specifically named as a defendant in *LAMCC v. NFL*. At the time, Tose's absence was a device to avoid the trap the NFL had tried to set for Joe Alioto. Now it meant that Tose had a way of escaping his $3 million worth of possible damages from the case and he was preparing to refuse to pay his share of the assessment whenever the damages were finalized in the appeals court.

Escaping that $3 million bill was of particular importance to Leonard Tose since he was still running downhill in front of a financial snowball. The 1982 strike had cost the Eagles $8 million in losses; his daughter Susan Fletcher's office reorganization had cost him $2.5 million in enforced contract buyouts. His abortive 1983 sale had cost him another $1.75 million to settle. On top of that were his gambling losses, which Tose himself claimed to be unable to quantify. "I never kept track," he explained. "I don't know any gambler who does." By the fall of 1984, his bankers at Crocker Bank were getting antsy about the $18 million owed them by the Eagles and the $12 million owed by Tose himself and secured by his Eagles stock. Tose had been attempting to find a minority partner in the meantime to pump in some fresh cash, but by October, had gotten nowhere. His remaining option was to use Year One to his best advantage.

For several months, Leonard Tose and Susan Fletcher had been engaged in secret back-burner discussions with Canadian real estate developer James Monahan. Monahan was a part-time resident of Phoenix and was interested in buying a minority share if the Eagles would move to Arizona as a condition of the deal. During the first week of November, Tose and Fletcher traveled to Phoenix, but Tose vehemently denied the trip had anything to do with the sale of his football franchise. He was in Arizona on business which "has nothing to do with that." Reports to the contrary were "ridiculous, ridiculous." He intended "to keep this club until the day I die and I'm not going to move them."

The Phoenix Metropolitan Sports Foundation, charged with bringing professional football to the Valley of the Sun, would say through its chairman only that "another situation is coming about involving an NFL franchise that is interested in relocating in Phoenix. It's a club—one that's in a stable situation—that no one would guess. There could be something happening shortly, but nobody wants to say anything until the end of the season for obvious reasons. We've heard rumors that something is going on with the Eagles and have had indirect talks about it, but have not talked directly to the Eagles." At the time, Leonard Tose's total debts were reported to be over $40 million. When pressed on whether or not her father was going to sell an interest significant enough to cause the franchise to move, Fletcher was evasive. "Do I know if the third world war's coming tomorrow?" she asked. "Who the hell knows. I don't know what life's going to bring."

By December, however, *The New York Times* reported that Crocker Bank "was making it abundantly clear" that "it wanted Tose to make good on his loans." Rumors about an Eagles move were now all over Philadelphia and Philadelphia's new black mayor, W. Wilson Goode, had already met with Tose on four different occasions to check them out. "Mr. Tose said to me he had in fact had discussions with the folks in Phoenix," Goode reported, "and there was a good deal of interest on the part of football owners in Phoenix, but that he had no plans to move the team." On December 10, however, Tose hedged somewhat. In seclusion in his suburban home, he let his PR man do his talking for him. "Mr. Tose is considering a move to Phoenix," the spokesman noted, "but nothing has been signed and no final decision has been made. There is nothing more I can tell you."

When Leonard Tose emerged momentarily from his seclusion three days later to get a haircut at the local barbershop, he was booed by other patrons as he left. By then, there had been significant further developments on two different fronts. The first, of course, was instigated by the city of Philadelphia. As soon as the possibility of a move had been confirmed, Mayor Goode began working frantically to put together a counteroffer. "I'd be delighted if he works something out," Tose claimed. "I'm not talking about matching the Phoenix offer. I'm talking about survival. You understand? Survival." The personal antipathy that had erupted toward Tose in Philadelphia as soon as news got out had apparently shaken him somewhat. "I guess it's a natural reaction," he admitted. "I didn't foresee it, but it doesn't really surprise me. . . . I don't feel very happy. I don't feel very good. I've heard the stories—'Keep the team and kill Tose.' " In his actual discussions with Goode, Tose would say only that there was a "50/50 chance" the team would stay. "I believe that the deal in Phoenix can reach a conclusion at any time," Mayor Goode warned.

So, of course, did Phoenix. There, the actual move was expected to be announced on December 17. Arizona Senator Dennis DeConcini's office confirmed as much when contacted for comment. The senator, his press aide explained, "is saying three things: One, it is our information the Eagles will move to Phoenix. Two, an announcement could come as early as [December 17]. And, three, when asked how sure he is, the response has been, 'Well, we'd be surprised if it did not go through.' " In fact, the deal had already been cut and agreed to. Only the signing was left. Monahan would buy twenty-five percent of the team for $30 million and some sources even claimed Tose had already received part of the cash. In addition, the Eagles would be marketed in Arizona by leasing seats in addition to selling tickets, each seat costing $3000 for ten years. "It's a rich community," Leonard Tose later observed. "I could have had $50 million in my pocket and kept the team in the family forever."

The other development cutting across Tose's path to Phoenix came from the League on December 14. After calling a special League meeting for December 18 to discuss Tose's situation, Rozelle chose to make a calculated gamble and filed suit in Philadelphia Federal District Court. "What began as a trickle in the wake of the Raiders case in California," a spokesman for the commissioner's office explained, "now threatens to become a flood if the Eagles leave the country's fourth largest market. Such a move would abandon a community that has supported its team superbly for more than half a century." The lawsuit asked that Tose be forced to "recognize contractual obligations to Philadelphia" and prevented from leaving without League permission. The suit also asked the court to declare ahead of time that "the NFL would not be violating any antitrust laws if the Eagles were forced to comply" with League regulations. While the suit offered little difference from the unsuccessful *LAMCC v. NFL,* the commissioner's calculation was based on a shrewd perception that Tose's shaky finances would make fighting a suit beyond his means. "I think they thought they had a defense," Mayor Goode said of Tose and the Eagles, "but I don't think he had the time."

While Leonard Tose was faced with this League roadblock, Philadelphia was offering a loan of $43 million it had arranged for Tose with local banks. Tose had consistently refused the proposal because the banks wanted, as in 1977, to take away his financial control. On Saturday, December 15, the logjam was broken by Rozelle. The commissioner informed Tose that the NFL was willing to consider "cooperation" in finding Tose the money he needed at its meeting on December 18. Any approval, of course, would depend on the Eagles remaining in Philadelphia. From that point on, discussions between Tose and Goode shifted to the possibilities for a new lease. When, late on Saturday night, Goode offered a deal that would increase the Eagles' annual revenues by $2 to $4 million, Tose accepted and signed an agreement to keep the Eagles at home. According to Tose, it was the invocation of Philadelphia patriotism by his wife and daughter that finally swayed him. "They told me," Tose remembered, " 'You can't move the team to Phoenix, it belongs here.' And I couldn't do it to Philadelphia. The people here have treated me well. They have supported me."

As for the NFL's reported loan offer, Pete Rozelle was vague. "It's a sensitive situation," he noted. "I'm not fully informed as to what they want from the League, and it's tough for me to talk about what they say is cooperation when I haven't talked to the twenty-seven guys who would have to pay for it." On December 17, Tose was scheduled to visit the League office and spell out what he wanted. The rumor was that Tose would ask for $12 million with which to get Crocker's personal loans off his back.

In the meantime, Leonard Tose insisted he had never led Phoenix to believe he was moving there and that he owed them no explanation. "I'm not saying we haven't talked to them," he explained. "I'm saying it wasn't finalized." Tose said he intended to call Monahan, the man with whom his deal there had been made, "in the next few days and tell him what I did." Monahan, of course, already knew from reading the papers and was outraged. "That son of a bitch," Monahan fumed. "I'm furious. I'm disappointed. I'm mad as hell. He used somebody before and he used me this time." Leonard Tose's Year One had yielded yet another former or would-be partner who now hated him.

It did not, however, solve his financial problems. "The jackals are still on my heels," the Eagles owner shrugged, "and will be until I die." The League meeting on December 18 did not loan Leonard Tose any money. Instead, the commissioner appointed a three-man committee "to help find a way to refinance the Eagles." The members were Pat Bowlen, leader of a group that had bought the Denver Broncos for $73 million shortly after the Cowboys sale, Ralph Wilson, and Hugh Culverhouse. "We have no time schedule," a League office spokesman explained. "They'll set their own calendar." The committee took its time with what was a "complicated situation." One of the complications in Tose's dilemma was that Chuck Sullivan had reportedly acted as personal guarantor of Crocker's $12 million, again in contravention to the constitution.

While the committee took its time, the pressures on Leonard Tose became acute. No Philadelphia bank would lend him anything without the right to control the franchise, and by February 3, 1985, according to *The New York Times*, Crocker Bank had refused to extend his loans, which were due in full by January 1986. In addition, the bank was concerned about the Eagles' declining net worth and gave Tose six weeks in which to demonstrate he was capable of retiring the loans in full or face foreclosure. Tose was now cornered and the League's committee did nothing.

His other options exhausted, Leonard Tose took the step he had struggled to avoid for sixteen years. On March 6, it was revealed Tose had made an agreement to sell his entire ninety-nine percent interest to Norman Braman, a south Florida businessman who was a native of West Chester, Pennsylvania. According to the terms of the sale, Braman would pay off Crocker's $18 million and $12 million loans and pay off another $12 million in deferred player salaries due shortly. In addition, Tose would receive $10 million cash on closing, plus $1.5 million for ten years, a $5 million payment at his death to his designated heir, and an extra $1.5 million "to pay off some taxes." The gross value of the deal was estimated at "more than $70 million." Pete Rozelle commented that he "felt sorry" for Tose, because he knew he "so desperately" wanted to stay in the League. "Leonard Tose has a lot of friends in the League who are sorry that he won't be part of the League anymore," the commissioner observed. "By the same token, the League has been concerned about the stability of the club. If everything checks out, the owners won't have to spend any more time on those financial problems.''

Leonard Tose himself claimed to be relieved. "I'm delighted," he said. "Nobody believes me when I tell them, but selling the team is like lifting a pack off my back. I had a hell of a run for sixteen years. Hey, listen, as a kid, I was a truck driver. My father couldn't read or write. He started a trucking company with a horse and wagon. I've had a hell of a run."

On May 17, 1985, the sale was finalized and Leonard Tose left the National Football League for good. One of his first stops afterward was a month's vacation on the French Riviera. "Hey," Leonard Tose grinned in parting, "this is not a case of walking away poor. I'm walking away rich. That's one of the reasons I can smile."

9

After Leonard Tose sold out, taking Susan Fletcher with him, the only woman who remained sitting in the NFL's inner circles was Georgia Frontiere.

Georgia's Year One began on both up and down notes.

The up note was the performance of her team. Despite banners in the Anaheim stands like "Thanks, Georgia, Now the Whole World Is Laughing at Us," the Rams rebounded from their disastrous two-win strike season to a record of nine to seven and made the playoffs for the first time since 1981 as a wild card. After winning their first playoff game, Mrs. Frontiere's team began 1984 with a game against Jack Kent Cooke's Redskins in the National Conference semi-finals. Georgia was enormously pleased by the turnaround and called a team meeting for the morning of the Redskins game in order to express her appreciation. When her players had gathered in a large hotel conference room prior to taking their buses to the stadium, Georgia thanked them all and said she wanted to give them a present. Next to her was a table piled high with Cabbage Patch Kids, that season's hottest children's toy. Each player was given one before filing onto the bus. When they got off the bus at Washington's R.F.K. Stadium, the Rams made their way through the swarms of rabid Redskins fans, clutching their dolls under their arms. The Rams lost, fifty-one to seven. They were a playoff team nonetheless, and would stay that way during 1984 and 1985.

The down note was the ongoing investigation by a Los Angeles grand jury of ticket scalping. Among those called to testify in the fall of 1983 was Don Klosterman. While still under contract to the Rams, he'd had nothing to do with running the team for almost two years while he waited for his contract to run out. Immediately after it did, Klosterman would take over the new Los Angeles Express franchise in the USFL. According to a source close to the investigation, the grand jury had asked Klosterman whether it was possible that five thousand tickets to the 1980 Super Bowl had been scalped and Klosterman had reportedly answered "right number, wrong year." Georgia bumped into Klosterman on December 1, 1983, when she and Dominic were in New York City and arrived at "21" for dinner. As the Frontieres were shown to their table, Klosterman was seated two tables away with broadcaster Pat Summerall and NFL Commissioner Pete Rozelle, Klosterman's boyhood friend. Self-consciously gracious, Georgia went over and said hello. Shortly thereafter, and before they'd even ordered, Klosterman and his party left. Rozelle, according to a source close to Georgia, was "flustered" at being seen with Klosterman.

When the Frontieres returned to Los Angeles, they walked into the strangest twist of all in the saga of the ticket scalping inquiry. This episode featured one H. Daniel Whitman and two men named Cohen. Whitman, part owner of exclusive Cyrano's restaurant on Sunset Strip and the Christiana Inn of South Lake Tahoe, was described by the *Los Angeles Herald Examiner* as "a longtime friend of Dominic Frontiere, husband of Rams owner Georgia Frontiere." The first Cohen was one Raymond Cohen. Raymond had been in the hands of the grand jury since April and had a lot to talk about. This Cohen told federal authorities that Whitman had introduced him to Dominic Frontiere and that Frontiere was in turn "the source of several thousand tickets" for the 1980 Super Bowl. Those tickets had been sold at some six times their value and, according to Cohen as reported in the *Los Angeles Times*, the money returned to Dominic, who allegedly had made no report of the transaction on his tax returns. Raymond Cohen was also scheduled to testify in an unrelated counterfeiting case against Jack Catain, the man who'd threatened Harold Guiver and Don Klosterman back in 1980. The second Cohen's name was Robert, and he was an old friend of Whitman's. Later Whitman's lawyer would also characterize Robert Cohen in court as "a small-time criminal who wanted to improve his standing in the underworld . . . hoped to get a better connection both for his cocaine trade and addiction, and wanted to prove to other criminals that he was able to have people murdered."

The drama began in fall 1983, when Whitman told his friend Robert Cohen that he needed someone killed. The someone was Raymond Cohen, who, Whitman told Robert, had to die because he was informing on several "heavyweights out of Chicago." In November 1983, Robert approached someone he knew and offered five thousand dollars worth of cocaine in exchange for Raymond's murder. The man he approached, however, was an FBI informant and, at that point, government investigators began to work their way back up the chain. FBI agents used a Hollywood makeup artist to phony a bullet hole in Raymond Cohen's forehead, took a picture of the "body," and had their informant give it to Robert Cohen and secretly tape their conversation about the deed that was supposed to have taken place on November 15. On December 2, authorities confronted Robert and he quickly turned informant himself. The next step was for Robert Cohen to strap on a secret tape recorder and meet with Whitman and tell him Raymond Cohen was dead. The government agents' apparent hope was that Whitman could in turn be made to implicate Jack Catain.

As it turned out, Whitman did less than that. "For whatever it's worth," he told the wired-up Robert Cohen, "if it means anything to you, let me just tell you that what was done was sanctioned." Cohen assumed the sanction had come from "organized crime," but Whitman never said who. "Remember one thing," Whitman continued, "that when you do a favor, you're owed a favor. . . . You're owed one. . . . And as you will find out, some of it can be done. I can reach high. . . . These things don't happen unless you get it cleared. You get some idea of where I can go if I have to." The conversation eventually changed to the man Whitman thought was dead and the informing he had done. Whitman noted that "I'm going to get myself killed if I testify, if I tell them anything about what I know." Whitman admitted to Robert Cohen that he had been approached by federal agents himself earlier in the year. "I said, 'You want to talk to me about Dan Whitman, sit down, I'll tell you everything you want to know,' " Whitman remembered. " 'You want to talk about Ray Cohen, Jack Catain, Dominic Frontiere . . . I don't want to talk to you guys about it.' "

H. Daniel Whitman was arrested on December 7 and charged with soliciting a homicide. At the time of his arrest, the owner of Cyrano's Restaurant was driving a stolen Mercedes-Benz and carrying a .22 caliber pistol. A U.S. Secret Service agent later testified that once in custody, Whitman had informed him that Jack Catain "was aware that Raymond Cohen was to be killed," but Whitman later denied saying any such thing. Whitman also specifically told investigators that Dominic Frontiere had no involvement in the murder whatsoever. When Whitman was arraigned on December 9, his attorney told the judge that he had already received "calls from two presidents of banks, and the head of a major film studio" offering to help his client make bail.

Whitman pled not guilty and was tried in March 1984, and convicted and sentenced to eight years in prison and a $100,000 fine. During his trial, the Los Angeles Times noted, "it was stated for the first time publicly that Dominic Frontiere, husband of the Los Angeles Rams owner, is a subject of the investigation into whether people who may have profited from the scalping failed to report the income for tax purposes." Dominic responded to the allegation through his attorney. "It is untrue," the attorney bristled. The attorney claimed to have known about Raymond Cohen's claims already and suggested the informant was lying. "Ray Cohen has been sitting with the government for quite a while," he pointed out, "telling them a lot of things about a lot of people." The Rams, on the other hand, had "provided an accounting to the government of virtually all of the Super Bowl tickets" from 1980. Only two hundred out of twenty-eight thousand had been untraceable. Dominic, he explained, "is very upset that these allegations have been made and believes the reason that they stay alive is that he is a celebrity in the community."

Apart from that, neither Mr. nor Mrs. Frontiere had anything to say about H. Daniel Whitman or either of the Cohens.

On June 19, 1986, Dominic Frontiere was indicted for making false statements on his 1980 tax return, making false statements to IRS investigators, and "corruptly endeavoring to obstruct an Internal Revenue Service investigation." The three felony counts carried total maximum sentences of eighteen years in prison and $20,000 in fines. Among other things, the indictment alleged that Frontiere failed to report hundreds of thousands of dollars from the resale of tickets to the 1980 Super Bowl.

10

The Sullivans found Year One discomforting.

Old Billy had made no secret whose side he was on in *LAMCC v. NFL*. He found losing to Al Davis a bitter pill to swallow, and remained a Rozelle partisan even when the issue was long since decided. He was also disturbed by the business's new economics. "The biggest problem in our game," Billy observed, "is that we have quite a number of people who inherited wealth and have never had to worry where the next slice of bread is coming from. Nothing in this world says you can't use your head, but we, as a League, haven't had much practice at it. Somewhere we have to look in the mirror and say who's at fault for this. The answer is the owners."

For Chuck, the discomfort was more intense. Year One was the year it was revealed that Chuck Sullivan did not possess the Midas touch. After a spectacular rise to influence in the football business, Chuck decided to expand into rock 'n' roll and significantly overreached himself. For Chuck, it must have felt like a natural progression. He had promoted concerts in college and organized Bob Hope tours as a captain stationed in Thailand during the Vietnam War. After buying the newly named Sullivan Stadium in Foxboro, he began staging shows there that featured the likes of David Bowie and the group, The Police. In spring 1984, he was looking to book the hottest proposed tour of the summer, the Jackson Family Victory Tour, featuring teen idol Michael Jackson, into his facility and met with Frank DiLeo, the vice-president of Michael Jackson's record label, on a visit to Los Angeles. DiLeo was about to leave the record business to become Jackson's personal manager and he told Sullivan that the tour's original promotion arrangement had fallen through and the Jacksons were looking for a new promoter for the tour itself. "Chuck went out to L.A. to talk about the stadium," one of the other Sullivans remembered. "The next thing I knew his banker was telling me he was going for the whole banana. I could hardly believe it."

To secure "the whole banana," Chuck Sullivan leaped into a bidding war with some of the more experienced tour promoters in the business. Forming a momentary partnership with Eddie DeBartolo, Sullivan wired an offer guaranteeing the Jacksons $40 million or sixty-seven percent of the gross, whichever was higher. In late April, he was summoned to Los Angeles by DiLeo. By then DeBartolo, worried over the financial risk, had dropped out. Chuck Sullivan returned from L.A. after his Stadium Management Corp., a music business unknown, had been named promoter of the tour that was expected to gross $70 or $80 million, at least twice the previous rock 'n' roll record. The deal he'd cut gave the Jacksons 83.44 percent of "gross potential ticket proceeds" and Sullivan 16.56 percent. The Jacksons' cut was some twenty-five percent above the industry standard. In addition, "gross potential ticket proceeds" meant they would be paid as though every seat in the house were filled, whether it was or not. Most of the expenses were Sullivan's and he also had to guarantee his stars at least $36.6 million, to be paid in advance. To make the down payment of $12.5 million, he put Sullivan Stadium up as collateral for a $12.5 million loan from Crocker Bank. The remaining $24.1 million was due within two weeks of the opening concert, scheduled for July 6.

Chuck used the NFL meeting in May 1984 to start putting the stops on his tour together. A number of stadium managers were there to make Super Bowl bids, and according to one of them, Chuck used his insider's knowledge to try to make comparable deals for the Jacksons. Doing so, was, of course, a music industry first. No one in rock 'n' roll had yet tried the football approach. From Sullivan's perspective, it was also a natural progression. He, too, had a seller's market and a product that would put any place it stopped on the map. The Jacksons were at that moment the hottest thing in music and Chuck was convinced that the frenzy of anticipation for their Victory Tour would provide leverage sufficient to make stadiums put themselves out to book a date. His terms were anything but modest. "If we had given in to Chuck's demands," one stadium manager noted, "we would have lost $300,000."

An example of Sullivan's rock 'n' roll cum football approach was his negotiation with Philadelphia over the city's JFK Stadium. Sullivan's talks were conducted with a mayor's task force. He wanted the city to furnish free hotel rooms for the tour's entire work force, provide free use of the stadium, and forego any of its usual cut of concessions sold at the Jacksons' events. In all, the subsidy Chuck asked for was in the neighborhood of some $400,000. Chuck argued that having the Jacksons in town would generate business well worth the price. Philadelphia found the argument hard to swallow, but other locations were quicker to deal. Lamar Hunt's Arrowhead Stadium in Kansas City got the tour's opening dates by agreeing to a flat fee of $100,000 for three concerts, rather than its usual twelve percent. Texas Stadium in Irving outside Dallas, the second stop, refused to reveal the terms of its agreement, but Jacksonville landed the tour's third stop by agreeing to provide $445,000 worth of goods and services gratis. There were also, however, omens of the disaster to come. Perhaps the most embarrassing of those was the refusal of the Foxboro city fathers, upset by disorderly conduct at previous Sullivan concerts, to issue a permit allowing a Jackson event to be held in the stadium that had been hocked to make the whole Victory Tour possible.

In truth, Chuck Sullivan had made several significant miscalculations. The first was over just how far his NFL-style approach to stadiums would carry him. It wore thin early, created several public relations disasters, and he was soon paying much closer to standard rates and losing money accordingly. The second miscalculation was over the Jacksons' box office staying power. The world's hottest item in June was just another traveling rock 'n' roll extravaganza by August and old news not long after that. Their concerts were not automatic sellouts, tickets cost $28 apiece, and Sullivan had to pay the Jacksons sell-out rates even if he had tickets left over. The third miscalculation was over just how much money something like the Victory Tour ate up as it went along. Just drawing up the Jacksons' contract cost $400,000 in legal fees. Sullivan's insurance premiums ran another $500,000. He also had to cover the standard expenses of electricity, production, ticket takers, ushers, and catering. His payroll included, under the terms of the Jacksons' contract, an "ambiance director," paid to provide "homey touches" to the $40,000 traveling parlor in which the group sat before and after shows, as well as some 250 other employees. At each stop, Sullivan had to erect and then tear down a 365-ton stage one third the size of a football field. To move the operation required more than thirty highway trailer rigs. From the start, overhead expenses ran in the neighborhood of $1 million a week, far beyond what Chuck had counted on.

Sullivan's first retrenchment was to beg out of the $24 million he still owed on the Jacksons' advance. Instead, the arrangement was renegotiated so that the Jacksons' share was reduced to seventy-five percent of "gross potential sales" and the advance was dropped. The respite that afforded Sullivan did not last long. Having projected earnings of as much as $14 million in June, Chuck had reduced his projection to $3 million by August. By October, when the Jacksons reached Toronto after some thirty appearances elsewhere, the numbers looked even worse. By then, according to the *San Francisco Chronicle*, some fifty thousand tickets had gone unsold, costing yet another $1.4 million that Stadium Management Corp. didn't have. After the last Toronto show, Chuck Sullivan stayed up all night with the Jacksons and their lawyers, fashioning yet another renegotiation. This time he wanted "gross potential sales" changed to "actual sales." By morning, the Jacksons agreed to work on that basis henceforth, but insisted on being paid some $600,000 for previously unsold tickets. Chuck agreed. "The bottom line," he announced, "is that if everything works out well, the profit for Stadium Management Corp. will be about $500,000."

But everything did not work out well. By the time the Victory Tour reached Vancouver and Los Angeles, the last two stops, in late November and early December, the extravaganza was a financial shambles. Sullivan and his stars were dealing through intermediaries and Sullivan was claiming to be running between $4 and $6 million in the red. On November 28, Sullivan stopped payment on a $1.9 million check he had given the Jacksons for the Vancouver performance and checked into a cardiac care hospital to recover from a mild heart attack. In order to save the final Los Angeles performance, Sullivan left his hospital bed to renegotiate, trading the $1.9 million for a bigger piece of the proceeds from the three Los Angeles dates. Sullivan got the concession but it didn't help much. The Jacksons finished their twenty-city, fifty-five engagement migration in a soggy December rain in Dodger Stadium, playing to conspicuous blocks of empty seats interspersed with an audience that ''barely applauded'' when they came on stage.

When all the bills were in and Year One drew to a close, Chuck's expansion into music promotion had cost Stadium Management Corp. a reported $13 million.

How much pressure those losses put on the Sullivans' relatively meager cash flow remained unknown, but members of the League who were ac-quainted with the details of Chuck's rock 'n' roll bellyflop were less surprised than others when Old Billy let the word out during the 1985 season that his family's football holdings, Stadium Management Corp., and the Patriots, were both on the market. The Sullivans' reported asking price was $100 million for the package—$99,975,000 more than it had cost Billy to get into the business in the first place.

That there was still some Sullivan magic left was apparent in his team's fortunes once word of a possible sale got out. A perennial also-ran or worse throughout the last two decades, the Patriots had not played for any kind of title since 1963, but in 1985 their eleven to five regular season earned a wild card berth in the playoffs. They then beat the Jets, the Raiders, and the Dolphins in succession and won a trip to Super Bowl XX in New Orleans, their first Super Bowl ever. The performance maximized the Sullivans' franchise value, but, even more important to Billy was the satisfaction. Most satisfying of all was the win over Al Davis's Raiders. Significant underdogs, Sullivan's team had delivered a twenty-seven to twenty thrashing to the architect of football's new age and the Sullivans found it hard to restrain themselves. Pat Sullivan, the franchise's general manager and Billy's youn-gest son, roamed the sidelines during the game, shouting insults at the Raiders players. After the Patriots victory, Pat got into an epithet match with Howie Long, a Raiders tackle, and grabbed the man's face mask. When Matt Milley, a nearby Raiders linebacker, saw the move, he swatted Sullivan across the head with his helmet, opening a gash over Pat's eyebrow. The scuffle was all over the front pages the next day.

''I didn't know him,'' Long claimed. ''He said, 'Let me tell you who I am.' I said, 'Wait a sec, big guy. You might have 30 million in the bank but you ain't tellin' me nothin'.' I faked like I was going to hit him, just to see him jump. I'm not going to let a classless, silver-spooned, nonworking son of a bitch like that tell me anything. For me, it's God, Al Davis, and my wife, not necessarily in that order. Sullivan doesn't sign my checks. He's the jellyfish of Foxboro. Anytime he wants to lock it up in a closet and waive all legal rules, he can give me a ring. I'm listed.''

"We have our pride too," Patrick Sullivan noted.

Old Billy endorsed his son's attitude. "Guys like Davis," he sneered, "I don't want any part of them. I like the term 'Fighting Irish.' If you fight one of us, you fight us all." Nor could Billy resist taking a parting shot. "Commitment to Excellence?" he crowed, "I like Commitment to Integrity better."

Having come in at the bottom, the Sullivans could now go out at the top.

11

For Art Modell, football's new age began right where he'd left off before his heart attack.

By 1984, the first round of Modell's desperate struggle to defend his "good name" was already working its way through the appeals courts. This was Gries II, the suit charging that Modell had violated the agreement made with Gries about representation on the Browns board. The common pleas court had ruled in Gries's favor, but in December 1983, the Ohio Appeals Court had reversed the decision. In 1984, the Ohio Supreme Court had reversed the appeals court and reinstated the common pleas court's ruling. In 1985, the United States Supreme Court would refuse to hear the case, in effect upholding its Ohio counterpart and the plaintiff, Robert Gries.

As much as losing that case would displease Modell, everyone understood Gries II was more annoyance than anything else. Gries I, challenging the legality of the sale of Cleveland Stadium Corp., was a much greater danger. When Year One began, it was scheduled for trial in June. In the meantime, both elements to the suit besides Modell—Cleveland Stadium Corp. and Robert Gries—had to be dealt with.

On the stadium front, Modell continued to try to slip out from under the aging structure he had set out to refurbish a decade earlier. This time, he became one of the leading community spokesmen for a proposal to build a new $150 million domed stadium on the Cleveland waterfront. "I civically cry out for the dome as the one single catalyst that can turn the city upside down," Modell told a January dinner of the sales and marketing executives of Cleveland at which he was named Cleveland's Business Executive of the Year. "In my twenty-three years in Cleveland, I haven't seen any project that has the dynamics of this one. I'm convinced that it can turn the city around. . . .

This dome could give Cleveland the opportunity to launch itself into the twenty-first century."

By March, the Dome had become a bond proposal on the May 1984 Cuyahoga County ballot and a campaign had been launched. "Now is the time to build the dome," one of the "vote yes" brochures argued. "Right now . . . when community leaders of both parties can put aside their differences to support the dome, it says one thing. It says, Greater Cleveland is on the way back. And it says, we're back to stay. We're tired of losing jobs and losing hope. We're finally working together and that's the beginning of real pride and real progress. It may be hard to believe it's happening—but it's sure great to see!" One of the community leaders referred to by the pamphlet was, of course, Art Modell. On March 16, he endorsed the measure and said he would commit the Browns to play in the new dome as long as two conditions were met. The first was that the city "make Cleveland Stadium Corp. whole" by paying it $12 million for the work it had done on the existing Cleveland Stadium. The second condition was "that the operator of the domed stadium be from the private sector, that it not be run by a governmental body. If the city knew how to run a stadium," he pointed out, "I wouldn't be in the stadium business to begin with." Modell admitted that his Stadium Corp. was the "logical prospect" to run the new stadium, but claimed he would support it even if it wasn't his to run.

The [Cleveland] Plain Dealer columnist Jim Parker greeted Modell's endorsement with a now jaundiced eye. "Anything Else, Art?" he asked derisively. "This Art Modell is one class act. As busy as he is . . . he finds the time to lend his 'unqualified support' to efforts to construct a property tax financed, $150 million domed stadium in downtown Cleveland. Unqualified, Modell says, so long as a couple conditions—otherwise known as qualifications—are met. Modell wants somebody to reimburse him for the $12 million in capital improvements he says his Stadium Corp. has put into the city-owned stadium and he wants his new domed playground operated by the private sector. . . . Who do you think Modell has in mind when he talks about the private sector? . . . This is not a bad deal, not too shabby at all. Modell picks up $12 million [and] moves his herd into some fully carpeted digs, courtesy of property owners and renters who pay their landlords' property tax."

On May 8, Greater Cleveland voters rejected Modell's dome idea by a margin of two to one.

Art Modell was equally unsuccessful at trying to shake his shadow, Robert Gries. The two knocked sparks off each other again on day one of Year One. That January 1, an interview with Gries was published in a local paper. Earlier Modell had publicly claimed he was "proud" of the franchise's record. "If he's proud of his record," Gries responded, "we see things differently. I'm embarrassed by the record over the last ten years." Modell did not take the crack lying down. "Modell's chief lieutenant wrote a letter to Rozelle," Gries remembered, "saying that I should be fined for criticizing a fellow owner publicly. I wrote back an answer and then I met with Rozelle about it. I said I had shown great restraint and that it was not the same as a direct criticism to comment on the team's record. Nothing was ever done about it.'' Modell and Gries clashed again at a summer banquet honoring the old 1964 Browns team that won the NFL championship, the last Browns team to do so. The dinner was held at the hotel on Public Square in whose note the Browns, thanks to Art Modell, owned a two-ninths share. At the ceremonies, the *Akron Beacon Journal* observed, "owner Art Modell, the man who literally sold Cleveland Stadium Corp. to himself for $6 million, sat proudly at the dais. Down on the floor of the grand ballroom, far to the left of the head table, sat Bob Gries.'' One of the main events of the evening was the showing of a commemorative slide show from the Browns' last championship season. The football slides were interspersed with advertising slides, purchased by individuals and corporations to help finance the banquet. Robert Gries bought one that was flashed on the screen. It contained his name and only his name. By this point, of course, he needed to say no more.

It seemed Robert Gries was blemishing Art Modell's reputation in every direction he turned and on that level, it was a relief for Modell finally to face off with his adversary when *Gries Sports Enterprises v. Cleveland Browns* came to trial in June 1984. Both men were reported to have spent more than $1 million apiece on legal fees. Gries paid his own and Modell's were charged to the Browns, meaning Gries paid for forty-three percent of the defense's case as well as one hundred percent of the plaintiff's. The trial lasted some two months and virtually all of it was spent dissecting the two-year-old transaction that Modell had used to pay off his burgeoning debts. "Time Has Stopped in 1982 for Browns Trial," the *Beacon Journal* noted. From Modell's perspective, it was, of course, a bad place to stop. Even if the judge ruled in his favor, he was still losing every day in the courtroom as his less than impressive finances were dragged into the open for all of Cleveland to see.

"Did you ever have a problem raising a million dollars for anything?'' Modell was asked under oath.

"No,'' he answered.

Both Art Modell and Robert Gries were in the courtroom virtually every day of the trial but the two did not exchange words, passing each other silently in the hallway outside. Modell kept a proud front, but by the time the case was taken by Judge John L. Angelotta to consider before ruling, it seemed Modell was in trouble. That sense was confirmed on August 2, when the judge issued a strongly worded letter telling Modell to settle the dispute by August 30 or else. If that settlement didn't occur, the court would void the Stadium Corp. sale. "A knowledgeable buyer," the judge noted, "under no restraint and without compulsion to act would not consummate this transaction.'' He suggested Modell separate the Strongsville land and the hotel note from the rest of the deal. Modell, however, would have nothing to do with it, calling the judge's letter "beyond comprehension.'' A source close to the case described the ruling as "just another nail in the coffin of Art Modell's ownership.''

That nail was driven home on August 30. Since no settlement had been reached, the judge entered his final judgment. "Defendants have failed to prove $6 million was a fair price," he observed. "The directors who voted in favor of the transaction abused their discretion." The deal benefited only Modell, "rather than serving the best interests of the Browns." The court ordered Modell to pay back the $6 million to the Browns plus interest calculated from March 1982, when the original transaction had been made. He also intended to appoint an accountant to determine if the Browns had lost any other money as a consequence of the Stadium Corp. acquisition. If they had, Modell would have to pay that as well.

Modell's attorneys immediately appealed the decision and got a stay of the judge's order. "Art wants his vindication," one of them noted, "and he'll get it."

In the meantime, Art Modell's reputation in Cleveland had taken a significant beating. When Ronald Reagan visited the city during the last days before his November 1984 reelection, Modell was one of the dignitaries on the platform at his appearance. When Modell was introduced to the crowd, he was greeted with boos.

On April 25, 1985, the Ohio Court of Appeals reversed the lower court in the matter of Gries I, ruling that the court was in no position to second-guess a corporate board. This time Robert Gries appealed. For his part, Art Modell stopped short of claiming vindication. "This thing has been beaten to a pulp already," he offered. "I'll let the decision of the court speak for itself."

New age or not, Art Modell still had a long way to go in making his "good name" whole.

12

Year One was, of course, Al Davis's year.

It surprised no one when he proved a less than magnanimous winner. "Rozelle needs to go to work and get out of the courtroom," Davis slashed upon receiving the news that his victory was complete, "get out of Congress, get off the tennis courts, get out of the race tracks, get out of the social circles, get out of his vendettas, and be the commissioner again for the League. I'm sure the National Football League has greatness in the future, even though the last five years have been a downer. . . . If during the last five years Pete Rozelle had channeled all the energies of the entire NFL and channeled all the money that was spent on the Raiders' case into promoting the League, we'd have a tremendous climate for professional football. I think for five years this guy has done nothing but carry on this vendetta. All this energy, instead of spending it on the player strike, promoting the game, new ideas, new concepts, this guy carried his vendetta to the ultimate.''

By this time, the *Los Angeles Times* observed, ''no football fan in America needs to be told who Al Davis is.'' His *LAMCC v. NFL* victory had set the Davis legend in concrete.

''If Al Davis had decided he wanted to be president,'' the man who gave him his first college coaching job observed, ''he could have done it. He's that brilliant.''

''I think Al Davis has the serial number of the unknown soldier,'' an NFL coach commented.

''Al Davis has spent most of his life looking for weaknesses in people,'' one of the losing attorneys in *LAMCC v. NFL* noted, ''because he believes in life there are only winners and losers.''

''Sure I like to win,'' Davis said of himself, ''and I do have this belief and commitment to excellence. Achievement is important to me. Achievement for the entire organization. If some say I'm hard-nosed, yeah, I am . . . I just hope that someday this team would be recognized, if it isn't already, as the greatest team of all time in any sport.'' Davis also dismissed all the commissioner's talk about anarchy. ''As Rozelle always does when he's defeated in court and he can't get his way,'' Davis claimed, ''he predicts doom, anarchy, free agency, all the words that are used to create fear in the minds of people, when in reality it's not true.''

What was true, according to Davis, was that the football business was changing and his move to L.A. had been no more than a response to a change that was already happening. ''I foresaw that in the eighties no longer would it be hard work and intelligence,'' he observed, ''but another factor was coming into professional sports that would determine who wins—economics. . . . I don't think that I'm any different than most other owners. I really don't. It's just that my life is professional football. Most of them, their lives are independent businesses and things like that.'' Whatever the rules of the game were and whoever might be playing, Al Davis still had few if any doubts about whether he would end up on top. ''I've always been on top ever since I was a kid,'' he pointed out. ''I think problems are normal in life. What most people call problems I would call something we've got to solve, something we've got to get a solution to and take care of in the normal course of business. Not respond to it as a special case. I treat problems as normal.''

Even with Year One in full sway, the League's diehards still had hopes that the problems Davis had in Los Angeles would not prove as tractable as he anticipated.

The first of those was the continued absence of a lease with the Coliseum. As 1984 began, the Raiders' negotiations with the LAMCC remained stalemated. ''We have gone through numerous drafts,'' one of the Coliseum's negotiators noted. ''New issues have been raised by the Raiders . . . and their legal staff has not come down for six to eight months to talk about them. They haven't come down.'' The impasse began to dissipate when Bill Robertson was reappointed to the LAMCC in June 1984, this time by Mayor Tom

Bradley. "I felt that ultimately the deal would be finalized," Robertson commented, "but some people felt I should be back on." Robertson quickly pointed out that the Raiders had "kept their moral obligations" by moving south on their own and argued that "they are looking for us to keep our contract." At issue specifically was a $6.7 million "loan," due to Davis that a number of commissioners described as a "gift" because of its extraordinarily favorable terms.

On November 15, the LAMCC put that issue to rest by agreeing to make the payment: $2.7 million would be paid as $675,000 a year rent credit already in place and scheduled to run through 1985. The remaining $4 million was handed over in cash on November 30. According to one source close to the negotiations, Davis's negotiating posture "greatly improved" once the payment was made. On December 9, he finally signed a ten-year lease with three five-year options. According to Robertson, its terms were "basically the same as the memorandum of agreement" first signed in March 1980.

Lease or not, there was still a question as to whether Davis could draw enough fans in his new hometown to make the move worthwhile. "Once the court case was resolved," Tex Schramm noted, "the Raiders are like any other franchise. They're new in town and they have no longterm following. The Raiders image may not work in L.A." That hope, too, was quashed in no uncertain fashion during the 1984 season. On November 4, Al Davis's franchise set an NFL regular season single game revenue record, selling 92,469 tickets to a game with the Denver Broncos, a gross of $1,596,000. Averaging over 70,000 in attendance for each of its eight home games, the Raiders also set a single season revenue record, grossing some $10 million. "After All the Hassles," the *San Francisco Examiner* headlined, "Davis Finds a Pot of Gold in L.A." Hopes that Al Davis's grip on L.A. would slip of its own accord were dead by 1985.

In their place, two last-ditch options remained. The first was Rozelle's favorite. According to this scenario, the damage award from *LAMCC v. NFL*, which the League was still appealing in a process separate from the decision itself, would finally be ruled upon by the appeals court. At that point, the decision could be rejoined to the damages and appealed again to the Supreme Court, which could then rule in the League's favor and thwart Davis in a dramatic last stand. Outside of the commissioner's immediate circle, however, there were few League members prepared to place any more hope in legal rescue. Many more hoped that, instead, Davis could be induced to settle the damages before they were finalized, reducing the League's financial obligation significantly. Throughout the process of appealing the damages, the award was growing by leaps and bounds. The legal expenses of Davis and the LAMCC, for which the League was one hundred percent liable, were expanding daily, and the award itself was subject to ten percent interest. By the time the League gathered for its 1985 annual meeting in Phoenix during the third week of March, the figure had reached somewhere between $70 and $80 million. "By our calculations," one owner pointed out, "if the courts grant the damages requested, we stand to lose $2.5 to $3 million per team. We are hoping to get that figure below $2 million. These aren't the best of times in this League, you know.''

Considerable tension surrounded that hope at the 1985 annual meeting in Phoenix on the afternoon of March 13, when Davis took the floor to address the rest of the League. He had been working intensely on his speech for several weeks and used a few notes while he made his points. ''I told them all the things I had talked about for five years,'' Davis explained. ''That they tried to beat me, that they're still trying to beat me, but nothing is going to change the fact that I'm in L.A.'' He also pointed out what he had won for all of them along the way. Because of his move, franchises' leverage in the superstadium game had made a quantum leap and that made everyone more money than they could have otherwise hoped for. Instead of thanking him, Davis complained, they did the opposite. Davis considered his speech ''tough talk'' and warned the rest of the League that it had better ''get me straightened out.'' The League was ''waving swords at windmills'' by continuing to pursue him. ''There are more important issues to address,'' he insisted, and ''this thing should be put to bed as soon as possible.''

The meeting at which Davis spoke was, by all accounts, a tense scene. ''There was so much bitterness in the room at times,'' one of those present noted, ''it's hard to believe these guys can run their other businesses one way, in an orderly fashion, and run the League like this.'' Hard to believe or not, bitterness was the NFL's new dominant mode. ''He has left a lot of open wounds,'' one NFL executive explained, ''and even if we settle for less out of court, I doubt anybody will consider it a magnanimous gesture by Al.'' The last estimate, of course, significantly underestimated the degree to which the League was worried about its mounting bill to him. Each day that passed with the *LAMCC v. NFL* judgment outstanding cost the League another fifteen thousand dollars.

''So what's the bottom line, Al?'' one owner finally demanded of Davis. ''Can we get this thing settled?''

Davis answered that he thought that is exactly what ought to be discussed.

In response, the assembled League gave Al Davis a standing ovation.

Alex Spanos, the new owner of the San Diego Chargers, spoke for the pro-Davis sentiment which emerged inside the League in response to Davis's opening. ''After all,'' Spanos pointed out, ''we have already lost the case, so let's clean up the rest of it as soon as possible. You know the man is outstanding in this business. I think he's the best there is. Just look at what he has said and look at what has happened. He's been right all along in many cases. I just hope they keep talking until this thing is resolved. I, for one, would prefer to be his ally rather than his adversary. It's hard enough to beat him on the field. We don't need the rest of this too.''

The conditions Davis placed on his offer to discuss settlement were that the League respond within seventy-two hours and that Rozelle be directly involved. For his part, Rozelle insisted that another owner be involved as well. The commissioner wanted no part of conversations with Davis that didn't include a witness. The witness chosen was John Nordstrom of the

Seattle Seahawks. During the last two days of the annual meeting, Rozelle, Davis, and Nordstrom met briefly on two occasions. "Davis invited discussion on a possible settlement," Rozelle admitted to reporters on March 16, "so I did meet with him. It's difficult to characterize the discussions at this point, other than to say there will be further talks."

That there had been talks at all was, of course, historic. After ten years of skirmishing and five years of outright war, it was the first time Al Davis and Pete Rozelle had ever discussed a formula for settling Davis's differences with the League. It must have been a satisfying moment for the managing general partner of the Los Angeles Raiders. He now had the upper hand and the commissioner had to come to him in pursuit of terms. It was a heady position for someone who had struggled so hard to reach it and what happened next, one NFL insider remembered, was that Davis "overplayed his hand."

After the annual meeting adjourned, Nordstrom and Davis met out on the Pacific Coast and then Rozelle, Nordstrom, and Davis had a conference call. Davis, Rozelle remembered, "threw down the gauntlet in a strident way." His offer was also, in financial terms, much less than his fellow owners had hoped for. "He wanted to settle at ninety-two cents on the dollar," Rozelle explained. "John Nordstrom and I informed the clubs that we couldn't recommend it. There was no interest by the clubs in the offer. It just wasn't a settlement worth considering. The most common response was, 'That's not settlement, that's capitulation.' "

By April 1985, the discussions about settlement had ended and both sides of *LAMCC v. NFL* resumed their wait for an appeals court ruling on the damages that ought to be assessed.

None of it changed Al Davis's attitude about Pete Rozelle one with. The commissioner, Davis observed, was still "scurrilous" and "a fraud."

On june 16, 1986, the Federal Appeals Court returned the Raiders' *LAMCC v. NFL* damage judgment to the lower court, ruling it excessive in light of the financial "windfall," provided the franchise by its move from Oakland to Los Angeles. It was Al Davis's first loss in ten years. "Obviously I don't feel good," Davis noted. "We would have liked to have won."

13

Pete Rozelle did not simply roll over in the face of the football business's new age, but there was little he could do save try to salvage whatever status and power remained to him. The commissioner's Year One both began and ended on the defensive and Year Two would be no different.

The opening defense of 1984 was in response to the irritated faction championed by Jack Kent Cooke. *The Boston Globe* described it as "the most

serious challenge Rozelle has had in his twenty-four years in office.'' At
Super Bowl XVIII in January, Cooke was claiming fifteen owners who were
''upset'' with the way Rozelle had run things. Spurred on by the League's
declining economics, Cooke's group blamed Rozelle for the Los Angeles
damage judgment hanging over their heads and, like Carroll Rosenbloom
years earlier, complained about how much of their money the commissioner's
office was spending. The Tampa Super Bowl had only exacerbated their anger.
There, Rozelle's office had spent $500,000 on a party for the press and the
commissioner and Carrie had stayed in a suite that cost $1500 a night. Adding
further to the owners' heat was the fact that Rozelle was now finishing the second
year of a new ten-year contract and, except for the three-man committee who
had awarded it to him, none of the men paying his salary even knew what it was.

If this rumbling among his employers was indeed what the *Globe* claimed
for it, the Cooke rebellion served only to demonstrate how entrenched in
office Pete Rozelle was. In truth, Cooke had ten votes at best to unseat
Rozelle, and the League's constitution required at least twenty-one votes in
order for the commissioner to be dismissed. Rozelle was in no danger of
losing his job. He was, however, quite obviously losing his control. The sole
victory of Cooke's rebellion symbolized as much. It took place at the March
meeting in Chicago at which Rozelle asked Robert Irsay to let him know as
soon as possible if and when he was leaving Baltimore. At that meeting, the
clamor to know what Rozelle's contract contained could no longer be ignored.
Being kept in the dark, the dissident minority complained, was an example of
the commissioner ''blatantly showing arrogance and power.'' At the March
meeting, Leon Hess, chairman of the committee that had negotiated that
contract, read it to the group. According to a knowledgeable NFL source, it
specified that Rozelle would receive $700,000 a year in salary and another
$25,000 a year in deferred income. Once Hess was finished with the recita-
tion, there was little else the Cooke dissidents could do but stand back and
watch the commissioner struggle against the tide.

By the end of Year One, examples of Rozelle's less than successful
flailings were piling up: Irsay left for Indianapolis, Eddie DeBartolo faced the
League down, the football business's economics began going berserk, and Al
Davis further entrenched himself in L.A. It was in the arena of franchise
movement that the commissioner's new impotence was most apparent. Irsay
was, of course, only the beginning. Leonard Tose's flirtation with Phoenix
came next. Though Tose's lack of cash and Philadelphia's willingness to
rewrite the Eagles' lease kept his franchise in Pennsylvania, Rozelle understood
there were only more such flirtations in the wings and, in most, the commissioner
might well lack the kind of leverage he had over Tose. In response, the
commissioner attempted to shore up what remained of his position.

The shoring up took the form of a new League policy on franchise
movement, promulgated by Rozelle in an attempt to at least partially replace
the outlawed Section 4.3. In it, the League committed itself for the first time
to a concrete list of procedures and standards that had to be followed if a
franchise wished to change home turfs. Rozelle distributed it to his employers
on December 21. It was, of course, a step Al Davis had been calling for since

1978. Specifically, the new doctrine required all franchises to file a "statement of reasons" by January 15 of the year in which they intended to move. The reasons had to include comparisons of the franchise's home revenues with League averages, ticket sales projections, information on the new site, and a description of the effects on other teams' travel expenses and the like. Included with the statement had to be a copy of the franchise's existing lease, audited financial statements for the preceding four years, a financial analysis of the new lease, and a projection of profits and losses for the next three years in the new location.

A spokesman for the commissioner described the new policy to *The New York Times* as one which "basically reaffirms the approach the NFL has always taken." Such criteria were only now being formalized, the spokesman observed, "because prior to 1980, there was no reason to billboard the objective factors that the League evaluated in any proposed transfer since no NFL team had seriously proposed to move for twenty years. If the League had promulgated 'standards' while the Raiders case was going through the appeals process, I'm sure critics would have falsely charged that this was an admission on our part that the old rule was illegal." Coming when it did, this new policy was "taking what the League feels is a proper course in handling an issue about which there is no consensus, on either a judicial or a legislative level." In fact, it was a somewhat galling act for Rozelle and one in which he had little faith. Rather than reducing the League's legal vulnerability, he worried it would only open up a multitude of further legal dilemmas. The policy, he pointed out, was only voluntary and "could easily be challenged" by any owner bent on going to court.

His doubts were confirmed less than a month after the policy was promulgated. In January 1985, two franchises gave official notification that Rozelle's promulgation was unacceptable and would be ignored. One of the franchises was the New Orleans Saints, owned by John Mecom. Mecom, the Saints owner since the team came into existence as the price Rozelle was prepared to pay to get the merger with the AFL through Congress, was in the process of trying to sell the club and wanted the latitude to extract the highest possible bid, either through forcing a renegotiation with his Superdome landlords or selling the franchise to another city. Mecom's attorneys dispatched a letter to Rozelle, shortly before Super Bowl XIX in San Francisco, notifying the League that the franchise "reserved the right" to relocate under the provisions of *LAMCC v. NFL* and would not recognize the new policy should the Saints choose to move. This potential challenge was short-lived and was resolved within two months when Mecom sold the franchise to a New Orleans auto dealer, Tom Benson, for $65 million. Part of the deal included a $15 million loan guarantee by the state of Louisiana and a significant reduction of lease costs. All told, it proved a short and lucrative venture in the League's continuing superstadium game.

The other challenge that confirmed Rozelle's doubts was not so easily resolved. It came from Billy Bidwill's St. Louis Cardinals. Bidwill's attorneys had been the first to file a letter of exception with the commissioner's office and to claim their rights under *LAMCC v. NFL*. The letter created an ironic juxtaposition. Bidwill owned the only franchise in the Rozelle era to transfer under the outlawed Section 4.3 and Bidwill had also served on the fact-finding committee that had investigated Al Davis's proposed move to Los Angeles and found it wanting. "He was on the committee that said I shouldn't move," Davis pointed out with a certain satisfaction, "but in recent weeks he has come up to me and said he shouldn't have done what he did. Now he realizes what I went through." Bidwill's move was prompted by his own superstadium game with St. Louis. Busch Stadium, the Cardinals' home field, had the second smallest capacity in the NFL, the franchise had the League's second lowest average attendance, and the fourth lowest season ticket sales, despite filling the stadium to an average of ninety-three percent of capacity. Bidwill wanted the city to build him a new eighty-thousand-seat stadium in the suburbs and the city wasn't going for it. As a consequence, Bidwill had begun discussions with both New York City and Phoenix about moving the Cardinals to either of those cities.

Those discussions lasted through 1985 without resolution, but the situation escalated anyway when, at the end of Year Two, Busch Stadium sued Bidwill to prevent him from breaking his St. Louis lease. That in turn led to a meeting between Bidwill, Rozelle, and their respective attorneys, early in 1986, at which Bidwill announced he was suing the League to prevent it from enforcing Rozelle's new policy and to insure that the *LAMCC v. NFL* precedent was applied to the Cardinals, should they choose to move. "I tried to dissuade him," Rozelle remembered. The attempt was unsuccessful and the suit was filed. By then, of course, Rozelle's disillusionment with his own policy had been significantly enlarged. "I implemented specific procedures in response to the appeals court decision in the Davis case," he explained, "but I really felt it was just a license to litigate. Bidwill's suit was the first example." In the old days, Pete Rozelle could have handled a relative nonentity like Billy Bidwill with a minimum of effort.

The old days, however, were long since dead in the NFL, even on TV. The commissioner who could do no wrong now seemed snakebit whichever direction he turned. Not only had his leverage evaporated, the video bonanza which had generated it had gone south with much of the rest of the Rozelle era as well. The news on the television front was perhaps the worst of football's new age. What had once seemed an insatiable demand for whatever the League broadcast was suddenly proving significantly less marketable. The "slippage" had begun in 1983, the first full season after the disastrous 1982 strike, when instead of climbing back to 1981 levels, ratings sank. CBS's Sunday games went from a 15.4 rating and a 39 share to 14.5 and a 36 share, NBC's dropped from 12.3 and 33 to 11.1 and 27, and ABC's Monday night prime time games collapsed from 21.1 and 37 to 17.8 and 31. Those most upset by the drop were, of course, the advertisers who were paying the networks between $220,000 and $370,000 a minute to display their products next to the League's. "If I had to guess right now," one ad agency executive observed of the 1983 figures, "I would think that the three networks will have some trouble selling football next year." To help ease the networks' burden, Rozelle exercised his remaining powers and unilaterally enlarged the ad space available on League broadcasts from twenty-four minutes a game to twenty-five. "There were no negotiations about it," Rozelle remembered. "I just gave it to them."

Nonetheless, the deterioration only continued in 1984. Two months into the season, CBS had fallen to a 12.6 rating and 31 share, NBC to 9.9 and 25, and ABC to 16.1 and 29. Super Bowl XIX drew more than 110 million viewers and Super Bowl XX drew 120 million, but the regular season was an ongoing disaster for the broadcasters who had bet $2 billion over five years that the ratings would go up instead of down. Even when the ratings improved in 1985, advertisers continued to shy away. "Each week during the 1985 NFL season," *Sports Illustrated* reported, "network ad salesmen held what became known as Friday afternoon fire sales. Like an airline selling standby seats at discount before a departure, the networks booked unsold commercial spots below their full price rates. Some commercial time was sold for less than 1983 and 1984 prices."

By the time 1986 began, the NFL, once a goose that laid golden eggs, was a network money-loser. Because of the exorbitant terms of the rights contract they had signed in 1982 and under which they had only one more year to broadcast, the 1985 NFL season cost CBS and NBC some $15 million each in red ink while ABC lost at least $25 million. ABC had even begun talking publicly about dropping prime time football altogether. Simply put, the NFL's advertising revenue base had diminished considerably, thanks to the plethora of other football games now available on cable and pay-for-view television. Worse still, the NFL's demography—an audience of males between the ages of nineteen and forty-nine—had decreased in value. Where once potential NFL viewers had bought almost all the nation's automobiles, for example, now at least half those cars were purchased by women who watched *Murder, She Wrote* or *Cagney and Lacey*. Whether Rozelle could get another $2 billion, five-year deal was suddenly very much up for grabs. In January 1986, Rozelle said he expected only a "modest increase" under the next contract. A month later, he declined to predict any increase at all. For their part, the networks claimed increase was out of the question.

One effect of the flattening of the League's video future was to close off yet another of the commissioner's dwindling number of options. Having lost the power base he had built with the escalation of television, he would not be able to regain it the same way. The saturation point had been reached and Pete Rozelle would have to turn in another direction if he were ever to put League Think back together. The direction he chose, however, was also familiar. From the beginning of Year One, the commissioner had begun commuting to Washington, D.C., in hopes of reviving the breakout strategy that had failed in 1981 and 1982. By April 1984, Congress was again, at Rozelle's urging, considering a professional sports team community protection act, proposing at least partial NFL exemption from the antitrust laws.

The 1984 version of the legislation had a very familiar look at first. It allowed the League to control franchise movement without interference from the Sherman Act and made such control retroactive to cover both the Raiders and the Colts. As in 1981 and 1982, however, this retroactive element made passage impossible. "It's ridiculous to push for retroactivity," one NFL owner complained. "We could get this thing passed in a minute if Pete would drop this vendetta against Al Davis." Senator Richard Lugar of Indiana confirmed that judgment. "This legislation won't get anywhere in its current form," he pointed out. With or without retroactivity, the renewed effort to break out made it readily apparent that Rozelle had lost his influence over the legislative process as well. By the time the 1984 Sports Community Protection Act was reported out of the Senate Commerce Committee by a nine to eight vote, it had assumed a form that the League couldn't stomach. The revised bill set up legal requirements for future team moves and established a three-member arbitration board, on which the NFL had only one seat, to rule on all such moves. The proposal, a spokesman for Rozelle noted in announcing the League's opposition, "is a quick-fix solution to a complex problem. It will complicate, not clarify, the question of sports franchise locations, which already is subject of conflicting states' and federal law."

Rozelle's once magic congressional touch succeeded only in keeping something worse off the books during 1984. In 1985 the picture was little different, even though the League's strategy changed somewhat. In his 1985 lobbying campaign, the commissioner dropped retroactivity once and for all. He also made it clear he was prepared to barter. "I personally," Rozelle told Congress, "and the other owners in the League feel a responsibility, when Congress passes something for you, to give a quid pro quo to show a sense of responsibility for that action." In this instance, the quid pro quo was NFL expansion by two, if and when the League's Sherman Act status was "clarified." While the offer was tempting, no such legislation was passed during 1985.

When 1986 began, however, the commissioner had managed to get "five or six senators" interested in what he called "a compromise bill." This legislation would subject the League to various criteria for the consideration of moves but give the League back the right to approve or disapprove by three-quarters vote. It also established their right to share their television money by three-quarters vote and the right to approve all new owners. The latter two were both areas in which Rozelle realistically expected to have to fight court cases in the decade to come. Robert Dole of Kansas, Senate majority leader, was prepared to bring the bill to the floor, but was stymied by the threat of a filibuster led by Senator Albert Gore Jr. of Tennessee. Gore's position was that expansion by two was insufficient and any exemption ought to net at least expansion by six.

"The NFL is rushing Congress to grant blanket antitrust exemptions," Gore argued, "that would give the League unprecedented power to control the marketplace. Fans want to watch football, but a majority of owners would rather play Monopoly. . . . In fact, [this legislation] would give the League even greater leverage to ignore loyal fans and shun market forces. Although it would please current owners, nothing would be done about the shortage of franchises that brought on the rush of team moves in the first place. . . . Never before has the NFL asked for so much running room. In the past, the League tempered its antitrust requests by agreeing to add new teams. . . . Yet in the years since the [AFL] merger, the NFL has expanded by only two teams—Tampa Bay and Seattle. There has been no expansion for ten years. So many cities are hungry for pro football that they have launched a bidding war to lure away established teams. . . . Instead of meeting the demand for more teams, the League seeks antitrust exemptions to give itself control over team movement and all team revenues. . . . This time they are privately promising to stop any more team moves. Senators from states that already have teams are understandably eager to secure such promises. But the underlying problem is the scarcity of teams and the only real answer is expansion."

Faced with Gore's roadblock, Rozelle simply stood his ground. Citing "all the unknowns on the part of the owners," specifically the upcoming 1986 labor negotiations and the television negotiations scheduled to be completed in 1987, Rozelle rejected the idea of six new franchises out of hand. "There is no way to expand on that basis," he declared. With that, stalemate once again descended on the commissioner's congressional front.

Pete Rozelle still pursued his agenda doggedly, but behind his brave front, football's new age was tinged with a deep weariness. "This job," he admitted in November 1984, "is not as much fun as it once was." There was little to break the omnipresent sense of collapse and disorder and even less in the way of good news. The best of it was personal. Though Rozelle had experienced a comedown from the glory days, he was at least assured that his place in history would be remembered. That assurance came on January 26, 1985, the first day of his twenty-sixth year as commissioner, when the Pro Football Hall of Fame's panel of judges selected him for induction.

The induction took place on August 3, 1985, in Canton, Ohio, home of the Hall of Fame and the long-demolished Hupmobile showroom where the NFL originated. Rozelle and the four former players inducted with him brought the total of men so honored to 128. Most were players or coaches but among the League's own past honorees were Bert Bell, the man Rozelle succeeded; George Halas and George Preston Marshall, the two men he'd had to face down to get control when still the "boy czar"; Art Rooney, the resident NFL saint and still Rozelle's staunchest backer; and Lamar Hunt, who'd been inducted in 1972 as an honor to the old AFL, the most successful competitor in the NFL's history. Rozelle himself called the induction itself "a big moment."

August 3 was typically muggy in Canton and the inductees were each introduced to the crowd gathered round the hall's front steps by a presenter of their choice. Rozelle selected Tex Schramm. The ceremony began with an invocation by the Reverend Peggy Ecia of Canton's Unity Church. "Father," she beseeched, "we are grateful for this wonderful day you have given to us. We are grateful for the great honor which you have given to each one of us to be here today and we especially pray for these enshrined today. We know that you have chosen them, you have selected them. We know that you have guided them through the years. . . .''

Next, Schramm presented his old friend Pete Rozelle. Speaking of the selection of Rozelle at the Kenilworth Hotel in 1960, Schramm observed that "when they made that decision, they probably didn't know it at the time, [but] they probably made one of the most important and wisest decisions that they could have made. Because . . . they selected a man for the times. A man that was prepared to lead [the NFL] through a new era and that man was thirty-three-year-old Pete Rozelle. We are now twenty-six years later honoring that man. But when he was selected, few people realized what they had obtained as their leader. . . . They had obtained a man of tremendous intelligence, foresight, patience, preparation, tenacity, a will to win, and a sense of class and he imparted that through the League and he also had the background to make it work because he was young and had grown with the new giant, television. . . . He handled all the threats to the integrity of the game and he handled them with dignity. He went through the pains of growth because no sport experienced the growth that the NFL did in the past twenty-five years. . . . From the very beginning he said, I don't care what it is, what it takes, we are going to do it with class and with style, something that we can be proud of. . . . He had the foresight. . . . So you have a man here that you are honoring very properly. A man that is very deserving. A man who has stood very tall and who you will look upon for many, many years when you think about the NFL. Probably the greatest commissioner the sport has ever had, the commissioner of the NFL, Alvin Ray Pete Rozelle.''

The crowd greeted the commissioner affectionately. Looking out at them, Rozelle was "surprised at how many of my friends and relatives from California had come. It was a time of a lot of memories. I reflected on all the changes and thought about the seriousness of it all.''

Little of that reflection came out in Rozelle's speech. "The commissioner's job, of course, is very unique,'' he observed. "You are hired by the owners, but you are called upon to make decisions that affect them. You can't please everyone, every time. . . . You simply have to do what you think in your judgment is in the best interest of the game. . . . When I became involved in the NFL, I realized that it was a great reservoir of talent, ability, and willingness to help. . . . I feel very fortunate to have always worked at what I love. I don't go out and stamp things on an assembly line. I was blessed. I was always able to work in sports, particularly the National Football League. I can only say that I feel very happy, proud, and so grateful to be here today.''

Once again, the crowd responded warmly. The applause was genuine. No one had the bad manners to spoil the moment by pointing out that the honor amounted to a consolation prize.

CHAPTER NOTES

The chapter notes that follow list the principal sources I have used in writing this book. They are by no means exhaustive but are intended to give the reader a general overview of my research.

1/1.

NFL minutes, 2/25/74, 3/20/72, 3/24/72, 4/2/73.
NFL constitution and bylaws.
INTERVIEWS:
    Gene Klein, 9/14/83.
    Pete Rozelle, 6/5, 6/6/84.
    Leonard Tose, 10/3/84.
    Jack Kent Cooke, 9/27/83.
    Tex Schramm, 9/15/83.
    Lamar Hunt, 9/22/83.
    Art Modell, 9/14/83.
    Bill McPhail, 9/7/84.
    2 NFL executives, confidential.
TESTIMONY:
    Edward Bennett Williams, *NASL v. NFL*, 4/7/80.
Official NFL Record and Fact Book. New York: Workman Publishing Company, 1985.
Noll, Roger [ed.], *Government and the Sports Business*, Brookings Institute, 1974.
New York Times Magazine, 1/15/84.
Sports Illustrated, 1/6/64.
Christian Century, 4/5/72.
Esquire, 11/72.
Time, 4/5/82.
New York Times, 7/20/73.

1/2.

INTERVIEWS:
    Pete Rozelle, 8/9/83, 8/25/83, 10/17/83, 6/6/84.
    Tex Schramm, 9/15/83.
    Wellington Mara, 10/17/84.
    Ken Macker, 9/26/83.
    Bill McPhail, 9/13/83.
TESTIMONY:
    Pete Rozelle, *LAMCC v. NFL*, 4/2/82.

SPEECHES:
    Pete Rozelle, 1985 Hall of Fame Enshrinement Program.
    Tex Schramm, 1985 Hall of Fame Enshrinement Program.
NFL Record and Fact Book.
Sports Illustrated, 1/6/64.
[Baltimore] *Sun,* 10/13/59.

1/3.

INTERVIEWS:
    Pete Rozelle, 8/9/83, 6/5/84.
    Dan Rooney, 9/19/83.
    Lamar Hunt, 9/20/84.
    Bill McPhail, 9/23/83.
    NFL owner, confidential.
TESTIMONY:
    Pete Rozelle, *LAMCC v. NFL,* 4/5/82,
        NASL v. NFL, 4/16/80, 4/21/80,
        Hearings before the Subcommittee on Monopolies and Commercial Law,
        U.S. Congress, 10/14/75,
        Hearings before the House Select Committee on Professional Sports,
        U.S. Congress, 6/23/76.
DEPOSITIONS:
    Pete Rozelle, *LAMCC v. NFL,* 8/27/80.
NFL Record and Fact Book.
Noll, *Government and the Sports Business.*
Rozelle, Pete, "NFL TV History," *New York Times,* 9/2/79.
New York Times Magazine, 1/15/84.
Sports Illustrated, 1/6/64.
New York Times, 4/18/82.

1/4.

INTERVIEWS:
    Pete Rozelle, 8/9/83, 8/25/83, 6/5/84, 6/11/84.
    Bill McPhail, 9/23/83, 9/7/84.
    6 friends of Pete Rozelle, confidential.
    NFL executive, confidential.
    Rozelle critic, confidential.

1/5.

INTERVIEWS:
    Gene Klein, 9/16/83, 9/14/84.
    Lamar Hunt, 9/22/83.
    Leonard Tose, 9/23/83.
    Art Modell, 9/14/83, 11/9/84.
    Tex Schramm, 9/18/84.
    Billy Sullivan, 10/19/84.
    Pete Rozelle, 6/5/84.

TESTIMONY:

Art Modell, *Gries Sports Enterprises v. Cleveland Browns*, 7/12/84.
Edward Bennett Williams, *NASL v. NFL*, 4/7/80.
Pete Rozelle, Hearings before the Committee of the Judiciary, U.S. Senate, 8/16/82.
Theodore Kheel, Hearings before the Subcommittee on Labor-Management Relations, U.S. Congress, 10/2/75.

DEPOSITIONS:

Al Davis, *LAMCC v. NFL*, 3/4/81.
Arthur Anderson & Co., *National Football League Management Council, Member Clubs of the National Football League—Pro Forma Combined Statement of Income for the 1973 Playing Season.*
Arthur Anderson & Co., *NFL Management Council, Member Clubs of the National Football League—Pro Forma Combined Statement of Income for 1974 Playing Season.*
Noll, *Government and the Sports Business.*
Esquire, 11/21/78.
Fortune, 3/73.
Time, 9/6/71.
Popular Mechanics, 11/73.
U.S. News and World Report, 4/12/74.
[Cleveland] *Plain Dealer*, 9/18/66.
Philadelphia Inquirer, 9/6/70.
Miami Herald, 7/8/76.

1/6.

INTERVIEWS:

Tex Schramm, 9/18/84.
Lamar Hunt, 9/20/84.
Pete Rozelle, 6/5/84.
Joe Alioto, 2/1/85.
NFL owner, confidential.
2 NFL executives, confidential.
Chipman, Donald, et al. *The Dallas Cowboys and the NFL*, University of Oklahoma Press, 1970.
Sports Illustrated, 6/20/66.
Dallas Morning News, 11/14/83, 11/16/83, 11/20/83.
Dallas Times Herald, 1/28/84.
Kansas City Times, 4/1/75.

1/7.

NFL Record and Fact Book.
Chipman, *The Dallas Cowboys and the NFL.*
Esquire, 9/72.
Dallas Times Herald, 5/25/75.
Dallas Morning News, 6/17/81.

1/8.

INTERVIEWS:

Art Modell, 9/14/83, 11/9/84.
Pete Rozelle, 6/11/84.
Robert Gries, 10/11/84, 10/12/84.
NFL executive, confidential.
NFL sportswriter, confidential.

TESTIMONY:

Art Modell, *Gries Sports Enterprises v. Cleveland Browns,* 7/12/84.
Robert Gries, *Gries Sports Enterprises v. Cleveland Browns,* 6/20/84.
Cleveland Browns press release, 4/78.
Akron Beacon Journal, 1/16/83, 1/17/83.
[Cleveland] *Plain Dealer,* 3/24/61, 9/18/66, 9/4/82.
Cleveland Press, 6/1/68.
Austin Statesman, 5/19/39.

1/9.

INTERVIEWS:

Robert Gries, 10/11/84, 10/12/84.
NFL executive, confidential.

TESTIMONY:

Art Modell, *Gries Sports Enterprises v. Cleveland Browns,* 6/18/84, 7/12/84.
NASL v. NFL, 4/23/80.
Point of View, 11/2/74.
[Cleveland] *Plain Dealer,* 8/23/72, 12/3/72, 2/4/73, 2/27/73, 3/8/73, 3/11/73, 5/10/73, 7/7/73, 7/13/73.
Cleveland Press, 8/24/72, 5/8/73.

1/10.

INTERVIEWS:

Steve Rosenbloom, 9/21/84, 10/11/84.
Wellington Mara, 10/17/84.
Gene Klein, 9/14/84.
Tex Schramm, 9/18/84.
Pete Rozelle, 6/6/84.
Ed Garvey, 9/24/83.

DEPOSITIONS:

Al Davis, *LAMCC v. NFL,* 3/4/81.
Pete Rozelle, *LAMCC v. NFL,* 10/11/79.
Pack, Robert, *Edward Bennett Williams for the Defense,* Harper and Row, 1983.
Parrish, Bernie, *They Call It a Game,* Dial Press, 1971.
Forbes, 9/13/82.
Esquire, 11/21/78.
Sports Illustrated, 1/6/64.

NFL press release, 7/16/63.
[Baltimore] *Sun*, 4/20/62, 10/28/62, 11/22/66, 12/16/66.
Los Angeles Times, 4/4/79, 9/25/79, 1/26/83.
Los Angeles Herald Examiner, 4/3/79.

1/11.

INTERVIEWS:
    Steve Rosenbloom, 9/21/84, 10/11/84.
    Art Modell, 11/9/84.
DEPOSITIONS:
    Pete Rozelle, *LAMCC v. NFL*, 8/27/80.
Chipman, *The Dallas Cowboys and the NFL*.
Sports Illustrated, 8/14/72.
Esquire, 11/21/78.
[Baltimore] *Sun*, 10/28/62, 3/18/71, 7/14/72.
[Baltimore] *News-American*, 4/1/82.
Los Angeles Times, 2/27/80.

1/12.

INTERVIEWS:
    Steve Rosenbloom, 9/21/84.
    Tex Schramm, 9/18/84.
    Lamar Hunt, 9/20/84.
    Gene Klein, 9/14/84.
    former LAMCC member, confidential.
DEPOSITIONS:
    Pete Rozelle, *LAMCC v. NFL*, 10/11/79.
    Al Davis, *LAMCC v. NFL*, 3/14/80.
Esquire, 11/21/78.
Los Angeles Times, 8/30/73, 11/26/73, 1/11/74, 1/17/74, 2/12/74, 10/3/79.
[Baltimore] *Sun*, 10/28/62, 10/5/72, 5/1/73.

1/13.

INTERVIEWS:
    Steve Rosenbloom, 9/21/84.
    Wellington Mara, 10/17/84.
    Gene Klein, 9/14/84.
    Wayne Valley, 9/25/84.
    George Ross, 10/11/84.
    NFL owner, confidential.
    NFL executive, confidential.
DEPOSITIONS:
    Al Davis, *LAMCC v. NFL*, 11/25/80, 3/4/81, *Barrero v. Davis*, 11/1/73.
    Mandell, Arnold, *The Nightmare Season*, Random House, 1976.

Sport, 1/81.
Look, 11/18/69.
Saturday Evening Post, 11/75.
Sports Illustrated, 11/4/63, 11/15/65.
New York Times Magazine, 12/13/81.
[Oakland] *Tribune,* 12/21/44, 11/6/46, 2/8/49, 11/17/55, 11/28/56, 3/15/60, 9/8/60,
     11/13/60, 2/21/62, 1/6/77.

1/14.

INTERVIEWS:
     Tex Schramm, 9/18/84.
     Wayne Valley, 9/25/84.
     George Ross, 10/11/84.
TESTIMONY:
     Al Davis, *Coggins v. New England Patriots,* 5/12/82.
DEPOSITIONS:
     Al Davis, *Valley v. Davis,* 8/23/73, *LAMCC v. NFL,* 11/25/80, 3/4/81.
Chipman, *The Dallas Cowboys and the NFL.*
Sports Illustrated, 11/15/65, 8/29/66.
Saturday Evening Post, 11/75.
Look, 11/18/69.
New York Times Magazine, 12/13/81.
[Oakland] *Tribune,* 8/11/66, 3/23/69.
New York Times, 4/27/69.

1/15.

INTERVIEWS:
     Tex Schramm, 9/18/84.
     Art Modell, 11/9/84.
     Pete Rozelle, 6/7/84.
     Steve Rosenbloom, 9/21/84.
     Wayne Valley, 9/25/84.
     Jim Kensil, 6/7/84.
     Jay Moyer, 6/7/84.
     George Ross, 10/11/84.
     NFL owner, confidential.
DEPOSITIONS:
     Al Davis, *LAMCC v. NFL,* 3/14/80, 11/25/80, *Valley v. Davis,* 8/23/73.
     Pete Rozelle, *LAMCC v. NFL,* 8/27/80.
New York Times Magazine, 11/13/81.
Look, 11/18/69.
New York Times, 4/23/83.
[Oakland] *Tribune,* 3/19/72.

1/16.

INTERVIEWS:
    Gene Klein, 9/14/84.
    Steve Rosenbloom, 9/21/84.
    3 NFL owners, confidential.
    NFL attorney, confidential.
Mandell, *The Nightmare Season.*
Forbes, 11/15/68.
Home, 9/25/75.
Business Week, 10/13/73.
[San Diego] *Tribune,* 1/13/72, 9/23/81.
San Diego Union, 2/24/72, 7/2/74, 8/2/74.
Los Angeles Times, 3/21/74.
Wall Street Journal, 12/4/70.

1/17.

NFL minutes, 6/26/73.
INTERVIEWS:
    Pete Rozelle, 6/6/84.
    Gene Klein, 9/14/84.
Mandell, *The Nightmare Season.*
Parrish, *They Call It a Game.*
Psychology Today, 6/75.
NFL press release, 4/26/74.
Los Angeles Times, 3/21/74.
[Oakland] *Tribune,* 7/8/75.

1/18.

NFL minutes, 2/25/74.
INTERVIEWS:
    Pete Rozelle, 6/25/83, 6/5/84, 6/7/84.
    Dan Rooney, 10/4/84.
    Lamar Hunt, 9/20/84.
    Wellington Mara, 10/17/84.
    Gene Klein, 9/14/84.
    Ed Garvey, 12/3/84.
Sherman Antitrust Act, Section 1.
Supreme Court Reports, *Federal Baseball Club v. National League,* 5/29/22.
Supreme Court Reports, *Radovich v. NFL,* 2/25/57.
Federal Supplement, *Mackey v. NFL,* 12/29/75.
Noll, *Government and the Sports Business.*
New York Times, 2/17/74, 2/22/74.

1/19.

NFL minutes, 2/26/74.
NFL constitution and bylaws.
INTERVIEWS:
    Wellington Mara, 10/17/84.
    3 NFL owners, confidential.
    NFL executive, confidential.
TESTIMONY:
    Chuck Sullivan, *NASL v. NFL,* 4/22/80.
DEPOSITIONS:
    Pete Rozelle, *LAMCC v. NFL,* 10/11/79.
Sports Illustrated, 9/25/72.
Newsweek, 9/6/71.
Time, 9/6/71.
New York Times, 8/27/71, 8/28/71, 1/18/74, 2/28/74, 3/14/76.

1/20.

NFL minutes, 2/28/74.
INTERVIEWS:
    Steve Rosenbloom, 10/11/84.
    2 NFL owners, confidential.
    NFL executive, confidential.
Colts Game Program, 9/30/73.
[Baltimore] *Sun,* 7/13/72, 9/17/72, 10/21/72, 10/14/73, 9/18/79, 2/16/84, 3/4/84.
[Baltimore] *News-American,* 7/14/72, 8/4/72.
Indianapolis Star, 6/17/84.

1/21.

NFL minutes, 3/20/67, 5/1/71.
NFL, Report of Special Committee on Membership Rules and Ownership Policy, Section 3(f), 5/15/70.
NFL, Confidential Memorandum to Members of the National Football League, 2/18/71.
Agreement of AFL and NFL, Section 4(m), 12/1/66.
TESTIMONY:
    Pete Rozelle, *NASL v. NFL,* 4/16/80, 4/17/80, 4/21/80.
    Edward Bennett Williams, *NASL v. NFL,* 4/7/80.
    Lamar Hunt, *NASL v. NFL,* 4/2/80.
    Joe Robbie, *NASL v. NFL,* 4/9/80.
    Bill Bidwill, *NASL v. NFL,* 4/22/80.
    Art Modell, *NASL v. NFL,* 4/23/80.
National Basketball Association, *Official Guide,* 1968–69.

1/22.

NFL minutes, 5/25/72.
INTERVIEWS:
     Pete Rozelle, 6/6/84.
     Tex Schramm, 9/18/84.
     NFL owner, confidential.
     NFL executive, confidential.
TESTIMONY:
     Edward Bennett Williams, *NASL v. NFL,* 4/7/80.
     Lamar Hunt, *NASL v. NFL,* 4/3/80.
     Joe Robbie, *NASL v. NFL,* 4/9/80.
     Leonard Tose, *NASL v. NFL,* 4/22/80.

1/23.

INTERVIEWS:
     Lamar Hunt, 9/20/84.
     Pete Rozelle, 6/6/84.
TESTIMONY:
     Lamar Hunt, *NASL v. NFL,* 4/2/80.
Chipman, *The Dallas Cowboys and the NFL.*
Texas Monthly, 4/78.
Forbes, 10/1/84.
Pro, 10/84.
Kansas City Times, 9/1/84.
Kansas City Star, 8/8/82.

1/24.

INTERVIEWS:
     Lamar Hunt, 9/20/84.
     Steve Rosenbloom, 9/21/84.
     3 NFL owners, confidential.
TESTIMONY:
     Lamar Hunt, *NASL v. NFL,* 4/2/80, 4/3/80.
     Edward Bennett Williams, *NASL v. NFL,* 4/7/80.
     Pete Rozelle, *NASL v. NFL,* 4/17/80.
letter, Lamar Hunt to Pete Rozelle, 10/16/67.
letter, Lamar Hunt to Pete Rozelle, undated.
letter, Lamar Hunt to Wendell Cherry, 10/8/73.
letter, Lou Spadia to Lamar Hunt, 11/73.
letter, Lamar Hunt to Pete Rozelle, 11/12/73.
letter, Pete Rozelle to Lamar Hunt, 11/19/73.
letter, Lamar Hunt to Pete Rozelle, 2/74.
note, Pete Rozelle to Lamar Hunt, 8/11/72.
Texas Monthly, 4/78.
Sports Illustrated, 9/3/73.

Kansas City Star, 8/8/82.
[Baltimore] *Sun,* 9/2/79.

1/25.

INTERVIEWS:
   3 NFL owners, confidential.
TESTIMONY:
   Leonard Tose, *NASL v. NFL,* 4/22/80.
   Pete Rozelle, *NASL v. NFL,* 4/16/80, *LAMCC v. NFL,* 4/6/82.
Philadelphia, 8/70.
[Philadelphia] *Bulletin,* 6/9/70, 5/4/72, 12/3/72.
Philadelphia Daily News, 3/11/69, 7/1/72.
Philadelphia Inquirer, 5/14/70, 6/8/70, 6/11/70, 6/12/70, 5/3/72.

1/26.

NFL minutes, 2/25/72.
INTERVIEWS:
   Leonard Tose, 10/3/84.
   3 NFL owners, confidential.
   NFL executive, confidential.
TESTIMONY:
   Leonard Tose, *NASL v. NFL,* 4/22/80.
NFL, *Official Record Manual,* 1983.
Philadelphia Inquirer, 8/8/71, 6/3/71, 12/16/71, 2/9/72, 7/15/72.
Philadelphia Daily News, 6/23/71, 8/2/71, 2/10/72, 2/16/72, 10/4/72.
[Philadelphia] *Bulletin,* 8/9/71, 2/9/72, 10/3/72, 12/3/72.
Jack Anderson column, *San Francisco Chronicle,* 6/12/70.

1/27.

INTERVIEWS:
   Billy Sullivan, 10/19/84.
   Bob Marr, 1/22/85.
   Leonard Tose, 10/3/84.
   NFL owner, confidential.
TESTIMONY:
   Chuck Sullivan, *NASL v. NFL,* 4/22/80.
   Pete Rozelle, *Coggins v. New England Patriots,* 5/6/82.
DEPOSITION:
   Pete Rozelle, *LAMCC v. NFL,* 8/28/80.
Boston Globe, 1/27/70, 3/5/70, 3/22/70, 5/27/70, 9/19/70, 9/24/70.
Boston Herald, 5/26/70, 12/9/76, 12/31/78, 7/9/79, 6/15/80.
Patriot Ledger, 8/3/71.

1/28.

INTERVIEWS:
    Billy Sullivan, 10/19/84.
    Bob Marr, 1/22/85.
    2 NFL owners, confidential.
TESTIMONY:
    Billy Sullivan, Hearings before Select Committee on Professional Sports,
        U.S. Congress, 6/23/76, *Coggins v. New England Patriots*, 5/3/82,
        5/10/82.
NFL, *Official Record Manual*, 1983.
Boston Globe, 1/18/74, 3/21/74, 4/7/74, 3/21/82.
Boston Herald, 5/26/70, 12/3/70, 3/27/74, 4/3/74, 6/5/80.

1/29.

INTERVIEWS:
    Pete Rozelle, 6/11/84.
    George Ross, 10/11/84.
    NFL owner, confidential.
    NFL executive, confidential.
TESTIMONY:
    Joe Robbie, *NASL v. NFL*, 4/9/80.
DEPOSITIONS:
    Al Davis, *LAMCC v. NFL*, 11/25/80.
Miami Dolphins, *Press Yearbook*, 1967.
Miami Dolphin Game Program, 11/27/66.
Sports Illustrated, 8/8/66, 12/15/69.
Miami Herald, 5/16/69.
Palm Beach Post Times, 12/17/72.

1/30.

INTERVIEWS:
    Pete Rozelle, 6/6/84.
TESTIMONY:
    Joe Robbie, *NASL v. NFL*, 4/9/80.
    Chuck Sullivan, *NASL v. NFL*, 4/22/80.
Shula, Don, *The Winning Edge*, Dutton, 1973.
Sports Illustrated, 12/15/69, 11/9/70, 7/27/81.
Miami News, 9/10/71, 12/11/75.

1/31.

TESTIMONY:
    Edward Bennett Williams, *NASL v. NFL*, 4/7/80.
    Lamar Hunt, *NASL v. NFL*, 4/2/80.
petition for temporary conservatorship, George Preston Marshall, 12/12/63.

Pack, *Edward Bennett Williams for the Defense*.
Washington Monthly, 6/78.
American Lawyer, 5/85.
New York Times, 10/25/83.

1/32.

TESTIMONY:
   Edward Bennett Williams, *NASL v. NFL*, 4/7/80.
Pete Rozelle, *NASL v. NFL*, 4/16/80.
Pack, *Edward Bennett Williams for the Defense*.
The Washingtonian, 9/82.
Forbes, 9/13/82.
San Francisco Chronicle, 1/6/84.

1/33.

NFL minutes, 4/2/73, 2/25/74.
INTERVIEWS:
   Pete Rozelle, 6/5/84.
   Steve Rosenbloom, 9/21/84.
   Leonard Tose, 10/3/84.
   Dan Rooney, 10/4/84.
   Tex Schramm, 9/18/84.
   Jay Moyer, 6/5/84.
Sports Illustrated, 10/23/72, 12/1/75.
New York Times Magazine, 1/12/75.

1/34.

National Football League constitution and bylaws.
INTERVIEWS:
   Dan Rooney, 10/4/84.
   Pete Rozelle, 6/5/84.
Stanford Research Institute, *Socioeconomic Information on Candidate Areas for NFL Franchises*, 1973.

1/35.

NFL minutes, 2/25/74.
INTERVIEWS:
   Pete Rozelle, 9/25/83, 6/5/84.
   Dan Rooney, 9/19/83, 10/4/84.
   Art Rooney, 9/16/83.
   Leonard Tose, 10/3/84.
   2 NFL owners, confidential.

Kowet, Don, *The Rich Who Own Sports*, Random House, 1971.
Fortune, 11/68.
Nation's Business, 9/80.
New York Times, 9/5/74.

1/36.

NFL minutes, 2/27/74.
INTERVIEWS:
    NFL owner, confidential.
    NFL executive, confidential.
[Baltimore] *Sun*, 3/1/74.

2/1.

INTERVIEWS:
    Ed Garvey, 12/3/84.
    Pete Rozelle, 6/5/84.
    Keith Fahnhorst, 12/6/84.
    Bob Moore, 2/8/85.
TESTIMONY:
    Joe Robbie, *NASL v. NFL*, 4/9/80.
    Ed Garvey, Hearings before the Subcommittee on Labor, U.S. Senate, 10/31/77.
    Sargent Karch, Oversight Hearings on National Football League Labor-
        Management Dispute, U.S. Congress, 9/29/75.
NFLPA Demands, 3/16/74.
Statement by Wellington Mara, 4/4/74.
Statement by Management Council, 4/4/74.
Sports Illustrated, 3/22/71.
Business Week, 8/8/70.
Newsweek, 8/3/70.
Ebony, 11/70.
New York Times, 8/2/70, 8/3/70, 8/4/70.

2/2.

INTERVIEWS:
    Pete Rozelle, 6/5/84.
Sports Illustrated, 4/15/74.
Time, 4/15/74.
New York Times Magazine, 1/12/75.
Fortune, 9/74.
Newsweek, 4/15/74.

2/3.

INTERVIEWS:
   Billy Sullivan, 10/19/84.
   Chuck Sullivan, 10/17/84.
   Bob Marr, 1/22/85.
   Sullivan acquaintance, confidential.
Fortune, 8/20/84.
Boston Globe, 3/21/74, 4/10/74.
Boston Herald, 4/10/74.

2/4.

NFL minutes, 4/23/74, 4/24/74, 6/4/74.
INTERVIEWS:
   Dan Rooney, 10/4/84.
   Pete Rozelle, 6/5/84.
   Gene Klein, 9/14/84.
   Tex Schramm, 9/18/84.
   Bob Marr, 1/22/85.
TESTIMONY:
   Joe Robbie, Hearings before Select Committee on Professional Sports, U.S.
      Congress, 6/23/76.
   Pete Rozelle, *LAMCC v. NFL,* 4/5/82.
DEPOSITIONS:
   Pete Rozelle, *LAMCC v. NFL,* 8/27/80.
Stanford, *Socioeconomic Information on Candidate Areas.*
Seattle Post-Intelligencer, 4/25/74, 4/26/74.
St. Petersburg Times, 4/25/74.
San Diego Union, 6/5/74.

2/5.

INTERVIEWS:
   Billy Sullivan, 10/19/84.
   Chuck Sullivan, 10/16/84.
   Pete Rozelle, 6/5/84.
   Bob Marr, 1/22/85.
TESTIMONY:
   Pete Rozelle, *NASL v. NFL,* 4/16/80, 4/22/80, *Coggins v. New England
      Patriots,* 4/7/82.
.LaSalle National Bank, Billy Sullivan Financial Workup, 10/28/75.
Rhode Island Hospital Trust National Bank, Billy Sullivan Credit Workup, 11/3/75.
NFL press release, 12/5/74.
Boston Globe, 6/2/74.
Seattle Times, 10/29/74.

2/6.

INTERVIEWS:
    Ed Garvey, 12/3/84.
    Wellington Mara, 10/17/84.
    Gene Klein, 9/14/84.
    Sargent Karch, 10/17/84.
TESTIMONY:
    Ed Garvey, Hearings before Subcommittee on Monopolies, U.S. Congress, 10/14/75,
Oversight Hearings on National Football League Labor-Management Dispute, 9/29/75.
    Leonard Lindquist, Oversight Hearings on National Football League Labor-Management Dispute, 9/29/75.
New York Times, 5/26/74, 7/1/74, 7/4/74, 7/11/74, 7/16/74, 7/18/74, 7/21/74, 7/29/74, 8/5/74, 8/7/74, 8/12/74, 9/14/74, 9/15/74, 11/15/74.
Los Angeles Times, 7/16/74.

2/7.

DEPOSITIONS:
    Pete Rozelle, *LAMCC v. NFL,* 8/27/80.
NFL, *Official Record Manual,* 1983.
Sports Illustrated, 7/22/74, 8/19/74, 10/7/74.
Time, 8/26/74, 11/4/74.
[Baltimore] *Sun,* 10/20/72, 10/21/72, 8/13/73, 11/13/73, 11/14/73, 5/3/74, 9/30/74, 10/3/74, 11/28/74, 3/4/84.
[Baltimore] *News-American,* 12/16/73, 12/21/75.

2/8.

NFL minutes, 10/30/74.
INTERVIEWS:
    Hugh Culverhouse, 9/18/83.
    Pete Rozelle, 6/5/84, 6/11/84.
    Steve Rosenbloom, 9/21/84, 10/11/84.
    Tex Schramm, 9/18/84.
    Dan Rooney, 10/4/84.
    Bob Marr, 1/22/85.
    3 NFL owners, confidential.
    NFL source, confidential.
    Culverhouse associate, confidential.
    Source close to Rams sale, confidential.
TESTIMONY:
    Al Davis, *Coggins v. New England Patriots,* 5/12/82.
    Pete Rozelle, *NASL v. NFL,* 4/16/80, 4/21/80.
    Leonard Tose, *NASL v. NFL,* 4/22/80.
letter, Wayne Field to Pete Rozelle, 10/28/74.

letter, Pete Rozelle to Lloyd Nordstrom, 11/13/74.
Complaint, *Culverhouse v. Los Angeles Rams*, 7/6/72.
Florida Trend, 9/78.
Associated Press, 10/29/74.
Tacoma News Tribune, 10/29/74.
Tampa Tribune Times, 12/3/74.
Bradenton Herald, 8/20/78.
Seattle Post-Intelligencer, 11/1/74.
St. Petersburg Times, 12/8/74.

2/9.

INTERVIEWS:
Robert Gries, 10/11/84, 10/12/84.
TESTIMONY:
Art Modell, *Gries Sports Enterprises v. Cleveland Browns*, 6/18/84, 7/12/84.
Robert Gries, *Gries Sports Enterprises v. Cleveland Browns*, 6/20/84.
letter, Anthony G. Gulotta to Art Modell, 2/26/74.
Akron Beacon Journal, 1/16/83.

2/10.

NFL minutes, 3/17/75.
INTERVIEWS:
Ed Garvey, 12/3/84.
TESTIMONY:
Ed Garvey, Inquiry Into Professional Sports, U.S. Congress, 6/23/76.
NFLPA, *Labor Organization Annual Report*, Department of Labor, 12/1/73 to 11/30/74.
Sports Illustrated, 5/1/72, 4/21/75.
New York Times Magazine, 1/12/75.

2/11.

INTERVIEWS:
Pete Rozelle, 6/5/84, 6/7/84.
Wayne Valley, 9/25/84.
Lamar Hunt, 9/20/84.
Gene Klein, 9/14/84.
Dan Rooney, 10/4/84.
Tex Schramm, 9/18/84.
Leonard Tose, 10/3/84.
Art Modell, 11/9/84.
Jay Moyer, 6/5/84.
George Ross, 10/11/84.
Davis associate, confidential.

DEPOSITIONS:
   Al Davis, *LAMCC v. NFL,* 11/25/80, 3/4/81.
Business Week, 6/9/75.
Overdrive, 9/74.
[Oakland] *Tribune,* 5/20/75, 6/1/75, 6/4/75, 6/5/75, 6/6/75, 6/12/75, 6/13/75,
   12/23/75, 5/25/78.
[New York] *Daily News,* 3/9/80, 3/11/80.
Miami Herald, 7/27/78.
Chicago Tribune, 5/31/83.
San Diego Union, 11/25/75, 12/20/75.
San Jose Mercury, 12/25/75.

2/12.

NFL minutes, 6/24/75, 6/25/75.
INTERVIEWS:
   Billy Sullivan, 10/19/84.
   Bob Marr, 1/22/85.
TESTIMONY:
   Edward Bennett Williams, *NASL v. NFL,* 4/7/80.
   Lamar Hunt, *NASL v. NFL,* 4/2/80.
Demand note, William Sullivan/LaSalle National Bank, 11/7/75.
Boston Globe, 8/1/75.
Boston Herald, 7/31/75.

2/13.

INTERVIEWS:
   Pete Rozelle, 9/25/83, 6/6/84.
   Steve Rosenbloom, 9/21/84.
   Mel Durslag, 10/18/84.
   NFL owner, confidential.
TESTIMONY:
   Pete Rozelle, Hearings before the Subcommittee on Monopolies, 10/14/75.
NFL, *Official Record Manual,* 1983.
Sports Illustrated, 9/30/74.
Los Angeles Times, 7/14/75, 7/26/75, 7/30/75, 7/31/75, 8/1/75, 8/2/75, 8/6/76,
   10/3/79.

2/14.

INTERVIEWS:
   Pete Rozelle, 6/5/84.
TESTIMONY:
   Leonard Lindquist, Oversight Hearings on National Football League Labor-
      Management Dispute, U.S. Congress, 9/29/75.
letter, Chris Hemmeter to Pete Rozelle, 10/22/75.

file memo, Jay Moyer, 10/16/75.
Sports Illustrated, 12/1/75.

2/15.

NFL minutes, 11/4/75.
INTERVIEWS:
> Chuck Sullivan, 10/17/84.
> Bob Marr, 1/22/85.
> Pete Rozelle, 6/11/84.

TESTIMONY:
> Chuck Sullivan, *NASL v. NFL,* 4/22/80.
> Billy Sullivan, *Coggins v. New England Patriots,* 5/4/82.
> Pete Rozelle, *Coggins v. New England Patriots,* 5/6/82.

letter, Peter Toulmin, Rhode Island Hospital Trust National Bank, to Chuck Sullivan, 11/4/75.
letter, Pete Rozelle to LaSalle National Bank, 11/7/75.
proxy, Mary Sullivan to Billy Sullivan, 11/6/75.
Financial workup, LaSalle National Bank, William Sullivan, 11/7/75.
Memorandum of Closing, LaSalle National Bank and William Sullivan, 11/7/75.
Credit risk offering, Rhode Island Hospital Trust National Bank, William Sullivan, 11/3/75.
Boston Globe, 11/11/75.

2/16.

NFL minutes, 11/6/75.
INTERVIEWS:
> Leonard Tose, 10/3/84.
> Steve Rosenbloom, 10/11/84.
> Gene Klein, 9/14/84.
> Wellington Mara, 10/17/84.
> Bob Marr, 1/22/85.
> Pete Rozelle, 6/6/84.
> Art Modell, 11/9/84.
> Bill McPhail, 9/23/83.
> NFL owner, confidential.

New York Times, 1/30/83.

2/17.

NFL minutes, 1/9/76, 1/10/76, 3/18/76.
INTERVIEWS:
> Ed Garvey, 12/3/84.
> Pete Rozelle, 6/7/84.
> Jim Kensil, 6/7/84.

TESTIMONY:
> Pete Rozelle, *Coggins v. New England Patriots*, 5/6/82, *NASL v. NFL*, 4/16/80, 4/17/80.
> Lamar Hunt, *NASL v. NFL*, 4/2/80.

Mackey v. NFL, 407 Federal Supplement 1000 (1975).

2/18.

NFL minutes, 3/15/76, 6/16/76.
INTERVIEWS:
> Jay Moyer, 6/6/84.

TESTIMONY:
> Pete Rozelle, *NASL v. NFL*, 4/16/80, 4/17/80.
> Joe Robbie, *NASL v. NFL*, 4/9/80.
> Leonard Tose, *NASL v. NFL*, 4/22/80.
> Lamar Hunt, *NASL v. NFL*, 4/3/80.
> Edward Bennett Williams, *NASL v. NFL*, 4/7/80.

2/19.

NFL minutes, 3/16/76.
INTERVIEWS:
> Pete Rozelle, 6/5/84.
> Tex Schramm, 9/18/84.

TESTIMONY:
> Pete Rozelle, *LAMCC v. NFL*, 4/5/82.

Associated Press, 5/29/84.
[Baltimore] *Sun*, 3/31/76, 6/15/79.
[Baltimore] *News-American*, 6/17/79.
Indianapolis News, 2/17/77.

2/20.

NFL minutes, 3/15/76.
INTERVIEWS:
> Pete Rozelle, 6/6/84.
> Gene Klein, 9/14/84.
> Steve Rosenbloom, 9/21/84.
> Art Modell, 11/9/84.
> 2 NFL executives, confidential.

NFL, *Official Record Manual*, 1983.
New York Times, 12/25/75.

2/21.

INTERVIEWS:
Robert Gries, 10/12/84.
TESTIMONY:
Art Modell, *Gries Sports Enterprises v. Cleveland Browns,* 6/18/84, 7/12/84,
   NASL v. NFL, 4/23/80.
Robert Gries, *Gries Sports Enterprises v. Cleveland Browns,* 6/20/84.
Point of View, 3/27/82.
Cleveland, 1974.
[Cleveland] *Plain Dealer,* 7/71, 2/22/77.
Cleveland Press, 9/2/72.

2/22.

memo, Rhode Island Hospital Trust National Bank, R. B. Baxter, re: William A.
   Sullivan and New England Patriots Football Club, Inc., undated.
memo, Bruce L. Dahltorp, LaSalle National Bank, to William Powers, Rhode
   Island Hospital Trust National Bank, re: February 20, 1976, meeting on New
   England Patriots, undated.
memo, Rhode Island Hospital Trust National Bank, P. N. Toulin to A. M.
   Anderson, re: Patriots loan, 2/12/76.
letter, Joseph H. B. Edwards to John S. Shapira, 8/19/76.
Boston Globe, 3/21/82.

2/23.

INTERVIEWS:
Gene Klein, 9/14/84.
Pete Rozelle, 6/11/84.
Mandell, *The Nightmare Season.*
San Diego Union, 2/17/76, 3/12/76, 3/13/76, 3/26/76, 12/28/79.
[San Diego] *Tribune,* 3/15/76, 6/8/77, 6/30/77, 1/29/80, 9/23/81.
Los Angeles Times, 3/21/74, 3/27/76, 10/6/76.
Seattle Post-Intelligencer, 7/11/74.

2/24.

NFL minutes, 3/18/76.
INTERVIEWS:
Dan Rooney, 10/4/84.
Wellington Mara, 10/17/84.
Pete Rozelle, 6/6/84.
Steve Rosenbloom, 9/21/84.
Bob Moore, 2/8/85.
TESTIMONY:
Pete Rozelle, Inquiry into Professional Sports, U.S. Congress, 6/23/76.

Ed Garvey, Inquiry into Professional Sports, U.S. Congress, 6/23/76.
New York Times, 3/19/76, 8/30/76.

2/25.

INTERVIEWS:
>   Dan Rooney, 10/4/84.
>   Pete Rozelle, 6/7/84.
>   Art Modell, 11/9/84.
>   George Ross, 10/11/84.
>   Bob Moore, 2/8/85.
>   Davis employee, confidential.

DEPOSITIONS:
>   Al Davis, *LAMCC v. NFL,* 11/25/80, 3/4/81.

Sports Illustrated, 12/2/74, 8/1/77.
[Oakland] *Tribune,* 4/4/75, 9/13/76, 9/15/76, 9/26/76, 10/6/76, 12/16/76.
San Francisco Chronicle, 4/12/75, 4/21/76.
New York Times, 3/19/76.

2/26.

INTERVIEWS:
>   Steve Rosenbloom, 9/21/84.
>   Pete Rozelle, 6/6/84.
>   Bill Robertson, 9/6/84.

DEPOSITIONS:
>   Al Davis, *LAMCC v. NFL,* 3/4/81.
>   Georgia Rosenbloom Frontiere, *LAMCC v. NFL,* 9/4/80.
>   Pete Schabarum, *LAMCC v. NFL,* 12/19/80.
>   Don Klosterman, *LAMCC v. NFL,* 1/14/80.

Los Angeles Coliseum, suite brochure, 1976.
Los Angeles Times, 4/20/76, 10/1/76.

2/27.

INTERVIEWS:
>   Wellington Mara, 10/17/84.
>   Pete Rozelle, 6/6/84.
>   Dan Rooney, 10/4/84.

Mackey v. NFL, Federal Reporter, 543 F. 2d 606 (1976).
NFLPA, *Labor Organization Annual Report,* Department of Labor, 12/1/75 to
>   11/30/76.
Sports Illustrated, 3/7/77.
United Press International, 2/16/85.
New York Times, 3/6/77.
Los Angeles Times, 3/31/77.

2/28.

letter, Association of Industries of Massachusetts to the Honorable Michael Dukakis, 8/13/76.

letter, Securities and Exchange Commission to F. Douglas Cochrane, re: New England Patriots Football Club, Inc., 9/17/76.

letter, Alfonso Puyama to New England Patriots, undated.

letter, Clifford F. Miller to New England Patriots, 11/23/76.

letter, Joseph H. B. Edwards to Douglas Cochrane, 8/20/76.

letter, LaSalle National Bank to William H. Sullivan Jr., 9/19/76.

letter, LaSalle National Bank to William Sullivan, 11/5/76.

handwritten note, Rhode Island Hospital Trust National Bank, "Attitude Change," undated.

memo, Rhode Island Hospital Trust National Bank, P. N. Toulmin, 7/14/76.

memo, Rhode Island Hospital Trust National Bank, P. N. Toulmin and R. B. Baxter, 6/21/76.

memo, Rhode Island Hospital Trust National Bank, Gordon T. Neal to William P. J. Powers, re: New England Patriots, 7/30/76.

memo, Rhode Island Hospital Trust National Bank, G. T. Neale to H. S. Woodbridge Jr., 9/9/76.

memo "for the record," Rhode Island Hospital Trust National Bank, re: New England Patriots loans, 10/8/76.

memo, Rhode Island Hospital Trust National Bank, re: New England Patriots/ Billy Sullivan, 10/29/76.

memo, Rhode Island Hospital Trust National Bank, H. S. Woodbridge Jr. to W. P.J. Powers, re: New England Patriots, 11/22/76.

Boston Globe, 11/3/74, 8/25/76, 12/5/76, 12/9/76, 3/21/82.

Boston Herald, 3/9/74, 12/9/76.

2/29.

NFL minutes, 3/16/76.

DEPOSITIONS:

Al Davis, *LAMCC v. NFL,* 11/25/80.

NFL, *Official Record Manual,* 1983.

Newsweek, 1/10/77, 1/24/77.

Time, 1/10/77.

Sports Illustrated, 1/17/77.

[Oakland] *Tribune,* 1/10/77.

3/1.

NFL minutes, 3/28/77, 3/31/77, 4/1/77, 6/15/77.

INTERVIEWS:

Gene Klein, 9/16/83.

Tex Schramm, 9/15/83.

Pete Rozelle, 8/25/83, 6/7/84.

Wayne Valley, 9/25/84.

George Ross, 10/11/84.
NFL owner, confidential.
3 Davis friends, confidential.
DEPOSITIONS:
    Al Davis, *LAMCC v. NFL*, 3/14/80.
    Tex Schramm, *LAMCC v. NFL*, 8/22/80.
press release, Leonard Tose, 12/2/76.
Sport, 9/79.
Inside Sports, cited *San Francisco Chronicle*, 6/19/81.
[Oakland] *Tribune*, 1/10/77.

3/2.

NFL minutes, 3/28/77.
INTERVIEWS:
    Wayne Valley, 9/25/84.
    Pete Rozelle, 8/25/83.
    Art Modell, 11/9/84.
    Steve Rosenbloom, 9/21/84.
    3 NFL owners, confidential.
TESTIMONY:
    Pete Rozelle, *NASL v. NFL*, 4/21/80.
    Al Davis, *Coggins v. New England Patriots*, 5/12/82.
DEPOSITIONS:
    Al Davis, *LAMCC v. NFL*, 11/25/80.
letter, Robert J. Schrieber to NFL, 3/8/77.
letter, Pete Rozelle to Edward J. DeBartolo Sr. and Edward J. DeBartolo Jr., 3/11/77.
Sports Illustrated, 4/18/77.
Business Week, 10/11/76.
Forbes, 9/13/82.
San Francisco Examiner, 4/5/77, 5/6/83, 3/20/84.
San Francisco Chronicle, 3/15/77.
Los Angeles Times, 4/2/77.
[Baltimore] *Sun*, 1/21/77.

3/3.

INTERVIEWS:
    NFL owner, confidential.
City of New York v. New York Jets Football Club, Inc., et al, 394 NY 2d 799.
Fortune, 1/70.
New York Times, 5/26/68, 8/7/68, 1/20/74, 3/20/74, 4/10/76, 2/2/77, 2/4/77,
    2/11/77, 2/12/77, 2/15/77, 2/16/77, 2/18/77, 2/19/77, 2/20/77, 3/17/77,
    3/18/77, 5/27/77, 3/3/81.

3/4.

NFL, *Official Record Manual*, 1983.
Miami News, 2/3/76, 7/8/76, 8/23/77.
Miami Herald, 1/21/76.
New York Times, 2/16/76.
Minneapolis Tribune, 5/13/74, 7/14/74.
Minneapolis Star, 2/6/76, 3/21/76, 5/11/77, 7/27/77.
St. Paul News American, 2/28/75.
[Baltimore] *News-American*, 9/26/77.
Indianapolis Star, 4/2/84.

3/5.

TESTIMONY:
        Leonard Tose, *Tose v. First Pennsylvania*, 6/25/80.
        Sidney Forstater, *Tose v. First Pennsylvania*, 6/17/80.
        John Bunting, *Tose v. First Pennsylvania*, 6/11/80.
        Edwin Rome, *Tose v. First Pennsylvania*, 6/18/80.
        Gerald Hays, *Tose v. First Pennsylvania*, 6/5/80.
        Dick Vermeil, *Tose v. First Pennsylvania*, 6/16/80.
        F. Anthony Newton, *Tose v. First Pennsylvania*, 6/10/80.
letter, Herb Barness to Leonard Tose, 9/76.
memo, Gerald Hays, 3/24/77.
Associated Press, 8/11/77.
Philadelphia Inquirer, 6/12/77, 8/7/77, 8/10/77, 6/20/80.
[Philadelphia] *Bulletin*, 8/10/77.
Philadelphia Daily News, 8/10/77, 8/11/77.

3/6.

INTERVIEWS:
        Pete Rozelle, 6/7/84.
        Gene Klein, 9/14/84.
        Jay Moyer, 6/7/84.
DEPOSITIONS:
        Al Davis, *LAMCC v. NFL*, 3/14/80.
Sports Illustrated, 8/1/77.
[Oakland] *Tribune*, 7/12/77, 7/19/77, 7/21/77, 7/22/77, 7/23/77.
San Francisco Chronicle, 3/11/80.

3/7.

NLF minutes, 10/13/77.
INTERVIEWS:
        Pete Rozelle, 6/11/84.
        Bob Moore, 2/8/85.

3 NFL owners, confidential.
NFL observer, confidential.
TESTIMONY:
    Pete Rozelle, *Coggins v. New England Patriots*, 5/6/82.
    Billy Sullivan, *Coggins v. New England Patriots*, 5/4/82.
    Al Davis, *Coggins v. New England Patriots*, 5/12/82.
Florida Trend, 9/78.

3/8.

INTERVIEWS:
    Pete Rozelle, 6/6/84.
    Steve Rosenbloom, 9/21/84.
DEPOSITIONS:
    Al Davis, *LAMCC v. NFL*, 11/25/80.
    James Kenyon, *LAMCC v. NFL*.
Stanford, *Socioeconomic Information on Candidate Areas*.
Los Angeles Times, 1/26/78, 1/27/78, 2/17/78, 8/9/78.

3/9.

INTERVIEWS:
    Leonard Tose, 10/3/84.
    Pete Rozelle, 6/11/84.
    Billy Sullivan, 10/19/84.
    Gene Klein, 9/14/84.
TESTIMONY:
    Pete Rozelle, *LAMCC v. NFL*, 4/6/82.
    Chuck Sullivan, *NASL v. NFL*, 4/22/80.
    Billy Sullivan, *Coggins v. New England Patriots*, 5/4/82.
    Roger Hillas, *Tose v. First Pennsylvania*, 6/20/80.
    Alex Krege, *Tose v. First Pennsylvania*, 6/10/80.
DEPOSITIONS:
    Pete Rozelle, *LAMCC v. NFL*, 8/28/80.
Philadelphia Journal, 2/1/78, 2/8/78.
Philadelphia Daily News, 1/17/78, 2/10/78.
Philadelphia Inquirer, 2/1/78, 2/10/78.
[Philadelphia] *Bulletin*, 2/10/78.
Associated Press, 2/2/78.
Boston Herald, 9/1/78.

3/10.

NFL minutes, 3/16/78.
INTERVIEWS:
    Pete Rozelle, 6/6/84.

Bob Moore, 2/8/85.

Jay Moyer, 6/7/84.

TESTIMONY:

Ed Garvey, Hearings before Subcommittee on Labor, U.S. Senate, 10/31/77.

Joe Robbie, *NASL v. NFL*, 4/9/80.

Chuck Sullivan, *NASL v. NFL*, 4/22/80.

Leonard Tose, *NASL v. NFL*, 4/22/80.

Pete Rozelle, *NASL v. NFL*, 4/17/80.

NFLPA, *Labor Organization Annual Report*, Department of Labor, 12/1/76 to 11/30/77.

NFLPA, *Labor Organization Annual Report*, Department of Labor, 12/1/75 to 11/30/76.

NFLPA, *Labor Organization Annual Report*, Department of Labor, 12/1/77 to 11/30/78.

Associated Press, 7/30/77.

Miami Herald, 5/15/77, 7/30/77, 8/2/77.

Miami News, 8/25/77.

Philadelphia Inquirer, 8/12/77.

3/11.

NFL minutes, 3/16/78.

INTERVIEWS:

Steve Rosenbloom, 9/21/84.

Art Modell, 11/9/84.

TESTIMONY:

Pete Rozelle, *NASL v. NFL*, 4/16/80, 4/21/80.

Leonard Tose, *NASL v. NFL*, 4/22/80.

Lamar Hunt, *NASL v. NFL*, 4/2/80, 4/3/80.

Chuck Sullivan, *NASL v. NFL*, 4/22/80.

Art Modell, *NASL v. NFL*, 4/23/80.

DEPOSITIONS:

Max Winter, cited *NASL v. NFL*, 4/22/80.

letter, Lamar Hunt to Pete Rozelle, 3/8/77.

notes, Robert Schulman, 3/16/78.

San Francisco Chronicle, 1/6/84.

Cleveland Press, 12/8/77.

3/12.

INTERVIEWS:

Bill Robertson, 9/6/84, 12/4/84.

TESTIMONY:

Pete Rozelle, *NASL v. NFL*, 4/21/80.

Lamar Hunt, *NASL v. NFL*, 4/2/80.

Bill Robertson, *LAMCC v. NFL*, 4/6/82.

James Kenyon, *LAMCC v. NFL*, 4/1/82.

DEPOSITIONS:
   Al Davis, *LAMCC v. NFL,* 3/4/81.
   Bill Robertson, *LAMCC v. NFL,* 6/8/79, 10/9/80.
   Pete Rozelle, *LAMCC v. NFL,* 8/27/80.
letter, Anaheim Stadium Associates to city of Anaheim, 4/17/78.
letter, William O. Talley to Lawrence N. Strenger, 5/1/78.
letter, Gerald Blakely to Carroll Rosenbloom, 5/31/78.
Los Angeles Times, 2/22/78, 3/30/78, 4/28/78.

3/13.

INTERVIEWS:
   Joe Alioto, 2/1/85.
   NFL owner, confidential.
Tose v. First Pennsylvania Bank, 492 F Supp 246 (1980).
Radovich v. NFL, 362 US 445 1L ed 2d 456, 77 S Ct 390.
Kapp v. NFL, 390 Fed Supp 73 (1974).
Philadelphia, 10/83.
Philadelphia Eagles press release, 5/5/78.
Associated Press, 4/19/78.
United Press International, 3/31/82.
Philadelphia Inquirer, 4/19/78, 4/20/78, 5/10/78, 6/8/78, 3/28/79, 6/20/79.
Philadelphia Daily News, 5/6/78.
San Francisco Chronicle, 3/11/80.
Boston Globe, 4/25/76.

3/14.

NFL minutes, 6/7/78.
INTERVIEWS:
   Tex Schramm, 9/18/84.
TESTIMONY:
   Pete Rozelle, *NASL v. NFL,* 4/16/80, 4/21/80.
   Joe Robbie, *NASL v. NFL,* 4/9/80.
   Edward Bennett Williams, *NASL v. NFL,* 4/7/80.
   Leonard Tose, *NASL v. NFL,* 4/22/80.
   Lamar Hunt, *NASL v. NFL,* 4/2/80.
   Art Modell, *NASL v. NFL,* 4/23/80.
   Chuck Sullivan, *NASL v. NFL,* 4/22/80.
notes, Don Weiss, 6/7/78.

3/15.

INTERVIEWS:
   Bill Robertson, 9/6/84, 1/24/85.
   Pete Rozelle, 6/6/84.
   Bradley adviser, confidential.

TESTIMONY:
   Bill Robertson, *LAMCC v. NFL*, 4/6/82.
   Pete Rozelle, *LAMCC v. NFL*, 4/1/82, 4/2/82, 4/6/82.
DEPOSITIONS:
   Bill Robertson, *LAMCC v. NFL*, 10/9/80.
   Pete Rozelle, *LAMCC v. NFL*, 8/28/80.
letter, Bill Robertson to Peter Schabarum, 7/26/78.
letter, Bill Robertson to Carroll Rosenbloom, 7/17/78.
letter, Pete Rozelle to Kenny Hahn, 8/15/78.
memo, J. Kenyon to J. Hines, re: Ram Deal/Anaheim, 7/10/78.
telegram, Kenneth Hahn to Pete Rozelle, 7/24/78.
Los Angeles Times, 7/26/78.

3/16.

NFL constitution and bylaws.
NASL minutes, 8/28/78.
INTERVIEWS:
   Pete Rozelle, 6/6/84.
   Lamar Hunt, 9/20/84.
TESTIMONY:
   Pete Rozelle, *NASL v. NFL*, 4/16/80, 4/17/80, 4/21/80.
   Lamar Hunt, *NASL v. NFL*, 4/2/80.
   Joe Robbie, *NASL v. NFL*, 4/9/80.
   Edward Bennett Williams, *NASL v. NFL*, 4/7/80.
   Leonard Tose, *NASL v. NFL*, 4/22/80.
memo, Pete Rozelle to NFL Executive Committee, 6/28/78.
NASL v. NFL, 505 F Supp 639 (1980).
Kansas City Star, 7/17/78.

3/17.

In both this chapter and the following one, I have re-created the NFL's Chicago meeting through the use of a number of different sources. In some cases, I have combined statements made at different points in time inside a single set of quotation marks, but only to amplify a point made on several different occasions and not to alter the thrust of the statement.
NFL minutes, 10/4/78.
INTERVIEWS:
   Steve Rosenbloom, 9/21/84, 10/11/84.
   Wellington Mara, 10/17/84.
   Joe Robbie, 9/27/83.
   Gene Klein, 9/14/84.
TESTIMONY:
   Pete Rozelle, *LAMCC v. NFL*, 4/1/82, 4/5/82.
   Bill Robertson, *LAMCC v. NFL*, 4/6/82.
DEPOSITIONS:
   Al Davis, *LAMCC v. NFL*, 3/14/80, 11/25/80, 3/4/81.

Pete Rozelle, *LAMCC v. NFL,* 10/11/79, 8/27/80, 8/28/80.
Gene Klein, *LAMCC v. NFL,* 9/17/80.
Ralph Wilson, *LAMCC v. NFL,* 12/4/80.
Art Modell, *LAMCC v. NFL,* 9/24/80.
Robert Schulman, cited *LAMCC v. NFL,* 4/1/82.
notes, Robert Schulman, 10/4/78.

3/18.

See note Chapter 3/17.
NFL minutes, 10/5/78.
INTERVIEWS:
    Pete Rozelle, 6/6/84.
    Steve Rosenbloom, 9/21/84.
    Leonard Tose, 10/3/84.
    Gene Klein, 9/14/84.
    Jay Moyer, 6/6/84.
TESTIMONY:
    Bill Robertson, *LAMCC v. NFL,* 4/6/82.
    Pete Rozelle, *LAMCC v. NFL,* 4/1/82, 4/5/82.
DEPOSITIONS:
    Al Davis, *LAMCC v. NFL,* 3/14/80, 11/25/80.
    Pete Rozelle, *LAMCC v. NFL,* 8/27/80, 8/28/80.
    Ralph Wilson, *LAMCC v. NFL,* 12/4/80.
    Robert Schulman, cited *LAMCC v. NFL,* 4/1/82.
report, Jim Kensil, cited *LAMCC v. NFL,* 4/5/82.
notes, Robert Schulman, 10/5/78.

3/19.

NFL minutes, 1/29/79.
INTERVIEWS:
    Bill Robertson, 9/6/84, 1/24/85.
    Gene Klein, 9/14/84.
    Mel Durslag, 10/1/84.
TESTIMONY:
    Bill Robertson, *LAMCC v. NFL,* 4/6/82.
DEPOSITIONS:
    Al Davis, *LAMCC v. NFL,* 11/25/80, 3/4/81.
    Bill Robertson, *LAMCC v. NFL,* 6/8/79.
    Ralph Wilson, *LAMCC v. NFL,* 12/4/80.
Los Angeles Herald Examiner, 7/26/78, 7/27/78, 8/2/78.
[Oakland] *Tribune,* 1/18/79.

3/20.

NFL minutes, 1/28/79.
INTERVIEWS:
Leonard Tose, 10/3/84.
TESTIMONY:
Leonard Tose, *NASL v. NFL*, 4/22/80.
Jimmy Murray, *Tose v. First Pennsylvania Bank*, 6/23/80.
Philadelphia, 10/83.
Philadelphia Inquirer, 11/20/78, 12/24/78, 1/18/81, 5/23/83.
Philadelphia Daily News, 1/4/80, 1/18/81.
[Philadelphia] *Bulletin*, 9/10/79.
[San Diego] *Tribune*, 8/13/83.

3/21.

NFL minutes, 3/14/79, 3/15/79.
INTERVIEWS:
Pete Rozelle, 6/11/84.
Bill Robertson, 9/6/84.
TESTIMONY:
Pete Rozelle, *LAMCC v. NFL*, 4/5/82.
Bill Robertson, *LAMCC v. NFL*, 4/6/82.
DEPOSITIONS:
Bill Robertson, *LAMCC v. NFL*, 6/8/79.
letter, Robert Bush to James Hardy, 1/24/79.
Miami Dolphins Ltd. v. City of Miami, Fla. App., 374 So. 2d 1156, 9/18/79.
Miami Herald, 3/17/79, 3/18/79.
Los Angeles Times, 3/13/79.
[Baltimore] *Sun*, 1/27/79, 1/28/79, 1/29/79, 1/30/79.
Minneapolis Tribune, 2/8/79, 3/14/79.

3/22.

NFL minutes, 6/6/79.
INTERVIEWS:
Steve Rosenbloom, 9/21/84, 10/11/84.
Pete Rozelle, 6/6/84.
Gene Klein, 9/14/84.
Source close to Rosenblooms, confidential.
NFL source, confidential.
NFL, Tribute to Carroll Rosenbloom.
Los Angeles Times, 4/12/79, 4/13/79, 5/8/79.
Los Angeles Herald Examiner, 4/3/79.
[Baltimore] *Sun*, 4/3/79.
Miami Herald, 4/3/79.

3/23.

INTERVIEWS:
  George Ross, 10/11/84.
  L.A. source, confidential.
DEPOSITIONS:
  Al Davis, *LAMCC v. NFL*, 11/25/80, 3/4/81.
  Bill Robertson, *LAMCC v. NFL*, 6/9/79, 10/9/80.
  Georgia Rosenbloom Frontiere, *LAMCC v. NFL*, 9/4/80.
  Al LoCasale, *LAMCC v. NFL*, 2/27/81.
  John Madden, *LAMCC v. NFL*, 2/25/81.
Minneapolis Star, 4/30/79, 5/22/79.
Minneapolis Tribune, 5/14/79, 5/19/79, 5/22/79.

3/24.

NFL minutes, 6/5/79, 6/6/79, 3/13/80.
INTERVIEWS:
  Pete Rozelle, 6/6/84.
  Jack Kent Cooke, 9/27/83.
  Art Modell, 11/9/84.
  Gene Klein, 9/14/84.
  Cooke friend, confidential.
TESTIMONY:
  Edward Bennett Williams, *NASL v. NFL*, 4/7/80.
  Pete Rozelle, *NASL v. NFL*, 4/17/80.
The Washingtonian, 9/82.
Los Angeles Times, 5/30/79.
New York Times, 5/30/79.
Washington Post, 8/3/79.

3/25.

INTERVIEWS:
  Steve Rosenbloom, 9/21/84, 10/11/84.
  Pete Rozelle, 6/11/84.
TESTIMONY:
  Pete Rozelle, *LAMCC v. NFL*, 4/5/82.
DEPOSITIONS:
  Georgia Rosenbloom Frontiere, *LAMCC v. NFL*, 9/4/80.
  Dominic Frontiere, *LAMCC v. NFL*, 2/13/81.
  Pete Rozelle, *LAMCC v. NFL*, 8/28/80.
  Mel Irwin, 10/8/80, 10/23/80.
memo, Georgia Rosenbloom to the staff of the Rams, 8/6/79.
Georgia Rosenbloom Frontiere, "The Future Is Suddenly Now."
Sport, 10/80.
Los Angeles Times, 4/4/79, 8/17/79, 10/3/79, 1/26/81.

[Baltimore] *Sun,* 12/9/79.
New York News Service in *Washington Post.*

3/26.

INTERVIEWS:
 Bill Robertson, 1/24/85.
 George Ross, 10/11/84.
 Los Angeles attorney, confidential.
 Source close to L.A. negotiations, confidential.
DEPOSITIONS:
 Al Davis, *LAMCC v. NFL,* 11/25/80.
 Bill Robertson, *LAMCC v. NFL,* 10/9/80.
 Pete Rozelle, *LAMCC v. NFL,* 10/11/79, 8/28/80.
letter, Bill Robertson to Football Search Committee, 9/19/79.
New York Times Magazine, 12/13/81.
[Oakland] *Tribune,* 8/13/79, 9/10/79, 9/11/79, 10/25/79, 10/27/79, 10/30/79,
 11/2/79.
San Francisco Chronicle, 4/7/80, 1/22/81.
Los Angeles Times, 3/14/80.

3/27.

INTERVIEWS:
 Pete Rozelle, 6/11/84.
 Gene Klein, 9/14/84.
DEPOSITIONS:
 Pete Rozelle, *LAMCC v. NFL,* 10/11/79.
Associated Press, 6/11/79, 9/22/79.
[Baltimore] *Sun,* 6/12/79, 6/13/79, 8/9/79, 8/10/79, 8/11/79, 8/16/79, 8/17/79,
 8/18/79, 8/30/79, 9/2/79, 9/27/79, 9/28/79, 10/16/79, 10/17/79, 10/27/79,
 10/29/79, 10/31/79, 11/1/79, 11/2/79, 11/4/79, 12/4/79, 3/4/84.
[Baltimore] *News-American,* 8/10/79, 8/17/79, 9/27/79.

3/28.

INTERVIEWS:
 Pete Rozelle, 8/25/83, 6/7/84.
 NFL source, confidential.
TESTIMONY:
 Pete Rozelle, *LAMCC v. NFL,* 4/5/82, 4/6/82.
DEPOSITIONS:
 Al Davis, *LAMCC v. NFL,* 11/25/80, 3/4/81.
 Pete Rozelle, *LAMCC v. NFL,* 8/28/80.
 Georgia Rosenbloom Frontiere, *LAMCC v. NFL,* 9/4/80.
 Dominic Frontiere, *LAMCC v. NFL,* 2/13/81.
 Mel Irwin, *LAMCC v. NFL,* 10/8/80.

AFFIDAVITS:
 James Hardy, *LAMCC v. NFL,* 1/8/80.
Hayward Daily Review, 1/3/80.
[Oakland] *Tribune,* 12/23/79.
Los Angeles Times, 12/17/79.

3/29.

INTERVIEWS:
 Pete Rozelle, 8/25/83, 6/7/84.
 Bill Robertson, 9/6/84.
 Jim Kensil, 6/7/84.
 Mel Durslag, 10/1/84.
TESTIMONY:
 Pete Rozelle, *LAMCC v. NFL,* 4/2/82, 4/6/82.
DEPOSITIONS:
 Al Davis, *LAMCC v. NFL,* 3/14/80, 11/25/80, 3/4/81.
 Pete Rozelle, *LAMCC v. NFL,* 8/28/80.
 Bill Robertson, *LAMCC v. NFL,* 10/9/80.
AFFIDAVITS:
 Bill Robertson, *LAMCC v. NFL,* 3/20/80.
letter, Pete Rozelle to Al Davis, 1/10/80.
[Oakland] *Tribune,* 1/5/80, 1/9/80, 1/11/80, 1/12/80, 1/13/80, 1/15/80, 1/18/80, 1/20/80.
Los Angeles Times, 1/16/80, 1/19/80.
Los Angeles Herald Examiner, 1/17/80.

3/30.

NFL minutes, 10/31/79.
INTERVIEWS:
 Steve Rosenbloom, 10/11/84.
 Don Klosterman, 9/27/83.
 Pete Rozelle, 6/11/84.
DEPOSITIONS:
 Mel Irwin, *LAMCC v. NFL,* 10/23/80.
 Dominic Frontiere, *LAMCC v. NFL,* 2/13/81.
 Don Klosterman, *LAMCC v. NFL,* 11/4/80.
 Georgia Rosenbloom Frontiere, *LAMCC v. NFL,* 9/4/80.
 Pete Rozelle, *LAMCC v. NFL,* 8/28/80.
 Harold Guiver, *LAMCC v. NFL,* 10/14/80.
 Al Davis, *LAMCC v. NFL,* 11/25/80.
letter, Harold Guiver to Georgia Rosenbloom, 11/13/79.
letter, Harold Guiver to Georgia Rosenbloom, 1/28/80.
handwritten note, Harold B. Guiver, 10/24/79.
Los Angeles Rams, *Media Guide,* 1978, 1979.
Time, 1/28/80.
Washington Post, 1/80.

Miami Herald, 9/19/79.
New York Times, 6/12/78.

3/31.

INTERVIEWS:
    Pete Rozelle, 8/9/83.
    Bill Robertson, 1/24/85.
    Davis source, confidential.
TESTIMONY:
    Pete Rozelle, *LAMCC v. NFL,* 4/5/82.
    Bill Robertson, *LAMCC v. NFL,* 4/6/82.
DEPOSITIONS:
    Al Davis, *LAMCC v. NFL,* 3/14/80, 3/4/81.
    Bill Robertson, *LAMCC v. NFL,* 10/9/80.
    Mel Irwin, *LAMCC v. NFL,* 10/23/80.
AFFIDAVITS:
    Al Davis, *LAMCC v. NFL,* 3/18/80.
Los Angeles Rams phone records, cited *LAMCC v. NFL,* 4/6/82.
LAMCC v. NFL, California Reporter, Volume 26, Number 52.
[Oakland] *Tribune,* 1/25/80, 1/30/80, 2/3/80, 2/4/80.
Los Angeles Times, 1/25/80, 3/5/80.
Los Angeles Herald Examiner, 1/24/80.

4/1.

NFL minutes, 3/3/80.
INTERVIEWS:
    Pete Rozelle, 6/7/84.
TESTIMONY:
    Pete Rozelle, *LAMCC v. NFL,* 4/2/82, 4/5/82.
DEPOSITIONS:
    Al Davis, *LAMCC v. NFL,* 11/25/80.
    Pete Rozelle, *LAMCC v. NFL,* 8/27/80.
    Art Modell, *LAMCC v. NFL,* 9/24/80.
AFFIDAVITS:
    Al Davis, *LAMCC v. NFL,* 3/18/80.
[Oakland] *Tribune,* 3/2/80.
San Francisco Examiner, 3/3/80.
Los Angeles Times, 3/4/80.

4/2.

INTERVIEWS:
    Art Modell, 9/14/83, 11/9/84.
    Bill Robertson, 9/6/84.
    Stephen Reinhardt, 10/9/84.

TESTIMONY:
   Art Modell, *Gries Sports Enterprises v. Cleveland Browns,* 6/18/84, 7/12/84,
      NASL v. NFL, 4/23/80.
   Pete Rozelle, *LAMCC v. NFL,* 4/2/82, 4/5/82, 4/6/82.
DEPOSITIONS:
   Al Davis, *LAMCC v. NFL,* 11/25/80.
   Art Modell, *LAMCC v. NFL,* 9/24/80.
   Pete Rozelle, *LAMCC v. NFL,* 8/27/80.
telegram, Al Davis to Pete Rozelle, 3/6/80.
Akron Beacon Journal, 1/18/83.
[Cleveland] *Plain Dealer,* 3/4/77, 9/26/78, 11/30/79, 1/13/81.
Cleveland Press, 3/27/80.
[Oakland] *Tribune,* 3/7/80, 3/8/80.

4/3.

NFL minutes, 3/10/80.
INTERVIEWS:
   Gene Klein, 9/14/80.
   Leonard Tose, 10/3/84.
   Joe Robbie, 9/27/83.
TESTIMONY:
   Pete Rozelle, *LAMCC v. NFL,* 4/2/82, 4/6/82.
DEPOSITIONS:
   Al Davis, *LAMCC v. NFL,* 11/25/80.
   Pete Rozelle, *LAMCC v. NFL,* 8/27/80.
Sports Illustrated, 3/24/80.

4/4.

INTERVIEWS:
   Tex Schramm, 9/15/83, 9/18/84.
   Stephen Reinhardt, 10/9/84.
   L.A. source, confidential.
TESTIMONY:
   Bill Robertson, *LAMCC v. NFL,* 4/6/82.
   Pete Rozelle, *LAMCC v. NFL,* 4/2/82.
AFFIDAVITS:
   Yvonne Burke, *LAMCC v. NFL,* 3/18/80.
letter, John Larsen to Al Davis, 3/3/80.
memo, Harry Hufford to Board of Supervisors, 2/26/80.
motion, Baxter Ward to Board of Supervisors, 2/26/80.
LAMCC v. NFL, Federal Register, Volume 26, Number 52, 12/24/82.
Sports Illustrated, 3/24/80.
Los Angeles Times, 3/18/80.
[Oakland] *Tribune,* 3/26/80.

4/5.

INTERVIEWS:
    Pete Rozelle, 6/6/84.
TESTIMONY:
    Lamar Hunt, *NASL v. NFL,* 4/2/80, 4/3/80.
    Edward Bennett Williams, *NASL v. NFL,* 4/7/80.
    Joe Robbie, *NASL v. NFL,* 4/9/80.
    Pete Rozelle, *NASL v. NFL,* 4/16/80, 4/17/80, 4/21/80, 4/22/80.
    Leonard Tose, *NASL v. NFL,* 4/22/80.
    Chuck Sullivan, *NASL v. NFL,* 4/22/80.
    Art Modell, *NASL v. NFL,* 4/23/80.
NASL v. NFL, 505 F Supp 659 (1980).
NASL v. NFL, 670 F. 2d 1249 (1982).
Texas Monthly, 4/78.

4/6.

TESTIMONY:
    Leonard Tose, *NASL v. NFL,* 4/22/80, *Tose v. First Pennsylvania Bank,*
        6/24/80, 6/25/80, 6/26/80.
NFL Record and Fact Book.
Tose v. First Pennsylvania Bank, 492 F Supp 246 (1980).
Philadelphia Inquirer, 4/5/80, 6/25/80, 6/27/80, 7/1/80.
[Philadelphia] *Bulletin,* 1/22/81.
Philadelphia Daily News, 1/4/80.

4/7.

INTERVIEWS:
    Gene Klein, 9/14/84.
    Pete Rozelle, 8/9/83, 6/11/84.
    Joe Alioto, 2/1/85.
    Jay Moyer, 6/6/84, 6/7/84.
    Bill McPhail, 9/23/83.
DEPOSITIONS:
    Al Davis, *LAMCC v. NFL,* 3/14/80, 11/25/80.
    Gene Klein, *LAMCC v. NFL,* 9/17/80.
[San Diego] *Tribune,* 2/14/80.
San Diego Union, 2/15/80.
[Oakland] *Tribune,* 10/25/79.
Los Angeles Times, 3/3/80.

4/8.

INTERVIEWS:
    Steve Rosenbloom, 9/21/84.

Pete Rozelle, 6/11/84.
NFL owner, confidential.
NFL source, confidential.
DEPOSITIONS:
   Al Davis, *LAMCC v. NFL,* 11/25/80, 3/4/81.
   Pete Rozelle, *LAMCC v. NFL,* 8/28/80.
   Dominic Frontiere, *LAMCC v. NFL,* 2/13/81.
   Bill Robertson, *LAMCC v. NFL,* 10/9/80.
   Mel Irwin, *LAMCC v. NFL,* 10/8/80, 10/23/80.
   Harold Guiver, *LAMCC v. NFL,* 10/14/80.
speech, Georgia Rosenbloom Frontiere, 4/15/84.
Georgia Rosenbloom Frontiere, "Cynics and Critics," *Los Angeles Times,* 9/4/81.
TV Guide, 12/17/83.
Los Angeles Times, 4/7/80, 7/22/80, 8/7/80, 9/25/80, 10/30/80, 12/11/80, 4/19/81,
   12/18/81.
Los Angeles Herald Examiner, 3/20/81.
Florida Ledger, 9/17/81.
Miami Herald, 12/26/80.

4/9.

DEPOSITIONS:
   Al Davis, *LAMCC v. NFL,* 11/25/80.
Sports Illustrated, 1/6/81, 1/19/81, 2/2/81.
Los Angeles Times, 1/9/81, 1/24/81, 1/29/81.
Los Angeles Herald Examiner, 1/5/81.
Philadelphia Daily News, 1/8/81.
[Oakland] *Tribune,* 1/16/81.

4/10.

INTERVIEWS:
   Robert Gries, 10/12/84.
TESTIMONY:
   Art Modell, *Gries Sports Enterprises v. Cleveland Browns,* 6/18/84, 7/12/84.
   William Huffman, *Gries Sports Enterprises v. Cleveland Browns,* 6/19/84.
Sporting News, 12/6/80.
[Cleveland] *Plain Dealer,* 5/23/82.

4/11.

TESTIMONY:
   Art Modell, *NASL v. NFL,* 4/23/80.
letter, Robert Irsay to Colts ticket holders, 1/16/81.
Playboy, 8/81.
[Baltimore] *Sun,* 9/16/79, 9/18/79, 3/1/80, 4/4/80, 4/10/80, 5/24/80, 12/19/80,
   1/3/81, 1/24/81, 2/11/81, 6/9/81, 6/11/81, 7/15/81, 9/3/81, 11/20/81.
[Baltimore] News-American, 11/12/78, 12/22/80.
Washington Post, 2/26/80.

4/12.

INTERVIEWS:
Joe Robbie, 9/27/83.
Tex Schramm, 9/15/83.
Pete Rozelle, 6/7/84.
Bill Robertson, 9/6/84, 1/24/85.
Jay Moyer, 6/7/84.
L.A. source, confidential.
Los Angeles Times, 1/14/81, 2/7/81, 3/17/81.
Los Angeles Herald Examiner, 4/6/81.
San Francisco Chronicle, 3/18/81, 5/9/81.

4/13.

In this, and the following two chapters that re-create the first trial of *LAMCC v. NFL,* I have used both the testimony as taken in the trial itself and the trial coverage of the following newspapers: *Los Angeles Times, San Diego Union, San Francisco Chronicle,* [Oakland] *Tribune.* In addition I have also used the following:
INTERVIEWS:
Pete Rozelle, 6/7/84.
Gene Klein, 9/14/84.
Jay Moyer, 6/7/84.
LAMCC v. NFL, Federal Reporter, Volume 26, Number 52, 12/24/82.
New York Times, 1/30/83.

4/14.

See note 4/13.
INTERVIEWS:
Federal Court source, confidential.
Georgia Frontiere, "Courting a Sport," *Los Angeles Times,* 9/4/81.
Riverside Press Enterprise, 6/9/81.
[Baltimore] *Sun,* 6/10/81.

4/15.

See note 4/13.
INTERVIEWS:
Leonard Tose, 10/3/84.
Jay Moyer, 6/7/84.
NFL source, confidential.
TESTIMONY:
Art Modell, *Gries Sports Enterprises v. Cleveland Browns,* 7/12/84.
[Cleveland] *Plain Dealer,* 7/10/81, 8/16/81.

4/16.

INTERVIEWS:
   Ed Garvey, 12/3/84.
   Jack Donlan, 10/17/84.
   Bob Moore, 2/8/85.
   Keith Fahnhorst, 12/6/84.
DEPOSITIONS:
   Al Davis, *LAMCC v. NFL*, 11/25/80.
NFLPA, *Labor Organization Annual Report*, Department of Labor, 12/1/78 to
   11/30/79, 12/1/77 to 11/30/78, 12/1/76 to 11/30/77.
NFLPA, *The Audible*, 1/82.
NFLPA, *Report to Members*, 9/81.
[Cleveland] *Plain Dealer*, 9/11/81.

4/17.

INTERVIEWS:
   Robert Gries, 10/12/84.
TESTIMONY:
   Art Modell, *Gries Sports Enterprises v. Cleveland Browns*, 6/18/84, 7/12/84.
   Robert Gries, *Gries Sports Enterprises v. Cleveland Browns*, 6/20/84.
   Jay C. Hall, *Gries Sports Enterprises v. Cleveland Browns*, 6/19/84.
   William Huffman, *Gries Sports Enterprises v. Cleveland Browns*, 6/19/84.

4/18.

INTERVIEWS:
   Art Modell, 11/9/84.
   Bill Robertson, 9/6/84, 1/24/85.
   Stephen Reinhardt, 10/9/84.
   Mel Durslag, 10/1/84.
   L.A. source, confidential.
   2 negotiations sources, confidential.
   Participant, confidential.
Los Angeles Times, 9/27/81, 9/28/81, 9/30/81.
[Cleveland] *Plain Dealer*, 3/28/82.

4/19.

INTERVIEWS:
   Billy Sullivan, 10/19/84.
   Bob Marr, 1/22/85.
   Jack Donlan, 10/17/84.
   Source at Miami meetings, confidential.
NFLPA, Bargaining Demands, 2/82.
United Press, 3/31/82.
Fortune, 8/20/84.

Boston Globe, 7/26/81, 7/28/81, 8/13/81, 11/6/81.
Boston Herald, 4/1/81, 8/4/81.
New York Times, 2/17/82, 2/19/82.

4/20.

INTERVIEWS:
    Steve Rosenbloom, 9/21/84.
    Paul Tagliabue, 6/7/84.
    Ben Zelenko, 9/5/83.
TESTIMONY:
    Pete Rozelle, Hearings before the Subcommittee on Monopolies, U.S. Con-
        gress, 12/10/81.
NFLPA, *The Audible,* 1/82.
Memphis Commercial Appeal, 1/22/82.
New York Times, 2/19/82, 3/26/82.
Los Angeles Times, 3/19/82.

4/21.

INTERVIEWS:
    Robert Gries, 10/12/84.
TESTIMONY:
    Art Modell, *Gries Sports Enterprises v. Cleveland Browns,* 6/18/84, 7/12/84.
    Robert Gries, *Gries Sports Enterprises v. Cleveland Browns,* 6/20/84.
    William Huffman, *Gries Sports Enterprises v. Cleveland Browns,* 6/19/84.
[Cleveland] *Plain Dealer,* 3/28/82.

4/22.

NFL minutes, 3/22/82.
INTERVIEWS:
    Pete Rozelle, 6/5/84.
    Gene Klein, 9/14/84.
    Leonard Tose, 10/3/84.
    Contract source, confidential.
TESTIMONY:
    Pete Rozelle, Hearings before the Subcommittee on Monopolies, U.S. Con-
        gress, 12/10/81, *LAMCC v. NFL,* 4/2/82.
    Art Modell, *Gries Sports Enterprises v. Cleveland Browns,* 7/12/84.
DEPOSITIONS:
    Al Davis, *LAMCC v. NFL,* 3/4/81.
Sports Illustrated, 3/29/82.
San Francisco Examiner, 3/12/80.
[Cleveland] *Plain Dealer,* 5/29/82.

4/23.

INTERVIEWS:
>Art Modell, 9/14/83.
>Pete Rozelle, 6/7/84.
>Jay Moyer, 6/7/84.
>NFL source, confidential.

Sport, 8/82.
[Cleveland] *Plain Dealer*, 5/8/82.
New York Times, 1/30/83.
Los Angeles Times, 3/30/82, 4/2/82, 4/7/82, 4/22/82, 5/8/82.
[Oakland] *Tribune*, 5/10/82.

4/24.

INTERVIEWS:
>Pete Rozelle, 6/7/84.
>Leonard Tose, 10/3/84.

TESTIMONY:
>Pete Rozelle, Hearings before the Judiciary Committee, U.S. Senate, 8/16/82.
>Al Davis, Hearings before the Judiciary Committee, U.S. Senate, 9/20/82.
>Ed Garvey, Hearings before the Judiciary Committee, U.S. Senate, 8/16/82.
>Bill Robertson, Hearings before the Judiciary Committee, U.S. Senate, 8/16/82.

Los Angeles Times, 5/22/82, 8/12/82.

4/25.

INTERVIEWS:
>Leonard Tose, 9/20/83, 10/3/84.
>Dan Rooney, 10/4/84.
>Pete Rozelle, 8/9/83, 6/6/84.
>Hugh Culverhouse, 9/19/83.
>Jack Donlan, 10/17/84.
>Bob Moore, 2/8/85.
>Keith Fahnhorst, 12/6/84.

NFLPA, flyer, undated.
NFLPA, *Because We Are the Game*.
Time, 10/4/82.
Sports Illustrated, 2/1/82, 9/27/82.
U.S. News and World Report, 9/6/82.
Associated Press, 11/9/82.
New York Times, 9/9/82, 10/1/82, 10/9/82, 10/10/82, 10/18/82, 11/1/82, 11/5/82, 11/7/82, 11/8/82, 11/15/82, 11/17/82, 11/19/82.
San Diego Union, 10/28/82.
St. Petersburg Times, 11/9/82.

4/26.

INTERVIEWS:
    Pete Rozelle, 8/9/83, 6/7/84.
    Gene Klein, 9/14/84.
    Chuck Sullivan, 10/17/84.
    Lamar Hunt, 9/22/83.
    Hugh Culverhouse, 9/19/83.
    Tex Schramm, 9/14/83.
    Art Modell, 9/14/83.
    Steve Rosenbloom, 9/21/84.
    Ed Garvey, 9/24/83.
    Keith Fahnhorst, 12/6/84.
    Rozelle friend, confidential.
NFLPA, *Labor Organization Annual Report,* Department of Labor, 12/1/82 to 11/30/83.
Sports Illustrated, 11/29/82.
Macleans, 11/29/82.
New York Times, 12/7/82, 1/9/83, 6/7/83.
San Francisco Chronicle, 9/14/83.

4/27.

NFL minutes, 3/21/83, 3/22/83.
INTERVIEWS:
    Dan Rooney, 10/4/84.
    Pete Rozelle, 8/25/83, 6/11/84.
    Gene Klein, 9/14/84.
    NFL source, confidential.
Philadelphia, 10/83.
[Cleveland] *Plain Dealer,* 3/20/83.
San Francisco Examiner, 5/6/83.
New York Times, 3/23/83.
Los Angeles Times, 4/14/83.

4/28.

NFL minutes, 3/22/83.
INTERVIEWS:
    Leonard Tose, 10/3/84.
    Art Modell, 11/9/84.
    Pete Rozelle, 8/9/83, 6/11/84.
    NFL source, confidential.
Sports Illustrated, 9/19/83.
Philadelphia, 83.
Associated Press, 1/12/83, 7/21/83, 9/21/83, 11/21/83.
Philadelphia Inquirer, 1/5/83, 1/29/83, 5/22/83, 5/23/83, 7/10/83, 7/13/83, 7/17/83, 8/7/83.
Philadelphia Daily News, 11/22/83.

4/29.

INTERVIEWS:
    Art Modell, 11/9/84.
    Pete Rozelle, 6/11/84.
    Robert Gries, 10/12/84.
DEPOSITIONS:
    Gabe Paul, *Cleveland Indians v. Cleveland Stadium Corp.*, 1/20/84.
letter, Art Modell to Robert Gries, 5/6/82.
letter, Robert Gries to Art Modell, 5/7/82.
letter, Art Modell to Gabe Paul, 1/20/82.
[Cleveland] *Plain Dealer,* 3/18/82, 6/10/82, 10/30/82, 11/13/82, 4/21/83, 4/27/83,
    5/3/82, 6/12/83, 9/4/83.
Cleveland Press, 3/18/82.

4/30.

NFL minutes, 5/25/83.
INTERVIEWS:
    Art Modell, 9/14/83.
    Pete Rozelle, 8/25/83, 6/11/84.
    Billy Sullivan, 10/19/84.
    Steve Rosenbloom, 9/21/84.
    Leonard Tose, 10/3/84.
    NFL owner, confidential.
    NFL source, confidential.
New York Times, 5/25/83.
San Francisco Examiner, 9/7/83.
Boston Herald, 2/21/83, 6/30/83.
Boston Globe, 6/30/83.
Los Angeles Times, 12/6/82, 3/13/83.
Riverside Press Enterprise, 12/19/80.
Palm Springs Desert Sun, 10/8/83.

4/31.

INTERVIEWS:
    Gene Klein, 9/14/84.
    Paul Tagliabue, 6/7/84.
    Jay Moyer, 6/7/84.
Sports Illustrated, 8/29/83, 9/5/84.
San Diego Union, 1/15/83, 10/13/83, 12/10/83.
[San Diego] *Tribune,* 11/9/83.
New York Times, 6/26/83.
San Francisco Chronicle, 6/1/83, 6/24/83, 6/28/83, 7/27/83.
San Francisco Examiner, 6/18/83, 7/22/83, 10/12/83.
[Oakland] *Tribune,* 5/83, 6/1/83, 7/22/83.
Los Angeles Times, 10/27/83.

4/32.

NFL minutes, 10/5/83.
INTERVIEWS:
    2 NFL owners, confidential.
Miami News, 12/13/82, 12/14/82.
Miami Herald, 9/1/83.
[Baltimore] *Sun*, 8/22/82, 6/3/83, 9/2/83, 9/28/83.
Indianapolis Star, 1/13/82.
New York Post, 9/29/83.
New York Times, 9/18/80, 12/5/80, 9/14/83, 9/29/83, 11/23/83, 2/5/85.

4/33.

NFL minutes, 10/5/83.
INTERVIEWS:
    Pete Rozelle, 8/9/83, 8/25/83, 6/11/84.
    Gene Klein, 9/14/84.
    Art Modell, 10/9/83.
    Rozelle friend, confidential.
San Francisco Chronicle, 10/5/83, 10/6/83, 10/7/83.
Peninsula Times Tribune, 10/6/83, 1/9/84.

4/34.

INTERVIEWS:
    Pete Rozelle, 6/7/84.
    Tex Schramm, 9/18/84.
    Art Modell, 9/14/83.
    Joe Robbie, 9/27/83.
    Leonard Tose, 10/3/84.
    Bill Robertson, 9/6/84.
    2 NFL owners, confidential.
    NFL source, confidential.
    Bradley source, confidential.
    NFL observer, confidential.
    NFL insider, confidential.
author's notes, Rozelle press conference, 1/20/84.
Sports Illustrated, 9/5/84.
Forbes, 10/1/84.
New York Times, 1/15/84.
Dallas Morning News, 12/14/83.
Washington Post, 1/23/84.
San Francisco Chronicle, 10/3/83, 10/27/83, 11/29/83, 1/24/84.
Los Angeles Times, 2/3/83.
Peninsula Times Tribune, 1/22/84, 2/28/84.
Tampa Tribune, 1/23/84.

5/1.

INTERVIEWS:
>   Tex Schramm, 9/18/84.
>   Pete Rozelle, 6/11/84.
>   Leonard Tose, 10/3/84.
>   Joe Alioto, 2/1/84.

Newsweek, 9/3/84.
Forbes, 9/13/82.
Dallas Times Herald, 11/15/83, 1/14/84, 1/22/84, 1/28/84, 3/3/84, 3/17/84.
Dallas Morning News, 11/14/83, 11/15/83, 12/14/83, 1/8/84, 1/18/84, 2/25/84,
>   3/10/84.
San Francisco Chronicle, 4/18/84.
Washington Post, 3/20/84.
New York Times, 3/5/85.
Wall Street Journal, 1/22/85.

5/2.

INTERVIEWS:
>   Pete Rozelle, 6/11/84.
>   Gene Klein, 9/14/84.

transcript, Robert Irsay press conference, 1/20/84, recorded by [Baltimore] *Sun*.
Jimmy Irsay, "Hoosier Heartland," *Sports Illustrated*, 11/19/84.
Newsweek, 4/9/84.
Sporting News, 1/21/85.
People, 1/86.
[Baltimore] *Sun*, 1/20/84, 1/21/84, 1/22/84, 3/2/84, 3/16/84.
[Baltimore] *News-American*, 1/21/84, 3/3/84, 3/15/84.
Indianapolis Star, 3/12/84, 3/31/84, 4/1/84.
Indianapolis News, 4/2/84.
San Jose Mercury, 3/21/84, 3/22/84.
Washington Post, 3/30/84, 4/8/84.

5/3.

INTERVIEWS:
>   Billy Sullivan, 10/19/84.

Game Day, 11/11/84.
Miami News, 1/27/84, 3/2/84, 3/6/84, 11/28/84.
Miami Herald, 3/6/84, 3/10/84, 3/14/84, 5/25/84, 6/23/84, 7/7/84, 7/29/84, 10/8/84,
>   11/15/84, 1/9/85.
San Francisco Examiner, 3/17/85.

5/4.

INTERVIEWS:
>   Gene Klein, 9/14/84.

Sports Illustrated, 1/16/84, 2/25/85.
Forbes, 11/5/84.
San Francisco Magazine, 3/84.
San Francisco Examiner, 3/10/84, 3/19/84, 3/20/84, 3/23/84, 3/27/84, 10/24/84, 12/9/84.
San Francisco Chronicle, 1/11/84, 7/23/84, 12/2/84.
San Jose Mercury, 3/6/84, 3/16/84.
New York Times, 3/23/84, 4/30/84, 10/18/84.

5/5.

INTERVIEWS:
     Gene Klein, 9/14/84.
     Pete Rozelle, 6/11/84, 2/18/86.
complaint, *Klein v. Davis*, 1/30/84.
San Diego Union, 3/23/84, 7/31/84, 8/1/84, 8/3/84, 8/28/84.
[Oakland] *Tribune*, 3/23/84.

5/6.

INTERVIEWS:
     Wellington Mara, 10/17/84.
     Art Rooney, 9/16/83.
     Dan Rooney, 9/19/83, 10/4/84.

5/7.

INTERVIEWS:
     Lamar Hunt, 9/22/83, 9/20/84.
Hearings, Committee on Government Operations, Subcommittee on Commerce, U.S. Congress, *Silver Prices and the Adequacy of Federal Actions in the Marketplace, 1977–80*, 3/31 to 5/22/80.
Commodity Futures Trading Commission, *Report on Recent Developments in the Futures Market*, 1980.
Fortune, 4/1/85.
Forbes, 10/1/84.
Newsweek, 3/11/85.

5/8.

INTERVIEWS:
     Leonard Tose, 9/20/83, 10/3/84.
NFL Record and Fact Book.
Associated Press, 1/30/84.
Philadelphia Inquirer, 3/27/84.
New York Times, 12/17/84, 12/30/84, 2/3/85, 3/6/85, 3/9/85, 3/11/85, 4/7/85.
Phoenix Gazette, 11/8/84.
San Francisco Examiner, 12/11/84, 12/14/84.
San Francisco Chronicle, 11/13/84, 12/13/84, 12/15/84, 12/17/84, 12/18/84.

5/9.

INTERVIEWS:
Source close to investigation, confidential.
Source close to Georgia, confidential.
Rams source, confidential.
TV Guide, 12/17/83.
Los Angeles Times, 12/9/83, 12/23/83, 3/1/84, 3/9/84, 3/10/84, 3/21/84.
Los Angeles Herald Examiner, 12/9/83, 12/10/83.
New York Times, 12/10/83.

5/10.

INTERVIEWS:
Billy Sullivan, 10/19/84.
Chuck Sullivan, 10/16/84.
Fortune, 8/20/84.
Sports Illustrated, 1/13/86.
CBS News, 1/13/86.
USA Today, 1/13/86.
San Francisco Chronicle, 10/28/84, 12/10/84, 1/6/86.
San Francisco Examiner, 6/30/84, 10/23/85.
Los Angeles Times, 11/30/84, 12/5/84.

5/11.

INTERVIEWS:
Art Modell, 11/9/84.
Robert Gries, 10/12/84, 10/24/84.
TESTIMONY:
Art Modell, *Gries Sports Enterprises v. Cleveland Browns,* 7/12/84.
brochure, Vote Yes on Issue 1.
[Cleveland] *Plain Dealer,* 3/16/83, 12/2/83, 1/7/84, 3/16/84, 3/17/84, 5/9/84,
8/3/84, 8/31/84, 4/26/85, 7/2/85.
Akron Beacon Journal, 7/4/84, 7/16/84, 8/3/84.

5/12.

INTERVIEWS:
Tex Schramm, 9/18/84.
Pete Rozelle, 2/18/86.
Bill Robertson, 1/24/85.
NFL source, confidential.
Davis associate, confidential.
Associated Press, 11/7/84.
Los Angeles Times, 9/17/84, 11/15/84, 11/25/84, 11/30/84, 12/9/84.
New York Times, 3/17/85.

San Francisco Chronicle, 3/23/84.
San Francisco Examiner, 1/15/84, 12/19/84, 3/17/85.

5/13.

INTERVIEWS:
    Pete Rozelle, 6/5/84, 2/18/86.
    NFL source, confidential.
invocation, Hall of Fame Enshrinement, 8/3/85.
speech, Tex Schramm, Hall of Fame Enshrinement, 8/3/85.
speech, Pete Rozelle, Hall of Fame Enshrinement, 8/3/85.
NFL Record and Fact Book.
A. C. Neilsen and Co., cited *New York Times,* 10/25/84.
Sports Illustrated, 2/24/86.
Boston Globe, 2/2/84.
San Francisco Examiner, 2/21/84, 6/13/84, 11/25/84.
San Francisco Chronicle, 1/27/85, 2/19/85.
San Jose Mercury, 4/28/84, 6/14/84.
[Oakland] *Tribune,* 11/6/84.
Washington Post, 1/21/85.
New York Times, 11/23/83, 10/25/84, 12/30/84, 1/19/85, 3/17/85, 1/19/86.

INDEX

ABC (American Broadcasting Co.), 14, 36, 530, 552, 643, 644
  Monday Night Football, 18, 436
  NFL contracts, 6, 15
Acapulco (Mexico), 295
Acme Packing Company, 154
Adams, Bud, 25, 93, 102, 103, 104, 105, 538
Adelphi College, 59, 395
Aetna Life Insurance Company, 218
AFL-CIO (American Federation of Labor-Congress of Industrial Organizations), 16, 317, 327, 520
Airport Marina Casino (Las Vegas, Nev.), 203
Akron Beacon Journal, 36, 37, 635
Akron Pros, 12
Aladdin (Las Vegas, Nev.), 471
Alameda County (Calif.), 250, 413, 427
  see also Oakland-Alameda County Coliseum
Alameda County Board of Supervisors (Calif.), 412
Alameda County Building Trades Council (Calif), 507
Alameda County Superior Court (Calif.), 201
Alaska Trainship Corporation, 179
Alexander, Lamar, 516
Alexander v. NFL, 498
Alioto, Joseph, Jr., 333–334, 410–411, 431, 437, 448, 455, 457, 458, 460, 461, 473, 485–487, 488–498
  passim, 511–512, 521, 526, 535–538, 539–540, 578, 585, 597, 622
Alioto, Kathleen Sullivan, 333, 512
All-America Football Conference, 48, 79, 197, 275
Allen, George, 532
All Star Games (strikers), 546
Alworth, Lance, 461
Amerada Hess, 282
Americana Hotel (Bal Harbour, Fla.), 3, 23
American Airlines, 320
American Bank and Trust Co., 556
American Basketball Association, 93, 150
American Conference (NFL), 591
American Football League (AFL), 14, 18, 49, 51, 61, 132–133, 144, 170, 218
  Davis as commissioner, 56–57, 62, 65
  demise, 66
  early history, 60, 102, 104
  feud with NFL, 3, 4, 105–106
  NFL merger, 17, 62–63, 65–66, 74, 147
  ownership, 450
American Metal Forming Company, 435
American Professional Football Association, 12
American Security Bank, 142
Americans. *See* Birmingham Americans
American Way, 320
Anaheim ("Big A") Stadium, 55, 307, 308–309, 329, 338, 340–341, 344, 465
Anaheim (Calif.), 152–153, 186, 253, 308–311, 465
  Rams move to, 326, 328–330, 338–343, 350, 356, 361–362, 368, 371, 375, 388, 391, 395, 413, 431, 438

Anaheim Stadium Associates, 310, 326, 329–330, 340, 465
Anaheim Southern California Sun, 149, 186, 215, 216
Anderson, Dick, 244–247, 273
Anderson, Gary, 575, 586
Anderson & Company, Arthur, 23, 567
Andrews, Vinnie, 36, 37
Angels. *See* California Angels
Anheuser-Busch, 91
Annual meetings
  1960, 11–12
  1972, 5–6, 95
  1973, 70
  1974, 3–7, 86, 89, 157–159
  1975, 199
  1976, 224–233 passim
  1977, 271–275
  1978, 320–325
  1979, 366–371
  1980, 439
  1982, 515, 528–533
  1983, 552–555, 559
  1984, 611–612
  1985, 611, 639
Antitrust cases, 16, 78–82, 147, 200–201, 213, 221–222, 255, 484, 516–521, 535, 537–542, 549, 555
  see also Sherman Act
Arab Banking Corp., 601
Argovitz, Jerry, 575, 586
Arizona, 230, 622
  see also Phoenix
Arizona Biltmore (Phoenix, Ariz.), 271, 528
Arizona State University, 175, 602
Armour Company, 327
Arrowhead Stadium (Kansas City, Mo.), 630
Asbury Park High School (N.J.), 282
Associated Industries of Massachusetts, 258
Associated Press, 396, 546
Association of Small Business Investment Companies, 197
Astrodome, 25
Atkinson, George, 249–251, 267, 273, 473
Atkinson v. Noll, 251, 267, 298–302
Atlanta (Ga.), 132, 193
Atlanta Falcons, 184, 185, 365
Atlantic City (N.J.), 556–557
Audible, The, 319
Austin Statesman, 27
Australia, 9

Babbitt, Bruce, 602, 605
Baer, Harold, 288
Bailey, James 476–477, 503, 506, 507, 526, 527
Baker, Howard, 148, 516
Bakersfield (Calif.), 604
Bala Cynwyd (Pa.), 13
Bal Harbour (Fla.), 163, 196, 607
Balmoral (racetrack), 278

Baltimore (Md.), 48–50, 52, 54, 88, 182, 186–187, 189, 291, 368–369, 377, 386, 398–399, 479–481, 581
Baltimore City College, 48
Baltimore Colts, 11, 13, 22, 44, 45–46, 59, 66, 86–88, 102, 136, 175, 179, 186–190, 194, 230–231, 239, 368, 376, 386, 416, 580–581, 593, 645
  city of Baltimore negotiations, 478–481
  move to Indianapolis, 602–607
  Rosenbloom buys, 48–53
  stadium negotiations, 89–90, 159, 396, 398, 401–402
Baltimore News-American, 87, 231, 399, 604
Baltimore Orioles, 385, 400, 479
Baltimore Sun, 50, 54, 87–89, 188–190, 230, 368, 371, 397–399, 401, 478, 479, 603
Baltimore/Washington International Airport, 478
Bank, Girard, 457
Bank of Honolulu, 199
Bankston, W. O., 599
Barber, George, 600
Barnes, Bill, 194
Barness, Herb, 113–114, 292–293, 294, 296, 313–314, 332, 363
Barnett Banks of Florida, Inc., 192
Barnett-Wilson Corp., 192
Bassett, John, 168, 169, 170, 176, 186, 200, 206, 215, 216, 222, 229, 239, 243
  Anderson lawsuit, 575–576
Bateson Co., Inc., J. W., 31
Beame, Abraham, 85, 284–287
Bears. See Chicago Bears
Beatty, Warren, 375
Bede Aviation Corp, 435
Bel-Air (Calif.), 52–53, 211, 387
Bel Air Hotel (Los Angeles, Calif.), 404
Bell, Bert, 10, 11, 13, 15, 16, 18, 48–49, 79–80, 102–104, 123, 124, 155, 230–231
Bengals. See Cincinnati Bengals
Benson, Tom, 642
Bentsen, Lloyd, 538
Bethlehem Steel, 35, 327
Beverly Hills (Calif.), 73, 241, 295, 358, 526
Beverly Hills High School, 8
Beverly Hills Hotel, 415
Beverly Hilton, 359, 361–362, 365, 368, 371
Beverly Wilshire Hotel, 379, 414, 483
Bidwill, Bill, 93, 231, 232, 239, 297, 617, 642–664
  NASL lawsuit, 452–453
  Raiders' move to Los Angeles, 433, 437, 439, 441
Bidwill, Charlie, 125, 156
"Big A" Stadium (Anaheim, Calif.). See Anaheim ("Big A") Stadium
Bills. See Buffalo Bills
Birmingham (Ala.), 123, 151, 178, 185, 186, 193, 216, 417
Birmingham Americans, 149, 186, 199
Birmingham Vulcans, 222, 228–229, 230
Bishop Realty Company, 40
Bissell, 123, 134
Blakeley, Jerry, 309
Blazers. See Florida Blazers
Blecher, Maxwell, 485, 493, 535
Blitz. See Chicago Blitz
Bloomington (Minn.), 289, 290, 371
Blue Chip Investors, 203, 205
Blue Cross, 523
Boe, Dick, 335
Boggs, Hale, 17
Bonwit Teller, 295
Booz, Allen & Hamilton, 318
Borough Park (Brooklyn, N.Y.), 35

Boston (Mass.), 123, 124, 553
Boston Bar Association, 258
Boston Braves, 122
Boston Bruins, 322
Boston Celtics, 179, 322
Boston College and Law School, 121–122, 124, 172
Boston Globe, 124, 125, 126, 129, 173, 209, 219, 258, 513, 640
Boston Herald, 127, 173, 262, 512, 571, 572
Boston Patriots, 103–104
Boston Pops, 572
Boston Red Sox, 123, 124, 322
Boston University Field, 124
Bowlen, Pat, 625
Boy's Club (Chicago), 239
Bradley, Tom, 328, 340–341, 375, 396–397, 411–412, 427, 507, 508, 509, 592, 637–638
Bradshaw, Terry, 269
Bramen, Norman, 625
Braves. See Boston Braves
Bright, Bum, 600–601
Broncos. See Denver Broncos
Brooke, Edward, 312–313
Brookings, Institution, 24
Brooklyn (N.Y.), 35, 36
Brooklyn Dodgers, 284
Brooks Ticket Agency, A1, 420
Broward County (Fla.), 175, 289
Brown, Jerry, 327, 396–397
Brown, Paul, 11–12, 223, 529
Brown Derby (Los Angeles, Calif.), 333
Browns. See Cleveland Browns
Bruins. See Boston Bruins
Brussels (restaurant), 332
Brussels-Lambert (Belgian bank), 297
Bryant, Cullen, 213, 215
Bryant v. NFL, 213
Buccaneers. See Tampa Bay Buccaneers
Budweiser (beer), 571
Buffalo (N.Y.), 187, 358
Buffalo Bills, 103, 174, 202, 203, 350, 558
Bulldogs. See Canton Bulldogs
Bulls. See Chicago Bulls
Bunting, John, 293–298, 314, 332, 334, 457
Burke, Yvonne Braithwaite, 446
Busch Stadium (St. Louis), 643
Business Week, 73, 202, 203
Byrd, Robert, 538
Byrne, Brendan, 285

Cabbage Patch Kids (toys), 626
Cabot, Cabot & Forbes, 309–310, 329–330, 340, 350
Caesars Palace (Las Vegas, Nev.), 471, 560, 604
California, 210, 577
California Angels, 152, 307
California Board of Medical Quality Assurance, 242
California First Bank, 601
California State Board of Medical Examiners, 77
California Sun. See Anaheim Southern California Sun
California Superior Court, 70, 427
Candlestick Park (San Francisco, Calif.), 614
Canning Company, K. S., 112
Canton (Ohio), 12, 16, 664
Canton Bulldogs, 12, 154
Canyon Hotel (Palm Springs, Calif.), 320
Cardinal Mooney High School (Youngstown, Ohio), 478
Cardinals. See Chicago Cardinals; St. Louis Cardinals
Carey, Hugh, 583, 585
Carothers, Hamilton, 348, 353, 356, 409
Catain, Jack M., Jr., 420–422, 573, 627, 628

CBS (Columbia Broadcasting System), 10, 13, 14, 15, 18, 28, 91, 530, 552, 643, 644
    NFL contracts, 6, 15, 249, 436
CC & F Stadium Properties, 310
Cedars of Lebanon Hospital, 486
Celtics. *See* Boston Celtics
Central National Bank of Cleveland, 236, 505–507 passim, 528
Central Penn National, 331
Central States Fund. *See* Teamsters Pension Fund
Chandler, Wyeth, 401
Chargers. *See* San Diego Chargers
Charities. *See* NFL Charities
Charlotte (N.C.), 178, 186, 417
Charlotte Hornets, 149, 215
Chase Manhattan Bank, 332, 457
Chavez Ravine (Calif.), 253
Chesapeake Restaurant (Baltimore, Md.), 400
Chesler, Louis, 45–46
Chessie System, 238
Chicago (Ill.), 13, 87, 152–153, 166, 177, 187, 188, 278, 361, 553, 605, 607, 608
Chicago Bears, 11, 16, 87, 93, 231, 239, 590
Chicago Blitz, 553
Chicago Bulls, 107, 110, 111, 321, 325, 619
Chicago Cardinals, 102, 230–231, 394
Chicago Cubs, 93
Chicago Tribune, 140, 187
Chicago White Sox, 554
Chicago Wind, 215
Chiefs. *See* Kansas City Chiefs
Chris-Craft Industries, Inc., 21
Christiana Inn (South Lake Tahoe, Nev.), 627
Christian Century, 3
Cincinnati (Ohio), 179, 193
Cincinnati Bengals, 147, 179, 443, 547, 590
Cincinnati Reds, 179
Citibank, 314, 331–332, 453
Citicorp Real Estate, 601
City Club Forum (Cleveland, Ohio), 502
City of New York v. New York Jets Football Club Inc., Leon Hess, Metropolitan Baseball Club Inc., Donald Grant, New Jersey Sports Authority, Sonny Werblin, National Football League, and Pete Rozelle, 287–288
City of Oakland v. Oakland Raiders, 576–580
Civil Rights Act, 520
Clark, James P., 112
Clark, Steve, 367–368
Cleveland (Ohio), 36–37, 39–42, 236–238, 278, 324, 434–436, 503, 563, 568, 633–636
    see also Greater Cleveland Growth Association
Cleveland Beacon Journal, 635
Cleveland Browns, 11, 22, 34, 40, 41, 66, 93, 197–198, 435–436, 474, 476, 477, 503, 522–526, 564, 565, 566, 567, 633–636
    Modell purchased, 36–39
    see also Robert D. Gries and Gries Sports Enterprises v. Arthur B. Modell
Cleveland Browns Football Company, Inc., 38, 198, 526, 633, 635
Cleveland City Council, 41, 42
Cleveland Clinic Hospital, 569
Cleveland Common Pleas Court, 563, 568
Cleveland Indians, 39, 198, 325, 435, 567–569
Cleveland Indians Co. v. Cleveland Stadium Corp, and Cleveland Browns, Inc., 569
Cleveland Indians Co. v. Cleveland Stadium Corp. and Servomation Corp., 568
Cleveland Municipal Stadium, 39–42
Cleveland Plain Dealer, 37, 40, 41, 237, 238, 511, 563, 566, 634
Cleveland Press, 325, 435
Cleveland Rams, 8

Cleveland Sports Media Association's Pride of Cleveland Award, 39
Cleveland Stadium, 400, 475, 563, 634
Cleveland Stadium Corporation, 41–42, 196–198, 234–238, 324, 435–436, 474–477, 503–507 passim, 522–523, 563, 565, 567–569, 633–636
Coggins v. New England Patriots, 261
Cohen, 420–421
Cohen, Raymond, 627–629
Cohen, Robert, 627–629
Cole, Richard, 235, 506, 522–523, 526
Colgate-Palmolive (co.), 144
Coliseum Commission. *See* Los Angeles Coliseum Commission
Coliseum, Inc. *See* Los Angeles Coliseum
Colts. *See* Baltimore Colts
COMEX (N.Y. Exchange), 620
"Commitment to Excellence" (Raider motto), 593, 633
Committee appointments, NFL, 303–304
Committee on Interstate and Foreign Commerce, Congressional, 76
Committee to Relocate the Rams to Orange County, 311
Compensation. *See* Rozelle Rule
Compton (Calif.), 416
Compton High School, 8
Compton Junior College, 8
Congress, 644, 645
    see also Antitrust cases; Sherman Act; names of committees and members
Connelly, John, 114, 115, 116, 117
Continental Bank and Trust, 601
Continental League, 14
Cook, Herman, 69
Cook, Marlowe, 520
Cooke, Carrie. *See* Rozelle, Carrie
Cooke, Inc., Jack Kent, 384
Cooke, Jack Kent, 4, 55, 93, 141, 142, 207, 210, 228, 253, 294, 323, 336–337, 346, 366, 382–385, 414, 452, 552, 590, 591, 593, 611, 626, 640
    biography, 143–144
    cross-ownership, 143–146
Cooke, John, 210, 383
Cooke, Ralph, 21, 383
Cooley, Benton, 364–365
Cosell, Howard, 571, 572
Costello, Frank, 139
Cotchett, Joseph, 482, 491, 492
Council of Colt Corrals, 291
Court of Common Pleas (Cleveland, Ohio), 542
Covington and Burling (law firm), 83, 99, 174, 222, 234, 336, 348, 356, 409, 437, 519, 520
Cowboys. *See* Dallas Cowboys
Coyne, James J., 155
Criswell, W. A., 598
Crocker Bank, 514, 556, 560, 622, 623, 625, 630
Crosby, Heafy, Roach & May, 424
Cross-ownership. *See* Ownership policy
Crowder, Randy, 315, 316
Crown Cork & Seal, 114
Csonka, Larry, 168, 169, 170, 200
Cubs. *See* Chicago Cubs
Cullum, Caroline, 455, 457, 458
Culverhouse, Hugh, 51, 179, 195–196, 223, 227, 279, 306–307, 322, 336, 356, 366, 373, 375–376, 398, 416, 456, 465, 511, 531, 538, 542, 546, 551, 556, 578, 590–591, 601, 610, 613, 625
    accomplishments, 589–590
    bid for Rams, 193–194
    directorships, 192

Culverhouse, Hugh (*continued*)
  on finance committee, 303–304
  and Georgia Rosenbloom, 460
  wealth, 193
Culverhouse, Joy (Mrs. Hugh Culverhouse), 193, 195
Curry, Bill, 166
Cushing, Cardinal, 207
Cuyahoga County (Ohio), 37, 634
Cyrano's Restaurant (Los Angeles, Calif.), 627, 628

Dade County (Fla.), 175, 289
Dade County Democratic Party. *See* Democratic Party—Dade County
Dade County Industrial Development Authority (Fla), 611
Dade County Metro Transit Authority, 134
Daley Memorial Award, Arthur, 211
Dallas (Tex.), 39, 48, 92, 101–102, 109, 110, 347–401, 431, 434
Dallas Cowboys, 4, 5, 21, 26–27, 28–29, 51–64, 92, 104, 232, 273, 308, 343, 597–598
  Bum Bright buys, 601
  history, 104–105
Dallas Morning News, 599
Dallas Texans, 103, 105
Dallas Times Herald, 599
Dallas Tornado, 107, 108, 321, 346
Davidson, Gary, 149, 150, 168, 169, 170, 176, 186, 199
Davis, Al, 23, 34, 43, 121, 136, 150, 157, 170, 191, 206–207, 216, 222, 223, 224, 229, 250, 263, 308, 337, 375, 572, 587, 590, 591–592, 606–607, 610, 613, 619, 632
  AFL commissioner, 56–57, 62, 65–66
  AFL-NFL merger, 62–63
  Anderson-Rooney agreement failure, 247–248
  annual meeting (1985), 639
  antitrust lawsuit, 367, 539–542
  and Atkinson, 249–251
  Atkinson v. Noll, 298–299
  City of Oakland v. Oakland Raiders, 576–580
  conflict with Klein, 448, 459, 471, 551, 574
  conflict with Modell, 434, 477
  conflict with Rozelle, 249–250, 272–273, 274, 448, 459, 463, 473–474, 521, 529, 549–552, 618, 636, 640, 645
  and cross-ownership, 323–325
  deals with Oakland Coliseum Commission, 377–380, 591–592
  early career, 58, 59, 395
  49ers' sale, 275–281
  friends, 66–67
  Gene Klein v. Oakland Raiders Ltd., Allen Davis, and John Does I through XX inclusive, 615–617
  and Glick, 202–205, 444–445
  homelife, 61, 395–396
  labor policy, 247
  LAMCC v. NFL, 413–414, 417, 432, 447–448, 455, 531, 533–538, 555, 581, 594
  on "League think," 100, 153
  and the Mafia, 460–461
  memorandum of agreement with Los Angeles, 444–446
  Modell on, 67
  NFL lawsuit victory, 555, 636–640
  NFL strike, 545
  Oakland Raiders sale, 60–61, 63–65, 69–70
  Philadelphia Eagles et al v. Oakland Raiders Ltd., 446–447
  Raiders publicity and promotion, 593
  Raiders receivership move, 447
  Raiders transfer fact-finding committee, 433

religious views, 274
reputation, 51, 58–61, 62, 64–65, 66, 224, 248–249, 274, 532
and Robertson, 371, 377, 379–380, 393, 415, 427, 446, 467
and Rosenbloom, 49, 56, 253, 326, 330–331, 372, 382, 415–417, 448, 459, 467, 469, 551
and Rozelle, 4, 66–68, 223–224, 303–306, 425, 434; *see also subhead* conflict with Rozelle
Super Bowl, 472–474, 593–594
on ticket scalping, 263–267, 417–418, 461–463, 469–470
USFL challenge, 531–532
and Valley, 58–59, 62, 70, 135, 201, 205–206, 274
Davis, Allen R. *See* Davis, Al
Davis, Carole (Mrs. Al Davis), 61, 273, 404
  heart attack, 395–396
Davis, Mark Clark, 61
Davis, Marvin, 435, 476, 504, 505, 509
DeBartolo, Eddie, Jr., 275, 278–281, 306, 323, 367, 375, 392, 491, 529, 547, 553–554, 569–570, 590, 593–594, 630, 641
  conflict of interest with father, 278–279, 586–588, 611–615
  Raiders move to Los Angeles, 350, 443
DeBartolo, Edward, Sr. (Mr. D.), 179, 277, 278–281, 323, 593–594
  buys into USFL, 553–554, 569–70
  conflict of interest with son, 278–279, 586–588, 611–615
DeBartolo Corp., 277–278, 279, 280, 554, 614
Decatur Staleys, 12, 154
DeConcini, Dennis, 538, 540, 623
del Coronado Hotel (San Diego, Calif.), 224, 228, 231, 243
DeLorean, John Z., 242–244
Democratic Farm Labor Party, 380
Democratic Party, 132
  California, 327
  Dade County (Fla.), 135, 175
Democrats for Ford, 241
Denver (Colo.), 35, 102, 304, 553
Denver Broncos, 93, 103, 589, 625
DeOrsey, Leo, 141
Department of Justice, 519
Department of Labor, 200
Detroit (Mich.), 149, 553
Detroit Lions, 25, 45, 79, 212–213, 297, 343, 456, 549
Detroit Wheels, 149, 186
Diamond Shamrock Corp., 238
Diamond Vision, 571
Diplomat Hotel (Miami, Fla.), 514
Dirksen Building (Washington, D.C.), 192
Disneyland, 309
Disneyland Hotel, 341
Dixon, Dave, 107–108
Dodgers. *See* Brooklyn Dodgers; Los Angeles Dodgers
Dodger Stadium, 55, 253, 632
Dole, Robert, 663
Dolphins. *See* Miami Dolphins
Donlan, Jack, 501–502, 514, 515, 544–547
Douglas, Kirk, 375
Drug use, 76–78, 242, 459
Dukakis, Michael, 240, 258
Dumont network, 13
Duquesne University, 157
Durslag, Mel, 357–362, 373–374, 394–395, 413, 423, 463, 467, 469–472, 483, 509, 534, 577, 590
Dusseldorf (W. Germany), 149
Dyke Stadium, 231

Eagles. *See* Philadelphia Eagles
Eastmont Mall Associates, 204–205, 248, 501
East Rutherford (N.J.), 85, 285
Eaton Corporation, 237
Ecia, Peggy, 646
Edelman, Ed, 446, 447
Edward Bennett Williams for the Defense, 140
Edwards, Don, 538
Egan (Minn.), 290
Ellington, Duke, 172
El Rancho Del Rayo (Klein's Calif. estate), 574
Empire City (racetrack), 156
Empress Productions, 465
Esquire, 31, 43
European American Bank, 601
Expansion, 17, 28, 132, 147–153, 157–159,
    174–179, 190–196, 222, 228–230, 243,
    343, 482–483, 516, 518, 535–536, 621, 645

Fabulous Forum. *See* Forum
Fahnhorst, Keith, 499–501, 550–551
Falcons. *See* Atlanta Falcons
Fallingbrook, 384
FBI. *See* Federal Bureau of Investigation
Federal Baseball Club, 79
*Federal Baseball Club of Baltimore v. National
    League of Professional Baseball Clubs*, 79
Federal Bureau of Investigation, 627–628
Federal Commodities Futures Trading Commission,
    620
Federal Reserve Board, 620
Federal Securities and Exchange Act, 259
Federation of Professional Athletes, 317, 319
Fencik, Gary, 500
Fenway Park (Boston, Mass.), 124
Ferre, Maurice, 289, 580, 608–609
Fidelity National Bank, 562
Field, Wayne, 179, 190
Fines (football), 76–78, 222, 250, 459
Finks, Jim, 437
Firestone, John D., 114, 295, 332
Firestone v. Tose, 295
First Federal Savings Bank, 601
First National Bank of Chicago, 239, 261, 262
First Pennsylvania Bank, 114, 116–120, 292–298,
    314, 332–334, 363, 365, 457–458
First Provident Bank, 313
Fletcher, Susan, 558–562, 622–623, 626
    see also Tose, Susan
Florida A&M, 151
Florida Blazers, 199
Fonda, Jane, 593
Forbes, 27, 43, 143, 277, 282, 591, 620
Ford, William Clay, 25, 212, 213–214, 297, 312,
    331, 456–458, 612, 613
Fordham University, 82–83
Ford Motor Company, 21, 327, 612
Forstater, Sidney, 292, 294, 296–298, 332, 363,
    457
Fort Belvoir (Va.), 59
Ft. Lauderdale (Fla.), 347, 610–611
Ft. Lauderdale Strikers, 317–318, 335, 346, 452
Fort Pitt Hotel, 155–156
Fortune, 25, 168, 172, 282–283, 612, 620
Forum (Inglewood, Calif.), 55, 145, 146, 253,
    382
Forzano, Rick, 213
Foss, Joe, 29, 62, 104, 132
Foundation for Children with Learning Disabilities,
    210
Fouts, Dan, 302
Foxboro (Mass.), 125–126, 208, 308, 571, 631
Foxboro High School, 126
Foxboro Raceway, 125

Franchises
    moves, 230–231, 308, 343, 346–356, 391–392,
        394, 396, 410, 431, 576–577, 593, 641–642
    worth 23, 51, 133, 145, 152, 155, 158, 169, 176,
        239, 260, 276, 296, 560–561, 600, 616,
        625, 632
    see also specific teams
Frank, Barney, 240
Frankovich, Mike, 509–510
Frank Youell Field (Oakland, Calif.), 58
Free agency, 80–82, 167, 212, 223, 245–246, 247,
    257, 499
    see also Rozelle Rule
Freebie and the Bean, 387
Freemont Hotel Casino (Las Vegas), 203
Frontiere, Dominic, 387–388, 390, 408, 416, 465,
    487, 489–490, 572–573, 627–629
    IRS investigation, 535
    ticket scalping inquiry, 573
Frontiere, Georgia. *See* Rosenbloom, Georgia
    (Frontiere)
"Future is Suddenly Now, The", 390

Gambling, 44–47, 118, 456, 556–557, 559
Game attendance, 5, 185–186, 439, 549, 552, 621,
    638
Game scheduling, 245, 445
Garner, James, 593
Garvey, Ed, 16, 80, 82, 83, 84, 234, 243, 248,
    255, 271, 316–319, 365, 498–502, 515,
    521, 539, 541–548
    NFLA negotiations, 1970, 80–81, 163–167
    NFLPA negotiations, 1974, 81–82
    NFLPA negotiations, 1976, 244–246, 247, 256
    NFLPA negotiations, 1977, 257
    NFLPA director resignation, 550
    NFL strike, 181–185
    Plan B, 200–201, 209, 222
Gator Bowl, 398, 400
Gelker, Thomas, 496–497
*Gene Klein, v. Oakland Raiders Ltd., Allen Davis,
    and John Does I through XX, inclusive*, 615
George Sargent Trust, 171, 208, 217–219
Georgetown University, 386
Georgetown University Law School, 140
George Washington Life Insurance Co., 192
Giants. *See* New York Giants
Giants Stadium, 285, 287, 584
Giorgio's (Beverly Hills), 295, 457
Girard Bank, 332, 457
Glick, Allen, 201–205, 248, 444–445, 460–461
Godbold, Jake, 398, 403
Golden Beach (Fla.), 372–373
Golden State Warriors, 275
Goldman Sachs, 477
Goode, W. Wilson, 623–624
Gore, Albert J., 645–646
Gracie Mansion (N.Y.C.), 286
Grand Duchess of Stadiums. *See* Los Angeles
    Memorial Coliseum
Grand Union (supermarket chain), 36
Grant, Cary, 375
Grant, Donald, 284–288, 583–584
Greater Cleveland Convention and Visitors' Bureau,
    435
Greater Cleveland Growth Association, 37, 41, 237
Greater Indianapolis Progress Committee, 230, 291
Green Bay (Wis.), 154–155, 498
Green Bay Packers, 45, 65, 92, 114, 154–155, 201,
    617
Green Mountain Park (Vt. racetrack), 156
Gries, Robert, Jr.
    family background 37, 38, 197
    and Modell, 38, 40, 42, 197–199, 234–236, 237,
        238

Gries, Robert, Sr., 37, 38, 197, 475–477, 504–507, 522–528, 563, 564, 566–569, 633, 634–635
Gries Investment Company, 197
"Gries I." *See Gries Sports Enterprises v. Cleveland Browns*
Gries Sports Enterprises, 38, 197, 198, 235, 506, 507, 633
Gries Sports Enterprises v. Cleveland Browns ("Gries I"), 635
"Gries II." *See Robert D. Gries and Gries Sports Enterprises v. Arthur B. Modell*
"Gries III." *See Robert D. Gries and Gries Sports Enterprises v. Arthur B. Modell and Cleveland Browns Football Company, Inc.*
Grizzlies. *See* Memphis Southmen
Grove Corp., 295
Grunyon's (Manhattan Beach, Calif.), 387
Guida, Louis, 560–562
Guider, Dorothy. *See* Williams, Dorothy Guider
Guiver, Harold, 265, 386, 417–422, 468–469, 488, 572–573, 627
Gumball Rally, 387
Gunny's Crab House, 188
Guren, Shelly, 42, 197
GWD Associates, 203–204

Hacienda Hotel and Casino (Las Vegas), 203
Hadl, John, 461
Hahn, Kenny, 342, 368–369, 395, 397, 411–412, 426, 444, 467, 592
"Hail to the Redskins" (song), 28
Halas, George, 11, 14, 16, 28, 87, 93, 155, 211, 221, 230, 239, 290, 617, 646
  conflict with Rozelle, 16
  Raiders move to Los Angeles, 433, 437, 442
Hale and Dorr (law firm), 180
Halpern (attorney), 441
Hamline College, 290
Hammond Pros, 12, 154
Hardy, Jim, 328, 368
Harris, Franco, 249
Harris, James, 302
Hilton, Barron, 73, 103, 105, 123, 242, 243, 244, 615, 616
Hilton Corp., 73
Hilton v. Klein, 243–244
Hitler, Adolf, 274
Hoffa, Jimmy, 139
Hogan and Hartson (law firm), 140
Holiday Inn, 277
Holy Cross University, 152
Hong Kong, 341
Honolulu (Hawaii), 124, 151, 158, 177, 360, 365, 370, 371, 420, 594, 600, 605, 611
Honolulu Hawaiians, 149, 216
Hoosier Dome, 581, 604, 625
"Hoosier Heartland" (Colts' song), 606
Hope, Bob, 172
Hornets. *See* Charlotte Hornets
Hotel Corporation of America, 127
Hotel del Coronado. *See* del Coronado Hotel
Hotel Navarro (N.Y.C.), 50
House Judiciary Committee, 517, 539
House Select Committee on Sports, 519
House Select Subcommittee on Professional Sports, 15, 520
House UnAmerican Activities Committee, 140
Houston (Tex.), 29, 56, 102–103
  see also Astrodome
Houston Oilers, 25, 93, 103, 205, 416, 547
Houston Texans, 186
Howsam, Bob, 102, 103
Hudnut, William, 604, 606
Huffman, William, 476–477

Hughes, Harry, 396, 399, 401, 479, 605
Hughes, Howard, 283
Humphrey, Hubert, 132, 285
Hunt, Bunker, 101, 105, 107, 108
Hunt, Caroline, 101
Hunt, Clark, 108
Hunt, Haroldson Lafayette III, 101
Hunt, Herbert, 101, 107, 108
Hunt, H. L., 100, 105, 106–107, 449–450
Hunt, Lamar, 5, 14, 22, 27, 54, 91, 94, 96, 98, 111, 113, 123, 125, 127, 132, 168, 179, 192, 201, 206, 207, 272, 276, 320–325, 326, 335, 337, 345, 346, 347, 362–363, 365, 367, 613, 619–621, 630
  AFL startup, 102–105
  early career, 101
  family, 100, 106–107, 449–450
  on Garvey, 81
  NASL lawsuit, 98–99, 448, 450
  negotiations with Schramm and NFL, 29, 56–57, 92
  NFL "planning committee," 223
  and Oakland Raiders, 58
  other sports interests, 92, 107, 108–110
  ownership policy, 226, 228
  personality and personal traits, 105, 106
  ticket scalping, 264
  and Tose, 225
Hunt, Lamar, Jr., 108
Hunt, Lyda Bunker (Mrs. H.L.), 100
Hunt, Margaret, 101
Hunt, Norma (Mrs. Lamar), 109
Hunt, Ruth Ray (Mrs. Lamar), 106–107, 449–450
Hunt, Sharon, 108
Hunt Oil Company, 107
Hurok, Sol, 384
Hyde, Henry, 538

I Love Lucy (TV program), 18
Indianapolis (Ind.), 151, 158, 229–230, 291, 398, 417, 552, 604–605, 625
Indianapolis Colts, 625
Indianapolis Star, 291, 604
Indians. *See* Cleveland Indians
Industrial National Bank of Rhode Island, 262
Inglewood (Calif.), 55, 145, 253
Inside Sports, 492
Internal Revenue Service (IRS), 125, 133, 168, 193, 276, 312
  Frontiere investigation, Ticket scalping
    and Rozelle, 47, 233–234
International Lawn Tennis Federation, 107
International Management Group, 168
International Metal Investments, 619
Irsay, Harriet (Mrs. Robert), 88, 89, 189, 402, 480, 625
Irsay, Jimmy, 88, 480
Irsay, Robert, 159, 186, 187, 194, 231, 277, 351, 353, 354, 375, 387, 467, 478–481, 581, 585, 593, 602–608, 641
  behavior, 86–87
  buys Baltimore Colts, 51–52, 87
  divorce, 625
  drinking problem, 90, 189
  early career, 87–89
  family life, 88
  interference with Colts, 189–190
  lies about background, 88–89, 188
  NFL expansion, 229, 230
  press criticism, 86, 88–89
  and Rosenbloom, 54, 86–87, 89–90, 186–188
  shooting, 625
  stadium negotiations, 291, 368–370, 396–403, 440
  and Thomas (Joe), 86, 89

Irsay, Roberta, 88, 89
Irsay, Tommy, 88
Irving (Tex.), 31, 308
Irwin, Dottie, 468
Irwin, Mel, 467–469, 485, 489
Iselin, Phil, 84, 207, 282, 283, 284
Ivanhoe Insurance, 192

Jackson, Henry (Scoop), 148
Jackson, Michael, 629
Jackson Family Victory Tour, 629–631
Jacksonville (Fla.), 179, 192, 193, 215, 477, 556, 631
Jacksonville Area Chamber of Commerce, 193
Jacksonville Sharks, 149, 186, 397
Jacksonville University, 193
Jessie, Ron, 212, 215
Jets. See New York Jets
JFK Stadium. See Kennedy Stadium, John F.
Jimmy Fund (Boston Charity), 122
Jimmy's Restaurant (Beverly Hills, Calif.) 421
Jimmy the Greek, 490
Jockey Club, 134, 137
John Mackey, et al v. National Football League.
    See Mackey v. NFL
Johnson, Lyndon, 172
Jones, Bert, 188
Jones, Day, Reavis & Pogue (law firm), 523

Kaiser Industries, 413, 414, 422
Kansas City (Mo.), 29, 105, 347
Kansas City Chiefs, 5, 22, 105, 322, 345, 416, 576
Kansas City Star, 345
Kansas City Times, 29, 105
Kapp v. NFL, 333
Karch, Sargent, 255, 256–257
Katz, Solomon, 114
Keating, Ed, 168, 169–170
Keland, Willard, 51, 134
Kenilworth Hotel (Miami, Fla.), 11–14, 19, 28, 44, 647
Kennedy, John F., 47, 600
Kennedy, Joseph, 47, 53
Kennedy Stadium, John F., 215, 630
    see also RFK Stadium
Kennel Club (Fla.), 156
Kensil, Jim, 355, 415
Kenyon, James, 309–310
Kheel, Ted, 255
Kidde Company, 560, 562, 621
Kiick, Jim, 168, 169, 170, 200
King, Milton, 141–142
King County (Wash.), 174, 175, 177
Kingdome (Wash.), 174, 175, 176
Kings. See Los Angeles Kings
Kingston Trio, 172
Kissinger, Henry, 569
Klein, Frances (Mrs. Gene), 71, 74–75
Klein, Gene, 6, 22–23, 92, 96, 191, 206, 271, 272,
    280, 305, 351, 353–356, 358–359, 373,
    375, 381, 385–386, 392, 402, 459, 460,
    470–472, 486, 492, 495, 529–531, 558,
    574–576, 587, 591, 610, 614
  buys into San Diego Chargers, 63, 73–74, 616
  Chargers' drug use, 76–78
  Chargers' strike, 183
  childhood, 71
  and Davis, 57, 66, 70–71, 75, 302
  early career, 71–73
  El Rancho del Rayo (Calif. estate), 574
  finances, 242
  on Garvey, 82
  Gene Klein v. Oakland Raiders Ltd., Allen Davis,
    and John Does I through XX, inclusive, 615

heart attacks, 486, 529
Hilton v. Klein, 243–244
leaves Chargers, 616
life-style, 74–75, 241–242
Los Angeles Raiders Ltd v. Eugene Klein, 615
Raiders move to Los Angeles, 414, 417, 423,
    439, 443, 448, 578
on Rosenbloom, 44, 220, 233
on Rozelle, 75–78
sells Chargers, 616
Klein, Joyce (Mrs. Gene), 75, 241
Klein, Nancy (Mrs. Gene), 241
Klosterman, Don, 408, 416–422, 427, 626, 627
  Raiders move to Los Angeles, 439, 443, 459
Knobel, Norma. See Hunt, Norma
Knowlton, Austin, 179
Koch, Ed, 582–585
Kowet, Don, 155
Kuharich, Joe, 10

Labor relations. See National Football League
    Players Association (NFLPA)
LaJolla (Calif.), 74
Lakers. See Los Angeles Lakers
LAMCC. See Los Angeles Memorial Coliseum
    Commission
LAMCC and Oakland Raiders Ltd. v. National
    Football League, Alvin Pete Rozelle, Eugene
    V. Klein, and Georgia Rosenbloom, 448
  see also LAMCC v. NFL
LAMCC v. NFL, 347, 348, 351, 358, 368, 410,
    413–414, 432, 447–448, 455, 460, 467,
    469, 473–474, 484, 502, 511, 518, 529, 531,
    533–542 passim, 549, 551, 554–555, 572,
    574, 581, 585–586, 590, 593–594, 597, 605,
    615, 622, 624, 629, 637–640, 642–643
Lampert, Ira, 560
Landy, John, 10
Lansky, Meyer, 45
LaSalle National Bank (Chicago), 208, 217, 218,
    238, 239, 240, 258, 262
Las Vegas (Nev.), 37, 219, 278, 295, 603–604
Laugh-In (TV program), 18
Laxalt, Paul, 591
"League Think" (concept), 13, 22, 24, 26, 34, 39,
    43, 50, 56, 67–68, 78, 81, 91–92, 93, 100,
    147, 150, 153, 154, 159–160, 163, 199, 216,
    283, 315, 325, 333, 334, 347, 384, 474,
    477, 483, 516, 529, 533, 539, 549, 591, 644
Leahy, Frank, 122, 123
Leahy, Marshall, 11
Learjet, 187, 188, 278
Leaseway Transportation, 324
LeBaron, Eddie, 570
Legion Field (Birmingham, Ala.), 123
Leonard Tose v. First Pennsylvania Bank et al, 333,
    410
Levanthal, Wally, 332
Liberty Bell (Phila. racetrack), 156
Liberty Bowl (Memphis, Tenn.), 401
Lillis, Don, 282
Lincoln Mortgage and Loan Company, 417
Lindsay, Gil, 328
Lindsay, John, 84–85
Lions. See Detroit Lions
LoCasale, Al, 274, 299, 303, 306, 307, 378, 379,
    380, 404–405, 413, 424–425, 592–593
  Raiders move to L.A., 437, 445
Loew's Anatole Hotel (Dallas, Tex.), 401–402
Lombardi, Vince, 114
Lombardi, Vince, Jr., 544
London (England), 149
Long, Howie, 650
Long, Russell, 17

Long Beach (Calif.), 54, 71, 328, 417
Long Beach Press Telegram, 8
Long Canyon (Calif.), 8
Look, 59, 64, 67
Los Angeles (Calif.), 8, 20, 52, 54–55, 65, 79, 85, 93, 103, 177, 326, 327, 329, 330, 338, 339, 341, 343, 355, 357, 358–362, 370, 371, 373, 377, 379, 391, 396–398, 406, 409, 422, 436–438, 441, 442, 444, 445, 477, 494, 497, 519, 553, 593, 626, 632
  see also Los Angeles Raiders
Los Angeles Biltmore (Los Angeles, Calif.), 537
Los Angeles City Council, 54, 327, 328, 368, 393, 411
Los Angeles Coliseum. *See* Los Angeles Memorial Coliseum
Los Angeles County Board of Supervisors, 54, 252, 327, 393, 411, 423, 444, 447, 460
Los Angeles County Council, 445
Los Angeles Dodgers, 307, 342
Los Angeles Dons, 79
Los Angeles Express, 644
Los Angeles Federal District Court, 212, 413, 427, 484, 534
Los Angeles Friars Club, 351, 358
Los Angeles Herald Examiner, 327, 357, 361, 362, 373, 413, 423, 459, 466, 469, 470, 627
Los Angeles Hilton, 420
Los Angeles Kings, 145, 382
Los Angeles Lakers, 145, 382
Los Angeles Memorial Coliseum, 8, 23, 43, 232, 291, 307, 311, 312, 328, 338–343, 346–351, 358, 362, 368, 377, 390–393, 406–411, 417, 459, 483, 496, 498, 540, 591
  Raiders move to, 432, 438, 445–446
  and Rams, 52, 54–56, 252–253
Los Angeles Memorial Coliseum Commission (LAMCC), 54–56, 232, 252–253, 308, 311, 326–330, 339–343, 346–351, 354, 357–358, 361–362, 369–370, 379–381, 393–395, 397, 401, 406–407, 411, 413–415, 417, 423, 427, 431–432, 437, 444, 447, 484, 502, 511, 519, 536, 638
  see also LAMCC v. NFL
Los Angeles Olympic Organizing Committee, 446
Los Angeles Raiders, 442, 468, 485, 538, 578, 592, 594, 601, 632, 637–638, 640
Los Angeles Raiders Ltd. v. Eugene Klein, 615
Los Angeles Rams, 10, 43, 73, 205, 211–214, 249, 307, 369, 373–376, 382, 386–391, 393, 408, 416–420, 461, 464, 535, 572, 626, 628
  Culverhouse attempt to buy, 193–194
  move to Anaheim, 308–311, 326–330, 339–342, 350, 356–357, 361, 371, 395, 396, 413, 535
  and Reeves, 55
  and Rosenbloom, 50–54
Los Angeles Recreation and Parks Department, 327
Los Angeles Sports Arena, 55, 145, 307, 311, 407
Los Angeles Times, 56, 74, 210, 212–213, 241, 254, 281, 307, 310, 329, 330, 338, 374, 375, 382, 386, 387, 405, 406, 411, 423, 432, 465, 470, 482, 485, 488, 490, 492–495, 508, 534, 536, 572, 592, 627–628, 637
Louisiana Downs (racetrack), 278
Lowell (Mass.), 127
Lugar, Richard, 649
Lukas, Wayne, 574
Luviano, John, 115
Lynn, Mike, 290
Lynwood (Calif.), 7–8, 416

Macker, Ken, 9, 10
Macker Company, 10

Mackey, John, 80–81, 163–165, 182, 222, 520
  see also Mackey v. NFL
Mackey v. NFL, 80–81, 165–166, 182, 184–185, 200, 205, 210, 212, 215, 221–224, 229, 245, 255, 257, 317, 498, 540
Madison Hotel (Washington, D.C.), 256
"Madison Street agreement, The," 231
Madrid (Spain), 149
Mafia. *See* Organized crime
Mahrishostrau (Austria), 290
Maier, Cornell, 441, 493
Major League Sports Community Protection Act of 1982, 538
Management Council Executive Committee, 166–167
Mandell, Arnold, 76–77, 242
Mangurian, Harry, 179
Manhattan. *See* New York City
Manufacturers National Bank, 297–298, 314, 331
Manufacturers Trust, 313
Mara, Ann (Mrs. Wellington), 83
Mara, Jack, 82, 83
Mara, Tim, 82, 83, 155
Mara, Wellington, 11, 14, 25, 56, 81, 92, 153, 159, 166–167, 183–184, 221, 255, 297, 306, 312, 315, 321, 570, 613, 617
  early Giants career, 82–83
  Giants move to New Jersey, 84–86, 284
  Raiders move to Los Angeles, 433, 440–441
  on Rosenbloom, 43, 220–221
Marine Corps, 188
Market Melodies (TV program), 35, 36
Marr, Bob, 128–129, 171–174, 176, 180–181, 208, 217–219, 220, 513
Marr, Dan, Jr., 125, 128
Marr, Dan, Sr., 127, 128
Marriott Corporation, 601
Marriott Hotel (Ft. Lauderdale, Fla.), 610
Marriott's Rancho Las Palmas (Palm Springs, Calif.), 439, 551, 553
Marshall, George Preston, 13, 16, 28, 141–146, 155, 156
Martha, Paul, 547, 554–555, 570
Martin, Clarence, 179
Maryland, 51, 187, 602, 606
Massachusetts Senate, 258
Massillon Tigers, 12, 154
Maui (Hawaii), 481
May Company, 197
McCarthy, Joseph, 139
McCaskey, Ed, 590, 613
McCloskey, Tom, 98, 109, 113, 179, 192, 193, 195–196, 277
McConnell, David, 128, 130, 171, 180, 208, 209, 217–218
McDonald & Company, 477, 503–504, 506, 523–525, 527
McElhenney, Hugh, 179
McGah, Ed, 59, 63, 68, 69–70, 202, 273
McGarvey, Robert J., 46
McKeigue, Jean Sullivan, 571
McLaney, Mike, 46, 47
McNamee, Frank, 11
McPhail, Bill, 13, 15, 16, 18, 19, 28, 209
Meadowlands (East Rutherford, N.J.), 84, 85, 86, 284, 287, 329, 582–585
Meany, George, 166
Mecom, John, 25, 462–463, 642
Mellon Bank, 279
Melvin, Richard, 46
Memorial Coliseum. *See* Los Angeles Memorial Coliseum
Memorial Stadium (Baltimore, Md.), 54, 187, 189, 480–481, 581

Memorial Stadium (Bloomington, Minn.), 480
Memphis (Tenn.), 148, 151, 158, 168, 174–178,
   186, 222, 228–229, 239, 290, 516, 553
Memphis City Council, 174
Memphis Commercial Appeal, 516
Memphis Grizzlies. *See* Memphis Southmen
Memphis Memorial Stadium, 174, 176
Memphis Southmen, 149, 168, 170, 176, 216, 222
Mencken, H.L., 48
Merrill Lynch Private Capital, Inc., 556, 560, 601
Metropolitan Oil Company, 123, 126, 218
Metropolitan Sports Facilities Commission, 290
Mets. *See* New York Mets
Meuli, Franklin, 275–276, 279
Mexico City (Mexico), 149
Miami (Fla.), 28, 46, 51, 102, 132–136, 138, 192,
   288, 315, 498, 580–581, 608–610
Miami Chamber of Commerce, 134
Miami City Commission, 608
Miami Dolphins, 51, 95, 99, 130, 133–138,
   168–171, 217, 239, 254, 288–289, 295,
   315–318, 335, 443, 581, 632
   Stadium, 608–611
Miami Dolphins, Ltd. v. City of Miami, 295
Miami Gatos, 138
Miami Herald, The, 134, 136, 608, 609, 610, 611
Miami International Merchandise Mart, 192
Miami News, 289
Miami Toros, 138, 317
Midlantic Bank, 331
Mid-South Grizzlies. v. NFL, 229
Midwest Federal Savings and Loan (Minneapolis,
   Minn.), 601
Milletti, Nick, 41
Miller, Alan, 164
Miller, Vance, 599–600
Milley, Matt, 632
Minneapolis (Minn.), 57, 80, 102, 104, 123, 133,
   179, 201, 290, 310, 326
Minneapolis Federal District Court, 81, 221
Minneapolis Lakers, 290
Minneapolis Tribune, 290
Minnesota House of Representatives, 290
Minnesota Kicks, 321
Minnesota State Legislature, 290
Minnesota Vikings, 21, 104, 201, 212, 265,
   289–290, 321, 440, 571
Minor League Executive of the Year award,
   144
Mode, Inc., 192
Modell, Art, 6, 21, 22, 23, 43, 71, 114, 125, 209,
   233–235, 251, 280, 297–298, 305–306, 307,
   323–325, 336, 434–435, 479, 497, 502, 532,
   547, 549, 551, 553, 563, 569, 589, 590, 616,
   633–634
   buys into Cleveland Browns, 36–37
   childhood, 35
   Cleveland Municipal Stadium renovation, 39–42,
      633
   Cleveland's Business Executive of the Year, 633
   Cleveland Stadium Corporation, 41–42, 196–197
   conflict with Davis, 67
   cross-ownership policy, 93, 94–95, 97
   dispute with Gries, 198–199, 563–567, 634–636
   early career, 35–36
   finances, 234–237, 476–477, 502, 504–507,
      522–528
   heart attack, 569
   marriage, 37–38
   NASL lawsuit, 452, 454
   negotiations with Gries, 560
   NFL-AFL merger, 65–66
   physical traits, 34
   public image in Cleveland, 37, 237

Raiders move to Los Angeles, 433, 440,
   493–494, 507, 510, 533, 534, 537–538
   on Rosenbloom, 49, 220
Modell, George, 35
Modell, Patricia (Mrs. Art), 37–38, 236, 527–528,
   569
Monahan, James, 622–625
Monday Night Football. *See* ABC (American
   Broadcasting Corporation)—Monday Night
   Football
Monmouth Park (racetrack), 281, 283
Moore, Bob, 317, 498–500
Morabito sisters, 276, 279
Morrison, Curly, 36, 37
Morton, Emil, 608
Moyer, Jay, 69, 228, 482, 537, 554, 556, 577
Muncie Flyers, 12, 154
Munich (W. Germany), 149
Murchison, Clint, 4, 28, 35, 39, 60, 105, 164,
   597–601, 619
   cross-ownership, 92, 93
   illness, 598
Murchison, Clint, Jr., 26–27, 31–32, 104
Murchison, John, Jr., 598
Murchison, John, Sr., 597–598
Murchison Brothers (partnership), 597
Murphy, Larry, E., 46
Murphy Stadium, Jack, 575, 628
Murray, Jimmy, 297, 314, 332, 558–559
Museum of Science and Industry (Los Angeles,
   Calif.), 54
Muskie, Edmund, 591
Narcotics. *See* Drug use
NASL. *See* North American Soccer League
NASL Players Association, 317
NASL v. NFL, 453, 455, 518, 554, 619
Nassau County (N.Y.), 151–153, 178
National Airlines, 501
National Basketball Association (NBA), 110, 145,
   151, 276, 519
National City Bank, 505, 507
National Conference, 65, 307, 589, 626
National Conference Championship Game, 529
National Football League. *See* NFL headings
National Football League Players Association
   (NFLPA), 16, 33, 80, 81, 164–165,
   199–201, 246–247, 256, 271, 315–319,
   498–499, 500, 520, 525, 539, 541,
   549–551, 553, 613
   1970 negotiations, 163–164
   1974 negotiations, 166–167, 181–185
   strikes, 181–185, 191, 542–548
National General Corporation, 72, 74
National Hockey League, 145, 278, 519
National Labor Relations Act, 183
National Labor Relations Board (NLRB), 257, 319,
   547
National Theatres and Television Corp., 71
NBC (National Broadcasting Co.), 14, 18, 643–644
   NFL contracts, 6, 15
Neilsen ratings, 271
Networks. *See* Television; specific networks
Nevada Gaming Control Board, 203
Newell, Pete, 9
New England Merchants Bank, 208
New England Patriots, 23, 62, 92, 121–130,
   171–173, 180–181, 217–219, 308, 513,
   549, 579–580, 632
   repurchase by Sullivans, 180–181, 207–208,
      237–238, 257, 260–262, 312–313
   see also Boston Patriots
New Jersey, 553, 584
New Jersey Sports Authority, 84, 86, 286–288,
   582–584

Newman, Julius, 560
Newman, Sandra, 560–562
New Orleans (La.), 17, 25, 65, 132, 257, 295, 324, 614
New Orleans Saints, 17, 25, 147, 176, 212, 547, 642
Newport Beach (Calif.), 330
News-American. See Baltimore News-American
Newspaper Guild, 327
Newsweek, 85, 170, 263, 597–598
New York City (N.Y.), 13, 14, 21, 25, 50, 62, 66, 71, 76, 77, 83, 84, 86, 124, 145, 153, 174, 283–288, 546, 582–585, 627, 643
New York Cosmos, 285, 324, 326
New York Daily News, 205
New York Giants, 11, 13, 43, 45, 71, 82, 83, 92, 152, 183–184, 284–285, 306, 329, 570
  move to New Jersey, 84–86, 308
New York Islanders, 335
New York Jets, 51, 65, 84, 152, 176, 207, 217, 281, 284–288, 306, 307, 329, 415, 592, 632
New York Mets, 283–284
New York Nets, 335
New York Post, 86, 585
New York Stars, 186
New York State Supreme Court, 288
New York Times, The, 15, 17, 65, 182, 183, 245–246, 255, 284, 285, 287, 305, 534, 545, 547–548, 550, 555, 582, 585, 623, 625, 642
New York Times Magazine, The, 199
New York Titans, 103, 104, 281
New York Yankees, 324
NFL championship, 37, 45, 108
NFL charities, 67–68, 273, 274
NFL constitution, 3, 153, 159, 337–338, 344–356, 409, 427, 441
NFL films, 299, 318
NFL finances, 589–591
NFLPA. See National Football League Players Association
NFL Properties, 30, 67, 68, 105, 274, 318
NFL Security, 77, 279
Nicklaus, Jack, 179
Nicoli, Anthony, 602–604
Ninth Circuit Court of Appeals, 586, 594
Nixon, Richard, 285
Noll, Chuck, 249, 250–251, 299–301
Nordstrom, Inc., 179
Nordstrom, Lloyd, 179, 191, 322, 639–640
North American Soccer League, (NASL), 92, 98, 99, 107, 108, 109, 138, 191, 276, 317–324, 326, 619
North Andover (Mass.), 545
North Dade (Fla.), 610
Northern State College, 131
Notre Dame University, 111, 118, 122, 138, 277
Novel and Greenough Academy, 129
NYU (New York University), 71

Oakes, Paul, 291
Oakland (Calif.), 57, 58, 59, 61, 63, 65, 204, 331, 553, 576–579, 585, 606–607, 614
Oakland-Almeda County Coliseum, 68, 302, 310, 432, 445, 533, 536
Oakland Chamber of Commerce, 59
Oakland City Council, 60
Oakland Coliseum. See Oakland-Alameda County Coliseum
Oakland Raiders, 4, 23, 43, 56, 68, 75, 201–202, 205, 207, 250, 272, 275, 299–302, 306, 432, 483, 503, 518–519, 533
  City of Oakland v. Oakland Raiders, 576–579
  move to Los Angeles, 330, 535, 537

Oakland Raiders Ltd., 68, 70
Oakland Superior Court, 437
Oakland Tribune, 58, 64, 66, 68, 202–205, 248, 273, 301
  on Davis, 248–249
Ocean Reef, 134
Office of Price Stabilization, 131
Ohio Court of Appeals, 633, 636
Ohio Supreme Court, 633
Oilers. See Houston Oilers
Old Guard (NFL), 154–155
Olejniczak, Dominic, 155
Oley Cooke and his Orchestra, 144
Olympics (Los Angeles, 1932), 39, 54
Olympics (Los Angeles, 1984), 252, 311, 328, 446
Olympics (Melbourne, 1956), 9
O'Melveny and Myers (law firm), 491
O'Neil, John, 135
O'Neill, F.J. (Steve), 324
O'Neill, Thomas P. (Tip), 126
Orange Bowl (Miami, Fla.), 51, 113, 132, 135, 136, 137, 288–289, 580–581, 608–609
Orange County (Calif.), 55, 152, 308, 311, 330
Oregon State University, 58
Organized crime, 45, 202, 204, 279, 420, 628
Organized Crime Strike Force, 203
Orlando (Fla.), 150, 178, 614
Owens, R.C., 182
Ownership policy, 50–51, 90–100, 109–111, 121–122, 138, 143, 145–146, 178, 191, 207, 217, 225–228, 276, 279, 317–326, 334–338, 344–348, 382–386, 448, 450, 455, 554, 569–570, 586–588, 614, 618, 619

Pacific Ocean, 211
Pack Robert, 45, 140
Paley, William, 15
Palm Springs (Calif.), 65, 73, 223, 320, 436, 532, 551–555, 559, 592
Pan American Airways, 134
Paradise Valley Shopping Center (Ariz.), 230
Parins Committee, 586
Paris (France), 149
Parrins, Robert, 570, 612
Parrish, Bernie, 45
Pat Joyce Tavern (Cleveland, Ohio), 168
Patriots, See Boston Patriots; New England Patriots
Patriots, Inc., 128–130
Patton, George, 282
Paul, Gabe, 567–569
Pay 'n Save Corp., 179
Pearl Harbor (Hawaii), 28
Pemberton, John, 294, 296–297, 457–458
Penn Racing Association, 156
Pennsylvania, 11
Penrod Drilling, 101
People, 607
Perk, Ralph, 42
Philadelphia (magazine), 111–112, 115, 116, 558
Philadelphia (Pa), 98, 118, 132, 179, 334, 553, 558–559, 610, 614, 621–625, 630
Philadelphia and Reading Corp., 49
Philadelphia Atoms, 195
Philadelphia Bell, 149, 150, 186, 215
Philadelphia Bulletin, The, 116, 117, 120, 297, 298
Philadelphia Court of Common Pleas, 115–116, 117, 119
Philadelphia Daily News, 119, 120, 313, 314, 332, 558
Philadelphia Eagles, 4, 10, 11, 22, 98, 112–120 passim, 179, 190, 193, 205, 276, 292–298, 313–315, 331–334, 556, 558–562, 621–626, 641
Philadelphia Eagles et al v. Oakland Raiders Ltd., 437–438, 446–447

Philadelphia Federal District Court, 292, 624
Philadelphia Flyers, 578
Philadelphia Inquirer, 98, 295, 296, 331, 458, 556–557, 561, 621
Philadelphia National Bank, 297, 332
Philadelphia Quartermaster Depot, 49
Phipps, Gerald, 93, 159
Phoenix (Ariz.), 148, 151, 158, 175–178, 230, 271, 290, 532–533, 553, 581, 602–606, 614, 622–625, 643
   annual meeting (1985), 611, 639–640
Phoenix City Council, 175
Phoenix Metropolitan Sports Foundation, 622
Piedmont (Calif.), 61
Pittsburgh (Pa.), 155–156, 322, 553–555, 570
Pittsburgh Civic Arena, 278, 554
Pittsburgh Maulers, 569, 587, 612, 614
Pittsburgh Penguins, 278
Pittsburgh Pirates (football team), 155
Pittsburgh Steelers, 5, 11, 13, 66, 80, 149, 154, 157–158, 232, 249–251, 263, 299–301, 524
Pittston Company, 218
Placid Oil Company, 100–101, 107
Plain Dealer. See Cleveland Plain Dealer
Planning committee, 223–224
Playboy, 169
Player-Club relations committee, 315–316
Player salaries, 543, 613
Pontiac (Mich.), 25
Pope, Ed, 136
Port Everglades Steel Corp., 192
Portland (Ore.), 65, 614
Portland Storm, 149, 186
Portland Trailblazers, 179, 191, 276
Powell, Adam Clayton, 139
Pregerson, Harry, 486, 488–489, 492–497, 507, 534
Premier Electric Company, 435
"Pride and Poise" (Raider motto), 64, 593
Pro (magazine), 105
Pro Bowl, 201
Pro Football Hall of Fame, 100, 646–647
Pro Football, Inc., 139, 141–143, 145
Pro Football Writers Association, 211
Pros. *See* Akron Pros
Provident National Bank, 332, 457
Public relations, 5–6, 8, 9–10, 249, 464, 542, 593

Racine Cardinals, 12
Radovich v. NFL. See William Radovich v. National Football League
Radovich, William, 79
Ralston Purina Corp., 91
Rams. *See* Cleveland Rams; Los Angeles Rams
Rancho Granada (Calif.), 585
Rancho Las Palmas Resort (Palm Springs, Calif.), 439, 551, 553
Rancho Sante. Fe (Calif.), 574
Ray, Ruth. *See* Hunt, Ruth Ray
Red Dog Investors, 203, 205
Red Lantern Bar (Folcroft, Pa.), 621
Reds. *See* Cincinnati Reds
Red Sox. *See* Boston Red Sox
Reeves, Dan, 10, 11, 14, 27, 50, 51, 55, 65, 193, 197
Reeves, Ken, 184
Reinhardt, Stephen, 441, 446, 447, 460, 508
Republican Party, 241
RFK Stadium (Washington, D.C.), 139
Rhode Island Hospital Trust National Bank, 208, 217, 238–240, 258–259, 262
Rich Who Can Own Sports, The, 155
Rickey, Branch, 14
Riviera (Las Vegas, Nev.), 471
Robbie, David, 138

Robbie, Elizabeth, 134, 137, 138, 452
Robbie, Joe, 51, 81, 130, 191, 200, 203, 217, 225, 228, 244, 443, 538, 552, 580–581, 585, 608–611
   childhood, 131
   cross-ownership, 95, 96, 99, 100, 146
   Danny Thomas partnership, 134
   Dolphin Stadium, 608
   early career, 131–132
   financial success, 135
   hires Shula as Dolphins' coach, 136–137
   NASL lawsuit, 452
   NFL expansion, 158, 175, 178
   NFLPA negotiations (1974), 166
   physical traits, 131
   purchases Miami franchise, 132–137
   Raiders move to Los Angeles, 448, 481
   and Sullivan, 130, 131
   and WFL, 168, 169, 171
   wife enters NASL management, 138
Robbie, Kathleen, 138
Robbie, Michael, 138, 443
Robert D. Gries and Gries Sports Enterprises v. Arthur B. Modell ("Gries II"), 566
Robert Irsay Company, *See* Irsay, Robert
Robertson, Bill, 437, 441, 445–446, 447, 459–460, 467, 482–483, 508–510, 539–540, 591, 638
Rochester Jeffersons, 12, 154
Rockefeller Center (N.Y.C.), 45, 47
Rock Island Independents, 12
Rome (Italy), 149
Rooney, Art, 5, 11–12, 80, 155, 156, 211, 646
Rooney, Art, Jr., 156
Rooney, Dan, 13, 21, 156, 223, 232, 245–247, 249–252, 263, 524, 587, 618
   and Davis, 272
   early career, 157
   and NFL expansion, 149, 150, 152, 153, 154, 155, 158, 175, 176, 178, 190, 195, 196
   NFL strike, 546–547
   Raiders move to Los Angeles, 444
Rooney, John, 156
Rooney, Kathleen (Mrs. Art), 156
Rooney, Pat (son), 156
Rooney, Patricia (Mrs. Dan), 157
Rooney, Tim, 156
Rose Bowl (Calif.), 263, 266
Rosenbloom, Carroll, 11–12, 22, 50, 57, 86, 87, 102, 145, 150, 158, 159, 163, 179, 203, 206, 249, 252–254, 263, 267, 431, 459, 466, 538, 589, 590, 617
   and antitrust exclusion, 80, 81
   buys Colts, 49
   childhood, 48
   and Culverhouse lawsuit, 194
   and Davis, 56, 488, 489–490
   death, 488
   early career, 48–49
   gambling, 45
   and Irsay, 89–90, 186–187
   life-style, 210–211
   Los Angeles Memorial Coliseum, 54–55, 85
   marriages, 52–53
   McLaney lawsuit, 46–47
   NFL-AFL merger, 65–66
   NFL expansion, 175, 195
   NFLPA negotiations (1974), 183
   personality traits, 23, 43–44, 186–187
   physical traits, 56
   Robbie dispute, 136–137
   and Rozelle, 44, 210–214, 219–221, 232–234, 254
   and Rozelle Rule, 182
   and ticket scalping, 265–266, 462–463, 469, 471

Rosenbloom, Carroll (*continued*)
  trades Colts for Rams, 50–52
  and WFL, 206, 215–216
Rosenbloom, Ed, 51
Rosenbloom, Georgia (Frontiere; Mrs. Carroll;
    Mrs. Dominic Frontiere), 54, 163, 234,
    448, 572, 589, 592, 610, 626, 629
  conflict with Davis, 459, 464
  IRS investigation, 572–573
  LAMCC v. NFL, 490, 574
  life-style, 466
  marriages, 53
  and the press, 464
  Raiders move to Los Angeles, 461, 464, 468,
    482, 484, 485, 487–488, 489, 492, 495
  remarriage, 465
  taping (bugging), 467, 468, 489
  ticket scalping, 469–470, 627
Rosenbloom, Solomon, 43, 48
Rosenbloom, Steve, 44, 47, 49, 53, 56, 136, 194,
    233, 254, 465, 466, 468, 521, 552, 573
  on his father, 55, 90, 195, 211, 220
  and NFL expansion, 148
  as Rams executive vice-president, 54
  replaces father as Colts president, 50
  stadium negotiations, 481
Rosenbloom, Velma, 52–53, 54
Ross, Don, 463
Ross, George, 205
Rozelle, Ann Marie, 9, 19
Rozelle, Carrie Cooke (Mrs. Pete), 20–22, 33, 159,
    210, 439, 484, 495, 586, 588
Rozelle, Jane (Mrs. Pete), 9
Rozelle, Pete, 13, 22–27 passim, 32, 34, 39, 48,
    51, 54, 58, 62, 71, 82, 86, 90, 106, 114,
    120, 218, 244, 249, 267, 271, 456, 465, 473,
    515, 528–531, 551, 554–555, 570, 594,
    597, 604–605, 607, 616–618, 622, 625, 627,
    634, 640–641, 644–645
  annual meetings, *see* Annual meetings
  and antitrust exclusion, 79, 80, 81, 516–522,
    538–539, 541
  as "boy czar," 14
  childhood, 7–8
  as commissioner, 3–5, 641–642
  conflict with Davis, 223, 272, 273, 274, 459,
    463, 473, 474,   *see also* subheads of
    Davis
  conflict with Halas, 16
  conflict with Marshall, 16
  contract, 641
  Culverhouse lawsuit, 194
  and Davis, 67, 68, 78, 204
  Davis contract dispute, 69, 70
  divorce, 19
  drug use in NFL, 76, 77–78
  early career, 8–10, 104
  father's death, 585–586
  football promotion, 5
  and Georgia Rosenbloom, 466
  and Hunt, 108
  Internal Revenue Service, 233, 234
  and Irsay, 231
  and Joe Robbie, 134, 138
  and Klein, 75
  "League Think" ideology, 13–17, *see also*
    "League Think"
  life-style, 210
  Mackey decision, 222–224
  and Mafia, 460
  NASL lawsuit, 448, 449, 452–453, 454–456
  and National Football League Players
    Association, 163–164, 165, 166, 185, 498, 501,
    502

NFL expansion, 147–149, 150, 152, 153,
    154–155, 156, 158, 159–160, 175–176,
    177, 178, 179
NFL-AFL merger, 17, 66
NFL gambling crisis, 44–47
NFL planning committee, 223–224
NFL strike, 545, 548–549
ownership policy, 91–96, 97, 98, 99, 100,
    110–111, 112–113, 121–122, 143, 146
Patriots move to Foxboro, 124, 125, 126
personal life, 19–22, 210
personal traits, 3–4, 178
Philadelphia Eagles et al. v. Oakland Raiders,
    437–438
philanthropy, 67
Pro Football Hall of Fame induction, 646–647
Raiders move to Los Angeles, 431–434, 439–441,
    445–448, 449–466 passim, 468, 480, 482,
    484–485, 499–516 passim, 534–537
Raiders transfer fact-finding committee, 433
and Rooney, 157
and Rosenbloom, 44, 49, 209–214, 219–221,
    232–234, 254
and Schramm, 28, 29, 30, 33
Seattle team ownership, 190–191
and Sullivan, 130, 180, 207
Tampa team ownership, 196
and TV, 13, 14–16, 18
and ticket scalping, 265–266, 462–463, 469–470
Tose's gambling, 557
Tose's purchase of Eagles, 114, 115, 117
Tose v. First Pennsylvania Bank, 457
voted NFL commissioner, 11–12
and WFL, 149, 168, 170, 206, 215–216
Rozelle, Ray, 7, 8
Rozelle Rule, 45, 80, 86, 166, 181, 182, 200, 209,
    212–13, 214, 215, 221–222, 245, 255–256
Rubin, Betsy (Mrs. Mickey), 119
Rubin, Mickey, 119
Rugo, Guido, 127
Rule of Reason standard, 221
Ruth, Babe, 465
Ruyanaidh (co.), 156

St. Louis (Mo.), 643
St. Louis Cardinals, 75, 87, 93, 230–231, 642
St. Petersburg Times, 196
St. Regis Hotel (N.Y.C.), 547
Saints. *See* New Orleans Saints
Salinas (Calif.), 576
San Antonio Wings, 216
San Bernadino-Riverside (Calif.), 152
Sanders, John, 575
Sanders, Stan, 509–511
San Diego (Calif.), 65, 71, 74, 182–183, 223,
    225–228, 232, 241, 610
San Diego Charger Football Club, 78, 639
San Diego Chargers, 22, 58, 59, 61, 63, 65, 70,
    73, 74, 105, 274, 460, 470, 471, 472
  NFL strike, 182–183
  drug use, 76–78
San Diego City Council, 575
San Diego Superior Court, 242
San Diego Tribune, 71, 74
San Diego Union, 243, 486, 495, 542, 574,
    616–617
San Dieguito River, 574
Sands (Las Vegas, Nev.), 471
San Francisco (Calif.), 11, 58, 153
San Francisco Chronicle, 144, 490, 496, 578–579,
    592, 612, 631
San Francisco Examiner, 554, 570, 612, 638
San Francisco 49ers, 58, 65, 73, 110, 148, 212,
    570, 587

San Leandro (Calif.), 58, 507
Sarasota County (Fla.), 193
Saratoga Development Corp., 202, 203, 204, 205
Saratoga (racetrack), 156
Sargent, Francis, 124, 126
Sargent, George, 127, 129, 207
Sargent, Hessie, 129, 130, 171, 172, 180, 207–209
Sargent, Lee, 129, 130, 172, 173, 209
Sargent Trust. *See* George Sargent Trust
Sarkowsky, Herman, 179, 191–192, 195, 196, 271, 272
  Raiders move to Los Angeles, 433, 436, 439, 440, 441, 453, 493
Saturday Evening Post, 57
Schabarum, Pete, 252
Schaeffer, Donald, 478, 479, 480, 582, 603–606
  buys into Cleveland Browns, 37, 38
Schaeffer Brewing Company, 125
Schaeffer Stadium. *See* Sullivan Stadium
Schramm, Marty (Mrs. Tex), 22, 33
Schramm, Tex, Jr., 10, 17, 21–22, 23, 24, 30, 32, 34, 51, 57, 62, 64, 65, 91, 105, 157, 164, 272, 229, 232, 434, 502, 529, 551, 572, 589, 597
  biography, 27–28
  cross-ownership, 92, 95–96
  and Davis, 66–67, 206, 223–224, 273
  Hall of Fame induction of Rozelle, 647
  negotiates sale of Cowboys, 599
  and NFL expansion, 148, 149, 158, 176
  obsession with football, 33
  physical traits, 33
  Raiders move to Los Angeles, 440, 443, 448, 482, 493, 509, 534
  on Rosenbloom, 44
  and Rozelle, 5, 9, 28, 29, 45
  status in NFL, 26, 27, 30, 34, 223
  temperament, 32–33
  as Washington Redskins general manager, 28–29
Schramm, Tex, Sr., 27
Schwartz, David, 240
Schwarz, F.A.O., Jr., 582–583
Scottsdale (Ariz.), 70, 148
Seattle (Wash.), 65, 92, 151, 219, 222, 229, 239, 272, 478
Seattle Kings, 179, 190–191
Seattle Post-Intelligence, 177
Seattle Professional Football, 191
Seattle Seahawks, 640, 646
  expansion team ownership, 179, 190–191, 195, 196
  NFL expansion choice, 148, 151, 158, 174, 175, 177, 178
Seattle Supersonics, 74
Seattle Times, 175
Secret Service (U.S.), 628
Securities and Exchange Commission, 146, 203, 260
  see also Federal Securities and Exchange Act
Selman, Dewey, 500
Senate Commerce Committee, 645
Senate Judiciary Committee, 539
Services Bureau Corp., 29
Servomation, Inc., 505–506, 523, 568
Sharks. *See* Jacksonville Sharks
Shea Stadium, 85, 217, 582–584
Sheraton-Belvedere (Baltimore, Md.), 50
Sherman Antitrust Act, 15, 84, 96, 102, 138, 147, 206, 255, 448, 449, 516, 537–538, 540, 553, 588, 612, 645
  Culverhouse lawsuit, 194
  defined, 78
  early litigation under, 79
  Haynes lawsuit, 579–580

and *Mackey v. NFL*, 80–81, 200, 212–214, 221
  NASL lawsuit, 229, 449, 450
  Tose v. First Pennsylvania, 457
Shreveport (La.), 150, 186
Shreveport Steamer, 186
Shula, Don, 136–137, 170, 203, 232, 610
Shulman, Sam, 74, 92, 179
Sibley, Harper, 138
Siegel, Herb, 21
Silverdome (Pontiac, Mich.), 25
Simmons Market Research, 6
Simon, Bill, 476
Simpson, Alan, 538
Sinatra, Frank, 593
Sisk (U.S. congressman), 519
Skalbania, Nelson, 513–514
Slaten, Carole, 496
Slick Trailers, 114
Smith, Rankin, 184, 538, 570
Snider, Ed, 560–561
Socioeconomic Information on Candidate Areas for NFL Franchises, 150
Soldier Field (Chicago), 231
Sonnabend, Paul, 127
Southern California Sun. See Anaheim Southern California Sun
Southern District Court of New York, 194
Southern Methodist University (Dallas, Tex.), 101, 480
Southmen. *See* Memphis Southmen
Spa, The (Palm Springs, Calif.), 460
Spadia, Lou, 65, 110, 148, 158
Spanos, Alex, 616, 617, 639
Sport (magazine), 271
Sporting News (magazine), 69
Sports Antitrust Broadcast Act, 14
Sports Arena. *See* Los Angeles Sports Arena
Sports Authority. *See* Tampa Sports Authority
Sports Community Protection Act of 1984, 645
Sports Illustrated, 5, 12, 14, 51, 83, 147, 248, 256, 249, 550, 593, 614, 644
  on Davis, 58, 59, 60
  on Giants move to New Jersey, 84–85
  on Miller, 164
  on NASL Philadelphia franchise, 109
  on NFL annual meeting (1980), 440
  on NFL expansion, 147
  on NFL gambling crisis, 44
  on Raiders, 470
  on Robbie, 130–131, 135, 137
  on television deal (1982), 530
  on WFL, 186, 215
Stadium Club (Texas Stadium), 31, 32
Stadium Corp. *See* Cleveland Stadium Corp.
Stadium Management Corp., 513, 630–632
Stadium Realty Trust, 125, 126, 128, 130, 512–513
Stadiums, 124–126, 236–237, 360
  leases, 24–25, 40–42, 54–55, 60, 283–288, 481
  Superstadium Game, 25–26, 31–32, 39–42, 84–86, 252–254, 288–291, 307–311, 326–331, 338–341, 367–371, 580–585, 602–611, 643
  see also specific stadiums
Staggers (U.S. congressman), 76
Staleys. *See* Decatur Staleys
Stanford Research Institute (SRI), 150–151, 152, 153, 158, 174–175
Stanford University, 498
Stanton, Frank, 18
Stardust Hotel-Casino (Las Vegas, Nev.), 203
Stark, Fortney, 538
Stars. *See* New York Stars
Steamer. *See* Shreveport Steamer
Stein, Gertrude, 57

Steinbrenner, George, III, 41, 42
Sterling, Scotty, 58
Stiles, Maxwell, 8
Stockholm (Sweden), 149
Storm. *See* Portland Storm
Stratford (Ontario), 144
Strauss, Robert, 520, 591
Strikers. *See* Ft. Lauderdale Strikers
Strongsville (Ohio), 40, 41, 197, 198–199, 236, 475–476, 503, 505, 506, 523–524, 527
Suffolk County Probate Court, 209, 217
Suffolk Superior Court, 171, 172
Sullivan, Billy, Sr., 23, 62–63, 81, 82, 92, 135, 237, 272, 511–514, 530–531, 571, 587, 589, 609, 619
    childhood, 122
    cross-ownership, 95, 98
    early career, 122–123
    and Joe Robbie, 131
    ouster from Patriots, 129–130, 171–173
    ownership dispute ruling, 121, 180, 181
    Patriots move to Foxboro, 124–126
    Raiders move to Los Angeles, 443, 447, 482, 534
    repurchase of Patriots, 207–209, 217–219, 260
    Schaeffer Stadium, 126–129
    starts Patriots, 103–104
Sullivan, Chuck, 82, 126, 172, 180, 181, 237–240, 456, 501, 513, 545, 547, 551, 556, 560, 578, 625, 629–631
    heart attack, 632
    Jackson Family Victory Tour manager, 629–632
    NASL lawsuit, 452, 454
    Raiders move to Los Angeles, 437, 439, 442, 493
    repurchase of Patriots, 207, 208, 218–219, 220, 237, 258–262
Sullivan, Joe, 122, 127, 128, 512
Sullivan, Kathleen, 126, 240, 512
    see also Alioto, Kathleen Sullivan
Sullivan, Mary, 128, 130, 181, 218
Sullivan, Mary T. (Mrs. Billy), 126, 129, 171
Sullivan, Nancy, 609
Sullivan, Patrick, 579–580, 632–633
Sullivan, Walter, 173
Sullivan & Cromwell (law firm), 172
Sullivan Stadium (Foxboro, Mass.), 126, 127, 129, 172, 208, 258, 261, 512–513, 571, 629
Summerall, Pat, 627
Summers, Carl, Jr., 616
Summit Hotel (N.Y.C.), 431, 432, 567
Sun. See Baltimore Sun
Sun Devil Stadium (Ariz.), 175
Super Bowl, 18, 51, 52, 65, 85, 90, 127, 135, 137, 187, 188, 212, 232, 238, 263–264, 266, 272, 273, 456, 464, 573, 578, 590, 602–603, 609, 610, 627
    ticket scalping, 263–264, 462–463, 468, 469, 573
    TV audience, 3
Super Bowl II, 263
Super Bowl III, 113
Super Bowl VII, 20
Super Bowl VIII, 3, 22, 130
Super Bowl XI, 263, 271
Super Bowl XIV, 439, 469
Super Bowl XV, 470, 472, 473, 474, 480, 482
Super Bowl XVI, 529
Super Bowl XVII, 552
Super Bowl XVIII, 588–589, 591, 593, 599
Super Bowl XIX, 642, 644
Super Bowl XX, 632, 644
Superdome (New Orleans, La.), 25, 642
Supplementary Merger Agreement, 92
Sutton Place Hotel (Toronto), 169
Swann, Lynn, 249–250
Syracuse University, 59

Tagliabue, Paul, 520
Tampa (Fla.), 50, 148, 158, 219, 222, 239, 589, 593, 610
Tampa Bay Bandits, 455, 576, 646
Tampa Bay Buccaneers, 223
    expansion team ownership, 179, 192–194, 195–196, 229
    NFL expansion choice, 174, 175, 176–177, 178
Tampa Sports Authority, 174, 175
Tampa Stadium, 174
Teamsters Union, 111, 112, 445
Teamsters Union Pension Fund, 203, 204
Teleprompter, Inc., 146
Television, 18, 22, 108, 148, 153, 200, 436, 614, 643–644
    NFL contracts, 6–7, 13–15, 23, 304–306, 515, 528–530
    Super Bowl success, 3, 439–440
    see also specific networks
Texans. *See* Dallas Texans; Houston Texans
Texas A&M University, 600
Texas Monthly, 100, 101, 106–107, 449
Texas Stadium, 31–33, 600, 630
Texas Stadium Corporation, 31
Thomas, Danny, 133, 134
Thomas, Joe, 51, 52, 86–87, 88, 89, 189–190
Thomas, Joseph, 503, 504
Tickets
    allocation, 263–264, 267, 272, 416
    scalping, 265–266, 417–419, 461–463, 469–470, 572–573, 627–629
Time (magazine), 6, 170
Titans. *See* New York Titans
Tokyo (Japan), 149
Toledo (Ohio), 151
Toolson v. New York Yankees, 79
Tornado. *See* Dallas Tornado
Toronto, 169, 170, 631
Toronto Conservatory of Music, 144
Toronto Maple Leafs, 168
Toronto Northmen, 176, 200
Tose, Andrea (Mrs. Leonard), 118, 119, 120, 456
Tose, Julia (Mrs. Leonard), 621
Tose, Leonard, 4, 22, 109, 135, 190, 192, 206, 271, 272, 538–539, 542, 545, 558–559, 561–562, 573, 589, 601, 610, 621–626
    buys Eagles, 113–117, 121
    divorce, 119
    early career, 111–112
    finances, 113–114, 116–117, 120, 458, 556–557
    First Pennsylvania Bank lawsuit, *see subhead Tose v. First Pennsylvania*
    gambling, 118, 556–558
    and Hunt, 225–226
    leaves Eagles, 625
    life-style, 117–118, 455–456, 457
    NASL lawsuit, 452, 453, 456
    NFL expansion, 148, 158, 176, 179
    ownership policy, 98–99, 109, 110, 111, 121
    Raiders move to Los Angeles, 437, 442, 443, 492–493
    on Rozelle-Rosenbloom conflict, 220
    sells Eagles to Norman Braman, 625
    Super Bowl XV, 472–473
    Tose v. First Pennsylvania, 457–458, 459
    and *Valley v. Davis*, 205
Tose Trucking Company, 111, 112, 116
Tose v. First Pennsylvania Bank, 455, 457–458
Trailblazers. *See* Portland Trailblazers
Trancas Beach (Calif.), 52, 53, 211
Tribune (Oakland). *See Oakland Tribune*
Twentieth Century Fox, 509
"21" Club (N.Y.C.), 145
Tye, Frania, 449

Ueberroth, Peter, 462, 463
Union Commerce Bank (Cleveland, Ohio), 36, 436,
    503, 505, 507, 521–522, 528
United Jewish Appeal, 118
United Parcel Service, 112
United States Football League (USFL), 531–532,
    554–555, 575, 613–614
  competes with NFL for players,
    553, 612
  DeBartolo, Sr., buys into, 553–554
Universal Studios, 483
University Hilton (Los Angeles, Calif.), 438
University of Alabama, 192
University of Alabama Law School, 193
University of California (San Diego), 76
University of California School of Medicine, 76,
    138
University of Illinois, 87, 89, 188
University of Mexico, 138
University of Nebraska, 613
University of Pennsylvania, 48
University of San Francisco, 9
University of South Dakota, 131
University of Southern California, 59
University of Tampa, 151, 179
University of Texas, 27
University of Washington, 151, 179
University of Wisconsin, 80, 154, 164
Upshaw, Gene, 247–248, 472, 473, 474, 501, 515,
    542, 547
  NFL strike, 544, 545
  succeeds Garvey as NFLPA executive director,
    551
U.S. Realty Co., 41, 197

Valley, Wayne, 58, 60, 63, 66, 104, 135, 224, 274
  on Davis, 59, 61, 62, 67
  Davis contract dispute, 68–70
  sues Davis, 70, 201–202, 205, 206
Valley v. Davis, 201–202, 205
Vancouver (British Columbia), 60, 631–632
Veterans Stadium (Philadelphia, Pa), 120, 192, 558,
    610
Victory Tour. See Jackson Family Victory Tour
Vietnam War, 126
Vikings. See Minnesota Vikings
Villanova University Law School, 558
Voinovich, George, 436
Vulcans. See Birmingham Vulcans

Waite Hill (Cleveland, Ohio), 38
Waldorf-Astoria (N.Y.C.), 81, 108
Wallace, George, 192
Wall Street Journal, 601
Walter Kidde & Company. See Kidde Company
Ward, Baxter, 444, 445
Warfield, Paul, 168, 169, 170, 200
Washington (D.C.), 15, 16, 17, 29, 30, 97, 141,
    183, 192, 501, 545, 551, 610, 644
Washingtonian, The, 144
Washington Monthly, 141
Washington Post, 139, 479
Washington Redskins, 4, 13, 16, 23, 28, 55, 93, 97,
    139, 141, 142, 145, 146, 156, 207, 532, 590
  NASL lawsuit, 450–451, 452

Wasserman, Lew, 483
WCT. See World Championship Tennis
Wells, Jack, 37
Wells Fargo National Bank, 601
Weinberg, Larry, 179
Werblin, Sonny, 51, 84, 86
Westchester County (N.Y.), 83, 209
Western Division Championship (AFL), 60
Wettenhall, Robert, 128, 129, 130, 171, 180, 208,
    209, 217–219
Wexler, Anne, 520
Wheels. See Detroit Wheels
White Plains, (N.Y.), 83
White Sox. See Chicago White Sox
Whitman, H. Daniel, 627–629
Whitney Land Company, 435
William Radovich v. National Football League, 79
Williams, Dorothy Guider (Mrs. Edward), 140
Williams, Edward Bennett, 4, 23–24, 91, 93, 94,
    109, 207, 478–479, 532
  early career, 140
  marriage, 140
  and Marshall's estate, 141–142
  NASL lawsuit, 450–454
  and NFL expansion, 158
  ownership policy, 91, 93, 94, 96, 97, 99, 143,
    226–228
  and Pro Football, Inc., 139, 141, 145, 146
Williams & Connelly, 141
Wilson, Lionel, 441, 493, 508–509, 576
Wilson, Ralph, 25, 103, 104, 174, 202, 203, 229,
    232, 625
Wind. See Chicago Wind
Wings. See San Antonio Wings
Winter, Max, 21, 57, 102, 104, 212, 265, 471, 571
Winton Place (Cleveland, Ohio), 37, 38
Wismer, Harry, 103, 104, 144, 145
Wittman, Dennis, 461
WJW Radio, 435
Wolfson family, 102
Wolman, Jerry, 112–113, 115, 179, 192
World Championship Tennis (WCT), 92, 107, 108
World Cup (soccer), 108
World Football League (WFL), 149, 168–170, 174,
    222, 271, 575, 612
  collapse, 150, 215–216
  financial troubles, 150, 186, 199
  merger suggestion, 206
  NFL expansion, 176
  NFL player raid, 150, 169
  opening games, 149, 185
"World Freebie League," 186
World Hockey Associations, 150
Wyman, Bautzer, Rothman, and Silbert,
    460
Wyman, Eugene, 460

Yale Bowl (New Haven, Conn.), 85
Yankee Stadium, 84, 85
Yonkers Raceway, 156
York, Marie Denise DeBartolo, 554

Zurn Industries, 88